| DATE | | | |
|---|---|---|---|
| | | 15.00 | |
| | | | |
| | | | |
| | | | |
| | | | |
| | | | |
| | | | |
| | | | |
| | | | |
| | | | |
| | | | |
| | | | |

© THE BAKER & TAYLOR CO.

# BALANCHINE'S

## Complete Stories

### OF THE

## Great Ballets

Also by George Balanchine and Francis Mason
101 STORIES OF THE GREAT BALLETS

# BALANCHINE'S

## Complete Stories

### OF THE

## Great Ballets

Revised and Enlarged Edition

BY GEORGE BALANCHINE
AND FRANCIS MASON

DOUBLEDAY & COMPANY, INC.
GARDEN CITY, NEW YORK

ISBN: 0-385-11381-1
Library of Congress Catalogue Card Number 76-55684
Copyright © 1954, 1968, 1975, 1977 by Doubleday & Company, Inc.
All Rights Reserved
Printed in the United States of America

"The Song of the Earth," translated by Alfred H. Meyer, from the book THE ANA-
LYTICAL CONCERT GUIDE, edited by Louis Biancolli. Copyright © 1951 by
Louis Biancolli. Reprinted by permission of the editor.

Excerpt from "Quicksilver" by Marie Rambert. Used by permission of St. Martin's
Press, Inc. and Macmillan & Co., Ltd.

Library of Congress Cataloging in Publication Data

Balanchine, George.
  Balanchine's Complete stories of the great ballets.

  Edition for 1968 published under title: Balanchine's New complete stories of the
great ballets.
  Includes index.
  1. Ballets—Stories, plots, etc.  I. Title.  II. Title: Complete stories of the great
ballets.
MT95.B3 1977    792.8'4

*Dancing is an action, showing outwardly the spiritual movements which must agree with those measures and perfect accords of harmony which, through our hearing and with earthly joy, descend into one intellect, there to produce sweet movements which . . . endeavor to escape and reveal themselves in movement.*

GUGLIELMO EBREO, "William the Jew of Pisaro,"
Italian Dancing Master of the Renaissance

*Vainest endeavor, to try to document dance, the most ephemeral of the arts. Suppose that you find the bricks and boards, the levers and pulleys of a theatre intact, and that your lunatic friend who loves the archives helps locate sources from which the scenic decoration, musical orchestration and plot evolution of a famous, forgotten ballet could be reconstructed. Suppose further that you were extremely fortunate in your friend and his treasure hunt uncovered even a precise, pre-Laban notation that enabled one to teach each pas to contemporary dancers. Still . . . Reason . . . would tell you that the essential movement would be missing. The trappings would be there, but you would not see the "dance urge" Heine saw watching Carlotta Grisi, or recognize with Kleist dance mannerism as a dislocation of the soul from the central still point of movement to the trajectory. Remember how different La Sonnambula seemed only a few years ago as Night Shadow? Today's dancers . . . attend that sort of party only in line of duty and then look obligingly uncomfortable. So you leave the past buried and go back to the new theatre to watch the business at hand, ballet as it is danced today—which is the living issue, not the death mask of ballet yesterday. You leave reluctantly; besides the ballet's immediate sensual beauty, and its brilliance in time and space as a medium of silent ideas, an urgent part of the reason you had worshiped it before all other arts was the simple wonder of seeing a human body moving in the same step for the same reason as did its predecessors a century or more ago.*

GEORGE JACKSON, "Notes Towards an Anti-History of Ballet in Vienna,"
in *Ballet Review*, 1967

*Each fairy tale is a magic mirror which reflects some aspect of your inner world, and of the steps required by our evolution from immaturity to maturity.*

BRUNO BETTELHEIM, The Meaning and Importance of Fairy Tales, 1976

To the Subscribers,
  those who come to the ballet today,
  know it and like it so much they will
  come also tomorrow

# PREFACE

This book attempts to tell the stories of ballets of lasting importance in the history of the art and to provide a record of significant new work performed in the past twenty-five years—ballets that are still a part of the contemporary repertory or ballets that made an enduring impression at the time.

Ballets of lasting importance—and by that we mean ambition fulfilled—ballets like *La Sylphide, Giselle*, and *Swan Lake,* have held the stage for more than a hundred years; *La Fille Mal Gardée* for almost two hundred. The new ballets that we see nowadays with increasing frequency all aspire to the same longevity. While few succeed, many remain in the active repertory longer than is imagined. A great number, like *Petrouchka*, come and go; others disappear entirely. (That has happened, naturally, to some of my own ballets; there is no point in insisting on keeping what doesn't work; there is also no point in reviving what cannot be properly recalled.)

The new pieces of the modern repertory, and now fortunately there are many of them every year produced by the growing number of ballet companies, are all candidates for lasting value and inclusion in the quasi-permanent repertory. Hopefully, many described in this book will last. Those that have not done so since *Balanchine's New Complete Stories of the Great Ballets* in 1968 have given place here to new ballets. We have tried to keep the stories of ballets likely to be revived one day, or ballets of interest from the point of view of music, choreography, design, or performance. In 1954, when the first edition of this book appeared, 131 ballets were described. In 1968, 241 were described in the second edition. Now, minus some 40 from the latter, there are 404.

The ballet audience has grown tremendously in recent years. In 1965 it was estimated that one million people attended dance performances in the United States. In 1975 that figure was fifteen million. It has been projected to reach twenty-five million in the near future. I believe it.

New audiences for ballet, of course, are not created by new dances that have just a passing interest. What makes an audience, what makes a newcomer committed is a dance that will cause him to ask, "When can I see that *again?*" Those are the ballets we are all looking for.

I have watched ballet grow wonderfully. When we began work on the first edition of this book, New York was lucky to see two months of ballet, domestic and foreign combined, all year. In a recent season, it was possible to see in a single year more than ten months of ballet performances by native and foreign ensembles. The result has been a marvelous proliferation of new work performed by an ever increasing number of gifted dancers.

When Lincoln Kirstein and I began to work together and started the School of American Ballet in 1934, we knew that our dancers would one day be admired throughout the world. This happened much more rapidly than we imagined. Now, many schools associated with ballet companies throughout the country are turning out talented young dancers.

The same thing has happened in England, where Ninette de Valois founded her school the same year; the Royal Ballet is the result. Now the Royal Ballet and the New York City Ballet dance next door to each other in Lincoln Center. Both of us sell out. There is no end to what trained talent can give.

Audiences cannot be trained, of course, only advised a little—most of all advised to go to the ballet and to keep on going. It is the closest the observer can come to the steady training required of the dancer in order to create the performance that will captivate him.

Years ago maybe it was possible to go to the ballet regularly and not experience a great evening on every occasion; today, there are many great evenings. This book is designed to help find them and to give some preparation to those who do not trust their eyes and ears in the theatre first. Much as reading about ballet may be useful after enjoying performances, it will scarcely substitute for the initial excitement of seeing and hearing performance in the theatre. But if it leads to the theatre, we are pleased. Francis Mason and I have enjoyed working toward that possibility.

We wish to thank Harold Kuebler and Debra Groisser for prolonged editorial assistance and patience. I have other jobs to do and it has not been easy to give this one priority.

We often wonder what Lawrence Sherman and Marion Patton, our first editors, must think of how the book we first planned with them has grown. It is maybe like the Christmas tree in *The Nutcracker*.

GEORGE BALANCHINE

# ACKNOWLEDGMENTS

Many have helped in the making of this book. First, those who made it possible to see the ballets described here—the press representatives of the ballet companies whose repertories we have made an effort to record. Second, the critics and other writers on dance whose work is often quoted in the text. When the first edition of this book was prepared in the early 1950s, the dance critics in the daily press in the United States could be counted on the fingers of one hand; now, with ballet and dance companies established in many cities or touring throughout the country, newspapers and magazines of repute have realized that they must have competent persons to write about them. (For the first time, in 1976, a Pulitzer Prize was awarded to a dance critic—to Alan Kriegsman of the Washington *Post*.) There has been a happy increase, too, in the number of dance magazines. What writers on dance have to say, in acute and informative reviews, is valuable not only as history but in giving here a round character to flat recollection.

The Dance Collection of the New York Public Library at Lincoln Center is the master source in the world, as I hope everyone now knows, for those who seek history and knowledge of the dance. It is also the liveliest archive in the world as it succeeds in holding for the future the most ephemeral of the arts. The Dictionary Catalogue of the Dance Collection, the major bibliography of all materials relating to dance, has recently been published in twelve large volumes. It is very simply a monumental dance index—a guide to who danced what when, in whose design, to what music, what was written about it, what the dancer recalled, perhaps, and what it looked like in photographs of the time or on film. The dancers, choreographers and designers, the collectors, historians, critics, and lovers of dance who have given to the Dance Collection over the years must take considerable pride in this rare jewel in the crown of the New York Public Library. What Genevieve Oswald, the Curator of the Collection, and her colleagues have done is not only to pin down the butterfly, but in many cases to make it fly again. For in the written and spoken word, in film, photographs, drawings, prints, the Collection is becoming increasingly valuable. Those who read these words and cherish their own collections and files of dance materials are urged to remember the Dance Collection's concern to keep such things permanent in a perishable world. The Collection is situated in the New York Public Library's Museum and Library of the Performing Arts at Lincoln Center, 111 Amsterdam Avenue, New York 10023. Don't throw anything away!

We are deeply grateful to the critics and writers on dance whose work is quoted in this book: Jack Anderson of *Ballet Review, Dance Magazine,* and the *Dancing Times;* Barbara Archer of *The Record;* Robb Baker of *FM Guide;* Clive Barnes, dance and drama critic of the New York *Times;* Patricia Barnes of *Dance and Dancers;* Ann Barzell of *Dance News;* Byron Belt of the *Long Island Press;* Elena Bivona of *Ballet Review;* Alexander Bland of *The Observer;* Jane Boutwell of *The New Yorker;* Erik Bruhn for his essay "Beyond Technique" (*Dance Perspectives* 36); Richard Buckle of *The Sunday Times* (London), founder and editor of *Ballet;* Mary Clarke, editor of the *Dancing Times;* Selma Jeanne Cohen, founder and editor of *Dance Perspectives;* William Como, editor-in-chief of *Dance Magazine;* the filmmaker Gardner Compton in *Dance Magazine;* the art critic and collector Douglas Cooper in *Dance and Dancers;* the conductor and writer Robert Craft; Clement Crisp of the *Financial Times* (London); Arlene Croce, dance critic of *The New Yorker,* founder and editor of *Ballet Review,* correspondent of the *Dancing Times;* Edwin Denby, poet, critic (for the New York *Herald Tribune, Modern Music* and *Dance Magazine*), author of *Looking at the Dance* and *Dancers, Buildings and People in the Streets;* George Dorris of *Ballet Review;* John T. Elson of *Time* magazine; Janet Flanner of *The New Yorker,* author of *Paris Was Yesterday,* edited by Irving Drutman; Joseph Gale of the *Daily News;* Joseph Galeon of *Dance News;* Nancy Goldner, author of *The Stravinsky Festival of the New York City Ballet;* Robert Greskovic of *The Soho Weekly News* and *Ballet Review;* John Gruen in the New York *Times;* Henry Haslam in *Ballet Review;* Doris Hering of *Dance Magazine;* Frances Herridge, dance critic of the New York *Post;* Allen Hughes of the New York *Times;* Michael Iachetta of the *Daily News;* George Jackson of *Ballet Review* and *Dance News;* Robert Jacobson of *Cue;* Lydia Jaffe of *Dance Magazine;* Deborah Jowitt, dance critic of *The Village Voice* and author of *Dance Beat;* Oleg Kerensky of *The New Statesman,* author of *Pavlova* and *The World of Ballet;* Lincoln Kirstein for innumerable sources, most importantly *Movement and Metaphor: Four Centuries of Ballet, The New York City Ballet,* and *Nijinsky Dancing;* Anna Kisselgoff of the New York *Times;* Vera Krasovskaya, the Soviet critic; Alan M. Kriegsman of the *Washington Post;* Herbert Kupferberg of the *National Observer;* Jean Battey Lewis of the Washington *Post;* John Martin, the first dance critic of the New York *Times;* Jacqueline Maskey of *High Fidelity;* Nancy Mason of *Dance Magazine;* Olga Maynard of *Dance Magazine;* Don McDonagh of the New York *Times;* Bob Micklin of *Newsday;* James Monahan of the *Dancing Times* and *The Guardian;* Sam Norkin of the *Daily News;* Patrick O'Connor of the *Jersey Journal;* John Percival, dance critic of the *Times* (London) and *Dance and Dancers;* Richard Philp of *Dance Magazine;* Andrew Porter of *The New Yorker* and the *Financial Times* (London), author of *A Musical Season;* Dame Marie Rambert, author of her autobiography *Quicksilver;* Alan Rich, music critic of *New York* magazine; Peter Rosenwald of the *Wall Street Journal;* Hubert Saal of *Newsweek;* Winthrop Sargeant of *The New Yorker;* Robert Sealey in *Ballet Review;* Marcia B. Siegel, dance critic of *The Hudson Review,* the *Soho Weekly News,* the Boston *Herald Examiner* and author of a collection of criticisms, *At the Vanishing Point;* Anna Greta

Stahle of *Dance News;* Walter Terry, dean of American dance writers, dance critic for the New York *Herald Tribune* and *The Saturday Review;* Rose Anne Thom of *Dance Magazine;* Arthur Todd of *Dance Observer;* David Vaughan of *Ballet Review* and author of *Frederick Ashton and His Ballets* (1977); the late James Waring in *Ballet Review;* William Weaver of the *Herald Tribune;* Anne Marie Welsh of the Washington *Star;* Thomas Willis of the *Chicago Tribune;* and Peter Williams, founder and editor of *Dance and Dancers.*

For permission to quote from books, we wish to express thanks to George G. Harrap Co., Ltd., London, for an excerpt from *Frederick Ashton, a Choreographer and His Ballets* (1971); Horizon Press for *Dancers, Buildings and People in the Streets* by Edwin Denby (1965); Macmillan and Co., Ltd., for "The Bumboat Woman's Story," from *Bab Ballads* by Sir W. S. Gilbert; Pellegrini and Cudahy, Publishers, for *Looking at the Dance,* copyright 1949 by Edwin Denby; Random House, New York, and Faber and Faber, Ltd., for *The Age of Anxiety* by W. H. Auden; Saturday Review Press for *At the Vanishing Point: A Critic Looks at Dance* by Marcia B. Siegel, 1972; the late Igor Stravinsky for *Stravinsky: an Autobiography;* the late Carl Van Vechten for "The Russian Ballet and Nijinsky" from *Interpreters* by Carl Van Vechten.

The press and public relations representatives of ballet companies have responded generously to frequent requests. We are especially grateful to Charles France, Director of Publicity and Public Relations for American Ballet Theatre, Elena Gordon, Assistant to Charles France, and Joan Ehrlich-White, Virginia Hymes and Irene Shaw of that company; Tom Kerrigan of the Brooklyn Academy of Music; Isadora Bennett, Rima Corben and Robert Larkin of the City Center Joffrey Ballet; Dick Hendriks and Rima Corben of the Dutch National Ballet; Winnie Sampson of the Dance Theatre of Harlem; Judith Jedlicka of the Harkness Ballet; Sheila Porter, General Press Representative, Hurok Concerts and John Gingrich, Associate Press Representative; Virginia Donaldson, Press Representative of the New York City Ballet and her associates: Leslie Bailey, Linda Cioffoletti, Marie Gutscher, Clarence Hart and Larry Strichman; and Vivien Wallace of the Royal Opera House, Covent Garden, London.

We are deeply grateful to William Como, editor of *Dance Magazine,* for permission to reprint entire the long interview between Jerome Robbins and Edwin Denby on the subject of the ballet *Dances at a Gathering,* and the filmmaker Gardner Compton's article on Robert Joffrey's *Astarte.* Also valuable have been interviews by Jane Boutwell in *The New Yorker* with Maurice Béjart, Leonard Bernstein and Jerome Robbins, and Kenneth MacMillan; in *Show* magazine with Rudolf Nureyev; and in *Dance and Dancers* with Eliot Feld. The invaluable books of Igor Stravinsky and Robert Craft and Eric Walter White's *Stravinsky: the Composer and his Works* (1966) have been consulted frequently. David Vaughan kindly permitted us to read part of the manuscript of his book of *Frederick Ashton and His Ballets* (Alfred A. Knopf, New York, 1977).

We wish to thank, too, the publishers of *Ballet Review,* Marcel Dekker, Inc., for permission to quote so frequently from the pages of that magazine.

For helpfulness and interest we should like particularly to thank Jane Allison of the Indianapolis *Star;* Frank Darvas; Darryl Dodson of American Ballet Theatre; Harvey Lichtenstein of the Brooklyn Academy of Music; Cora Cahan of the Eliot Feld Ballet; Richard Philp of *Dance Magazine;* Karel Shook of the Dance Theatre of Harlem; Betty Cage, Barbara Horgan, Edward Bigelow, Robert Cornell, Carole Deschamps and Mary Porter of the New York City Ballet; Nathalie Molostwoff and Elise Reiman of the School of American Ballet; Robert Irving, Music Director of the New York City Ballet; and the staff of the Dance Collection of the New York Public Library at Lincoln Center, especially Genevieve Oswald, Curator, Reynaldo Alejandro, Natalie Bassein, Paul LePaglia, Lacy McDearmon, Winifred Messe, Madeleine Nichols, Andrew Wentink, and Henry Wisneski.

Henry Wisneski's counsel and advice on the photographs in this volume were invaluable and we are much indebted to him. The arrangement and presentation of the photographs, so important in a book on ballet, have been done by Randall Mize, to whom we wish to express special appreciation.

Words are insufficient for the thanks we owe the photographers whose work appears in this book. Unlike the dance writer and critic, whose work exists in print and does not perish, the dance photographer takes thousands of valuable photographs, many of which never see the light of day and all too few of which are published. The photographers are the unsung heroes and heroines of ballet, recording its history in frozen moments of performance we strive to recall in words that only approximate reality.

We wish also to thank most warmly for editorial assistance throughout the book Shields Remine. Harold Grabau has prepared the final text in exemplary fashion.

FRANCIS MASON

# CONTENTS

# ILLUSTRATIONS

# PART ONE

## *Stories of the Great Ballets*

## ABYSS

*Music by Marga Richter. Choreography by Stuart Hodes. Costumes by André Delfau. First presented by the Harkness Ballet at the Casino, Cannes, France, February 21, 1956, with Lone Isaksen and Erik Bruhn in the principal roles.*

Based on a story by Leonid Andreyev, *Abyss* shows what might happen when an innocent young couple encounter bestial forces. One of Russia's great writers whose work in many ways resembles that of Edgar Allan Poe, Andreyev relates in his story a disturbing incident that is presented here in dance terms. A young girl and boy, not yet old enough to be seriously in love but close since childhood and certain one day to marry, walk one day alone in the forest. There they are suddenly attacked by three menacing figures. The boy is powerless to protect the girl and she is carried off by two of the men. When the boy eventually finds her again, she is distraught and half out of her mind. He is about to leave her in horror at what the attackers have done. But he finds himself also curious and attracted. The abyss opens before him and he, too, seizes the girl.

## ADAGIO HAMMERKLAVIER

*Music by Beethoven. Choreography by Hans Van Manen. Set and costumes by Jean-Paul Vroom. Lighting by David K. H. Elliott. First presented by the Dutch National Ballet, October 4, 1973. First presented in the United States by the Pennsylvania Ballet.*

Inspired by the choreographer's listening to a recording by Christoph Eschenbach of the Adagio from Beethoven's *Hammerklavier Sonata*, this is a dance ballet. Eschenbach's performance, especially slow in tempo, stretches the possibilities of playing pianissimo to its extreme. His recording is used to accompany *Adagio Hammerklavier*, a dance for a boy and a girl, accompanied by two other couples.

Writing of a performance by the Dutch National Ballet in Canada in 1975, the critic Rose Anne Thom said in *Dance Magazine* that a pas de deux by Alexandra Radius and Hans Ebbelaar "communicated a sense of balance and confidence that was reassuring not only technically, but emotionally . . . It was the quiet understatement that made *Adagio* work . . ."

## AFTER CORINTH

*Music by David Gagne. Choreography by Walter Raines. Scenery by Gary Fails. First presented by the Dance Theatre of Harlem at the Uris Theatre, New York, April 29, 1975, with Virginia Johnson, Melva Murray-White, M. Elena Carter, and Roman Brooks.*

A new perspective on the story of Jason and Medea, *After Corinth* takes the view that Jason's new wife, Glauce, victimizes his first, Medea. It will be recalled that in the dominant classical version of this story in the Greek drama of Euripides, Medea, enraged at Jason's desertion of her, devises the murder of Glauce. Medea then murders her own children by Jason. The ballet imagines that, after death, Jason and Medea return to earth and that Glauce is then seen as the murderess.

## AFTER EDEN

*Music by Lee Hoiby. Choreography by John Butler. Scenery by Rouben Ter-Arutunian. First presented by the Harkness Ballet at the Broadway Theatre, New York, November 9, 1967, with Lone Isaksen and Lawrence Rhodes.*

*After Eden* is a dramatic ballet about Adam and Eve after the Fall and the expulsion from the Garden of Eden. It shows in dance terms, with no narration, something of the agony, regret, defiance, and resignation of the two lovers as they face the fate they had not imagined. In the process, their dependence on each other varies and it is this that makes the drama of the piece: Will they, after what they have come through, be able to stay together? At the start of the dance they are united in their misery and therefore mutually dependent. Later, realizing their new, appalling freedom, it seems briefly possible for them to separate or to entertain that notion. But not for long, for they have survived much and cannot go their separate ways. They are like magnets, alternately attracting and repulsing as they turn in different directions. In the end, they are newly united and apparently resolved to encounter the future together.

*After Eden* was revived by the City Center Joffrey Ballet, March 21, 1972, with Starr Danias and Dennis Wayne. Writing of this revival in the New York *Times*, the critic Anna Kisselgoff said that "Mr. Butler's symbolic images are so strong and so psychologically apt that he succeeds almost beyond belief in taking a specific emotional situation and generalizing it into a commentary on the universal human condition . . . Mr. Wayne and Miss Danias give a very strong performance . . . Miss Danias' Eve is fragile; she is much closer to the state of innocence just left behind than her partner. Mr. Wayne's Adam reacts through instinct, logically stressing the irrationality with which man often reacts to a new situation."

## THE AFTERNOON OF A FAUN

*Choreographic tableau in one act. Music by Claude Debussy. Choreography by Vaslav Nijinsky. Scenery and costumes by Léon Bakst. First presented by Diaghilev's Ballets Russes at the Théâtre du Châtelet, Paris, May 29, 1912, with Vaslav Nijinsky as the Faun. First presented in the United States by Diaghilev's Ballets Russes at the Century Theatre, New York, January 17, 1916, with Leonide Massine as the Faun.*

The music for this ballet was written by Debussy as a *Prélude* to a poem by Stéphane Mallarmé. Nijinsky's idea of portraying a languorous faun whose rest is disturbed by beautiful nymphs is thus related to Debussy's inspiration. Debussy wrote of his score: "The music of this prelude is a very free illustration to Stéphane Mallarmé's beautiful poem. It does not follow the poet's conception exactly, but describes the successive scenes among which the wishes and dreams of the Faun wander in the heat of the afternoon. Then, tired of pursuing the fearful flight of the nymphs and naiads, he abandons himself to a delightful sleep, full of visions finally realized, of full possession amid universal nature."

When the curtain rises on the ballet we see a faun idling away a hot summer afternoon. He lies on a hillock, playing the flute and eating grapes. It is apparent that his wants are simple and innocent. Dressed in light brown tights dotted with brown patches below the waist, he seems to be half boy, half animal.

A group of seven lovely nymphs on their way to bathe in a lake near by enter the faun's domain. They move in a line, forming a likeness to a Greek frieze, their bodies always turned to the audience, their faces always in profile. The faun has never seen such beautiful creatures before and climbs down from his hillock to observe the naiads with the golden hair and soft, gauze tunics more closely. The nymphs, in turn, are astonished by this creature who seems to be a handsome boy spotted like a goat with small horns growing from his forehead. What can he be? they wonder. Soon, as the playful faun leaps about them, the startled nymphs flee to the forest.

When they return, the faun tries to ingratiate himself with them. But still the naiads are frightened, and again they run away. All except one. This nymph is less embarrassed than her sisters and more anxious to discover the faun's secret. The faun is emboldened to make playful amorous gestures. The nymph allows him to touch her; she seems to respond to him, but then she eludes his grasp. She is frightened and rushes off to join the others. As she leaves, a silken scarf from her garment falls to the ground.

The faun, no longer playful, is sad at her departure. He picks up her scarf and holds it as if it were a treasure. He returns to the hillock, holds the scarf in his hands as if it were a woman's face, and touches it tenderly. Now he lays the scarf down softly and as he caresses it, imagines it to be the naiad he frightened away. With his possession of the scarf, the faun is content with his afternoon revery. It is as if the nymphs had never appeared, as if he had dreamed of their presence and in his dream possessed utterly the most beautiful of them all.

NOTES  *The Afternoon of a Faun* was Vaslav Nijinsky's first ballet. In its choreography and in its dancing the work completely rejected traditional forms. It was not a ballet in the accepted sense; it was a "choreographic tableau," a moving frieze, a work to be seen only from the front, a two-dimensional ballet. In his imitation of Greek paintings, Nijinsky was faithful to the spirit and to the letter; the traditional movements of classical ballet were altogether rejected in favor of an angular rigidity that would make possible a new expressiveness for the dancer's body.

Since Nijinsky's first performances, many dancers have taken the leading role in *The Afternoon of a Faun,* among them Leonide Massine, Serge Lifar, David Lichine, Igor Youskevitch, Leon Danielian, and Jean Babilée. Dame Marie Rambert, who knew Nijinsky well, has written of his achievement in her autobiography *Quicksilver:* "One is often asked whether his jump was really as high as it is always described. To that I answer: 'I don't know how far from the ground it was, but I know it was near the stars.' Who would watch the floor when he danced? He transported you at once into higher spheres with the sheer ecstasy of his flight.

"The most absurd theories were put forward about his anatomy. People said that the bones in his feet were like a bird's—as though a bird flew because of its feet! But, in fact, he *did* have an exceptionally long Achilles' tendon which allowed him with his heels firmly on the ground and the back upright to bend the knees to the utmost before taking a spring, and he had powerful thighs. As to his famous posing in the air, he indeed created the illusion of it by the ecstasy of his expression at the apex of the leap, so that *this* unique moment penetrated into every spectator's consciousness, and seemed to last. His landing, from whatever height he jumped, was like a cat's. He had that unique touch of the foot on the ground which can only be compared to the pianist's touch of the fingers on the keys. It was as subtle and as varied.

"And then there was his unique interpretation. He wafted the perfume of the rose in *Spectre de la Rose;* he was the very spirit of Chopin in *Les Sylphides;* he looked like a Hamlet in *Giselle;* his Petrouchka broke your heart with his sorrow, and his Faune had the real breath of antiquity.

"As to his choreography, I would not hesitate to affirm that it was he, more than anyone else, who revolutionized the classical ballet and was fifty years ahead of his time. Fokine was a logical development of Petipa, but Nijinsky introduced completely new principles. He produced three ballets in all: *l'Après-midi d'un Faune, Jeux,* and *Sacre du Printemps.* For each of them he established a basic position strictly adhered to all through the ballet. For *Faune* he took his inspiration from Greek vases and bas-reliefs. The body was facing front while the head and feet were always seen in profile. The deportment had to be classical, yet the head had independent movements not connected with deportment in the classical vocabulary, and so had the arms. It was an orchestration of the body, with each part playing a totally different melody. There was nothing you could do automatically. The walking was all done on one line parallel to the footlights, the whole foot on the ground. It was an incredibly difficult position to achieve, let alone use in walking, or changing direction, or combining with highly stylized arm movements. He did not explain why he wanted them thus, but he showed again and again the way they had to be done until he obtained a perfect copy of his own movement. His method of creation was diametrically opposed to Fokine's. Fokine always took the dancers into his confidence and allowed them, even encouraged them, to participate in the creation of a character. Not so Nijinsky. When once I was extolling the virtues of *Petrouchka* to him, saying it was Fokine's masterpiece, he said that it *was* so, as far as the three main characters went, but the crowd was treated too loosely, and everybody did what they wanted within the space indicated to them. Nijinsky on the contrary did not allow the slightest freedom of movement or gesture and exacted only a perfect copy. No wonder it took some 120 rehearsals for *l'Après-midi d'un Faune,* lasting about ten minutes, to be achieved as he wished, since not a single movement could be done spontaneously, each limb having to be studied separately. He required a perfect ballet technique and then broke it down consciously to his own purpose—and then it proved a masterpiece. Each nymph looked a goddess. Although they were incapable of understanding Nijinsky's intentions, the mere fact of faithfully copying his unique movements gave them the requisite style. He told them: no expression in the face, you must just be as though asleep with your eyes open—like statues.

"Once when a new girl had to learn Nijinsky's sister's part, in which the Nymph suddenly sees the Faune, turns away and walks off—he said to her: 'Why do you look so frightened?'

"She said she thought she was meant to be. Thereupon, quite in a rage, he said that the movement he gave her was all that was required of her, he was not interested in her personal feelings. And how right Nijinsky was for his particular choreography! It acquired an impersonal, remote character—just like the paintings on Greek vases or bas-reliefs—not that he ever attempted to copy any particular poses from these, but created them by the profoundest penetration into their very spirit. The walking was done not strictly to the music, but rather loosely as though walking 'through' the music."

In 1936 Edwin Denby reviewed a performance by David Lichine:

"The *Faun* is an astonishing work. After twenty-three years it is as direct and moving as though it had been invented yesterday. It gathers momentum from the first gesture to the last like an ideal short story. From this point of view of a story, the way the veil is introduced and re-emphasized by the nymph is a marvel of rightness. From the point of view of visual rhythm the repetition of the nymph's gesture of dismay is the perfection of timing. It is, of course, because so few gesture motifs are used that one can recognize each so plainly, but there is no feeling of poverty in this simplification. The rhythmic pattern in relation to the stage and to the music is so subtly graded that instead of monotony we get a steady increase in suspense, an increase in the eyes' perceptiveness, and a feeling of heroic style at the climax.

"It is true that most of the gestures used have prototypes in Greek reliefs and vase paintings, but, in addition to that intellectual association with adolescence, the fact is that when the body imitates these poses, the kind of tension resulting expresses exactly the emotion Nijinsky wants to express. Both their actual tension and their apparent remoteness, both their plastic clarity and their emphasis by negation on the center of the body (it is always strained between the feet in profile and the shoulders *en face*)—all these qualities lead up to the complete realization of the faun's last gesture. The poignancy of this moment lies partly in the complete change in the direction of tension, in the satisfying relief that results; and the substitution of a new tension (the incredible backbend) gives the work its balance. But besides, the eye has been educated to see the plastic beauty of this last pose, and the rhythmic sense to appreciate its noble deliberateness. That it is so intensely human a gesture, coming after a long preparation of understatement, gives it, in its cumulative assurance, the force of an illumination. This force of direct human statement, this faith in all of us, is the astonishing thing about the *Faun*. It is as rare in dancing as in the other arts. These last moments of the *Faun* do not need any critical defense. But they have been so talked about that I am trying to point out for intellectuals that they are not a sensational tag, but that the whole piece builds up to them, and reaches in them an extraordinary beauty.

"The De Basil company danced the *Faun* beautifully. Lichine in the title role excelled. It is a part that demands exceptional imagination as well as great plastic sense. And Lichine had besides these a fine simplicity."

*Music by Claude Debussy. Choreography by Jerome Robbins. Set and lighting by Jean Rosenthal. Costumes by Irene Sharaff. First presented by the New York City Ballet at the City Center, New York, May 14, 1953, with Tanaquil LeClercq and Francisco Moncion.*

Mallarmé's poem that inspired Debussy's music *Prélude à l'après-midi d'un Faune* describes the reveries of a faun and his real or imagined encounter with nymphs. In 1912 Nijinsky presented his famous ballet, drawing his ideas from both the music and the poem, among other sources. This *pas de deux* is a contemporary variation on those themes.

The scene is a room with a mirror, very much like a modern ballet studio with one wall a mirror so that dancers can watch themselves. The mirror wall is the imaginary wall toward the audience, so that when the dancers stare out at us they are really looking at their own reflections. The setting, with walls and ceiling of transparent cloth against a blue sky, seems to float in space; it is as remote and silent as the sylvan scene of Nijinsky's work. On the floor of the room a boy, naked to the waist, lies asleep. At the call of the music, he stirs, rolls over, arches his back, stretches like a cat. He sits up and stares out at us with such interest and objectivity that we know he appraises himself in the mirror. He stands, watching himself, adjusts his belt, poses to the sensuous music, gestures, then slowly somersaults and lies on the floor again, languorous and satisfied with himself. He falls asleep. A girl in white practice dress approaches the room. She pauses at the door, prepares her ballet shoes for the work to come and looks at the mirror. From the door she is drawn toward her image—and does not notice the boy. She has eyes only for her own reflection. She poses at the mirror, then kneels. She then begins to exercise at the *barre*. The boy wakens like a startled faun and watches her. She observes herself closely. When she comes to an open pose the boy steps in and lifts her up and away from the *barre*, as if she were coming up for air. The boy holds her in poses that please her image, both always looking into the mirror and never directly at each other. She likes the way she looks as he supports her, misses his hand at her waist when he is not there. She luxuriates for a moment, then stands and looks at the floor. He comes to her, his hands touch her hair, but she rises immediately into a formal *attitude*, rejecting any contact except what will make her more lovely to herself.

The enchanted boy, now watching only her in the mirror, lifts her now to his shoulder; she descends, her loose hair falling about her face. They separate then to opposite sides of the room, watching each other in the mirror. Their cool concentration on the invisible reflections before them is so intense that we know when one of them is watching the other. They approach each other slowly, reaching out. They stand side by side for a moment. The boy makes a circle of his arms and the girl slips through them, held there full length, swimming in the air. Then her body collapses as if a spell had been broken. She kneels on the floor, the boy beside her. He now looks at her directly while she still watches in the mirror. He leans toward her, his face comes close, he kisses her cheek. Her hand slowly moves up to her cheek. She stands and still looking straight ahead in the mirror, walks backward out of the room, her hand still at her face. He watches her in the mirror. She is gone. The boy lies down on the floor, pushes himself up on his arms and descends slowly again into sleep.

NOTES   Since this ballet was first performed, it has been danced throughout the United States and many countries overseas by the New York City Ballet, by the Royal Ballet, and by Jerome Robbins' Ballets: U.S.A. The latter performed it at the White House, April 11, 1962, following a state dinner given by President and Mrs. Kennedy for the Shah and Queen of Iran.

Soon after the first performance of *Afternoon of a Faun*, Doris Hering wrote in *Dance Magazine:* "*Afternoon of a Faun* is a work of great awareness and wry insight and one that shimmers with atmosphere from beginning to end . . .

"There is a wonderful sense of theatrical rightness in Mr. Robbins' choice of the antiseptic studio atmosphere for history of nascent love vying with narcissism—not only because dancers live in a world of mirrors, but because this particular format allowed him to concentrate on the rich mood relationship between the music and his own choreography. And instead of making a 'dance' in the formal sense of the word, he allowed the movement to flow out of the materials of the classroom, which are often more beautiful than their embellished stage versions. And he found two exceedingly sensitive performers in Francisco Moncion and Tanaquil LeClercq."

## THE AGE OF ANXIETY

*Dramatic ballet in six scenes. Music by Leonard Bernstein. Choreography by Jerome Robbins. Scenery by Oliver Smith. Costumes by Irene Sharaff. Lighting by Jean Rosenthal. First presented by the New York City Ballet at the City Center, New York, February 26, 1950, with Tanaquil LeClercq, Francisco Moncion, Todd Bolender, and Jerome Robbins in the principal roles.*

Inspired by Leonard Bernstein's Second Symphony, *The Age of Anxiety*, and the poem by W. H. Auden on which this music is based, this ballet concerns the attempt four people make to find themselves. The ballet follows the sectional development of the poem and music.

THE PROLOGUE    The curtain rises on a scene that might be a public place in any part of a large modern city. A man enters on the left and walks slowly to the center of the stage. A girl appears on the right and walks toward him. Two men join the couple. All are strangers. The four figures stand opposite each other to form a small square, as if they were standing about a table. They sit together, become acquainted, discover mutual interests and a common problem, and with quiet, implicit understanding agree to set out on a journey together.

It is clear that each of these four people has something to fear. Their gestures and smallest movements are timorous and tentative. Because they do not know each other well, they seem always to be seeking something in their relationship to make it seem less odd that four strangers should meet and instantly, instinctively, feel a need to share each other's thoughts. Strangers they certainly are, but in their immediate awareness of a common problem their relation assumes an interested tenderness, a feeling of relief that companionship is still possible. All are humble in the face of this unstated problem, which seems at first to be loneliness. The journey they take together is a metaphor, a figure in dance terms, of the long exploratory conversation they begin to have in order to learn more of themselves and their age. The dance mirrors their talk.

THE SEVEN AGES    The four characters show us the life of man from birth to death in a set of seven variations. In the first variation, one of the men learns to stand, to walk, to articulate. In the words of Auden's poem:

Behold the infant, helpless in cradle and
Righteous still, yet already there is
Dread in his dreams at the deed of which
He knows nothing but knows he can do,
The gulf before him with guilt beyond,
Whatever that is, whatever why

> Forbids his bound; till that ban tempts him;
> He jumps and is judged: he joins mankind . . .

The girl comes forward and dances the second age. Her movements are warm and open, joyously happy. The girl is not only conscious of herself, but conscious of life about her, and displays an eagerness to participate in that life: she sacrifices part of herself to the world.

In the third variation, the four strangers meet love—the inevitable consequence of knowing and discovering something outside the self. It is love on an elemental, physical level, the love of extreme youth that recalls Auden's lines:

> Since the neighbors did,
> With a multitude I made the long
> Visitor's voyage to Venus Island . . .

The fourth age shows us the plight of social man, man thrust into the world of ambitions. Here he becomes aware for the first time of what he must do to climb the road to his ideal, how this road sometimes diverges and how he is perhaps deceived about his goal. Here he faces the problem of realizing a dream in an apparently dreamless world: which fork in the road shall he choose?

Now, in the fifth age, the dancers find material success and discover the price paid to achieve it. Here we imagine very easily a great modern city where nature is entirely absent, where everything moves on a fixed schedule, and where citizens are mere readers of timetables, conforming religiously to the demands of a huge machine that they have no power to control.

The sixth age shows us a reaction to this superhuman condition—disillusionment, a brief effort to rise above it, a danced argument as to which is better: to give in to the determinism of the city or to fight against it fearlessly. The four strangers split into two groups and take these differing points of view. At the end, one of the dancers tires. His fist moves to his mouth to stifle a yawn. He sits, curled up like a child.

In the final age, man has abandoned hope, abandoned his rage at human error, and ceased to have any reason to act. The dancer walks slowly, is ignored by passers-by. He reaches out, collapses, and is carried off. Slowly a figure moves across the stage, dragging behind him a long piece of crepe. The end has come. Man is dead and no longer a member of the minority.

THE SEVEN STAGES   The four figures come together again. They stand in a close line and move together awkwardly, reaching out in unison toward an invisible goal. They separate and look about, then start on a dream journey to find happiness.

Four figures dressed exactly like them, but with masks covering their faces, enter. Lines of masked creatures file in and dance between the four characters and their doubles, who imitate precisely the movements of the four.

One by one, and with different partners, the four strive for a goal where they will have no doubts and feel secure. They wander in a maze, lose their way, lose each other, then meet again safely. Nothing definite has been gained, but together they have had a harrowing common experience. They repudiate their doubles, pushing them aside. Now the four not only subconsciously know each other very well, but they are friends, too.

THE DIRGE   The four friends fall flat on their faces as the All-Powerful Father enters. This father symbol is depicted as a huge figure on stilts, a tin man of faith. He beckons to them with mechanical movements and stalks forward. They take courage and touch him. Other people enter and pay homage to the Father. It is interesting that he moves awkwardly, that he requires the assistance of his disciples. He is not so much a religious as a political figure: a representation of power that exists not through his own will alone. He sits on the shoulders of the crowd. The girl dances before him ecstatically, fascinated with the new-found rapid grace in movement his presence gives her. She reaches out to him supplicatingly. The Father responds to her plea by falling over, collapsing. The four regard him as the god that failed.

THE MASQUE   The exhausted girl falls against one of the boys. There is silence for a moment. Then carefree music blares out. The music simulates jazz, and the four characters cavort about the scene forgetting their problem in playful versions of jive. But soon their vigorous efforts to be cheerful begin to pall. One of them stops dancing and stomps in raging despair: it is the kind of protest of the half-intoxicated, the man who knew that drink would solve nothing at all. The girl curls up on the ground.

EPILOGUE   One of the men seems to die. The girl and another man go to him and help him. Now all four stand together as at the beginning of the ballet. They kneel together, then rise. The girl reaches out to the men, as if she wants to ask a final question the answer to which is very important to her. But they all have such questions. Gradually they turn and walk toward the four corners of the stage from which they came. Just before they exit, they turn and bow slightly to each other in gratitude for the faith they have given each other in the anxious age.

NOTES   W. H. Auden's *The Age of Anxiety: A Baroque Eclogue* was published in 1946. *The Age of Anxiety*, Leonard Bernstein's *Symphony No. 2 for Piano and Orchestra*, on which the ballet was also based, was first performed by the Boston Symphony Orchestra, Serge Koussevitzky conducting, on April 8, 1949. The composer was the piano soloist. At that time Bernstein offered a description of his work and its source, the poem by Auden. "The essential line of the poem (and of the music) is the record of our difficult and problematical search for faith. In the end, two of the characters enunciate the recognition of this faith—even a passive submission to it—at the same time revealing an inability to relate it personally in their daily lives, except through blind acceptance . . . If the charge of 'theatricality' in a symphonic work is a valid one, I am willing to plead guilty. I have a deep suspicion that every work I write, for whatever medium is really theatre music in some way . . ."*

* Program notes of the Philharmonic-Symphony Society of New York, 1949–50.

Jerome Robbins, who had collaborated with Bernstein on two ballets for Ballet Theatre, *Fancy Free* (1944) and *Facsimile* (1946), was inspired by the music to choreograph a new work, his second as Associate Artistic Director of the New York City Ballet. Robbins has pointed out, however, that his ballet is different from both the poem and the score: "It is a ritual in which four people exercise their illusions in their search for security. It is an attempt to see what life is about."

## AGON

*Music by Igor Stravinsky. Choreography by George Balanchine. Lighting by Nananne Porcher. First presented by the New York City Ballet at the City Center, New York, November 27, 1957, with Diana Adams, Melissa Hayden, Barbara Walczak, Barbara Millberg, Todd Bolender, Roy Tobias, Jonathan Watts, Arthur Mitchell, Roberta Lubell, Francia Russell, Dido Sayers, and Ruth Sobotka.*

While the New York City Ballet has in its repertory many works by Igor Stravinsky, *Agon* is the third Stravinsky ballet composed especially for our company. Lincoln Kirstein and I had always wanted a new Stravinsky work to follow *Orpheus*, and at first it seemed possible that this might be based on another Greek myth. We looked into a number of possibilities, but none of them seemed to work out. We began nevertheless to discuss possibilities of a new ballet with the composer. It was Stravinsky who hit upon the idea of a suite of dances based on a seventeenth-century manual of French court dances—*sarabandes, gaillards, branles*—he had recently come across. We all liked the idea, especially as Kirstein and I recalled Stravinsky's other masterful treatment of polkas and other dance forms, including ragtime rhythms. The title of the ballet, *Agon*, the Greek word for *contest, protagonist,* as well as *agony* or struggle, was a happy inspiration of Stravinsky's. It was to be the only Greek thing about the ballet, just as the dancing manual, the point of departure, was to be the only French.

Stravinsky and I met to discuss details of the ballet. In addition to the court dances, we decided to include the traditional classic ballet centerpiece, the *pas de deux,* and other more familiar forms. Neither of us of course imagined that we would be transcribing or duplicating old dances in either musical or dance terms. History was only the takeoff point.

We discussed timing and decided that the whole ballet should last about twenty minutes. Stravinsky always breaks things down to essentials. We talked about how many minutes the first part should last, what to allow for the *pas de deux* and the other dances. We narrowed the plan as specifically as possible. To have all the time in the world means nothing to Stravinsky. "When I know how long a piece must take, then it excites me." His house in California is filled with beautiful clocks and watches, friends to his wish for precision, delicacy, refinement. We also discussed in general terms the character each dance might have and possible tempos.

When we received the score I was excited and pleased and set to work at once. Sounds like this had not been heard before. In his seventy-fifth year Stravinsky had given us another masterpiece. For me, it was another enviable chance to respond to the impulse his music gives so precisely and openly to dance.

Music like Stravinsky's cannot be illustrated; one must try to find a visual equivalent that is a complement rather than an illustration. And while the score of *Agon* was invented for dancing, it was not simple to devise dances of a comparable density, quality, metrical insistence, variety, formal mastery, or symmetrical asymmetry. Just as a cabinetmaker must select his woods for the particular job in hand—palisander, angelique, rosewood, briar, or pine—so a ballet carpenter must find dominant quality of gesture, a strain or palette of consistent movement, an active scale of flowing patterns which reveals to the eye what Stravinsky tells the sensitized ear.

I was fascinated by the music, just as I had been fascinated and taught by Stravinsky's *Apollo* in the 1920s. As always in his ballet scores, the dance element of most force was the pulse. Here again his pulse built up a powerful motor drive so that when the end is reached we know, as with Mozart, that subject has been completely stated. Stravinsky's strict beat is authority over time, and I have always felt that a choreographer should place unlimited confidence in this control. For me at any rate, Stravinsky's rhythmic invention gives the greatest stimulus. A choreographer cannot invent rhythms, he can only reflect them in movement. The body is his medium and, unaided, the body will improvise for a little while. But the organizing of rhythm on a large scale is a sustained process, a function of the musical mind. To speak of carpentry again, planning a rhythm is like planning a house; it needs a structural operation.

As an organizer of rhythms, Stravinsky, I have always thought, has been more subtle and various than any single creator in history. What holds me always is the vitality in the substance of each measure. Each measure has its complete, almost personal life; it is a living unit. There are no blind spots. A pause, an empty space, is never empty space between indicated sounds. It is not just nothing. It acts as a carrying agent from the last sound to the next one. Life goes on within each silence.

*Agon* was written during the time of Stravinsky's growing interest in the music of Anton Webern and in twelve-tone music. He has said: "Portions of *Agon* contain three times as much music for the same clock length as some other pieces of mine." The score begins in an earlier style and then develops. The piece contains twelve pieces of music. It is a ballet for twelve dancers. It is all precise, like a machine, but a machine that thinks.

Like the score, the ballet is in three parts, performed without interruption. The first part consists of a *pas de quatre* for four boys, a double *pas de quatre* for eight girls and a triple *pas de quatre* for all twelve dancers. The curtain goes up before the music begins. There is no setting, only a plain backdrop. Four boys in practice clothes stand facing the back. They turn toward us quickly; as they step forward, the music begins, with a bright trumpet fanfare. The boys soon give way to eight girls. To a faster rhythm they, too, seem to be warming up. Then the boys come back and as the music, now a variation and development of the previous section, becomes more familiar and Stravinsky gives short solo passages to some of the principal instruments, the dancers stand in a state of readiness. Supported by the full confidence of the orchestra, all twelve dance.

There is another fanfare and three of the dancers, two girls and a boy, face us. They dance a *pas de trois*. The boy then dances a *sarabande*. Stravinsky's scoring is for solo violin, xylophone, tenor and bass trombone. This seems an odd combination on paper, but it is lovely in fact, and the contrast between the instruments is very interesting to the ear. The music changes then and we have the two girls dancing a *gaillard* featuring three flutes, chimes, mandolin, harp, and the lower strings in marvelous combinations. This gay dance with leaping steps merges into a coda for all three, as the boy comes back. The coda is the first piece in twelve-tone style and, now that our ears have been tuned in, we are ready for its complexities.

After a fanfare and a brief orchestral interlude again, the first *pas de trois* is replaced by another and the second part of the ballet begins with three *branles*. Descriptions of many old *branles* are available in dance histories, but my dances of course are improvisations. The two boys show off the girl, lifting her, balancing her, then she leaves.

Robert Craft says in his notes to the recording of *Agon* that Stravinsky saw an engraving in the old French manual depicting two trumpeters blowing accompaniment to a *branle simple* and that suggested the brilliant combination of those instruments for the next part, which is canon form. The two boys each take the part of one of the trumpets.

The *branle gai* is a solo for the girl, dominated by the rhythmic sound of castanets and the sort of dance style they suggest. The full orchestra then intervenes and the boys rejoin the girl for a final *branle double*.

Next comes the *pas de deux*, again after the fanfare and a short interlude. The music of the adagio is scored for strings, with a concertante part for the solo violin. There are variations for the boy, the music of which recalls the second *branle*, and the girl, and a coda. A brief quartet for mandolin, harp, violin, and cello is especially memorable in the score.

Four horns then recall the opening fanfare. The music for the first movement of the ballet is repeated and the piece ends as it began, with four boys dancing alone. They face the backdrop as the curtain falls.

In his book *Movement and Metaphor: Four Centuries of Ballet* (1970), Lincoln Kirstein, who commissioned *Agon* from Stravinsky for the New York City Ballet, has written interestingly about the background of the first production and given his impressions of the ballet. He writes that "the innovation of *Agon* lay in its naked strength, bare authority, and self-discipline in constructs of stressed extreme movement. Behind its active physical presence there was inherent a philosophy; *Agon* was by no means 'pure' ballet 'about' dancing only. It was an existential metaphor for tension and anxiety . . ."

Edwin Denby, the poet and critic, in *Dancers, Buildings and People in the Streets* (1965), fortunately now available in paperback, has written at length of "The Three Sides of *Agon*."

## ALBORADA DEL GRACIOSO

*Music by Maurice Ravel. Choreography by Jacques d'Amboise. Costumes by John Braden. Lighting by Ronald Bates. First presented at the New York City Ballet's Hommage à Ravel at the New York State Theatre, Lincoln Center, May 22, 1975, with Suzanne Farrell and Jacques d'Amboise in leading roles. Dedicated to Richard Boehm. Conducted by Robert Irving.*

Ravel composed this piece of music as "an experiment in writing music that would sound improvised." Written first for the piano, and later orchestrated, it was originally part of a suite called *Miroirs* which consisted of pieces dedicated to five friends of the avant-garde, the "Apaches."

An *alborada* is an instrumental early Spanish folk form translatable as "dawn song" or "morning serenade." A *gracioso* is a comic or grotesque lover, perhaps like Don Quixote. Later, the *alborada* developed into a kind of dance especially popular in the Spanish province of Galicia near the Basque country of Ravel's ancestry. This is the structure upon which Jacques d'Amboise based his ballet.

Writing after its premiere the critic Herbert Kupferberg reported to *The National Observer* that this ballet is "Jacques d'Amboise's most notable achievement."

## ALLEGRO BRILLANTE

*Classic ballet. Music by Tchaikovsky. Choreography by George Balanchine. Costumes by Karinska. Lighting by Jean Rosenthal. First presented by the New York City Ballet at the City Center, New York, March 1, 1956, with Maria Tallchief and Nicholas Magallanes; Carolyn George, Barbara Fallis, Barbara Millberg, Barbara Walczak, Arthur Mitchell, Richard Rapp, Jonathan Watts, and Roland Vasquez.*

Tchaikovsky's first piano concerto is played so often that many forget his other compositions for piano and orchestra. If my ballet to his second piano concerto, *Ballet Imperial,* has made that work better known, I am delighted. The music of his unfinished third piano concerto, Opus 75 in E Flat, has also seemed to me most appropriate for dancing. This was in fact the last music Tchaikovsky composed; he died less than a month after finishing the orchestration of the first movement, *Allegro Brillante,* on October 15, 1893. The composer had originally projected this music for use in a symphony, but after dismissing that idea, he rewrote the first movement for piano and orchestra and discarded the rest. As its marking suggests, the score is brisk and declarative but it is also deeply contemplative, I think.

The ballet is arranged for two principals and an ensemble. I had no narrative idea for the work, only wishing to have the dancers complement the music as best I could. The leading dancer of the work follows the piano in the cadenza, but her cavalier also has his important part, as do the supporting dancers, in conveying what I hope is the spirit of the work.

## L'AMOUR ET SON AMOUR (Cupid and His Love)

*Ballet in two scenes. Choreography by Jean Babilée. Music by César Franck. Settings and costumes by Jean Cocteau. First presented by Les Ballets des Champs-Élysées, at the Théâtre des Champs-Élysées, Paris, December 13, 1948, with Jean Babilée and Nathalie Philippart in the title roles. First presented in the United States by Ballet Theatre at the Metropolitan Opera House, New York, April 17, 1951, with Jean Babilée and Nathalie Philippart as* Cupid *and* Psyche.

The story is told in mythology of Psyche, the daughter of a great king, who was so beautiful that the goddess of love became jealous of her. Wrathful Venus thereupon sent to earth her son, Cupid, to excite the girl with a passion for a hideous and hateful man, as a penalty for thus emulating the most beautiful of all the goddesses. Cupid came to Psyche to fulfill Venus' designs, but was so enchanted by the girl's loveliness that he fell in love with her. Secretly he came to earth every night to visit Psyche, taking leave of her before the break of day to conceal his identity, lest Venus discover his treachery in love.

Psyche's sisters knew of these visits and in their jealousy instilled doubts within the girl's heart: why should a lover conceal himself in the dark? The next night Psyche vowed to see her lover. As he slept, she lighted a lamp and saw the handsome god. But a drop of oil from the lamp fell on Cupid's shoulder, and he awoke to see her watching him. The youthful god rose up, told Psyche that her lack of faith had spoiled their love, and vanished into the night.

The desperate girl waited night after night, but her lover never returned. She went in search of him, beseeching the help of all the gods and goddesses. At last she came to the temple of Venus and humbly invoked her aid. The goddess swore vengeance and devised for Psyche a series of tasks she must accomplish before she could find her love. Venus' instructions were so difficult to carry out that Psyche almost died in her efforts to fulfill them. But Cupid, observing her plight, encouraged and aided his love from afar.

Venus became reconciled to the girl's beauty and no longer despised her. Psyche joined Cupid in the heavens, and the two lived happily ever after. Psyche is the Greek word for soul, and the girl in this myth thus represents the human soul that strives and labors through insuperable difficulties to reach the supreme happiness of Olympus.

*L'Amour et Son Amour* does not recount the details of this story. Instead, the ballet strives to present the quality of the love that gave rise to the myth, to portray in movement the reunion of the god with the earth-bound girl and the attachment that made that reunion possible. The ballet carries a motto by

Jean Cocteau: "Love has no explanation—do not seek a meaning in love's gestures." The music is César Franck's *Psyché* Suite.

The subdued music begins slowly. A drop curtain, white against a misty violet, depicts the profile of a youth whose eyes are directed toward a small opening in the painted frame that contains his image. The music heightens slightly and subsides again as the violet of the curtain changes to green. The curtain rises. A bright backdrop, painted in the sunny colors of the Mediterranean, pictures an imaginary map; it is framed by a Greek design. The scene is earth.

Psyche enters on the right. A flesh-color, skintight bodice reveals the beauty of her body. About her waist she wears a dark net skirt. Her long dark hair reaches to her shoulders. She moves slowly, almost listlessly. The graceful poses she assumes become an impressionistic rendering of the flow of the music. She moves as in a dream.

A man enters on the left, then another. The two approach Psyche, kiss her hands, and pay tribute to her beauty. They lift her gently, and the girl moves in mid-air between them. They hold her as she poses ethereally, like a drifting cloud. She stands alone for a moment, enchanted by some distant reality the men know nothing of. They come close to her again, and the three dance. The girl's arms stiffen. Holding her hands, one of her partners lifts her to the other. Psyche leads the dance with soft gestures, as if to instruct her admirers in the realm of her imagination. Her arms gesture with tender voluptuousness.

The men leave her, and Psyche stands alone, her arms at her sides. The music whirs to announce the arrival of seven zephyrs, who enter breathlessly. Their misty green gowns float in the air behind them. They surround Psyche in a wide semicircle. She responds to them with a gesture of sudden awakening. The zephyrs kneel and bow their heads, and Psyche dances alone. The zephyrs rise, and she dances among them, taking their hands as they weave in and out into a close circle that encloses her. Their hands flutter over Psyche's head to the accompaniment of the harp. Psyche falls back in the arms of one of the zephyrs. Another comes and lifts her legs, and three zephyrs carry her off toward Olympus. The other zephyrs fly into the twilight. The drop curtain falls.

After a brief interlude, the scene changes. Now we are high in the heavens. It is night. White lines sketch in the outlines of great constellations made by twinkling stars. The sky is warm, midnight blue. Psyche enters on the left. She marvels at the spacious beauty of the scene, its limitless starry light. The zephyrs stand behind her as she dances with them. Psyche senses that her dream is about to come true. The zephyrs rush her off.

Cupid leaps in, seemingly sustained in the air by the white wings he wears. He circles the stage in bold and daring flight. He becomes thoughtful and kneels. He looks toward the left and beckons with a noble godlike gesture toward the light. He leaves the scene. Just as he steps off, Psyche enters with the zephyrs; she moves in retarded, slow motion. The glow of the sky darkens. Psyche lies down. The stars black out.

Cupid appears in a circle of soft white light that seems to emanate from his person. He moves his arms slowly, as if he were pulling effortlessly invisible wires. Psyche attempts to rise. Cupid goes to her. Now she stands, holding onto his shoulder for support. The young god puts his arm about the girl's waist in recognition, and the two dance, softly and slowly, backward and forward. The music mounts to a crescendo. The two lovers kneel together. Cupid rises, turns with tremendous speed. Psyche imitates his movement. He holds out his arms, and the girl rushes toward him. He catches her foot in his hands and carries her back swiftly as she hovers over him.

Psyche steps down and poses against Cupid's back. He kneels, and the girl walks around him as he holds her hand. The music gradually loses its intensity. The two dance together gently. The light dims. Cupid holds up his left hand. The girl circles the stage and disappears. The light fades. Cupid stands in his domain, governing the light of the stars with his hands. The stars lose their luster; the circle of light about the god narrows to a pin point.

# ANASTASIA

*Scenario and choreography by Kenneth MacMillan. First performed in a one-act version by the Ballet of the Deutsche Oper, Berlin, June 25, 1967, with Lynn Seymour in the title role. Music by Bronislav Martinu (Symphonic Fantasy). Introductory score by the Studio for Electronic Music of the Berlin Technical University. Designed by Barry Kay. Film scenes from the Aero Film production From Tsar to Stalin. Conducted by Ashley Lawrence. First given in three-act version by the Royal Ballet at the Royal Opera House, Covent Garden, London, July 22, 1971, with Lynn Seymour as Anastasia, Derek Rencher and Svetlana Beriosova as the Tsar and Tsarina, and Antoinette Sibley and Anthony Dowell as Kschessinska and her partner. Music for Acts One and Two by Peter Ilyich Tchaikovsky (Symphonies Nos. 1 and 3). Scenery and costumes by Barry Kay. First presented in the United States by the same ensemble with the same principals at the Metropolitan Opera House, New York, May 5, 1972.*

*The nursery was the center of all Russia's troubles.*
SIR BERNARD PARES

*Anastasia* tells the story of the royal Russian princess who survived, some believe, the Bolshevik Revolution to live on and recall her past. Robert Massie in his book about the last Russian Tsar and his wife, *Nicholas and Alexandra,* quotes an older relative of the real Anastasia, who knew the child well, the Tsar's sister, Grand Duchess Olga: "My telling the truth simply does not help in the least, because the public simply wants to believe the mystery." This three-act ballet relates the young Anastasia's early life in the Russian imperial family and concludes with a scene in a Berlin hospital in 1920 where A Woman Who Believes She Is Anastasia looks back on her story. The same dancer depicts both. Through Anastasia's personal history the Russian past and cataclysmic public events are telescoped and recaptured.

Tsar Nicholas II came to the Russian throne in 1894 at the age of twenty-six. His wife, Alexandra, bore him four daughters—Olga, Tatiana, Marie, Anastasia—and one son, his first heir, the Tsarevitch Alexei, a hemophiliac. The

Tsarina believed implicitly in the power of the Russian priest and mystic, Rasputin, to treat her son's bleeding.

The boy's tutor, the Swiss Pierre Gilliard, later wrote: "The illness of the Tsarevitch cast its shadow over the whole of the concluding period of Tsar Nicholas II's reign and alone can explain it. Without appearing to be, it was one of the main causes for his fall, for it made possible the phenomenon of Rasputin and resulted in the fatal isolation of the sovereigns who lived in a world apart, wholly absorbed in a tragic anxiety which had to be concealed from the world." And Alexander Kerensky, the Russian revolutionary leader removed by the Bolsheviks, declared: "Without Rasputin, there could have been no Lenin."

In March 1917 the Tsar abdicated as a result of the outbreak of revolutionary activity and, following the Bolshevik October Revolution that same year, the imperial family was imprisoned. On the night of July 16/17, 1918, the Tsar and his family were killed by Bolshevik forces at Ekaterinburg.

It was in 1920 that a woman patient in a Berlin hospital was recognized by some as one of the daughters of the Tsar. Since then this woman has endeavored to prove her identity as the Grand Duchess Anastasia.

ACT ONE: IN THE COUNTRYSIDE, AUGUST 1914   The imperial family is at a picnic in a birch grove by a lake with guests, who include the Tsarina's great friend Madame Vyrubova, Rasputin, and a group of naval officers. The party ends as the Tsar receives news of the outbreak of World War I.

The royal family is seen here to be a loving, close-knit group who have a congenial but necessarily distant relationship with the officers and courtiers who surround them. On this informal occasion, a picnic in the country, where the young can romp and play, where the Tsar can relax and take snapshots of his children, there is an illusion of tranquility broken only by the presence of young officers. Dominating the scene is the Tsarina's concern for her son and her faith in Rasputin's power to keep him from any dangerous accident. One of her relatives later recalled: "The Empress refused to surrender to fate. She talked incessantly of the ignorance of the physicians. She turned toward religion, and her prayers were tainted with a certain hysteria."

Anastasia, in a sailor blouse, enters on roller skates. She soon establishes a forthright, playful character, yet is considerate of others. She dances with three of the young officers who attend the family and, later, dances with her mother, who shows her the steps of an old Russian dance. When a telegram is brought to the Tsar and news of war breaks the calm, the soldiers and sailors in attendance begin to practice drills and maneuvers. The Tsar dances reassuringly with his wife, Rasputin leads them all in prayer, and there is a hope of victory. But one senses that it is a thin hope. The critic Peter Williams, remarking on the silver-birch setting of the scene, noted that some of the trees "have been cut down, with just their stumps showing, to suggest that the ballet opens where Chekhov's *Cherry Orchard* left off—a warning wind symbolic of the passing order."

ACT TWO: PETROGRAD, MARCH 1917   Despite rapidly growing unrest, the

Tsar is giving a ball to celebrate the coming out of his youngest daughter, Anastasia. He has invited his favorite ballerina—with whom he had a liaison before his marriage—to dance for his guests. Anastasia is puzzled by the outburst of revolutionary activity.

The setting of the ballroom, like the first act, is circular in form, with a circular staircase descending like a vortex just off-center. Before the ballroom, however, an outside scene, with slogans and discontent in the streets, reminds us of unrest among the Russian people.

In the ballroom itself, which contrasts vividly with the poverty we have just seen, there are ceremonial dances for the Tsar, the royal family, and their guests. Anastasia, who has come of age, looks lovely and has a new maturity. The ballerina Mathilda Kschessinka, one of the great Russian ballerinas, first dancer of the Maryinsky Theatre for more than twenty-five years, enters and with her partner performs a *pas de deux* to the second movement of Tchaikovsky's symphony. Favorite of the Tsar before his accession to the throne and later the wife of the Grand Duke Andrei, the real Kschessinkaya in fact left Russia to live in Europe, where she danced triumphantly and taught for many years. Margot Fonteyn, and numerous other dancers were among her students. She died in Paris, in 1971, at the age of 99.

Later, when the ballerina has changed from her costume to a ball gown and joined the party, there is a *pas de quatre* in which she appears with the Tsar, the Tsarina, and Rasputin. Kschessinkaya's partner later joins in that dance, where old and new relationships excite the participants. The young Anastasia watches her parents and their friends and is bewildered; coming of age is more complicated than she has imagined if life, and love, are like that. An officer who tries to involve Anastasia herself is repulsed.

Now the action shifts back to the unrest in the streets of St. Petersburg. Soon the populace and troops outside the palace interrupt the processions and formal dances of the ballroom. They invade the premises and the ball ends in disaster.

ACT THREE: SOME YEARS LATER   For the woman who believes she is Anastasia, past and present intermingle. She relives incidents from the years since the massacre of the Tsar and his family; her rescue by two brothers; the birth of her child; her marriage; the death of her husband; the disappearance of the child; her attempted suicide; the confrontation over the years with relatives of the imperial family who deny her identity as the Grand Duchess Anastasia.

The scene here is a Berlin hospital, where Anastasia sits on a white iron bed. She has recovered from a long period of unconsciousness and, reliving the past, is trying to find out who she is. Is she a plain person named Anna Anderson who has suffered simply a series of personal tragedies, or is she the Grand Duchess Anastasia who, in addition to personal misfortune, symbolizes another world? Filmed flashbacks of the past aid her memory of historic events, shown in newsreels and still photos, while her personal history and relationships are danced and depicted on stage. We see her rescue, the man who becomes her lover, their child, their happiness. This, too, is destroyed by another firing squad, for her husband is shot. She escapes yet again with his brother. Inter-mingled with the recapitulation of history and personal tragedy are confron-tations the girl endures with members of the imperial family who refuse to rec-ognize her as Anastasia. She herself, however, has no doubt; transcending all of her prolonged personal misfortune is her vivid recollection of the lovely past, when families might picnic under the silver birches and a young girl in a sailor suit might be so beloved by her parents that she would surely have a happy life. The ballet ends as we see Anastasia poised high at the foot of her hospital bed. The bed begins to move, coming toward us like an open royal limousine, it progresses; Anastasia, still and triumphant, receives silently the homage of the world.

Reflecting on Kenneth MacMillan's achievement in the three-act ballet form, Arlene Croce wrote in *The New Yorker* in 1974: "Of the three full-evening ballets MacMillan has produced so far, *Anastasia* seems to me the best, not so much because of what it achieves as because of what it attempts. In *Romeo,* MacMillan had before him both Leonid Lavrovsky's version for the Bolshoi and Cranko's for the Stuttgart; in *Manon* he is working à la Cranko. But in *Anastasia* he produced a personal fantasy about a global cataclysm entirely from nothing. I don't think he was being pretentious, and the insults that were showered upon him for missing the mark themselves missed the mark. Mac-Millan's taste, musical instinct, and technical skill place him first among those British and European choreographers whose careers began in the fifties."

## APOLLO (Apollon Musagète)

*Ballet in two scenes. Music and book by Igor Stravinsky. Choreography by George Balanchine. Scenery and costumes by André Bauchant. First pre-sented by Diaghilev's Ballets Russes at the Théâtre Sarah Bernhardt, Paris, June 12, 1928, with Serge Lifar as Apollo, Alice Nikitina as Terpsichore (Alexandra Danilova alternated with Nikitina in this role in the original production), Lubov Tchernicheva as Polyhymnia, and Felia Dubrovska as Calliope. First presented in the United States by the American Ballet at the Metropolitan Opera House, New York, April 27, 1937, with scenery and costumes by Stewart Chaney. Lew Christensen was Apollo; the three Muses were danced by Elise Reiman, Holly Howard, and Daphne Vane.*

To the Greeks, the god Apollo was many things: he was the god of prophecy, the god who punished wrongdoers, the god who helped those in trouble, the god of vegetation and agriculture, and the god of song and music. Apollo re-ceived different epithets, different names, for each of his various powers. Be-cause of his powers of song and music, he was also closely associated with the Muses, goddesses who represented the different arts and derived inspiration from Apollo's teaching. This ballet concerns itself with Apollo, leader of the Muses, the youthful god who has not yet attained the manifold powers for which he will afterward be renowned among men.

The three Muses of the ballet were selected for their appropriateness to the choreographic art. In the words of the composer, "Calliope personified poetry and its rhythm; Polyhymnia represents mime; Terpsichore, combining in herself both the rhythm and the eloquence of gesture, reveals dancing to the world and thus among the Muses takes the place of honor beside Apollo."*

The ballet begins with a brief prologue that depicts the birth of Apollo. Before the opening curtain, the string orchestra intimates the theme that will become identified with the god as the ballet progresses. This theme receives a rhythmic accompaniment from the lower strings, and the curtain rises.

The scene is Delos, an island in the Aegean Sea. It is night; stars twinkle in a dark blue sky. Back in the distance, in a shaft of light, Leto gives birth to the child whom the all-powerful Zeus has sired. She sits high on a barren rock and holds up her arms to the light. The music quickens, the woman buries her face in her hands, a hurried crescendo is cut off sharply, the strings are plucked, and Apollo is born. Leto disappears, and in the shaft of light at the base of the high rock stands the infant god, wrapped tightly in swaddling clothes. He hops forward stiffly to a swift, flowing melody.

Two handmaidens leap softly across the stage and come to Apollo. The newborn god falls back in their arms; his mouth moves in an inarticulate cry for help, and the two women begin to unwrap his swaddling clothes. They circle the god, unwinding the rich cloth, but before they can finish, Apollo spins suddenly and frees himself of the garment and looks about the dark world, not seeing clearly, not knowing how to move. After this burst of energy, he is frightened. His head is crowned with golden vine leaves and his body is endowed by nature with sinuous strength, but the young god is bewildered.

The two handmaidens bring to him a lute, sign of his future greatness in music. Apollo does not know how to hold the instrument. They place it in his hands and stand behind him, reaching out their hands to pluck the strings. Apollo follows their example and finds the first clue to his immortality. There is a blackout.

The musical statement that marked Apollo's birth is repeated sonorously. When the lights come on again, the scene is brilliant, as if a flash of lightning had been sustained and permanently illuminated the world. Apollo, dressed now in a short gold tunic, stands in the center of the stage. To the music of a solo violin, he plays upon the lute. He whirls his arms around and around in a large circle over the strings, seeming to draw music from the instrument with his youthful strength. Other strings now accompany the solo violin softly. Apollo places the lute on the ground and dances alone. He reaches out to the lute for inspiration and moves tentatively, carefully, but with a new-found ease. Now that he has proved his potential grace in movement, Apollo picks up the lute again. He turns slowly in attitude, holding the lute before him. The solo violin concludes the theme.

Three Muses appear to Apollo, walking slowly and respectfully toward him from three corners of the stage. With a godlike gesture, the god welcomes them. The young goddesses bow to him, then in unison bend in low arabesques

* From Igor Stravinsky, *An Autobiography*, Simon and Schuster, Inc., New York, 1936.

about the lute he holds high in his hands. They break this pose and stand together. The melody is strong yet moving, vigorous yet simple, like the youthful, inexperienced quality of the dance that now begins.

Apollo reaches out and, touching their hands gently, draws the Muses close to him. The three girls stand close together, one behind the other. Apollo takes their hands one by one. They pose in arabesque for an instant and move to the center of the stage. He motions two of the girls aside; Terpsichore, Muse of song and dance, falls back in his arms. He leaves her kneeling alone and, enclosing the other two girls in his arms, he lowers them slowly to the ground so that they also kneel.

Terpsichore rises and, dancing on point, slowly takes the hands of her sister Muses and encircles their kneeling figures. Now the three Muses stand again in a close line. The lower strings play the poignant theme with deep strength, and Apollo circles the stage in broad, free leaps as the girls move their arms in rhythm to the music.

The god returns to the Muses and supports each as she turns close to the ground. The girls form a line behind Apollo and move across the back of the stage, their bold, youthful figures imitating the dance of their leader. The girls pause and kneel, then rise at once. Apollo, arms outstretched, supports them as they hold hands and form a circular tableau.

When this tableau is broken, the Muses form a close line in front of Apollo. This line moves backward as one, the young god and goddesses shuffling awkwardly on their heels. The line comes to a rest. The three girls stand motionless; Apollo bends down and tenderly pushes them into motion with his shoulder. Led by Terpsichore, the Muses dance alone. The melody ends.

Apollo presents each of the Muses with the symbol appropriate to her art. To Calliope, Muse of poetry, he presents a tablet; to Polyhymnia, Muse of mime, a mask that symbolizes unearthly silence and the power of gesture; and to Terpsichore, Muse of dancing and song, he gives a lyre, the instrument that accompanies those arts. The Muses accept these gifts with delight and respect, form a line, and hop like pleased children to the side of the stage. Apollo commands the Muses to create and sits to watch what they will do.

Calliope comes forward with her tablet. She holds it out before her, then clutches it to her heart. Placing the tablet on the ground, she dances. The melody she moves to is based in form on the Alexandrine, the classical heroic measure of French poetry. Her dance is emotional, yet not weakly so; as she circles the stage before Apollo, her leg boldly sweeps the air before her. She is scribbling hastily on the palm of her hand when her dance nears its end, wondering if she has done well. She becomes a little sad, the music seems to cry out softly with her, and she goes to show Apollo what she has written. He does not approve.

Brilliant chords herald the dance of Polyhymnia, who soon puts her mask aside and dances rapidly to a sprightly, rhythmic melody. The girl holds her finger to her lips throughout the dance, as she tries to maintain the dignity of her mask, but her youthful enthusiasm gets the best of her: she forgets—as she responds to the happy, worldly music—and before she knows what has happened, her lips have moved and she has spoken. Terrified, she claps her hands over her mouth, punishing her own naughtiness, but Apollo sees what she has done and censures her.

Terpsichore comes forward and dances in profile with her lyre. She holds the instrument high above her head, her curved arms suggesting the shape of the lyre, and her feet pluck at the ground as if they played upon it. She moves adroitly and sharply, with assured grace; the gestures she makes with her arms as she poses in a series of balanced arabesques show us that her whole body is coordinated to beauty. The music she dances to is similar in melody to Calliope's, but the rhythm is different; like her dance, it is more pointed, less romantic. Of all the Muses, she alone dances perfectly, and Apollo commends her.

Now the young god dances alone. Majestic chords announce the theme of his variation. He reaches his arms up toward Olympus, leaps grandly into the air, then kneels. To the quiet rhythms of the music, Apollo performs with ideal perfection, setting an example to the Muses and reminding us that he himself has acquired the skill he demands of them.

As his dance ends, Apollo sits on the ground in a graceful, godlike pose. Terpsichore appears before him and touches his outstretched hand. The young goddess steps over his arm and bends low in extended arabesque beside him. Now the girl rises and sits on Apollo's knees. He holds his arm up to her, she takes it, and both rise to dance a muted *pas de deux*. The melody is softly lyrical, but at the same time strong; it depicts in sound an awakening of Olympian power and strength, beauty and grace.

Apollo supports Terpsichore in extended arabesque, lifts her daringly high so that her body curves back over his shoulder, holds her as she extends her legs and sinks on the ground to rise on point in graceful extensions. She pirouettes swiftly and sharply in his arms then entwines herself around Apollo. The music brightens, they separate, dancing playfully, then meet again. Both kneel. Apollo puts his head in Terpsichore's open hands. Now, at the end, she falls across Apollo's back as the god bends down to give the Muse a short swimming lesson as a reward for her beautiful dancing. Her arms push the air aside as if they were moving in the water. When Apollo rises, Terpsichore's body is curved against him.

Calliope and Polyhymnia rush in and join Apollo and Terpsichore in a joyous coda in which the Muses surround Apollo with their new-found pleasure in movement. The young god, in their midst, holds out his arms; two of the girls grab hold, and he swings them through the air. The quick grace of the Muses is accompanied by lively, shifting rhythms in the music that rushes to a finish. Apollo takes them by the hand and drives all three across the stage in a swift chariot race. As the music ends, Apollo stands alone. The three girls walk toward him together and in unison clap their palms. Apollo leans down and places his head against their hands.

From on high, Zeus calls his son Apollo home with mighty crescendos of sound. Apollo stands motionless, as if under a spell, listening. The three Muses sit upon the ground. Apollo walks slowly around them. As he stands in back of them and reaches out over them, the three girls lift their feet to meet his hand. Apollo blesses them with a noble gesture. The Muses reach their arms up, and

Apollo lifts them up beside him. For a moment the arms of the four figures are entwined, then the three Muses pose in arabesque behind Apollo's profiled figure to form a tableau in which the goddesses are as one with him.

Now Apollo takes their hands and draws them like a chariot across the stage. He takes them to the foot of the high rock, then walks forward and begins to climb to the summit, pointing the way to Olympus. The Muses follow. The four figures are silhouetted against the sky, holding out their arms to the sun. Leto, Apollo's mother, falls back in the arms of his handmaidens as she reaches up to her son in farewell.

NOTES  *Apollo* is not the kind of ballet most people expect to see when they know its name. When the ballet was first performed, a French critic said that this was not Apollo at all, that the choreographer had cultivated the deliberately odd, that Apollo would never have done this, or this, or this, etc. When the critic was asked how he knew what Apollo would have done, he had no answer. He was thinking of some familiar statue of Apollo, the Apollo Belvedere perhaps, and imagined that a ballet about the god would personify sculptural representations. But *Apollon Musagète* is not Apollo Belvedere; he is the wild, half-human youth who acquires nobility through art.

Stravinsky's *Apollon Musagète* was originally commissioned by Elizabeth Sprague Coolidge and received its first performance at the Library of Congress in Washington on April 27, 1928, with choreography by Adolph Bolm, who danced the principal role. Ruth Page (Terpsichore), Elise Reiman (Calliope), and Berenice Holmes (Polyhymnia) were the three Muses. After this first performance, Stravinsky offered the score to Diaghilev, who assigned the ballet to me.

This was the second time I had worked closely with Stravinsky's music (*Le Rossignol* was a first attempt, an exercise set me by Diaghilev in 1925). *Apollo* was a collaboration. As I wrote in *Stravinsky in the Theatre*, "I look back upon the ballet as the turning point in my life. In its discipline and restraint, in its sustained oneness of tone and feeling, the score was a revelation. It seemed to tell me that I could, for the first time, dare not use all my ideas; that I, too, could eliminate. I began to see how I could clarify, by limiting, by reducing what seemed to be myriad possibilities to the one possibility that is inevitable.

"In studying the score, I first understood how gestures, like tones in music and shades in painting, have certain family relations. As groups they impose their own laws. The more conscious an artist is, the more he comes to understand these laws and to respond to them. Since working with Stravinsky on this ballet, I have developed my choreography inside the framework such relations suggest."

Stravinsky, in his 1936 *Autobiography*, notes that the invitation to compose a ballet for a contemporary music festival in Washington gave him an opportunity to carry out an idea that had long appealed to him, "to compose a ballet founded on moments or episodes in Greek mythology plastically interpreted by dancing of the so-called classical school . . . I had especially in my thoughts what is known as the 'white ballet,' in which to my mind the very essence of this art reveals itself in all its purity. I found that the absence of many-colored effects and of all superfluities produced a wonderful freshness. This inspired me to write of an analogous character. It seemed to me that diatonic composition was the most appropriate for this purpose, and the austerity of its style determined what my instrumental ensemble must be. I set aside the ordinary orchestra because of its heterogeneity . . . and chose strings.

"On June 12, 1928, I conducted the first production of *Apollo* . . . in Paris . . . George Balanchine, as ballet master, had arranged the dances exactly as I had wished—that is to say, in accordance with the classical school. From that point of view it was a complete success, and it was the first attempt to revive academic dancing in a work actually composed for the purpose. Balanchine . . . had designed for the choreography of *Apollo* groups, movements, and lines of great dignity and plastic elegance as inspired by the beauty of classical forms . . .

"As for the dancers, they were beyond all praise. The graceful Nikitina with her purity of line alternating with the enchanting Danilova in the role of Terpsichore; Tchernicheva and Dubrovska, those custodians of the best classical traditions; finally, Serge Lifar, then still quite young, conscientious, natural, spontaneous, and full of serious enthusiasm for his art—all these formed an unforgettable company."

The importance of *Apollo* to the history of ballet has been described by Lincoln Kirstein: "*Apollon Musagète* introduced to ballet in its time a spirit of traditional classicism absent since Petipa's last compositions almost thirty years before. It demonstrated that tradition is not merely an anchorage to which one returns after eccentric deviations but the very floor which supports the artist, enabling him securely to build upon it elements which may seem at first revolutionary, ugly, and new both to him and to his audience. *Apollon* has now lost for us the effects which offended, irritated, or merely amused an earlier public. We forget that much of the 'modernism' of adagio movement in our classic dance derives directly from *Apollon;* that many ways of lifting women, of turning close to the floor, of subtle syncopation in the use of *pointes,* of a single male dancer supporting three women, were unknown before *Apollon.* These innovations horrified many people at first, but they were so logical an extension of the pure line of Saint-Léon, Petipa, and Ivanov that they were almost immediately absorbed into the tradition of their craft.

"Glenway Wescott said that instead of *Apollo, Leader of the Muses,* the ballet should have been entitled *Apollo's Games with the Muses.* The mimed athletics, the strenuous atmosphere of violent physicality recall the nervousness of runners before a race. Each variation seems a training for the final translation to Olympus. In the chariot-race finale which evokes memories of the profiles on Roman coins and cameos and of the decathlon, visualized in the newly extended idiom of Russian ballet, a transformation of the Olympic games into contemporary dancing takes place. Of all Balanchine's works *Apollon* is the most significant historically, the most compact, the most influential . . ." (In "Balanchine Musagète," *Theatre Arts,* November 1947.)

North German Television in 1967 made a film of rehearsals and a performance of *Apollo.* A spoken commentary by John Drummond described the occasion, in which Stravinsky and I participated. The dancers were Jacques d'Am-

boise as Apollo, Suzanne Farrell as Terpsichore, Gloria Govrin as Calliope, and
Patricia Neary as Polyhymnia.

# APPARITIONS

*Dramatic ballet in three scenes with prologue and epilogue. Music by Franz
Liszt. Choreography by Frederick Ashton. Book by Constant Lambert. Sce-
nery and costumes by Cecil Beaton. First presented by the Sadler's Wells
Ballet at the Sadler's Wells Theatre, London, February 11, 1936, with
Robert Helpmann as the Poet and Margot Fonteyn as the Woman in Ball
Dress. First presented in the United States by the Sadler's Wells Ballet at
the Metropolitan Opera House, New York, October 25, 1949, with the same
principals.*

The inspiration of a poet is the subject of this romantic ballet. Here the poet
derives his work not from real life, or from anything connected with it, but
from the realm of the fantastic imagination, from apparitions. The ballet thus
depicts the poet as character rather than creator, as a victim of the apparitions
he finds it necessary to invoke. The scenario of *Apparitions* was suggested by
the synopsis Hector Berlioz wrote for his *Symphonie Fantastique*. The music,
orchestrated by Gordon Jacob, was selected from the later works of Franz
Liszt by Constant Lambert.

PROLOGUE   The curtain rises on a scene representing the poet's study. It is
an immense, dark, high-ceilinged room with great leaded windows—the kind of
room in which we think instantly of hidden shadows lurking in the corners. It
is night. On the right, a lamp stands upon a desk. Seated at the desk is the
poet. He is evidently engrossed in composition, for at first he does not look up.
Soon, however, he rises and gestures impatiently. His poem is not progressing
as he would wish; he seems to require a fresh stimulus to continue.

The poet is astonished as light appears outside the windows. He is amazed
further when he observes in the window frames mysterious apparitions. There
stands a beautiful young woman in a formal ball dress, there a handsome hussar, and there a monk. Immediately the poet is enamored of the woman, who
smiles at him in recognition. He sees in her an idealized version of all women,
a picture of the perfect romance, and for a few moments he imagines that he
has the key to the end of the poem he has been writing. But the woman and
the other figures disappear. He reaches out toward them, then turns and sits
again at his desk. Now his inspiration is so intense that words will not come.
His mind is preoccupied with the source of his inspiration rather than the lines
she might assist him to create. His mind whirls with romance. He gives up in
impatience, abandons the poem, and takes a potion to induce sleep. The curtain falls.

SCENE ONE: A BALLROOM   Now the scene shifts to the locale of the poet's
dream. The curtain rises on a ballroom, where fashionable couples are danc-

ing. The poet enters, observes the scene, and wishes to participate in the discreet gaiety, but the dancers look through him as if he were the empty air. At a pause in the dancing, the lovely woman in the ball dress enters the room. All the men—particularly a handsome, swashbuckling hussar—are deferential to her dark beauty and vie for her favor. The dancing recommences. In this new dance, the women change partners constantly, and suddenly the poet is holding in his arms the apparition that delights him. But she is unaware that she has seen him before and turns her head away to catch sight of the hussar. She leaves the scene when the hussar rejoins her, and soon the ballroom is empty. The poet, alone, despairs.

SCENE TWO: A SNOW-CLAD PLAIN    The dream changes, and the poet finds himself in the lonely winter forest. He longs for the reappearance of the woman, but imagines that she will again reject him. He hears bells in the distance, wonders what they are for, and dancers who wear skirts shaped like bells move around and around him, giving vivid expression to his romantic hallucination.

A funeral procession enters. Cloaked figures carry the body of the deceased on a bier. The poet is startled to see that the procession is led by the monk who appeared in the window of his study. Now he has seen again all three: the girl, the hussar, and the monk. Is this the end? What will happen? Will his dream be resolved?

He is drawn to the bier. Before the monk can prevent it, he snatches away the burial cloth and discovers the face of his beloved. Again he despairs. The monk reprimands him. The procession moves on. The poet falls to the ground to weep and to pray.

SCENE THREE: A CAVERN    The scene now is a dark, secluded cavern. Creatures in red costumes have gathered here to practice some secret, magical rite. The poet joins them, seems to be accepted among them, rejoices, then falls back aghast as he sees before him the creature of his imagination, her face defaced, grotesque, ugly. The poet disclaims responsibility for his dream and seeks to escape. The woman is now attracted to him and will not let him go. The poet faints. As he passes into deep unconsciousness, her face miraculously takes on its previous apparent beauty.

EPILOGUE    The final curtain rises on the poet's study. He is still asleep. Gradually he wakens. He cannot shake off his dream, and as he pieces it together, he sees the dream as a telling, romantic poem on his own pursuit of romanticism—a perpetual destruction of the self in the seeking of the unattainable. He kills himself.

The woman of his imagination enters and grieves. She turns her face away as cloaked figures take up the poet's body.

# ARENA

*Music by Morton Subotnick. Choreography by Glen Tetley. Lighting by John B. Read, executed by Gilbert V. Hemsley, Jr. First presented by the Netherlands Dance Theatre at the Royal Theatre, The Hague, February 4, 1969. First presented in the United States by the Stuttgart Ballet at the Metropolitan Opera House, Lincoln Center, New York, June 4, 1975, with Richard Cragun, Egon Madsen, and Dieter Ammann in leading roles.*

When *Arena* was first danced, the choreographer has recalled, critics tried to read into it the Cretan myth of the Minotaur—doubtless because the composer of its electronic score, Morton Subotnick, had given his work the title *The Wild Bull.* "But I did not consciously intend any such meaning," Tetley has said. "The relationships that I tried to portray arose solely from the kinds of movement that I wanted to use, and from tensions implicit in the music. However, for the sake of those who find it hard to get by without some kind of 'plot,' let me essay the following interpretation: The ballet seems to me rather like a set of variations on the theme of might, dominance, pure power. When people are forced into close proximity, the mutual tensions can lead to an explosion of violence, which may manifest itself on either a physical or spiritual plane. These were the thoughts that had been suggested to me by the music."

The action of *Arena,* which is danced by six men, takes place in an undefined space from which there is apparently no clear escape. A struggle develops between two of the men; jealousy and love in varied ways are displayed until one of the major participants, in understandable rage, begins to throw chairs around the stage.

The dancer and writer James Waring reported to *Ballet Review* in 1971, after the ballet's premiere: "*Arena* is about self-doubt, and self-confidence, and their oscillation. The six men are gladiators of some sort, in a circus of the mind. Three of them function mostly as decor. Of the other three, Frans Vervenne (sometimes, Harmen Tromp) sleeps on a pile of nesting chairs. Hans Knill is a final challenger who overcomes the principal figure, Jon Benoit. The ballet unfolds in a series of physical challenges, alternating with periods of retreat."

# ASTARTE

*Created and choreographed by Robert Joffrey. Music performed by Chamberlain, conducted by Hub Miller. Commissioned score composed by Crome Syrcus. Lighting design and set by Thomas Skelton. Costumes by Hugh Sherrer. Film created and photographed by Gardner Compton. Produced by Midge Mackenzie. First presented by the City Center Joffrey Ballet at the City Center, New York, September 20, 1967, with Trinette Singleton and Maximiliano Zomosa.*

Astarte, moon goddess of love and fertility, borrowed from the Babylonian-Assyrian Ishtar by the Greeks, is the heroine of this multimedia work. Astarte gave herself to all men, but was owned by none. She has been called the patron goddess of Women's Liberation, lover and destroyer, bestower of both life and death. The ballet that celebrates her powers uses music (an acid-rock score specially commissioned) amplified dramatically, lights (incandescent and strobe), film, and dance in the first combination of these elements in the theater of ballet. Techniques and impressions familiar in the discothèque are here, melded with dance to produce a dramatic *pas de deux* unlike any seen before.

What happens in general is simple. As the music starts full volume, the darkened theater is suddenly filled with varied kinds of light. A steadily blinking strobe stares out from the front of the stage so that no one in the audience can see for a moment of necessary adjustment; the stage itself begins to have some light on it, and searching spotlights are aimed at the audience, trying to find we know not what.

We soon find out. The backcloth of the setting on stage is a tightly stretched white cloth pulled in at the center like a belly button, and, against a drop farther back, a frantic film is being projected, of frantic birds and a hypnotic girl —the goddess Astarte. The seeking spotlights find a boy seated on the aisle in the audience as the eye of the goddess winks. He rises, transfixed by her glance, and slowly makes his way down the center aisle of the theater as we all watch. He crosses then to the right, toward steps to the stage, meanwhile looking at the stage at the goddess who has materialized before us. He goes up on stage and, standing there, still staring alone at the eyes of the goddess, begins to take off his clothes—all of them, down to his briefs, as her image looms huge above him on the screen. Soon his image, too, is seen to merge with hers. The rock singer has begun to sing, and the boy puts his clothes tenderly on the ground under the watching eye of the mysterious girl. He now goes to her, holding out his hands and, reaching her, molding them to her body. She steps forward then, and he begins to hold her in a dance that is anticipated, gesture by gesture, by the film that wraps around them and shows through them. The dance is slow, cool, collected, as the music blasts, and the boy and the goddess who controls him are in a different world, out of all contact with those who watch. There is no appeal here for attention to the spectator; there is only attention to each other, and the spectators are beyond reality. The boy in his dance worships the girl as he maneuvers her, lifts her, touches her. He attempts in mounting frenzy for a moment to control and subdue her as an erection rises in the stretched jersey of backcloth, and to kiss her. Then the music quietens. In the film we see his body branded with the impress of the goddess's as his passion is spent. She lets down her hair, and the dance of engulfment continues relentlessly, he, as always, powerless to resist her beauty and powerless, too, completely to claim her. He falls back, and, in the film, we see him somersault in pain and fall forward so that she in triumph can cause him to writhe at her feet.

She hovers over him as the rapid pulse of the strobe illumines them. She raises her leg over him, and the boy crouches there below her. Then, holding her above him, he rises and, before we realize it, he is carrying her and displaying her curved body aloft, as the filmed image has already anticipated, her legs locked about his head, his hands clasping her ankles. It is a posture of glory for the remote goddess and proud submission for the boy. He kneels at last so that she can step down. Before he realizes it, she is gone. The backdrop dissolves, and the boy walks back, back, through the back wall of the stage, where huge, high doors open for him, through the storage of scenery and props, to the exit to the street. These doors, too, open for him and, still transfixed by the goddess and his joy in her, he moves out into the light and traffic, perhaps to rejoin the world.

NOTES  Gardner Compton, who created the films for *Astarte*, has had some interesting things to say about its composition. Writing in *Dance Magazine*, he said: "The discothèque is the temple of electricity with its light shows, audio-visual devices such as film (which, in essence, is merely the reproduction of light), and other visual effects. In these new temples, some dance to electronic music while others sit in small groups on the floor watching the God Electricity (Light) perform on the walls and ceilings. The milieu of *Astarte* was precisely this new house of worship.

"One of the elements of this new creed is the use of multimedia devices to obtain involvement. *Astarte* sought to bridge the gap between the loose, unrefined area of the happening and a legitimate art form—in this case, ballet. What Robert Joffrey and I tried to avoid was the looseness of form characteristic of the happening. Our concept was more classical in nature. The choreographer was using movement in a magnificent sustained counterpoint to the amplified acid-rock music. It was the dancers who were receiving the audio massage, a massage that tuned them *out* on the world of the audience. In so doing we hoped that the fantasy of the film media combined with the reality of the dancers would tune *in* the audience on the ritualistic milieu of the discothèque.

"But *Astarte* was merely a beginning, a primer for what is to come. It is only one of the first steps in the direction of a totally involved multi-media theatre experience. And I believe this will be a vital concept of the whole.

"In order for choreo-cinema to be successful, there must be a perfect blending of these concepts to form one unified artistic viewpoint. . . . I remember Martha Graham giving an image in class that made first position a reality to me. The essence of that image was as follows: Your arms are carried from the back as though you are standing in a shower and the water is like energy draining down the arm and off the middle fingers of the hands. A cameraman should film a dancer so that the last object to leave the frame is that portion of the body that moves the energy from space to space. The camera itself should also move the energy from one space to another, or it is not contributing. Timing and framing are the essential tools of a dance cameraman. One must frame on space and let the dancer move into it. Space is the dancer's canvas, whether on stage or on film. Both space and movement, too, may have to be modified or distorted to make the choreo-cinema effective to an audience.

"The camera is the eye of the audience, the establisher of the involvement, the point of view, the movement. Why should the joy of movement be limited to the dancers? The members of the audience, too, can enjoy it, but only if the camera works for them. Thus if someone were to ask me the difference between a *pas de deux* on stage and a *pas de deux* on film I would answer as follows: A *pas de deux* on stage is a dance for two people (usually a boy and a girl), whereas a *pas de deux* on film is a dance for a boy, a girl, *and* camera. If cinematographic movement techniques are used successfully with dance, a successful marriage can result. One must wed the movement of one art to the movement of the other in order to achieve a true choreographic end.

"In *Astarte*, Robert Joffrey choreographed for the stage. What I filmed was Joffrey's choreography (even the abstract images are derived from images of the dancers themselves). However, I selected and chose for my camera, making the film very different from what the dancers were doing on stage. Often to reach a total choreographic concept, I borrowed the fugue form from music. I repeated themes in such a way that the movement would start with the live dancers and then be repeated and built through film, although the dancers on stage were then doing something altogether different. At other times the film would initiate the theme and then the dancers would echo it and build it to climax which the film would again pick up. . . ."*

## AS TIME GOES BY

*Music by Franz Josef Haydn. Choreography by Twyla Tharp. Lighting by Jennifer Tipton. Costumes by Chester Weinberg. Assistant to Miss Tharp: Harry Berg. First presented by the City Center Joffrey Ballet at the City Center, New York, October 24, 1973. Conducted by Seymour Lipkin.*

*As Time Goes By* is a dance ballet to wonderful music by Haydn—the third and fourth movements of the *Symphony No. 45 in F-Sharp Minor*. Mozart once said, I think, that Haydn's music had given him immense amusement and also the deepest reflections. Mozart, as usual, was right. The music here is the famous *"Farewell" Symphony*, where the players get up and leave the stage one by one. What the choreographer does with that situation, and with other plots and developments of the music, is her own special business. The critic Marcia B. Siegel described it for *Dance Magazine:* "Beatriz Rodriguez' opening solo in silence is allegro ballet laced with those odd dislocations of body parts, those big transformations with smooth, almost lazy recoveries that we've come to think of as Tharpian. As Haydn's minuet begins, five other dancers join her and they slip through a long chain of decorous attitudes and preparations that melt or click into surprise partnerships. Haydn leaves the music dangling on an unfinished cadence, and the dancers redeploy themselves to begin The Four Finales, a glorious rout in which you can just pick out elements of various overworked dance endings, exits, and climaxes, all overlapped and out of joint and meticulously mistimed. Finally, to Haydn's famous adagio, where the musicians leave one by one, Larry Grenier spins out an extraor-

* Reprinted by courtesy of *Dance Magazine*.

linary solo in one long, sinuous, self-involved phrase of movement, while the stage fills with dancers and empties again. You can't remember where he came from and you can't imagine where he'll stop. The curtain goes down while he's still dancing.

"I'm not inclined to take the title of *As Time Goes By* too seriously—it might have come about by accident. A harried person from the Joffrey publicity department runs into the studio a week before the première and pleads: 'Twyla, time is going by. The papers are screaming. We've got to have a title for your ballet!' Without taking her eyes off the rehearsal, Tharp mutters: 'Okay, call it *As Time Goes By*. Now don't bother me.'

"However that was, the ballet seems more concerned with continuity than with time itself. It shows us the bridges between things, the awkward foldings that precede the beautiful unfoldings, the movements that connect rather than the poses that separate. The beginning is the end is the beginning. Amen."

Arlene Croce, dance critic of *The New Yorker,* has written of Twyla Tharp's work in the November 19, 1973, issue of that magazine:

"Twyla Tharp is the Nijinska of our time. *Deuce Coupe,* an unidealized portrait of American youth in the nineteen sixties, is her *Les Biches,* and *As Time Goes By,* an abstract fantasy about individuals against the blank canvas of a tribal society, is her *Les Noces.* Of course I'm generalizing, but not, I hope, idly. *As Time Goes By,* created this season for the Joffrey Ballet and employing an all-Joffrey cast and Haydn music, is a study of classical dancing. Its 'tribal' ethos is that of young, hard-working New York-American dancers, subspecies Joffrey, and its light-speckled fancies and serene inversions of classical principles are as far from the iron wit of *Les Noces* as the heterogeneous home-style social dances of *Deuce Coupe* are from the monolithic encounters of that Parisian salon in *Les Biches.* Nevertheless, the parallel persists between Twyla Tharp and ballet's greatest woman choreographer. I think that, like Nijinska's, Twyla Tharp's work exacts a primitive force of expression from its subject, which is classical ballet. It seems to seek out first principles and turn them over with curiosity, finding new excitement in what lies on the other side of orthodoxy. And it gains a secondary kind of raw power from what seem deliberate lapses from ballet decorum and refinement. Sometimes, a classical step is resolved with a new twist; it forms itself and then re-forms itself backward. But sometimes the step isn't all there; it seems truncated or only half-quoted; the effect is of a surgical cut, a slash at the fat body of unusable style. The negations and distortions of Nijinska's choreography cut away rhetorical flab. The turned-in toes and obsessive stiff pointwork of *Les Noces* were a radical distortion, necessary if women's feet and not simply their points were to become significant once more on the stage. In much the same way, Twyla Tharp is moving toward a new quality of plain speech in classical choreography. At times, she seems to be on the verge of creating a new style, a new humanity, for classical-ballet dancers. If she doesn't go all the way to a full enunciation of that style, that is probably because the ballet is not long enough. Time, in this ballet, goes by much too fast.

"*As Time Goes By* is in four sections, quasi-dramatic in their progression. Beginning with the Individual, it moves on to the Group, then to the Mass, and finally back to the Individual. (These designations are my own; I prefer them to the unevocative titles in the program.) The opening solo is danced by Beatriz Rodriguez in silence. It is a concise statement of the material that will be developed, a ball of string that will be unwound. We see semaphore arms, snake hips, pirouettes stopped in mid-whirl, a paroxysm of flexions in *relevé*. Rodriguez, who looked childlike in *Deuce Coupe,* is transformed again. She is monumental, like a Nijinska iron woman. Three boys and two girls join her (Adix Carman, Henry Berg, William Whitener, Eileen Brady, and Pamela Nearhoof) and the music begins—the Minuet and Trio of Haydn's *'Farewell'* *Symphony.* The dance that accompanies it is not one dance but six—one for each member of the sextet. All six dances go on at the same time, now linking up, now separating, and the whole moving from one tight cellular cluster to another. This sextet, which builds up the fascination and the deadpan humor of a clockwork toy, is a classical arrangement of the Tharpian group dance and typically democratic. The multifocal viewpoint makes a special event of the partnering (which keeps changing hands). It also eliminates the conventional hierarchy of the ballet ensemble. No one here is a ballerina; anyone may partner or be partnered. The sextet builds up pressure, too. The little hexagonal unit seems to become more and more confining, but the sweet musicianship of the choreography keeps the scene clear, its density unharrowing.

"The music breaks off, and one of the girls does a little walk-around in silence as new dancers enter. The Presto movement of the symphony starts. Suddenly, the stage seems to expand to unbelievable size. Dancers pour on and spread out. The broadened pattern has released us, but the tempo has stepped up the pressure, and we redouble our concentration. Now, against a complex background of moving dancers, solo variations occur; one, for Nearhoof, is galvanically funny, though at this breathless speed the laughs can't keep up with the jokes. Nor can we keep up with the ballet. There is no time to ponder the new logic of the steps—new in the way they combine close musical fit with a 'natural' loose look suited to each individual dancer; there's just time enough to enjoy it. One would like the key to that new logic; what makes it work at this tempo? Whatever it is, the result is a hyperkinesthesia that takes hold of the audience and doesn't let up until, once more, Haydn waves his wand and the dancers stroll nonchalantly away.

"The end of the piece is as Haydn would have wished it. To the Adagio finale of the *'Farewell'*—so called because the instrumentation thins out until only two violins are left—a dancer (Larry Grenier, whose attenuated lyrical style is itself a statement of slackening force) moves alone while others set about disappearing in a fashion that is unpredictable and sometimes chancy. A girl leaves, only to return a moment later. A boy lifts a girl off, turning her twice in the air, so another girl has to duck three times to avoid being hit. Ultimately, Grenier is *all* alone, having spun out the last thin skein of movement.

"As *Time Goes By* is not a pretentious enough ballet to make people feel that they have witnessed a heroic new undertaking in choreography. Its fifteen minutes are loaded with interest, but, like all of Twyla Tharp's work, the piece is peculiarly horizonless. Although each work she has made is self-contained and perfectly lucid in its own terms, each seems almost accidentally bound by the rise and fall of a curtain, and to be part of a larger continuity that exists out of time—out of the time, that is, of this ballet we have just seen. Somewhere, perhaps, there are unseen dancers unrolling the patterns and following up every implication, but we in the audience are spared their tortuous zeal. Twyla Tharp makes us feel that a ballet is nothing more than divisions of a choreographer's time. Although she understands cheap sensation and uses it well, there is no gloss, no appeal for attention, no careerism in her work. It's amusing to think of what a promoter like Diaghilev would have done with her. First, I think, he would retitle the sections of this ballet *Ariadne, Athens, The Labyrinth,* and *Theseus.* Cocteau would write the program notes and design the costumes. (The ones we have, by the Seventh Avenue designer Chester Weinberg, are examples of modest chic in shades of taupe.) Diaghilev would call the whole piece *The Minotaur,* because there's no Minotaur in it, and he would proclaim 'La Tharp' the herald of a new age. Which she is."*

## AT MIDNIGHT

*Music by Gustav Mahler. Choreography by Eliot Feld. Décor by Leonard Baskin. Costumes by Stanley Simmons. Lighting and scenic supervision by Jean Rosenthal. First presented by American Ballet Theatre at the New York State Theatre, Lincoln Center, December 1, 1967, with Bruce Marks, Christine Sarry, Terry Orr, Cynthia Gregory, and Eliot Feld in the principal roles. Sung by William Metcalf. Conducted by Kenneth Schermerhorn.*

Danced to four of the "Five Rückert Songs" of Mahler, lyrics arranged by the composer to poems by Friedrich Rückert, *At Midnight* is named for the first of those songs. But the ballet is not based on what the songs say. They are rather an accompaniment to a danced narrative that reflects the motto of the ballet, a quotation from Thomas Hardy: "In the ill-judged execution of the well-judged plan of things, the call seldom produced the comer, the man to love rarely coincides with the hour for loving. Nature does not often say 'See!' to her poor creature when seeing can lead to a happy doing or answer 'Here!' to a body's cry of 'Where?' till the hide-and-seek has become an irksome, outworn game."

The curtain rises on a dark stage. Illumined in the back is a painting of a face in torment surrounded by two ravens. We make out on stage toward the left a crouching group of men. A half-naked boy climbs onto their bent backs, lying there for support in an hour of need in the middle of the night. He stretches out and rolls off onto the floor as the baritone begins the song "At Midnight." The men cluster around the boy, covering his face with their hands. He is lifted high and then let down to dance alone. At the end, he leaps back into the arms of the men, where he first curls up, then stretches, his arms reaching out in an agony that has not gone away.

The backdrop changes to a painting of a figure crouching in despair. To the song "Ich atmet' einen Lindenduft" (I breathed a fragrance soft and sweet), a

* "A Moment in Time," by Arlene Croce. Reprinted by permission; © 1973 The New Yorker Magazine, Inc.

boy and girl, she in flowing yellow, he in gray, move in an intense yet lyric dance. Two extraordinary catches at the end of this buoyant *pas de deux* yield to a high lift, and the boy carries the girl away as she rides on his shoulder.

A boy, lost and never a part of a group of other boys and girls who dance happily and unaware about him, laments his loneliness and tries to imitate them. The music is the song "Ich bin der Welt abhanded gekommen."

The second song is now repeated. To its music, a girl joins the couple of the second song. There is no real communication between them, however, as she dances along and the couple, preoccupied, stands and sits together. They remain after the girl leaves and seem to waken from their reverie. Four other couples join them now, as do the lone girl of the last song and the boy of the third. Here, too, each of the single figures is so engrossed in trouble and separation that they have no eyes for each other. Amidst all these persons there is no new personal contact. They remain on stage as the song ends, alone as we first saw them.

NOTES    Anna Kisselgoff of the New York *Times* has called *At Midnight* a "landmark ballet, poetic in its depth but accessible to everyone on its theatric level." Reviewing the ballet in the *Dancing Times,* the critic P. W. Manchester wrote that Eliot Feld's "first ballet, *Harbinger,* premièred in the 1967 spring season, indicated that a new talent had arrived. *At Midnight* more than confirmed the promise of *Harbinger.* Feld has set it to four of Gustav Mahler's songs. The first one provides the title for the ballet and is also the finest part of the work. It is a study in man's aloneness. The choreography, marvelously interpreted by Bruce Marks, aches with the doubts and loneliness of the fears that come only in sleeplessness. The second song . . . is a *pas de deux* for young lovers, done with exquisite, unsentimental sweetness by Christine Sarry and Terry Orr. . . . *At Midnight* is both moving and masterly. And . . . Feld is entering on his career as a choreographer while he is also just beginning his best years as a dancer. . . . His closeness to his company as colleague as well as choreographer may well be a major factor in what everyone is hoping will truly be a new era for American Ballet Theatre, one in which it will at long last have its own choreographer, creating for its particular talents, moulding its special and unique style."

Writing of the première in the *Jersey Journal,* the critic Patrick O'Connor said: "It is a unique privilege to be present at the first presentation of a great American work of art. But that's what happened to me last night at the American Ballet Theatre. In truth, there's no such thing as an American work of art. There are only works of art sometimes, too rarely, I'm afraid, composed, put together, by an American. Last night it was *At Midnight* by Eliot Feld. I won't say choreographed. It seemed much more than a dance composition. Feld is involved in what Doris Humphrey once called the art of making dances.

"Movement is, of course, the essential element but so is the painter's brush, the dynamics of stillness, the sacrifice of the mass, the crucifixion, the resurrection, the healing power of love. The whole piece was bathed in love and so was the audience; they knew it, felt it and were grateful.

"It seems almost profane to talk about the dancing. It wasn't dancing; it was another kind of activity—exalted movement. Cynthia Gregory in pentecostal lavender made one weep, and Christine Sarry in pentecostal yellow sustains stillness miraculously. She also danced brilliantly. Bruce Marks—as the Christ figure?—gave a shattering performance. Feld the dancer served Feld the choreographer like a ministering angel. A rare privilege, an historic occasion, something to tell my grandchildren."

Reviewing a 1975 performance by the Eliot Feld Ballet with Lawrence Rhodes, the English critic John Percival wrote in *Dance and Dancers:* "Rhodes, perhaps the greatest of American male dancers today, for some reason has never settled down with one of the major companies, and nowadays combines membership in Feld's company and the Pennsylvania Ballet. He has a slight, supple physique and the ability to make every movement eloquent. *The Consort* shows him to be capable of a show-off solo, but a role like the central figure of *At Midnight* suits him even better . . . He gives it great bitterness."

## AUREOLE

*Music by George Frederick Handel. Choreography by Paul Taylor. Lighting by Thomas Skelton. First presented by the Paul Taylor Dance Company at Connecticut College, New London, Connecticut, August 4, 1962.*

A dance work that has happily entered the repertory of the Royal Danish Ballet and been seen in presentations by Paul Taylor's ensemble with Rudolf Nureyev, *Aureole* has proved itself a most distinguished work in the contemporary repertoire. Paul Taylor, regarded by Clive Barnes as "one of the most talented and innovative choreographers this country has ever produced," has danced it with his own company at home and abroad. It was my pleasure some years ago to work with Paul Taylor in the New York City Ballet's *Episodes*.

*Aureole* is a dance for five—two boys and three girls. Its content is a most original response to Handel's lyric and expressive score (the *Concerto Grosso in G* and the fourth movement of *Alexander's Feast*).

## BACH SONATA

*Music by Johann Sebastian Bach. Choreography by Maurice Béjart. First presented by the Ballet of the Twentieth Century, 1970, with Suzanne Farrell and Jorge Donn. First presented in the United States by the same ensemble at the Brooklyn Academy of Music, New York, January 29, 1971, with the same principals.*

A *pas de deux* set to Bach's *Sonata No. 5 for Violin and Harpsichord*, and designed to show the artistry of the two principals, *Bach Sonata* is not the usual display piece for the ballerina and her partner. Instead, it poses the problem of how an infatuated boy can encircle and win a girl who appears to be indifferent to everything he does.

## LE BAISER DE LA FÉE (The Fairy's Kiss)

*Ballet-allegory in four scenes. Music and book by Igor Stravinsky. Choreography by George Balanchine. Scenery and costumes by Alicia Halicka. First presented by the American Ballet at the Metropolitan Opera House, New York, April 27, 1937, with Gisella Caccialanza as the* Bride, *William Dollar as the* Bridegroom, *and Kathryn Mullowney as the* Fairy.

Stravinsky dedicated this ballet "to the memory of Peter Tchaikovsky . . . It was his Muse (like our Fairy heroine) whose fatal kiss, imprinted at birth, made itself felt in all the work of that great artist, and eventually led him to immortality. Thereby does our ballet (with a similar tale) become an allegory." The story of the ballet is derived from a tale by Hans Christian Andersen—"The Ice Maiden." Stravinsky selected elements from this long and beautiful fairy tale to compose his scenario. Here, the Ice Maiden comes down from the sky to claim for her own a hapless youth. When he is a child, abandoned in the snow, the fairy kisses the boy coldly with a fatal kiss that seals his eternal devotion to her. The babe becomes a man and, with no recollection of the fairy's power over him, is engaged to be married. The Ice Maiden returns to fulfill the prophecy of her kiss and to carry him away to the ends of the earth.

FIRST TABLEAU: PROLOGUE—THE SNOWSTORM  The curtain rises soon after the orchestra has begun to play softly a lilting lullaby. The scene is deserted, barely lit. Snow begins to fall. A woman enters, carrying a child. She dances across the stage, her hood flowing behind her. She lifts the child in her arms lovingly and covers it with her cape. At first she does not appear to be alarmed at the snow, but the lullaby to which she dances changes to an ominous melody presaging a severe storm and the woman is frightened for her child. She covers it more carefully, holds it close to her breast, and continues on her way. Winds leap across the stage from right and left, passing close to her, then circling about her as if to enclose her with their freezing force. She cowers in terror. Myriad snowflakes enter behind her, hover over her, and leave her shivering on the ground. The piercing winds return, their frigid capes streaming from their shoulders; the snowflakes re-enter and surround the mother. She rises helplessly and attempts to flee, but the snowflakes divide into groups and block her escape. The music increases its ominous force. The snowflakes force her to the front and drown her with freezing snow. As the mother cowers beneath them, she thinks only of her child. She dies. The winds remove her body, and the child is abandoned to the snowflakes, who pass over the pathetic bundle as they vanish.

The winds pull in a swift white sleigh that brings onto the scene a beautiful fairy, the Ice Maiden. A spotlight catches her imposing figure. She stands in statuesque pose, holding high a wand of ice; her noble head is crowned with a star of white jewels; her dress is white, long, and full. She steps down from the sleigh, presents her wand to her escorts, and directs them away. Immediately she begins to dance. Each one of her open, flowing movements is imitated by a figure in black, who stands in the distance like a shadow to remind us that the beauty of the fairy is bewitching. The fairy dances close to the child. She stands over him; her flowing white dress seems to cover him as she turns brilliantly on point. She bends over the child, reaches out, draws him close to her face. She kisses him tenderly, yet coldly, and places the child on the ground. Now that she has sealed the fate of the helpless child, the fairy dances away slowly on point. Her shadow disappears with her.

The scene darkens. A peasant enters, carrying a lantern. He is followed by a group of mountain climbers, who help him as he seeks to recover the lost child. The music imitates their anxieties. At last one of the men sees the small bundle in the snow. The light is brought nearer, and the other men hold him as he reaches down and picks up the child while the orchestra sounds climactic chords of pathos. The scene blacks out as they hurry off.

SECOND TABLEAU: THE VILLAGE FESTIVAL   Twenty years have passed. Befriended by peasants, the child has grown up to become the most popular young man in the village. He is to be married soon to the miller's daughter.

After a brief orchestral interlude, the lights come up on a colorful mountain scene overhung with fir trees; snow-capped peaks are seen in the distance. Boys and girls of the village dressed in gay Swiss costumes stand in a wide circle dancing a folk measure to a rhythmic, holiday tune. A group of boys then move to the center, where they are surrounded by the smiling girls. They all gather behind the village bandsmen and parade around the stage.

A high-spirited boy carrying a gun runs into the crowd. This is the bridegroom. Everyone welcomes him, particularly the girls, and it is clear that he has the affections of them all. He dances forward with two of the girls to the light rhythm of the music, which soon becomes strong and robust. Everyone joins them in their youthful dance. When the dance is over, the young man calls one of his friends and directs him to shoot at a distant target. The boy aims and misses. Another boy tries and misses. The bridegroom seizes his gun, shoots, and hits the target, to the delight of the girls, who playfully congratulate him.

The bride enters, surrounded by six of her bridesmaids. She dances briefly before the company, and then the boy joins her for a happy duet that reflects their mutual joy. Several of the village girls start a yodeling contest, which is interrupted for a final festival dance by the bride, the bridegroom, and all their friends. The peasants encircle the bride and bridegroom and begin to leave the stage. The bride goes off with her friends. The boy seems to depart with the rest, but as the stage empties, we see that he has remained. He sits on the ground in quiet meditation. One of his friends tries to persuade him to continue with the celebration, but the boy refuses. He is alone.

On the right a beautiful gypsy enters. She is dressed in black and white. The boy does not notice her as he looks at the ground thoughtfully. The gypsy crosses the stage in a determined stride, her arms gripped at her sides. The jewel she wears on her forehead catches the light for an instant; her face is a frigid mask. It is the face of the Ice Maiden, who has disguised herself to discover the boy. She approaches him, circles him several times, as if to be sure of his identity, then sits down close beside him and looks up straight into his face. The orchestra sounds a sharp chord; she grips his wrist fiercely and examines his open palm to foretell the fate she herself has planned for him.

The boy is completely passive to the strange gypsy fortuneteller. His body falls back as she circles his hand before her savagely. She rises, throws his hand away from her in a gesture of triumphant recognition, and dances before him. The boy watches as she steps with fascinating, malevolent vigor, flinging her loose black hair over her face. He responds to her exotic dynamism and comes to her. He holds the gypsy obediently while she walks forward as if she were driving her points into the ground. Now they cross the stage to the right, the gypsy whirling rapidly, the boy following and falling at her feet as she extends her leg to lash the air above him. He rises to embrace her, but she shoves him away contemptuously, then seizes him violently and passionately. The boy is obedient to her every gesture as he realizes her power to fulfill his fortune. She turns him around, stands in back of him, points her arm forward over his shoulder, and pushes him in its direction. The boy does not resist; he walks in a dream as the gypsy directs him toward his destiny. Blackout.

THIRD TABLEAU: INSIDE THE MILL   A group of peasant girls are arranged in an open triangular tableau as the lights illuminate the interior of the bride's home. The rough wood walls are decorated with wreaths; candles hang low from the ceiling; there are two large windows at the back. The scene is framed with old Swiss lace. The day of the wedding is approaching, and all of the bride's friends have gathered to prepare for the occasion. The peasant girls dance gaily to a blithe melody, led by a girl in a bright yellow skirt, whose energy and enthusiasm are expressed in precise, rapid steps.

The bride enters and dances in front of the group. Dressed all in white, she wears a small wreath of white flowers in her hair. The girls in back of her imitate her movements. The bride walks back to welcome her friends; some of them form a circle around her. She bows, then bows to another group that surrounds her. She blows kisses to them all and exits.

The peasant girls dance again; the bride returns just before the music ends and she stands in the center of a beautifully posed group her friends form about her. The girls run off and leave the bride alone. The orchestra begins to play quietly a lovely, sweeping melody. The bride circles the room, goes to the window, looks out expectantly, but sees nothing. She is waiting for the bridegroom. She walks over to the other window, her back turned to the room. The bridegroom enters. The bride does not see him. He circles the room looking for her. She moves away from the window as if she felt his presence, but does not find him, for the boy has walked behind her. Both stand in the center of the room, their arms held out, seeking. Their backs almost touch and they move away in opposite directions to circle the room again. The boy kneels. The girl sees him, runs up behind him softly, and leans over his shoulder to welcome him playfully. He rises. Their *pas de deux* begins.

The couple cross the front of the stage together, extending their arms to the side in rhythm to the flow of the music. The bride falls back in the boy's arms. The music changes, as a clarinet states the theme of their adagio. The boy holds the girl about the waist as she dances quickly but softly, like a sylph. He lifts her as they move together, and her points continue their dance in the air. The bride kneels and watches the boy dance. Then both circle the stage. The girl beckons to him and whispers something. They stand together in the center of the stage. They bow low to each other. The boy holds out his hand and, as the orchestra states the climax of the theme, the girl takes his hand and poses in a low, deep arabesque. She rises and falls back against his arm. He raises her off the floor with low lifts in which the girl bends her knees softly. He holds her under her arms, and the girl sits on his knee, smiling happily, her legs extended before her.

The bridegroom stands aside and watches the girl dance alone to a fresh, piquant theme. She dances flirtatiously, flouncing her skirt high. She mimes her intense happiness, feigning intoxication from her joy. The black shadow of the Ice Maiden suddenly appears before her and points menacingly. The boy does not see the apparition, who disappears before the girl has rushed backward into his arms. The bride looks toward the vanished shadow and moves her hand in front of her face in innocent, unbelieving astonishment.

A pounding drum announces a sharp, accelerating dance melody. The peasant girls re-enter to take up its rhythm, and the bride and bridegroom leave the stage. The bridegroom returns to dance a short, brilliant variation. He is followed by the bride, who comes down the stage diagonally, dancing smartly on one point, extending her other leg straight out to the side with every step. She finishes her dance with a series of rapid turns that delight the whole company, then runs across the stage at full speed toward the bridegroom, who catches her daringly in midair.

The couple leave the stage to the dancing peasants for a moment, then return to join them in a final ensemble. At its conclusion one of the girls brings out the bride's veil and throws it playfully over her head. The girls gather about the bride and separate the two lovers. The bride leaves the stage with her playful friends. The bridegroom remains alone. The light dims.

The bridegroom turns rapidly; as he comes out of his spin, he sees on the right a girl dressed in white, her head and shoulders covered with a long white veil. As he recognizes his fiancée, he seems also to be remembering slowly and with effort that he must have known her like this always—tall, beautiful, and in white. He moves toward her, fascinated by his illusory recollection and the new loveliness she has for him. The girl does not move; she remains motionless, drawing the boy toward her with mysterious and bewitching magnetism. He stands in front of her, reaches around her strongly, and holds her tightly by the waist, his face buried in the frigid whiteness of her veil. Thus holding her, he lifts her feet off the floor; her body arches back, and he carries her walking slowly backward. Now the orchestra states fully but quietly the melody of Tchaikovsky's "None But the Lonely Heart," which was suggested softly at the beginning of the scene.

The boy lets the girl down gently and falls helpless against her. His limp

body falls to the floor at her feet. The girl bows over him, opens her arms
wide, takes his hand, and pulls him up as she circles about him. They move a
short distance together; then the boy kneels. He stretches his arms back; the
girl takes his hands. He crawls forward. The girl stands against his back, her
body in arabesque, her face falling over against his. Her white veil envelops
his face in a glacier of tenderness. The tragic melody, now at its height, accompanies them as they move across the stage.

The boy falls forward on the ground. The girl bends down and covers him
with her veil. He rises under it, throws the veil back over her head, and stands
transfixed as he beholds her face—the face of the Ice Maiden and gypsy in one.
The Ice Maiden stands regally as we saw her in the first scene, her lovely,
noble head crowned with a star of shimmering crystals. The boy backs away
from her in terror at his recognition, then draws close to her again in helpless,
passionate longing. He rests his head on her breast. The Ice Maiden stands
rigid, head back, her arms stretched out behind her. Slowly she lifts her arms
and touches the boy's head with a retarded and considered gesture that seems
to freeze the gentleness of her touch and turn him to ice. Now she moves her
hand down the boy's trembling arm, takes his hand, and leads him away. The
scene blacks out.

FOURTH TABLEAU: EPILOGUE   The lights come up on the same scene. The
bride enters the room, searching for her fiancé. She circles the stage, looks out
of the windows from which she has so often seen him come to the mill. He is
nowhere to be found. She waves her veil over her head sadly and begins to despair. Then suddenly, in the back, the wall of the room disappears and the
bride beholds in the sky a scene that makes her tremble. High up, far away in
the distance, the Ice Maiden sits in the cold blue winter sky holding out her
arms to the bridegroom, who strives to reach her. He stretches out his arms to
the magical fairy, who seems to enfold him. They rise together in the sky. The
bride kneels and, weeping, waves her wedding veil in farewell.

NOTES   At the end of 1927, when he was finishing the music of *Apollo*, Igor
Stravinsky was asked by Madame Ida Rubinstein to compose a ballet for her.
Bronislava Nijinska was to be the choreographer, Alexandre Benois the designer. Stravinsky writes, in his autobiography: "The idea was that I should
compose something inspired by the music of Tchaikovsky. My well-known
fondness for this composer, and, still more, the fact that November, 1928, the
time fixed for the performance, would mark the thirty-fifth anniversary of his
death, induced me to accept the offer. It would give me an opportunity of paying my heartfelt homage to Tchaikovsky's wonderful talent.

"As I was free to choose both the subject and scenario of the ballet, I began
to search for them, in view of the characteristic trend of Tchaikovsky's music,
in the literature of the nineteenth century. With that aim, I turned to a great
poet with a gentle, sensitive soul whose imaginative mind was wonderfully
akin to that of the musician. I refer to Hans Christian Andersen, with whom in
this respect Tchaikovsky had so much in common. To recall *The Sleeping
Beauty*, *The Nutcracker*, *Swan Lake*, *Pique Dame*, and many pieces of his

symphonic work is enough to show the extent of his fondness for the fantastic.

"In turning over the pages of Andersen, with which I was fairly familiar, I came across a story which I had completely forgotten that struck me as being the very thing for the idea which I wanted to express. It was the very beautiful story known to us as the 'Ice Maiden.' I chose that as my theme and worked out the story on the following lines. A fairy imprints her magic kiss on a child at birth and parts it from its mother. Twenty years later, when the youth has attained the very zenith of his good fortune, she repeats the fatal kiss and carries him off to live in supreme happiness with her ever afterwards. As my object was to commemorate the work of Tchaikovsky, this subject seemed to me to be particularly appropriate as an allegory, the Muse having similarly branded Tchaikovsky with her fatal kiss, and the magic imprint has made itself felt in all the musical creations of this great artist.

"Although I gave full liberty to painter and choreographer in the staging of my composition, my innermost desire was that it should be presented in classical form, after the manner of *Apollo*. I pictured all the fantastic roles as danced in white ballet-skirts, and the rustic scenes as taking place in a Swiss landscape . . ."

The ballet was performed for the first time November 27, 1928, at the Opéra, Paris, with the composer conducting. It was performed in other European capitals and, in 1933, at the Colón Theatre in Buenos Aires. November 26, 1935, Frederick Ashton choreographed a new version of the ballet for the Sadler's Wells Ballet. This version, designed by Sophie Fedorovitch, featured Pearl Argyle, Harold Turner, and Margot Fonteyn—her first created role. Frederick Ashton, interestingly enough, had danced in the original Nijinska production. I staged the ballet in 1937 for the American Ballet's Stravinsky Festival in New York.

Certain parts of the story of the ballet are hard to make clear on the stage. At the beginning of the Second Tableau, for example, how is the audience to know that the bridegroom is the child of the Prologue? Believing that everything must be clear on the stage, I have tried to indicate this in a number of ways in different revivals of the ballet, as I have also endeavored to make it obvious that the gypsy is, in reality, the fairy disguised. The finale of the ballet also presents a mechanical difficulty. Ideally, the ending should have a magical effect: the fairy should appear to be suspended and the bridegroom, just below her, must seem to be swimming through space, as it were, to reach her. The Ice Maiden drags the boy down into the lake with her, and in recent revivals I have tried to indicate that the two figures are moving together in the water, but limited audience visibility of the back of the stage has prevented this plan from attaining real success. There is no question but that the final Tableau requires a stage high and deep for the achievement of full illusion.

*The Fairy's Kiss* has been revived twice by the Ballet Russe de Monte Carlo: on April 10, 1940, at the Metropolitan Opera House, with a cast headed by Alexandra Danilova as the bride, André Eglevsky as the bridegroom, and Mia Slavenska as the fairy; and on February 17, 1946, at the City Center, New York, with Alexandra Danilova, Frederic Franklin, and Maria Tallchief. It was staged for the Opéra, Paris, July 2, 1947, when Tamara

Toumanova, Alexandre Kaliujny, and Maria Tallchief took the principal roles. At its revival by the New York City Ballet November 28, 1950, the leading roles were danced by Tanaquil LeClercq, Nicholas Magallanes, and Maria Tallchief.

Although his version of the ballet is unfortunately unknown in the United States, Sir Frederick Ashton choreographed *Le Baiser de la Fée* for the Sadler's Wells Ballet at the Sadler's Wells Theatre, London, November 26, 1935. The production was designed by Sophie Fedorovitch and the leading dancers were Pearl Argyle, Margot Fonteyn, and Harold Turner. An excerpt from this ballet, a *pas de deux*, was performed at the Royal Opera House, Covent Garden, in July 1970, at the Gala Performance in Ashton's honor.

The Royal Ballet revived *Le Baiser de la Fée* in a new version by Kenneth MacMillan at the Royal Opera House, Covent Garden, April 12, 1960, with Svetlana Beriosova, Donald MacLeary, and Lynn Seymour in the principal roles. This production, designed by Kenneth Rowell, was introduced to the United States by the Royal Ballet at the Metropolitan Opera House, New York, September 27, 1960, with the same principals.

In 1972, for the New York City Ballet's Stravinsky Festival, our celebration of the composer's ninetieth birthday, I arranged new dances for music from this ballet under the title *Divertimento from Le Baiser de la Fée*. This was based on Stravinsky's symphonic suite from the ballet, which uses just under half the score and which he called *Divertimento*. The dances were new ones, though some remembered gestures and movements were retained as I wished. The piece was presented without a setting and without a story line, as a dance ballet, for the first time on June 21, 1972, at the New York State Theatre, with lighting by Ronald Bates. Robert Irving was the conductor and the leading roles were danced by Patricia McBride, Helgi Tomasson, Bettijane Sills and Carol Sumner.

Writing about the staging of the *Divertimento* for the Stravinsky Festival in *The Nation*, Nancy Goldner said: "One of my favorite moments was a sequence of jumps for Helgi Tomasson in the *Divertimento from Le Baiser de la Fée*. All the sequence amounted to was a variation on something very commonplace: a preparatory sliding step with a little spring in it, called a *glissade*, followed by a moving jump in which one leg is thrown forward and the other backward. Usually, after the *glissade* the weight is on the front foot. This gives the dancer the momentum to jump off the floor on the front foot, with the back one swinging forward and up into the jump. His back is straight and he faces the line of direction. But that is not what Balanchine had Tomasson do. Instead of springing naturally off the front foot, he jumps off the back foot. Instead of facing the line of direction, his whole body is almost at right angles to it. He does these jumps in a circle, leading with the 'wrong' foot and at the 'wrong' angle. The effect is that of a car skidding around a corner on its outside wheels. Tomasson was so skimming and elegant in this unnatural deployment of momentum and balance that he seemed like those flying saucers that reportedly can veer at a right angle without slowing down."

The critic Anna Kisselgoff, reviewing a performance in the New York *Times* in 1974, said: "In Helgi Tomasson, the New York City Ballet has one of the best classical male dancers in the world today. No wonder then that George Balanchine chose him as the dancer upon whom to create one of the most unusual and poetic male solos in the Balanchine repertory.

"Saturday night at the New York State Theater, Mr. Tomasson's special combination of elegance and virtuosity was evident again in that solo, in the short ballet entitled *Divertimento from 'Le Baiser de la Fée,'* choreographed by Mr. Balanchine for the 1972 Stravinsky Festival . . . Perhaps it might be wiser to forget the now-discarded story line for the first Balanchine version of *The Fairy's Kiss* (the ballet's English title), and to view the current divertissement as a plotless pure-dance excerpt. Yet the fact that Stravinsky's original scenario had a hero and not a heroine as the protagonist might help explain why the choreography for the male dancer tends to overshadow the ballerina's.

"In this bright, joyful and tender *pas de deux,* backed by an ensemble, Mr. Balanchine has reserved the most inventive sequences for Mr. Tomasson. The man's variation, with its unexpected changes of direction, suggestions of swoons and a series of jumps followed by falls to the knee, appears totally original. In the coda, the extraordinary way Mr. Tomasson seems to be off balance when he is not is a tribute to both the imagination of the choreographer and the rock-firm technique of the dancer. At the same time, Mr. Tomasson is one of dance's most finished classic stylists."

*Music by Igor Stravinsky and Peter Ilyich Tchaikovsky. Choreography and book by John Neumeier. Costumes and sets by Jürgen Rose. Lighting by Jennifer Tipton. First presented by the Frankfurt Ballet in 1974. First presented in the United States by American Ballet Theatre at the New York State Theatre, Lincoln Center, in 1975.*

The choreographer John Neumeier has devised a new libretto, with a flashback technique, for his ballet on this theme. In addition to Stravinsky's score he uses two short works of Tchaikovsky in his score: the "Feuillet d'Album," Op. 19, No. 3, and "None But the Lonely Heart," Op. 6, No. 6—a principal element, of course, in Stravinsky's.

The action of the ballet follows this libretto:

PROLOGUE: THE WEDDING CELEBRATION   The marriage of Rudi and Babette is being celebrated at a party with their friends. Among the guests is a stranger who sings a lovely, melancholy song, at the end of which she gives Rudi a kiss. Her song, and the kiss, awaken in him the memory of an old desire, as intangible but as haunting as perfume. With the memory, Rudi feels an inexpressible yearning, disturbing the happiness he hopes to find with Babette.

SCENE ONE: REMEMBRANCE (BALLET BLANC)   Rudi's *Sehnsucht* (his subconscious yearning self) takes him back to his childhood and the memory of an experience. In a clear, white world, Rudi, as the child he once was, is entranced by the vision of beautiful dancing creatures. One of these, the most dazzling of all, gives the boy a kiss, then disappears among the others. Rudi searches in vain for her, in an agony of love and longing that will haunt his life.

SCENE TWO: THE WEDDING CELEBRATION CONTINUES   Rudi realizes that the mysterious singer is the same beautiful creature from the pure, white world of his childhood for whom he has searched his entire life. Rudi's longing once more takes him in search of her.

SCENE THREE: IN THE GARDEN   Stealing away from the party, Babette finds Rudi in the garden, where she again expresses her love for him. They are interrupted by the departing guests, making their adieux. Together again, Rudi turns to Babette, feeling in her presence the strength of a love great enough to overcome his yearning for the unattainable. Reassured, Babette re-enters the house to prepare herself for their wedding night.

SCENE FOUR: TOWARD ETERNITY   Alone in the garden, Rudi's *Sehnsucht* grows stronger and stronger, overpowering Rudi's will . . . It compels him to obey the unearthly summons of the Fairy. Rudi goes in quest of his glorious tormentress, leaving Babette to wait in vain for his return.


# BALLADE

*Dramatic ballet in one act. Music by Claude Debussy. Choreography by Jerome Robbins. Scenery and costumes by Boris Aronson. Costumes executed by Karinska. Lighting by Jean Rosenthal. First presented by the New York City Ballet at the City Center, New York, February 14, 1952, with Tanaquil LeClercq, Janet Reed, Nora Kaye, Roy Tobias, Robert Barnett, Louis Johnson, John Mandia, and Brooks Jackson.*

This ballet's program note reminds us that a *ballade* (or *ballad*) is "a musical composition of poetic character . . . a dancing song, a poem of unknown authorship which recounts a legendary or traditional event and passes from one generation to another." The legendary or traditional event in the ballet is enacted by the legendary and traditional characters Harlequin, Columbine, and Pierrot, who find themselves in a band of other, more modern, theatrical characters. The music for *Ballade* is Debussy's flute solo *Syrinx* and the same composer's *Six Antique Epigraphs*, orchestrated by Ernest Ansermet.

Snow is falling on a quiet scene as the curtain rises. Seven people lie asleep in chairs that are grouped about the stage. In the back is a drop curtain that depicts the sun and moon surrounded by clouds of ice. The people take no notice of the snow; their bodies lie limply in the chairs, and they seem like so many rag dolls.

To the quiet music of a flute, a strolling musician enters, carrying balloons. The snow stops falling. Slowly he goes to each of the chairs and at each one he leaves a balloon. When he has distributed balloons to all seven, he watches as the hands that hold them are drawn mysteriously upward. Gradually all the figures waken and rise toward their balloons. They bow to the strolling player and look up at the balloons he has left them as he leaves the scene.

One of the girls steps out. She is dressed in Harlequin's traditional costume of varicolored diamond patches. Slowly she turns; the others move the chairs back and run about the stage with their balloons. Now they tie the balloons to the chairs and come forward to dance in a semicircle.

The rest of the group retire as three boys dance forward rapidly and, like clowns and tumbling artists, execute a rushing, circusy number. When they finish, the girl dressed as Harlequin comes forward. She reaches down, takes her foot in her hand, brings it around behind her back, and turns. Now she somersaults and her movements take on an angular quality. As the music becomes faster, she leaps wildly, circles the stage, revolves in bouncing turns, and goes back to her chair.

A girl in pink, her cheeks spotted with circles of bright red rouge, begins to dance. This is Columbine. A boy, also dressed in pink, kisses her hand. He kneels before her as she begins to dance to quick, subtle music. The girl is indifferent to the boy and wanders almost accidentally into his arms. He tries to get some reaction as he declares his love, but the girl, like a rag doll, looks at him stupidly. Finally he embraces her and kisses her throat. The girl reaches into her dress to find her heart and brings out a handful of sawdust. The astonished youth retires, and the girl sits on the floor at the left.

Now a girl representing Pierrot takes the center of the stage briefly. The melody sounds hauntingly. Pierrot collapses and dies. Two boys take up her loose, disjointed body and carry her. The others grieve. Pierrot is given a balloon and slowly she rises. She wonders at the balloon's magical force in bringing her to life again. The strange figures watch breathlessly as she ponders this mystery and makes a decision. The music stops. Pierrot stares up at the balloon, then deliberately allows it to slip through her fingers. In stunned silence her fellow actors imagine that she has sacrificed her life. Everyone watches as the balloon disappears overhead.

Forgetful of Pierrot's sacrifice, the whole troupe dances a happy ensemble. Suddenly the lights begin to go down. The strolling musician returns, and the players return to their chairs. As he takes their balloons away, each collapses and becomes lifeless again. The strolling musician stares at Pierrot, who stands alone without a balloon. Slowly he leaves the scene. Pierrot looks after him for a moment, then goes to each of the chairs, trying to waken their occupants. She cannot stir them. Snow begins to fall again, and the curtain descends as Pierrot, sad that she alone possesses a life outside the magic of the theatre, stares off into the distance.

## BALLET IMPERIAL (TCHAIKOVSKY CONCERTO NO. 2)

*Classic ballet in three movements. Music by Peter Ilyich Tchaikovsky. Choreography by George Balanchine. Setting and costumes by Mstislav Dobou-*

*jinsky. First presented by the American Ballet at the Hunter College Play-
house, New York, May 27, 1941, with Marie-Jeanne, Gisella Caccialanza,
and William Dollar in the principal roles. Revived by the Ballet Russe de
Monte Carlo at the City Center, New York, February 20, 1945, with Mary
Ellen Moylan, Maria Tallchief, and Nicholas Magallanes in the leading roles.
Revived by the Sadler's Wells Ballet at the Royal Opera House, London,
April 5, 1950, with scenery and costumes by Eugene Berman and a cast
headed by Margot Fonteyn, Michael Somes, and Beryl Grey. Revived by
the Ballet of La Scala, Milan, with scenery and costumes by Eugene Berman, March 25, 1952, with Olga Amati, Gilda Maiocchi, and Giulio Peru-
gini in the principal roles.*

Great ballets of the past are directly associated with great composers of the
past. *The Sleeping Beauty,* the masterwork of the great nineteenth-century
choreographer Marius Petipa, survives not only for its dancing, but also for its
music. Petipa created more than sixty full-length ballets during a half century
of work as ballet master at the Imperial Russian Theatre. Few of these works
are performed today. This is not because the dancing in these ballets was not
good; it is because their music was not good enough to inspire the dancing to
new heights. Audiences have wished to forget the bad music and, consequently, the dances that went with it.

Since the death of Petipa, in 1910, much has happened to the classical
dancing he developed into so high a form in his famous ballets. The basic vocabulary is the same, but we have added new words, new phrases; classical
dancing today is much more difficult, more complex, more intricate, more demanding. Oftentimes people are inclined to think that the great dancers of the
past were incomparable and that dancers today are as nothing beside them.
This is not true. The great dancers of the past were incomparable for what
they did. Today we do something else.

*Ballet Imperial* is a contemporary tribute to Petipa, "the father of the classic
ballet," and to Tchaikovsky, his greatest composer. The ballet is set to Tchaikovsky's *Piano Concerto No. 2 in G.* It is a dance ballet and has no story.

FIRST MOVEMENT: ALLEGRO BRILLANTE   The orchestra and piano introduce
the opening theme, a brilliant and noble melody. The piano develops this
theme alone, and a quick rush on the strings signals the second theme. The
curtain rises. Eight couples in classical costume stand in a diagonal, the boys
facing the girls some distance apart. They begin to dance. The stage frame is
draped with blue velvet trimmed with ermine. We are in the room of a palace.
In contrast to this sumptuous warmth, in the distance there is a view of the
snow-covered Fortress of Peter and Paul. The royal gates that direct our eyes
to this view are embellished with the imperial eagle. The dancing is quick and
formal, bright and dignified.

Eight girls join the eight couples, and after them comes a soloist, a beautiful
young girl who prepares the stage for the ballerina. The ballerina enters,
dances to a piano cadenza, and by her loveliness in performance convinces us
that we are watching a queen among dancers. At first she dances alone,

finishing her variation in open rapid turns that encircle the stage. The music is softer, has now a stately romantic quality, and the ballerina dances with a cavalier. Now the ballerina and the *corps de ballet* leave the stage and the soloist performs a *pas de trois* with two boys. The second theme has returned with the same signal from the strings, it has merged with the first, and the music gathers to a flourishing finish. The ballerina and the *corps de ballet* dance to this music with young, regal splendor, and the movement is over.

SECOND MOVEMENT: ANDANTE NON TROPPO   After a brief introduction, the piano plays alone the principal theme. This is music of sentiment, pathos, and high feeling—slow, almost retarded, in its romantic commitment. A solo violin plays the theme accompanied by the piano. The ballerina enters with her cavalier. Eight girls form a maze through which the ballerina and her partner move. Now she and her partner are lovers. They appear to be happy, but then the man pleads with her intently and we understand that their love is not perfect. But soon the ballerina responds to her lover's plea and dances with tender intimacy. The *corps de ballet* dance protectingly around the couple and lead them gently into the wings.

THIRD MOVEMENT: ALLEGRO CON FUOCO   The music is gay and assertive with a fiery brightness and crispness. The ballerina is carried in high on the shoulders of her partner. He sets her down softly, and she dances with ravishing quickness to the brilliant music. She and her partner leave the stage for a moment to the *corps de ballet*, but return again and again to lead the dancing. The ballerina's partner dances a variation, the soloist is seen briefly leading the crowded stage of dancers, and the ballerina comes back to finish with her court the final, electric flourish of ensemble movement.

NOTES   *Ballet Imperial* has been danced by a number of companies in recent years. The Royal Ballet mounted a new version, in a setting by Carl Toms, October 18, 1963, and the New York City Ballet on May 19, 1964, presented its own production, staged by Frederic Franklin. Its scenery by Rouben Ter-Arutunian and costumes by Karinska suggests the splendors of the Imperial capital in Russia, Peter the Great's "Window on the West," the city of canals and painted stucco that recalls the heroic grandeur of Italy. In the background, across the broad Neva River, framed by the rostral columns celebrating Russian naval supremacy, is the lancet spire of the Peter-Paul fortress. The azure draperies reflect the color of the Maryinsky Theatre of Opera and Ballet for which Tchaikovsky composed his great theatrical scores.

On January 12, 1973, with its name changed to *Tchaikovsky Concerto No. 2*, the ballet was presented in a new version by the New York City Ballet at the New York State Theatre, Lincoln Center. Patricia McBride, Peter Martins, and Colleen Neary were the principals. The setting was a plain cyclorama and the costumes much simplified. So also was the Second Movement, where the pantomime of the cavalier was eliminated. I made these changes because the times have changed since the ballet was first done. Our audiences these days don't require elaborate costumes and decoration in a ballet, and rightly so. We see dancing better than we used to and prefer to see it directly, unencumbered. The music and the dancing themselves are enough here, I hope, to form illusions that scenery and costumes only made specific.

## BALLET SCHOOL

*Music by Liadvov, Shostakovich, and Glazunov. Choreography by Asaf Messerer. First presented by the Bolshoi Ballet at the Metropolitan Opera House, New York, September 17, 1962.*

This work originated from a collection of dances presented by pupils of the Bolshoi Ballet School upon their graduation. It shows in compressed form the years of training and work required to become a classical dancer. The ballet was made by the ballet master at the Bolshoi, Asaf Messerer, who has said of his work: "I endeavored to show to the audiences the richness of the Russian classical school and give some insight into the training of its dancers—from the initial steps of the child pupils to the mature masters of ballet. I tried to avoid brilliance of technique as an end in itself and did not wish to turn the performance into a mere display of the skill of the soloists. I aimed also at introducing to the public many of our promising and gifted dancers. Thus, not only such stars as Maya Plisetskaya and Fadeyechev dance in it, but some of the younger members of the company, among them Nina Sorokina, Natalia Bessmertnova, and Mikhail Lavrovsky."

Before the leaps and the pirouettes lie long hours of systematic practice at the *barre*. Before the child is given exercises in the center of the classroom, she must be taught the five basic positions at the *barre. Rond de jambe, arabesque, grands battements,* each *pas* is learned under the discerning and exacting eye of the ballet master. The children learn the small leaps, the *changement de pieds,* the *entrechats.* And finally in *adagios* and *pas de deux* they are able to demonstrate such taxing exercises as the *grande fouettée.* Groups of male dancers leap across the stage. To the familiar strains of Glazunov's music the *jetté* is displayed.

## UNE BARQUE SUR L'OCÉAN

*Music by Maurice Ravel. Choreography by Jerome Robbins. Costumes by Parmelee Welles. Lighting by Ronald Bates. First presented at the New York City Ballet's Hommage à Ravel at the New York State Theatre, Lincoln Center, May 29, 1975, with Victor Castelli, Daniel Duell, Laurence Matthews, Jay Jolley, and Noland T'Sani.*

A dance for five boys dressed in white and blue who move against a vibrant sea color in the background, this ballet responds to the music without specific narrative. The boys move like waves and eddies or submarine currents, reacting to water and wind, the forces and whims of nature.

Reflecting the work of Impressionist painters, Ravel, like Debussy, was interested in water movement: its perpetual shifts and shimmering colors. By orchestrating *Une Barque*, as Lincoln Kirstein has written, Ravel enlarged his theme so that "as the music gathers resonance the arpeggios grow to sweeping splashes of harp and the whole orchestra seems to vibrate as much with color and with physical motion of the waves." Jerome Robbins, I have heard, calls his ballet *Sailing*.

## BARTÓK NO. 3

*Music by Béla Bartók. Choreography by John Clifford. Costumes by Ardith Haddow. Lighting by Ronald Bates. First presented by Los Angeles Ballet Theatre, March 27, 1974.*

This is a dance ballet to Bartók's last work, the *Piano Concerto No. 3*. There are three movements, the first led by three girls with accompanying corps de ballet, the second a romantic *pas de deux* supported by six girls, the finale an ensemble for the entire group.

When *Bartók No. 3* was danced in New York, by the New York City Ballet (May 23, 1974), Bob Micklin of *Newsday* wrote that he liked Clifford's ballet "very much. It is the best work he's done to date."

## LA BAYADÈRE

*Ballet in four acts. Music by Ludwig Minkus. Book by S. N. Khudekov. Choreography by Marius Petipa. First presented at the Maryinsky Theatre, St. Petersburg, February 4, 1877. First presented (Act IV) in the United States by the Kirov Ballet at the Metropolitan Opera House, New York, September 14, 1961, with Kaleria Fedicheva as Nikiya, and Sergei Vikulov as Solor.*

The libretto for this ballet, which is still active in the Soviet repertory, tells the story of a hapless Indian bayadère—a temple dancer—named Nikiya. The bayadère is loved but badly treated by Solor, a young warrior who breaks his pledge to her and marries another. Nikiya is poisoned by a confidante of her rival and dies. In the final act, the repentant Solor dreams that he seeks his beloved in the "Kingdom of the Shades." Though, like Orpheus and Albrecht, he finds her, she eludes him, despite his pledge that he will never forsake her again.

But the important thing about Act IV of *Bayadère* is not the story but the dancing. What happens is that the wraithlike inhabitants of the "Kingdom of the Shades" descend upon the stage down a long ramp at the back, parallel to the audience, all in profile in *arabesque penché* at each step. There are thirty-six Shades. These and their ensuing steps, while basically simple for dancers to perform, so direct the attention by their repetition that an otherworldliness results. Next there is a *pas de trois* for three of the Shades, followed by variations for each. Solor now dances a variation that reasserts his humanity in this atmosphere of immortals. The *pas de deux* between the two lovers ties them together as it were by a long diaphanous scarf. As Nikiya holds one end of the scarf with one hand, Solor at the other end supports her in a series of turns that is rivaled only by the lifts in the final act of *Giselle* for an expression of close spirituality.

NOTES   Rudolf Nureyev's fine production of *La Bayadère* for the Royal Ballet has become well-known in the United States. Another production, by Natalia Makarova, was presented in July 1974 by American Ballet Theatre. Arlene Croce wrote in *The New Yorker:* "It is an astounding success—more evidence that self-exiled Russian stars have as much to give as to gain in the West. *La Bayadère* (short for *La Bayadère,* Act IV: The Kingdom of the Shades) is an old Petipa classic of which most Westerners were unaware until the Kirov Ballet toured it in 1961. When Rudolf Nureyev, who defected on that same tour, produced it two years later for the Royal Ballet, it seemed that a miracle of transposition had taken place. Makarova has wrought an even greater miracle. She's not only reproduced a masterpiece of choreography, she's taken Ballet Theatre's corps and recharged it from top to bottom.

"The process of transformation is as yet incomplete, but never in my experience had the company danced a classical piece in so strict a style, on so broad a scale, and with such clarity of rhythm. Without these qualities, *La Bayadère* wouldn't be fun—it wouldn't even be *La Bayadère*—and what's *most* fun about this production is that every girl on the stage seems to be aware of the sensational progress she's making. . . . What matters . . . is that the motor impulse is there, solidly pumping energy into the right channels.

"Makarova's direction has been faithful and revealing. That motor impulse is basic to Petipa's exposition of movement flowing clean from its source. It flows from the simple to the complex, but we are always aware of its source, deep in the dancer's back, and of its vibration as it carries in widening arcs around the auditorium. This is dancing to be felt as well as seen, and Petipa gives it a long time to creep under our skins. Like a patient drillmaster, he opens the piece with a single, two-phrase theme in adagio tempo (arabesque, cambré port de bras), repeated over and over until all the dancers have filed onto the stage. Then, at the same tempo, with the dancers facing us in columns, he produces a set of mild variations, expanding the profile of the opening image from two dimensions to three. Positions are developed naturally through the body's leverage—weight, counterweight. Diagonals are firmly expressed. Returning to profile, the columns divide and flutter one by one to the rear. The final pose is of two long columns facing the wings with annunciatory arms. Now, to a collection of beer-garden tunes (the composer is Ludwig Minkus), Petipa sets dances for five soloists—a ballerina, a danseur, and three principal Shades—while behind them the vast, tireless corps responds in echoes, diverges, vanishes, regathers into garlands, into gateways, tosses, and freezes. The choreography is considered to be the first expression of grand-scale symphonism in dance, predating by seventeen years Ivanov's masterly designs for the definitive *Swan Lake*. But our first reaction is not to how old it looks but to how modern. Actually, the only word for this old-new choreography is immemorial. *La Bayadère* (1877) looks like the first ballet ever made: like man's—or, rather, woman's—first imprint in space and time.

"The subject of 'The Kingdom of the Shades' is not really death, although everybody in it except the hero is dead. It's Elysian bliss, and its setting is eternity. The long, slow repeated-arabesque sequence creates the impression of a grand crescendo that seems to annihilate all time. No reason it could not go on forever. And in the adagio drill that follows, the steps are so few and their content is so exposed that we think we'll remember them always—just like dancers, who *have* remembered them for a hundred years and for who knows how long before Petipa commemorated them in this ballet. Ballets, passed down the generations like legends, acquire a patina of ritualism, but *La Bayadère is* a ritual, a poem about dancing and memory and time. Each dance seems to add something new to the previous one, like a language being learned. The ballet grows heavy with this knowledge, which at the beginning had been only a primordial utterance, and in the coda it fairly bursts with articulate splendor. My favorite moment comes in the final waltz, when the three principal Shades are doing relevé-passé, relevé-attitude cambré to a rocking rhythm, and the corps, seeing this, rush to join them in the repeat. They—the corps—remember those cambré positions from their big dance.

"It's the corps' ballet—a fact the management should recognize by allowing a company call after, as well as before, the soloists have taken their bows. But the soloists in the performance I saw—Cynthia Gregory, Ivan Nagy, Karena Brock, Deborah Dobson, and Martine van Hamel—deserved their applause. Gregory was at her greatest. She took her grand port de bras the way it was meant to be taken—straight up out of the floor and through the body. Van Hamel, who may be the most talented of the company's younger ballerinas, did her variation the hard way by not coming off point until she was well up and into arabesque, and the excessively slow tempo made it even harder. Nagy has a way of filling a role superlatively without actually doing the steps. In his variation, he gathered himself powerfully and unfurled something that started like double assemblés and ended halfway to double sauts de basque. In the *pas de deux* with the veil, he didn't parallel the ballerina's steps and poses— but this is one of the differences between Makarova's staging and Nureyev's. Another difference is that she doesn't stroke the upbeat, or break the path of a gesture in order to point it. The way these two have staged the piece corresponds to their styles as performers—hers, musically more fluid; his, more emphatic. Also, her arabesques are not penchées, the solos are arranged in a different order, and she ends the ballet with the corps stretched along the floor in a semicircle rather than backbent in a sunburst. I prefer the Royal Ballet's orchestration, with its drumrolls and its protracted climax that accompanies the sunburst, and I think I prefer the sunburst, but apart from those things there's little to choose between these productions. They're both marvellous. Marcos Paredes' costumes for Ballet Theatre are in the Victorian style traditional to this ballet, and I liked his headdresses for the women—beaded circlets à la Anna Pavlova."*

In *Baryshnikov at Work*, the dancer Mikhail Baryshnikov calls *La Bayadère* "one of the great, if not the greatest, classical works in the history of ballet. It is Petipa's idea of life in the beyond . . . Poetically, it is unmatched in the classical repertory."

## LE BEAU DANUBE

*Ballet in one act. Music by Johann Strauss. Choreography by Leonide Massine. Scenery and costumes by V. and E. Polunin, after Constantin Guys. Costumes by Comte Étienne de Beaumont. Book by Leonide Massine. First presented in a two-act version by Comte Étienne de Beaumont's Soirée de Paris, Paris, May 17, 1924, with Lydia Lopokova as the Street Dancer. First presented in the final one-act version by the Ballet Russe de Monte Carlo at the Théâtre de Monte Carlo, April 15, 1933, with Alexandra Danilova as the Street Dancer, Leonide Massine as the Hussar, Tatiana Riabouchinska as the Daughter, Irina Baronova as the First Hand, and David Lichine as the King of the Dandies. First presented in the United States by the Ballet Russe de Monte Carlo at the St. James Theatre, New York, December 22, 1933, with the same principals.*

This famous character ballet takes place in a public park, the Prater, in old Vienna. Nowadays we are somewhat used to ballets that are set in parks—where policemen romance with governesses, where children rollick and get into mischief, and where the perennial gigolo tries to interest the young, innocent girl. These are all adaptations of *Le Beau Danube* (*The Beautiful Danube*) and a tribute to its popularity. Roger Désormière arranged and orchestrated the pieces by Johann Strauss that make up the ballet's score.

The curtain rises on a charming wooded park in Vienna. It is Sunday afternoon, about a hundred years ago. A gardener is tidying up the grounds, a young artist is painting at an easel; we hear the sound of a Strauss waltz and we believe the pretty picture we see on the stage. Strollers soon enter and enjoy the beauty of the scene: a family with two daughters, ladies of the town, seamstresses and dandies.

The artist is attracted to the first hand, the seamstress, and flirts with her as he sketches her portrait. The girl is pleased with the artist until the King of the Dandies rushes in and whisks her away from him.

Now a dashing hussar, in immaculate uniform, promenades with one of the daughters of the family. He is deferential to her family and is apparently formally engaged to her, for when he dances a mazurka with the girl their romance appears to be permanently happy. They leave the scene hand in hand.

* From "Makarova's Miracle" by Arlene Croce. Reprinted by permission; © 1974 The New Yorker Magazine, Inc.

A small band of street entertainers enter and set up to amuse the crowd that has gathered. The manager of the troupe points with pride to his principal artiste, a dancer, and the beautiful girl begins a lively solo that thrills the crowd. The manager and an athlete with bulging muscles join her; the dance becomes hilarious and everyone applauds them.

The hussar and his fiancée stroll back into the park at this point, and the hussar is embarrassed to see his past catch up with him. The street dancer instantly claims him as a former devoted lover and, to his fiancée's horror, pretends that the hussar has deserted her! The poor girl swoons during this scene of simulated jealousy and her family escort her out of the park, vowing vengeance on the ne'er-do-well hussar. The street dancer, not to be outdone by her rival, pretends to swoon also.

The hussar is distressed at what has happened, but he could hardly control the whims of the street dancer and there is nothing else for him but to take up with her again! The crowd wanders off and they are alone. The first familiar bars of the *Blue Danube* Waltz are heard. The hussar is moved to dance; quietly and slowly the music accompanies his recollection of his romance with the dancer, and he opens his arms to her. He waits, not moving. She too remembers. She feels false jealousy no longer, and they begin to dance, their initial restrained steps building gradually to an ebullient and joyful whirling with the persistent swell of the waltz.

But just as the former lovers seem to be reunited, the hussar's fiancée returns. She has run off from her raging family and insists on claiming the hussar: after all, she loves him. Why should she give him up so easily? The hussar, who has never seen such determination in a woman, is charmed by her completely and again forgets the street dancer. The *Blue Danube* has ended.

The young girl's family race in and try to separate their daughter from the fickle hussar, but the younger daughter steps in, cajoles and persuades, and tears turn to laughter. The hussar is properly deferential again to his fiancée's family; the father blesses the handsome couple; and the crowd in the park dance in celebration of the happy resolve. The street dancer, too, congratulates them with a final display of high-spirited dancing, and the charming park becomes a place where nothing unpleasant can ever happen.

## BEAUTY AND THE BEAST

*Dramatic ballet in two scenes. Music by Maurice Ravel. Choreography by John Cranko. Scenery and costumes by Margaret Kaye. First presented by the Sadler's Wells Theatre Ballet at the Sadler's Wells Theatre, London, December 20, 1949, with Patricia Miller as Beauty and David Poole as the Beast. First presented in the United States by the Sadler's Wells Theatre Ballet at the Denver Auditorium, Denver, Colorado, November 14, 1951, with the same cast.*

Ravel's *Mother Goose* Suite is made up of five movements, each based on a famous fairy story. The familiar tale of "Beauty and the Beast" inspired the fourth movement of the suite, but the English choreographer John Cranko has been inspired to use this dramatic theme as an accompaniment to almost all of Ravel's score.* The ballet is an intimate drama, actually a long *pas de deux* for the two principal characters.

The curtain rises soon after the music has begun. The scene is the forest where the beast is king. The light, almost transparent, cloth on which the trees of the forest are painted is cut into strips, giving a jungle effect. The light is dim. The beast reclines alone in the forest. He seems to be sleeping; he wakens and rubs his eyes with his long, clawlike hands. Then we see that he is weeping. His whole body shakes with violent sobbing.

Behind him, a beautiful young girl enters the forest. The beast does not see her, and the girl, unaware that she has happened upon a dangerous wood, moves in and out among the trees. The beast rises, sensing a strange presence. He wishes to welcome the girl, but knows he will frighten her. As her back is turned, he reaches out to her plaintively. The girl moves off into the forest, and the beast follows her. She begins to feel that she is not alone.

The ragged trees rise, and the scene changes to another part of the forest. Here in the center of the jungle is a dark clearing. A little light penetrates the darkness through an entrance formed by curving trees. Here the girl enters. Now she is thoroughly lost and frightened and she does a little dance to allay her fear—a kind of whistling-in-the-dark variation. Gradually she tires and sits down to rest. Soon she falls to the ground and sleeps.

Light begins to fill the jungle through the grottolike entrance formed by the trees. The girl wakens and looks about. She observes birds in the trees, dances happily, gesturing lovingly to the surrounding forest. She approaches one of the trees to pick fruit. As she takes the fruit, she sees that it is held in the hairy paws of the beast, who has been observing her secretly.

The girl faints. The beast picks her up and holds her carefully. The girl sobs in his arms and releases herself. She attempts to flee the forest, but at the entrance, branches of trees reach out to restrain her. The door of the cage has been shut, and the girl looks at the beast in terror.

The beast tries to convince her that he means no harm. Gently he kneels before her and holds out a red flower. Again the girl wishes to escape. The beast grovels on the ground, then crawls helplessly. He drops the flower and begins to cry. The girl goes over to him, but she is still too frightened to indicate her pity. She turns to run through the entrance, where the confining branches have disappeared. She passes through, out into the light, but her hand still holds the side of the entrance: she is uncertain and returns.

She dances back into the jungle. Now she is completely unafraid. She stands over the beast and helps him rise. He lifts her high in his arms and holds her so that she almost stands above him. The girl reaches down and holds his face in her hands. The music rushes magically; the beast releases her; and we see that his face is no longer the fierce mask of a ferocious beast, but the face of a handsome young man. The girl caresses his face, and the two lovers dance a

* The section *"Laideronette, Impératrice des Pagodas"* is omitted in the ballet.

flowing *pas de deux* in which the changed beast holds the girl secure as her feet gently touch the ground. At the end, the lovers reach out to each other and the curtain falls.

## BHAKTI

*Based on a Hindu theme and musical setting. Choreography by Maurice Béjart. Costumes by Germinal Casado. First presented by the Ballet of the Twentieth Century in 1968. First presented in the United States by the same ensemble at the Brooklyn Academy of Music, New York, January 25, 1971.*

A Hindu love poem in dance, *Bhakti* is a ballet in three parts. The themes of those parts have been described by their creator, Maurice Béjart: "It is through love that the worshiper identifies with the divinity; and each time he relives the legend of his god, who is himself only one of the faces of the supreme and nameless reality." The three parts of the work are *pas de deux* between certain girls and their heroes:

RAMA   an incarnation of Vishnu. His love affair with Sita, symbol of purity, is related in the celebrated Hindu epic *Ramayana*. This poem forms the basis of every classical dance or theatrical production in India.

KRISHNA   another incarnation of Vishnu. He is the God of Youth and Beauty, the divine Player of the Flute whose affairs with the shepherdesses and the lovely Radha are sung in the *Gita Govinda*. He is also the teacher par excellence, and it is he who speaks in the *Bhagavad-Gita*, one of the most important books of all.

SHIVA   the third person in the Hindu Trinity (*Trimurti*): Brahma, Vishnu, Shiva. As the "Destroyer," he kills illusion and personality. God of the Dance, his wife Shakti pursues the vital energy that flows from and returns to him, immobile, yet forever in motion.

Introduced by three young men, the ballet proceeds to representations of these gods and their ladies, each supported by appropriate ensembles.

## LES BICHES

*Ballet in one act. Music by Francis Poulenc. Choreography by Bronislava Nijinska. Scenery and costumes by Marie Laurencin. First presented by Diaghilev's Ballets Russes at the Théâtre de Monte Carlo, January 6, 1924, with a cast that included Vera Nemtchinova and Anatole Vilzak, Alexandra Danilova, Bronislava Nijinska, Felia Dubrovska, Ninette de Valois, Alice Nikitina, Lubov Tchernicheva, Nicholas Zverev, and Leon Woicikowski. First presented in the United States by the Marquis de Cuevas' Grand Ballet*

*at the Century Theatre, New York, November 13, 1950, with a cast headed
by Marjorie Tallchief, George Skibine, and Olga Adabache.*

Two ballet companies have preferred to call this ballet *The House Party* and
*The Gazelles.** It is certainly about a house party. There is a hostess, a woman
considerably older than her youthful guests; she seeks to form an attachment
with one of the young men at her party. The relations of some of her guests
are similarly romantic. The ballet thus has a romantic theme rather than a
specific plot; the characters are dancers. The ballet is in eight parts, corresponding to the divisions of the score: "Rondo," *"Chanson dansée,"* "Adagietto," *"Jeux,"* "Rag Mazurka," "Andantino," *"Chanson dansée,"* "Finale."

Before the curtain rises, the orchestra plays a short introduction; slow at
first, the music becomes smartly quick and pulsating and reminds us of the vitality of youth. The curtain rises on an enormous room that bears the mark of
the fashionable interior decorator. Painted blue curtains at the back enclose a
window. A large blue couch stands at the rear. Twelve girls enter and dance
pertly to the rhythm of the music. Their long, cool pink dresses whirl about
them in innocent contrast to the sophistication of their steps. The girls kneel,
rise, circle on point, bend back seductively, and choose partners as the music
hastens to a brisk finish. They run off in gushing, schoolgirl fashion.

Three boys in bathing trunks enter to the strong, choppy beat of the *"Chanson dansée."* They dance in a line; their movements are assertive and angular.
They thrust out their chests and display their biceps in a dance that stylizes
athleticism. The two boys on the side imitate the turns of the dancer in the
center. They kneel. The twelve girls run in. The boys continue their dance for
the girls' benefit, while the girls try to attract them. They surround each of the
three boys, then stand in a semicircle behind them. The boys kneel before the
girls, but seem to be disinterested.

A girl dressed like a page boy in white tights, blue tunic, and white gloves
enters on the right and interrupts the scene. She crosses the stage on point,
holding her hand up stiffly, as if she were on some secret errand. She takes no
notice of the guests, but the boys are fascinated. The girl leaves and, abandoning all hope of winning the boys, four of the girls flounce away and arrange
themselves decorously on the sofa. The others continue their flirtation with the
boys, who abandon them again when the girl enters as before. One of the
youths is attracted to her; she dances off, and the flighty girls take up with the
other two boys. The strange girl recrosses the room, but pauses this time to
dance briefly. Her hands are joined and she holds out her arms as she poses;
her movements are softly angular. Two of the boys have gone off with the girls
in pink, and one of the boys watches the girl in blue as she dances alone, apparently oblivious of his presence. He comes up behind her as she finishes her
variation, comes close and holds her arms; the two exit together.

The two boys return with the girls and begin a rollicking game. The boys

* Literally, *les biches* means *the hinds,* but colloquially it also means simply *girls,*
or *young ladies.*

slide the couch forward. They stand on it, lifting the girls over it; then the girls dance across the couch one by one and hop off the arm onto the floor. The boys walk off. The sofa is turned with its back to the front, and the girls hide behind it as the girl in blue re-enters with her partner. They dance briefly and exit when they see they are being watched. The boys come back to find the girls. They move the couch back near the window, and all leave the stage.

A woman in an elaborate yellow dress enters and crosses the stage with mannered steps. This is the hostess. She brandishes a long cigarette holder pointedly, as if she were posing for a stilted advertisement, and at the same time nervously belies her pose by playing with her long pearl necklace. Her hands are constantly in motion; she cannot remain still for an instant. Her dance is the dance of a woman who can never imagine herself alone; it is the perpetual and desperate performance of a woman who has to be seen to appreciate herself. No one interrupts her parody of a youthful dance, and she stops. She arranges herself languidly on the couch.

The two young men enter suddenly. They dance proudly, asserting their masculine strength. They approach the hostess, stomping their feet. She is delighted and joins them in a dance to the "Rag Mazurka." Vigorous at first, their *pas de trois* slows down. The hostess is enamored of both her partners. Both boys offer their arms. She doesn't know which to choose. She takes a chance and breaks free. Both boys follow her off.

The girl in blue meets her partner in the center of the stage for a *pas de deux* to the "Andantino." Their gestures and steps are strangely discontinuous; they move, pause, move again—formal, but intimate. Their dance ends as the boy holds the girl straight in his arms; then, with an intricate twist of both their bodies, the girl is poised high on his shoulder. They leave the stage.

To a sprightly tune two young girls enter and dance a lively duet in which each tries to outdo the other in expressing their attachment. Their dance becomes secretive when they imagine they are not alone. They blush and exit hurriedly.

In different groups that turn rapidly as they cross the stage, the entire ensemble gradually returns for the finale—first the girls, then the boys, followed by the hostess and the girl in blue. All romantic attachments seem to be forgotten as the ensemble joins together for a final fling.

NOTES   One of the popular ballets of the Diaghilev era, *Les Biches* is regarded by its choreographer as the modern equivalent of *Les Sylphides*. It has been revived since its first production by the Markova-Dolin Ballet, when Alicia Markova danced the part of the girl in blue and Anton Dolin danced her partner; and by the Grand Ballet of the Marquis de Cuevas, where the production met with critical and popular approval, both in Europe and New York.

The composer, Francis Poulenc, noted in the English magazine *Ballet* (Volume 2, No. 4) that *Les Biches* "is a ballet in which you may see nothing at all or into which you may read the worst . . . In this ballet, as in certain of Watteau's pictures, there is an atmosphere of wantonness which you sense if you are corrupted but which an innocent-minded girl would not be conscious of."

Nijinska revived *Les Biches* for the Royal Ballet December 2, 1964, with Svetlana Beriosova, Georgina Parkinson, David Blair, Keith Rosson, Robert Mead, Maryon Lane, and Merle Park in leading roles. This revival was first presented in the United States at the Metropolitan Opera House by the Royal Ballet the following spring.

## THE BIG CITY

*Music by Alexander Tansman. Book and choreography by Kurt Jooss. First presented by the Jooss Ballet at the Opera House, Cologne, November 21, 1932. Costumes and lighting by Hermann Markard. First presented in the United States by the City Center Joffrey Ballet at the City Center, New York, February 28, 1975. Staged by Anna Markard. Costumes and lighting by Hermann Markard, re-created by Ray Diffen and Jennifer Tipton. Pianists: Stanley Babin and Mary Roark. Conducted by Sung Kwak.*

*The Big City* was originally presented just four months after Kurt Jooss' masterwork, *The Green Table*, had won first prize in an international dance competition. Although the ballet is often described as the first dance composition to deal with social criticism, Jooss maintains that this was not his intention. He has described the work as an "attempt to portray the loneliness of city people by means of dramatic dance." He was inspired by the "bustle of city life, backyard gloom and the glamour of dance halls." The Joffrey Ballet version, taken from the final 1935 version, was staged by Jooss' daughter, Anna Markard.

The action of the ballet is compressed into three graphic scenes accompanied by music (Tansman's *Sonatine Transatlantique*) that recalls the time of Europe's first appreciation of *le jazz hot*. The plot: "In the hurrying throng of a continental city are seen a young Girl and a young Workman, her sweetheart, homeward bound after the day's work. A Libertine, in search of new conquests, follows the young Girl to her home. Dazzled by the promise of adventure, she fares forth on his arm to the dance halls, where disillusion awaits her."

Writing of the American revival of *The Big City* in *The Village Voice*, the critic Deborah Jowitt said that "the life of this city is a bitter cartoon of what we can imagine life in a German city at the edge of World War II to have been like." . . . What makes the ballet absorbing and moving is not the sad little plot or the social message, but the delicate way Jooss was able to suggest characters, social backgrounds, occupations of people through the ways he made them move. What he gives you in many cases seem like rapid sketches of something he means to develop later—but what sketches!"

Interviewed in the New York *Times* by Anna Kisselgoff at the time of the Joffrey revival, Kurt Jooss said that *The Big City* "must be seen now as a period piece of the nineteen-twenties . . . I am not a social-protest choreographer . . . I consider myself a choreographer first."

# BILLY THE KID

*Ballet in one act. Music by Aaron Copland. Choreography by Eugene Lo-*
*ring. Book by Lincoln Kirstein. Scenery and costumes by Jared French. First*
*presented by Ballet Caravan at the Chicago Opera House, Chicago, October*
*16, 1938, with Eugene Loring as* Billy, *Marie-Jeanne as the* Mother *and*
*Sweetheart, Lew Christensen as* Pat Garrett, *and Todd Bolender as* Alias.

The story of Billy the Kid is already a legend in America, a part of the larger
legend we know as the Opening of the West. The facts known about him—that
his real name was William H. Bonney; that he was born in New York City in
1859; was taken to Kansas when he was three; killed his first man in Silver
City, New Mexico, when he was twelve; and by the time he was hunted down
and shot, at the age of twenty-one, had killed a man for every year of his life—
these facts remind us of a gangster movie. But actually these facts do not tell
us the whole story of the Kid. They do not tell us that, although Billy the Kid
was regarded as the most dangerous desperado of his time, he was loved and
admired as much as he was feared, and that the Far West after the Civil War
was a place where these emotions could interchange and resolve—to make of
his life the heroic myth it has since become. This ballet is not, therefore, a simple biography of a wild West killer: it is the story of the life of Billy the Kid as
it became a part of the life of his time.

PROLOGUE    The first, slow notes of the music are subdued and eerie, like
sounds in the wilderness at night. The curtain rises. Across the front of the
stage a spotlight shines, making a path of brilliant orange light. The rest of the
stage is suffused in a semidark glow, as if bathed in the light of the golden
sun. An arid khaki-colored desert and tall, branching cacti are seen in the distance. From the right, a man dressed in a cowboy outfit steps boldly into the
path of light. Later we shall learn that this is Pat Garrett, the sometime friend
of Billy the Kid who becomes sheriff and kills him. But at the moment he is
simply any American pioneer, moving westward toward the blaze of the setting sun. He moves stiffly, with determination; for each step forward he will
take none back. Then his progress becomes a dance, the movements of which
remind us of the frontiersman's work: he circles his arm high over his head to
lasso invisible cattle; he pulls back roughly on invisible reins to halt a covered
wagon, then drives the horses on with a lash of a whip; he kneels motionless,
gun pointed, to catch the imaginary Indian. The music gains in strength with
his vigorous movements. It becomes stronger still, as Garrett is followed by another man and a woman. The man copies every one of his leader's gestures,
while the woman sets a dance pattern for the pioneer mother who rocks her
children to sleep even when danger surrounds her. Other couples enter, and
the orchestra builds gradually to sound a mighty processional as the pioneer
figures follow their leader in this formalized march to the West. Now Garrett
thrusts his arms forward, pushing back the frontier. He faces directly into the

light. He pirouettes rapidly, spine in the air, and repeats these movements as all the men in the caravan follow his lead. All the dancers catch the full vitality of the music, which itself pushes forward to a resistless, persistent climax. Then, at its fullest volume, the music is cut off sharply. There is a blackout.

STREET SCENE When the lights come up again, the backdrop still depicts, as it will continue to do, the same arid desert, but before the curtain move a group of particular characters—not pioneers simply—who place this episode in the hot and sunny main street of an early Western town, just north of the border. Woodwinds play an old Western tune that the rest of the orchestra takes up gaily and playfully. A smiling, sinuous Mexican in a wide-brimmed hat struts about, pawing the street with his boots like a tame but unbridled stallion. Pioneer women, dressed for the town in close-fitting bonnets, pass him by, their arms crooked to carry invisible burdens. The Mexican ignores them. Cowboys ride across the scene, spurring on the imaginary horses they straddle. Three dancing girls enter, their hands on their tightly corseted hips in an impudent attitude. Two women look them up and down and, noting their high-buttoned gold shoes and garish red tights, turn up their noses in disapproval, sniff at the air, and walk away. Eight cowboys ride on, and there is a short rodeo. At the end three of them stop and take up with the dance-hall girls. A group of lovely Mexican girls come onto the scene, and now the street seethes with activity. The people stand about, some talking, some flirting, others going about their private business.

Then suddenly the music is quiet. An oboe sounds a theme, and on the left a small, attractive woman comes in. She is dressed in city clothes and is clearly a stranger to the community. A big, gangling boy, dressed only in overalls and a straw hat, hangs onto her skirts, and they move through the crowd. This is Billy the Kid. The boy looks about and appears to want to stop, but his mother walks on ahead and they exit. The Mexican and the four Mexican girls dance together briefly, and then the Kid and his mother return. This time the Kid shows off his strength by softly lifting his mother around for several measures. She pushes his cheek to tell him how silly he is, and he turns his face away, blushing, but he persists at the game and the two waltz off.

Meanwhile something has happened to the crowd. They stand closely packed together, watching an argument between the Mexican and a man in red. The argument becomes a fight. They hit each other in slow motion, neither falling. The music accompanies their blows with retarded rhythm that increases in volume and speed as the fight becomes serious. The people in the crowd begin to sense that they should stand back. Now, as a trumpet sounds the theme militantly, the Kid enters with his mother. Both of them are fascinated by the brawl and stand on the fringe of the crowd. Just as they join the group, the Mexican pulls a gun. The man in red turns quickly to defend himself and steps against the crowd, right next to Billy and his mother. The Mexican fires. He misses. Billy's mother doubles up in agony. She falls against her son, who stands transfixed, staring straight ahead, not comprehending. She grasps his arm, slides down slowly to the ground, and dies. The people are horrified, but they, too, are motionless. They remain still and shocked as the

Kid shakes off his dream, grabs a knife, and dashes over to the Mexican. Billy kills him with one quick stab in the back. He topples over. Everyone steps back, unbelieving. Billy looks about wildly, wondering where to go. Pat Garrett steps in to help him, but the Kid ignores him and runs off. Already he has chosen his way.

One of the men stoops to pick up the body of the Kid's mother, and the whole crowd leans over in unison, expressing the common grief. Another man kneels down beside the dead Mexican, throws him over his shoulder, and carries him off. But the Mexican will reappear. He becomes Alias, a character of many disguises who haunts the Kid constantly throughout his life and finally helps to kill him.

The crowd begins to disperse. Couples walk away, shaking their heads, still stunned by the two murders. But instead of leaving the stage, they mill about, circling slowly, and we see after a few minutes that perhaps they are not the same men and women who saw Billy the Kid's first crime. The men lift their women affectionately, just as Billy lifted his mother, but everyone is wary and suspicious. The people have changed. They have grown older and, as we have been watching them, years have passed in the street. Finally, one by one, the couples leave and the stage is empty.

THE DESERT    The Kid enters in the back. He is no longer a child. He is dressed in black and white striped riding breeches, boots, a wide-brimmed hat; there is a skull on his shirt pocket. He dances alone. In this dance we understand a little of how the Kid has grown up. The proud pose that begins and ends the dance is confidently self-assertive, and in between the Kid performs a series of difficult movements with ferocity rather than grace. He stomps loudly with his heavy boots, circles an imaginary foe with his gun ready to fire, spins swiftly in the air, lands, and kicks out at his victim. He is going through the only vocabulary he possesses, and we realize that all of his life, every waking moment, is a practiced preparation for the next time he will have to kill. His dance gesture for shooting is a quick aim at the target, then a spin in the air that matches the speed of a bullet, and finally a vicious kick. It is the gesture of a man who hates his dead foe and the whole world. And there follows inevitably the same pose of self-assertion. Never does this man doubt that he has done the right thing, never has he supposed himself guilty of a crime. Shooting happens to be his way of living: a murder is just like lighting a cigarette.

As the Kid nears the end of his soliloquy, he is interrupted by the arrival of a small posse. Three men canter across the stage in formation, circle, and try to close in on the Kid. He hides. Then he aims, spins, and kicks. The leader of the three men falls dead. The Kid prances slowly and softly, then draws himself up to his full height and stands triumphant. The scene blacks out.

A spotlight at the front of the stage comes on. Sitting close to the footlights, around a campfire, the Kid and Pat Garrett are playing cards. Garrett is now sheriff, but still a friend to the Kid. The light from the fire makes enormous silhouettes of their figures against the backdrop. The orchestra plays a quiet, wistful melody. The Kid shuffles the cards and deals. The two men draw their cards. A man and two cowgirls, all friends of Billy, approach the fire. The man stoops down to watch the card game. Garrett is distracted for an instant, but turns back to find the Kid cheating. He protests. The Kid is patient with him at first, denies cheating, and attempts to humor him. Pat continues to protest, but when he sees that the Kid will not accept his friendship, will not even admit to overt cheating, he rides off into the night. Billy's three friends gather about the fire and take up the cards while the Kid stands aside. His rage mounts. Pat has got the better of him. He stomps angrily, regretting that he did not kill his friend. The group at the fire turn and stare at him; they are frightened at what he may do. But the Kid does not have time to act. Shooting is heard in the distance, and before he can flee, the stage fills with people. The drums boom with gunfire as Pat Garrett leads a posse on in pursuit of the Kid. Billy moves to defend himself, shoots wildly as his friends gather about him and his attackers fall on their faces to protect themselves. A fierce gun battle ensues, during which the Kid continues to shoot out indiscriminately at all comers. He and his friends are hemmed in by two lines of gunfire. They are all killed except Billy. As he is about to fire another round, he trips over the body of one of his own men. Two men move in to hold him. One of them is Alias. The Kid kills Alias. The other is Pat Garrett. Pat is quick: he sticks a gun in the Kid's back and rides him off to jail. The Kid does not seem to care in the least.

The posse that has helped capture Billy—cowgirls and cowboys—now join together to celebrate and dance joyfully. In the midst of their frolic, the Kid's sweetheart, a beautiful Mexican girl, walks in and tries to find her lover. No one pays any attention to her. She leaves the scene disconsolate. The celebration is blacked out.

THE JAIL   Billy stands on one foot, shuffling cards. Naked above the waist, he wears a kerchief about his neck, arm bands, and black riding togs over white tights. His jailer, Alias, stands at his side, ready to receive his cards. Billy bides his time, shuffles the cards slowly, and shifts to the other leg. The jailer grows impatient and turns away for an instant. Billy moves openly to grab his gun, as if the jailer expected him to. The jailer, of course, sees the move but ignores it. He suggests that it is all part of the game and that Billy won't do anything wrong. He walks away. The Kid sneaks up on him softly and this time does grab his gun. The jailer turns back, expecting the Kid to hand it over. The Kid laughs. He kills the jailer and stands again triumphant. Blackout.

THE DESERT   The Kid gallops across the stage to his hide-out. He disappears. A posse follows, but they are unable to pick up the trail. Billy enters again, screened by two Mexican girls, who stand between him and the posse. Alias, now disguised as an Indian guide, leads him away. The Kid arrives at a quiet spot, and Alias leaves him. Pat Garrett and his riders pass by, but see nothing. Billy takes his hat off and undresses to go to sleep. He is so tired he seems to be asleep already. He crouches on the ground to the right and stacks his clothes automatically, as if in a dream. His sweetheart enters on the left, behind his back. She dances on point, formally. He does not turn and see her, but looks up, seeing her in his mind's eye. He looks back down at his clothes. The girl touches his shoulder and poses briefly. He stirs, first swings his right leg out and back from his crouching position—a movement in stylized keeping with the girl's remote intimacy. She stands close beside him, but he is never aware of her real presence. He rises, stretches; the girl holds onto him and poses again beautifully, and they begin a short *pas de deux* to a sensuous waltz. He lifts her gently and swings her body slowly, not looking at her at all; he might be dancing with any girl and she with any man. Almost immediately he abandons her and goes back to stretch out to sleep. The girl dances off as quietly as she came, with no protest. The dream is over.

Pat Garrett, led by Alias, comes in and watches Billy asleep. Billy has not heard them, but wakes up as if warned by something. He reaches for his gun, holds it ready. The night is black: he sees nothing. For an instant he is afraid. Garrett and Alias stand stock-still, holding their breath. Billy calls out "*¿Quien es?*" ("Who is it?"), his voice hoarse with fear. There is no answer. He waits. Still no sound. He laughs to himself, silently. To reassure himself, he laughs harder; his body shakes with laughter. He stops, takes out a cigarette, strikes a match, and illuminates his face for a flickering moment. Garrett fires. Billy falls. He is dead.

Long-robed Mexican women enter and stand over his body. They pass by slowly, mourning, to music of lamentation, and the light fades.

EPILOGUE   The setting sun shines across the stage, and Pat Garrett walks in boldly, as he did at the beginning of the ballet, leading a host of pioneers. All march facing west, then turn back east, then west again, as the music impels them forward.


## BIOSFERA

*Music by Marlos Nobre. Choreography by Arthur Mitchell. Scenery and costumes by Fred Barry. First presented by the Dance Theatre of Harlem at the ANTA Theatre, New York, March 10, 1971.*

*Biosfera* is a dramatic *pas de deux,* not the usual display piece for two dancers but an opportunity for the two artists to become involved in a situation beyond themselves. The curtain rises on a dark stage where we gradually make out a girl and a boy, posed on platforms at opposite sides of the scene. The girl is dressed all in white, he in black. They leave their platforms to dance in a spotlight in the center. The music is lightly electronic, mysterious. The dance has a kind of detached romanticism about it. At the end, the girl and the boy return to the platforms at either side of the stage.

Reviewing *Biosfera* in the New York *Times* in March 1971, Clive Barnes said of the dancers: "Sheila Rohan is the girl, dancing with a crisp clarity, and the man is the distinguished and elegant Walter Raines, who at one point has to stand on his hands for what seems like two minutes . . . Mr. Mitchell has gotten himself the makings of a first-rate American classic ballet company."

# BIRTHDAY OFFERING

*Music by Alexander Glazunov. Choreography by Frederick Ashton. Costumes by André Levasseur. First presented at the Royal Opera House, Covent Garden, London, by the Sadler's Wells Ballet on May 5, 1956, with Margot Fonteyn, Beryl Grey, Violetta Elvin, Nadia Nerina, Rowena Jackson, Svetlana Beriosova, Elaine Fifield; Michael Somes, Alexander Grant, Brian Shaw, Philip Chatfield, David Blair, Desmond Doyle, and Bryan Ashbridge in the principal roles. First presented in the United States by the same company at the Metropolitan Opera House, New York, September 11, 1957.*

*Birthday Offering* was the Sadler's Wells Ballet's danced celebration of its twenty-fifth anniversary. Set to music from Glazunov's *The Seasons, Ruses d'amour,* and other works, as arranged by Robert Irving, the ballet displayed the special gifts of the first dancers of the company and was a tribute to the tradition and practice that had made the ensemble famous. That *Birthday Offering* is more than a *pièce d'occasion* was suggested by a revival in 1960 when it was danced by young aspiring ballerinas. Mary Clarke wrote in *The Dancing Times:* "This quality of youth and freshness gave the ballet a different kind of charm. Choreographically, it is a wonder. Each of the solos is a small masterpiece and the flow and patterns of the ensemble work are marvelously smooth yet delicate. Ashton here, in a Maryinsky mood, proved himself to be the equal of Petipa."

The score was taken from the following compositions of Glazunov: Entrée: *Valse de Concert, No. 1;* Grand Adagio: *Scènes de Ballet;* Fifield's Variation: *Scènes de Ballet;* Jackson's Variation: Winter (*Les Saisons*); Beriosova's Variation: Winter (*Les Saisons*); Grey's Variation: Summer (*Les Saisons*); Fonteyn's Variation: *Ruses d'amour.*

# BLUEBEARD

*Comic ballet in two prologues, four scenes, and three interludes. Music by Jacques Offenbach. Choreography by Michel Fokine. Book by Michel Fokine. Scenery and costumes by Marcel Vertès. First presented by Ballet Theatre at the Palacio de Bellas Artes, Mexico City, Mexico, October 27, 1941, with a cast headed by Anton Dolin as Bluebeard, Alicia Markova as Hermilia, Irina Baronova as Boulotte, Ian Gibson as Prince Sapphire, Antony Tudor as King Bobiche, Lucia Chase as Queen Clementine, Miriam Golden, Jeannette Lauret, Nora Kaye, Rosella Hightower, and Maria Karnilova as Wives of Bluebeard, and Dimitri Romanov, Donald Saddler, Annabelle Lyon, Jerome Robbins, and Hugh Laing as the Queen's Lovers. First presented in the United States by Ballet Theatre at the Forty-fourth Street Theatre, New York, November 12, 1941, with the same principals.*

*Bluebeard* is a comedy with a double plot. Its characters are everywhere at once, and if you don't have a clear idea of who they are and what they're up to, the ballet doesn't turn out to be as funny as it might be. The music, arranged and orchestrated by Antal Dorati, is taken from Offenbach's operetta *Barbe-Bleue* and other scores by that composer. The time is the beginning of the sixteenth century; the place is the mythical kingdom of King Bobiche.

FIRST PROLOGUE   There is a rousing, thumping overture. The curtain rises. King Bobiche, a tottering old man in purple robes and ruby crown, enters the scene carrying an infant. This is his daughter, Hermilia, who must be exiled because she is not a son. The old king doesn't know quite how to go about this, but he is determined that the child's birth shall be kept secret. Count Oscar, his chancellor, brings on a basket. The dejected monarch secures a necklace about the child's throat to identify her royal lineage; the two men place her carefully into the basket and sneak off to set her adrift in the river. Blackout.

SECOND PROLOGUE   Count Bluebeard sticks his head through the curtains and steps out quickly. He tweaks his beard, rolls his eyes, smacks his thigh, and appears to be a real devil of a fellow. He embraces a girl who comes along and kisses her so passionately that she collapses. This is his first wife. The same thing happens to two other maidens. A fourth girl is so overcome by the mere sight of Bluebeard that she falls in a trance before he can grab her. The fifth wife drinks with her husband. When she dies of the poison prepared by Bluebeard's henchman, Popoloni, Bluebeard stands over her body with an eager and how-was-that-for-killing-them-off leer.

ACT ONE: THE PALACE OF KING BOBICHE   The drop curtain rises on a medieval castle. Huge battlements rise up in the distance. It is night, some eighteen years after King Bobiche cast his daughter into the stream. On the right is a garden bench.

Queen Clementine dances in, followed by a page of the court. The page immediately begins to make love to the queen on the garden bench. The queen does not seem to care in the least. Bobiche interrupts them, parts the two lovers as if he'd spent his life dealing with his wife's infidelities, and then storms about with pretentious jealousy.

The queen pleads with him, but the king is adamant and orders that the page be hanged. When the poor lad is dragged off by the king's soldiers, the king chases his queen about the garden. They disappear for a moment. By the time the queen returns, two more suitors, dashing Spaniards with castanets and guitars, are ready to pay court to her. She is enchanted and watches with pleasure as the two men draw swords and fight for her affection. The two men readily see, however, that the queen is generous and can love them both. They put down their swords and alternately she kisses them as she joins them in a *pas de trois*.

Again the king interrupts and again we have tears, royal insistence, and an order for two more executions. This process goes on until five of the queen's many lovers have been caught in the act and sent off to be hanged. But still the king is not satisfied. He can certainly not expect his wife to love him and his mind goes back to the daughter he might have loved so much. He turns his back on the queen and weeps. He must get his daughter back, if by some miracle she is still alive!

The king orders his chancellor to search every corner of the kingdom for Hermilia and then condescendingly takes the hand of the queen. Members of the court kneel as the royal pair leave the garden. The drop curtain falls.

FIRST INTERLUDE: A CITY STREET   On his way to carry out the king's order, Count Oscar encounters the lovers of the queen, who are being led by their executioner to the gallows. He takes pity on them and inquires if they have any money. Luckily, they have. Good old Oscar empties their pockets and pardons them. The five men dance for joy while the chancellor counts his money.

ACT TWO: THE COUNTRYSIDE   With a roll of the drums, the curtain rises on a bright scene in the country. Scarecrows look out over the wheat fields in the distance, and the sun shines with an intense, glowing yellow. Peasant girls and boys dance together happily, circling and forming a chain, moving in vigorous, youthful harmony. One of the girls we notice right away because she is the prettiest of them all and because everyone seems to admire her. This is Floretta, in reality Hermilia, the daughter of King Bobiche. As if this weren't enough, the shepherd with whom she dances a romantic *pas de deux* is actually no shepherd at all but Prince Sapphire!

As Floretta sits on her shepherd's knee, a stunning blond girl comes in and berates the shepherd. She brags of her jealousy in a big emotional display, stamps her foot at Floretta, and the two lovers fly from her rage. Boulotte follows them.

Popoloni, the old alchemist who has helped Bluebeard kill off his wives, comes onto the scene. He tells the peasant girls that Bluebeard needs a new wife and that he will choose one of them for his bride. Bluebeard follows him almost immediately in an absurd chariot, and the girls quake at the sight of him. A few of the more courageous girls surround him, while others manage to form a line. Bluebeard looks the girls over one by one as if he were examining fresh meat. He doesn't like what he sees and pouts. As all the girls circle him, Boulotte re-enters. Bluebeard is just another man to her. She smacks him on the back, tweaks his beard, and treats him as if he were a rough and ready peasant. Ready Bluebeard obviously is: no woman has been so bold with him in years. He dances with her and soon proposes. Boulotte instantly consents, and Bluebeard carries her to his chariot. All wave as they exit.

Now the two plots of the ballet cross. Count Oscar, the chancellor, enters with one of the king's men. He is searching for the king's lost daughter. Popoloni engages Oscar in conversation, and as they talk, Floretta and her shepherd pass by. The shepherd bids the girl a hurried good-by as soon as he sees the count, who would expose his disguise. Count Oscar approaches her, asks politely to see her necklace, and Floretta is revealed as Princess Hermilia! Floretta fears that her shepherd might not love a Princess and wants to make sure of his affections. But, of course, Prince Sapphire is off sulking with similar thoughts. The drop curtain falls.

SECOND INTERLUDE    Bluebeard and Boulotte are racing across the stage to celebrate their marriage when their chariot passes Count Oscar and Hermilia. The fickle Bluebeard eyes the princess, and already he has had enough of the bouncing blonde. He must marry her, he decides, and vows to set a new plot in motion.

ACT THREE: A CELLAR IN BLUEBEARD'S CASTLE    The scene is dark as a dungeon. This is the laboratory of the alchemist Popoloni. On the left, at a table, chemicals burst into flame as he mixes them together. He chuckles to himself, delighted that his master has given him a new project. On the right are five vaults, each bearing the name of one of Bluebeard's dead wives! A sixth grave, as yet uncovered, is ready to receive another wife.

Bluebeard stalks in to give Popoloni his final orders: Boulotte must die! Boulotte enters and slaps him on the back. Bluebeard, out of all patience, tells Popoloni to be hasty. Boulotte takes one look at the five graves and clasps Bluebeard frantically in her arms. He pushes her off and Boulotte rolls about on the floor in despair. She rises and hangs on Bluebeard's neck, pleading with him to save her. "No!" he answers, and leaves her alone with her poisoner.

Boulotte goes over to Popoloni and tries to flirt with him. But the old man pushes her off his knee and tells her to leave off. He tells her that he has something for her and bids her drink from two goblets. Boulotte looks toward the open grave and refuses to drink. When Popoloni turns his back for a moment, she picks up a goblet from his table and drinks that one, instead. Poor girl, all the goblets are filled with the same poison! She falls to the floor.

Popoloni pretends grief; he is joined in his sorrow by Bluebeard, whose body shakes with sobs. He kneels beside his beloved and then, suddenly, he is up dancing as if he is absolutely delighted! He leaps over the body and dashes off in pursuit of the Princess Hermilia.

Old Popoloni's grief turns out to be genuine. He takes a feather, touches it to Boulotte's face, and she is alive again. Then, at a clap of his hands, all the graves open and we see that all the other wives have been similarly brought back to life by the alchemist. Bluebeard's first five wives surround Boulotte and pay tribute to the kindly Popoloni in a happy dance. The scene blacks out.

THIRD INTERLUDE    Bluebeard, too, has his qualms. The ghosts of his murdered wives circle around him as he recalls his crimes. For a moment, he is sorry.

ACT FOUR: THE COURT OF KING BOBICHE    King Bobiche leads his queen to their great, ermine-draped throne, and both prepare to welcome the Princess Hermilia to her true home. They embrace their daughter, who is strangely unhappy. They find out why when the king proposes that she marry a prince named Sapphire. Hermilia doesn't want a prince; she wants her shepherd. She storms about the court, refusing to consent to her father's wish. In despair, the

Anna Pavlova in *La Fille Mal Gardée*. Dance Collection, N.Y.P.L. at Lincoln Center, Astor, Lenox and Tilden Foundations.

Tamara Karsavina and Vaslav Nijinsky in *Le Spectre de la Rose*. Dance Collection, N.Y.P.L.

Clockwise from top left: Vaslav Nijinsky in *Giselle, Scheherazade, Jeux,* and *Afternoon of a Faun*. All photos from the Roger Pryor Dodge Dance Collection, New York Public Library.

Galina Ulanova in *Romeo and Juliet*. Collection of Rosemary Winckley.

Galina Ulanova in *Swan Lake*. Collection of Rosemary Winckley.

Alicia Markova and André Eglevsky in *The Nutcracker*. Photo by Maurice Seymour, from the Dance Collection, N.Y.P.L.

Alicia Markova in *Giselle*. Photo by Fred Fehl.

Alexandra Danilova and Frederic Franklin in *The Nutcracker*.

Alicia Alonso and Igor Youskevitch in *Giselle*. Photo by Fred Fehl.

king calls for Prince Sapphire, and when he appears, Hermilia cannot believe her eyes. Everyone rejoices.

But not for long. Bluebeard, no longer remorseful, is determined to wed Hermilia. He dashes in and flourishes his sword. The king is terrified and hides behind the throne. Prince Sapphire, the only fearless member of the court, suggests a duel. They begin to spar with their swords. Bluebeard tricks the prince and stabs him in the back. Bluebeard chuckles as his rival falls dead. Hermilia mourns her lover while the heartless Bluebeard wipes his sword and turns to her. Now, indeed, she must marry him!

Popoloni enters the court leading five masked women. Bluebeard is so busy sitting in Hermilia's lap that he doesn't pay much attention. Poor Hermilia can do nothing but cry. When Bluebeard looks up, the five women unmask: he sees all his dead wives! He leaps high into the air and runs for his life. The wives close in and beat him soundly. He frees himself and threatens Popoloni. But he observes that one of his former wives was really worth saving, after all. He drops the sword and goes to embrace her.

But King Bobiche has other ideas. The queen's five lovers have returned from the dead, too, and something must be done quickly: so he pairs them off with Bluebeard's wives. Old Popoloni recalls Prince Sapphire to life, and Hermilia is happy. The royal couple parade with Bluebeard and Boulotte, trumpets blare, Boulotte whirls around and around and around, and the colorful assembly of courtiers and peasantry rejoice.

## BOURNONVILLE DIVERTISSEMENTS

*Music by various composers indicated below. Choreography by Auguste Bournonville. Staged by Stanley Williams. Costumes by Ben Benson, after the original designs. Lighting by Ronald Bates. First presented by the New York City Ballet at the New York State Theatre, Lincoln Center, February 3, 1977, with Nichol Hlinka and Daniel Duell; Patricia McBride and Helgi Tomasson; Merrill Ashley, Robert Weiss and Kyra Nicholas; Suzanne Farrell and Peter Martins; Colleen Neary, Adam Luders, Victor Castelli, Muriel Aasen, Wilhelmina Frankfurt, Heather Watts and Bart Cook.*

I hope that by this time everyone knows the Danish ballet is built on a technique established in the nineteenth century by the great August Bournonville (1805–79), himself a remarkable dancer and choreographer, creator of many lasting works in the repertory of the Royal Danish Ballet. Bournonville was a pupil of Auguste Vestris, the first universally renowned male dancer in Europe, and brought superb technique to Denmark which he afterward modified in his own way. We see the result of his teaching in every ballet the Danes dance and whenever Danes dance. I have known and respected Bournonville's work ever since I worked at the Royal Danish Theatre in 1929 as guest choreographer.

Stanley Williams of our School of American Ballet is a much respected authority on Bournonville and we thought it would be good for our dancers, and for our audiences, to come to know well some of Bournonville's finest dances. Stanley Williams then put together a most entertaining ballet.

The ballet is in five parts, the first the *Ballabile* from the first act of *Napoli*, 1842, Bournonville's masterwork, with music by Paulli. Next, the *Pas de Deux* from Act I of *Kermesse in Bruges*, 1851, with music by Paulli. The third dance is a *Pas de Trois* from *La Ventana*, 1854, with music by Lumbye. The two concluding pieces are the famous *Pas de Deux* from *Flower Festival in Genzano*, 1858, with music by Helsted, and the *Pas de Sept* from *A Folk Tale*, 1854.

As Svend Kragh-Jacobsen observed in our program at the New York City Ballet, these five pieces made up a well-varied program with which to present Denmark's grand old master to a new audience.

## BOURRÉE FANTASQUE

> *Classical ballet in three parts. Music by Emmanuel Chabrier. Choreography by George Balanchine. Costumes by Karinska. Lighting by Jean Rosenthal. First presented by the New York City Ballet at the City Center, New York, December 1, 1949, with Tanaquil LeClercq and Jerome Robbins, Maria Tallchief and Nicholas Magallanes, Janet Reed and Herbert Bliss as the principals.*

This dance spectacle in three movements has no story, but each of the three parts has its own special character and quality of motion to match the buoyant pieces by Chabrier that make up the ballet's score. Each movement of the ballet is danced by a different *premier danseur* as principals. The "Joyous March" that serves as the overture sets a festival pace for the proceedings: loud, cheerful chords, crashing cymbals, and themes so blatantly vivacious that our senses are prepared for the high-spirited geniality with which the ballet both begins and ends.

BOURRÉE FANTASQUE   The curtain rises just before the overture finishes its final crescendo. Transparent white gauze curtains are draped across a blue background, and from the ceiling of the stage hang three black chandeliers, each holding differently colored candles. To the extreme right, standing in a straight line at right angles to the footlights, are four couples waiting for their cue. They are dressed in smart, crisp black; the girls fan themselves with small black fans. The sprightly music begins. The couples join arms and dance across the stage with jaunty, playful steps. The boys encourage the girls, who turn rapidly as their movements become more complicated. Four girls enter at the back; the couples stand back on either side as the newcomers move downstage, dancing in unison a series of bright, high steps. All the dancers are manifestly enjoying themselves immensely as they execute the precise, sparkling routine, yet they all maintain a firm, dead-pan expression, which makes their dancing absurdly comic. The boys leave their partners and pull the girls into their line. Everyone bows low.

A tall girl and a boy much shorter run out onto the stage and dance together briskly. The girl wears flowers high in her hair and fans her face impatiently. They stop suddenly; the music hesitates. The girl turns her back on the boy and looks down at her fan, which clearly amuses her more than he does. The boy tries to make a graceful pose and grabs hold of the ballerina's waist for support. She looks down at him with bored contempt; apparently he will think anything funny. He puts out his leg and looks on incredulously as the ballerina steps across it with little, mincing steps. He smiles at her gratefully; every one of her gestures is marvelous to him. She collapses in his arms and dances frantically. She holds her leg high, and he obligingly supports it under the knee. He stoops down close to the floor to watch her feet closely. The ballerina is determined to exploit his patience at every opportunity and when the boy supports her in attitude, she throws her leg up behind him and kicks him in the back of the head. The boy continues, however, to fancy that she is perfection itself. He moves to sit down, but the ballerina jumps into his lap before he reaches the floor. He tries to engage her flirtatiously, but she will have none of it; he nods his head beseechingly, but she shakes her head insistently. They rise and exit with a flourish.

The eight girls and four boys dance briefly. Like the ballerina's partner, the boys crawl on the floor to admire the girls' dancing feet. Then they move between the two rows of girls and join them in witty steps to the staccato verve of the music.

The ballerina and her partner return and enliven the fun to a high pitch of merriment. The boy holds the ballerina about the waist and squats low behind her as she hops toward the back on one point. Then he joins the other four boys in a dance that becomes intensely brisk. The ballerina fans herself calmly. The girls come forward and rejoin the boys, and the ballerina's partner twirls her about. He catches her in a tight embrace, but she bends her body back, trying to escape. He attempts to put his arms around her neck, but she holds his hands; their arms tangle hopelessly. The two move close to the footlights and forget all classical pretensions as they turn swiftly around and around on one foot, like circus performers. They both stop this exhibition simultaneously and join the group in a final round of merriment that ends abruptly on a note of rampant gaiety.

PRELUDE  The gauze curtains are pulled slightly higher over the empty stage. Eight girls enter from the wings and cross the stage fleetingly, softly, devising a fragile, romantic mood to the new sensuous melody. They arrange themselves in two striking poses about their leaders. A lovely girl walks out slowly from the back. She is looking for someone; she approaches like a sleepwalker and notices no one. A boy emerges from the opposite side. He, too, moves as if he were in a dream. The boy and the girl wander in different directions, weaving in and out among the other dancers as if caught in a labyrinth that will never lead them to each other. Each appears to sense the other's presence, but as they pass closely, their hands almost touching, their reverie does not allow them to see and after a pause they continue on their search.

At last the boy discovers the girl. Her back is turned to him. He places his hand on her shoulder; at his touch she poses gracefully. The boy takes his supporting hand away; the girl stands motionless on point for an instant until he has moved in front of her. She places her arms on his shoulders, and the boy assists her as she displays her comeliness in open turns that cause her black dress to flow about her. Their contact is intimate but also remote, warm yet formal; they recognize each other only in the perfection with which they dance together. She falls back in his arms.

The boy turns briefly to support two of the other girls, but returns to the ballerina. She pirouettes rapidly with her arms high over her head; the boy catches her still turning figure and circles with her. He lifts her tenderly. Momentarily, he is separated from the ballerina and the other girls group themselves around him. He kneels and they cover his head with their arms possessively so that he does not see his lover approach him. She moves away listlessly, returns, retires, then moves back toward him determinedly, in a running leap. The boy looks up and catches her falling body tenderly as the other girls back away. He lifts the ballerina high, and they move forward diagonally across the stage, two girls following along closely, their arms stretched up to clasp the ballerina's outstretched hands. The other girls move by in the opposite direction, passing under their arms swiftly and creating an impression of effortless speed. Now the boy moves backward with the ballerina and the group moves forward beneath her. He lifts her down and for an instant he loses her. The sumptuous music nears its fullest statement as he finds her again. He holds her hand, she rises on point and extends her leg slowly but firmly. Her extended point seems to pierce the richness of the melody.

With an elegant flourish, the ballerina bends low before the boy in a formal gesture of gratitude and acceptance. She rises to turn rapidly in attitude; the boy steps forward quickly and catches her about the waist as she turns full circle. The movement is repeated several times, after which the lovers stand close together, her head on his shoulder. They move apart; the girls glide in between them, forming the same intricate pattern that separated them at the beginning. They look about, seeking, wandering in and out; they pass, pause, but do not find. Both walk off as they came, preoccupied with their private dreams. The others dance slowly into the wings.

FÊTE POLONAISE   To the tune of a lively fanfare, a girl and a boy run out onto the stage. The boy kneels, takes the girl's hand, and holds her secure as she races around him. They are followed by three couples, who repeat this routine while the orchestra hurries its preface to the principal theme. Two other couples join the group. These two girls place their hands on their hips and look out into the audience with the gay impudence of chorines. A loud beat is sounded on the drum, and the exhilarating polonaise begins as the two girls are thrown high by their partners.

The other couples join the dance; the boys kneel around the girls in a circle and with a whipping motion encourage their cavorting. Directly all the dancers have caught the vivacity of the music, the ballerina enters to make the scene more animated still. Her grace and high good humor infect the dancing with fresh lightness. She seems astonishingly light as her partner swings her high about him. Finally, he catches her in a breath-taking leap and the two exit.

There are now eight couples on the stage, who dance together briefly before the ballerina and her partner return. This time the boy swings the ballerina about him on one arm; her legs beat together in midair. The girls circle them; the ballerina is turned rapidly by her partner as the girls dance around them; then she kneels. She leaves the stage, and the romantic ballerina of the prelude enters with her group of dancers. Soon all three ballerinas and their partners are assembled with the entire *corps de ballet*. The *corps de ballet* form concentric circles about the romantic ballerina, who is lifted high above them, and for a few moments the entire scene whirls with movement as each circle of dancers runs around and around.

All the boys dance a short routine with boundless energy, and the three ballerinas come to the front of the stage with their partners. Now it is almost like a competition between them. The ballerinas gather with their different groups. They take turns leading the groups of eight girls across the stage diagonally with broad, running jumps. The groups crisscross in midstage as the music nears a climax of jubilation. Then all the ensemble is reunited for the height of the festivity. Their ensembles are grouped behind the three ballerinas in a spectacular pose as the music ends and the curtain falls.


## LA BOUTIQUE FANTASQUE (The Fantastic Toyshop)

*Ballet in one act. Music by Gioacchino Rossini, arranged and orchestrated by Ottorino Respighi. Choreography by Leonide Massine. Scenery and costumes by André Derain. First presented by Diaghilev's Ballets Russes at the Alhambra Theatre, London, June 5, 1919, with Enrico Cecchetti as the Shopkeeper, Lydia Lopokova and Leonide Massine as the Cancan Dancers, and a cast that included Lydia Sokolova, Leon Woicikowski, Stanislas Idzikowski, Vera Nemtchinova, Lubov Tchernicheva, and Serge Grigoriev. First presented in the United States by the Ballet Russe de Monte Carlo at the Majestic Theatre, New York, March 20, 1935, with a cast that included Alexandra Danilova and Leonide Massine (Cancan Dancers), Eugenia Delarova, Tamara Grigorieva, Nina Verachinina, Yurek Shabelevsky, Roland Guérard, David Lichine, and Serge Grigoriev.*

Like *Coppélia, La Boutique Fantasque* is based on the charm of the mechanical doll. Here, in a great fantastic toyshop in southern France, dolls from all over the world entertain customers from all over the world, who have come to see the detailed and charming workmanship of a master dollmaker. The time is the 1860s.

At the rise of the curtain, the sunny shop is empty. It has been closed for lunch. The shopkeeper and his helper return and open the doors for business. While they are busy preparing for their work, a dirty little boy comes in and attempts to steal gold lace from one of the shopkeeper's prize dolls. The thief is apprehended and, fleeing, bumps into two prospective customers, an English old maid and her companion.

The old maids want to see the best dolls and when the shopkeeper has shown them the mechanical peasant dolls on display, they ask to see more. New customers, an American family with two children, charge in. The family know the English ladies and after all the customers have exchanged greetings, the American turns to the shopkeeper and asks to see his dolls.

The shopkeeper obsequiously consents, and two tarantella dancers are wheeled in. When the customers have examined them, the two dolls, an Italian girl and her sweetheart, break into an animated tarantella to the lively accompaniment of rattling tambourines. Then, as if their mechanism had run down, the dancers collapse.

Next there is a mazurka, danced by dolls representing the Queen of Clubs, the Queen of Hearts, the King of Diamonds, and the King of Spades.

A Russian couple enter with their four children. The English ladies resent the intrusion of these foreigners and take their leave.

The next set of dolls displayed by the shopkeeper represent a snob and a melon hawker, a combination of the rich and the poor. The snob bustles about busily while the melon hawker slices a melon and presents it to him. Then the melon hawker shines the shoes of the snob, who trips over the hawker, only to rise again in a mechanical miracle.

The customers are now convinced that they are seeing a great and marvelous entertainment. Their mutual enthusiasm makes them all friendly and they watch with delight as more dolls perform.

Five Cossack dolls led by a chief perform a rapid dance next. Then the chief Cossack is joined by a Cossack girl doll, who kisses him while the soldiers snap to attention. The porters of the fantastic toyshop drill the Cossacks off.

Now two dancing poodles display their skill by walking on their hind legs. The female dog tries to attract the male dog by her cavortings and the male dog, in his enthusiasm for her dancing, rushes around and around her. The American couple are shocked at this amorous display and blindfold their children.

The shopkeeper now informs his prospective customers that they are about to see the most ingenious dolls of all: the cancan dancers. The couple who are wheeled in dance with such gusto that all the spectators are bound to agree. As the girl doll abandons herself in the cancan, her partner is so delighted that he performs marvelous gravity-defying tricks.

Now both families who have been watching the dolls want to buy the cancan dancers. The American children like the male doll best, the Russians the girl. Their fathers talk to the shopkeeper, agree to pay his price, and leave, saying that they will call for the dolls in the morning.

Night has fallen. The shopkeeper and his assistants lock up and leave.

Now that they are alone, all the dolls in the shop emerge from their boxes and become more animated than ever. They are very happy to be dancing so freely, but they are also sad. The cancan dancers are to be separated tomorrow. The two lovers dance together for what seems to be the last time, and the other dolls dance about them, celebrating their love. At the end of the revels there is a general cakewalk, danced by all the dolls.

When morning comes and the shop is reopened, all appears to be as it was the night before. But when the American and Russian families call to pick up the dolls they have engaged to buy, something is amiss: the cancan dancers have disappeared from their boxes! The children howl, the fathers berate the shopkeeper, and the mothers rage. The shopkeeper and his assistants are beaten, and the whole toyshop is attacked by the disappointed customers.

Just when it seems likely that the irate foreigners will destroy the shop completely, the toy dolls come to the rescue. The poodles attack the Russian mother; her husband and children are set upon by the card toys; and the Americans are routed by kicking ballet-dancer dolls. Finally the Cossacks drive the customers from the shop.

Unbelieving, the Americans and Russians stand outside and look back through the window. They see all the dolls in the shop dancing together a brilliant ensemble, a final happy dance. The shopkeeper and the cancan dancers shake hands. All the dolls rejoice that the two lovers are still together.


# BRAHMS QUINTET

*Music by Johannes Brahms. Choreography by Dennis Nahat. Costumes by Willa Kim. Lighting by Nananne Porcher. First presented by American Ballet Theatre at the Brooklyn Academy of Music, New York, December 1969, with Cynthia Gregory, Ivan Nagy, Mimi Paul, Gayle Young, Naomi Sorkin, Ian Horvath, Eleanor D'Antuono, and Terry Orr as principals.*

This dance ballet to a masterpiece by Brahms uses the score for its narrative. The music critic Donald F. Tovey referred to the Brahms *Quintet in G Major, Op. 111,* as "an immensely powerful outburst of high spirits. . . . The first movement seems unlimited in its capacity for expansion. The adagio . . . is one of Brahms's tragic utterances. Its tempo is slower than that of any other piece of classical music since Beethoven's C Minor Concerto." Tovey found the third movement to be an "exquisite plaintive little scherzo and trio" and the finale "vigorous. . . . At the end its coda breaks away into a completely new dance tune, the phrases of which reel down in bacchanalian irregularity to explain themselves with impudent assurance as connected with the main theme by ties as intimate as a borrowed visiting card." (From *Cobbet's Cyclopedic Survey of Chamber Music,* 1963.)

Reviewing the ballet for the Washington *Post,* the critic Jean Battey Lewis said that "Nahat's *Brahms Quintet* is one of those flowing, floating dance works so appealing to us these days. It has a lovely, curving wind-swept quality and an abstraction that still celebrates the affection between the dancers."

## BRAHMS-SCHOENBERG QUARTET

*Music by Johannes Brahms, orchestrated by Arnold Schoenberg. Choreography by George Balanchine. Scenery by Peter Harvey. Costumes by Karinska. First presented by the New York City Ballet at the New York State Theatre April 19, 1966, with Melissa Hayden and André Prokovsky, Patricia McBride and Conrad Ludlow, Allegra Kent and Edward Villella, and Suzanne Farrell and Jacques d'Amboise in leading roles.*

In talking about music that is good for dancing I have often said that most string quartets are not suitable—they are too long, they are full of repeats, and of course they are meant for smaller audiences. This quartet of Brahms, the *Piano Quartet in G minor, Opus 25*, I have always liked a great deal but it never occurred to me to use it for a ballet until Robert Craft told me about Schoenberg's orchestration.

This undertaking was of course most unusual for Schoenberg. But in a letter to Dr. Alfred Frankenstein, Schoenberg gave his reasons: "1. I love the piece. 2. It is seldom played. 3. It is always very badly played, as the better the pianist, the louder he plays and one hears nothing of the strings. I wanted for once to hear everything and this I have achieved."

I liked hearing everything too, and wanted to see the piece danced. The result is a dance ballet, with only a musical narrative. The movements are marked *Allegro, Allegro ma non troppo, Andante,* and *Rondo alla Zingarese: Presto.*

## BROUILLARDS

*Music by Claude Debussy. Choreography by John Cranko. First presented by the Württemberg State Ballet at the Opera House, Stuttgart, March 8, 1970. First presented in the United States by the same ensemble (the Stuttgart Ballet) at the Metropolitan Opera House, New York, April 30, 1971.*

Nine piano preludes by Claude Debussy are the inspiration for *Brouillards* ("Mist"). The choreographer, John Cranko, said: "Mist, snow, heather and sails are the transient pictures in Debussy's music: the mist dissolves, the snow melts away, the heather fades, and the sails grow slack—leaving behind remembrance and regret only because of their beauty. Every day passes away—like all human relations." While thus a ballet without a narrative, *Brouillards* may be said to have a mood plot set to music.

The piano begins and the curtain rises on a dark scene where we gradually discern a chain of dancers in white. They swirl and gather in the center, undulate in the mist, separate, return and cluster. A girl and three boys, to the music of *La Puerta del Vino* ("The Gate of Wine"), perform a bright dance in which, first riding on the back of one, then dancing an adagio with another, and finally turning to respond to the third, the girl shows that she likes all three. The boys leave her, sulking, at the end.

To *Voiles* ("Sails"), a girl and boy dance, responding to the music with daring lifts, slides, and turns, he going in one direction with the wind, as it were, she in another. Next, a *Cakewalk*, a comic turn to quick, witty music for three boys. *Bruyères* ("Heather"), which follows, is a dance for a boy who is enamored of a sleeping beauty who lies nearby on a bench. He kneels at her feet, kisses her, dances for her, but she does not respond. When, finally, he shakes her in exasperation, she rises and coolly walks away.

Two girls dance to the music of *The Fairies Are Exquisite Dancers* and make of it a joyful competition of held poses and leaps. To *Dead Leaves* there is another *pas de deux*, a passionate adagio. *Homage to S. Pickwick, Esq.* is a tribute to John Bull, armed with bowler hat and umbrella, by six boys who kid him and rag him until he collapses. They cover him up, the bowler on the umbrella remaining as a kind of gravestone.

*Footsteps in the Snow* is for a girl and two boys, both of whom seem to follow in pursuit of the girl, and the *Finale,* again, is an ensemble piece, the group of dancers filling the surface of the stage with swirling mist.

# BUGAKU

*Music by Toshiro Mayuzumi. Choreography by George Balanchine. Scenery and lighting by David Hays. Costumes by Karinska. First presented by the New York City Ballet at the City Center, New York, March 30, 1963, with Allegra Kent and Edward Villella in the leading roles.*

Over the years the New York City Ballet has had a happy association with Japan. The company danced there in 1958, and in 1959 the musicians and dancers maintained by the Imperial Household known as *Gagaku* came to the United States and appeared with great success on the regular programs of the New York City Ballet. The *Gagaku* is the oldest dance company in the world, with an uninterrupted tradition of repertory and performance extending almost a hundred years. Having heard the *Gagaku* and seen their fine dancers with so much pleasure, I asked the gifted young Japanese composer Toshiro Mayuzumi to write the music for a ballet. The work was commissioned by Mrs. Norman LaSalle. Our idea was that the piece would be in the style of Japanese court music (*Bugaku*), but for Western orchestration.

Mayuzumi's score I liked very much when we received it. Just as the composer had transposed the Japanese court music into a Western vocabulary, I attempted in the dances to transpose the classic Western academic ballet into a style suggested by the music.

The setting is a severely simple arena-like stage typical of formal Japanese presentations. The costumes are a free fantasy on traditional Japanese court dress. The dance is in three main parts. At the beginning, before any dancers appear, the ear takes in the strange sounds of the orchestral introduction. Five girls enter and dance with grave formality, following the lead of a girl in a rose-petal skirt. They are joined by five boys, who file on to the vigorous sound of drums. Later, these couples return in ceremonial robes to escort the boy and girl who have led them. The diaphanous ceremonial robes of the girl flow behind her as the boy lifts her in a dance of praise. But love here is as ritualistic as the setting. The attendants remove the ceremonial robes of the couple. They continue their dance, now unencumbered by the costumes. Their dance is a *pas de deux* of discovery. After the adagio, the girl dances joyously, then the boy, but then the music slows down. The attendants return to dress them again in their robes and there is a stately procession at the end of which all kneel.

## THE CAGE

*Ballet in one act. Music by Igor Stravinsky* (Concerto Grosso in D for Strings). *Choreography by Jerome Robbins. Costumes by Ruth Sobotka. Lighting by Jean Rosenthal. First presented by the New York City Ballet at the City Center, New York, June 10, 1951, with Nora Kaye as the* Novice, *Yvonne Mounsey as the* Queen, *and Nicholas Magallanes and Michael Maule as the* Intruders.

This ballet is a dramatic demonstration of a phenomenon common to insect and animal life and to Western mythology too: the phenomenon of the female considering the male as prey. The mantis devours her partner after mating; the spider kills the male unless he attacks first; and the Amazons, in Greek mythology, were a cult of warlike females who did not associate with men, except for procreation. The Amazons despised their male children and maimed or destroyed them. Woman was sufficient; Man was accidental. *The Cage* shows us such a tribe of women.

Before the ballet begins, the auditorium is completely dark. The footlights come up before the curtain, then go out; the lights in the orchestra are extinguished. There is no music. The curtain rises. The light is obscure and misty, but we see hanging over the stage a tangle of multicolored strands, like the web of some huge spider. Mysteriously, as if it were a living thing, the web rises, stretches, and hangs over the floor. On the left stand a group of female figures arranged in a tight tableau; they are clustered together like bees in a hive.

The music begins with three notes sounded sharply on the strings. The women stir. In the center of the group sits the queen of the tribe. The lights come up gradually. A still, shrouded creature is drawn out from between the queen's legs; the novice has been born. The queen strips the confining membrane from the novice's body. The new member of the tribe crouches slightly. Her body is marked with endless, tangled viscera. Her face is still covered. She is motionless. The queen stands behind her, extending her arms grotesquely, seeming to enclose the novice with her long talons.

The orchestra begins a vibrant march. The twelve members of the tribe turn their backs, rise on point, and commence a grotesque ceremonial dance. As their bodies turn, we see that their backs are insectlike: strands reach out from their black spines to cover their backs, and they seem to resemble scuttling beetles. The queen leaves the novice and dances among the tribe. The women circle her and bow low obediently as she dances. The novice remains inert.

Now two of the women go to the novice and drag her to the center, before the queen. The queen tears off the membrane covering her face. The novice's hands reach up to protect her eyes from the sudden light. Her face is a mask; her hair, dark and wet, clings to her head. The queen is well pleased at her ugliness. The birth rite is over; the queen and her creatures leave to watch the novice from the surrounding darkness. Just as she departs, the queen touches the novice's dark head in blessing.

The melody changes; the music slows in tempo. The novice's untrained limbs do not yet know how to move and she squats alone. She tests her arms and legs, pushes her body up on them, rises on point. Her gestures are sudden and sharp, her body angularly contorted. Her fingers are clawing and knifelike blades cutting at the air tentatively; her arms are sinuous, serpentine. She walks with knees open and bent, arms ready to enlace her prey.

The music breaks into a loud, rapidly rhythmic burst of sound. A man rushes in and seizes the novice by the waist. She twists away in revulsion. The intruder attempts to pull her close to him and falls to the ground. The novice falls upon him, and they roll over together. The exhausted intruder lies quiet as the novice rises and steps upon his chest with the sharp point of her foot. Now she straddles his body, grabs his head between her legs, clenches her fists, tightens and twists her body, and cracks his neck with her knees. He is dead.

The music quietens. The novice kicks the body over on its face. As the orchestra resumes the opening march, she dances alone, her knees rising high, driving her feet hard against the ground. Her head is thrown back and her mouth hangs open in a shriek of triumph.

The queen leads the tribe back to the novice. The hideous women stalk into the light, surround the novice, and congratulate her. She has met the test, her instinct has obeyed the law of the tribe: she has killed her first male. The novice kicks at his body contemptuously, and he is dragged off.

The queen embraces the novice. Other women in the tribe pair off and rest together. The women are content with their own society and relax without fear of intrusion. Then the music sounds a warning. The couples separate. The light dims. The queen signals the others to hasten away. The novice, suddenly afraid, is running off after them as her swift body is caught up in the arms of a dark, handsome intruder. Her legs try to kick her body free as he holds her, but she cannot loosen his grasp. The warning in the music ceases; the melody flows yieldingly. The novice is now unsure. Gradually she succumbs to the superior strength of the intruder and dances with him a romantic love duet. He holds her on his knee, and she sharpens her claws together, not for battle now, but for love. Their bodies separate and their fingers approach and entwine like bristling antennae. She tries to make herself graceful as she dances and falls back into the intruder's arms. He catches her body between his legs; her face turns up toward his, and their arms embrace in a cocoon. The novice's feet beat at the floor as the intruder becomes her lover.

The lights go down for a moment. The music whirrs ominously. The frightened intruder moves and the woman falls to the ground. The two lovers cower together, trying to conceal each other in the darkness, as the queen and the tribe enter. Then, as the intruder sees the women who would claim the novice, he revolts and pushes the woman, now hideous to him, into the arms of her Amazon queen.

This is what the tribe have waited for. The queen directs her creatures to attack the intruder as the novice is held secure. The women climb upon the intruder like ants on a stick of candy. He is released briefly and rolls helpless on the ground. The novice's native instinct begins to return. She falls upon him, straddles him, and slides her body over the passive male. She squats guiltily as the women seize him and carry him aloft. The queen orders her fellow creatures to carry the novice on their shoulders and hold her poised above him. The novice's claws are straight and sharp for the kill. She aims carefully and deliberately and slashes.

The body of the intruder lies again on the ground. The hungry women crawl over him, devouring his limbs. The novice strangles him between her knees. His body curls for a moment, then straightens. He is dead. His body is rolled across the stage. The victorious women leap over it as they dance triumphantly.

The novice cleans her talons. The queen joins her to accept her as a true member of the tribe. The two grotesque figures whirl together, then stand motionless, their deformed bodies dominating the dark cage. The music stops. The great spidery web loosens and falls about them to the ground.

NOTES  When *The Cage* was presented during the New York City Ballet's Stravinsky Festival in June 1972, the critic Sam Norkin wrote in the *Daily News:* "A hit since its premiere 21 years ago, this ballet is a 16-minute spellbinder . . . The driving music that accompanies the ballet was danced sensationally by Melissa Hayden as the novice. Here was a great ballerina in full mastery of her role. Gloria Govrin and Nicholas Magallanes were convincing in their roles as the queen and intruder respectively."

# CAKEWALK

*Ballet in three parts. Music adapted and orchestrated by Hershy Kay after music by Louis Moreau Gottschalk. Choreography by Ruthanna Boris. Scenery and costume by Robert Drew. Lighting by Jean Rosenthal. First presented by the New York City Ballet at the City Center, New York, June 12, 1951, with a cast headed by Janet Reed, Patricia Wilde, Yvonne Mounsey, Herbert Bliss, Frank Hobi, Tanaquil LeClercq, and Beatrice Tompkins.*

*Cakewalk* is an American ballet based on the minstrel shows. The great era of the minstrel show began to end toward the turn of the century, but this ballet reminds us of why this form of entertainment, native to America, was once so universally popular: like the original, it has humor, sentiment, magic, and liveliness. *Cakewalk,* being a ballet, doesn't have the two sets of bones, the two banjos, the two tambourines, and the singers that every real minstrel show used to have. These musical elements are taken care of by the orchestra, which plays in special arrangements a group of pieces and songs by Louis Moreau Gottschalk, the American composer and pianist whose music was so popular among original minstrel show artists: such works as "Bamboula," "Maiden's Blush," and "Won't You Buy My Pretty Flowers?" On stage, the dancers imitate the conventional minstrel show turns in dance terms that combine folk dancing with an enlivened classical technique. Like all proper minstrel shows, *Cakewalk* is divided into three parts.

PART ONE   The orchestra strikes up a loud, ebullient overture. The curtain rises. At extreme left and right are entrance doors on to the stage. In the back hangs a drop curtain that shows a huge Mississippi side-wheeler plying up the stream. Already, before the dancers appear, we have a vivid sense of the atmosphere in which the original minstrel show flourished.

One by one, the performers make their entrance to begin the "Grand Introductory Walkaround." They strut across the stage rapidly, led by the interlocutor, giving us a hint of the novelties to come. Finally, when all have disappeared in the door at the left, the drop curtain rises and we see the stage set for the minstrel show. In the back stands a long platform with ramps leading forward down to the stage. Gold chairs and torches are lined up on stage and platform. The "Grand Introductory March" reaches a climax of happy anticipation, and the artists—the center performers, the semicircle, the auxiliary ladies and gentlemen, and the two end men—move to their seats. A tambourine claps for order as all sit down at the interlocutor's signal.

The interlocutor leads forward a dainty girl, whose old-fashioned curls and somber countenance presage a dance of great seriousness. The orchestra sounds the first notes of a "Pathetic Ballad" in slow waltz time; the girl moves forward on point and renders a dance of absurd tragedy. She is all alone; the four boys who dance with their partners in a semicircle around her will not pay any attention to her. She is doomed to be a perpetual wallflower. Yet all the time the girl maintains in her steps and gestures an indifference to ordinary mortals that exposes her addiction to pathos. She loves to be sad, and sad in the grand manner. She clasps her hands and raises them in supplication; she kneels, begging for help in her distress; she turns beseechingly to the happy couples for succor. No one will help her! The girl raises a pointed hand to her temples and fires. The saccharine music expires, and the unfortunate creature is free to be happy again. She takes her seat, rises disconsolately to the audience applause, and sits down again, her eyes downcast.

The interlocutor, his black cane in hand, comes forward and performs "Sleight of Feet," a rhythmic jumping specialty that makes him a magician in movement. He tries to attract our attention to his hands, his coattails, and his cane as his feet perform quick marvels. The end men run forward with a chair, and he falls back, exhausted by triumph.

The interlocutor is followed by the two end men, one short, the other tall, who rise from their places at each end of the line and dance "Perpendicular Points." This number displays their adroit sharpness in dancing almost continually on their toes to curtly paced music that would trip them up if it could. Their long swallow-tailed coats bounce in the air as their points hit every beat of the music. As their number ends, they rush over to the left and end up sitting in the lap of the surprised interlocutor.

The lights go down. A bright spotlight catches a girl in a shining red dress who rushes out and dances a vigorous "Freebee" to a fresh, rousing theme. All the performers clap their hands in rhythm to the music; the girl dances faster; the whole troupe catches the contagious liveliness of her movement and the members come forward to join her. They parade across the platform as the girl in red is lifted high between two boys and carried around the stage. But the instant her feet touch the floor, she is on fire again with movement and leads all in a jumping, turning ensemble that increases in speed and dizziness. All fall flat on the floor, exhausted.

PART TWO   The dancers rise and carry out the chairs and benches. The drop curtain falls, and some of the performers come forward and sit to watch the show themselves. The stage is now empty and dark. The music warns of mysterious events. Three capes—red, green, and purple—seem to move across the stage unsupported, sweeping the air before them. Then the capes are dropped and we see that they are worn by Louis, the Illusionist, and his two assistants, Moreau and Lessau—the interlocutor and the two end men in disguise.

Louis and his two assistants make magic signs, gather close in a line, their capes before them. The drop curtain rises. The three cloaked figures slide off into the wings, miraculously leaving before us, in the center of the stage, the goddess Venus, gamboling on the green with three Graces. When they have danced their bit, the magician and his helpers return. They enclose the four mythical figures in their capes and they disappear.

Next Louis brings forth a wild pony, transmigrated from its native hills. The wild pony, danced by the leader of the frenzied "Freebee," cavorts and bucks about her unnatural surroundings with stubborn, bold abandon. The magician tries to tame her, pulling the reins taut, but the pony's mane switches the trainer's face and he at last releases her.

Tinkling music is heard. Perched on a seat hung with flowers, Hortense, Queen of the Swamp Lilies, swings into view and off again. Her garlanded swing brings her back, however, and she is lifted down to earth by Harolde, the young poet, who joins her in a *pas de deux*. To the music of a solo violin and the harp, the idealized lovers dance with considered, prolonged languor, never hurrying, never reaching their goal.

PART THREE   The lights come up. The magician has materialized his last illusion and he and his assistants leave the scene stealthily, their cloaks wrapped about them. The orchestra begins a catchy march, and all the participants parade the stage in a spirited, strutting, gala cakewalk that moves rapidly to a boisterous, rollicking conclusion. All the dancers wave responsive greetings to the audience as the curtain falls.

## CAPRICCIO ESPAÑOL

*Ballet in one act. Music by Nikolai Rimsky-Korsakov. Choreography by Leonide Massine, with the collaboration of Argentinita. Book by Leonide Massine. Scenery and costumes by Mariano Andreù. First presented by the Ballet Russe de Monte Carlo at the Théâtre de Monte Carlo, May 4, 1939, with a cast that included Argentinita, Alexandra Danilova, Michel Panaieff, and Leonide Massine. First presented in the United States by the Ballet Russe de Monte Carlo at the Metropolitan Opera House, New York, October 27, 1939, with Mia Slavenska, Alexandra Danilova, André Eglevsky, and Leonide Massine in the leading roles.*

*Capriccio Español* is a ballet about Spain, rather than a Spanish ballet. Just as Spanish dance themes provided Rimsky-Korsakov with melodies for a bright and colorful orchestration, the choreography here uses Spanish dance steps to create a romantic and colorful representation that some of us might imagine to be Spain. The ballet, therefore, has no particular story to tell; instead, it tries through a series of dances to create an atmosphere, a feeling that something real has been touched.

The ballet begins with a dance called the alborada, a morning serenade. We find ourselves in the public square of a small Spanish town whose inhabitants are preparing for a festival. The music is almost uncontrolled in its loud, blaring enthusiasm. Boys of the village dance with wild abandon to this music. Soon they are joined by a group of girls. But instead of choosing the boys for their partners, the girls turn to the elders of the village and dance with them playfully and charmingly. The girls are aware that only these older men, who have seen so many beautiful women in their lives, have a real and knowing appreciation of their loveliness, and the older men, in turn, are charmed by the fact that the girls know this. The music is quieter, occasionally bursting into crescendos, as it varies the more gentle secondary theme.

The turbulent first movement is now repeated, and the boys again take up their dance. There is a roll on the drum, which the brasses build into a fanfare, and a stunning gypsy comes into the square. This is the fortuneteller. She begins to dance, enchanting all the village with her fiery, sinuous movements. A gypsylike melody inserts itself between solos for various instruments as the fortuneteller continues to hold everyone's attention. She is joined by a partner and in the rapid stampings, quick whirls, and persistent rhythms of their dance, the bodies seem to make the whole square vibrate. The strings are plucked like guitars, and the couple bring their duet to a close with a fandango.

Another couple come forward and, in the midst of the excited crowd, now overflowing with the spirit of the festival, this peasant boy and girl lead all the natives in a tempestuous ensemble. The fortuneteller returns with her partner to join the peasant couple as the festival reaches a peak of excitement. All the people have now forgotten that they are moving in a dance, for their dancing derives from a holiday impulse that makes everything but dashing and turning movement impossible. Inspired by the dazzling display of the two lead couples, the villagers become intoxicated with joy at their own brilliant facility and dance with their leaders a final, uproarious ensemble as the opening theme of the ballet triumphantly returns.

## CAPRICHOS

*Ballet in four episodes. Choreography by Herbert Ross. Music by Béla Bartók. Costumes by Helene Pons. First presented by the Choreographers' Workshop at the Hunter Playhouse, New York, January 29, 1950. Presented by Ballet Theatre at the Center Theatre, New York, April 26, 1950, with Charlyne Baker, Jenny Workman, Nana Gollner, John Kriza, Ruth Ann Koesun, and Mary Burr as the principals.*

This ballet derives its inspiration from the comments the Spanish artist Goya made on a series of his etchings. The choreographer has taken four of these comments and visualized opinion. The ballet is performed to Béla Bartók's *Contrasts for Piano, Clarinet, and Violin*. A blue backdrop is the only scenery.

There are two girls on stage as the curtain rises. They are dressed in brief white nightgowns. They wear black crucifixes about their necks and long black gloves. Goya's comment is: "These good girls have seats enough and nothing to do with them better than carry them on their heads." The girls are not good at all. Their principal pleasure consists in pulling their dresses up to their necks as often as possible. They carry two stools and try to amuse themselves by playing with them as they cavort about the stage. Finally the girls realize that they are boring themselves to death. One stands holding a stool on her head; the other falls to the ground in an idiotic posture.

"No one ever escapes who wants to be caught" is Goya's second comment. The two girls remain on stage to watch. One fans her dress back and forth to cool her body; the other relaxes with her head in her hand. A woman in black enters, her head concealed by a blue shawl. She is followed by two men in cloaks. The woman moves over to the two girls, who observe her with preoccupied, gum-chewing expressions. The woman begins to dance. The men close in. She pretends to detest them and to want to be alone. The men are delighted by the pretense at resistance and allow her to fascinate them. They move in and caress her boldly, and the three dance together, the woman clapping her hands with simulated Spanish pleasure. The two men lift her up to their shoulders, then each holds her and swings her body around and around. As one of the men embraces her, the other picks up her feet. They lay the woman on the ground. Now something has happened that the two girls can understand; they move over to the woman. The men walk away. The girls frolic about the stage. The woman rises and disappears, her blue shawl whirling with her movement.

The girls are dejected again. A young widower enters. He mourns his dead wife and holds his hand before his eyes as he sees the lascivious girls. He moves over toward them, his face determined to be sad. Then he goes to the back of the stage and stands close to the wings. He holds out his arms in supplication. Suddenly, as if he were holding out his arms to catch a potato sack, his dead wife falls into his arms. Her body is limp, absolutely lifeless. The man kneels. He attempts to bring his love to life, but her loose body resists his efforts. If he does not hold her, the girl falls over on her face. The young man gets a little annoyed and tries to dance with his rag doll of a wife. He is forced to push her legs ahead of him. Now he is embarrassed. He shows the girls that his wife really is dead. There is no use pretending. Goya's comment is: "If he were more gallant and less of a bore, she would come to life again." He carries his wife off.

The color of the backdrop changes to a bright green. The two girls rise from their siesta as four hooded figures enter slowly, carrying long brooms of straw. The girls are suddenly respectful in the presence of these mysterious, religious men. Two of the men carry a plank; a woman sits upon it, resigned to her fate. ". . . They are determined to kill this saintly woman. After judgment has been pronounced against her, she is dragged through the streets in triumph. She has indeed deserved a triumph, but if they do it to shame her, they are wasting their time. No one can make her ashamed who has nothing to be ashamed of . . ."

The triumphal procession is over. The men stand the plank upright and fix its base in the ground. The girls stand on their stools at the back to see better. The saintly woman is tied to the plank. Red light appears at her feet, and from the movement of her toes it is apparent that she is uncomfortable. She tries to escape the licking flames by lifting one tortured foot, then another away from the fire. One by one, the four men toss their brooms of straw at her feet. The woman trembles all over. The light on the backdrop becomes brilliantly red. With a hideous gesture, the woman at the stake claws at her flesh, seeming to pull it up over her face like a mask. One of the men stands behind the stake and extends his arms straight out, sanctifying the project. The woman's body falls forward. Her bonds still hold her to the stake. Everyone is still but the two girls, who move about slowly. One finally rests on her stool and amuses herself alone. The other girl, on the right, imitates crudely the sufferings of the saintly woman. The curtain falls. A voice says, *"El sueño de la razón produce monstruos"* ("The dream of reason produces monsters").

# CAPRIOL SUITE

*Ballet in one act. Music by Peter Warlock. Choreography by Frederick Ashton. Scenery and costumes by William Chappell. First presented by the*

*Marie Rambert Dancers at the Lyric Theatre, Hammersmith, London, February 25, 1930. First presented in the United States by the Sadler's Wells Theatre Ballet at the War Memorial Opera House, San Francisco, California, December 5, 1951, with a cast that included Patricia Miller, Donald Britton, and David Poole.*

This entertainment ballet is a twentieth-century version of dances that were popular four hundred years ago. In 1588, the Frenchman Thoinot Arbeau set down in writing a record of sixteenth-century dances with the music that accompanied them. This book, called *Orchesographie* (writing dancing), appeared seven years after the presentation of the first modern ballet, the first ballet to unify in one entertaining spectacle the theatrical elements that had amused the courts of Europe for many centuries.

Arbeau's book is a dialogue, in the classical manner. He and a novice at the dance, a young man named Capriol, talk about dancing—how it came to be so popular among mankind, the different kinds of contemporary dancing, and the proper music to accompany the different forms. Peter Warlock, the English composer, arranged a number of the tunes set forth by Arbeau in an orchestral suite, and Frederick Ashton, in turn, devised the appropriate sixteenth-century dances as described by Arbeau to young Capriol.

The curtain rises and the orchestra begins a sprightly tune. The setting is simple and formal: a low stone railing topped with urns curves about the back of the stage. The back cloth is light green. Two couples dressed in the sixteenth-century French fashion perform a basse danse, a light but dignified measure. When they finish, the lights dim and two boys lead on a girl dressed in a long skirt. The orchestra plays a stately pavane, and the girl begins to dance between her escorts. Soon she pauses and sits on the knee of one of the boys. He presents a red rose to her. She sweetly refuses to accept it and when the other boy offers her a scroll, upon which he has written a poem to her, she will have none of him. She rises, and the boys stand on each side of her contemplating the gifts she has rejected.

The lights brighten, and to gay, bouncing music a girl and a boy dance a tordion, a court dance that is nevertheless playful and uninhibited in enthusiasm. The dancers who performed the pavane watch the dancing couple. Another girl enters. When the tordion finishes, those two couples come forward. The dancing, which has mostly been confined to the floor, now rises as the boys perform *pieds en l'air* to entertain the girls. When the dance is over, the boys kneel and the girls fall back over their shoulders. They leave the stage.

The music becomes bright and brisk. Four boys jump out onto the stage and dance a mattachins, a vigorous sword dance. Three of the boys lift the victor high over their heads as this dance ends. Gradually all the dancers return and perform different versions of the branle, a sixteenth-century court dance so popular that there were different versions for different age groups. The music increases in gaiety. The more ebullient dancers enclose in a moving circle the more stately couples, and the curtain falls.

## CARACOLE (see DIVERTIMENTO NO. 15)

## CARD GAME (Jeu de Cartes)

*Ballet in three deals. Music by Igor Stravinsky. Choreography by George Balanchine. Book by Igor Stravinsky, with the collaboration of M. Malaieff. Scenery and costumes by Irene Sharaff. First presented by the American Ballet at the Metropolitan Opera House, New York, April 27, 1937.*

The characters in this ballet represent the cards in poker hands. There are twenty-six cards for the whole ballet, representing portions of the four suits, plus the joker. Fifteen of these cards—one always the joker—are dealt out to make up three separate hands of poker for each of the three scenes in the ballet. The ballet is prefaced by this translation from a poem by La Fontaine:

One should ever struggle against wrongdoers.
Peace, I grant, is perfect in its way,
But what purpose does it serve
With enemies who do not keep faith?

FIRST DEAL   The orchestra plays a sonorous and playful march. The curtain rises on an empty stage. The scene is enclosed in a green felt façade. A great crystal candelabra stands at the left, representing one corner of a card table. The green tabletop stretches back up against the backdrop, where another candelabra is suspended at the opposite corner of the table; the stage thus becomes the table itself.

Fifteen dancers trip out from the right and form in a line straight across the stage. All hold large yellow-striped cards before them, concealing their identity. The joker is among them. Easily identified by his yellow costume striped with bright orange and his silly fool's cap, he steps out of line and runs about, trying to find the best hand. The cards turn and move close together in a shuffling movement. Then the hands are dealt out by an invisible player. The first five cards on the left jump out of line over to the left; the remaining cards form hands at the center and on the right. All the characters still hold the cards before them, but the joker can be distinguished in the hand on the left.

The hand on the right throw the placards over their heads to reveal themselves as the Ace and Queen of Hearts, the Queen of Clubs, the Jack of Spades, and the Jack of Diamonds—a two-pair hand. All the cards are easily identifiable in their resplendent costumes. The Ace of Hearts, his head covered like some medieval armored knight, flourishes his powerless sword in the air, and the smiling Queen of Hearts is surrounded by her dancing partners. The cards fall back in line and bow to the hand at the left.

The second hand turns out to be two kings and two eights—with the joker, a full house. The four cards and the joker step out proudly, the joker flagrantly boasting about the two kings. Now the members of the back hand throw off their placards. The joker holds his nose in contempt as he sees a pair of sevens, but he is stunned along with everyone else as they see three aces with the two sevens—another full house, which beats the joker's hand unaided! The joker comes forward, laughing hilariously to music that accompanies his dance. He grips his sides and bends over as he laughs. His loose, disjointed figure cavorts about the stage in short, jerky steps, running to the left, then to the right. He pirouettes like a top and circles the stage in wide, distorted leaps, turns in the air, slaps the table with his hands, and exits. The three hands spread out and close. All the cards choose partners and slowly dance off. The last couples to leave the stage are the two disconsolate kings with their two eights hanging limply on their arms.

SECOND DEAL   The introductory march to the ballet heralds the second scene. A new line of cards run out from the left, holding up before them large blue-striped placards. They form in a line down the center of the table, shuffle, and form three hands as before. From the hand at the left two jacks step out and dance. They bow and scrape before the three kings in their hand, carrying their trains and saluting them endlessly to a comic martial tune. They fall back into line and bow ceremoniously to the right after they have danced a courtly measure.

The Queen of Hearts steps out of the second hand, bounces in royal attitude, and dances a sprightly variation to a vivacious tune while throwing kisses gaily to everyone. She resumes her place, and the Queen of Clubs emerges and dances alone. She spins rapidly with her arms extended and as the whirring tune finishes, she stands with her hands on her hips while the Queen of Diamonds performs a difficult series of steps to a fresh melody. The Queen of Spades follows her, and then all four queens stand and watch the Jack of Hearts, their one remaining card, perform his variation. He bows to the queens; they all dance together and resume their places. They gesture toward the hand arranged in the center. Four aces and the ubiquitous joker come forward, the joker walking arrogantly, congratulating himself on the good luck he brings. But his hand has won the deal on its own merit, without his help.

The joker dances with the four queens as all the other cards leave the stage. He pulls them around in a line as he kisses the hand of the Queen of Hearts, then tags onto the end of the line. The joker stands in the middle of the line and dances lackadaisically with the queens, amusing himself at their silly posturings and leading them in a dance that burlesques their charm. Finally he pushes them all into the wings.

THIRD DEAL   The same march begins the third deal. A line of cards, their identities concealed as before, file out from the right; the cards are dealt into three hands. The hand on the left—a flush of Hearts, the five, six, seven, eight, and nine—walk to the front and dance pertly but modestly. They retire, and the joker dances forward with the hand on the right—the seven, eight, nine, and ten of Spades—with the joker, a higher flush than the first hand. The joker tries to play off his Spades against the Hearts, but the first hand moves away to stand in front of the final hand, which is still unrevealed. The joker and his Spades form a huddle to decide on the best method of play, then the five cards form a line, with the joker at the end. He bumps the girls forward and dances with them playfully as the orchestra mimics a bright melody of Rossini's.

The Hearts move forward; the joker and his Spades run back to see the final hand and stand aghast as they behold a royal flush: the ten, Jack, Queen, King, and Ace of Hearts! The joker grips his head in despair: he can laugh no longer when the joke is on him. He falls on his back, the music laughs at him, he rolls over and crawls off.

The royal flush marches forward to a delightful tune. The jack holds up his hand, trumpeting their arrival; the king and queen raise their hands in greeting and congratulate each other that the royal family is reunited. The queen jumps and everyone jumps. All the cards in the three deals gather behind them. They blow kisses to all her family and everyone else in sight and they all bow to her in mock humility. The other cards come to shake the hands of the lucky hand, and the king and queen welcome them. The king orders all the Hearts in the deck to come forward with the royalty. The other suits form lines behind the Hearts and all dance a courtly measure to the king's command. The deck of cards form a tableau about the queen. She is lifted high above them; the surrounding multitude fall forward in obeisance to her; and as the lights go out, all the cards are seen scrambled together in the middle of the table, shuffled together for a new game.

NOTES   *Card Game* was the first collaboration between Stravinsky and myself in the United States. In 1936, when Lincoln Kirstein and I decided upon a Stravinsky Festival for the American Ballet, we wanted to present a new Stravinsky ballet. We wrote to Stravinsky in Paris, commissioning him to write a new ballet. We told him to write anything he wanted. He decided on a dance with playing-card characters, a poker-game ballet.

Soon after the score arrived in New York and I had begun rehearsals on the new ballet, Stravinsky himself arrived. As always, the ballet was a collaboration. Lincoln Kirstein has noted that Stravinsky possesses "the profound stage instinct of an amateur of the dance, the 'amateur' whose attitude is so professional that it seems merely an accident that he is not himself a dancer."

In *Card Game*, Stravinsky and I attempted to show that the highest cards— the kings, queens, and jacks—in reality have nothing on the other side. They are big people, but they can easily be beaten by small cards. Seemingly powerful figures, they are actually mere silhouettes.

*Card Game* was revived by the Ballet Russe de Monte Carlo at the Fifty-first Street Theatre, New York, October 14, 1940, with Frederic Franklin as the joker and a cast that included Alexandra Danilova, Nathalie Krassovska, Alicia Markova, André Eglevsky, and Igor Youskevitch. In the most recent revival by the New York City Ballet (first performance February 15, 1951), Todd Bolender and Janet Reed have danced the joker and leading parts have been danced by Janet Reed, Patricia Wilde, Doris Breckenridge, Jillana, Francisco Moncion, Frank Hobi, Michael Maule, and others.

Another version of Stravinsky's score was choreographed in 1945 by Janine Charrat and had its first performance by the Ballets des Champs-Élysées in Paris, with Jean Babilée as the joker.

John Cranko's production of *Jeu de Cartes* was first presented at the Würt-

temberg State Theatre, Stuttgart, January 22, 1965, with scenery and costumes by Dorothee Zippel and lighting by Gilbert V. Hemsley, Jr. The ballet,
introduced to the United States by the Stuttgart Ballet at the Metropolitan
Opera House, New York, June 17, 1969, has been staged by the City Center
Joffrey Ballet.


# CARMEN

*Dramatic ballet in five scenes inspired by the opera by Meilhac and Halévy.
Music by Georges Bizet. Choreography by Roland Petit. Scenery and costumes by Antoine Clavé. First presented by Les Ballets de Paris de Roland
Petit at the Prince's Theatre, London, February 21, 1949, with Renée Jean-
maire and Roland Petit in the principal roles. First presented in the United
States by Les Ballets de Paris at the Winter Garden, New York, October 6,
1949, with the same principals.*

SCENE ONE: A PUBLIC SQUARE IN SEVILLE   What seems to be a building with
an outside staircase stands at the back of the square, and from it a long
clothesline hung with multicolored garments suggests that it is a cheap public
square. Three men play at cards on a plank that has been set up between two
high ladders. Couples mill about the square in a casual and desultory manner,
smoking, dancing occasionally with simulated high spirits, but in general im-
plying that if they wait about long enough, something important may happen.
They are not disappointed. Upstairs in the building someone is making a
ruckus. Everyone listens attentively. Down the stairs runs an unfortunate girl
who is clearly having difficulty with her pursuer. We understand why when
we see that her pursuer is Carmen.

Everyone in the public square knows Carmen, every woman and especially
every man. By experience and reputation fierce in love, Carmen is also fierce in
jealousy, and although no one knows or cares what she is fighting with this
other girl about, all the people in the square assume that the fight is worth
watching. They take sides. Between two groups who egg them on, Carmen
and the girl scratch each other and tear each other's hair out and kick each
other around. The crowd is delighted with their ferocity and cheers spitfire
Carmen when she succeeds in throwing her opponent to the ground. Just as
they begin to express their enthusiasm for her victory, Don José, cape flying,
enters on the run. Everybody seems to know him, too.

Don José is an official of some sort, a man from another part of the town,
perhaps a policeman in mufti. He does not approve of what is going on and
tries to break up the crowd. He takes pity on the prostrate girl, but then he
sees her conqueror. The music sounds an ominous theme; the drum beats
warningly. Don José is transfixed, immediately attracted to Carmen, as all the
men seem to have been. He takes in her long and supple body, her boyish bob,
her defiant eyes, her wide red mouth that seems a brilliant slash across her
white round face, and doesn't know what to do. Then he remembers his duty.
He seizes Carmen by the shoulder, coldly, officially, to admonish her. Carmen
responds by glaring up at him and yanking down her blouse to expose the vo-

luptuousness of her other shoulder. Don José is confused. Instead of arresting her, he allows Carmen to make a rendezvous with him. He dashes off, and the spectators nod to themselves knowingly.

SCENE TWO: A TAVERN   The stage is dark as the curtain rises on the second scene. Gradually a line of paper lanterns light up across the scene, and behind the lanterns is a tavern: tables and chairs, a bar in the back, and steps leading to an upstairs room. A number of steady customers are disposed about the tavern. A couple are making love, indifferent to their surroundings, and other habitués sit on the wooden chairs in an attitude of boredom. Some of them get up and start a kind of dance—wiggling and stomping and turning cart wheels and revolving the chairs on one leg—signifying their willingness to make the evening a deliberate, if not a spontaneous, success. Back near the bar, a man cloaked in black dozes.

Don José enters the room. He enters it just as he entered the public square: officiously, disapprovingly. But in the tavern, he senses that this will not be tolerated. After all, he has come on his own account, not on any official business, and everyone happens to know his particular business. And so, he joins the steady customers to prove that he is a regular fellow. He dances all by himself to prove also that he is a dashing fellow, while the crowd stands back and sings to the rhythm of his stomping the "Habañera." Although this song, with its warnings of rebellious love that can never be tamed, accompanies Don José's solo, he is sensitive only to its rhythms, which the spectators accentuate with militant clapping of hands. Don José is thinking of his meeting with Carmen.

Carmen has apparently been hiding behind the bar all this time. Suddenly, we see her sitting on top of it. Two gallants lift her down, and she commences a dance of her own. She carries a small black fan, which she holds close to her breasts. Her naked shoulders and her hair are covered with shiny spangles that fall from her body as she turns in powerful spins. Carmen's dance has more dash and strength than Don José's, and everyone watches her long legs as she traverses the tavern with steps that reveal her character as an untamable lover. Don José observes her more intently than the rest. At the end of her dance, Carmen kneels at his feet, her arms open in a gesture of welcome that is both public and intimate.

Don José goes to her. Carmen pretends that she is indifferent and fans herself nonchalantly. A pickpocket tries to rob Don José, but he brushes him aside. He picks Carmen up, holding her knee in his arm. He carries her closely, possessively, as if she had never been carried by a man before. He turns and carries her upstairs; Carmen relaxes in his arms.

When the two lovers have disappeared, two men and a girl begin a tempestuous dance that attracts all the customers. All join in the dance and whip themselves into a frenzy of happiness. Carmen's rendezvous has been a success, Don José has been seduced, and there is cause for rejoicing: they need fear officials no more. Carmen and Don José run down the stairs and lead the dance. The crowd fall on their knees around the lovers and beat the floor to the hysterical rhythm of their feet. At the climax of the music, Don José enfolds Carmen in his cape and runs off with her.

SCENE THREE: CARMEN'S ROOM; IT IS THE MORNING AFTER   Don José pulls back the yellow curtains that conceal the boudoir from the audience, and bright sunlight from an open window fills the room. Carmen lies on a disordered iron bed, sucking a plum. She rises lazily, stretches, and slowly goes into a dance. Don José pours water in a basin, washes his hands, dries them on the curtains, and seems not to notice the increasing sensuous pleasure Carmen derives from her own seductiveness. He sits and watches her disinterestedly. She caresses her body, her hands moving from her hair over her face to her shoulders, her breasts and her thighs, and up again to her face. Don José shows no signs of interest and, tired of self-love, Carmen turns away with disgust toward the balcony outside the window. The noise of the street attracts her. Instantly, Don José is on his feet. Really, he isn't tired at all. He wishes her to stay! Carmen moves to leave the room, but Don José pulls her back. Carmen, however, will be detained only by love. The lovers kiss and begin a dance together.

Don José lifts Carmen up to his shoulder, then holds her as her body comes down full length in his arms. Carmen's interest in him is renewed and gradually she compels Don José to share her passion. His body falls back to the floor and he braces himself on his arms and legs as Carmen poses aggressively above him, her knee resting between his. Carmen's breathing is now as lusty as her movements, and Don José responds fully. The climax of her passion approaches. She lies upon him. Don José raises his knees, and Carmen's legs stretch out straight from her curved body in an attitude of diving. The tenseness in their bodies relaxes as the music ends and the two lovers lie exhausted.

Barely has their passion subsided than three of Carmen's friends enter to persuade them to come out into the street. The friends whisper secretively to Carmen, and she motions to Don José to follow them. Now he will follow her anywhere.

SCENE FOUR: A STREET IN SEVILLE   It is night again. The scene is abandoned. Old cart wheels stacked against posts constitute the only scenery. Carmen and Don José, followed by her friends, walk on carefully, not wishing to be overheard. Cloaks disguise their identity. There is a brief conference. They are giving Don José his final instructions. Carmen puts a dagger in his hand. He listens and nods; the others leave and he is alone. The orchestra again sounds the theme that marked the first, fateful meeting of Carmen and Don José, and the drum now beats the rhythm of death. Don José stomps his feet in unison with the drum and waits. On the right, a man in a purple cloak enters. Don José seems to recognize him, stands motionless as he passes, then throws himself upon him. He stabs the man in the back. The man falls flat on his face. Don José reaches for his purse. Carmen and her bandit friends run out from hiding, grab for the money, and run off. Don José kicks the body over and follows them.

SCENE FIVE: IN FRONT OF THE PLAZA DE TOROS  Now that Don José has become a part of Carmen's life and has made the ultimate sacrifice and killed for her, Carmen begins to lose interest in him. She must always be taming someone to her will; once they have given in, she must seek new conquests. At the beginning of the fifth scene a crowd of lovely girls dressed colorfully but formally stand outside the arena, the Plaza de Toros, waiting for the bullfight to start—but waiting, too, for the arrival of the handsome toreador. The toreador, brought in on the shoulders of his admirers, gets down smartly and welcomes the greetings of the girls. As he flirts with them, he notices Carmen standing away from the crowd. She stares at him. She wears a veil, and the toreador prefers her indifference to the open affection of the young ladies. Don José enters and observes this silent exchange between Carmen and the toreador. The bullfight is about to begin; the toreador turns away from Carmen regretfully, and the crowd follows him into the arena. Carmen starts to join them.

Don José rushes up to her, tears off her veil, and grasps her throat in a passion of jealousy. He holds her face between his hands, and Carmen defies him. They separate, take positions at either side of the stage, and stand for a moment facing each other with so deep an anger that they become animal in their hatred. One of them must tame the other. The drum sounds slowly in a staccato beat; spotlights magnify and double the shadows of Carmen and Don José against the side of the arena. They approach and separate in a manner very similar to the fight in progress inside the ring, daring each other on, determined that one of them shall die. The drum beats faster and louder; Carmen circles Don José. He pulls out the dagger, rushes her quickly, and stabs her in the heart. He holds her about the waist as her body writhes back. She reaches up a trembling arm and caresses the face of her lover. She can stand no longer. Don José holds her to him still, and her legs vibrate with her heart's last beat. She falls limp. The music sounds brilliantly. Hats are thrown in from the arena. The fight has been won. The love has been lost.

*Ballet in two acts. Music: a Bizet collage by Wolfgang Fortner in collaboration with Wilifried Steinbrenner. Choreography by John Cranko. Scenery and costumes by Jacques Dupont. Lighting by Gilbert V. Hemsley, Jr. First presented by the Stuttgart Ballet at the Württemberg State Theatre, Stuttgart, February 28, 1971, with Marcia Haydée, Egon Madsen, and Richard Cragun in the principal roles. First presented in the United States by the same ensemble at the Metropolitan Opera House, New York, April 28, 1971, with the same principals.*

The ballet, in seven scenes, conveys in dance terms the plot of Bizet's opera. The locale is Spain, about 1820. The first scene takes place in a cigarette factory where Carmen, a beautiful, sultry girl who works there, has an argument with the woman in charge and scratches a cross on her back. She is arrested by a sergeant, Don José, a country boy who is immediately attracted to her. In the next scene, at the barracks jail, Carmen gets Don José to free her. He is stripped of his rank and jailed. In Scene Three, at a gap in the town wall of

Seville, Carmen persuades Don José, who is on guard, to let the smuggler band to which she belongs pass out of the city. Don José follows them. In the final scene of the first act, in the gypsy camp of the smugglers, there is a love scene between Carmen and Don José. Soldiers arrive to arrest Don José, who has deserted. He stabs the officer in charge.

Act Two of the ballet opens at an inn on the beach. Here Carmen dresses for her dance and sends Don José away on an errand. The toreador arrives with a group of friends and is fascinated by Carmen. Don José returns and is fiercely jealous. The desert region is the next scene, where Carmen's fate is revealed to her in a game of cards. Don José feels that he is losing her. A traveling Englishman is robbed and killed by the smugglers. Now an outlaw and a murderer, hunted by soldiers, nearly rejected by Carmen, Don José becomes desperate as he watches Carmen leave on the arm of the torero. In the final scene, outside the arena in Seville, Carmen accompanies the torero to the bullfight. She sees Don José there and has a presentiment of her fate. After the corrida has begun and they are alone, Don José pleads with her to come back to him. Knowing her fate, she still refuses. Don José stabs her.

## CARMEN SUITE

*Music by Rodion Shchedrin. Choreography by Alberto Alonso. First presented by the Bolshoi Ballet at the Bolshoi Theatre, Moscow, in 1967, with Maya Plisetskaya in the leading role. First presented in the United States by the same ensemble at the Metropolitan Opera House, New York, 1974.*

The first ballet to be choreographed especially for the celebrated Soviet ballerina Maya Plisetskaya, *Carmen Suite* presents the familiar story of Mérimée's novella as a mortal combat in a simulated bullring. It emphasizes character rather than plot. While we see Carmen, Don José, and the toreador assume their expected roles, the ballet is dominated throughout by Fate in the form of a bull. A huge head of a bull painted on a backdrop high over the arena dominates the decor. The program says: "Carmen is a beautiful woman who is free, true to herself, and completely honest. Don José lies, and thus he loses her. The Bull represents Fate. Therefore Carmen and the Bull die at the same time because she and her Fate are one." The final *pas de deux*, a danced contest between Carmen and Don José, is a simulated bullfight in which the ballerina assumes the combined roles of heroine and Fate in the form of a bull.

## CARMINA BURANA

*Music by Carl Orff. Choreography by John Butler. First presented by the New York City Opera at the City Center, New York, September 24, 1959, with Carmen de Lavallade, Veronika Mlakar, Scott Douglas, and Glen Tetley in the principal roles.*

*Carmina Burana,* a choral theater piece based on poems discovered in the library of an ancient Bavarian monastery, is a secular rather than a sacred work. The thirteenth-century poems and songs composed by minstrels and monks who had freed themselves of monastic discipline were set by Carl Orff to vigorous, compelling music. The chorus of monk-clad singers stands at both sides of the stage.

The ballet, which begins after the First Chorus, is an abstract landscape of movement, not a realistic retelling of the poems. The Prologue regrets the ever-changing fate of man, first riding the Wheel of Fortune with success, then ground under by it. The first part relates the joys of spring. The second celebrates the pleasures, extravagances, and despairs of tavern life. The third part is a series of love poems. The Epilogue returns to the plaintive bemoaning of the ruthless Wheel of Fate.

Leopold Stokowski, a champion of the score, characterized it as "a synthesis of beauty of melodic line, remarkable rhythmic variations; lusty vitality; immense range of mood, humor, frenzy; folk-like simplicity, satire, mystery, spontaneous eloquence and tranquility . . ."

Fernand Nault created a *Carmina Burana* for the Colorado Concert Ballet in Denver, in 1962. This version, with decor by Robert Prevost, was presented by Les Grands Ballets Canadiens at the Salle Wilfred Pelletier, Montreal, June 24, 1967.

Writing of the first presentation of John Butler's ballet, the critic Arthur Todd in *Dance Observer* said that "All of the movement for the four dance principals is composed in honor of eroticism . . . Most notable of the four is Scott Douglas, notable heretofore chiefly for his classical balletic style."

## CARNAVAL

*Romantic ballet in one act. Music by Robert Schumann. Choreography by Michel Fokine. Scenery and costumes by Léon Bakst. Book by Michel Fokine. First presented at Pavlova Hall, St. Petersburg, 1910, with Tamara Karsavina as* Columbine, *Vera Fokina as* Chiarina, *Ludmilla Shollar as* Estrella, *Bronislava Nijinska as* Papillon, *Leonide Leontiev as* Harlequin, *Vsevolod Meyerhold as* Pierrot, *Enrico Cecchetti as* Pantalon, *and Joseph Kchessinsky as* Florestan. *First presented in Western Europe by Diaghilev's Ballets Russes at the Théâtre National de l'Opéra, Paris, June 4, 1910, with the same principals except for the following substitutions: Vaslav Nijinsky as* Harlequin, *Adolph Bolm as* Pierrot, *and Ivan Kussov as* Florestan. *First presented in the United States by Diaghilev's Ballets Russes at the Century Theatre, New York, January 1916.*

First performed as a *divertissement* for a benefit in St. Petersburg, *Carnaval* was later revived and presented in Paris by Diaghilev. It became one of the most popular ballets in his repertory and one of the most popular works in the repertories of ballet companies that have since performed it, though it must be admitted that contemporary revivals have hardly retained the spirit of the original. The music is an orchestration of Schumann's *Carnaval* Suite for piano. The principal characters—Pierrot, Columbine, etc., are drawn from the *commedia dell' arte,* the popular early Italian street comedies.

The scene is an antechamber to a ballroom. At the rise of the curtain, we are introduced to the atmosphere of the ball that is taking place in the next room. Girls run by, pursued by their escorts. Dancing couples from the ball take refuge in the empty spaces of the anteroom and waltz. Chiarina and Estrella, two charming girls, enter with their partners. Two lovers kiss in passing and return to the ball.

Pierrot, the sad clown, pokes his head into the room. He steps into the room carefully, lest anyone hear or see him, his long, loose sleeves flapping dejectedly at his sides. He moves with slow melancholy; he seems to be saying that he is the only one in the world who will not dance and enjoy himself at the ball. Aware of his ugliness and awkwardness, he is filled with self-pity.

Harlequin bounces in, notes the melancholy Pierrot, and taunts him for not joining in the fun the music calls for. Unmercifully the energetic Harlequin pokes at the helpless clown, who falls to the floor. The irrepressible Harlequin leaves him in disgust.

Couples from the ball dance through the anteroom again. Pierrot looks at them and takes himself off before he can be chided once more.

Now the romantic poet Eusebius enters. He sits on a settee and wistfully contemplates a vision he has of an ideal lady. The lady materializes in the form of Chiarina, who gives him a rose. Estrella, ambitious and flirtatious, enters pursued by the eager Florestan, who beseeches her to grant him the favor of some small attention. Estrella pretends to disapprove of his advances, but then links her arm in his; the two exit for a dance.

Eusebius and Chiarina dance, or rather Chiarina dances and Eusebius observes her with adoring eyes. They leave the scene together.

Papillon, a girl whose varied, busy movements suggest a perpetual giddiness, rushes in. Pierrot discreetly follows her, hoping to make a conquest at last. He watches her from behind a settee, then bounds out into the room to catch her. When poor Pierrot thinks he has finally found a partner, Papillon escapes his grasp and leaves. The helpless clown is alone again.

Now there is an interval of dancing by Chiarina and two of her girl friends, who are masked. Florestan, still in pursuit of the coquettish Estrella, comes into the room. The girls playfully try to detain him, but the determined youth flees.

Columbine, gay and flirtatious, enters with Harlequin. They play together amorously. Though she seems to like him very much, the girl refuses Harlequin's invitation to elope. Their rendezvous is interrupted by the foppish Pantalon, who sits on a settee and reads with relish a note. Columbine goes to the back of the settee and puts her hands over Pantalon's eyes, while Harlequin snatches the note away from the intruder.

Pantalon, who was only reading the note to attract attention, tries to ingratiate himself with Columbine, who toys with him amusingly and then suggests that he join her and Harlequin in a *pas de trois.* At the end of the dance, she and Harlequin send Pantalon on his way.

Harlequin sits on the floor and indicates to Columbine that his heart lies at her feet. The fickle girl goes to the settee, where Harlequin sits adoringly in front of her.

The dancers return and, observing Harlequin and Columbine, congratulate them on their love. Columbine is suddenly nice to everyone. She comforts the pompous Pantalon and permits poor Pierrot to kiss her hand. All join in a happy dance.

The joviality is cut short by a crowd of busybodies, proper people who think that the people in the anteroom are not behaving with decorum. The gay dancers mock them and shove them about until they take flight. In the melee, the trickster Harlequin sees that Pierrot and Pantalon are pushed together. Before the two can separate themselves, Harlequin has tied Pierrot's long sleeves together around Pantalon. While Pantalon tries to release his bonds, all the other dancers gather about Columbine and Harlequin to form an admiring tableau.

## CELEBRATION

*Ballet by Jerome Robbins. Music and choreography as specified below. Scenery by Rouben Ter-Arutunian. First presented by the Festival of Two Worlds at the Teatro Nuovo, Spoleto, Italy, July, 1973, with Antoinette Sibley and Anthony Dowell (England), Violette Verdy and Jean-Pierre Bonnefous (France), Carla Fracci and Paolo Bortoluzzi (Italy), Patricia McBride and Helgi Tomasson (United States), and Malika Sabirova and Muzafar Bourkhanov (Soviet Union).*

Subtitled "The Art of the *Pas de Deux*," *Celebration* combined in a few historic performances classical *pas de deux* of the past with contemporary dance. The basic idea was to show the classic *pas de deux* in all its glamor but to show, too, the depth of feeling of contemporary ballet duets. The original intention was for *Celebration* to begin with a brief talk and demonstration of the art of the *pas de deux* by Anton Dolin, the famed partner of many ballerinas. Jerome Robbins decided instead to introduce his ballet himself, saying simply that it would be a "celebration of dancing by dancers."

The dancers are five couples from England, France, Italy, the United States, and the Soviet Union. Heralds carrying flags introduce the action. All five dancers enter to a fanfare and dance to the music of a Tchaikovsky waltz. Then one by one, the couples performed some of the great *pas de deux*. First, Sabirova and Bourkhanov in *The Corsair Pas de Deux*, then Fracci and Bortoluzzi in the love duet from *La Sylphide*, the oldest work of the evening. A *grand pas classique* for Verdy and Bonnefous came next, followed by Robbins's own *Afternoon of a Faun* by McBride and Tomasson. The *grand pas de deux* from the final act of *The Sleeping Beauty* by Sibley and Dowell concluded the first act of the presentation.

The second part consisted of the Balanchine *Tchaikovsky Pas de Deux* (McBride and Tomasson), the Ashton *Pas de Deux* from *Thaïs* (Sibley and

Dowell), the Petipa/Minkus display piece from *Don Quixote* (Sabirova and Bourkhanov), Robbins's new *Bagatelles* to music from Beethoven (Verdy and Bonnefous), and the celebrated final *pas de deux* from the Mérante/Delibes *Coppélia*.

The finale was an arrangement by Jerome Robbins for all five couples of the Ivanov adagio from *Swan Lake*, Act Two.

NOTES  Robbins's *Bagatelles,* called then simply *A Beethoven Pas de Deux,* had been performed initially at a preview in New York, May 16, 1973, at the New York City Ballet's Annual Spring Gala. It was danced by Violette Verdy and Jean-Pierre Bonnefous to *Four Bagatelles* of Beethoven, played by the pianist Jerry Zimmerman: Nos. 4, 5, and 2 from *Opus 33* and No. 4 from *Opus 126.* The costumes were by Florence Klotz and the lighting by Ronald Bates.

Reporting to the New York *Times,* the critic John Gruen wrote of the première of *Celebration* at the Spoleto Festival: "Bringing together five celebrated ballet couples (by no means an easy feat), and devising a work that would focus on international ballet styles, Robbins made clear both his magnetism as one of the world's great choreographers and his deep love of classical traditions."

The Ashton *pas de deux,* to the Meditation from the opera *Thaïs* by Jules Massenet, was first performed by Antoinette Sibley and Anthony Dowell at a gala ballet performance at the Adelphi Theatre, London, March 21, 1971. The critic Peter Williams wrote about the performance in *Dance and Dancers* magazine: Ashton "has created one of those oriental dream sequences that so reflect the whole mood of occidental awakening to the orient of the mid-nineteenth century. At least I imagine that Sibley must have been a dream figure, since she first appears with a light veil over her face as she approaches the kneeling Dowell. Everything about this dance evoked Pavlova, whom Ashton adored without reservation and whom he delighted in imitating until once, while staying at a country house, he seriously damaged his foot in an impromptu performance of *The Dying Swan.* But although the accident put a stop to any further imitations, Pavlova continued to cast a loving shadow over his life. This new *pas de deux* is all drifting and swooning and some fiendishly difficult lifts which have to look as though she is a wraith, and in which Dowell managed to make Sibley look as though she was. . . . It was lovely, and they were lovely, and to those that remembered, it must have brought on waves of nostalgia for Pavlova with Mordkin. . . ."

Writing after the first repertory performance of *Four Bagatelles* by the New York City Ballet, January 10, 1974, with Gelsey Kirkland and Jean-Pierre Bonnefous, Anna Kisselgoff said in the New York *Times:* "The very structure of *Four Bagatelles* follows the conventional sequence of the nineteenth-century classic *pas de deux:* adagio, variation for the man, then the woman, coda. In the first part, Mr. Robbins throws out almost subliminal quotes from three styles. A fleeting reminder of Denmark's Bournonville school, as in *Flower Festival at Genzano,* occurs in the beginning with the girl's *penchées arabesques,* head tilting and the man's leaps. Later, as Miss Kirkland slowly extends her leg to the side from on-toe position, while Mr. Bonnefous supports her in an image directly culled from the *grand pas de deux* of *The Sleeping Beauty,* there is a flashing allusion to the Russian style of Petipa.

"The adagio ends with Miss Kirkland down on one knee and Mr. Bonnefous behind her, in a reversal of the traditional pose that closes the adagio of Act Two of *Giselle*—a nod toward French Romantic ballet.

"These are, of course, whiffs of history wafting through a contemporary work, and the allusions are absent from the solos. Mr. Bonnefous's variation has folk touches that are echoed in the coda and some interesting experiments in phrasing. It is a tricky solo, somewhat short on transitional steps, and Mr. Bonnefous could not quite conceal the effort involved. Miss Kirkland, obviously most suited to the Robbins choreography, danced with brilliant technique and demure appeal. Mr. Zimmerman played with his customary excellence."

## CELLO CONCERTO

*Music by Antonio Vivaldi. Choreography by Gerald Arpino. Lighting design by Thomas Skelton. First presented by the City Center Joffrey Ballet at the City Center, New York, September 6, 1967. Cellist: Nellis De Lay. Conducted by Seymour Lipkin.*

A dance ballet to Vivaldi's *Concerto for Cello, Strings, and Continuo in E Minor,* this is Gerald Arpino's second work to the music of Vivaldi for the City Center Joffrey Ballet. It is in four movements.

While an ensemble figures at the beginning of the first movement, it is in fact dominated by the adagio *pas de deux* of the girl and boy who finish it. The second movement, brisk in style, is again an ensemble, led at first by a girl who performs a brilliant variation.

The third, quiet, movement is danced by two couples, who perform two adagios to the lyric score; the girls are lifted high into the wings at its close.

Bright again in tempo and atmosphere, the final movement features brisk variations by a boy and his girl against the animation of the ten supporting dancers.

## CHABRIESQUE

*Music by Emmanuel Chabrier. Choreography by Gerald Arpino. First presented by the City Center Joffrey Ballet at the City Center, New York, February 1, 1972.*

A dance ballet to Chabrier's *Trois Valses Romantiques, Souvenirs de Munich,* and *Cortège Burlesque, Chabriesque* is arranged for fourteen dancers. Writing of the ballet's performance in Chicago, the critic Ann Barzell said in *Dance News:* "*Chabriesque* is a classical suite in the high key of exhilarating virtuosity to which Arpino stretches his most virtuosic dancers. The choreographer delights in spaciousness and his fourteen dancers are seldom on stage all at the same time. His designs are not group tableaux, but groups flowing in ever-changing patterns. Arpino's inventiveness is boundless as he finds new ways to fly and whirl, to lift a partner or catch her coming or flipping from on high. There are new combinations of steps, new interweavings and through it all he maintains a style, romantic in mood and airy in movement. The girls wear white leotards with a cloud of sequin-spattered tulle for skirts. The men are in dark-blue tights and shirts.

"No matter how many unique roles dancers star in they feel the need to appear in what is nearest to them, the basic classicism of the daily class. So, it is understandable that Christian Holder has a pivotal role in *Chabriesque*, perhaps to prove that serenity of classicism is in his range. He danced with exemplary style, partnering the excellent Pamela Johnson. Starr Danias and Glenn White were notable throughout and after one stunning *pas de deux* set audiences cheering into the next dance. Francesca Corkle, recovering from an injury, brought her special bounce to several dances partnered by Scott Barnard, always excitingly precise."

## CHACONNE

*Music by Christoph Willibald Gluck. Choreography by George Balanchine. Lighting by Ronald Bates. First presented by the New York City Ballet at the New York State Theatre, Lincoln Center, January 22, 1976, with Suzanne Farrell and Peter Martins in the leading roles. Conducted by Robert Irving.*

It is no secret that I have loved Gluck's music for *Orpheus and Eurydice* almost all my life. Soon after I came to America, when Lincoln Kirstein and I took our new, young American Ballet to the Metropolitan Opera, I did a ballet to all of his music for the opera. The opera became, in fact, a ballet, with the dancers taking the stage and the singers performing with the orchestra from the pit. That production, designed by Pavel Tchelitchew with settings and costumes we could never produce today, is part of history. My next involvement with *Orpheus* was with Stravinsky, with whom I did the ballet of that name in 1948. But I returned to Gluck and his opera in Hamburg, in November 1963, when Rolf Liebermann of the Hamburg Opera kindly invited me to stage the work there. To conclude the production of the opera, which was brilliantly designed by Rouben Ter-Arutunian in a high baroque style of extraordinary extravagance, I had an opportunity again to do dances to Gluck's music. I repeated them in 1973, after Liebermann moved to the Paris Opéra and invited me to produce *Orpheus* there, too. The present ballet is an adaptation of what was first done for Hamburg, plus the introductory *pas de deux*. Brigitte Thom, who danced in the Hamburg production, helped me to revive it.

The chaconne of the title of course refers to an old-style dance, now centuries old, but it also was the popular name for ballet music used to end an opera. Basically, the ballet is a set of two *pas de deux* with other *divertissements*—a duet, a trio, a dance for five, with an ensemble. There is no story. Listen to the music first, if you can. Words you might try to use to describe it—mysterious, reflective, contemplative, plaintive, noble, etc.—are not enough for Gluck's lyric masterpiece.

The critic George Jackson has written: "Vainest endeavor, to try to document dance, the most ephemeral of the arts."

## CHANSONS MADÉCASSES

*Music by Maurice Ravel. Choreography by Jerome Robbins. First presented at the New York City Ballet's Hommage à Ravel at the New York State Theatre, Lincoln Center, May 28, 1975, with Patricia McBride and Helgi Tomasson, Debra Austin and Hermes Conde. Conductor: Robert Irving.*

The music here is three songs for soprano, piano, flute, and cello. The work was commissioned by Elizabeth Sprague Coolidge of Washington, D.C., and first performed in 1926. Ravel used poems by the Creole poet Evariste-Désiré de Parny, who lived in India and collected folk songs of Madagascar: "which may give an idea of their customs and habits. They possess no verse; their poetry is nothing but an elaborate prose. Their music is simple, gentle and always melancholy."

Ravel once said he believed this music introduces a "new element, dramatic —indeed, erotic, resulting from the subject matter of Parny's poems."

Jerome Robbins set the three songs in an individual way. The first is a love song; the second, where the action of the ballet principally focuses, expresses doubts about the white man and his role in Madagascar's past; and the third song depicts a hero husband lying in the heat of the shady tree, wondering what's for dinner.

## CHECKMATE

*Dramatic ballet in one scene with prologue. Music by Arthur Bliss. Choreography by Ninette de Valois. Scenery and costumes by E. McKnight Kauffer. First presented by the Sadler's Wells Ballet at the Théâtre des Champs-Élysées, Paris, June 15, 1937, with June Brae as the Black Queen, Robert Helpmann as the Red King, Pamela May as the Red Queen, Harold Turner and William Chappell as the Red Knights, Richard Ellis and Michael Somes as the Black Knights, Frederick Ashton and Alan Carter as the Two Players, and a cast that included Margot Fonteyn and Leslie Edwards. First presented in England by the Sadler's Wells Ballet at the Sadler's Wells Theatre, October 5, 1937, with the same principals. First presented in the United States by the Sadler's Wells Ballet at the Metropolitan Opera House, New York, November 2, 1949, with Beryl Grey as the Black Queen, Leslie Ed-*

*wards as the* Red King, *Gerd Larsen as the* Red Queen, *Alexis Rassine and John Field as the* Red Knights, *Kenneth Melville and Philip Chatfield as the* Black Knights, *and a cast that included Pauline Clayden, Rosemary Lindsay, Rowena Jackson, Kenneth MacMillan, and John Cranko.*

Checkmate is an allegory, a story of the battle between love and death told in terms of a chess game. It is apparent from the beginning who will win, but the contest, with its determined conflicting forces, creates a dramatic situation that often precludes prediction and the spectator, like the quiet chess player, finds himself deliberating the outcome.

The terms of the allegory are introduced in a prologue. The music is ominous, doomful, without relief in its projection of the battle to come. The curtain rises on a chess game. Two players in armor, Love and Death, sit opposite each other at a small table in the center of the stage. The chess game begins as Love makes a move. Death watches, deliberates, and moves his skeletonlike hand over the table. He moves. Love tries to analyze the situation, will not move again as he sees that the situation is hopeless: it is checkmate and there has not been any game at all. Blackout.

A backdrop rises, and we see that the stage is covered with black and white squares, as on a chessboard. The red chessmen enter and begin to take their places on the board. First come the eight pawns, danced by girls, gay and lighthearted pages to the royalty to come. The two red knights march in from opposite sides of the board and practice their fierce skill in combat. Two black knights, sent by the enemy to report on the strength of the other side, herald the entry of the black queen, whose omnipotence over all the pieces on the board is soon apparent. She beats off one of the red knights who will not submit to her attractions. To make himself attractive to her, the other red knight dances a vigorous mazurka. When he finishes, she rewards him with a red rose —Death's symbol of the blood she will spill before she is through. The pawns leave the board, followed by the conquering black queen and the black knights. In their absence, one of the red knights dances the praises of the black queen. Two red bishops parade in ceremoniously, followed by two red castles. Finally the red king and queen enter. Both knights salute them. The red king, old and doddering, can hardly make his way about the board and it is clear he can win nothing, while the queen is anything but a matriarch. The red pieces are now all in place, and the game begins in earnest.

The black queen leads the onslaught. The red king tries to maneuver his forces to prevent a frontal attack, but the black queen sees an opening and dashes through the enemy line. Even the two red bishops cannot hold off the black pieces. The red queen begs for mercy for her king, but the relentless black queen delivers her into the hands of her two knights.

The red knight, who imagined himself powerful in love, even with the black queen, attempts to rally his king's forces. For a time the contest is equal, for the knight's love of his king appears to be a match for his passion for the enemy queen. But when he must choose, when he has the chance to slay the queen, when she is kneeling helpless before him, he naturally hesitates. The black queen laughs in his face and cuts him down. The red king despairs.

Death enters. The body of the defeated red knight is held high by the red pieces, and Death leads the cortege off the board.

The red king has been abandoned; he is alone on the board with the black queen. She toys with him like a snake. He cannot escape: wherever he turns, a new black piece appears to block his path. He makes a pathetic figure—but then, from the beginning he has seemed weak and powerless—and the black queen's game with him becomes a protracted mercenary exhibition of power. She looks at him as if wondering whether the game were worth winning after all, he being such a contemptible creature. He is backed into his throne. Now, with nothing to lose, the king fights back with vigor for a brief moment. The black queen admires his mettle so much that she condescends to kill him. It is checkmate indeed.

## CHOPINIANA (see LES SYLPHIDES)

## CHORAL VARIATIONS ON BACH'S "VOM HIMMEL HOCH"

*Music by Igor Stravinsky. Choreography by George Balanchine. Scenery by Rouben Ter-Arutunian. Lighting by Ronald Bates. First presented by the New York City Ballet at the Stravinsky Festival, 1972, at the New York State Theatre, Lincoln Center, June 25, 1972, with Karin von Aroldingen, Melissa Hayden, Sara Leland, Violette Verdy, Anthony Blum, and Peter Martins in the principal roles.*

The Christmas hymn *"Vom Himmel Hoch Da Komm' Ich Her"* is familiar today as it was in Bach's own time. Its inspiriting music derived from a time during the Reformation when popular feeling gained an ascendancy in church music, and even today it is possible to find reflected in its melody an open, confident, but at the same time tender conviction to match the words:

| | |
|---|---|
| *Vom Himmel hoch da komm' ich her,* | From heaven high I come to you, |
| *Ich bring' euch gute neue Mähr.* | I bring you tidings good and new, |
| *Der guten Mähr bring' ich so viel,* | Good tidings of great joy I bring: |
| *Davon ich sing'n und sagen will.* | Thereof will I both say and sing. |

In 1747, Bach wrote canonic variations on the hymn for two-manual organ and pedals as a submission to a learned society. In 1955, Stravinsky began to compose instrumental and choral variations on Bach's masterwork. The score, for mixed chorus and orchestra, was dedicated to Robert Craft, who conducted its first performance at Ojai, California, May 27, 1956.

I myself first learned about the music from Stravinsky when he was working on the first two variations in New York at the end of 1955. When we were planning the Stravinsky Festival at the New York City Ballet after the composer's death, in 1971, one of the first works that I wanted very much to include was this one. Robert Irving conducted the first performance at the last night of the festival.

Those who will want to know more about the music will wish to read Robert Craft's exposition for Stravinsky's own recording of the work. As for the ballet, it is very simple.

There are five variations in the score. Brass proclaims the melody of the hymn as twelve young girls dance. All wear white. The background is a high chevron of white and brass rods, an imaginative simulation of pipes of the baroque organ.

In the four variations that follow, one is led by a ballerina and eight girls; another by four couples in which a *pas de deux* figures; another by a girl and boy against a background of twelve boys; and a finale with four *pas de trois* and eight girls, ending with the entire group of forty-six dancers. All forty-six dancers are on stage throughout the ballet, those not participating in the action standing aside.

It is boring, I think, to describe in any kind of detail what appears on the stage in a ballet that has only the music as its subject. What matters is the music itself and the more we can all be familiar with it, the better we are, both before seeing and afterward, too. This score is such an especially beautiful one that I hope you will hearken to it, but as always it is perhaps best to like it first without caring to, without preparation. I mean, many of the loveliest works of art are surprises we enjoy because we like them themselves, not because others alert us to them. Which is, of course, the point of the open mind, the open ear, the open eye!

## CHOREOGRAPHIC OFFERING

*Music by Johann Sebastian Bach. Choreography by Ballet of the Twentieth Century. First presented by that ensemble at the Brooklyn Academy of Music, New York, January 25, 1971.*

The Artistic Director of the Ballet of the Twentieth Century, Maurice Béjart, has written in his *Notebook* about the philosophy behind this and other works by his company:

"Dancer-Choreographer collaboration / Choreography, like love, is done in pairs / In a choreographic work, the dancer is more important than the choreography, for it is the dancer who is author of the work; the choreographer merely fits it together / To the extent that the choreographer strives to understand the shape, rhythm and will of the body one may create a work that appears original. The dancer's body, which is the interpretator, is always right. When I say body, I mean the whole intuitive and spontaneous being, and not the mind of the dancer. The dancer should be carefully observed, not only for the steps he makes, which he believes favor him, but because, despite what he says or thinks, his whole being is impelled to express itself in that very particular way / By listening to both the music of the bodies and that of the musical work, one could very well create a work. But taken on the whole, the work is not one's own, since it exists only because of its parts: the music and dancer / After all is said and done, the important thing is that something happens, regardless of who creates it / The dance is visual music."

The music for *Choreographic Offering* consists of eight canons from Bach's *Musical Offering*, orchestrated by Münchinger, with percussion episodes. Bach composed his work on a theme by King Frederick of Prussia. For almost a full hour, the regal theme supports a prodigious suite of canons, which imitate the theme, fugues and sonatas. Béjart's ballet, choreographed by his dancers, uses as its theme an adagio exercise used by the great Italian dancer and ballet master Enrico Cecchetti (1850–1928), teacher to pre-eminent Russian dancers. Béjart writes: "Within the eight central canons of the work there is a development which takes the form of a musical discourse; a countersubject, which is developed by the dancers and the percussion, follows; the theme meshes with a classic dance motif, modifying, supplementing and parodying it. These two basic elements seem to struggle to dominate the work, which appears about to fall apart. 'Life' enters and supplies a conclusion. This ballet has no other meaning, no other purpose, than to present, or to 'offer' the public the quality called 'Twentieth Century Ballet.'"

Following Béjart's scenario, the theme is danced by a boy, classically presented, but at once there is an "anti-theme" by another boy, who dances in a completely contemporary way, in vivid contrast, to the music of drums, chimes, and an "Iguanaphone." The ballet is full of surprises, seemingly improvised by the dancers, although there are the expected sequences in canon, with couples repeating dances by their predecessors. The contrast between the old and the new would appear to be the point, plus a useful and novel way to introduce a ballet company to a new public who might wonder what it represents.

Interviewed in *The New Yorker* magazine (February 6, 1971), the choreographer said of *Choreographic Offering*: "It's a discourse between the two main elements in my work—classical ballet, which is choreographed to Bach's *Musical Offering*, and modern dance, which appears during percussion passages, to interrupt and parody the traditional steps. There is a struggle between the two styles but we don't resolve it. We end with a young girl holding out a rose to the audience. That's our way of saying, 'In New York, you have the best choreographers and dancers, so we don't dare offer you a finished ballet. Come to your own conclusions.'"

## CINDERELLA

*Ballet in three acts and seven scenes. Music by Sergei Prokofiev. Choreography by Rotislav Zakharov. Libretto by Nikolai Volkov. First presented by the Bolshoi Ballet at the Bolshoi Theatre, Moscow, November 15, 1945, with Olga Lepeshinskaya in the title role. Designed by Pyotr Williams. Presented in a new version with choreography by Konstantin Sergeyev at the Kirov State Theatre of Opera and Ballet, Leningrad, April 8, 1946, with*

*Natalia Dudinskaya in the title role. A new production, revised by Sergeyev, was presented at the Kirov Theatre, July 13, 1964, with Irina Kolpakova. Designer: Tatiana Bruni. This production was first presented in the United States by the Kirov Ballet at the Metropolitan Opera House, New York, September 11, 1964, with Irina Kolpakova and Yuri Soloviev.*

Prokofiev wrote that he conceived of *Cinderella* "as a classical ballet with variations, adagios, *pas de deux*, etc. I see Cinderella not only as a fairy-tale character but also as a real person, feeling, experiencing, and moving among us." The Russian composer began work on the score in 1940, but because of other commitments during World War II did not finish the orchestration until 1944.

ACT ONE: A ROOM IN CINDERELLA'S HOUSE   It is evening and Cinderella's stepsisters—Krivlyaka (Affected) and Zlyuka (Furious)—are embroidering a silk scarf while their mother dotingly looks on. Cinderella sits alone at the fireplace, polishing a pot. The two sisters begin to quarrel over the scarf; their tempers are so bad that the mother can resolve the fight only by cutting the scarf in two. They now tease Cinderella, whom no one, not even her loving father, will defend. When they leave her alone finally, she sets about her routine of cleaning up the room. She finds a piece of the scarf and, forgetting herself, dances. But a mirror brings her back to reality; she sees her miserable dress and realizes that such a scarf is not for her. Her sadness induces memories of her beloved mother; she shuns the portrait of her cruel stepmother and tries to cover it with a curtain.

Her father returns and wants to comfort Cinderella. She sits on his knee and cries. But he fears his wife more than he loves his daughter, and, observing the covered portrait of his spouse, is apprehensive. Meanwhile, Zlyuka and Krivlyaka, who have been watching, alert their mother, who rushes in in a rage. She attacks her husband and taunts Cinderella mercilessly, finally collapsing in a fit of anger.

A beggarwoman appears, asking for alms. While the stepmother and the two sisters want to chase the woman away, and the father is too frightened to do anything, Cinderella turns and gives her a piece of bread.

Now preparations begin for the gala ball to which the family—all except Cinderella—have been invited. Dressmaker, hairdresser, dancing master, and musicians come to prepare the ladies. When everything is ready, they all depart for the castle, and Cinderella is alone.

Wishing also to be at the ball, Cinderella lets herself be carried away by unattainable dreams. She curtsies, as if before the prince himself. Suddenly the old beggarwoman appears again, but this time as Cinderella's fairy godmother. She promises to make the girl's dreams come true in gratitude for Cinderella's kindness. The fairy presents the girl with a pair of crystal slippers and orders four fairies representing the seasons of the year to prepare and dress Cinderella for the ball. The fairy of Spring brings her a gossamer dress, light as a cloud; Summer brings lovely roses; Autumn a splendid cloak glowing like the sun; and Winter diamonds and jewels, glistening like icicles. Dressed and ready now for the ball, Cinderella is truly a princess out of a fairy tale.

Before she leaves for the castle, however, the fairy godmother warns her that she must return home exactly at twelve o'clock, or she will turn back into her original state forever. She will be reminded of the approach of midnight by twelve dwarfs whom the fairy godmother will cause to emerge from the ancient clock at the castle. The fairy godmother wishes her godspeed and leaves, as a golden coach magically appears before Cinderella to take her to the ball.

ACT TWO: THE BALL AT THE PRINCE'S CASTLE   While waiting for their host to appear, the splendidly dressed ladies and gentlemen dance a stately measure. The stepmother and her two daughters arrive and, grotesquely imitating the manners of their betters, attract considerable attention. Two men are finally persuaded to ask the two sisters to dance.

The prince appears, greets his guests, and ascends the throne. As the ball continues, a new strain of enchanting music is heard, and, accompanied by attendants, a lovely young girl enters. The prince cannot take his eyes off her, and asks her to dance. The court is curious about her identity. No one, not even her own family and least of all the ugly stepsisters, realizes that the beautiful guest is Cinderella.

When Arab boys present Cinderella with three oranges, she is so moved by the envious glances of Krivlyaka and Zlyuka that she gives the fruit to them. The prince and Cinderella are then briefly alone. They have both fallen in love at first sight and dance together to declare their love.

When the guests return, the court festivities continue. But at the height of the celebration, before she has even contemplated that such an evening should ever end, the clock strikes twelve. True to the fairy godmother's word, twelve dwarfs emerge from the clock. Cinderella, terrified, flees the castle. The prince runs after her. The prediction of the fairy godmother is fulfilled: Cinderella is again as she first was, and only the crystal slippers remain from her ball dress. She loses one slipper as she dashes home, and the prince, as he pursues her, finds it. He comforts himself that to find the girl all he has to do is find the owner of the slipper!

ACT THREE, SCENE ONE: COURTYARD OF THE CASTLE   In an effort to find the maker of the shoe, the prince summons cobblers throughout the kingdom. No one can name the shoemaker and the prince decides to set out himself on his search for his beloved.

ACT THREE, SCENE TWO   The prince searches far and wide, and every lovely girl in the land weeps that the slipper will not fit. The prince remains determined to find his true love.

ACT THREE, SCENE THREE: A ROOM IN CINDERELLA'S HOUSE   Cinderella sleeps, pressing the remaining slipper to her breast. The slipper falls to the floor. Waking up the next morning, she recalls the splendid ball and her meeting with the prince. She decides that it must all have been a dream. But in the course of going about her daily chores, she finds the glass slipper. So it was not a dream after all! She cannot believe it.

The stepsisters come and relate the fine time they had at the ball, how popular they were, and how a princess gave them oranges.

Noise from the street heralds the arrival of the prince, who is going from house to house in search of the unknown beauty. When he enters, both stepsisters try in vain to force their feet into the shoe, and even their mother tries her luck. Then the prince notices Cinderella standing in the corner. She is so stunned by her lover's presence that she does not know what to do. She becomes so confused that she drops the other slipper. There is now no doubt as to who she is! Her fairy godmother appears and blesses Cinderella and her prince.

ACT THREE, SCENE FOUR: A FLOWERING GARDEN   Cinderella and the prince have found each other. They celebrate their reunion and live happily ever after.

*Ballet in three acts. Music by Sergei Prokofiev. Choreography by Frederick Ashton. Scenery and costumes by Jean-Denis Malclès. First presented by the Sadler's Wells Ballet at the Royal Opera House, Covent Garden, London, December 23, 1948, with Moira Shearer as Cinderella, Michael Somes as the Prince, Robert Helpmann and Frederick Ashton as Cinderella's Stepsisters, Pamela May as the Ragged Fairy Godmother, Nadia Nerina, Violetta Elvin, Pauline Clayden, and Beryl Grey as the Fairies, and Alexander Grant as the Jester. First presented in the United States by the Sadler's Wells Ballet at the Metropolitan Opera House, New York, October 18, 1949, with Margot Fonteyn as Cinderella and the same principals.*

*Cinderella* is a story everybody knows and in the past it has attracted a great number of choreographers—French, Russian, and English. This particular ballet on the story, however, is important for a special reason: it is the first classic English ballet in three acts, the first full-length English work in the style and manner of the great nineteenth-century classics. But *Cinderella* is entertaining as well as important. Here the familiar tale is embellished with dramatic and comic differences, with *divertissements,* and with the grace and warmth of the grand academic style.

ACT ONE: A ROOM IN THE HOUSE OF CINDERELLA'S FATHER   The curtain rises on a somber scene. Cinderella crouches on the hearth of a high stone fireplace on the right. On the left, at a plain table, her father sits reading. Near him sit Cinderella's two stepsisters, busily sewing a scarf. They are elderly and hideous, and there is an obvious tension in the room. Cinderella is sitting by the fireplace because she is not allowed to sit anywhere else. Dressed in worn, unbecoming brown, she makes a pathetic figure. The light shines on her face and, despite her sadness, we note that she is beautiful. The music is quiet but expectant; strings are plucked rapidly to sound curiously like the clicking of knitting needles.

The stepsisters, old maids that they are, have been invited to a ball this very night and they work at their sewing with some haste. They finish the scarf and begin to fight about who shall wear it. Cinderella glances at them as if their bickering were all too familiar: in this house there is either quarreling or silence. But she is afraid to interfere. She is no longer the daughter of the house but its servant. The daughters of her father's second wife now rule the house, and she, like her father, can exist only by conforming to their wishes.

The father tries to calm his stepdaughters, but abandons hope when they ignore him. Each tugs at her end of the scarf, and it is torn in two. The stepsisters leave the room, still quarreling, and he follows after them despondently. Cinderella is alone. She takes up a broom and moves wistfully about the room, posing gracefully. She is thinking of happier days, when her mother was alive and there was love for her to respond to. She picks up a piece of the scarf her stepsisters have left behind and puts it around her shoulders: now she is a lady, the lady her mother would have wanted her to be. She takes a candlestick from the table, crosses the darkened room, lights the candle at the fireplace, and holds it high to look upon her mother's portrait, which hangs above the mantel. The father returns, sees his daughter's despair, and attempts to cheer her. But he, too, is sad. The ugly stepsisters come in and reprimand him for keeping Cinderella from her housework. They warn the girl to return to her cleaning.

The orchestra sounds a new, magical melody. The stepsisters hear it, too. Cinderella looks up expectantly, and into the room hobbles a hunchbacked woman in rags. Her face is grotesque, her rags are filthy, but Cinderella seems to welcome her. The old hag begs for money, and the two stepsisters go into a tizzy of silly fear, running away to the other side of the room. Cinderella would like to comfort the old hag, but she knows that she has nothing to give. When the woman begs from her, Cinderella can only give her a bit of bread. The elder stepsister is annoyed at this generosity and threatens the woman. But, like an omen fulfilled, she is suddenly seized with a toothache and flees back to her sister. As Cinderella watches, wishing she could help more, the old hag glances at her gratefully and gently and disappears.

No sooner has the father reminded his two stepdaughters that they must begin to dress for the ball, than purveyors arrive—a tailor, dressmakers, a shoemaker, a jeweler, a hairdresser, a dancing master, each taking advantage of the sisters' new-found popularity to sell all their wares and talents. The old women are delighted at this attention, costly as it may be, and titter constantly like debutantes. Soon they are decked out in extravagant dresses. At this point the dancing master reminds them of the courtly steps in which they must be perfect. The women practice their bows and try to dance, as two violinists play a gavotte. The elder stepsister, old as she is, manages to execute the gavotte more or less to the dancing master's satisfaction, while the meek, shy sister despairs of learning. The dancing master sees that neither will ever learn and finally pretends that both are perfect.

The time of the ball is drawing near, and the stepsisters hurry with their makeup, primping extravagantly, as if all the powder and rouge in the world would reduce their ugliness. Their coach is announced, there is a final flurry of activity, and the sisters, absurdly proud in their bearing, depart.

Again Cinderella is alone. She looks into the fire. The women did not even bother to say good night to her. She wonders what the ball will be like, what any ball is like. She dances again with the broom, holding it before her as if she were not waltzing alone, and moves happily about the room, imagining herself at the ball. Soon she sees how silly she is being, puts the broom down, and goes back to sit at the hearth.

The harp is plucked gently, and again the eerie, high, piercing cry that heralded the arrival of the old beggarwoman causes Cinderella to look up and smile. The music is magical, like the loveliness of a dream; it grows in volume as the lower strings sound a full, promising melody. The room in which Cinderella sits seems to disappear, its walls vanishing. The old woman stands in the center of the room. She looks at Cinderella, and then something more extraordinary happens. In a flash, the old hag is transformed into a lovely, kind fairy: the ragged cretin becomes a beautiful creature dressed in a shimmering gown.

Cinderella cannot believe her eyes and when her fairy godmother tells her that she must prepare for the ball, that now, really, she *is* going to the ball, the lonely girl almost cries with happiness. The fairy godmother waves her wand, calling forth four fairies to dress Cinderella for the ball.

First comes the fairy Spring, then the fairies Summer, Autumn, and Winter. One by one, the fairies each dance a variation. After each one appears, the accompanying backdrop vanishes and Cinderella's room stretches back into the distance farther and farther. The scenery is transformed completely for each fairy, changing in color from green to icy blue, in surroundings from abundant garlands to a pinnacle of ice, and the fairies and their attendants are dressed charmingly in the habits of their seasons.

Cinderella sits on the floor at the feet of her fairy godmother, taking in the full magic of her great powers. Now she understands. The fairy godmother tells her to bring a pumpkin. Before the girl's astonished eyes, she changes the pumpkin into a magnificent coach. Cinderella is surrounded by the fairies, who present gifts to her and dress her for the ball. Almost at their touch, the lonely girl becomes as beautiful as a fairy tale princess, dressed splendidly in white and gold, wearing a crown and a long, flowing cape with a high pearl collar that encloses her shining face.

Her godmother tells Cinderella not to delay, that a newfound happiness awaits her at the ball. But she warns the girl that she must leave the ball before the clock strikes twelve. If she remains after midnight, the magic will vanish as mysteriously as it came and she will be just a lonely girl again, dressed in shabby clothes. Cinderella promises that she will not tarry and bows to her in gratitude. The fairies and a multitude of stars surround Cinderella as she goes to her coach and proceeds to the ball.

ACT TWO: A BALL AT THE PALACE   The ball has already begun when the curtain rises. Members of the court are dancing a formal measure in a ballroom that has been set up in the palace garden. Two great trees and their overhanging branches enclose the festive scene. To the left and right, spectators watch the ball in low stage boxes. In the back, on either side of a flight of low steps, are two high elegant structures, pavilions set up especially for the ball. On the ground floor of these pavilions we can see other guests amusing themselves. Farther back, by the light of a distant chandelier, we can make out a splendid formal garden. At the top of the steps is the prince's throne. The prince has not yet arrived, and the court jester sits on the royal stool.

Cinderella's stepsisters make an absurdly grand entry in keeping with the elegance they have assumed for the occasion. Cinderella's father accompanies them and is made visibly ill at ease by their pretensions. The older sister is determined to enjoy herself and acts unimpressed by the beauty of the palace garden: it is all her due, designed for her enjoyment, and she imagines herself attractive. The younger sister is more honest and cannot so easily disguise the fact that all this elegance is strange to her. She tugs plaintively at her sister's dress and wants to go home. She is, of course, refused and resolves to see the evening out only when a courtier begins to pay her some attention, thus reviving her spirits. She is disenchanted when her jealous sister takes her suitor away.

Now, as another courtly dance commences, the two sisters have a chance to perform the measures the dancing master taught them. The older sister watches with disgust as the younger dances. She starts out well, and for a moment we think she is really going to make it, but her steps become tentative and it is apparent that she's forgotten every step she knows. The older sister laughs, executes the dance with grotesque accuracy, and then, to show off, tries to balance on one foot. The younger sister is terrified, and, of course, the show-off begins to topple over. The jester catches her as she stumbles about trying to keep from falling flat on her face.

Four friends of the prince enter and prepare the guests for the arrival of their host. The handsome prince enters with a regal but lively flourish, and all the guests bow to him. The two sisters attempt to make their reverence so that the prince will take particular notice of them, but he does not even glance at them. The prince's companions dance a *pas de quatre*, which is followed by another general dance by the court.

One guest has not yet arrived. The light, mysterious music that heralded the first appearance of Cinderella's ragged fairy godmother interrupts the court music, and everyone pauses. The jester, at the prince's order, goes to welcome the newcomer in the garden. The twelve girls representing stars and the four fairies with their pages enter at the rear, and the court wonders what to expect with such an elaborate preparation. All look toward the entrance to the ballroom as the prince awaits the guest. Finally the royal coach of Cinderella draws up to the garden gate. The girl steps out, and all are dazzled by her natural beauty and the loveliness of her costume. The prince, who is immediately charmed, takes Cinderella's hand and leads her forward. Two pages hold Cinderella's train while the stars and fairies kneel about their mistress. Wishing to discover more about this ravishing girl, the prince escorts her for a walk through the palace grounds.

The other guests, who have watched the entrance of Cinderella from the boxes at the sides of the ballroom, now mingle on the dance floor and begin a masked dance. The ugly stepsisters, of course, have not recognized Cinderella and accept her simply as visiting royalty. Soon the prince returns alone and dances a variation, after which he leaves the scene. Now Cinderella dances and in her movements she conveys the youthful and tender joy she feels at the ball. It is as if she belonged there, for she is unembarrassed and confident in her natural graciousness.

The two sisters, alone for a moment, spend their time gossiping about the unattractive girl who has gained the prince's favor. The two lovers return. The harp is plucked against a deep, flowing melody, and they begin a *pas de deux*. The dance is soft and considerate, yet strong in its regal elegance and the personal elegance of the handsome young pair. The prince kneels before Cinderella as their dance finishes. She responds to his love by dancing a variation that reflects her new-found pleasure in loving and being loved. She is so happy that she has no memory of her misery at home; she pirouettes rapidly, and her two stepsisters are a million miles away.

A Negro page brings to the prince an orange on a silver tray. This is the most highly prized fruit in all the kingdom and the finest gift he can give Cinderella. She accepts it graciously. Then the prince turns to the ugly stepsisters and bestows an orange on each of them. Instantly they begin to quarrel about whose orange is larger, and the dominating sister snatches the choice one away from the timid creature.

Cinderella and the prince lead the court in an ensemble dance. The music is a bright, sparkling waltz that gradually gains in sonorous force, and all the guests are caught up in the spirit of romance. Suddenly—as the waltz gains relentless force, cymbals shimmer, and we hear the loud ticking of a clock—a flourish of trumpets announces the approach of midnight. The cymbals crash, to warn Cinderella that she must hasten. The girl rushes from the prince's arms. He watches, astonished, as she tries to make her way through the crowded guests to the gate. The girl is desperate lest her secret be discovered. When she arrives at the gate, midnight has come. Her beautiful dress becomes her ragged work clothes, and she flees into the night, leaving behind one of her slippers. The prince cannot understand; he looks after her as the orchestra restates the theme of their *pas de deux* and the curtain falls.

ACT THREE, SCENE ONE: AFTER THE BALL    When the curtain rises on the first scene, again Cinderella is seen sitting by the fire in her father's house, just as she was at the entrance of the fairy godmother. She is asleep. She wakens, looks about, and thinks she has dreamed of the ball. Only the slipper she finds hidden in her apron convinces her that she really was there, that there was a handsome prince, and that he did love her. She dances again with the broom, reflecting in her steps her unhappiness before the ball, her recollection of her first love, and her resignation to her everyday life.

Her sisters return. They are so tired that they don't even wish to gossip until they have undressed and cast off the weight of their excessive finery. They sigh as they remove their shoes from their swollen feet. But soon they are taunting Cinderella with tall tales about the ball, the prince, and his attentions to them. They toy with the oranges he gave them, and Cinderella is thinking too much of what the ball was really like to care much about their prattling.

The women hear a disturbance in the street. Townswomen rush in and excitedly announce that a royal procession is waking everyone up, that the prince, enamored of a girl he cannot find, is determined to discover the owner of a shoe left behind at the ball. He vows that he will marry the girl whom the shoe fits.

The sisters are apprehensive lest the prince visit their house when they are not fully dressed and scurry about putting on their formal gowns and their tight shoes again. The prince enters with the jester and an entourage. He holds Cinderella's lost slipper in his hand and declares that the woman it fits shall become his wife. He does not notice the girl in rags who crouches at the fire. The stepsisters do obeisance before the prince, who responds to them so graciously that they imagine one of them might be the chosen one. First, the shy stepsister tries on the shoe. She knows it is silly to pretend that it will fit and gives up wistfully. The other sister is delighted at her failure, but has no more luck herself, despite much straining and pinching in an effort to force her foot into the shoe.

When it is apparent that she, too, is a misfit, Cinderella helps her pull the shoe off. As the girl kneels before her sister, the other slipper falls from her apron pocket. The prince sees it and asks the girl if she will try on the shoe. Her stepsisters rail at her, but the prince insists. The shoe fits perfectly. At first the sisters cannot believe it, but when the prince announces that Cinderella will be his bride, they attempt in several reverential gestures to make up for the years of misery they have caused the girl. Cinderella understands them, pities them, and touches them lovingly as they bow before her. The prince and Cinderella embrace. The fairy godmother appears and raises her wand.

ACT THREE, SCENE TWO: AN ENCHANTED GARDEN    The scene is transformed. We find ourselves in a magical place, a colorful garden where the light seems to sparkle. There a great boat awaits the arrival of the lovers. The prince's friends and the fairies dance together, and Cinderella and the prince enter. Six of the stars surround them as they dance, the fairies pose gracefully with their cavaliers, and the music sounds soaringly the theme of ideal romance that marked the couple's first recognition of love. The fairy godmother and all the magical creatures wish the lovers godspeed, and they step into the waiting ship. The surging music falls off into soft measures that predict eternal joy. The prince holds Cinderella in his arms as they sail off on a happy voyage that will never end.

Yet another important version of this ballet came into the American repertory in 1970:

*Music by Sergei Prokofiev. Staged and choreographed by Ben Stevenson. Scenery by Edward Haynes. Costumes by Norman McDowell. First presented by the National Ballet at the Lisner Auditorium, Washington, D.C., April 24, 1970.*

The synopsis of this version of the ballet is close to others, but has some important differences:

ACT ONE   Cinderella's father watches his two stepdaughters embroidering scarves to be worn to a ball given that evening by the prince. The cruel stepdaughters tease their stepfather with the scarves. Cinderella enters and stops them. The stepsisters are furious and order Cinderella to clean the kitchen as they drag their father from the room. Her only friend now seems to be the broom.

Cinderella, remembering a picture of her mother, takes it from its hiding place and sits gazing at it. Her father enters and is overcome with remorse when he sees how much Cinderella resembles his first loving wife. She tries to comfort him when the stepsisters enter and are enraged to see Cinderella in her father's arms. They pull them apart and snatch the picture away. Suddenly the door opens and an old beggarwoman enters. The stepsisters decide to give her the picture, but the old woman sees the resemblance between the picture and Cinderella and returns it to Cinderella. Cinderella gives the old woman her last crust of bread.

The dressmaker and the wigmaker arrive to ready the stepsisters for the ball. A dancing master also arrives with the impossible task of teaching the stepsisters how to dance. Cinderella is alone again, pretending she is at the ball, and dances with the broom, then bursts into tears realizing it is only a daydream. The old beggar returns and much to Cinderella's amazement is transformed into a beautiful fairy godmother. The kitchen changes into a magic glade with dragonflies swooping among the trees. The fairy godmother asks Cinderella to find a pumpkin and four lizards and gives them to one of the dragonflies, who darts off into the trees. The fairy godmother gives a pair of glass slippers to Cinderella. The fairies of Spring, Summer, Autumn, and Winter arrive and dance for Cinderella, changing the seasons as they do. Cinderella's rags become a beautiful dress. The fairy godmother shows Cinderella a magic clock and warns her that at midnight her magic clothes will turn again into rags. The fairy godmother changes the pumpkin and lizards into a coach and horses and Cinderella drives to the ball like a princess.

ACT TWO   A jester greets the guests as they arrive in the ballroom. The guests are amazed when the ugly stepsisters arrive. The prince enters, and he too is amused by the sight of the sisters; however, he asks them each in turn to dance with him to the amazement of the crowd. Cinderella arrives in her coach, and the prince falls in love with her at first sight. He offers his guests oranges, as they are the very rarest fruit in the land. One of the sisters is left without an orange; Cinderella sees this and gives up her own. The stepsister accepts without recognizing Cinderella.

While the prince and Cinderella are dancing together, the clock strikes midnight and Cinderella's beautiful clothes turn to rags. The prince rushes after her to find only one of her glass slippers on the stairs.

ACT THREE   Cinderella waits among the cinders in the kitchen thinking the ball only a dream until she finds the other glass slipper in her pocket. She quickly hides it as the ugly sisters arrive. They show Cinderella the oranges they received from the prince. Suddenly the jester enters the room, heralding the arrival of the prince and two of his friends who have with them the glass slipper. The stepsisters vainly try to squeeze their big feet into the tiny slipper. The prince sees Cinderella sitting by the fire and asks her father if she may try it. As Cinderella gets up from the stool, she drops the other glass slipper. The prince is overjoyed! The stepsisters beg Cinderella's forgiveness and the fairy godmother arrives, accompanied by the fairies of the seasons.

The prince returns the glass slippers to them and the kitchen once again changes into a magic glade. Cinderella and her prince dance a romantic *pas de deux*, and at its conclusion, the guests arrive for the coronation of Cinderella, the cruelly mistreated girl who rose from the cinders to a royal throne.

NOTES  Reviewing this production of *Cinderella* in the British magazine, *Ballet Today*, Kay Rinfrette wrote: "Ashton's *Cinderella* for the Royal Ballet influenced Stevenson's ballet in several aspects. Like Ashton, Stevenson employs the English pantomime tradition by having the stepsisters played *en travesti*, and he excludes the stepmother who usually appears in Russian productions. Also, Stevenson omits the prince's search around the world. Unlike Ashton, Stevenson changes the sequence of musical numbers in the ballroom scene to give the *grand pas de deux* a traditional, formal structure. (The adagio is followed by the man's, then the ballerina's variation.) The choreography, especially effective in solos and group work, and character development are Stevenson's exciting, original conceptions (with only a few distant reverberations of some Ashton choreography).

"The choreographic structure of the ballet—Stevenson's use of thematic materials—is magnificent. Two primary movement themes (motifs), used separately and in combination, are introduced in the four-seasons sequence in Act One: (1) sudden or unexpected changes in direction of movement, and (2) traveling lifts which give an impression of weightlessness. The feeling of lightness created in this sequence emphasizes a fairy-tale quality and contrasts to the heaviness of the previous fireside scene (the cumbersome, heavy awkwardness of the stepsisters, the figurative 'burden' falling on Cinderella's shoulders).

"Specifically, the thematic movements include the 'dragonflies' transporting the fairy godmother in multiple traveling lifts with quick changes of direction —at one point she is carried back and forth across the stage three times without pause—and the sudden direction changes in the solos for Spring and Autumn. The same movement themes appear in the ballroom scene, especially in the *corps de ballet* work: many lovely lifts in unexpected directions, often backwards; at the waltz's climax, the girls, arching their backs, fall forward sequentially into their partners' arms, only to be weightlessly lifted and wafted away. The ballroom grand adagio, with its many extend traveling lifts (in fact, some lifts looked awkward and unnecessarily difficult), is also a part of weightless fantasy—the ballerina is swept away by the fairy-tale grandeur both literally and figuratively.

"The adagio in the last act is less involved with fantasy, closer to a real-life love relationship. This meaning is underscored by the choreography which includes thematic elements but in different combinations: there are fewer lifts, more *terre à terre* work, including swift runs with sudden direction changes, as if the lovers were blown by the wind. Structurally, this adagio is the climax of the ballet, combining and reconciling the literary themes of fantasy versus reality and the choreographic motifs of floating lightness versus heaviness or a sense of weight. In the final coronation scene, heavy-looking imperial crowns are placed on the heads of Cinderella and the prince—the fantasy (lightness) becomes a reality (weight).

"Character and dancing aspects are well balanced in this production, meaning that the stepsisters do not monopolize the show. Their hilarious antics are most clever in sequences with the dancing master and at the ball when they 'send-up' ballet steps—such as one sister holding an *attitude* for several seconds and then collapsing in a heap. The polarization of characters is clearly established in the beginning, when the stepsisters angrily snatch away from Cinderella a painting of her mother, and when Cinderella is kind to the old hag visitor (fairy godmother in disguise). The father, depicted as a multiple-henpecked man unable to cope, is a kind of transition figure between the 'good' Cinderella and the 'evil' stepsisters. Even minor characters are sharply drawn—the snobbish, prim dancing master and the eccentric, dissatisfied wigmaker."

Reviewing this new production of *Cinderella* in the New York *Times*, the critic Clive Barnes wrote: "The result is most pleasing. This is a good *Cinderella*. The settings by Edward Haynes and the costumes by Norman McDowell are simple but elegant, and Mr. Stevenson's unaffectedly classical choreography is a model of good taste.

"This is a formidable undertaking for a small company—it does not have so many dancers as the City Center Joffrey Ballet—and it survived grandly. Mr. Stevenson's choreography is strongly influenced by Frederick Ashton—Mr. Stevenson being a former member of the Royal Ballet—yet not slavishly so. Often he has gone to some lengths to be different from the Ashton version of the score, and his concept is always attractive.

"It is the kind of choreography that suits dancers—graceful and understated. He is not afraid of virtuosity, and certainly Mr. Stevenson has made more demands upon these Washington dancers than any previous choreographer. He cannot prevent the first scene of Cinderella and her sisters from appearing prosey—it always does in any production—but he does give his two lovers the most intricately stylish *pas de deux*.

"The dancing was splendid. Mr. Stevenson has mounted his ballet on two couples, Gaye Fulton and Desmond Kelly, and Marilyn Burr and Ivan Nagy. At the performance I saw it was given by Miss Fulton and Mr. Kelly.

"Miss Fulton, a delicate figurine of a princess in hiding, made an enchanting Cinderella, and Mr. Kelly, elegant and assertive, was the most perfect of Princes.

"Another young man of more than usual promise is Kirk Peterson, from the Harkness Youth Company, who was dancing the Jester. He had a brilliant technique and was very cleverly used by Mr. Stevenson. I also admired the roistering humor of Frederic Franklin (the company's director) and Larry Long as the Ugly Sisters, and the style of Judith Rhodes and Christine

Knoblauch among the fairies. But the entire company extended and excelled itself."

## CIRCLES

*Music by Luciano Berio. Choreography by Glen Tetley. Decor and costumes by Nadine Baylis. First presented by the Netherlands Dance Theatre at the Royal Theatre, The Hague, March 5, 1968. First presented by the same ensemble at the City Center, New York, April 19, 1968.*

This dance ballet uses the Luciano Berio score *Circles* for female voice, harp, and two percussion. The score's libretto is three poems by e. e. cummings (*Numbers 25, 76,* and *22*). The ballet is for six dancers, all of whom appear at the beginning of the piece, moving, exercising, warming up in silence. A boy and girl separate themselves from the group and, to the first of the three songs, dance together. Another *pas de deux* accompanies the second song while the third is more of an ensemble that recalls what has gone before.

Reviewing the ballet after its American premiere, Clive Barnes said in the New York *Times:* "Mr. Tetley's *Circles* is a lovely work. It is curious—perhaps shameful—that while Mr. Tetley has an enormous reputation in the Netherlands and England, in his native land he goes as a prophet if not unhonored at least remarkably unrecognized . . .

"The dancing flickers, ebbs and flows in all directions at the happily wayward command of the music. The six dancers interweave their patterns with a kind of creative expertise, certain in its technique yet diffident in its artistic assurance. The impression is of golden people dancing in a golden landscape, yet a gold not without the threat of devaluation and a landscape not without the danger of erosion. Nothing here is quite so certain as the actual dancing—what lies behind could be another story."

## CIRCUS POLKA

*Music by Igor Stravinsky. Choreography by Jerome Robbins. First presented by the New York City Ballet at the Stravinsky Festival, 1972, at the New York State Theatre, Lincoln Center, June 23, 1972.*

Stravinsky's *Circus Polka* was composed precisely for the circus—for the Ringling Brothers, Barnum and Bailey Circus in 1942. The circus impresarios wanted to do a ballet for elephants. They asked me to arrange the dance and told me I could choose the composer. Who else but Stravinsky? I telephoned him, not giving away the whole story. "What kind of music?" he asked. "A polka," I said. "For whom?" he wanted to know. "Elephants." "How old?" "Young!" "Okay, if they are very young, I'll do it." What he did served its purpose very well, and our ballet for *Fifty Elephants and Fifty Beautiful Girls,* staged by John Murray Anderson, with costumes by Norman Bel Geddes, and

Vera Zorina riding at the head of the troupe at the first performances, was done no less than 425 times.

Jerome Robbins in his ballet took an entirely new direction, and the work was one of the happiest inventions during our Stravinsky Festival at the New York State Theatre in 1972. Robbins chose for his cast young girls from the School of American Ballet and put them, the youngest first, through their paces. As ringmaster of the troupe, in formal top hat and swallow-tail coat, he led forty-eight of our talented children to Stravinsky's brisk measures. At the end, at his direction, the children formed the Stravinsky initials, *I. S.*, with periods. The ballet was such a hit that the whole piece had to be repeated at once.

## CLOCKWISE

*Music by Jean Françaix. Choreography by Bruce Marks. Costumes by Stanley Simmons. Lighting by Jules Fisher. First presented by the American Ballet Company at the Brooklyn Academy of Music, New York, October 24, 1970, with Karen Kelly, Christine Kono, Elizabeth Lee, Christine Sarry, Cristina Stirling, Larry Grenier, Edward Henkel, Daniel Levans, Richard Munro, John Sowinski, Kenneth Hughes, Kerry Williams, Olga Janke and Eve Wallstrum.*

This first ballet by a premier danseur of American Ballet Theatre is a dance work arranged to a composition about a clock of flowers, by the French contemporary Françaix. The piece is in seven parts, as is the ballet, where different combinations of dancers suggest the fleeting passage of time. A central *pas de deux*, to a pensive romantic melody, suggests permanent affection, too, but that soon yields to convivial ensemble, and the work ends as it began, with a simulation of a clock.

NOTES  The critic Clive Barnes, in the New York *Times*, said that Bruce Marks "has produced a graceful, charming work . . . that bodes well for his future as a choreographer. This elegant first ballet . . . was neatly danced, with Christine Kono, Christine Sarry, Daniel Levins, Elizabeth Lee and John Sowinski all to the fore."

## THE CLOWNS

*Music by Hershy Kay. Choreography by Gerald Arpino. Costumes by Edith Lutyens Bel Geddes. Lighting by Tom Skelton. Assistant to Mr. Arpino: James Howell. First presented by the City Center Joffrey Ballet at the City Center, New York, February 28, 1968, with Robert Blankshine, Frank Bays, Erika Goodman and Maximiliano Zomosa in principal roles. Special effects by Vernon Lobb and Kip Coburn. Conducted by Hershy Kay.*

*The Clowns* is a dramatic metaphor about life as it is lived by those perennial reflectors of the human spirit—the floppy white clowns of the *commedia dell' arte*. The piece begins with a bang, as if all the world had exploded, and a lone clown, battered and bruised, appears to be the only remnant of civilization. But he is not quite alone, for bodies begin to fall out of the sky like hail, bodies of fellow clowns. Mournfully but doggedly determined and not stopping to grieve, the survivor piles them all up into a kind of pyre. But mysteriously, at least one of them is alive, for a girl emerges to join the clown. The two clowns dance together joyously. Their dance is a dance of renewal and liveliness and the life is contagious: before we know it, the whole pile of bodies is revived and the clown tribe lives again.

Not content, however, with renewal and resumption of their old funny and antic roles, the clowns now reveal their human side, too. They begin to plot against each other and to employ weapons—big balloons that seem to envelop the opposition. The original survivor, however much he tries not to get involved in this dark side of human nature, is soon caught up in it, too. The fellows he has helped revive turn hostile and he is the victim. In retaliation, he brings in the biggest balloon imaginable, a huge, long cylinder that becomes a transparent tunnel. What this instrument soon becomes is a clown catcher and all the opposition are entrapped in it, beating against its walls, helpless to get out. They can *see* out and the walls of the prison are soft but they cannot penetrate them. They are all sucked down into it. Except for one. The first survivor, who again survives.

## LE COMBAT (*see* THE DUEL)


## CON AMORE

*Classic ballet in three scenes. Music by Gioacchino Rossini. Choreography by Lew Christensen. Libretto by James Graham-Luhan. Scenery and costumes by James Bodrero. Scenery executed by James Martin. First presented by the San Francisco Ballet, March 10, 1953, at the War Memorial Opera House, San Francisco, with Sally Bailey, Nancy Johnson, and Leon Danielian in the principal roles. Presented by the New York City Ballet at the City Center, New York, June 9, 1953, with a cast headed by Sally Bailey, Nancy Johnson, Herbert Bliss, and Jacques d'Amboise.*

Con Amore is a ballet about love as it was frequently depicted in nineteenth-century European engravings. It is about love as it was regarded a hundred years ago and about love as it is frequently still regarded today. The ballet is in three scenes, each of which has for its music an overture by Rossini: the overtures to *La Gazza Ladra, Il Signor Bruschino,* and *La Scala di Seta.*

SCENE ONE: THE AMAZONS AND THE BANDIT  After a musical introduction, the curtain rises on a stylized rustic scene. Here a company of Amazons, handsome and robust girls in smart military uniforms, are drilling under the command of their captain and her lieutenants. The girls move briskly and sharply, and it is apparent from their severe military bearing that they have never known love and wouldn't even entertain the idea of it. They are perfectly happy watching their beautiful captain as she sets an example of the brilliant skill in dancing and drill that they themselves hope to attain.

Love, however, asserts itself. A bandit invades the wood and dances among them. The girls treat the handsome intruder with disdain at first, but his uncontrolled gaiety and charm eventually pierce their hearts. But the vagabond bandit will have none of them. He will not be tied down by love and spurns their affections. He even dares to resist the charms of the lovely captain. At this point the perennial wrath of woman scorned holds the bandit at bay. The Amazons aim their muskets at him and he kneels before them, helpless. Blackout.

SCENE TWO: THE HUSBAND'S RETURN    After a short musical interlude, the curtain rises on the boudoir of a fashionable lady. She is alone in the room and is obviously preparing for a tryst. This turns out to be a series of trysts. The lady's husband is away at the moment, and all of her suitors have chosen this night to visit her.

First, a man about town knocks at her door. The lady admits him. The man attempts to embrace her, but the lady eludes him. It is clear, however, that she does not wish to elude him long. But before she can succumb, there is another knock at the door. The man about town hastily conceals himself, and the lady admits a sailor, who relentlessly chases her about her apartment, breathing lustily. He has almost worn down the lady when there is still another knock. The lady hides the sailor in her closet and admits a young student. This lad, instead of being eager for the lady's affections, finds her charms distasteful. She is obliged to make the advances, which the young man, knees quivering, just manages to escape. The man about town and the sailor, who have been watching all this, emerge from their hiding place to berate the student and resume their attack. There is another knock at the door. The lady's husband enters. He sees his wife with the three men and stares at them with his mouth open in astonishment. Blackout.

SCENE THREE: A TRIUMPH OF LOVE    In the final scene, we return to the finale of Scene One, where the bandit still kneels at the mercy of the angry Amazons. Amore (Cupid) enters in a chariot and with her skill attempts to remedy the situation. Hardly has she begun to do so than we are again presented with the dilemma of the finale of Scene Two. What is Amore going to do with all these men who seem to be in love with the same woman? But Amore solves everything. She draws her bow; her arrows pierce the hearts of all the men. As the curtain falls, the bandit, smitten finally with love for the Amazon captain, holds her in his arms; the lady is reunited with her husband; the man about town and the sailor embrace the Amazon lieutenants; and the timorous student, struck by love at last, rushes to claim Amore herself.

## THE CONCERT

*A charade in one act. Music by Frédéric Chopin. Choreography by Jerome Robbins. Costumes by Irene Sharaff. First presented by the New York City Ballet March 6, 1956, at the City Center, New York, with Tanaquil LeClercq and Robert Barnett in principal roles.*

Jerome Robbins subtitles this ballet "The Perils of Everybody" and writes in a program note: "One of the pleasures of attending a concert is the freedom to lose oneself in listening to the music. Quite often, unconsciously, mental pictures and images form; and the patterns and paths of these reveries are influenced by the music itself, or its program notes, or by the personal dreams, problems, and fantasies of the listener. Chopin's music in particular has been subject to fanciful 'program' names such as the Butterfly Étude, the Minute Waltz, the Raindrop Prelude, etc."

During the overture to the ballet, we look at an amusing drop curtain, by Saul Steinberg, depicting the interior of an old-fashioned concert hall. When the curtain rises, a pianist crosses the stage, dusts the piano, and slumps down in meditation. Finally, he begins to play, and the audience begins to arrive, each carrying a folding chair: a man in a scarf who sits and meditates seriously, then two girls who clearly disturb him, then a girl in a huge wide-brimmed hat. She is so enthralled by the music that she snuggles right up to the piano and embraces it. A very serious student indeed follows, and then a husband and wife and a man on tiptoe. An usher tries to straighten out a mix-up over seats. When everyone is quieted down a bit, their fantasies begin to take over.

The husband envisages the murder of his wife and dreams of her substitute nearby. As the pianist pounds out a Mazurka, he sees himself as a brave hussar carrying off his beloved. His beloved, meanwhile, only wants to be a poor butterfly and acts that way. The wife intervenes, the poor girl is put down, and her husband is compelled to back down.

These are but some of the jokes that are played and acted out by these people to Chopin's music. To reveal all of them is to miss the fun of seeing the ballet, called by Patricia Barnes, in *Dance and Dancers*, "dance's funniest creation."

NOTES  *The Concert* was extensively revised for Jerome Robbins's Ballets U.S.A. presentation at the Spoleto Festival June 8, 1958, with settings by Saul Steinberg that were used in the New York City Ballet revival (first presented December 2, 1971, at the New York State Theatre with Sara Leland, Francisco Moncion, Bettijane Sills, Shaun O'Brien, Robert Weiss, Bart Cook, Stephen Caras, Gloriann Hicks, Delia Peters, and Christine Redpath in principal roles. Jerry Zimmerman was the pianist).

*The Concert* was mounted for the Royal Ballet at the Royal Opera House, Covent Garden, London, on March 4, 1975, with frontcloths designed by Edward Gorey. Principal roles were taken by Lynn Seymour, Michael Coleman, and Georgina Parkinson. Writing in *Dance and Dancers* magazine, the English music critic Noël Goodwin said: "When I first saw *The Concert* in the inaugural Festival of Two Worlds at Spoleto in 1958, I ventured the opinion that this was one of the few deliberately comic ballets which could round off a program without anticlimax . . . Let me now amend that in the light of later experience and its welcome addition to the Royal repertory: *The Concert* is one of the few successful comic ballets on any count, and one that I still find the most hilarious I have ever seen."

## CONCERTO

*Music by Dimitri Shostakovich. Choreography by Kenneth MacMillan. First presented at the Deutsche Oper, West Berlin, November 30, 1966. First presented in the United States by American Ballet Theatre at the New York State Theatre, New York, May 18, 1967, with Eleanor D'Antuono and Scott Douglas, Toni Lander and Bruce Marks, and Cynthia Gregory in the principal roles. Decor and costumes after designs by Jürgen Rose. Lighting by Jean Rosenthal.*

This is a dance ballet arranged to Shostakovich's *Concerto No. 2 for Piano and Orchestra*. Its plot is the music. The choreographer has said: "I just listen and listen and dig into the music. I don't do any actual preliminary work at home like some other choreographers, and so it can be a tricky business. Every choreographer has his own method of working, but I invent my ballets directly, in the rehearsal room. When there, I again listen to the music, this time with the dancers, and then start experimenting and inventing."

The first movement is led by a brightly dancing girl and boy, the second is dominated by a serious dance for two lovers, while the third is led by a charming girl. The mood and temper of the dances reflect a vision of the music.

The British critic Clement Crisp has written that *Concerto* has "a fresh, 'open' style that matches the exhilarating textures of the score with complete assurance."

## CONCERTO BAROCCO

*Classic ballet in three movements. Music by Johann Sebastian Bach. Choreography by George Balanchine. Scenery and costumes by Eugene Berman. First presented by the American Ballet at the Theatre of Hunter College, New York, May 29, 1940, with Marie-Jeanne, Mary Jane Shea, and William Dollar in the principal roles.*

The only preparation possible for this ballet is a knowledge of its music, for *Concerto Barocco* has no "subject matter" beyond the score to which it is danced and the particular dancers who execute it. Set to Bach's *Concerto in D minor for Two Violins,* the ballet tries to interest the audience only by its dancing, its treatment of the music, just as Baroque art and architecture interested people not because of their subjects but because of the decorative treatment that embellished those subjects.

Bach's great concerto can stand alone. Some people then wonder, why arrange a ballet to such music? Why not arrange ballets to music that is more dependent, music that dancing can "fill out"? The answer is that bad music often inspires bad dancing, bad choreography. It is not an accident that the dance masterpieces of Saint-Léon, Petipa, and Fokine all have scores that are also masterworks. *Coppélia, The Sleeping Beauty,* and *Petrouchka,* with their scores by Delibes, Tchaikovsky, and Stravinsky, suggested to each one of these choreographers an advance in the development of ballet.

Choosing pieces of music for dancing is a matter for the individual choreographer. A choreographer disinterested in classical dancing will not care to use scores by Bach and Mozart except for theatrical sensational reasons; he will select music more to his immediate purpose. But if the dance designer sees in the development of classical dancing a counterpart in the development of music and has studied them both, he will derive continual inspiration from great scores. He will also be careful, as he acts on this inspiration, not to interpret the music beyond its proper limits, not to stretch the music to accommodate a literary idea, for instance. If the score is a truly great one, suitable for dancing, he will not have need of such devices and can present his impression in terms of pure dance.

FIRST MOVEMENT: VIVACE   The curtain rises. The music begins. There are eight girls on stage. Dancing variously as one group, as two groups, and in duets, the girls correspond to the music the orchestra plays, but not in any strict or literal sense; they do not mirror the music, rather they move in accordance with its length, the space between its beginning and end being filled by a dance picture of the music. Just as the portrait is different from the news photograph, so the dance picture tries to tell something independent of an exact, bar-by-bar, rhythm-by-rhythm, mirror image of the music.

As the two violins take up their parts in the music, two soloists enter. Singly, together, and with the *corps de ballet,* they become a part of the dance orchestration. They support each other as the music of one violin entwines the other; they depict and develop dance themes that recur with the repetition and development of themes in the orchestra.

SECOND MOVEMENT: LARGO MA NON TANTO   Now the soloists leave the stage. The orchestra sounds the touching, lyrical melody. One of the soloists returns, accompanied by a male partner, who lifts her softly and slowly, turns her as the *corps de ballet* bend low before her, and leads her in and out of a maze formed by the *corps.* The music is tender, but it possesses a warm nobility and strength that the ballerina's partner allows her to imitate as its development proceeds. When the music gathers toward a full statement and the theme repeats again and again, climbing with each repetition to a climactic rest, the ballerina's partner lifts her without pause high over his head, over and

over again, to the accumulating sound. Then, toward the end of the movement, the boy slides the girl low across the floor in three daring movements.
The ballerina rises each time in an open pose that reflects the strength underlying the lyricism of the theme.

THIRD MOVEMENT: ALLEGRO   The music is now quickly rhythmic. All ten
dancers seem to respond to it spontaneously, marking the beat of the music
with soft, light jumps, crisp arm gestures, and syncopated groupings. As the
joyous music ends, all the dancers kneel.

## CONCERTO FOR JAZZ BAND AND ORCHESTRA

*Music by Rolf Liebermann. Choreography by Arthur Mitchell and George
Balanchine. Lighting by Ronald Bates. Conducted by Robert Irving. First
presented by the New York City Ballet at the New York State Theatre, Lincoln Center, May 7, 1971, with dancers from the Dance Theatre of Harlem
and the New York City Ballet.*

This ballet, which received its one and only performance at a special gala occasion, will never be done again in all probability but is worth remembering
and recording. It was a wonderful thing for me to collaborate on the choreography with Arthur Mitchell, who had become, in the New York City Ballet,
our first black *premier danseur,* the first black first dancer in *any* major ballet
company.

In 1968, at the time of the assassination of Martin Luther King, Jr., I did a
memorial ballet, for one performance, to Stravinsky's *Requiem Canticles.*
Arthur Mitchell, at that time disturbed by King's death and its meaning, determined that he would make it possible for other blacks to become fine dancers.
The Dance Theatre of Harlem, and its associated school which he subsequently founded, is one of the great breakthroughs in the arts in America. To
work with his dancers and our own on one ballet was, therefore, a special
pleasure.

The music for the ballet, by the distinguished impresario and musician Rolf
Liebermann, alternates a big jazz band (Doc Severinsen and the *Tonight
Show* Orchestra) with a symphony ensemble. It is in six parts: *Introduction
and Jump, Scherzo I, Blues, Scherzo II, Boogie Woogie,* and *Interludium.*
Those who saw the ballet that night seemed to enjoy it very much and to ap-
preciate the special quality of the occasion. It made me, personally, as it did
Lincoln Kirstein, prouder than ever to be an occupant of the New York State
Theatre.

## CONCERTO FOR PIANO AND WINDS

*Music by Igor Stravinsky. Choreography by John Taras. Costumes by Rou-
ben Ter-Arutunian. Lighting by Ronald Bates. Pianist: Gordon Boelzner.*

*Conducted by Robert Irving. First presented by the New York City Ballet
at the Stravinsky Festival, 1972, at the New York State Theatre, Lincoln
Center, June 20, 1972, with Bruce Wells in the leading role.*

This wonderful score by Stravinsky, too seldom heard in the concert hall, has
been used twice by John Taras for ballet. His first version, *Arcade*, was done
for the New York City Ballet at the City Center, New York, March 28, 1963,
with Suzanne Farrell and Arthur Mitchell in the leading roles. His second
ballet to this music was presented during the Stravinsky Festival at the New
York City Ballet in June 1972.

The ballet starts shortly after the orchestra begins, the curtain rising on
fourteen boys, all in red costume. Different groupings take up the accent of
the music, precise and percussive, as the piano, like a percussive instrument,
plays a toccata-like theme. There are no strings in this orchestra, we remember, as the definitive gesture and movement point to vital and supple action rather than reaction.

The second movement, which is very slow and pulsating, has an entirely
different character. The stage darkens and three spotlights point to three boys
kneeling. They rise slowly in answer to the music, as do the lights, and in
poses and groupings complement the piano and wind instruments' accompaniment. At the end, they again kneel in the dark.

Under bright lights, the dancers to the music perform a variety of brisk response that includes references back to the first part, a fugue, and a lively
finale.

# CONCERTO FOR TWO SOLO PIANOS

*Music by Igor Stravinsky. Choreography by Richard Tanner. Costumes by
Stanley Simmons. First presented by the New York City Ballet at the New
York State Theatre, Lincoln Center, January 21, 1971, with Gelsey Kirkland and John Clifford, Colleen Neary and James Bogan, and David Richardson as principals.*

This work, the first by Richard Tanner for our repertory, was later performed
at the New York City Ballet's Stravinsky Festival, on February 23, 1972.
Stravinsky's music had its first performance in 1935, with the composer and his
son Soulima as soloists. The concerto is in four movements: 1. *Con moto*, 2.
*Notturno—Adagietto*, 3. *Quattro variazioni*, and 4. *Preludio* and *Fuga;* the
ballet follows this same pattern, basing its movement on the score's development. The plot of the music is the ballet's narrative.

One of the remarkable aspects of the score, as Eric Walter White notes in
his indispensable volume on Stravinsky, is its second movement, the *Nocturne*
—"a slow movement of exquisite tenderness and feeling, closely related in style
to the slow movements of the Piano Sonata and the Capriccio."

# CONCERTO GROSSO

*Music by George Frederick Handel. Choreography by Charles Czarny. Costumes by Joop Stovkis. First presented by the Netherlands Dance Theatre at the Circustheatre, Scheveningen, Holland, January 29, 1971. First presented in the United States by the same ensemble at the Brooklyn Academy of Music, New York, April 1, 1972.*

Handel's music for the *Concerto Grosso No. 5* and the *Allegro* from the *Concerto Grosso No. 12* accompany this dance ballet based on gymnastics and athletics. The first part, begun by four boys in gym suits, is a warm-up for exercises and games to come. Four girls join them. The second part, *Obligatory Exercise,* is for three dancers. In *Shadow Boxing,* in silence, eight dancers wearing red mittens fight with each other in a gentle way. Following a sequence for skating, a line is drawn on stage to represent a tightrope, on which the dancers balance and perform. Next, in bright striped costumes of red and white, two boys play at soccer, each embodying opposing sides. All four couples join together again for the finale, a *Karate Minuet.*

# CONCERTO IN G

*Music by Maurice Ravel. Choreography by Jerome Robbins. Sets and costumes by Rouben Ter-Arutunian. Lighting by Ronald Bates. First presented by the New York City Ballet at the Hommage à Ravel at the New York State Theatre, Lincoln Center, May 14, 1975, with Suzanne Farrell and Peter Martins as principals. Conducted by Manuel Rosenthal.*

One of the real hits of the New York City Ballet's Ravel festival in 1975, *Concerto in G* is danced to music that has an association with the United States. Ravel, at the peak of his fame and popularity, had just returned from a triumphant American tour when he began work on the piece. His hope was to compose a work that he could play himself, in order to fulfill the many requests that had accumulated for personal appearances. In the end he asked Marguerite Long, an old friend, to play as he conducted. Together they performed the concerto to great acclaim throughout Europe.

Janet Flanner attended the first performance and reported, under her pen name "Genêt," enthusiastically to *The New Yorker,* as Irving Drutman has recalled in *Paris Was Yesterday, 1925–39* (The Viking Press, New York, 1972).

Robbins's ballet to the *Concerto in G* is a dance piece without a story. There are three movements. While the first and third parts of the ballet, like the music, respond to jazz influences, a central sinuous adagio for the two principals creates an enduring impression.

Frances Herridge in the New York *Post* called *Concerto in G* "another gem for the repertory in a class with Robbins's *Dances at a Gathering.*"

Writing in *Dance and Dancers* magazine, the critic Patricia Barnes wrote that Robbins's "opening and closing movements, inventive, fresh and lively, used the ensemble of boys and girls with a vitality that earlier characterized his *Interplay* and in its jazz-tinctured rhythms showed Robbins in his very best Broadway mood; but it was the adagio movement for Suzanne Farrell and Peter Martins that was the work's real heart. Robbins has used Farrell's exquisite body to fabulous effect, exploiting her length of limb, her whole-hearted approach to dancing, in a pas de deux of genuine tenderness. The blend of daring lifts, swoops and swirls is contrasted with wonderfully effective little pauses, moments of telling stillness."

## THE CONSORT

*Music by Dowland, Neusidler, Morley, and anonymous composers. Orchestrated by Christopher Keene. Choreography by Eliot Feld. Costumes by Stanley Simmons. Lighting by Jules Fisher. First presented by the American Ballet Company at the Brooklyn Academy of Music, New York, October 24, 1970, with Marilyn D'Honau, Christine Kono, Elizabeth Lee, Olga Janke, Cristina Stirling, Larry Grenier, Kenneth Hughes, Daniel Levans, Richard Munro, and John Sowinski.*

Seventeenth-century music, mostly English, with some bawdy German songs for salt, provides the musical base for this dance ballet, orchestrated by the then musical director of the American Ballet Company, Christopher Keene. There is no plot here, and at first it appears that we shall be watching simply a stately but vigorous period piece, expressive of the Elizabethan age. But a curious thing happens. The long, formal dresses of the girls yield to short shifts, and before we know what has happened, the boys are whirling them about, courtiers have become peasants and, perhaps, themselves. While the stylization of the dances suggests a time long ago, the best of the orchestration and its demanding rhythms suggest the music of our own time, too, which is reflected in a rustic dance difference. Set for ten dancers, there are combinations of ensembles, boys and girls alone as well as *pas de deux* and solos, that merge the two styles of dancing.

NOTES  Writing about *The Consort* in the *Village Voice*, the critic Deborah Jowitt said: "The first part of *The Consort* is courtly, restrained, with that faint undercurrent of unpleasantness that you feel in a real pavane. Within the elaborate ritual, everyone is sizing up his partner and engaging in an almost invisible thrusting and parrying. Feld keeps the feeling of social dance; many instances of couples doing unison movement based—very remotely—on period dances. There are a few interludes that are more irregular. For example, there's an interesting bit in which Olga Janke dances very slowly and minimally, involved with her own skirt and a path that she is not quite progressing along, while John Sowinski keeps circling her lightly, but not lightheartedly—doing some of the subtly complex Feld steps that Sowinski performs with such luminous intelligence. They are aware and yet not aware of each other, and you are not quite sure which is the moth and which the star.

"As the court section ends, some of the women begin to help each other undress on stage. Quietly and naturally, they remove headdresses, take off boleros, loop their skirts up to above their knees. Daniel Levans examines and strokes his feathered cap for quite a time before tossing it into the wings. Again there is something faintly sinister in the air. When all the dancers are ready, the peasant section begins and begins mildly, with some of the same steps from the court part. You almost feel that these could be the same aristocrats playing at being peasants. Yet the stage gets more crowded (five couples as opposed to the three who began the piece), the dancers' bodies begin to look more weighty and sprawling, the harp (Keene's lute surrogate) is less noticeable, and the brasses begin to bray. These are still social dances, but with a coarseness and an increasingly ribald air. Two men do a fast rowdy dance, each with two girls, to Hans Neusidler's marvelously strange "Der Juden Tanz." *The Consort* ends with a debauch—the men wobbling like scarecrows, clutching the women to them; just drunk enough to be singlemindedly lecherous and with enough control left to do something about it. As the curtain comes down, the women have their legs about the men's waists and are being tossed and worried at. It reminded me of one of those Breughel scenes: you feel that because most of the time the peasants must have worked so hard, their appetites for play and drunken oblivion must have been immense, simple, and quickly sated."

## COPPÉLIA (The Girl with Enamel Eyes)

*Classic ballet in three acts. Music by Léo Delibes. Choreography by Arthur Saint-Léon. Book by Charles Nuitter and Arthur Saint-Léon, after a story by E. T. A. Hoffmann. First presented at the Théâtre Impérial de l'Opéra, Paris, May 25, 1870, with Giuseppina Bozacchi as Swanilda and Eugenie Fiocre as Franz. First presented in the United States by the American Opera at the Metropolitan Opera House, New York, March 11, 1887, with Marie Giuri and Felicita Carozzi in the leading roles. First presented in England at the Empire Theatre, London, May 14, 1906, with Adeline Genée as Swanilda.*

Just as *Giselle* is ballet's great tragedy, so *Coppélia* is its great comedy. Both ballets are love stories and both have their roots in real life as well as in fantasy. In *Giselle* there are ghosts to test the quality of the hero's love for the heroine, and in *Coppélia* there is another romantic device by which the heroine makes sure of her lover's devotion. This device is the beautiful, lifeless doll, whose quiet, mechanical beauty contrasts with the charming liveliness of the real-life heroine. Because the hero in *Giselle* can only meet his lost love briefly in fantasy, and thereafter she is lost to reality, the ending of the ballet is tragic. But in *Coppélia* the inadequacy of the fantastic wax doll leads the hero back to his real love, and the ending is happy. And where Albrecht in *Giselle* learns an unhappy lesson from which he will never completely recover, Franz in *Coppélia* learns a lesson that makes his life happy forever after.

ACT ONE: THE SQUARE   A spacious overture sets the tone for the whole ballet. The music begins with a melody of quiet dignity, first stated by the horns, then swept up by the strings. A muffled drum sounds, and the mood changes spontaneously to open gaiety as the orchestra plays a spirited robust mazurka. At its conclusion, the curtain rises.

The scene is a square in any small town in Central Europe; the time is a sunny afternoon several hundred years ago. A small house in the back faces the audience; on the side, a higher dwelling with a balcony projecting from the second floor dominates the street. Other buildings cluster about the square in a pleasantly haphazard fashion. All the façades are clean and painted in bright colors, and the walls and roofs seen in the background confirm our impression of an old village whose charm has not been worn away by changing times. The square is empty. An old man, bent with age, hobbles out of the door of the house on the right. This is Dr. Coppélius, the town's most mysterious citizen. He is said to dabble in alchemy and magic, but no one knows precisely what he does. Coppélius looks up at the balcony of his house, and we see that a lovely young girl is sitting there, reading a book. She is hidden a little from the full light of the sun, is wholly preoccupied with her reading, and takes no notice of the old doctor. Coppélius points up at the studious girl, rubs his hands with satisfaction as if he were a delighted chaperone, and re-enters his house.

The door of the little house in the back opens in a moment, and Swanilda emerges. She is dressed in bright colors particularly becoming to her dark beauty. From her movements we know almost immediately that she is very young and very much in love. The music to which she dances is piquant in the unembarrassed fullness of its melody, and Swanilda dances to it with obvious pleasure at some inner happiness. She walks rapidly on point, looking about the square anxiously to see that she is alone. She is expecting someone, but has some business of her own to attend to first. She glances up at the balcony of the large house and sees there the charming young girl, just as attractive as she is. The girl is intensely occupied and, holding the book rigidly before her, she does not look down to see Swanilda waving to her. Swanilda is annoyed. First of all she is annoyed because the girl is clearly snubbing her, but she is chagrined mostly because she has noticed that Franz, her fiancé, has also waved at this strange girl and has never mentioned it to her. Everyone calls the girl Coppélia. She is said to be the old man's daughter, but Coppélius has never appeared with her in the streets of the town and their relationship is just as unfathomable as Coppélius himself. Swanilda imitates her, holding an imaginary book before her. Then she bows low to Coppélia, in mock ceremony. Still the girl will not notice her. Swanilda stamps her foot in annoyance and dances briefly. She does not understand why Coppélia sits there reading on such a beautiful day and suspects she might be in a trance. On the other hand, she might be waiting for Franz! Swanilda approaches the house to see the girl more closely, shakes her fists at her, but quickly turns away as she hears Franz coming down the street. She is carefully hidden by the time he enters and she observes him secretly.

Franz is a high-spirited young peasant dressed in country costume. Like Swanilda, Franz is open and carefree by nature, but his heartiness masks a certain conceit: he seems not to have a care in the world and would not think it odd if every girl in the village adored him as much as Swanilda does. He does not go directly to Swanilda's door, but strides over to the house of Coppélius. After making sure that he isn't being watched, he glances up at the balcony. He waves to Coppélia flirtatiously, but also casually, as if he were in the habit of greeting her every time he passed. He points to Swanilda's door and remembers his love for her in the midst of this new infatuation. He clearly enjoys not knowing which lovely girl to choose. He clutches his heart as he looks up at Coppélia, then blows a kiss to her. Swanilda's worst suspicions of Franz's fickleness seem to be justified. Her suspicions become fears when Coppélia looks up from her book and waves back to Franz. Neither she nor Franz can see that behind the girl Coppélius stands concealed. He watches the flirtation with obvious disapproval, steps forward quickly, and closes the window curtains in Coppélia's face. Franz is abashed by this sudden disappearance of his new love. He is so distressed that he doesn't notice Swanilda, who has come into the square and stands right behind him. Swanilda refuses to attract his attention when he won't even turn away from the balcony; she walks off.

Now Franz consoles himself by remembering his rendezvous with Swanilda. But he does not have time to reach her door before Swanilda returns, bringing a beautiful butterfly she has just caught.

Franz takes the butterfly from her and pins it to his shirt. To Swanilda, this harmless gesture is a stab at her own broken heart. She bursts into tears and angrily accuses Franz of being unfaithful to her. He demurs, but she has no patience with his offhand answers and suggests that they come to him just as readily as his flirtations. Now that he sees how serious she is, Franz sincerely denies that he loves anyone else. But Swanilda is firm in her disbelief; she will not listen. Now Franz begins to lose his temper: how can she fail, he wonders, to see that he loves only her? Swanilda leaves the square, and Franz hails a party of peasants, their friends, who are unaware of the tension between the two lovers. They dance the rollicking mazurka that the orchestra first played in the overture, and when Swanilda joins them, her anxieties are momentarily dispelled. But she is determined to keep clear of Franz and, even at the sacrifice of her happiness, will accept no explanations.

The dancing of the peasants halts as the burgomaster enters the square. Everyone stands aside to make room for him and listens attentively as he tells them that on the next day the village will receive a great new bell for the town clock as a gift from the lord of the manor and that they must prepare themselves for the celebration attendant upon the ceremonies. The peasants are delighted at the idea of an unexpected festival. Their pleasure is so great that they do not pay much attention to strange noises emanating from the house of Coppélius.

The burgomaster goes on to say that the gracious lord will present handsome dowries to the girls who marry on the festival day. Several couples look at each other expectantly, but Swanilda is unmoved. Franz watches her closely. The burgomaster turns and asks her if she will be wed tomorrow. Unwilling to expose her broken heart to her friends and perhaps still hoping that she may be wrong about Franz's love, Swanilda resorts to fate and takes up an ear of wheat which the burgomaster offers her and shakes it near her ear, looking at her fiancé. The custom is—if she hears anything, her lover "loves her true"; if the wheat is silent, her lover "loves her not." Franz supports Swanilda in lovely deep poses as she bends low to listen to the wheat. Swanilda hears nothing. Franz, who thinks this pretense is silly, also hears nothing. She beckons to a friend and shakes the wheat again. The friend claims there is a sound, but Swanilda will not believe it. She throws the straw to the ground and announces that she and Franz are no longer engaged. Franz stalks away in disgust at the ways of women, while Swanilda joins her friends to dance a bright, gay tune as if nothing had happened to disturb their good time. A drum roll sounds, and Swanilda's friends dance a czardas, a Hungarian folk dance that starts out with slow, formal dignity and then increases in both speed and humor to become delirious with joy. The light grows darker and the group soon disbands. The stage is empty as night falls.

The door to Coppélius's house opens, and the wizened old man totters out. He pulls out a large key, locks the door, tries it several times, puts his key away, pats his pocket, and proceeds slowly across the square, leaning heavily on his cane. Obviously reluctant at leaving his house, Coppélius is easily frightened by a band of pranksters who rail at him good-humoredly, dance about him, and boisterously try to overcome his reluctance to join in. He loses his temper, which only encourages the fun. As they push him about, Coppélius drops his key. The villagers do not notice this and soon leave him. He shuffles across the street on his errand, shaking his head at their impertinence.

Swanilda and a group of her friends pass him as they enter on their way to supper. Swanilda is delighted to find that he has lost his key. She looks back toward Coppélius, who has now disappeared, and then at his house. Her friends easily persuade Swanilda to try the key in Coppélius's door. At last she will discover the illusive Coppélia alone! She goes to the door, fits the key to the lock, and signals pleadingly to her friends to follow. She steps in. She backs out hurriedly, frightened at her own audacity and the dark interior. Her friends line up behind her in single file, trembling with fear, and one by one they enter the house.

The square is deserted for a moment, then Franz comes in, armed with a ladder. The petulant youth is determined to have his love acknowledged by Coppélia, now that Swanilda has renounced him, and he places the ladder against the house. He is climbing up to a window when Coppélius, who has finally missed his key, rushes in to look for it. He apprehends Franz, attacks him with his walking stick, and chases him off. He then continues to search for the key. When he fails to find it and discovers that his door is wide open, he throws up his hands in despair and with great agitation runs into the house. The persistent Franz re-enters, places his ladder again, and climbs toward the mysterious Coppélia. The curtain falls.

ACT TWO: COPPÉLIUS'S HOUSE    The scene is a large room with dark walls. There is a large window at the back, and on the left is a curtained enclosure. Curious immobile figures, staring straight ahead, sit and stand about the stage in fixed attitudes, each as if cut off in the middle of a gesture. But there is not time to observe them before Swanilda and her friends walk in on tiptoe. The girls take in the weird room and are clearly sorry that they have let Swanilda talk them into coming. A small light throws their shadows against the walls, and they retreat into the center of the room. More curious than afraid, but still treading softly, Swanilda roams about looking at the woodenlike characters.

They seem to be dolls, but they are all life-sized and the suspended gestures in which they are fixed are alarmingly human. On the right, seated on a cushion, sits a tall Chinaman dressed in a richly embroidered native costume. A one-man band in resplendent parade dress stands with arm out, ready to strike the huge drum he carries. An astronomer in long black robes and a high, peaked hat, a poised juggler in the middle of one of his tricks, a Harlequin in typical diamond-patched costume, and a king holding scepter in hand—all these characters occupy Coppélius's room as if it were their home. [In the Sadler's Wells Theatre Ballet production, the figures are a Chinaman, a Crusader, Pierrot, an astrologer, and an Oriental dancer.] They are all individuals, each seems to exist apart from the others, yet to Swanilda and her friends the silent, still figures have no animate existence at all and resemble nothing so much as oversized dolls. Still, the girls are terrified by the darkness and the strange silence. Swanilda is instinctively moved to investigate the curtained alcove, for nowhere does she see Coppélia. She goes over, starts to peep through the curtain, and then runs back to her friends. Her knees are trembling so much that one of the girls holds her shaking legs. The girls force Swanilda to return to the curtain, and this time she is a little bolder. She looks behind the curtain, runs back to her friends, and gestures with automatic movements to music that might accompany the dance of a mechanical toy! Coppélia is a doll! One of the girls accidentally collides with the sitting Chinaman, and the interlopers are aghast as the Chinaman throws out his arms like an automaton, wags his head knowingly, and does a little rhythm act. The terrified girls approach him carefully, but the Chinaman does not change his position. He is a doll, too, but a wonderful mechanical doll, so close to reality that the girls have never imagined his like before. They stare rapturously at his jerky, automatic gestures, laugh delightedly, and search for the hidden clockwork that makes him move. They find nothing. The music peters out. The doll stops as he began.

Swanilda and her friends examine the doll Coppélia. Swanilda reaches out tentatively and touches her. Coppélia is cold as ice, utterly lifeless, a wax doll like all the rest! Swanilda takes her book away, and the frozen girl sits as before, her stilted hands grasping nothing. Swanilda can make neither head nor tail of the book and turns back to be absolutely certain that the lovely girl will not look up and wave to her, as she did to Franz. She leans over to feel her heart. She feels nothing. Sure now that the charming creature of whom she was so jealous is merely an absurd doll, Swanilda gathers her friends about her and laughs with glee at the prospect of Franz paying court to her.

All the girls are tremendously relieved that they have no one to fear in the empty house and prankishly run to each one of the dolls. They wind the dolls up, and soon all the mechanical creatures are in motion. The one-man band plays his music, the juggler commences his act, the astronomer lifts a telescope to his eye—and the fascinated girls can't decide which they like best. They are so enchanted by the dolls that they do not hear Coppélius enter. The music imitates his fierce anger.

He runs in, cape flying behind him, speechless with rage. He shakes his stick at the intruders and rushes about to catch them. All the girls retreat toward the door—all of them except Swanilda, who sneaks into Coppélia's booth while the toymaker shakes his stick at her fleeing friends and pulls the curtains closed. Coppélius comes back into the room and makes straight for the curtains to see if the girls have harmed his most cherished creation. A window opens at the back, and Coppélius stops. Another intruder! He stands close against the back wall, ready to pounce on the stranger. Franz climbs into the room. Coppélius waits patiently until the youth cannot return to the window and then sets upon him. Franz pleads that he means no harm, that he has entered merely to see the girl he loves, and that he will die unless he talks with her.

Gradually Coppélius realizes that Franz is quite serious and he ceases to threaten him. He wants to hear more and astonishes Franz by becoming quite friendly. Coppélius insists that he stay, telling him that his daughter will be in very shortly, and invites the unbelieving youth to sit down and have a drink. When the drink is poured, Franz has no more apprehension and accepts it with relish. The toymaker chatters constantly, pretends to drink too, and Franz —gloriously happy now that he has neared his goal—fails to see that Coppélius is providing him with one drink after another. He tries to describe the beauties of Coppélia to the old man with drunken gestures, and his host nods repeatedly in agreement as Franz's intoxication is increased by a potion he has poured into the drink. Franz's head falls back against the chair, his arms hang limp in sleep, and in this room filled with dolls he is almost like a doll himself.

Coppélius checks to be sure that he is unconscious and wrings his hands in glee in anticipation of his next move. He takes out a huge leather volume, puts it down on the floor, and hurriedly leafs through the pages looking for a secret formula he has never used before. He finds it, leaps up, looks back at Franz, and approaches the drawn curtains of Coppélia's closet. He yanks back the curtains, peers in, and examines carefully every feature of Coppélia's face and dress. The clever Swanilda no longer resembles herself as she sits rigidly in Coppélia's costume, holding up her little book. Coppélius goes behind her chair and wheels Swanilda into the middle of the room as the orchestra sounds a beautiful melody on piercing, muted strings. He glances down at the book and makes magical gestures in Swanilda's face. Swanilda does not blink. Now the toymaker runs over to Franz and, moving his hands down the youth's body from head to foot, seems to pull the power of life from him like a magnet. Coppélius holds the life force tight in his hands and goes back to the doll, whom he tries to endow with this potency. He consults the book again and repeats the ritual. To his astonishment and happiness, Swanilda tosses away the book, and Coppélius believes his wooden doll has actually come to life.

Swanilda's arms move stiffly as the music mimics the mechanics of her strength. She raises her head and stands up, her body still bent over in a sitting position. The delighted Coppélius straightens her up, and she stands still for a moment. Her face is expressionless. Then she begins to try out her arms and legs, pushing her feet out before her in a simulated walk. Coppélia's master encourages Swanilda's every step with more incantations; the girl is excited at her success in deceiving him. She looks over at Franz and can hardly wait until he wakens. Meanwhile she lets Coppélius imagine that he alone is responsible for her new-found vitality. Her stance is rigid and her face assumes an equally artificial smile. At Coppélius's command, her legs move less mechanically, and soon she is dancing to a light, sparkling waltz, perfecting her steps as she circles about. Now that he has taught her to dance, the toymaker wishes her to continue showing off his magical powers. The doll smiles ingratiatingly, but instead of dancing she walks about the room, as if she were exploring it for the first time. She goes over to Franz, shakes him, sees the discarded wine mug, and raises it to her lips. Coppélius snatches it from her in the nick of time. He is beginning to find out that this live doll can be as exasperating as any young girl.

Swanilda keeps up her fun with him, but still maintains her mechanical characteristics. Like a child, she pretends in each one of her tricks merely to be doing what her teacher has told her to do in the first place. The tormented Coppélius beseeches her to dance again; she stares at him dumbly. Finally, to keep her out of any more mischief, he distracts her by placing a black mantilla about her shoulders. Swanilda responds instantly by dancing a bolero. The music is subdued, but the girl intensifies the impassioned Spanish dance as the tempo mounts. Coppélius now supposes that there is nothing he cannot make her do; he experiments further by investing the doll with a Scottish plaid. Sure enough, as the orchestra pipes a sprightly jig, she follows its rhythms like a good Scottish lass. At the end of this dance, however, Swanilda has had enough. She kicks the pages of his magic book and runs berserk about the room.

She tries to awaken Franz from his stupor. Coppélius, fraught with anxiety lest she harm herself as well as the other dolls, finally succeeds in grabbing her. He sets her down hard on her chair, shakes his finger in her face, and rolls the chair back into the curtained alcove. Franz stirs, stretches, and looks about. Coppélius allows him no time for questions and tells him to get out. Franz leaves eagerly, climbing back out of the window. Swanilda, no longer a doll, pushes the curtains aside and dashes about the room knocking over every one of Coppélius's precious toys except the king, who stands in ridiculous majesty over the chaotic scene. Then, all too lifelike, Swanilda escapes through the door to catch up with Franz.

The shocked Coppélius cannot believe his eyes. He pulls back the curtains, and there, thrown across her chair, he sees the naked, limp body of his beloved Coppélia.

ACT THREE: THE WEDDING   The festival day has arrived, and all the villagers have gathered in the sun on the manor house lawn to take part in the celebration. The town's new bell has been blessed, and the lord of the manor awaits the presentation of dowries to those who will marry on the holiday. Swanilda, radiant in her wedding costume, and Franz, also in formal array, approach the lord with the other couples. Franz cannot take his eyes off Swanilda, who has taught him the lesson he unconsciously yearned to know. He knows now that, as his wife, she will be to him all women—all the other girls the beautiful Coppélia represented. The assembled villagers share the exuberant joy of Franz and Swanilda. The lord of the manor congratulates them and presents the dowries.

The irate and pathetic Coppélius marches in and upsets the happy throng by reminding them of the damage he has sustained. Coppélius is so intent on securing compensation, rather than explanations and apologies, that the crowd does not sympathize with him readily. The only one who sympathizes is Swanilda, who steps forward understandingly and offers him her dowry. The sullen Coppélius is about to take it, but the lord of the manor motions Swanilda away and rewards the toymaker with a bag of gold. The old man leaves the scene, wondering whether it will ever be possible for him to create a doll as lovable as his ill-fated Coppélia.

The pageant of the day now commences. The peasants dance the familiar "Dance of the Hours," in which the arrangement of the performers imitates the progress of the hours around an enormous clock as the hurdy-gurdy music tinkles the time away. The twelve girls form a circle like the face of an enormous clock, kneel toward the center, and one by one rise, pirouette, and kneel again, telling the time away.

Soft woodwinds herald the arrival of Dawn, danced by a lovely young girl. Her dance, with the music, is at first slow and tentative, like the gradual approach of light; then her body responds to bright wakening music and she celebrates the rising sun.

Now Prayer—a demure girl who clasps her hands before her and turns slowly in deep arabesques—delights the villagers. She kneels as the harp ends the music for her dance.

A peasant couple perform a vigorous betrothal dance to rhythmic, piping music. They bow to the lord of the manor, and all await the arrival of the bride and groom.

Franz bows and holds out his hand to Swanilda. Together they dance a moving adagio to a deep melody from the strings. Franz carries Swanilda high on his shoulder, sets her down gently, and the girl kneels before him. She rises on point, pirouettes swiftly in his arms, is lifted again, released, and caught as her lover holds her across his knee. He turns her in arabesque, and the dance that symbolizes their reconciliation and pledged happiness comes to an end. Their dance together and the variation each now performs alone reveal the youthful strength and tenderness each possesses for the other. When they have finished, all the villagers join the smiling couple in a fast, constantly accelerating dance in which the whole company becomes a part of the breathless happiness reflected in the shining faces of Swanilda and Franz.

American Ballet Theatre revived *Coppélia*, in a new production by Enrique Martinez, during their 1968 season at the Brooklyn Academy of Music in New York. Carla Fracci and Erik Bruhn danced the first performance. Others dancing the principal roles were Cynthia Gregory and Gayle Young, Alexandra Radius and Ted Kivitt, and Eleanor D'Antuono and Ivan Nagy. When she joined the company, Natalia Makarova danced the role of Swanilda.

In 1974 I decided that we should stage *Coppélia* at the New York City Ballet (we needed another evening-long ballet) and asked the ballerina and teacher Alexandra Danilova, celebrated for many years for her Swanilda, to collaborate with me on the choreography. Rouben Ter-Arutunian designed the scenery and costumes, which were executed by Karinska. The ballet was first presented by the company July 17, 1974 at the Saratoga Performing Arts Center, the New York City Ballet's summer home at Saratoga Springs, New York.

*Coppélia* was first danced, of course, in France. It was introduced in Russia in 1884, with Marius Petipa's own version of Saint-Léon's original choreography. I remember very well performances by the Russian Imperial Ballet of *Coppélia* and as a member of the company danced in the mazurka. (It is said that the czardas and the mazurka were first introduced into ballet in *Coppélia* and, from then on, divertissements based on national and folk dances became very popular in ballet.)

I have often said that Delibes is one of my favorite composers for dance. In our new *Coppélia*, we used the entire score of the three-act version. The first dance drama of really uniform excellence deserves no less! No part of the ballet is subordinate to any other; most important of all, ballet music in *Coppélia* participates in the dance drama as never before, Delibes' charming, melodic music assisting the plot and unifying the music and dance. As we know, Tchaikovsky was directly inspired by Delibes' scores to write his own ballet music. Delibes is the first great ballet composer; Tchaikovsky and Stravinsky are his successors.

The first American performance of *Coppélia*, though greeted with applause by press and public in 1887, was not as memorable as a later one, when Anna Pavlova, making her début in the United States, appeared as Swanilda at the Metropolitan Opera House, New York, February 28, 1910.

Most major ballet companies round the world dance *Coppélia* and many distinguished dancers have performed its leading roles. The Ballet Russe de Monte Carlo staged the ballet for Alexandra Danilova who was identified with it for many years. The noted dance critic and poet Edwin Denby called her "the most wonderful *Coppélia* heroine in the world." Madame Danilova now teaches at the School of American Ballet in New York, where we began our work on our production.

Writing of the first performances at Saratoga, the critic Arlene Croce said in *The New Yorker*:

"In the New York City Ballet's new *Coppélia*, which had its première at the company's summer home in Saratoga, Patricia McBride gives a great and a great *big* performance—big in scale as well as spirit. The role comes as a climax to the present and most exciting phase of her career. The scale on which she has been dancing this year is a new development in her style, and to reach it she hasn't sacrificed any of her speed or sharp-edged rhythm or subtlety of intonation. And although the role of Swanilda gives her plenty of unaccustomed material (such as extended pantomime), she sweeps through it without ever once looking like anyone but herself. She persuades you that Swanilda is Patricia McBride and always has been. This is a remarkable triumph for an artist whom the world knows as the flag-bearer of the New York City Ballet, the embodiment of its egoless-star ethic. McBride is fundamentally inscrutable. She doesn't exist outside her roles, and when you try to place her among her peers in world ballet—Gregory and Sibley and Makarova and the other great Russians whose names mean more to the public than McBride's does—her image dissolves in a succession of ballets: *Donizetti Variations, Rubies, La Valse, Brahms-Schoenberg Quartet, Who Cares?, Dances at a Gathering, Harlequinade.* McBride doesn't throw us cues to let us know how we ought to take her; she doesn't comment, doesn't cast herself as an observer of life. All she knows about life she seems to have learned through dancing, and all she has to tell she tells through dancing. How durable a bond of communication this is she proves once again in *Coppélia,* and in the very first moments.

"Swanilda's *valse lente* is the opening dance. By custom, it's a straight classical solo, and it gives us the ballerina in full flight almost as soon as the curtain has gone up. But in the New York City Ballet version McBride runs down to the footlights and, on the first notes of the waltz, addresses the audience in a passage of mime. 'This one up there,' she says, pointing to Coppélia on her balcony, 'she sits and reads all day long. That one, who lives over there, is in love with her, but she never notices him. Me, I just play.' And she plays (dances), first for her own pleasure, then for Coppélia's, with enticing steps that seem to say, 'Come down and play with me. See how nicely I play.' The structure of the waltz is mime, dance, dance-mime; in one stroke the means by which the story of *Coppélia* will be told are laid before us, and the fact that it's all done to an unvarying waltz rhythm lets us see easily how these different effects—of a mime gesture or a dance movement or a dance movement that functions as a mime gesture—depend for their force and clarity on having a different relation to an over-all rhythm. 'Mime' time is not 'dance' time, and each has to be established to musical time in a different way. This isn't as elementary as it sounds. The big catch in keeping the time values disparate is that the rhythm which connects them may disintegrate, and the worst danger of *that* is that the dancer will seem to be switching personalities on us, much as if she were a singer whose speaking voice didn't resemble the voice she sang with. (A lot of the modern distrust of mime comes from the schizoid effect of miscalculated rhythm.) In McBride's variation, and through her whole radiant performance, she plays excitingly close to the danger point. But the values of dance and mime, distinct in their time sense, are equalized in their scale—the largest scale that one could hope to see. So the meanings that are conveyed by all these sharply differentiated rhythms are always absolutely

clear; they fly at you and away, or loom and settle, but there's no break in her
consistency. She 'reads' at every moment. She is a character. McBride has
never struck me as a particularly strong actress, and her method baffled me for
years. How else, if not by acting, could she have made her character in 'La
Valse' so vivid—a character unlike anyone else's who does the part? But for
McBride acting is not the key; dancing is. And now that she's become so grand
I don't see how anyone could miss that. She is a great dancer and a great star.

"The new production of *Coppélia*, staged by George Balanchine and Alexandra Danilova, is a combination of old and new choreography, the old being
a first and second act built largely around the excellent 'after-Petipa' version in
which Danilova used to star for the Ballet Russe de Monte Carlo, and the new
being a glittering Act III, all of it Balanchine's except for the grand adagio and
the ballerina's variation, which belong to Danilova-Petipa. Balanchine's dances
are not uniformly masterpieces, but, taken all together, they ought to extend
the life of this ballet another hundred years. In their unique blend of light
irony and ingenuousness, they are a mirror of the music—serious music that
was not meant to be taken too seriously.

"For his third act, Delibes envisioned a village wedding, with the villagers
putting on an allegorical pageant of man's works and days. Most productions
get through Dawn and Prayer and then give up in confusion, either reassign-
ing the rest of the music (Work, Hymen, Discord and War) or dropping it altogether. Balanchine uses all the music Delibes wrote, and he does not mistake
its spirit. His choreography really does present a plausible (though not a realistic) village pageant stuck together with metallic threads and parchment and
candle wax, but noble nonetheless, with an anti-grand-manner grandeur. The
Waltz of the Hours, that sublime gushing fountain of melody, is danced by
twenty-four grinning little girls in gold tunics, who line the path of the soloist,
Marnee Morris, and form choral borders for the solos that follow: Dawn (Merrill Ashley), Prayer (Christine Redpath), and Work, or La Fileuse, here called
Spinner (Susan Hendl). The entrance of these three graces—posed motionless
as beauty queens in a carriage that circles the stage twice—is one of the most
piercing visions in the ballet. And the solos for Ashley and Hendl are outstanding—complete summations of their gifts. There's a dance for Four Jesterettes in
padded motley sewn with bells. (In the Monte Carlo production, this entrée—
originally Hymen—was called Follies, which seems more to the allegorical
point than Jesterettes.) Discord and War is a romp for boys and girls in
horned helmets, a flourish of capes and spears waved as idly as pickett signs—a
witty number, shakily danced. Then, after the bridal *pas de deux*, comes an
exhilarating finale, with climax piled on smashing climax. Best of all is the
ballerina's fish dive into her partner's arms, instantly followed by the only
thing that could top it—the return of the twenty-four golden tinies cakewalking
on in a wide curve, with Morris in the lead tearing off *piqué-fouetté* turns.

"Balanchine's hand is evident elsewhere in the production, too—in that first-
act entrance of Swanilda, and in the Mazurka and Czardas, which surely have
never before been so thick and bushy with (musical) repeats, so fertile with
invention. Their one weakness is that they are isolated from the action and
don't serve any purpose. But the weakness is very likely not a permanent one.

This is not a finished production, and by the time it reaches New York, in November, Balanchine is sure to have taken over more of it—filling up gaps in the staging, refurbishing or replacing some of the less effective old dances, and straightening out a few discrepancies, such as the sudden, unmotivated shift to a sunnier mood that follows Swanilda's solemn ear-of-wheat dance. Possibly he'll find more for the hero to do, too. At present, Franz has only one dance— an interpolation in the third act which old-timers will recognize as Eglevsky's variation from the *Sylvia Pas de Deux*. It's nice to have this great solo back again, especially as danced by Helgi Tomasson, but Tomasson, who is a charming Franz, doesn't get a chance to display his true dance power until the finale. I hope, too, that a way can be found to make the meaning of the ear-of-wheat episode (a direct descendant of the petal-plucking scene in *Giselle*) at least as clear to a modern audience as it is in the Ballet Theatre version.

"The part of the ballet that is, right now, just about perfect is the second act. Here, again, Balanchine has obviously been at work; you can almost feel him assuming command of the action the moment Coppélius enters his workshop to find it overrun by Swanilda and her friends. Coppélius is Shaun O'Brien, giving the performance of his career. He is not a buffoon, and Swanilda is not a zany. He's a misanthrope, a tyrant, believably a genius who can create dolls everyone thinks are alive. She is a shrewd, fearless girl who grows into womanhood by accepting as her responsibility the destruction of Coppélius. She must break his power over gullible, romantic Franz, who has chosen the perfect woman, the doll Coppélia, over the natural woman, herself. The conflict between idealism and realism, or art and life, is embedded in the libretto of *Coppélia*, and Coppélius's passion is in the music. I enjoy burlesque versions of the second act (and in this tradition there's no Swanilda more enjoyable than that gifted zany Makarova), but the heart of the music isn't in them. Balanchine's Coppélius is kin to other Balanchine artist-heroes—not only Drosselmeier of *The Nutcracker* but Don Quixote and Orpheus and the Poet of *La Sonnàmbula*. And when he raises Swanilda-Coppélia onto her points and she remains locked there, upright or jackknifed over them, he's the strangest of all alchemists, seeking to transform his beloved twice over: doll into woman, woman into ballerina. Swanilda must become as totally manipulatable, totally perfectible, as a Balanchine ballerina. She must be a work of art, and then burst out of her mold. I once saw a brilliantly horrifying performance given by the Royal Danish Ballet, in which Solveig Østergaard and Frank Schaufuss confronted each other as monsters equal in might if not in cunning. But there was nothing in it like Shaun O'Brien's 'speech' to McBride, conveyed in a paroxysm of joy: 'I have made you and you are beautiful.'

"Rouben Ter-Arutunian's costumes are attractive, and his scenery is modest and quite pretty in several styles. Act I is like a child's pop-up picture book, with exaggerated perspectives. Act II, a cutaway of Coppélius's lab, ranges from Ensor to Burchfield, but the backcloth for Act III looked sketchily realized. A number of bells hanging above the stage (the pageant celebrates, along with everything else, a *fête de carillons*) bear the monograms of those associated with the original production—the choreographer, Arthur Saint-Léon; the librettist, Charles Nuitter; and E. T. A. Hoffmann, whose tale of Coppélius inspired the ballet—and those responsible for the present one. The largest bell, for which I forgive this somewhat presumptuous idea, is inscribed 'J'étais créé par Léo Delibes, 25 Mai 1870.' It is Coppélia herself who speaks. G.B., for George Balanchine, happen to be the initials also of Giuseppina Bozzacchi, who has no bell of her own. She was sixteen when she made her début at the Paris Opéra, appearing as the first Swanilda. Giuseppina took Paris by storm. Then Discord and War came in earnest. Six months later, in the siege during the Franco-Prussian War, she died of smallpox on the morning of her seventeenth birthday."*

In February 1975 Erik Bruhn, Resident Producer of the National Ballet of Canada, mounted for that company a new production of *Coppélia* which Clive Barnes in the New York *Times* (March 2, 1975) described as "unusual in its style and manner." This *Coppélia* was first presented in the United States by the same ensemble at the Metropolitan Opera House, New York, July 24, 1975, with Veronica Tennant, Rudolf Nureyev and Jacques Gorrissen as the principals.

Reviewing a performance in January 1975 of *Coppélia*, the critic Robert Greskovic wrote in *The Soho Weekly News:* "Swanilda, the lead in Balanchine/Danilova's *Coppélia*, was made on McBride. At this matinee she was sensational. The lusciously brocade layers of her dancing and the free, spunky spirit of her manner make hers the yardstick of interpretation for this role. McBride's physical response to the role's musical and choreographic demands is immediate and enchanting. She's the 'favorite daughter' of the village by virtue of the mental and physical prowess she brings to her almost constant presence in all three acts. Her mime, simple and clear with opera-house scale, is melded, like her dancing, with spontaneity, giving a fully articulated account of the music. McBride doesn't now act and then dance her characterization—she is always this Swanilda.

"Her large dark eyes create a focus that comments on her dancing. She *takes* everyone in, onstage and off, as she 'tells and shows' us what she's up to. Her strong and accentuated arm and leg joints stretch, curl and angle her limbs in a constant state of flirtatious flux. She elaborates her story as she responds to her music. As McBride's *batterie* cuts the air along a diagonal line, she proudly rivets her attention to the precise and generous activity of her feet. As she maintains her place to execute a series of multiple and varied turns, she sparkles, glances up and out; each time her head snaps around, she reverberates another wave of ecstatic after-energy.

"By the time she's dancing in celebration as the guest of honor at 'The Festival of the Bells' (Act III), she's fully matured. She doesn't rest on her laurels, her dancing scatters them in the wind of her joyous triumph. The conflict of her emotions in Act I and the calculation of her scheme in Act II are clearly behind her, here she's free and riding the crest of her popularity. This role is richly designed with some of Balanchine's finest dancing ideas, and McBride's

* "I Have Made You and You Are Beautiful" by Arlene Croce. Reprinted by permission; © 1974 The New Yorker Magazine, Inc.

pungent glamour and full-range dance power yield a Swanilda who is at home and home free."

## LE CORSAIRE

*Music by Adolphe Adam. Choreography by Mazilier. Scenery by Desplechin, Cambon, Thierry, and Martin. First presented at the Théâtre Impérial de l'Opéra, Paris, January 23, 1856, with Carolina Rosati, Mlle. Couqui, and Segarellu in the leading roles.*

Based on Byron's poem, *Le Corsaire* was originally a three-act ballet that served as a useful vehicle for ballerinas such as Taglioni, Pavlova, and Karsavina. It was long in the repertory of the Russian theatres. Over the years, the work was much revised, with new music by Minkus and Drigo as well as new choreography by Marius Petipa and Vakhtang Chabukiani. A *pas de deux* from the complete ballet has frequently been performed by Soviet companies and by the Royal Ballet. Chabukiani's version, after Petipa, was first performed in the United States at Madison Square Garden by soloists of the Mali Opera Theatre, Leningrad, in July 1959. Margot Fonteyn and Rudolf Nureyev introduced the work to London at the Royal Opera House, Covent Garden, November 3, 1962.

In her *Autobiography* (1976), Margot Fonteyn describes the first performance of the *Corsaire pas de deux* with Rudolf Nureyev in New York in 1964. The applause lasted at least twenty minutes. "No one has ever danced *Corsaire* like Rudolf, and it is permissible in this case to use the adjective 'sublime.'"

When the Dance Theatre of Harlem took its version (by co-director Karel Shook) of the *Corsaire pas de deux* to London for a season at the Sadler's Wells Theatre in 1974, Peter Williams wrote in *Dance and Dancers* of the performance by Paul Russell and Laura Brown: "Russell gave one of the most exuberantly extrovert performances I have ever seen in this showy pas de deux. Looking for all the world like the Gold Slave from *Scheherazade* (naked torso, glittering baggy pants and bandeau round the brow), he bounds about, ripples his muscles, dives into head-to-floor back-bends in a manner which I feel Fokine originally intended for his Slave . . . Laura Brown had a few tricks in store, particularly in a dazzling manège of turns and a remarkable extension . . . At every performance I saw, this duet justifiably brought the house down in a manner I have seldom known in Rosebery Avenue."

In a long essay on the Dance Theatre of Harlem in *Ballet Review*, in 1974, the critic Robert Greskovic commented on this ballet:

"Shook's restaging is splendid. Laura Brown's princess manner is delicate enough to convey her character and strong enough to configure her choreography. The most finished of her 'finished' manners are showcased here. She projects smiles and knowingly wondrous eyes that gleam their brightest satisfaction at the top of her balances, lifts and posé arabesques. Her ear-high développé à la seconde reaches its height quickly as she holds a sharp steady balance. Her manège of: piqué turn, piqué (changing arms), piqué again, and fouetté turn in the coda is a clearly spotted and securely jumped ride around the world. In Russell's extraordinary, steady one-handed lifts, she's relaxed and regal.

"The delicacy and finesse of her performance is a perfect counterbalance and motivation for Russell's pirate. Paul Russell is Le Corsaire—Russian, French, exotic and proud, with a touch of American athleticism. The only other American dancers I've seen who succeeded in impersonating this swash-buckling bandit have been John Prinz and Edward Villella. Prinz ultimately failed by his lack of technical control and I've seen Villella only on television, but Russell is completely alive and breathing, full on stage. His rush-on en-trance is immediately authoritative. His alert, darting eyes are seeing his space before they're looking for a partner. He takes us all in before he takes flight. His enthusiasm and freedom on stage suggest someone who's been on the seas for months and this is his first return to solid earth. He's found one of earth's treasures, and, as Brown enters, rises through ¾ point and folds himself to the ground in a sinking révérence. He approaches her and handles her with won-dering care. The mechanics of the partnering gain drama from Russell's daz-zling concentration. He must handle this beauty, now. He must lift her, he must catch her, he wants to hold her. He makes his job his passionate desire. And when he's alone and in his variations he's wanting to celebrate. When he takes his first attitude balance atop strong ¾ point, he dégagés back for a spinning cocked-leg double tour, landing on one knee with the other leg ex-tended; then whips around a twisting sous-sus turn to stand full height again. These sous-sus turns with his hands on his shoulders are lusciously plastic in the smooth, changing tilt his shoulders take to propel his turn and stop it at an opposite angle to its beginning. Shook has set a clearly musical series of embo-îtés en tournant that travel into preparation for the long spine-tingling axis of Russell's double tours. Coming out of even chaîné turns there is a tour that folds kneeling to the floor and unfolds instantaneously as, with a brazen slap of one hand to his stage, Russell springs to arabesque posé on ¾ point, perfectly placed, leanly arced—like an arrow's vibrating contact with the bull's-eye of a target. This is no formidable youthful debut as Le Corsaire, it's an electrifying (by any standards) triumph of theater."

# CORTÈGE BURLESQUE

*Music by Emmanuel Chabrier, orchestrated by Hershy Kay. Choreography by Eliot Feld. Decor by Robert Munford. Costumes by Stanley Simmons. Lighting by Jules Fisher. First presented by the American Ballet Company at the Festival of Two Worlds, Spoleto, Italy, June 27, 1969, with Christine Sarry and John Sowinski. First presented in the United States by that en-semble at the Brooklyn Academy of Music, New York, October 21, 1969, with the same dancers. Conductor: Christopher Keene.*

A *divertissement* to Chabrier's *Cortège Burlesque* and *Souvenirs de Munich,* arranged for orchestra, this ballet featured the dancing of the two principals of the new American Ballet Company, Christine Sarry and John Sowinski, when the group made its debut. The *pas de deux* is danced against a fantastic backdrop that recalls the circus, its animals and amusements. The dance reflects the circus atmosphere as the boy and girl dance their bouncing display piece in open competition, the boy supporting the girl but acting, too, very much the soloist who won't be upstaged by any ballerina, however famous. Not as often as he can help it, that is, which isn't much, for the girl takes over the scene steadily, yielding only to real perseverance from her partner.

NOTES  Reviewing the ballet in *Dance and Dancers,* Patricia Barnes wrote that "*Cortège Burlesque* is one of those ballets that laughs at itself while exploiting the technical skill of its dancers. Sarry was a joy . . . and in the New York performances the two dancers really went to town, sending up the manners and egos of ballerinas and their partners with wit and some bold, assertive dancing. The piece is enhanced by yet another excellent backdrop by Robert Munford, portraying a circus atmosphere precisely right for its purpose."

## CORTÈGE HONGROIS

*Music by Alexander Glazunov. Choreography by George Balanchine. Decor and costumes by Rouben Ter-Arutunian. Lighting by Ronald Bates. First presented by the New York City Ballet at the New York State Theatre, Lincoln Center, May 16, 1973, with Melissa Hayden and Jacques d'Amboise, Karin von Aroldingen and Jean-Pierre Bonnefous in the leading roles. Conducted by Robert Irving.*

I did this ballet for Melissa Hayden, who had been dancing with our company twenty-four years—when she decided in 1973 to retire. "Why not stop before you begin making excuses?" she said. "Why not stop when you're still enjoying everything?" The idea behind the ballet was simply to give Melissa Hayden yet another opportunity to enjoy herself and give our audiences pleasure.

The music is a collection of pieces by Glazunov (1865–1936), best-known for his ballet *Raymonda.* The finale of the ballet features a *pas classique hongrois,* where Hungarian gesture and dance are combined with the academic classic dance.

There is no story to *Cortège Hongrois*: it is simply, as its name suggests, a procession of dances in the Hungarian manner. There is a grand promenade at the start, which introduces two sets of dancers—first a group in colorful peasant costume, and then a group of courtiers led by the ballerina and her cavalier. The scene is a large formal ballroom.

Four of the courtly couples begin a dance in which others join. Next, eight couples, to a plaintive melody, dance a supported adagio.

In vivid contrast, the peasants, led by a vigorous couple, dance a czardas, a

Hungarian folk dance of perennial popularity. Four of the courtly girls follow, for a whirring, accelerating *pas de quatre*.

Variations for some of the courtiers are now presented; first one for a girl, another for four of the boys, a third for another girl, and the finale, what we have been waiting for, a *pas de deux* for the leading courtly couple. Dressed in white embellished with gold and wearing a crown, the ballerina performs in the grand manner, dancing with her partner to a deep, stirring melody that gradually builds. There are variations for the two dancers, hers a character dance with much folk gesture. The courtiers rejoin the royal couple; the peasants come, too, to participate in the festivities, and there is a flourishing finish.

Finally, the two groups combine in a folk dance, heels and spurs clicking, and that seems to be the end. But there is another promenade, the lights go down, and only on the ballerina does the spotlight shine. A crown of lights illumines the stage and all kneel, acknowledging her radiance.

NOTES    At the time of the ballet's premiere, when ballerina Melissa Hayden was presented by Mayor Lindsay with the Handel Medallion, New York City's highest cultural award, Lincoln Kirstein wrote of her career in the New York City Ballet's program: "If one had to define one essential gift with which a dancer needs to be endowed, there might be a rush of answers. A beautiful body, grace of line, graciousness of spirit, joy in the work, ability to please, unswerving integrity, relentless ambition towards some abstract perfection. Certainly all these factors determine a dancer's character, and every element exists in some combination within the performing artist's presence. These factors and elements are never evenly, nor even justly distributed. The first lesson dancers approaching any wisdom about themselves learn is how little they can depend on any single attribute or even combination of a few of them.

"Perhaps the most essential gift donated by those forces who care for careers, cosmically or supernaturally, is an ability to animate, magnetize and dominate those factors which one likes least in oneself. The mirror is the first to tell us no one is perfect, but there is always a terrible temptation to whittle down our notions of perfection in order to accommodate what we imagine our mirrors reflect. Dancers are accustomed to look to their mirror for correction, criticism and even comfort from their earliest days in a classroom. Strong dancers never succumb to the blindness of narcissism. Dancers are not narcissistic; their selves are their material. These must be kept under constant scrutiny; their own eyes and minds are finally their closest friend and severest critic. The best performers know themselves better than anyone else. Whatever face they may put upon their image, they know exactly what face, best face and worst fits them.

"This kind of realism is not easily endured. In the best sense, it becomes a method, an analytical attitude towards performance. It is a strict school, a stoic attitude, but it has advantages. It permits survival. Of all the dancers with whom I've had the honor and pleasure of working, Melissa Hayden has been strongest and lasted longest. In the twenty-two years that she has been associated with Balanchine and myself, there has been no one whose strength surpassed hers. This is not alone in muscle, although one can mark little deterioration in her fantastic energy since the first season we danced at Covent Garden in 1950. To say that she has never missed a performance is less important than to realize that no single performance has ever been below her extraordinary level of efficiency. Whether or not the audience recognized it, her steely spine and wiry resilience, even under the attack of cruel strain or sprain, gives stamina to colleagues who know only too well what pain and strain are.

"Melissa has been the nearest thing to a 'star' in our starless company. We have never encouraged stardom on programs, posters or publicity; managers can't make stars; the public does. There has been a good deal of unobservant cant about a creature vulgarly entitled 'the Balanchine dancer.' When one takes the trouble to inspect the personnel of our company as it is now constituted, one can easily mark the corporeal distinction between Gelsey Kirkland and Gloria Govrin, between Peter Martins and John Clifford, between Karin von Aroldingen and Helgi Tomasson. Melissa Hayden was never a Balanchine-dancer, but she supported his repertory for over twenty years. In consideration of his much bruited intolerance or prejudice, this must mean something; Milly must have been doing something right.

"What she has given, and still victoriously gives, is a sense of security, a conviction that she knows what she's doing, how it should be done, and to what complete degree of energetic expenditure she can do it. The ballet, like *bel canto* voice production, is an area of extreme virtuosity; remove the element of physical electricity and acrobatics, the hazards of the arena overcome, and you delete most public curiosity. Ballet is a spectator sport; its very economics depend on mass appeal. For more than a century, whatever its association with kings and queens, courts lost or in decline, it is the big opera-house public that has justified its expense and problems. Intellectuals may analyze their pleasure, but it is fortunately not left to their tender mercies. Melissa Hayden is and has been a popular figure; she pleases, satisfies, thrills and amuses a big public which may make no very delicate judgment, but which in its instinct can not be fooled into thinking that boredom or dissatisfaction with emptiness is entertaining or instructive.

"From her own account, she has been dancing for forty years in schools and on stages, all over the world. Mathematically, considering the hours of practice, rehearsal, performance—plus a private life with a family, children and friends—this is staggering. Less accident-prone than almost any professional, she has probably made more appearances before a public than any other performer of the period. Her pleasure in performance has been so complete that it has been transmitted to her muscular organism like some blessed sun lamp, to keep her fit in spite of any mischance or fatigue.

"To stop dancing, to abandon the habit of a lifetime, to foreswear performance in a frame that has become familiar as one's bed and breakfast, is not the worst thing that can happen to a dancer. When the decision is made, as in the case with Melissa, there is the new adventure of energy reapplied. Her energy is no less; it will simply be channelled otherwise. Anyone who has heard her demonstrate in lectures knows that charm is a weak word for her didactic method. She has been a crusader for ballet as a language and a skill and now she will direct her experience, taste and information towards a wholly new audience—that of potential students, scholars and enthusiasts. The husbanding of energy that has been her greatest gift permits no waste of effort. Hysteria is an artificial additive that lack of control sometimes substitutes for temperament. Hysteria is not part of her nature, since she has always been a realist and she realizes, from observation of colleagues less fortunate than she, that irrational indulgence costs mind and muscle of which no one has too much to spare. Her warmth is humane; she has had her fair portion of the world's grief. She has not been given everything she may have desired or even deserved. However, in situations in which she has found herself, and indeed in which she has chosen to find herself content, she did better than most."

## DANCES AT A GATHERING

*Music by Frédéric Chopin. Choreography by Jerome Robbins. Costumes by Joe Eula. Lighting by Thomas Skelton. First presented by the New York City Ballet at the New York State Theatre, Lincoln Center, May 8, 1969. Pianist: Gordon Boelzner. Dancers: Allegra Kent, Sara Leland, Kay Mazzo, Patricia McBride, Violette Verdy, Anthony Blum, John Clifford, Robert Maiorano, John Prinz, and Edward Villella. Dedicated to the memory of Jean Rosenthal.*

*Dances at a Gathering* is a ballet for ten dancers to piano pieces by Chopin. Five girls and five boys dance in an open space as a pianist plays to the left of the stage. He plays mazurkas, waltzes, études, a scherzo, and a nocturne— eighteen pieces in all—as the dancers, distinguished in the program by the color of their costumes, respond to the music.

The curtain goes up on a bare stage with a background of blue sky and amorphous clouds; we are outdoors in a clearing, a field, a meadow, a grove. A boy enters on the right, informally dressed in open white shirt, brown tights, and boots. He walks slowly, quietly looking the place over, glancing up at the sky, thinking. Then he is lifting his arm and his walk becomes a stride, a dance, as the piano begins, *Mazurka, Opus 63, No. 3.* His dance reflects a pleasure in being where he is on a day like this. As the music ends, he leaves, meditating.

A girl and a boy enter and dance to the *Waltz, Opus 69, No. 2,* moving arm in arm, at first a bit tentatively as if nothing will come of it, but the music changes all that as they follow its flow in lifts, leaps, and a rushing exit with the girl poised high on the boy's shoulder. Another girl and boy come in and dance a little more formally, responding to the character of the *Mazurka, Opus 33, No. 3,* with arm gestures, too. But they, too, get carried away with the music and she, too, is lifted off in a rushing conclusion.

A girl enters alone and dances fast to the staccato beat of a new, more demanding *Mazurka, Opus 6, No. 4.* She is still on stage as the next part begins.

Six dancers in different groupings respond to the music of four fresh *Mazurkas, Opus 7, Nos. 5* and *4, Opus 24, No. 2* and *Opus 6, No. 2.* There are two boys, dancing back to back in a kind of jig, one of the boys interested in one girl, who watches, the other in another. And not the same ones they were dancing with earlier. Rhapsodic as particular partnerships become, in the group commitments dissolve with no regrets and everyone begins again. In the dancing and watching of dances, in the joining in, partnerships shift. The dances become full of character and there is a feeling that we are in real Mazurka country as gesture identifies with music and place. There are friendships between the girls, too, and both boys and girls play at posing each other in groups for photographs.

Now to the *Waltz, Opus 42*, a girl and boy try to outdo each other in speed and virtuosity, each showing off to the other, he cartwheeling to victory, all of it a serious but affectionate competition. She touches his hand and he lifts her up to his shoulder, wrapping her about his head closely as they leave.

Three girls dance the *Waltz, Opus 34, No. 2*, entering in a dim light, strolling, doing solos, then all three dancing together. A boy comes to lift one girl away. They dance together as the other two watch. These two look into the distance. Then as quietly as he came the boy is gone, leaving his girl kneeling. She rises to join her two friends, they pose in a group, then separate with separate dreams, only to join arms and leave together.

The lights come up and two boys compete now to the music of *Mazurka, Opus 56, No. 2*, each trying to outdo the other, throwing each other about, making dramatic exits backward.

As the lights fade, a girl enters to dance thoughtfully alone to the *Étude, Opus 25, No. 4*.

To the big *Fourth Waltz, Opus 34, No. 1*, six couples dance, responding dramatically to the pulse of the music. There is an exhilarating series of slides and lifts, at the end of which the boys line up to pass the girls down a diagonal line, lifting them so that the next boy lifts them higher still to the demanding rush of the piano.

Now in dimmer light come a boy and girl. She clearly likes him and tries to make it clearer. He leaves her but another boy enters. She dances all around him, surrounding him with attention but he ignores her and goes off. With a third boy she has the same result, but more amused than despairing, she flicks her wrist and goes off.

Next a *pas de deux* to the *Étude, Opus 25, No. 5*, then a fast solo for a boy to the *Étude, Opus 10, No. 2*. The *Scherzo, Opus 20, No. 1* involves six dancers in dramatic declarations, fulfillments, and disappointments. As the three girls fall back in the boys' arms, they are a bit embarrassed and leave in a rush.

For the final piece, the *Nocturne, Opus 15, No. 1* and its slow melody, the lights come down. Gradually all ten dancers appear, singly and in couples, together now for the first time. One of them, the boy who began the dances at this gathering, touches the ground of the place. They all look at him and then up at the sky, which they watch intently. They pair off then and walk away. All move forward as the music dramatizes their situation. Then they look to the ground and raising their arms start a dance that does not develop. They go to the back of the stage, the boys to one side, the girls on another, and bow. The curtain falls.

NOTES *Dances at a Gathering* came about in an interesting way. "I started out to do a *pas de deux* for Eddie Villella and Pat McBride," Jerome Robbins told Hubert Saal of *Newsweek*. "Then I got turned on by the music. It all started to pour out as if some valve inside me had opened up and the purity of working with dancers took over. I had to find the form. Usually I work with a structured music, as in Stravinsky's *Les Noces*, where the literary material is built in. In this case I took whatever appealed to me and let it happen, trusting it. It's nice to work loosely and intuitively."

Shortly before the première, Robbins said to Clive Barnes of the New York *Times*, "I'm doing a fairly classical ballet to very old-fashioned and romantic music, but there is a point to it. In a way it is a revolt from the faddism of today. In the period since my last ballet (*Les Noces*, 1965), I have been around looking at dance—seeing a lot of the stuff at Judson Church and the rest of the avant-garde. And I find myself feeling just what is the matter with connecting, what's the matter with love, what's the matter with celebrating positive things? Why, I asked myself, does everything have to be separated and alienated so that there is this almost constant push to disconnect? The strange thing is that the young people are for love. Is that bad?"

Shortly after the première of *Dances at a Gathering*, Robbins was interviewed for *Dance Magazine* by the critic Edwin Denby. The complete text of the article, reprinted by courtesy of *Dance Magazine*, follows: "Robbins's *Dances at a Gathering* is a great success both with dance fans and the general public. And it is a beautiful piece. But it wasn't planned as a sure-fire piece—it wasn't planned at all beforehand and began by chance, as Robbins explains in the interview (taped shortly after the official première) which appears on the pages that follow.

"The ballet is set to Chopin piano pieces and the program lists ten dancers but tells you little more. The curtain goes up in silence on an empty stage. It looks enormous. The back is all sky—some kind of changeable late afternoon in summer. Both sides of the stage are black. Forestage right, a man enters slowly, deep in thought. He is wearing a loose white shirt, brown tights and boots. He turns to the sky and walks slowly away from you toward center stage. You think of a man alone in a meadow. As he walks you notice the odd tilt of his head—like a man listening, inside himself. In the silence the piano begins as if he were remembering the music. He marks a dance step, he sketches a mazurka gesture, with a kind of pensive vigor he begins to improvise and now he is dancing marvelously and, in a burst of freedom, he is running all over the meadow at its edge. Suddenly he subsides and, more mysterious than ever, glides into the woods and is gone. Upstage a girl and boy enter. At once they are off full speed in a double improvisation, a complexly fragmented waltz, the number Robbins speaks of as the 'wind dance.'

"As one dance succeeds another—the ballet lasts about an hour—you are fascinated by the variety and freshness of invention, the range of feeling, and by the irresistibly beautiful music which the dance lets you hear distinctly—its mystery too. You see each dancer dance marvelously and you also see each one as a fascinating individual—complex, alone, and with any of the others, individually most sensitive and generous in their relationships. The music and the dance seem to be inventing each other. For a dance fan, the fluid shifts of momentum are a special delight. For the general theater public, Robbins's genius in focusing on a decisive momentary movement—almost like a zoom lens—makes vivid the special quality of each dance, and all the charming jokes.

"But it is a strange ballet.

"Our talk began before the tape machine arrived. Robbins had been telling me how the ballet developed. He had been asked whether he would care to do a piece for the 25th Anniversary City Center Gala, May 8. Delighted by the way Patricia McBride and Edward Villella had been dancing *The Afternoon of a Faun,* he thought he would like to do a *pas de deux* for them—perhaps to Chopin music—and he accepted. As he listened to records and became more and more interested in the possibilities—it occurred to him to add two more couples—and he began rehearsal. In the course of rehearsals, however, all the six dancers he had chosen were not always free, so he went on choreographing with four others, using those who happened to be free. Gradually he made more and more dances, but without a definite plan for the whole piece. When about two-thirds of the ballet was done, he invited Balanchine (who had just returned from Europe) to rehearsal. At the end of it he turned to Mr. B and said, 'Don't you think it's a bit long?' Mr. B answered, 'More. Make more!' He did.

"Robbins said to me, 'As you see, there are still never more than six dancers dancing at once.' He told me that as the dances and relationships kept coming out of the different pieces of music and the particular dancers available, he began to feel that they were all connected by some underlying sense of community (he said, laughing, 'Maybe just because they were dancers') and by a sense of open air and sunlight and sudden nostalgia perhaps.

"We spoke of one of the many lovely lifts—this one at the end of Eddie's *pas de deux* with Pat where it looks as though he were lifting a sack onto his shoulder and, up on his shoulder, the sack suddenly changes into a beautiful mermaid. Robbins explained how it came out of a sudden metamorphosis in the music. And he illustrated how the lift is done.

"We were talking of Villella's gesture of touching the floor in the final minutes of the ballet, and Robbins mentioned that he was perhaps thinking of the dancers' world—the floor below, the space around and above. I was saying that I liked that gesture better the second time I saw it because it was slower and I wondered if he (Robbins) had changed it. At that point the tape begins:

"ROBBINS  No, that's just a very subtle thing of acting and where the human being is at the time. I think two weeks ago at the preview, Eddie was under more difficulties and pressures—down more—and perhaps that made the difference.

"I think the ballet will seem different in almost every performance, not vastly, but shades like those you saw, they will happen, depending on the dancers. You said it, I remember, way back—the dancers read (in a review) what the ballet is about, then they change because now they *know* it (they know it in words)—before they just *did* it. And that can happen—there was a modesty and a sort of not knowing in the first showing. They may start to think now that maybe they should do it more like what everyone says it is. I don't know what to do about that except to ask them not to.

"I always tell them to do it for themselves, and to think of 'marking' it—Don't think of doing it full out.

"DENBY   Well, that's another quality the ballet has. I was very happy to see that with Eddie, who is used to 'doing it full out'—he does that very beautifully, it's not vulgar selling at all—he's not forcing it. But the inner business he also does very well—in *Giselle*. He's remarkable, you know, wonderful.

"ROBBINS   I like watching ballets, anyway, best of all at rehearsals when a dancer is just working for himself, really just working. They are beautiful to watch then. I love to watch George's (Balanchine) work that way. Just love to.

"DENBY   How beautiful everything is before it gets its name. Did I hear you say that Melissa (Hayden) will be covering Violette (Verdy)?

"ROBBINS   Yes, I think she'll be marvelous.

"DENBY   And so is Verdy. Someone told me that you're working to add a much longer number for her. So I said, 'Oh, wonderful.'

"ROBBINS   I haven't been around ballet for so long, I forget how scuttle-butty it gets around here. If you say to someone, 'I want to work with you tomorrow,' the next day someone asks you, 'Are you doing a new ballet?' It already has gotten that big.

"But it was nice working with them. I did enjoy it very much. Patty McBride, I just *love* working with her.

"DENBY   Yes, she's remarkable. . . . And I am very happy about what you did with Bob Maiorano. Because this year he's suddenly become a very good dancer wherever I look at him. He was beginning last year and, all of a sudden, there he is—now you can really see it.

"ROBBINS   Yes.

"DENBY   He has a marvelous Italian beauty of gesture. Maybe he was afraid of it all this time. The arm is so heavy the way he moves it. But the weight is right for all of them—the boys especially.

"ROBBINS   Bobby Weiss, have you seen him? In one of the performances he is going to do Johnnie Clifford's part.

"DENBY   He was wonderful in a school performance last year, too. Especially in the end of *Sylphides,* when he lost his nervousness in the finale. He looks as though he were not letting go as much as is his nature.

"ROBBINS   He is beautiful when he lets go. In rehearsal, I just made him go.

"DENBY   Clifford was remarkable too; he is so positively there. But it's not so simple. There is also something private about it. And Tony's (Blum) great—so much livelier than he's been . . . often.

"ROBBINS   That's the fun of having another choreographer work with the dancers. Like in Ballet Theatre, Eliot Feld was doing a ballet, and I looked at his dancers and thought, Now, those are people I bypassed, but he saw something in them and brought out another whole aspect of them. It's always charming. But every choreographer—Agnes (de Mille) has people she works with I can't see—people I work with that she can't see. That's nice for the dancers, isn't it?

"DENBY    And for the choreographers if you are going to travel around. You should try out your dances on the Russians. I'm sure they would like to have a dance of yours, they like to gather things—archives in their minds. It would be so much fun.

"ROBBINS    I'm going to Russia. I *would* like to see if I can get it either to the Bolshoi or Kirov. I would like to see them dance this. I really would. It might finally turn out to be a peasant parody, you never know (*laughter*)—that folk part of it—I was surprised.

"DENBY    I was surprised that people made so much of it, because the dancers are always so elegant. They might be landowners, if they were anybody in Europe.

"ROBBINS    At first I also thought they were very elegant people, maybe at a picnic, maybe doing something—their own thing.

"And also to me—and this I'm very careful about—I don't want it to be a big thing—but the boys and the whole period are very hippie-ish.

"DENBY    At first you had the beards, I was quite pleased with that.

"ROBBINS    The boys still had them at rehearsal because of the long lay-off. Tony had long hair and a moustache and John Prinz had long hair and a beard and it was marvelous looking. It really affected what I was doing. I liked the boots—and the sketches are much more hippie than they appear on stage, in the sense of belts and open blouses for the boys and long hair and ballooning sleeves. There is something in the nature of knowing who they are and having love and confidence in them.

"DENBY    Competence? . . .

"ROBBINS    Confidence—which I feel is in the work, finally. Loving confidence in themselves and in the other people.

"DENBY    That is in there very strongly.

"ROBBINS    It has some strangenesses in it too, I'm sure, but I can't yet quite see it. Every now and then I look at a step and think that is a very odd step. There is a strange step that Eddie does in his solo—he should play with it the way one does this (*hand gesture*).

"DENBY    There was an eight-year-old Negro boy in the street and he was running; he suddenly started throwing his feet around—with such pleasure.

"ROBBINS    I saw something nice in the park. Near Sheep Meadow there was a black boy and a white boy, both happened to be wearing blue. The black boy had a blue sweat shirt and the white boy had a blue sweater and open collar. They were running toward each other and it was more than a game. They ran and reached out hands. Not just shook hands, because that's what it was about, but they took hands and swung around each other with their heads thrown back with laughter. And then let go and embraced each other. Oh, it was so beautiful, I was thrilled by it. There was so much rapture and ecstasy and friendliness and openness about it. Then they quieted down and began talking, (*laughs*).

"DENBY    There are things in the ballet that are a bit gruesome. And, you know, very interesting.

"ROBBINS    Gruesome?

"DENBY   It's partly in the lifts, partly sometimes in the way the boys treat a girl.

"ROBBINS   Well, opening night there was an accident. I want to be sure you know that it was an accident. There was a place where Sally (Sara Leland) was being swung around and they fell off the lift and it turned into a—it looked like she was in outer space—like she'd been released from a capsule. She was just swirling around. Horrifying for a moment. But there are?—I don't know, I can't tell.

"DENBY   It's definitely in the music. It's much stranger than one. . . .

"ROBBINS   Yes, than one thinks.

"DENBY   Than one is supposed to think.

"ROBBINS   There's a nocturne. I began late listening to one nocturne—it was like opening a door into a room and the people are in the *midst* of a conversation. I mean, there's no introduction, no preface; it's like a cut in a film; it's almost like Chopin had finished the previous nocturne, finished it properly, and there was a fade-out. And suddenly (*clap*) you're on somebody's face who's talking. But in the middle of a sentence! You don't even get 'and then,' it's right in the middle of a word and he's very strange, really quite strange. He knew a lot, I think. Much more than I thought before I began. It was fascinating that way—just like some connection happened between all those sounds that he thought of, and where I was at.

"DENBY   The movement through a piece is always so interesting, and that you catch so well and do so many things with.

"ROBBINS   I listened to a lot of recordings, different people playing the same piece. I used mostly Rubinstein and Novaes and some Brailowsky. I listened to some of the Dinu Lipatti. Then it was enough for me and after that I knew I would start to get confused. There are hardly any liberties taken at all —I would say none. Only one where at the end of Eddie's first dance it's marked *fortissimo*—da da da *whoosh*—I don't even know if it's Chopin's indication—I choreographed it that way—and Eddie was gone, *whoosh*. I didn't like it, it was a little obvious, like I was trying for a hand and the piece was trying for a hand, I thought there was something else there, so I took it on retard and soft, and let him take that poetic thing he does there. The dancers are beautiful.

"DENBY   Gordon (Boelzner) plays it very well because he also plays it for movement, without those extra questions of pianism.

"ROBBINS   There are no sentimentalities.

"DENBY   If you were listening to the music at a concert you might want more nuances, but this way you don't because the dancers are doing it, the nuances.

"ROBBINS   And he's tireless, that boy. It's fantastic. He plays it all day long, and does the other rehearsals, too. Some of those pieces are killers. I suddenly thought, Look at a Chopin concerto—they play a piece and go off and rest. They do maybe half an hour or twenty minutes and go and have a fifteen-minute intermission. But he's tearing off those *Études* written for these two fingers. You know about the one Eddie dances to—the little fast one—sort of chromatically going up and down the scale? Well, Chopin devised it to give these two fingers which are the weakest, a workout.

"DENBY  I am so glad you didn't orchestrate it. Not that it would be possible, but there's that temptation.

"ROBBINS  I got worried for a while before we got it down on the big piano because it began to sound very hollow to me. And I thought, Well when people come to this big theatre and they have just seen a big ballet with a lot of marvelous sounds, the piano is going to sound like a little rehearsal piano. But it doesn't, where it is. It seems it fills the house and sustains—a good combination, I think, between what you are seeing and what you hear.

"DENBY  It isn't miked?

"ROBBINS  No, not at all!

"DENBY  And you're so glad to see him, too. I wondered whether he can see the dancers.

"ROBBINS  Most of them, but not the ones on the side of the stage he is on. But there is a place where we have a mirror—rigged way up high on the wings so that if he looks up he can see someone come in for just a cue. And I thought Tom Skelton did a very good job in a very little time. He did the lighting.

"DENBY  Some of it looks ominous, sometimes. I mean weather. It changes. I suppose you wanted that too. I liked it.

"ROBBINS  I didn't mean it to look ominous, but I suppose that vast sky, it is almost like nature changing on you. You're a little worried about what is going to happen next, it doesn't matter if it goes up or down. It's just that it changes. Everything changes.

"I didn't know it was going to be that long a ballet or what it was going to be. I originally thought, we'll do it using the wings and the cyclorama because it's just going to be a *pas de deux*. But by the time it was all done, I thought, Wow, who should do a set? Is it Jane Freilicher, or is it one of those watery sort of places, or is it—? Now I'm used to the way it is. I don't know if I want a set, or anything softer around the edges. That's a very hard line, those black wings. But once it starts, I don't suppose you are particularly aware of it any more.

"DENBY  When you watch you realize that there are woods there, and you're in a meadow and there are trees.

"ROBBINS  Isn't that funny, odd how that all got evoked. My names for the dances themselves, for instance, the second dance for John Prinz and Allegra (Kent), I call it 'wind waltz' because to me they are like two things that are on the wind that catch up with each other. There is something about air—breezes which are clawing them and pushing them almost like two kites. And 'walk waltz' or 'the three girls' to me is somehow in the woods. On a Chekhov evening. It just is. I can't see it any other way. It has that quality.

"DENBY  The whole piece is a Chekhov piece. There are so many things suggested and not explained. The business of looking around at the end is the trickiest. I didn't like it at all the first time. Yesterday I didn't mind it so much. It is like looking at an airplane, I think of missiles and war.

"ROBBINS  They must do it very softly. That is almost one of the hardest parts to be able to do. It is very hard for them just to walk on and be confident and just raise their heads or eyes and look at something without starting to make it dramatic. I keep telling them, 'Relax, don't be sad, don't get upset, just see it, just whatever you want to pick, just see. It's a cloud passing, if you want. Take it easy on it, don't get gloomy.'

"DENBY    It's because they all do it together.

"ROBBINS    Together—right—they all follow one thing. And that upset you? You thought it was airplanes and missiles?

"DENBY    The atom bomb comes in and everything else. The sort of thing about Hitler attacking Poland. Your mind gets full of ideas that you don't want, that don't have anything to do with the piece.

"ROBBINS    If I had to talk about it all, I would say that they are looking at —all right—clouds on the horizon which possibly could be threatening, but then that's life, so afterwards you just pick up and go right on again. It doesn't destroy them. They don't lament. They accept.

"DENBY    That's what I told myself. It must be that they are looking at clouds—clouds rarely go that fast, but it might be a storm coming up and they're wondering if it's going to happen.

"ROBBINS    That section, it was the last piece I did, though. I spent about two weeks after I finished the bulk of the choreography—it was almost all done about two weeks before the eighth of May. But that last two weeks I spent in arranging, trying to get the right order. Not only who danced what, but also that sense of something happening—making the dances have some continuity, some structure, whether I knew specifically what it was or not. At one point I had the scherzo finishing the ballet and the grand waltz opening it. All different sorts of ways. It was just—it was a marvelous sort of puzzle. Here I have all these people and these situations and I know they belong to each other—now let me see how. It was almost like rearranging *things*. And suddenly a picture was there. I am surprised by a lot of it. I am very surprised by the reaction to it. I didn't expect it at all. Something is there that I didn't know I was doing.

"DENBY    The reaction?

"ROBBINS    To the ballet.

"DENBY    That everybody liked it so much.

"ROBBINS    So much. The questions you are asking me about it seem to—I was originally going to call it *Some Dances*. That's all they are, just a series of dances. But something else takes over.

"DENBY    I don't know that the title is exactly the best.

"ROBBINS    It's a hard one to find. I was going to say *Dances: Chopin, In Open Air*, but that isn't the right title. In French *Quelques Danses* is nice, but in English *Some Dances* is sort of flat. If you say *Eighteen Dances* or *Nineteen Dances*, it divides them into compartments.

"DENBY    And it's of no consequence. Once you see the piece, you figure it is a piece. That end is quite prepared for all along when it happens. You really didn't want a big dance at the end. Since they are walking so much anyway, it is natural to make the end out of that.

"ROBBINS    Also the end of it had to come out of the scherzo, that very restless piece which ends with them all sort of *whoosh* running out—disappearing like cinders falling out into the night, and it couldn't end there, either. That's not the end of it, that's not how I feel about these people—that they went *whoosh* and disappeared. They are still here and they still move like dancers. They are a community. They take—what's the Italian word?—'a *passegiata*'— they take a stroll, like in an Italian town, around the town's square at sundown. They may have felt a threat, but they don't panic, they stay.

"I was very touched by Maria (Tallchief) last night. She was moved by the ballet, and I suddenly realized how much it meant to me that she *was* and that it pleased her, because she is such an image in my mind of what a dancer should be, and I can't think of her as a cinder which went *whoosh* and was gone.

"So coming back after the scherzo to the stage and the floor that we dance on, and putting your hand on it—if it's the earth or a ballet dancer's relationship to a wood floor—*that* somehow is the ending I knew I had to get to somewhere. Very little of this was conscious, Edwin. I don't like to make theory afterwards. I'm just trying to get at it—there may be seven other reasons I'm not mentioning, well, you understand.

"DENBY    I don't want to pull it out of you—

"ROBBINS    Well, besides, you have your thoughts about it anyway.

"DENBY    Of course. Everyone is very happy that you've done a ballet again.

"ROBBINS    So am I.

"DENBY    And the dancers are happy. And it's nice you want to do some more.

"ROBBINS    I'm surprised. I didn't know which I would do or how I would do. It's almost like an artist who has not been drawing for a long time. I didn't know how my hand would be. And I was so surprised that the dances began to come out and began to come out so gushing, in a way. And I worked in a way I hadn't worked before. Whether I knew the details or not, I pushed through to the end of the dance. I sort of knew where it was going, and then I'd go back and clean it up and fill it up. Quite often the dancers weren't even sure how they got through the steps to the next step. But they went with me. Well, what I started to say was that I was pleased to be choreographing again and to have it coming out, and it's given me a sort—it's unplugged something. And I want to do a lot of ballets. I want to go on and see if I can work a little bit more the way I've worked this time—that sort of trusting the intuition more than self-controlling the intuition. I'd like to see what happens with some other kind of music now. That music I feel I am very identified with and always have been. It may go all the way back to my sister's dancing days as a Duncan dancer. I think a lot of that's in there.

"DENBY    I imagined you and your sister at the piano—you were seven or eight. The first thing that came from it was *The Concert* which, the first time, I was quite offended by.

"ROBBINS    (*laughs*) I made up for that.

"DENBY    I miss it now. I'd love to see it. But your jokes this time are adorable.

"ROBBINS    I love them in the section where they're posing, just love them. . . . I had a researcher call me from a magazine to ask me some questions. The first one was something very close to this: 'Where do you place your newest ballet in the mainstream of the trend of abstract dancing today?' (*laughter*) I've also been asked, 'What is the relationship between *Les Sylphides* and your ballet?' Well, I guess we used the same composer.

"DENBY   Did you use any of the same pieces?

"ROBBINS   No, I didn't, except one, the adage that Tony and Pat do, the third dance. Evidently, that music was used as the man's variation at one point, which I didn't know. It's a lovely piece.

"DENBY   You told me that you are going to do another Chopin ballet.

"ROBBINS   I've finished one nocturne and I've about three-quarters of another one, and I have an idea for a third. I've started them and want to see how they come out. One for Millie, one for Allegra, and I think one for Kay Mazzo.

"DENBY   She's beautiful.

"ROBBINS   Isn't she lovely?

"DENBY   Sally is wonderful. She gets more and more of that giving-without-thinking.

"ROBBINS   She has a kind of toughness, not tough as much as a practical quality. But then I'll say something and can see in her eyes that she's suddenly grasped it, and you can see it explode inside her—such joy.

"DENBY   The dance of the girls comes off so wonderfully. Allegra is wonderful all through.

"ROBBINS   That's the way about all of them. At so many rehearsals, they didn't dance all out. They sort of walked. That's how I got Eddie to do that first variation the first night. He came into rehearsal and had to save himself for the performance and just marked through it. I ran back and said, 'Now, that's what I want.' The same with Allegra—when she marks something, she shows you what it is. I don't think they realize how trained they are—so clear. Like someone with a great voice who can whisper and you hear it. And that's what you see. And that's what they do.

"DENBY   They are so completely clear, it's extraordinary how clear they are because whatever is passing through is never a blur or an uncertainty or a conventionalism.

"[Postscript from Robbins to Denby (sent the following day from Stockholm where Robbins was supervising final rehearsals of *Les Noces* for its June 6 première with the Royal Swedish Ballet. He went from there to Moscow to attend, by invitation of the U.S.S.R., its International Ballet Competition.)]

May 27, 1969

"Dear Edwin:

"Something bothered me terribly after we met—one of your remarks about the people looking up and watching something cross the sky at the end of the ballet. You said something about planes—A bomb—war today, etc., and it jarred me very much. I couldn't figure out 'the why' right away—but then I did on the trip over. First of all I feel you are imposing a terribly out-of-context meaning to what they are seeing. The ballet stays and exists in the time of the music and its work.

Nothing is out of it, I believe; all gestures and moods, steps, etc. are part of the fabric of the music's time and its meanings to me. I couldn't think of planes—A bomb, etc. Only clouds—and the flights of birds—sunsets and leaves falling—and they, the people's reactions are all very underplayed, very willing to meet whatever threat is *in the music.*

"Well, those people knew their disasters—felt them, maybe felt that at a certain time their being would come to an end—but they faced it as a part of living.

"I hadn't thought of *all* of this when I did it. All I knew is that they weren't afraid, had no self-pity, and stayed—didn't leave.

"And I do feel that last piece is the logical end of the whole ballet. To me it is very much the only possible result of all that's come before.

". . . Stockholm is lovely, limpid skies at midnight—looking clear and blue as a New York fall—It was so good to see you—J"

*Dances at a Gathering* has been acclaimed in the United States and in London, where it was first performed by the Royal Ballet, October 19, 1970. Marcia Marks in *Dance Magazine* found it "the most significant work for many a season. For Robbins, it is the most spontaneous outpouring of sheer creative force in his balletic career, and for the dancers, it is an unexpected revelation." Patricia Barnes in *Dance and Dancers* magazine said, "*Dances at a Gathering* is, by general consent, a masterpiece. . . . It has been interpreted by different people in different ways, but all seem agreed on one aspect. This is a ballet about people, recognizable human beings rather than mere ciphers. There is no story, but a strong mood and atmosphere are present. There are ten dancers, five boys and five girls—they could be Americans, Poles, Danes or Russians. Their nationality is unimportant. What is significant in the fluent, utterly captivating series of dances is a love of humanity, an observation and understanding that is remarkably conveyed by the dancers involved. It seems impossible to leave the theatre having seen *Dances at a Gathering* and not feel one's soul uplifted."

In London, where the first performance was danced by Rudolf Nureyev, Monica Mason, Antoinette Sibley, Anthony Dowell, Laura Connor, Ann Jenner, David Wall, Lynn Seymour, Michael Coleman, and Jonathan Kelly, the editor of the *Dancing Times,* Mary Clarke, wrote: "Genius is a word to be used sparingly in the small artistic world of ballet but genius is the only word for Jerome Robbins, as choreographer and man of the theatre. . . . It may sound exaggerated to say that this ballet, just about people dancing, is profoundly moving but it is true. There is more dancing than in some three-act ballets and certainly more emotion because it is happening here and now. It is an hour of delight and if you catch it on a program with Ashton's *Enigma Variations* or *The Dream,* your faith in ballet will be restored. The Press has been unanimous in praise. I echo Clement Crisp of *The Financial Times:* it is a ballet 'that will enrich our lives for years to come.'"

In 1972, Jerome Robbins wrote to *Ballet Review* the following letter, which is of general interest:

To the Editor:

For the record, would you please print in large, emphatic and capital letters the following:

THERE ARE NO STORIES TO ANY OF THE DANCES IN DANCES AT A GATHERING.
THERE ARE NO PLOTS AND NO ROLES. THE DANCERS ARE THEMSELVES DANCING
WITH EACH OTHER TO THAT MUSIC IN THAT SPACE.

Thank you very much.

New York, N.Y.

Jerome Robbins.

The pianist Gordon Boelzner, interviewed by Arlene Croce and George
Dorris in *Ballet Review* (Vol. 3, No. 4.), has many interesting comments on
*Dances at a Gathering, In the Night* and *Who Cares?*

## DANSES CONCERTANTES

*Classic ballet in five parts. Music by Igor Stravinsky. Choreography by
George Balanchine. Scenery and costumes by Eugene Berman. First pre-
sented by the Ballet Russe de Monte Carlo at the City Center, New York,
September 10, 1944, with a cast headed by Alexandra Danilova and Leon
Danielian.*

Stravinsky's *Danses Concertantes* was first performed as a concert piece, but
the composer had conceived the work with the choreographer and had intended his score to be used in the theatre. When the work was first played
(1942), it was apparent that the music embodied dancing—not only dance
rhythms, but specific poses and gestures for a group of dancers—so that to hear
*Danses Concertantes* was also to visualize a ballet. The plot of the ballet
*Danses Concertantes* is the plot of the score: "Introductory March," "*Pas
d'Action,*" "Four Variations on a Theme," "*Pas de deux,*" and "Concluding
March."

The curtain rises on a handsome, ornate drop curtain. Between two high
columns draped in rich cloth, the legend of the ballet is sketched out and we
read the name of the ballet, its composer, choreographer, and designer. The
orchestra commences a rhythmic, witty march. The dancers, in bright costumes, parade before the curtain at the music's command. There are fourteen
of them—eight girls, four boys, and the *premier danseur* and the ballerina, who
enter toward the end of the march and finish it with a flourish.

The drop curtain rises. The ballerina dances before the *corps de ballet,*
which is arranged in four groups, in each of which a boy partners two girls.
The colorful, spangled figures of the dancers are outlined boldly against the
dark back cloth. The ballerina dances with sweet, lyric grace, but also with
humor, for the music contrives to interrupt and cut short its soft melody with
sharp accents in surprising places. You get the impression that you might get
from reading a lyric poem whose lines are sometimes truncated in the middle
of words but nevertheless flow on to graceful conclusion.

The majestic opening of this second section is heard again, and the full orchestra plays a lively, precisely accented conclusion that merges directly into a
new theme that is quiet, tender, and romantic. The ballerina has left the stage,

and each of the four groups of dancers comes forward and dances a *pas de trois* to variations on the theme.

The first and second variations are rigorous in rhythm, and the musical phrases seem to balance about a center, as the two girls cluster and move away from the boy. The third variation, Andantino, is softer, more wistful; the fourth, happy and boisterous.

The dancers now leave the stage to the ballerina and her partner, who dance a *pas de deux*. The dancers are almost personified in the music, which demands at first beauty in slowness, then a quiet, pointed wit that ascends to an elevated, noble manner. The *pas de deux* ends on a note of tenderness.

All the dancers return. The opening march is resumed, and the entire group dances to its buoyant rhythm. The music ends sharply and unexpectedly. All rush forward and bow low to the audience as the curtain falls behind them.

NOTES Frederic Franklin later took the role first danced by Leon Danielian. Maria Tallchief, Ruthanna Boris, and Mary Ellen Moylan were among the dancers in the first performance.

In 1972, for the Stravinsky Festival at the New York City Ballet, which we planned in order to celebrate the composer's ninetieth birthday, I did a new version of *Danses Concertantes*. It was not only that I did not remember what I had done the first time; it was that I wanted, with the new dancers I was working with, to do something different.

It often happens: we forget. I don't think that is so bad when we have in the present so much to do! How in the world is it possible—really for me, it is not—to create a ballet first done many years ago, with young dancers who are very different? Writers think with words; I think with bodies and the ballets I work on necessarily have a great deal to do with the here and now, not a recollection or a notation or someone's idea of accuracy of the past. That is perhaps a proper function in a ballet company for some ballet masters, to reconstruct, but it is not for me; I am too busy making for now. I think ballet is now. I remember saying to an interviewer, Louis Botto, as we were preparing for the Stravinsky Festival, precisely this—that ballet is about people who are now, not about what will be. Because as you don't have these bodies to work with, it's already finished. This is not a question of what the story is, or what the costumes are, or preserving the ballet of 1972 for future generations. I'm staging ballets for today's bodies. For people who are here now. And you admire the way he or she looks and how they move. It's this person today—not just *anybody*.

And so I enjoyed very much doing *Danses Concertantes* again.

The outline of the ballet is just as it was in the first version, but the details are radically different. The first performance of the new *Danses Concertantes*, by the New York City Ballet at the New York State Theatre, was danced by Linda Yourth and John Clifford, with a group of twelve dancers. The orchestra was conducted by Robert Irving. Scenery and costumes, as before, were by Eugene Berman.

# DANTE SONATA

*Dramatic ballet in one act. Music by Franz Liszt. Choreography by Frederick Ashton. Scenery and costumes by Sophie Fedorovitch. First presented by the Sadler's Wells Ballet at the Sadler's Wells Theatre, London, January 23, 1940, with Margot Fonteyn and Robert Helpmann among the principal dancers. First presented in the United States by the Sadler's Wells Ballet at the Metropolitan Opera House, New York, September 23, 1950, with Margot Fonteyn, Moira Shearer, and Michael Somes among the principals.*

This ballet is based on appreciations of Dante's *Divine Comedy* by the poet Victor Hugo and the composer Franz Liszt. Liszt used Hugo's poem "After a Reading of Dante" as an eloquent statement of his own appreciation of that poet and wrote a composition for piano on its theme. This ballet, like Liszt's music, depicts an embattled conflict between the forces of good and the forces of evil.

The curtain rises on a decorative backdrop that indicates with a few white lines the fiery fumes of purgatory hovering above parallel lines reminiscent of ascending steps. There are two groups of people in the ballet: the Children of Light and the Children of Darkness. The former are dressed in innocent white, most of the latter in black. Black, shining snakes coil about the bodies of the two principal Children of Darkness, a man and a woman.

The Children of Light, apparently those who have understood their sins and repented, dance joyfully alone. Soon they are invaded by the Children of Darkness. The evil men and women attack the purified ones with determined concupiscence. The Children of Light try to beat them back, but some are seduced.

The Children of Light move flowingly, without suddenness, while their opposites fill the stage with violence. The efforts of the innocent to save themselves, to prevent any one of their number from yielding to this violence, enforce a constant tension. But finally their resistance is in vain: physically they become slaves to the powers of evil.

The Children of Darkness are not enlightened by their triumph and regard it with displeasure even as it is achieved. The curtain falls as the leaders of the Children of Light and the Children of Darkness, on opposite sides of the stage, are held up by their fellows in simulated crucifixion, their limbs twitching with agony.

# DAPHNIS AND CHLOË

*Dramatic ballet in three scenes. Music by Maurice Ravel. Choreography by Michel Fokine. Book by Michel Fokine. Scenery and costumes by Léon Bakst. First presented by Diaghilev's Ballets Russes at the Théâtre du Châtelet, Paris, June 8, 1912, with Tamara Karsavina as Chloë, Vaslav*

*Nijinsky as Daphnis, and Adolph Bolm as Dorkon. Revived, with choreography by Catherine Littlefield, for the Philadelphia Ballet, 1937. Revived, with choreography by Frederick Ashton, by the Sadler's Wells Ballet at the Royal Opera House, Covent Garden, London, April 5, 1951. Scenery and costumes by John Craxton. Margot Fonteyn, Michael Somes, Violetta Elvin, John Field, and Alexander Grant danced the principal roles. This is the version described below.*

The two orchestral suites *Daphnis and Chloë,* now so familiar to us, are derived from an original ballet score designed for this ancient tale of youthful romance. Actually, two suites Ravel made of this music were performed in concert form before the ballet was produced. *Suite No. 1*—"Nocturne," "Interlude," and "Warriors' Dance"—begins at the end of Scene One of the ballet, after Daphnis has collapsed, and concludes with the end of the general dance of the pirates in Scene Two. *Suite No. 2*—"Daybreak," "Pantomime," and "General Dance"—is the music for the whole of Scene Three.

In its outlines, *Daphnis and Chloë* is not radically different from many ballets with stories that relate the love of young people who are finally reunited after some difficulty, some obstruction, has seemed to rule out a happy ending. This is naturally the way of ballet stories, as it is with all fiction, for unless there is some kind of obstruction, we are not apt to have a story: love, alone, is not enough. But it is the different quality of the love—the difference in the affection of Tristram for Iseult in *Picnic at Tintagel,* of Franz for Swanilda in *Coppélia,* of Amyntas for Sylvia in *Sylvia,* and in the way these lovers react to any interference—that make all these stories interesting. If we care about the kind of affection these lovers have for each other, what their gestures are, and how they look together, we are apt to be disturbed if any obstruction is put in their way and we are delighted at the end if the lovers seem to be happy and forgetful in their understanding of what has come between them. The two lovers in the story *Daphnis and Chloë* are very young; they are youthful innocents. We are made to see this and resent immediately the interference they endure. We are happy at the end because their initial innocence is not seriously violated: they still love, but with a difference that will make them happier.

SCENE ONE: A SACRED GROVE    On this day young people of a Mediterranean isle are paying tribute to the god Pan and his nymphs, whose grotto stands at the left. Daphnis, the handsome shepherd, and Chloë, the girl he has loved all his life, are among the worshipers. Their affection has become so accepted by the other young people that some of the maidens don't seriously believe in it. Still hoping that Daphnis will notice one of them, the maidens join him in a dance. Chloë reacts with appropriate jealousy and does not repulse the advances of another shepherd, Dorkon. All this is in the spirit of fun; the lovers have taken a vow to be faithful to each other, and their friends are amusing themselves a little because of the seriousness of the romance. Dorkon, however, is serious too, and Daphnis tells him to leave his girl alone. But Dorkon is not to be easily routed. Daphnis becomes angry, and his friends try to make light of the situation by suggesting that the two begin a dancing contest for Chloë's favor.

Dorkon's dance is as crude and awkward as his advances toward Chloë have been, and Daphnis, in a splendid dance with his shepherd's crook, easily defeats him. Chloë rewards Daphnis with a kiss, Dorkon departs, and her friends take Chloë away.

Daphnis is alone. He lies down on the ground and daydreams of his perfect love. He has almost fallen off to sleep when he is joined by the temptress Lykanion. Daphnis is indifferent to her beauty, but strangely attracted also. Lykanion is sure of her knowledge of love, and the inexperienced youth is disturbed. But Lykanion is too anxious to instruct Daphnis. He senses instinctively the evil in her advances and dismisses her.

Now the youth is roused by a battle cry. A band of pirates have invaded the island, and the natives have risen in arms against them. The defenseless girls seek the safety of Pan's grotto, but the pirates, disrespectful of the god, pursue them. Bryaxis, leader of the pirates, captures Chloë and carries her off swiftly before Daphnis can act. Daphnis cannot understand how this has happened. He despairs and rails at the power of gods who would permit her abduction.

The music is quiet and mysterious. Suddenly one of the stone nymphs of the grotto comes to life in a magical blaze of light. As the chorus begins to chant along with the music, this girl and two other nymphs begin to dance. Daphnis does not see them. Now they go to him, rouse him, and lead him before the grotto of Pan. At the nymphs' call, an image of the god fills the sky. Daphnis prays that the powerful god will restore Chloë to him.

SCENE TWO: THE PIRATES' HIDE-OUT   On the shore of another island, the pirates are celebrating their victory at night. They dance joyfully and divide among themselves the day's profits. Chloë, her wrists bound together with rope, is brought in, and Bryaxis, the pirate captain, commands her to dance. The helpless girl is afraid to refuse, but soon, as she dances, she lifts her bound wrists in supplication, begging to be released. Bryaxis only laughs at her. The terrified girl trembles at the thought of intimacy with such a man. Bryaxis is about to approach her when the seacoast is suddenly illuminated by brilliant, flashing light. The pirates cower at this miracle and stare, astonished, as the great god Pan appears in a vision. He orders the pirates to free Chloë. The brigands flee to the hills.

SCENE THREE: ANOTHER PART OF THE SACRED GROVE   The orchestra is silent as the curtain rises. Daphnis, lying alone, grieves over Chloë's loss. Gradually the music imitates the sounds of the breaking day; the sun rises. Fellow shepherds come seeking Daphnis. But he does not wish to join them; only by praying to the god may he help his love to be rescued. Chloë's friends appear and tell him that she has returned. The ecstatic Daphnis searches for her. At first sight of Daphnis, Chloë runs into his arms, and the two lovers rejoice.

Lammon, an old shepherd, tells Daphnis that his prayers have indeed been answered but that Pan acted in his favor because of the god's memory of his own love for the Syrinx. Daphnis and Chloë, in their gratitude for Pan's intervention, re-enact the god's romance for their friends. Daphnis, as Pan, vainly pursues the lovely nymph, who flees from him. He pleads with her, but she will not acknowledge him. She hides and, at Pan's persistence, casts herself into a brook and drowns. The god takes a reed from the brook and makes of it a flute, which he names for Syrinx. He plays upon the flute. At its sound, Chloë begins to dance with tenderness and joy.

The ensemble joins the two lovers in a final general dance that celebrates their reunion and their lasting love.

NOTES   Serge Diaghilev commissioned Ravel to compose a ballet in one act on the story of Daphnis and Chloë. The work was to be performed in 1911, and during the ensuing delay, Ravel arranged two suites from his score, both of which were performed in the concert hall before the ballet's first performance. The ballet at last saw the stage June 8, 1912, with Tamara Karsavina and Vaslav Nijinsky in the title roles. Fokine, the choreographer, had had in mind a ballet on the Daphnis and Chloë legend for eight years. In 1904, in St. Petersburg, he had submitted a scenario for such a work to the director of the Imperial Theatre, along with a preface that detailed the reforms to be embodied in his work, reforms that he regarded as crucial for the art of ballet: "The dance need not be a mere *divertissement*, introduced into the pantomime. In the ballet the whole meaning of the story can be expressed by the dance. Above all, dancing should be interpretive. It should not degenerate into mere gymnastics. It should, in fact, be the plastic word. The dance should explain the spirit of the actors in the spectacle. More than that, it should express the whole epoch to which the subject of the ballet belongs . . . The ballet must no longer be made up of 'numbers,' 'entries,' etc. It must show artistic unity of conception . . . a unity which is made up of the three elements—music, painting, and plastic art . . . The great, the outstanding feature of the new ballet . . . shall be but one thing—the aspiration for beauty . . ."

But the reforms suggested in Fokine's manifesto were largely ignored and his project for a ballet was refused. Part of his original scenario was staged for the Diaghilev Ballets Russes after many of his reforms had been realized, in *Les Sylphides, Firebird,* and *Petrouchka.*

This production of *Daphnis and Chloë* was a considerable success. Tamara Karsavina, who created the part of Chloë, has written that the ballet was, to her mind, Fokine's masterpiece. "In it, Fokine explored to the full the recesses of neo-Greek choreography as originally revived by Isadora Duncan."

Successful as it was, however, the production of *Daphnis and Chloë* created a quarrel between the choreographer and the impresario. Fokine had difficulty obtaining adequate rehearsal time and new costumes for his new ballet, and since Nijinsky, in his staging of *The Afternoon of a Faun,* was being rewarded with both, the older choreographer felt slighted. Soon after, he left the Diaghilev company for two years.

The *Daphnis and Chloë* of Catherine Littlefield, pioneer in American ballet, was a completely new choreographic venture, first produced in 1937 for her Philadelphia Ballet.

Two new productions of *Daphnis and Chloë* were given in New York in

1975. The first, with choreography by John Taras, costumes and production by Joe Eula, and lighting by Ronald Bates, was part of the New York City Ballet's Hommage à Ravel and received its first performance at the New York State Theatre, Lincoln Center, New York, on May 22, with Robert Irving conducting. Peter Martins, Nina Fedorova, Karin von Aroldingen and Peter Schaufuss were the principals.

The second new production, choreographed by Glen Tetley for the Stuttgart Ballet and first presented at the Württemberg State Theatre, Stuttgart, May 17, 1975, with scenery and costumes by Willa Kim and lighting by John B. Read, was first presented by the same ensemble in the United States at the Metropolitan Opera House, Lincoln Center, on June 12, 1975 (lighting executed by Gilbert V. Hemsley, Jr.), with Stewart Kershaw conducting the orchestra and chorus. Richard Cragun, Marcia Haydée, Birgit Keil, and Egon Madsen were the principals.

## DARK ELEGIES

*Music by Gustav Mahler. Choreography by Antony Tudor. Scenery and costumes by Nadia Benois. First produced by the Ballet Rambert at the Duchess Theatre, London, February 19, 1937, with Maude Lloyd, Antony Tudor, Walter Gore, John Byron, Agnes de Mille, Hugh Laing, Daphne Gow, Ann Gee, Patricia Clogstoun, Beryl Kay, and Celia Franca. First presented in the United States by Ballet Theatre at the Center Theatre, New York, January 24, 1940, with scenery and costumes by Raymond Sovey after the Benois originals. The principal dancers were Nina Stroganova, Miriam Golden, Antony Tudor, Hugh Laing, Lucia Chase, and Dimitri Romanoff.*

*Dark Elegies* is a dance ballet to the *Kindertotenlieder* (Songs of Childhood Death) of Mahler. The singer on stage tells of the grief of a father over the death of his children. The setting is somber, rough, jagged, with lowering clouds over water and mountains and trees that seem to have been lashed relentlessly by the wind. As the music laments, a small group of villagers begin to dance. Their grief over a disaster that has befallen them all is communal and also private. We do not know what the tragedy is, there are no specifics, but with the expression and gesture of the dancers, we have no need. Their movement universalizes the particulars of Mahler's songs and we watch, as at a religious rite, the unfolding of desperate grief to mourning, to resignation and perhaps hope.

Dame Marie Rambert, in whose ballet company this ballet was created, has recalled in her biography *Quicksilver:* "Tudor told me he was anxious to do a ballet to Mahler's *Kindertotenlieder*. He had already suggested it two years before, but at that time I did not think he was mature enough to tackle such a tragic subject. I had also been perturbed by the main idea of a disaster that would kill all the children and leave the parents alive. I kept reasoning with Tudor that except for the Massacre of the Innocents such a special calamity

Tanaquil LeClercq and Francisco Moncion in *Afternoon of a Faun*. Photo by Fred'k Melton.

Nora Kaye in *Pillar of Fire*. Photo by Fred Fehl

Janet Reed and Jerome Robbins in *Fancy Free*. Photo by Fred Fehl.

Jerome Robbins in *Prodigal Son*. Photo by George Platt Lynes, from the Dance Collection, N.Y.P.L.

Erik Bruhn in *The Nutcracker*. Photo by Fred Fehl.

Cynthia Gregory and Ivan Nagy in *Giselle*. Photo by Louis Péres.

Fernando Bujones in *Le Corsaire*. Photo by Martha Swope.

Martine van Hamel in *The Sleeping Beauty*. Photo by Martha Swope.

Daniel Levans in *Billy the Kid*. Photo by Jack Mitchell.

had never happened and would seem *too* contrived. But now in 1937 he seemed very sure of the way to treat it. I asked him to show me one finished song and realized how profound the choreography was. He had seen at an exhibition of Nadia Benois a landscape which he was sure would be the right setting, and when I saw the painting I agreed with him. So we invited her to design the scenery and the costumes, which she did perfectly. The ballet was not purely realistic. It had lovely words and music, and the dances were classical for the soloists and in folk-dance style for the ensemble. Yet he managed to keep the style homogeneous.

"He called this ballet *Dark Elegies*. It was in two scenes: 1. Bereavement; 2. Resignation. It was like a mourning ritual accompanied by a singer on the stage. Singly or in groups, the bereaved parents express their sorrow in a slow dance at having lost their children when their village was stricken by calamity. They try not to show their pain, but it breaks through at moments. All was said in classical language, and this severe form made the expression more poignant when despair burst through it.

"When we performed this ballet in 1966 to a new young public, many of them thought that it was all about the Aberfan Disaster, to such a degree had the most unforeseen of calamities happened in reality.

"*Dark Elegies* was Tudor's masterpiece and has remained the greatest tragic ballet of the English repertoire so far.

"In addition to our own dancers he used a guest dancer, the American Agnes de Mille, a most remarkable artist."

Agnes de Mille's own recollections of *Dark Elegies* are recorded in a long interview with the critic Clive Barnes (see his book *Inside American Ballet Theatre*, 1977).

NOTE *Dark Elegies* has been in the active repertory of the Ballet Rambert since it was first performed. It is now danced by the National Ballet of Canada and other companies. Jerome Robbins has said: "Fokine inspired me as a performer; he made me feel I could really dance. Tudor didn't; he made it complicated. He brought psychological motivation into ballet; he conveyed through movement emotions that could not be put into words. And he had the courage to persevere along this line in the face of adverse criticism. But he did wonderful things in pure dance, as well. *Gala Performance* and *Dark Elegies* stand alone, and I think they will last longest because they are more formal in structure . . . Tudor had a great influence on my early work and a great influence on all contemporary ballet."*

## LES DEMOISELLES DE LA NUIT (The Ladies of Midnight)

*Dramatic ballet in three scenes. Music by Jean Françaix. Choreography by Roland Petit. Book by Jean Anouilh. Settings and costumes by Léonor Fini. First presented by Les Ballets de Paris at the Théâtre Marigny, Paris, May 21, 1948, with Margot Fonteyn, Roland Petit, and Gordon Hamilton in the*

* From "Antony Tudor" by Selma Jeanne Cohen, in *Dance Perspectives 18*, 1963.

*leading roles. First presented in the United States by Ballet Theatre at the Metropolitan Opera House, New York, April 13, 1951, with Colette Marchand, John Kriza, and Eric Braun.*

This ballet rightly assumes that when a young man marries a cat, things are going to be pretty difficult around the house. How the young man meets the cat, how he is enamored of her feline grace, how his love transforms her for a time into a beautiful young girl, and how, despite his love, his wife is unable to conquer an irresistible inclination to scamper on the rooftops, the ballet chooses to relate in three scenes.

SCENE ONE: A HOUSE IN THE COUNTRY  Low, moaning music is heard from the orchestra as a brief overture begins. The curtain rises. The scene is a large, high room whose walls are papered with yellowing, peeling newspapers. Cats sit about the room in relaxed attitudes: some polishing their nails, some resting against a ladder. A black kitten reclines on a white couch at the right. On the wall, partially obscured by a wispy rag, hangs a portrait of a big, beautiful white cat. A doorway in the center is hung with tattered and torn cloth; innumerable cats must have sharpened their claws on it.

A young musician enters. He pushes aside the dusty drapes and steps carefully into the room. He has been invited to this house in the country to play at a wedding and is astonished to see that no ordinary preparations for such an occasion have been made. He observes the curious cats and walks over to the portrait. He turns in the air in surprise at what he sees there. The entire house is occupied by cats!

Two black-and-white cats in handsome livery, pages to the household, dart out and grab the musician's hat. The tempo becomes brisk. The light brightens. He chases after them unsuccessfully. The black cat rises from the couch; she and three of the kittens surround the musician. The cats dance about the boy, scratching at his face. The black cat curls up at his feet. He dances for a short time with the kittens. They leave. Agatha, the beautiful white cat at whose portrait the musician has marveled, enters quickly, expectantly. Agatha is the bride of the month. The cat baron who rules over the house marries one of his harem every month, and it is Agatha's wedding that the musician has been invited to attend. Tall and graceful, with long, lithe legs, she immediately attracts the young man. She is dressed in white, with short gloves; a blue ribbon is tied about her throat. The music changes; an oboe plays a wistful, yet playful, melody to the accompaniment of plucked strings.

Agatha begins to dance. The musician watches, fascinated. The music becomes rhythmic. He compares the cat to her portrait. He goes up to Agatha. She circles him on point, and the strings commence a flowing theme. The boy turns swiftly and kneels at her feet. Now he rises and holds her close. The cat responds experimentally. Gradually Agatha becomes as interested in the musician as he is in her. He lifts, holds, and embraces her for a duet that lasts five minutes. The music whines plaintively. The other cats look on with horror. What will the cat baron do? They attack the boy and try to pull him away, but

Agatha climbs up on his back. Cymbals and brass simulate the contest. The boy embraces the cat. The music is silent for a moment.

The cat baron enters, his fur bristling. A lovely black cat, whose costume is embellished with the skeleton of a fish, separates the lovers rudely. She is evidently the cat baron's principal aide. Footlights throw the shadows of the two lovers and the jealous cat baron against the back wall. The baron dances in gleeful anticipation of his wedding. Agatha dances with him, not unwilling at first, but she breaks away and gestures to the boy, who stands on the opposite side of the stage, holding out his arms to her plaintively. She goes to the boy. The cat baron pulls them apart and dances furiously. He threatens the musician with his long claws.

The black cat takes Agatha's hand and pulls her toward the baron. A white veil is thrown over the bride's head before she can protest. Daringly she pulls it off and rejoins the boy. The cat baron makes a last effort to dominate her passions. The pages hold the cat couple high on their shoulders in a wedding parade. But Agatha falls down into the musician's arms. The desperate cats scuttle off. Suddenly Agatha is no longer a kitten; her face is the face of a beautiful girl.

SCENE TWO: AT HOME    The orchestra plays a protracted interlude of hurried music. The curtain rises on a boudoir scene. A white bed canopied in white gauze stands on the left. At the right is a large window, looking out on to a dark-blue night. A bird cage stands near the window. Agatha, in a becoming white costume, her light hair shining, stands alongside her new husband. They embrace. The girl goes over to the bird cage, takes out a bluebird, fondles it, and dances as she holds it before her. The boy sits at the foot of the bed and watches her adoringly. Odd, this passion of hers for birds.

He rises, stands by the window, then goes over to the right wall. As he steps back into the room, the cat baron follows him closely. Agatha is agitated. Her lover tries to throw the intruder out, but the baron is so delighted to see his sometime fiancée again, even if she is a real girl now, that he forces her to dance with him. When the boy separates them, the cat jumps up onto his back and scratches at him fiercely. Both claim Agatha. Finally the musician succeeds in throwing the baron out.

Agatha seems to be grateful. To a quiet, deep melody, she stands behind the boy and wraps her arms about his neck. They begin to dance. In the midst of their *pas de deux*, the girl's limbs seem to quicken. The boy takes her to the bed. There he lifts her high on his shoulder. He lets her down slowly, and the girl's body curves backward. He rocks her back and forth, his knee a fulcrum to her seesawing body. The boy falls back, exhausted. Agatha falls over his knees.

Prolonged, mournful cat calls are heard. Agatha raises her head. The sounds persist. As she moves off the bed onto the floor, a cymbal crashes. Her movements are catlike. She looks back at her lover, despairs, and climbs out the window. The musician awakens. The orchestra plays the haunting music of the ballet's overture. Where has Agatha gone? Out on the roof again, presumably. He takes a candle and follows her.

SCENE THREE: THE ROOFTOPS   The theme of the overture persists throughout the interval. The scene, as the curtain rises, is a red rooftop against a blue sky. Four dormer windows penetrate the roof from within. There is a gutter at the front. Agatha and the cat baron stand poised against two of the windows. They run to each other and embrace in the gutter. The musician climbs onto the roof through the window at the left. Other cats crawl over the roof and stand ready to attack him behind the window. They pounce on him. The boy falls. Agatha and the cat baron lead a train of cats over the roof, in and out among the windows. The boy tries to follow and slides into the gutter. When he rises, the cats gather behind each of the windows and menace him as he tries to gain the top of the roof. He holds Agatha desperately for a brief moment. The cat baron pulls her away and leads her to the peak of the roof. There the other cats place her on the baron's back. He races down toward the gutter. Agatha falls. The musician has been slapping about in the gutter like a fish fresh out of water. He squirms over to the girl. He sits up. Agatha poses against him; then both fall back. Their bodies arch away from each other, their hands and feet joined. They move close and lift their legs so that their toes touch. The boy dies. The girl looks down at him and dies. Their heads fall back and their arms dangle over the edge of the roof. Their curious love is happy in death.

NOTES   After its performance by Ballet Theatre, *Les Demoiselles de la Nuit* was called by John Martin of the New York *Times* "in many ways the best of Petit's ballets to be seen in this country. Though it has his characteristically theatrical approach, it has also much more of a choreographic basis than any of his other pieces." Petit had originally planned to include this ballet in the repertory of his own Ballets de Paris during one of its New York seasons, but had been unable to do so. Colette Marchand had succeeded Margot Fonteyn in performances of the principal role in Paris when the ballet was first produced; in New York, Marchand repeated her earlier success. The ballet has been considerably revised since its first American performance. Mary Ellen Moylan has danced Agatha with both critical and popular approval.

# DESIGNS WITH STRINGS

*Music by Peter Ilyich Tchaikovsky. Choreography by John Taras. First presented by the Metropolitan Ballet at Wimbledon, England, February 6, 1948. First presented in the United States by Ballet Theatre at the Center Theatre, New York, April 25, 1950, with costumes by Irene Sharaff.*

*Designs with Strings* is a dance ballet to the second movement of Tchaikovsky's *Trio in A minor,* arranged for piano and string orchestra. Instead of a story it has a mood, a character that arises from the dancing. There is no scenery; all the dancers wear simple black classical costumes and it is only in what they dance that they become individuals rather than performers.

The piano plays the stately, sentimental opening theme. There are six dancers—two boys and four girls. When the curtain rises, they are grouped together and stand motionless in silhouette against a plain backdrop. Their arms are extended slightly as they stand together; all the dancers appear to have a common relation and when they respond to the music and begin to move slowly in and out among themselves, they create an impression of unwinding of latent, quiescent energy.

The lights come up, the full string orchestra takes up the theme, and three of the dancers leave the stage. The remaining three, a boy and two girls, dance softly to the music. Their movement, like the melody, is romantic—a little sad, a little wistful. Their three companions return and circle the stage rapidly, as if to show that there is happiness in romance also. All six dance together briefly, and suddenly the melody quickens and the music becomes tinkling and light and gay. The dancers duplicate this change of pace and temper with whirling acceleration and with steps that are sharply fast and precise.

At the climax of this openly joyous sequence, the dancers leave the stage and a girl dances with a boy alone. The theme changes for this *pas de deux*, which is not at first so much romantic as it is matter-of-fact. But the dancing soon alters this, and we see as they move together that the girl and the boy are surprised and pleased to be by themselves, apart from the group. He lifts her off into the wings on the left; the first theme returns accompanied by a newly accented rhythm. Three girls rush out and dance brightly for a moment, to break the romantic spell, and leave the stage.

Another theme, noble and lowing, is heard on muted strings. The ballerina returns with two boys, who support her in a short dance. The wistfulness and playfulness have disappeared; the ballerina and her partners display a proud, youthful dignity. The new-found dignity breaks into pathos, however, upon the return of the other dancers. The six try to dance together as before, first the girls, then the boys. The first theme is heard again, poignantly on piercing strings. The ballerina separates herself from the group, and a boy supports her in a series of slow, extended movements across the stage. The other dancers move forward and separate them. The girl runs to the boy, seeming to plead with him and to claim him. But when she places her arms on his shoulders, he slips away from her and goes to rejoin the others. Slowly the girl follows him. The lights go down. The dancers stand as they were at the beginning, their figures silhouetted in a close group that seems now inseparable.


## DEUCE COUPE

*Music by the Beach Boys. Choreography by Twyla Tharp. Setting by United Graffiti Artists. Costumes by Scott Barrie. Lighting by Jennifer Tipton. First presented by the City Center Joffrey Ballet at the City Center, New York, March 1, 1973, with Erika Goodman, Twyla Tharp, and dancers from the Joffrey Ballet and the Twyla Tharp Company.*

Described as a juxtaposition of classical ballet and choreography based on social dances of the 1960s, *Deuce Coupe* was the first major work to be staged with an important ballet company by the modern dancer and choreographer Twyla Tharp, who appeared in the piece with members of her company. The title refers both to an automobile and to the piece *Little Deuce Coupe* by the Beach Boys, the rock group whose music, on tape, is featured in the ballet. Another major feature of the ballet is the setting—a background of three high strips of translucent paper (at first they look like windows we can't see out of) that a group of young people gradually fill with graffiti. As they inscribe the long sheets of paper, the paper is rolled up until the full height of the stage reflects their handiwork.

What happens on stage can be simply suggested but inadequately described. While a ballet dancer, Erika Goodman, performs an alphabetical but not-so-straightforward rendition of steps from the classical ballet dictionary, beginning with *Ailes de pigeon*, the rest of the dancers, in various combinations and permutations, perform dances both ancient and modern.

There are nineteen dances: *Matrix I, Ailes de pigeon* through *Attitude*, for the ballerina type and a couple; *Little Deuce Coupe, Balancé* through *Ballon*, with eighteen dancers and the persistent ballet performer; *Honda I, Balloné battu* through *déboulés*, for a *pas de trois* and the ballet girl; *Honda II, Changement de pieds* through *Dégagé à la quatrième devant en l'air*, for a couple and the girl; *Devoted to You, Dégagé en tournant* through *Failli*, for two couples and the girl; *How She Boogalooed It, Faux* through *Manège*, for the girl and a large ensemble; *Matrix II, Pas de basque sur les pointes* through *Pas de chat*, for the girl and six; *Alley Oop, Pas de cheval* through *Répétition*, for the girl plus eight; *Take a Load Off Your Feet, Retire* through *Sissone Tombée*, for three girls and two boys; *Long Tall Texan, Six* through *Suite*, for three girls; *Papa ooh Mau Mau*, for six; *Catch a Wave*, for five; *Got to Know the Woman, Temps de cuisse* through *temps lié*, for two girls; *Matrix III, Temps lié grand* through *Voyage*, for the ballet girl; *Don't Go Near the Water*, for six girls; *Matrix IV*, for a girl and boy; *Mama Says—"Eat a Lot, Never Be Lazy,"* for five boys and a girl; *Wouldn't It Be Nice*, for ten; and *Cuddle Up*, a finale for the whole company.

NOTE   Writing on the première in the *Daily News*, the critic Joseph Gale said that *Deuce Coupe* "is all the sadness, joy, cynicism and flavor of the beat generation . . . and the ballet is a smash.

"It is never less than exciting in crazy whorls of frenzied choreography that races, expires, picks up, jets ahead, pauses, and finally lays itself bare in unshed tears of last hopes.

"Through it all, there is the shining thread that holds it together and is the ballet's signature. That is Erika Goodman, unruffled and serene, who goes through a fair lexicon of classical dance, from *ailes de pigeon* through *pas de cheval*, while the world breaks up around her. She is the symbolic glory and salvation, the one who, after all else has failed, proffers hope in the palm of her outstretched hand. . . .

"There is also the schizoid passion of Miss Tharp's own dancing and, too, the United Graffiti Artists, who scrawl up a wall with the best decor of the season."

See comments on *As Time Goes By,* another Twyla Tharp ballet, for other views of this choreographer.

In the City Center Joffrey Ballet's spring season, 1975, the ballet became *Deuce Coupe II,* with the removal of Twyla Tharp's own dancers from the ensemble, a revision of the dances, and a new backdrop. Writing in *New York* magazine, the critic Alan Rich said that "the new work creates its own joy. Its scenario is entirely new; instead of being a work about pure dance, with its central soloist re-enacting the classic steps in alphabetical order, it is now a work about style. It spends its 40-or-so minutes as a steady wash, its pop steps from early on slowly oozing into romantic elegance as its dancers learn to unbend their knees and walk upon earth as adults. It is also, therefore, about growing up. Its music track, still a pastiche of the Beach Boys's greatest hits, is stronger, more poignant, altogether splendid."

## DIM LUSTRE

*Music by Richard Strauss. Choreography by Antony Tudor. Scenery and costumes by Motley. First presented by Ballet Theatre at the Metropolitan Opera House, New York, October 20, 1943, with Nora Kaye and Hugh Laing in the leading roles.*

The dancer Hugh Laing has defined the theme of this ballet to Richard Strauss's *Burleske in D minor* for piano and orchestra: "Two people find they have been caught up with memories, not with each other, and they part." The scene is a ballroom. The atmosphere is heavy with recollection of another era. There a couple are attracted to each other and dance. He kisses her on the shoulder, she recalls the past, the action freezes, there is a blackout, and a girl dancing a reflection of the lady relives her first innocent romance with a young boy. When the young boy kisses her on the shoulder, the past dissolves and the present dance resumes. Now the man is reminded suddenly by a tap on the shoulder of a time spent with three coquettish girls. The action dissolves again into the past and we see his double relive the earlier time (which was the one he loved?). This emerges again into the present at the tap of a shoulder. Other memories converge upon the dance of the couple, there are flashbacks of a girl with an unforgettable perfume, of a man with a white tie. In the end, the lovers part, aware that what attracts them to each other is not themselves so much as pieces of the past. They cannot make for themselves a new memory.

*Dim Lustre* was revived by the New York City Ballet on May 26, 1964, with costumes, scenery, and lighting by Beni Montressor. Patricia McBride and Edward Villella danced the principal roles.

# DIVERTIMENTO NO. 15

*Music by Wolfgang Amadeus Mozart. Choreography by George Balanchine. Costumes by Karinska. Scenery by David Hays. First presented by the New York City Ballet at the American Shakespeare Festival Theatre, Stratford, Connecticut, May 31, 1956, with Tanaquil LeClercq, Diana Adams, Patricia Wilde, Melissa Hayden, Allegra Kent, Nicholas Magallanes, Herbert Bliss, and Roy Tobias in principal roles.*

This ballet is a complete reworking of *Caracole*, a ballet to the same music, Mozart's *Divertimento No. 15 in B flat major* (*K. 287*), that was first presented by the New York City Ballet in 1952. Although *Caracole* had real success when it was first done, we did not dance it for several years and when the dancers and I began to work on a revival in 1956, we found we could remember very little of the original. So many new ballets had intervened that I had to start work all over again! That was not altogether a misfortune, for this score is one I admire most in the world.

Mozart wrote the *Divertimento* when he was twenty-one. He composed many similar works, pieces designed for special social occasions, large garden parties, carnivals, balls. All of these pieces were written to divert and charm audiences that expected to be entertained. Very often people danced to them. This particular divertimento is probably the finest ever written.

The ballet follows the different movements of the score. There is no story. It is designed for five principal girls, three boys, and a *corps de ballet* of eight girls. First movement—Allegro. Second—Andante Grazioso—Theme and Variations. Third—Minuet. Fourth—Andante. Fifth—Allegro Molto—Andante.

The ballet was danced for the first time at the bicentennial celebration of Mozart's birth that Lincoln Kirstein arranged at the American Shakespeare Festival Theatre. It then became a part of the repertory of the New York City Ballet.

# DONIZETTI VARIATIONS

*Music by Gaetano Donizetti. Choreography by George Balanchine. Costumes by Karinska. Lighting by David Hays. First presented by the New York City Ballet at the City Center, New York, November 16, 1960, with Melissa Hayden and Jonathan Watts in the leading roles.*

This is a dance ballet, pure and simple, to some pleasant music by Donizetti. It was originally produced as part of "Salute to Italy," a dance program at the New York City Ballet honoring the one-hundredth anniversary of the formation of the Italian state. The program was planned around works with music by Italian composers, beginning with *Con Amore* (Rossini) and continuing with *Monumentum* (Stravinsky/Gesualdo) and *La Sonnambula* (Bellini). To contrast with the seriousness of these last two, we needed another, cheerful and sunny work. We found just what we wanted in music from a little-performed opera by Donizetti, *Don Sebastian*. The ballet features a central *pas de deux* for a ballerina and her partner—entrée, adagio, two variations and coda, plus variations and ensembles for the corps of six girls and three boys.

## DON JUAN

*Ballet by John Neumeier. Music by Christoph Willibald Gluck and Tomás Luis de Victoria. Choreography and staging by John Neumeier. Decor and costumes by Filippo Sanjust. Text by Max Frisch, translated by John Neumeier. Narrated by Sir Ralph Richardson. First presented in New York by the National Ballet of Canada at the Metropolitan Opera House, Lincoln Center, April 26, 1974, with Rudolf Nureyev in the leading role.*

The romantic hero Don Juan is no stranger to ballet. Gluck's great music, so important for its time, is thought to be the first truly dramatic score for dance, designed to conform to a projected scheme of character, time, place, and situation. The first choreographer for the score was Angiolini (Vienna, 1761). Michel Fokine staged it for René Blum's Ballet Russe in London in 1936, with Anatole Vilzak as the hero and André Eglevsky as the Jester. Sir Frederick Ashton also choreographed a *Don Juan,* but to the score of Richard Strauss. This production, with Robert Helpmann, Margot Fonteyn, and Moira Shearer, was staged by the Sadler's Wells Ballet in London in 1948. Its theme was "The love that caught strange light from Death's own eyes," taken from Gautier's poem *"La Morte Amoureuse,"* and Ashton depicted the hero pursuing many loves but discovering that Death is his true beloved.

John Neumeier's ballet pursues a similar conception in a dramatic narrative accompanied not only by Gluck's music but also by the *Requiem Mass* of Victoria. Like a contemporary film, the ballet cuts back and forth in theme and music in such a way as to suggest motivations and insights the choreographer wishes to bring out, interweaving solemnity and celebration, action and passion, love and death. The context of the narrative is the familiar aftermath of Don Juan's murder of the father of a girl he has seduced.

When the curtain rises we discern behind a scrim a Lady in White. She is watched by a man who stands with his back to us, a mysterious creature in a long black cloak and black hat. It is November 2, the Day of the Dead in the Spanish calendar. A funeral procession passes. Commander Don Gonzalo de Ulloa is being carried to his grave, mourned by his daughter Doña Ana. After the bier has passed, the man in black reveals himself as Don Juan Tenorio, her father's killer. Doña Ana, still beguiled by the Don, is heartbroken as he rebuffs her. The Don proceeds to a banquet, accompanied by his servant and collaborator Catalinon.

In the next scene, a huge ballroom, Catalinon engages a troupe of dancers to present, in a series of *divertissements,* the amorous adventures of his master. Catalinon himself assumes the role of the legendary seducer, Don Juan. The

Don and the ladies of the party watch with amusement as a placard announces the theme of the play, "Don Juan and the Ladies," which is enacted on a small stage at the back of the hall. There the Don is observed in successful pursuit of three girls. Next, in the scene "Don Juan Serenades Doña Ana," we flash-back to his conquest of that lady, whose fierce passion soon exhausts him. When her father enters unexpectedly, sword in hand, a duel ensues. After he has killed her father, Don Juan wipes his sword on Doña Ana's skirt.

Now the Lady in White appears, but only to Don Juan, who reaches out to her. They dance, he fascinated by her blond coolness, in a duet in which she rejects him. She seems to be leading him away in a direction he cannot deter-mine. For the first time, a woman has not succumbed to his charm. Mysteri-ously, she disappears and there is no one in his arms. In one of the moments of silence in the ballet, the hero composes himself. A voice says, "Don Juan is a narcissist who loves only himself . . . He is not a lover, he remains alone . . . Disguising his true self, Don Juan is his role."

Then the music resumes and Catalinon is organizing things again, this time with "A Peasant Wedding," where the rustic lovers dance a *pas de deux*. Watching the dance and eying the peasant girl, Don Juan, to reassure himself after the incident with the Lady in White, determines to seduce her. In the midst of the Don's conquest of the girl, Doña Ana enters and watches. She knows everything that is happening at once but is so in thrall to the Don that it does not seem to matter. The Don amuses himself by playing the two ladies against each other.

As a climax to his satirical presentation, Catalinon and the dancers present "The Damnation of Don Juan," which develops into an orgy involving all the guests.

Don Juan leaves the party, pursuing the Lady in White. He passes a proces-sion of mourners carrying the empty bier. Doña Ana is there, weeping. Gradu-ally he realizes that this is his own funeral cortege. As the Lady in White now beckons to him, he recognizes her as the Angel of Death.

Clive Barnes wrote in the New York *Times* after the New York premiere that "Mr. Nureyev is superb as Don Juan—from the nervous, preening way he pats his hair, to his smiling yet supercilious disdain, to his slightly nervous pride . . . The entire portrayal, morose, disenchanted and just a little foolish, is remarkable.

"The ballet shows the National Ballet of Canada at its very best and the whole performance could not have been bettered."

# DON QUIXOTE

*Ballet in four acts, eight scenes, and a prologue. Music by L. Minkus. Chore-ography by Marius Petipa. First presented by the Bolshoi Theatre, Moscow, December 26, 1869. First presented in the United States by the Bolshoi Ballet at the Metropolitan Opera House, New York, April 21, 1966, with Petipa's choreography revised by Aleksandr Gorsky and Rostislav Zakharov. Scenery and costumes by Vadim Rindin. Maya Plisetskaya appeared as Kitri,*

*Vladimir Tikhonov as* Basil the barber, *Pyotr Khomutuv as* Don Quixote, *and Nikolai Samokhvalov as* Sancho Panza.

Miguel Cervantes's masterpiece *Don Quixote* has a long ballet history. Beginning with a danced version by Noverre in the mid-eighteenth century, the story has attracted dancers and choreographers many times. The two principal versions of Cervantes's novel are described below.

PROLOGUE: DON QUIXOTE'S STUDY Don Quixote's servants, anxious about his growing obsession with ancient chivalry, are seen trying to throw his books away. He enters, reading, and sits at his table. He rejoices in heroic tales of brave knights and beautiful ladies. In a vision, he beholds the lady of his dreams, Dulcinea. Sancho Panza enters, pursued by angry shopkeepers from whom he has stolen a goose. The Don rescues him, appoints him his squire, and sets out on his adventures.

ACT ONE: THE SQUARE IN BARCELONA Basil, a barber, is in love with the innkeeper's daughter, Kitri, but her mother wishes her to marry Gamache, a foppish nobleman. Don Quixote arrives with Sancho. The Don assumes that the inn is a famous castle. Sancho is teased by the townsfolk and tossed in a blanket. Don Quixote rescues him. Don Quixote now sees the beautiful Kitri. He is bewitched and acclaims her as his Dulcinea.

ACT TWO, SCENE ONE: INSIDE THE INN Kitri's mother, still determined to marry her daughter to the nobleman, so distresses Basil that he pretends to stab himself. As he lies dying, he begs Kitri's parents to unite them.

ACT TWO, SCENE TWO: A GYPSY ENCAMPMENT Gypsies and strolling players, alerted to the imminent arrival of Don Quixote and Sancho, prepare to trick the knight. Don Quixote enters and pays homage to their leader as king. The leader then calls for dances to begin. This is followed by a command performance of the puppet theater. Watching the play, Don Quixote mistakes the heroine for Dulcinea, sees her under attack, and rises to assault the puppet stage. Pursuing her further to windmills nearby, he imagines Dulcinea is being concealed. Mistaking the windmills for menacing giants, he tilts at them, only to be caught up in one of the wings and tossed in the air. Sancho revives and comforts him.

ACT THREE, SCENE ONE: A FOREST The Don and Sancho lie down to rest in a wood. But still stunned from his fight with the windmill, the Don is troubled by fantastic dreams where he sees himself a knight in shining armor surrounded by lovely ladies.

ACT FOUR: PROLOGUE Hunting horns proclaim the arrival of the Duke of Barcelona, who has heard about Don Quixote and wishes to see the curious knight himself. He awakens the Don and invites him to accompany a *fiesta*. The Duke then persuades Basil to dress up and pretend to be a Knight Errant to play a trick on Don Quixote.

ACT FIVE: THE MAIN SQUARE OF BARCELONA   It is *fiesta* time. The Duke and the Duchess and the Don watch the dancing. Suddenly the Don thinks that he recognizes his Dulcinea in a girl carried on by mysterious figures guarded by a strange knight. The Knight challenges the Don to a duel and the old man is soon vanquished. His opponent, removing his disguise, reveals himself as Basil the barber. The Don is so crestfallen by this trickery that the Duke and Duchess have pity and comfort him. Kitri and Basil then celebrate their betrothal in a *grand pas de deux*. Don Quixote realizes that he has not yet found his Dulcinea and with Sancho sets off for more adventures.

NOTES   This *Don Quixote* includes the *grand pas de deux* that is often presented independently in various versions on ballet programs. The part of Kitri has been performed over the years by many famous ballerinas, Pavlova and Karsavina among them. Pavlova produced a shortened version of the ballet for her tours. Rudolf Nureyev produced his version of the Petipa ballet for the Vienna State Opera on December 1, 1966, himself appearing as *Basil* with Ully Wuehrer as *Kitri*, Michael Birkmeyer as *Don Quixote*, and Konstantin Zajetz as *Sancho Panza*.

In 1970, Nureyev staged his version of the ballet with the Australian Ballet in a production designed by Barry Kay. This production was first presented in the United States by the Australian Ballet in San Francisco, January 4, 1971. In 1972, Nureyev and Robert Helpmann made a film of this production.

Interviewed by Laura Bell for *Show* magazine in 1971 about certain aspects of his production of *Don Quixote*, Nureyev commented about the duel between the Don and his foppish rival Don Gamache: "The duel is mine but the stabbing is all in the original Petipa, and in the book. There, you may remember, it is even broader. Basilio has a bladder of sheep's blood hidden under his arm and when he stabs it, blood spurts everywhere. I decided this was going a bit far in literalness, and it would be messy. The duel, though, was originally between the knight and the heroine's father, an innkeeper. But I think it proper Don Quixote should fight his own kind, not a commoner, so I have him fight Don Gamache, who, in the bargain, is wearing the proper white gauntlets to throw down. I try all through to keep the six main characters together, playing off each other, as in *commedia dell'arte*—you can even match up characters. Quixote is Pantalon, Kitri is Columbine; Basilio, Pierrot, and so on. I wanted the story not to be about Don Quixote but about how people react to him, how they take advantage of him and devise ways to mock and laugh at him. Yet they go crazy doing this, they are as fanatic as the knight is.

"And Don Quixote himself . . . At first, I hated him quite a lot. I didn't understand for a long time. I was on the side of the people. To me he was just a clown. And then I read the book! There is so much there, but in a ballet you can only skim the surface. I tried to put in a lot of things I felt about the book, like impressions of the Callot lithographs, but you daren't put too much comment in. It really is largely a lot of dances and great zest and comic spirit . . . and yet, everybody seems to think of this ballet as kind of foolish.

"I can't take any credit for these productions which I do only to provide another vehicle for myself and to preserve what is left of Petipa. With *Don Qui-*

*xote* I wanted a comic part and since no choreographer has ever offered me one, I did this. With original choreography you have to sit down and think and spend a lot of time. I do *not* like improvisations. If you want to create a ballet, you have to have a certain point of view, something you want to say, not just steps or variations that just 'come' to you. And even with *Raymonda* and *Don Quixote,* they took a lot of working out and research. Perhaps in time . . ."

A film of Nureyev's production of *Don Quixote* was made in Australia in 1972 with the Australian Ballet. Codirected by Nureyev and Sir Robert Helpmann, the film starred Lucette Aldous as Kitri-Dulcinea and Nureyev as Basilio. It was first presented in the United States, November 1, 1973, at a Gala Benefit for the Dance Collection of the New York Public Library.

*Ballet in three acts. Music by Nicolas Nabokov. Choreography by George Balanchine. Scenery, costumes, and lighting by Esteban Francés. Assistant to Mr. Francés: Peter Harvey. Costumes executed by Karinska. First presented by the New York City Ballet at the New York State Theatre, May 27, 1965, with George Balanchine as* Don Quixote, *Suzanne Farrell as* Dulcinea, *Deni Lamont as* Sancho Panza, *and the entire company.*

I first read Cervantes in Russian, but I have read parts of *Don Quixote* many times since, in English and French as well. The idea of doing a ballet about the Don has always seemed to me natural and inevitable, something I would want to do whenever time and opportunity came. Other ballets to *Don Quixote* I had perhaps seen but scarcely remembered. The Petipa ballet, with music by Minkus, was in the repertory of the Maryinsky when I was a boy (I danced in this production in 1916, when I was twelve), but it was not a serious work and not one of my favorites. Twenty years ago I discovered that my friend the composer Nicolas Nabokov had a similar enthusiasm for *Don Quixote.* He had written an orchestral suite on the Don and Dulcinea which I liked. We then spoke of doing a full-scale ballet on the subject one day, but it was some years before this came about. We began to work out a scenario in detail. We did several scenarios, in fact, arriving at a final one in June 1964. Throughout the composition of the score we were in frequent communication and saw each other as often as possible to discuss the music and the action. As a musician with a deep knowledge of ballet, Nabokov knew what he was getting into. Three-act ballets are difficult compositions. Nabokov's score has everything, it *has* to have everything to do its job properly, for music written to accompany a danced narrative with *divertissements* cannot preserve the unities designed for the concert hall. Nabokov worked within three traditions, the musical one, the ballet tradition, and the dramatic. His score in essence amounts to symphonic dance variations.

The action of the ballet follows closely the scenario Nabokov and I worked out together.

The form the novel took for us naturally does not follow the sequence of the book, but I must say we never had any difficulty in our ideas. The problem was always what we had to cut and put aside. Don Quixote's anguished search for human perfectibility, the intricate shifts from fantasy to reality that take place in his mind, are vividly expressed through his adventures and the dream of the Lady Dulcinea, who appears in many guises to him. Guises these always are—the Magdalen, the Virgin Mary, the Shepherdess Marcela, the Lady of the Silver Moon—and although he gives his whole life for her, he never really sees her. He is, if you like, a kind of secular saint whom no one believes in. Finally, his death brings him face to face with himself, seemingly defeated, but having lived as he believed.

PROLOGUE: DON QUIXOTE'S STUDY    Don Quixote sits alone and reads his books about chivalry. He searches through them for the answers to his dreams of knight errantry. He falls off to sleep. A mist covers the stage and strange figures from his dream take over the scene: a girl seems to materialize right out of the pages of a book; a dragon appears. The Don rescues the girl. He rests. A young girl, a maidservant, enters and washes his feet, drying them with her hair. He kisses her forehead and she leaves and Don Quixote rises.

Sancho Panza enters carrying the Don's clothes, does a pratfall but quickly rises to dress his master. The Don, with sword held high, follows the girl toward the brilliant sun she has let into the room. This is the only sun he will see. As Cervantes said, "Misfortunes always pursue men of talent." Don Quixote's study is now transformed, becoming:

ACT ONE, SCENE ONE: LA MANCHA    Don Quixote stands alone surrounded by earth and sky. Windmills in the distance. In the piercing light of midday there appears to him a vision of the Madonna, a girl with a resplendent headdress standing on a cart much as if a statue of the Virgin being carried in a village procession has suddenly come to life. It is the servant girl of the Prologue. He kneels before the vision, takes the oath of a knight, and receives the Madonna's blessing.

Don Quixote encounters a child being beaten by a man. He challenges the man and chases him off. The rescued child runs away, mocking the Don. Next he comes upon a group of prisoners being led in chains. He attacks the jailers and frees the men, who thereupon set upon the Don and Sancho and give them a good trouncing.

ACT ONE, SCENE TWO: A VILLAGE SQUARE    There are folk dances in front of an inn. Sancho runs out, pursued by guards and fishwives from whom he has stolen a huge fish. He is caught, beaten up, and tossed in a blanket. Don Quixote appears on his horse, dismounts and liberates Sancho. Sancho kneels at his feet, weeping. The Innkeeper brings food and the Don comforts Sancho. A cortege enters. A poet is being mourned. A beautiful country girl, Marcela, is seized and accused of causing his death. We see that she is the same girl as in the first scenes, dressed now as a shepherdess with a long crook. She is grateful to the Don and dances. In Cervantes, she explains that she is not to be blamed for the poet's death: "If every beauty inspired love and won hearts, men's fancy would become vague and bewildered and not know where to stop, for as beauty is infinite, desire must likewise be infinite. If this is so, as I believe it to be, why do you ask me to surrender my will under pressure for no other reason than that you say you love me? For beauty in a modest woman is like distant fire or a sharp sword; the one does not burn, the other does not cut the man who does not go near it. Now if modesty is one of the virtues and the fairest ornament of the body and the soul, why must the woman who is loved for her beauty lose it to gratify the desires of a man who, for his pleasure alone, tries with all his strength and ingenuity to rob her of it? I was born free, and to live free I chose the solitude of the fields. The trees of those mountains are my companions; with the trees and the brooks I share my thoughts and my beauty. I am the hidden fire and the distant sword . . ."

Now a puppeteer comes into the courtyard with his cart and arranges his puppet show. In the midst of the show Don Quixote becomes indignant about what he sees. Here again is the tiny blond heroine who emerged from his books. To him, she is Dulcinea and when he sees her being persecuted by Saracens, he charges the puppet show with his sword. The puppet theater falls down on his head. Just then, to solemn music, heralds announce the arrival of the Duke and Duchess of the region. The Duchess observes the wreckage of the theater and orders it cleared out. She congratulates the Don on his victorious adventure with the puppet. Supported by Sancho, Don Quixote kneels before her. Recognizing him from Cervantes's book, the Duchess gives him wine and invites him to come to the castle. He is lifted onto his horse, Sancho mounts the donkey, and the villagers wave them farewell.

ACT TWO: THE PALACE    The curtain rises on the sumptuous ballroom of the Duke's palace. Don Quixote enters with the Duchess, who places him to her right as she sits on the throne. He stands by her side like a true gentleman. Courtiers enter and as they bow to the royal couple, they also pay mocking deference to Don Quixote, sensing the joke the Duchess is playing on the knight. The courtiers and their ladies now dance a stylized courtly ballet: first, a sarabande by the entire assembly, then a series of danced *divertissements: a danza della Cacia*, a *pas de deux Mauresque*, a *Courante Sicilienne*, a *Rigaudon Flamenco*, and a *ritournel*. Now eight masked men enter. The Duchess whispers to the Duke. All salute as Don Quixote escorts the Duchess down to the dance floor to dance a *pavane*. The court has decided to end the charade they have been playing with the Don. Sancho senses this and tries to take the Don away, but the courtiers close in on them. They are blindfolded, tickled by ladies' fans, pricked by swords. A wooden horse is brought in, they are placed on it, fireworks are set off in its tail and at the explosion Don Quixote and Sancho fall to the ground, where they are beaten. There then appears to Don Quixote a vision of Dulcinea. The whole court freezes like waxworks. She gestures to him, seems to be calling to him to renew his adventures. He lays his sword at her feet and kneels before her. Dulcinea helps him up and just as Don Quixote is about to follow her, a masked lady approaches and beards him with whipped cream, a final mockery. He ignores her scorn and in a trance stumbles after Dulcinea to start again on his quest.

ACT THREE, SCENE ONE: A GARDEN OF THE PALACE    The Don and Sancho enter. They lie down to rest under an old oak tree. He sleeps and begins to dream. Masked courtiers arrive and cover him with a fishing net. Dulcinea appears. In his dream he sees a ballet in the Elysian fields. In the midst of the dancing is the Lady of the Silver Moon in whom is embodied "all the impossible and chimerical attributes of beauty which poets give to their ladies." There follows a classical *pas d'action*, consisting of a set of four variations, a *pas de deux* and a coda. Dulcinea is challenged by a girl in black, the Night Spirit, reminiscent of the Duchess, and tormented by the magician Merlin. She goes to Don Quixote, and he rouses himself to help her. As he does so, dragging the net behind him, the magic landscape of his dream vanishes. He is alone on an empty field with mills turning their big wheels in the wind and seeming to move ominously toward him and Dulcinea.

ACT THREE, SCENE TWO    A huge giant bears down on Don Quixote as high as a windmill. The Don attacks him but his long lance is caught in a sail of the windmill and he is tossed high into the air and falls back to earth. Sancho runs to him and binds his head. Strange creatures cross the stage; like pigs they swarm all over the place. Now four courtiers of the Duchess disguised in masks bring in a wooden cage. Don Quixote crawls into it like a wounded dog. Weeping, Sancho follows, holding his master's sword.

ACT THREE, SCENE THREE: DON QUIXOTE'S STUDY    To a *pavane funèbre* the Don is carried to his home. He is taken from the cage and undressed for bed. He asks for the last rites of the Church. In his delirium he sees a procession of Bishops, Cardinals, monks, earls, and dukes, all hooded figures, march in to a Gloria. His books are burned by these Inquisitors. Then, in another vision, he sees again the vision with which his adventures began, the Madonna of the cart, the lovely blond girl with a halo. He reaches out to her yearningly, rises high in his bed as if by a miracle, she looks at him, then vanishes. The hooded figures are grouped around his bed as in the painting of the burial of the Count d'Orgaz by El Greco. But in a changing light, they are changed into the simple people of his village, the serving girl, the priest, Sancho. He recognizes them, blesses them, and dies quietly as the first lights of dawn come through the open window. The servant girl makes a cross of two sticks, places it on his body, and kneels to weep at his side. ". . . If he like a madman lived, at least he like a wise man died," said Cervantes.

NOTES    My interest in *Don Quixote* has always been in the hero's finding an ideal, something to live for and sacrifice for and serve. Every man has a Don Quixote in him. Every man wants an inspiration. For the Don it was Dulcinea, a woman he sought in many guises. I myself think that the same is true in life, that everything a man does he does for his ideal woman. You live only one life and you believe in something and I believe in that.

For criticism of this ballet, readers may wish to consult "The Story of 'Don Quixote'" by Elena Bivona in *Ballet Review*, Vol. 2, No. 2; and Andrew Porter's review of the 1973 performances of the ballet in *The New Yorker*, reprinted in his book *A Musical Season*.

The composer Nicolas Nabokov contributed to the January 1973 edition of the New York City Ballet program *Playbill* an entertaining and informative essay about his career and our collaboration on this ballet. His autobiography *Bagazh*, like his earlier book of recollections, *Old Friends and New Music*, is a fascinating account of his remarkable career.

## DOUGLA

*Music by Geoffrey Holder, arranged by Tania Leon. Choreography by Geoffrey Holder. Scenery and costumes by Geoffrey Holder. First presented by the Dance Theatre of Harlem at the ANTA Theatre, New York, April 20, 1974.*

*Dougla* is a colorful, exotic dance ballet about an Asian and African marriage— a mix of Hindu and African ritual set to drumming music. The theme is: "Where Twains meet, where Hindu and African tangle, their offspring are called Dougla."

There are five parts to the ballet: "Dougla People," "Woman in Green," "Pas de Deux," "Women in Black," and "Acrobats," with the full company again on stage for a "Dougla People" finale.

When the Dance Theatre of Harlem conquered London in their first appearances there in 1974, the critic Peter Williams wrote in *Dance and Dancers* magazine: "What was shown during the season was quite enough to prove Arthur Mitchell's point which is that black dancers *can* take their rightful place in all areas of dance; it also proved what an incredible feat it was to have achieved all this in five years."

## THE DREAM

*Ballet in one act. Music by Felix Mendelssohn, arranged by John Lanchbery. Choreography by Frederick Ashton. Scenery by Henry Bardon. Costumes by David Walker. Lighting by William Bundy. First presented by the Royal Ballet at the Royal Opera House, Covent Garden, April 2, 1964, with Antoinette Sibley as Titania, Anthony Dowell as Oberon, Keith Martin as Puck, Alexander Grant as Bottom, Carole Needham as Helena, Vergie Derman as Hermia, David Drew as Demetrius, Derek Rencher as Lysander, and Alan Bauch as the Changeling Indian Boy. First presented in the United States by the Royal Ballet at the Metropolitan Opera House, New York, April 30, 1965, with the same cast, with Rennie Dilena as the Changeling Indian Boy.\**

Frederick Ashton arranged his ballet to *A Midsummer Night's Dream* for the Royal Ballet's observance of the four-hundredth anniversary of Shakespeare's

\* See also A MIDSUMMER NIGHT'S DREAM.

birth. Based on Shakespeare's play, using Mendelssohn's music, the ballet tells the magical story of the quarrel between the King and Queen of Fairyland and its outcome.

The King and Queen, Oberon and Titania, quarrel over the Changeling Indian Boy. Whom shall he belong to? Oberon sends his sprite Puck through the forest to pluck a strange flower, the juice of which when dropped in the eyes during sleep brings love for the first living thing seen on waking. Oberon plans to use this drug to spite Titania. Into the forest meanwhile have strayed a happy pair of lovers, Lysander and Hermia, and their unhappy friends Helena and Demetrius. Helena's desire for Demetrius is unrequited, for he mistakenly desires Hermia. Oberon has watched these mortals, and when Puck returns with the magic flower he sends him with the potion to charm Demetrius into love with Helena.

Now Oberon drops some of the charm into his Queen's eyes and causes her to be awakened by a rustic called Bottom on whom the returning Puck, to heighten his master's revenge, has fixed an ass's head. On waking, Titania at once falls in love with Bottom the Ass, but Puck, for all his cleverness, has complicated the affairs of the other, mortal lovers by charming the wrong man, Lysander, into love with Helena. Oberon commands Puck to create a fog, under cover of which all that is awry is magically put right. Titania, released from her spell, is reconciled to her master and the mortal lovers are happily paired off. Bottom, restored to human form but with dreamlike memories of what lately happened to him, goes on his puzzled way.

NOTES    *The Dream* was staged by John Hart for the City Center Joffrey Ballet in 1973. The first performance, at the Wolf Trap Performing Arts Center in Virginia, near Washington, D.C., August 9, featured Rebecca Wright, Burton Taylor, Russell Sultzbach, Larry Grenier, Alaine Haubert, Charthel Arthur, Robert Talmage, Robert Thomas, Richard Coleman, Robert Estner, Phillip Hoffman, Jeffrey Hughes, Ted Nelson, Donna Cowen, Denise Jackson, Eileen Brady, Diane Orio, and Vinod Sahl. Writing of this production after its first New York performance (October 9, 1973), Clive Barnes said in the New York *Times:* "Ever since Ashton created *The Dream* for Britain's Royal Ballet nearly ten years ago, it has been one of that company's special treasures. This new production, authoritatively staged by John Hart, is a charmer, full of the original's mixture of Shakespeare, poetry, Mendelssohn, moonshine and fun. It is an extraordinarily English ballet, but the New York dancers have adopted it for their own.

"The costumes, fanciful and glamorous, are the same as David Walker designed for the original production, but Mr. Walker has devised a completely new setting to replace the earlier scenery by Henry Bardon. The setting, a sylvan glade, looks appropriately Victorian, but does not have the full romantic exuberance of the Royal Ballet's first staging. Yet what is more important is the style of the dancing, and here the Joffrey company does splendidly.

"Rebecca Wright made a Titania of glistening eyes and the most entrancing delicate footwork. It was a performance of gossamer and thistledown. As Oberon, Burton Taylor—making his welcome return to the stage after nearly two years off through injury—danced cleanly and forcefully. His presence was admirable, his partnering secure and his elegance always completely natural."

## DRUMS, DREAMS AND BANJOS

*Music by Stephen Foster; variations and orchestrations by Peter Link. Choreography by Gerald Arpino. Set by Rouben Ter-Arutunian. Costumes by Stanley Simmons. Lighting by Thomas Skelton. Vocalist: Charles Leighton. First presented by the City Center Joffrey Ballet at the City Center, New York, October 9, 1975, with a cast headed by Charthel Arthur and Dermot Burke. Conductor: Seymour Lipkin.*

"He set a nation singing," wrote Harold Vincent Milligan in his biography of Stephen Foster; *Drums, Dreams and Banjos* is the Joffrey Ballet's bicentennial tribute. In 1951, President Truman issued a proclamation designating January 13, 1952, and each succeeding January 13 throughout the years as Stephen Foster Memorial Day, calling upon all to observe that occasion with appropriate ceremonies, pilgrimages to the shrines of this beloved composer, and musical programs featuring his compositions. Gerald Arpino's ballet celebrates the Stephen Foster achievement, expressing in both dance and music the sentiment as well as the energy and ebullience of his work.

A Joint Resolution of the House of Representatives some years ago referred to Foster and his work as "a national expression of democracy through his clear and simple embodiment of American tradition" and called him the "father of American folk music and the true interpreter of the fundamental spirit of music."

Recalling as it does the charms of an earlier America, Foster's music has extraordinary appeal. Born in Pittsburgh on the fiftieth anniversary of the Declaration of Independence, Foster lived to hear his music flourish throughout the land. His infectious songs, introduced by such groups as the Christy Minstrels, quickly became a part of our heritage. They were sung by pioneers on the long trek westward, hummed by harvesters in the fields and by workers laying the first railroad lines. The forty-niners whistled "Oh! Susanna" while prospecting for gold in California; his songs were favorites of soldiers on both sides during the Civil War.

Besides his own large body of work, Foster arranged the songs of some of the great European contemporaries—Bellini, Donizetti, Strauss—for inclusion in his anthology *The Social Orchestra*. One of the aims of that successful volume was to "improve the taste of the community for social music."

The Stephen Foster songs that are danced to in the ballet are "Angelina Baker," "Old Folks at Home," "Oh! Boys Carry Me 'Long," "Nelly Bly," "Farewell My Lilly Dear," "Plantation Jig," "Open Thy Lattice, Love," "Anadolia," "Some Folks," "I Will Be True to Thee," "Ah, May the Red Rose Live Alway," "Eulalie," "Oh! Susanna," "Camptown Races," "Jeannie with the Light Brown Hair," "Old Black Joe," "Ring de Banjo," "My Old Kentucky Home," "Beautiful Dreamer," "Soiree Polka," and "Tioga Waltz." Taken from

*The Social Orchestra* are "Oh! Summer Night" by Donizetti and a waltz by Strauss.

The dance and dramatic action of the stage panorama to the vivid score that was arranged to this memorable music reminds us not only of the familiar tunes but the times they were created in and the times they have lived through. As such, it reminds us of years of war as well as peace, years that Foster has made memorable.

## THE DUEL (Le Combat)

*Ballet in one act. Music by Raffaello de Banfield. Choreography by William Dollar. Costumes by Robert Stevenson. Lighting by Jean Rosenthal. First presented by the New York City Ballet Company at the City Center, New York, February 24, 1950, with Melissa Hayden and William Dollar, Val Buttignol, Walter Georgov, Shaun O'Brien. This ballet is an extensive revision of the same choreographer's* Le Combat, *which was performed for the first time in the United States by Les Ballets de Paris at the Winter Garden, New York, October 6, 1949.*

This short, dramatic ballet tells the story of the brave Christian warrior Tancred and the pagan girl Clorinda: how they meet, fall in love, separate, and meet again for a final, fatal encounter. A low beating of the drum and subdued fanfares—heard as if from some distant battlefield—introduce the warlike rhythms that dominate the ballet.

The curtain rises on a scene that might represent any barren field. Rocks are clustered on the left, there are no trees, and a bright sky exposes the wasteland. Four Crusaders stand poised for action against any intruder. All are armored and wear high-plumed helmets with visors that conceal their faces. One of them, the warrior in red, is the leader, Tancred. They begin to dance, holding out their arms to control invisible reins, jumping and turning, practicing their skills in battle. They are all obedient to Tancred's command.

A strange warrior enters and approaches. The four Crusaders stand in line, ready to attack. The stranger is dressed in black. This is Clorinda, the beautiful Saracen. From her golden helmet streams a green scarf lined with red. Her movements are direct and unafraid; she is not in the least terrified of the enemy. She comes nearer to the group. The men stand motionless until finally the daring Clorinda challenges one of the Crusaders. He moves out of line and engages her in battle; the other men observe their code of honor by refusing to assist him. The two warriors rush each other swiftly, jumping high as they pass back and forth. Clorinda gains the upper hand and wounds her opponent mortally; and he falls over on his face. She dances around his body on firm points, her head held high. During the duel, her helmet had fallen off, and the long black hair that hangs down to her shoulders accentuates her proud beauty. Tancred walks toward her, obviously moved both by her bravery and her loveliness. He takes off his helmet and bows in tribute. Clorinda does not respond. She leaves the scene. Blackout.

Tancred enters alone. He dances, to reveal his superior strength and agility as a prince of warriors, and exits. Clorinda follows him. Now she is dressed in full battle array, with a visored helmet topped with a black plume. She leaps around the stage lightly, glorying in her own adroitness. Suddenly she stops; she senses danger. Two Christian warriors appear before her. She leaps into the air as they rush by closely, trying to enclose her. The drum beats in staccato rhythm. Clorinda does not hesitate in her attack, and soon the Crusaders weary of their effort to maneuver her into a dangerous position. She drives them off.

Clorinda relaxes for a moment and briefly shows herself to be a beautiful and pathetic girl, exhausted by the strenuousness of war. She holds her hand up beseechingly and opens her arms wide, as if she were praying for relief from the life she has chosen. She holds her head in her hands despairingly for an instant, but then she is alert again, listening for anyone who might be watching her. She crosses the stage slowly in an arrogant posture. A drum beats, loudly and suddenly. Clorinda leaps off.

Tancred enters, seeking out the enemy. He follows Clorinda. She reenters the field, the Crusader close behind. Neither recognizes the other. They begin to fight, standing close together at first, then separating to each side of the stage, then approaching each other warily. Tancred supports Clorinda and turns her as she assumes first a tight, aggressive pose, then an open arabesque. Now the duel becomes earnest as the two adversaries dodge and jump aside from their strong thrusts. Clorinda wounds Tancred, but this only encourages the Crusader. He stabs the girl as they engage in close contest. She falters in pain. They separate, preparing for the finish. They approach slowly. The girl falls. Tancred stands back. She pulls off her helmet. He sees her face; his own face is shocked with recognition. He holds out his hands helplessly, then takes off his own helmet and goes to her. He lifts her to him, and in her agony and love Clorinda's body curls in his arms. Tancred stands and pulls Clorinda up. She leans against him, her head on his shoulder, and he turns her in arabesque. Her movements are now automatic. She seems not to have the strength to move at all, and yet she wishes to reassure Tancred of her own love. But she is tired. He carries her in his arms; her body stiffens, her legs beat in a final spasm, and she is dead. Tancred places her body on the ground softly and stands over her. As he grieves, he remembers the long battle he has just begun. He picks her up and carries her off.

# DUMBARTON OAKS (A Little Musical)

*Music by Igor Stravinsky. Choreography by Jerome Robbins. Costumes by Patricia Zipprodt. Lighting by Ronald Bates. First presented by the New York City Ballet at the New York State Theatre, Lincoln Center, June 23, 1972, with Allegra Kent and Anthony Blum in the leading roles.*

Dumbarton Oaks is the name of a nice old house in Washington, D.C., with magnificent gardens. Actually, all the house is not old, only a bit of it, but there have been important additions (the place houses a superb museum of pre-Columbian sculpture, a center for Byzantine studies, and a great library). Mr. and Mrs. Robert Woods Bliss, who bought this property and endowed it, were wonderful patrons of the arts for Washington and for the nation. In 1937 they commissioned Stravinsky to write a piece for their thirtieth wedding anniversary. The first performance was led by Nadia Boulanger at Dumbarton Oaks, May 8, 1938, and Stravinsky's *Concerto in E Flat* for chamber orchestra has been named for the place ever since.

The score is in three movements. The instruments of the chamber orchestra are treated as solo instruments and there is much variety in what Eric Walter White calls a work that "is gay and exhilarating in its effect."

The ballet is a dance to this music, with a theme. The theme is a recollection of time past, perhaps the 1920s, when a house like Dumbarton Oaks enjoyed a new lease on its lively history. The setting is wicker chairs, garden trellises with Japanese lanterns, and a tennis court in the background.

The piece begins with an ensemble of six couples, boys and girls in various combinations, who wear typical sporting dress of the 1920s (headbands for the girls, etc.). As they leave, a couple keen on tennis come into the picture. They put aside their tennis rackets and dance a vivacious *pas de deux*, syncopated and responsive to the music of the score's *Allegretto*. What starts out to be, at one point, sentimental, in the love duet returns to the flirtatious. From a recumbent posture, the girl picks up her tennis racket again and, as if a match were ended, shakes hands with her partner. Serious though it has seemed to be, the game is still the thing.

In the last movement, marked by Stravinsky *Con moto,* six boys tap-dance to a march with six girls. The lead boy then rushes in, finds the lead girl, and together they and the ensemble conclude a brisk finale to a *Fugato* climax.

NOTES   It is of interest that during the composition of this work, Stravinsky studied and played Bach regularly. He was greatly attracted, he writes in *Themes and Episodes,* to the Brandenburg Concertos, especially the third, "which I have also conducted. The first theme of my concerto is, of course, very much like Bach's in that work, and so is my instrumentation—the three violins and three violas, both frequently *divisi a tre,* though not chordally as in Bach. I do not think, however, that Bach would have begrudged me the loan of these ideas and materials, as borrowing in this way was something he liked to do himself."

The original costumes for this work were abandoned soon after its first performances during the New York City Ballet's Stravinsky Festival. It has been performed since in practice clothes.

Reviewing the ballet's entry into the regular repertory of the New York City Ballet, February 9, 1973, Clive Barnes wrote in the New York *Times:*

"On Friday night the New York City Ballet at the New York State Theatre gave everyone a surprise. A small surprise, but a surprise. It was the first repertory performance of Jerome Robbins's ballet *Dumbarton Oaks.* When this was originally given last summer at the Stravinsky Festival, it had an anyone-for-tennis setting. Now the work has been transposed to the ballet studio. Tennis rackets are out, and toe shoes are in.

"This strong but lighthearted work has taken the transposition well. The setting, which had a definite air of improvisation to it, could be improved and should be, for this is a most agreeable work. There is a playful flirtatiousness to the choreography, which is perfectly apt for this breezy, jazz-tinctured score. The ballet was fluently danced by a cast led by Allegra Kent and, dancing the role for the first time, Jean-Pierre Bonnefous."

## DUO CONCERTANTE

*Music by Igor Stravinsky. Choreography by George Balanchine. First presented by the New York City Ballet at the Stravinsky Festival, 1972, at the New York State Theatre, Lincoln Center, June 22, 1972, with Kay Mazzo and Peter Martins as the dancers, Lamar Alsop and Gordon Boelzner as the musicians. Lighting by Ronald Bates.*

This work for violin and piano was composed by Stravinsky in the early thirties. It is a short piece in five movements and a marvelously lyrical one in several of its parts. It is not surprising that the composition of the *Duo Concertante* was associated in Stravinsky's mind with a book on the classical poet Petrarch by his friend Cingria, which appeared about the time he was writing this music. Stravinsky in one of his recollections quotes this passage from Cingria: "Lyricism cannot exist without rules, and it is essential that they should be strict. Otherwise there is only a faculty for lyricism, and that exists everywhere. What does not exist everywhere is lyrical expression and composition. To achieve that, a craftsman's skill is necessary and that must be learned."

This is exactly a thought I have tried so unsuccessfully to say myself on a number of occasions and it is wonderful to find it so finely expressed in connection with a composition I so much admire.

I am trying to recall the first time I heard the *Duo Concertante*. It was, I think, in France in a performance by Samuel Dushkin, the violinist, and the composer himself, both of whom in the early thirties toured Europe performing Stravinsky's music. It has always been a favorite of mine and when we were planning the Stravinsky Festival at the New York City Ballet, I decided to make a ballet to the music.

The less I say about the ballet, the more I think you may enjoy watching it. It is nothing very unusual, only two dancers, a girl and a boy, standing on stage next to a piano, where the two musicians begin to play. The dancers listen intently; we listen to them. The music for piano and violin is questioning at first, then declarative, open; it then tightens in rhythm and assertiveness of melody. Before we know it, the dancers are moving to the music. Sometimes they stop to listen. The second movement, Ecloque I, begins with a jocular tune and develops into a brisk dialogue between the two instruments. In Ecloque II, the violin takes the lead and in a slowly paced cadenza sings an idyll. For the fourth movement, there is a vigorous and lively Gigue. The stage darkens for the finale, the Dithyramb. Eric Walter White calls this a "noble rhapsody . . . a movement of grave beauty. The high-pitched violin part leads the piano into an increasingly elaborate passage. . . . The effect is that of an exalted threnody." The stage darkens for this music, one spotlight shining on the two musicians, another on the two dancers. The lights close down about the artists as the music ends.

A girl and a boy, a piano and violin. Perhaps, as Lincoln Kirstein says, that is what ballet is all about.

NOTES  Reviewing this ballet in *The Nation*, Nancy Goldner wrote: "*Duo Concertante*, for piano and violin, is one of the most beautiful duets Balanchine has ever done. As a metaphor on the idea that the festival celebrates music, Mazzo and Martins listen to the musicians, who are on the stage, almost as much as they dance. Watching them listen is a theatrical experience in itself. Their faces speak a multitude of unknown thoughts, but the intensity and sweet concentration with which they listen suggest that the notes are running through their bodies. Finally, they are moved to dance. At first they stick closely to the music's beat, almost 'conducting' it with arms and legs; torsos are still.

"Becoming more free, the dance turns into a melting duet, each phrase winding down on slightly bent knees, as in a whisper. They dance with seeming spontaneity. Even when Balanchine arranges an unusual means of partnering—as when Martins scoops her from the floor holding only the underside of her thigh—the movement spins off them with utter simplicity and naturalness. In other sections, they occasionally stop dancing to listen. At those times, Martins firmly takes hold of her hand or slips his arm around her waist. She is shy, but the music pleases her and so does he. She does not move away. They listen in repose, arm in arm. In the last part, the stage darkens except for a white spotlight. She places her arm in the light and raises it above her head. No longer is it her arm; it exists independently, like a segment of a statue. He kisses the back of her hand, a supplicant at the throne of beauty. She is now a goddess-ballerina; he, her servant. She steps out of the light. He steps into it. Not finding her, he leaves. She returns. He kisses her hand again. The jump from intimate hand-holding to ceremonial hand-kissing is theatrically daring. It is also inevitable, and those who cannot accept the leap or the brazen display of sentiment cannot ultimately accept one of the underlying themes of Balanchine's work. In his most noble ballets, he elevates the dancer into an image of love, a Muse-ballerina who inspires but is unreachable. And so this ending is an apotheosis of Balanchine's art."

# DYBBUK VARIATIONS

*Music by Leonard Bernstein. Choreography by Jerome Robbins. Scenery by Rouben Ter-Arutunian. Costumes by Patricia Zipprodt. Lighting by Jennifer Tipton. First presented by the New York City Ballet at the New York State*

*Theatre, Lincoln Center, May 15, 1974, with Patricia McBride and Helgi*
*Tomasson as the principals and a cast headed by Bart Cook, Victor Castelli,*
*Tracy Bennett, Hermes Conde, Daniel Duell, Stephen Caras, Nolan T'Sani,*
*Peter Naumann, Muriel Aasen, and Stephanie Saland. Conducted by Leon-*
*ard Bernstein. Baritone: David Johnson. Bass: John Ostendorf.*

The composer Leonard Bernstein and the choreographer Jerome Robbins first
conceived of the idea of a ballet to the dybbuk theme in 1944, at the time of
their first brilliant collaboration, *Fancy-Free*. A dybbuk, in Central-European
Jewish folklore, is a dead but restless spirit that enters and persists in the body
of a living person. The possessed body acts and speaks with the voice and behavior of the dead one. The most famous treatment of the theme is the play by
S. Ansky, *The Dybbuk*, renowned in its original Yiddish version and through
many subsequent international productions, among them the Habimah presentation in New York in the 1940s. The restless spirit dominates the action.

Jerome Robbins has said that the ballet is not a retelling of Ansky's play,
"but uses it only as a point of departure for a series of related dances concern-
ing rituals and hallucinations which are present in the dark magico-religious
ambience of the play and in the obsessions of its characters."

An understanding of the play is useful background to the ballet. It tells the
story: In friendship, two young men pledge that their children will wed each
other, should one have a son and the other a daughter. The friends part and
go out into the world, where each marries and has a child, boy and girl, as
hoped for. Chanon and Leah meet when grown and, unaware of their parents'
commitment, fall in love. But because Leah is from a wealthy family and
Chanon is a poor but devoutly orthodox theological student, their love is un-
declared. Chanon is also regarded as a wanderer and seeker of truths that are
perhaps best always hidden.

Leah's father arranges a suitable match for her; Chanon desperately turns to
the Kabbala, book of mystic wisdom and dark magic. (This text, developed by
rabbis from about the seventh to the eighteenth centuries, was based on a
mystical technique of interpreting Scripture; by this method the initiated were
empowered to foretell the future and penetrate sacred mysteries.) He seeks in
the Kabbala for a way in which to win Leah for himself. As a last resort, he invokes the powerful but dangerous other-worldly formulae of ancient usage. At
the supreme moment of discovering the secret words that unleash the dark
forces, he is overwhelmed by the enormity of it, faints and dies.

At Leah's wedding, Chanon returns to her as a dybbuk and, claiming her as
his rightful bride, clings to his beloved. Finally, through prescriptive counterrit-
uals instituted by elders of the religious community, Chanon is placed under formal ecclesiastical curse and the dybbuk is expelled. Leah, unable to survive
without her predestined bridegroom, dies to join him.

Throughout the Ansky play, a supernatural being called "The Messenger"
is an omniscient and prophetic witness to each evolving phase of the drama.

The action of the ballet is divided into eleven parts: 1) IN THE HOLY PLACE:
Variations for Seven Men; 2) THE PLEDGE: Male duet; two couples; three couples; 3) ANGELIC MESSENGERS: Variations for three men; 4) THE DREAM: *Pas de*

*deux;* 5) INVOCATION OF THE KABBALA: the quest for secret powers; VARIATIONS:
a. Solo with six men; b.c.d.e. Soli; f. Solo with six men; 6) PASSAGE; 7)
MAIDEN'S DANCE; 8) TRANSITION; 9) POSSESSION: *Pas de deux:* allegro, adagio;
10) EXORCISM: Entire cast; 11) REPRISE AND CODA.

NOTES   Talking with *The New Yorker* about the ballet shortly before its
première, the composer, Leonard Bernstein, described how he and Jerome
Robbins had approached the dybbuk legend. "Ansky's story is a kind of ghetto
version of *The Ring of the Nibelung.* Greed versus love. A compact that is broken. Two young men pledge that their children will marry, but one of them
eventually disregards the oath because he wants a wealthy husband for his
daughter, Leah. Chanon, the son of the other man, becomes a wandering
scholar, a very *farbrente* Talmudist, and a Cabalist. He comes to this little
town, sees Leah, and, even though he doesn't know about the pledge, falls in
love and desperately tries to find Cabalistic ways of winning her. In (one)
dance . . . Chanon calls on the dark powers to help him, and at the moment
of revelation he dies, because no human vessel can contain that much fire and
knowledge and survive. His soul becomes a dybbuk and finds its resting place
in the body of his beloved. And when the rabbi exorcises the dybbuk from her
body, Leah joins him in oblivion.
   ". . . You have to remember that this is a story about ghetto people who
have nowhere to go, no professions they can be in, no place in the world except the isolated provincial town in which they live. They are forced in on
themselves, and they turn to their Torah and live their whole lives in terms of
that. And they get to such a point of intensity, of concern, of concentration on
their relationship with God that they come to believe the whole universe
depends on it. That is the reason behind all the diagrams, the mysticisms, and
the calculations. Where else could these people look except to heaven? Jerry
suggested a marvellous line for the program note. He said that this ballet deals
with the visions, hallucinations, and magical religious manifestations of an
oppressed people. And that's exactly it. All they had for centuries was a book
with the words of God."*
   Writing after the première of *Dybbuk Variations* in *Newsweek,* the critic
Hubert Saal said: "Robbins's ballet does not tell the detailed story . . . of
S. Ansky's 1914 play, a classic of the Yiddish theatre . . . but extracts highlights
of the drama, making a superdrama of such abstractions as the conflict between light and dark, the individual and society, love and law. Sometimes what
occupies a long scene in the play takes a moment in dance—and vice versa. In
reorganizing what Ansky called a 'realistic play about mystic people,' Robbins
and Bernstein have created a work that is theatrical without being showy,
stylized without being stilted and Hebraic without being parochial.
   "The eleven scenes, starkly and effectively designed by Rouben Ter-Arutunian, begin with the important mood setter, the dance of the seven elders,
who with pious grace assume the shape of a Menorah, the Jewish candela-

---

* From "Possession" by Jane Boutwell in "The Talk of the Town." Reprinted by
permission; © 1974 The New Yorker Magazine, Inc.

brum. Throughout the ballet they act as an irresistible force in their faith and fanaticism, embodying the inexorable power of Jehovah's Law and of social custom. Among the most dramatic scenes are the brilliant, complex variations for Chanon and his fellow scholars, who vainly try to dissuade him from the cabalistic investigation that ends in his death. Of all the dance sequences, perhaps the most satisfying is the long *pas de deux* in which the dybbuk takes possession of Leah. Their agitated bodies, trying to adjust to the violent collision of two souls, gradually fuse into one, through their love for each other.

"The climax is spine-tingling, with some magical stagecraft, as the exorcising elders force Chanon to leave the body of Leah and she abandons her own flesh to join him as pure spirit in the hereafter. As this Jewish Romeo and Juliet, the brilliant Helgi Tomasson and the radiant Patricia McBride dance with fire and tenderness.

"No one could have provided Robbins with a more resilient musical floor than Bernstein, who has remained in close touch musically with his Jewish origins. His first symphony, the 'Jeremiah,' was dedicated to his father, a noted Talmudic scholar, and his third symphony is called 'Kaddish.' With obvious eagerness, Bernstein has seized this opportunity to invent music with old-fashioned Hebrew lilt and cadence, an intonation that is part laughter, part tears, and a range from simple folk tunes to complex inversions of tone rows. . . .

"Robbins and Bernstein, two 55-year-old partners and friends, are complementary opposites. . . . Robbins emphasized that the new work 'is a ballet, not a play. It says things that the play doesn't. There are whole areas in the play that are non-verbal.' Bernstein was amazed by the performance of the New York City Ballet Orchestra. 'They're fantastic,' he exclaimed, 'the most wonderful theatre orchestra in the world.'

"Both men remembered the time 30 years ago when the idea for *Dybbuk Variations* came to them—standing on the stage of the old Metropolitan Opera House after the triumph of *Fancy Free*. 'I love the dark, lyric quality of Ansky's play,' says Robbins. 'The astonishing faith. Of all kinds.' Two years ago they isolated themselves in Jamaica and devoted a concentrated three weeks to finding an approach that lay between Robbins's feeling for the abstract and Bernstein's for the concrete drama. 'After that,' Bernstein says, 'I just wrote music and played it for Jerry and he would say that excites me or it doesn't.'

"Earlier Robbins had said, 'Choosing the *Dybbuk* had nothing to do with my being Jewish.' Now Bernstein said, 'In a larger sense what success we've had is based on our experience of Jewishness. Isn't that right, Jerry?' Robbins paused and said, 'I don't know,' and then smiled and added: 'But we are what we are and that feeds into it.'"


## THE DYING SWAN (Le Cygne)

*Music by Camille Saint-Saëns. Choreography by Michel Fokine. First produced at a concert in the Nobleman's Hall, St. Petersburg, Russia, in 1905, with Anna Pavlova. First presented in the United States at the Metropolitan Opera House, New York, March 18, 1910, by Anna Pavlova.*

Perhaps the most famous of all dramatic solos for the ballerina, *The Dying Swan* shows the last minutes in the life of a stricken swan. Slowly, trembling, trying to hold on to life for a brief last flight but then giving up, she dies. It only takes about two minutes to perform. When Pavlova first danced it at the Metropolitan, Carl Van Vechten wrote that it was "the most exquisite specimen of her art which she has yet given to the public."

The choreographer, Michel Fokine, recalled that the dance was composed in a few minutes. One day Pavlova came and asked him to do a solo for her for a concert being given by artists from the chorus of the Imperial Opera. She had just become a ballerina at the Maryinsky Theatre. Fokine was at that time a mandolin enthusiast and had been playing at home—to the piano accompaniment of one of his friends—Saint-Saëns' *Swan*. He said right then, "What about Saint-Saëns' *Swan?*" She immediately realized, Fokine wrote, that a swan would be a most suitable role for her. "As I looked upon the thin, brittle-like Pavlova, I thought—she is just made for the *Swan*." A rehearsal was arranged and the dance completed very quickly. "It was almost an improvisation. I danced in front of her, she directly behind me. Then she danced and I walked alongside her, curving her arms and correcting details of poses.

"Prior to this composition, I was accused of barefooted tendencies and of rejecting toe dancing in general. *The Dying Swan* was my answer to such criticism. This dance became the symbol of the New Russian Ballet. It was a combination of masterful technique with expressiveness. It was like a proof that the dance could and should satisfy not only the eye, but through the medium of the eye should penetrate into the soul" (*Dance Magazine*, August 1931).

In 1934 in Paris, Fokine told Arnold Haskell (see his *Balletomania*): "Small work as it is, and known and applauded all over the world, it was 'revolutionary' then, and illustrated admirably the transition between the old and the new, for here I make use of the technique of the old dance and the traditional costume, and a highly developed technique is necessary, but the purpose of the dance is not to display that technique but to create the symbol of the everlasting struggle in this life and all that is mortal. It is a dance of the whole body and not of the limbs only; it appeals not merely to the eye but to the emotions and the imagination."

The French critic André Levinson has written of *Le Cygne:* "Arms folded, on tiptoe, she dreamily and slowly circles the stage. By even, gliding motions of the hands, returning to the background from whence she emerged, she seems to strive toward the horizon, as though a moment more and she will fly— exploring the confines of space with her soul. The tension gradually relaxes and she sinks to earth, arms waving faintly as in pain. Then faltering with irregular steps toward the edge of the stage—leg bones aquiver like the strings of a harp—by one swift forward-gliding motion of the right foot to earth, she sinks on the left knee—the aerial creature struggling against earthly bonds; and there, transfixed by pain, she dies."

The dancer and teacher Hilda Butsova, who became Pavlova's leading dancer (1912–25) in the company that toured the world, has recalled with Marian Horosko in *Dance Magazine* the joy and hardships of those days: "It was not that she wanted to make money or had a big ego. She wanted people to see dance. . . . It was Anna Pavlova, and no one else, who opened the world to ballet. It was she who did the back-breaking work of pioneering. It was Pavlova who found and cultivated audiences for contemporary ballet companies. Her service to ballet is priceless. No other single human being did more for ballet than she. To all the millions of people for whom she danced, she brought a little of herself; she brought a little happiness to them all. Her genius was as intangible as the legacy she left behind. What remains of Pavlova today is not a movement in the art, not a tendency, not even a series of dances. It is something far more concrete, but possibly far more valuable: inspiration."

## EARLY SONGS

*Music by Richard Strauss. Choreography by Eliot Feld. Costumes by Stanley Simmons. Lighting by Jules Fisher. First presented by the American Ballet Company at the Brooklyn Academy of Music, New York, April 5, 1970. Soprano: Eileen Shelle. Baritone: Steven Kimbrough. Pianist: Gladys Celeste Mercader.*

*Early Songs* is a dance ballet arranged to fourteen songs by Richard Strauss, songs of the composer's youth, when he wrote with fervor and passion to accompany poems he admired about love, dreams, separation, longing, despair, night. *Early Songs* can be said to be about love and the way different young couples are involved in it, how they show it, hide it, seek it, find it, languish in it, rejoice in it. There is no story, only the dance and gestural images we seek on stage. Sometimes they are reflective of the music; sometimes they suggest things beyond the music.

The music is sung by a soprano and a baritone, accompanied by the piano. The words are not directly relevant to the danced picture which is best seen beyond words, in the theater. Successful dance ballets are the hardest things in the world to describe outside their own language!

The ballet is in fourteen parts that flow together, accompanying the Strauss songs. While an understanding of the words of the songs, which are sung in German, is certainly not essential to enjoyment of the dances, you may wish to listen to recordings before coming to the theater.

The curtain rises in silence on two boys and a girl. The music is quiet as the baritone starts to sing of meadows at twilight and the pursuit of a beautiful woman "Dream at Twilight." As the song continues in that vein, rising slowly in intensity, one of the boys, in green, responds to the girl and the others among the couples who materialize about him. He would be with them, but is not, as they come and go. He is left, seeking but not finding, but not absolutely forlorn; after all, they have not rejected him: perhaps it is the other way round.

To the tempo of the rapid "Serenade," sung by the baritone, the boy dances with a girl quick in movement and flirtatiousness. He kneels at her feet and they dance together. Her legs tremble at the beauty of it. Two other couples, the girls responding similarly to the romantic ambience, appear to attend them; the boy then lifts the girl to his shoulder and takes her off into the wings. It is not surprising that the song should invoke the nightingale dreaming of kisses and a rose that, in the morning, should remember and shine with the recollection of the night.

Four couples dance pensively to a poem about "The Star." Next, in the fourth dance, again a *pas de deux* ("Tomorrow"), a young couple move quietly together as the soprano sings of a tomorrow that will unite happy persons, who will look into each other's eyes with muted recognition of their joy. Gently, the boy carries the girl off into the wings.

The baritone sings now a bright tune ("To What End, Maiden?") in which he wonders amusingly at the deceitfulness of a young maiden. There is a dance for three couples, then just one, where the boy seems to question the girl and to find her wonderful at the same time.

"Strolling at Night" follows, under a silvery moon, where an enraptured couple dance of their intense happiness. He falls at her feet. Now, two boys and a girl, hand in hand, dance to a song ("Beautiful, Yet Cold"); the soprano sings about the beautiful but cold stars of heaven that cannot compare to the eyes of the beloved.

Next, a girl moves toward dancing couples, seeming to see a vision of her own ideal and truly finding him in her thoughts, if not in reality ("Rest, My Soul"). The girl in lonely torment is joined by a boy who makes an effort to make her forget. Gentle at first, he fails to comfort her and then almost forces her to forget. She is then in torment, held by him agonizingly and turning her face from him. They leave, her arms folded and her hands curled over her face.

Bright light comes up and five couples rush on to celebrate with the baritone the coming of spring ("Sir Spring"). Next, a boy alone dances, introspectively and thoughtful ("All My Thoughts"). Then he faces three girls. He tries to lead them in a dance ("Ah, Woe Is Me, Unhappy Man!"), partnering them one after another, but does not succeed. He is alone again at the end.

A radiant couple swirl to a song by the baritone about the uselessness of descriptions of his beloved ("Nothing"). What do we know about the sun, the giver of life and light?

Two other lovers dance their joy as the soprano recalls the magic of the time they first looked into each other's eyes and love showered down on them ("Ever Since Your Eyes"). The girl leans against the boy as the lights dim. He touches her hand. Other lovers join them as the song speaks of night, which may steal one's love away ("Night").

NOTES  Writing about *Early Songs* in the New York *Times*, the critic Clive Barnes said that the ballet "is a picture of a world lost, a world full of gentle nuance, of literary feeling, of a rapture impassioned by the poetry of poetry rather than the poetry of life. Love is pure here, and its heartbeat is a kind of exquisite stylization of lust. It is the end of a civilization, and empty-handed cavaliers bearing silver roses are about to be everywhere. . . . It is a fantastically beautiful work; it lilts, it rises, it flies like a kite above our all-too-average dance works. . . . Feld offers a choreographic viewpoint that extends our view of the dance."

Walter Terry wrote in *The Saturday Review:* "*Early Songs,* tastefully costumed by Stanley Simmons and sensitively lit by Jules Fisher, is a work of superior craftsmanship choreographically, but more, it is an art experience that lifts the spirit. At its première, it was faultlessly danced by its cast of thirteen, including Feld himself, (Christine) Sarry, Elizabeth Lee, John Sowinski, and Richard Munro among the most impressive."

## ECCENTRIQUE

> *Music by Igor Stravinsky. Choreography by Eliot Feld. Scenery by Oliver Smith. Costumes by Frank Thompson. Lighting by Jennifer Tipton. First presented by American Ballet Theatre at the City Center, New York, January 18, 1972, with Elizabeth Lee, Christine Sarry, and John Sowinski in leading roles.*

This is a dance ballet to two works by Stravinsky—the *Four Studies for Orchestra* (1928) and the *Orchestral Suites 1 and 2* (1917–25). The first part of the ballet is for a group of girls and a leading dancer; the second, in a setting inspired by the image of Harlequin, is for a boy and girl and accompanying corps de ballet.

## ECHOING OF TRUMPETS

> *Music by Bohuslav Martinů. Choreography by Antony Tudor. Scenery by Birger Bergling. First presented by the Royal Swedish Ballet at the Royal Opera House, Stockholm, September 28, 1963. First presented in the United States by the Metropolitan Opera Ballet at the Metropolitan Opera House, New York, March 27, 1966.*

The theme of *Echoing of Trumpets* is closely related to another composition by Martinů, *Memorial to Lidice,* but the choreographer, Antony Tudor, was not aware of this until later. He chose instead Martinů's *Symphonic Fantasies Symphony No. 6* for his ballet about domination and war, about humanity under the heel of the conqueror.

The action takes place in an occupied village that has been ravaged by war. There the women whose husbands have been killed are in immediate conflict with the invaders. They are violated and killed. A refugee returning to the village to see his sweetheart is caught and killed. The girl dances a lament with her dead lover.

Many have seen in this ballet resemblances to the destruction of Lidice by the Nazis. The choreographer has denied that this is the theme of his work. "Perhaps it's more about how people always seem to want to dominate people. Everyone knows that's a stupid thing to do. Yet they keep on doing it. They never stop torturing each other with a kind of mild viciousness."

## ELITE SYNCOPATIONS

*Music by Scott Joplin and others. Choreography by Kenneth MacMillan. Costumes by Ian Spurling. First presented by the Royal Ballet at the Royal Opera House, Covent Garden, London, October 7, 1974, with Merle Park, David Wall, Monica Mason, Michael Colman, Jennifer Penney, Carl Myers, Vergie Derman, Wayne Sleep, Wayne Eagling, Jennifer Jackson, Judith Hower, David Drew, and David Adams in leading roles. First presented in the United States by the same ensemble April 27, 1976, at the Metropolitan Opera House, New York.*

This is a dance ballet to Scott Joplin's music. The pieces that are illustrated by dance are the *Sunflower Slow Drag, Elite Syncopations, The Cascades, Hothouse Rag, Calliope Rag, Ragtime Nightingale, The Golden Hours, Stop-time Rag, The Alaskan Rag, Bethena*—a Concert Waltz, *Friday Night,* and *Cataract Rag.*

## EMBRACE TIGER AND RETURN TO MOUNTAIN

*Music by Morton Subotnick. Choreography by Glen Tetley. Decor by Nadine Baylis. First presented in the United States by the Royal Swedish Ballet at the City Center, New York, November 21, 1974.*

Fourteen centuries ago, the Chinese developed a system of calisthenics and shadowboxing called T'ai-Chi. The object in T'ai-Chi is to empty out all extraneous thoughts in order to gain an intense inner concentration. Today in China and on Taiwan persons gather in parks every morning to do these thirty-seven exercises. In the West, too, T'ai-Chi has become extremely popular with persons who seek a thoughtful but not exhausting form of exercise. The names of the thirty-seven exercises typify the action so that participants will remember the sequence. The seventeenth exercise is called Embrace Tiger and Return to Mountain. It is this that the choreographer Glen Tetley has seized upon in order to evolve a work that fuses Eastern and Western attitudes to movement. It is danced to an electronic score by Morton Subotnick and performed on a mirrored floor that adds a further dimension to the visual impression of the piece. What the dancers do is not determined by a story. The stances they take, the gestures they make, and the steps they perform suggest variations on exercise (for combat?), shadowboxing (illusions?), tracking (prey?), and hunting.

*Embrace Tiger* is also part of the repertoire of the Eliot Feld Ballet.

## L'ENFANT ET LES SORTILÈGES (The Spellbound Child)

*Lyric fantasy in two parts based on a poem by Colette. Music by Maurice Ravel. Choreography by George Balanchine. First presented by Raoul Guns-bourg at the Théâtre de Monte Carlo, March 21, 1925. Conducted by Victor de Sabata. First presented in New York by Ballet Society at the Central High School of Needle Trades, November 20, 1946. Costumes and scenery by Aline Bernstein. Conducted by Leon Barzin. The Child: Joseph Connolly. Presented in a third version by the New York City Ballet at the Hommage à Ravel, May 14, 1975, at the New York State Theatre, Lincoln Center. Costumes and sets by Kermit Love; supervising designer, David Mitchell. Orchestra, singers, and chorus conducted by Manuel Rosenthal. The Child: Paul Offenkranz.*

"The essence of Ravel's genius is found in this sympathetic and somewhat sentimental masterpiece," writes the musician Arbie Orenstein in *Ravel: Man and Music* (1975). I very much agree, as will probably be clear from the number of times I have worked on this opera-ballet! The title has been variously translated—everything from *Dreams of a Naughty Boy* to *The Spellbound Child*, but I have preferred to stay with the original. Which is where I began, having worked on the first production with Ravel. The composer has always meant a great deal to me.

Ravel, who was fond of George Gershwin's music, wrote that *L'Enfant et les Sortilèges* "was composed in the spirit of an American musical comedy." The hero of the piece, a young boy, both sings and dances. He is about six or seven years old. Colette's text sets the scene in a country house in a room looking out on a garden. There are a large Armchair, a tall Grandfather's Clock, a round squirrel cage by the window, a boiling kettle in the fireplace, and a purring Cat. It is afternoon.

The boy is supposed to be studying, but he is bored and would rather do anything else. His Mother comes in and scolds him but he sticks out his tongue at her. For punishment, she gives him bitter tea and dry bread and says he has to stay alone until dinner. Alone, the boy stamps his foot and shouts that he hates everyone and will be as naughty as he likes. Proving it, he breaks the teapot and Cups, tries to torture the squirrel, pulls the Cat's tail, overturns the kettle, rips the wallpaper, stops the Clock and tears up his schoolbooks. He declares that he may be naughty but he is also free!

What he has also done, however, is to free the room and the objects in it. Animated by his naughtiness, they all begin to come to life and to sing and dance. First the Armchair, then the Grandfather's Clock, then the Teacups followed by the figures on the wallpaper, Shepherds and Shepherdesses. A Princess emerges from one of his schoolbooks, complaining, "Now that you have torn up the story, what will happen to me?" He vows to protect her from evil enchantment but she disappears. As he despairs, other books come to life and the Child is suddenly faced with arithmetic and other problems! This is followed by a duet for two Cats, who retreat into the garden. The boy follows them.

Now the room disappears, the walls giving way, and the boy is alone in the garden with the Cats. There the music of Dragonflies, Moths, Bats, Frogs, and rustling Trees greets him. Much as he wants to join in the enchanted world of the lively garden, he sees that they delight in their freedom and in their love for each other. He realizes that they are forgetting him; he cries, "I'm alone! . . . Mother!"

In chorus the Animals turn on the boy, attacking him as the naughty lad who had always tormented them. They are so anxious to strike him and to get in the first blow that they begin to fight each other. In the process a small Squirrel is wounded. He goes to the Child, crying in pain. The boy puts a bandage on him. The Animals observe this and are astonished at his kindness. They cannot believe it. Then they observe that they have hurt the boy, too. As they wonder what to do they recall that he was calling someone. Who? Mother! They encircle the hurt Child and all call "Mother! Mother!" Then, getting no response, they take him to his nest. Dawn begins to rise. Proclaiming the boy to be good and kind and their friend, they leave him as he reaches out for home and his Mother.

# ENIGMA VARIATIONS

*Music by Edward Elgar. Choreography by Frederick Ashton. Scenery and costumes by Julia Trevelyan Oman. First presented by the Royal Ballet at the Royal Opera House, Covent Garden, London, October 25, 1968, with Derek Rencher, Svetlana Beriosova, Stanley Holden, Brian Shaw, Alexander Grant, Robert Mead, Vyvyan Lorrayne, Anthony Dowell, Georgina Parkinson, Desmond Doyle, Antoinette Sibley, Wayne Sleep, Leslie Edwards, and Deanne Bergsma in the principal roles. First presented in the United States by the same ensemble, with the same cast, at the Metropolitan Opera House, Lincoln Center, April 22, 1969. Conducted by John Lanchbery.*

Subtitled, in the composer's words, "My Friends Pictured Within," *Enigma Variations* is a dance portrait of the artist among friends and family in Victorian England. The ballet is based on its score, which characterized thirteen friends and relations "who were there," and a fourteenth, "absent on a sea voyage" at the time, who remains the "enigma."

Describing one aspect of his composition, Elgar said it was "written at a time when friends were dubious and generally discouraging as to the composer's musical future." The action of the ballet, which is set in an English country house in the Cotswolds in 1898, occurs at a point when the composer needed friends most. It follows very closely the true story that Elgar had sent the completed score of his *Variations* to the celebrated Viennese conductor Richter, in the hope of interesting him in the work. Elgar's various friends, who visit him during the trying period of his awaiting a reply, pass an afternoon in the customary, relaxed pursuits of a Victorian autumn day. Only his wife, a constant source of inspiration and encouragement throughout his life, understands and watches over him to offer comfort. One by one the friends enter the action, identifying their separate personalities with each danced variation to the music Elgar wrote to characterize them. A chamber-music comrade, an amateur cellist, a tricycle-riding crony, a contemplative scholar, a romantic young girl, a gracious and sedate lady, and an eccentric dog lover all pass in review. Those closest to him, his wife and his friend "Nimrod" (who also knew the conductor Richter), continually reflect their understanding and the significance of the anxious waiting period. From time to time, Lady Mary Lygnon appears and reappears as a mysterious background figure, symbolic of the enigma of the long anticipated reply. At the end of the ballet, a telegram arrives for "Nimrod" from Richter, announcing that he will indeed conduct the first performance of *Enigma Variations*.

NOTES   Unanimously regarded as a masterpiece when it was first presented in England, the ballet was called by John Percival, in the *Times*, "a rare and moving expression of the quality of friendship." It received wide acclaim after its U.S. première. Writing in the *Village Voice*, the critic Deborah Jowitt said: ". . . I am astonished at its power to move me. The key—or one of them—to the enigma of the ballet's beauty is the nostalgia inherent in certain things. Lorca once wrote that a flock of sheep bears nostalgia about with it; it need not matter whether one has longings at all relevant to a flock of sheep. I don't think that one needs to have known era, place, or people involved in Ashton's ballet to be beguiled.

"The setting is Elgar's house in Worcestershire in the late years of Victoria's reign and of the nineteenth century. Everything about the ballet has an air of lateness: the composer's lateness in achieving recognition, the ripe late-Romantic music, the autumn garden, the amber of the sunlight. Julia Trevelyan Oman's set and costumes are carefully and poetically authentic. It's the kind of set I loved as a child—so super-real that it's hard to believe that there actually is a backstage area and not just more lawns and paths. There is a brick entrance, a cutaway view of an interior stairway, hammocks, bicycles, trees from which occasional yellow leaves float. Those friends of Elgar's cryptically enshrined in the musical variations are conveniently brought together. . . . They wander about . . . each emerging to do his (or her) variation and then strolling off. At the end a telegram is brought. . . . Elgar's friends rejoice in his good fortune.

"I see most clearly in this ballet what Ashtonophiles rave about. He is best at being quiet; his effects are modest, unflamboyant, but extremely sensitive to the nuances of character. . . . Sometimes he creates character through rhythm and through subtle gestural grafts onto the ballet vocabulary. Other times . . . he suggests eccentricities by requiring an eccentric manner of performing straightforward classical steps. He has a fine way with small understated lifts that seem to come with no preparation; the girl's feet make shy conversational steps barely off the ground. There are several of these in the bittersweet duet for Elgar and a very young girl (beautifully done by Derek Rencher and Antoinette Sibley), and in one of more promise of fulfillment between Matthew

Arnold's son and Isabel Fitton (Robert Mead and Vyvyan Lorrayne). I especially liked two delightfully brusque, erratic solos performed by Alexander
Grant and Anthony Dowell; some affectionate conjugal passages between
Elgar and his wife (Svetlana Beriosova); and a dignified . . . touching duet
between Elgar and a friend (Desmond Doyle) to the famous *Nimrod* variation."

In a long essay on the work of Frederick Ashton in *Ballet Review* (Vol. 3,
No. 4), the critic Jack Anderson has written:

"Man is capable of being better: he can dream, he can work, he can try
harder. Such assumptions may seem old-fashioned and unduly optimistic. But
they have not yet been proven totally wrong, and I can conceive of no satisfactory social relationships without them.

"One of Ashton's most unusual ballets on these themes is *Enigma Variations*. Formally, *Enigma* is daring—much more so than many ballets which os-
tentatiously proclaim their originality. For one thing, it is filled with "non-
dance." Elgar studies a manuscript. Two eccentrics ride bicycles. Lady Elgar
examines a score. Nevinson yawns. Elgar and Jaeger gesticulate as though actually conversing in the "Nimrod" variation, which concludes with the men
and Lady Elgar walking, arms linked, backs to the audience. The telegraph
boy is tipped and the ballet ends with the taking of a photograph. Amidst
these gestures—distillations of character traits akin to those Ashton uses in his
comedies—passages of heightened movement occur like surges of feeling, as in
"Nimrod" where the weighted stride of "real" walking gives way to low lifts
and the long, eloquent line of classical ballet, only to subside back into walking. A master of choreographic repose, Ashton knows when not to move a
dancer. In the passages for Elgar and his wife a movement is usually allowed
to come to rest before a new movement begins, which makes these actions
seem to arise from deep founts of emotion.

"The ballet is a quiet ode to friendship, to people one loves. The characters
are not necessarily Elgar's friends as they were historically, they are his friends
as he might have remembered them—an altogether different matter, since we
glorify their virtues and convert their failings into eccentricities. And we see
all in the light of affection.

"The hero is a successful artist. What an unlikely subject for a ballet! For,
as Ashton shows, artistic creation is untheatrical—a matter of solitude, work,
and worry, interspersed with conversations with neighbors and confidences
shared with wife and friends. Elgar is often alone. But his work and solitude
are not in vain. The telegram from Richter arrives. A party is held and friends
take photographs. And tomorrow the new work begins.

"Art. Friendship. Meaningful work. Graciousness. Tranquility. These are
some of the things Ashton's ballets celebrate."

In a long interview with Don McDonagh in *Ballet Review* (Vol. 3, No. 4),
Frederick Ashton was asked if he had a preference for works with a narrative
continuity or works that are lyrical abstract statements.

"A: No, it depends on the music. For instance in *Enigma Variations* I could
have taken the music and done a series of dances. But this somehow didn't appeal to me. Then I hit upon the idea of using the actual people who were writ-

ten about musically and this began to fascinate me. I did a lot of study on them and read biographies to try and get under the skin of it. When Elgar's daughter, who is now a very old lady, came to see it she said, 'I don't understand how you did it because they were exactly like that.' And she said, 'I never liked any of them except Troyte.'

"McD: There is very little dancing by Elgar himself and yet he is apparent everywhere. Just his presence as he stands upstage is very important. It focuses the piece.

"A: He needs to be that kind of solid character. I started by making him dance more but it seemed wrong, so I cut it out. Even when he does a few steps it kind of jars on me. When he and Jaeger have the conversation they're supposed to have had, about Beethoven's quartets, they do a bit of dancing there, and I tried to do it like question and answer. Even that I kept to minimal dancing."

David Vaughan's complete account of the creation of *Enigma Variations* in the book *Frederick Ashton and His Ballets* is strongly recommended.

## EPILOGUE

*Music by Gustav Mahler. Choreography by John Neumeier. Costumes by Mitchell. Lighting by Nananne Porcher. First presented by American Ballet Theatre at the New York State Theatre, Lincoln Center, New York, July 9, 1975, with Natalia Makarova and Erik Bruhn. Conducted by David Gilbert. Dedicated to Vera Volkova.*

*Epilogue,* as the title suggests, is a dance narrative supplementing an earlier dramatic action. What that action was is never made clear. What is clear, as the curtain rises, is that there has been Trouble in the autumnal years. There is as yet no music. A spotlight shines from above and in it brown leaves can be seen to fall to the ground. A girl crouches. A man stands nearby. There appears to be no communication between them; but then the visible tension suggests these two know each other, are lovers in fact, and have had a serious quarrel that disallows contact. They want to make it up, but how? They bow to each other in curious ways, without acknowledgment. Then, as the man stands with his back to the girl, she goes to him, standing close. The music starts: the *Adagietto* of Mahler's *Symphony No. 5.* The dance now recapitulates the Effort at Reunion, the Difficulty in Giving In, Making Allowances, Permitting Forgiveness. Yet tensions persist. Long dances by each display varying degrees of anguish and being wronged; sometimes neither sees what the other suffers. Toward the end, in capitulation, the man falls at the girl's feet. She touches his head. As she falls back in his arms, the leaves again descend.

# EPISODES

*Music by Anton Webern. Choreography by Martha Graham and George Balanchine. Scenery and lighting by David Hays. Costumes by Karinska. First presented by the New York City Ballet at the City Center, New York, May 14, 1959. Episodes I, with choreography by Martha Graham, was danced by Miss Graham, Bertram Ross, Sallie Wilson, Helen McGehee, Ethel Winter, Linda Hodes, Akiko Kanda, Richard Kuch, Dan Wagoner, David Wood, Kenneth Peterson, James Gardner, and Robert Powell. Episodes II was danced by a cast headed by Violette Verdy and Jonathan Watts, Diana Adams and Jacques d'Amboise, Paul Taylor, Melissa Hayden, and Francisco Moncion.*

In the 1950s Stravinsky began to tell me about the music of Anton Webern, the Austrian composer (1883–1945). Stravinsky called him a great composer and was so enthusiastic that I thought he must be very good indeed, although I was not then much interested in atonal music, except maybe Schoenberg's. To me, Schoenberg was the Einstein of twelve-tone music; I didn't see how he could be surpassed. But within the next few years, Robert Craft, Stravinsky's friend, recorded all of Webern's work. Everyone who cares about music must always be grateful to him. I listened to everything and liked it. The songs were the best of all, but they were written to be listened to. The orchestral music, however, fills air like molecules: it is written for atmosphere. The first time I heard it, I knew it could be danced to.

To understand Webern better, I transcribed several of the instrumental pieces for piano and played them over and over. The music seemed to me like Mozart and Stravinsky, music that can be danced to because it leaves the mind free to *see* the dancing. In listening to composers like Beethoven and Brahms every listener has his own ideas, paints his own picture of what the music represents. Beethoven did not have this in mind, I am sure, but he does seem to be painting a picture and people like to put themselves in that picture. Now how can I, a choreographer, try to squeeze a dancing body into a picture that already exists in someone's mind? It simply won't work. But it will with Webern. This kind of music, which Mozart and Stravinsky have also written, is like a rose—you can admire it deeply but you cannot inject your personal feelings into it.

Lincoln Kirstein shared my interest and admiration for Webern and we thought we should try to do dances to all of the orchestral pieces. They are not many and last altogether less than an hour. We decided to invite Martha Graham to collaborate on the undertaking and she happily agreed. We accordingly divided the scores and got to work. Miss Graham did her dance on a theme of Mary Queen of Scots while I began to do a ballet without a story. Miss Graham's part of *Episodes* has unfortunately not been seen for some years. It is our hope that one day it will be danced again.

EPISODES I    The music is the *Passacaglia, Opus 1*, and the *Six Pieces for Orchestra, Opus 6*, both composed in 1909 before Webern had used Schoenberg's idea of the twelve-tone row. The dance is based on the final moments of Mary Queen of Scots. It recapitulates her last thoughts as she mounts the scaffold.

The setting is austere, a black platform across the back of the stage with steps on both sides approaching it; in the center of the platform stands a black box and a high halberd-like heraldic device. The music begins with an ominous plucking of strings. Mary, in black, stands below, tense. Her stiff dress seems both to armor and to imprison her. Suddenly high on the platform, she is free of it, stepping out as a young girl in white to meet her lover Bothwell. She comes down again and her black dress remains standing like an empty cage, on the platform accusing her worldliness. She rejects the crown-craving Bothwell, the love of her life, and is in torment.

Four girls now dress Mary in blood red and she begins her long contest with Queen Elizabeth of England. The music shifts to the *Six Pieces for Orchestra*. The black box on the platform becomes a throne. Elizabeth sits there in burnished gold. She descends. The two queens play a fateful game of tennis, a formal court tennis.

As Elizabeth wins, she is lifted high. Mary then sits for a moment on the throne. But now the throne is the scaffold. Mary kneels before it, the tall halberd, now an ax, turns in the air and a bright red light illumines her cast-off queenly garb.

EPISODES II    The music for this part of the ballet, which, like the first part, can stand alone, consists of Webern's other orchestral works.

To the *Symphony, Opus 21*, there is an ensemble. The curtain rises before the music begins. Four couples stand on stage. As the music starts, dryly and carefully, the boys touch the girls on the shoulder; they join hands then, pose briefly, and begin to move together. One couple leads the others but soon, just as the instrumentation shifts and develops, the other pairs react to the music differently. The dance is about the music; it is meant to look that way. Stravinsky has said that nothing in contemporary music has haunted him more than the coda of this symphony.

The second part, to the *Five Pieces, Opus 10*, is a *pas de deux*. The lights dim to darkness. Two figures emerge in spotlights, a boy dressed in jet black, a girl in white. She moves toward him slowly. He catches her, her body collapses over his arm and stays there, bent over, as he moves away. He leaves her there, then goes to find her again. Schoenberg said of Webern's music that it expresses an entire novel in a gesture, a joy in a breath. Although I did not know he had said that when I was working on this ballet, I believed it myself.

Some people watching this part of the ballet in the theatre laugh a little. That is, here at home, not on our tours of Europe or Russia. I sometimes think Americans feel obliged to laugh too much when there is not any reason to.

The third part, to the *Concerto, Opus 24*, is again a *pas de deux* for another couple, with four girls accompanying them. The boy moves the girl as the composer moves his instruments. Speaking of some of Webern's music, Robert

Craft says that "at first the listener might be reminded of a switchboard sporadically lighting up, but the plot of wires between the lights is what must be illuminated." Which is what I try to do.

*The Variations for Orchestra, Opus 30.* The original production of *Episodes* continued at this point with a dance performed by Paul Taylor, then appearing as a guest artist with our company. Just as Sallie Wilson from the New York City Ballet appeared in Miss Graham's part of *Episodes,* Mr. Taylor appeared in mine. The piece consists of a theme and six variations. Webern wrote of the *Variations:* "The motivic development uses much crab-wise movement with augmentation and diminution . . . By changing the center of gravitation within the two forms by augmentation and diminution the character and meter of the piece is constantly changing . . ."

The final part of *Episodes* is performed to Webern's tribute to Bach, the *Ricercata for Six Voices from Bach's Musical Offering.* The dances here, as elsewhere in this work, praise the music. The further Webern goes, the more active and lean the music becomes. The energy it has is that of free polyphonic voices, each equally individual and expressive. They keep shifting in balance and so do the dances. In Virgil Thomson's phrase, the music turns out to be "a dialect of Bach."


# EPITAPH

*Music by György Ligeti* (Atmosphères *and* Volumina). *Choreography by Rudi van Dantzig. Scenery and costumes by Toer van Schayk. First presented by the Dutch National Ballet, June 25, 1969, in Amsterdam, Holland. First presented in the United States by the same ensemble at the Minskoff Theatre, New York, November 9, 1976.*

The Dutch critic Luuk Utrecht has rightly observed that *Epitaph* is "a gloomy comment on the life of man, like an inscription on a tomb." Love and death govern the action and there is never any doubt that the latter will win out. Two brides in spotless white symbolize, according to the choreographer, Rudi van Dantzig, "the illusions and ideals after which mankind always strives; sometimes unattainable, then senseless or cruel, sometimes ridiculous and often so overwhelming that generations sacrifice themselves or are offered to them." The two boys who devote themselves to the two brides perish, dancers are encased in black boxes and to the sound of a roaring organ all the ensemble collapses in a heap. The brides tidily close them all up in a box and kneel to weep at the loss.


# L'ESTRO ARMONICO (Cycle of Harmony)

*Music by Antonio Vivaldi. Choreography by John Cranko. First presented by the Stuttgart Ballet at the Württemberg State Theatre, Stuttgart, Ger-*

*many, April 27, 1963. First presented in the United States by the Stuttgart Ballet at the Metropolitan Opera House, New York, May 30, 1973.*

*L'Estro Armonico* ("Cycle of Harmony") is a dance ballet to three concerti by Antonio Vivaldi, arranged by Kurt-Heinz Stolze, the *Concerto in A Major,* the *Concerto in A Minor,* and the *Concerto in D Major.* The choreographer, John Cranko, said of his ballet that it "uses a selection from the twelve concertos of Vivaldi. Personally I should have liked to choreograph all twelve, but to avoid boring the public I have chosen three. These concertos have been choreographically linked: the themes propounded in the first two concertos have been taken up and developed in the third." A woman is the center of the ballet, the male soloists supporting and revolving about her.

## THE ETERNAL IDOL

> *Music by Frédéric Chopin. Choreography by Michael Smuin. First presented by American Ballet Theatre at the Brooklyn Academy of Music, December 4, 1969, with Cynthia Gregory and Ivan Nagy.*

A romantic narrative ballet, *The Eternal Idol* is appropriately set to the *Larghetto* of Chopin's *Concerto No. 2 in F Minor.* The theme and inspiration for the ballet is Rodin's famous sculpture "The Eternal Idol," where a boy kneels at a girl's feet and rests his head on her breast. The ballet begins that way, reminding us of the pose of the sculpture. It then explores in a *pas de deux* for the lovers the beginnings and growth of their love for each other. As the critic Walter Terry has noted, the ballet evokes such images as Bernard Champigneulle speaks of in his book *Rodin:* ". . . Songs and sighs of love, cries of pleasure and pain, cries of pain and pleasure mingled, the eternal call of woman, the call of man . . . all found expression in Rodin."

## ÉTUDES

> *Music by Knudager Riisager (after Czerny). Choreography by Harald Lander. Scenery by Erik Nordgreen. First presented by the Royal Danish Ballet at the Royal Theatre, Copenhagen, January 15, 1948. First presented in the United States by the American Ballet Theatre at the Metropolitan Opera House, New York, October 15, 1961, with Toni Lander, Royes Fernandez, and Bruce Marks in the leading roles. Scenery and costumes by Rolf Gerard.*

This ballet is the choreographer's tribute to the dancer and may perhaps be considered as a representation of the work that must be accomplished by young dancers throughout the long and difficult preparatory years. We see in the ballet the first elementary exercises at the *barre* by young pupils, then work in the center of the stage, away from the *barre*, followed by a *pas de trois*, a *pas de deux*, a *pas de quatre*, a *pas de six*, and ensemble work. At the end of the ballet, the soloists display their skill individually and collectively.


## EUGENE ONEGIN

*Ballet in three acts and six scenes after Alexander Pushkin. Music by Peter Ilyich Tchaikovsky, arranged and orchestrated by Kurt-Heinz Stolze. Chore-ography by John Cranko. Scenery and costumes by Jürgen Rose. First pre-sented by the Stuttgart Ballet at the Württemberg State Theatre, Stuttgart, Germany, April 13, 1965, with Marcia Haydée and Heinz Clauss in the principal roles. First presented in the United States by the same ensemble at the Metropolitan Opera House, Lincoln Center, New York, June 10, 1969.*

The ballet tells the story of Pushkin's great poem. The music, by Tchaikovsky, is not from that composer's opera *Eugene Onegin*, but has been arranged from his lesser-known compositions.

How is it possible for me to speak of Pushkin's poem *Eugene Onegin* with-out emotion? It is like asking an Englishman to speak of Shakespeare without emotion. Alexander Pushkin produced the first great Russian poem, or "free novel" in verse, in *Eugene Onegin* (1823–30). His work is the beginning of greatness of the Russian language. There are problems about the translation of *Eugene Onegin* into English. Many have tried to render the poem into Eng-lish. Vladimir Nabokov's complete version is the best we have, but for the reader with no Russian, it is difficult to explain the poem's greatness. For it is not what we think of as an epic or a huge, classic poem. It is a story, first of all, a work in poetry in a language that was unknown before, a language that became with Pushkin the Russian language of literacy and spoken liveliness. At any rate, John Cranko chose to make a ballet of this narrative, having known it as a poem, and also as an opera in Tchaikovsky's profound version. He arranged his ballet not to the music of Tchaikovsky's opera, but to other work by Tchaikovsky researched, arranged, and orchestrated by Kurt-Heinz Stolze.

Interviewed by *The New Yorker*, Cranko spoke of his ballet: " 'I see *Onegin* as a myth in the same way that Charlie Chaplin is a myth. . . . Myths always have double meanings, and in this sense Chaplin is both funny and terrifying. Onegin is a young man who has everything—good looks, money, charm—and yet he adds up to nothing. Which makes *him* terrifying. His problem is a very contemporary one—lack of recognition. Then, of course, the plot of the Pushkin poem is balletic—explainable in three different dance styles. The first act is a youthful peasant dance, the second is a bourgeois party, the third is an elegant St. Petersburg ball. And like a thread going through the labyrinth you have your soloists, with their problems, their stories.'

"Mr. Cranko . . . added that when he choreographed a ballet he tried to create visual images that speak for themselves. 'A diamond has no color, but it takes light, and when you look at it you see red, blue, green, and yellow,' he said. 'A ballet image should be like a diamond. No meaning. No color. But hard, not sloppy. I have a specific feeling which maybe I can only shape for myself. So the ultimate definition of the images comes from the eyes of the public, not from my eyes.'"

A synopsis of the ballet follows:

ACT ONE, SCENE 1: MADAME LARINA'S GARDEN  Madame Larina, Olga, and the nurse are finishing the party dresses and gossiping about Tatiana's coming birthday festivities. Madame Larina speculates on the future and reminisces about her own lost beauty and youth. Girls from the neighborhood arrive, their greetings and chatter are interrupted by gunshots.

Lensky, a young poet, engaged to Olga, arrives and tells them there is no cause for alarm; he was hunting with a friend from St. Petersburg. He introduces Onegin, who, bored with the city, has come to see if the country can offer him any distraction. Tatiana, full of youthful and romantic fantasies, falls in love with the elegant stranger, so different from the country people she knows. Onegin, on the other hand, sees only a coltish country girl who reads too many romantic novels.

ACT ONE, SCENE 2: TATIANA'S BEDROOM  Tatiana, her imagination aflame with impetuous first love, dreams of Onegin and writes him a passionate love letter which she gives the nurse to deliver.

ACT TWO, SCENE 1: TATIANA'S BIRTHDAY  The provincial gentry have come to celebrate Tatiana's birthday. They gossip about Lensky's infatuation with Olga and whisper prophecies of a dawning romance between Tatiana and the newcomer. Onegin finds the company boring. Stifling his yawns, he finds it difficult to be civil to them: Furthermore, he is irritated by Tatiana's letter which he regards merely as an outburst of adolescent love. In a quiet moment, he seeks out Tatiana and, telling her that he cannot love her, tears up her letter. Tatiana's distress, instead of awaking pity, merely increases his irritation.

Prince Gremin, a distant relative, appears. He is in love with Tatiana, and Madame Larina hopes for a brilliant match; but Tatiana, troubled with her own heart, hardly notices her kindly and elderly relative.

Onegin, in his boredom, decides to provoke Lensky by flirting with Olga who lightheartedly joins in the teasing. But Lensky takes the matter with passionate seriousness. He challenges Onegin to a duel.

ACT TWO, SCENE 2: THE DUEL  Tatiana and Olga try to reason with Lensky, but his high romantic ideals are shattered by the betrayal of his friend and the fickleness of his beloved; he insists that the duel take place. Onegin kills his friend and for the first time his cold heart is moved by the horror of his deed. Tatiana realizes that her love was an illusion, and that Onegin is self-centered and empty.

ACT THREE, SCENE 1: ST. PETERSBURG  Years later, Onegin, having traveled the world in an attempt to escape from his own futility, returns to St. Petersburg where he is received at a ball in the palace of Prince Gremin. Gremin has recently married, and Onegin is astonished to recognize in the stately and elegant young princess, Tatiana, the uninteresting little country girl whom he once turned away. The enormity of his mistake and loss engulfs him. His life now seems even more aimless and empty.

ACT THREE, SCENE 2: TATIANA'S BOUDOIR   Tatiana reads a letter from Onegin which reveals his love. Suddenly he stands before her, impatient to know her answer. Tatiana sorrowfully tells him that although she still feels her passionate love of girlhood for him, she is now a woman, and that she could never find happiness or respect with him. She orders him to leave her forever.

NOTES   The critic Walter Terry, reviewing a performance of *Eugene Onegin* in New York in 1971, wrote in *The Saturday Review:* "How Cranko tells a story in dance! He is a theater man through and through, as was his illustrious predecessor of two centuries ago in Stuttgart, Jean-Georges Noverre, whose revolutionary esthetics carried the ballet away from mere steps to *ballet d'action*—that is to say, to dramatic ballet, to movement with dramatic meanings.

"Cranko's *Onegin* has its virtuosic steppings—the cross-stage leaps by the company at the close of Act One, Scene 1, or the great pinwheel pattern in the ballroom scene—but of equal importance are the acted, not danced, duel and death scene that takes place way at the back of the stage (the late Doris Humphrey, among the great choreographers of our age, once stated that tragedy worked best in upstage remoteness and that comedy was for downstage familiarity), the finale in which the heroine stands alone center stage, and the remarkable mirror dance that combines acting and dancing as Tatiana literally draws her dream lover from the image in her mind and has him step from behind her own reflection in the mirror and into her arms.

". . . Marcia Haydée was Tatiana, a role identified with her very special artistry as both an actress and a dancer, and Heinz Clauss was Onegin, stern, strong, remote yet romantic. . . ."

# EVENING DIALOGUES

*Music by Schumann. Choreography by Jonathan Watts. First presented by the Joffrey City Center Ballet at the City Center, New York, October 22, 1974, with Francesca Corkle, Beatriz Rodriguez, Russell Sultzbach, and Burton Taylor as principals.*

One of Schumann's great works for piano, the *Davidsbündlertänze*, is played throughout this ballet to inspire and accompany dances by vulnerable and susceptible young persons who listen and respond. They care deeply about what they hear and react with fervor to the intensity of concentration of the short, vivid dance pieces. Their dances express the joy and disappointments of love and youth.

## AN EVENING'S WALTZES

*Music by Serge Prokofiev. Choreography by Jerome Robbins. Costumes by Rouben Ter-Arutunian. First presented by the New York City Ballet at the New York State Theatre, Lincoln Center, May 24, 1973, with Patricia Mc-Bride and Jean-Pierre Bonnefous, Christine Redpath and John Clifford, Sara Leland and Bart Cook in leading roles.*

The music for this dance ballet is five waltzes by Prokofiev from his *Symphonic Suite of Waltzes*. There is no story, only these persons dancing to these waltzes. Each of the waltzes is different, and a different atmosphere and mood are established for the dances. The three leading couples as well as the soloists and *corps de ballet* are formally dressed, as if they were attending a formal party.

Writing in the *Wall Street Journal* about the ballet, Peter J. Rosenwald said that "it has so much beautiful movement that it could almost bring back ballroom dancing as a national pastime. . . . From beginning to end it has that Robbins romantic style, warm and eloquent, full of effortless and thrilling lifts which are never showy for their own sake."

Deborah Jowitt in the *Village Voice* wrote: "Over the decorous unison waltzing of the *corps*, pairs of soloists enter one at a time to make violent small talk in dance. Small outbursts of movement, sudden changes of heart and direction interrupt the smooth surface of the waltzing. These couples are, perhaps, dancing out the thoughts and the verbal exchanges that occur at grand parties such as these, where a current of fashionable melodrama flows through the ballroom. The duet for Redpath and Clifford (replacing the injured Gelsey Kirkland and Helgi Tomasson at the last minute) is particularly effusive, with a hint of drastic coquetry."

## EVERY NOW AND THEN

*Music by Quincy Jones. Choreography by William Scott. Costumes designed by Hutaff Lennon and Jack Cunningham; costumes executed by Zelda Wynn. Lighting design by Gary Fails. First presented by the Dance Theatre of Harlem at the Uris Theatre, New York, April 26, 1975.*

The ballet *Every Now and Then* was made by the ballet master of the Dance Theatre of Harlem, William Scott. His dances play with black folk dance, jazz, and ballet, mixing them together and merging the styles. Designed and laid out to be danced, the steps often appear spontaneous and improvised, like sudden expressions of a personal fantasy. The critic Arlene Croce of *The New Yorker* once noted in young amateur dancers on the "Soul Train" television program: "Every now and then, one of the boys will hurl himself into a *saut de basque*—playing at ballet."

# FAÇADE

*Ballet in one act. Music by William Walton. Choreography by Frederick Ashton. Scenery and costumes by John Armstrong. First presented by the Camargo Society at the Cambridge Theatre, London, April 26, 1931, with a cast that included Lydia Lopokova, Alicia Markova, and Frederick Ashton. First presented in the United States by the Sadler's Wells Ballet at the Metropolitan Opera House, New York, October 13, 1949, with Moira Shearer and Frederick Ashton in featured roles.*

The music to *Façade* was originally written as a setting to certain poems by Edith Sitwell. The poet recited her verses accompanied by the music. The ballet has nothing to do with the poems and uses only the music, to which the choreographer has arranged a series of nine comic *divertissements* that poke fun at their subjects. The scene shows the façade of a large, light-colored house of the Victorian era.

First, two girls and a boy amble out on stage and dance a "Scottish Rhapsody" in appropriate native costume. This is followed by a number called "Yodeling." A milkmaid enters with a stool. Soon she is disturbed by three mountaineers, who turn her around as she stands posed on the stool and pay tribute to her fresh beauty. There is a yodeling contest, in which the girl enters with gusto. The music ripples and laughs with the happy young people. Next comes a "Polka," danced by a smart young lady.

Now two couples dance a "Fox Trot," which is followed by a "Waltz" executed by four girls. Two vaudeville dandies take up the "Popular Song" and perform it with quick, funny precision. The "Country Dance" features a silly country girl, a yokel, and an irate squire. A gigolo, overslickly dressed in evening clothes, and a debutante, who wears a long red dress and an absurd feather in her hair, now come forward and dance the "Tango." The gigolo bends the debutante backward, dips her low, runs a scale down her back with his fingers, and with a devilish air tries to overexploit her good nature. The debutante is amenable to any treatment, however, and finishes the dance considerably disheveled. All the dancers come forward now and join in a "Tarantella Finale."

# FACSIMILE

*Choreographic observation in one scene. Music by Leonard Bernstein. Choreography by Jerome Robbins. Scenery by Oliver Smith. Costumes by Irene Sharaff. First presented by Ballet Theatre at the Broadway Theatre, New York, October 24, 1946, with Nora Kaye, Jerome Robbins, and John Kriza.*

A naturalistic ballet of ideas, *Facsimile* takes up a problem which is not only contemporary, but ageless. It is the problem of what modern man shall do with his time. Often apparently immune to authentic feeling, he takes refuge in the constant company of his fellow men, where he can conceal his lack of security. He arranges his life not only to conceal his real identity from his friends, but to hide it from himself. The ballet's program note reads: "Small inward treasure does he possess who, to feel alive, needs every hour the tumult of the street, the emotion of the theatre, and the small talk of society."

The scene of the ballet is a lonely stretch of beach. There is an improvised bathing tent at the left. On the right, disappearing in the distance, is an irregular line of pilings, marking the shore line. When the curtain rises, there is but one figure on stage: a woman in a bathing suit, who is idling away her time. The music is quiet and as lonely as the scene.

We see that the woman is bored. She seems to have nothing to wait for and walks about trying to find something to amuse her. She takes no pleasure in the scene and tosses away inanimate objects. Finally she goes over to her bathing tent, pulls the awning across it, and amuses herself slightly by watching her own shadow. Her own shadow is better than no society at all.

The woman turns and looks down the beach. Someone is coming! She is delighted and childishly runs behind the awning to surprise the stranger. A man strolls onto the scene. He does not see the woman and, just as she has done, tries to find something to amuse him. He plays with his beach towel, looks up and down the beach, thinks of nothing. He wonders why he is there. Now he sees the woman's shadow on the awning.

She steps out coyly. Both these vacuous personalities try to make something of themselves. Alone, they may be nothing, but together, they must pretend that this is not true. They introduce themselves, chatter, begin to flirt. They have nothing else to say to each other and grasp at flirtation like a straw. They therefore take their love very seriously.

But soon they tire even of this recourse. They come to life again as another man strolls toward them. Both imagine that the newcomer might be self-sufficient enough to amuse them. He turns out to be just as insecure as they are.

Now that they are a triangle, one woman and two men, the idlers try to make something out of nothing. The first man pretends to be annoyed at the intrusion of the second and claims the girl's whole attention. The girl plays along with him, and the intruder sees that this might be an interesting game after all. He flirts with the woman and tries to win her from his rival.

The woman now has a situation that amuses her immensely. She plays with the two men adroitly and watches closely to see their reactions. She knows that the important thing is to be so charming that the game will never end, for if either suspects that she is insincere, both will desert her. The men participate in the game for a short while, but the first man finally insists that she stop this nonsense and be his. The woman says, "No." Finally she has to take some way out and confesses that she likes the second man best. Her first lover storms at her and acts furiously jealous. He takes the woman and his rival and drags them across the beach. Soon all three are fighting together, their bodies tied in a writhing knot on the beach.

The woman is through. She cries out, "Stop!" The three figures untangle themselves, and when they see that the girl is really serious and actually prefers neither one of them, the two men leave the scene. The first man acts as if he had been hurt and misunderstood; the second tries to shrug off the incident: what difference could it possibly make to him? Now the woman is alone again. The incident has not made any difference to her, either. As she strolls away from the beach, there is a real question as to whether anything will ever make any difference to her.

# FALL RIVER LEGEND

*Ballet in eight scenes, with prologue. Music by Morton Gould. Choreography by Agnes de Mille. Scenery by Oliver Smith. Costumes by Miles White. First presented by Ballet Theatre at the Metropolitan Opera House, New York, April 22, 1948, with a cast headed by Alicia Alonso, Diana Adams, Peter Gladke, and John Kriza.*

This modern melodrama is founded on fact. Fall River, Massachusetts, in the summer of 1892 was the scene of a hideous crime that attracted the attention of the nation. In that city, a respectable spinster by the name of Lizzie Borden was said to have hacked to death with an ax her father and her stepmother. Lizzie Borden was subsequently tried for this double murder. The jury, however, acquitted her, and she went back to her father's house and lived as a recluse until she died. The murderer was never found.

In *Fall River Legend*, Lizzie Borden is hanged. Here she is called the Accused, and in the prologue of the ballet she faces the gallows.

PROLOGUE   Before the curtain rises, the music begins with loud shrieks of sound that forebode terror. The orchestra quiets down, the curtain rises, and we are about to be witnesses at an execution.

The gallows stands stark and bare, its rope dangling, against a dark, blue-green sky. The Accused, in black, stands on the right with her pastor. Near them is a black, leafless tree. On the left, the speaker for the jury mechanically intones the jury's bill: that the jurors on oath present that on August 4, 1892, the Accused with a certain weapon, to wit, an ax, did assault and kill her stepmother and father with twenty mortal wounds. The Accused stands in a spotlight on the right. She holds the pastor's hand and seems immune to feeling. The speaker for the jury recalls aloud that the house where she committed these murders was the house where she was born. As he remembers that she lived there once with her father and mother in happiness, the drop curtain rises, the gallows slides back to support a corner of the house, and the lights rise on a typical Victorian home set back off the street. Except for the stoop and the front door, the façade of the house is torn away to expose the interior. On the left, we notice a tree stump set for chopping wood. We are to see the Accused in her childhood.

SCENE ONE: THE HOUSE OF THE ACCUSED—THE PAST   The sky that hangs over the house is washed in hideous green. The Accused, dressed now in dark green, stands before her room and watches time go back to the days of her girlhood. Old neighbors and townspeople pass by. Her father and mother are there. The Accused holds out her hands to them longingly, trying to claim their attention, but they do not notice her. A young girl in white appears. We know immediately that she is the Accused as a child. The Accused goes to her, hovers over her as if to protect her, and follows her girlish dance steps to hurdy-gurdy music.

The child runs to her mother. The mother caresses her daughter; the Accused pathetically fingers her mother's white shawl. A strange woman enters. Her back is straight as a ramrod, her chin is held high; she is dressed in severe black with a black boa about her shoulders. This woman marches, rather than walks, and watches with the determined interest in everyone else's business that only the spinster can have. The child is frightened of this woman; the Accused articulates this fright in a sudden tightening of her gestures: as the mature child, she is not only afraid, she knows why she fears. Instinctively the Accused goes to her father and kneels before him to guard him against this woman. But the adamant spinster comes forward; the father welcomes her and shakes her hand, not seeing his daughter as she kneels between them.

The spinster turns on the child and scolds her, apparently for no reason at all, but we see instantly that the spinster is acutely aware of the child's hatred that the Accused has expressed. Just as we note the woman's rudeness in scolding the girl in the presence of her mother, we see that the mother is indifferent. She is ill. She clutches at her heart and faints. A crowd gathers. The father and the child rush to her and hold her lovingly; they are helpless in their fear and shock. The spinster orders the child away from her mother and takes charge like a schoolteacher. The Accused, who has seen it all before, trembles; she holds her hands in front of her face to erase this memory. The child cries.

The mother recovers slowly from the attack, and the father leads her to the house. He turns at the door and bows to the spinster. The crowd disperses. The spinster walks proudly and primly down the street alone. The Accused turns her back on this woman.

The lights go down and a little time passes. When the stage is lit again, we see the child sitting on the steps by the door watching her mother and father dance. The Accused watches, too, as her parents move gracefully in a soft love duet. The child goes to her father, who holds her tenderly; then the mother lifts the girl into her arms. We are watching the ideally happy family. The Accused joins in the reliving of her childhood and with the girl dances gaily about her loving parents. She seems to lose all her hardness and bitterness; she forgets about the future as she and the child become one in their movements and one in their affection for the mother and father.

But the joyous dance is too much for the mother. She has another attack. Two passers-by run for help. The father lifts her carefully and carries her into the house. The Accused and the girl pray together for their mother. The spinster enters and goes immediately into the house. Two women come to the girl and dress her in black: her mother is dead. The Accused clutches the side of the house, hides her agony, and represses the hatred that must soon be asserted.

The father comes out into the street, looking for his daughter. The spinster stands beside him. The child runs to her father's arms and weeps. He attempts to console her, but the child breaks away from him and moves to enter the house. She cannot go in: the spinster, now in complete control, stands in the doorway.

The child returns to her father and kneels at his feet, begging him to allow her to see her mother. The woman in black marches up to the child and, taking her shoulders in her hands, shakes her viciously. The grieving father does not understand. He tries to separate them, then buries his face in his hands. He bows to the woman's authority and falls on his knees at her feet.

In the background, the Accused has turned to watch. Her grief and indignation are uncontrollable; her body writhes obscenely. The spinster sees the mother's white shawl lying on the ground. She goes to pick it up. As she does so, the Accused runs across the stage and leaps to her father's back, claiming him, denying him everything but grief. But he does not feel her presence. The spinster puts the white shawl over her shoulders. The father lifts her in his arms and takes her across the threshold. The door slams shut in the face of the Accused.

SCENE TWO: THE HOME OF THE ACCUSED—THE PRESENT   Many years have passed. The child has disappeared, and the Accused now lives her own part in the tragedy. She is a woman now, a young woman who ought to have been married years ago. As the lights come up, we see her father and her stepmother in the living room of the house. They sit opposite each other, rocking back and forth, reading books that they hold out stiffly in front of them. There is no music. In this oppressive silence, the Accused enters. She takes a chair between the two. All three rock in unison. The silence becomes taut and music begins quietly.

The house is moved forward to the front of the stage. The Accused rises from her chair and snaps her fingers desperately, demanding an end to this sitting and staring. Her father and stepmother do not pay any attention to this outburst. For a moment the Accused sits down again, then, nervously, almost without control, she runs up the stairs and down again, apparently for no reason at all. The stepmother glances up knowingly from her book and whispers to her husband. The Accused returns to sit and rock and stare. She gets up to look out of the window, but the woman in black follows her and snaps the window shade shut in her face. The Accused goes to her father and embraces him, but the woman pulls her away.

The Accused can bear it no longer; she goes out into the yard. The suspicious stepmother follows her for a moment, but sees she is alone and returns to the sitting room. Her husband places the white shawl about her shoulders and stands behind her chair.

In the yard the Accused meets her pastor. He is young and pleasant-looking, slightly deferential to her, and she is plainly attracted to him. They dance together, the girl participating in the dance with a kind of desperate and abandoned joy. She has no other companionship, no one knows the secret agonies and longings of her heart, and she does not know how to be happy in a normal way. The pastor is sufficiently acquainted with her family situation to be sympathetic and kind. The dance over, the two shake hands formally, both of them a little conscious of the absurdity of this convention.

The father opens the door and comes out to look for his daughter. He has acquired now the sternness and brusqueness of his wife. He disapproves of the rendezvous and tells the girl to come in. She does so reluctantly, and the pastor leaves the scene.

Back in the parlor, the family sit rocking again. The Accused moves from her chair and goes into the back hall. She re-enters the room with an ax in her hand. The orchestra sounds a sharp shriek on the strings. The stepmother cringes and seeks protection from her husband. The girl does not understand why she should be afraid and smiles to herself. She goes out into the yard, chops wood, and buries the blade of the ax in the chopping block. She goes back into the house with the wood, wipes her hands, and sits down again. Everything is still the same.

SCENE THREE: THE STREET BEFORE THE HOUSE    The house is moved back. We hear light and gay music, and young happy couples fill the street and dance together. The Accused opens the door and comes out to watch; her family remain seated in the parlor. Sitting on the doorstep, the girl observes wistfully the open happiness of youth. A soft and romantic *pas de deux* is danced by one couple who find themselves alone for a moment; then they are joined by other couples and leave the stage.

The Accused is alone and despondent. She thinks she must hate what she cannot have. The music snarls; she rises, leaps, and turns down the stage in a rapid diagonal. She almost runs into the ax, which still stands buried in the tree stump. She touches the handle. The music cries out in warning, and the girl creeps away from the ax in terror. She falls to the ground. As she rises, her eyes turn, fascinated, back to the ax. She moves toward it; her hand trembles. She is revolted by her thoughts and moves away.

Just as she does so, the young pastor enters with a bouquet of red roses. The music is low and tender. The girl takes the flowers and smoothes her hair. The pastor picks her up and holds her briefly as if she were a child. They begin to dance, and the girl forgets that romance seemed impossible for her five minutes before. The pastor asks her to come with him on a church picnic, and the girl responds eagerly.

Her happiness is short-lived. Her father and stepmother come out of the house and see her with the pastor. The parents creep up on the innocent lovers. The stepmother stares at the girl. The Accused falls to the ground and kicks her feet in an uncontrolled, childish tantrum. She rolls across the stage and finds herself looking straight at the ax. Meanwhile the stepmother is whispering to the pastor about the girl's abnormalities, telling him that she is perhaps insane. The pastor is respectful to the woman, but disbelieves her. The Accused rushes at her stepmother, scratching at the air in front of her. The woman accepts this as but another sign of the girl's insanity and threatens her. Then she and her husband beckon to the girl to come with them back to the house. The Accused gives them a quick look of appraisal, glances at the house, hesitates, and quickly, spasmodically, grabs at her mother's white shawl. Placidly she now goes to the pastor and takes his arm. They walk off together. For the first time in her life, the Accused has defied in action what she has always defied in her mind.

SCENE FOUR: A PRAYER MEETING   The lights go down; the house turns. Over the house, the green sky darkens ominously. But when the lights come up, we find ourselves at a prayer meeting. The pastor stands in the midst of his congregation. The Accused looks on like an outsider: these happy people are like the lovers she saw dancing in front of her house, and she doubts that she can become one of them. The pastor perceives her thoughts, welcomes her, and the women of the church gather about the Accused and befriend her. One of the women kisses her and smiles. The Accused cannot believe her eyes. The congregation divides into two groups, dancing joyously to simulated organ music. The Accused hesitates to participate, but no longer watches as if she were an outsider.

Suddenly the congregation leaves the scene. The Accused and her pastor are alone. The music becomes dispassionately sentimental. The Accused falls to the floor and curls up like a child: never since childhood has she known such kindness as this. She rises; the pastor goes to her and takes her hand. Still the girl is afraid. The Accused looks into his eyes and sees there none of the deception, none of the duplicity she fears. Now she submits wholly to the young man's tender feeling for her and, all doubt gone, allows him to give her hope in a triumphant dance. The music mounts steadily in volume; the two figures move faster, circling and leaping. Then, with a quick cut in the music, the melody becomes soft and yielding. The girl kneels against her lover. He lifts her in his arms, and she curls up against him. He releases her for a moment, and they stand together, side by side, as the other couples in the congregation return.

To fresh, vibrant music, the Accused dances among the other lovers in an ensemble dance strongly reminiscent of a country revival meeting. She is carried high off the ground by two boys and shakes hands with the girls. Knowing happiness, she now has the right to participate. Her joy is open and she moves with quick spontaneity.

Her stepmother enters. When the Accused sees her, her body stiffens, her face contorts in pain, as if her heart were slashed with a knife. She falls to the ground, hysterical in her agony. The pastor reaches out to help her, but the woman in black draws him aside. The Accused sees them whispering together and, losing all control, seems to become as mad as her stepmother imagines her to be. The music whirls insanely. The congregation closes in on her in a semicircle of slow motion. The Accused writhes on the ground, rises, and walks in a trance.

The stepmother and the pastor come to her. The pastor puts her mother's white shawl about her shoulders and politely says good-by. The girl turns to stare after the pastor. She holds out her hand to him in one last plea. He does not see her. The stage darkens. The church turns, to become the house again. The stepmother leads her to the door. Her last hope is gone.

SCENE FIVE: INSIDE THE HOUSE   When the lights come up, the stepmother has gone into the house. The Accused remains on the doorstep. From this position she watches the happy young couples of the town move before her. Changed entirely, she observes them from the private distance of her mind. Her face is a mask. Her father and stepmother sit rocking in the parlor. She can no longer envy the lovers, because the possibility of being like them has been destroyed. Now she moves like an automaton, as if her every step were predetermined. She walks directly to the chopping block. Two cheerful girls walk down the street. The girl does not know they are there. She touches the ax, then picks it up and turns back toward the house. She has no doubt about what she must do. When she enters the parlor, her father and stepmother jump up in terror. The Accused merely looks at them. As the scene blacks out, her free hand moves up to cover her face.

SCENE SIX: THE PRESENT AND THE PAST   A drop curtain falls, to enlighten us on the goriness of the crime. We see depicted here the parlor suspended in mid-air, its chairs overturned; on the floor of the room streams of blood meet to form a red flood.

The Accused enters. She has removed her dress; her petticoat is spattered with blood. Her mother appears. The Accused begins to act out the wish she imagines to be fulfilled by her terrible crime. The mother must approve of the double murder; it is for her that the Accused has killed.

Her mother embraces her, and the girl rests content in her arms. But then the mother notices the red stains. The girl, now again the small child of the ballet's first scene, tries to hide the stains with the hem of her skirt. The mother slaps her hand. She examines the stains and sees that her daughter is covered with blood. She slaps the girl's cheek and pushes her forward. The child's arms hang limp, her fingers flutter. The mother rocks the naughty child against her breast. She smiles a little as she upbraids the Accused and vanishes in the night.

SCENE SEVEN: THE HOME OF THE ACCUSED   The drop curtain rises and the house is seen again. In time, this scene follows immediately after Scene Five. No longer dark, the sky in back of the frame dwelling is now hideously and grossly red. There is no sound, yet the atmosphere is tense, expectant. Neighbors are running up and down the street, frantically trying to locate the source of the ghastly outcries they have heard.

The Accused can be seen emerging from the back hall under the stairs. The orchestra is still quiet. She tries to straighten up the parlor hastily, but stops when she sees that people are looking in the window at her. Then quickly, in a desperate rush, she dashes for the front door. When she appears on the doorstep, the orchestra crashes and blares. The girl runs into the crowd and circles the street. The orchestra continues to play fortissimo as the girl cries out to the world the horror of her home.

Meanwhile townspeople have entered the house. Two men bring forward the bloody ax and the mother's white shawl, laced now with blood. They confront the girl. Her hands quiver before her face. Moving as in a dream, she takes her mother's shawl and holds it to her lips.

The pastor makes his way through the crowd to the Accused. He holds her, lifts her gently as if to protect her. The girl's feet kick at the air in a spasm of desperation. Then she collapses at the pastor's feet.

SCENE EIGHT: THE GALLOWS    The house of the Accused disappears except for a piece of its framework, which forms the gallows we saw in the prologue. She stands with the pastor, awaiting her execution. The people of the town pass by and stare at her. She is not disturbed, for she is preoccupied with her own frantically rapid memories of her crime and what led up to it: the blissful childhood, the loving mother, the father destroyed in his weakness by the demon spinster, the love she has wanted to give all her life, and the love that must now die. She holds out her hand, grasping at her memories, kneels, and opens her arms. The pastor comforts her.

A mother and her small daughter, perhaps the Accused herself, come to see the condemned woman. Ironically, the child shakes her fists at the Accused. Contented couples pass and watch. The Accused lets her head rest briefly on the pastor's shoulder. There is not much time left. He kisses her and leaves her alone. The girl turns to the gallows and opens her arms, as if to welcome the hangman's noose. Her body twitches grotesquely; her neck breaks. The music finishes like thunder. The Accused has been hanged until she is dead.

# FANCY FREE

*Ballet in one act. Music by Leonard Bernstein. Choreography by Jerome Robbins. Scenery by Oliver Smith. Costumes by Kermit Love. First presented by Ballet Theatre at the Metropolitan Opera House, New York, April 18, 1944, with John Kriza, Harold Lang, and Jerome Robbins as the three Sailors; Muriel Bentley, Janet Reed, and Shirley Eckl as the three Passers-by.*

This modern American ballet tells what happens to three sailors who go out on liberty in New York City. The time is "the present": any hot summer night. The scene is a side street in Manhattan.

The music is quiet when the curtain rises. Outlined against the dark city night is the interior of a bar. The entrance to the bar, on the right, leads out onto a street corner. There a bright street lamp shines down on the sidewalk. Inside the bar there are no customers; the lone bartender lazily dries and polishes beer glasses. He begins to read a newspaper. In the background the myriad lights of distant skyscrapers penetrate the sultry night like stars.

Through the side windows of the bar we can make out three sailors walking toward the corner. The music blares out. They rush toward the corner, pivot on the lamppost, and begin to dance in the street in front of the bar. Dressed in clean summer whites, the sailors are out to make the most of the night. They preen a little, adjust their hats to jazzy angles, and strut along the pavement in anticipation of the good time that must naturally come their way. Their dance is like an improvised vaudeville act; it's clear that the three are friends and that they can kid each other and laugh about it. If they have their way, this is going to be an evening to beat all the rest. They try to outdo each other with brief trick dance steps and laugh. Two of them push the third high up in the air between them. Inside the bar the bartender smokes and reads his paper.

The rowdy music that accompanies the sailors' dance slows down and softens. The three men know from experience that simple determination isn't going to get them a good time. They straighten their jackets, readjust their hats, and wonder what to do next: which do they want first—women, drink, or music? One of the sailors leans against the lamppost to consider the problem seriously. One of his pals joins him. Before these two have made up their minds completely, the third sailor enters the bar. His friends race in after him.

The three sailors strut up to the bar with a special salty air for the bartender's benefit. They order three beers, clink their glasses together, down the drinks in unison, and slam the glasses back down on the bar. The bartender eyes them suspiciously: who's going to pay? The sailors look at each other as if such a thought had never entered their heads. Finally one of them is tricked into paying by the other two. As he puts down the money, he tries to shrug off the fact that he always ends up with the short end of the stick.

Now that they've had one drink, the sailors remember that they don't want to drink alone. They look around the empty bar with amused disgust, hitch up their pants, and head for the door. The music is moody, waiting for something to happen. The sailors are getting slightly tired of each other; they wonder if the evening is going to turn out to be a bust, after all. One of them pulls out a stick of gum. He starts to unwrap it, then remembers his friends and splits it with them. The three chew thoughtfully and, one by one, flick the pieces of gum wrapper out into the street to see which one can flick it farthest. The winner wonders what difference it makes.

At this point, just as the three are about to relax into boredom, they straighten up as if lightning had struck. The music breaks out into loud, rhythmic boogie-woogie, and a terrific-looking girl walks by. She wears a tight-fitting blouse and skirt, high patent leather shoes, and carries a red handbag. The girl knows she is being watched; she smiles and by her walk suggests all the things the sailors are imagining. The sailors are struck numb; standing close together, they move as one body—bending so far forward to watch the girl that they almost fall on their faces.

The girl pretends that she hasn't seen them, which sends the boys into action. Suddenly they are three very different individuals, each trying to interest the girl in his own special way. They imitate her walk, laugh at her, grab her purse and toss it around, and all but lie at her feet to get the girl to recognize their existence. The girl wants to be angry and tries to act as if she is, but the boys sense that she's just kidding. When she laughs in warm, friendly recognition, the three sailors smile back and wonder—who saw her first? A small fight breaks out. Two of the boys lift the girl high. She kicks free and stomps off impatiently. The battle has left one sailor lying in the street. He watches as his two friends follow the girl, then lazily picks himself up.

He smoothes out his uniform and starts to go back into the bar. Then, as in a dream, he bumps into a small, cute girl, younger than the first. He apologizes for his clumsiness, smiles winningly, looks her up and down adroitly, and introduces himself. The girl smiles back. The sailor looks over her shoulder to be sure his friends have disappeared and asks her into the bar for a drink. The girl consents.

Inside, the bartender is still reading. The sailor and his girl climb up on two stools and order drinks. He is feeling his way with the redhead, but decides on the old routine. The music stops as he gives her a dazzling, rapid display of What-I've-Been-Through. His hands circle the air and zoom down to attack imaginary ships, and his body vibrates to machine-gun fire as he describes the terrors of life at sea. When the girl takes this in and doesn't laugh at him, just watches, the boy decides that she's not only cute, she's adorable. He asks her to dance.

The orchestra plays a low blues number as they move together slowly. The *pas de deux* they dance is instinctively intimate, and the intimacy—their mutual liking and attraction—is so natural and unforced that formality and doubt would be out of place. This is a made-for-each-other dance that makes sense in its alternate casualness and conviction. He dances with her as he would with any girl, then holds her closely, and she responds warmly to this way of showing how special she is. When the dance is over, he bends down and kisses her softly. The girl smiles and wipes her lipstick off his face. They move together back to the bar.

The sailor picks the girl up and sits her on a stool. He has started to pay for the drinks when a roaring rattle of sound breaks the romantic spell and ushers in his two friends. The two gobs barge into the bar with the first girl and stop dead in their tracks when they see him with a date. He grabs his girl and pulls her toward the door to avoid the intruders. But the girl stops him. The girls are old friends, apparently, and begin to carry on together as girls will.

The boy sees that the situation is hopeless and goes to join his pals at a table. More drinks are ordered. The girls sit down. There are only four chairs, and one of the sailors is left standing. He tries to sit on the first girl's lap—she seemed more experienced and tolerant—but she pushes him off. Two of the sailors dance with the girls, and the boy who found the redhead sits alone for a moment. Now he cuts in. The snare drum signals the quarrel that ensues: who's going to dance with whom? The situation is hopeless. One of the boys has got to clear out or the night will be ruined.

The three sailors finally get together and agree that they'll have a contest to see which one of them can dance best. The girls will be the judges of the two winners, and the third man will scram. Two of the sailors join the girls at the table, and one of the boys begins a solo.

His dance is rowdy and energetic as he tries to outdo all the steps he thinks his friends might try. The girls are delighted at his fresh and arrogant skill and begin to applaud as he finishes his number by jumping up on the bar with one leap. There he poses for an instant, then jumps down, grabs up a beer, and flourishes his glass. The other two sailors razz him as the girls clap their hands.

The next variation is danced by the cute girl's first partner. His dance is subtler, relying more on sinuous, flowing rhythm than boisterousness, more on false modesty than overt bragging. The girls respond to his quiet dance with a sigh, and his friends hold their noses. He lies on the floor with his legs in the air as his number ends. The last sailor tries to combine the two styles of his friends and succeeds brilliantly in a snaky, Latin dance at the end of which he jumps down from a bar stool to kneel on the floor before the girls.

The girls don't know which ones to choose! They argue about it; then the boys argue with them and start to fight among themselves. The competition that began when the first girl passed by on the street turns into anger and rage, and they begin to tear each other apart. The girls cringe against the bar, thinking at first that this can't be serious, but as the battle goes on in earnest, they decide to get out of there fast. The sailors dive behind the bar in a tussle and don't notice that the girls have walked out on them. When they pause and wake up to this fact, they look at each other frantically and dive for the door. Out on the street they can't find the girls. They look at each other with amused disgust, straighten out their uniforms, nurse their aches and pains, and relax again.

What are they to do now? Maybe another drink will help. They re-enter the bar, down a drink apiece, and again the same sailor pays. The friends head back for the street. They stand there under the lamppost, as they did before they first entered the bar at the beginning of the evening. They split another piece of gum three ways; they tear off the paper and flip it into the street.

The music sounds noisily, and a beautiful babe promenades across the street —terrific, you understand? As before, the three bodies slant in unison as they follow her every step and wiggle. The girl struts off down the street on the left. The sailors seem to recover from her fascination and remember the bruises of the battle royal the last girls got them involved in. Each watches the others carefully, to be sure that this feeling is unanimous. This is just a stall. They begin to idle away from each other, laughing the blonde off, when one sailor strikes off like a streak of lightning after the girl. His friends follow. The cycle is endless.

NOTES   Lincoln Kirstein, in his book *Movement and Metaphor* (1970), which analyzes fifty seminal ballets in the history of the art, reminds us that *Fancy Free* "remains the sturdiest characteristic national work" in the American repertory.


# FANFARE

*Classic ballet in one act. Music by Benjamin Britten. Choreography by Jerome Robbins. Lighting by Jean Rosenthal. First presented by the New York City Ballet at the City Center, New York, June 2, 1953, with a cast headed by Yvonne Mounsey, Todd Bolender, Frank Hobi, and Michael Maule.*

*Fanfare,* which had its first performance on Coronation Night 1953, is a visualization of *The Young Person's Guide to the Orchestra,* a well-known work by the contemporary English composer Benjamin Britten. Britten's score consists of variations and a fugue on a theme by Henry Purcell, from *Abdelazor.* These variations and the final fugue illustrate, one by one, the different musical instruments, or group of instruments, that make up the modern symphony orchestra. The ballet is a set of dances arranged to these variations and fugue. A narrator stands at the side of the stage to introduce the ballet and the different instruments.

When the curtain rises, all the dancers who will later represent the different instruments of the orchestra are gathered together on stage under heraldic flags that depict ancient instruments. As Purcell's theme is played by the orchestra, the dancers imitate by noble gestures and attitudes the solemn dignity and nobility of the music. The dancers' costumes differentiate by color the four families of the symphony orchestra: the woodwinds are dressed in blue, the strings in orange, the brass in yellow, and the percussion in black. Each dancer's costume is embellished with a design that identifies the instrument portrayed. Each wears a crown.

After the opening theme has been stated, all the dancers exit. Now the narrator introduces the instruments. First, the woodwinds. The variation of piccolo and two flutes is characterized by a *pas de trois,* danced by three girls. Next, the clarinets, who are represented by a *pas de deux* for a boy and a girl. A lone girl dances to the music of the oboe. She moves in slow, beautiful adagio to its music. Next, two boys dance comically to the variation for two bassoons.

The strings now take the stage. The first and second violins are represented by groups of girls. They are followed by a girl and a boy who dance to the music of the violas. Two girls depict the cellos, while a boy mimes and dances the difficulties of the double bass. Finally the harp, represented by a ballerina all in white, fills the eye with precise and flowing grace to tingling arpeggios.

Next the brass—horns, trumpets, tuba, and trombones—are depicted. Finally, the percussion—drums, cymbals, gongs, etc. The variation which these instruments play is represented by three boys who characterize by horseplay and wit the sudden booms, rattles, crashes, and slaps of the percussion instruments.

Now that all the instruments of the orchestra have been demonstrated, the narrator tells us: "We have taken the orchestra to pieces. It remains to put it back together again. We shall do this in the form of a fugue."

The first voice of the fugue is taken by the woodwinds, one by one; next come the different strings; then the brass; and, at the end, the percussion. The four great families of the orchestra mingle on stage, depicting by a massive dance the cumulative power of all the instruments. The original theme by Purcell is again sounded by the entire orchestra, and all the dancers accompany the music with triumphant, noble flourishes.

*Fanfare* was revived by the New York City Ballet January 15, 1976, at the New York State Theatre, Lincoln Center, New York.

## FANTASIES

*Music by Ralph Vaughan Williams. Choreography by John Clifford. Costumes by Robert O'Hearn. Lighting by Ronald Bates. First presented by the New York City Ballet at the New York State Theatre, Lincoln Center, January 23, 1969, with Kay Mazzo, Sara Leland, Conrad Ludlow, and Anthony Blum.*

A dramatic dance ballet for two couples, *Fantasies* is about reality and the ideal—the real persons we meet and the imagined ideal we sometimes make them into. The music is Vaughan Williams' *Fantasia on a Theme by Thomas Tallis.*

The Chicago critic Thomas Willis said: "The ballet is at once tender and passionate, joyful and wistful, *Romeo and Juliet* in a skewed mirror."

Writing after its première, Clive Barnes said in the New York *Times* that the twenty-one-year-old John Clifford, "the City Ballet's wunderkind, produced his second work for the company and it fascinated . . . It is a very good piece . . . and reveals a choreographer of more than usual interest . . . Here he is concerned with choreography that combines Soviet-style partnering with a very Tudoresque awareness of the psychological motivation of movement. It is a good work, arresting and moving . . . It was a privilege to be there in the theatre when Mr. Clifford's future first became apparent."

## FEAST OF ASHES

*Music by Carlos Surinach. Choreography by Alvin Ailey. Costumes by Jack Venza. First presented by the Robert Joffrey Ballet at the Fashion Institute of Technology, New York, September 30, 1962, with Françoise Martinet, Lisa Bradley, and Paul Sutherland in leading roles.*

This dramatic ballet is based on García Lorca's famous play *The House of Bernarda Alba.* The story, narrated in modern dance techniques, tells the tragic plight of a young girl, Adella, who tries to escape the fatal decisions of her matriarchal family. Her love for her elder sister's fiancé causes a family disaster.

The music for the ballet is Surinach's *Doppio Concertino* and part of his *Ritmo Jondo.* The choreographer has said that he chose these scores "because of their texture, rhythm, color, and dynamics in relation to the theme of the dance drama. Also because, like the work itself, they are a stylization of real Spanish themes—both secular and religious. I have tried in the texture of the movement to re-create, with stylized modern movements, the quality of Lorca's drama—to start as the playwright and actor do with the natural gesture and meaning and to extend these into the intense and telling emotional language of modern dance. I have tried to suggest and comment upon Lorca's view of his Spanish milieu rather than imitate it. I have also tried through this movement to universalize this drama of matriarchal domination. And, last of all, I have tried to remain as faithful as one can in a transposition of this sort to the great play upon which it is based."

Reviewing *Feast of Ashes* in the Washington *Post*, the critic Jean Battey found it "a stunning work of theatre . . . It is magnificently conceived, moving from the daughter's relationship to her mother and family to the inner torment of her lover . . . The dance idiom is strongly that of modern dance (no one is on point), with strong use of Spanish dance to underline the brooding Spanish mood."

## LA FÊTE ÉTRANGE

*Ballet in two scenes. Music by Gabriel Fauré selected by Ronald Crichton. Book by Ronald Crichton. Choreography by Andrée Howard. Scenery and costumes by Sophie Fedorovitch. First presented by the London Ballet at the Arts Theatre, London, May 23, 1940, with Frank Staff, Maude Lloyd, and David Paltenghi in the principal roles. First presented in the United States by the Royal Ballet at the Metropolitan Opera House, New York, with Donald MacLeary, Anya Linden, and Ronald Hynd in the principal roles.*

Based on an episode in a chapter in Alain Fournier's novel *Le Grand Meaulnes, La Fête Étrange* is a ballet about "the tragedy of sensitive adolescence, symbolized not only by the sequence of events, but by the gradual though pronounced change of mood; anticipation leading through happiness to ecstasy, which in its turn fades into sadness and disillusion." These words by Ronald Crichton, whose idea the ballet was, reflect the narrative action, which shows an adventure a country boy has one winter day with the inhabitants of a strange château.

There he wanders early one morning and is fascinated to find a lovely young girl, who mistakes him for a moment for her fiancé, a young nobleman she has come out of the house to meet. She returns to the house, her fiancé arrives, and the boy is about to leave when he meets with guests on their way to the wedding at the château. He joins them and in the second scene, on the terrace of the château, he again meets the lovely young girl. She and all the guests are kind to him, and excited by their warmth and elegance, the boy is happier than he has ever been. But this cannot last. The fiancé, jealous of the bride's kindness to the boy, denounces her and leaves her. The boy is heartbroken and tries in vain to console the girl, who goes into the house alone. The boy leaves and goes back into the country.

Reassessing this ballet after many years, the critic James Monahan wrote in *The Dancing Times* that it was still a beautiful work because "it carries just the sort of 'story-line'—and no more—which a ballet can well support. Ballet is the lyric poetry among the dramatic arts; it is at its weakest when it tries to be most dramatic and at its strongest either when it relies most on 'pure' dance or when, like lyric poetry, it is evoking mood and atmosphere rather than telling a story. There is very little story in *La Fête Étrange;* it is all, or almost all, mood and atmosphere—wonderfully evoked by Fedorovitch and Fauré, gracefully sustained by Andrée Howard."

## FÊTE NOIRE

*Music by Dimitri Shostakovich. Choreography by Arthur Mitchell. Scenery and costumes by Bernard Johnson. Lighting by Fred Barry. Pianist: Craig Sheppard. Conducted by Isaiah Jackson. First presented by the Dance Theatre of Harlem.*

When the Dance Theatre of Harlem presented *Fête Noire* at the Spoleto Festival in July, 1971, the critic William Weaver called the ballet "a kind of black version of *Graduation Ball,* danced with precision and brio," and so indeed it is. The music is the *Concerto No. 2 for Piano and Orchestra* by Shostakovich. The setting is a huge ballroom where, responsive to the developing themes and moods of the music, the dancers celebrate an important occasion that demands of them their very best.

## FIELD FIGURES

*Music by Karlheinz Stockhausen. Choreography by Glen Tetley. Scenery and costumes by Nadine Baylis. First presented by the Royal Ballet, November 9, 1970, at the Theatre Royal, Nottingham, England. First presented in the United States by the same ensemble at the Metropolitan Opera House, Lincoln Center, New York, May 22, 1972, with Deanne Bergsma, Rudolf Nureyev, Vergie Derman, Michael Coleman, Sandra Conley, Wayne Eagling, and Peter O'Brien.*

A dramatic dance ballet, *Field Figures* is performed to two pieces of music by Karlheinz Stockhausen: *Setz die Segel zur Sonne* ("Set Sails for the Sun") and *Verbindung* ("Connection"). They consist of instrumental improvisations that are variously processed by electronic techniques at the time they are played.

The setting is an abstract one of vertical rods and there is about the piece a sense of the magnetic field—what happens when certain bodies in certain situations attract and repel, satisfy and frustrate. The three girls and the four boys in the ballet are variously paired but there is one principal couple.

Writing in *The Times* of London, the critic John Percival said: "There is nothing pretty about *Field Figures,* but it is, to my mind, extraordinarily beautiful."

Richard Buckle in the *Sunday Times* of London said that *Field Figures* "is one of the most important creations of our time." Writing in the *Financial*

*Times,* Andrew Porter called it "one of the most perfectly shaped, impressive and enthralling works in the repertory."

## LA FILLE MAL GARDÉE (The Unchaperoned Daughter)

*Ballet in three scenes. Music by Ferdinand Hérold. Choreography by Jean Dauberval. First presented at Bordeaux, France, 1789, and at the Grand Theatre, Paris, July 1, 1789. First presented in the United States in various versions beginning in 1794. Revived by Ballet Theatre, with music by Wilhelm Hertel and choreography restaged by Bronislava Nijinska and Dimitri Romanoff, at the Center Theatre, New York, January 19, 1940, scenery and costumes by Serge Soudeikine.*

Many people who go to the ballet and chance to come across a work that was originally presented more than a hundred and fifty years ago imagine that such a ballet must be sad—perhaps an antique tragedy. But *La Fille Mal Gardée* is a comedy. The earliest of all the ballets in the current repertory, its universally comical situations are no doubt responsible for its survival.

Soon after the music begins, a painted drop curtain depicts the principal characters of the ballet. On the left are Lisette and Colin, the two lovers. A rotund Cupid painted at the top of the scene directs a pointed arrow at the heroine. Lisette's mother, Madame Simone, dominates the scene, trying to watch her daughter and be pleasant to the suitor she has chosen for her. The story contained in this picture gradually unfolds as the drop curtain rises. The ballet is set in a small provincial French town. The time is about two hundred years ago.

SCENE ONE: THE FARM OF MADAME SIMONE   Alongside the steep-roofed house of Madame Simone, a "rich farmerette," is the family barnyard. In back, a rushing stream cascades down a hill. Madame Simone sits on a bench at the left, whiling away the time of day. Two neighbors join her to gossip. She bustles off with them.

The music suggests the arrival of the heroine, and Lisette enters on the left. Dressed in a light-blue skirt with a red bodice, with blue ribbons in her hair, she is the picture of innocent, country prettiness. The day has just begun, and because she is supposed to be busy at one task or another, Lisette pretends to arrange several flowerpots on the bench. She bows to several of the village boys, bound for the fields with their scythes, as she waters the flowers. Colin, a good-looking farmer, enters on the left, carrying a rake. He sits down on the bench, and Lisette, anxious to be surprised by his arrival, absent-mindedly waters his head. Colin jumps up, and he and Lisette immediately begin to dance together. Their dance reveals that the two have been attracted to each other for some time, that this is not their first rendezvous. Colin lifts Lisette boldly, yet gently.

The love duet is interrupted by Lisette's mother. Directly she approaches, the two lovers rush to hide behind the bench. Madame Simone discovers them,

however, and chases Colin around the stage. Hastily he embraces Lisette and
rushes off. Madame Simone, in a high temper, proceeds to lecture her daughter on her duty to make a proper marriage. Lisette protests that she is absolutely innocent of any flirtation, but her mother persists in her rage. The two
neighbors come in to watch the scene. Lisette finally secures her mother's forgiveness by offering her, with a sweet smile, one of her own flowers.

Trumpets announce the arrival of four of Lisette's friends. They are followed by a group of villagers. The young people want Lisette to join them.
Dutifully she asks her mother's permission and she begins to dance. Colin
sneaks in at the back and conceals himself in the crowd. He runs out and takes
Lisette's hand when her mother stalks off. The two dance a lively duet, surrounded by their friends. The music is gay and sparkling. The conviviality is
short-lived, however, for Madame Simone returns, sees Colin, and sends him
packing. She makes a point of her daughter's idleness by presenting scythes to
her four friends.

Lisette attempts to console herself by dancing with her friends as they celebrate the harvesttime. She tries to leave with them when they go, but her
mother pulls her back. Lisette herself is now in a temper. She stomps, shakes
her fists pathetically, cries, and hides her face in her hands. Her mother takes
her hands away and tries to make amends. Colin has entered quietly and
stands in back of Madame Simone. That is consolation enough for Lisette. She
waves to him. Her mother notes the gesture, but cannot find a reason for it.
Colin does not conceal himself for long, however. The impetuous girl rushes to
him. They embrace briefly before Madame Simone leaps at them to drag
Lisette back toward the house.

She sits her daughter down on the bench. Lisette rises and brings out a butter churn. Her mother fills the churn with cream and orders her daughter to
work. Lisette churns away, and her mother leaves the scene. Colin leaps in
behind Lisette. He places his hands on hers and easily persuades her to stop
her work. He sits down on the bench beside her; Lisette, suddenly embarrassed at being alone with her lover, rises and dances. She turns softly and
slowly, beguiling Colin with her sweet motion. When she finishes her dance
with a series of rapid turns, Colin throws out to her a long blue ribbon. Lisette
catches it and, holding the flowing ribbon above their heads, the two dance together romantically. Lisette tosses the ribbon back to Colin, who fixes it halter-
fashion around her shoulders, after which the girl performs her steps as if by
his command. Lisette pirouettes into his arms, Colin ties the ribbon about her,
and the girl poses against her lover. The two then leave the stage.

Thomas, a vinegrower, enters with his son, Alain. Come to see Madame
Simone by appointment, the obese Thomas is decked out in a bright-green
suit; he is determined to be formal and correct. His son, determined to be
playful and completely oblivious to his surroundings, leaps about the stage trying to catch butterflies in a net. Thomas reprimands him and pulls him to a
bench.

Madame Simone, dressed in her best purple, arrives to greet the guests.
With ceremonious gestures, she and Thomas discuss the suitability of a marriage between their children. Madame Simone is readily persuaded of Alain's

eligibility when Thomas dangles a bag of gold in her face. The woman approaches to examine the young man, ascertains that he is sound of limb if not of mind, and gives her approval. She drags Lisette out to meet her fiancé. Dutifully the girl has changed her clothes for the occasion, but she has no idea of its real meaning. Both parents push their children toward each other. Both children step back in horror as they realize the meaning of their parents' interview. Each tries to escape, but the parents hold them secure. The curtain falls as they both kneel, their faces turned away from each other. Lisette's white dress and pink ribbons are for the wrong man. Madame Simone stands over them in an attitude of supreme happiness. During the scene change, Thomas and Madame Simone, accompanied by the neighbors, drag the engaged couple off to the village notary to make the marriage settlement final.

SCENE TWO: THE VILLAGE GREEN   On the painted backdrop, wheat fields are seen in the distance. Sheaves of freshly cut wheat are propped up where the workers have left them. A windmill stands over the fields on a hill at the back. On the right is a great tree; two cows meditate nearby. The workers of the village, colorfully dressed girls and their companions, pause for a general dance. Lisette and Alain are pushed into the scene by their parents. Despite all their complaining, the two are made to stand close together. They are able to separate only when Thomas asks Madame Simone to dance. The aged couple cavort grotesquely about the green; it has suddenly occurred to Madame Simone that she, too, might be quite a match, and she flirts with the vine-grower.

Meanwhile Colin has entered quietly on the right. He sees that his sweetheart has been promised to another and turns away. Madame Simone and Thomas race off to pursue their flirtation elsewhere, and some of Lisette's friends, noticing Colin's plight, encourage the girl to comfort the poor lad. Lisette touches his arm. By her soft, endearing gestures the girl convinces him that she herself has had nothing to do with the proposed match. Colin puts his arms about her, and their foreheads touch. He kneels, and the two begin an adagio to the melody of solo strings and an accompanying harp. The villagers sit on the ground to watch the lovers. Lisette leaves the scene after the dance is over, and Colin performs a bright, dazzling variation. Lisette returns for a winsome, engaging dance in which she lifts her skirt softly, with innocent coquetry. Her variation increases in momentum; at the end she turns brilliantly and cuts her movement off suddenly with a swift, pert pose.

Alain, who has been off chasing after butterflies, runs onto the scene, brandishing his net before him. He circles the stage in long, high leaps. Two of the girls try to engage his attention. The youth ignores their flattery, but the girls persist and dance on either side of him. Alain abandons them, jumping off into the wings in pursuit of his hobby.

Thunder is heard and the scene darkens; lightning flashes illumine the hurried dashing back and forth of the villagers. Lisette and Colin follow as their friends run for cover. Alain rushes in, trembling with fright at the lightning. He hides his head under a girl's skirts and pushes her off toward safety. The drop curtain falls.

SCENE THREE: MADAME SIMONE'S HOUSE   Lisette enters quickly to escape the storm. Her mother follows and bustles about the room. Lisette pours coffee for her, then sits at her feet as Madame Simone begins to work at her spinning wheel. Lisette tries to sneak away, but her mother orders her to read a book she gives her. Lisette looks at a page or two, then asks her mother the meaning of one of the words. Madame Simone is horrified: she has given her daughter the wrong book! A romantic novel, no less! The girl succeeds in crawling away a few feet until Madame Simone seizes her from behind and draws her back to her chair. She takes up her sewing again.

Colin opens the transom above the door and throws in a flower to Lisette. Lisette turns around and sees him. Immediately her mother senses her agitation and commands her to be still. Colin, by passionate signs, beseeches her to dance for him. The girl persuades her mother to play the tambourine so that she can practice her dancing. Lisette dances flirtatiously for Colin's benefit. The old woman tires of the tambourine and falls off to sleep. Lisette approaches her on tiptoe. As the girl takes her key, her mother wakens and beats the tambourine. Lisette continues her dance, and at its conclusion Madame Simone kisses her in reward.

Boys and girls of the village enter, bringing with them sheaves of wheat, which they stack against a table. Lisette would like to follow them off, but her mother commands her to take her turn at the spinning wheel. Lisette stamps her foot and throws herself down in the chair to sulk. Her mother leaves the room.

The orchestra repeats the melody to which she and Colin danced so happily, and Lisette imagines what it would be like to be married to the man of her own choice. She puts her hands on her heart and blows a kiss toward the door. She sees herself surrounded by Colin's children, whom she scolds; she rocks her arms as if they held a child.

To Lisette's embarrassment, Colin is there in the room watching her. The sheaves of wheat are thrown aside, and her lover sits smiling at her. She sits beside him for a moment, then jumps up as he proposes to her seriously. Colin pleads with her—after all, she has just imagined herself as his wife—but the girl in her embarrassment and confusion denies her love and shoves the boy toward the door. Colin begins to lose his temper at her stubbornness and is delighted to find her even more flustered when she finds that the door is locked!

Lisette runs to the chair and sees that she can keep up the pretense no longer. Colin kneels at her feet and places his head in her lap. The two trade their scarves as a pledge of their love. Madame Simone can be heard approaching. Lisette tries to hide Colin—under the little table, in a small chest. In desperation, she pushes him into the hayloft and slams the door shut just as her mother enters.

Lisette thinks she is safe but she has forgotten Colin's scarf. Madame Simone spots it instantly and fetches a large switch to beat the girl. Lisette runs, but the old woman catches up with her, spanks her soundly, and, as an additional penalty, locks her in the hayloft!

Visitors are heard outside. Madame Simone admits Thomas and Alain, the village notary and his secretary following in their wake. Villagers accompany them to witness the marriage contract. The notary buries his face in his registry, the parents rejoice, and the preoccupied Alain toys with the spinning wheel. Madame Simone presents him with the key to the hayloft and tells the youth where to find his bride. Alain unlocks the door. Lisette and Colin step out sheepishly, their clothes and hair covered with hay.

Madame Simone is scandalized. Before all the village, her daughter has ruined the family's reputation. Lisette begs her to understand. Colin joins Lisette, and both lovers kneel before her. At first Madame Simone refuses to listen. Then she realizes that the notary can quite easily make another marriage contract and consents. Lisette kisses her joyfully. Colin kisses her. The two lovers kiss, and Madame Simone embraces them both.

*Ballet in two acts. Music by Ferdinand Hérold, freely adapted and arranged by John Lanchbery. Choreography by Frederick Ashton. Scenery and costumes by Osbert Lancaster. First presented by the Royal Ballet at the Royal Opera House, Covent Garden, January 28, 1960, with Nadia Nerina, David Blair, Stanley Holden, and Alexander Grant in the principal roles. First presented in the United States by the Royal Ballet at the Metropolitan Opera House, New York, September 14, 1960, with the same principals.*

Although other versions of the ballet are often danced, Frederick Ashton's re-creation of *La Fille Mal Gardée* is now permanent in the modern repertory. In 1960 Tamara Karsavina, the ballerina who danced in the ballet in Russia, recalled an earlier production in the Covent Garden program: "This production we now regard as the turning point in the history of ballet; a break-away from the formal, pseudoclassical tradition; a ballet of action instead of a succession of conventional dances which use the plot as a peg on which to hang a succession of *entrées, pas seuls, pas d'ensemble . . .* The story lends itself admirably to ballet treatment; there is not a dance in it that does not flow directly out of a natural situation. It is a charming period piece singularly compatible with the artistic trends of today . . ."

The music for the ballet, entirely restudied and arranged by John Lanchbery after consulting varied scores for the ballet by Hertel, Feldt, and others, is based on the 1828 score of Ferdinand Hérold, then chorus master of the Paris Opéra. After a pleasant overture, the curtain rises. An inner drop curtain depicts a charming rural landscape with a village in the distance. Arnold Haskell in the Covent Garden program describes the action when this inner curtain rises:

ACT ONE, SCENE ONE: THE FARMYARD   "Lise, the only daughter of Simone, a widow and owner of a prosperous farm, is in love with Colas, a young farmer, but her mother has more ambitious plans.

"The dawn of a busy day on the farm is heralded by the cock and his attendant hens. Lise, disappointed at not seeing Colas, leaves a ribbon tied in a lover's knot, as a token of her devotion. He finds it and ties it to his staff. The lovers meet, but are interrupted by Simone, who sets her daughter a task of churning butter. Colas, in hiding in the loft, joins her. The work is shared and then forgotten as they declare their love.

"The farm girls summon Lise to play, but her mind is elsewhere. Her suspicious and ever-watchful mother catches hold of her and chastises her. Just then Thomas, the prosperous and wealthy proprietor of a vineyard, arrives with his son Alain. Simone, aware of their mission, dismisses Lise. Thomas asks her hand for his son, and when Lise returns, Alain, coy and clumsy, shows off his paces. She is amused and a little shocked by his antics, but definitely not interested. They set off for the harvest.

ACT ONE, SCENE TWO: THE CORNFIELD   "It is harvest time, and after working in the fields the harvesters, led by Colas, relax in a joyful dance. Lise and Alain dance, but Colas intervenes, and the young girl makes it clear where her preference lies. One of the harvesters plays the flute to the general merriment, and Alain thinks he will have a turn, but the harvesters mock him and he is rescued from their horseplay by his indignant father.

"The field is now left for the triumphant Colas, who dances with Lise. Simone joins in the merriment. But suddenly they are interrupted by a storm that drenches them, scattering them far and wide.

ACT TWO: INTERIOR OF THE FARM   "Mother and daughter, soaked by the storm, return to the farmhouse. They sit down to spin: work, thinks the mother, should keep Lise out of mischief. But she is overcome by sleep and Lise, who has seen Colas through the gate, tries to take the key from her. Simone awakes and, in order to remain watchful, plays the tambourine for Lise to dance. But the tap grows feebler, she begins to nod, and now she is fast asleep. Lise runs to the door and makes love to Colas through the unfriendly bars. The knocking of the harvesters, coming for their pay, awakens Simone. Colas enters with them and conceals himself in a pile of straw. Simone tells her daughter to get on with her chores as she leaves to give the harvesters a drink. Lise, thinking she is alone, dreams of the delights of married life. Colas cannot resist, and comes out from hiding. She is bashful at first having been taken by surprise, but once again they declare their love, exchanging scarves as a token.

"As Simone reappears, Lise hustles Colas into her bedroom. The ever-suspicious mother realizes that the lovers have been meeting, and in her turn hustles Lise into the bedroom, locking the door.

"Alain and his father now arrive with a notary to complete the marriage contract. When it is signed, Simone hands Alain the key to the bedroom. After a moment of idiotic indecision, he opens the door, and to everyone's dismay, Colas and Lise emerge. The lovers fall on their knees to ask Simone for forgiveness and a blessing. In spite of the fury of Thomas and Alain, urged on by the notary and the villagers, she finally gives in amidst general rejoicing."

NOTES   Andrew Porter, music and dance critic of *The Financial Times*, London, has said of this ballet: "The first act, in two parts, lasts just over an hour; the second, thirty-six minutes. There is not an ounce of padding. Invention tumbles on invention, and the whole thing is fully realized in dance. The second act, in fact, is continuous, *durchkomponiert;* there is no possible break for applause except between the sections of the *grand pas de deux* just before the final gigue. The choreography is wonderfully fresh, and the shape of the scenes is beautifully balanced.

"There is comedy, sentiment, jollity, romance, flowing one into another. There is a clog dance for Widow Simone, brilliantly sustained; a 'parade' before the drop curtain which must be the most delightful of its kind ever done; a *valse des moissoneurs* in the first act which one would like to be twice as long; a stave dance; breathtaking 'Russian' lifts; passages which seem to be inspired by the virtuosity of the Georgians.

"Ribbons run like a motif through the first two scenes. They are used in a score of ingenious and beautiful ways, reaching their climax in a great maypole where the fleeting kaleidoscope of stage patterns is recorded by the plaited thread.

"To a far greater extent than any of the classics as we now know them, *La Fille Mal Gardée* seems to be all 'highlights,' without any of the stretches that we sit through for the sake of the best bits. And this cunningly varied and ceaseless flow of dance is constantly enlivened by the most brilliant inventions by the way, comic or touching, that give fullness to the ballet—far more of them than can be taken in at once."

Interviewed by the critic Don McDonagh in *Ballet Review* (Vol. 3, No. 4), Frederick Ashton observed that *La Fille Mal Gardée* is a really English work. "It has the Lancashire clog dance which is almost like a folk dance. *Fille* came about in a very odd way because of Karsavina. She was always after me to do it. I didn't particularly like the idea and I didn't like the music to the traditional version, by Hertel. I went back to Hérold, who did it originally . . . It was mostly a matter of selecting and curtailing. I always work out the structure of a ballet before I start—who's doing what and for how long. I don't do any steps until I'm with the dancers. The structure for *Fille* I worked out with John Lanchbery, marking the music. I have a great instinct for the right length of things. And I set that very tightly. It's a kind of minutage. And after I set that, in the case of *Fille* at least, it went very easily. Everything just flowed."

Readers are referred to David Vaughan's *Frederick Ashton and His Ballets* for more details on the genesis of *Fille Mal Gardée*. Vaughan has written in *Ballet Review* about Ashton and this ballet:

"He is a great comic choreographer. *La Fille Mal Gardée* is a perfect expression of his artistic benevolence. The dramatic complications are ingenious and of great concern to the characters involved. Yet the problems can be solved, the mistakes can be mended and the mistaken forgiven. As in Molière, all balance which can be attained is attained (the lovers marry) and any remaining sources of imbalance are neutralized (Molière's hypochondriac becomes a doctor himself, Ashton's Alain goes off with his umbrella).

"Each set of characters has its distinct style. The young lovers dance in a now playful, now softly melting classicism. The farmers' choreography combines classicism with folk dance borrowings to suggest the union of man with nature and a love of meaningful work. Simone, Thomas, and Alain derive from farce, pantomime, and music-hall. The dancing chickens, which some ballet-goers find annoyingly "unrealistic," may be there to be deliberately artificial, to emphasize right from the start that this ballet, however homely its subject, is not photographic naturalism, but instead uses the exaggerations of comedy to point to certain human truths."*

# FILLING STATION

*Ballet-document in one act. Music by Virgil Thomson. Choreography by Lew Christensen. Book by Lincoln Kirstein. Scenery and costumes by Paul Cadmus. First presented by Ballet Caravan at the Avery Memorial Theatre, Hartford, Connecticut, January 6, 1938, with Lew Christensen, Marie-Jeanne, Erick Hawkins, Michael Kidd, Todd Bolender, Eugene Loring, and Fred Danieli in the principal roles.*

*Filling Station* is not only one of the first modern ballets on a familiar American subject, but one of the first ballets to employ American music, scenery, and costumes by an American, and American dancers. It was the first ballet on an American subject commissioned by Lincoln Kirstein for his Ballet Caravan, a small American company founded in 1936 which, with the Balanchine-Kirstein American Ballet, was to be the precursor of the present New York City Ballet.

*Filling Station* is an attempt to discover an American hero, a hero equivalent to the heroes of classical European ballets. The makers of the ballet have chosen a filling station attendant as their hero. The fact that the ballet succeeded in its aim was recently demonstrated by the marked success of its revival, which clearly indicated that the popular American myth of 1938 was still viable fifteen years later.

After a robust overture, the curtain rises on the interior of Mac's filling station. It is night. A neon sign advertising gas is seen in reverse against the large plate-glass window on the left. In the rear, there is a door leading to the station rest room.

Mac, the station attendant, is whiling away the lonely hours of the night reading a tabloid. He puts down the paper and begins to dance. He moves about the stage with vigorous leaps and turns. His dance is interrupted by a motorist who comes into the station to ask for directions. The motorist is dressed like a golfer in a comic strip: he wears violently colored checkered knickers, straw hat, and smokes a cigar.

Mac tries to direct him to his destination by pointing out the route on a map. When the motorist fails to understand, Mac produces a huge enlargement of the map to set him right. Behind this map, two truck drivers, friends of Mac, sneak into the station while Mac gives the motorist final directions.

As soon as the motorist departs, the two truck drivers greet Mac and the three men dance an athletic *pas de trois* that features cartwheels and somer-

* Reprinted by permission of *Ballet Review*, Marcel Dekker, publisher.

saults. Their good fellowship is cut short by the arrival of a state trooper, who accuses the truck drivers of speeding. The men deny this, and the state trooper leaves after warning them severely.

The motorist in knickers returns, this time with his family and his golf gear. His wife, a huge blonde in unbecoming slacks, towers over her husband and constantly berates him. Their daughter, a constantly whining child, is clearly in need of the rest room. While his wife and daughter disappear into the rear of the station, the motorist entertains Mac and the truck drivers by practicing golf. He is not happy for long, however. When wife and daughter return, they combine to make life so miserable for him that he happily leads them back to their car outside.

Now an intoxicated young couple drop by on their way home from a party at the local country club. The girl stumbles in first, followed by her escort. She is in no condition to dance, but insists on doing so. The boy supports her in adagio poses, holding the girl's almost limp body upright when she collapses in his arms.

As the couple finish this comic adagio, they are joined by Mac and the truck drivers. By this time, the girl wants to dance with everybody. All the men join her in a dance that is climaxed as she is tossed from one man to another and thrown high into the air. When the unhappy motorist, who has momentarily escaped from his wife and child, re-enters the station, the dance is at fever pitch. Noting the newcomer, the girl jumps into his arms just as his wife comes in after him.

The motorist tries to stay on the opposite side of the stage from his wife as all join in the "Big Apple." But the celebration is soon broken up. A gangster enters. He lines all the people up and instructs them to place all their jewelry and cash in a bag he snatches from the motorist's wife. Everyone conforms to his wish except Mac, who sneaks outside and turns out the lights.

Directly the lights go out, the stage is in confusion. Mac enters with a flashlight, and soon the stage is filled with the beams of flashlights carried by the others as they try to help Mac track down the gangster. Blinded by their lights, the gangster shoots.

When the lights come up, it can be seen that the girl from the country club is dead. All gather around her body. The state trooper enters and takes the gangster off to prison. The girl's body is lifted high and carried off in solemn procession. Just as the ballet seems about to end in a tragedy, the girl wakes from the dead and waves at Mac as her cortege moves out of the station. Mac saunters about for a moment, then returns to his newspaper.

NOTES   *Filling Station* was revived by the New York City Ballet on May 12, 1953, at the City Center, New York. Jacques d'Amboise, Janet Reed, and Michael Maule danced the principal roles.

# FIREBIRD

*Dramatic ballet in three scenes. Music by Igor Stravinsky. Choreography by Michel Fokine. Scenery and costumes by Golovine and Bakst. First presented by Diaghilev's Ballets Russes at the Théâtre National de l'Opéra, Paris, June 25, 1910, with Tamara Karsavina as the* Firebird, *Michel Fokine as* Prince Ivan, *and Enrico Cecchetti as* Kastchei.

*Firebird* marks Igor Stravinsky's entry into the field of ballet music. Perhaps his most famous score, the original ballet to the music remained dormant for many years. In 1954, to commemorate the twenty-fifth anniversary of the death of Diaghilev, under whose auspices the original had been created, the Royal Ballet produced in London a reconstruction of the original, with scenery and costumes by Natalie Gontcharova. This was made possible by Serge Grigoriev, Diaghilev's régisseur for many years, Lubov Tchernicheva, and Tamara Karsavina. The revival was first presented at the Empire Theatre, Edinburgh, August 23, 1954, with Margot Fonteyn as the *Firebird,* Michael Somes as *Prince Ivan,* Svetlana Beriosova as the *Tsarevna,* and Frederick Ashton as *Kastchei.* This production was first given in the United States at the Metropolitan Opera House, September 20, 1955, with the same principals.

Fokine has described in his book *Memoirs of a Ballet Master* how he envisaged the action of the ballet, and the background to the collaboration that produced the final work. In the Royal Ballet revival, the curtain rises on the enchanted garden of the sinister Kastchei. A high golden fence protects his golden fruit and the lovely princesses he has captured. The Firebird now appears, followed by Prince Ivan. The Firebird attempts to steal the golden apples from Kastchei's magic tree but Ivan captures her. He vows that he will not let her go unless she gives him one of her feathers. With her feather as talisman, he is assured of her magic intercession if he should ever need it. The Firebird yields to his entreaties and leaves.

Now in the growing darkness Ivan learns from the most beautiful of the captive maidens held prisoner by Kastchei how the evil magician entraps innocent travelers and turns them into stone. Ivan is attracted to the lovely creature who tells him this strange story and they dance. At dawn they kiss and part, the girl warning him not to follow her.

Ivan does not heed the warning. Following after his beloved, he opens the gate to Kastchei's magic garden and alarms sound, bells peal, and swarms of monsters rush out. Kastchei emerges, his enslaved creatures do him homage, and he approaches Ivan menacingly. The wicked magician tries to turn him to stone but just then Ivan remembers the Firebird's feather. He waves the feather in Kastchei's face and the Firebird instantly reappears. She compels Kastchei's monsters to dance until they collapse. Then, remembering the great egg that holds the soul of the magician, she orders Ivan to steal it. Finding it, Ivan throws the egg into the air. As it falls and breaks, Kastchei dies. Ivan then is free to marry his princess. All at the ceremony rejoice. The Firebird flies away forever.

*Music by Igor Stravinsky. Choreography by George Balanchine. Setting by Marc Chagall. Lighting by Jean Rosenthal. First presented by the New York City Ballet at the City Center, New York, November 27, 1949, with Maria Tallchief as the* Firebird *and Francisco Moncion as* Prince Ivan.

The composer of *Firebird*, Igor Stravinsky, once said that Russian legends have as their heroes men who are "simple, naïve, sometimes even stupid, devoid of all malice, and it is they who are always victorious over characters that are clever, artful, complex, cruel and powerful." Prince Ivan in this ballet is such a hero: he is a simple hunter who stumbles into the eerie garden of an evil monster, there falls in love with a beautiful princess held captive by the ogre, and rescues her with a supernatural power granted him by a magical bird of fire.

SCENE ONE: A FOREST   As the music to the ballet begins, we have that first suggestion of the mystery and magic that will control Ivan's destiny. No sooner has the orchestra—with its low, throbbing strings and baleful trombones—given us a hint of darkness and foreboding, than the curtain rises to present us with an enormous painting of the ballet's heroine, the Firebird who will help the prince to free the world of one of its monstrous evils. The Firebird is depicted as bright, glorious, and triumphant—a fantastic creature, half bird, half woman. She has the face and arms of a charming young girl and a body of shimmering feathers that tapers off in orange-speckled flame. This colorful figure is painted against a background of amorphous, purple shapes. The music now suggests unimagined giants plodding across the earth and a fairyland peopled with primeval beings sadly singing an accompaniment.

Now the painted curtain rises. It is dark, and as the stage brightens slightly, we can see in the background trees so thickly crowded that the sun can scarcely penetrate. Here in the forest we are transported visually to the world of fantasy at which the music has hinted, and when the prince enters, his bow stretched tightly, ready to destroy any creature concealed in the thicket, we understand why he hunts with care. Ivan wears a costume more becoming to an untutored Russian peasant than to a royal prince, but this serves only to remind us that we are watching a story of a time before the primitive court of the Tsar was altered by European opulence.

Subdued, half-uttered cries come from behind the dark trees. Ivan looks about him, searching for the beasts that may lie waiting in the shadows, when a low, steady drum, followed by an answering horn, indicates that he is about to meet his prey. Suddenly the music whirs rapidly and brightly and from above a bright amber light races around and around the prince. Ivan, almost blinded, throws up his arms in astonishment and tries to avoid the shadow the light makes of his startled figure. He runs off, seeking the safe darkness. The music increases its speed, and on stage to its swift accompaniment dances the dazzling Firebird.

Her entrance is as strong and brilliant as the bright red she wears. As she crosses the stage in a series of swiftly executed leaps and poses, followed by that same amber light which announced her arrival, glints of light catch her figure in various attitudes to reveal the long red feather that rises high on her head. Her arms and shoulders are speckled with gold dust, and the shimmering red bodice reflects spangles of brilliance about her moving form. She dances frantically, in continuous movement, to music that mirrors her great joy in displaying vivid images of flight. Even here, in the secluded forest, the Firebird refuses to be earth-bound and seems to resist nature by performing dashing movements that whip the very air about her.

The prince emerges from the shadows to watch unseen. Wishing to capture this creature who moves so magnificently, he reacts with wonder as he discovers that this marvelous bird is also a ravishing woman. He follows her surreptitiously while the Firebird, unaware of the hunter who pursues her, darts about the stage climaxing her solo with rapid turns on point across the stage. This movement increases in momentum with the music, and just as her accelerating spin reaches its fullest force and the music its highest pitch, Ivan dashes forward and reaches out to catch the Firebird about the waist. Brought down to earth, she freezes at his touch, all movement ceasing. Slowly she backs away, in terror of the hunter, in modesty at sight of the man. She turns to escape, but Ivan, fascinated at her daring now that she is in his power, holds her secure. The Firebird, rigid with fear, her arms stiff across her body, falls back against him reluctantly, apparently resigned, but now her arms fly out and beat the air in a frantic effort to free herself.

Ivan will not release his prey, and the frightened Firebird, certain of death by his hand, pleads for mercy. The prince is moved to pity by this appeal for freedom and gently loosens his grasp. He holds out his arm, and the Firebird, in extended arabesque, falls across it, bending her head so that her headdress almost touches the floor at the prince's feet as she bows in tribute to his pity and courtesy.

Encouraged now by the prince's tenderness, the Firebird moves back to dance again. When she turns full circle, Ivan comes forward to support her. Moved by his compassionate strength, as Ivan is moved by her unclaimed love, the Firebird walks toward this man so strange to her. He holds her hand high, then she runs toward him, her body falling back full-length in mid-air. Ivan catches her swooping body and supports her again, as she repeats this movement of ultimate sacrifice and trust. Assured of his sympathy, the Firebird now dances with the prince.

Standing behind her, Ivan supports her arms with his own as the Firebird, standing on point, bends her knees to the floor, then rises to his embrace. Legs spread wide, she slides across the stage as Ivan holds her. The haunting melody of their *pas de deux* soars to its height as the Firebird is held motionless on point, her right leg extended in stillness. Then she falls back, and Ivan swings her around and around in great circles as her free arm flutters in flight. Reminded by this of her greater freedom in the air, the Firebird moves as if to leave the prince. He bows to her formally in homage, and in gratitude for his generosity in releasing her, the Firebird takes from her breast a brilliant red feather. She indicates to the prince that this feather is a magic charm: he need only wave it in the air and she will come to his aid, should he ever require it. Ivan, in respectful deference to the truly supernatural being he now understands the Firebird to be, thanks her and watches regretfully as she turns and leaps gloriously into the wings. The prince follows, transfixed as the music ends in enchanted serenity.

SCENE TWO: KASTCHEI'S GARDEN   While Ivan remains in the shadows, marveling at his encounter with the Firebird, we hear a gay melody from the orchestra. Ten young princesses run in, happily dancing to its tune. They wear long peasant dresses with little caps, and their innocent, carefree gambols make it impossible for us to believe that they are, in reality, captives of the monster Kastchei who rules over the forest. Two of the young girls carry scarves and, as the group dances with simple but elegant grace, these two playfully direct the dancing of the others. They are all dancing together when Prince Ivan startles them. Shocked at the intrusion of a stranger in their dangerous world, the princesses gather together and whisper excitedly. Ivan is amused at their fear and approaches them. From a respectful distance, in mock seriousness and formality, he beckons one of the maidens to come to him. The princesses are agitated by this request and wonder at Ivan's audacity. Ivan insists, and one of the girls at last leaves the group. Ivan bows to her, then whispers softly in her ear. The girl is shocked by what he says to her and runs back to tell her friends. The maidens confer, and then the most beautiful one of them all, in sweet and nervous modesty, steps forward to greet the prince.

The two bow formally and, linking hands, lead the group in a *khorovod* or Russian round dance, to the accompaniment of folklike themes. The chorus of girls become so entwined about their two leaders that it is impossible for the prince and the princess to remain long together. They close their arms about one another, but their partners come amusingly to break their embrace. The two lovers dance with their friends until the light begins to fade. A trumpet is heard in the distance, and the girls gather together quickly in fear. The princess then hastily bids Ivan farewell and runs off with her companions. Ivan stands alone, bewildered at their behavior, as the music takes on mysterious darkness and hints of things unseen.

Ivan stares into the dark thicket about him and is suddenly afraid, but before he can leave the threatening darkness that seems to close in on him, a sharp crash of sound comes from the orchestra and dozens of weird monsters leap with a single bound into the stage and surround him. Green, brown, and multicolored creatures with hideous features and maimed limbs cavort about Ivan to fierce, militant beats from the orchestra. The monsters—some masked with the head of animals—divide into four groups and race backward and forward and sideways, each group trying to outdo the others in grotesque gestures of threat. One of the creatures is held upright, then thrown straight up into the air and caught by the others, only to be tossed up again. The music subsides, and all the creatures of this fantastic underworld fall on their faces as their master, Kastchei, enters menacingly. He is surrounded by the princess and her friends. Kastchei flourishes his dark cap at his creatures, and we glimpse his skeletonlike body. On his head he wears a spiked crown of burning gold. His fingernails, long as his hands, clutch at the air for victims to satisfy an insatiable appetite.

As Kastchei's slaves surround him in frantic attitudes of homage, Ivan moves to flee. But then he remembers the pledge of the Firebird, remembers that he need fear no danger, and brings out the magic feather. He runs, weaving in and out among the monsters, waving the charm in the air. The monsters try to close in on him. Kastchei stamps the earth in indignation and vows to kill the prince. To the theme to which they danced so playfully just a few moments before, the princesses encircle their evil lord and plead for mercy for Ivan. Kastchei dismisses them with curt disgust, but the prince, encouraged by the confusion he is causing among the monsters, races about with the brilliant red feather. The ogres step back, astounded at his fearlessness in the presence of the all-powerful Kastchei. Enormous snarls from the orchestra follow the prince as he provokes the demons to madness. Kastchei moves in to attack. Then a quick whir in the music proclaims the imminent arrival of the Firebird, come to Ivan's rescue.

The Firebird runs onto the scene with a magnificent leap, carrying over her head a naked golden sword. She hurriedly presents the sword to Ivan, then circles the stage in so rapid and fierce a spin that all the monsters are set to twirling with her. She exits quickly as Ivan falls upon Kastchei with the golden sword. The monster falls dead and Ivan, bathed now in the Firebird's brilliant light, holds the gleaming sword high in triumph as the music sounds his victory in a final crescendo.

The stage is dark. The prince stands alone among the fallen bodies of the monsters. The Firebird approaches. Harp strings are plucked gently. The prince finds the princess; he helps her rise. Both bow low before the beautiful Firebird, thanking her for saving their lives. The princess' friends rise and do obeisance before the magical bird, and the Firebird bows to them in return.

Free now of mortals, the Firebird dances alone. The stage is completely dark save for the light that follows her. She rises on point, extends one leg straight out, and whips the air in daring turns. The Firebird now revives the fallen monsters. She gestures over them as the harp sounds swooping arpeggios and consigns them to an endless sleep. The orchestra plays softly a flowing lullaby. The mysterious eerie forest of Ivan's adventure becomes serene as she sets all at peace with graceful, birdlike movement. Her mission over, the Firebird moves across the stage in a flowing dance, now turning, now stepping softly. Her feet tremble to release her body back into the air. Compelled to leave the earth, she moves away, her body thrown back. The last we see of her is her golden hand fluttering against the dark curtain at the side of the stage. The scene blacks out.

SCENE THREE: THE COURT OF PRINCE IVAN   The music begins a quiet, subdued statement of an ancient Russian folk song. The melody that seems simple at first is changed gradually into a majestic song of thanksgiving. The music mounts in dignity and volume as light slowly comes up to show us a blue-green drop curtain. On this curtain are represented all those figures in fairyland who never will have any trouble in living happily ever after. Now that the music has asserted itself fully in praise and gratitude, we see two guards enter. They stand at attention in front of the curtain. The stage is fully lighted. Courtiers enter and bow to each other with each mighty chord from the orchestra, then join hands with the princesses who trip in to meet them. Now the drop curtain rises. Before another curtain of magical deep red, Ivan and his princess stand together. Pages enter with royal standards. A crimson carpet is pulled down the center of the stage, and onto it step Prince Ivan and his bride, in regal costume. All pay homage to the royal couple, and a page comes running out to present to the prince and princess a great wedding cake, aglow with hundreds of candles. The curtain falls as he kneels before them with his gift.

NOTES   The New York City Ballet production of *Firebird* has been revised over the years, like all ballets of any interest, and most importantly perhaps by Jerome Robbins and me at the New York State Theatre, May 28, 1970. Marc Chagall had wanted for some time to do new designs for the costumes and to make other changes. The new *Firebird* was an attempt, in fact, to present Chagall's paintings in action, with Stravinsky's accompaniment. This provided an opportunity to make changes, too, in the choreography. Jerome Robbins and I shared the work, he taking responsibility for the scenes involving large ensembles. Gelsey Kirkland, Jacques d'Amboise, and Gloria Govrin were the principal dancers in this revival. Barbara Karinska's costumes to Chagall's designs were acknowledged masterpieces of art and craft, like all her marvelous work. Karinska's supremacy was appropriately acknowledged at this period by an exhibition of her designs at the Library and Museum of the Performing Arts, New York Public Library, Lincoln Center.

*Music by Igor Stravinsky. Choreography by Maurice Béjart. First presented by the Paris Opéra Ballet at the Palais des Sports, Paris, October 31, 1970, with Paolo Bortoluzzi in the principal role. First presented in the United States by the Ballet of the Twentieth Century at the Brooklyn Academy of Music, New York, January 25, 1971.*

To the choreographer Maurice Béjart, *Firebird* is a revolutionary act, a Maoist gesture. Béjart writes: "The Firebird is the Phoenix reborn from ashes. The Bird of Life and Joy, immortal, whose splendor and strength remain indestructible, untarnishable. . . ."

Referring to the original version of the *Firebird*, Béjart says: "Since then, the . . . ballet seems lame. What remains now is pure music that is true to a certain choreographic vision, but inappropriate to the complicated wanderings of the complete scenario" of the original. "There is no question about replacing one story with another or even transforming the original. Instead, let us try to free the emotion that fills the succession of scenes in a reduced version, and therein find the two major elements that startled at the creation: Stravinsky, Russian musician; Stravinsky, revolutionary musician. Let the dance become the abstract expression of these two elements that are always present in the music: a profound feeling of Russia and a certain rupture with traditional music, translated above all by an inhabitual rhythmic violence. The Firebird is the Phoenix reborn from ashes. The Poet, like the revolutionary, is a Firebird."

Interviewed in *The New Yorker* magazine (February 6, 1971), Béjart was even more specific about his viewpoint on *Firebird:* "The music is so strong, so modern, so full of life, but the Russian legend on which the ballet was based—the magical Firebird who enables a Prince to rescue a Princess from a wicked sorcerer—is impossible to translate on the modern stage. So I thought there must be a way to reach the spirit of the music. The ballet was composed shortly before the Russian Revolution, and as I started to read revolutionary poets such as Esenin and Mayakovsky, I discovered that there was a small group of avant-garde writers, artists, composers, and dancers working in this period who called themselves the Firebird. So I did an abstract ballet but tried to give the feeling of young intellectuals grouped around one boy searching for something new in life. The Firebird leader is a phoenix. He is destroyed, but he rises from the ashes and lives again. That is why we have two men dancing the Firebird instead of one ballerina. . . . Ballet has been a woman-dominated art since the middle of the nineteenth century, but in every folklore the male dancer is more important. In seventeenth-century France and Italy, where ballet was born, women were at first not even allowed to participate. For example, Louis XIV was a very good dancer, but never his queen. They called him the Sun King because he always took the part of the sun in his ballets. In the classic repertoire, we have the *entrechat*, the jump in which the dancer changes the position of his feet several times. The *entrechat-trois* is always called *le royal*, because the Sun King performed it exceptionally well. I think the day of the prima donna in dance, theater, and opera has passed into the history of our civilization. Now we begin to go in the other direction."*

Following this conviction, the action of the ballet depicts the history of a vigorous revolutionary band: their rise, fall and, miraculously, their rise again at the will of a dynamic boy. A group of young partisans in dungarees declare their faith in a revolt, making a pledge of faith in blood in a red spotlight. One of the group, a vigorous boy, discards his denims for a red costume and asserts leadership. He is hailed by the group and leads them in battle. While he loses the fight and his army is defeated, he rises from the dead, hailed by his band of Firebirds.

In his book *The World of Ballet*, the English critic Oleg Kerensky describes another version of *Firebird:* "John Neumeier, a young American dancer and choreographer who became director of the ballet in Frankfurt in 1970, launched his regime with a new version of Stravinsky's *The Firebird* in a science-fiction, outer-space setting. The translation of the wicked Kastchei

* From "Béjart" by Jane Boutwell in "The Talk of the Town." Reprinted by permission; © 1971 The New Yorker Magazine, Inc.

from a sinister Russian magician into an enormous robot with a television screen for a face, and of the hero from a peasant-prince into a white-suited space explorer, gave the ballet a new life, creating much the sort of shock and naive fantasy effect which the original Fokine-Golovine production must have had in Paris sixty years ago. Neumeier, who is still in his twenties, resembles John Clifford in his versatility as a choreographer (he has also done an abstract Bach ballet for Frankfurt) and as a dancer (he replaced Richard Cragun in Cranko's difficult Webern ballet, *Opus I*)."

The Harkness Ballet presented a production of *Firebird* at the Kennedy Center, Washington, May 24, 1972, with choreography by Brian Macdonald and settings and costumes by Rouben Ter-Arutunian. Jeanette Vobdersaar and Manola Asensio alternated in the title role.

## FIRST AERIAL STATION

*Music by Louis Spohr. Choreography by Toer van Schayk. Scenery and costumes by Toer van Schayk. Lighting by Howard Eldridge (Theatre Projects Services Ltd.). First presented by the Dutch National Ballet at Amsterdam, Holland, October 6, 1976. First presented in the United States by the same ensemble at the Minskoff Theatre, New York, November 9, 1976.*

A vivid contrast between a forgotten time and the present, *First Aerial Station* tells the story of a minor revolution in the dance world. The past is represented by the phrase *First Position on Point*, what the choreographer, Toer van Schayk, calls "an antiquated and obsolete ballet terminology from the early years of the past century." The time is around 1813, when Louis Spohr wrote the *Nonet in F Major* that accompanies the ballet. The contrast here, before the triumph of the romantic ballet later in the nineteenth century, is between the leftover "genre noble" dancers who hang on tenaciously to the rigid, frozen style of performance established since the days of Louis XIV, and the "genre/grotesque," the avant-garde dancers who were determined to seek new ways of moving.

The action all takes place in a ballet classroom, where a portrait of Napoleon on the wall comes and goes as victory follows defeat. The eventual victory of the avant-garde permits the dancers to leave the earth and take off in flight.

## FIVE DANCES

*Music by Sergei Rachmaninoff. Choreography by Christian Holder. Costumes by Christian Holder. Lighting by Jennifer Tipton. First presented by the City Center Joffrey Ballet at the City Center, New York, October 16, 1975, with Denise Jackson and Russell Sultzbach. Pianist: Stanley Babin.*

The dancer Christian Holder for his first ballet chose some wonderful piano pieces by Rachmaninoff. The five dances arranged to them are for a girl and a boy, alone and together, in moods and transports that show different aspects of character. Each dances alone, for the first four dances, so that we have an idea of their personalities before they meet for the final *pas de deux*. The focus at the beginning is on the girl who appears in a long dress in a spotlight, her back to us. She responds to the elegiac music of the piano with a dance of some passion and then rushes off. Next, the boy, in white, dances lyrically on a bright stage. His dance becomes tempestuous, then assumes a stillness, and the lights fade. To fast, rippling music the girl returns. The boy's second dance which follows is decisive and assertive in strength and confidence. Now, on a darkened stage, the boy carries the girl. She turns softly in his arms and to quiet music that grows in intensity of passion they dance. At the end, the boy lifts the girl high in declaration of his love and the light fades.

The music by Rachmaninoff for *Five Dances:* Élégie and Mélodie, Op. 3, Nos. 1 and 3; Preludes No. 9 in E flat minor, Op. 23, No. 6 in F minor, Op. 32, No. 1 in F sharp minor, Op. 23.

In a review entitled "Aptly Original" in the New York *Times,* Clive Barnes said that "clearly Mr. Holder has a choreographic fluency, and it was particularly obvious in the gentleness and intricacy of the final duet."


# FLAMES OF PARIS

*Music by Boris Asafiev. Choreography by Vasili Vainonen. Book by Nicolai Volkov and Vladimir Dimitriev. Decor by Vladimir Dimitriev. First presented at the Kirov Theatre, Leningrad, November 7, 1932, with Vakhtang Chabukiani, Olga Jordan, Nina Anisimova, and Galina Ulanova in principal roles.*

Long celebrated in the Soviet Union as a full-length four-act ballet, *Flames of Paris* tells a story that takes place at the time of the French Revolution of 1789. Full of revolutionary fervor, the ballet features not only the march of the Marseillais on Paris but the storming of the Tuileries. The decadence of the court of Louis XVI is portrayed, counterrevolution is exposed, and a brave young girl personifies the triumph of the people.

Scenes from the ballet have been seen on film, one of them featuring the Soviet virtuoso danseur Chabukiani in a popular *pas de deux* from the last scene of the ballet. It is this *pas de deux* that American Ballet Theatre introduced on January 13, 1973, at the City Center, New York, in a version staged by David and Anna-Marie Holmes. The costumes were by Marcos Paredes, the lighting by Nananne Porcher, and the conductor was Akira Endo. Eleanor D'Antuono and John Prinz were the dancers. The central dance takes place in the atmosphere of a celebration over the taking of the Tuileries. The *pas de deux* is ebullient and pyrotechnic in character, political but personable.

## LES FLEURS DU MAL (The Flowers of Evil)

*Music by Claude Debussy. Choreography by Maurice Béjart. Scenery and costumes by Joëlle Roustan and Roger Bernard. First presented by the Ballet of the Twentieth Century, September 3, 1970, at the Théâtre de la Monnaie, Brussels. First presented in the United States by the same ensemble at the City Center, New York, January 26, 1971, with Suzanne Farrell, Jaleh Kerendi, Angela Albrecht, Jorge Donn, Floris Alexander, and Dyane Gray-Cullert.*

In 1968 the choreographer Maurice Béjart created a full-evening ballet, *Baudelaire*, in which seven dancers played the part of the poet Charles Baudelaire and attempted to re-create his world. *Fleurs du Mal* ("Flowers of Evil," the title of the French poet's masterpiece) is an adaptation of part of that ballet. Set to *Le Jet d'Eau* ("The Fountain") as arranged by Debussy, the ballet treats different aspects of love.

There is a floorcloth of black, swirling waves on a white background that climbs up into the backcloth. Large mirrors right and left reflect the movement as dancers emerge to respond to the poem that is being recited. The girls wear long, trailing dresses and in the atmosphere there is a feeling of a bygone era. The girls discard the trains of their gowns and join three boys in a dance as the music begins. They dance in pairs, a girl and boy, then girl and girl, boy and boy. What we have is three impassioned *pas de deux*. The dancers cluster together at the end.

## LES FORAINS (The Traveling Players)

*Ballet in one act. Choreography by Roland Petit. Music by Henri Sauguet. Book by Boris Kochno. Scenery and costumes by Christian Bérard. First presented by Ballets des Champs-Élysées, Paris, March 1945, with Roland Petit, Janine Charrat, and Ethéry Pagava in principal roles. First presented in the United States by Les Ballets de Paris at the National Theatre, New York, October 8, 1950, with Polajenko, Belinda Wright, Danielle Darmance, Simone Mostovoy, Jack Claus, Gordon Hamilton, Elise Vallée, and Nina Bibikova.*

The overture to *Les Forains* blares out with trumpets, drum rolls, and crashing cymbals—appropriate music for a parade, a vaudeville show, or a circus. The ballet that follows is something like all of these things. Although never familiar in America, bands of strolling players have entertained people in Europe for centuries, performing on street corners, on highways, and in remote villages, attracting such crowds as they could and living as their casual audiences rewarded them. *Les Forains* shows us what happens to one particular group of such players one night in a city street.

The stage is dark as the ballet begins. There is no decoration, only a plain backdrop. From the left, a young girl enters. She wears a simple costume, but carries a black-and-silver fan and dances across the stage oblivious of anyone who might be watching her. A troupe of poorly dressed young people trudge wearily onto the scene behind her, pulling along with them a battered wheelbarrow packed high with what seems to be a rolled-up tent. One man follows a little behind, supporting with his left arm a girl who sits on his shoulder. He appears to be the leader of the group. He lets the girl down, consults with the others, claps his hands, and the relaxed scene is transformed instantly into breathless activity.

The wheelbarrow is moved toward the back of the stage; several of the men begin to unpack it hurriedly while the other members of the troupe energetically practice their routines. They throw off their overcoats, and we see that they are wearing costumes. We see a clown and several acrobats; the rest are dancers. The boys support the girls as they warm up for performance; one of the acrobats cartwheels around the stage; while in the back a primitive stage is constructed of crude lumber and cloth. There is a white curtain across the stage proper; colored curtains conceal the wings. Several passers-by pause to watch. The company runs in back of the miniature stage, the lights are lowered, and our attention is fixed on the white curtain.

An intense green light is thrown against the curtain from behind, and we see the silhouettes of a man and a woman engaged in amorous dalliance. The light changes; a clown and a girl come out, bringing with them a chair; and there is acrobatic display. The girl does a running jump onto the chair, where the clown catches her and lifts her down. Next there appears a girl wearing a long white dress of gauze, with long, full sleeves. She dances slowly, to accentuate her movements with the airy movement of her costume. Then the clown enters again, this time to do his specialty, which consists of brisk acrobatics executed as clumsily and as amusingly as possible. Now the curtains part for the Siamese twins, two girls bound together in what appears to be one *tutu*. They step down from the stage and dance side by side, each indicating hopelessly the impossibility of ever dancing otherwise.

The magician who now takes his turn we recognize as the leader of the troupe. He is dressed formally now, in long black evening coat. He waves his wand, and the stage is filled with confetti and paper streamers. Then he approaches the stage, pulls the curtains aside, and brings to life a beautiful girl who lies there motionless in a glass case. The girl is under his power and obeys the magician, with the stiff movements of a mechanical doll. The magician now does his final trick: two live doves fly from his hands and circle the stage until they are retrieved by one of the men.

The whole company joins in for a finale. Each of the performers dances a short variation alone, then all participate in a final chorus, surrounding the magician, whose rapid spins in the air set an increasing tempo for the others to follow. The dance ends with everyone in the group cheerfully exhausted. The small crowd that has been watching applauds lightly, and the magician passes his hat. But each member of the audience turns away as he approaches, and soon the players are left alone.

The youthful ebullience with which they had produced their show collapses almost at once; they are angry because they have received nothing for their entertainment and sad at their public's indifference. They take down the stage, pack up the cart again, and move off in the same melancholy manner with which they entered. The troupe seems to have forgotten the two white doves, which flutter against their cage as the light darkens. One of the girls comes back to find them, picks up the cage, and runs with it back to her friends.

## FORCES OF RHYTHM

*Music: traditional and contemporary. Choreography by Louis Johnson. Costumes by Zelda Wynn. Lighting by Fred Barry. First presented by the Dance Theatre of Harlem at the Hunter College Playhouse, New York, December 11, 1971.*

The dance audience has often imagined a work that would combine the styles of classical ballet, modern and ethnic dance. The choreographer Louis Johnson has made such a piece using the gifts of the Dance Theatre of Harlem. The choreographer's idea here is to capture the essence of ballet and ethnic dancing styles in such a way as to display the rapport, beauty, and relationship between the two. This is accomplished in a number of ways.

The curtain rises on twelve dancers as a voice speaks above the music, "We're in a difficult situation. We're going to have to live together." Some of the girls are in long white cotton dresses with bandannas in the hair, an attire reminiscent of the old South; others are in toe shoes and short white ballet costumes; while the boys, too, are in ballet rehearsal costume, T-shirts and tights. This costume combination reveals the ballet's content as the three groups dance together. It is enlarged in the next part, "Roots and Rhythm," by four boys in red loincloths who display the vigor of native African dance.

The sixteen dancers play a kind of counterpoint against each other with the music. Ranging from the heroic measures of affirmation in the Tchaikovsky symphonies to folk, blues, rock, and jazz, the dances reveal variations on these musical themes in dance expression. Six movements follow: "Rhythm and Strings," to Tchaikovsky's music; "Distress," for four girls; "Shout," a solo for a girl to a plaintive, demanding rhythm; "Forces of Rhythm," a dance for three; "Harlem Rhythms," for a boy soloist; and a "Coda" for all sixteen dancers. From bare foot to toe shoe, recollections of minstrel days with derby hats and white socks, the ballet traces a historical development within a dance entertainment.

Arlene Croce wrote of Paul Russell's performance in *Forces of Rhythm,* in *The New Yorker* in 1973: "Russell is the greatest performer the company has . . . He has the greatness and the naturalness to remind you of something in real life."

Writing of *Forces of Rhythm* as it was performed in 1974, the critic Robert Greskovic said in *Ballet Review:* "Using a tape track that sounds patched together from twirling a radio dial, the dances range from soul-felt, revivalist surges through Balanchinian concerti forces to mimetic African arm-flapping rituals. The costumes match each dance's style with long, white ruffled muslin shifts and kerchiefed heads for the revivalists, basic black and white dancewear for the Balanchinians, and loin-bikinis, ankle bells and head bands for the tribal artists. There is a jumbled pas de trois for McKinney and Williams (as a *Barocco* couple) with Bryant in his red loin wrap. The joke here is a 'ballet' one with McKinney distracted from her lyric duet with Williams by the foot-stomping and arm-waving Bryant. We've seen partners compete for the ballerina before, but never with such outrageous contrast. And, of course, in 'There Is a Rose in Spanish Harlem,' Paul Russell, in loincloth, derby, socks and ballet slippers, provides one of the most delicious performances of the season. I saw Russell in '72 and again (twice) this season, and it amazes and thrills me every time to see him take this recorded music and fill it out to bursting with show biz know-how and genuinely amusing style. During his dancing, which is a cross between bravura pyrotechnics and gyrating Broadway jives, he has some 'takes' that confront his audience with generous wit and unabashed joy. He is a comic and a comet; his body is all singing, all dancing. He's a genius. There is an interchangeable male/female solo for either V. Johnson doing a sweetly abandoned skirt-whirling freak-out à la Jamison in *Revelations*, or William Scott biting the music with purposeful rock/bop attack. It has something from (for) everybody and all of it's dancing by a company that loves what (ever) it's doing."*

## THE FOUNTAIN OF BAKHCHISARAI

*Choreographic poem in four acts. Music by Boris Asafiev. Choreography by Rotislav Zakharov. Book by Nikolai Volkov, based on the poem by Alexander Pushkin. Scenery by V. M. Khodasevich. First presented by the Kirov Ballet at the Kirov State Theatre of Opera and Ballet, Leningrad, September 28, 1934.*

This ballet in four acts follows closely the action of Pushkin's poem. The action takes place in Poland and Bakhchisarai during the eighteenth century.

ACT ONE: AN ANCIENT PARK NEAR THE CASTLE OF THE POLISH PRINCE POTOTSKY The prince is celebrating the birthday of his beautiful daughter Maria by giving a ball. Maria and Vatslav, a young nobleman, dance together, oblivious to their surroundings. Hand in hand they go off into the park.

Out of the darkness a scout from the army of the Crimean Khan Girei steals into the park. He is not observed.

The prince and his daughter lead their guests in a polonaise, which is followed by a lively kracovienne. The guests enjoy themselves hugely. Vatslav plays the harp and to its song Maria dances. He responds with a dance of his own. At the conclusion of a *pas de deux*, the guests join in a mazurka. The

* Reprinted by permission of *Ballet Review*, Marcel Dekker, publisher.

merriment of this dance is quickly dispelled, however, by the sound of an approaching army on horseback. The castle guard, mortally wounded, enters to warn the prince of a surprise attack by the Tartar horde:

> . . . multitudes of Tartars
> Pour forth into Poland like a river;
> not with such terrible swiftness
> does fire spread through the harvest.

The guests disperse and return to engage the forces of Girei in combat. Many are slain and the Poles are soon overwhelmed. The castle is ablaze. Vatslav attempts to lead Maria to safety, but the khan himself blocks their escape. Vatslav challenges Girei and appears to succeed, but then we see that he has been stricken by a blow from a concealed dagger. Maria, in despair, hides her face in her scarf. Girei tears it away and, dazzled by her beauty, adores her.

ACT TWO: GIREI'S HAREM IN BAKHCHISARAI, CAPITAL OF THE CRIMEAN TARTARS  The many lovely young wives of the khan play and chat in the morning sunlight. The khan's favorite, the Georgian girl Zarema, "star of love, beauty of the harem," demands the attention due her position. She and the other wives impatiently await the khan's return and prepare themselves excitedly when trumpets announce the arrival of Girei and his troops from Poland.

Warriors rush in. Maria is carried in on a litter. Girei enters, takes off his armor, dons a golden robe and reclines on his couch. Zarema dances for him, but he is indifferent to her. The girl is distraught, but persists; she cannot believe that he has lost interest in her.

Maria enters, carrying the harp Vatslav played for her. With her fair hair and delicate features she is a curiosity to the other women. Absorbed with her own thoughts of home, of her lost lover, she ignores Girei, who cannot comprehend her aloofness. The other wives try to divert the khan, but neither they nor Zarema can claim his attention. He thrusts Zarema aside and leaves the room. The other wives ridicule the rejected Zarema and rejoice in her downfall. When Girei returns and she embraces him, he again repulses her, this time more coldly.

ACT THREE: MARIA'S BEDCHAMBER IN GIREI'S PALACE  Alone with an old servant, Maria strums the harp that Vatslav left behind. Girei, transfixed by an unearthly love unknown to him, enters the room. Haunted by her presence, wishing to possess her, but realizing also that as the murderer of her beloved he cannot hope to win her, Girei does not know where to turn. Maria, appalled by the force of his desire, is desperately afraid. He sees her fear and spares her, leaving the room.

Maria, relieved and alone, dreams of the past, of her lover Vatslav, of their longed-for marriage. The old servant takes her to bed, and, falling asleep on a carpet at the door, stands guard over the girl.

Zarema, the favorite of the harem, enters, skirting the old woman's carpet. She begs Maria to return the khan to her, his rightful beloved: she cannot live without him. The servant wakens and summons the khan. He enters the room with a guard just as Zarema threatens to stab Maria to death. Girei, in a frenzy, dashes to Zarema, trying to catch her hand, but she eludes him and stabs Maria, who dies like a flower cut off in full bloom. Maddened by this act, the khan threatens to kill Zarema. But the girl, welcoming death as an alternative, goes to meet his blow. He then instructs the guard to take the girl away.

ACT FOUR: A FOUNTAIN COURT IN THE PALACE  Girei watches as one of his generals returns from a fresh campaign with trophies, banners, and new captives for the harem. He is unmoved by these triumphs. Zarema is dragged before him. He is merciless, thinking only that Maria one day would have yielded to him except for this girl's wicked jealousy. She begs him for mercy with her eyes but he cannot bear to look at her. She is led across to the battlements and forced over the steep precipice to her death. A fierce dance by the khan's warriors does not assuage his grief. He finds solace only at the "fountain of tears," which he has erected in the courtyard to the memory of his "sorrowful Maria."

> The water murmurs in the marble
> and drops like cold tears,
> never falling silent.

In the magical sound of the fountain Girei seems to see the image of Maria. But when he reaches out to touch her, she is not there.


# FOUR LAST SONGS

*Music by Richard Strauss. Choreography by Maurice Béjart. First presented by the Ballet of the Twentieth Century. First presented in the United States by the same ensemble at the Brooklyn Academy of Music, February 10, 1971.*

While Richard Strauss did not write his four last songs to be performed as a group, that is the way they have turned out in musical history. Not so much in subject matter as in temper and retrospective attitudes to life, the four songs lend themselves to appreciative contemplation. Dancers have found that, too, and to the fancy of Maurice Béjart the four songs—*"Frühling"* ("Spring"), *"September," "Beim Schlafengehen"* ("Going to Sleep"), and *"Im Abendrot"* ("In the Evening")—suggest the four loves of a dying man.

The curtain rises in silence and we see a boy in the distance in a spotlight. As he walks toward us, four girls, from the four corners of the stage, approach him. All five join hands, the music begins, and he in the midst of the girls is caught up in recollection of his past loves. A series of *pas de deux* then follows, each recalling the drama of a particular passion, while the other girls watch from a symbolic distance. His final love and partner is Death.

The critic Don McDonagh in the New York *Times* wrote that "The ballet beautifully succeeds in detailing each encounter with respect for and rapport with its music . . . Each of the duets displays the tonality of the Strauss song that accompanies it and conveys its romantic interlude with soft spoken surety."

*Music by Richard Strauss. Choreography by Lorca Massine. First presented by the New York City Ballet at the New York State Theatre, January 21, 1971.*

The first of Lorca Massine's ballets in America (the dancer and choreographer had previously composed fifteen ballets for his own company in Europe), *Four Last Songs* was first arranged for students at the School of American Ballet, a number of whom appeared in the ballet's performances. Writing of the ballet, Nancy Goldner, dance critic of the *Christian Science Monitor,* described it as "an utterly strange and utterly beautiful ballet . . . The music is Richard Strauss; it is perhaps the most difficult kind of music to work with, for it lacks a tight rhythmical structure. Dynamically, the music ebbs and crests."

So does the action, taking place in a rehearsal studio where small and larger groups of dancers move together, break apart, recombine, isolate each other, come together again. There is a feeling of community achievement but of great individuality, too. Art is a product of being alone and working and the beautiful dances we sometimes see emerge from such a place as this.

Persons who saw *Four Last Songs* as it was first done with students at the School of American Ballet in New York say they will never forget it.

## FOUR SCHUMANN PIECES

*Music by Robert Schumann. Choreography by Hans van Manen. Scenery and costumes by Jean-Paul Vroom. First presented by the Royal Ballet at the Royal Opera House, Covent Garden, London, January 31, 1975, with Anthony Dowell in the principal role. First presented in the United States by the National Ballet of Canada at the Metropolitan Opera House, New York, August 4, 1976, with Rudolf Nureyev in the principal role.*

Danced to the music of Robert Schumann's *String Quartet in A Major,* Op. 141, No. 3, which is played in the orchestra pit, *Four Schumann Pieces* is a dramatic ballet without a story. It shows a man who stands alone but who is surrounded by persons he would wish to know, though he often has strength only to ignore them. Of the five couples who dance with him, he appears to know none. Gradually, however, his courage is emboldened and he tries to join them. He despairs, however, at the first opportunity and just keeps on watching. Later, he dances with one of the girls, then with one of the boys, and appears to be bereft, preferring a lone splendor until he again goes back to join the group.

## FOUR SEASONS

*Music by Antonio Vivaldi. Choreography by Flemming Flindt. Scenery by Jorgen Mydtskov. Costumes by Charlotte Clason. First presented by the Royal Danish Ballet at the Royal Theatre, Copenhagen, April 10, 1975. First presented in the United States by the same ensemble at the Metropolitan Opera House, New York, June 5, 1976.*

Vivaldi's great musical work, envisioned by many as *musique dansante*, has attracted many a choreographer. The Danish ballet master first essayed a ballet to this score in 1971 but revised his conception definitively four years later. Commencing with the open expressiveness of the "Spring" concerto, the action in dance/dramatic terms moves to the harmony and invention of an impassioned "Summer." The color of the scene shifting into "Autumn," the dances take on a commitment to hunting, and in "Winter" there is dedication by the assembled dancers to the omnipotent Snow Queen that melts into a renewed expectation of "Spring" and the circle of the year is closed.

## THE FOUR TEMPERAMENTS

*Classic ballet in five parts. Music by Paul Hindemith. Choreography by George Balanchine. Scenery and costumes by Kurt Seligmann. Lighting by Jean Rosenthal. First presented by Ballet Society at the Central High School of Needle Trades, New York, November 20, 1946, with Gisella Caccialanza, Tanaquil LeClercq, Mary Ellen Moylan, Elise Reiman, Beatrice Tompkins, Todd Bolender, Lew Christensen, Fred Danieli, William Dollar, José Martínez, and Francisco Moncion as the principal dancers.*

Subtitled "A Dance Ballet Without Plot," *The Four Temperaments* is an expression in dance and music of the ancient notion that the human organism is made up of four different humors, or temperaments. Each one of us possesses these four humors, but in different degrees, and it is from the dominance of one of them that the four physical and psychological types—melancholic, sanguinic, phlegmatic, and choleric—were derived. Greek medicine associated the four humors and temperaments with the four elements—earth, water, fire, and air—which to them composed the human body as well as the world.

Although the score is based on this idea of the four temperaments, neither the music nor the ballet itself make specific or literal interpretation of the idea. An understanding of the Greek and medieval notion of the temperaments was merely the point of departure for both composer and choreographer.

The ballet is in five parts that correspond to the divisions of the score. The first section, Theme, features three couples, who dance three *pas de deux* to different statements of the basic musical theme. The music is languidly paced at first; the strings carry the melody carefully, but effortlessly. The bright assertiveness of the piano interrupts this passage, and the music becomes syncopated, with a quick, tinkling brilliance. In the third statement the string orchestra and the piano combine to state the theme fully.

Melancholic, the first variation on the theme, begins sadly and slowly; a solo violin sings despondently against the piano's accompaniment. A dancer performs a helpless, despondent, and lonely variation. The tempo changes, and he is joined by two girls as the full orchestra plays with muted strings. Four mysterious girls stalk in fiercely, majestically, to the tune of a strong and vibrant march in which the piano joins percussively.

The second variation, Sanguinic, is bright and effusive in its waltz tempo. A ballerina and her partner dance with open gestures that are alternately sharp and flowing. A secondary group of four dancers accompanies them.

To the third variation, Phlegmatic, a dancer dances at first alone. His mood changes suddenly with the music. He is joined by four girls and with them dances a sequence of adroitly measured lightness to a gay, humorous melody.

After a brief variation by a ballerina who represents the choleric temperament, the entire ensemble returns to the stage for a recapitulation of their dances; this merges with the music for a finale characterized by high, extended lifts.

NOTES    Arlene Croce, in *The New Yorker,* December 8, 1975, reviewed at length the New York City Ballet revival of *The Four Temperaments* with Bart Cook in Melancholic, Merrill Ashley in Sanguinic, Jean-Pierre Bonnefous in Phlegmatic, and Colleen Neary in Choleric.


# GAÎTÉ PARISIENNE

*Ballet in one act. Music by Jacques Offenbach. Choreography by Leonide Massine. Book by Comte Étienne de Beaumont. Scenery and costumes by Comte Étienne de Beaumont. First presented by the Ballet Russe de Monte Carlo at the Théâtre de Monte Carlo, April 5, 1938, with Nina Tarakanova as the Glove Seller, Eugenia Delarova as the Flower Girl, Jeannette Lauret as La Lionne, Leonide Massine as the Peruvian, Frederic Franklin as the Baron, and Igor Youskevitch as the Officer. First presented in the United States by the Ballet Russe de Monte Carlo at the Metropolitan Opera House, New York, October 12, 1938, with Alexandra Danilova as the Glove Seller; the other principals were the same as those who danced the première in Monte Carlo.*

The trumpets and snare drum, which begin the overture to this ballet with loud and persistent good humor, proclaim a tale of the night life of old Paris, a story of romance, convivial dancing, and perpetual high spirits. The jubilant rhythm and sparkling melody of the music remind us of a time when love was brief and casual, but intense, of a time when the day began at nine o'clock in the evening.

The curtain rises on the most popular room of a fashionable restaurant in nineteenth-century Paris. High green draperies are looped back against brass pillars; brass chandeliers flood the room with light. Marble-topped tables and gold chairs stand at the back. Four waiters and four cleaning girls are preparing the *salon* for the evening's entertainment. The boys flick the tables and chairs with their towels and dance comically to amuse the girls. They run forward and sit at the front of the stage at the end of their act.

A girl with flowers in her hair enters gaily. She shakes hands with the waiters, who gather around her adoringly. This is the flower girl. She presents each boy with a bouquet. They reward her with a drink, and the flower girl joins them in a dance in which she toasts her admirers. One of the boys lifts her up to his shoulders and another kneels below her.

Three ladies of easy virtue—the *cocodettes*—enter with their escorts. The girls are dressed cheerfully in loud, candy-striped dresses; their companions wear black jackets and berets. The flower girl sets up her tray of flowers and leaves with the waiters. The *cocodettes* dance a lively mazurka with their partners. The waiters return to watch, but soon the company is distracted by the entry of the ballet's heroine, the beautiful glove seller. The men desert their partners and cluster around her. She carries a basket of gloves on her arm and tries to attend to her business, but the men insist that she dance with them. She is lifted high, then circles the stage as all stop to admire her. The glove seller is not as pert and flirtatious as the flower girl, yet her beauty is more striking.

Everyone is watching her when the gay Peruvian, just arrived in Paris, hustles in to a whistling tune. He has been so eager to get to the café and enjoy the proverbial night life that he has brought his bags with him. He scuttles about the stage in uncontrollable excitement at the possibilities of the evening, amusing the girls, who know that—though his pockets may be filled with gold—he is incapable of stopping long enough to spend it on any one of them: he will always pursue pleasure, but never enjoy it. Finally he drops his bags and goes over to the flower girl, who places a *boutonnière* in his white lapel. He wiggles with delight as the girls watch him. Only the glove seller does not notice him. The Peruvian is fascinated. He sneaks up on her and asks for a pair of gloves. The girl obliges and tries to fit him. The Peruvian dances even as he stands still.

The baron enters. A waiter takes his cape, and the flower girl, attracted by his handsome uniform, immediately goes over to him. The baron, however, has seen the glove seller; gently ignoring the other girl, he turns to her, introduces himself modestly, and asks her to dance. The glove seller responds graciously, and the guests retire as the two come forward and dance to a romantically rhythmic waltz. The couple move together not as if they had just met, but as if they were predestined to know one another; their dance is touching, in its quiet, flowing warmth.

In the background the jovial Peruvian entertains the *cocodettes*. With a flourish, he ceremoniously orders a bottle of champagne. He sips a glass, spits, and stamps his feet. The girls encourage him as he orders another bottle. He approves the new wine and offers it to the ladies. His flirtations are interrupted by the arrival of five soldiers and an officer, who strut into the café as if they expected all the girls to notice only them. The girls oblige them. The couples perform a martial dance at the conclusion of which the girls hang about the soldiers' necks in mock farewell as the soldiers salute them.

All are startled by the sudden entrance of La Lionne, the fashionable beauty of the day. She sweeps into the café in her red velvet dress and greets the group condescendingly; the girls are furious, the men anxious to please her. La Lionne's escort, the duke, is unable to make up his mind whether to be pleased or annoyed. Her companion, the lady in green, seeks an alliance among the men.

La Lionne makes eyes at the officer, who abandons his attempt to take up with the beautiful glove seller. The Peruvian returns. He douses himself liberally with perfume and approaches the glove seller. As he whispers in her ear, she plagues the baron by pretending to agree to the Peruvian's suggestion. The baron is furious with her. The duke is furious with La Lionne. Both fight with their rivals, and the guests, who seem to have been waiting for such an outbreak, take sides and join in the contest. The scene becomes riotous. It is too much for the Peruvian, who crawls under a table, his limbs quaking. The restaurant is cleared. The waiters return and see the Peruvian, who doesn't dare look up. They pound on the table, and the terrified playboy rushes off, carrying the table on his head.

The baron and the glove seller re-enter and, to a sumptuous waltz, dance together. Their mutual love now assured, the two dance in reunited harmony. No sooner have they finished than the café comes to life again. The dazzling cancan dancers enter with their dancing master, and all the guests regather to watch them display their high, bold kicks. The girls form in a line as the dancing master commands, one by one they fall to the floor in a split. The crowd is delighted and everyone joins in the boisterous dance, some taking the cancan girls for their partners. The Peruvian enters with his top hat. The girls circle him and rotate his hat about their slippers.

The whole cast is assembled on the stage for the finishing bars of the heated dance. All the girls are lifted high; their legs fall back in the air. The girls fan themselves briskly. The lights dim; wraps are brought. The girls take their partners' arms; the music becomes soft and mellifluous; and the couples glide away as if they were carried by quietly moving gondolas into the night—the baron with the glove seller, the flower girl with the duke, La Lionne with the officer. The glove seller, her hair covered with a black mantilla, waves farewell and falls back in the baron's arms. The Peruvian is left alone. The couples wave at him. He sulks.

## GALA PERFORMANCE

*Ballet in two parts. Choreography by Antony Tudor. Music by Sergei Prokofiev. Scenery and costumes by Hugh Stevenson. First presented by the London Ballet at Toynbee Hall, London, December 5, 1938, with Maude Lloyd, Gerd Larsen, Peggy van Praagh, Hugh Laing, and Antony Tudor in principal roles. First presented in the United States by Ballet Theatre at*

*the Majestic Theatre, New York, February 11, 1941. Scenery and costumes
by Nicolas de Molas. The cast was headed by Nora Kaye, Nana Gollner,
Karen Conrad, Hugh Laing, and Antony Tudor.*

*Gala Performance* is a comedy, telling a joke about ballet and three different
ballerinas. Today many of us are inclined to stay away from ballet because we
think it's made up of silly mannerisms. *Gala Performance* shows us these mannerisms (exaggerates them in the style of its period) and makes us laugh.
Three famous ballerinas—the Queen of the Dance (from Moscow), the Goddess of the Dance (from Milan), and the Daughter of Terpsichore (from
Paris)—are performing on the same stage for the first time in their lives. In
their attempts to outdo each other, the dancers invoke every trick of their
trade: they not only compete in respect to their dancing, but resort to any ruse
that will secure the most applause.

The time of this *Gala Performance* is about sixty years ago; the place is the
Theatre Royal in London. The music is by Prokofiev: the first movement of the
*Concerto No. 3 in C for Piano* (for Part One) and the *Classical Symphony* (for
Part Two).

PART ONE    The curtain rises on a backstage scene. The closed curtain of the
Theatre Royal is the backdrop of the setting, and in the harsh light before the
performance begins we watch the nervous, hurried preparations for an unprecedented program of ballet. Two *coryphées* come out through the wings and
begin to warm up. Others join them. These girls are members of the Theatre
Royal's *corps de ballet*, the chosen few who will have the honor of appearing
with the three guest ballerinas. They are quite naturally frightened and wait
apprehensively for the arrival of the great dancers. They practice dance steps,
turn their backs to us, and pose in the direction of the audience behind the
curtain. Other girls and a number of boys—attendant cavaliers to the ballerinas
—come on stage.

A woman in black, the theater dresser, enters and adjusts the costumes of
the *coryphées*. Next comes the ballet master, who watches the *corps de ballet*
as they quickly run through the steps they will dance when the curtain rises.
All the company turn expectantly as the Russian ballerina approaches the
stage. She walks commandingly. Everyone on stage is beneath her notice, and
she accepts the homage of the company with marked indifference. Then, as
she scrutinizes the *corps de ballet*, she notices that one of the *coryphées* is
wearing a necklace. She motions to the girl, reprimands her, and orders her to
remove it. She herself is loaded down with jewelry, to which she now directs
her attention while the distraught girl dashes off, weeping.

The ballet master and the conductor hover about the ballerina. The conductor promises to heed her warning about the proper tempo, while the ballet
master can only assure her that his *corps de ballet* will be impeccably unob-
trusive. The Queen of the Dance makes final adjustments in her richly embroidered red dress, fixes the high feather in her hair, and turns toward the curtain
to rehearse her bows. Her way of acknowledging applause seems to be more
important than the dance that will apparently receive it, and the girls and boys

are secretly amused at the number of kisses she expects to throw to her audience. She is watching out of the corner of her eye, however; she snaps her fingers at the *corps* and orders them to practice their routine.

This severe scene is interrupted by the arrival of the Daughter of Terpsichore, the sparkling French ballerina, who bounds onto the stage in a fluffy, delicate costume appropriate to her exuberance. She can hardly keep still long enough to be introduced to her Russian peer, who naturally scorns her, and has no time to be regal and domineering. But she has time to be demanding and takes the conductor aside to instruct him about the tempo *she* will require. Where the Russian ballerina will make her every wish a command, the scatter-brained French dancer imagines that everything will be all right because everyone loves her and wants to please her. We are suddenly thankful that this is a ballet and not a play, for the silly French ballerina must surely never stop talking.

But if we think that the Russian and French ballerinas are vain and absurd, we have not yet seen their peer in mannerism. The Italian ballerina, the famed Goddess of the Dance, now enters. She is dressed in dignified black and walks across the stage with slow, studied elegance; her steps are carefully measured: every time she puts a foot forward, it seems to hesitate, as if it were considering the worthiness of the floor she deigns to walk upon. Automatically she holds out her hand to be kissed. The cavaliers, prompted by the ballet master, pay tribute to her. Now she orders the dresser to hold up a mirror so that she can make final adjustments to her coiffure and elaborate headdress. The dresser's attention wanders for a moment, and the Goddess of the Dance rewards her with a smack.

The ballet master huddles with the *corps de ballet*, giving them their final instructions. The stage lights come up; some of the dancers make a final rush to the rosin box so that their shoes will not slip on stage; others wish themselves luck by repeating private superstitious gestures; and one wonders how the performance will ever begin. But suddenly everyone is miraculously in place. The drop curtain rises, and the scene blacks out.

PART TWO: GALA PERFORMANCE  When the lights come up again, we are the audience at the Theatre Royal. Instead of the backstage picture, we now see an ornate setting, draped in orange and red, that might represent any regal hall. Eight *coryphées* are on stage. They wait tremulously for their cue and begin to dance. They are nervous, but not too nervous to try to ingratiate themselves with the audience: each tries to outleer the others with absurd chorine smiles.

Four cavaliers lead the Russian ballerina on stage. They bow and leave the stage. The ballerina comes forward slowly, almost to the footlights, and begins to dance when she has played upon the anticipation of the audience to establish what she doubtless imagines is a personal, lovable relation. In her dance she attempts to hit the audience between the eyes with the most elementary pirouettes, staring them down, *daring* them not to like her. And she wins our applause. When she leaps off into the wings, one of her cavaliers, invisible to the audience, catches her, and she poses in endless midflight. She accepts applause with no modesty whatsoever and finds it difficult to leave the stage for an instant while it continues.

Now the Italian ballerina comes on. She comes forward to the footlights, tantalizing us with possibilities, rises on point as if it were the supreme sacrifice, and nods curtly at the conductor. The dance she executes is an adagio, in which she eschews the assistance of her partner. No one can serve her great art but herself; the audience should be grateful to be watching her. She balances as long as possible in every pose and is coldly indifferent to gasps of amazement from the audience: to her, nothing is impossible. When her dance ends, she allows a cavalier to lift her off into the wings. As she returns for her curtain calls, she walks with the measured steps of her backstage entrance. After obligingly taking applause with the company and her cavaliers, she finally shoos them off so she can acknowledge her due alone.

The French ballerina now takes the stage and covers it with rapid leaps. She responds to applause by inflicting upon the audience an ingratiating and somewhat irritating charm.

The solos are over, and the three ballerinas appear together in the coda. They come out on stage and stand together and for a moment they are equals, but directly they begin to dance, competition is rampant. The French and Russian ballerinas try every means to attract the attention of the audience and thereby lose the contest, for the Italian "goddess" makes the audience love her by treating them as if they were idiots. She is surely in command of the whole situation and only at the final curtain does she give any sign of respecting any gift the audience might bestow on her. When the three ballerinas receive flowers, she manages to grab more bouquets than the other two. Not to be outdone, the French ballerina steps in front of the curtain to pick up more bouquets which the audience has thrown to her. But when the curtain rises again, the Italian still has the most flowers. The other two ballerinas look at her and then at us and smile and smile and smile.

# GAMES

*Choreography by Donald McKayle. Decor by Paul Bertelsen. Costumes by Remy Charlip. First presented at the Hunter College Playhouse, New York, May 25, 1951, with Esta Beck, Eve Beck, Louanna Gardner, Remy Charlip, John Fealy, George Liker, John Nola, and Donald McKayle.*

The music for this dance is traditional songs, sung at the first performance by June Lewis and the choreographer. Donald McKayle has divided *Games* into three parts—Play, Hunger, Terror. "The streets are their playground, through all their play runs a thread of fear—'Chickee the Cop.'"

Writing of *Games* in *Dance Magazine*, the critic Doris Hering said: "In his group work *Games*, Mr. McKayle captured with uncanny perception the shadowed happiness of little children in the city." Seven children play, get frightened, terrified, fantasize, find their own kind of happiness.

*Games* was revived by Eliot Feld's American Ballet Company at the Brooklyn Academy of Music, New York, October 22, 1969.

## GARTENFEST

*Music by Wolfgang Amadeus Mozart. Choreography by Michael Smuin. Scenery by Jack Brown. Costumes by Marcos Paredes. Lighting by Jean Rosenthal. First presented by American Ballet Theatre at the Brooklyn Academy of Music, December 18, 1968, with Sallie Wilson and Paul Nickel, Ted Kivitt and Ivan Nagy, and Cynthia Gregory in principal roles. Conducted by Jaime Leon. Solo violinist: Guy Lumia.*

*Gartenfest* is a dance ballet to Mozart's early *Cassation No. 1 in G* (he was but thirteen at the time), music suitable for use in the open air, where much great eighteenth-century music was performed. The scene is appropriately, therefore, a garden, where dancers perform a series of diversions, varying in character with the music. There is no plot, only the inherent dance quality of the score and its design. The ballet is in six movements: *Menuetto,* for a lead boy and girl and four couples; *Allegro,* a bright and vigorous dance for two boys who compete in varied complex combinations of steps, beats, and jumps; *Andante,* a solo for a ballerina, supported by an ensemble of six girls; *Menuetto,* a dance for three couples; *Adagio,* a *pas de trois* for a ballerina and two boys; and *Finale: Allegro assai,* a dance for the ballerina who introduced the ballet, with the entire cast.

NOTES  Reviewing *Gartenfest* in *Dance and Dancers* magazine, Patricia Barnes said that "Ballet Theatre has been lucky enough to find within its ranks another young man, Michael Smuin, who with his latest work shows himself to have genuine choreographic potential. . . . *Gartenfest* was a genuine success, most notable for the way in which it exploited the talents of its dancers, mostly drawn from the younger principals and the most promising soloists. . . . The choreography had the same fluent charm as the score."

## GASPARD DE LA NUIT

*Music by Maurice Ravel. Choreography by George Balanchine. Scenery and costumes by Bernard Daydé, execution supervised by David Mitchell. Lighting by Bernard Daydé in association with Ronald Bates. Solo pianist: Jerry Zimmerman. Conducted by Robert Irving. First presented at the New York City Ballet's Hommage à Ravel at the New York State Theatre, Lincoln Center, May 29, 1975, with Colleen Neary, Victor Castelli, Karin von Aroldingen, Nolan T'Sani, Sara Leland, and Robert Weiss as principals.*

Gaspard is a manifestation of the evils of Night. Lincoln Kirstein has written that this composition was the first of Ravel's major works in which "he expressed his attraction to the turbulent, mysterious, bewitched world of the supernatural." Robert Craft has said, too, that Ravel "is essentially a musical story teller, more inspired by poetry, and more inspired by words, syllables, literary programs, than by the problems of traditional musical form."

The music accompanies three poems: "Ondine," "The Gibbet," and "Scarbo." "Ondine" evokes the spirit of the water nymph in her enchanted watery kingdom where "each current is a path that winds its way towards my palace, and my palace is built aqueously at the bottom of the lake, in a triangle of fire, of earth and of air."

"The Gibbet" recalls the sounds of night "or the hanged man who breathes a sigh on the forked gibbet . . . and the corpse of a hanged man that is reddened by the setting sun."

The poem of Scarbo, who is an obscure devil-dwarf, begins with "O, many a time have I seen and heard him, Scarbo, when at midnight the moon shines in the sky like a silver shield upon an azure banner sown with golden bees."

The celebrated French pianist and conductor Alfred Cortot said that "these three poems enrich the repertory of our time by one of the most astonishing examples of instrumental ingenuity ever contrived by the industry of a composer."

The ballet I made to these songs is not a narrative affair illustrating each poem but an attempt to complement the music and works by visual gesture.

## GEMINI

*Music by Mahler. Choreography by Vicente Nebrada. First presented by the Harkness Ballet at Brooklyn College, New York, October 7, 1972, with Christopher Aponte and Darrell Barnett.*

A *pas de deux* for two boys to the *Adagietto* from Mahler's *Fifth Symphony*, *Gemini* explores varied aspects of the relationships between the protagonists. Writing in *Dance and Dancers* magazine, the critic Patricia Barnes wrote: "Undeniably evoking homosexual love, the bodies of the two men twine and curve around each other. Numerous lifts are used but I found it neither acrobatic nor vulgar. Aponte and Barnett brought a control and strength to their movements that prevented the work from descending to sensationalism or sentimentality."

*Music by Hans Werner Henze. Choreography by Glen Tetley. Scenery by Nadine Baylis. First presented by the Australian Ballet with Marilyn Rowe, Alida Chase, John Meehan, and Gary Norman. First presented in the United States by American Ballet Theatre at the City Center, New York, 1975, with Cynthia Gregory, Martine van Hamel, Jonas Kage, and Charles Ward.*

The twins of this *Gemini* are two couples who resemble each other. Often the dances they do appear to be a kind of mirror-image. But it is not always so and, like true twins, there is a similarity of movement but an inner difference of feeling that materially alters behavior. No two couples can be the same, love in the same way, make the same commitments, or fulfill their destinies identically. The ballet shows us variations on these themes.

Writing of the performance of July 9, 1975, the critic Anna Kisselgoff reported in the New York *Times:* "Mr. Tetley works in a totally international style . . . *Gemini* is one of the best examples of this genre, and it was danced on this occasion with a thrilling blend of virtuosity and emotional depth by Cynthia Gregory, Martine van Hamel, Jonas Kage and Charles Ward."

## GISELLE

*Fantastic ballet in two acts. Music by Adolphe Adam. Choreography by Jules Perrot and Jean Coralli. Book by Vernoy de Saint-Georges, Théophile Gautier, and Jean Coralli. Scenery by Pierre Ciceri. Costumes by Paul Lormier. First presented at the Théâtre de l'Académie Royale de Musique, Paris, June 28, 1841, with Carlotta Grisi as Giselle, Lucien Petipa as Albrecht, Adèle Dumilâtre as Myrtha, Queen of the Wilis, and Jean Coralli as Hilarion. First presented in England at Her Majesty's Theatre, London, March 12, 1842, with Carlotta Grisi and Jules Perrot in the principal roles. First presented in Russia at the Bolshoi Theatre, St. Petersburg, December 30, 1842, with Elena Andreyanova as Giselle. First presented in Italy at the Teatro alla Scala, Milan, January 17, 1843, with choreography by A. Cortesi and music by N. Bajetti. First presented in the United States at the Howard Atheneum, Boston, January 1, 1846, with Mary Ann Lee and George Washington Smith in the leading roles.*

*Giselle* is such an important and popular ballet that people who know something about dancing are always talking about it. They speak of Pavlova's Giselle, Karsavina's Giselle, Spessivtzeva's Giselle, Markova's Giselle, and those who are unfamiliar with ballet think it strange: it's as if the habitual theatre-goer spent all of his time talking about *Hamlet,* without paying much attention to modern plays.

But there is good reason for the balletgoer to be preoccupied with *Giselle.* Like *Hamlet, Giselle* is a classic: it is not only important historically, it also happens to be good. It is just as popular today as when it was first performed, more than 130 years ago. People go to see *Giselle* and to see new ballerinas dance it for the same reason we go to see new interpretations of *Hamlet:* the work is such a good one that we always discover something in it we hadn't seen before, some variation in performance that brings out an aspect that seemed previously concealed; we learn something new.

There are many ballets important to history: the ballet in which the ballerina first discarded her heeled slipper, the ballet in which she first stood on the tips of her toes, and the ballet in which she jumped dangerously but effortlessly from a height of twenty feet to be caught in her lover's arms. But these ballets, with all their innovations, haven't come down to us; they are important

Rudolf Nureyev in *Petrouchka*. Photo by Rosemary Winckley.

Natalia Makarova in *Don Quixote*. Photo by Rosemary Winckley.

Mikhail Baryshnikov in *Don Quixote*. Photo by Kenn Duncan.

Vladimir Vasiliev in *Spartacus*. Photo by Rosemary Winckley.

Nina Sorokina and Vladimir Vasiliev in *Spartacus*. Photo by Beverley Gallegos.

Nadezhda Pavlova and Vyacheslav Gordeyev, February 1973, Moscow Competition.
Photo by Judy Cameron.

Vyacheslav Gordeyev. Photo by Kenn Duncan.

Mikhail Baryshnikov in Pushkin's class at the Kirov school, Leningrad, 1968. Photo by Patricia Barnes.

only in a narrow academic sense. *Giselle* has come down to us, has been performed by one ballet company or another ever since its first performance, because it combines innovation with drama and dancing that make us forget all about history.

*Giselle*'s innovation is its summing up of what we know as the Romantic ballet. To be romantic about something is to see what you are and to wish for something entirely different. This requires magic. The mysterious and supernatural powers that romantic poetry invoked to secure its ideal soon became natural to the theatre, where dancers attired in billowy white seemed part of the world and yet also above it. Marie Taglioni in the ballet *La Sylphide* (see page 603), popularized this fashion so completely that the sylph became ballet's symbol for romantic love—the girl who is so beautiful, so light, so pure that she is unattainable: touch her, and she vanishes.

Poets and novelists of the time were all interested in stories of the romantically supernatural, stories that told of lovely young girls whose love was never fulfilled because of intervening powers. One of these stories told of girls known as Wilis, who were engaged to be married yet died before their wedding days. In the evening they rose from their graves and danced alone in the moonlight. Their dancing was impassioned with their anger at death; but, dressed in their flowing bridal gowns and endowed with unearthly gifts of movement, their ghostly forms seemed never to touch the ground.

The Wilis were so beautiful that it was simple for them to attract young men into their midst. But they were as dangerous as they were irresistible. They danced with the young men who came only to trap them: their suitors were compelled to dance until they died.

This story of the Wilis seemed to be ideal for ballet: it made the story of *La Sylphide* look like merely the first step in the attainment of the romantic ideal. For the heroine of that ballet was purely a creature of the imagination, a figure in the hero's dream. We had admired her beauty and pitied her, but she was too illusory a character to make us feel deeply. What would accomplish this, what would make us care about such a character, would be to give her a basis in real life, to make her real and unreal at the same time—like the Wilis.

The poet, novelist, and critic Théophile Gautier read the story of the Wilis as it was related by Heinrich Heine, and thought it would make a good ballet and would be particularly fine for Carlotta Grisi. Gautier had seen Grisi's début in Paris and had fallen in love with her. Under the tutelage of her husband, Jules Perrot, the great dancer and choreographer, she had become the potential rival of Marie Taglioni and Fanny Elssler.

However, the story of the ballet required considerable work before it was resolved. There was the problem of how the heroine would become a Wili, under what circumstances would she die? Gautier presented this difficulty to the popular librettist Vernoy de Saint-Georges. Within three days they had contrived a suitable story and the libretto had been accepted at the Paris Opéra. Within a week the score had been written and the ballet was in rehearsal. At its first performance, a few days later, *Giselle ou les Wilis* was proclaimed the triumphant successor to *La Sylphide* and the greatest ballet of its time. For the Giselle he created for her, Grisi owed Gautier her greatest triumph and Gautier's attachment later obliged the ballerina to leave Perrot.

ACT ONE: A VILLAGE ON THE RHINE   The first curtain is preceded by a brief overture. The contrast between the strong, virulent opening measures and the light romantic melody that follows gives us an indication of the pitiless fate that will govern this love story. When the curtain rises, we see a part of a wooden village on the Rhine. It is vintage time, and the people of the village are preparing to celebrate. Peasant couples cross the stage, talking to each other affectionately; a few girls enter alone, wave in greeting to their friends, link arms, and follow them off to the left, near the entrance to a cottage. This is the cottage of Giselle, the lovely village maiden who lives with her mother, Berthe. On the right we discern the entrance to another cottage.

The stage is empty for an instant. Trumpets sound a warning. Hilarion, a gamekeeper, enters. He is dressed somewhat rudely and his gestures are not refined, but he is a man of genuine feeling. Almost directly he walks over to the door of Giselle's cottage. He is in love. Hilarion is about to knock on the door when he hears someone approaching. He looks around hurriedly and hides behind Giselle's cottage to watch.

Two men enter. They are Albrecht, Duke of Silesia, a handsome young man who wears a royal cape over his peasant clothes, and his squire, Wilfrid. Albrecht, too, goes to Giselle's door. Hilarion, who watches the scene jealously, is interested in the cape and sword that Albrecht wears, for Hilarion, like Giselle, knows this young man only as Loys, a peasant. Albrecht stands before Giselle's cottage and holds his hands over his heart. He, too, is in love and has put on peasant disguise in order that his love may be returned. Wilfrid, his attendant, is not in favor of his master's love for Giselle and begs him to come away. Albrecht refuses. He gives his cape and sword to Wilfrid and dismisses him. Wilfrid conceals the cape and sword in the cottage on the right and reluctantly withdraws.

Albrecht, at the door of Giselle's cottage, listens, then knocks. The music anticipates. He runs and hides. Giselle emerges from the house. She is expecting Albrecht and runs out happily. She dances joyfully and beautifully, as if she wanted to be watched. But no one is there! She looks about, acts as if she were indifferent, and begins to dance again. Now she hears something. She stops and poses as she listens carefully. Albrecht is blowing kisses to her! But still he will not show himself. Giselle is annoyed at this teasing, stamps her foot impatiently, and prepares to go back into the house. At this point Albrecht steps out before her. Giselle frowns and pretends that she is not glad to see him. He nudges her shoulder, and she bows low before him, still unsmiling. She runs to the cottage door, lest her pretense break down. Albrecht stands before the door to prevent her escape, then reaches out and gently takes her wrist. Now she smiles, looking up at him with amused reproach.

The two lovers dance across the stage together and sit on a crude wooden bench at the right. Albrecht tries to sit close to Giselle, but she edges away every time he moves closer. Again she tries to go back into the house, and again Albrecht prevents her.

Suddenly Albrecht is completely serious. He expresses to Giselle his eternal love and vows that he will always be faithful to her. Giselle acts as if she did not take him at his word and, to prove this, she picks a flower and begins to pluck its petals in a game of he-loves-me-loves-me-not. Albrecht vigorously nods his head when the petals say he-loves-me, but the last petal she chooses to pick turns out to be loves-me-not. Giselle throws the flower to the ground and begins to cry. To comfort her, Albrecht picks up the flower again and declares that the last petal is really he-loves-me. Giselle is fully consoled and, linking her arm through Albrecht's, dances again with him.

The lovers are so absorbed in each other that they do not notice Hilarion, who has emerged from his hiding place. The gamekeeper boldy interrupts their rendezvous and separates them. Before they know what has happened, Hilarion is attacking Albrecht and warning him not to make love to Giselle. Giselle thinks that Hilarion is simply jealous and upbraids him for eavesdropping. Hilarion kneels before her and assures her that he alone truly loves her. Her anger mounting, Giselle dismisses Hilarion with rude laughter. The gamekeeper regards Albrecht with suspicion and hatred and, as he leaves the scene, shakes his fists at him.

Giselle is still shaken by this scene. Albrecht holds her in his arms and reassures her softly. They walk together. Village girls now enter, carrying huge baskets of grapes. They are all friends of Giselle's, and when they begin to dance, she joins them, dancing in their midst to a bright, melodious waltz. Albrecht watches Giselle from the bench nearby. She soon runs over and asks him to join in. Boys join the girls as Albrecht and Giselle dance around the stage. The two lovers blow kisses to each other as the music accompanies their dance with a soft, hesitant theme that tinkles gently. The waltz ensemble ends as Albrecht holds Giselle on his knee.

Berthe, Giselle's mother, opens the cottage door and steps out. She does not wish to interfere with the festivities, but she is genuinely worried. Giselle playfully hides behind her friends, but her mother discovers her. She upbraids her daughter for dancing so much and reminds her that her heart will fail. Berthe attempts to impress Giselle with the truth of what she says by warning her that if she dies, she will become one of the Wilis, one of those creatures doomed to dance forever, even in death.

Giselle's friends take Berthe's tale more seriously than her daughter does. She wishes to dance again and goes to Albrecht. Berthe, however, takes her by the hand, and together they go into the cottage. The door closes. The disappointed Albrecht wanders off, and the villagers disperse.

Now that the stage is empty, Hilarion, bent on vengeance, approaches Giselle's cottage. He does not know how he can convince the girl that she is being deceived. A hunting horn sounds in the distance. Hilarion hears a hunting party come his way and seeks concealment in Albrecht's cottage.

Wilfrid, Albrecht's squire, is the first of the hunting party to enter. He looks about apprehensively, lest his master still be present. The prince of Courland and his daughter, Bathilde, follow with huntsmen and members of the court. The prince gestures to Wilfrid that they are in need of refreshment and rest and orders him to knock at Giselle's door.

Berthe responds to Wilfrid's knock. Seeing the prince and his daughter, she bows low before them and invites them to partake of whatever humble refreshment she can offer. She signals inside the house, and two girls bring out a table and stools, metal goblets, and a pitcher of wine.

Giselle steps out of the house and is astonished to see the royal party. She bows to Wilfrid, thinking him a prince. Wilfrid indicates the true prince; Giselle curtsies to him and his daughter and tries to assist in their entertainment. Bathilde is kind to the girl and indicates to her father, "How beautiful she is!" Wilfrid pours the wine, and the prince and Bathilde drink. While they sit at the table, Giselle kneels surreptitiously at Bathilde's feet and touches the hem of her long dress. Giselle has not seen such expensive fabric before and remarks its beauty when Bathilde looks down and sees her. Bathilde takes Giselle aside and asks her how she spends her day. "Weaving and spinning," Giselle replies. "But are these the things you like to do best?" Bathilde wonders. "No," Giselle indicates, "I like best to dance," and so saying dances several steps before Bathilde.

Giselle's mother disapproves and is about to reprimand her daughter, but the dance is quickly over. Bathilde wishes to express her admiration for the peasant girl by giving her a present. With the prince's consent, she takes off her necklace and, calling Giselle to her, places it about the girl's neck. Giselle, in rapture, kisses her hand and proudly shows the necklace to her mother.

The hunting party now accepts Giselle's invitation to rest within the cottage. Wilfrid remains without, ready to rouse the prince with the hunting horn should there be good cause for the hunt to continue. Wilfrid dismisses the huntsmen and follows after them.

Hilarion comes forth from Albrecht's cottage. He carries Albrecht's sword in his hand. He looks about quickly, sees no one, and gestures in triumph: now perhaps Giselle will believe him! He exits as the peasant girls and boys return to resume their dancing. They knock at Giselle's door and finally persuade her mother to allow her to join them. The girls and boys recline in a semicircle about Giselle, who dances a brilliant solo. Albrecht appears as the girls dance. He and Giselle join her friends, and as the dance ensemble ends, the lovers embrace.

The music crashes ominously. Hilarion runs out, tears the lovers apart, and tells Giselle what he has learned: "You might love this man, but he is an impostor." He rushes out, retrieves Albrecht's sword, and places it in Giselle's hand. Albrecht is motionless with horror. He knows that the gamekeeper is right, but he knows that this is not the way for Giselle to learn the truth. She will never believe him again, never believe his love. Giselle seems to think Hilarion is lying; it does not occur to her that her lover has wronged her.

Wilfrid enters and attempts to protect his master. Hilarion persists in reminding Giselle that the sword is Albrecht's. She goes to Albrecht. With great faith she asks him if the gamekeeper is speaking the truth. Albrecht bows his head; he cannot speak. Then, looking up at Hilarion, who imagines that a duke cannot love as truly as a gamekeeper, seizes the sword and attacks him. Only Wilfrid prevents him from murdering the gamekeeper. The sword falls to the ground. Hilarion is glorying in his revenge so much that he does

not notice what he has done to Giselle. He takes down the hunting horn and blows on it to summon the prince. Sobbing in her mother's arms, Giselle cannot yet believe what she has learned.

The prince and his daughter come out of the house with their party. The prince is surprised to see Albrecht in peasant's clothes; Bathilde goes to Albrecht and asks him what is wrong, why he is dressed like this? Giselle watches him closely. When he kneels before Bathilde and kisses her hand, Giselle tears herself from her mother's arms and accosts Bathilde. Albrecht tries to caution Bathilde, but before he can prevent it, she has pointed to the ring on her finger: she is engaged to Albrecht, Duke of Silesia.

Giselle, her heart broken, is so defenseless that her reason begins to disintegrate. Fiercely she tears the necklace Bathilde gave her from her neck and dashes it to the ground. She falls before her mother. Berthe comforts her as best she can and tries to quiet her and loosens her hair. Albrecht attempts to speak to her, to assure her of his love, but she will not listen. The girl is so stricken with grief, so helpless without the love she lived by, that all present, courtiers and peasants alike, pity her.

Giselle staggers to her feet. She moves about the stage slowly and pathetically, reliving her moments of happiness with Albrecht. With her reason gone, this is all she can think of. She picks up an imaginary flower and to herself plays another game of he-loves-me-loves-me-not. She circles the stage, and all the people stand back. Suddenly Giselle sees Albrecht's sword lying forgotten on the ground. She runs to it and, taking it up at the pointed end, holds it in front of her. Hypnotized by her madness, her friends do not move. Giselle bends low and drags the sword about with her, its handle rattling as she trails it around the stage at the feet of her friends. Then, before anyone can move, she raises the sword high and forces its point into her heart. Albrecht leaps across to her and seizes the sword.

The prince and Bathilde withdraw. Here they can only cause agony. Giselle, dying in her mother's arms, rises and goes to Albrecht. Her mind is now completely gone and she imagines that there has never been anything wrong, that he is her lover as before. She begins to dance with him, and again the soft, hesitant theme of romance that accompanied one of their happy dances together is repeated. Giselle awkwardly, falteringly, repeats the steps that she formerly danced with such grace. Then, in the midst of the dance, she is frightened. She runs to her mother, but falls to the ground before she can reach her embrace. Albrecht despairs as Berthe bends over her daughter. But Giselle asks for him. He comes to her and looks down into her eyes, which even now seek only his. He declares again his imperishable love. Giselle reaches up to touch his face in a gesture of forgiveness; then her hand falls. She is dead.

Albrecht rises and drags Hilarion to see what his jealousy has accomplished. As the gamekeeper weeps and kneels beside Giselle, Albrecht seizes the sword and again tries to kill him. Wilfrid again prevents him. Albrecht weeps beside Giselle. The dead girl lies before him, her arms crossed on her breast. The villagers turn their faces away to hide the grief they share.

ACT TWO: WITHIN A FOREST GLADE AT MIDNIGHT   In the second act we pass
to a scene and a mood entirely different from that of Act One. Our first hint of
this comes in the music. The strings sing softly against a rippling harp; all is
quiet and ethereal. The curtain rises on a scene misty with the dewy night. The
moon penetrates the thick trees occasionally; its light is reflected in a nearby
lake, and in this dimness we discover Giselle's grave at the left. Her name is
inscribed on a large cross that stands above the grassy mound. In the dark-
blue sky, small shimmering lights appear.

Three huntsmen with a lantern enter to rest. They sit down near the lake.
Hilarion joins them. Soon the men are disturbed by the eerie atmosphere of
the place. They have heard tales that Wilis danced here and they fear the
place is haunted. The lights in the sky are not constant, they appear to
shimmer at will. Hilarion, aware that Giselle's grave is close by, becomes apprehensive. He approaches the grave. The men warn him to leave. Hilarion is
reluctant, but joins his friends as they depart.

Across the back of the stage a veiled figure in a long white dress moves
flowingly. She is Myrtha, Queen of the Wilis. She enters, crosses the stage rapidly, and again appears at the back. At her second entry, she has removed her
veil. She bows, poses in deep, still arabesque, and begins to dance. Her movements are confident, controlled, beautiful, but they possess no warmth. The supernatural powers Myrtha possesses allow for nothing but perfection. She
moves more rapidly now; the quickness of her dancing is brilliant and hard,
like a diamond. She gathers two fern branches from the lakeside, throws them
into the forest to dedicate the place to her awful purpose, and circles the
stage in a brilliant display of virtuosity.

Now, with her wand, she calls forth the Wilis. Instantly obedient to her
command, they appear on either side of the stage, their hands crossed over
their breasts. Myrtha orders them to remove their white veils. They obey her
and arrange themselves for a dance. Led by two attendants to the queen, the
Wilis move with a perplexing, almost automatic, grace, as if they danced only
at Myrtha's will. Myrtha dances among them, dances with relentless, abandoned force, as if she could not restrain herself, then orders the dancing to
end. All the Wilis turn toward Giselle's grave, kneel, and bend low. A new
creature is to be initiated.

Myrtha bends over the grave with a magical branch. The earth parts, and
Giselle rises from the mound. She is dressed in white, veiled, her arms crossed
over her breast. Instinctively, as if hypnotized, she responds to Myrtha's commands. She walks toward the queen and stands motionless as Myrtha removes
her veil. Now Giselle opens her eyes. Following Myrtha's example, she begins
to dance, imitating her movements exactly. Myrtha declares that she is now a
member of the ghostly tribe and orders Giselle to dance alone. The girl suddenly seems to come to life and, turning around and around, rejoices in her liberation from the grave.

Surrounded by her sisters, Giselle dances as they, too, have danced at their
first appearance from their graves—before the dreadful power of the queen
dominated them completely. Giselle leaves the scene at the end of her dance,
and Myrtha orders the Wilis to conceal themselves.

The stage is empty when Albrecht enters. He moves slowly, dejectedly. He has come to visit the grave of his beloved and is filled with memories of her tragic death. Wilfrid follows his master and attempts to dissuade him from reminding himself of Giselle. Albrecht dismisses him and kneels before Giselle's grave. As he thinks of her, Giselle appears. Albrecht cannot believe it; he looks again; she was not there, after all. He rises and looks about the scene. Now Giselle runs fleetingly in a swift diagonal before him. Albrecht catches her in his arms briefly, lifts her in midflight, and again she disappears. Albrecht's brief touch is like a glance; he thinks that he must be dreaming, yet prays that the dream is true.

As he kneels in prayer, Giselle re-enters and dances about him. He does not see her. Then Giselle walks up in back of him and lovingly touches his shoulder. Albrecht rises and watches her. Joyful that his prayer has been answered, he wishes to touch her. They begin to dance together, Giselle leading the way. Then suddenly she vanishes.

She returns, picks two white lilies, and, dancing in swift diagonals, throws the flowers back over her head. Albrecht, pursuing her closely, picks up the flowers and follows her into the forest as she exits.

Hilarion returns to the scene. No sooner has he done so than Wilis appear before him. He turns to escape them, but in every direction other winged creatures enter and surround him. Myrtha enters with her attendants to examine the captive. At her command, all the Wilis encircle Hilarion, then stand in a long diagonal line, reaching from the right front of the stage to the lakeside. Myrtha stands at the right, at the head of the line. Hilarion, now sure of her intent, begs her for mercy. The queen gestures grandly, "No." Hilarion rushes down the line, beseeching the Wilis to intervene for him. They all refuse. Myrtha declares that he must die. She points to the lake. Hilarion is turned around and around as he is thrust down the long line of Wilis. At the end, two Wilis seize him and cast him into the lake.

Myrtha, unrelenting and triumphant, crosses the stage in light, unremembering leaps and exits at the rear. Two by two, all the Wilis follow her, imitating her step precisely. When Myrtha leads them back on stage, Albrecht confronts the queen. He, too, asks that his life might be spared, and again the queen denies the request. Giselle pleads in his behalf, but her intervention serves only to increase Myrtha's anger. Giselle, determined to save Albrecht at all costs, gestures to him to take refuge beneath the cross at her grave. Myrtha quickly orders the Wilis to intercept Albrecht, but he succeeds in reaching the cross in spite of their efforts to ensnare him. Giselle stands before him in an attitude of protection, and the queen is helpless.

Determined that Albrecht shall die, and offended at this sudden curtailment of her power, the queen orders Giselle to descend from the cross and dance. The girl obeys her, dancing alone between the Wilis, who are arranged in lines down the sides of the stage.

At the conclusion of the dance, Albrecht leaves the protective cross, steps down, and the two lovers go down the lines of Wilis, pleading for their intercession. All obstinately refuse. Now Giselle and Albrecht begin a *pas de deux*. As Albrecht supports Giselle in the adagio, Wilis contrive to come between them and separate them. But the two are now so reunited, so reassured of their lasting love, that they escape these Wilis without even noticing them.

Myrtha commands Giselle to dance alone again. This is followed by a variation for Albrecht. Giselle rejoins him. He lifts her again and again, higher and higher, straight into the air, her phantomlike body seeming a part of the air. Giselle dances another solo. The queen of the Wilis knows that Giselle will never tire, that, like all Wilis, she has a passion for dancing. She knows also that Albrecht will wish to please Giselle and will dance with her. Albrecht will dance to his death.

Albrecht commences another variation. When he has finished, he pleads with the Wilis to make him dance no longer. They ignore his request and, in the midst of continuation of the dance, he falls exhausted to the ground. Giselle tries to help him up, but he cannot move. Giselle turns to the queen and dances to divert her. Finally Albrecht stirs as Giselle beckons to him. They resume their dance; Albrecht makes a new plea to Myrtha, and the dance is resumed as she again denies him. When Albrecht collapses and kneels on the ground, Giselle stands over him protectively. She humbly approaches Myrtha and when the queen obstinately rebuffs her, Giselle asks each of the Wilis to help her. They can do nothing; they are all in the queen's power.

Albrecht attempts to leave the scene, but the watchful Wilis prevent his escape and force him to dance again. He leaps again and again high into the air, then falls to the ground.

Dawn approaches. Four o'clock sounds in the distance. The Wilis must vanish, for with the coming of day, they are powerless. Giselle rejoices that Albrecht has been saved! The Wilis again bow at Giselle's grave, consigning her back to the earth. Giselle embraces Albrecht as she kneels beside him. She knows that this is farewell. The Wilis rush away into the coming dawn, followed by their queen. Albrecht succeeds in rising. Giselle, with mysterious longing, yearns to return to the earth. She goes to her grave. Albrecht follows her, but before he reaches the tomb, she has fallen back and been covered with earth. Albrecht despairs and falls to the ground where he first knelt beside the grave of his beloved.

NOTES   Two recent performers of the title role in *Giselle* have attracted special attention, both in the Royal Ballet's production. Writing in the New York *Times* of Merle Park's performance of May 10, 1970, at the Metropolitan Opera House, New York, Clive Barnes said: "She is gorgeous—one of the greatest Giselles I have ever seen and to be ranked with Ulanova, Markova, Alonso, or Chauviré. Miss Park conveys all of Giselle—her innocence, her simple love of play-acting, her vanity, her nervousness, her compassion. Her portrayal is not only beautiful in its dramatic detail—never in my life have I seen a more consummately convincing mad scene—but is also marvelously danced. Once again, as with Antoinette Sibley, with these classic English ballerinas, one looks to Leningrad for their peers, and here you find Natalia Makarova. Makarova has more elevation, more ethereality. Park has more force, more honesty, and more technical finesse. Miss Park is a Giselle for people who never want to see that ballet again."

In June 1972, Natalia Makarova danced *Giselle* with the Royal Ballet in London. Peter Williams reviewed her performance in *The Observer:* "The first time that Natalia Makarova ever danced *Giselle* with her parent company, the Kirov, was in London. In this city, some years later, she broke the umbilical cord and decided to remain in the West. It was right that in *Giselle* she should return to dance as guest with the Royal Ballet at Covent Garden, since the company has its roots deep in the Leningrad School.

"Giselle is probably the most deceptive role in all classical ballet since sheer dancing ability is simply not enough to make it work. The ballerina has to be totally convincing as a human and, later, as a supernatural being. It is the conviction Makarova brings to both aspects of the part, combined with her great schooling, that makes her possibly the finest interpreter of our time.

"She *is* the simple village girl, overpowered by the attentions of Albrecht, whom she believes to be a swain of peasant stock; her trust in him is complete and touching. Her madness, following the moment of truth, is achieved by none of those contrived ballerina gestures but with the inconsequential movements of a deranged mind—she scrabbles at the ground for imagined flowers; in her aimless wandering she already imagines the Wilis; she is a lost soul with just the right glimmer of confused recognition as she confronts one of the figures in her tragedy.

"In the opening moments of the first act, Makarova had a bit of trouble with the tempi; gradually, as the ballet progressed, she and conductor Lanchbery moved together until, in the second act, any disparity was smoothed out. Her control, never overstepping the bounds of the role, is wonderful: slow turns which even leave time for extra beaten steps in their progress; a softness that is never coy; a quiet exultation in all her phrasing. Her arms are so expressive that, in the second act, their fluidity seemed to become a part of the mists encircling her unhallowed grave.

"There is no doubt that Makarova's performance was enriched by the accord which existed between her and Anthony Dowell's anti-hero Albrecht. What for him started as a flirtatious game gradually developed into true tenderness; his partnering all through became a moving expression of a love that believably went beyond death and the grave. Dowell's dancing and subtle playing matched so perfectly with Makarova's that this might well be the beginning of an historic partnership."

Writing of his famous roles, the *premier danseur* Erik Bruhn recalled his impressions of Albrecht in the essay "Beyond Technique" for *Dance Perspectives:* "I think I consider Albrecht as something of a playboy, with a definite background that James (in *La Sylphide*) does not have. He is just James. He could be a peasant boy from the country with not much sophistication. Albrecht belongs to the aristocracy. A marriage has been arranged for him, as was customary at that time, and he accepts this without protesting or rebelling. At the same time he feels that he is free to do what he wants to do as well. So here is this playboy playing with something as lovely, as innocent, as serious as Giselle. Yet there is a certain innocence in Albrecht too, or he would have been smart to conceal the fact of his disguise as a peasant and nobody could have discovered that he had a fiancée already. His fancy for

Giselle is earnest enough as long as he can keep it secret. For he is quite prepared to do what he is supposed to do and marry his proper fiancée and continue the family tradition. He does not dream that Giselle will take his attentions so seriously.

"She is attracted to him because he is different. After all, she has plenty of peasants to choose from. Whether the audience sees him first dressed as a count or as a peasant does not matter. There is something different about him. It is like we see someone on the subway and he may stand out because of his mod clothes and long hair (though even that we pass by now), or he may dress like anyone else and we don't know why but suddenly we turn and look. Giselle recognizes his difference though she doesn't know where he comes from.

"After she dies from the shock of Albrecht's deception, he realizes some sincerity in life that he might not otherwise have known. His awareness of guilt makes him mature. His going to her grave at night is like a nightmare. The wilis, of course, are not real because today we cannot believe in terms of wilis flying around. They are in Albrecht's mind. They are all the things we are afraid of, that we have tried to escape. In his nightmares a man's wrong deeds come back to him, carrying a message that he must look at right in the face. Then he can accept his guilt without pushing it away; he can face reality. Albrecht survives because he can admit his guilt and realize his responsibility. After that night he will go into the future with an awareness that makes him mature. And this proves a strength in him too.

"My first *Giselle* was with Alicia Markova in 1955 and, unlike my first *La Sylphide,* it was a success. We did it in three days. I had never done *Giselle* before but I had seen it and maybe I wanted to do it for years. Markova was so clear in what she told me about the ballet that I felt ready to go on stage that night after only one rehearsal. She never had to repeat herself and she said once, 'We seem to speak the same language.' Thanks to her, it worked out just right. Some things were sketchy because we had worked alone and there was just one runthrough before the performance with everyone on stage, and suddenly I realized that people were there in those places and they were all moving. I chose to do nothing rather than try to act something I didn't know anything about. Yet I later relied on the work I had done with Markova and based my future performances on it.

"It seemed there was nothing wrong with my first *Giselle;* in fact it set me up like I was supposed to be *the* Albrecht. But if I had not on occasions revived my idea about Albrecht, I couldn't do the character today and the memory of my Albrecht would belong to the books. It had only a momentary truth that worked for a time as life. Now I can bring more to a role. I can go back to roles I have done for ten years to get a picture of how I see James or Albrecht today. When I first did them I had less of a past to return to and therefore was not able to give that much to a role. I think the more experience you have got the more need there will be for you to use it. And there will be a youth and vitality in the characterization that it didn't have originally. In a more mature state, one has more imagination as to what a youth would do. When I was his age I could only be me which was the beginning of a James. Now I can give a more complete portrayal of James and Albrecht because I have used my imagination. And the portrayal of the character is always true as long as we bring to it what we have within us."

In a review headlined "Fairy-Tale Debut," the critic Clive Barnes wrote in the New York *Times* of Gelsey Kirkland's first performance in this role with American Ballet Theatre at Washington's Kennedy Center, May 18, 1975: "Partnered by Mikhail Baryshnikov, she made her debut in the title role of *Giselle* and the debuts of few ballerinas can have been more memorable. It was the coming together of a dancer and a role that had been made for each other . . . Since her school days, Miss Kirkland has understandably been the darling of the ballet's cognoscenti, but here irrefutably was the emergence of a great American ballerina. She did not put a foot, a hand or even a gesture wrong—it was the fairy-tale debut little girls dream about . . ."

The Kirkland-Baryshnikov *Giselle* was reviewed in detail by Arlene Croce in *The New Yorker* after its New York presentation in August 1975. The critic, pointing out that we have lacked a great American-born Giselle ever since the ballet became a part of the active repertory in the United States, said that Gelsey Kirkland "may be the first totally creditable Giselle since the ballet was first danced here," in 1846.

When Galina Ulanova visited New York in 1975 with the Bolshoi Ballet, whose young dancers she enjoys training, the critic Anna Kisselgoff interviewed her in the New York *Times:*

". . . The difference between Miss Ulanova's approach to a ballet and that of a younger generation was illustrated during the interview when she cleared up a specific dramatic point in the Bolshoi's current production of *Giselle* that is not included in Western productions.

"At the close of the second act, Giselle (a peasant girl who is now a spirit) is cradled by Albrecht, the aristocrat who has betrayed her. The action seems puzzling. Is the ghost of Giselle so corporeal that she can be picked up like a parcel?

"No, replied Miss Ulanova, explaining that the original dramatic meaning of the moment had been lost.

"'In the original production by Leonid Lavrovsky, it was different. Giselle had returned from the grave and was joyful. She was a live spirit, as there are in fairy tales.

"'As dawn breaks, however, she must leave and it was then that Albrecht tried to prolong this moment. She would lean back and it was here that he would carefully pick her up as she was "fading away."

"'He would touch her skirt'—here Miss Ulanova moved her arms and lifted her head in an instant that brought the action to life—'and Albrecht would feel Giselle's presence as if it were a breeze.

"'Now they pick Giselle up and just rock her. Well, you know young people —they are lightheaded.' Miss Ulanova smiled as she used a Russian expression that could be literally translated as 'They have the wind blowing through their heads.'"

Readers interested in discovering the motivations and rationale of dancers will wish to know that Mikhail Baryshnikov, in his book *Baryshnikov at Work*, has described with Charles Engell France the background of his first appearances as Albrecht. He analyzes *Giselle* in detail from the point of view of the part as he sees it—a man in love, caught up by fate, innocent, not a faithless, plotting aristocrat.

Shortly after the Kirkland-Baryshnikov *Giselle*, another debut in the title role was given by Bronwyn Thomas, aged fifteen, in the U. S. Terpsichore production at the Marymount Manhattan Theatre, New York, on August 13, 1975. Her Albrecht was Daniel Levans, the Myrtha Marrisa Benetsky. The role of Giselle's mother was taken *en travestie* by David Vaughan. This modest presentation, with piano accompaniment, was modeled after Anton Dolin's production, made so familiar in performances by that *danseur noble* and Alicia Markova.

On June 2, 1977, the American Ballet Theatre production of *Giselle*, with Makarova, Baryshnikov and Van Hamel, was seen live on PBS television direct from the Metropolitan Opera House in New York.

## GLINKAIANA

*Music by Michael Glinka. Choreography by George Balanchine. Scenery, costumes, and lighting by Esteban Francés. First presented by the New York City Ballet at the New York State Theatre, Lincoln Center, November 1968, with Violette Verdy and Paul Meija, Mimi Paul and John Clifford, and Patricia McBride and Edward Villella in the principal roles.*

Glinka is the Mozart of Russia; before him there was no real Russian music. From my earliest years I have always loved his music. In the New York City Ballet's days at the City Center Theatre, we did a ballet, a short one, the *Mazurka* from *A Life for the Tsar*, one of Glinka's great operas, which Vida Brown and I danced in. But I go back further than that with Glinka, having danced in his opera *Russlan and Ludmila* at the Maryinsky Theatre in St. Petersburg when I was a student. I remember those days (this was during the Revolution or just afterward) very well: sometimes it was so cold the men in the orchestra wore overcoats and mittens without fingers. We froze on stage. Still, I loved every note of that music.

*Glinkaiana* is simply a series of dances to four works by Glinka: a *Polka*, orchestrated by Vittorio Rieti, *Valse Fantasie* (this music was used for an earlier New York City Ballet production, in 1951), *Jota Aragonesa*, and *Divertimento Brilliante.*

## THE GODS AMUSED

*Music by Claude Debussy. Choreography by Eliot Feld. Costumes by Frank Thompson. Lighting by Jennifer Tipton. First presented by the American Ballet Company at the Brooklyn Academy of Music, New York, April 28, 1971, with Daniel Levans, Elizabeth Lee, and Christine Sarry.*

*The Gods Amused* is a dance ballet for three deities set to Debussy's *Danses Sacrée et Profane*. A young god and two young goddesses disport and amuse themselves on a day brilliant with light and reflection. The boy is the leader, and the girls are watchful of him. The nobility of these Olympian creatures gives them a certain detachment and while they might openly admire each other, there is no commitment in a personal sense; after all, all gods are beautiful. When the game is over, the three rest a bit, but at the end remind us in a statuesque pose of their immortality.

## GOLDBERG VARIATIONS

*Music by Johann Sebastian Bach. Choreography by Jerome Robbins. Costumes by Joe Eula. Lighting by Thomas Skelton. First presented by the New York City Ballet at the New York State Theatre, Lincoln Center, May 27, 1971. Pianist: Gordon Boelzner. Part I: Theme, Renée Estopinal and Michael Steele. Variations, Gelsey Kirkland, Sara Leland, John Clifford, Robert Weiss, Robert Maiorano, and Bruce Wells; Bryan Pitts, David Richardson, Delia Peters, Christine Redpath, Bettijane Sills, Stephen Caras, Hermes Conde, Richard Dryden, Francis Sackett, Suzanne Erlon, Gloriann Hicks, and Virginia Stuart. Part II: Variations, Karin von Aroldingen, Susan Hendl, Patricia McBride, Peter Martins, Anthony Blum, and Helgi Tomasson; Merrill Ashley, Rosemary Dunleavy, Renée Estopinal, Johnna Kirkland, Deborah Koolish, Gail Kachadurian, Colleen Neary, Susan Pilarre, Giselle Roberge, Polly Shelton, Marjorie Spohn, and Lynne Stetson; Stephen Caras, Victor Castelli, Hermes Conde, Richard Dryden, Bryan Pitts, David Richardson, Francis Sackett, Nolan T'Sani.*

Because this dance ballet is based on its music, Bach's *Goldberg Variations*, it might be well to consider the score first. The popular name of *"Goldberg" Variations* attached itself to the work because of the circumstances of its composition. It was hoped that they would be a sure cure for the insomnia of one Count von Kayserling. As the story goes, Bach was commissioned by the count, the Russian ambassador to the Dresden Court, who suffered badly from insomnia, to write some pieces "of a smooth and lively" character in order to relieve the tedium of his sleepless nights. Johann Theophilus Goldberg, a pupil of Bach, was harpsichordist to the count. He was the one who played the finished variations for the count and his name has attached itself to the work ever since.

Published in 1742, the *Goldberg Variations* consist of an aria or theme and thirty variations. It is the only work of Bach's in the form of a theme and variations. But it differs from most compositions of this work in an important respect. We usually think of a series of musical variations as an exploitation or development of a theme or melody that is stated at the beginning of the piece; we expect the same music to appear again and again in different dress. Bach's variations, however, are harmonic variations, rather than melodic; they develop the bass of the original aria rather than its melody. The result is that in

the thirty variations that follow, the melody of each is always fresh while the
original bass accompaniment is developed anew underneath. The fundamental
pattern in the bass can be heard in the first few bars of the aria, a *sarabande*
that Bach wrote for his wife.

But first of all, the *Goldberg Variations* are a pleasure. The pianist Charles
Rosen writes in the notes to his recording: "It is the most open and public of
Bach's keyboard works, the one that most absorbs and transforms the popular
styles of his time. The *Goldberg Variations* are, in fact, an encyclopedia: a survey of the world of secular music . . . a social work: it was meant mainly to
delight, and it instructs only as it charms. . . . There are canons, a fugue, a
French overture, a *siciliana*, a *quodlibet*, accompanied solos and a series of inventions and dance-like movements."

A hearing of a recording of the work is certainly not essential before seeing
the ballet (Bach's music is immediately likable in any case), but it is enjoyable
to listen to so entertaining and danceable a masterpiece. Come to think of it, I
would suggest, if the piece is not familiar to you already, that you hear it first as
you see the ballet. In this case, both what you see and what you hear will be
marvelous.

What you see begins, and ends, with a *sarabande* or stately dance. Two
dancers in eighteenth-century costume perform an elegantly simple *pas de
deux* at the beginning. They are still as the curtain rises, posing formally, then
they step toward us as the music begins. Their somewhat courtly manner of
movement and gesture sets the style for much that follows. Their dance is
slow, a bit grave, "yet happy, tranquil and at the same time vibrant with inter-
nal life," as Wanda Landowska described the music.

The theme stated, dancers in modern attire come to accompany the inventiveness of the score: there is a trio for a girl and two boys, then a series of
variations for different groupings—solos, quartets, *pas de deux*, a sextet, in a
continuing flow of dance discovery of the music.

After the fifteenth variation, a middle point is reached. The second part of
the ballet has a different character from the first, as do the costumes, which
become more formal. Dominated by the dancing of three couples, with solos
by the principals, and a *corps de ballet* of twenty, the new part is an exploration of the classic *pas de deux* and concentrates more on the few rather than
the many. Just before the end, all the dancers return, and in costumes recalling
eighteenth-century court dress, celebrate the final variation. The restatement of
the opening aria at the end is danced by the couple we saw first at the start of
the piece, but dressed now in contemporary costume. The circle is closed.

The general outline I have tried to give here is all you need, assuming, in
fact, that anything is needed but open eyes and ears. Those who want to recollect some details after they have seen *Goldberg Variations* may find the following map useful:

The piece begins, and ends, with an aria, a *sarabande*. The harpsichordist
Ralph Kirkpatrick calls the whole work "an enormous *passacaglia* . . . framed
as if by two monumental pylons, one formed by the aria and the first two variations, the other by the two penultimate variations and the *quodlibet*, the variations are grouped like the members of an elaborate colonnade."

After the aria is stated by the piano, the curtain rises on a girl and boy, she in a white ballet dress, he in eighteenth-century attire with black knee britches, white stockings, and a white ruffled shirt. They are quite still for a moment, posing formally, then they move toward us. Their dance is slow, a bit grave, yet, in Wanda Landowska's words about the music, "happy, tranquil and at the same time vibrant with eternal life." The boy kneels before the girl briefly.

1. A girl in a light olive-green tunic and two boys in tank suits replace the first couple as the introductory aria finishes and we are in another century altogether. The music is brisker, too, within the flowing melodic line and after the girl begins, the boys dance too, at her signal. She joins them at the close.

2. In what Landowska calls a "serene and pastoral mood," a girl in violet and two other boys dance; it is a friendly, thoughtful occasion, both boys lifting the girl to the trills of the score.

3. A boy, like a watchful teacher, leads four couples in an ensemble. One of the girls joins him. As he takes her off, the music changes, becoming openly declarative, with a kind of flourish.

4. These "jocose imitations" (Landowska) are danced by three couples and a boy who gesture in formal greeting and thanks.

5. The music, very fast, a contest for the performer, is for crossed hands (crossed keyboards on the harpsichord), an "outburst of irrepressible joy," in George Malcolm's words; two boys compete in the dance.

6. To new, slower music, the boys rest, lie down, stretch, look up briefly at the sky, then at each other. Then they sit up, rise, approach each other in a friendly way and begin to dance.

7. Their dance is a *saltarella*, a kind of jig, the rhythms of which were very popular in old French ballets. They greet a group of newcomers.

8. Six boys who watch a girl dance to tripping rhythms. She bows to them and goes. A boy in green leads the boys in a dance, girls join them and there is an ensemble.

9. As the music slows down four beats to the bar, the lead boy moves toward the lead girl, as do other couples in the group. They face each other across a circle of dancers. They simply walk, aimlessly, without any intention. The circle is broken; they are individuals again, then the walk becomes a promenade and they are all moving together and it is a dance. For twelve dancers.

10. A *fughetta*. Here, as George Malcolm puts it, the solemn *aria* melody is "slyly turned into a lithe and witty subject" for a little fugue. A dance for four boys, somersaults, cartwheels, and rolls.

11. To very rapid runs on the keyboard, three girls and three boys dance like the wind.

12. Three other couples dance to a stately measure in a dim light, then the six dancers from (11) return for varied combinations and separations. The boys watch the girls a bit and there is a final ensemble.

13. To a *cantilena* with a delicately ornamented upper melodic line, two girls and two boys dance. The light is subdued, the atmosphere friendly and thoughtful. There, hinting, in the words of the critic Emory Lewis, "at the

differing ways of love," the two boys dance together, as the girls watch, then the girls dance together, as the boys relax. Then again the boys dance with the girls.

14. Again the boys dance with the girls. The lights come up. To brilliant music of crossed keyboards, there is an ensemble led first by the boy in green.

15. The mood quietens again and the first of the variations in a minor key is danced by six girls, who back in from the right, and six boys, who back in from the left. They become a group of varied partnerships. The girls are lifted off gently into the wings at the close.

16. One boy remains, his arm raised before his face when suddenly to the right, to flourishing music, a phalanx of twelve girls ushers in three couples. In George Malcolm's words, this is "a specially grand variation and acts as a prelude to the second half, taking the form of an overture in the French style with the typical pompous opening and lively fugato. The aria is transformed by great technical skill into a splendid piece of Baroque grandeur."

17. A group of girls in blue begins this sparkling variation in which the music seems to cascade across the stage. The three couples who are to dominate this last half of the ballet take over but the girls return to finish the dance.

18. To a marchlike rhythm, a girl in pink and her partner dance an exhilarating, witty *pas de deux* in which the two dancers openly enjoy the mocking laughter in the music. Four boys and four girls watch.

19. Another *pas de deux* to music of gentle syncopations that floats, in Landowska's phrase, "like a barcarolle."

20. Excitement returns and the same two dancers seem to counteract the impulsive rhythm of the music by deliberately slow movement. The lights dim and before we know it they seem to have caught up with the music in rapid combinations of motion and gesture. The dancers perhaps embody George Malcolm's description of the music here, where "differing voices take up a living pursuit of each other."

21. The light darkens. A supported adagio for the third couple, this variation in G minor is reflective of the tragedy and pathos implied in the score.

22. A "massive" variation to Landowska, "its voices interlacing after the fashion of Palestrina," is danced by the boy who, left alone, dejected, seeks comfort in expression, then returns to his memories.

23. The lights come up. Brilliant again and almost "vertiginous in its joy" (Landowska), this variation accompanies a swift dance for four couples; the boys, then the girls racing diagonally across the stage, then all leaving together.

24. Calm again and in a stately dance rhythm, the music accompanies the girl who left the boy. She dances a variation. Three of her friends are with her and appear to want to be soloists, too.

25. The last variation in a minor key, somber, restless, romantic, a "richly ornamented adagio that overwhelms us" (Landowska), is danced by the girl in pink and her partner.

26. This sparkling variation is a combination of 18/16 time in one hand and 3/4 in the other, the two hands temporarily changing places once in a while.

Girls and boys in new costumes, like the eighteenth-century couple at the start, enter and watch as the other two lead couples dance.

The 27th variation (Landowska saw "humor and malice" here), the 28th (memorable for its tinkling trills), and the joyful 29th bring all six of the principals before us as each dances before the *corps de ballet*. All now are dressed in eighteenth-century costume.

For the 30th variation, a *quodlibet*, or fantasia, involving two folk tunes as well as the fundamental base melody, the dancers cluster at the center of the stage. They stand there briefly in a quiet pose. The lights come down; they all seem to promenade off. But as the aria is played again, the first two dancers, now in modern dress, come back to show again the beginning.

NOTES    Few ballets have been so praised, and at such articulate length, as *Goldberg Variations*. After a performance of what the choreographer called a "work in progress" at the Saratoga Performing Arts Center on July 23, 1970, Don McDonagh wrote in the New York *Times* that "the New York City Ballet has presented many premières in its history but none has had the informal and charming intimacy of *Goldberg Variations*."

After the New York première, *Variety* said the ballet was not only "a pinnacle of 20th century art but gave rise to the notion that it may be the most perfect dance work ever made. No better dancing can be seen than in this work. . . . Few other companies could have provided such superior execution by 42 dancers. . . . It is difficult to overestimate the contribution of pianist Gordon Boelzner, who played the immense work with brilliance, insight and rhythmic subtlety."

Winthrop Sargeant in *The New Yorker* called *Goldberg Variations* "a magnificent spectacle. . . . The ballet is abstract in the sense that music is abstract, but, like music, it contains moods ranging from sombre to playful. Mr. Robbins's feeling for the music is extraordinarily sensitive, and his treatment of rhythmic movement is—like his treatment of stage space—fluid, sometimes eccentric, but always deeply conscious of musical values. The première of the *Goldberg Variations* was to me the high point of a busy ballet season, and it places Mr. Robbins among the great, original masters of the art."

In *The Saturday Review,* the critic Walter Terry, admiring the ballet, recalled that Jerome Robbins had used the harpsichord at the working rehearsal of *Goldberg Variations* at Saratoga. "At a subsequent matinee, the harpsichord was tried again. In both forms of accompaniment, Gordon Boelzner was the admirable, laudable musician. Robbins himself says that he prefers the support of the piano since 'I worked with the piano in rehearsal when the ballet was being created, and it is closely related to those sounds. As for the length of the ballet . . . I could not violate the music. It is there, all there, and if the mind wanders, let it rest and then come back.'"

Writing in *Dance and Dancers* magazine, the critic Patricia Barnes described many of the performers:

"The first variations are dominated by the performances of the six soloists— among the company's most brilliant. The two girls are rewardingly contrasted. Sara Leland, lithe, daring and intensely musical, has an abandon and fearlessness that is exciting to watch; while Gelsey Kirkland, more restrained in her personality, offers us dancing that is as delicately precise as the finest embroidery. Her manner is touching too. Just 18, she is poised on the threshold of womanhood, but retains the charming innocence of a young girl. She has one solo, outstandingly danced, sympathetically watched by six young men casually seated on the floor, that perfectly catches in its unselfconscious coquetry her individuality and special grace.

"John Clifford, Bruce Wells, Robert Weiss and Robert Maiorano have equally enhanced their reputations. Each has had his artistry extended in this work. Clifford has never looked so elegant, while losing nothing of his appealing ebullience. Wells, a sure *premier danseur* in the making, is superb, smooth and effortless in everything he does, demonstrating a perfect line, buoyant elevation and a radiant personality.

"Another dancer who has caught the eye ever since he joined two years ago has been Robert Weiss. His brio, neat footwork and fine *ports de bras* are always in evidence, and Robbins has here exploited his mercurial gifts to splendid advantage. A slight stiffness in his upper torso at present prevents this slim and promising young dancer from total elegance, but this should come.

"One of Maiorano's first major opportunities came with *Dances at a Gathering*, and he has once more found himself in a Robbins ballet that gives him a chance to shine. His developing stage presence and ever-improving technique need this sort of exposure, for when given the opportunity he has shown himself most capable. . . .

"It would be impossible, in this dense and lengthy ballet, to describe fully the variations in detail, so isolated examples must suffice. One particularly striking section for four dancers, two boys and two girls, stands out. The two boys (Bryan Pitts and David Richardson) dance together, watched by the two girls (Leland and Kirkland), and while they relax the two girls dance.

"My own favorite variation is performed by two couples. Maiorano with Leland and Weiss with Kirkland, while Wells and Clifford slowly, in musical counterpoint, walk around them. The dance turns into two pas de trois, as the two boys weave their way in and out of the dancers to form two trios. The subtle transition is so beautiful, natural and elegant that one almost holds one's breath at Robbins's dazzling craftsmanship. . . .

"The final half of the ballet revolves around the six dancers, supported by the ensemble, and is far more formal in its construction while the choreography is more intricate. There is room only for the mention of highlights.

"The opening couple, McBride and Tomasson, backed by the ensemble, reflect in their pas de deux something of the bucolic humours of the 18th century, as hands on hips, backs to the audience, their bodies seem to shake with merriment, but this humour is touched with a 20th-century jazziness that perfectly fits the music's rhythms. The pas de deux from Blum and Hendl, at the start cool and classical, deploys Hendl's clean lines and Blum's strong presence. There is a gradual and subtle change of mood as the choreography becomes more sensual. The convolutions of the two dancers as they entwine around each other, while within the framework of the classic technique, succeeds in looking very new and very arresting.

"The loose-limbed and pliant qualities of von Aroldingen are shown off well in her quirkily individual solo, backed by three girls, but even better is the appearance of Peter Martins. He has never seemed more spirited, more dexterous. He was a joy to watch as he revelled in the musical rhythms and choreographic complexities. This elegant and beautiful dancer has sometimes in the past appeared a little too reserved. In *Goldberg* he was a powerhouse of excitement and physical strength. . . .

"Musically the work is yet another gift to City Ballet by its remarkable pianist, Gordon Boelzner. As in the previous Robbins masterworks, Mr. Boelzner, calm and implacable, is at his keyboard on a platform to the left of the proscenium arch and, as always, playing with modest majesty. He has become one of City Ballet's gilt-edged assets. Typically, when for one performance he was asked as an experiment to play on the harpsichord rather than the piano, he was willing, able and of course brilliant."

Admirers of *Goldberg Variations* must also be referred to Elena Bivona's indispensable essay on the ballet in *Ballet Review*, Vol. 3, No. 6, 1971.

## GRADUATION BALL

*Ballet in one act. Music by Johann Strauss. Choreography by David Lichine. Scenery and costumes by Alexandre Benois. Book by David Lichine. First presented by the Original Ballet Russe at the Theatre Royal, Sydney, Australia, February 28, 1940, with Tatiana Riabouchinska and David Lichine in the leading roles. First presented in the United States by the Original Ballet Russe at the Fifty-first Street Theatre, New York, November 6, 1940, with the same principals.*

*Graduation Ball* is the story of a party. Young girls at a fashionable school in Vienna put on a gala entertainment to fete the graduates of a nearby military academy. The girls and boys meet, amuse themselves by performing a series of *divertissements*, discover a secret romance, and dance until the headmistress of the school ends the party. The music for the ballet—chosen, arranged, and orchestrated by Antal Dorati—is selected from the works of Johann Strauss.

The ballet is set in the high, formal drawing room of the girls' school. There the girls are excitedly preparing for the ball, which is clearly their one real social occasion of the year. The senior girls primp excessively and try out their newly acquired fashionable manners, while their more numerous juniors, in simple frocks and pinafores, laugh at their affectations. Soon they are all ready to receive their guests from the local military school. The headmistress, an absurd and bustling busybody danced by a male dancer, rushes in and makes sure that her pupils look their very best.

Loud martial music announces the arrival of the cadets, who march in boldly to the staccato drums. Although the boys stand rigidly at attention when they halt, and face straight forward, their roving eyes size up their young hostesses in short order. The elderly general who leads the boys finally allows them to relax, and the young people are suddenly embarrassed: with all their pretense at worldly knowledge, they don't really know how to get the ball under way. The boys stay on one side of the room, the girls on the other, and there is a momentary stalemate.

The pompous old general has been immediately attracted to the headmistress and escorts her off for a rendezvous. The young people are unchaperoned and don't know quite what to do. A young girl, deciding to give the senior girls their comeuppance, leaves her friends and approaches the formation of boys. The cadets greet her with such loud heel-clicking and deference that the girl is terrified: she finds herself sitting smack in the middle of the floor.

The ball at last gets under way when the cadets elect a leader and order him to choose a partner and begin the first dance. Of course, he is more timid than his fellows and steps out of line only because of military discipline. The girls feel so sorry for him that before he can really make a choice, a partner is dancing with him. With this example, the other cadets take partners and all dance.

The headmistress and her general return to supervise the entertainment they have so carefully rehearsed—first comes a *divertissement* by one of the cadet drummers, then a romantic Scottish *pas de deux* that recalls the spirit of such old ballets as *La Sylphide*. The young girl who tried to start the dance is enchanted by this dance of ethereal love and improvises an impromptu dance of her own.

Next comes a dance-step competition in which the girls try to outdo each other in the number of *fouettés* they can execute, and there is a final *perpetuum mobile* in which all dance. The romance of the headmistress and the general has progressed during these entertainments, which they have hardly watched. The girls and boys leave the room seeking refreshments; the older people dance together and declare their love. They are in the midst of a passionate embrace when their students come back. The young people laugh and congratulate them, and the party hastens to a high-spirited conclusion. Despite their discovered romance, the headmistress and the general are compelled to end the dance. The cadets bid the girls a fond farewell and sadly take their leave. The lights dim.

The ballroom is now deserted. One of the cadets is seen trying to sneak back, to bid his girl a more private farewell. We are a little amused to see that this is the same cadet who was so hesitant about beginning the ball; no longer bashful, he is now bold. For a moment it appears that he'll be able to effect his rendezvous, but the headmistress darts out and shoos him off. He was only trying!

# GRAND PAS ESPAGNOL

*Music by Moritz Moszkowski. Choreography by Benjamin Harkarvy. Costumes by Joop Stokvis. First presented by the Netherlands Dance Theatre at the Empire Theatre, Sunderland, England, November 7, 1963. First presented in the United States by the Harkness Ballet at the Music Box Theatre, New York, January 17, 1969, with Elisabeth Carroll, Marina Eglevsky,*

*Lone Isaksen, Finis Jhung, Helgi Tomasson, and Lawrence Rhodes. Conducted by Krasimir Sipusch.*

This *divertissement* in the Spanish manner is a dance ballet for three girls and three boys. The music, by a German composer much admired in Russia, recollects, like the style of movement and gesture, familiar Spanish attitudes from folk dance and bullfight that recall, too, an affection the Russian classic dance developed for Spain. There are opportunities for vivid ensembles, a pensive duet for two of the girls, a vigorous trio for all three boys, and a flourishing finale.

*Grand Pas Espagnol* was presented by the City Center Joffrey Ballet at the City Center, New York, October 12, 1972. Lighting by Jennifer Tipton. Seymour Lipkin was the conductor and the dancers were Francesca Corkle, Rebecca Wright, Pamela Nearhoof, Glenn White, Paul Sutherland, and William Whitener.

Writing in *Dance and Dancers* magazine, Patricia Barnes wrote of the first performances by the Harkness Ballet: "This is an excitingly conceived *pas de six* reminiscent of the days of Petipa and Minkus—a display of that ballet—Spanish variety of classical dancing that can still be seen in such ballets as *Don Quixote* . . . To ensure that these classical variations should have the authentic flavor of the Imperial Russian Ballet, Harkarvy studied for a period with Madame Anderson Ivantzova, a former ballerina of the Bolshoi, who taught him the particular style he required as his base."

## THE GREEN TABLE

*Dance of Death in eight scenes. Book by Kurt Jooss. Music by Fritz Cohen. Choreography by Kurt Jooss. Costumes by Hein Heckroth. First presented by the Jooss Ballet at the Théâtre des Champs-Élysées, Paris, July 3, 1932. First presented in the United States by the City Center Joffrey Ballet at the City Center, New York, March 9, 1967.*

One of the most renowned dance works of the century and now a part of the American repertory, Kurt Jooss's ballet about war and death was first performed in the United States by his own company in the 1930s. Memories of World War I were still fresh and apprehensions of another war dominated many people's thoughts. Although naturally influenced by the time of its creation, *The Green Table* has been successfully presented ever since, testifying to the power of its theme and presentation. The English critic John Percival has written: *"The Green Table* must be one of the most *shocking* ballets ever created, in the proper sense of the word, but its impact remains the same after repeated performances."

Subtitled "A Dance of Death," the ballet is about diplomacy and war, the seeming uselessness of talk, the horror of battle. The table of the title is the green baize table to be found in a diplomatic conference room, where the ballet begins. There men in morning dress negotiate at the table. The two sides cannot agree about the matter under discussion, evidently one of great seriousness. Formal pleasantries persist for a while as each side takes up a series of attitudes, but it is clear that they are getting nowhere. In the final argument, the diplomats pull out guns and fire them across the table, and war is declared.

We now see the result of the fruitless discussions and watch as Death, stalking throughout the ballet like a relentless demonic force, claims his victims. There is a scene of parting, as soldiers leave for war, scenes of carnage in battle and refugees fleeing, a scene in a brothel and the home-coming of the few survivors. Death claims everyone: the fighting men, an old mother, a young girl in a brothel, a war profiteer. Then the action returns to the beginning and we are at the conference table again. Signifying peace, the diplomats fire their revolvers into the air and get on with the discussion.

## GROSSE FUGE

*Music by Ludwig van Beethoven. Choreography by Hans van Manen. Scenery by Jean-Paul Vroom. Costumes by Hans van Manen. First presented by the Netherlands Dance Theatre at the Circus Theatre, Scheveningen, Holland, April 8, 1971. First presented in the United States by the same ensemble at the Brooklyn Academy of Music, New York, April 1, 1972.*

This dance ballet arranged to the *Great Fugue* of Beethoven and the *Cavatine* from the *B Flat Quartet* is for eight dancers, four boys and four girls. While there is no narrative, the ballet develops a set of themes established by the dancers. At first, apart, the girls and boys seem not to care about each other while in fact that is what their dancing is about—display pieces to excite interest. That accomplished, the four couples pair off, the girls attaching themselves to the boys, clinging to large buckles that hang from the waists of the boys' trunks. Together, each pair of lovers celebrates the joy found in sensuality.

NOTES  The dancer and choreographer James Waring reported from Europe to *Ballet Review* in 1971: "Hans van Manen has made a ballet to the "Great Fugue" of Beethoven, with a postlude, a slow movement from one of the late string quartets. It looks nothing like Ashton's *Symphonic Variations*, yet it has a similar kind of watertight construction. Hans's style is not so lyric nor so expansive, yet, after Ashton, he is the best choreographic craftsman I've seen in Europe. *Great Fugue* . . . is a formal piece, very musical, a very personal kind of musical response. The dancing observes the rhythms of the music, but with constant slight shifts of focus in and out of Beethoven's phrases. The Netherlands Dance Theatre dance it beautifully, with passion and precision. An elegant piece."*

* Reprinted by permission of *Ballet Review*, Marcel Dekker, publisher.

# THE GUARDS OF AMAGER

*Music by V. C. Holm. Choreography by Auguste Bournonville. Scenery and costumes by Bjorn Wünblad. First presented by the Royal Danish Ballet at the Royal Theatre, Copenhagen, February 9, 1871. Revived for the contemporary repertory by Hans Brenaa, assisted by Lizzie Rode. First presented in the United States by the Royal Danish Ballet at the Metropolitan Opera House, New York, June 3, 1976.*

A ballet about a forgotten incident in history, *The Guards of Amager* takes us back to 1808, when Napoleon had all Europe in thrall. Determined to protect themselves against a menacing English fleet, the Danes set up a volunteer corps to protect themselves. The story of the ballet, a *demi-caractère* comic affair, deals with the possible unfaithfulness to his wife of a young lieutenant posted on the island of Amager to protect Copenhagen. Enamored of the peasant girls there, Édouard seems to have another alternative when his wife, Louise, on a visit, perceiving this possibility, disguises herself to become the belle of a local ball. When Édouard fails to recognize her, despite his enchantment with her charms, she reveals her identity but forgives him. The atmosphere of this ballet and the design of its choreography suggest an achievement of *ballet comique* unimaginable a hundred years ago, much less today.

# THE GUESTS

*Classic ballet in one act. Music by Marc Blitzstein. Choreography by Jerome Robbins. Lighting by Jean Rosenthal. First presented by the New York City Ballet at the City Center, New York, January 20, 1949, with Maria Tallchief, Nicholas Magallanes, and Francisco Moncion in the principal roles.*

This ballet concerns itself with prejudice: with "the patterns of adjustment and conflict between two groups, one larger than the other." What happens when these two groups meet and find themselves absolutely opposed? The ballet presents this problem socially, at what seems to be an ordinary party.

The curtain rises on a formal setting. High black columns in the back suggest a large ball. The host comes forward formally and prepares to welcome a group of guests. The guests enter in two distinct groups. At first it would seem that they are not distinct at all, for the boys and girls wear the same kind of clothes and move in the same way, but gradually we see that they never commingle, that the dances that now get under way are arranged in block patterns, and that the two separate groups instinctively avoid close contact. The host is not disturbed by the difference between the two. He leads the party on without nervousness, aware that the two groups have lived amicably side by side for a long time and cannot possibly achieve closer contact. Both sides of the party feel this almost naturally, the girls dancing only with partners from their group, gathering together and speaking together, but never paying attention to what the other side might be doing; they do not even acknowledge each other's existence beyond politely moving aside when they wish to pass each other. It is apparent, however, that the smaller group is more deferential to the larger.

The party proceeds. The host brings out masks and passes these favors out to members of the larger group of guests. Several masks are left over and put aside. The masked couples begin to dance, while the smaller group stands aside and watches. The dance has not proceeded long before we notice that the discarded masks have disappeared; two of the dancers are obviously wearing them. But the host does not note this breach of etiquette, and the dancing couples, unaware of true identities, continue to enjoy themselves.

One girl and boy in particular are strangely attracted to each other. They move together with a soft, relaxed ease as if they had been dancing together all their lives. The boy steps forward slightly and reaches out his hand, pointing the way to some distant happiness. The girl imitates this gesture. They stand facing each other; when their hands touch, the contact is electrically romantic. Yet their dance is not intimate; it is, rather, the dance of two people who are living a dream. There is no sudden passion, no questions need to be asked; the boy supports and lifts the girl tenderly, and she responds to this with soft grace.

The ensemble dance ends, and the host orders the guests to remove their masks. The guests discover that the boy and the girl who are so much in love belong to different groups; one of them has worn the mask in error! Chaos breaks out. The two groups drag the boy and the girl apart and make them dance separately. When the two groups pass, the boy and girl hold out their hands to each other longingly.

Finally they can bear the separation no longer. They defy convention and meet. The boy lifts the girl high and carries her away into the distance. The astonished guests look at each other in horror. The curtain falls.

## HAMLET

*Dramatic ballet in one act. Music by Peter Ilyich Tchaikovsky. Choreography by Robert Helpmann. Scenery and costumes by Leslie Hurry. First presented by the Sadler's Wells Ballet at the New Theatre, London, May 19, 1942, with Robert Helpmann as* Hamlet *and Margot Fonteyn as* Ophelia. *First presented in the United States by the Sadler's Wells Ballet at the Metropolitan Opera House, New York, October 12, 1949, with the same principals.*

This *Hamlet* is not an adaptation of Shakespeare's play for ballet; rather, it is a ballet version, a ballet interpretation of Shakespeare's subject. It does not follow the action of the play precisely, but rather recollects the plot of the play in its own drama. The ballet *Hamlet* is prefaced by these lines from the play:

For in that sleep of death, what dreams may come
When we have shuffled off this mortal coil
Must give us pause.

These lines warn us to expect dreams, impressions, perhaps even flash backs of
Hamlet's life and tragedy. The music for the ballet is Tchaikovsky's fantasy-
overture *Hamlet*.

At the rise of the curtain we see a ghostly sight. A thin, bright shaft of light
shines down on Hamlet's face. He is dead. Four pallbearers carry him slowly
to his grave; the end of the play is the ballet's beginning. And still it is
different, for the pallbearers are not the captains appointed by Fortinbras to
bear Hamlet; they are hooded monks.

The monks bear Hamlet off, and the scene brightens. The scene is not literal, not so much a section of a Danish castle as a projection of Hamlet's imagination. It is ghastly and bloody and mad. A huge creature depicted on the
backdrop rushes toward murder, a jagged knife poised in readiness. Over a
portal at the left, a great detached hand holds a dagger casually, as if it were a
cigarette. The scene is possessed with violence.

One by one, characters familiar to Hamlet appear—first the gravedigger. As
we are remembering what he said to Hamlet and what Hamlet said to him, the
Prince of Denmark himself enters. He watches the scene as we watch it; he is
observing himself. Detached in death, he looks back over his life.

He does not like what he sees; his anticipation of vile deeds suffered and
vile deeds done causes him to hide his face from view. Now he watches the
gravedigger play with Yorick's skull, throwing it into the air, rolling it along
the ground.

A crowing cock heralds the arrival of the ghost of Hamlet's father, who instructs Hamlet in the manner of his death: how he was murdered by his
brother with the connivance of his queen. Hamlet's guesswork has proved true
in a way he had not imagined, and the evil of the present king and Hamlet's
mother, the queen, has new justification. Hamlet promises the ghost that he
will seek revenge.

Old Polonius and Laertes appear, followed by the king and queen. The lusty
king makes love to the queen while her son rages openly. But the king ignores
him and turns his attention to Laertes, granting the youth permission to go to
France. Polonius warns the king to beware of Hamlet. When the doddering
chamberlain has promised him to spy on Hamlet, the king departs.

Hamlet watches his mother and approaches her. Mysteriously, Ophelia steps
before the queen, and the two women are confused. Hamlet falls to the floor,
moves his hands frantically in front of him as if to separate this double image,
but still the two women shift before his eyes. When they leave the scene,
Hamlet prays.

Now Laertes dances gaily with his sister, Ophelia. Soon they are interrupted
by Polonius, who wishes his son a lengthy Godspeed. Laertes departs for
France, and Polonius takes his daughter to Hamlet. He wishes to observe them
and conceals himself as the prince courts his daughter sweetly and sincerely.
But then Hamlet senses that something is rotten; he catches the king spying on
him with Polonius and throws Ophelia to the ground.

Next Hamlet watches the play-within-a-play. All members of the court enter, and a page announces that the entertainment is about to begin. In the play, parts are taken not by professional actors but by the creatures of Hamlet's imagination: Ophelia is the player queen, the ghost of Hamlet's father is the player king. When the player king is to be murdered, both Hamlet and Claudius approach his sleeping figure. Both pour poison in his ear.

The king, again the spectator and no longer the murdering actor, is horrified at this re-enactment of his crime and goes to pray. Hamlet is about to seize this opportunity to kill his archenemy, but then rationalizes that it is the wrong occasion. But there is occasion for another death: Polonius is plotting with the queen; Hamlet stabs him.

Laertes returns to avenge his father's death and accuses the king. The queen points out the youth's error, and all turn to watch sadly the beautiful Ophelia, gone mad with grief at her father's death and her lover's inconstancy. Ophelia's madness spurs Laertes to seek out Hamlet.

Hamlet stands aside to watch a funeral procession. Ophelia is dead, and he would accompany her to her grave. But the pallbearers are not carrying Ophelia, his dead love; it is the queen they carry. Again Hamlet cannot distinguish the two in his affections. Laertes, who is marching in the procession, sees Hamlet and immediately attacks him. The prudent king pulls Laertes back and suggests to him another plot.

This plot is now set in motion. We watch another courtly scene, where all the principals are present. The king and Laertes are in concert, while Hamlet is apparently reconciled with his mother. Now the king offers Hamlet wine, which is poisoned. Hamlet will not accept it and turns away in wrath at such a social grace from such a man. The queen attempts to pacify her son by drinking a toast to him with the wine. The king, paralyzed with anxiety at her foolish act, draws her aside.

Laertes sneaks up on Hamlet and stabs him in the back. The wounded prince returns the thrust, and Laertes dies. Now Hamlet attacks the king. The queen watches, horrified, as her son kills her husband. Then she, too, dies.

The gravedigger returns, and the ballet has come full circle. Now that there is no need for him to live, now that revenge is done, Hamlet succumbs to his wounds. He falls to the ground. The monks come in, take up his body, and raise it high over their heads. The scene grows dark. Soon all we can see is Hamlet's face, ghostly white in the pin-point spotlight; his beginning is, after all, his end.

# HARBINGER

*Music by Sergei Prokofiev. Choreography by Eliot Feld. Setting by Oliver Smith. Lighting by Jean Rosenthal. First presented by American Ballet Theatre at the New York State Theatre, New York, May 11, 1967, with Christine Sarry, Edward Verso, Paula Tracy, Cynthia Gregory, Marcos Paredes, and Eliot Feld in leading roles.*

*Harbinger* tells no story; its plot is outlined by the music of Prokofiev's *Concerto No. 5 in G for Piano*. Usefully for the listener and spectator, both the composer and the choreographer have given notes on their own impressions of this work.

Prokofiev writes: "The first movement is an *Allegro con brio* with a *Meno mosso* as middle section. Though not in sonata form, it is the main movement of the concerto and fulfills the function and maintains the spirit of the traditional sonata form. The second movement has a march-like rhythm. I would not think of calling it a march because it has none of the vulgarity of commonness which is so often associated with the idea of march, and which actually exists in most marches. The third movement is a toccata. This is a precipitate, displayful movement of much technical brilliance and requiring great virtuosity; it is a toccata for orchestra as well as for piano. The fourth movement . . . is the lyrical movement of the concerto. It starts off with a soft, soothing theme; grows more and more intense in the middle portion, develops breadth and tension, then returns to the music of the beginning. The finale has a decided classic flavor. The coda is based on a new theme, which is joined by the other theme of the finale. There is a reference to some of the material of the preceding movements in the finale."

The choreographer and dancer Eliot Feld described his view of the work in an interview with Jack Anderson in *Dance Magazine*. He said that in choreographing *Harbinger*, he wishes to "explore certain patterns of human relationships. . . . The first movement, in which a solo boy ambles lazily among a group of girls, is about 'being by yourself and having fantasies.' The impetuous second movement is conceived as a chase. The third movement is a slightly melancholy duet with *corps de ballet* serving as background. . . . The fourth movement, a competitive trio for two boys and a girl, is 'just what it appears to be.' The finale is composed of movement motifs taken from the preceding sections. 'I guess that in all of *Harbinger* I'm talking about myself and the people I know. It's like showing some of the kinds of personal games we play.'"

*Harbinger* attracted considerable attention when it was first presented in New York. Clive Barnes of the New York *Times* wrote that Mr. Feld was "the most important indigenous talent in classic ballet since Jerome Robbins."

Interviewed by the British magazine *Dance and Dancers*, Eliot Feld was asked when, as a dancer in American Ballet Theatre, he got the idea of doing choreography. He replied: "I don't really know. When I started to try out choreography I really had no idea of doing a ballet. I had listened to the Prokofiev fifth piano concerto for some time and I had the idea of doing this duet—very allegro, very short. I worked with a dancer just as a favour and we choreographed this dance, which turned out to be the eventual duet in *Harbinger*, my first ballet. It took us about 300 hours of rehearsal time to choreograph two minutes of choreography. I don't indulge in that way of working any longer. Then I got another idea for another of the movements and I began to choreograph that, but it became difficult because I needed three people, and Royes Fernandez helped me out at that time. Gradually I realised that I had a ballet, but I don't really think that I had thought of myself as wanting to be a choreographer before that. Before *Harbinger* I had never put any steps together. I have a lot to thank Robbins for, because after I had completed about four minutes of choreography he came in and saw what I had done and seemed very excited about it. He asked me what I intended to do, and I told him it depended a lot on what he could do for me; would he be willing to speak to Lucia Chase about producing the ballet? He did, and on the basis of his approval it was put on by Ballet Theatre."

## HARLEQUINADE

*Ballet in two acts. Music by Riccardo Drigo. Choreography by George Balanchine. Scenery, costumes, and lighting by Rouben Ter-Arutunian. First presented by the New York City Ballet at the New York State Theatre, February 4, 1965, with Edward Villella and Patricia McBride in the leading roles.*

Most of us know the old *commedia dell'arte* story of how Harlequin wins Columbine from her rich father.

The original ballet to this story, *Harlequin's Millions*, was first presented at the Hermitage Theatre in St. Petersburg in 1900. It was the last success of the brilliant creator of dance, Marius Petipa. I remember very well dancing in this production when I was a student at the Imperial Ballet School. What I liked about it was its wit and pace and its genius in telling a story with clarity and grace. It was a very different kind of ballet from *The Sleeping Beauty*, and showed the range of his genius.

*Les Millions d'Arlequin* had a great deal of influence, I think, on ballet history, becoming the model for comedy narrative. It is the other side of the coin from *Swan Lake*, if you like. I don't of course remember details of the old production. In 1950 I arranged a *Harlequin pas de deux* for Maria Tallchief and André Eglevsky that used some of Drigo's music in a *demi-caractère* display piece. I remember thinking at the time that one day we should try to do the whole ballet. That came about in the usual accidental way when it was suggested that the settings Rouben Ter-Arutunian had designed for the New York City Opera production of Rossini's *Cenerentola* might be usable for a full-length *Harlequinade*. We were able to borrow the scenery, which the designer adapted for the ballet, and I began to work.

During the overture we see a drop curtain painted in the style of Pollock toy theaters with boxes right and left and a paper proscenium. When this rises the scene shows the exterior of the house of the rich merchant Cassandre, father of the beautiful Columbine. The action shows how Harlequin, helped by La Bonne Fée, succeeds in rescuing Columbine from the wealthy suitor her father has picked out for her. The enraged Cassandre tries to have Harlequin killed but is foiled. The Good Fairy brings a cornucopia of gold pieces, Harlequin outbids his rich rival, and the lovers are united. There is a dance celebration of their love in an enchanted park.

NOTES When I was studying ballet in Russia, I much admired Petipa's original version of this ballet (*Les Millions d'Arlequin,* first performed at the Hermitage Theatre, St. Petersburg, February 10, 1900). The fun and slapstick as well as the occasional deeper meaning of the popular Italian comedy, the *commedia dell'arte,* have always appealed to me with their strength and warmth, and in *Harlequinade* I have attempted to remain faithful to the spirit of Petipa's dances and drama without reproducing any of the actual steps of his time. Who, in fact, remembers them?

As I often do with my ballets, I changed *Harlequinade* somewhat in 1973, adding sequences at certain points and filling out the piece so that, hopefully, with one intermission, it makes for an evening-long diversion. Among the additions are a tarantella in Act One and a polonaise in Act Two. Children are used among the dancers, and the music is now the complete score by Riccardo Drigo.

The critic Nancy Goldner described the revision in *Dance News:* "*Harlequinade* is now filled out so that it fills an evening. The main addition is a 'ballabile des enfants' for polichinelles, little harlequins, scaramouches, and pierrots and pierettes—in other words, small editions of all the adult roles. They do a series of *divertissements* in the beginning of Act II, and, as is his way, Balanchine gives them simple but utterly charming steps. Their dances most closely resemble the polichinelle dance in *Nutcracker;* in fact, the *Harlequinade* polichinelles are now wearing the *Nutcracker* costumes. At the end of the variations, all the children do a grand polonaise, and they do it with more style and belief than the adults. Watching all 32 children dancing with proper deportment and happy faces is enchanting. Inevitably, it reminds one of Balanchine's childhood and his statements about how exciting it was to appear on stage. So here is Papa giving his kids what he had. That knowledge gives an extra charm to the ballet.

"There is also a new blaze-of-color ensemble dance for adult revelers in the first act. The idea is to cram hordes into a small area, so that all you see are many bright colors in squished motion. But the costumes are garish, the paper lanterns carried by the dancers kept falling off, and it went on too long.

"Gelsey Kirkland was beautifully shy and sweet in her solemn way as Columbine. Her delicate articulation suits the choreography well, yet this is still Villella's ballet. His brute strength is here quieted by humor and something that is almost lyricism, especially in the beautiful serenade dance. His strength is still felt, but from the underside. It is very compelling."


# HARLEQUIN IN APRIL

*Pantomime with divertissements in two acts, with prologue, entr'acte, and epilogue. Music by Richard Arnell. Choreography by John Cranko. Scenery and costumes by John Piper. First presented by the Sadler's Wells Theatre Ballet at the Sadler's Wells Theatre, London, May 8, 1951, with David Blair as Harlequin, Patricia Miller as Columbine, and Stanley Holden as Pierrot. First presented in the United States by the Sadler's Wells Theatre*

*Ballet at the Eastman Theatre, Rochester, New York, October 25, 1951, with the same principals.*

This dramatic ballet tells a modern story in terms of old characters. Here the old, typed characters—Harlequin, Columbine, and Pierrot—who have come down to us from Greek mythology and the *commedia dell'arte* and who figure in such ballets as *Carnaval,* are used to represent new notions while at the same time preserving much of their original symbolism. Here Harlequin is human aspiration reborn after fire and devastation. Harlequin returns to life among the flowers of April, earth-bound and self-sufficient creatures from whom he escapes. Columbine is Harlequin's love, the representation of the ideal he aspires to. Pierrot stands between the two; he is the perpetual fool, and we laugh at him until he interferes too much.

PROLOGUE   The curtain rises on an inside drop that depicts another, smaller stage hung with a tattered curtain. This interior theatre has not simply fallen into disrepair through age and use; it has been burned out and destroyed, and stands as a symbol of human wreckage where no human can flourish.

Pierrot, superhuman fool of the gods, ambles in carrying a bag. His face is painted white to match the loose white costume that hangs about his loose-jointed figure. He takes a sheet of music from the bag and opens his mouth to sing. When he discovers that he cannot sing, that he can make no sound, he hides his face behind the music. Now he tries again, a little more successfully, then puts the music back in his bag of tricks and exits. The lights grow dim.

ACT ONE: APRIL   When the lights come up, the drop curtain has disappeared and we are backstage in the interior theatre. Groups of girls dressed like plants lie about the stage. Pierrot enters with a watering can and goes about watering the plants. One of the groups begins to rise; the center group stirs. There is a fluttering of hands, and the plants in the center group huddle together closely, as if protecting something. Now the girls kneel, and Harlequin rises in their midst, born anew in the ashes of destruction. Naked to the waist, Harlequin wears a black mask across his eyes. He walks in and out among the flowers and plants, who celebrate his birth.

Pierrot takes from his bag a jacket for Harlequin. Harlequin puts on the coat and removes the mask. Now fully dressed in his traditional diamond-patched costume, Harlequin comes fully to life. A drum sounds loudly; he chases Pierrot off and dances, turning again and again to a persistent drum roll. The plants, which have remained lifeless, now rise and leave the scene. As the last plant moves off, Harlequin restrains her and the two dance a *pas de deux*. This is largely a dance of resistance, as the self-sufficient plant struggles to be free of this strange being who demands and requires her company. Harlequin tears the flowery mask from her face and for a moment she is just a young girl, but she reaches out trembling hands to retrieve the mask.

Harlequin kicks at the mask and throws it aside. The other plants begin to return; they find the mask and place it again on the face of the frightened girl, after which they form a line and leave the scene. Harlequin kisses the last girl, the girl he has danced with, and finds himself alone.

Harlequin is angry. He falls to the ground in his rage. Pierrot comes and tries to comfort him. Harlequin, armed now with a sword, watches astonished as a unicorn, traditional guardian of chastity, crosses the stage. Even now, Harlequin is aware that the unicorn will attempt to separate him from his ideal. He threatens the strange animal, but the proud unicorn stalks away. The drop curtain falls.

ENTR'ACTE   Pierrot comes out before the drop curtain and dances. Then he takes from his white bag a violin and a bow and plays the instrument. Like the song he tried to sing at the beginning of the ballet, Pierrot's violin concerto is not of high quality. Rather impatient with the unobliging violin, he kneels and plays it as if it were a cello. Then he thrusts it aside, returns it to the bag, and leaves the scene.

ACT TWO: THE SKY   The light is dim when the drop curtain rises again. Gradually the light rises. Now the interior backdrop is streaked with clouds. Harlequin, still carrying his sword, enters and watches the unicorn. Pierrot hides behind Harlequin, egging him on. The unicorn nods its head in assent to a command that Harlequin has made to it and returns, carrying on its back a lovely young girl—Columbine. Immediately in love, Harlequin kisses her. Pierrot pulls him away from the girl, and Columbine comes down from the unicorn's back. She seems to have some power over the creature, for at her order the unicorn goes to sleep.

Columbine goes directly to Harlequin and they dance. Harlequin pushes Pierrot away when he attempts teasingly to interfere. Columbine falls back in Harlequin's arm, and he buries his face in her breast. The two lovers fall to the ground and kiss. Columbine's arms reach up around Harlequin's head, and Pierrot rushes in to pull them apart. They are separated for a moment, but again Harlequin embraces the girl. He lifts her, and as he holds her aloft, her extended leg trembles. The lovers lie down again to fulfill their passion.

Pierrot, now fully alarmed, wakes the sleeping unicorn. The unicorn, militant and unfeeling, pulls Columbine from Harlequin's close embrace. Harlequin stabs at the unicorn, but the scene is filled with magical duplications of the unicorn and Harlequin is helpless against this multiple representation of chastity. Some of the unicorns claim Columbine as others stalk Harlequin down and stand over him. She is lifted onto the back of one of the unicorns, then lifted high into the air by the others. Harlequin climbs up on the strange creatures to reach her; at the pinnacle he is pushed off and falls to the ground.

Columbine disappears. Harlequin goes off in search of her as the unicorns leave the scene. Harlequin returns, with a rag-doll representation of Columbine in his arms. Pierrot bows to him, and Harlequin begins a wild, frantic dance that expresses his rage at his loss. He beats Pierrot, the interfering fool who has deprived him of the ideal, and chases him off.

To quiet, moving music, Harlequin holds the model of Columbine in his arms and kisses its hands. The plants return, gather about Harlequin, and enfold him. They place the black mask about his eyes and take off his jacket. The plants huddle over him closely, and as they kneel, he disappears in their midst.

EPILOGUE   Pierrot returns. He sees Harlequin's jacket lying on the ground and picks it up. For a moment he considers the loss of his friend, but not for long. He begins to try on the jacket. It is too small for him, he can get only one arm in, but so dressed he poses arrogantly, an absurd masquerade of Harlequin, while the real Harlequin sleeps.

## THE HAUNTED BALLROOM

*Dramatic ballet in three scenes. Music by Geoffrey Toye. Choreography by Ninette de Valois. Book by Geoffrey Toye. Scenery and costumes by Motley. First presented by the Vic-Wells Ballet at the Sadler's Wells Theatre, London, April 3, 1934, with a cast that included Robert Helpmann, Alicia Markova, and William Chappell. First presented in the United States by the Sadler's Wells Theatre Ballet in Buffalo, New York, October 23, 1951, with David Poole in the principal role.*

The drama of this ballet is based on its mysterious locale and the destiny that haunts the people who inhabit it. Set in the ancient ballroom of a Scottish castle, the ballet calls up those venerable but terrifying demons and ghosts which control the fate of a family. In two graphic scenes, *The Haunted Ballroom* displays the inscrutable power of these creatures and the helplessness of those who live in perpetual dread of their appearance.

The overture is low in volume, eerie and mysterious in mood. The music warns us of incipient danger—a danger that does not come suddenly, but quietly and patiently waits to pounce upon its helpless prey. There is a rush of sound from the harp, the orchestra plays a low, murmuring waltz, and the curtain rises.

The scene is dark, almost pitch-black. Slanting wings enclose a large, cavernous space. At the back, centered in the black wall, is an arched doorway. From the ceiling hangs a chandelier festooned with cobwebs. Long strips of rotting black cloth are draped from the chandelier to the corners of the room.

We are in an abandoned ballroom, a place seldom used by its owner. In the back, the door opens. Young Tregennis, son of the master of the house, enters. He is dressed in black velvet with a red sash about his waist. The youth looks about the room apprehensively, and we sense that even in some typical childish prank he would never choose to enter it alone. Three ladies in long, trailing evening dresses follow him into the musty ballroom. They flutter their large fans nervously and examine the ballroom with no little curiosity; it is clear that, during a ball that is being held elsewhere in the castle, they have asked the boy to show them this hidden room.

One by one, the ladies tap the boy on the shoulder with their fans, playfully commanding him to dance with them. As he moves about the dark ballroom with the ladies, the trains of their dresses drag along the floor and whirl the dust about their waltzing figures. But the youth is in no mood for dancing. He breaks away from the women and stands with his head in his hands. He seems to be aware of something the women cannot see and trembles like a small child.

The ladies still wish to be amused, however, and again tap him with their fans. The boy remains motionless. He knows that he should never have given in to their whim and, most of all, that he should not have come here himself. As the teasing women begin to lose all patience with their young host, his father is seen standing in the doorway.

The master of Tregennis is astonished to find the door open and shocked to find his guests in this part of the house. He observes his son standing in the corner. The youth cowers away from his father. He orders the boy to leave the room. The boy runs to his father, begging for forgiveness, but imperiously the father gestures him away. The boy flees.

Now the master of Tregennis turns and bows to the ladies. A waltz melody is heard. The master apologizes to his guests for his strange behavior and tells them the cause of his anxiety. He indicates to them that this is truly a haunted ballroom: his father died here and his father before him—indeed, all of his family have perished in this room. The ladies cover their faces with their fans to conceal their embarrassment and fear. Now that they understand, they bow to the master of Tregennis, take up their trains, and leave the room.

Alone, the man stands in the center of the haunted ballroom and stares into the dark corners. He is afraid and fascinated at the same time; he cannot move. The room darkens and a light shines upon him. He looks into the light, trying to control his fear, but his hand reaches out to ward off some unseen terror. The light has caused his frightened figure to be thrown against the back wall in immense silhouette. The curtain falls as he stands helpless in the sight of the fate he must someday meet.

During a brief interval, the orchestra recapitulates the happy dance theme to which the three ladies danced with young Tregennis. The harp interrupts this music to sound a warning, there is a muffled trumpet call, and the curtain rises again.

The ballroom is now almost completely dark. Gradually the lights come up, and we note that the door in the back wall is open. Into the room dances a strange figure dressed in somber black with a black mask. He plays upon a flute and then thrusts the flute into the air as if it were a sword. Ghostly creatures in white follow him and form a tableau. Their faces are veiled, their long white sleeves dangle from their arms to give their figures a disjointed, unearthly quality. Two veiled women, dressed similarly to two of the ladies who invaded the ballroom in the first scene, enter and dance at the command of the strange figure in black.

Just as we are wondering where the counterpart to the third lady might be, she enters and dances as the masked stranger plays upon his flute. The ghostly creatures collapse and form weird groupings that remain still throughout her demoniac dance. She is joined by the other two women, and all three move together until the strange player halts the dance suddenly: at his command, each ends her movement in an arabesque.

Now the strange player moves about the room, obviously preparing the scene for some portentous event. The master of Tregennis stumbles into the room. He wears a long white dressing gown, and a mysterious call seems to have demanded his return to the room. He observes his uninvited guests and rudely asks the strange player for an explanation. The master of Tregennis is told that a group of dancers have come to his ballroom and that they are eager to dance if he will be good enough to lead them.

The master apparently accepts this explanation, for he bows to the ghostly creatures. The music roars in violent crescendo. The master takes off his dressing gown to move more freely and enters into a violent dance. His strange guests surround him like flies, encouraging him to increase the tempo of his movements. The master is tired and wishes to stop, but is helpless to do so. Finally he collapses in the stranger's arms.

One of the ladies encourages him to renew his dance, and he moves with her about the room as figures cloaked in white robes weave in and out between them. The orchestra sounds the music of the dance fiercely and relentlessly. The master of Tregennis can move no more. He falls to the floor, dying. The lady is held poised above him. He reaches out and is caught up in the arms of the ghostly creatures. He struggles helplessly in their grasp. Weird women gather close about him; the music cries out with piercing pathos. He is carried aloft.

For a brief moment the master manages to free himself. He rushes away from his attackers, running to the front of the stage to cling to the proscenium. He knows now who they are and that he must soon be one of them. The time for his own death in the haunted ballroom has come, and he is powerless to resist.

A clock begins to clang. The ghosts who have made him one of themselves form a final tableau, and he dies. The curtain falls. The strange player in black emerges with three creatures in white and across the front of the stage, in step with the striking clock, they carry the body of the master of Tregennis to his forebears.

Once more the curtain rises on the ballroom. Two footmen enter by the door, carrying lanterns. A butler follows them, and the three men search the room for their master. When they discover his body, his son, dressed in a white dressing gown similar to his father's, stumbles into the room. He hastens to his father and turns away in grief and terror. The master of Tregennis, his lifeless arm dangling in the air, is carried out by his two footmen.

Three women, evidently members of his family, try to comfort the boy. He accepts their condolences, but then turns away from them. They know what he is thinking—that he will be next. They leave him alone. The light that shone upon his father makes of his startled figure a frightening silhouette against the dark wall of the ballroom; he clutches at his throat in terror and acknowledges his destiny.

# HELEN OF TROY

*Comic ballet in three scenes, with prologue. Music by Jacques Offenbach. Choreography by David Lichine. Book by David Lichine and Antal Dorati. Scenery and costumes by Marcel Vertès. First presented by Ballet Theatre in Detroit, Michigan, November 29, 1942, with a cast headed by Irina Baronova as Helen, André Eglevsky as Paris, Jerome Robbins as Hermes, and Simon Semenoff as Menelaus.*

This ballet is a comic treatment of the legend of Helen of Troy: how the beautiful queen deserted her aging husband, Menelaus, and sailed away with Paris to far-off Troy. The music, by Offenbach, was arranged and orchestrated by Antal Dorati.

PROLOGUE    After a jubilant, rousing overture, the curtain rises on a mountain scene. A drop curtain depicts rocks and trees. Half a dozen sheep kneel about the youthful Paris, who is sleeping. The shepherd rises, yawns, stretches, and begins to dance. A lamb joins him, and Paris holds her lovingly in his arms. Now all the sheep sit in a semicircle about Paris as he displays his youthful vigor. They applaud him when the dance is over.

Hermes, messenger of the gods, enters, idly chewing an apple. Three goddesses accompany him. The great Zeus, apparently, has a problem. Each one of these goddesses, Hera, Pallas Athena, and Aphrodite, has claimed a golden apple inscribed "To the fairest," and since only one of them can finally possess the apple, the ladies have been brought before Paris. Hermes tells him he will judge for Zeus which is the fairest.

Paris doesn't have much trouble making up his mind. Hera is the oldest and a little too grimly determined. Pallas Athena can't take her nose out of a book. Aphrodite, the goddess of love, promises Paris that he shall have the fairest of all women for his wife, and the shepherd immediately rewards her with the golden apple. The sheep circle about them, and Paris starts to leave with Aphrodite. But he has forgotten the lamb, who runs up and reminds Paris not to forget her. Paris takes her by the hand, and all exit. Hermes is left alone, still eating his apple. He reaches up and pulls down the curtain.

SCENE ONE: THE COURT AT SPARTA    Under the patronage of Aphrodite, Paris has come to Greece. We are at the palace of Menelaus. The aged king sits on his throne as the court entertains him. His beautiful wife, Helen, dances before him. Paris watches her closely. This must be the woman Aphrodite promised him! When her dance is over, Helen runs to the throne and kisses Menelaus, but it is clear that she has eyes only for the strange shepherd.

She dances again, this time with garlands. Paris comes forward and supports her in the dance. Menelaus is preoccupied with court business and only waves to her from time to time. All the men of the court seek to partner Helen, but she always chooses Paris. The two lovers approach Menelaus. Helen kisses her husband, and the jealous old man shoves Paris aside.

Courtly couples in white dance before the king and queen. Helen is bored. When the time comes for Menelaus to dance before his court, she ridicules him like all the rest. His absurd exhibition is cut short by a cramp. Paris is amused and comes forward to dance. The brilliant strength and graceful ease of his dance dazzle the court. He kneels to Helen.

There follows another courtly entertainment, in which Paris' pet lamb participates. Helen is now sitting at Menelaus' feet. The old man has dozed off. Hermes jumps into his lap, and the king embraces him. Helen is delighted at the success of this idiotic ruse and joins Paris for a *pas de deux* in which they acknowledge their love for each other. Paris lifts her high, to his shoulders, and carries her across the stage.

Menelaus is warned that his country is at war. He wakes up, pushes Hermes off his lap, and tries to recover his dignity. He straightens his crown and staggers blindly across the stage. His men drive on the stage in a chariot, and Menelaus, hastily decked out in battle dress, drives off to battle. All wave to him. Hermes sits on the royal throne of Sparta.

Paris caresses Helen. The members of the court form a great semicircle, and Helen, in their midst, dances. Now Hermes presents Helen with a duplicate to the key to her chamber. Helen gives it to Paris, who kneels before her. Helen's lady in waiting presents another duplicate to another adorer of her mistress, Orestes. Now that the stage is set for further complications, Hermes, back on the throne, gestures in comic triumph.

SCENE TWO: HELEN'S BEDCHAMBER   Before a drop curtain, the lady in waiting hastily provides Orestes with a dress similar to her own. Then she peeks behind the curtain. She takes Orestes by the hand, and the curtain rises. We are in Helen's private apartment. There is a screen on the left; the darkened room is dominated by a great canopied bed.

Helen enters, dressed in diaphanous white. The two maids help her prepare for bed and go behind the screen. Now Orestes declares himself. Discarding the attire of a lady in waiting, he assures Helen of his love, embraces her, and forces her to dance with him. Helen protests. Hermes wanders in, reading a book. When he sees what's going on, he wonders where the devil Paris is. He draws his arm back as if to strike Orestes, and the intruder, stricken by this godlike gesture, falls to the ground. Hermes pushes him out of the room.

Helen sprays herself liberally with perfume and is ready now for her true lover. Hermes unlocks the door, and Paris comes in. His pet lamb scurries behind the screen as he takes Helen in his arms. Hermes starts to knit. At first he pays no attention to the lovers, but when their mutual demonstrations become passionate, he rises and discreetly places the screen in front of them. The screen begins to vibrate.

And who should come in at this point but good old Menelaus, back from the wars. He carries a bouquet of roses for Helen. He assaults Hermes and tells him to get out. Then he observes the trembling screen. He rushes behind the screen. Paris runs out, followed by Helen, disguised in the lamb's coat. The poor lamb shivers in her underwear as Menelaus pursues Paris vainly, dashing hither and thither about the room. Paris and the pet lamb escape. Hermes blows a policeman's whistle to direct the busy traffic, stands behind Menelaus, and Helen pushes her deluded husband over his back. She stands over him as Hermes sits knitting on her bed. The drop curtain falls.

SCENE THREE: THE PORT  Menelaus emerges from his wife's boudoir and weeps despairingly. Ladies of the court join him, wring out his wet handkerchief, and try to cheer him up.

The drop curtain rises on a seaside scene. Ladies of the court gambol about the beach. A girl enters, leading a faun on a leash. The faun cavorts across the beach obligingly among the ladies and leaps off into the wings when they have had enough.

Courtiers come onto the scene, followed by Helen. She dances, surrounded by all the sheep in Paris' flock, who lift her to their shoulders. Menelaus puffs in and pleads with her.

Now Hermes sails up in a great barge of war. He takes out a Yo-yo and plays with it adroitly as Helen and Paris are confronted by Menelaus. The music laughs and chortles, and all the courtiers gather for a razzle-dazzle dance of farewell to the lovers. Menelaus is carried helplessly above the swirling crowd, and before he knows what has happened, Paris and Helen have climbed into the barge and set sail for distant Troy. All wish them Godspeed save Menelaus, who vainly tries to board the vessel.

# HI-KYO

*Music by Kazuo Fukushima. Choreography by Jaap Flier. Costumes by Joop Stokvis. First presented by the Netherlands Dance Theatre at the Stadsschouwburg, Amsterdam, Holland, June 30, 1971, with Arlette van Boven and Hans Knill. First presented in the United States April 1, 1972, by the same ensemble at the Brooklyn Academy of Music, New York, with the same principals.*

There are at least eight meanings for the Japanese *hi-kyo*, and this ballet is about all of them: hidden place, place where no one lives, the moon, flying mirror, sly, unfair, adversity, and distress. *Hi-kyo* is a dance for two people, an extended *pas de deux*, with the flutist on stage with the dancers. The music is a work of the same title for flute, piano, and strings by the contemporary Japanese composer Kazuo Fukushima. *Hi-kyo* was the first new work created by the dancer and ballet master Jaap Flier after he became artistic director of the Netherlands Dance Theatre.

The dance takes place in a setting hung with black rope so that we seem to be in an impenetrable forest. A boy enters and appears to move easily through the thicket. A girl, who enters from the opposite side, encounters difficulty but pulling herself up on the strands of rope, seems to swim among the branches. The boy joins her now and the two become close and inseparable, tangled like the ropes they dance among. They wish to escape, are captured again by the ropes, but then the girl is released and leaves the scene. The boy remains, caught in the forest, which now, the ropes still, looks like a cage.

## L'HISTOIRE DU SOLDAT (The Soldier's Story)

*Narrative ballet in five scenes; to be read, played, and danced. Music by Igor Stravinsky. Words by C. F. Ramuz. Choreography by Ludmilla Pitoev. First presented at Lausanne, Switzerland, September 28, 1918, with Gabriel Rossel, George Pitoev, and Ludmilla Pitoev in the principal roles. Scenery and costumes by René Auberjonois. First presented in the United States by the League of Composers at the Jolson (later Century) Theatre, March 25, 1928. Pantomime by Michio Ito. Scenery and costumes by Donald Oenslager. Tom Powers was the Reader; Blake Scott and Lilly Lubell were the principal characters.*

*L'Histoire du Soldat* is a composition for eight instruments, a narrator, and dancers. The small orchestra and the narrator are on stage with the dancers, who perform in a separate central area. The story is taken from an old Russian fairy tale which tells of a soldier who gives up his violin, the instrument that "speaks like his own heart," to the devil.

SCENE ONE: A WOOD   Before the action begins, the narrator tells us that there is a soldier who is going home to his village on leave. He has walked all the way.

The scene reveals a wood, through which there runs a stream. The soldier enters. From his gear he takes out a holy medallion, a snapshot of his girl back home, and a violin, his favorite personal possession. He begins to play, sitting idly by the stream.

The devil comes to him, disguised as a harmless elderly man. He asks if he may buy the violin. The soldier, who knows that the instrument is really a poor one, cannot understand; he does not want to sell it anyhow. The man insists, and the soldier finally agrees to trade his violin for a book the man tells him is of great value. The soldier is illiterate and does not know whether this is true, but the man's claim that the book will surely make him rich convinces him that the exchange is a good one. The man persuades him to teach him how to play the violin and to visit his home for several days.

SCENE TWO: THE VILLAGE   The narrator informs us that Joseph, the soldier, visited the devil and then resumed his homeward march. But when he got home, no one welcomed him. His girl had married someone else and had two children, and his mother was so frightened of him she would not come near him.

The action is renewed. The devil, disguised now as a cattle merchant, stands in the center of Joseph's native village. Joseph, outraged at his unpleasant homecoming, blames the barter of his violin for the mysterious book on the stranger. He attacks him with a sword. The devil, unmoved, commands him to become a civilian and to find the valuable book. As he takes out the book, the devil takes out his violin.

The narrator goes on to tell us how Joseph became a wealthy man by following the lessons of the devil's book. He is wealthy but miserable, able only to take money for additional orders for business.

SCENE THREE: JOSEPH'S OFFICE   Joseph is seen behind a great desk, reperusing the devil's book. A ragged old woman, the devil in disguise, enters and tries to sell him junk from her scavenger's bag. She lays before him his holy medallion, the photo of his girl, and his violin. He demands to know the price of the violin. The old creature tells him he'd better try to play the violin first: maybe it doesn't work well. Joseph takes up the instrument, but though he bows the strings frantically, no sound emerges. The hag has disappeared. Joseph destroys the violin and the book he received for it from the devil.

SCENE FOUR: A FOREIGN LAND—THE PALACE   The march that heralded the beginning of the soldier's story is heard again, and the narrator tells us that Joseph has tried to begin life anew. After destroying the book, he abandoned his wealth and went to a new country near by. There, in Joseph's new land, the king's daughter is dying of an unknown disease. The king has promised that the man who cures her shall marry her, and Joseph hopes to do this. Briefly the devil appears, this time as a gentleman in evening dress.

Joseph is seen sitting in a room at the palace, trying to determine what he should do by consulting a deck of playing cards. The cards augur well for him, but he is certain that he has not escaped Satan.

The narrator interrupts and tries to persuade Joseph to put up everything he has and gamble, all or nothing, with the devil. The soldier agrees and sits down to a game of cards with the devil. Although the devil wins each draw, he becomes strangely tired. Joseph forces him to drink, and he passes out in a stupor. Joseph seizes his violin and plays upon it the old, familiar music.

The narrator now tells us that Joseph will surely cure the ailing princess. Joseph is seen playing his violin before the princess, who lies back on a couch. She is revived by the music and rises to dance with him. Joseph embraces the princess.

Satan, all disguise thrown off, enters and demands the violin. Desperately, on all fours, the devil tries to snatch the instrument. Joseph begins to play upon it. The devil dances to this music until he collapses. The princess and Joseph drag him away.

They return to talk of their love. The devil, from outside, vows vengeance. He indicates that if Joseph remains in the princess' kingdom, he will survive, but that if he goes beyond the borders of the land, he will again be Satan's victim.

Again the narrator intervenes. He tells us how the princess, wishing to know more about her beloved, persuades him to take her on a visit to his native village. He realizes that this trip outside the kingdom will be fatal, but he cannot resist her demand.

SCENE FIVE: THE VILLAGE   In this scene, the soldier's old village and the border of his new home are both seen. When Joseph crosses the border of the princess' kingdom, the devil attacks. The devil now plays upon the violin. The princess calls to Joseph, but he cannot answer. He is now the devil's perpetual slave.

NOTES   Notable among the many other ballets to this score is that of Eliot Feld, who abandoned the original libretto for a new one. This depicts the sexual initiation of a young soldier as it is manipulated by a pimp and two whores. The soldier here is not only the victim of the military situation but also the victim of a human situation war has encouraged and accelerated.

*Music by Igor Stravinsky. Choreography by Eliot Feld. Costumes by Frank Thompson. Lighting by Jennifer Tipton. Conductor: Akira Endo. First presented by American Ballet Theatre at the City Center, New York, January 7, 1972, with Daniel Levans, Eliot Feld, Sallie Wilson, and Paula Tracy in leading roles.*

Reviewing Eliot Feld's version of the ballet in *Dance News*, the critic Nancy Goldner wrote: "It is a true theater piece, perhaps the purest of its genre. In place of the traditional story, Feld has substituted the theme of corruption, and the ballet ends with a strong anti-war statement. The corruptors are the pimp (Feld) and his whores (Sallie Wilson and Paula Tracy); they do in the soldier (wonderfully done by Daniel Levans). The dance style is as stylized as can be without becoming mimetic. Character is introduced and almost mercilessly sustained by emblematic movement, the most pungent of which is the pimp's rolling palms. Even the soldiers' dance, because it is repeated several times, becomes emblematic . . ."

Eliot Feld presented a revised version of his ballet *A Soldier's Tale* at the New York Shakespeare Festival Public Theatre, October 18, 1976. Lighting was by Thomas Skelton, costumes by Theoni V. Aldredge.

## HOLBERG SUITE

*Music by Edvard Grieg. Choreography by Arthur Mitchell. Costumes by Zelda Wynn. Lighting by Gary Fails. First presented by the Dance Theatre of Harlem at the Festival of Two Worlds, Spoleto, Italy, in June 1971.*

When Arthur Mitchell founded his Dance Theatre of Harlem, he was concerned to show the great gift his dancers have for classical ballet. *Holberg Suite* happily accomplished that result for the company's first performances and the work soon entered the repertory. *Holberg Suite*—named in honor of Norway's great playwright, for whom Grieg wrote the music as a tribute—is a dance ballet in five parts: a lyric "Opening" (for nine dancers); "pas de

Neuf"; a quick and playful "Pas de Trois"; a moody "Pas de Deux"; and a jolly "Finale."

NOTES Writing of the production by the Dance Theatre of Harlem in *Ballet Review*, the critic Robert Greskovic said: "'Holberg Suite' (like 'Fête Noire') is one of Mitchell's program openers and as such it remains his best suite. It's a solid, varied and impressive introduction of the company to its audience. In addition to its lineups of group work, it contains some perky solos for dancers who, grateful for the chance, take it with daring aplomb. With the men in pale blue blouses, darker tights and light knee socks, and the women in filmy pale blue shifts, there is a Bournonville brightness to the stage which restates itself in the hops, beats and jumps of the ensemble sections. The dances are bright and fluid presentations of this sunny, 'up' music by radiant young performers. Dances for nine, three, and two precede a group finale (with a lead couple). Virginia Johnson's largesse of stature proves accomplished and virtuoso-sweet in some cool, breezy pirouettes and sparkling batterie. The easy manners she projects as Russell and Bryant carefully support her in the pas de trois prove her power to enchant. She has opportunities to release (and quick change) her long legs in lifts and splits. Russell and Bryant present her with smiling authority and individual, double-escort manners. There is some sound and articulate supported work in the pas de neuf with Raines, Gerald Banks, and Scott handling two ballerinas each with deft calm. Susan Lovelle's upcurving back and star-reaching gaze as she's transported in arabesque look superb. She reposes in stilled flight with a proud, private smile from her pixie face, her eyes glistening competition with her rhinestone earrings. In moments like this I want to say 'Hold it. You're there!' Here she was, not just a gifted dancer's body, but a young ballerina-hopeful. Ronald Perry and Roslyn Sampson lead the Finale with knowing-we-made-a-conquest ease. By this time the audience is theirs, and Sampson and Perry gratefully respond by not resting on their predecessors' laurels. They seize the chance with gracious attack, Sampson springing jumps and flashing sous-sus turns with impish glee, and Perry, ice-blue sleeves billowing, taking to the air with easy legs and carefully pointed sharp, multiple beats.

"'Holberg Suite' is a clear, handsome piece that makes suitable demands on the company and breezes about the stage with musical authority and theatrical purpose."*

# HOMAGE TO ISADORA

*Music by Brahms. Choreography by Frederick Ashton. First presented at the Hamburg Ballet's Nijinsky Gala, Hamburg, Germany, June 22, 1975, with Lynn Seymour. Pianist: Christoph Eschenbach. First presented in the United States with Lynn Seymour by American Ballet Theatre at the Ken-*

* Reprinted by permission of *Ballet Review*, Marcel Dekker, publisher.

*nedy Center of the Performing Arts, Washington, D.C., April 6, 1976.*
*Pianist: Howard Barr.*

Initially called *Brahms Waltzes,* this work is Frederick Ashton's recollection of the impression made by Isadora Duncan as he saw and admired her. Set to the Brahms Waltzes No. 15, Op. 39, which are played by the pianist on stage, the dances re-create a memory of a legend. John Percival wrote in *Dance and Dancers* that Ashton told the opening of the ballet, "with Seymour coming forward and scattering flower petals, was exactly as he remembered Isadora, the rest being a re-creation based on his memories. It certainly had an entirely authentic look to it, bringing the beautifully curved line of the many Duncan drawings into a seamless flow of movement . . . ."

In an interview with Don McDonagh in *Ballet Review* (Vol. 3, No. 4) Frederick Ashton recalled what Isadora Duncan was like "in London, in 1921, I think. It was before she went to Russia. She did a series of matinees in London at the Prince of Wales Theatre to practically empty houses. She was a marvelous mover. She ran wonderfully. Even when she was galumphing around she was still very impressive. I must have been about fifteen or so when I saw her and that's a very bad age at which to see an aging, fat woman. I was completely taken by her. I saw about three or four performances. She would do a whole program of Wagner one afternoon, and then she would do a whole program of Chopin another afternoon, and then she would do Schubert or Liszt. She had a very good pianist who would play pieces while she got into another drape. She had a marvelous tragic impact and she had enormous grace. Marvelous use of the head and arms. The hands were beautiful. I don't think she did very much, I'm sure she didn't. And it's quite difficult to do a recital, you know. You have to be somebody pretty big to interest an audience for a whole afternoon . . . She had a quality I can only describe by saying that when she moved she left herself behind. And she did very simple things. In one Brahms waltz I remember she had her hands full of petals and as she ran forward the petals streamed after her. It sounds terribly corny but it was wonderful. Then she could be quite dramatic. In Chopin's Funeral March she would come in with a huge cloak around her and would just stand there. And you'd think, My goodness, how much longer is she going to stand there. Then slowly she would open the cloak and she had a whole armful of lilies inside. She had grace and she had power. She was also like a sort of highbrow striptease, because she would start her program in a great long garment and then after she did a dance she would take something off and hang it on the piano and so on 'til she finally ended up in a short thing up to here. Big legs, she had."

Anna Duncan's recollections of Isadora, as recorded in an interview with Parker Tyler in *Ballet Review* (Vol. 3, No. 1), are also of interest to those who would wish to know more about the great American dancer.

## HOMAGE TO THE QUEEN

*Music by Malcolm Arnold. Choreography by Frederick Ashton. Scenery and costumes by Oliver Messel. First presented by the Sadler's Wells Ballet at the Royal Opera House, Covent Garden, London, June 2, 1953, with Nadia Nerina, Violetta Elvin, Beryl Grey, and Margot Fonteyn in leading roles. First presented in the United States by the Sadler's Wells Ballet at the Metropolitan Opera House, New York, September 18, 1953.*

Presented in London on Coronation Day, 1953, *Homage to the Queen* was ballet's tribute to Queen Elizabeth II. Arranged in four tableaux and an apotheosis, the Queens of the four elements, Earth, Air, Fire, and Water, enter with their consorts and attendants. Then in separate scenes the monarchs dance, epitomizing their special characteristics. Their attendants also perform a *pas de six*, a *pas de trois*, and a *pas de quatre*. At the end, in an apotheosis, Queen Elizabeth I is seen in gold brocade at the top of a flight of steps, where she gestures to the young queen who stands below.

## ILLUMINATIONS

*Dramatic ballet in one act. Music by Benjamin Britten. Words from Arthur Rimbaud. Choreography by Frederick Ashton. Scenery and costumes by Cecil Beaton. Lighting by Jean Rosenthal. Soprano soloist, Angelene Collins. First presented by the New York City Ballet at the City Center, New York, March 2, 1950, with a cast headed by Nicholas Magallanes as the* Poet, *Tanaquil LeClercq as* Sacred Love, *Melissa Hayden as* Profane Love, *and Robert Barnett as the* Dandy.

A sequence of danced pictures or charades, *Illuminations* was inspired by prose poems written in 1871–72 by the French symbolist poet Rimbaud and by certain incidents in the short, violent life of the poet. Rimbaud lived to be thirty-seven, but he wrote no poetry we know of after he was nineteen. What he wrote before then is contained principally in two works, of which *Les Illuminations* was the first.

The title of this book and its meaning relate not only to the poems, but to the poet. For it was Rimbaud's special idea that the poet should be a seer, a visionary, one who arrived at a new, fresh illumination through the disordering of the senses, one who participated fully in darkness in order to see the light. His poems recollect the process by which this light is discovered, and in them we see sudden flashes of light illuminating the darkness the poems enclose. Throughout the ballet, selections from *Les Illuminations* are sung in French.

FANFARE   The music begins with loud, strident cries from the strings. The curtain rises. About the stage, reclining in various postures, are mysterious white figures. All of them are asleep. In the center, in waistcoat, high white collar, and striped pants, lies the poet. The soloist sings:

> "J'ai seul la clef de cette parade sauvage."

The poet rises, falls back, rises again, and wakes, wakes the sleepers, turning their drowsy bodies. Now he puts on a hat and encourages the strange people to dance. The soloist sings portions of these impressions of the poet.

Now the people leave the stage and the poet is alone. The music is quiet and expectant. The poet throws gold stardust into the air to the song:

> "J'ai tendu des cordes de clocher à clocher; des guirlandes de fenêtre à fenêtre; des chaînes d'or d'étoile à étoile, et je danse."

Stars glow brightly on the backdrop as the poet seems to string pearls between the distant steeples.

Two women come to the poet. One is all in stark white—even her face is a white mask; the other, also in white, wears her clothes loosely, voluptuously. The pure white figure, Sacred Love, leaves the poet alone with her opposite. Profane Love and the poet join in a ferociously passionate dance to a new song:

> "Gracieux fils de Pan! Autour de ton front couronné de fleurettes et de baies, tes yeux, des boules précieuses, remuent. Tachées de lie brune, tes joues se creusent. Tes crocs luisent. Ta poitrine ressemble à une cithare, des tintements circulent dans tes bras blonds."

As the lovers embrace, they look up and see a parade enter, led by a drummer and a trumpeter. There follow two acolytes, a bishop, and a royal couple whose long trains are held out behind them. The parade moves to the center, and the royal pair are crowned king and queen by the bishop. They kneel together. The poet watches this procession and ceremony as if he couldn't believe it. The soloist sings:

> "Un beau matin, chez un peuple fort doux, un homme et une femme superbes criaient sur la place publique: 'Mes amis, je veux qu'elle soit reine!' 'Je veux être reine!' Elle riait et tremblait. Il parlait aux amis de révélation, d'épreuve terminée. Ils se pâmaient l'un contre l'autre.
> "En effet, ils furent rois toute une matinée, où les tentures carminées se relevèrent sur les maisons, et tout l'après-midi, où ils s'avancèrent du côté des jardins de palmes."

Finally the poet can bear it no longer. When the procession begins to leave the scene, he rushes upon it, throwing himself on the king's back. He knocks off the crowns of the royal pair and sends the whole parade packing. Alone, he takes up the king's crown and puts it on his head. Profane Love enters and throws herself at his feet. The poet ignores her. The girl grovels in the dirt for a moment, then reaches out her hands and tries to crawl up to his shoulders. The poet repulses her and begins to walk away, and the girl, refusing to give up her hold on him, is dragged along behind him. The poet, now enraged, strikes her in the face. She leaves the stage, promising vengeance. The poet lies at the front of the stage.

The scene darkens. Two spotlights show us the figure of Sacred Love, who enters with four men. The song is renewed as the poet lies dreaming.

Supported by the four men, Sacred Love is turned around and around in graceful poses, lifted high above the stage, and carried across it as the men form a chariot beneath her. As the dream subsides, she is lifted off in a long, quiet rush toward the wings.

The poet rises. He tosses his crown away. The curious crowd that peopled the stage in the first scene now fills the stage. Its members grab the poet, toss him about, turn him upside down and attack him.

The strange creatures chase the poet and surround him. Hidden for a moment in their midst, he is then lifted high above them. Profane Love enters to watch the scene with pleasure. Back in the distance we see the figure of Sacred Love soaring across the landscape. The poet is helpless and beckons to Profane Love for help. She laughs and orders one of the men to shoot the poet.

A man draws a pistol, aims it, and fires. The poet is wounded in his wrist, just as the real poet, Rimbaud, was wounded by his sometime mentor and guide, the poet Verlaine.

Profane Love, now wishing to be forgiven, falls at the poet's feet. He does not even look down at her. He grasps his wounded arm and steps over her body. Blood spills from the wound. The poet turns and slowly moves backward toward the transparent backdrop, where Sacred Love can still be seen in flight. The poet steps through the backdrop, the front of the stage darkens, all the curious people collapse again in sleep, and we see the hero walking alone beneath a blazing sun.

# IMAGINARY FILM

*Music by Arnold Schoenberg. Choreography by Glen Tetley. Designed by Nadine Baylis. First presented by the Netherlands Dance Theatre at the Circustheater, Scheveningen, Holland, May 5, 1970. First presented in the United States by the same ensemble at the Brooklyn Academy of Music, March 28, 1972.*

The titles of the pieces of music by Arnold Schoenberg used for the ballet give us an indication of things to come: Danger Threatening, Fear and Catastrophe; Forebodings, the Past, Climax or Turning Point. The Schoenberg scores are *Incidental Music for a Film Scene (Begleitungsmusik zu einer Lichtspielszene,* Op. 34), which is played through twice in the ballet, and *Five Pieces for Orchestra,* Op. 16.

*Imaginary Film*'s title tells its story, in fact a free fantasy on film drama and melodrama and also on what dance sometimes imagines itself to be when it takes itself too seriously. Everything seems to happen in it: a girl in evening dress on roller skates shoots one of two struggling men; a huge shaggy creature like King Kong moves in and out, even umpiring a tennis match. The choreography catches the action and violence we are used to in films and stops it down, as it were, to comedy, so that we can reflect on it, and ourselves.

# INCUBUS

*Music by Anton Webern. Choreography by Gerald Arpino. Costumes by Lewis Brown. First presented by the Robert Joffrey Ballet at the Fashion Institute of Technology, New York, September 28, 1962, with Lone Isaksen, Brunilda Ruiz, Paul Sutherland, Helgi Tomasson, Nels Jorgensen, Suzanne Hammons, and Lawrence Rhodes in leading roles.*

"According to a legend originating in medieval times, a demon or spirit was thought to lie on sleeping persons, especially young women, inducing agonizing nightmares." The ballet, set to Webern's *Six Pieces for Orchestra,* is a journey into madness for such a young girl, who goes to sleep in torment one night, having been rejected by her mother. She clutches a rag doll. She dreams of others with whom she might identify—and whom she fears: a boy who wants to kiss her, a minister intent on dealing with the devil, a group of acrobats who seem to represent the free spirit she wishes to become. The lead acrobat falls and dies. The girl collapses into madness, indifferent now even to the rag doll. She is taken away and the doll alone remains.

The choreographer has said that he chose Webern's music "because he anticipated his time in music, and today I feel his music in 'our time.'"

# INITIALS R.B.M.E.

*Music by Johannes Brahms. Choreography by John Cranko. Décor by Jürgen Rose. First presented by the Stuttgart Ballet at the Württemberg State Theatre, Stuttgart, Germany, January 19, 1973, with Richard Cragun, Birgit Keil, Marcia Haydée, Heinz Clauss, and Egon Madsen in principal roles. First presented in the United States by the same ensemble with the same principals at the Metropolitan Opera House, New York, May 30, 1973. Conducted by Stewart Kershaw. Piano solo by Katsurako Fujiwara.*

This dance ballet is named for its principal dancers—Richard Cragun, Birgit Keil, Marcia Haydée and Egon Madsen, the stars of John Cranko's Stuttgart Ballet. Cranko called it "a ballet for four friends to music of Johannes Brahms, whose passionate feeling for friendship and love is confirmed by his compositions, in his letters and by the testimony of others."

The first movement of the Brahms *Piano Concerto No. 2,* to which the ballet is arranged, was set for Richard Cragun; the second for Birgit Keil. Marcia Haydée and Heinz Clauss are featured in the third movement and Egon Madsen in the fourth. Each of the sections is supported by the *corps de ballet.*

NOTES   Writing of this ballet's success on the Soviet tour of the Stuttgart Ballet (1973) in *Dance Magazine,* Lydia Jaffe notes that each of the four stars of *Initials R.B.M.E.* are "all dancers with whom Cranko has had a long and friendly association at the Stuttgart. They started with him as beginners, and his guidance brought them to artistic accomplishment.

"The ballet was enthusiastically acclaimed, and Vera Krasovskaya, the Soviet ballet critic, remarks: 'What a wealth of fantasy! The dancers execute these virtuosities with precision, discipline and feeling. It is an homage to the whole company.'"

## IN NIGHTLY REVELS

*Music by Bach. Choreography by Peter Darrell. First presented by the Jacob's Pillow Dance Festival, Lee, Massachusetts, July 3, 1973, with Margot Fonteyn. Harpsichordist: Jess Meeker.*

*In Nightly Revels* is a dramatic dance for a lady. A harpsichord is at the left; three candelabra stand in what appears to be a deserted ballroom. A boy enters with a taper to light one of the candelabra. A man enters then and sits at the harpsichord. He begins to play music, from Bach's *Well-Tempered Clavier*. Now comes a beautiful lady, rushing on in a black cape. She wears a tiara and a pink gown. Expectant, she gestures graciously for the other candles to be lit and signals to a boy to take her cape. She seems to have arrived at a party; no one else is there; it is perhaps her own.

Now pensive, the woman nods at the harpsichordist, who begins to play. The measures he plays are sad and stately, and the woman reaches up her arms as if sacrificing something. Her hands descend down her body as if bathing it in her own tears as the dance threnody continues. She seems to be recovering from an experience that still controls her being. It is the reverse of another ballet, *Le Spectre de la Rose,* where a young girl returns from a ball to fall asleep in a chair to dream of a spectral hero. This woman of experience has had her dream, and there is a suggestion that it is one of many broken ones. She consoles herself with the music and the luxury of her surroundings. The back of the room disappears and the forest surrounding the room beckons to her. Looking out on the birch trees in the soft moonlight, she is renewed in body and spirit. A new experience awaits her. She again takes up her cape, stands briefly at the harpsichord, thanks the player, and disappears into the night.

## INTERMEZZO

*Music by Johannes Brahms. Choreography by Eliot Feld. Costumes by Stanley Simmons. Lighting by Jules Fisher. First presented by the American Ballet Company at the Festival of Two Worlds, Spoleto, Italy, June 29, 1969, with Christine Sarry, Elizabeth Lee, Cristina Stirling, David Coll, John Sowinski, and Alfonso Figueroa. Pianist: Gladys Celeste Mercader. First presented in the United States by the American Ballet Company at*

*the Brooklyn Academy of Music, New York, October 23, 1969, with Olga
Janke replacing Cristina Stirling in the original cast.*

*Intermezzo* is a set of dances to piano music by Brahms—the *Op. 117* and *118
intermezzos* and some of the *Op. 39* waltzes. The piano is on stage to accompany the dances throughout the ballet. The story is what the dancers do.

They are seen entering gradually onto a darkened scene, three couples in
formal dress. They listen to the first bars of the music as the light rises. Then a
girl begins to move to the music. The others follow, responding to the flow of
the music in speed and stillness. Two couples leave, and the remaining one
dances a *pas de deux* to a romantic sequence. They yield the stage to another,
faster duet, this one buoyant and full of brio; then the third couple returns and
all six finish the piece.

This is the ballet's pattern, a series of duets and ensembles, all of them distinct in character with the music, all of them a contrast. There is a tempestuous waltz, and, in one duet, the boy is distracted by the girl so much that
she seems to blind him. After another duet in which the dancers appear to be
driven in the demanding pace of the music, a girl dances pensively alone. The
*pas de deux* resume, their variety accumulating with shifts in the music. Toward the end, as the lights begin to fade, the three girls are cradled in their
lovers' arms. They realize it is late and say good night.

NOTES   *Intermezzo* was the new major work created by Eliot Feld for the
first performances of his American Ballet Company. Writing about these performances in *Dance and Dancers*, Patricia Barnes said:

"For a choreographer still only in his middle 20s to create within a couple
of years six ballets is an achievement in itself; that they should all be interesting, and at least three of them major works by any standard, sets Feld up in
the ranks of the leading contemporary choreographers. Choreographed during
the spring of 1969 and seen for the first time in Spoleto, *Intermezzo* is a real
beauty. Performed to a backdrop of curtains and with the piano placed to the
left of the stage, the dances have a flow and musicality that is both subtle and
natural. Using just six dancers and varying his work with ensemble, *pas de
deux* and solos, the choreography has an ecstasy and technical dexterity that is
gorgeous . . . it is Feld's genuine invention and originality that make *Intermezzo* so rewarding. He dares a great deal in his choreography and asks almost impossible things of his dancers. Lifts abound in his work, some like none
I have ever seen before. When performed by dancers such as the nimble
Christine Sarry and David Coll, who is, quite simply, one of the best partners I
have ever seen, the effect is dazzling.

"Another striking *pas de deux* is that created for Elizabeth Lee and John
Sowinski, which is strongly atmospheric, a tiny choreographic gem almost
complete in itself. With Sowinski's arm protectively round her waist, Lee
seems to perceive strange and fearful visions. Sowinski gently removes her
hands from her eyes and tenderly, reassuringly, he helps her face life. This
small sequence is danced with a beauty, gravity and compassion that is altogether memorable."

Writing of the ballet in the *Village Voice*, the critic Deborah Jowitt said, "*Intermezzo* . . . is all ardent swoops and dips, runs and waltzes, light and breathless lifts. Occasionally a mysterious melancholy comes in like gathering dark. John Sowinski reaches toward the invisible while his partner, Elizabeth Lee, tries gently to turn him back toward her. They and the other two couples (Christine Sarry and David Coll, Olga Janke and Alfonso Figueroa) do not so much formally replace each other on stage in *pas de deux* as sweep in and out as if flashing different facets of a relationship between two people."

## INTERPLAY

*Ballet in four movements. Music by Morton Gould* (American Concertette). *Choreography by Jerome Robbins. First presented by Billy Rose, in* Concert Varieties, *at the Ziegfeld Theatre, New York, June 1, 1945, with a cast headed by John Kriza, Janet Reed, and Jerome Robbins. First presented by Ballet Theatre at the Metropolitan Opera House, New York, October 17, 1945, with settings by Oliver Smith and costumes by Irene Sharaff; Janet Reed, John Kriza, and Harold Lang headed the cast of dancers.*

*Interplay* is an American ballet for eight dancers: four boys and four girls. It has no subject matter and no locale; but directly the dancing and music begin, it is apparent that it could only be an American work. The setting is simple: a plain colored backdrop and wings of differently colored cloth. The costumes are informal. So is the music. Loud and brassy at the beginning, the score is overtly raucous and playful.

FIRST MOVEMENT: FREE PLAY A boy dances out onto the stage. He is followed by three companions. He dances alone for a few seconds, showing off. The others join him. The boys take turns jumping over each other's backs and horsing around. They all end up lying on the floor with their legs in the air.

A girl enters. The boys sit and marvel at her. Three other girls follow, and now the boys are moved to action. They get up, take partners, and the four couples, one after the other, execute a number of turns in a quick, graceful, athletic fashion. The lead boy runs through, under the arms of the dancers, and takes them to the front of the stage. There are no footlights, and the modern jive motions of the couples are silhouetted against the backdrop.

Now the couples move back and form a wide circle. The boys toss the girls around, and the music becomes quieter as the dancers stand in a straight line. The dancers seem to be playing a game that they all understand. There is some competition among the couples in the execution of conventional pirouettes and arabesques, but the game isn't really that serious. They are all having a jazzy good time. They all clap hands, the boys roll the girls over their backs, and the first dance ends with the four boys sitting on the floor; their girls stand in back, holding their hands.

SECOND MOVEMENT: HORSEPLAY After a brief pause, the music resumes.

Though still modern in its rhythm, the melody now has a buoyant lightness. A few of the couples sit lazily on the stage; the others stand apart. One of the boys begins to dance alone. His solo is quietly comic, like the music, and amusingly impertinent in its imitation of some conventional movements in classic ballet. The dance increases in pace. The boy circles the stage, spins rapidly in the air, and finishes his solo. He kneels and opens his arms to two of the girls.

THIRD MOVEMENT: BYPLAY   The lights dim, and the piano begins a slow, sentimental blues. All the couples stretch and rearrange themselves about the stage. The lead boy and lead girl commence a *pas de deux*. Their dance is openly romantic, but has no particular intensity. Love is a game, too, they seem to say. The boy lifts the girl high over his head as she maintains an open position, pushes her forward across the floor on her toes as if she were a toy cart, then holds her close. The girl wraps herself around the boy, then both sit down on the floor and hold hands, like two children sitting on the beach.

FOURTH MOVEMENT: TEAM PLAY   The light brightens; the music returns to a fast, vigorous tempo. Now the dance becomes a contest. Two of the boys choose sides, and the two sides go into huddles to decide on tactics. They line up opposite each other. All turn cartwheels, then soloists from the two sides try to outdo each other in complicated movements. The boys vie with one another to see who can do the most turns in the air without stopping. Two girls, one from each side, begin to turn around and around on point as the game comes to a heated close. All the boys and girls run back and turn about the stage in a circle. The girls dash forward to the footlights. The boys sprint after them. With the last crash of the music, the boys take a running fall on the floor and slide under the girls' legs. Blackout.

# IN THE NIGHT

*Music by Frédéric Chopin. Choreography by Jerome Robbins. Costumes by Joe Eula. Lighting by Thomas Skelton. Pianist: Gordon Boelzner. First presented by the New York City Ballet at the New York State Theatre, Lincoln Center, January 29, 1970 with Kay Mazzo and Anthony Blum, Violette Verdy and Peter Martins, Patricia McBride and Francisco Moncion.*

At the time of his ballet *Dances at a Gathering*, Jerome Robbins said, "There is more Chopin that I like—the nocturnes, for example—that I may use for another ballet." *In the Night* continues the exploration of Chopin's music, using for its score the Chopin *Nocturnes, Opus 27, No. 1; Opus 55, Nos. 1 and 2*; and *Opus 9, No. 2*.

When we speak of a nocturne, the critic Harold Schonberg has pointed out in his fine book on Chopin and Schumann, we think automatically of Chopin's "night pieces." They were, in the composer's lifetime, his most popular compositions, captivating all of Europe from the amateurs who found them comparatively easy to play, to the connoisseurs who liked their dreamlike form. "We live in a non-sentimental age, or pretend to," Schonberg remarks, and the nocturnes are not now so much played. Perhaps after this ballet we will listen to them more. Many consider the first nocturne used in the ballet to be Chopin's greatest; the last, *Opus 9, No. 2,* is surely the most popular of the twenty works in this genre.

*In the Night* consists of dances for three couples. They dance in sequence and then appear together briefly. The curtain rises on a starry night. A boy and a girl enter to the slow introductory music. Their dance develops with the pulse of the score, which quickens dramatically, then returns to simplicity and melody. The boy lifts the girl into the wings.

There is a more formal atmosphere for the second *pas de deux,* a suggestion of chandeliers above the stage. The music is tender, but in the midst of the dance the girl breaks away from the boy. When she returns, their dance has a real abandon until holding the girl upside down as her limbs tremble, passions subside. At the end, he lifts her, facing him, and away.

In the third *pas de deux,* almost melodramatic in response to the piano, there are declarations, rejections, pleadings, rapid swings from one emotion to another. She hangs onto the boy. He leaves her and she seems helpless. But after a short reunion, both leave. She returns, to walk across stage, kneel before him, and touch him. He cradles her in his arms.

To the most familiar nocturne, the three couples enter, meeting as if accidentally at a dance. The girls acknowledge each other, then the boys, but all clearly have eyes only for each other and do not know quite what is happening. Each couple goes its own way.

Deborah Jowitt wrote in the *Village Voice:* "I shall not vex myself with wondering whether Jerome Robbins intended his new ballet, *In the Night,* as a companion piece to his *Dances at a Gathering* or as a sequel, prelude, epilogue, cadenza. I think that it is probable that Robbins simply had more Chopin in his ears and more movement ideas in his head so he made another ballet—not as long as *Dances at a Gathering* but equally astonishing.

"The two ballets are certainly related. The movement has the same beautiful ease in space. We do not notice 'choreography,' but see dancing. Even ballet steps that we know melt into the long phrases before our eyes can freeze them. The special kind of contemporary Romanticism that Robbins is interested in is expressed in dance that burgeons and branches and grows like leaves—startling, perhaps, by its eventual shape, but never seeming inorganic. . . .

"Kay Mazzo and Anthony Blum perform the first duet. The gracious rapture of their relationship is punctuated by little confrontations. They appear to leave each other for the pleasure of rushing together again.

"The chandelier projection creates a half-indoor feeling—a ballroom with all the doors and windows flung open. In this duet for Violette Verdy and Peter Martins, there is a delight in each other, but also a slight and charming decorousness. Occasionally they do little steps arm in arm as if they were at a dance, or remembering a dance. She looks very small, very trusting beside him.

"The third duet is full of passion and artifice. The lovers, Francisco Moncion and Patricia McBride, are being melodramatic for each other. One minute they are involved in flashy, tempestuous lifts; the next minute one of them disappears from sight. Their very anger seems to be exciting them. Even her final kneeling at his feet to touch him is extreme as well as truly humble.

"At the end the three couples, still alone, occupy the same fragrant patch of night. The women come together and are surprised to see each other: you can almost see them blinking awake. The men greet each other. Then the couples separate and again take their own paths.

"The choreography serves the dancers, and they in turn serve it beautifully. Each seems completely real in what he is doing. Ballet technique disappears as artifice and becomes—as it rarely does—a means to dancing, a transparency for spirit to be seen through."

*In the Night* has also been described, with an interesting commentary, by the critic Robert Sealy in *Ballet Review,* Vol. 3, No. 3.

## INTRODUCTION AND ALLEGRO FOR HARP

*Music by Maurice Ravel. Choreography by Jerome Robbins. Costumes by Arnold Scassi. Lighting by Ronald Bates. First presented by the New York City Ballet at the Hommage à Ravel at the New York State Theatre, Lincoln Center, May 22, 1975, with Patricia McBride and Helgi Tomasson as principals. Solo harp: Cynthia Otis. Conducted by Robert Irving.*

A dance ballet to some lovely music composed by Ravel in 1905–6, this work is arranged for a girl and a boy and six couples. A small-scaled work for harp, string quartet, flute, and clarinet, the *Introduction and Allegro* has a bright, luminescent lyricism. The harp seems to ask a question the dancers attempt to answer in a rush of delight.

## THE INVITATION

*Scenery and costumes by Nicholas Georgiadis. Music by Matyas Seiber. Choreography by Kenneth MacMillan. First presented by the Royal Ballet at the New Theatre, Oxford, November 10, 1960, with Lynn Seymour, Christopher Gable, Anne Heaton, and Desmond Doyle in the principal roles. First presented in the United States at the Metropolitan Opera House, New York, May 10, 1963, with the same principals.*

Speaking about his ballet, the choreographer Kenneth MacMillan has said, "The story is realistic, set at the beginning of this century. I combined two ideas—from a South American book called *House of the Angel* and Colette's *Ripening Seed*. But I made the characters people I know, not the characters in the books. An older, unhappy married couple meet two young people whose love for each other is gentle and tender. The older couple destroy this innocence. The story does not resolve itself. When one loses innocence and grows up, it can be a shattering experience without resolution. I hope the spectators may see things in the ballet which they've felt in their lives."

The scenario for the ballet follows: "In a grand house live a wealthy widow and her three daughters. The two elder daughters of marriageable age are strictly guarded by their mother. The youngest daughter has invited her boy cousin and some young friends to stay with her, along with their parents. In the party there is an unhappily married couple who were friends of the widow's husband.

"The youngest daughter and her cousin are drawn towards each other, but she is also attracted to the married man after dancing with him. After the children have gone to bed, entertainers arrive to perform for the guests. The girl creeps down and secretly watches. At the end of the performance the married couple quarrel and the man rushes off in anger followed by the girl. The cousin appears in search of the girl but instead finds the wife alone. Timidly he succumbs to her. At the same time the girl discovers the man walking by the lake, but his affectionate approach to her changes to violence and she is left weeping.

"The house party ends and the married couple continue their indifferent relationship. The boy tries to resume his courtship of the girl but she rejects him."

## IRISH FANTASY

*Music by Camille Saint-Saëns. Choreography by Jacques d'Amboise. Scenery and lighting by David Hays. Costumes by Karinska. First presented by the New York City Ballet at the Greek Theatre, Los Angeles, August 12, 1964, with Melissa Hayden, André Prokovsky, Anthony Blum, and Frank Ohman in the leading roles. First presented in New York at the New York State Theatre, October 8, 1964, with the same principals.*

*Irish Fantasy* is a dance ballet on an Irish theme set to music from Saint-Saëns's opera *Henry VIII*. The opening music even has occasional strains of the traditional Irish tune "Johnny I Hardly Knew You." A lace-curtain drop curtain sets the light, bantering tone of the piece, which is dominated by girls in green, boys in brown, and a girl in pink, the heroine. The girl in pink is admired by several of the boys, but is finally won, after a vigorous dance of conquest, by the leading *danseur*. The quality of the movement tells the story of the piece, which is bright, competitive, and ebullient.

## IVAN THE TERRIBLE

*Ballet in two acts. Music by Sergei Prokofiev, arranged by Mikhail Chulaki. Scenario and choreography by Yuri Grigorovich. Scenery and costumes by Simon Virsaladze. First presented by the Bolshoi Ballet at the Bolshoi Theatre, Moscow, February 20, 1975, with Yuri Vladimirov and Natalia Bess-*

*mertnova in the principal roles. First presented in the United States by the*
*same ensemble at the Metropolitan Opera House, Lincoln Center, New York,*
*April 29, 1975. Conducted by Algis Zhyuraitis.*

Persons unacquainted with Russian history and knowing no Russian might suppose that Ivan was a terrible Tsar. Actually, the Russian word *grosniy* means formidable, threatening, menacing, stern, as well as terrible. This ballet about his life goes back to sixteenth-century Russia to provide the background for what we know of his character. The action tells of a difficult and troubled time when, torn apart by civil strife and foreign invasion, "Russia rang like an alarm bell with a call to unite the country." The scenes of the ballet tell of the young Tsar Ivan IV, of his beloved Anastasia who was poisoned by treacherous Boyars, and of Prince Kurbsky who betrayed his homeland. They tell of "the Russian people, who withstood all the ordeals, survived and emerged victorious."

The choreographer Yuri Grigorovich has said that the ballet is not a literal representation of history but "seeks to re-create an image of the period. The essential theme is the nature of the Russian character, the traditions of loyalty and heroism, the ethics and morals of the individual Russian . . .

"Many aspects of Ivan's complex nature are portrayed. On the one hand he is shown as a man who passionately and faithfully loves his wife Anastasia, and detests the treachery of the Boyars. On the other hand, he is shown as the mighty Tsar, himself treacherous and cruel.

"The ballet is conceived as a historical chronicle in which the action develops through the juxtaposition of contrasting scenes, which are not necessarily subject to the strict development of the plot. Lyric, dramatic, even humorous scenes, set side by side, reveal a many-faceted panorama of the period. Thus the ballet becomes not 'episodes in the life of a Tsar' but scenes of a complex and tormented time in sixteenth-century Russia."

The action of *Ivan the Terrible* is presented in two acts of nine scenes each.

ACT ONE, SCENE ONE: INTRODUCTION; THE BELLRINGERS SUMMON THE PEOPLE   Agitated chords commence the action. Six Bellringers holding ropes that ascend to huge bells overhead are encircled by crowds of people. The Bellringers kneel. In the back behind a scrim, we discern leading members of the Tsar's court, all dressed in long robes.

ACT ONE, SCENE TWO: THE BOYARS AND IVAN   The scrim opens. On a high throne sits Ivan. He rises. All kneel as he dances. His movements and gestures are as percussive as the declarative music that accompanies them; we witness an assertion of power so strong it appears to be a natural force. At the end he climbs back up to the throne as if it were Everest to conquer.

ACT ONE, SCENE THREE: IVAN'S ENCOUNTER WITH ANASTASIA   Girls in diaphanous gowns decorated with pearls approach the throne. Fierce in his black and gold robes, the Tsar grips the arms of his throne but watches. Soon he descends. Enthralled with one of the girls, he touches her head. She is frightened

and backs away but the Tsar is transfixed and will not let her go. Prince
Kurbsky, a leading courtier and chief of the Boyars, instinctively kneels to the
Tsar's new favorite and with the others discreetly withdraws. Alone with the
Tsar, Anastasia kneels before him. He declares his love openly. They bow
deeply to each other, then walk toward us to begin a dance of quiet joy at his
discovery.

ACT ONE, SCENE FOUR: KURBSKY'S DESPAIR   The leading courtier is outraged
at Anastasia's sudden ascendancy and mimes his displeasure at being side-
tracked after all he has done for the Tsar in the past. Alternately whining and
attacking, tearing his hair and banging on the door, Kurbsky finally determines to get even with the Tsar and attack him where it will hurt most. He is
deflected by an invasion from abroad.

ACT ONE, SCENE FIVE: THE BATTLE WITH THE FOREIGN ENEMY   The
Bellringers return in red boots, sound their bells, and cluster in the center.
Crowds of people enter to lament the coming war but the invaders must be
repulsed. Now the very battle comes onto the scene, Kurbsky leading the Russians in pursuit of the Moslems. Ivan even more vigorously at the head of the
battle declares his will for victory and kisses his sword as trumpets blare.
Among scythes of death which surround him as he dances, he proceeds to
battle and overcomes the enemy in a blaze of glory.

ACT ONE, SCENE SIX: ANASTASIA'S MEDITATION   In the throne room of the
Kremlin, Anastasia descends to dance to lyric strings of an increasing fear. She
is afraid for her husband and the country and longs for his return.

ACT ONE, SCENE SEVEN: VICTORY CELEBRATION   The Bellringers, now in the
white of peace, lead the victory parade. The Boyars are welcomed home by
their ladies, then Anastasia greets Ivan. They dance jubilantly in a *pas de deux*
at the end of which he carries her off into the wings. Kurbsky and the others
continue the celebration.

ACT ONE, SCENE EIGHT: IVAN'S ILLNESS   The courtiers kneel before Ivan, who
is seated on his throne in torment. Anastasia is at his feet. In severe exhaustion
he rises. She tries to help him and he leans on her.

ACT ONE, SCENE NINE: THE TSAR'S ANGER   Emboldened by the Tsar's illness,
a group of Boyars plot together. In the Tsar's absence, one of the wily courtiers goes to the throne. Ivan suddenly appears in back of the throne, seizes
him, throws him down the high flight of steps, following him as he falls. The
Tsar then turns and climbs back up to the throne as if he were making an attack on a craggy mountain. At the top he confronts the revolting courtiers and
hurls down in their midst his golden spear. They cower in terror.

ACT TWO, SCENE ONE: IVAN'S HAPPINESS   This is a dance of love to quiet music in the royal bedchamber. Treacherous Boyars watch and wait for the time to strike.

ACT TWO, SCENE TWO: THE BOYARS' CONSPIRACY   The wily courtiers assemble with their women and plot against the Tsar. In a drink that is passed among them, they pledge their new allegiance. Kurbsky enters. They hold out the cup to him. He cannot take it. Yet in an ensuing dance, he deliberates the alternatives and succumbs, seizing the cup in a frenzy.

ACT TWO, SCENE THREE: ANASTASIA'S DEATH   The Tsarina Anastasia is now given the cup. She drinks, is poisoned, and begins to die. She dances limply, helplessly as all watch in despair, collapsing finally in Kurbsky's arms. All shun him. Kurbsky puts down the body. Incredibly, Anastasia rises. She reaches out for vengeance and dies as Kurbsky trembles.

ACT TWO, SCENE FOUR: THE PEOPLE'S REVOLT   Again in red boots, the Bellringers return. The people who surround them cry havoc and protest.

ACT TWO, SCENE FIVE: IVAN MOURNS FOR ANASTASIA   Alone, the Tsar gives himself up to grief and despair, an intensification of his earlier illness. Voices sing as he lies spread-eagled. In the midst of the choir and candles, Anastasia seems to come back to him. She kneels to bless him.

ACT TWO, SCENE SIX: KURBSKY'S ESCAPE AND THE ROUT OF THE BOYARS   Ivan attacks the drunken, celebrating Boyars, cracking a long rope like a whip. There is a frenetic chase but with halberds and axes the traitors are closed in.

ACT TWO, SCENE SEVEN: THE OPRICHNIKI   A dance of death re-enacts the murder of Anastasia and the Boyars are ensnared by the Tsar's private secret police and vigilantes, the Oprichniki. The Devil forces Kurbsky, who has finally been caught, to drink from the cup of poison he had given to Anastasia. Devilish minstrel clowns, the Skomorokhi, hang the Boyars. The Devil himself, his jaw wagging hideously, suddenly tears off a mask and rips off his costume. It is Ivan.

ACT TWO, SCENE EIGHT: IVAN'S MEDITATION   The Tsar appears to be exultant in victory over his enemies but we see at once, as he pounds his staff into the ground, that his life force has begun to leave him. The scepter of power has now become a burden, weighing him down, oppressing him beyond measure. He lies again spread-eagled on the ground. Figures presaging death torment him but miraculously he rises. He dances with a newfound ferocity and is determined to persevere.

ACT TWO, SCENE NINE: FINALE. THE TRIUMPH OF THE RUSSIAN PEOPLE   The Bellringers return, leading a mass of people. As the bells resound, Ivan seizes the ropes and is pulled up by them toward the bells. Ensnared there, he glares out at us, implacable, unforgiving, determined on yet another victory.

NOTES  The Soviet composer Mikhail Chulaki, who arranged Prokofiev's music for the ballet, has recalled that the idea for a dance-drama about Ivan came originally from the conductor A. L. Stasevich, who had worked on Prokofiev's music for the Eisenstein film *Ivan the Terrible*. Stasevich had arranged the film music as a cantata and drew Grigorovich's attention to its great potential as a ballet score.

Chulaki continues: "Unfortunately, Stasevich died before he could evolve the score for the ballet. But Grigorovich's imagination had already been fired by this deeply expressive music. The ballet began to form in his mind as an independent work, which did not slavishly follow the plot of the film, but drew its theme from the quality of Prokofiev's music.

"The thematic material from the film *Ivan the Terrible* became the basis for the ballet score. In certain episodes other stylistically related works by Prokofiev were used: The *Russian Overture*, three sections from the *Third Symphony*, and a fragment from the cantata *Alexander Nevsky*. This additional music gave Grigorovich a broader psychological spectrum to work with—from Ivan's unbounded happiness with Anastasia, to his horrifying visions."

The choreographer Yuri Grigorovich has said that "Prokofiev's music for the film *Ivan the Terrible* is an outstanding achievement . . . I considered it essential that this music, so full of vivid imagery, lyric beauty, and heroic grandeur, be brought back to life; not only to be heard again, but this time to be interpreted choreographically because Prokofiev's music seems to demand expression in direct, human terms."

Writing in *Ballet Review* (Vol. 5, No. 2), the critic Robert Greskovic commented on a performance of *Ivan the Terrible* in 1975 by Vladimir Vasiliev: "Vasiliev is magnetically magnificent. He has both a manly and a boyish quality that makes him unique. He represents the first male Bolshoi dancer to have the charisma heretofore held by Bolshoi ballerinas. Though the Bolshoi is touted for the power of its male dancing, it has not, like the Kirov—which has produced stars aplenty starting with Nijinsky—produced a male classical star of household-word stature. Vasiliev gives off a personable power that keeps his audience as interested in him as in what he's doing. You can almost sense the audience around you growing more keenly perceptive as Vasiliev grows more potent. If he were to become a regular visitor to our country, Vasiliev could develop a following similar to that of Nureyev."*

## IVESIANA

*Music by Charles Ives. Choreography by George Balanchine. Lighting by Jean Rosenthal. First presented by the New York City Ballet at the City Center, New York, September 14, 1954. Janet Reed and Francisco Moncion, Patricia Wilde and Jacques d'Amboise, Allegra Kent and Todd Bolender, Diana Adams and Herbert Bliss, Tanaquil LeClercq and the entire company.*

* Reprinted by permission of *Ballet Review*, Marcel Dekker, publisher.

The great American composer Charles Ives died May 19, 1954, at the age of seventy-nine. Four months later, our company performed for the first time a ballet of some of his music, music that was then little known. Fortunately that situation has since changed and with fine performances and recordings of Ives's major works, most of us know something about the music that was seldom played during the composer's lifetime. I remember hearing about Ives's music in 1934, I think from Roger Sessions, but it was then almost impossible to hear his music. Leon Barzin gave me my first chance with a performance by the National Orchestral Association. Fascinated as I was by the music, it seemed to me incredibly difficult, far too complex for dancing. Some years later, however, after refreshing myself with the music of Schoenberg, Berg, and Anton Webern, I turned again to Ives. After finishing a ballet to Schoenberg's *Opus 34*, I began to work my way into Ives's music and with increasing respect and admiration. It saddens me that I never met him or told him I wanted to use his music: he seemed inaccessible. Lincoln Kirstein brought Mrs. Ives to the first performance of our ballet and I was very moved.

Ives's music is most interesting to me for its rhythms. The choreographer has little music that can twist him out of his habitual methods of design, but I found in Ives's work the shock necessary for a new point of view. Since the ballet was first done, I have revised it several times, adding a new piece I have discovered, omitting another. The music I find hard *not* to work with. In homage to the composer, we called the ballet *Ivesiana*.

1. *Central Park in the Dark*. As the names Ives gave to his music so vividly describe them, I would hope that they also tell what the dance might be about. Ives wrote that this piece "purports to be a picture in sound of sounds of nature and of happenings that men would hear . . . when sitting on a bench in Central Park on a hot summer night. The strings represent the night sounds and silent darkness—interrupted by sounds from the Casino over the pond—of street singers coming up from the Circle, singing— . . . of pianolas having a ragtime war in the apartment house 'over the garden wall' . . . a streetcar . . . a fire engine . . . wayfarers shout—again the darkness is heard . . ." That is the musical background to the dance event, which is a meeting between a girl who is lost and a boy and how they become lost together, in the dark in a place like Central Park.

2. *The Unanswered Question* calls for a double orchestra. "The strings . . . are to present 'The Silences of the Druids' who know, see, and hear nothing. The trumpet intones 'The Perennial Question of Existence' and states it in the same tone of voice each time. But the hunt for the 'Invisible Answer' undertaken by the flutes and other human beings becomes gradually more active, faster and louder. The 'Fighting Answerers,' as time goes on . . . seem to realize a futility, and begin to mock 'The Question'—the strife is over for the moment. After they disappear, 'The Question' is asked for the last time, and the 'Silences' are heard beyond in 'Undisturbed Solitude.'" The dance of course does not follow these interesting remarks of the composer but from them and from the music, which is in effect a dialogue or argument between the trumpet and the woodwinds against the background of the strings, I derived the idea of

a girl all-knowing like a sphinx to whom a man might turn. But I try to say too much and in words begin to limit what I hope the dance conveys.

3. *In the Inn.* This is as informal as its music, with a dance by two young people. As the music echoes old-time dance rhythms, the dancers' steps do too. They act exhausted at the end, shake hands and part.

4. *In the Night.* This short piece of Ives's composed in 1906, and what I have arranged to it, must speak for themselves in the theatre.

Other music by Ives that has been used in *Ivesiana* includes "Hallowe'en," which was originally the second of the danced pieces; "Over the Pavements," originally the fourth (after "The Unanswered Question"); "Arguments," which replaced "Hallowe'en" in 1955; and "Barn Dance," which in 1956 replaced "Arguments."

# LE JEUNE HOMME ET LA MORT (The Young Man and Death)

*Dramatic ballet by Jean Cocteau. Music by Johann Sebastian Bach. Chore- ography by Roland Petit. Scenery and costumes by Georges Wakhevitch. First presented by Ballets des Champs-Élysées at the Théâtre des Champs- Élysées, Paris, June 25, 1946, with Jean Babilée and Nathalie Philippart in the title roles. First presented in the United States by Ballet Theatre at the Metropolitan Opera House, New York, April 9, 1951, with the same cast.*

This modern fable of love pictures the plight of a young man whose passion for a girl is requited only in death. The boy is the typical young romantic Parisian painter, thinking and dreaming only of the girl who does not love him: of the girl who never comes, but for whom he constantly waits. The ballet is performed to an orchestration of Bach's *Passacaglia and Fugue in C minor.*

The orchestra states the music's dominant theme deeply and softly. The curtain rises. The scene is a corner of a Paris garret. Dirty walls on both sides converge at the rear. In the center, a high stanchion supports a rafter. A rope hangs down from the rafter, tied in a noose at the end. Alongside it stands an iron stove. There is a door at the left. The stark furnishings of the room—a bare table, a stool, half a dozen old wooden chairs—are illumined by the harsh light of a bare electric bulb shaded with newspapers. Against the right wall stands a cot, partially covered with a red silk cloth. A young man in paint-covered overalls lies sprawled back on the cot, smoking slowly, languidly, apparently relaxed. His body tightens, becomes tense. He looks at his watch, sits up. His eyes watch the door as he mashes out the cigarette; his feet move restlessly. The boy rises and moves toward the door, where he poses adroitly and turns swiftly in the air to indicate his increasing anxiety. When he has examined his watch again, he turns away angrily and throws himself on the cot.

The door opens slowly. A dark girl in a yellow dress and black gloves stands there in the doorway. Her feet vibrate against the floor arrogantly as she watches the boy across the room. There is a brief moment of recognition, and he runs across the room to leap to her side. He attempts to embrace the girl;

she is reluctant, cold in his grasp. They begin to dance together around the room. The boy is indifferent to anything but the girl. They move rapidly and roughly, banging chairs aside. The girl dances with fierce stiffness, like a violent mechanical doll.

The girl pushes the boy away and sits down on a chair and crosses her legs. He stands in back of her, declaring his love for her with generous, open gestures. The girl ignores him. The boy tries to force her to dance with him again. The girl joins him for a moment, but it is apparent that he is not content merely to dance. The girl turns stiff in his embrace and pushes him to the floor. She dances over to the table. He jumps onto the table and crouches for an instant above her. The girl shoves him to the floor and sits nonchalantly against the table, watching him writhe on the floor.

The boy reaches out for a chair, pulls himself up, and sits with his back to the girl. She lights a cigarette. The smoke drifts over to him. He points his leg out toward her and rises, hypnotized. He moves toward her like a toy soldier, his movements imitating the quality of the girl's gestures. He stands close, his face against hers. The girl blows smoke in his face. The boy angrily knocks the cigarette out of her hand and stamps on it. Now the girl moves around the table, and he cannot seem to catch her. He decides on a more careful approach.

The girl sits in a chair, absolutely oblivious to him, as if she were at a cocktail party and he was only one of the many people who were quite naturally looking only at her. The boy takes a chair and walks it over beside her. He steps up on the chair, and the girl moves away. He chases after her and dances with bold, desperate leaps in the air, pleading for her love. The girl does not notice. He turns rapidly and comes close to her. The girl slaps him off fiercely, and he falls away in the slow motion of agony. Now he moves about the room frantically—back to the corner and to his love again. Kneeling behind her, he embraces her legs. The girl wrenches herself free and pushes him away. The boy falls against the table.

He has lost control of his will and only wishes to be close to her. He lies on the floor and reaches out to caress her. She kicks him in the face savagely. His body reacts in agonizing, painful slow motion as his face falls against the floor and his feet describe a high arc in the air. Twice more he attempts to touch her, and twice more she kicks him away.

The boy rises and chases the girl back to the corner of the room. The music approaches a crescendo. They meet and move forward. The music softens. Suddenly the girl responds to the boy's embrace. She caresses his face softly; he is motionless in her gentle arms, oblivious to the violence they threaten. She leads him to a chair. The boy moves in a dream. He sits down, his head falls forward, and the girl raises his arm high in a wide arc of slow movement. She moves away. The boy seems to be asleep; his arm hangs pendulously over the back of the chair.

The girl moves a high stool to the foot of the post in the center of the room, steps up on it, and adjusts the noose that hangs from the rafter. Carefully she sets the noose swinging. Then she moves back to the boy. Her cold hands touch his neck. The boy wakens, startled. She twists his head around toward the noose. As he lifts his arms in terror, the girl pushes him backward. The chair clatters to the floor. The boy's foot trembles. The girl runs through the door, triumphant.

The boy leaps after her, but she has vanished. He takes a chair, swings it wide, and throws it against the wall. He jumps upon the table, turns briskly in his anger and fear, then falls, helpless. He rises. He is standing beside the table, and his line of sight crosses the swinging noose. He drags the table with him as he moves forward stiffly. His body arches back as he holds the table, and he topples to the floor. He rises, leaps boldly and assertively to regain his courage, and moves stiffly toward the noose. He grabs the stool and backs away, circling the post. His frantic, nervous shadow is seen reflected against both converging walls. Slowly, inevitably, he sets the stool down firmly at the foot of the post. He climbs up, fixes the noose about his neck, and pushes the stool away with his feet. The stage darkens. Two crossing beams of light are focused on his hanging body. His leg trembles spasmodically as he dies.

Mysteriously, the walls of the garret fall back and the night sky line of Paris is seen in the distance. The room is illumined by the light of the city. A woman wearing the white mask of death enters on the left from over the roof-tops. Her arm points forward. As if by her command, the boy's body stirs. He releases the noose and slides down the post to stand beside her. The strange figure removes her mask and places it on the boy's face. Her own face is revealed as the face of the girl he loved. The girl points forward, and the boy moves magically through the wall before her. As the curtain falls, the two are seen moving against the rooftops of the dark sky line.

*Le Jeune Homme et la Mort* was revived for Mikhail Baryshnikov and Bonnie Mathis by American Ballet Theatre at the City Center, New York, 1975.

# JEUX (Games)

*Ballet in one act. Music by Claude Debussy. Choreography by Vaslav Nijinsky. Book by Vaslav Nijinsky. Scenery and costumes by Léon Bakst. First presented by Diaghilev's Ballets Russes at the Théâtre des Champs-Élysées, Paris, May 15, 1913, with Tamara Karsavina, Vaslav Nijinsky, and Ludmilla Shollar. First presented in the United States by Ballet Theatre at the Center Theatre, New York, April 23, 1950, in a new choreographic version by William Dollar, with Nora Kaye, Igor Youskevitch, and Norma Vance. Scenery and costumes by David Ffolkes.*

For his second ballet, the famous dancer Vaslav Nijinsky chose a modern subject. Today, when we are accustomed to ballets about garden parties (*Lilac Garden*) and sailors on liberty (*Fancy Free*), the new ballet without a modern subject is a rarity, but in 1913 the opposite was the case. Nijinsky was the first choreographer to create a ballet related to the modern world. His subject is love as it is revealed in a tennis game.

The curtain rises on a formal garden of a large estate. The sky is dark-blue; it is almost night. A tennis ball bounces onto the stage, and after it comes a young man leaping in pursuit. He is dressed in tennis clothes and carries a tennis racket, but is clearly somewhat bored with the game. He searches half-heartedly for the ball and welcomes the distraction of two girls who enter the garden. With the approach of night they, too, have left off a game of tennis.

The boy begins to flirt with the girls, at first casually, then more seriously. He dances with them playfully, as if he were continuing with each of them a game of tennis. After he has partnered the two girls singly, he dances with both of them together. He lies down on the grass between them and then, rising, touches their faces tenderly.

Now the boy does not know which girl to choose. He wants both; both are beautiful. The girls long for him to make a choice, but at the same time know how unhappy such a choice will make one of them.

Another tennis ball bounces in from the nearby court. The boy leaps to retrieve it, and the girls follow him as he abandons the game of love for tennis.

NOTES *Jeux* has been restored to the modern repertory in a production by John Taras for the New York City Ballet. The ballet, with choreography by Mr. Taras to Nijinsky's original libretto, was first presented at the New York State Theatre on April 28, 1966, with Edward Villella, Allegra Kent, and Melissa Hayden. Scenery and costumes were by Raoul Pène du Bois, lighting by Jules Fisher, and the costumes were executed by Karinska. Writing about the ballet in the New York *Times*, Clive Barnes said that the choreographer "has managed to sustain the mood of a hot summer evening, where secrets are told and emotional corners turned, one of those evenings with thunder in the air . . . Interestingly, the one major change Mr. Taras has made in the Nijinsky scenario is to make the relationship between the girls more serious than in the original . . . While flirtation still abounds, the relationship of the girls is no longer merely flippant."

For a full understanding of this ballet of Nijinsky's, the account in Richard Buckle's biography of the dancer-choreographer and that in Lincoln Kirstein's *Nijinsky Dancing* are recommended.


# JEWELS

*Ballet in three parts. Music by Gabriel Fauré, Igor Stravinsky, and Peter Ilyich Tchaikovsky. Choreography by George Balanchine. Costumes by Karinska. Scenery by Peter Harvey. Lighting by Ronald Bates. First presented by the New York City Ballet at the New York State Theatre, April 13, 1967, with Violette Verdy and Conrad Ludlow; Mimi Paul and Francisco Moncion; Patricia McBride, Edward Villella, and Patricia Neary; and Suzanne Farrell and Jacques d'Amboise in the leading roles.*

This is a dance ballet in three parts to music by three different composers. The music for the three parts is very different and so are the dances. The dancers for each part of the ballet are dressed like jewels, emeralds for Fauré, rubies for the Stravinsky, and diamonds for the Tchaikovsky. (I thought of using sapphires, too, and had Schoenberg in mind, but the color of sapphires is hard to get across on stage.) The idea for a new ballet using jeweled costumes came about some years ago when my friend Nathan Milstein introduced me to Claude Arpels, the jeweler. I saw later the splendid stones in his collection in New York. Of course I have always liked jewels; after all, I am an Oriental, from Georgia in the Caucasus. I like the color of gems, the beauty of stones, and it was wonderful to see how our costume workshop, under Karinska's direction, came so close to the quality of the real stones (which were of course too heavy for the dancers to wear!).

The first part, "Emeralds," is arranged to music by Fauré, from *Pelléas et Mélisande* and *Shylock*. It is danced by two leading couples, three soloists, and a *corps de ballet* of ten girls. There is first of all a *pas de deux* to soft, melodious strings with eight girls accompanying, then a variation for a girl to light, lilting music. This is followed by a dance by the other leading girl. There is a *pas de trois* and then to music of muted strings another *pas de deux*, quiet and alone. All the dancers join in the finale.

To try to describe for you the dances themselves would be boring, for they have no literary content at all. I suppose if this part of the ballet can be said to represent anything at all, it is perhaps an evocation of France, the France of elegance, comfort, dress, perfume.

Others seem to have found the second part, "Rubies," representative of America. I did not have that in mind at all. It is simply Stravinsky's music, which I have always liked and which he and I agreed to use, arranged for a leading couple, a soloist, and a *corps de ballet* of girls and boys. The couple and the soloist alternate in leading the ensemble.

Stravinsky's *Capriccio for Piano and Orchestra* was first performed in 1929, with the composer as soloist. The work is in three movements, *Presto, Andante rapsodico*, and *Allegro capriccioso ma tempo giusto*. In naming this piano concerto *Capriccio*, Stravinsky relates in his *Chronicle* that he was thinking of definitions of a *capriccio* given by Praetorius: "he regarded it as a synonym of the *fantasia* which was a free form made up of *fugato* instrumental passages."

"Diamonds," the final part of the ballet, is danced to Tchaikovsky's *Symphony No. 3 in D major*, which has five movements. I did not use the first movement, which is not really suitable for dancing, and concentrated on the remaining four, which include two scherzos, a slow movement, and a superb polonaise. This ballet is arranged for a girl and her partner, a group of soloists, and a large *corps de ballet*. The movements are marked: 2. *Alla tedesca, Allegro moderato a semplice*; 3. *Andante elagiaco*; 4. *Scherzo, Allegro vivo*; and 5. Finale: *Allegro con fuoco (tempo de Polacca)*. The first is danced by twelve girls and two soloists, the second is a *pas de deux* for the two principals, the third an ensemble with variations for the two principals, and the finale a polonaise for the entire group of thirty-four dancers.

Dancers in our ballets are always changing and sometimes I change the dances, too. April 30, 1976, I made some new ones for the "Emeralds" part of *Jewels*. Violette Verdy and Jean-Pierre Bonnefous were the dancers.

# JINX

*Ballet in one act. Choreography by Lew Christensen. Music by Benjamin Britten (Variations on a Theme by Frank Bridge). Scenery by James Stewart Morcom. Costumes by Felipe Fiocca. First presented by Dance Players at the National Theatre, New York, April 24, 1942, with Janet Reed, Lew Christensen, and Conrad Linden in principal roles. Revised and presented by the New York City Ballet at the City Center, New York, November 24, 1949, with Janet Reed, Francisco Moncion, and Herbert Bliss in leading roles.*

*Jinx* is a dramatic ballet about superstition, in particular a superstition that comes to dominate the lives of performers in a small circus troupe. The setting for the ballet is simple. Two white poles on either side of the stage reach up toward the center of an invisible tent. The back curtains are drawn aside slightly for an entrance to the circus ring. Gaily colored performing boxes stand in a pile on the left, and in the center of the stage, on top of one of these boxes, stands a young girl dressed in pink. Sitting at her feet is a young bareback rider who obviously admires her. He takes the girl's hands and turns her in arabesque slowly, as if they were performing before a quiet but attentive imaginary audience. He lifts her down, and the two change places. From above, he supports the girl as she continues her modest display. Then he pulls her up to him, and they embrace warmly but gently. They sit together for a moment, and the boy goes off.

A clown enters on the right and watches the girl. She does not notice his presence, but it is apparent that he, too, admires her. He dances for a moment, assuming attitudes that make him appear grimly sad, rather than pathetic. The girl gets up to leave, the clown approaches her, and she accidentally runs into him. He catches her before she can fall and holds her in his arms, but only for an instant, for the girl breaks away in terror at this intimacy and runs off. Two men, the ringmaster of the troupe and one of the wire walkers, have come in quietly and observed this scene with interest.

Three girls enter as these men turn and leave the ring. Two of the girls are bareback riders and they go through a rehearsal of their act. The grotesque clown joins the wire walker and the boy whom we saw first on the stage, and the three men turn cartwheels in a vigorous athletic routine. In the middle of one of their tricks, the clown bumps into the boy and he falls. The wire walker helps him up and looks long and suspiciously at the clown. From this point on, the clown is Jinx to the whole troupe.

The ringmaster runs in, and, at a flourish of his whip, the company goes into an ensemble dance. They all exit, and through the entrance to the ring walk three girls in long capes. Their backs are to the audience. One by one, they turn and perform brief specialty numbers. The first girl drops her cape, to be revealed as the Tattooed Lady; the second is the muscled Strong Lady; and the third girl, the Bearded Lady, conceals her face as long as possible with a large orange ostrich feather. They dance together briefly, put their capes back on as if they were great ladies, and walk off in a stately fashion.

Next the bareback riders put on their act. The ringmaster stands in the center, and around and around him the two girls and the boy ride their imaginary horses. They finish and bow. Now Jinx is rolled in on a wheelbarrow, where he sits smelling a bouquet of rotten flowers and vegetables. The wire walker presents parasols to his two female partners, and in a straight line across the stage each does a turn on an imaginary wire. The lovely young girl in pink displays her skill first. Jinx climbs up on the boxes to watch her performance more closely. The girl is nervous at his nearness, but finds reassurance in the presence of the boy she loves, who stands at the other end of the wire. Jinx cannot take his eyes off her; after each of the wire walkers has done a turn and the three have begun their finale, his attention grows intense. Suddenly the girl slips and begins to fall. She is caught in the nick of time, and Jinx rushes to comfort her. He touches her, and the frightened girl jerks away from him. The bareback rider takes up the ringmaster's whip and chases Jinx out of the ring.

Now the entire troupe is thrown into confusion and terror. Jinx runs in. The boy is cracking the whip close behind him. They run around the group at top speed until Jinx stumbles and falls. The boy brings his whip down on him, lashing the clown over and over again to rhythmic chords from the orchestra. The troupe steps back and turns away in horror as the clown curls up in agony, straightens out, and, with a final spasmodic tremble, dies. The Bearded Lady comes to him and grieves for him in a slow dance that reveals her pathetic attachment. The Tattooed Lady and the Strong Lady try to comfort her, but she is inconsolable. The boy brings in the wheelbarrow, and when Jinx is placed on it, the troupe forms a procession. They march slowly behind the body, bowing their heads rhythmically. When they have placed the body high up on the boxes, the Bearded Lady collapses and all bow their heads.

The music now becomes ghostly. The company senses that something is wrong and turns to look at the body. It is not there. They separate the boxes and take them down, but Jinx has disappeared. As they gesticulate in astonishment, Jinx enters from the other side of the stage, where they cannot see him. He walks stealthily to pick up the forgotten whip and cracks it at the feet of the boy. Everyone turns and steps back in fright. Jinx follows them and, cracking the whip in the center of the ring, forces them to dance around him. He urges them to dance faster and faster, and gradually the whole troupe collapses from exhaustion. Jinx then revives them with a beseeching gesture, and all leave the stage but the boy and the girl. The boy holds the girl up and lifts her high over his head, but she cannot stand by herself. She stands on point for a moment, but falls forward over his supporting arm in an attitude of complete and pathetic helplessness. The boy himself loses his strength and dies. Jinx takes the girl's hands to claim her, but at his touch she, too, expires, falling across her lover's body. The rest of the circus troupe has come in and looks on this scene with dread. The clown turns and stares at them intently without moving. A jinx is something you cannot kill, he seems to say, and the curtain falls slowly.

# JIVE

*Music by Morton Gould. Choreography by Eliot Feld. Costumes by Wilma Kim. Lighting by Jennifer Tipton. Conducted by Seymour Lipkin. Clarinet solo: David Weber. First presented by the Joffrey City Center Ballet at the City Center, New York, February 21, 1973.*

The name of the ballet and its four parts—*Warm-up, Blues, Rag,* and *Ride-out* —says all that needs to be said in words about a new dance piece that mirrors not only its music—Morton Gould's *Derivations for Clarinet and Band*—but aspects of the world as young people are observed in it. The light is bright at the start as eight couples in brilliantly dyed shirts and tights/stockings warm up in tennis shoes. There is a kind of challenge in the air. Team against team. After a romantic blues piece for three couples in a cool, impassioned dance, the mood brightens to a syncopated *Rag* for three other couples. The finale, *Ride-out,* for the whole company, features mock heroics to the clarinet and knees set vibrating by the music. The dancers shout exultantly at the end.

NOTES   Writing in *The Village Voice*, the critic Deborah Jowitt said that *Ride-out* "is the best moment in the ballet—a phrase with quaking knees, a rock to one side, a big scooping leg gesture that leads into a turn, and I forget what else. It looks wonderful, as if the dancers are trying to keep their balance, and their cool, on a slippery log."

After the premiere, Clive Barnes wrote in the New York *Times*:

"Mr. Feld's use of rhythm is subtle and humorous, and he has never been so happy with it as here. He takes Mr. Gould's lightly jazzy music, and rides it out with dances of remarkable fluency. It is almost like an improvisation, except that improvisations are rarely lucky enough to look like improvisations.

"Mr. Feld has not worked very much in the jazz-dance idiom before, but here he does show a new talent.

"The dancing was very hip and hep. Pamela Nearhoof, who is really becoming a most interesting dancer, had her best chance so far. And, dancing with Christian Holder, especially in the 'Blues' section, she had a lovely and flip elegance. She moves her hips beautifully, and has a lovely slow smile.

"In addition to these two—for Mr. Holder is also exuberantly effective— probably Rebecca Wright and Gregory Huffman were the most prominent, and they were both joyous and relaxed. But the whole company does this sneakers tribute to time past with a Saturday-night high school gymnasium fervor. The dancers pick up Mr. Feld's style and carry it."

# JOB

*Masque for dancing in eight scenes. Music by Ralph Vaughan Williams. Choreography by Ninette de Valois. Book by Geoffrey Keynes. Scenery and costumes by Gwendolen Raverat. Wigs and masks by Hedley Briggs. First presented by Camargo Society at the Cambridge Theatre, London, July 5, 1931, with Anton Dolin as Satan and Stanley Judson as Elihu. First presented in the United States by the Sadler's Wells Ballet at the Metropolitan Opera House, New York, November 2, 1949, with scenery and costumes by John Piper. Robert Helpmann was Satan and Alexis Rassine was Elihu.*

The subtitle of this ballet, *Being Blake's Vision of the Book of Job,* tells us that this "masque for dancing" is based on the *Illustrations to the Book of Job* that William Blake published in 1825. The ballet's book is based directly on Blake's twenty-one engravings, as is its music; and the choreography, in its groupings and tableaux, aims at a projection of Blake's imagination into the theatre.

SCENE ONE   Before a decorative back cloth Job sits with his family in a group on the right. With him are his wife, his seven sons, and three daughters. Job is content, materially prosperous, with no complaint in the world. He and his wife watch as his children—first the boys, then the girls, then all together—perform a light pastoral dance which symbolizes in its ordered balance and harmony the respect and love that bind the family together.

Night begins to fall. The family gathers about Job, and he gives thanks on this day for his earthly blessings. His children pray with him. There is no servility in their attitude toward their father. Prayer is natural to them as it is to him. Job and his wife bid the children good night, and the parents are left alone. They sleep.

Satan enters. His spirit hovers over Job and his wife, and their sleep is disturbed. Satan invokes evil dreams for this good man and his wife, appealing to heaven that Job's faith be tested. As Satan makes his appeal, heaven is depicted before us by a broad, high flight of steps at the top of which sits the Godhead, Job's spiritual self. The children of God dance before the Godhead, moving between him and Satan, who rests below. The Godhead gestures toward Satan, to include him in his family, but Satan will not be one of them. He proposes to Job's spiritual self that Job's material self be tested by temptation. The Godhead consents, and Satan, satisfied, leaves the scene, which darkens as the children of God pay homage to their king.

SCENE TWO   When the lights come up, the scene again is heaven. Satan is alone, standing before the throne of the Godhead. Delighted with the opportunity to tempt the faithful Job, he commences a triumphant dance, demoniac in its impudent power, frightening in its strength. His dance over, he leaps to the throne. His leg coils beneath him and he looks out over the scene gloatingly. We think of Milton's lines:

High on a Throne of Royal State, which far
Outshon the wealth of Ormus and of Ind,
Or where the gorgeous East with richest hand
Showrs on her Kings Barbaric Pearl and Gold,
Satan exalted sat . . .

The children of Job enter, observe Satan in his exaltation, and gather together in a group, anticipating the trouble to come.

SCENE THREE   We return to the first scene, but now we see Job's family as Satan would wish us to see it. Job's sons and their wives and his daughters are wining and dining in an evil bacchanal, yielding to temptations of the flesh. Satan descends from the throne he has usurped and kills the children of Job.

SCENE FOUR   Now we see enacted the terrible dreams that Satan causes Job and his wife to experience in their sleep. Visions of war, pestilence, and famine appear to torment the God-fearing pair.

SCENE FIVE   Satan's worst is yet to come. Three messengers come to Job and dance before him. They inform him of the death of his children and the loss of all his material goods. Satan enters briefly to warn Job of his end and disappears. Three Comforters, insidious creatures of Satan, replace their leader and attempt to insinuate themselves into Job's confidence. They pretend at first to be sympathetic, to grieve with him over his loss, then they rail at him. Job cannot contain his grief and cannot understand that these things can be visited upon him. He rebels, as if crying out, "Let the day perish wherein I was born." He appeals to heaven, but when heaven opens before him, he sees Satan on the throne. Dark angels are gathered about Satan.

SCENE SIX   A handsome young man, Elihu, pure and beautiful in his simple holiness, appears to Job and in a dance indicates to the old man his error in accusing God of injustice. Job comes to see that he has done wrong and comprehends his sin of complacent materialism. Elihu is kind to him. Again Job appeals to heaven, and this time he sees the Godhead on the throne, surrounded by angels.

SCENE SEVEN   Satan reappears before the throne of the Godhead, claiming that Job has failed the test and demanding the fruits of his victory over him. The Godhead orders Satan to come to him. As he draws near to the throne, Satan kneels and kisses his flowing robe. The Godhead will not endure this absurd flattery. He extends his arm, and Satan rises to fall back, full-length, down the great flight of steps tumbling into darkness.

SCENE EIGHT   Again, as in Scene One, Job and his family rest together, but this time—in realization of spiritual, rather than material, wealth—Job blesses his wife and his children with new meaning.

# JOURNAL

*Music by Burt Alcantara. Choreography by Louis Falco. Décor and costumes by William Katz. First presented by the Netherlands Dance Theatre at the Royal Theatre, The Hague, October 27, 1971. First presented in the*

*United States by the same ensemble at the Brooklyn Academy of Music, New York, March 30, 1972.*

*Journal* is a dance narrative with music and words, a collage with a new dimension. The words, like news headlines or quick entries in a diary, punctuate the action, rising over and above the music and the action, sometimes reflecting the action, sometimes calling attention to a complementary feeling or situation; they do not literally describe it or cogitate it; like *Strange Interlude*, they accompany the action. The action is about men and women and what they seem to mean to each other and what they might really mean. The dance endeavors to expose, often comically, actual situations that are concealed from the participants, sometimes by themselves.

NOTES  Deborah Jowitt in the *Village Voice* wrote of *Journal:* "The dancers engage in monologues, dialogues, bouts of screaming. Some of the material is autobiographical, and it's all angry. Much of the movement is casual, scrambling. Some of it more formal—non-specific but colored by the arguments and flung by dancers at other dancers as if it were cursing. Many of the dialogues have to do with male-female bickering, and in one extremely effective final scene between one couple, other dancers stand for the possessions that she is taking with her when she leaves. The dancers stumble off with her like good little animals. The dance is scraps of human hostility jumbled together, spilling out of the bright, bitter little games Falco has set them. Grownups on a playground, using the swings to bash each other. . . ."

# THE JUDGMENT OF PARIS

*Music by Kurt Weill. Choreography by Antony Tudor. Scenery and costumes by Hugh Laing. First presented by the London Ballet at the Westminster Theatre, London, June 15, 1938, with Therese Langfield as Juno, Agnes de Mille as Venus, Charlotte Bidmead as Minerva, Antony Tudor as the Client, and Hugh Laing as the Waiter. First presented in the United States by Ballet Theatre at the Center Theatre, New York, January 20, 1940. Scenery and costumes by Lucinda Ballard. Viola Essen as Juno, Agnes de Mille as Venus, Lucia Chase as Minerva, and Antony Tudor and Hugh Laing.*

This is a comic ballet on a classic theme. Using music from Kurt Weill's *Threepenny Opera*, the choreographer has made a clip joint the scene of a modern version of the judgment of Paris, on who was the most beautiful goddess, Juno, Venus, or Minerva. A besotted customer arrives at a sleazy bar. Three ladies of the evening try to ensnare him, each doing her own dance. Although, like Paris, he prefers Venus in the end, he is too drunk to give her a proper prize. The ladies and the waiter pounce upon his wallet as he passes out.

*The Judgment of Paris* has been in the active repertory of the Ballet Rambert for many years, and is regularly presented on its programs of Tudor ballets that also include *Lilac Garden, Dark Elegies,* and *Gala Performance,* other works originally created by the choreographer with this company.

## KETTENTANZ

*Music by Johann Strauss and Johann Simon Mayer. Choreography by Gerald Arpino. Costumes by Joe Eula. Lighting by Thomas R. Skelton. First presented by the City Center Joffrey Ballet at the City Center, New York, October 20, 1971.*

*Kettentanz* (Chain Dance) is a ballet of six couples who begin the piece, hands joined, to a vigorous *galop* by Strauss. It is Strauss's music (and a finale by his contemporary Johann Mayer) that gives the ballet its character, although it is used here through no sentimental screen of Old Vienna. It is, rather, the zest and energy of the polkas, galops, and other dances that have been used, with gestures of the past, to show new dances of contemporary interest. There are nine dances in all, performed in an unbroken chain: Strauss's *Gitana Galop, Opus 108; Annen Polka, Opus 137; Erste Kettenbrucke Walzer, Opus 4; Eisele und Beisele Sprunge, Opus 202; Chineser Galop, Opus 21; Seuzer Galop, Opus 9; Hofball Tanze, Opus 51; Cachucha Galop, Opus 97;* and Mayer's *Schnofler Tanz.*

NOTES  Writing in *Dance Magazine,* the critic Doris Hering said that "superlatives are the province of second-rate movie critics, but I can't resist one in connection with Gerald Arpino's *Kettentanz.* It is his loveliest ballet. . . . Arpino has soared blithely above the music to create a suite of tender miniatures, all growing out of an opening chain formation and eventually returning to it with the gleaming casualness of a meadow stream filtering through cluster after cluster of brightly nodding flowers."

In the *Christian Science Monitor,* Nancy Goldner wrote of the dances in *Kettentanz:* "They are . . . purely virtuoso essays. As such they are immensely enjoyable . . . as in a pensive duet for Rebecca Wright and Dermot Burke; a bobbing, sprightly exercise in small and quick footwork for Scott Bernard and Glenn White; and a brilliant *Cachucha Galop* for Susan Magno and Miss Wright, a dance that Fanny Elssler made famous about a century ago. . . ."

Reviewing *Kettentanz* in the *Daily News,* Joseph Gale said that the ballet "is one of Arpino's half-dozen or so neoclassical masterpieces. It is folk—perhaps even countryside—Viennese. . . . It is all ravishing—gay, insouciant, tender, frothy, and as is characteristic of Arpino's works of this genre, bravura."

# KONSERVATORIET (Conservatory)

*Music by H. S. Paulli. Choreography by Auguste Bournonville. First presented by the Royal Danish Ballet at the Royal Theatre, Copenhagen, May 6, 1849. First presented in the United States by the Royal Danish Ballet at the New York State Theatre, 1965. Revived by the City Center Joffrey Ballet at the City Center, New York, February 20, 1969, in a staging by Hans Brenaa, with Barbara Remington, Pamela Johnson, and Paul Sutherland in principal roles. Scenery by William Pitkin.*

Most students of ballet are familiar with the name of the great Danish ballet master, Auguste Bournonville, whose work has been familiar to audiences for 150 years. We know it in the dancing of great stars like Erik Bruhn, who was schooled at the academy set up by Bournonville and who has written a book about it. We know it in the repertory of Bournonville's own Royal Danish Ballet and we know it, too, in fortunate revivals like this one of *Konservatoriet* —which is simply the Danish word for what we mean by conservatory, or a place of study.

The place of study here is a school of ballet, where a ballet master is in charge of a group of brilliant pupils. The dance style of the ballet is what Bournonville learned in France from Auguste Vestris, the *premier danseur* of his time. In the setting of an old Paris ballet studio, with crystal chandelier, covered with cloth to protect it from dust, and to the accompaniment of a violinist (the violin, we realize, was the instrument for ballet classes in those days), we watch a ballet master put his students through their paces.

NOTES   The fact that *Konservatoriet* is, in fact, the first act of a much longer ballet (called *A Proposal of Marriage Through a Newspaper*) need not divert us, for that ballet tells the story of two girls, Elisa and Victorine, who come to Paris for adventures, beginning with the study of ballet. The ballet master prompts them to show their best form and he, too, shows them what he means by form, by dancing a solo of his own.

Writing of *Konservatoriet* in *Ballet Review* in 1969, Henry Haslam described the work's importance for both history and the present: In this particular work, he said, "could be seen the quintessence of the French school. It was choreographed by Bournonville in 1849 from memories of his stay in Paris more than twenty years earlier as a student of the great Vestris, a brilliant dancer in the age of male supremacy in the ballet world. Bournonville taught the French school of Vestris in his classes in Denmark. One of his students, Christian Johannson, went to St. Petersburg, where his teaching combined with the influence of the Italian school, which was then reintroduced to Paris and western Europe in 1909 by the Diaghilev Ballet. This Russian school is the background of many of the great teachers in America today. But the branch of the French school remained in Denmark, cut off from the mainstream of the dance world until the early 1950s.

"Hans Beck, a pupil of Bournonville who succeeded him as director of the company, was responsible for the revival of *Konservatoriet*. Hans Brenaa, who was dancing under Beck, is one of the foremost authorities on Bournonville and staged *Konservatoriet* this year for the City Center Joffrey Ballet. The ballet was originally in two acts, titled *Konservatoriet or A Proposal by Advertisement*. It had a very complicated plot about dancers and their adventures and flirtations in Paris. It is regrettable that the second act did not survive, for in it was a *can-can*, which was probably one of the first times such a dance appeared on a ballet stage. Only the first act remains, in which the ballet master, Victorine, and Elisa are introduced—the leading roles which still use the names but have lost their distinct characterizations. The scene is a ballet studio, with the ballet master conducting a class that contains a series of *enchaînements* which are exacting both technically and stylistically.

"I was delighted that an American company had obtained *Konservatoriet* for its repertoire, and I applauded Robert Joffrey, artistic director of the City Center Joffrey Ballet, for his decision to have the ballet staged for his company by Brenaa, who is a fine teacher and coach. The dancers were privileged to be able to work with him in a style and technique not part of their background."

## LADY FROM THE SEA

*Music by Knudage Riisager. Choreography by Birgit Cullberg. Costumes and scenery by Kerstin Hedeby. Lighting by Jean Rosenthal. First presented by Ballet Theatre at the Metropolitan Opera House, New York, April 20, 1960, with Lupe Serrano, Royes Fernandez, and Glen Tetley in the leading roles.*

Inspired by Ibsen's play of the same name, *Lady from the Sea* tells the story of Ellida, who loves a sailor. The sailor leaves her and returns to sea. After much soul-searching, Ellida marries a widower, father of two daughters, but feels miserable in her new home. She dreams that she rejoins her sailor-lover at the bottom of the sea. When the sailor actually returns, her husband offers Ellida her freedom, but she does not leave him. The truth is, the sailor, like the sea, represents for her a romantic yearning, an escape from reality.

## LAMENT OF THE WAVES

*Music by Gérard Masson. Choreography by Frederick Ashton. Costumes by Derek Rencher. Projection sphere by Bill Culbert. Lighting by William Bundy. First presented by the Royal Ballet at the Royal Opera House, Covent Garden, London, February 9, 1970, with Marilyn Trounson and Carl Myers.*

The theme of this dramatic dance for a girl and a boy is stated by the choreographer, Frederick Ashton: "Two young lovers are drowned." What we see in

THE LEAVES ARE FADING

the ballet is not only the act of drowning but the reliving in their last moments of the love that has bound the lovers together. Projections and other intricacies of modern stagecraft are used to give an undersea setting. The music is the *Dans le Deuil des vagues* of Gérard Masson.

The English critic Peter Williams wrote in *Dance and Dancers* magazine after the premiere: "As you drown your whole life passes before you. . . . There they are, two lovers gradually floating down to the seabed with their movements already following the undulations, and caught up in the eddies, of the swirling waters. In the flickering shafts of submarine light they recall their love for each other. When they first sink to the floor of the sea they are separated; gradually they reach for each other and then in a series of comings-together they re-enact their moments of tenderness, of passion and of occasional antagonism until they become conscious of a vast flickering sea anemone shape, sinisterly emerging from the glooms, which brings realization of their lack of infinity. They lie down and tremulous waters descend to cover them forever."

## THE LEAVES ARE FADING

*Music by Antonin Dvořák. Choreography by Antony Tudor. Scenery by Ming Cho Lee. Costumes by Patricia Zipprodt. Lighting by Jennifer Tipton. First presented by American Ballet Theatre at the New York State Theatre, Lincoln Center, New York, July 17, 1975, with Kim Highton, Marianna Tcherkassky, Amy Blaisdell, Nanette Glushak, Linda Kuchera, Kristine Elliott, Hilda Morales, Elizabeth Ashton, Christine O'Neill, Michael Owen, Raymonda Serrano, Charles Ward, Richard Schafer, Clark Tippet, Gelsey Kirkland, and Jonas Kage. Conducted by Akira Endo.*

While *The Leaves Are Fading* appears to be a danced recollection of a time past, it soon becomes clear that it might become a future time, too; it is a dance ballet with a definitive program; its inventiveness permits alternative views on final meanings. The music of the piece consists of selections from little-known works by Dvořák: the *Cypresses,* or *Evening Songs;* and other chamber music for strings written in the 1880s, the *String Quartet,* Op. 77, the *String Quartet,* Op. 80, and part of his *Terzetto.*

The critic George Jackson has called this ballet an E. M. Forster novella. The frame of the action of the dance is far simpler than what follows. We are in a wood after summer but before the autumn, when the leaves begin to fade but before they fall. A branch overhead to the right bears leaves that are still dominantly green but give signs of changing with the season. The background of heavy green is also tinged with brown. A woman walks into this wood, a mature person in a long green summer dress. She looks about slowly; we know she is in familiar surroundings. She walks across the scene with a faint kind of recollective introspection and regret and seems to retreat into its shadows. The dancers who follow are perhaps shadows of her own past.

First girls come, eight of them, then four boys, and there is an ensemble of pastoral creatures under a fading sun. There are varying combinations, a young couple dancing in a state of real joy that quiets down a bit, later a brilliant dance by a boy, followed by another ensemble. All of the dancers appear to know each other; the world they inhabit seems to be familiar and the knowing smiles and gestures they make are friendly without being insistent or flirtatious. The girls and boys seem to have special commitments the others acknowledge.

A new girl enters now to dance with a boy to expansively lyric music. The two lovers are so content in their lively, mutual joy that the dance does not pause for sentimental gestures or declarations. Yet there is no rush. The dramatic lifts and large, expressive movements that follow often stop suddenly for thoughtfulness. The entire *pas de deux* appears to be inner-directed, an expression of rapturous feeling rather than a display of brilliantly executed lyricism. Other couples enter. The girl hesitates; she wants to touch the boy's face, but then she notices others are present.

After an ensemble another *pas de deux* follows. This third pair of lovers dance their own tender commitment, a dance brief but full, too, of effulgent happiness. At the close of their dance, the girl greets another girl who has just come in. She and her partner celebrate their love in a dance that seems to seize on every passing moment. The leaves are fading . . .

In the music for the ensuing ensemble there are certain hints of warning, yet tempered joy dominates. The light darkens. The lovers return, there is a kind of leave-taking, and the woman in green who began the piece comes back. She carries now a red nosegay, looks about the scene again, and, her memories refreshed, goes away.

After the premiere of *The Leaves Are Fading*, the English critic Alexander Bland wrote in *The Observer* that one of American Ballet Theatre's triumphs was "to mount a new Tudor ballet after many years, *The Leaves Are Fading*. Characteristically it was totally uncharacteristic—neither enigmatic nor dramatic but gently charming and lyrical in a wistful English way. To a tuneful Dvořák score young people meet and flirt and part, visions in the memory of an older woman. Deft and fluent, it opens up a fascinating and promising new Tudor vein."

## LEGEND OF LOVE

*Ballet in three acts. Music by Arif Melikoff. Libretto by Nazim Hikmet. Choreography by Yuri Grigorovich. Scenery and costumes by Simon Virsaladze. First presented at the Kirov State Theatre of Opera and Ballet, Leningrad, 1961.*

ACT ONE, SCENE ONE: A ROOM IN THE PALACE OF QUEEN MEKHMENEH BAHNU The queen's youngest sister, Princess Shyrin, is mortally ill and the queen, her attendants, and the vizier are in despair. Warriors usher in a stranger who claims he can cure the princess. When the vizier offers him gold and the queen her crown if he will cure Shyrin, the stranger says no; he demands only that the queen shall sacrifice her beauty to save her sister. She consents and the stranger restores the princess to health. When she rises from the bed she does not recognize her sister the queen, whose face has become disfigured.

ACT ONE, SCENE TWO: THE GARDEN OF THE PALACE  A group of artisans, among them a young painter in blue named Ferkhad, are decorating an arch in the garden when the queen, her face now veiled, and the princess enter at the end of a long procession. They are both attracted at once by Ferkhad, and the procession halts as he dances for them. But the vizier orders the work to proceed. The royal attendants dance an ensemble, Ferkhad then emerges alone and the princess calls to him. They are irresistibly drawn to each other and dance a *pas de deux* of mutual praise and joy in which the boy never touches the princess. For he has learned that he has given his heart to a princess and that it is hopeless for him, a humble artisan, to aspire to her hand. She leaves and he lies in the garden, yearning for her.

ACT TWO, SCENE ONE  The people of the country, who stand around a spring which has run dry, lament the lack of water in the kingdom. A high mountain must be cut through to bring water to the valley from upland streams, but the task is beyond human effort. Water is brought from afar, but only for the palace, where the queen is tormented by her passion for Ferkhad.

ACT TWO, SCENE TWO  The court jester tries to distract the queen, who sits alone. The veiled figure, her body splendid and beautiful, rises and dances in despair. Her face has been disfigured to secure her sister's life and she knows that her love will never be returned by Ferkhad.

ACT TWO, SCENE THREE: SHYRIN'S ROOM  Ferkhad enters and he and the princess dance together passionately. The princess decides that she cannot leave her lover and resolves to leave the palace and follow him. Learning of the flight, the vizier informs the queen, who at once orders the lovers to be seized and brought back. Warriors overtake the couple. The princess begs her sister not to separate them but the queen is unrelenting. She holds out one hopeless possibility: that if Ferkhad will succeed in cutting an opening into the mountain so that water might come to the valley, then may Shyrin be his wife.

ACT THREE: THE MOUNTAINS  Alone at night, Ferkhad, exhausted from work, imagines that he has succeeded in his task and that water gushes from the mountain. In the flowing water he fancies he sees his beloved. Back in her chamber at the palace, Mekhmeneh Bahnu has lost her peace of mind. In her fevered fantasy, she sees herself as lovely as she was only a short time ago and finds that Ferkhad loves her. But her sister runs into the room, shattering her dream. The princess implores the queen to go with her into the mountains to Ferkhad.

Hope has brought the people to the mountains. If Ferkhad accomplishes his task, their sufferings will end! The queen and Shyrin arrive. Ferkhad is joyous and he and the princess are happy for a brief time. They think that the queen will permit her to remain with him. But the queen is crafty and says that her sister can remain only if Ferkhad abandons the task she has set him. But Ferkhad knows that it is impossible for him to betray the hopes that the people have in him. Shyrin understands this, too. The two lovers dance a *pas de deux* of farewell and part forever.

## THE LESSON (*see* THE PRIVATE LESSON)

## LIEBESLIEDER WALZER

*Music by Johannes Brahms. Choreography by George Balanchine. Scenery by David Hays. Costumes by Karinska. First presented by the New York City Ballet at the City Center, New York, November 22, 1960, with Diana Adams, Melissa Hayden, Jillana, Violette Verdy, Bill Carter, Conrad Ludlow, Nicholas Magallanes, and Jonathan Watts.*

"Brahms and waltzes! The two words stare at each other in positive amazement on the elegant title page of the score. The earnest, silent Brahms, a true younger brother of Schumann, and just as north German, Protestant, and unworldly as he—writing waltzes!" So wrote the music critic Eduard Hanslick when Brahms published his first group of *Liebeslieder Walzer* in 1869. Brahms had written them during his first year in Vienna and they were so successful that five years later he wrote a new series. They have been popular ever since, in the concert hall and in the home but most of all at home, for this music for piano, four-hands, and a quartet of voices was perhaps designed for the pleasure of performers. All the *Liebeslieder Walzer* performed together last about an hour, which is a very long time to hold an audience's attention in the theater, especially if the music is all in three-quarter time. But I felt I had to do dances, set to this music. And the music would seem to me the best preparation one can have for watching the dances, unless one wants simply to be naturally surprised at what might happen. What happens on stage is dancing and gesture and music. The setting is a ballroom of an earlier time. There are small tables with candles at the side. A piano stands on the left, a man and a girl in evening dress sit down to play and four singers join them. Four couples in formal dress stand in this ballroom. As the music starts, they begin to dance. The music is a waltz in slow time, the words are about love. The waltz does not last long. Neither does the second, which is more vigorous. It is sung first by the baritone and is then taken up by the other singers. Two couples dance this one, as the others watch. And so it goes, one waltz after another, all different, for changing combinations of voices, for changing couples, for changing aspects of love.

Sometimes friends ask me why we do not print the words to all of these long songs in the program so that everyone will understand the original German. I always answer that the words really have nothing to do with the dances; to print them would suggest that the dances were illustrations and I never had that in mind.

After the eighteenth waltz and the end of Brahms's first group of *Liebeslieder*, the curtain comes down for a few minutes. When it rises again, there is a new setting, still a ballroom, but one without walls and illumined by the stars. The dancers are dressed differently, too, in costumes for ballet dancing. The atmosphere here is more theatrical, if you like, than the intimacy of the first part. So, I think, is the music.

At the end, after fourteen waltzes, the dancers leave the stage. The last song is to words by Goethe:

> Nun, ihr Musen, genug!
> Vergebens strebt ihr zu schildren
> Wie sich Jammer und Gluck
> Wechseln in liebender Brust

(*Now, Muses, enough! You try in vain to portray how misery and happiness alternate in a loving heart.*)

As these words are sung, the dancers come back and listen. That is all.
The words ought to be listened to in silence.


## LIEUTENANT KIJÉ

*Music by Sergei Prokofiev. Choreography by Alexander Lapauri and Olga Tarasova. Libretto by Andrei Veitsler, Alexander Lapauri, Alexander Misharin, and Olga Tarasova. Scenery and costumes by Boris Messerrer. First presented by the Bolshoi Ballet at the Bolshoi Theatre, Moscow, February 10, 1963.*

The ballet began as a historical anecdote about a nonexistent Lieutenant Kijé appearing in the army lists through the oversight of a court official and brought to life by a flourish of the Tsar Paul's pen. As time went on, promotions and titles were showered on this fictitious character until he rose to the very top rank of the Russian Imperial Army. From this story, Yuri Tynianov, a Soviet writer, devised the plot for a satirical novel. A film of the same name was also produced, with music by Prokofiev, who later made a symphonic suite of his score. The suite and the film music are both used for the ballet.

It is interesting that Prokofiev's music was used by Fokine for his last completed ballet, *Russian Soldier*, presented by Ballet Theatre at the Metropolitan Opera House, New York, April 6, 1942, with Yurek Lazowski in the title role. The ballet was dedicated to the gallant Russian soldiers of World War II.

## LILAC GARDEN

*Dramatic ballet in one act. Music by Ernest Chausson. Choreography by Antony Tudor. Setting and costumes by Hugh Stevenson. First presented by the Rambert Ballet Club at the Mercury Theatre, London, January 26, 1936. Maude Lloyd, Hugh Laing, Peggy van Praagh, and Antony Tudor were the principals. First presented in the United States by Ballet Theatre at the Center Theatre, New York, January 15, 1940, with Viola Essen, Hugh Laing, Karen Conrad, and Antony Tudor in the principal roles.*

This ballet is a tragedy of manners. It portrays the problem of a young woman who is about to marry a man she does not love. The time is the latter part of the Victorian era. It does not occur to the girl that her marriage can be put off: that she can escape from its "convenience." *Lilac Garden* depicts her mute acceptance in the kind of world where confession of any difficulty would be impossible. The drama of the ballet arises from a social situation that seems to demand confession and release.

The name of the girl is Caroline. She is giving a party for all of her friends and relations before the wedding. The scene is a lilac garden; the time is evening. The music is Chausson's *Poème*, for violin and orchestra.

When the curtain rises, Caroline and the man she must marry are standing together in the center of the garden. Giant shrubs of lilac surround the small open space. The light is misty. The girl wears a long white dress and white flowers in her hair. Her fiancé wears a formal suit with a long, formal coat reaching to his knees. There is a boutonnière in his buttonhole. They are a handsome couple, but each is preoccupied; they seem to have nothing to say to each other, no gestures to make. The man looks off to the left as if he were searching for someone. On the right, Caroline's lover enters. As she sees the man she really loves, the girl motions him away. The dark young man in uniform turns away. Caroline takes her fiancé's arm and they walk off, side by side. She glances back over her shoulder as they disappear. Another guest arrives at the party, a woman in a slate-blue dress. This is the former mistress of Caroline's husband-to-be. Other women come onto the scene. Caroline reenters. She greets the newcomer. She does not know that this woman loves her fiancé. Now Caroline is alone. She moves backward toward the right. Her lover emerges; she falls back against him. He slips his arms under hers, and the two begin to dance. Their steps are so in harmony that it is apparent they have danced together many times before. Now the occasion is different. Caroline nervously looks to left and right whenever they pause in motion.

The woman in blue, her back turned, moves ominously across the back of the garden. The boy kisses Caroline's hand. The girl draws her hand back quickly; the woman in blue turns around. Caroline nervously introduces her two guests. Her hand moves to her lips; perhaps she should have kept them apart. The three dance forward together. As soon as she dares, Caroline draws her lover aside, and they dance away. Two men leap onto the stage and exit with the woman in blue.

Caroline re-enters, alone. She dances plaintively to the threnody of the violin's romantic theme. She holds her hand to her forehead in a gesture of hopelessness. As a group of her guests disturb her solitude, the girl moves her hand slightly, pretending that she is smoothing her hair. The melody mounts in intensity. The guests leave as two of the girls are lifted high by their escorts. Caroline pirouettes desperately toward the other side of the garden. Her lover appears while she turns frantically, and he catches her in his arms. He lifts her high above him, then the two kneel together. Then Caroline is afraid, suddenly, and hurries off.

Three couples and a girl come into the garden. Caroline's lover takes the girl for a partner, and the couples separate and bow, preparatory to a formal dance. Caroline disturbs the pattern by entering swiftly and dancing down the line between the couples. She moves off to the right.

The woman in blue joins the couples. She is searching for Caroline's fiancé, her former lover. By common instinct, the other women turn away and leave the garden. The woman bows to Caroline's lover. He turns away and follows the other men off. One man is attracted to the woman and remains until it is apparent that she will not notice him.

Caroline's fiancé steps out into the garden. The woman in blue runs to him, though the man turns aside, afraid to acknowledge her. He catches her as she leaps toward him, and the woman is poised for an instant high over his shoulder, looking down on his head. She has been his mistress, he has loved her, perhaps still does. He wishes to see her, but not here. He releases the woman he has renounced for Caroline, and they move together, mutually fearful of the consequences. The guests rush across the garden, and their rendezvous is interrupted swiftly. In what is apparently a single movement, the woman is lifted high and carried by Caroline's lover as Caroline is caught up in mid-movement by her fiancé.

All the guests dance together in a wide circle, as if nothing had happened. All leave the stage but Caroline and her lover. Her arms are rigid as she falls back into his arms. They dance forward; the music builds to a climax. He lifts the girl up straight and catches her body at full length as he lets her fall. He dips her body gently toward the ground and releases the girl to kneel at her feet.

Two of the older married women at the party see the lovers together. The boy rushes off. One of the women whispers to her companion, revealing Caroline's secret. Now she bows to Caroline. She approaches her softly and takes her hand, and the two move back to the rear of the garden. The woman reassures Caroline by her sympathy for her situation: all women, she suggests, love the man they do not marry. Caroline buries her face in her hands for a frantic instant. This is the first sympathetic advice she has ever received about her lover; she understands, to her horror, the sympathy that she in turn may someday give to someone else. The girl pulls her hands away from her face before she can weep. Caroline walks off.

Her lover re-enters. He gestures after Caroline, his hands clasped before him, hoping. The woman who has befriended Caroline and two other women repeat his gesture, then stand aside with bowed heads as the man sees that he can do nothing. They try to comfort him, but Caroline returns. The women leave the lovers alone. Now the music of the violin piercingly responds to the unhappiness of their passion; their fear that it will be perceived increases. Their ecstasy in being close is destroyed as they turn away from each other curtly and cruelly, lest they be seen. They stand apart, holding hands, as Caroline's fiancé enters. Her lover releases her, and the engaged couple walk away together. Now that all seems to be known, the boy rushes off alone.

The fiancé's former love, the woman in blue, dances into the garden, her movements quick, unyielding, and desperate. She leaves as Caroline and her own lover approach with two other couples. The three couples dance with stilted, subdued steps. The woman in blue tries to approach her lover. Fiercely he motions his former mistress away with his hand. The other couples walk away. He is afraid that Caroline may see, but directly the woman approaches her fiancé, Caroline disappears. The man is desperate: he has lost them both. He follows after the woman in blue, his hand shaking in anxiety.

Caroline and her lover enter and dance frantically, oblivious to their surroundings, and go off together. The entire orchestra takes up the theme of the violin fully. As the music gathers volume, the fiancé enters. The woman in blue leaps to his arms. Caroline and her lover run across the back. When they enter the garden, Caroline's fiancé turns away from the woman in blue and catches Caroline about the waist to lift her high above him. Caroline's arm points straight up over her head; she will not touch him. He lets her down. The other guests have come in; the orchestra sounds the climax of the melody. Caroline's fiancé bends down to kiss her hand. The girl stands beside him in stiff resignation; all movement is frozen: the guests are caught, with the engaged couple, in a tense, frigid tableau.

Caroline is the first to break the spell. Her fiancé stands holding the hand of an imaginary girl as she moves out to her lover; the music subsides. The guests move, the woman in blue approaches the fiancé, and all four lovers move forward in a slow line—Caroline and her lover at either end, reaching out into space. The two couples dance, the rejected lovers moving in unison with Caroline and her husband-to-be. The dresses of the girls flow with their retarded movement.

Suddenly the fiancé walks away. The woman in blue opens her arms. Caroline's lover runs off and returns to present to her a bouquet of lilacs. He kneels and kisses her hand. Caroline holds the flowers listlessly in her hand. Her fiancé returns with her cloak. He places it about her shoulders. The girl in white steps toward her and places her head on Caroline's shoulder in farewell. Caroline gestures to all of her guests, bidding them good-by. The violin mirrors her movement. As she reaches out her hand to her lover, her fiancé draws her hand back to her side. Caroline takes his arm and walks away with the man she must marry. The other guests depart. Her lover remains in the garden, his back turned.

NOTES  *Lilac Garden* was one of the first ballets by the English choreographer and dancer Antony Tudor to be staged in the United States. It immediately became popular and has been so ever since. The New York City Ballet staged a new production of it on November 30, 1951, at the City Center, New York. This production provoked the following remarks from John Martin of the New York *Times: "Lilac Garden,* a modern classic, begins a new phase of its existence with the notable restudying it has received. Antony Tudor has given it back its choreographic substance . . . All its esthetic values have been deepened; so, too, have its emotional values. Nora Kaye, who has danced her role many times, has found new warmth, new womanliness, new quiet eloquence of movement and of spirit, and Tanaquil LeClercq, who has never danced the role of the other woman before, illumines it with electric tensions that are taut and tragic. As a crowning glory, Horace Armistead has provided a setting that actually participates in the drama by its subtly authoritative establishment of the mood and the mores of the action."

Alicia Markova, Nora Kaye, Diana Adams, and Alicia Alonso have all danced the part of Caroline. Maria Tallchief danced the part of the other woman in guest appearances with Ballet Theatre in 1949. Tanaquil LeClercq and Yvonne Mounsey danced it in the New York City Ballet revival. Hugh Laing and Antony Tudor resumed their customary roles in first performances of that revival; Tudor's role was danced later by Brooks Jackson.

Dame Marie Rambert, in whose ballet company *Jardin aux Lilas* (*Lilac Garden*) was created, has recalled its beginnings in her book *Quicksilver:* "Tudor wrote *Jardin aux Lilas* in 1936. The subject was suggested to him by Hugh Stevenson, who did a perfect, though obvious, setting of clumps of lilac bushes and beautiful costumes, very expressive of the various characters. Here is the synopsis as printed in the program: Caroline, on the eve of her marriage to the man she does not love, tries to say farewell to her lover at a garden reception, but is constantly interrupted by guests and in the end goes off on the arm of her betrothed with hopelessness in her eyes. The situation is complicated by the presence of her betrothed's former love.

"The interplay of feelings between these characters was revealed in beautiful dance movements and groupings, with subtle changes of expression, which made each situation clear without any recourse to mime or gesture. It could be called a *'ballet psychologique'* on the same ground as Stendhal's *'roman psychologique.'* It had one quite startling moment: at the height of the drama the movement froze and the music continued alone for several bars. It made you hold your breath. The whole ballet was perfect and has become a classic. Although it had been composed on the small stage of the Mercury, it bore transference to the Metropolitan Opera House in New York. In fact, as I have indicated, those of our Mercury ballets that were good became even better on big stages, because the dancers could take wing after the restricted space of our own stage—and the integrity of the work itself shone the brighter."

## THE LITTLE HUMPBACKED HORSE

*Ballet in three acts. Music by Cesare Pugni. Choreography by Arthur Saint-Léon. First presented at the Bolshoi Theatre, St. Petersburg, December 27, 1864. Revised and presented in a new version at the Bolshoi Theatre, Moscow, 1959. Music by Rodion Shchedrin. Libretto by Vasili Vainonen and Paval Malyarevsky. Choreography by Alexander Radunsky. Sets by Boris Volkiv. First presented in the United States by the Bolshoi Ballet at the Metropolitan Opera with Maya Plisetskaya and Vladimir Vasiliev in the leading roles.*

In the Russian repertory for more than a hundred years, this is one of the first ballets to be based on a Russian theme. It has had two major revisions, the first at the turn of the century, by Gorsky, and a new one with an original score that is now in the Bolshoi repertory.

Vigorous chords begin the overture of rousing music. A piping of pastoral music signals the rise of the curtain.

ACT ONE, SCENE ONE: A HUT   Once upon a time there was a peasant who had three sons, Danila, a clever lad, Gavrila, not so bright, and Ivan, a fool. Ivan is lonely as his brothers play with friends. Alone, he plays on his pipe. His brothers ridicule him. The bearded father enters and though the brothers try to exclude Ivan from what he has to say to them—that they must keep watch for a thief who is stealing their corn—Ivan listens and cares.

ACT ONE, SCENE TWO: A FIELD AT NIGHT   Watching and waiting for the thief, the brothers drink and pass out. In the lovely lonely night Ivan enters. He finds his brothers, throws away their bottle, removes their boots and covers them up. He marvels at the stars. As the night draws on, a whirlwind is heard over the field and with it the neighing of a horse. A white horse with a red mane leaps across the sky. Ivan grabs her waving tail and leaps onto her back. She implores him to let her go free. Ivan agrees and in gratitude she gives him two gold-maned horses and a little one, barely six inches high, with two humps on its back and ears down to the ground. She tells Ivan that he can sell the two large horses but must never part with the humpbacked horse, who will be forever his friend. Suddenly, as firebirds fly overhead, one of them drops a feather, which the little horse warns Ivan not to pick up because of the possible trouble it will bring. Ivan ignores the warning and chases it. The two brothers now return to steal the two golden-maned horses and take them off to market. Ivan returns, cannot believe it. The humpbacked horse is sympathetic, gathers up Ivan's brothers' boots, and takes him off into the sky.

ACT ONE, SCENE THREE: A MARKET   A huge walled castle with church spires looks down upon the market place, where an old violinist plays for dancing. The two brothers enter with their horses. Trumpeters and a drummer herald the arrival of the Tsar, who enters on a dilapidated horse followed by an escort. The Tsar sneezes and descends from his horse, but gets tangled up in his cloak. He sees the horses then and is not so ridiculous after all when he admires them and makes an offer. But Ivan arrives at this point with his little humpbacked horse and explains that he is the owner and will take for them two bags of gold, thank you. He returns his brothers' boots and knocks their heads together. The Tsar shows his crown imperiously and, after he has purchased the two horses, makes Ivan chief of his stables. Obviously no one else can handle these curious horses. The Gentleman of the Bedchamber in the Tsar's entourage is angered by this and vows to avenge himself on Ivan.

ACT TWO, SCENE ONE: THE TSAR'S BEDCHAMBER   Trumpets and a drum roll herald the arrival of the Tsar. He eats and sleeps. A fly settles on his forehead and Ivan is the only one who dares to kill it. This naturally annoys the former head groom. One day a Gentleman of the Bedchamber, anxious to discover how Ivan is looking after the horses, goes to the stables and finds the firebird's feather. He steals it and reports Ivan to the Tsar for hiding such a treasure. The old Tsar is fascinated by the feather and, touching a painting of sea birds with the feather, is astonished that they should come alive. He is so delighted that he decides thus to touch the portrait of the maiden-Tsar. She, too, comes to life, but only long enough for the Tsar to fall in love with her. Then she vanishes. That old Gentleman of the Bedchamber, bent always on Ivan's downfall, swears that Ivan has boasted that he can bring her back. The Tsar summons Ivan and gives him an ultimatum to secure her return. Ivan weeps as the Tsar insists, but his little humpbacked horse consoles him.

ACT TWO, SCENE TWO: A SILVER MOUNTAIN BY THE SEASHORE   The little horse takes Ivan to the Silver Mountain, where at night the maiden-Tsar appears in a silver boat. She dances a long quiet variation. At last, with the help of the little horse, Ivan captures her in the midst of her flurried escort of maids. She tries to hide her face in her hands but Ivan takes them away. He is astonished at her beauty and plays his pipe for her. She dances to his music and then they dance together, but the little horse will not permit them to fall in love and interrupts their rendezvous. He lulls the maiden-Tsar to sleep and Ivan sets off with her on the journey to the palace.

ACT TWO, SCENE THREE: THE TSAR'S BEDCHAMBER   We see the Tsar sitting on a high throne, close to a portrait of the maiden, for whom he pines. An announcement is made, he prepares for the arrival of his beloved. The Tsar begs her to marry him but she won't unless a ring she lost in the ocean can be found in three days. Ivan is ordered to find it. Again it is clear that the maiden loves Ivan and is not moved by the Tsar in any way. When the Tsar at the end tries to snatch her hand, she pulls it away.

ACT THREE, SCENE ONE: THE UNDERWATER KINGDOM   The little horse leads Ivan into the kingdom with a silver moon the maiden has given him. Ivan offers the silver moon to the empress of the water sprites in exchange for the ring. She says that only the perch can find it for him but that he is away. While they look for him, the sea creatures amuse Ivan with dances that embody the liveliness of the water kingdom. Ivan is so pleased that he gets down from his sea shell and dances too. Finally the perch is found and brings up a chest with the ring.

ACT THREE, SCENE TWO: THE TSAR'S PALACE    Peasants carrying a suckling pig and other foods prepare for the Tsar's wedding. The Tsar plays hide-and-seek with the maiden, placing the crown at her feet. Ivan enters, greets her, and presents the Tsar with the ring. The Tsar puts the ring on her finger, but it is perfectly clear that she prefers Ivan. She tells the Tsar that she will not marry him unless he can become young and handsome. The Tsar threatens to cut off Ivan's head. The maiden informs the Tsar that he himself can become young and handsome if he will jump into a caldron of boiling milk. The Tsar says no, Ivan must go first. Ivan, emboldened by the promises of the little horse, says all right, takes off his shirt and jumps in. The Tsar is about to claim the maiden as his own forever when Ivan emerges from the caldron. He is handsomer than ever, the maiden adores him more than ever, and the Tsar is so furious that he jumps into the pot himself. He never comes out. The nobility anxiously peer into the caldron but nothing happens. The poor Tsar has been boiled alive.

ACT THREE, SCENE THREE: THE PALACE    Feted by the people, Ivan and the maiden rejoice in their happiness. They welcome the peasants who encircle them and dance in their midst, she in lyric and folk gestures and then he in a variation that ends at her feet. Now the little humpbacked horse enters and brings flowers to the couple as all hail them. He then flies away into the sky.

NOTES    Reviewing the first performance of this ballet in London in 1963, Andrew Porter wrote in the *Financial Times:* "It seems that Vladimir Vasiliev will conquer London on this Bolshoi visit as decisively as Soloviev did on the Kirov one. It is not just that he moves rapidly, jumps high, turns stunningly, lands precisely, has extension, energy, and control. Not just that he is a captivating actor, with a charming presence. It is that all these gifts are contained in a personality that projects itself, unforced, naturally, in a way that tells instantly of a great dancer."

## A LITTLE MUSICAL (*see* DUMBARTON OAKS)

## LE LOUP

*Music by Henri Dutilleux. Choreography by Roland Petit. Book by Jean Anouilh and Georges Neveux. Decor and costumes by Jean Carzou. First presented by Les Ballets de Paris de Roland Petit at the Théâtre de l'Empire,*

*Paris, March 17, 1953, with Violette Verdy and Roland Petit in the principal roles. First presented in the United States by the same ensemble, January 19, 1954.*

*Le Loup*, a dramatic ballet in several scenes, tells the remarkable story of a young bride who is enchanted by a wolf. This comes about after her husband leaves her for a Gypsy girl; the bride, distraught, imagines that her beloved has turned into a wolf. When she later finds out that she is deceived, she has become so devoted to the wolf that she will not leave him—despite the perils of the hunt, which now confront the wolf, and the opposition of the villagers. He and she are hunted down and killed.

## MADRIGALESCO

*Music by Vivaldi. Choreography by Benjamin Harkarvy. Costumes by Nicolaas Wijnberg. Lighting by Nicholas Cernovitch. First presented by the Netherlands Dance Theatre July 5, 1963, at Gravenhage. First presented in the United States by the Pennsylvania Ballet at the Walnut Street Theatre, Philadelphia, February 15, 1973, with Alba Calzada and Michael Lucci in leading roles.*

A work for twelve dancers, *Madrigalesco* is named for the first of two concertos by Antonio Vivaldi that accompany the action: the *Concerto in D Minor, Madrigalesco*, and the *Concerto in D Minor*, Op. 3, No. 11. The ballet evokes a world of manners, attitudes, and sentiments suggested by various paintings of the Italian Renaissance. The dress of the dancers is formal, as is the way they present themselves, but the situations they suggest have the variety of the extraordinary art they imitate in action.

## THE MAIDS

*Music by Darius Milhaud. Choreography, based on the play by Jean Genet, by Herbert Ross. Designed by William Pitkin. First presented by Ballet Theatre Workshop at the Phoenix Theatre, New York, May 13, 1957.*

Revived in 1969 and 1973 in New York and 1970 in London, *The Maids* tells a story that was regarded as too controversial for the general public in 1957, when it was first presented. A famous play by Jean Genet, the story involves the contrast between servants and master as a way of looking at a split in the world between the individual and society. The program note, by Jean-Paul Sartre, reads: "Genet suggested the maids be played by two boys, hoping by this device to confuse the audience, and thereby to force upon them that effect of ambiguity which terrorizes the maids. For Genet, theatrical procedure is demoniacal. Appearance, which is constantly on the point of passing itself off as reality, must constantly reveal its profound unreality."

The choreographer took Genet's advice; the two maids, Claire and Solange, are played by boys. As they act out in effect two different aspects of one servant, the two portray the games of master and servant to which their lives have become accustomed. In the end these games are intolerable and in what Clive Barnes has called the "most terrifying death I have ever seen in dance," one maid smothers another with a pillow. The charade and self-destructive slavery of the servant are seen to be, literally, impossible.

NOTES  *The Maids* was revived by Eliot Feld's American Ballet Company in 1969 and by American Ballet Theatre in 1973. It was staged by the Royal Ballet at the Wimbledon Theatre, London, October 19, 1971. Reviewing a performance of the revival of *The Maids* by American Ballet Theatre (January 16, 1973, at the City Center, New York), the critic Anna Kisselgoff wrote in the New York *Times:* "A superlative performance, danced straight from the gut, was offered by Daniel Levans and Gayle Young. Mr. Young and particularly Mr. Levans as Claire consistently caught the fierce desperation and violence of the Jean Genet play that inspired the ballet. Mr. Levans's characterization—both his acting and his movements—was always sharp, and its aggressiveness was appropriate. Mr. Young was properly conspiratorial, and . . . the result was electrifying and dramatic tension."

## MA MÈRE L'OYE (Mother Goose)

*Music and scenario by Maurice Ravel. First staged by Jacques Rouché at the Théâtre des Arts, Paris, January 28, 1912. First presented in the United States by the New York City Ballet at the Hommage à Ravel at the New York State Theatre, Lincoln Center, May 22, 1975. Choreography by Jerome Robbins. Costumes by Stanley Simmons. Lighting by Ronald Bates. Conducted by Robert Irving.*

Jerome Robbins subtitles his ballet "Fairy Tales for Dancers," giving us the key to his own *Mother Goose*. While Ravel's subtitle to his music's scenario might be "What the Sleeping Beauty Dreamed," Robbins extends the idea so that we have "What the Sleeping Beauty as Dancer Dreamed on Stage at the New York City Ballet." For what this new and fascinating version of Ravel's script does, in fact, is to take Ravel's wonderful concept of imagining the dreams of the Sleeping Beauty but to see the Sleeping Beauty *as a dancer* and all the other characters, too, as dancers who know the old fairy stories so well, having done them so abysmally often, that finally they have a chance to get even and to portray the stories as *they* wish. We have not only a fairy story within a fairy story but the performers' own variations. The dancers, in Deborah Jowitt's phrase, "look like children who have ransacked the attic to find costumes and props for a game of charades." The result is a remarkable entertainment for those who know Ravel's intention, know ballets like *The Sleeping Beauty* and *The Nutcracker*, etc., and know something of the New York City Ballet's scenery and costumes. And our dancers, too! *Ma Mère l'Oye* is an in-house joke for our faithful audiences.

Ravel originally composed his *Mother Goose* as five piano pieces. Later, in 1911, writing a scenario of his own, he added more pieces plus connective transitions. His script, charming and wittily detailed as the score itself, contains delightful invention. To the spellbound Sleeping Beauty (the Princess Florine, a character, of course, in a fairy tale by Perrault) he gives dreams of other fairy-tale characters (also by Perrault or his imitators).

Ravel's script might be summarized as follows:

PROLOGUE    Stories are told, then enacted.

ONE: DANCE OF THE SPINNING WHEEL    The Princess Florine is celebrating her birthday. During the festivities she accidentally pricks her finger on a spindle. According to the curse of the Bad Fairy she now must die. But through the intervention of the Good Fairy, her death is altered into a one-hundred-year sleep from which she will be awakened only by the kiss of someone who loves her. The court prepares her for bed and departs.

TWO    To entertain her during her long sleep, the Good Fairy decides to provide her with dreams, and she evokes for the Sleeping Princess a series of fairy tales:

BEAUTY AND THE BEAST    Beauty breaks the evil enchantment which has changed a prince into a Beast by accepting his love.

HOP O' MY THUMB    An impoverished woodcutter has purposely lost his seven little sons in the forest. Hop o' My Thumb, the youngest, seeks to avoid their fate by leaving a trail of crumbs to lead them back home.

LAIDERONNETTE, EMPRESS OF THE PAGODAS    Cursed by a demon, Laideronnette has been changed into the ugliest woman in the world. Similarly, her paramour, once a handsome young man, has been transformed into a Green Serpent. After bathing in waters whose magical powers they are unaware of, the two are restored to their former selves and all celebrate.

THE FAIRY-TALE GARDEN    The dreams of the Princess are interrupted by the arrival of Prince Charming led by Cupid, who breaks the Sleeping Beauty's spell, and the Prince is happily married to the Princess in the presence of the joyous court and attendant dream figures.

Jerome Robbins in his choreography follows Ravel's script closely but gives it special character within the New York City Ballet ambience. It is of interest that when Jerome Robbins first joined City Ballet, he made his debut in *Mother Goose Suite*, Todd Bolender's ballet, dancing Hop o' My Thumb.

Writing at length of the premiere in *The New Yorker*, Arlene Croce said that in the poetic style of *Ma Mère l'Oye*, Jerome Robbins "returns to those qualities which first defined him as a unique theatre artist."

## MANIFESTATIONS

*Music by Primous Fountain III. Choreography by Arthur Mitchell. Scenery and lighting by Gary Fails. Costumes by Zelda Wynn. First presented by the Dance Theatre of Harlem at the Auditorium Theatre, Chicago, February 25, 1976.*

A modern parable on the Adam and Eve story, *Manifestations* is set in Eden before the Fall. The Serpent is the first to appear, somewhat dramatically as he dangles down from on high to interrupt the action of love below. Adam and Eve nevertheless persist in their impassioned devotion. The wit with which their situation is appreciated not only by themselves but by the Serpent gives character to what John Percival, in the *Times* of London, called a "highly entertaining . . . classical ballet cabaret."

## MANON

*Ballet in three acts. Music by Jules Massenet, orchestrated and arranged by Leighton Lucas with the collaboration of Hilda Gaunt. Produced by Kenneth MacMillan. Choreography by Kenneth MacMillan. Designs by Nicholas Georgiadis. First presented by the Royal Ballet at the Royal Opera House, Covent Garden, London, March 7, 1974, with Antoinette Sibley, Anthony Dowell, David Wall, and Derek Rencher in principal roles. First presented in the United States by the same ensemble, May 7, 1974, at the Metropolitan Opera House, New York.*

Based on Abbé Prévost's great eighteenth-century romantic novel *Manon Lescaut* and not on the famous operas derived from that work, this ballet tells the story of a girl who has much charm but little character. She suffers accordingly, but not before she has brought down with her a lover who persists in finding in her charm a character no one else can see. The choreographer, Kenneth MacMillan, has said that what interested him from the start was Manon's amoral nature, which shifts from scene to scene, and within scenes.

ACT ONE, SCENE ONE takes place in the courtyard of an inn near Paris. The music that introduces it is not the familiar music by Massenet we might expect from that composer's opera to this story; indeed, all of Massenet's music used in the ballet comes from any work of his except his opera *Manon*. This particular inn is frequented by actresses, gentlemen, and the demimonde from Paris; it is artificially gay, a set-up and a snare for the unwary; it is not surprising to find a ratcatcher one of the principal personages in the courtyard. Coaches come and go, depositing pretentious ladies with large muffs who are escorted by gouty gentlemen. In the crowd we begin to distinguish a young man, Lescaut by name, who seems to know what everything is all about and has it all under control; he dances a vigorous solo. After an interlude featuring a bunch of ragpickers, we notice, too, a young divinity student who walks about in a broad-brimmed hat reading, preoccupied with his holy studies. This is Des Grieux, a handsome boy who seems to shun the world. The worldly persons who dominate the courtyard are Lescaut, who is there to meet his sister, Manon, on her way to join a convent, and Monsieur G.M., a wealthy Parisian. A coach arrives bringing Manon and an old gentleman who has been very much attracted to her. Manon is young, about sixteen she seems (as in Prévost), and much dazzled by the bustle of the courtyard. But it is clear that she has the old gentleman under control and shuns his advances. Des Grieux does not notice her, nor she him, at first; he sits reading. Monsieur G.M. does notice her and wants her as much as the old man does; he asks Lescaut to intercede on his behalf and secure Manon's favors for him. Lescaut is happy to oblige and all but auctions his sister off between Monsieur G.M. and the old man. In the midst of this undertaking, Manon is horrified to see a ratcatcher in the crowd. Des Grieux, watching a bit now, moves over to a table on the right, fanning his face with his hat and removing his jacket. He and Manon, both all innocence, watch as a courtesan dances for Lescaut and G.M. Then suddenly Des Grieux has forgotten his book and is staring at Manon. The old man kisses her hand. Des Grieux rises. The old man gives money to Lescaut. Manon is suddenly face to face with Des Grieux. The lights dim; they seem to be all alone; he dances for her, then kneels at her feet and kisses her hand. She is embarrassed, touched, and clearly attracted. To soft strings, he openly adores her. When she rises, he takes her in his arms and they begin to dance together of their growing passion. The dance is cool, detached from its environment.

Manon and Des Grieux, now much in love, decide to escape to Paris with the help of the money she has meanwhile taken from the old gentleman. Lescaut and the old gentleman, having made a bargain about Manon, emerge from the inn. To their dismay, Manon has gone: Des Grieux has mounted the driver's seat in the coach and taken her away. Monsieur G.M., always eager to join the crowd, at this point informs Lescaut that he, too, is interested in Manon. G.M.'s wealth is known to Lescaut, who promises to find his sister and persuade her to abandon Des Grieux and accept the rich G.M.

In SCENE TWO, Lescaut remarkably succeeds. The setting is Des Grieux's rooms in Paris, where he writes a letter, by candlelight, to his father asking him for money. Manon, languishing near the large bed at the left, does not like to be unattended and tries to interrupt her lover. They dance, reassuring each other of the depth of their love. Manon then helps Des Grieux into his overcoat and he goes off to mail the letter. In his absence, her brother, the perpetual fixer, arrives with Monsieur G.M. When the latter presents her with a fine gown and jewelry, it is as if she had never been a sweet sixteen-year-old on the way to any convent. She forgets Des Grieux, although she does hang on to the bed draperies a bit in fleeting recollection. There is a *pas de trois* in which her brother guides the girl and with G.M. swings Manon between them as if she were a toy. Lescaut swings her up to G.M.'s shoulder and, seeing the self-satisfaction that has matured between the two "lovers," asks for payment from G.M.

Manon says "adieu" to the bed and leaves with G.M. while Lescaut jiggles the purse he has received. Des Grieux returns and, sharing the purse with him, Lescaut tries to persuade him that they will all be rich if he, Des Grieux, will sanction the liaison between Manon and G.M. Lescaut is thoroughly in control of this situation and the impoverished Des Grieux consents.

In ACT TWO, the first scene is a gambling house and bordello, a *"hôtel particulier* of Madame." This Madame bustles about in her hall of mirrors and shiftily clad young girls making matches with the men who turn up. It is all *ancien régime* and polite; the men put their swords away upon arrival and even with the raucous music there is an agreed on code of behavior that prevents the expression of true feeling.

Lescaut, drunk, brings in Des Grieux, who is horrified at it all. Lescaut dances brilliantly of his spirited exhilaration and the girls try to close in on Des Grieux. When Manon arrives on the scene with G.M. and finds Des Grieux there, she gradually is seen to be torn between the wealth of her present lover and her recollection of the impetuous youth who saved her from the convent. Wearing a black and gold dress of rich embroidery and brilliant jewelry, Manon dances with her assembled admirers at the party while Des Grieux watches. She is manipulated in the *sarabande* and passed from one man to another as G.M. watches. Finally, she is lifted to G.M. and placed at his feet.

Although Manon is increasingly shattered by Des Grieux's presence and tries to avoid him, he at length tries to persuade her to leave with him. She tells him that the time is not right and engineers an arrangement for Des Grieux to cheat at cards with G.M. Her older lover is highly suspicious, however, and in the midst of the card game catches Des Grieux cheating. Des Grieux and Manon rush away.

In SCENE TWO, back at Des Grieux's lodgings, he and Manon once again declare their love for one another. She touches the curtains of their bed. G.M. interrupts them, however, just as Des Grieux has succeeded in reminding Manon that if she is to stay with him, she must give up the jewelry G.M. has lavished on her. It is precisely the jewelry's return that G.M. in his vengeance seeks. Lescaut is brought in, in handcuffs, and G.M. is triumphant. In the ensuing struggle and her arrest as a prostitute, Manon's brother is killed. Manon and Des Grieux look on in horror. Monsieur, holding Manon's arm, is gleeful.

In ACT THREE, the scene shifts to New Orleans, then a penal colony for the French. In his office, the jailer of the penal colony has a rendezvous with his girl. Two soldiers enter to remind him of certain duties and he leaves for the port.

The port dominates the second scene, busy with the unloading of ships. Cargo and passengers descend onto the dock while the soldiers and natives watch. Many of the exiled prisoners are girls, prostitutes like Manon, who lament their lot in a dance. Yet the jailer flirts with them and, above all, with Manon, who enters with Des Grieux. The jailer's girl despairs of her lover and tries to deflect his attention from the new riffraff from France, but the man persists and she is dragged away by his soldiers. Manon is also taken away to his room. Here the jailer, strangely drawn to this pathetic emaciated creature who has seemingly lost all her charm, is completely captivated. He is a displaced G.M. all over again and can offer her much. The dance he compels her to perform is done passively on her part and she appears to despise the man. He does not notice, however, and places a bracelet on her wrist in gratification. Des Grieux enters and stabs him. Manon throws the bracelet on the jailer's body and flees with Des Grieux.

Trying to escape capture, the lovers hide in a swamp, where mists and menacing foliage envelop their passage. Exhausted from their flight, Manon and Des Grieux rest. In a kind of delirium, the girl recalls her past and sees it travel in the mist before her—the jailer, the Madame of the bordello, the ratcatcher, G.M. Roused by her delirium, Des Grieux tries to comfort her. The two perform an impassioned dance in which Manon seeks a comfort as yet unknown; in a turmoil of abandonment, she is flung high into the air and spins there hysterically, only to be caught again in her lover's arms. All her former notions of wealth and splendor have been renounced for her love for Des Grieux. As she gradually expires, the demented man tries to revive her and to prop her up, but he cannot succeed. She has given up the ghost and Des Grieux laments.

NOTES   The music for *Manon* by Massenet, arranged by Leighton Lucas and Hilda Gaunt, is taken from the operas *Le Cid, Griselda, Thérèse, Cinderella, Cléopâtre, Don Quixote, Eve, Thaïs, Bacchus, Ariane,* and *Le Roi de Lahore,* the orchestral works *Scènes alsaciennes, Scènes pittoresques, Scènes dramatiques, La navarraise, Valse très lente, Chanson de Capri,* and *Aubade de Chérubin.*

The music for the Prelude to the ballet is from *Le dernier sommeil de la Vierge* and the *Cantata de la Vierge.* The score for Act One, Scene One is derived from *Aubade de Chérubin, Scènes dramatique, Scènes pittoresques, Le Cid, Crépuscule, Pastorale* from *L'esclaramonde, First Orchestral Suite, Scènes dramatiques, Si tu le veux, mignonne*—a song, *Griselda, Thaïs, Ariane, Élégie, Menuet d'Amour* from *Thérèse.* Act One, Scene Two: *Cendrillon, Ouvre tes yeux bleus*—a song, *Cendrillon,* and a salon piece.

Act Two, Scene One: *Scènes dramatiques, Au Cabaret*—*Scènes alsaciennes, Ariane, Bacchus,* a salon piece, *Don Quixote, Cléopâtre, Le Roi de Lahore, Crépuscule, Air de ballet, La navarraise, Élégie, Il pluvait*—a song, *Griselda, Cléopâtre.* Scene Two: *Adam and Eve, Bacchus.*

Act Three, Scene One: *Cendrillon, Griselda, Don Quixote, Cendrillon, Don Quixote, Don Quixote, Crépuscule, Sappho,* and *Adam and Eve.* Scene Two: Symposium of hallucinations. Scene Three: *La vierge, La vierge.*

Interviewed in *The New Yorker* in 1974 about *Manon,* Kenneth MacMillan said: "The characters fascinate me. You have a sixteen-year-old heroine who is beautiful and absolutely amoral, and a hero who is corrupted by her and becomes a cheat, a liar, and a murderer. Not exactly our conventional ballet plot, is it? One of the intriguing things about Prévost's Manon is that there doesn't seem to be any logic in the way she thinks. One minute, she tells Des Grieux that she loves him, the next minute she's deceiving him with an elderly count. My clue to her behavior is her background of poverty. Manon is not so much afraid of being poor as *ashamed* of being poor. Which brings me to the other theme of the ballet—the contrast between great wealth and great poverty in eighteenth-century France. . . ."[*]

## MARGUERITE AND ARMAND

> *Ballet in one act. Music by Franz Liszt, orchestrated by Humphrey Searle. Choreography by Frederick Ashton. Scenery and costumes by Cecil Beaton. Lighting by William Bundy. First presented by the Royal Ballet at the Royal Opera House, Covent Garden, March 12, 1963, with Margot Fonteyn, Rudolf Nureyev, Michael Somes, and Leslie Edwards in the principal roles. First presented in the United States by the Royal Ballet at the Metropolitan Opera House, New York, May 1, 1963, with the same principals. Present orchestration by Gordon Jacob.*

This dramatic ballet in four scenes and a prologue is Frederick Ashton's version of *The Lady of the Camellias* by Dumas *fils*, the famous novel about a Parisian courtesan, beautiful but fatally consumptive, who renounces her lover to save his reputation. The dance narrative is so arranged that in the last stages of her fatal illness Marguerite relives some incidents of her tragic life. The music is an orchestration of Liszt's *Sonata in B minor*.

In the Prologue, as Marguerite lies dying, she looks back in her delirium on her life with Armand. Huge projections of the two lovers are thrown against the background to the scene, and we see in a series of flashbacks her recollections. Meanwhile, Armand enters and moves like a distracted mourning spirit before visions of his life with Marguerite. When she sees his face in her fever she reaches out frantically and tosses in agony on her couch. Then, in a moment, through a gauzy curtain their time together is recaptured realistically on stage: on the same couch Marguerite sits in a stunning red dress, camellias at her breast and in her hair, surrounded by a group of admirers. As the orchestra sounds fully a major theme of Liszt's sonata, Armand enters, handsome, excited, intense. Marguerite is interested in him at once. The duke, her present lover and protector, watches with the others as Armand kisses her hand. The two begin then to dance. It is a dance of gay abandon with an undertone of seriousness. She coughs suddenly but it is only a passing thing. They are alone briefly, the others returning just as she falls back into Armand's arms. The duke angrily breaks in, takes her away; as she leaves, Marguerite tosses a camellia to the floor near Armand. Another man starts to pick it up but sees Armand's interest. Armand takes it and dashes off.

In a flash it is spring; the two lovers are living an idyllic life in the country. They dance joyously. Armand then goes off riding and Marguerite sits alone in lovely profile, contemplating a happiness she had not thought possible. Just then his father enters. The music portends his stern moral character. He bears down on her insistingly, but Marguerite is so astonished that she does not at

[*] From "MacMillan's Manon" by Jane Boutwell in "The Talk of the Town." Reprinted by permission; © 1974 The New Yorker Magazine, Inc.

first understand what on earth he can be saying. Then in agony, she comprehends: she must give up Armand, free him for the life his father wants. She prays, beseeches the father not to make such a demand, but he is unrelenting. The music quiets, she sits exhausted on the couch, touches a pillow, tries to rise but falls fainting almost into the father's arms. She seems then to gather courage; her body, her forced posture, suggest that, but this crumbles in a moment and she pursues the father to relent. He exits. She takes to her bed and when Armand returns she hides her face from him. But they dance, this time with savage passion; he flings her body about him again and again and faster and faster. He sits on the couch and she is at his knee. He lies back and she joins him, but of a sudden she rises and rushes out in a flurry of movement. Blackout.

The lights are on again in a moment and we are in another room with candelabra. The duke escorts Marguerite into the room, she in diamonds and a black dress with a spray of camellias on velvet at her skirt. She goes quickly to the couch. She coughs and it is apparent that she is now seriously ill. Armand enters, shocked at finding her again in such a place and she shocked that he should see her so. He tears off her diamond necklace and flings it away. She tries to flee but he throws money in her face. He stands there, gesturing desperately, seemingly cleansing himself of her, and she cannot bear it. Armand's father enters. Marguerite quivers but rejects the father's help.

In the final scene a nurse and Armand's father are in Marguerite's apartment. He tries to comfort Marguerite. She begins in her fever to see only Armand, who runs in in a black cloak. He seizes his beloved in ecstasy. They kiss and she on hobbled point is lifted up, swimming in a kind of final hope as she dies. Armand places her on the floor. His father turns his back as his son in anguish lifts Marguerite's hand uncomprehendingly. It falls away from him to the floor.

NOTES  Reviewing *Marguerite and Armand* in the *Times* of London, Clive Barnes said that "the swiftness of the ballet gives it an hallucinatory quality and sense of flying passion, of a tragedy fitfully illuminated by flashes of Keats' 'spangly doom' . . . Here is the true Romantic agony distilled into a brief ballet, far more pungent in its effect than any *Giselle*." Writing in *Dance and Dancers*, Barnes said of the performances: "For Fonteyn, like Ashton, ever expanding and developing, this role is something new. It shows as never before Fonteyn the dance actress . . . The power she first tested out in *Ondine* and later in *Giselle* is here seen at full-stretch . . . Even to a greater extent than Fonteyn's Marguerite, Armand is derived from Nureyev . . . He has never been seen to such advantage in the West . . . He goes through *Marguerite and Armand* like a fiery arrow shot by destiny. The wild theatricality of Nureyev, the charge he can give the simplest pose or movement, the impact of his dancing, are used to telling effect."

The critic Dale Harris has written a long essay of great interest on Margot Fonteyn's career in *Ballet Review* (Vol. 4, No. 6). The essay, "Snowflake to Superstar," reviews the book *Fonteyn: The Making of a Legend* by Keith Money (London, 1973). Margot Fonteyn has since written her own book, *Au-*

*tobiography* (London and New York, 1976). Reviewing the volume in the New York *Times*, the critic Anna Kisselgoff said that "in the future it can be said that Dame Margot Fonteyn wrote the way she danced. Her autobiography has the same attention to form, interlaced with emotion, as her most memorable performances."

## MEADOWLARK

*Music by Franz Joseph Haydn. Choreography by Eliot Feld. First presented by the Royal Winnipeg Ballet, October 3, 1968, at the Manitoba Centennial Concert Hall, Winnipeg, Canada. First presented in the United States by the American Ballet Company at the Brooklyn Academy of Music, New York, October 23, 1969, with scenery by Robert Munford, costumes by Stanley Simmons, and lighting by Jules Fisher. The principal dancers were Elizabeth Lee and John Sowinski, Christine Sarry and Richard Munro, Olga Janke, Edward Verso, and Alfonso Figueroa. Conductor: Christopher Keene.*

A dance ballet to music by Haydn (selections from the flute quartets arranged and orchestrated by Hershy Kay), *Meadowlark*, like its title, suggests a perpetual spring of good humor, competition, and love. The ballet is in seven parts, the first three a series of *pas de deux*. The backdrop, a huge watercolor of flowers, cliffs, and the sea in the distance, evokes the pastoral atmosphere of warmth and otherworldliness that the dances make specific in their different ways. Pledges are made, possibly serious betrayals seem imminent, consolations are promised, and there is gentle mockery of useless lamentation in other dances. The girls are courted, one of the boys is disappointed, and there are some humorous regrets. Civilized behavior sets everything in order and a varied, complex finale brings the ballet to a joyous finish for all concerned.

*Meadowlark* was produced by Festival Ballet at the Hippodrome, Bristol, England, December 9, 1968, and by the City Center Joffrey Ballet at the City Center, New York, in 1972.

Readers who wish to know more about the early work of Eliot Feld will wish to read the book *At the Vanishing Point*, by Marcia B. Siegel. She wrote: "He is important because he is the first choreographer of this generation to break with the idea that ballet is about another world—a universe peopled with invincible beautiful beings who are possessed of superhuman powers. Feld's ballet is about this world."

## MEDEA

*Music by Béla Bartók, orchestrated by Herbert Sandberg. Choreography by Birgit Cullberg. First presented by the Royal Swedish Ballet at the Princes Theatre, London, February 12, 1951. First presented in the United States by the New York City Ballet at the City Center, New York, November 26, 1958, with costumes by Lewis Brown, lighting by David Hays. Melissa Hay-*

den (Medea), *Jacques d'Amboise* (Jason), *and Violette Verdy* (Creusa) *danced the principal roles.*

Based on the Euripides drama, *Medea* tells the classic story of the revenge of the beautiful Medea, skilled in magic, for her husband Jason's desertion. Medea murders the two children she has had by Jason and slays his new wife Creusa with a poisoned garment. The music is thirteen piano pieces by Bartók, arranged by Herbert Sandberg.

The ballet is in five scenes. In Scene I, Medea and Jason lie together with their two children. They play with the children. Before the happy family interlude is over, however, Jason is attracted by the beauty of Creusa, daughter of Creon, King of Corinth, and follows her. Jason woos Creusa in Scene II and their romance is approved by Creon. Medea in Scene III hears of Jason's faithlessness. He returns to ask her forgiveness but she rejects him. Jason returns to Creusa. In Scene IV he is married to Creusa in Creon's palace. Medea enters, feigning homage to the bride, and presents her with a crown of gold and a rich veil. Admiring these gifts, Creusa puts them on. She dies thus attired, for the gifts are poisoned, and Jason will not have a new bride. In the final scene, the grief-stricken Jason returns to his home and attempts to take his children. Medea drags them into the house and, while a crowd rages outside, kills them.

# MEDITATION

*Music by Peter Ilyich Tchaikovsky. Choreography by George Balanchine. Costumes by Karinska. First presented by the New York City Ballet at the New York State Theatre, December 10, 1963, with Suzanne Farrell and Jacques d'Amboise.*

*Meditation* is a dance for two people, a dramatic *pas de deux* rather than a formal *divertissement*. The drama is the music, one of a set of three pieces for violin and piano, Opus 42, No. 1, by Tchaikovsky, orchestrated by Glazunov. I called the piece *Meditation* because it is contemplative. The Tchaikovsky music is thoughtful too. A friend of mine once called the dance very sad and very Russian. He said he thought there was a kind of pleasure in unhappiness in it, what he called a kind of Russian pleasure. I disagree, although there is of course pleasure and happiness in meditation.

# MEDITATION FROM "THAÏS"

*Music by Jules Massenet. Choreography by Frederick Ashton. First presented by the Royal Ballet at a gala performance at the Adelphi Theatre, London, March 21, 1971, with Antoinette Sibley and Anthony Dowell. Costumes by Anthony Dowell. First presented in the United States by the Royal Ballet with the same cast at the Metropolitan Opera House, New York, 1972.*

A dramatic *pas de deux*. The *Meditation* is set to music used at one time by Anna Pavlova's company. It is a romantic work, typified by the unveiling of a quasi-Oriental figure by her admirer soon after their entry. He adores her, displays his love in splendid thrusts of his lady into the air, daringly, only to catch her with dashing courage. David Vaughan, in his biography of Frederick Ashton, says that no matter what her position, the heroine "had to be like a disembodied weightless spirit."

## MENDELSSOHN SYMPHONY

*Music by Felix Mendelssohn. Choreography by Dennis Nahat. Costumes and scenery by Peter Farmer. Costume supervision by David Guthrie. Lighting by Nananne Porcher. First presented by American Ballet Theatre at the New York State Theatre, Lincoln Center, July 19, 1973, with Martine van Hamel, Fernando Bujones, and Ian Horvath in leading roles.*

This dance ballet was designed to the music of Mendelssohn's *Italian Symphony* (*No. 4 in A Major, Op. 90*), a popular work in the concert hall that serves equally well as a base for dancing. The scene is abstract—a colorful perspective that stretches into the distance—and the costumes are not suggestive of any time or place. These dances to this music are the subject.

The first movement, *Allegro vivace,* is performed by twelve girls, who develop the several lively themes and fantasia. Six of them remain at the end, to be supported by six boys in the *Andante*. In their midst, a girl emerges to lead the dance in this somewhat mournful and dejected sequence (the second movement of this symphony has been called the "Pilgrims' March"). She dances alone to the melancholy music, others return, and the dance ends as a boy in white enters to hold her in a final submissive pose.

The boy remains for the sweetly singing third movement, a minuet and trio (*Con moto moderato*). The lights dim and the temper is thoughtful, introspective, as the dancer explores his gifts of accent, rhythm, and line to the graceful flow of sound. The finale is a bright *saltarello*—a characteristic Roman dance, like the Neapolitan *tarantella,* in triple time, performed by another boy who leads the entire cast to a flourishing finale.

## MESSE POUR LE TEMPS PRÉSENT

*A ceremony in nine episodes. Percussion and sound effects under direction of Maurice Béjart, with special composition by Pierre Henry. Choreography by Maurice Béjart. First presented by the Ballet of the Twentieth Century at the Avignon Festival, August 3, 1967. First presented in the United States by the same ensemble at the Brooklyn Academy of Music, New York, January 27, 1971.*

This *Mass for Today* has as its motto a quotation from Nietzsche: "I could

Margot Fonteyn and Rudolf Nureyev in *La Bayadère*. Photo by Anthony Crickmay.

Rudolf Nureyev in *The Sleeping Beauty*. Photo by Houston Rogers.

Margot Fonteyn in *Homage to the Queen*. Photo by Houston Rogers.

Merle Park and David Wall in *Walk to the Paradise Garden*. Photo by Anthony Crickmay.

Svetlana Beriosova and Derek Rencher in *Enigma Variations*.
Photo by MIRA, courtesy Hurok Concerts.

Antoinette Sibley and Anthony Dowell in *The Sleeping Beauty*. Photo by Anthony
Crickmay.

Natalia Makarova and Anthony Dowell in *Swan Lake*. Photo by MIRA, courtesy of Hurok Concerts.

Lynn Seymour and Anthony Dowell in *A Month in the Country*. Photo by Beverley Gallegos.

Lynn Seymour in *Homage to Isadora*. Photo by Beverley Gallegos.

only have faith in a God who knew how to dance." Its theme is love, militarism, alienation. Perhaps its most famous part, *The Jerk,* with rock music by Pierre Henry, energizes its dancers into a frenzy of display. The remainder of the ballet, which occupies the whole evening, recapitulates in dance terms "the history of the West in the past thirty years."

## METAPHORS

*Music by Daniel-Lesur. Choreography by Hans van Manen. Scenery and costumes by Jean-Paul Vroom. First presented by the Netherlands Dance Theatre at The Hague, Holland, December 6, 1965. First presented in the United States by the Dutch National Ballet at the Minskoff Theatre, New York, November 9, 1976.*

A dance ballet set to the *Variations for Piano and Orchestra* of Daniel-Lesur, *Metaphors* had been popular in Europe for some years before it was first introduced to America. The ballet has a basic theme that we begin to discern as the dance progresses—everything is in twos, two groups, two soloists. No dancer stands alone and a preoccupation with duality and duplication emerges. Two couples dominate the piece, first two sets of a girl and a boy and then a dance for the two boys. They dance a *pas de deux* very much in the classic style of reliance and support, dependence and strength. This is followed by a duet for the girls and other combinations in which soloists and groups reflect each other. The music is bright and the accent sharp but occasionally lyrical. Everything is good-humored but we take seriously the suggestion in the dualities depicted that mutual help and respect are essential aspects of living as well as performing.

## A MIDSUMMER NIGHT'S DREAM

*Ballet in two acts and six scenes. Music by Felix Mendelssohn. Choreography by George Balanchine. Scenery and lighting by David Hays. Costumes by Karinska. First presented by the New York City Ballet at the City Center, New York, January 17, 1962, with Arthur Mitchell as Puck, Jillana as Helena, Edward Villella as Oberon, Melissa Hayden as Titania, Roland Vasquez as Bottom, Francisco Moncion as Theseus, Patricia McBride as Hermia, Nicholas Magallanes as Lysander, Bill Carter as Demetrius, Gloria Govrin as Hippolyta; Violette Verdy, Conrad Ludlow, and the entire company.\**

Shakespeare's *A Midsummer Night's Dream* has always been a favorite of mine ever since I first saw it and appeared in the play as a child in Russia. I was an elf in a production at the Mikhailovsky Theatre in St. Petersburg when

\* See also THE DREAM.

I was about eight years old. I suppose it was then that I came to know so many lines from the play; even now I can recite in Russian speeches like the famous one of Oberon's beginning:

> I know a bank where the wild thyme blows,
> Where oxlips and the nodding violet grows . . .

I worked on a production of the play at the Shakespeare Memorial Theatre in Stratford, Connecticut, in 1950, arranging some dances. But what has really interested me more than Shakespeare's words in recent years has been the music that Mendelssohn wrote to the play, and I think it can be said that the ballet was inspired by the score.

Mendelssohn did not, however, write music for the whole play. To fill out the danced action that developed as the ballet was being made, I selected other scores of Mendelssohn's that neatly fitted into the pattern we were making. (The pieces incorporated along with the incidental music in the first act are the overtures to *Athalie, The Fair Melusine, The First Walpurgis Night;* in the second act the *Symphony No. 9* and the overture *Son and Stranger.*)

The story of the ballet, of course, concerns the adventures and misadventures of a group of mortals and immortals in their resolutions of the confusions and problems of loving and being loved. It is called a "dream" because of the unrealistic happenings that occur to the characters . . . real yet unreal events such as crossed loves, meaningless quarrels, forest chases, and magic spells woven by the infamous Puck. I think it is possible to see and enjoy the ballet without knowing the play. At least that was my hope in creating the piece.

The first act takes place in a forest near the duke's palace. Oberon, King of the Fairies, and Titania, his queen, quarrel. Oberon orders Puck to bring the flower pierced by Cupid's arrow (which causes anyone coming under its influence to fall in love with the first person the eyes behold), and while Titania is asleep and unknowing, he casts the flower's spell over her.

Meanwhile, Helena, wandering in the wood, meets Demetrius, whom she loves but who does not love her. Demetrius rejects her and goes his way. Oberon watches and tells Puck to use the flower on Demetrius that he may return Helena's affection.

Another couple, Hermia and Lysander, very much in love, are also wandering in the forest. They become separated. Puck, eager to carry out Oberon's orders, mistakenly anoints Lysander. Helena appears and Lysander, under the flower's spell, at once and to her amazement tells her how much he loves her.

Hermia now returns. She is astonished and then dismayed to see Lysander paying attention only to Helena. Puck manages to bring Demetrius, too, under the flower's spell, much to the delight of Helena, who doesn't care for Lysander at all.

Demetrius and Lysander, now both in love with Helena, begin to quarrel over her. Puck, at Oberon's order, has separated Bottom, a weaver, from his companions, transformed his head into that of an ass, and placed him at the sleeping Titania's feet. Awakening, Titania sees Bottom, thinks him fair, and pays him close and loving attention. At last Oberon, his anger over, has Bottom sent away and releases Titania from her spell.

Hermia now gets no attention, Helena too much. The men, completely at odds, quarrel seriously and begin to fight. Puck by his magic causes them to separate, lose one another and wander apart in the forest, until exhausted they fall asleep, with Puck arranging for Helena to fall asleep beside Demetrius and Lysander (his spell removed) by Hermia.

The duke and Hippolyta discover the lovers asleep in the forest, awaken them, find their differences are resolved and proclaim a triple wedding for themselves and the two couples.

The second act opens in the duke's palace with parades, dancing, and *divertissements* in honor of the newly married couples. When the celebrations are over and the mortals retire, we return to the demesne of Oberon and Titania, who are now reunited and at peace. And at last Puck having put order into disorder sweeps away the remnants of the night's doings. The fireflies twinkle in the night and reclaim the forest.

## MISS JULIE

*Ballet in four acts. Music by Ture Rangström, arranged and orchestrated by Hans Grossman. Choreography by Birgit Cullberg. Scenery and costumes by Allan Friderica. First presented by Riksteatern at Västerås, Sweden, March 1, 1950, with Elsa-Marianne von Rosen and Julius Mengarelli in the principal roles. First presented in the United States by the American Ballet Theatre at the Metropolitan Opera House, New York, September 18, 1958, with Violette Verdy and Erik Bruhn in the principal roles. Scenery and costumes by Sven Erixon.*

Based on the play of the same name by the Swedish master August Strindberg, *Miss Julie* portrays the downfall of a young woman of noble birth who is bent on willful conquest. On Midsummer Night, Julie, the daughter of a count, rejects the suitor her father has chosen and joins the local villagers and the castle servants at a barn dance, where she captivates the head butler, Jean. In the next scene, in the castle kitchen, she seduces him. The next morning, finding that the servant has become the master, she contemplates flight with him. But portraits of her ancestors torment her with guilt. Suicide is offered as the only way out. The butler returns and assists her death.

NOTES   *Miss Julie* is also in the repertory of the Royal Danish Ballet. Clive Barnes, reviewing a performance by this company in New York in 1965, wrote: "Erik Bruhn as Jean is superlative. This is probably his finest role . . . His portrayal is not only breath-catchingly well danced, but his whole characterization is among the greatest pieces of ballet acting we have ever seen. Servile, common, attractive, brutish, arrogant, the whole spectrum of Strindberg's remarkable character finds a place in Mr. Bruhn's portrait. His stiff little bows from the waist with his arms stiffly curved at the side, his nervous pulling down of his jacket, his sly sexuality, his sudden shifts of manner, everything he does or looks makes a contribution to the whole."

## MOMENTUM

*Music by Peter Ilyich Tchaikovsky. Choreography by Dennis Nahat. Lighting design by Jean Rosenthal. First presented by American Ballet Theatre at the Walt Whitman Auditorium of Brooklyn College, New York, March 15, 1969.*

A dance ballet to Tchaikovsky's *Souvenir de Florence,* and the first work by the dancer Dennis Nahat, *Momentum* is arranged in two parts, each for three girls and two boys. Writing in the New York *Times,* the critic Don McDonagh said that in the first movement Mimi Paul, with "her long, supple and dynamic style was an interesting contrast to that of the two couples who formed an undulating background to her solo. Eleanor d'Antuono led the group in the second movement with clean vigor."

## MONOTONES 1 AND 2

*Music by Erik Satie. Choreography and costumes by Frederick Ashton. Monotones 1, Trois Gnossiennes, orchestrated by John Lanchbery, first presented by the Royal Ballet at the Royal Opera House, Covent Garden, April 25, 1966, with Antoinette Sibley, Georgina Parkinson, and Brian Shaw. Monotones 2, Trois Gymnopédies, orchestrated by Claude Debussy and Roland Manuel, first presented by the Royal Ballet at the Royal Opera House, Covent Garden, March 24, 1965, with Vyvyan Lorrayne, Anthony Dowell, and Robert Mead. It was revived on April 25, 1966, with the same cast, and presented with Monotones 1. Monotones 1 and 2 first presented in the United States by the Royal Ballet at the new Metropolitan Opera House, May 3, 1967, with Michael Coleman replacing Brian Shaw.*

This is a dance ballet for six people, three in each *Monotone. Monotones 2,* first given as a *pièce d'occasion* in 1965 for the Royal Ballet Benevolent Fund Gala, was so admired that it was supplemented the following year and introduced into the company's regular repertory.

There is no plot, no decor. The dancers perform against a black background. This major lyric dance, which must be seen to be properly appreciated, was staged by the City Center Joffrey Ballet in 1975. Writing about it in *Dance and Dancers,* the critic Patricia Barnes said: "A real coup for Joffrey was his acquisition of Ashton's exquisite *Monotones.* A small-scale masterpiece, the choreography makes visible the cool melodic line of Satie's music to perfection, flowing as it does from one exquisite pose to another. There is a simplicity here, an inevitability, that is seen only in the greatest art. The lambent purity of these lovingly arranged attitudes and arabesques with their always complementary ports de bras move one not just by the beauty of their design but also by the uncluttered freshness of Ashton's vision.

"The first pas de trois (the second of Ashton's creations) to the *Trois Gnossiennes* was just slightly less effective than the second trio to *Trois Gymnopédies*. By the season's end, however, Rebecca Wright, Starr Danias and Burton Taylor were already beginning to get to the work's still centre. Pamela Nearhoof, supported by Kevin McKenzie and Robert Thomas, could hardly have been better. Her serene assurance and long-legged elegance were just right."

# A MONTH IN THE COUNTRY

*Ballet in one act. Music by Frédéric Chopin, arranged by John Lanchbery. Choreography by Frederick Ashton. Scenery and costumes by Julia Trevelyan Oman. First presented by the Royal Ballet at the Royal Opera House, Covent Garden, London, February 12, 1976, with Lynn Seymour as Natalia Petrovna, Alexander Grant as Yslaev, Wayne Sleep as Kolia, Denise Nunn as Vera, Derek Rencher as Rakitin, Marguerite Porter as Katia, Anthony Conway as Matvei, and Anthony Dowell as Beliaev. First presented in the United States by the same ensemble at the Metropolitan Opera House, New York, April 27, 1976.*

In a laconic note to his ballet, based on Turgenev's masterpiece, Frederick Ashton has written that "the action takes place at Yslaev's country house in 1850. Beliaev, a young student, engaged as a tutor for Kolia, disrupts the emotional stability of the household. Finally Rakitin, Natalia's admirer, insists that he and the tutor must both leave in order to restore a semblance of order to Yslaev's family life.

"The ballet is dedicated to the memory of Sophie Fedorovich and Bronislava Nijinska, Chopin's compatriots and my mentors."

Frederick Ashton first saw Ivan Turgenev's masterpiece of a play forty years and more before he was able to make a ballet to it, but he always wished to. Reading the play is of course the best preparation for the ballet, especially as Ashton's work might be called the distillation—in Ashton's words the "pill"—of the Russian master's drama. Those who wish to explore the life of Turgenev and the inspiration for the action of the play will be rewarded by a most moving story: the Russian writer is in fact the Rakitin of the drama, the man who says there that "all love, happy or unhappy, is a disaster when you give way to it."

The action of the ballet is all a giving way, posed against a responsive will to control and survive. The central figure, a young man of twenty-one, Beliaev, tutor to Yslaev's young son Kolya, is adored not only by the family's ward, the seventeen-year-old Vera, but by the lady of the house, Natalia Petrovna, twenty-nine. Natalia Petrovna in her turn has been for many years beloved by Rakitin, who has watched and still continues to observe her detachment from emotional life.

The ballet's compression of this drama takes place in a splendid drawing room in the Russian countryside. The family life, and the life of their perpetual house guests, appears to be an idyll of existence. The admirer of Natalia, Rakitin, knows his place, the limits beyond which he cannot go. In the midst of the summer, Natalia herself, challenged by her young ward's love for the tutor of her son, goes to an unspeakable limit and permits a declaration of love for the younger man. Observing the return of her passion, and Natalia Petrovna's possible doom, Rakitin rescues her by taking himself and the tutor away. In an ultimate expression of regret that their passion cannot be fulfilled, Beliaev kisses the ribbons of Natalia's dress.

The music for the ballet consists of Chopin's *Variations on "La ci darem la mano,"* the *Fantasy on Polish Airs,* and the *Andante Spianato and Grande Polonaise.*

## MONUMENT FOR A DEAD BOY

*Music by Jan Boerman. Choreography by Rudi van Dantzig. Scenery and costumes by Toer van Schayk. First presented by the Het National Ballet, 1966. First presented in the United States by the Harkness Ballet, November 3, 1967, with Lawrence Rhodes in the principal role.*

This ballet traces the history of a young boy who, at his death, looks back. It is preceded by a quotation from Truman Capote: "Unafraid, not hesitating, he paused only at the garden's edge where, as though he'd forgotten something, he stopped and looked back at the bloomless, descending blue, at the boy he had left behind." Verbal themes for the eight parts of the narrative are derived from *The Inner Wallpaper* by Hans Lodeizen. The music is an electronic score by Jan Boerman.

Six huddled dark figures, perhaps the furies who haunt the boy's life, are seen in shadow as the ballet begins. The mature boy and his younger self, portrayed by a smaller dancer, enter and move together, identifying and differing in gesture and emphasis. ("I am playing with the sad rope of time.") Then suddenly the older boy is lifted away to watch the youth. ("Springtime makes doors, the wind is an open hand, we must yet begin to love.") His parents enter and soon, in an excess of affection, they all but tear the child in two in a tug-of-war. ("Soon we will all have died; What is memory? What is love?") The boy seeks refuge in the arms of his older self. Where can I go, he seems to ask, but to myself?

Two visions now haunt him, one a girl in blue ("As I am standing in the yellow night on the blue floorcloth of my heart"), the other a girl in white. ("In a block of buildings I live as a child, suspecting fingers everywhere, darkness and kisses.") Both attracted and repelled, the boy finds alternating comfort, understanding, and tenderness with another boy at school. (". . . happiness with you means the past.") Next, a painting of a playground, the back wall embellished with graffiti and five boys spaced in front of it, comes suddenly alive. The hero is attacked, hurt, humiliated. (". . . like jellyfish on a beach, they soil the horizon.") The Girl in Blue finds him. They dance together in sympathy and passion but it is too late. Back at home, the boy watches in horror the aggressive lust of his parents. At this point the older boy and his youth portray his despair, a hopelessness that finds release only in death. (". . . like a curtain I jerked open darkness, to see the night.") As the hero dies, his younger self grieves, hailing him, celebrating him forever, in a silent lament, and remembering.

NOTES   Revived by American Ballet Theatre at the City Center, New York, January 11, 1973, *Monument for a Dead Boy* starred Ivan Nagy as the Boy. Scenery and costumes were by Toer van Schayk. Lighting by George Bardyguine.

The critic Robb Baker of *FM Guide* wrote of this revival: *Monument for a Dead Boy* "is a powerful psychological dance drama depicting a teenaged boy looking back at his own homoerotic fantasies." Rudolf Nureyev and Helgi Tomasson have danced the principal role in this ballet. The English critic Oleg Kerensky has said in his book *The World of Ballet* that "it is a powerful theatrical work. . . . It grips its audience at least as much by its subject matter, its psychological interest, and its skillful staging as by its dance content."

## MONUMENTUM PRO GESUALDO (*see* MOVEMENTS)

## MOON REINDEER

*Music by Knudager Riisager. Choreography by Birgit Cullberg. Scenery and costumes by Per Falk. First presented by the Royal Danish Ballet, Copenhagen, November 22, 1957, with Mona Vangsaae, Henning Kronstam, and Fredbjørn Bjørnsson in the leading roles. First presented in the United States by the American Ballet Theatre at the Fifty-fourth Street Theatre, New York, October 2, 1961, with Lupe Serrano, Royes Fernandez, and Felix Smith in the leading roles.*

Based on an ancient Arctic legend, *Moon Reindeer* tells the story of a lovely young girl, Aili, who, rejected by the man she loves, seeks the aid of Naiden, the Witch Doctor. Naiden agrees to help her but in return she must provide him with a human sacrifice to appease the gods of the underworld. Aili thus assumes by the light of the moon the guise of a white reindeer who so enchants young men that they fall over a precipice and perish. When the Laplanders try to avenge these deaths, the Moon Reindeer is killed and Aili resumes her human form.

## THE MOOR'S PAVANE

*Music by Henry Purcell (arranged by Simon Sadoff). Choreography by Jose Limon. Costumes by Pauline Lawrence. First presented by Jose Limon and Company at the Connecticut College American Dance Festival, Palmer Auditorium, New London, Connecticut, August 17, 1949, with Jose Limon, Betty Jones, Lucas Hoving, and Pauline Kohner. First presented by American Ballet Theatre at the New York State Theatre, Lincoln Center, June 27, 1970, with Bruce Marks, Sallie Wilson, Royes Fernandez, and Toni Lander. Assistants to Mr. Limon: Daniel Lewis, Clive Morgan, and Jennifer Muller. Conducted by Akira Endo.*

Long acknowledged as a masterwork of modern dance and performed in the United States and abroad by Jose Limon and his company, *The Moor's Pavane* is fortunately available to the public also in the repertories of American Ballet Theatre, the City Center Joffrey Ballet and other ensembles. Subtitled "Variations on a Theme of Othello," it is assumed that the spectator is familiar with Shakespeare's play. Here all subplots, or non-essentials of that story, are eliminated, and in a stately quadrille, the four principals—Othello, Desdemona, Iago, and Emilia, called here the Moor, his wife, the Friend, and his wife, dance a minuet of love, comradeship, jealousy inflamed, betrayal, death, and discovery.

NOTES  Reviewing this revival of *The Moor's Pavane* in the New York *Times*, Clive Barnes wrote: "*The Moor's Pavane* is a totally engrossing work and likely to remain among Mr. Limon's most enduring ballets. . . . What Mr. Limon has set out to do is to picture the corrosive force of jealousy and the destruction of good by evil, and to encapsulate this into the patterns of a ballroom dance.

"The dance starts simply enough, with bows and graces, and all manner of Elizabethan furbelows. But as it proceeds, the undercurrents of feeling beneath the courtly observances make themselves felt, the dance takes on a new urgency, moves into a new dimension. . . . Mr. Limon has been fortunate here in an ideal cast. I will never forget Mr. Limon himself and Lucas Hoving as the original Othello and Iago. They were fantastic—a bull and a matador come to judgment. Yet now Bruce Marks and Royes Fernandez are no less impressive. Mr. Marks, bearded, noble, anguished, and with all the passion and agony of the world on his broad shoulders, is brought low by a sinuously insinuating Mr. Fernandez, a very proper villain with the graceful movements of a snake.

"This admirable cast is completed by Sallie Wilson as the wicked Emilia (Mr. Limon is less charitable with her than is Shakespeare) and Toni Lander as the yielding and wronged Desdemona. It is a shrewd and subtle work that will be a credit to Ballet Theatre."

Writing in the Washington *Post* of Jose Limon's work after his death in

1972, Jean Battey Lewis said: "Perhaps his best-known work is *The Moor's Pavane*, his conception of the Shakespearean tragedy of Othello. He and his company danced the work at the White House before President and Mrs. Johnson in 1967 and the dance is in the repertoire of several ballet companies here and abroad. (It was danced at the Kennedy Center last season by American Ballet Theatre.)

"Eric Bentley once said that of all the works created on the American stage the one he would choose above all others to send abroad as a showcase of our art would be *The Moor's Pavane*.

"Describing himself as 'either the most atheistic of Catholics or the most Catholic of atheists,' Limon was often inspired by Biblical themes—*The Traitor*, based on the betrayal of Jesus; *There Is a Time*, and *The Exiles*, a dance about Adam and Eve, are among them. *A Choreographic Offering* to the music of Bach was his tribute to his mentor, Doris Humphrey.

"A few years ago the dancer declared, 'I try to compose works that are involved with man's basic tragedy and the grandeur of his spirit. I want to dig beneath empty formalisms, displays of technical virtuosity, and the slick surface; to probe the human entity for the powerful, often crude beauty of the gesture that speaks of man's humanity.

"'I reach for demons, saints, martyrs, apostates, fools, and other impassioned visions. I go for inspiration and instruction to the artists who reveal the passion of man to me, who exemplify supreme artistic discipline and impeccable form: to Bach, Michelangelo, Shakespeare, Goya, Schonberg, Picasso, Orozco,' he continued.

"This wrestling with elemental themes is obviously not a currently fashionable approach in an art that in recent years has leaned toward abstraction, impersonality and a structure based on chance. Talking to Limon last year after a rehearsal at Juilliard School in New York it was clear that he had no use for fashion in the arts.

"He was working at the time on a new dance, *Dances for Isadora*, which he said he was composing in memory of his wife.

"*Dances for Isadora* is a study of Isadora Duncan, the first great revolutionary American dancer. Somewhat as a companion piece (*Isadora* was a dance for five women), Limon was completing *The Unsung*, a suite of male solos on eight American Indian chieftains—our unsung heroes.

"Of his choice themes, Limon said at the time, 'What are we here on earth for if not to illuminate our experience, for ourselves and others?'"

# MOTHER GOOSE SUITE

*Classic ballet in five scenes. Music by Maurice Ravel. Choreography by Todd Bolender. First presented by the American Concert Ballet at the Central High School of Needle Trades Auditorium, New York, October 1943, with a cast headed by Mary Jane Shea and Francisco Moncion. Revised and presented by the New York City Ballet at the City Center, New York, No-*

*vember 1, 1948, with Marie-Jeanne, Francisco Moncion, Todd Bolender, and Beatrice Tompkins in the principal roles.*

This ballet is based on Ravel's score *Ma Mère l'Oye,* rather than on the "Mother Goose" fairy tales of Perrault that inspired Ravel to compose his well-known suite. The choreographer has devised a fantasy in which an older woman dreams of her adventures as a young girl. Her dreams are presented by groups of dancers, who portray in mime and movement certain flash backs of her youth, while the woman herself watches from the side lines. The parts of Ravel's suite are played in the following order: "Pavanne," "Enchanted Garden," "Hop o' My Thumb," "Enchanted Princess," "Beauty and the Beast."

The stage is dimly lighted as the curtain rises. A girl stands in a soft blue spotlight. She bows slowly, as if waking from some romantic reverie, and circles the stage on her points. Clouds drift by, enclosing the girl in her dream. The music is quiet and illusive. A strange woman enters in a stiff, long dress. Her face is veiled; she carries a fan. She does not see the girl at first, but turns to look at her lingeringly. The strange woman crosses over to the small theatre box at the side of the stage. She sits carefully under a small crystal chandelier. As she looks out to the stage, the clouds return to perpetuate the dream she watches.

The young girl, the spectator's second self, stands alone in the center of the stage. Four girls in red join her and support her as she poses in arabesque. The girls weave in and out under her extended arms. They bow to her, and she returns their greetings.

The music of the "Enchanted Garden" begins to build to a sumptuous, flowing climax. Four other girls enter, then four boys, who partner the girls alternately in a continuous dance in which they surround the young girl. She chases them, imitates the girls to attract the attention of the boys, and stands sad and helpless as the couples seem unaware of her existence. The girl goes over to the spectator and gestures questioningly: what is she to do? The spectator has no answer. Now desperate, the girl goes to each couple and asks to be recognized. The music pulsates. To its rhythms, the boys lift their partners high and carry them off over the girl's head. The girl stands with bent head. All is quiet again.

Hop o' My Thumb enters. This character is derived from the fairy-tale hero who dropped bread crumbs as he went away from home, imagining that they would lead him back. Here in the ballet, he is accompanied by the bird who ate his crumbs and caused him to lose his way. The bird-girl drapes her long blond hair over the boy's head, ensnaring him. The boy is undisturbed.

The young girl watches, astonished. The bird leaves the boy. He looks after her longingly, then begins to dance with the young girl. They kneel together and look at each other's hands, reading their fortunes. In the background, the bird can be seen crossing the stage in open flight. The boy and girl stare at each other, then rise to stand in front of the spectator. The girl stands motionless as the clouds flow in, envelop the boy, and carry him back to his true love. The girl leaves the stage.

Four girls in red, with long green gloves, enter with a Chinese prince who is dressed in brilliant gold. The orchestra plays a tinkling, Oriental tune, and the prince dances blithely. The young girl re-enters. Momentarily she is blinded by the strange, foreign spectacle. The prince approaches her deferentially and takes her hand, but she refuses to believe that a real prince has appeared to her. The prince takes her hands from her eyes, and now the girl dances with him gaily. He lifts her high, and the two dance before the group. Just as the girl has begun to enjoy herself thoroughly, the magical prince and his escort hop off into the wings.

A young man with the hideous and frightening head of a lion comes in. Before she knows what she is doing, the girl leaps to his shoulder; he lets her down softly. The beast looks into her eyes; the girl is terrified and backs away. The beast falls to the floor and, as the music moans and groans his agony, he mimes his misery and ugliness. Still frightened, the girl approaches the spectator. What can she do with the pathetic creature? The spectator presents her with a magic ring.

The girl runs about the stage rapidly, then puts her hand gently on the beast's shoulder. They dance. Clouds drift in and surround the beast. When they have passed by, he has become a handsome youth. He holds the beautiful girl softly and possessively. The spectator rises and leaves her box. The girl's fairy godmother intervenes and stands over the couple. The boy kneels, holding out his arms. The girl falls against him. He lifts her and carries her out. The spectator exits slowly, openly rejecting her own dream. The clouds drift by. The spell of the dream is still with her.

## MOVEMENTS

*Ballet in two parts. Music by Igor Stravinsky. Choreography by George Balanchine. Part I*, Monumentum pro Gesualdo, *first presented by the New York City Ballet at the City Center, New York, November 16, 1960, with Diana Adams and Conrad Ludlow in the leading roles. Decor by David Hays. Part II*, Movements for Piano and Orchestra, *first presented by the New York City Ballet, April 9, 1963, with Suzanne Farrell and Jacques d'Amboise in the leading roles. Scenery and lighting by David Hays and Peter Harvey.*

The two ballets *Monumentum* and *Movements*, first presented separately, have been performed together since 1963. Both have music by Stravinsky, both are short works, and it has been convenient for our audiences, and for us in the New York City Ballet, to see them combined. Their music is also an interesting contrast. In the first, Stravinsky was inspired by the music of the Italian composer Don Carlo Gesualdo, 1560–1613, "Prince of Madrigalists." In *Movements for Piano and Orchestra*, one of Stravinsky's first complete works in serial style, we have the composer speaking directly, in terms of his own preoccupations.

*Monumentum* was composed in 1960, to commemorate the four-hundredth anniversary of Gesualdo's death. Stravinsky's self-discovery here in the work of another composer works to the same advantage as it has done on other occasions, as we recall from his working to the inspiration of Tchaikovsky in *Baiser de la Fée* and to Pergolesi's example in *Pulcinella*. Stravinsky and his collaborator Robert Craft have prepared a splendid recording of some of Gesualdo's music that concludes with the *Monumentum*.

The music consists of three madrigals for five voices "re-composed for instruments." Like the music, the short ballet is in three parts, arranged for a leading dancer, her partner, and six couples. Each of the three sections is very brief, lasting just over two minutes.

At the conclusion of *Monumentum,* there is a short pause and *Movements* begins. Stravinsky has said that my ballet might also have been called "Electric Currents." It is, as he says, a double concerto for male and female solo dancers, both identified with the piano solo. There is an accompanying *corps de ballet* of six girls. The ballet is in five parts, lasting eight and a half minutes. Each part begins with a short instrumental introduction. Two groups of three girls set the tone for each section and the lead couple takes up the music as the piano enters. I seriously think that the best preparation for seeing this ballet is to listen to Stravinsky's recording of it a number of times. Its complexity and compression are remarkable. Eric Walter White has said that the composition "has the specific gravity of a tonal work of three times that duration.*
I myself had to see it, to make a ballet of it, to understand it. Nothing gave me greater pleasure afterwards than Stravinsky's saying the performance "was like a tour of a building for which I had drawn the plans but never explored the result."**

## MOVES

*A Ballet in Silence about Relationships. Choreography by Jerome Robbins. First presented by Jerome Robbins's Ballets: U.S.A. at the Festival of Two Worlds, Spoleto, Italy, July 3, 1959. First presented in the United States by Ballets: U.S.A. at the ANTA Theatre, New York, October 8, 1961.*

Jerome Robbins has called his ballet without music or scenery a "ballet in silence about relationships." Without a score to fall back on, the eye is focused in a new way on stage action. As the choreographer explains, "the score supports, conditions, predicts, and establishes the dynamics, tempo, and mood not only for the dance but also for the audience. Music guides the spectators' emotional responses to the happenings on the stage and creates a persuasive atmosphere for reaction. *Moves* severs that guidance . . . I wanted the audience to concentrate on movement. I wanted to do two things: one, an exploration of movement that the audience can interpret only as movement . . . two, I

---

* *Stravinsky, the Composer and His Works,* by Eric Walter White, University of California press, Berkeley, Calif., 1966.

** *Themes and Episodes,* by Igor Stravinsky and Robert Craft, Alfred A. Knopf, New York, 1966.

wanted to do a ballet about relationships between people—man and woman, one and another, the individual and the group."

The dance narrative explores, without a story, relationships and disconnections between dancers. They first appear coming at the audience in single file from the back of the stage. Different things happen. A boy and a girl dance together and we understand what they are about. Five boys dance and while four of them are doing classical *entrechats* the fifth does the "frog sag." Three couples dance. With no music, the dancers establish their own personal rhythms; they seem moved by their own impulses. At the end, the company files off just as it entered.

NOTES   Reviewing *Moves* in *The Dancing Times* in 1961 after its first London performances, Mary Clarke said: "A distinct and disturbing emotion of involvement in the whole human predicament is created by these silent movers, in their casual clothes on a bare stage. I don't think dancing has ever said so much, speaking alone and in its own language."

## MOZART CONCERTO

*Music by Wolfgang Amadeus Mozart. Choreography by John Cranko. Lighting by Gilbert V. Hemsley, Jr. First presented by the Stuttgart Ballet at the Württemberg State Theatre, Stuttgart, March 26, 1966. First presented in the United States by the same ensemble, June 20, 1969, at the Metropolitan Opera House, New York.*

This dance ballet to Mozart's *Concerto for Flute and Harp in C Major* (K. 299) is arranged for four soloists—two girls and two boys—and a supporting group of ten boys. The soloists, the two girls, like the flute and harp in the score, lead the work but there is no one-to-one correspondence. The ballet is in three movements. The finale, a *Rondo,* the critic Abraham Veinus has said, "is furnished with enough melodies to fit out at least two ordinary concertos."

Writing of this ballet in the New York *Times,* Clive Barnes said, "The effect is most interesting. For one thing this new arrangement leads to a greater flexibility in the work's structuring, for the two ballerinas can not only be partnered by their cavaliers but also by the ensemble. It also places a new and rather more glamorous emphasis on the two girls, who instantly become objects of seemingly universal admiration."

## MUTATIONS

*Music by Karlheinz Stockhausen. Choreography by Glen Tetley. Cinechoreography by Hans van Manen. Film visualization by Jean-Paul Vroom. Production designs by Nadine Baylis. Costumes by Emmy van Leersum and Gijs Bakker. Lighting by John B. Read. First presented by the Netherlands Dance Theatre at the Circustheater, Scheveningen, Holland, July 3, 1970.*

*First presented in the United States by the same ensemble at the Brooklyn
Academy of Music, New York, March 29, 1972.*

With the presentation of *Mutations,* New York saw a nude ballet performed
for the first time by a major company on a major stage. In addition to nudity,
unusual aspects of the work include film episodes, shown on three screens at
the back of the stage while live dancers perform in front of them, and action
which extends from the stage along a ramp into the center aisle.

The first of the ballet's films is of naked Gérard Lemaitre and is in such slow
motion that his body appears to float freely and effortlessly through space. The
final scene is a nude *pas de deux* danced by Anja Licher and Lemaitre while
all three films are shown behind them. The *pas de deux* repeats in part some
of the filmed choreography as well as sections of the live choreography.

The ballet is not entirely nude, for it also concerns the emotional influences
of costume. The clothed dancers have movements that are correspondingly
rigid. Those half-undressed use their freedom for aggression and competition.
And finally, the totally nude dancers explore the possibilities of fluid, unencumbered motion.

NOTES   Glen Tetley says, "You construct a game, you set your own restric-
tions, and then you challenge yourself to find your way through these restric-
tions."

Writing after the first performance of *Mutations* in London, in 1970, the
critic Alexander Bland said in *The Observer:* ". . . It is sincere, shapely, rich in
those plastic movements which Tetley excels in. . . . Nudity is used in this
ballet as a stimulating but serious ingredient which completely justifies itself
artistically. The scene is a kind of arena (by Nadine Baylis) into which white-
clad figures gradually fight their way. Once arrived, the mood changes. A nude
figure appears dancing on film, and this is followed by a nice trio for girls . . .
and some all-in applications of red paint suggesting violence. A couple dance,
clad and unclad on screen and stage, to gently variegated electronic sounds by
Stockhausen; more join in and the film triplicates until some mysterious figures
in transparent suits sweep the action off stage—naked and strangely vulnerable
—alone as the lights fade."

NOTES   The choreographer Hans van Manen has described the evolution of
*Mutations* in detail in an account by Glenn Loney published in *Dance Magazine,* February 1974. Asked to do a ballet to mark the twenty-fifth anniversary
of the liberation of the Netherlands from the Nazis, he responded: "I thought
it would be ridiculous to do a ballet symbolizing twenty-five years of freedom
from the Germans. After twenty-five years? If the ballet has to be about freedom, then we should make the ballet completely *free.* That's the best symbol
of freedom. We must be completely free in what we are doing." In the end,
the ballet was worked out with Glen Tetley, then closely associated with the
Netherlands Dance Theatre, Tetley creating the live part and van Manen the
film.

# NAPOLI

*Romantic ballet in three acts. Music by E. Helsted, Gade, and Paulli. Chore-*
*ography and book by Auguste Bournonville. Scenery by Christensen. First*
*presented by the Royal Danish Ballet at the Theatre Royal, Copenhagen,*
*March 29, 1842.*

*Napoli* is the great ballet by Auguste Bournonville, the dancer, choreographer,
and ballet master of the Royal Danish Ballet for many years and the founder
of its famous continuous tradition of training and performance. Since 1829,
when Bournonville mounted his first ballet in Copenhagen, ballets by him have
been danced by the Royal Danish Ballet more than four thousand times.
*Napoli,* the finest of them, is but a year younger than *Giselle;* but unlike
*Giselle, Napoli* has not been changed by succeeding generations of choreographers, dancers, and musicians: it is still danced in Copenhagen today as it
was more than one hundred and twenty-five years ago.

ACT ONE: NAPLES, BY THE BAY OF SANTA LUCIA; EVENING   Three boys are in
love with the beautiful Teresina, the daughter of a watchful widow. Teresina
loves only one, a fisherman, Gennaro. Her two suitors—Giacomo, who sells
macaroni in the town, and Peppo, who sells lemonade—try to persuade her
mother that Teresina will be better off married to one of them. Teresina, the
mother indicates, will make up her own mind. Teresina ignores her suitors as
she waits for Gennaro, who is returning to port with all the other fishermen of
the town.

Soon the fishermen return. Gennaro embraces Teresina, and her mother reluctantly consents to their marriage. A monk, Fra Ambrosio, enters and asks
the fishermen and the assembled townsfolk for alms. Gennaro and Teresina
both contribute. Teresina's suitors, Giacomo and Peppo, still persist in bothering her and her mother; they try to make the girl jealous as Gennaro jokes
with a girl who has come to buy fish from him. But when Gennaro places an
engagement ring on her finger, Teresina is convinced that her happiness lies
only with him.

The two lovers go out into the bay in order to be alone. After they have
been gone for some time, thunder and lightning fill the air. A violent storm
breaks over the Bay of Santa Lucia. Gennaro, out in the bay, rows frantically,
trying to reach shore. His fellow fishermen go to help him, and he is rescued.
But Teresina has been swept overboard by the giant waves, and no one can
find her. Gennaro curses his destiny. The girl's mother accuses him of drowning Teresina, and all the people of the town abandon him.

Gennaro is alone. He is about to despair, but then he prays beneath a likeness of the Madonna. Fra Ambrosio comes to him and, giving him an image of
the Madonna to carry with him for protection from harm, tells Gennaro not to
give up hope: he must take a boat and go out to sea and there find his love.
Gennaro goes to find a boat. Fra Ambrosio kneels in prayer.

ACT TWO: CAPRI; A BLUE GROTTO   In Act Two, the scene changes to an entirely different world. Here, in a blue grotto, we are in the abode of Golfo, a powerful sea sprite who rules over the sea around and about him. Two of Golfo's naiads approach the grotto in the great sea shell they use for a boat. They bring to their master Teresina, whom they have rescued. Teresina still holds the guitar she was playing to Gennaro in the fishing boat before the storm broke over Naples.

Teresina asks Golfo to return her to her home, but the sea sprite is fascinated by the girl's beauty and wishes to keep her by him. Over her head he pours the magical water of the grotto, and the girl becomes a naiad; she forgets entirely that she was ever a mortal.

All of Golfo's naiads and Tritons forgather and celebrate the initiation of the newcomer. Golfo himself makes love to her, but Teresina repulses his advances.

Gennaro's boat enters the grotto. Golfo signals his slaves to disappear: he, alone, will deal with the intruder. Gennaro beaches the boat and looks about him. He sees Teresina's guitar. He knows now that she is alive! Golfo tries to induce him to leave the grotto by causing fire to engulf the grotto, but Gennaro refuses to go. He asks for Teresina, and finally the other naiads bring the girl to him.

Of course, since she is no longer a human being, the girl does not recognize her lover. Gennaro tries to bring back her memory by speaking of their life together in Naples and by playing upon her guitar, but still the girl is unmoved. Gennaro is about to give up, when he remembers the image of the Virgin which Fra Ambrosio gave him. He beseeches the Madonna that Teresina's memory may be restored. Slowly Teresina recognizes him. She remembers their love, and the two lovers embrace.

Golfo, enraged at the reconciliation of the lovers, contrives to kidnap Teresina. But the girl will not leave Gennaro. The Tritons and naiads cannot separate them. Teresina realizes though, that they will never be able to return home unless Golfo's rage is calmed. She holds up the image of the Madonna and commands Golfo and his sea creatures to bow to the Queen of Heaven. Golfo and his Tritons and naiads submit, and the two lovers set sail for Naples in a boat weighed down with gifts.

ACT THREE: MONTE VIRGINES, NEAR NAPLES   The people of the city are gathered together on a religious pilgrimage outside Naples, when Teresina appears with her mother. The people are astonished. Gennaro arrives, and Teresina informs her friends that her lover rescued her. But her friends, who believed her dead, find that such a claim is too mysterious: perhaps witches are at work. Teresina's mother separates her from Gennaro.

Gennaro rails at Teresina's mother for believing such nonsense. The people flee in fear of witchcraft. Only Fra Ambrosio can set them right. He is sent for, blesses Gennaro, and tells the crowd how Teresina was rescued through the power of the Virgin.

Everyone believes the monk instantly, and all gather about Teresina and Gennaro. They dance to celebrate the reunion of the lovers, and Teresina and

Gennaro are lifted into a cart, in which their friends draw them toward their home, marriage, and a happy life together.

NOTES The critic Kitty Cunningham, who attended the Royal Danish Ballet festival in 1973, has written an interesting essay, "Watching Bournonville," in *Ballet Review* (Vol. 4, No. 6), in which the Bournonville ballet technique is discussed historically and also from the point of view of present dance practice. Commenting on that technique in the essay, the dancer Ellen Everett, who has danced in American Ballet Theatre's arrangement of *Divertissements from "Napoli"* (staged by Hans Brenaa), said: "Bournonville is a different language. Using the floor is stressed. This kind of dancing helps you jump and it helps you use your feet better. The way you carry yourself and the weight of the body falling helps you to do the movement. The *epaulement* is different too—especially the way you tilt from the waist and look under your arm. Every movement finishes and then melts into a *port de bras* for the real finish. But the phrasing and rhythms are the main difference. Everything feels up even when it is down."

For further reading on Bournonville technique, the volume by Lillian Moore and Erik Bruhn, *Bournonville and Ballet Technique* (London, 1961), is recommended. The writer Walter Terry is preparing a complete syllabus of the Bournonville classes and technique.

## N.Y. EXPORT, OP. JAZZ

*Music by Robert Prince. Choreography by Jerome Robbins. Decor by Ben Shahn. Costumes by Florence Klotz. First presented by Jerome Robbins's Ballets: U.S.A. at the Festival of Two Worlds, Spoleto, Italy, June 8, 1958. First presented in the United States by Ballets: U.S.A. at the Alvin Theatre, New York, September 4, 1958.*

When *N.Y. Export, Op. Jazz* was first performed in England, the critic Richard Buckle called it "an epic of our time." He wrote that the ballet is about young people of today "and addresses these mistrustful creatures in their own language." Describing the work in a program note, the choreographer wrote: "There has always been a tremendous amount of popular dancing in America. At this time its vitality has reached a new high, developing and expanding in form and style from the basic and major contributions of the Negro and the Latin American. Because of a strong unconscious emotional kinship with those minority roots, the teenagers particularly have popularized these dances. Feeling very much like a minority group in this threatening and explosive world into which they have been born, the young have so identified with the dynamics, kinetic impetus, the drives and 'coolness' of today's jazz steps, that these dances have become an expression of our youths' outlook and their attitudes toward the contemporary world around them, just as each era's dances have significantly reflected the character of our changing world and a manner of dealing with it. *N.Y. Export, Op. Jazz* is a formal, abstract ballet based on the kinds of movements, complexities of rhythms, expressions of relationships, and qualities of atmosphere found in today's dances."

The dance action is divided into five parts. There is first of all a drop curtain proclaiming the title in bold colors and design. When this rises, we watch a group of young dancers performing against a backdrop of television aerials. They are cool, detached, staring at the audience as if we should quietly drop dead. They then ignore us and dance in their own way of forgetting. But they cannot ignore a warning in the sky which threatens to envelop them. They fall flat on their faces. The next dance, "Statics," takes place on a rooftop, where five boys have a good time with one girl. When they are through with her, they throw her out before they have to look at her. In "Improvisations," we are in a playground or a dance hall where everyone can relax and show off without adult interference. "Passage for Two," the fourth sequence, is a blues *pas de deux* for two young lovers who meet casually, become interested in each other, embrace but then separate as if nothing at all had happened. The final section, "Theme, Variations, and Fugue," is a celebration of contemporary dance rhythms and styles, beginning with formal dignity and quickening into variations and a fugue of final hopefulness and defiance.

NOTES  Reviewing the London performances of *N.Y. Export, Op. Jazz,* Mary Clarke wrote in *The Dancing Times:* "It is a stunning work; it lifts you in your seat with excitement and admiration for the way it is danced and leaves you breathless with wonder about a choreographer who can orchestrate group movement so brilliantly . . . There is a kind of poetry, too, particularly in the Passage for Two when two solitary creatures make love without, you feel, even knowing each other's names . . . There is a lively sense of sympathy yet rivalry between the choreographer and the composer, Robert Prince, and a nice sense of fitness about the backcloths by Ben Shahn." In his collaboration with Robert Prince, from whom he commissioned the score, Jerome Robbins worked first with music that had been composed, secondarily with music written to conform to specific dance ideas he had in mind and—at the beginning of the last section—with no music at all. In that last section the composer wrote the theme and the first three or four variations after the dances had been set. After that, according to Robbins, the composer took over and the choreographer followed.

At the invitation of the President and Mrs. Kennedy, *N.Y. Export, Op. Jazz* was performed by Ballets: U.S.A. at the White House, April 11, 1962, in honor of the Shah and Empress of Iran.


# NIGHT SHADOW (La Sonnambula)

*Ballet in one act. Music by Vittorio Rieti, after Bellini. Choreography by George Balanchine. Book by Vittorio Rieti. Scenery and costumes by Dorothea Tanning. First presented by the Ballet Russe de Monte Carlo at the City Center, New York, February 27, 1946, with Alexandra Danilova as the*

Sleepwalker, *Nicholas Magallanes as the* Poet, *Maria Tallchief as the* Coquette, *and Michel Katcharoff as the* Host.

This dramatic ballet was suggested by the opera *La Sonnambula* (*The Sleepwalker*) by Vincenzo Bellini. *Night Shadow* has a dark, romantic mood appropriate to the suppressed and clandestine loves that dominate the story. The time is long ago, a time of rigid conventions that the romantic spirit aimed to destroy.

The ballet begins with a masked ball in the garden of a great house. The host, an elderly man, welcomes his guests, who bow to him deferentially. Near the host stands the coquette, a beautiful young girl, who tosses her head quickly and seems to have a decided hold on his affections. Her controlled vivacity appears slightly out of place in this gathering. All join in a general dance led by the host and his partner.

The poet enters. He is a handsome young man, renowned for his work, and all the guests turn to look at him. There is a pause in all movement, and the atmosphere is expectant. Finally, reluctantly and carefully, the host introduces the poet to his mistress.

All the guests have arrived, and the host orders the entertainment to begin. The couples stand aside and watch two peasant couples in a pastoral dance, a Moorish dance by two blackamoors, followed by a harlequin, who performs an amusing, grotesque solo. The guests applaud the entertainers and gradually move out of the garden to go to supper.

The coquette and the poet watch as the others depart. Both remain on the scene. They approach each other and dance a *pas de deux* that shows us the mutual attraction they feel. The poet is somewhat passive as the willful coquette claims him. Their love duet is cut short by the return of the party. The host goes immediately to the coquette and claims her attention. He is angry. The guests sense an embarrassing tension and turn away. The coquette smiles at the host, reassures him, and takes his arm. They follow the guests and leave the poet alone.

As he is bemoaning his misfortune, he sees what appears to be a ghost coming toward him slowly. The figure is all in white and carries a tall lighted candle in one hand. As it comes closer, the poet sees before him a beautiful woman walking in her sleep. Her long black hair hangs about her shoulders, her face is composed in sleep, and she moves as in a dream, rapidly but softly, dancing across the garden on point, never descending to the ground.

The poet is instantly enamored of this strange, lovely creature, who seems to be a part of his own dream, and he approaches her. But the woman does not waken. The poet dances around her, lies before her on the ground, encircles her, begging her to waken and respond to his love. The woman does not notice him and walks alone in her own dream, stepping over his recumbent body as if he were merely a stone. She begins to drift away, out of the garden. The poet, now desperate, follows.

The coquette returns at this point for a quick rendezvous and sees her lover following the woman in white. She is furious. The host returns to the garden with his guests. The coquette takes him aside and whispers to him. The host looks up, startled and enraged. The coquette leaves him and joins the other guests in a formal ensemble dance. During the dance, we watch the host, dagger in hand, leave the garden unobserved.

When the guests have applauded a final *divertissement,* the poet runs into the garden. He staggers in pain and clutches at his heart. Blood streams through his fingers. The couples stand back, horrified. The coquette watches him and does not move. The poet falls to the ground and dies. The guests stare at the beautiful woman in white, who moves, still in her sleep, across the garden. They follow her. She is the wife of the host.

NOTES   Bellini's *La Sonnambula* (1831) merely provided the subject matter for the ballet *Night Shadow* and not its plot. The opera tells the story of a romance between a farmer and a miller's daughter who is addicted to walking in her sleep. The score for the ballet is an arrangement of music from *La Sonnambula* and *I Puritani,* by the same composer.

*La Sonnambula*—as it is now usually called—is danced by the New York City Ballet, the Washington National Ballet, the Royal Danish Ballet, the Ballet Rambert in London, and by a number of other companies for which John Taras has staged the production. The New York City Ballet *La Sonnambula,* in a setting by Esteban Francés, was first presented January 6, 1960, with Erik Bruhn, Allegra Kent, Jillana, Edward Villella, Suki Schorer, and William Weslow. The costumes were by André Levasseur, obtained from the Marquis de Cuevas production in which Marjorie Tallchief and George Skibine appeared for some years.

Soon after the ballet was first presented, the American critic Edwin Denby wrote, in *Looking at the Dance:* "Mysterious in the interaction of its elements; the vapid ballroom dances; the winsome exhibition numbers that have a perverse and cruel undertone; the elaborate, encircling artifices of the coquette's *pas de deux;* the directness and space of the sleepwalking scene . . . The progress of the piece is 'romantic'—it is disconcerting, absurd and disproportionate; but its effect when it is over is powerful and exact. It gives you a sense—as Poe does—of losing your bearings, the feeling of an elastic sort of time and a heaving floor. As a friend of mine remarked, 'When it's over, you don't know what hit you.' "

# NIGHTWINGS

*Music by John La Montaine. Choreography by Gerald Arpino. Decor by Ming Cho Lee; Associate Designer, Holly Haas. Costumes by Wilma Kim. First presented by the City Center Joffrey Ballet, September 7, 1966, with Lisa Bradley, Michael Uthoff, and Nels Jorgensen in principal roles.*

*Nightwings* is set to music from *Birds of Paradise,* a score by the American composer John La Montaine. The repeated yet varied incantations of the birdcalls are suggestive of the timelessness in nature. The composer has said that the musical ideas on which the score is based "are taken from sounds of nature heard in remote places: in woods and forests, at the ocean shore, in the mountains. That other world of strange sounds, not man-made, the true primeval music, is both the subject matter and the poetical idea of the piece: the rustlings, the murmurings, the sudden silences, the sustained shrill excitement of vociferous birdcalls, their merriment, and their mourning; the simplicity and the purity of the single voice, and the incalculable random complexity, the cacophony of the total aural impression, a veritable 'caldron of sound.' In the runic repetitious incantations of birds, seemingly always the same, but in fact always different, some sense of the meaning of timelessness can be felt."

In the ballet a young man sleeps on a cot in a poor room in the city on a hot summer's night. The window curtain blows in a slight breeze. A bird cage stands on the floor. He dreams. The electric signs and water towers of the surrounding cityscape rise into the heavens and the boy seems to fly too, with them. A girl-like flying creature is brought to him. He watches her carefully, then seizes her to dance. Although she, frantic and frightened at being caught, at first seems to yield to the boy's fascination, her creatures do not permit such independence. They hold her above the boy and do not permit him to come closer. Then, in a quick shift from passion to unfulfilled action, she falls on the boy and chokes him to death. He is carried beneath her back to his cot and set to rest as she hovers over him full-length, bidding him farewell. The night-winged bird is then lifted off high to disappear as the boy writhes in his sleep and the cityscape returns. The light bulb above him flickers and his dream is over. Golden clouds descend.


# NIJINSKY—CLOWN OF GOD

*Ballet by Maurice Béjart. Music by Pierre Henry. Costumes by Joelle Roustan and Roger Bernard. Lighting by Roger Bernard. Sound direction by Pierre Henry. First presented by the Ballet of the Twentieth Century at the Forest National Auditorium, Brussels, October 8, 1971, with Jorge Donn as* The Clown of God, *Paolo Bartoluzzi as the* Rose, *Daniel Lommel as the* Golden Slave, *Jorg Lanner as the* Faun, *Micha Van Hoecke as* Petrouchka, *Suzanne Farrell as the* Girl in Pink, *Angele Albrecht as the* Nymph, *Jaleh Kerendi as the* Woman of the World, *Cathérine Verneuil as the* Ballerina, *Hitomi Asakawa as the* Doll, *and Pierre Dobrievich as* Diaghilev *in the principal roles. First presented in the United States by the Ballet of the Twentieth Century at the Felt Forum, Madison Square Garden, New York, October 24, 1972.*

The ballet is given in two parts, the whole consisting of eleven scenes. During the work, extracts from *The Diary of Vaslav Nijinsky* are read over the loudspeaker. It is largely upon this book, which Maurice Béjart reread in 1971, that his ballet on the life of the most renowned of all dancers is based. Béjart has said: "Of all the famous names connected with that rich and strange era of Diaghilev and the Russian Ballet, the person of Nijinsky is perhaps the most perplexing and fascinating. Even to those not particularly interested in ballet, the name and the phenomenon of this great dancer must be familiar. It is generally known that he was one of the most spectacular dancers the world has ever seen, that he was especially renowned for his sensational leap, and that his career was tragically curtailed by madness. Yet Nijinsky's personality and the forces that led to his madness are widely unknown.

"In one of his works Henry Miller, alone on an island, talks about the books he could not live without; among the two or three great titles which he cites appears *The Diary of Nijinsky*. He adds: 'I never grow tired of reading it.' The key to Nijinsky is in that *Diary*—a disturbing document about an exceptional human being.

"The *Diary* was written as his total madness was approaching and records his most inward feelings, emotions, and fantasies. In life, Nijinsky was described by his contemporaries as quiet, slow, and rather awkward, yet when he emerged upon the stage his personality was transformed and his body expressed grace, poetry, and dynamic energy. In the *Diary* yet another side of his personality is revealed—a quick, restless, and highly cultured mind reacting with intensity to the events and people around him. The *Diary* is a frightening yet uplifting book, for we watch Nijinsky's mind gradually giving way under the pressure of its own sensitivity to the horrors of the First World War, to Diaghilev's cruel treatment of him after his marriage, and to the artistic pressures of creativity. Yet beyond all this we feel his burning conviction in his role as 'Clown of God' and in his need to preach the gospel of universal love.

"This ballet does not attempt to be a biographical reconstruction of Nijinsky's life, but, taking its inspiration from the *Diary*, it tries to create a marginal note, a secret path where the heart, ideas, emotions, memories, and fantasies can live and dance an imaginary ballet on lines similar, perhaps, to those of his own thoughts during the last conscious moments of his life. Imaginative and allegorical figures come alive and enact the conflicts in Nijinsky's mind—representations of characters from his ballets and from his life. Most important among these are the three principal characters in the action: NIJINSKY HIMSELF—the artist and poet in search of Truth, who sees himself as the apostle of universal love, a mystic messenger of God; WOMAN—not just Nijinsky's own wife, but a symbol of love and poetry, a vision and a creature of the spirit; DIAGHILEV—Nijinsky's master, father, creator. In short, his God, at once feared and adored."

The setting of the ballet is a large open stage dominated by a large black cross. From left and right, high ramps descend to the open area. Everything is dark. A voice sounds: "The world was made by God, Man was made by God. It is impossible for man to understand God, but God understands God."

Béjart's "Clown of God" theme for this work is also taken from Nijinsky's *Diary:* "I will pretend to be a clown, because then they will understand me better. I love Shakespeare's clowns—they have a lot of humor, but nevertheless they express hate, they are not from God. I am a clown of God, and therefore like joking. I mean that a clown is all right when he expresses love. A clown without love is not from God."

A synopsis of the ballet follows.

PART ONE: THE NIJINSKY OF THE RUSSIAN BALLET 1. *The Creation of the World:* Inert, naked, and faceless bodies cover the stage. Under God's eyes they become animated, organized, breathing. The circle is formed. Life!

A being detaches itself from the anonymous mass and places itself in the center of the Circle. God gives him a face. It is man: The Clown of God. Slowly the Creator forms him, teaches him to live, to walk, to jump, to *Dance.*

2. *Earthly Paradise:* God creates Earthly Paradise for his most favored creature. . . . It is the age of the Russian Ballet, that torrent of images of Paradise, that revelation of color, sound, and light which, in five years, was to conquer the world. As a companion, God gives him *Dance,* personified by the Ballerina and, for friends, four guardian angels, four fantastic creatures: a Rose, a Faun, Petrouchka, and a Golden Slave, symbols of the four elements: Air, Earth, Water, and Fire.

3. *The Woman:* But his craving for a great and constant love, and his tenderness force him to create a new image of love. A woman, unreal at first, grows in his soul. Little by little she takes a tangible shape and he seeks in her the support of a creature of flesh and blood. The face of his dreams suddenly becomes the face of one woman—his WIFE.

4. *The Fall:* Nijinsky is tempted during the absence of God. He marries suddenly in South America and incurs the wrath of Diaghilev, who, when informed of the event, banishes him from the Russian Ballet. Earthly paradise crumbles. It is 1914—the end of an era.

PART TWO: THE NIJINSKY OF GOD The search for love, for true love, is long. Diaghilev is no longer God. A god who rejects his own creation, a god who will not pardon is not a god of love, not a true god.

His companion is by his side, but she cannot follow him in his search for the Divine, in his love of Humanity. He is alone, and alone he has to suffer a long Calvary at this time, troubled as it is by the horror of war; it is this that will lead to the famous day which he called his "Marriage with God," the day of his last dance recital on January 19, 1919, when in a series of sublime improvisations, he portrayed in mime the horrors of war, the absurd, senseless, and grotesque features of his times, and his love of God and Humanity. Vaslav Nijinsky no longer exists, but may this ballet help the world to love and know this unique, angelic being, in whom physical grace reflected spiritual grace, and whose technique and genius were immense because they serve God and brotherly love.

NOTES Writing of the ballet *Nijinsky* in the *Wall Street Journal,* Peter J. Rosenwald said: "'People want to have sports and mystery,' says Maurice Béjart, an innovative Belgian whose Ballet of the Twentieth Century comes to New York tomorrow. Mr. Béjart's company will be performing a controversial work called *Nijinsky, Clown of God,* but not at Lincoln Center or some other chaste establishment of the dance.

"Rather, *Nijinsky, Clown of God,* will get its first New York viewing at that midtown palace of cheers, boos, sweat, and liniment, Madison Square Garden's Felt Forum. As in Europe, where this ambitious work also has played in large sports arenas—such as the 5,000-seat Palais des Sports in Paris—Mr. Béjart hopes to attract some new converts to the dance from among people who might know more about Nijinsky, the race horse, than Nijinsky, the dancer. The ballet has drawn enthusiastic, animated crowds in Europe, even though it has been alternately praised and damned by European critics.

"In a masterpiece of dance theater, Mr. Béjart has fashioned a work which perfectly uses the many talents of his versatile company to tell factually and metaphorically the story of the great Ukrainian dancer, Vaslav Nijinsky, from his discovery by choreographer Serge Diaghilev of the Ballet Russe to his agonizing death in 1950, insane and lonely, believing himself to be incarnate God. Using extracts from Nijinsky's diary, the work concentrates on Nijinsky the man, Nijinsky the dancer, and Nijinsky's deeply religious yearnings. Said Nijinsky in his diary, 'I appear as a clown to make myself better understood. . . . I think that a clown is only perfect when he expresses love, otherwise he is no longer a clown of God.'

"What gives the work its vitality (and what seems to offend most academic critics) is the fusion of Nijinsky the man and the four most famous roles he portrayed: The Rose in *Spectre de la Rose*, the Golden Slave in *Scheherazade*, the Faun in *L'Après-Midi d'un Faun* and Petrouchka, the puppet with a soul, in the ballet of the same name. Not only has Mr. Béjart created five Nijinskys who often appear on the stage at the same time but he has given each of them a clown whose purpose is to symbolize their inner souls.

"From the moment when a giant papier-maché figure of Impresario Diaghilev points its finger at a mass of dancers and chooses Nijinsky, the stage is a whirl of action. Giant crosses rise from it, whole ballets within the ballet seem to take the focus of activity. The music varies from the familiar strains of Tchaikovsky's *Pathétique* Symphony to contemporary Pierre Henry's electronic score.

"There is a brilliant madness in Mr. Béjart's superimpositions of sight and sound, past and present, real and imagined, to produce a surprisingly integrated and intimate picture of Nijinsky's strange genius, his search for the relationship between art, love, and religion and an ultimate sense that the world which rejects his gifts of love is to blame for his madness and his death. Perhaps it is.

"If Mr. Béjart is sometimes excessive in his symbolism and uneven in his choreography, his dancers more than make up for these failings with stunning performances which give life to the characters and credibility to their actions. Jorge Donn's Nijinsky, Clown of God, and Suzanne Farrell as the Girl in Pink, who becomes Nijinsky's wife, are memorable and unique expressions of dance theater at its best.

"If *Nijinsky, Clown of God* has a major flaw, it is in proving that nothing exceeds like excess. It is so rich that it sometimes overwhelms itself and the spectacle overcomes its meaning. But it is never dull, never intellectual for its own sake, and never uninteresting."

## LES NOCES (The Wedding)

*Cantata with dances. Music and words by Igor Stravinsky. Choreography by Bronislava Nijinska. Scenery and costumes by Nathalie Gontcharova. First presented by Diaghilev's Ballets Russes at the Théâtre Gaîté-Lyrique, Paris, June 14, 1923, with Felia Dubrovska as the Bride and Leon Woizikowski as the Bridegroom. First presented in the United States by the League of American Composers at the Metropolitan Opera House, New York, April 25, 1929, with scenery and costumes by Serge Soudeikine and choreography by Elizaveta Anderson-Ivantzova.*

Stravinsky's dramatic cantata *Les Noces* depicts the ancient Russian peasant marriage ritual. Singers on the stage sing words which the dancers accompany with meaningful movement.

SCENE ONE: BENEDICTION OF THE BRIDE; THE TRESSES   The voice of the bride is heard chanting before the rise of the curtain. The scene is the interior of a peasant home in old Russia. The bride stands in the center of the stage, surrounded by her mother and her friends. Her friends help to calm the grief she feels at leaving her home, her fear of life with a man who seems to her now a stranger, and her hatred of the person who has arranged the match. The women tell her that her husband's father will accept her in their home and that her life will be much as it has been, that she must go through with everything for her own parents. At the bride's request, the women comb and bind her hair. They tell her that the birds outside the house are singing happily. Can't she be happy too? They ask God to bless her marriage.

SCENE TWO: BENEDICTION OF THE BRIDEGROOM; THE BRIDEGROOM'S HOUSE   The bridegroom's father and friends help him to prepare for his wedding. His hair, too, is combed and anointed. All wish him good luck. The parents of both the bride and the bridegroom lament the loss of their children, who are no longer children. The friends of the families congratulate the parents.

SCENE THREE: THE BRIDE'S DEPARTURE; THE WEDDING   The bride is prepared to go forth from her house to meet the bridegroom at the church. Her friends tell her she is a princess this day. At the church, the bridegroom kisses the cross. The best man declares his friend is present to greet his bride. The guests pay tribute to the bridegroom's love for his parents. The bride enters, and the wedding ceremony takes place. As the couple leaves, all congratulate them. Their parents lament.

SCENE FOUR: THE WEDDING FEAST   At the wedding feast, the father of the bride presents her to the assembled guests. Men in the company inform her of the household duties she must perform. The bridegroom is informed of his responsibilities to his wife. Everyone drinks and is joyous.

An older married couple is selected, from among the guests, to warm the marriage bed. There is a toast to the young couple, after which they are conducted to the door of their room. The older couple returns to the feast.

The guests gather about the parents of the bride and the bridegroom as they sit beside the door to their children's room. The bridegroom sings of his love for his wife.

NOTES  *Les Noces* was first performed in the United States in concert form, at Aeolian Hall, New York, in February 1926, under the auspices of the International Composers Guild.

Leopold Stokowski conducted the first United States performance of the complete cantata with dances. Marc Blitzstein, Aaron Copland, Louis Gruenberg, and Frederick Jacobi were the four pianists on this occasion.

Bronislava Nijinska's staging of *Les Noces* was first presented in the United States by the Ballet Russe de Monte Carlo in 1936, with Irina Baronova and Yurek Shabelevsky in the principal roles.

Nijinska's ballet was revived by the Royal Ballet in London March 23, 1966, with Svetlana Beriosova and Robert Mead in the principal roles. This production was first presented in the United States at the new Metropolitan Opera House, New York, May 2, 1967. After the London première, Mary Clarke reported in *Dance News* that the London press "has never acclaimed a ballet so unanimously." Alexander Bland wrote in *The Observer:* "The curtain rises on the Bride flanked by her companions holding her long ritual pigtails. 'Oh fair tress of my hair' sings the soprano—and this could be the motif of the whole ballet. The score weaves a crisp embroidery of words and music, poetry and slang. On the stage, in place of delicate classical curlecues and filigrees, Nijinska plaits her dancers together, kneads them into knotted mounds, tugs them backwards and forwards like lengths of thick hemp.

"The patterns are stiff and new as linen. The steps are complicated but rough, repeating like a sampler pattern. The groups are blunt and tight and rounded. Without a hint of rural charm, she evokes a peasant world where a wedding means . . . a vow, a bed, having children, dying and leaving them money and a cow. *Les Noces* is a superb example of the Diaghilev ideal—contributions of individual, almost independent merit, bound together into a single perfect skein."

*A dance cantata. Music by Igor Stravinsky. Choreography by Jerome Robbins. Set by Oliver Smith. Costumes by Patricia Zipprodt. Lighting by Jean Rosenthal. First presented by the American Ballet Theatre at the State Theatre, New York, March 30, 1965, with Erin Martin as the* Bride *and William Glassman as the* Bridegroom.

Preparing program notes for *Les Noces*, Jerome Robbins wrote: "Stravinsky used as material for *Les Noces* the ritualistic elements found in the ancient customs and traditions of Russian peasant weddings, but reserved the right to use them with absolute freedom, paying little heed to ethnolographical considerations. His purpose was not to reproduce the wedding or show a stage dramatization with descriptive music, but rather to present a ritualized abstraction of its essences, customs, and tempers.

"The text is adapted from folk songs and popular verse, typical wedding remarks, clichés of conversations, but again they are not used realistically but rather as a collage of the words spoken or sung during these traditional rites. The first half of the 'scenic ceremony' deals with the preparations, and revolves around religious elements. Alternating with these intense invocations and blessings are continual lamentations by the parents for the loss of their children, and by the bride against the matchmaker, on leaving home, and on losing her virginity.

"In the second half (the wedding feast) the grief and religious elements are forgotten in robust celebrations with food, drink, songs, toasts, boasts, bawdiness, rough jokes, etc. A married couple is selected to warm the bed and finally the marriage is allowed to be consummated while all sit outside the nuptial chamber."

The composition is divided into four tableaux which run without interruption:

TABLEAU I: PREPARATION OF THE BRIDE  Before a backdrop with two huge ironlike figures of saints, the musicians, four pianists, and a chorus file on stage. Then from both sides of the stage come the dancers in rough brown and white peasant dress. They bow to each other, to the musicians, and begin to dance. The bride flings out her two long braids on both sides and the women take up the strands and begin to plait her hair. The bride weeps and laments, her father and mother are entangled in the strands. Her tresses sing: "In the evening my mother braided you with care, she combed you with a silver comb, she combed you, she braided you. Ah, poor me, poor me. Alas, poor me." Then she is picked up like a child and taken out.

TABLEAU II: PREPARATION OF THE GROOM  The bridegroom is pushed out before the guests by his friends. As his mother berates him, we see that he is indeed her child as he crouches while his friends dance. Then one of them insists that he join them. There is a dance with his parents. Two bass voices sing: "Bless me, my father, my mother, bless your child who proudly goes against the wall of stone to break it."

TABLEAU III: DEPARTURE OF BRIDE; CODA: LAMENTATION OF MOTHERS  The bride enters in a white dress trimmed with orange and with an orange bow. She crouches in *plié*, then as her friends dance about her, she is lifted up and carried off in triumph. The lights dim and the two mothers lament: "My own dear one, child of mine, do not leave me, little one."

TABLEAU IV: WEDDING FEAST  When the lights come up, the bride and bridegroom are seen in the center. During a ritual dance both are raised high and then set down. The chorus sings realistic advice: "Love your wife, cherish her like your soul, shake her like a plum tree." The girl then dances to her friends and the boy to his. Then, after their bed has been warmed, they are placed together on a platform like two lost children and the marriage is consummated in quick trembling. The pianos and a bell strike a bell chord fortissimo and a solo bass sings, as a bridegroom would sing to his bride: "Dear heart, my own little wife, let us live in happiness so that all men may envy us." The bell chord tolls throughout his song, he finishes, the pianos alone take the chord, we hear it on every eighth beat, then there is no more singing, the pianos stop and we have only the persistent bell chord. The time between its sounding measures an infinity of happiness.

NOTES    Jerome Robbins's ballet was acclaimed by all the critics after its first performance. Allen Hughes in the New York *Times* called it "an overwhelming fusion of animal energy, ritualistic ardor, and rhythmic attack." Doris Hering in *Dance Magazine* said that the dancers in performance were in "what might be called a state of rhythmic grace . . . The dancers bowed . . . and then the surge began! They were drawn into a relentless sea of stamping, jumping, and somersaults. Sometimes there were brief allusions to national style in the use of squared arms or the digging of one heel into the ground and curving the feet outward. Always they seemed to be caught in something jubilant and ominous at the same time."

## NOMOS ALPHA

*Music by Iannis Xenakis. Choreography by Maurice Béjart. First presented by the Ballet of the Twentieth Century, at Royan, April 2, 1969, with Paolo Bortoluzzi. First presented in the United States by the same ensemble at the Brooklyn Academy of Music, New York, January 26, 1971.*

This dance for the *premier danseur* of Béjart's Ballet of the Twentieth Century was designed to exploit fully the capacities of two instruments, cello and dancer, within two structures, one musical, the other choreographic, "both extending to the utmost the potentials of the two."

A boy dressed in a bright red costume stands in a cone of brilliant light. He quivers in response to the music, and moving in and out of the light, alternates styles of dance, shifting from "classical" to "demi-caractère," taking up suggestions by the cello and sometimes making fun of them. When the cello sounds like a cat meowing, the dancer makes like a cat. But there appears to be a seriousness, too, about the piece as the dancer and music interact.

Writing about *Nomos Alpha* in *Dance and Dancers* magazine, the critic John Percival said: "The solo Béjart has made by Bortoluzzi is entirely unexpected. The music, for solo cello, is supposed to drive the player to the furthest extremes of his instrument's range, and Béjart does the same for the dancer . . . There is a fantastic variety here: walking, stretching, signalling in semaphore, now fast, now slow, now smooth, now jerky, nothing repeated, all

done with marvelous clarity and beautiful plastique, and nothing ever repeated although the solo lasts, I think, the best part of twenty minutes."

# THE NUTCRACKER

*Classic Ballet in two acts. Music by Tchaikovsky. Choreography by Lev
Ivanov. Book by Lev Ivanov. Scenery by M. I. Botcharov. First presented
at the Maryinsky Theatre, St. Petersburg, December 17, 1892, with An-
toinetta Dell-Era and Paul Gerdt as the Sugarplum Fairy and the Prince.
First presented in Western Europe by the Sadler's Wells Ballet at the Sadler's Wells Theatre, London, January 30, 1934, with Alicia Markova and
Harold Turner. This version was staged by Nicholas Sergeyev, after Ivanov.
First presented in the United States in an abbreviated form by the Ballet
Russe de Monte Carlo at the Fifty-first Street Theatre, New York, October
17, 1940, with Alicia Markova and André Eglevsky. Scenery and costumes
by Alexandre Benois. Presented in the United States in complete form by
the San Francisco Ballet, 1944, with choreography by William Christensen.
Presented by the New York City Ballet, with choreography by George Balanchine, February 2, 1954, with Alberta Grant as Clara, Susan Kaufman
as Fritz, Michael Arshansky as Herr Drosselmeyer, Paul Nickel as the Nutcracker and Maria Tallchief and Nicholas Magallanes as the Sugarplum
Fairy and her Cavalier. Scenery by Horace Armistead. Costumes by Karinska. Masks by Vlady. Revived in a new production by the New York City
Ballet with scenery by Rouben Ter-Arutunian and costumes by Karinska at
the New York State Theatre, December 11, 1964.*

It is another sign of how popular ballet has become that today many companies perform *The Nutcracker*. It has almost become a kind of annual Christmas ritual in many American and Canadian cities. Of course this was not always so. We used to rely on a touring company to give us a truncated version
of this full-length work, a ballet people used to call *Nutcracker Suite* because
they knew the music better than the ballet. Now that is all different. I have
heard that more than fifty groups do this ballet. The one we do in New York
every Christmas was first presented in 1954 and we have been doing it every
year since. There have been changes in the production (I am always making
them) but in its main outlines the story and the action are about the same.

I have liked this ballet from the first time I danced in it as a boy, when I
did small roles in the Maryinsky Theatre production. When I was fifteen, I
danced the Nutcracker Prince. Years later in New York, when our company
decided to do an evening-long ballet, I preferred to turn to *The Nutcracker*,
with which American audiences were not sufficiently familiar. I accordingly
went back to the original score, restored cuts that had been made, and in the
development of the story chose to use the original story by E. T. A. Hoffmann,
although keeping to the outlines of the dances as given at the Maryinsky. A
prologue was added and the dances restaged.

The three scenes of the ballet are arranged in two acts. In the first act, we are in the real world but begin a journey to the magical kingdom of the second.

The overture to the ballet is bright and delicate. Pizzicato strings and tinkling triangles create a light, intimate atmosphere that sets the stage for the action.

ACT ONE   When the curtain goes up, we are in a hallway of a large house looking at the door to the living room. This is the home of Dr. Stahlbaum, a city official, and his wife. It is Christmas Eve. Their children, Marie and Fritz, have fallen asleep by the door as their parents decorate the Christmas tree. Behind the keyhole, the parents and the maid are putting the finishing touches to the tree and arranging presents underneath. The children awaken and eagerly await the arrival of the guests. For there is to be a Christmas party, a family affair for relatives and close friends, but most of all a party for children.

Soon the other children arrive with their parents, and the doors are opened. All rejoice in the large, lighted tree. The grown-ups greet each other and there is much speculation among the children about what is in the packages. Now the parents organize things. Dr. Stahlbaum divides the children for games and dances. The boys do a brisk march and then there is a polite formal quadrille for the girls and the boys. Some of the grown-ups join in. Soon grandparents come to join the party, refreshments are served, and, most important of all, presents are given out.

The children are sitting quietly looking at their presents when suddenly everyone looks up. Something seems to have gone wrong. The lights flicker and over the huge grandfather clock a terrifying old owl flaps his wings as the hour is sounded. Then at the door an old gentleman looking very much like the owl comes in. This is Herr Drosselmeyer, an old family friend who is also Marie's godfather. He wears a black patch over one eye. He is a mysterious man, a marvelous inventor of moving toys, and he has brought with him three large boxes and also his handsome young nephew. Drosselmeyer kisses Marie and introduces her to his nephew, whom she likes at once. The gifts in the huge boxes delight everyone—a Harlequin and Columbine and a Toy Soldier who dance to jolly tunes. Then Drosselmeyer brings out a large Nutcracker, a soldier, for Marie. He shows everybody how it works and Marie is clearly delighted with it. She is so pleased with it that Fritz is furious. He grabs the Nutcracker and stamps on it. The nephew chases him away as Marie weeps. Drosselmeyer plays doctor and ties a handkerchief around the Nutcracker's head.

Marie and her friends sit and rock their dolls to sleep, only to be interrupted by the rowdy boys, who disturb them with drums and bugles. The nephew brings Marie a toy bed for the Nutcracker and he is tucked in and put under the tree. All the children are tired and upset and clearly in need of sleep. Dr. Stahlbaum and his wife now lead all the guests in a final dance, Marie dancing with the nephew. At the end, they shake hands solemnly, reluctant to say good night to each other, hoping that they will meet again soon. Everyone goes off to bed, the room darkens, and only by the lights of the Christmas tree can we make out the empty space.

It is midnight. Marie enters in a white nightgown. She comes slowly into the room, being careful not to make any noise. She goes directly to the Nut-cracker, takes him up and cradles him in her arms. Then she goes to her bed and sleeps. Drosselmeyer enters, takes the Nutcracker from her, and fixes his jaw with a screwdriver. He restores the Nutcracker to her. There is a rustle, the Christmas tree lights flash on and off. Marie wakes. She puts the Nut-cracker back in his bed and just then old Drosselmeyer from on top of the clock flaps his arms like the owl and Marie is thoroughly terrified. What is he doing in the house, anyhow, at this time of night? Marie just manages to hide behind a curtain when a big fat rat comes in. She dashes to the couch and huddles there. Suddenly the Christmas tree and everything under it seem to be growing—even the toy soldiers. The walls of the room grow. The tree grows taller and taller, to a huge height. The mice are big too, and it is good that the soldiers are there to protect her. They battle the mice, but the mice, led by their fierce king, seem to be winning. Then the Nutcracker, grown to life size, rises from his bed and leads the soldiers.

The Nutcracker orders cannon brought and candy is fired at the mice. Marie throws her slipper, which hits the king of the mice by surprise. The Nut-cracker runs him through with his sword, and the battle is won.

Marie falls onto the bed, which begins mysteriously to glide out of the room into the snowy evening. She arrives at the Kingdom of Snow and is met by the Nutcracker, who before her very eyes suddenly turns into a handsome young prince. He bows to Marie, gives her the crown taken from the king of the mice and leads her away on a magic journey. In a snowy forest, snowflakes dance.

ACT TWO: KONFITUERENBURG (THE LAND OF SWEETS) When the curtain rises, we are in the inside of a huge box of candy. Twelve angels enclose the stage, each dressed in white and gold. The Sugarplum Fairy, who rules over this Kingdom of Sweets, makes a regal entry. She dances a charming variation to the tinkling celesta. The angels enclose her in a semicircle of love. Then leading the angels off, the Sugarplum Fairy welcomes the full candy box: Chocolates and Coffee and Tea sweets, Candy Canes, Marzipan, Polichinelles, and lovely Dew Drops. At this point, to majestic heralding music, a walnut boat arrives bringing the Nutcracker Prince and Marie. The prince escorts Marie to the shore and introduces her to the Sugarplum Fairy. The fairy then asks the prince what happened. The prince then relates in pantomime how they came from far away, how the Mouse King and his men attacked Marie and the toy soldiers, how the mice were defeated finally when Marie at just the right moment threw her slipper and the King of Mice had his crown cut off, which was given as a present to Marie. The Sugarplum Fairy congratu-lates the prince warmly on his victory and escorts him and Marie to a candy throne high on a dais. Before the pair are placed numerous sweets and creams to eat as they watch the entertainment that has been arranged for their pleasure.

We now watch a series of dances by the creatures of the candy kingdom. When they are finished, the Sugarplum Fairy and her cavalier perform the grandest dance of all, a *pas de deux* to climax the occasion. This is exactly the kind of dance that Marie would like to do, too, one day, and she and the prince rejoice in the splendid tenderness of the royal couple. All of the candies then come back in as the Sugarplum Fairy and her cavalier bid the young couple farewell. Marie and her prince step into a royal sleigh drawn by reindeer and before our very eyes the sleigh rises right into the sky and away.

*Ballet in two acts after the story "The Nutcracker and the Rat King" by E. T. A. Hoffmann. Music by Tchaikovsky. Choreography and production by Rudolf Nureyev (the Prince's variation in Act Two by Vassily Vainonen). Scenery and costumes by Nicholas Georgiadis. First presented by the Royal Swedish Ballet at the Royal Swedish Opera House, Stockholm, November 17, 1967. Presented by the Royal Ballet at the Royal Opera House, Covent Garden, London, February 29, 1968, and introduced by that ensemble to the United States at the Metropolitan Opera House, New York, May 10, 1968.*

ACT ONE   It is Christmas Eve early in the nineteenth century. The wealthy mayor, Dr. Stahlbaum, is giving a party for his friends and their children. The children are dancing and playing in excited anticipation of the approaching Christmas festivities and of their presents. Herr Drosselmeyer, an old friend of the family, arrives bringing the children gifts and amuses them by his conjuring tricks. He gives Clara, his favorite, a Nutcracker, which delights her. Her brother Fritz spitefully breaks it but Herr Drosselmeyer mends it for her. After the grandparents arrive and join in the dancing Clara becomes very tired and falling asleep in her chair, has a vivid dream. The room and the Christmas tree seem to grow . . . from the wainscot a swarm of rats appears trying to capture the Nutcracker, but Clara rushes to his rescue, throwing them her favorite dolls in an effort to distract them from him. From their toy fort an army of soldiers led by the Nutcracker (who suddenly springs to life) comes to help the fight against the rats and their leader, the Rat King. A company of Hussars and another of marines fight the rat army but are overwhelmed. The Nutcracker and the Rat King are left on the battlefield. Desperately Clara flings her shoe at the Rat King. As it strikes him he falls dead and a sudden transformation takes place revealing the Nutcracker as a young, handsome prince.

ACT TWO   Together the Nutcracker Prince and Clara are carried away to an enchanted grotto. There Clara becomes frightened by bats but when the prince comes to protect her she realizes that they are actually her family and friends transformed by her nightmare.

The grotto mysteriously changes into Clara's own toy theater where she finds many of her favorite dolls brought to life. The mood changes to one of happiness and everyone dances. As Clara's dream closes she is found still sleeping in her chair. Her mother and father waken her and, as the guests take their leave, the party comes to an end. Clara is left alone, enthralled by memories of her adventures.

NOTES   Rudolf Nureyev's version of *The Nutcracker* for the Royal Swedish

Ballet was reviewed for *Dance News* by Anna Greta Stahle: "The Christmas party takes place in a palace—suggesting old St. Petersburg. The parents and children are dressed in directoire style, and the old people, like Drosselmeyer, keep to the fashion of their youth and are in rococo. The acting and miming is staged with imagination and humor; it is indeed an elegant and lively party.

"Clara is a girl of an age between child and woman, and consequently her dreams are both childish and tinged with an erotic element. Nureyev has omitted the visit to the Kingdom of Sweets and has built the *divertissement* entirely on dreams in which Clara's family and Drosselmeyer appear in different shapes. The same dancer is seen as Drosselmeyer, the Rat King, and the Prince. Clara is herself all through the ballet, dancing the usual Sugarplum Fairy *pas de deux* with the Prince as though it were a dream of herself as a princess."

*Ballet in two acts. Music by Tchaikovsky. Production conceived, directed and choreographed by Mikhail Baryshnikov. Choreography for "Snowflake" dance by Vasily Vainonen. Decors by Boris Aronson. Costumes by Frank Thompson. Lighting by Jennifer Tipton. First presented by American Ballet Theatre at the Kennedy Center for the Performing Arts, Washington, December 21, 1976, with Marianna Tcherkassky as* Clara, *Alexander Minz as* Drosselmeyer *and Mikhail Baryshnikov as the* Nutcracker-Prince.

This *Nutcracker* is not child's play, though it is about a young girl growing up. It is different from other productions of this ballet in its focus on the two men who are central to the life of young Clara—Drosselmeyer, her godfather in real life, and the Nutcracker-Prince, the dream figure who is created by Drosselmeyer's magic. Here the child Clara is on the point of growing up. Aided by her godfather, a dream of love materializes only to cause later doubts. This psychological drama is set within the conventional frame of *The Nutcracker:* the names are the same but the action of the ballet varies dramatically.

In the Prologue, it is Christmas Eve, a time when dreams may become reality. Drosselmeyer, godfather to Clara Stahlbaum, prepares gifts and magic dolls for the annual Christmas party at the home of her parents. Clara is to be the ballet's heroine.

ACT ONE, SCENE ONE   The Stahlbaum household prepares for Christmas. Clara, her brother Fritz, their parents and grandmother are all much involved in entertaining guests while at the same time enjoying the festivities themselves. Suddenly, Drosselmeyer appears and produces a magic puppet show. The puppets act out the fairy tale of the beautiful young Princess and two suitors—the handsome Prince and the wicked Mouse King. To everyone's delight, the Prince wins the Princess. Then Drosselmeyer produces three magic life-size dolls, plus his very special gift for Clara, a small Nutcracker doll. Nobody but Clara likes this rather strange toy but she is so delighted with it that she begs her godfather Drosselmeyer to make him life-size as he did with the other big dolls. A tipsy guest accidentally breaks the little toy Nutcracker and Clara binds his broken jaw with her handkerchief. As the guests finally depart, Clara asks to be allowed to take the toy to bed with her, but her father makes her leave it underneath the Christmas tree.

SCENE TWO   It is the middle of the night. Clara steals down to see her Nutcracker and is frightened by the bat-like shadow of Drosselmeyer, who is still there in hiding. Suddenly she sees some odd creatures around the tree. They seem to be like the guests in her parents' Christmas party who have turned into giant mice, the subjects of the Mouse King. She confronts them bravely. Suddenly Drosselmeyer causes the Christmas tree to grow to an immense height and then, before her very eyes, the Nutcracker doll grows to life size and begins to move. The Nutcracker is immediately pitched into battle with the Mouse King and his army. Another army of toy soldiers appears, who also remind Clara of her little friends from that evening's festivities, and the battle is on. Clara saves the day by hurling her candle at the Mouse King. He is distracted and the Nutcracker defeats him. Drosselmeyer appears as if to remind Clara, "You wanted him to grow up. Look, I am going to give you what you begged for (what you wanted) as a reward for your kindness and love for the Nutcracker." Drosselmeyer transforms the Nutcracker into the handsome young Prince, who beckons Clara to follow him to a land of magical dreams. Once again, Drosselmeyer waves his hands and the beautiful Christmas forest appears. The dancing Snowflakes guide the Prince and Clara to the Prince's castle.

ACT TWO   The Prince takes Clara to his kingdom. When they are met at the gates by his subjects, the Prince relates the story of his victory over the Mouse King. Soon they enter the Prince's court, which is filled with beautiful puppets that spring to life at the Prince's command and dance for him and Clara. Both the Prince and Clara join in when the entire court dances the Rose Waltz. Then, mysteriously, a strange atmosphere is sensed; the happiness of the scene seems to vanish. Everything in the court begins to disappear, as if an invisible hand were destroying an illusion. Clara is disturbed and confused and even more so when Drosselmeyer appears and tells her that this "dream" is over and she must go home. Clara does everything to keep her handsome Prince and his magic kingdom. To the music generally known as the Grand Pas de Deux from the ballet, she and the Prince resist Drosselmeyer's attempt to withdraw her from her dream in a dramatic *pas de trois*. Victorious, the two young people dance happily. But as the glorious procession of the Prince's subjects concludes, Clara is unaware that she must wake up anyhow. Little by little her dream world fades away and she finds herself in the streaming sunlight of early morning.

Alan M. Kriegsman, dance critic for the Washington *Post*, called the Baryshnikov production "not only a commercial triumph but an artistic coup as well." He observed that while a child's Christmas dream is the basis for this version of the ballet, here "the child is older—a girl on the verge of adolescence—and the dream branches out to become, not just the wish-fulfillment of a candy kingdom, but an envisagement of mature love, incarnate in the Nutcracker-Prince."

When Baryshnikov's *Nutcracker* was first performed, in Washington, the critic of the Washington *Star,* Anne Marie Welsh, interviewed the dancer and choreographer and appraised his achievement: "*The Nutcracker* of Mikhail Baryshnikov is a strange and wonderful ballet.

"The ballet is all sweetness and modesty, a sensitive and serious look at the 1892 Tchaikovsky classic which, for nearly 30 years, has been a Christmas entertainment for American children.

"This version is different, and although at first it may appear less appealing to children, in the long run it deserves to be considered. For Baryshnikov—and the production—have the real dreams of children at heart.

"In his debut as a choreographer, Baryshnikov has given American Ballet Theatre more than a mere innovation. He has given them a lasting work, and a production on a scale so appropriate to ABT's younger dancers that they have seldom looked better. He has given them choreography that is consistently pure and open. All the characters of *The Nutcracker*—partygoers and children and mice and dolls and flowers—seem in touch with the ballet's essential mystery, and become essential to a single imagined vision.

"And he has given Marianna Tcherkassky, his opening night Clara, a role so lovely and so right that she has triumphed.

"The 15-minute ovation that thundered after the poignant close of last night's premiere may have been partly sentimental, but Baryshnikov—as choreographer, producer and dancer—richly deserved it.

"There are no children in this production, no tinsel-wrapped gifts, no red, white and green. In fact, there is little of the Christmas Eve realism we've come to expect from *The Nutcracker*.

"The first act of the production is focused upon what Clara, a 10- or 12-year-old, sees: Drosselmeyer, her mysterious godfather; the nutcracker he gives to her, and the cruel adult who breaks this toy she loves. The dream that soon unfolds for her is truly a child's—scary at first, then heroic, and, finally, if only for the visionary moment, fulfilled.

"Baryshnikov's most significant and stunning departure from productions which have become standard is to turn the second act *pas de deux* into a *pas de trois* for Clara, the Prince and Drosselmeyer. The melody is one of Tchaikovsky's simplest and most haunting—just the G major scale played top to bottom—and the new dance for three is perfectly attuned to its musical impulse.

"Two kindred spirits hover about American Ballet Theatre's new *Nutcracker*. E.T.A. Hoffmann, the German romantic whose fairy tale of 1816 is the basis for the ballet, wears the face of Drosselmeyer, godfather to the story's heroine. Mikhail Baryshnikov, the gifted dancer who choreographed and produced the ballet, wears the face of a prince, the object of the heroine's affection.

"When he discusses the production which had its world premiere here last night, Baryshnikov says, 'This is Drosselmeyer's evening. It is his ballet. He makes this experience of the dream for Clara because he likes her. He wants to help her grow up, but he also wants to protect her from tragedy.'

"Baryshnikov sees Hoffmann as a benevolent story teller, a giver of dreams like the Drosselmeyer this *Nutcracker* celebrates. 'His tales,' says Baryshnikov, 'are full of his own cartoons and full of his own incredible feeling about being an artist.' In fact, Hoffmann was a frustrated artist, misunderstood by his public and unhappy in his personal life.

"His stories are riddled with the grotesque and the violent, and they end, more often than not, in merciless imaginative revenges upon fictionalized enemies. The benevolence of *Nutcracker* comes partly from the lyric strain in Hoffmann, partly from Alexandre Dumas, who rewrote the original tale and changed its ending, and partly, of course, from Baryshnikov's own fertile imagination.

"The revenge motif remains, giving this *Nutcracker* its most significant difference from all previous American productions, and bringing it a step closer to Hoffmann. Clara does dream of getting back at the adults who have hurt and frustrated her. Also, the psychoanalytic meaning of the work's title has been clarified by the changes Baryshnikov has made. But the grand difference is that for Clara, unlike Hoffmann, living well, or at least dreaming of living well, is the best revenge.

"Most versions of the ballet allow Clara to fade into the background after the first act party and her subsequent dream of the nutcracker vanquishing mice. She usually becomes a passive spectator in a series of *divertissements* that satisfy her child's desire for sweet dreams; in psychological terms, for oral gratification.

"'I wanted to find a way to connect the two acts of the ballet,' says Baryshnikov, and since he envisions Clara as a 10- or 12-year-old, he solved the artistic problem by having her dream of and dance with her nutcracker-turned-prince. Hers is now a vision of adult sexual satisfaction.

"Hence, Clara dances to the *grand pas de deux* music usually reserved for the Sugar Plum Fairy. Baryshnikov makes the dance a *pas de trois* with Drosselmeyer lending moral support to the girl, who isn't quite old enough to live happily ever after with her prince.

"'Clara is just on the line of growing up,' says Baryshnikov. 'This is the first move of her child's soul. The most important moment for her is when she saves her nutcracker. It is a little miracle, and, because she is good, Drosselmeyer can give her her dream of fulfillment.'

"All the other changes Baryshnikov has made move the ballet in this same direction—towards greater psychological explicitness and coherence. He discussed those changes the other day this way:

"Drosselmeyer gives a puppet show in the first act that shows a prince rescuing a princess from the clutches of a mouse king. 'I want Clara's dream to be a collage of impressions from the party,' says Baryshnikov, 'and one of those ideas in her excited imagination comes from Drosselmeyer's little entertainment.'

"A drunken adult rather than her mischievous brother breaks Clara's nutcracker. 'Yes,' said Baryshnikov, 'this fellow is an adult, so she can have the dream about adults. I can't say the idea is particularly mine, but it is part of my experience and makes the dream more real.'

"The men at the opening party are transformed into the truly scary mice of her dream. Gone are the funny, domestic rodents of most versions. 'Again, I can't say this is my idea independently,' says Baryshnikov, 'but I want the scene to be quite frightening and terrible. I remember my own dreams as a child, my own nightmares. This is a way to connect all her impressions after the party. She is very excited by the party, and the music here is very unusual and strange.'

"The Arabian variation, 'Coffee,' is deleted from the second act *divertissements*. 'I was trying to think what I wanted to do here, and though it is a beautiful piece of music, it slows things down. I want to keep things moving. Four little dances are enough, and this way the focus can stay on Clara.'

"The ending includes Drosselmeyer in the background and Clara looking quite bereft rather than joyous. 'She is involved very much with her nutcracker,' says Baryshnikov. 'But Drosselmeyer knows she is not ready and wants to protect her from any tragedy. He is explaining the dream to her. She wants to be with her nutcracker, but she has lost him. She is in that moment between reality and sleeping and it is all fading away. "That's it," Drosselmeyer is telling her; "it's morning, it's time to come back to the world." Yellow morning light is coming through the window. It is over for her, this vision that Drosselmeyer has given to her. He's mysterious, but he is warm and loving just as the Tchaikovsky score is. He has made this experience for her because he loves her and now he will help her to understand it.'

"Given this pattern of dramatic details, it's impossible to resist the obvious question. Baryshnikov has no hesitancy in answering it. 'Yes, I am a Freudian,' he says, laughing. 'But not in my everyday life.'"*

## OCTUOR

*Music by Igor Stravinsky. Choreography by Richard Tanner. First presented at the New York City Ballet's Stravinsky Festival at the New York State Theatre, Lincoln Center, June 21, 1972, with Elise Flagg, Delia Peters, Lisa de Ribera, Deborah Flomine, Tracy Bennett, James Bogan, Daniel Duell, and Jean-Pierre Frohlich. Conducted by Robert Irving.*

Stravinsky's famous *Octet for Wind Instruments* was first performed in Paris, October 18, 1923, at one of the Concerts Koussevitsky, the composer conducting. The following year, in an article about the piece, Stravinsky said that "form, in my music, derived from counterpoint. I consider counterpoint as the only means through which the attention of the composer is concentrated on purely musical questions. Its elements also lend themselves perfectly to an architectural construction."

Four couples are featured in Richard Tanner's ballet to the *Octuor*. There are three movements to the work, *Sinfonia, Tema con variazioni*, and *Finale*.

* Reprinted by permission of the Washington *Star*.

NOTES   Writing after the premiere in the *Daily News*, the critic Sam Norkin said: "The four skilled couples in simple summary costumes bounded through this jazzy, bustling and contrapuntal piece in a carefree manner, keenly aware of its structure. Elise Flagg was outstanding in this highly enjoyable new ballet."

## ODE

*Music by Igor Stravinsky. Choreography by Lorca Massine. First presented at the New York City Ballet's Stravinsky Festival, June 23, 1972, at the New York State Theatre, Lincoln Center, with Christine Redpath, Colleen Neary, Robert Maiorano, Earle Sieveling, and ensemble. Conducted by Robert Craft.*

Stravinsky's *Ode*, written in 1943 in elegaic commemoration of the death of Natalia Koussevitsky, is a lovely score too little known. The young choreographer Lorca Massine happily arranged dances to it for the New York City Ballet's Stravinsky Festival in 1972. After the premiere, Clive Barnes wrote in the New York *Times* that *Ode* "has its statuesque moments of sculptural identity, moments out of time when, Béjart-like, the choreographer ignores the music and creates a certain dramatic effect. This is perhaps the best thing we have seen in New York from Mr. Massine."

## OFFENBACH IN THE UNDERWORLD

*Music by Jacques Offenbach, arranged and orchestrated by George Crum. Choreography by Antony Tudor. Decor and costumes by Kay Ambrose. Lighting by Jennifer Tipton. First presented by the National Ballet of Canada in Toronto, Canada, February 1, 1955. First presented in the United States by the City Center Joffrey Ballet in Lewiston, New York, August 14, 1975.*

The action of this diverting ballet takes place in the 1870s in a fashionable cafe at an international capital. Visiting celebrities come to see, to be seen, and to amuse themselves. Among them are a famous operetta star and one of her admirers, a grand duke. A debutante of good family, accompanied by three friends, arrives veiled in order not to be recognized in a place that is "out of bounds." There is, too, a young painter, a regular patron, had he the money, who haunts the place night and day; he tries to earn a meager living by drawing sketches of the cafe's patrons. There is no story to the ballet, for the flirtations that arise at such a place at such a time are most often half forgotten by the next morning. There is neither a sad ending nor a happy ending, but only a closing time.

When the ballet was revived for New York, Celia Franca staged it. The decor was re-created by Edward Burbridge and the costumes re-created by

Ray Diffen. The City Center Joffrey Ballet production was dedicated to the memory of Kay Ambrose.

# OLYMPICS

*Music by Toshiro Mayuzumi. Choreography by Gerald Arpino. Setting by Ming Cho Lee. First presented by the Robert Joffrey Ballet at the City Center, New York, March 31, 1966, with Luis Fuente as the Torch Bearer, and Jon Cristofori, Richard Gain, Ian Horvath, John Jones, and Michael Uthoff as the Athletes.*

*Olympics* is the choreographer's tribute to the Greek ideal of the athlete as "the complete man," proud of his prowess, openly competitive in games but also dedicated to the gods and a human ideal. It is an all-male work, dominated by the runner who carries the torch from Olympus to signal the beginning of the ritual games. The dancers compete, running, wrestling, executing gymnastic feats in a series of swift displays to the gods.

# ONCE MORE, FRANK

*Music by Carson C. Parks, Harold Arlen and Johnny Mercer, Dean Kay and Kelly Gordon. Choreography by Twyla Tharp. Costumes by Santo Loquasto. First presented by American Ballet Theatre at the New York State Theatre, Lincoln Center, July 12, 1976, with Twyla Tharp and Mikhail Baryshnikov.*

Named for Frank Sinatra, whose recordings of three songs are played for the ballet, the ballet was a special piece for a gala performance. It is a dance for a boy and a girl who are both lost in the songs and coolly detached from them in bemused recollection of another time when they loved them first. The songs are "Something Stupid," "One for My Baby" and "That's Life." In his book *Baryshnikov at Work*, Mikhail Baryshnikov suggests that the dance was about the particular dancers involved, each with different backgrounds and styles, trying to find with Sinatra's help the ideal middle ground.

# ONDINE

*Music by Hans Werner Henze. Scenario freely adapted by Frederick Ashton from the story by Friedrich de la Motte Fouqué. Choreography by Frederick Ashton. Scenery and costumes by Lila de Nobili. First presented by the Royal Ballet at the Royal Opera House, Covent Garden, London, October 27, 1958, with Margot Fonteyn, Michael Somes, Julia Farron, and Alexander Grant in the principal roles. First presented in the United States by the Royal Ballet at the Metropolitan Opera House, New York, September 21, 1960.*

"This is the story of Palemon and Ondine telling how Palemon wedded with a water sprite and what chanced therefrom and how Ondine returned to her element beneath the Mediterranean Sea."

ACT ONE, SCENE ONE: OUTSIDE BERTA'S CASTLE  Berta, returning from a hunt, is courted by Palemon, who offers her an amulet, which she scorns. She rejoins her friends, and Palemon is left alone in meditation. Suddenly, out of a fountain in the garden of the palace, a strange being, Ondine, appears, a mortal girl for the first time. She sees her shadow and, enchanted, dances. Palemon is captivated but the water sprite is alarmed at his interest and flees to the forest. Palemon follows her.

ACT ONE, SCENE TWO: A MYSTERIOUS FOREST  Tirrenio, lord of the Mediterranean, and wood sprites lie in wait for the lovers. Tirrenio tries to separate them. He warns Palemon that should he be unfaithful to Ondine, he must forfeit his life. Ondine defies Tirrenio and the lovers seek out a hermit who marries them. She gains her soul and is no longer a mere water sprite. The scene ends with Berta distraught at the acts of Tirrenio, who tries to impede her pursuit of the lovers.

ACT TWO: A PORT  After their marriage, Palemon and Ondine come to a port where they decide to embark on a ship. Berta, following, sees the lovers and bribes the captain to take her unseen on board. Not knowing of their marriage, Berta is moved by jealousy when she sees Palemon, in a transport of love, offer Ondine the amulet he once offered to her. She reproaches Palemon. Ondine at once gives the jewel to Berta. Suddenly the outraged Tirrenio rises out of the sea and snatches the amulet from Berta. Ondine runs to the side of the ship, dips her hands into water and produces an exquisite necklace which she presents to Berta. Horrified at the supernatural gift, Berta throws it at Ondine's feet. The sailors who have witnessed this magic regard Ondine with doubt and awe; they threaten her. Tirrenio, again rising from the sea to protect Ondine, beckons to her. He creates a storm and, rising on the crest of a wave, seizes her and drags her to the bottom of the sea. The storm increases.

ACT THREE: PALEMON'S CASTLE  Saved from the shipwreck, Palemon and Berta arrive from their wedding. Berta gives Palemon a present, a portrait of herself, and leaves to prepare for their guests. Palemon, in a reverie, has a vision of Ondine. Berta returns and disturbs his dream. The guests arrive and the festivities begin, but at their height strange and sinister things happen. Tirrenio, true to his warning, appears seeking vengeance. Berta is dragged out by a swarm of water sprites. Ondine appears at Tirrenio's command. Palemon now realizes that she is his only love. Ondine warns him that owing to his lack of faith, her kiss can only mean his death. Finally, sadly, she kisses him and he falls dead. She takes his body back to the sea, there to hold him in an eternal embrace.

NOTES  *Ondine* has been a favorite theme of ballet since Fouqué wrote the original story in German in 1811. The theme, like that of *La Sylphide, Swan*

*Lake, Giselle,* and other romantic stories, tells the story of a magic being from another world who comes to earth and loves a mortal, with dire consequences to them both. The part of Ondine was associated for many years with Fanny Cerrito, just as today it has become famous through the interpretation of Margot Fonteyn. Cerrito first danced the role in Jules Perrot's ballet to the story on June 22, 1843, in London. For her shadow dance in the first act theatrical lighting was used for one of the first times. Other dancers who have appeared in the role are Carlotta Grisi (in Russia in 1851, in Perrot's ballet with music by Pugni) and Anna Pavlova.

## ONTOGENY

*Music by Karel Husa. Choreography by Dennis Nahat. Setting and costumes by Willa Kim. Lighting by Nananne Porcher. First presented by American Ballet Theatre at the City Center, New York, January 6, 1971.*

One dictionary defines the word "ontogeny" as "the development of the course of an individual organism." Not so much human as protozoic, the ballet begins by showing us, in fact, how chromosomes combine to make a man. He appears, pursued by his mother. He gradually acquires knowledge in his childhood, matures, and begins to understand himself. The life cycle continues. The music for the ballet is the *Third String Quartet* by Husa.

## OPUS LEMAITRE

*Music by Bach. Choreography by Hans van Manen. Sets and costumes by Jean-Paul Vroom. First presented by the Netherlands Dance Theatre, with Gérard Lemaitre. First presented in the United States by the Pennsylvania Ballet at the Academy of Music, Philadelphia, February 1974, with Lawrence Rhodes in the principal role.*

A major work for the *premier danseur,* named for and dedicated to the choreographer's colleague Gérard Lemaitre, *Opus Lemaitre* provides the male dancer with abundant opportunity to display balance, stillness, and a personal declarative style to match the grandeur of Bach's *Toccata and Fugue in D Minor.* The leading dancer is accompanied by five couples. He stands motionless among them for the entire length of the toccata, beginning to dance at the commencement of the fugue.

## OPUS ONE

*Music by Anton von Webern. Choreography by John Cranko. Lighting by Gilbert V. Hemsley, Jr. First presented by the Stuttgart Ballet at the Württemberg State Theatre, Stuttgart, November 7, 1965. First presented in the*

*United States by the same ensemble at the Metropolitan Opera House, New York, April 30, 1969, with Birgit Keil and Richard Cragun in the principal roles.*

A program note by Franz Willnauer reminds us that "genuine ballet art—like all genuine art—is ambiguous. It can be interpreted in many ways—from the stylized order of movements to the code of an incarnate calligraphy, to the symbolic dance drama of the human couple whose love and life are destroyed by the angel of death."

Set to Webern's *Passacaglia*, Op. 1, the ballet shows a life cycle in dance. A man is born. Curled up at first, he extends, is released, dances, finds a girl who comes down from above. They dance an impassioned *pas de deux* and then they are surrounded by a threatening group. Though they rejoin briefly, the girl is soon carried aloft. He reaches up for her but cannot reach her and, in despair, curls up on the ground, as at his beginning.


# ORPHEUS

*Ballet in three scenes. Music by Igor Stravinsky. Choreography by George Balanchine. Scenery and costumes by Isamu Noguchi. Lighting by Jean Rosenthal. First presented by Ballet Society at the New York City Center, New York, April 28, 1948, with Nicholas Magallanes as Orpheus, Maria Tallchief as Eurydice, Francisco Moncion as the Dark Angel, Beatrice Tompkins as the Leader of the Furies, Tanaquil LeClercq as the Leader of the Bacchantes, and Herbert Bliss as Apollo.*

This ballet is a contemporary treatment of the ancient myth of Orpheus, the Greek musician who descended into Hades in search of his dead wife, Eurydice. With his music, Orpheus charms the God of the Dead into returning Eurydice to him. He promises not to look at her until they have reached the earth again. Eurydice, unknowing, persuades Orpheus to break this promise, thereby bringing about her irrevocable death. The ballet tells this story and its aftermath as simply as possible with its music, its dramatic action, and its dancing.

SCENE ONE: THE GRAVE OF EURYDICE    The first notes of the orchestra remind us that Orpheus's instrument was the lyre. A harp sounds descending scales in a slow, mournful rhythm accompanied by quiet strings. Eurydice is dead, and Orpheus cannot console himself with his own song. The curtain rises. Orpheus stands alone beside Eurydice's grave with his back turned. His arms hang limp, his lyre is discarded at his feet, and his head is bowed to the intensely blue sky that would pierce his sorrow with brightness. Three friends enter on the left, cross over to the grave, and place upon it relics of Eurydice. Orpheus does not notice them; he remains motionless when they place their hands on his shoulder to console him. He ignores their departure. The music ceases its slow lamentation, and Orpheus wakens from his grief. He takes up his lyre and begins a dance that expresses physical grief as well as mental anguish. He raises the lyre high above him in supplication, then holds the instrument in one hand as he dances. The song of the lyre is inadequate to his bereavement; yet the lyre is the only possession Orpheus has left, and in his dance he tries to make the instrument a partner to his woe. This effort fails, and Orpheus places the harp on Eurydice's grave, where he beseeches it to speak for her. Then he falls in despair at the grave and reaches out to pluck the lyre's strings. At this sound, a satyr and four wood sprites leap out from behind rocks in the background and attempt to distract Orpheus. Orpheus rises to meet these creatures who have been moved by his song and he darts in and out among them for a moment, but soon leaves them, to dance alone with his lyre. His misery is unabated and his pathetic figure seems to demand the sympathy of the gods he invokes to aid him. Again he stands beside Eurydice's grave with downcast eyes.

Now the prayers of Orpheus are answered. In the back, against the vivid blue sky, appears a strange, dark figure whose body is enveloped in black coils. The Angel of Death poses briefly, then moves forward toward the grieving poet. He approaches softly, so as not to disturb Orpheus in his reverie, and touches him. Orpheus stands immobile. The Angel of Death frees himself of the black coil that represents his power in Hades, raises Orpheus's arms high, and entwines the coil between his outstretched hands. As he wraps the coil about the silent musician, the Angel of Death by his intimate presence endows Orpheus with the power to accompany him on the long journey across the River Styx to Eurydice. The angel stands away from Orpheus and dances triumphantly for a moment, then prepares for the trip into Hades. He frees Orpheus of the bonds of death, then places over the minstrel's eyes a golden mask which must not be removed until the journey is over. Then he picks up the lyre, slips his arm through it, and beckons to Orpheus. Orpheus moves toward him hesitatingly; pliantly he stretches out his hand to grasp the angel's upturned palm. The open, widespread fingers of the angel close about his hand with the strength of steel. A trumpet sounds. The angel moves the lyre down his arm to rest on their clasped hands and begins to lead Orpheus on the downward journey. The music is slow and spacious as the two figures move toward the front of the stage. From above, a flowing white gauze falls in slow motion, and in front of this curtain the Angel of Death leads the blinded Orpheus on the tortuous journey. The progress in their descent into Hades is marked by bright objects that can be seen moving upward in back of the transparent curtain. The passage becomes difficult as the two figures cross the stage toward the left, and as they disappear, the angel, exhausted, pulls Orpheus over the ground. When they have gone, mysterious figures in back of the gauze push the curtain forward with a movement similar to the helpless beating of wings against a cage.

SCENE TWO: HADES   The gauze curtain rises swiftly, and crouched about the stage in fearful attitudes are the Furies, creatures of Hell who would destroy those who enter the Land of the Dead unlawfully. Bright cones of light from above illuminate their hideous and fantastic attire. The leader of the Furies proceeds to direct them harshly in a rapid, rhythmic dance. Orpheus and the angel enter on the left. The leader of the Furies turns and points at them menacingly, followed by her weird creatures. But the angel and Orpheus stand motionless. The Furies finish their dance, and their leader directs them to gather in a group. Tortured souls who have remained in the background now stir with great effort. They carry heavy burdens of rock on their shoulders and bend painfully under the strain. They set boulders down behind the group of Furies, as if to protect themselves, and all turn toward the two interlopers.

The Angel of Death moves away from Orpheus, slips the lyre from his arm, and, standing in back of the minstrel, places the lyre for Orpheus to play. But Orpheus does not understand—he cannot see—and the angel moves his hands so that they touch the strings of the harp. The angel plucks the strings, and now Orpheus comprehends and begins to play. His music is accompanied closely by two oboes and the orchestra. The lovely, soft melody of his lyre enchants the Furies, who are lulled to silence and rest. Yet Orpheus is still reluctant to play the harp as he once did, before Eurydice died, and the angel continues to exact the music from him. He knows that only by his great music will Orpheus persuade the ruler of Hades to release Eurydice. The two figures dance to the beautiful song, the angel constantly encouraging Orpheus to prolong the melody. The burdened, tortured souls move closer to hear more perfectly, and the music reflects their agony, which Orpheus's song has temporarily relieved.

But now the song is over. Orpheus bows stiffly in obeisance toward the back. In the dark recesses of the stage a strange shape begins to turn toward him. This is Pluto, God of the Underworld. Standing before him, her hands resting on his shoulders, is Eurydice. Orpheus does not move. Although he cannot see, he senses her presence and waits for Pluto's answer to his prayer. Eurydice moves forward, haltingly at first, with a slight limping motion, then more freely as her dance becomes syncopated. She turns to Pluto and beseeches him to come forward. Eurydice's arms move constantly to express her desire for freedom, and Pluto moves toward her. The Furies take Orpheus by the hand and bring him to Eurydice. Pluto joins their hands, and for a moment the two stand motionless before the god as Orpheus pledges not to look at his wife until they have ascended to earth. A blue stalactite descends from on high to symbolize the reunion, and the Dark Angel comes forward to lead Orpheus and Eurydice back to earth. He takes Orpheus by the hand, and all the inhabitants of the underworld circle the three figures, who move with hands joined to the front of the stage. The gauze curtain falls behind them, and the Dark Angel proceeds ahead, holding out Orpheus's lyre as a guide to the couple.

Orpheus and Eurydice dance together to a sumptuous melody as their journey begins. At first Eurydice merely follows Orpheus, imitating his steps as he leads the way. But the ascent is difficult, and their dance becomes for a short time a kind of portrayal of the hardships they undergo in passing unseen obstacles. Orpheus is blind, and when Eurydice is not holding him by the hand, she is lost to him. Eurydice puts herself in his way constantly: she longs increasingly for Orpheus to see her. Her longing is infinitely tender and appealing because of the warmth of the love in her own eyes; she therefore seems to tempt Orpheus to tear the mask from his face not so that he can see her, but so that she can see him as she remembers him. She wishes to help him as they proceed along the way, but the one way in which she cannot help him is by showing her love for him. Eurydice is tormented momentarily by the fact that, although they are really together once again, they are actually remote to each other: Orpheus, because he cannot see; Eurydice, because she cannot be seen by the man she loves.

The tempo and the theme of the dance change briefly as Eurydice moves away and dances before the blind Orpheus a gay and pleasant measure. She holds in her hands an invisible pipe, and plays upon it in celebration of their reunion. Orpheus catches the mood of her dance and joins her in it. Both are attempting to suppress the impassioned longings they feel so deeply. But Orpheus becomes even more intently aware of his lack of sight as Eurydice beguilingly dances out of his reach, and the principal theme of their *pas de deux* returns, this time prefaced with a short musical warning from the harp. On the extreme left, the arm of the Dark Angel still holds out the guiding lyre, and the two lovers turn to follow it. They start out as before, Orpheus leading and Eurydice duplicating his movements, but now Eurydice moves close to him in intimate contact. Orpheus tries to hold her, but she slides down to the floor, where his arms reach out desperately to find her. The melody mounts to a brief crescendo. Now that he cannot touch Eurydice, Orpheus abandons all patience and takes his head in his hands. Eurydice stands beside him, her face close to his, and he tears the mask from his eyes. There is absolute silence. Instantly she falls against him and dies. At first too stunned to move, Orpheus stretches out his arms, eager to touch her and to feel her touch. Invisible creatures of Hades push forward the gauze curtain to make good their promise and slip Eurydice away. Orpheus kneels alone, his open arms clasping the empty air.

Now that he has lost Eurydice until he himself shall die, Orpheus is afraid. Horns sound in terrifying judgment upon his fatal error. He remembers that the Angel of Death is still with him, just ahead, and he turns, half crawling, half running, to grasp his lyre. But just before his fingers reach the lyre, it disappears. Powerless now in the Land of the Dead, Orpheus knows that he is powerless, too, on earth; he crawls off in search of his lyre.

The gauze curtain rises rapidly when Orpheus has left the stage. Here again on earth the sky is still blue, but now it is bathed also in blood-colored lights. There is a small hillock in the background. At the crash of a drum, there comes in from the left a tall Thracian woman with long red hair. This is the leader of the bacchantes, pleasure-seeking women who have not known love. She stalks the scene as if seeking desirable prey, moving with quick thrusts of legs and arms, looking to the right and left. She is soon followed by eight bacchantes, all with brilliant yellow hair. Orpheus enters carrying his mask. Immediately the bacchantes surround him. Their leader seems to demand his favor. Orpheus repulses her, indignant that she should try to sully his grief. The woman smiles her contempt and tries to take the mask from him. He runs, but the bacchantes are all around him. The leader embraces Orpheus savagely with her long arms, and the two fall to the ground. They roll over and over, and Orpheus frees himself, but the bacchante rises in triumph, holding his mask. Her face contorted with demoniac delight, she throws the mask out of sight. Orpheus cannot escape. The entire orchestra imitates his terror and the ferocity of the bacchantes with frenzied, rhythmic fortissimos. The bacchantes move in for the final attack. They push Orpheus back toward the hillock. He does not resist. They push him again. His head is bowed, his body listless. The bacchantes raise his arms, and for a brief moment they seem open in supplication. The leader stalks in on Orpheus and cuts off his right arm, then his left. He raises his head; she decapitates him. The body of Orpheus lies behind the hillock, torn to pieces. The bacchantes exit, strutting proudly, unregretfully.

SCENE THREE: APOTHEOSIS   The stage is empty. Gradually the red disappears from the blue sky and the earth is bright once more. Again we hear the harp play the theme that opened the ballet, but now the accompaniment is different: this seems but a mere imitation of Orpheus's music. Apollo comes in slowly and approaches the grave of Orpheus. He kneels beside it and takes from behind the hillock a golden mask of the minstrel's face. Apollo holds the mask high, invoking the spirit of Orpheus as the God of Song, then holds it gently with his arm, as Orpheus held his lyre. The harp sounds as Apollo plucks the air before the mask, but the music—accompanied as it is by two horns—makes us all the more aware of the death of Orpheus and of Apollo's inability to call forth his music alone. Finally Apollo sets down the mask and stands poised over the grave of Orpheus. Slowly he moves his arm upward, and from the grave rises the lyre of Orpheus entwined in a long garland of flowers. The lyre rises higher and higher, carrying with it for the ages the tenderness and power of his song.

## OTHER DANCES

*Music by Frédéric Chopin. Choreography by Jerome Robbins. Costumes by Santa Loquasto. Lighting by Gilbert V. Hemsley, Jr. First presented at a Gala for the benefit for the Library of the Performing Arts at Lincoln Center at the Metropolitan Opera House, New York, May 9, 1976, with Natalia Makarova and Mikhail Baryshnikov. Pianist: Jerry Zimmerman.*

Created for a special occasion, this dance for two has become a part of the permanent repertory. Jerome Robbins, in *Dances at a Gathering* and *In the Night*, had made enduring ballets based on Chopin's piano music. This work is an extension of his interest in that music, as reflected in an admiration for the two principal dancers. The music is four mazurkas and a waltz—the same waltz used years ago by Michel Fokine for the first solo in *Les Sylphides*.

# PAGANINI

*Ballet in seven scenes. Music by Sergei Rachmaninoff. Libretto and choreography by Leonid Lavrovsky. Scenery by Vadim Rindin. First presented by the Bolshoi Ballet at the Bolshoi Theatre, Moscow, April 7, 1960. First presented in the United States by the Bolshoi Ballet at the Metropolitan Opera House, New York, September 17, 1962, with Garosin Sekh in the title role.*

The choreographer has written: "For many years I dreamed of making a ballet about Paganini. Perhaps this wish derived from the impressions I formed in my youth from reading the memoirs of Paganini's contemporaries and biographers, who described his uncanny expressiveness and the remarkable plastic quality of his body, hands, and face. In the summer of 1959 I obtained a recording of Rachmaninoff's *Rhapsody on a Theme of Paganini*. I was deeply moved. The beautiful and convincing treatment of the musical work dedicated to Paganini insistently called me, a choreographer, to respond in my own professional language."

The ballet depicts Paganini's recollections of his life, from which the violinist emerges as an inspired artist wrestling with evil forces. What are described in the seven scenes are not actual facts of his life, but Paganini's meditations on them. The scenes are marked: "First Improvisations," "Enemies," "A Meeting," "Loneliness and Despair," "Love and Consolation," "The Joy of Creative Work and Death," "Finale—Stronger than Death."

In portraying Paganini, the choreographer was largely governed by Rachmaninoff's own wishes expressed in a letter written to Fokine. He wanted to see Paganini with a violin, not a real one but a fantastic one that could be impressed on the imagination. "Thus I felt that to bring Paganini to the stage," noted Lavrovsky, "the dancer performing his part must have his body and movements tuned like a perfect instrument, thus symbolizing the beauty and power of music itself. In this way the dancer's body, arms, fingers, his 'singing' face, could help to create on the stage a vision of the fantastic violin Rachmaninoff so longed to see."

# PAQUITA

*Music by Léon Minkus, orchestrated by John Lanchbery. Choreography by Rudolf Nureyev "after the original by Marius Petipa." Staged by Marika Besobrasova. Costumes by Freddy Wittop. Lighting by Nananne Porcher. First presented at the Theatre Royal, Drury Lane, London, November 1965, with students of the Royal Ballet School. First presented in the United States by American Ballet Theatre at the New York State Theatre, Lincoln Center, July 6, 1971, with Cynthia Gregory and Michael Denard as the principals.*

This entertaining dance ballet is all we now see of an original story ballet of two acts that enjoyed success for many years in France and Russia (*Paquita* is still in the Soviet repertory). First danced in Paris at the Opéra on April 1, 1846, by Carlotta Grisi, five years after her historic success in *Giselle*, the original choreography was by Mazilier and the music by Deldevez. The story tells of a Spanish gypsy Paquita who loves Lucien, a French nobleman. Their marriage appears to be impossible because of the difference in their social positions but all turns out well when Paquita discovers that she is, in fact, the daughter of a nobleman. The first Lucien was Lucien Petipa, brother of the great choreographer and ballet master Marius Petipa.

There have been a number of *divertissements* made from either the choreography or music of the Russian version of the French original, which had revised dances by Marius Petipa and music by Léon Minkus. Alexandra Danilova staged a one-act *Paquita* for the Ballet Russe de Monte Carlo, September 20, 1949, at the Metropolitan Opera House, New York, with Danilova and Oleg Tupine in the principal roles. The Grand Ballet of the Marquis de Cuevas from 1948 and, from 1951, the New York City Ballet for some years danced a *pas de trois* arranged to some of Minkus' music to *Paquita*. The latter, with Maria Tallchief, Nora Kaye, and André Eglevsky, was first presented at the City Center, New York, February 18, 1951, with costumes by Barbara Karinska.

The *divertissement* as arranged by Nureyev, exuberantly Spanish in character, has as its principal feature six variations for soloists, ballerina, and *premier danseur*. Enclosing these solos are group ensembles. The first introduces all the girls, who herald the arrival of the ballerina. Next, as the lights go down and the girls arrange themselves in a long diagonal across the stage, her partner enters to lead her in a dance. An interesting aspect of this *pas de deux* is that the girls who accompany the leading dancers reflect in their movements the steps and gestures of the ballerina. Eight girls and the soloists dance now to the playful rhythms of castanets. The harp now introduces the first of the six variations and it is always very interesting to see these Petipa dances. Like the variations in another of his masterworks, *The Sleeping Beauty*, they remind us of his great achievement in the classic ballet. We do not make dances like this now, perhaps, but we could make nothing if we had not had dances like these by Petipa to teach us.

After variations by two of the soloists, the *danseur* and the ballerina perform their individual dances. The circle is closed by brilliant dances for two more girls. The ballet ends in a joyous finale, the ballerina performing a dazzling variation.

NOTES  Reviewing *Paquita* in the Washington *Post*, the critic Jean Battey Lewis wrote that Cynthia Gregory, in the ballerina's role, "used her extraordinary technique to dance with a wonderful freedom. Balances were held with elegant aplomb, phrases were finished with a triumphant flourish, and she tossed off 32 fouettés, punctuated by double fouettés, with breezy precision." (October 30, 1972)

Writing of the first *Paquita* and its great ballerina Carlotta Grisi, Théophile

Gautier wrote in *La Presse,* Paris, on April 6, 1846: "This ballet, where the action is perhaps a little too melodramatic, is a complete success. The richness
and strangeness of the Empire costumes, the beauty of the decor, above all the
perfection of Carlotta's dancing, are responsible for this success. Her final steps
in the piece are of unimaginable daring and difficulty: these are a kind of hopping on the very tip of the toe with a sudden turn made with a dazzling
quickness which inspires a mixture of pleasure and fear, for its execution appears impossible, although she repeats it some eight to ten times. Thunderous
applause greeted the ballerina, who was called on to perform the dance twice
again after the fall of the curtain."

Readers who wish to know more about Carlotta Grisi, the first Giselle, and
other great ballerinas, should read *The Ballerinas* by Parmenia Miguel.

## PARADE

*Music by Erik Satie. Book by Jean Cocteau. Choreography by Leonide Mas-
sine. Scenery and costumes by Pablo Picasso. First presented by Diaghilev's
Ballets Russes at the Théâtre du Châtelet, Paris, May 18, 1917, with Leonide
Massine, Lydia Lopokova, Nicholas Zverev, Maria Chabelska, and Leon
Woizikowski in leading roles. First presented in the United States by the
City Center Joffrey Ballet at the City Center, New York, March 22, 1973,
with Gary Chryst, Eileen Brady, Gregory Huffman, Donna Cowen, and
Robert Talmage in leading roles.*

Renowned collaboration of the Diaghilev era, unique combination of the gifts
of Satie, Cocteau, Massine, and Picasso, *Parade* proves yet again in the 1970s
the genius of the Diaghilev Ballets Russes in generating artistic collaboration
of the highest order. When relatively few of the ballets created under Diaghilev's direction can be seen in our theaters (only *Petrouchka, Firebird*—in another version, *Spectre de la Rose, Apollo,* and *Prodigal Son*), in a recent season, it is refreshing to have the impresario's incomparable gifts demonstrated
again for a new generation. Until its American revival, *Parade* had not been
seen for forty-seven years.

*Parade* has long been considered a landmark for its introduction of cubism
into the theater. The idea of the ballet was Jean Cocteau's. It was he who persuaded Satie and Picasso, who had never worked with the Ballets Russes, to
collaborate on this undertaking in the midst of World War I. Subtitled a "Realistic Ballet," the work was intended to heighten realism; Guillaume Apolli-
naire, writing in the program, put the word *surrealism* onto the printed page for
the first time to describe *Parade.* This would seem to point to a contrast the
ballet makes visible on the stage—a contrast between performers in a traveling
circus, the real people, and their managers or impresarios—public relations
men who attempt to persuade the public to enjoy their arts.

Street circuses used to be common in Paris, and it is one of these that is the
subject of the ballet, where the huckstering managers parade their talent to

passers-by before the start of the show, with the hope that they will pay to come inside.

Massine, *Parade*'s choreographer, has said, in describing his method of making ballets, that it is sometimes the music, sometimes the theme, or the period and atmosphere of the action. With *Parade*, "the music was supreme, although the theme, too, interested me." Satie's score, like Picasso's settings and costumes visually, radically reflected new directions in sound and sense, mixing everyday noises, the real, with the imaginative expectation.

The action of the ballet is direct and straightforward, with none of the mystery associated so often with the avant-garde. After a series of almost solemn, quasi-religious chords in a brief musical prelude, there is a brief quiet that reveals a drop curtain of "early Picasso" portraying a rustic backstage scene of players relaxing before a performance. This inner curtain rises to show a scene by the same artist that is clearly different: a curtained booth, askew but making sense at once as a stage for the public to view a performance. Here parades an odd creature, the like of which has never been seen walking—a huge, pipe-smoking man made up of angles and planes and no softness. This is the French Manager, who introduces the Chinese Conjuror, who emerges from the curtained booth to amuse us with tricks—sword swallowing, etc.—to simulated oriental music. In a splendid multicolored costume he fairly dazzles us with his entertainment and then disappears behind the curtain.

There is a flourish and another huckster comes out, this the Manager from New York, his costume an amalgam of skyscrapers and curious angles. He carries a megaphone and a sign reading PARADE. He consults and commiserates with his French colleague, then introduces his specialty, a Little American Girl, a perpetual child in white middy blouse with a bow in her hair. To the menacing sound of multiple typewriters and gun shots, she dances a machine-age number, all winsomeness and cute charm. But her dance is more than that—it epitomizes, in small compass, the European image of America as heard by an acute ear and reflected by an acute eye in 1917. The imagery is almost totally derived from popular songs and movies. As the music imitates American dance rhythms, the little girl runs the gamut of stock U.S. melodrama—cops and robbers, rescue from a storm at sea, etc., at the end of which she bounces off as cheerily as she entered. At the end, her Manager is just as disappointed as his predecessor: no audience responds enough to come into their theater. He and the French Manager cannot understand this indifference.

Now in silence comes a brown-and-white Horse, grinning from ear to ear. Somewhat bashfully he entertains us, too, and prances out. The curtains close behind him. When they part again, we see two Acrobats, a girl and a boy, who dance a circuslike *pas de deux*, simulating tricks of the ring and high wire.

After the Acrobats finish, to the sound of a screaming siren the two Managers and the American Girl return. Next, the Horse and the Conjuror, finally the Acrobats, all in a reprise of their acts. In unison, they urge us, the audience, to come into their theater to see more. When we do not, they form a kind of cortege and the Horse lies down. The curtain falls as the music of the beginning is heard again.

NOTES   There are many accounts of the origins of *Parade* but none more complete than those in *Cocteau*, Francis Steegmuller's biography of the librettist, in Leonide Massine's autobiography, and in Douglas Cooper's book, *Picasso Theatre*. Cooper, Picasso's collaborator, assisted the revival by the City Center Joffrey Ballet, and also wrote about it at length in *Dance and Dancers* magazine. He said of the presentation, which had been re-created by Leonide Massine himself:

"The famous drop curtain, revealed during the opening section of the music, showed one of the most romantically evocative and tender of all Picasso's circus compositions. But behind it lay a surprising and colorful contemporary reality. A proscenium opening, decorated with scrolls and a lyre, was painted red and yellow, and set among whitish buildings, with dark windows, and some dark-green foliage. The Chinese Conjuror had a scarlet tunic, strikingly patterned in yellow and grey, over black trousers with a yellow pattern. The two Acrobats had sky-blue tights with bold ornamental motifs in white, while the Little American Girl had a dark-blue middy jacket over a white skirt.

"Each of these turns was presented successively by one of the two so-called Managers, dancers raised to eleven-foot-high figures by an elaborately carpentered, descriptively symbolic superstructure rising from their shoulders. Both wore a sort of formal evening dress and a top hat, but were equipped with buildings and other attributes to establish their national character: thus the American had the Woolworth building, a megaphone and some flags, while the French Manager had houses, trees, a staff and a long-stemmed pipe.

"Massine cleverly characterized each role in his choreography, which made much use of mime. The subtly emphasized rhythms beaten out by the four legs of the Horse, in an enchantingly comic, acrobatic dance without music, was a triumph of his invention. While the Managers were made to convey the force of their huckstering and despair by ungainly movements, by demonstrative and angry steps and by towering over all around them.

"Massine had the good fortune to find in the Joffrey Ballet a marvelous group of young dancers who worked with him brilliantly in this recreation of *Parade*. For it is a ballet which requires the performers to show style, precision of movement, perfect timing, athletic prowess, great powers of mime and especially a sense of enjoying what they are doing. Gary Chryst, assuming Massine's original role (the Chinese Conjuror), displayed that nervous intensity, speed, suavity, and air of mystery which is required for the character. His flickering hands, his shuffle, his leaps and especially his elevation were superbly timed and amazing to watch, as were the mimed passages of his dance where he finds an egg in his pigtail, digests it and recovers it from the toe of his shoe, or swallows a sword or eats fire.

"Donna Cowen, the first native-born American ever to dance the role of the Little American Girl, showed a marvelous sense of ragtime and was by turns pert, droll and captivating as she danced and mimed her way through the episodes of the ungainly typewriter, of the encounter with Indians, of the wreck of the *Titanic* or of the rosy dawning. The graceful and wistful *pas de deux* for the two Acrobats, who tumble, climb ropes, perform trapeze and walk a tightrope, was danced with great feeling and dexterity by Brady and Huffman. The Managers and the Horse gave their numbers with great distinction and all the fun and noise of the fair. The music was rendered in strict accordance with Satie's published score so that the incidental sound effects were confined to a typewriter, a ship's siren and some revolver shots at the appropriate times."

Cooper recalls that in staging the ballet, Massine was able to consult with dancers living in New York who had once appeared in various roles, notably Maria Chabelska, Vera Nemtchinova, Lydia Sokolova, and Michel Pavloff, while Boris Kochno also made a contribution from Paris. Lydia Sokolova in her memoirs had written prophetically: "*Parade* was so delightful that I am sure it would be a favorite if it could be done today."

## PARADISE LOST

*Music by Marius Constant. Choreography by Roland Petit. Libretto by Jean Cau. Scenery by Martial Raysse. First presented by the Royal Ballet at the Royal Opera House, Covent Garden, London, February 23, 1967, with Margot Fonteyn and Rudolf Nureyev. First presented in the United States by the Royal Ballet at the New Metropolitan Opera House, New York, May 10, 1967, with the same cast.*

This ballet is based not on John Milton but on a poem by Jean Cau: "Every paradise is found in order to be lost." What happens is that we first see a huge egg, outlined in neon, then in lights a countdown that flashes 5 . . . 4 . . . 3 . . . 2 . . . 1 . . . and then the birth of Man who turns out to be Adam. He walks down a ramp and the dancing begins.

In the words of Alexander Bland of *The Observer*, the action "is traced in a long series of solos and duets which make the first half of the ballet one of the most stimulating dance experiences in a long time—Adam exploring his nature and powers; his first intimation of pain and the birth of Eve; their mutual suspicion thawing into complete harmony; the change wrought by the Serpent, Eve twisting into seduction and Adam into aggressive sexuality, ending in a denouement as theatrically breath-taking as Nijinsky's leap in *Spectre de la Rose.*" The hero runs and jumps headfirst into a huge mouth of Eve.

Innocence is further destroyed by an attacking crowd and God's wrath finally descends. Peter Williams wrote in the *Sunday Times* of London: "The fall is frozen in yet another sublime 'fallen-angel' composition—Man crashed to earth with his body curved across the neck of the sorrowing Woman."

## PAS DES DÉESSES

*Music by John Field. Choreography by Robert Joffrey. First presented by the Robert Joffrey Ballet Concert at the Kaufmann Auditorium, Y.M.H.A., New York, May 29, 1954, with Lillian Wellein (Taglioni), Barbara Gray (Grahn), Jacquetta Kieth (Cerrito), and Michael Lland (Saint-Léon).*

Inspired by a romantic lithograph of 1846 by Bouvier, *Pas des Déesses* re-creates the ballet style of that day. At the start, four dancers are seen in the pose of this famous print. Each represents a famous dancer of the romantic era in ballet and each of the dances that follow displays the qualities made famous by the quartet—the languorous Danish ballerina Lucile Grahn, the darting Italian, Fanny Cerrito, and the floating Marie Taglioni, all strongly supported by the gallant Arthur Saint-Léon. The air of competition among the three ballerinas echoes the delicate rivalry which existed among these celebrated dancers.

The music for the ballet is by the Irish piano virtuoso John Field (1782–1837), who originated the name and style of the Nocturne. The ballet uses selected nocturnes, rondos, and waltzes.

The first *Pas des Déesses* was performed at His Majesty's Theatre, London, during the 1846 season by Taglioni, Cerrito, Grahn, and Saint-Léon. Choreography was by Jules Perrot.


## PAS DE DIX

*Classic ballet. Music by Alexander Glazunov. Choreography by George Balanchine. Costumes by Esteban Francés. Lighting by Jean Rosenthal. First presented by the New York City Ballet at the City Center, New York, November 9, 1955, with Maria Tallchief and André Eglevsky; Barbara Fallis, Constance Garfield, Jane Mason, Barbara Walczak, Shaun O'Brien, Roy Tobias, Roland Vasquez, and Jonathan Watts.*

The music for this dance for ten (two principals plus four girls and four boys) is taken from a ballet score I have always liked since my student days in Russia, Glazunov's *Raymonda*. I danced in Petipa's original production of this ballet at the Maryinsky Theatre when I was studying at the Imperial Ballet School. Some years ago, for the Ballet Russe de Monte Carlo, Alexandra Danilova and I put together our version of Petipa's last act—the nuptial festivities of the Hungarian lady Raymonda and the Count Jean de Brienna—a dance ballet that follows the narrative.

Except for one brief variation, all the music for the *Pas de Dix* is taken from this same act, but there is no attempt here to approximate Petipa's original, which no one remembers accurately, anyway. What I have done instead is to try to make an entertaining spectacle with no story, simply a series of dances for a ballerina, her partner, and a small ensemble. The music will be familiar, I think, to those who know the Russian repertory.


## PAS DE DUKE

*Music by Duke Ellington. Choreography by Alvin Ailey. Scenery and costumes by Rouben Ter-Arutunian. First presented by the Alvin Ailey City*

*Center Dance Theatre at the City Center, New York, May 11, 1976, with Judith Jamison and Mikhail Baryshnikov.*

Created for a special gala occasion and to honor the late Duke Ellington, this ballet was a *pas de deux* for two performers with radically different preparations—one a star of a modern dance company, the other a star of classic ballet. The choreographer brought the two together for a jazz ballet and made for the classic dancer a modern role he had not thought possible. The result was a memorable duet.

Clive Barnes recalled afterward in the New York *Times* that "it was remarkable how well Mr. Baryshnikov had absorbed the Ailey technique, and how well the two of them went together. It was sheer fun and Mr. Ailey was at his most persuasively inventive. It is always a delight to see Mr. Baryshnikov doing jazz movements—he performs a little naughtily, like a bright child talking faultlessly in a foreign language with a charming and slightly accentuated accent."

## PAS DE QUATRE

*Divertissement. Music by Cesare Pugni. Choreography by Jules Perrot. First presented at His Majesty's Theatre, London, July 12, 1845, with Marie Taglioni, Carlotta Grisi, Fanny Cerrito, and Lucile Grahn.*

This short ballet is probably the most famous *divertissement* in the history of dance. It displayed in one work four of the greatest ballerinas of its time, bringing these talents together for several memorable performances that have excited the curiosity of dance lovers for more than a hundred years. At this distance, it is impossible for us to tell exactly what *Pas de Quatre* looked like as a ballet, but information about what it resembled, and the unprecedented occasion it undoubtedly was, has come down to us in lithographs and reviews. If the greatest ballerinas of the United States, France, England, and the U.S.S.R. were to appear together in a ballet today, we should have some approximation of the excitement caused by the original *Pas de Quatre*. If such a *Pas de Quatre* seems impossible today, we must remember that it also seemed impossible in 1845.

Among all artists there is bound to be competition, and in the 1840s it seemed unlikely that any four of the great ballerinas would consent to dance on the same stage. Marie Taglioni had been acknowledged the finest dancer in the world when she created the title role in *La Sylphide* in 1832, and even thirteen years after her first famous role, she was still considered supreme in the realm of the romantic ballet that she had helped to create. But with the coming of the romantic era, there were also other ballerinas who danced in similar ballets: exceptional among these dancers were Fanny Cerrito, who was acclaimed in the early 1840s, Carlotta Grisi, who danced in 1841 the first performance of *Giselle*, and the Danish ballerina Lucile Grahn, who had successfully danced Taglioni's role in *La Sylphide*. The fact that each ballerina had danced *Giselle* (Taglioni, Cerrito, and Grahn undertook Grisi's original role in 1843) gives us an indication of their rivalry. There was, in short, so much natural jealousy between these four—and each faction of the public showed so great an amount of enthusiasm for its chosen goddess among them—that it appeared unlikely that the ballerinas would expose themselves to any common venture.

The man who thought otherwise and acted with persistence until he achieved his goal was the enterprising manager of His Majesty's Theatre in London, Benjamin Lumley. "The government of a great state was but a trifle compared to the government of such subjects as those whom I was *supposed* to be able to command," he recollected almost twenty years after the event. "These were subjects who considered themselves far above mortal control, or, more properly speaking, each was a queen in her own right—alone, absolute, supreme."

Lumley was encouraged to assemble the four ballerinas by a success he had brought off in 1843, when Fanny Cerrito danced at his theatre in a *pas de deux* with Fanny Elssler, the fifth great ballerina of this period. Why Elssler was not invited to participate in Lumley's assembly of ballerinas in 1845 is perhaps partially explained by this earlier triumph, but not altogether so. For Elssler's fame equaled, if it did not actually exceed, Taglioni's. No doubt that is exactly the point. Taglioni's superiority was unquestioned throughout Europe until Elssler made her début at the Paris Opéra in 1834. From this point on, the rivalry between the two was bitter. Elssler taunted Taglioni and her admirers by threatening to dance *La Sylphide*, which no other dancer yet dared to do. When Elssler essayed Taglioni's famous role in this ballet in 1838, open war broke out, and seven years later it must have been clear even to Benjamin Lumley that between these rivals there could never be peace. Théophile Gautier, who was to become the originator of *Giselle*, the friend and critical sponsor of Carlotta Grisi, wrote in 1837 that Fanny Elssler's dancing had a special quality that distinguished her from all other dancers and proceeded to make his point clear in a fashion that must have made the rivalry between the newcomer and the "Sylphide" intense: ". . . it is not the aerial and virginal grace of Taglioni, it is something more human, more appealing to the senses. Mademoiselle Taglioni is a Christian dancer, if one may make use of such an expression in regard to an art proscribed by the Catholic faith; she flies like a spirit in the midst of transparent clouds of white muslin with which she loves to surround herself, she resembles a happy angel who scarcely bends the petals of celestial flowers with the tips of her pink toes. Fanny is a quite pagan dancer; she reminds one of the muse Terpsichore, tambourine in hand, her tunic, exposing her thigh, caught up with a golden clasp; when she bends freely from the hips, throwing back her swooning, voluptuous arms, we seem to see one of those beautiful figures from Herculaneum or Pompeii which stand out in white relief against a black background . . ."

And Elssler was not praised only in Europe. She came to the United States in 1840 for a three-month tour and did not return to Europe for two years— two years during which she became the toast of the nation. She was welcomed by President Martin Van Buren, escorted by his son, entertained by Congress, carried on the shoulders of adoring crowds, and so universally acclaimed that she could declare, with accuracy, that "never was an artiste more completely seated in public sympathy." In nineteenth-century America she anticipated the exclusive success enjoyed by Anna Pavlova seventy years later.

But Benjamin Lumley also had grounds for being discouraged. His predecessor at His Majesty's Theatre had announced, but had been unable to present, Taglioni, Cerrito, and Elssler in a special performance. Circumstances, too, contrived against him. He had chosen Jules Perrot, the former partner of Taglioni and the choreographer who had collaborated on *Giselle,* to arrange the dances for the *Pas de Quatre,* and everyone was ready to begin—except one of the ballerinas. Carlotta Grisi, Perrot's wife, seemed unable to fulfill her engagement on time. She was dancing in Paris; how was she to get to London for rehearsals? Lumley tells us how: "A vessel was chartered . . . to waft the sylph at a moment's notice across the Channel; a special train was engaged and ready at Dover; relays of horses were in waiting to aid the flight of the *danseuse,* all the way from Paris to Calais."

When Grisi arrived, Perrot began to work on the most difficult assignment a ballet master ever had. He had not only to invent an ensemble that the four ballerinas would perform together, he had also to devise individual dances that would display ideally the particular artistry of each performer without distracting from the excellence of her sisters. In Lumley's words, "no one was to outshine the others—unless in their own individual belief." Perrot had worked closely on other projects with each of the four dancers previously and knew their temperaments; as the finest *danseur* of his time and a choreographer of equal fame, he also knew his job.

He seemed to succeed. The ballerinas were content with what they were to dance together and pleased with their variations; the costumes were ready, the theater sold out. And then came the problem of who was to dance first—or, rather, last, for the final variation in every ballet, as in regal processions, according to Lumley, is performed by the superior artist. Cerrito, Grisi, and Grahn agreed that Taglioni, because of her unprecedented fame, should occupy this place of honor. But as to the penultimate variation, the ladies disagreed: who was to be closest to Taglioni? Cerrito and Grisi vied for the position and quarreled on stage. Finally Grisi lost her temper, called Cerrito "a little chit," and the two ballerinas vowed they would never appear together.

Perrot, in despair, told the bad news to the manager. Lumley recalled what the choreographer said: "*Mon Dieu!* Cerrito won't begin before Carlotta, nor Carlotta before Cerrito, and there isn't anything that will make them change their minds: we're finished!" And Lumley also recalled what he replied: "The solution is easy . . . In this dilemma there is one point on which I am sure the ladies will be frank. Let the oldest take her unquestionable right to the envied position."

Perrot returned to the stage to try this ruse. When he told the two ballerinas the manager's decision, everything suddenly changed: they "tittered, laughed, drew back, and were now as much disinclined to accept the right of position as they had been eager to claim it." The trick worked! Taglioni was at this time forty-one, Cerrito was twenty-eight, and Grisi twenty-six: the reverse order was thus established, with Grahn, who was twenty-four, leading with the first variation. Lumley says that "the *grand pas de quatre* was finally performed on the same night before a delighted audience, who little knew how nearly they had been deprived of their expected treat."

What this audience saw was recorded by several critics, and approximations of the performance have been given us in modern representations of this *divertissement*. When the curtain went up, the four ballerinas appeared before a romantic background. They entered in a line, holding hands; each was dressed in billowing muslin and each wore in her hair a crown of white flowers, except Cerrito, who wore flowers in the knot at the back of her head. The ballerinas smiled, walked to the footlights, and bowed. The audience could not believe it. One member of the audience did not want to believe it and threw down from the gallery a shower of placards that declared Cerrito the peer of all dancers in the world. The audience was embarrassed and frightened of the possible consequences, but then someone laughed, the dancers smiled, and the music began.

The *Pas de Quatre* commenced in soft stillness as the four ballerinas moved toward the backdrop and arranged themselves in charming tableau about Taglioni, who looked down upon her sisters with an expression of sincere sweetness. Even the slightest display of jealousy was impossible now, for each artist was thoroughly aware that the ballet would surely fail if any of them failed to be as perfect as Perrot imagined they were and that they would be responsible. And so they knelt about Taglioni, opened their arms to her in a gesture of affection and respect, and smiled as innocently as she did. They changed their position, and the graceful Taglioni seemed to fall back in their welcoming arms.

The actual dancing began with a short variation by Grahn to quick, lively music. This was followed by a *pas de deux* by Cerrito and Grisi, which came to an end as Taglioni crossed the stage in high, light leaps that seemed to make her a part of the air. This introduction was merely a hint as to what was to follow in the four virtuoso variations. Grahn came first, dancing quickly, lightly, turning and hopping on point, moving about the stage with the controlled vigor of shining youth. Next, as the music changed, Carlotta Grisi stepped forward and danced with a sharp but airy vibrancy, a solo that summed up in a few short minutes her great fame.

Taglioni and Grahn, the oldest and the youngest, now danced together to a brief romantic measure. Cerrito was posed gracefully on stage with them, apparently waiting for them to finish their duet. Suddenly she cut this dainty and quiet sequence short, darting forward like an arrow released from the taut bow and describing a long, swift diagonal of accelerated turns. She finished her variation in a display of still, balanced poses contrasted with unparalleled verve and speed.

Taglioni, as the last of these great dancers, had the most difficult variation of all: she had to show the audience that what they had rejoiced in so far could be climaxed. And this she did, not by dancing in any fashion novel to her, but in a manner that epitomized her reputation: she moved with supreme lightness and she moved effortlessly, dazzling the audience with controlled poses even in midflight. And she moved with unquestioned authority, with the highest knowledge of her great gift and of her own faithful obedience to it, pausing in perfect balance with the grace and refinement of the mature artist.

Now, at the end, the three other ballerinas joined her. They all danced together, each trying to outdo the others in a final display of virtuosity. Then, as if they all understood that competition was in vain, they arranged themselves again in the tender tableau with which they had begun. Taglioni raised her arms over her head and looked down upon the other three, who gathered about her quietly and looked toward the audience with pensive, beguiling smiles, as if they had never moved.

NOTES   And what was the critical opinion of this *Pas de Quatre?* The *Times* of London called it "the greatest Terpsichorean exhibition that ever was known in Europe . . . Never was such a *pas* before. The excitement which a competition so extraordinary produced in the artists roused them to a pitch of energy which would have been impossible under other circumstances, and hence everyone did her utmost, the whole performance being a complete inspiration . . . The whole long *pas* was danced to a running sound of applause, which, after each variation, swelled to a perfect hurricane . . . Bouquets flew from every point, an immense profusion, as each *danseuse* came forward, so that they had to curtsy literally in the midst of a shower of floral gifts. Cerrito's wreaths and nosegays were more than she could hold in both her arms . . . The front of the stage was almost covered with flower leaves."

The critic of the *Illustrated London News* reported: "No description can render the exquisite, the almost ethereal, grace of movement and attitude of these great dancers, and those who have witnessed the scene may boast of having once, at least, seen the perfection of the art of dancing. . . ."

The best accounts of three of the four ballerinas are given by their contemporary Théophile Gautier. Gautier did not review the *Pas de Quatre,* but he speaks here of Taglioni the year before the London *divertissement:* "Mademoiselle Taglioni is not a dancer, she is the embodiment of dancing . . . Fortunate woman. Always the same elegant and slender form, the same calm, intelligent and modest features; not a single feather has fallen from her wing; not a hair has silvered beneath her chaplet of flowers! As the curtain rose, she was greeted with thunders of applause. What airiness! What rhythmic movements! What noble gestures! What poetic attitudes and, above all, what a sweet melancholy! What lack of restraint, yet how chaste!"

Gautier speaks of Cerrito two years after the *Pas de Quatre:* "Fanny Cerrito's principal qualities are grace of pose, unusual attitudes, quickness of movement, and the rapidity with which she covers ground; she bounds and rebounds with an admirable ease and elasticity; there is a charming grace about her whole body. . . . She radiates a sense of happiness, brilliance, and smiling ease which know neither labor nor weariness. . . ."

Of Carlotta Grisi, Gautier had this to say at the time of her début at the Paris Opéra (1841): "She is possessed of a strength, lightness, suppleness and originality which at once place her between Elssler and Taglioni." Two years later he was to write that "Grisi's dancing has a quite special style; it does not resemble the dancing of either Taglioni or Elssler; each one of her poses, each one of her movements, is stamped with the seal of originality."

*Pas de Quatre* with its original cast was performed only four times (July 12, 15, 17, and 19, 1845). Queen Victoria and the Prince Consort attended the third performance. Three of the original cast—Taglioni, Cerrito, and Grisi—danced in a revival of the *divertissement* that was performed twice in Lumley's theater: on July 17 and 19, 1847. Carolina Rosati replaced Lucile Grahn in these performances. Rosati at this time was only twenty years old; fifteen years later, in Russia, she was to dance the leading role in *The Daughter of Pharaoh* (Pugni), the first great success of the ballet master Marius Petipa.

A year after the first performance of the original *Pas de Quatre,* Taglioni, Grahn, and Cerrito danced together at Lumley's theater in a ballet called *The Judgment of Paris* (Pugni-Perrot). The ballerinas danced the parts of three goddesses in this *divertissement,* which was hailed almost as loudly as *Pas de Quatre. The Judgment of Paris* was Marie Taglioni's last new ballet.

Marie Taglioni retired soon after she danced the revival of *Pas de Quatre* and died impoverished in Marseille, France, in 1884, at the age of eighty. Fanny Cerrito, at the time of her appearance in London, had yet to achieve her fullest fame and in the 1840s and 1850s secured for herself additional triumphs. She died in 1909 at the age of ninety-two. Carlotta Grisi had new successes after the famous *divertissement,* creating the title role in *Paquita* (Mazilier-Deldevez) in 1846 and dancing at the Imperial Theatre in St. Petersburg. She was seventy-eight when she died in 1899. Lucile Grahn, the youngest of the *Pas de Quatre* ballerinas, had danced in Russia before she came to London for Lumley's *divertissement.* Trained in her native Denmark by the great Danish ballet master Auguste Bournonville, Grahn made her début at the Royal Theatre, Copenhagen, in 1835. In this theater Grahn danced a version of *La Sylphide* created for her by Bournonville (1836). This production of the famous ballet has been in the repertory of the Royal Danish Ballet ever since it was first performed. Grahn died in 1907 at the age of eighty-six.

Another historic presentation of *Pas de Quatre* took place January 24, 1972, at the City Center, New York, at the Gala Performance for the Dance Collection of the New York Public Library. Anton Dolin, who had reconstructed the ballet for American Ballet Theatre in 1941, did so again, this time bringing together Carla Fracci as Taglioni, Violette Verdy as Grisi, Patricia McBride as Cerrito, and Eleanor D'Antuono as Grahn.

## LES PATINEURS (The Skaters)

*Ballet in one act. Music by Giacomo Meyerbeer. Choreography by Frederick Ashton. Scenery and costumes by William Chappell. First presented by the Vic-Wells Ballet at the Sadler's Wells Theatre, London, February 16, 1937, with a cast headed by Margot Fonteyn, Robert Helpmann, and Harold Turner. First presented in the United States by Ballet Theatre at the Broad-*

*way Theatre, New York, October 2, 1946. Scenery and costumes by Cecil Beaton. Nora Kaye, Hugh Laing, and John Kriza danced the leading roles.*

Some people watch ice skating and say how like dancing it is. *Les Patineurs* shows us how dancing, among other things, can imitate ice skating. The ballet has no story; it simply organizes what any of us might see at a skating rink into a series of nine *divertissements*. The music, arranged by Constant Lambert, is based on selections from Meyerbeer's operas *L'Étoile du Nord* and *Le Prophète*. The Ballet Theatre production is described here.

The music is whistling, thumping holiday fare. The scene is any secluded skating pond, the time, night. Snowy branches of barren trees hang over the pond; brightly colored paper lanterns light up the forest. Four couples skate across the scene. Two pretty girls follow them, slipping and turning on the ice. One of the boys in the skating party falls; his girl brushes him off, and they exit. A boy in bright green rushes in and treats us to a quick, dazzling display of virtuosity and skates off as though he'd done nothing at all.

The harp signals a romantic melody, and two lovers enter. The boy carries the girl high on his shoulder, sets her down, and she turns close to the ground. The couple are dressed in white and seem at home in the snow-laden scene. They circle the stage, the boy lifting the girl softly to the right and left. For a moment they separate; then they rejoin, and the boy spins the girl around and around. They skate away, hand in hand.

Eight couples—the girls in bright red and the boys in yellow and blue—fill the skating area. Two girls take over the pond and dance brightly to a tinkling tune. The lovers join the eight couples and dance with them a gay ensemble. The boy in green circles the stage, then leaves. Now the ensemble moves with a slower grace. The boy in green now shows off among them, and all watch him. When he is finished, they turn to watch four girls who are skating apart from the crowd; then all skate off in a circling line.

The boy in green and the two girls who danced the first *divertissement* perform a *pas de trois*. Soon they are followed by two other girls, who do an incredible number of fast, accelerated *fouettés*. The boy in green hails the others in the party to come back, and everyone promenades. Snow begins to fall. The girls resume their *fouettés*, whirling away faster than ever as the exhilarating music comes to a climax. The boy in green is challenged by their skill to turn faster than ever and he is spinning like a top when the curtain falls.

# PAVANE

*Music by Maurice Ravel. Choreography by George Balanchine. Lighting by Ronald Bates. First presented by the New York City Ballet at the Hommage à Ravel at the New York State Theatre, Lincoln Center, May 29, 1975, with Patricia McBride. Conducted by Robert Irving.*

This work of Ravel's, the *Pavane pour une Infante Défunte*, or *Pavane for a Dead Child*, is perhaps the best-known of his compositions after the ever popular *Boléro*. This popularity is perhaps due to the name of the piece; everyone feels sentimental about the mere idea of it. Yet Ravel himself felt that the work owed its success to its "remarkable interpretations." He wrote: "Do not attach to the title any more importance than it has. It is not a pavane for a dead child but, rather, an evocation of the pavanes that could have been danced by such a little princess as painted by Velásquez at the Spanish court."

The dance to this music is arranged for a girl who responds to a ghostly idea among the living. The dictionary defines a pavane as a slow, stately dance. So does this girl perform it, in a flowing white gown, gossamer and a preparation for the shroud.

As the curtain rises, the girl, veiled, stands at the back of the stage. She shields her eyes in grief, then begins to dance. Cradling her hands as if to hold a child, the girl moves like the wind, yet royally, in a processional manner. In control of her long train, she lets it swirl about her, then covers her face with it and stands alone, grieving.

NOTES   The critic Byron Belt wrote after the premiere, in the *Long Island Press*: "*Pavane* is an undulating treatment of mourning, at once poignant and sensuous. Patricia McBride, swathed in white, uses a long scarf in the manner of an Art Nouveau Isadora Duncan, but it is carried off with such fragile beauty that the work seems astonishingly fresh and strong . . . *Pavane* . . . was created for a dancer magnificently able to dominate the stage completely with her virtuosity."


# PELLÉAS AND MÉLISANDE

*Music by Arnold Schoenberg. Choreography by Roland Petit. Scenery and costumes by Jacques Dupont. First presented by the Royal Ballet, March 26, 1969, at the Royal Opera House, Covent Garden, London, with Margot Fonteyn, Rudolf Nureyev, and Keith Rosson in the principal roles. First presented in the United States by the same ensemble at the Metropolitan Opera House, Lincoln Center, New York, May 5, 1969. Conducted by John Lanchbery.*

The choreographer of this ballet, Roland Petit, has written his own synopsis of the action and a comment:

"Mélisande is lost in the forest. Golaud finds her and falls in love. She senses that another destiny awaits her and when Pelléas, Golaud's brother, arrives, he and Mélisande instantly recognize that it has come.

"Golaud leads her away, but she returns to Pelléas with her long hair streaming round her. Golaud becomes tormented by jealousy and, seeing the lovers together, he stabs Pelléas. Mélisande dies of a broken heart. Reunited in death, the lovers are resurrected for Eternity from their forest grave.

"Pelléas and Mélisande like Romeo and Juliet are part of a legend which has through the centuries taught subsequent generations about love. The forces that unite or divide, that kill or revive them still constitute the very substance of love.

"Today love does not have to come under the same judgment as of old, nor to surmount the same obstacles, but love itself is the same, with fewer frills and furbelows, even, perhaps, stripped naked. This is why I have chosen to play down the circumstances that we connect with Pelléas and Mélisande. Instead, I have attempted to portray them as they appear in us. Hounded by an identical destiny, we see in them what we feel happening in ourselves."

The ballet is arranged to the tone poem of the same name by Arnold Schoenberg, who wrote that "inspired entirely by Maeterlinck's wonderful drama, I have tried to mirror every detail of it."

Reviewing *Pelléas and Mélisande* after its first performance, in *The Observer* of London, the critic Alexander Bland noted that the ballet was featured at a gala to celebrate Margot Fonteyn's thirty-fifth year with the Royal Ballet: "It has been an incredible career which has seen her steadily progress to that peak of artistry where, like a mature draughtsman, she can express everything with almost nothing. She packs richness into simplicity, conceals technique under nonchalance and melts emotion into classical economy and integrity . . . There is one effective moment when Mélisande dominates the stage with a tent of gauzy tresses . . . in which Pelléas becomes voluptuously entangled."

## LA PÉRI

*Music by Norbert Burgmüller. Choreography by Jean Coralli. Book by Théophile Gautier and Jean Coralli. First presented at the Théâtre de l'Académie Royal de Musique, Paris, July 17, 1843, with Carlotta Grisi and Lucien Petipa. Presented in a new version by Frederick Ashton, by the Royal Ballet at the Royal Opera House, Covent Garden, February 15, 1956, with Margot Fonteyn and Michael Somes. Music by Paul Dukas. Scenery by Ivor Hitchens. Costumes by André Levasseur. First presented in the United States by the Royal Ballet, September 26, 1957, at the Metropolitan Opera House. Presented in a new version by George Skibine to the Dukas score at the Opéra, Paris, December 1966, with Calire Motte and Jean-Pierre Bonnefous. Setting by Robert D. Mitchell. Costumes and lighting by Nicholas Cernovich. First presented in the United States by the National Ballet of Washington, with Andrea Vodehnal and Steven Grebel, at the Lisner Auditorium, Washington, February 26, 1967.*

According to Persian mythology, *péris* are fallen angels who assume the form of elfin sprites. There have been many ballets created around the story of Iskender and his search for the lotus, the flower of immortality, and his encounter with a *péri*. Iskender wanders far and wide searching for the flower, which he finds at last in the hand of a lovely sleeping *péri*. He steals the flower but cannot leave, for he adores the girl he sees lying before him. When she wakens, the *péri* senses his want, and dances to play upon his desire so that she may regain the flower. Iskender is bewitched and in exchange for a kiss would give her the world. He returns the flower. "Then the lotus seemed like snow and gold like the summit of Elbourz in the evening sun. The form of the *péri* appeared to melt into the light emanating from the calyx. Iskender saw her disappear. And realizing that this signified his approaching end, he felt the shadow encircling him."

This story and its heroine have fascinated choreographers and dancers for more than a hundred years. There have been many dances based on the original two-act ballet with Théophile Gautier's scenario. Grisi, Pavlova (in a version by Clustine, 1921), Spessivtzeva (in the ballet by Leo Staats, 1921), Markova (in Frederick Ashton's first version, 1931, for the Ballet Club, London), Yvette Chauvire (in the version by Serge Lifar, 1948), and others. The Dukas score was commissioned by the Russian ballerina Natalia Trouhanova and first performed by her in Paris, April 22, 1912.

## PERSEPHONE

*Melodrama in three scenes. Music by Igor Stravinsky. French text by André Gide. Choreography by Kurt Jooss. Scenery and costumes by André Barsacq. First presented by Ballets Ida Rubinstein at the Opéra, Paris, April 30, 1934, with Ida Rubinstein in the title role. Revived in a new version by the Royal Ballet, with choreography by Frederick Ashton at the Royal Opera House, Covent Garden, London, December 12, 1961. Scenery and costumes by Nico Ghika. Svetlana Beriosova appeared in the title role.*

The ballet tells the story of Persephone, daughter of Zeus and Demeter, goddess of fertility, who was taken away to the Underworld by Pluto, its king. In the first scene, "The Abduction of Persephone," Persephone on "the world's first morning" is warned not to pick the narcissus, for whoever breathes its fragrance must come to see a vision of Hades. But Persephone admires the flower and as she smells it she glimpses the sorrowful Shades of the Underworld, who must endlessly wander until the end of time. She has pity on them. Eumolpus, the high priest, tells Persephone that if she will go to the Underworld the lot of the Shades will be happier. Pluto claims Persephone, who descends to the Underworld.

In the second scene, "Persephone in the Underworld," she has become Queen of the Shades. With her descent, Pluto has banished spring from the earth. Biting a pomegranate presented to her by Mercury, she recalls the earth above, her mother, and her earthly husband, Demaphoon. Eumolpus relates that the earthly winter will not last forever and that it is Demeter's plan to cause Demaphoon to teach men to till the soil, thereby bringing them salvation. Through his intercession, Persephone is reborn and goes to rejoin her earthly husband.

"Persephone Reborn," the final scene, shows the goddess reunited with her mother and husband; spring returns to the earth. Having restored the seasons, Persephone realizes that her destiny lies with the Shades and that she must again return to rule over them at Pluto's side. Taking a torch offered her by Mercury to light her way back into the darkness, Persephone makes her farewell.

# PETROUCHKA

*Ballet burlesque in one act, four scenes. Music by Igor Stravinsky. Choreography by Michel Fokine. Book by Stravinsky and Alexandre Benois. Scenery and costumes by Benois. First presented by Diaghilev's Ballets Russes at the Théâtre du Châtelet, Paris, June 13, 1911, with Vaslav Nijinsky as* Petrouchka, *Tamara Karsavina as the* Ballerina, *Alexandre Orlov as the* Moor, *and Enrico Cecchetti as the* Charlatan. *First presented in the United States by Diaghilev's Ballets Russes at the Century Theatre, New York, January 25, 1916, with Leonide Massine, Lydia Lopokova, and Adolph Bolm in the principal roles.*

*Petrouchka* tells the story of a puppet with a human heart, a creature of straw who comes to life only to be disbelieved. Characters similar to Petrouchka, half comic, half tragic, have been common to popular theatrical tradition in Europe for hundreds of years—characters such as Pierrot and Puck, clowns no one will ever take seriously, funny men who are always unlucky but who somehow manage to have in the end more wisdom than anybody else; funny men such as Charlie Chaplin's tramp. *Petrouchka* is ballet's representation of this universal character, of what the creators of the ballet knew in their youth as the "Russian Punch and Judy Show." At first the puppet is happy to be a mere automaton. Then he falls in love with a beautiful dancer and tries to win her, though all the world seems against him. He loses her, dies, and everyone laughs. He wins by returning for the last laugh himself.

SCENE ONE: THE SHROVETIDE FAIR   The first scene of the ballet is set in a great public square in old St. Petersburg. The year is 1830; the season, winter —the last week before Lent, when all the populace gather together for final feasting and celebration. Even before the curtain rises, the orchestra tells us it is carnival time, as the cheerful blatancy of the music swells and varies to bring up images of a surging festival, where everyone is determined to have a good time in his own way. Peasants, gypsies, soldiers, and well-dressed folk, all in holiday attire, mingle in the snow-covered square. Fair booths decorated with bright bunting and flags surround an open area, and in the back stands the largest booth of all. It has blue curtains drawn across it like a stage. Above the booth, in Russian, are the words "Living Theater." Behind it are the spires of government buildings topped with flags. The crowd tries to keep warm by moving constantly; its members stamp and throw their arms around their chests as they talk to each other; some buy hot tea at a booth with a large, steaming samovar. But the cold weather serves only to intensify their good spirits. Everyone seems to be happy and carefree in the pursuit of a traditional pleasure all can share. The open, undisguised merriment of the music whirls with the circling crowd and its quick-changing rhythms accentuate the variety of noises that refuse to blend into one tune—the loud, comradely greetings, the laughter, the shrieking of persistent barkers, the vigorous dancing of three enthusiastic peasants.

The crowd hears a barrel organ grinding away in the distance, but its small sound is almost immediately drowned out by the hubbub in the square. The organ-grinder enters, playing a street song, and the people stand aside to watch his approach. With him comes a girl who carries a little rug under her arm and a triangle. She spreads the rug over the snow, strikes the triangle in a steady beat to secure everyone's attention, and begins to dance to a gay tune. Her dance is clearly designed to show the crowd how rapidly she can turn on one point without stopping; and as people begin to be impressed by her virtuosity, the organist shows off too, by grinding out the song with one hand and duplicating it on a cornet he holds with the other. When he finishes, he begins to play again his rather mournful street song, while on the other side of the stage a rival team of entertainers has appeared to attract the crowd away. There another dancer begins to turn to the tune of a hurdy-gurdy, and a new group forms about the girl and her accompanist. The organist and his partner glance over at the newcomers and speed up the tempo of their act. The two dancers and the two instruments compete openly: each of the girls imitates the other's movements, and the crowd watches first one and then the other as if they were looking at a tennis match. Finally the girls have spent all their energy and the contest is over. Both end their dances in identical positions; the spectators applaud, reward both couples, and everyone is delighted.

The square is now packed with people, who mill about greeting one another and conversing as the orchestra renews the raucous overture. Rowdy peasants come in and dance an animated Russian folk dance to the amusement of some of the crowd. The scene is now feverish with liveliness and hearty good spirits, and the music reaches a high volume to duplicate this enthusiasm. Two drummers step out from behind the blue-curtained stage at the rear and walk forward. The crowd stands back. The drums roll commandingly; everyone looks toward the stage; a loud chord from the orchestra is cut off sharply. A man with a high-peaked hat pokes his head through the curtains. This is the Charlatan, the showman in charge of the "Living Theater." Everyone is silent as they watch him. He is a showman who entertains by magic, and when he steps out from behind the curtains, no one is quite certain what he will do. His long black robe decorated with mysterious signs, his white face, and his menacing gestures attract the crowd strangely. He takes out a flute. The orchestra sounds a few weird bars suggestive of incipient evil. Then the Charlatan surprises us by playing on his instrument not an Oriental incantation, but a pleasant melody, beseeching in its repetitions. This is his magic song, the music that will bring to life the unseen show behind the closed curtains. The crowd waits, fascinated. The Charlatan gives a sudden imperious signal. The curtains fly back. We see a stage separated into three small compartments. In each compartment rests a motionless puppet, staring out at the audience with blank expression. The three figures are supported by high armrests. In the center is the prima Ballerina, with perfect, Dresden-china features and pink cheeks. She poses rigidly, waiting to be wound up. On the left is the Moor, with white eyes and a white mouth set in a coal-black face. He wears a turban, a bright blouse with a sash about his waist, and trousers of gold brocade. On the right, completely relaxed, is Petrouchka. His face is a white mask, his body is limp, like that of a rag doll. His costume has no conventional design: the loose-fitting trousers that hang down over black boots, the blouse ruffled at the neck, the haphazard cap—all make his figure absurd. While the ballerina and the Moor hold themselves erect, Petrouchka's head lolls to the side. Of the three, he is the least eager to move or to be moved. Lifeless as he is, Petrouchka therefore seems to be more natural. The ballerina and the Moor are posed tensely, ready to spring into activity, but Petrouchka's attitude suggests that perhaps he is tired of being a puppet.

The three puppets remain still as the Charlatan finishes his invocation to his magical gods. The ensuing music is low and mysterious. The Charlatan cuts it short by sounding his flute three times, whereupon Petrouchka, the ballerina, and the Moor instantly wake up and move their feet to the sharp and lively rhythms of a Russian dance. The puppets still stand, and their feet move so fast on and off the floor that their bodies seem suspended. They have come to life so spontaneously, and their feet mark each accent of the dance with such energetic unison, that it is difficult to believe they were inert but a moment before. The music becomes more demanding in its tempo, but the puppets follow the dance perfectly, as if they were toy soldiers obeying the beat of a snare drum. Now they abandon their armrests and step down. The crowd gives them room, and, to the great pleasure of the spectators, the puppets act out a dumb show almost as mechanically as they danced. Both the Moor and Petrouchka are enamored of the ballerina. The Moor flirts with her, and the ballerina seems to favor him, upon which Petrouchka, in a jealous rage, attacks his rival. The Charlatan signals for the drama to stop, and the three puppets involuntarily return to their dance routine. The stage grows darker, and the crowd begins to wander off. The Charlatan makes another signal, and the puppets immediately cease all movement and become rigid and still. The curtain falls.

SCENE TWO: PETROUCHKA'S ROOM    Now we are taken behind the scenes, into the private lives of the puppets. Petrouchka's room is a barren cell. The peaks of icy high mountains are painted all along the walls, near to the floor, while up above, near the ceiling, is a border of puffy white clouds. The room has been decorated, the set implies, for a character not altogether of this world. On the right wall hangs a large portrait of the Charlatan. A door on the left is embellished with satanic figures carrying pitchforks. Petrouchka is suddenly tossed into the room through this door by the Charlatan. The door slams shut. Petrouchka makes a feeble effort to pick himself up, but wonders whether it is worth it. His wooden gestures indicate that everything is hopeless. Here he is in prison again, with nothing to look at but a picture of his master. A piano takes up a despondent theme that embodies Petrouchka's despair, while the rest of the orchestra tries to drown it out. He moves about the room helplessly, he tries to open the door, he pounds on the walls, hoping that someone will release him. Then, all alone, he rages against the world that ignores him. As trumpets blare a loud fanfare, Petrouchka turns to the portrait of the Charlatan and shakes his fists in challenge to the evil magician who limits his life to public performances.

As if to prove that he is worthy of a better fate, Petrouchka then does a little dance in which he imitates human expression of feeling. The piano accompanies him. His arms are stiff, but when he holds them close to his heart and then opens them in a gesture of hope, we see that the puppet understands more than the dumb-show version of love. He is a marionette who might become human, but cannot because of the Charlatan who made him. His hatred of the Charlatan is his hatred of his inarticulate self, that part of his dual nature that can but pathetically copy the human gestures for the human emotion his other nature feels so intensely. He arouses our pity because we see that his rage against the world is also his rage at himself. His clumsy wooden limbs try in vain to express their freedom, and his white face is a mask of sorrow.

But Petrouchka's whole attitude changes when he turns to see that the ballerina has entered his prison. Now the music is gay and lighthearted and Petrouchka jumps about joyfully. The ballerina, who stands motionless on point, registers shock at this inelegant expression of pleasure. She makes the appropriate formal gestures of delicate disapproval and turns to go. Petrouchka is beside himself with anxiety and proceeds to increase the ballerina's distaste by leaping higher to attract her attention. Clearly, the ballerina has had enough of the uncontrollable puppet. She turns and leaves.

Once again Petrouchka is in despair and again, to the accompaniment of the piano and the overpowering orchestra that represents the world he fights against, he gives himself up to his grief. The Charlatan will always think him a mere puppet; the ballerina will never regard him as anything but an idiotic buffoon. He flings his exhausted body about the room, bangs against the walls, finally succeeds in tearing open a large hole in the right wall, and collapses when he sees that it leads nowhere.

SCENE THREE: THE MOOR'S ROOM   The Moor, too, has been imprisoned by the showman, but his abode is ornately decorated and sumptuously furnished. Everything is splashed with color. A large couch, covered with the skin of a tiger and backed with cushions, is on the left. Tall, bushy palm trees are painted on the walls. Serpents and ferocious beasts depicted in bright colors peer out into the room through thick jungle foliage. On the right is a door ornamented with a snake rampant. On the couch lies the Moor. He is playing idly with a coconut. The music is slow, almost lazy, as the Moor amuses his indolence by tossing the coconut and catching it. Unlike Petrouchka, the Moor is satisfied with his abode and appears happy whiling away the time of day like the caged beast contentedly resigned to an imitation jungle. He is also unlike the clown in his inhumanity: he is all puppet. He is soon bored with his simple pastime and tries to vary it with complications: by grasping his toy with his feet and letting it fall, by catching it in many ways. But this is not sufficient for the Moor's entertainment. He grows angry with the coconut. He shakes it, as an animal would shake the head of a helpless victim. He hears something inside, but he cannot break the coconut. He pulls out his scimitar, places the coconut on the floor at his feet. The music crashes with his effort to break the coconut in two, but it is hard as a rock. The Moor is astonished. He stares at the mysterious object that can withstand his mighty blow and decides that it must be magical. He kneels then, bows and worships his plaything as he would worship a god.

The door moves aside, and a roll on a drum signals the entrance of the ballerina. She dances in, horn held to her lips, and steps gaily about the room, the beat of the drum accompanying the tune she plays. The Moor forgets his fetish and watches her with great pleasure, a pleasure which the music expresses with brief cries. The ballerina is charmed by this simple response, so different from the open approval of Petrouchka, and obliges the Moor by dancing a waltz. He is delighted beyond mere approval by this performance and insists upon dancing too. His motions are primitive alongside her elegant steps, but he nevertheless tries to make his crude dance fit the rhythm of the ballerina's waltz. He fails miserably and persists in his own private rhythm as the orchestra imitates the chaos of their duet by opposing different melodies. The Moor is now infatuated with the dainty ballerina and demonstrates his affection by pulling her toward the couch. The ballerina pretends to be aghast at this behavior, but secretly she is charmed also and scarcely resists when the Moor holds her on his lap. Their amorous dalliance is interrupted, however, by strange noises from outside. One of Petrouchka's melodies is proclaimed on the trumpet, and the clown thrusts his arm in at the door in an effort to wedge himself into the room. He has imagined the plight of the ballerina and has come to her aid! The couple jump guiltily as he forces his way in; they spring apart. The jealous Petrouchka berates the Moor for his behavior and approaches him menacingly as the music resounds his rage. The Moor recovers from the surprise of Petrouchka's sudden appearance and replies with animal grunts. Then he draws his scimitar and begins to chase the clown around the room. The ballerina faints on the couch, the Moor closes in on Petrouchka, whose end seems certain until he makes a quick dash for the door and escapes. The Moor is about to pursue the interloper, when he remembers the ballerina. He drops his sword, goes back over to the couch, and pulls the ballerina back onto his lap. The curtain falls as his head bobs up and down in savage satisfaction. The private lives of the three puppets have turned out to be almost identical to the dumb show they acted before the public: Petrouchka always loses.

SCENE FOUR: GRAND CARNIVAL   The Shrovetide Fair, the outside world, has gone on while we watched the inner drama backstage, and the music now takes us back to the festivities. Very little time has elapsed, for the stage is not yet dark and the celebrating crowd is by no means ready to go home. The puppet theater in the back is dark and silent. Stimulated by their continuous refreshment, the peasants are all laughing and whipping themselves up to a final high pitch of excitement. A group of nursemaids emerge from the multitude, line up, and start a traditional dance to a Russian folk song that is exhilarating in its open melody; the crowd sways to the rhythm of the dance. The nursemaids' round is interrupted by deep, plodding notes from the orchestra, which herald the arrival of a trained bear. The bear swaggers clumsily onto the scene, led by his trainer, who laughs at the fears of the spectators and directs the bear in a few simple tricks. Then follows the dance of the coachmen, whose performance outrivals all the others in color and vigor. The theme to which the nursemaids danced is heard again, and the nurses join the coachmen. The couples seem to exhaust themselves in joyous abandon, but gain fresh strength with each step. Garishly dressed masqueraders—a demon, various animals—scurry about in the square trying to frighten people, but almost everyone is involved in the dance, in watching it at first, then imitating it while standing still, then participating fully, so that the stage gradually becomes a mass of whirling color. The frenzied beat of the music, and its increasingly raucous volume, intoxicates the dancers, and—as night descends on the scene and snow begins to fall—their movements in this picture frame of old Russia surge with a final expression of carnival fervor.

The enthusiasm of the revelers has not allowed them to notice that in the back, within the puppet theater, there are signs of activity behind the drawn curtains. They all turn, as they hear strange noises inside the theater, and wait expectantly. Petrouchka comes running out, the music sounds his fanfare, and we see that he is trying to escape from the Moor, who dashes out after him. The crowd is struck dumb by this apparently spontaneous life in the puppets and looks on, fascinated, as the clown tries to avoid the blows of the Moor's scimitar. The Moor's animal strength overpowers Petrouchka. The clown is cornered. He covers his head with his arms, shaking with fright. The Moor, with one blow of his sword, strikes him down. Petrouchka doubles up in pain. The music reflects his agony and his great effort to remain alive, but his legs stretch out, his whole body quivers spasmodically, and he is dead.

His death has been so realistic that the people who surround his body cannot believe that he is a mere puppet; a crime seems to have been committed. Someone calls a policeman, who observes the dead clown and hauls out the Charlatan to give an account of the strange goings on. The Charlatan is much amused at his suspicions and picks up the body to show everyone they are mistaken. Petrouchka is now a limp rag doll, a creature who could never have been anything but lifeless. The policeman is satisfied, people shake their heads, the crowd begins to leave slowly. The Charlatan remains alone, holding the puppet, and the stage is almost completely dark. He turns to re-enter the theater—perhaps to put the errant clown back in his cell—when Petrouchka's fanfare blares out loudly to stop him in his tracks. He looks up: on the top of the theater the ghost of Petrouchka shakes his fist at the Charlatan—and at everyone else who will not believe he is real.

NOTES   The idea of *Petrouchka* was first of all a musical idea. Stravinsky had finished *Firebird* and was about to begin work on his next project for Diaghilev—*The Rite of Spring*—when he interrupted his plans to compose a purely nonballetic piece. He wanted to write a piece for piano and orchestra in which the piano would seem to be attacked by the mass of instruments. It would fight back, flourish a bit, but then the large orchestra would win out.

Stravinsky began to think of this composition as a contest between a puppet, represented by the piano, and the orchestra. After he had finished it, he tried to find an idea that would express the image that had been in his mind as he composed. He found it in a word, *Petrouchka,* "the immortal and unhappy hero of every fair."

He conveyed his idea to Diaghilev, who, upon hearing the music, decided to produce a ballet on this theme as soon as possible. The painter and designer Alexandre Benois collaborated with the musician and the impresario on the story, which Michel Fokine choreographed for Nijinsky, Karsavina, Orlov, and Cecchetti.

Although it is perhaps the most famous ballet in the modern repertory, *Petrouchka* has but recently been revived with sufficient competence to remind us that its first production was a very great one indeed. Stravinsky has written in his *Autobiography* (1936): "I should like . . . to pay heartfelt homage to Vaslav Nijinsky's unsurpassed rendering of the role of Petrouchka. The perfection with which he became the very incarnation of this character was all the more remarkable because the purely saltatory work in which he excelled was in this case dominated by dramatic action, music and gesture. The beauty of the ballet was greatly enhanced by the richness of the artistic setting which Benois had created for it. My faithful interpreter Karsavina swore to me that she would never relinquish her part as the dancer, which she adored. But it was a pity that the movements of the crowd had been neglected. I mean that they were left to the arbitrary improvisation of the performers instead of being choreographically regulated in accordance with the clearly defined exigencies of the music. I regret it all the more because the *danses d'ensemble* of the coachmen, nurses and mummers, and the solo dances, must be regarded as Fokine's finest creations.

Carl Van Vechten describes Nijinsky's Petrouchka in this way: "He is a puppet and—remarkable touch—a puppet with a soul. His performance in this ballet is, perhaps, his most wonderful achievement. He suggests only the puppet in action; his facial expression never changes; yet the pathos is greater, more keenly carried over the footlights, than one would imagine possible under any conditions. I have seen Fokine in the same role, and although he gives you all the gestures the result is not the same. It is genius that Nijinsky puts into his interpretation of the part. Who can ever forget Nijinsky as Petrouchka when thrown by his master into his queer black box, mad with love for the dancer, who, in turn, prefers the Moor puppet, rushing about waving his pathetically stiff arms in the air, and finally beating his way with his clenched fists through the paper window to curse the stars? It is a more poignant expression of grief than most Romeos can give us."

Many famous dancers have since appeared in the role—Massine, Woizikowski, Jerome Robbins, Michael Kidd, Børge Ralov. Fokine revived the ballet for the Royal Danish Ballet in 1925, and for Ballet Theatre, October 8, 1942.

*Petrouchka* was revived by the Royal Ballet on March 26, 1957, with Alexander Grant, Margot Fonteyn, and Peter Clegg in the principal roles. Rudolf Nureyev danced the role for the first time with this company on October 24, 1963. Nadia Nerina was the doll and Keith Rosson the blackamoor. Mary Clarke wrote in the *Dancing Times:* "Let it be said at once that Nureyev captures to perfection the sawdust quality of the part. His first fall in the opening scene is just a crumble of a puppet body and all the way through one feels that the gloves contain no hands, just useless stuffing. This, of course, heightens the pathos of the character, the little pigmy soul that aspires to human loves and fears without a human body to support them. The scene in Petrouchka's cell is, as yet, only sketched; it will develop with more performances . . . but the final moment on the top of the booth, when the immortal soul asserts itself for the last time, is marvelously done. Everybody's heart must have trembled just a little bit when watching this."

*Petrouchka* is a ballet for which I have some sentimental recollection. In the Diaghilev production, whenever anyone was sick or unable to dance I took his part in the ballet. At one time I thought I had danced almost every male part in the ballet!

*Petrouchka* was revived in New York, March 13, 1970, by the City Center Joffrey Ballet under the supervision of Leonide Massine, assisted by Yurek Lazowski and Tania Massine. The principal roles were taken by Edward Verso, Erika Goodman, Christian Holder, Yurek Lazowski, and Zelma Bustilio. Noting that the ballet had not been seen in New York for twelve years, the critic Anna Kisselgoff wrote in the New York *Times* that "the spell of the decor, based on the original designs of Alexandre Benois, the magic of Igor Stravinsky's miraculous score and the radically expressive choreography of Michel Fokine are as strong as ever."

American Ballet Theatre revived *Petrouchka* June 19, 1970, at the New York State Theatre, with Ted Kivitt, Eleanor D'Antuono, and Bruce Marks in the principal roles. Clive Barnes in the New York *Times* called this production, staged by Dimitri Romanoff and Yurek Lazowski, "A sumptuous and authentic new staging that is part homage to the past and part reaffirmation of Ballet Theatre's historically classic role in American dance's future."

# PICNIC AT TINTAGEL

*Dramatic ballet in three scenes. Music by Arnold Bax. Choreography by Frederick Ashton. Scenery and costumes by Cecil Beaton. Costumes executed by Helene Pons. Lighting by Jean Rosenthal. First presented by the New York City Ballet at the City Center, New York, February 28, 1952, with Francisco Moncion as the Husband (King Mark), Diana Adams as the Wife (Iseult), Jacques d'Amboise as her Lover (Tristram), and Robert Barnett as the Caretaker (Merlin).*

Today, on the west coast of England, stands "wild Tintagel by the Cornish seas," a rocky promontory reaching out into the water. Here we find the ruins of an ancient castle celebrated by poets and chroniclers for centuries as the stronghold of King Arthur and his Knights of the Round Table. One of King Arthur's trusted knights was Tristram, who brought the beautiful Irish maid Iseult to Cornwall to be the wife of his uncle, King Mark. The love story of Tristram and Iseult has inspired writers from the time of Geoffrey of Monmouth to the times of Tennyson, Swinburne, Wagner, Hardy, Edwin Arlington Robinson, and Jean Cocteau.

This modern ballet recalls the story of Tristram and Iseult in a setting that is centuries later. The time is 1916, the year Sir Arnold Bax composed *The Garden of Fand,* the ballet's score. The place is Tintagel.

SCENE ONE   The curtain rises as the music begins. The melody is soft and magical, weaving in sound a mysterious spell. The scene is dominated by arches of gray, slatelike stone, the ruins of the castle where the romance of Tristram and Iseult took place almost a thousand years ago. A man is on stage. He is the caretaker. Dressed in green tweeds with a cap, he moves about the scene as if only he understood it, as if he shared some secret with the ancient castle that tourists could not understand.

Tourists enter on the right. They are a motoring party, dressed in the long dusters of the time. We see a man, his wife, and another man. Two other men follow behind. The husband looks about and goes over to the caretaker. As soon as he turns his back, the second man goes to the wife and takes her hand in his. She glances nervously at the other two men in their party, who are watching them, and cautions him to be discreet. The husband comes to take his wife on a tour of the castle, and they exit. As they leave, the wife waves to the second man, who walks off in the opposite direction.

The woman's maid enters, followed by her master's chauffeur and footman, who carry picnic baskets. A cloth is laid on the ground, the baskets are opened, goblets and a bottle of wine are set out, and the servants leave. The second man enters and asks the caretaker if he has seen the woman. He leaves. Now the woman inquires after the man and goes off in search of him.

The caretaker, alone, looks about quickly and takes up the bottle of wine. He opens the bottle, reaches into his pocket, gestures magically over the bottle, and then replaces it on the picnic cloth. All the picnickers return. The maid pours wine for her mistress and the second man, who stand together as the others sit on the ground. The two lovers look in each other's eyes, make a toast, and drink. As the glasses touch their lips, a trumpet is heard and the music bursts into thunderous sound. The party is alarmed, and all leave the stage.

SCENE TWO   The chauffeur and footman, magically transformed into two heralds, rush in bearing the flag of King Mark. The caretaker turns around and around in the center of the stage as the scene, almost at his command, is magically transformed. The ruins disappear, and in their place, rising from the ground, stands a colonnade that graced a room in King Mark's castle. The caretaker's wish has come true: the man and the woman have drunk the magic potion, to become Tristram and Iseult, and again he is Merlin, the magician, who can stand aside and watch the workings of his mysterious art.

Merlin leaves the scene, and King Mark enters with Iseult and Tristram. Except for their costumes, they are the same as before: two men in love with the same woman. King Mark knights Tristram with his sword, and Tristram kisses the hand of his king. Then, for a brief moment, Tristram is alone with Iseult.

The lovers snatch at the opportunity to be together. They are unaware that one of King Mark's knights watches them from the colonnade in the rear. Tristram lifts Iseult lovingly in his arms. Brangaene, Iseult's maid, rushes in and separates the lovers. She warns them to be careful, that the king approaches.

King Mark enters, and Brangaene dances with Tristram so that the king will suspect nothing. Two knights propose a hunt to the king. Mark assents and asks Tristram if he will join them. Tristram, anxious to be alone with Iseult, pleads some excuse. The two knights watch this and whisper together. Iseult observes their suspicions and separates the two talkers. Now Iseult herself whispers to Brangaene how delighted she is that she and Tristram can be alone at last.

King Mark thinks it strange that Tristram will not accompany them, but leaves the scene for the hunt. His knights and heralds follow. Iseult, alone, seeks Tristram, running in and out among the arches of the colonnade. She is unaware that one of the king's knights has entered surreptitiously and concealed himself behind one of the columns to watch her. The music is quiet, expectant.

Tristram enters, and the two lovers run together from opposite sides of the stage. The orchestra commences a restrained, almost suppressed, romantic melody that gains gradually in intensity. Tristram kneels, and Iseult falls back over his shoulder. They kneel together. The spying knight moves to watch them more closely. As the melody gathers to a soaring crescendo, Tristram lifts Iseult straight into the air.

The lights dim and the music quietens. The lovers are almost motionless, content merely to be alone together, but their passion returns. To the call of a flute, Iseult entwines her body about Tristram, and the two fall to the ground in a close embrace.

The quiet of the music is broken by a sudden, shocking fortissimo. The false knight rushes out. Tristram attacks him. Brangaene, much alarmed, goes to her mistress. A herald enters with two crossed swords, and the flags of King Mark return. Mark, who has been forewarned, enters and points accusingly to Tristram. Iseult goes to her husband to plead with him, but he brushes her aside. The two knights suggest to the king that he engage Tristram in a duel. Tristram accepts the challenge, and the two men take swords from the herald and begin to fight. As she tries frantically to separate the duelers, Iseult is stabbed. The heralds holding the flags of the king let them fall to the ground. King Mark renews his attack upon Tristram and wounds him fatally. As he falls, Tristram grasps the arm of the king and sinks slowly down. King Mark moves over to stand over Iseult's body.

SCENE THREE   The lights dim. Merlin returns, and the principals in the ancient tragedy disappear. Darkness envelops the scene briefly. When light returns, the castle has vanished and in its place we see again the ruins—dark fingers of stone against the sky. The wife and her lover stand together in their motoring coats, as we left them, about to drink the magic wine. They still look into each other's eyes, and for an instant we feel that they will never cease being Tristram and Iseult. But the husband steps in. He pushes his friend away. His wife's lover stands there, not understanding, holding out his glass: what has he done, he wonders?

The caretaker comes forward, and the stage darkens about him. Alone now in the castle, he holds up the crossed, gleaming swords of Tristram's mortal combat for Iseult. The curtain falls as the music that began the ballet returns us to the twentieth century, suggesting also that, at Merlin's command, the cycle might begin all over again.

NOTES  Frederick Ashton's first ballet for the New York City Ballet, *Illuminations,* had been such a success in 1950 that the American company immediately asked the distinguished English choreographer to return to the United States and mount a second work. Ashton's obligations as principal choreographer of the Sadler's Wells Ballet made it impossible for him to do this until two years later. In the meantime, however, he had agreed with the directors of the New York City Ballet on a subject: a modern treatment of the legend of Tristram and Iseult. Ashton and Cecil Beaton, who was to design the work, traveled to Tintagel, in Cornwall, England, where they observed the ruins of the ancient castle associated for centuries with the love story of Tristram and Iseult.

Ashton wished to use as a score for his new ballet *Iseult at Tintagel* (1915), by Sir Arnold Bax, Master of the Queen's Musick. The score, however, was found to be too short for his needs, and consultation with the composer suggested alternative music—Bax's *The Garden of Fand* (1916), which had had its first performance in the United States, by the Chicago Symphony Orchestra under Frederick Stock. Ashton adopted this score, cast the ballet, and in a very short space of time staged his new work.

Walter Terry reported in the New York *Herald Tribune* that "*Picnic at Tintagel*—musically, pictorially, choreographically, dramatically," was a "theatre piece of which the New York City Ballet may be justly proud . . . Not only has Mr. Ashton used well the dramatic urgency of time but he has also choreographed with craftsmanlike shrewdness and considerable artistry . . . The love duet itself is a work of great beauty . . ." On the occasion of the New York City Ballet's first presentation of *Picnic at Tintagel* in Europe, at the Edinburgh Festival in August 1952, the New York *Times* reported that the ballet "was swift, exciting and dramatic, and is likely to occupy a permanent place in British ballet."

# THE PIED PIPER

*Ballet in two parts. Music by Aaron Copland. Choreography by Jerome Robbins. Lighting by Jean Rosenthal. First presented by the New York City Ballet at the City Center, New York, December 4, 1951, with a cast headed by Diana Adams and Nicholas Magallanes, Jillana, Roy Tobias, Janet Reed and Todd Bolender, Melissa Hayden and Herbert Bliss, and Tanaquil LeClercq and Jerome Robbins.*

*The Pied Piper* is a dance ballet set to Copland's *Concerto for Clarinet and String Orchestra;* its title has nothing to do with the famous Pied Piper of Hamlin and refers instead to the clarinet soloist. Copland's score (1948) was not written with a ballet in mind, but *The Pied Piper* derives its inspiration directly from the music, so that we are always being reminded visually of what we are listening to.

Many people imagine that ballets without stories, ballets that are based simply on music—and music which was not composed for ballet in the first place—are a dull prospect. Of course, it is natural for all of us to like stories; but with a little careful listening and watching, it is just as natural for us to be entertained by a visual spectacle based on a musical narrative. After all, we begin to like stories first because we hear them, listen to them, before we learn how to read. If we listen to music in the same way, we find ourselves just as entertained: we don't have to know how to read it. *The Pied Piper* is another ballet that proves how much fun we can have if we recognize this.

Before the music begins, the curtain rises. The stage is dark, and as our eyes try to see what is there, we can barely discern a man walking out from the side toward the center. He is wearing a plain business suit and carrying a clarinet. He looks around him at the bare stage, where there is no scenery—only ladders left propped up against the back wall by stagehands, and a few idle, unpainted flats standing at the left. He looks up, where a little light filters down to illuminate the plain back wall and the radiators that cling to it. He plays a few testing scales on the clarinet and ambles across the stage to the right-hand corner. There he finds a music stand, a lamp, and a high stool. He turns the music stand so that it faces the stage, adjusts the lamp, opens the music, and sits down. Harp strings are plucked softly. Low strings reflect their chords, and the piper begins to play.

The clarinet melody is slow, quiet, sounding lonely and lyrical on the empty stage. Slowly two great doors in the back wall begin to open, and a bright slash of light widens and fans out from the doorway, making an aisle of light across the stage. Two dancers, a girl and a boy, stand silhouetted in the doorway. They are listening to the mysterious music, which seems to come from nowhere. Attracted by its sweet melancholy, they walk forward, holding hands. Both of them wear rehearsal clothes. The door closes behind them. They bow their heads as they stand facing the soloist, then their bodies fall back into a dance that responds irresistibly to the plaintive romance of the music.

The boy supports the girl in low turns and high, soft lifts. The *pas de deux* is tender and yearning, the pace slow, the steps wide, open, and reaching. The dancers pause as a spotlight at the front of the stage throws their shadows against the back wall, then move over to the right, seeking refuge at the source of the music. Another girl enters on the left with a boy. They watch their shadows on the wall. The first couple cross the stage and the boy lifts the girl high over his head as the strings piercingly sound the climax of the melody. Now they join the other two for a moment. All bow low to their shadows on the back wall. A group of dancers wander in and, with the intruding couple, watch as the lovers finish their dance. In the slow rhythm of the dance and the

music, lights come up and fade one by one to make the whole stage picture
balance in the romantic mood. Lights at the back, against the wall, and on the
sides shine directly onto the stage, making a carpet of yellow light. The scene
grows dark again, and the boy lifts the girl off into the wings toward the disappearing yellow light.

The dancers who have been standing quietly, watching the love duet, look
at the soloist. The stage is now lighted, and we see that all the dancers wear
rehearsal clothes—shirts and sweaters and tights of varied colors. The piper begins a cadenza as the romantic music fades behind, and gradually the dancers
gather together to listen. Others straggle on, see the group, and listen too. This
is music that seems to be asking a question, in quick, lively, darting phrases.
The atmosphere is expectant. Instinctively the boys and girls are attracted by
the piper's song, and their bodies, almost uncontrollably, begin to answer its
phrases. A blond girl's hand shakes to the music, and she holds it out at the
end of her arm as if it didn't belong to her. The hand creeps around to the
back of her neck, and soon her whole body is miming the music.

The solo ends after a swift climbing scale; the music is curtly and demand-
ingly rhythmic. A redhead seems to go crazy with the insistence of the piper's
call. Mysteriously she finds herself climbing on a boy's shoulders. Another boy
begins to chase her. Other boys crowd in, there is a scuffle—the boys fighting,
but not touching, pointing their fingers like guns.

Drawn to the scene by the light, driving melody, another couple enter. They
join the redhead and her partner. The boys and girls separate into two groups
and follow their leaders. When a final lead couple is seen to emerge, the boy
chases the girl in mock seriousness, turns, and she chases him. Now the whole
group is dancing, responding to the music with spontaneous and spasmodic
jerkings and jivings as it becomes brisker and hysterically carefree. In different
groups, they run back and forth, crisscrossing the stage. Then, suddenly, all
the dancers are flat on the floor. Their bodies remain quiet for a minute, but
then the music drives at them again with sharp, shrieking calls and they
bounce on the floor. Their arms reach up into the air, then their legs. The
redhead tries to control her dancing legs by pressing down on the top of her
head, as if to put a lid on the vitality created by the music, but her whole
body begins to vibrate. The others rise automatically to the music's call, and
the stage is a mass of hurried, comic twitchings to the loud beat of the music.

Now the song of the clarinet above the music attracts the dancers like a
magnet, and they gather round the piper. But his music drives them back
across the stage. Grouped closely together on the side, they reach up their
hands to the clarinet's high, piercing song and bow down low when the piper
sounds a low note. This low note begins a fast ascending scale and propels
them again into motion, and in one movement all the dancers dash across the
stage toward the piper. They fall at his feet in a wave, and the music explodes
on a final high note.

## PIÈGE DE LUMIÈRE (Trap of Light)

*Ballet by Philippe Hériat. Music by Jean-Michel Damase. Choreography by John Taras. Scenery by Félix Labisse. Costumes by André Levasseur. First presented by the Grand Ballet du Marquis de Cuevas at the Théâtre de l'Empire, Paris, December 23, 1952, with Rosella Hightower, Vladimir Skouratoff, and Serge Golovine in leading roles. First presented in the United States by the New York City Ballet at the City Center, New York, October 1, 1964, with Maria Tallchief, André Prokovsky, and Arthur Mitchell in leading roles. Supervision and lighting by David Hays.*

The creator of the idea for this ballet, Philippe Hériat of the Academy Goncourt, has described the background and action:

"From time to time, escaping convicts reach the heart of the virgin forest. Forever lost to a civilization whose stern laws alone await them, they form their own communities, living on the spoils of the hunt—the skins of wild beasts, serpents, exotic birds, and giant butterflies. This existence, cut off from the world, furnishes the ballet's theme: the scene is set in such an encampment.

"A young convict joins the band of runaways. They welcome him to their midst and, as night falls, they build a fire to lure from hiding those butterflies who appear at twilight. Species of every kind swarm through the forest. The most agile, the Iphias, and the most beautiful, the Morphide, linger a while together; but even love cannot distract them from the fatal flames. Before this trap of light the massacre begins. The young convict snares the Morphide, and the Iphias sacrifices himself to save her. She escapes, leaving with her captor the glittering traces of their encounter—gold pollen from her wings. Now, like his insect prey, he, too, becomes a hunted creature."

## PILLAR OF FIRE

*Ballet in one act. Music by Arnold Schoenberg. Choreography and book by Antony Tudor. Scenery and costumes by Jo Mielziner. First presented by Ballet Theatre at the Metropolitan Opera House, New York, April 8, 1942, with Nora Kaye as Hagar, Hugh Laing as the Young Man from the House Opposite, Lucia Chase as the Eldest Sister, Annabelle Lyon as the Youngest Sister, and Antony Tudor as the Friend.*

This ballet tells a story to a piece of music that was inspired by a story. Schoenberg's *Verklärte Nacht* (*Transfigured Night*) is based on a nineteenth-century German poem called *Weib und die Welt* (*Woman and the World*), which had a theme daring for its time. In the poem there are two characters, a man and a woman who walk together in a cold, moonlit wood. They are lovers. First the woman addresses the man. She tells him that she has sinned, that she is going to have a child that is not his. All this happened, she tells her lover, before she was sure of his affection, at a time when she was desperate for any kind of security. She has learned since that sensuality is no security at all and that her new love for him is the blessing she really sought. The man replies that she must not feel guilty, that their mutual love is so great that even her child will be unblemished, that it will be in reality his child. He says that, as the light of the moon embraces the dark night, her love for him will transfigure the child, just as his love for her has transformed him. There is no need for forgiveness: they have love.

Such is the story of *Pillar of Fire;* but because it is a ballet, it takes this story and presents it dramatically, introducing additional characters, giving us a picture of the community in which such an event can take place, motivating the principal characters and their actions as completely as possible. The time is about 1900. The place is any town. The curtain rises to a low throbbing of strings. We see a wide street, lined with houses, under a darkening sky. The street narrows and vanishes in the distance. In the foreground, on the right, stands a high, narrow house, its woodwork embellished with Victorian scrolls. On the front steps a girl sits, brooding. She is plainly, almost severely, dressed; her long dark hair is braided about her head. She sits absolutely erect, her whole body seeming to delight in an intense placidity that is belied only by the clenched fists in her lap. This is Hagar, who lives in this house with two sisters.

The music is dark, heavy, oppressive; yet within this gloom, the principal melody cries out yearningly. Hagar watches the townspeople pass by in the twilight. Young people walk in the street, young people in love, and we sense immediately that Hagar has never been like them. Spinsters walk down the street with exaggerated daintiness, and Hagar turns away in disgust. She herself is not a young girl, but already she is frightened: she cannot be like the beautiful young girls in love, and the spinsters suggest the only alternative. She smooths back her hair, and we see that she is not unattractive.

Her two sisters emerge from the house. One is older, prim, and straitlaced; the other is young, a blond girl with long curls, soon to become a woman. The contrast between these two is apparently the same as the difference Hagar has noted in the passers-by. The younger sister is obviously spoiled, and when the older sister seems to reprimand Hagar for sitting apart from them, the young girl pokes fun at her. A young man comes across the street to their door. Hagar is delighted to see him. He is her only friend, and she is in love with him. Now she is no longer moody, but she hesitates to display her true feelings before her family. She knows them too well. The friend observes this and, being a very polite, conventional young man, is pleasant to her sisters.

The sisters, in turn, are more than civil to him. They are thoroughly aware that he has come to the house mainly to see Hagar, but the one—older, strong, possessive—and the other—young, demanding, accustomed to having anything she wants—soon draw his attention to themselves while Hagar watches. The young sister sidles up to him, flirting with cunning innocence. The friend observes her manner, is charmed by her blind youth, and ignores Hagar. The spinster is delighted at this sudden success of her favorite and asks the friend into the house. He goes in, and Hagar again is alone. It occurs to no one that she would enjoy going with them.

Hagar's despair turns to anger and hatred. It is not enough that her sister has dominated her family; she must also dominate all those who come in contact with it. The girl sees her last hope of freedom gone: her friend is hopelessly ensnared. And so she tries to forget her hope that he will respond to her love. The house across the street aids her forgetfulness. Lights come up inside the house, and Hagar sees through the walls all she has imagined must take place within it. For this is a place where love is celebrated all night long, where bold, unpolite men come to meet their women.

Shadows of lovers embracing are thrown against the walls of the house, and Hagar reaches out in open longing. She is taken aback when a man comes out of the house and glares at her. He walks jauntily, confidently, putting himself on display a little. She pretends to be embarrassed when he looks at her boldly and openly. Under any other circumstances this man would seem absurd to her, but now he embodies all the longings that Hagar cannot satisfy in a normal way, and she is attracted to him and the mysterious life in the house across the street. The man gives her a final look and goes back inside.

Now Hagar's young sister returns with the friend. The friend observes Hagar and has no understanding of her dilemma. Instead of questioning her, instead of helping her, it is much easier for him to succumb to the designs of the younger girl. Now more a woman than a child, the girl curls herself around his affections with the sinuousness of a cat. Hagar sees that her older sister has succeeded in making of the younger a frightening, pretty projection of her own willful selfishness and turns away in horror at the contrast between the girl's innocent beauty and inner evil. Should she warn the friend? How can she? He would laugh and not believe her. And so she watches as the girl takes her friend's arm and goes off with him for a stroll in the moonlight.

As they disappear, Hagar is frantic. She despises not only her sisters, but the man who will be duped by them. She contorts her body obscenely to express the depth of her disgust. Feeling now completely severed from all she might hold dear, she turns instinctively toward the mysterious house. The man who watched her in the street sees that she is still alone and leaves the house to join her.

Hagar welcomes him, and the two dance together. The girl loses all sense of modesty and decorum and for the first time in her life gives open expression of her feelings. The man encourages her passion. When Hagar leaps across the stage, he seizes her in mid-air, cutting short her flight of freedom, directing her warmth only to himself. He takes her by the hand and leads her to the house. Now eager to learn its secrets, Hagar enters ecstatically.

When she leaves the house a little later, she is alone. The conventions she renounced to discover love renew their hold on her to expose her act as sin, and she is filled with remorse. Now she has nothing, for she has rapidly learned the inadequacy of the kind of life led by the bold young man.

Her older sister enters and sees the guilt on Hagar's face. Neighbors passing by seem to know of her guilt, and Hagar, bitterly ashamed, seeks some friendly response from the crowd. She is shunned by everyone, even by the sordid people who frequent the house she has just left. These lovers-in-ex-perience look at her in contempt while the youthful lovers-in-innocence scarcely see her.

The younger sister and the friend return from their walk. While the older sister mingles with a group of spinsters, confirming the shame Hagar has brought on the family, the young girl cavorts with new playmates from the house across the street. She is delighted to discover how nice they are.

The tormented Hagar can turn to no one. Obediently, like a child, she goes with her sisters toward the house. The two women say good night to her friend, as if to apologize for her behavior. The scene blacks out.

The street and the houses have vanished when the scene is lit again. The three sisters find themselves outcasts from society because of Hagar's indis-cretion. Secretly her two sisters are delighted at her defection; but they are angry at what it has cost them and they repudiate her. The friend comes to her with his sympathy and help, but Hagar cannot bear to confront him with her evil. She seeks recognition instead from the townspeople, from the loose women, from men like her seducer. All are aghast at her downfall and will not help. Finally, in desperation, she reaches out pathetically to the seducer him-self. He looks at her as if he'd never seen her.

Seeing her final despair, the friend returns. Hagar twists away to flee, but now the young man will not let her go. He holds her strongly, yet tenderly, tells her that she has forgotten his love and that he is there to stand by her and welcome her as his own. The girl is overwhelmed with his loving kindness and dances with him a *pas de deux* that is not only passionate, but tender. Hagar now possesses the permanent love that she despaired of finding. The lovers disappear for a moment, then we see them again, walking away in the dis-tance, their hands clasped, their shoulders touching. They move slowly away out of sight in a deep green forest to the singing romantic music.

NOTES  In 1973 American Ballet Theatre filmed for television the full-length *Pillar of Fire* under the supervision of Antony Tudor. Sallie Wilson, Gayle Young, Marcos Paredes, Bonnie Mathis, and Ellen Everett were the prin-cipal dancers.

The ballerina Sallie Wilson, who has excelled in the title role of this ballet, had a number of interesting things to say about working with the choreog-rapher Antony Tudor in an interview with the writer John Gruen, first pub-lished in *Dance Magazine*, March 1975. Excerpt: "Tudor makes you aware of the fact that when you are stepping on the stage, you're not coming in from the wings, but from where you are . . ."

## PINEAPPLE POLL

*Comic ballet in three scenes. Music by Sir Arthur Sullivan, arranged by Charles Mackerras. Choreography by John Cranko. Scenery and costumes by Osbert Lancaster. First presented by the Sadler's Wells Theatre Ballet at the Sadler's Wells Theatre, London, March 13, 1951, with Elaine Fifield as* Pineapple Poll, *David Blair as* Captain Belaye, *and David Poole as* Jasper. *First presented in the United States by the Sadler's Wells Theatre Ballet at the Buffalo Theatre, Buffalo, New York, October 23, 1951, with Maryon Lane as* Pineapple Poll *and David Blair and David Poole in their original roles.*

*Pineapple Poll* is a Gilbert and Sullivan ballet, based on one of the *Bab Ballads* of Gilbert and on a selection of Sullivan's music from the famous operettas that he wrote with Gilbert's collaboration. Like *H.M.S. Pinafore* and *The Pirates of Penzance, Pineapple Poll* is typically and charmingly British. It is the first ballet to exploit the universal fame of the Royal Navy and, like our own native ballets *Rodeo* and *Fancy Free,* gives us a story that is both happy and sentimental.

The story of the ballet takes its cue from Gilbert's ballad the *Bumboat Woman's Story.* (A bumboat is a boat carrying provisions, vegetables, trinkets, and so forth, to ships at anchor.) This ballad tells the history of the bumboat woman, Pineapple Poll, who joyfully recalls her past by saying:

> My cheeks were mellow and soft, and my eyes were large and sweet,
> Poll Pineapple's eyes were the standing toast of the Royal fleet!

> A bumboat woman was I, and I faithfully served the ships
> With apples and cakes, and fowls and beer, and half-penny dips,
> And beef for the general mess, where the officers dine at nights,
> And fine fresh peppermint drops for the rollicking midshipmites.

SCENE ONE: PORTSMOUTH; A PUBLIC SQUARE    Poll's history in the ballet begins one day in spring in a public square at Portsmouth, the great port in South England. Painted statues of the god and goddess of the sea stand on either side of the stage, framing the scene. The buildings—shops and naval supply stores—are clean and brightly painted. In the distance, over the shoulder of the statue of an admiral that stands in the background, we see the pointed roofs of warehouses and masts of anchored ships. On the right stands a pub, the Steam Packet. Jasper, potboy at the pub, is busy polishing the window that advertises wines and spirits.

Jasper turns and watches longingly as two pretty girls come into the square, dancing with a sailor. The sailor is dressed in a typical British seaman's uniform of the late nineteenth century; the girls wear colorful summer dresses. Two other tars enter the Steam Packet; a crowd of girls come in with a group of sailors, take partners, and dance. Two girls who are left without partners go to the door of the pub and knock. Two sailors come out to join them, and the waltzing couples pause for refreshment. The sailors call Jasper to bring them pots of beer, and the potboy runs frantically back and forth from the pub to the street with tankard after tankard. Finally he, too, is in need of refreshment and downs two mugs of beer before he reaches the sailors. The hearty tars toss him about, and he retreats to the door of the Steam Packet to watch them renew their dance. The vigorous dance ends with all the girls sitting on their partners' knees.

The music is bright and merry, a triangle tinkles, and Pineapple Poll dances into the square. She is dressed in a candy-striped dress and wears green ribbons in her red hair. She carries on her head a basket filled with flowers and trinkets, and soon all the sailors are surrounding her. Poll sells most of her wares and begins to dance. From the door of the pub, Jasper waves to her. She does not acknowledge his greeting, and he places his hand over his heart, signifying his love for her. He, too, would like to buy a trinket from Pineapple Poll and goes through all his pockets, one by one, searching for the one coin he knows he possesses. He finds a piece of silver and approaches Poll hopefully, but she treats him like any other customer and when he gives her the flower he has purchased, she throws it on the ground. Poll, however, consents to dance with him briefly, and Jasper holds her in his arms until he sees that his love is not requited; he returns to the pub.

The girls and the sailors promenade about the square, and Poll, without a partner, picks up the flower Jasper gave her and for a moment reconsiders. Then she tosses it away again and circles the stage. She and all the girls stop their dancing at this point and watch breathlessly the entrance of Captain Belaye:

> Of all the kind commanders who anchor in Portsmouth Bay,
> By far the sweetest of all was kind Lieutenant Belaye.
> Lieutenant Belaye commanded the gunboat, *Hot Cross Bun,*
> She was seven and seventy feet in length, and she carried a gun.

The tars salute their captain while the girls begin to swoon. Captain Belaye, dark and handsome, wears a blue jacket, white duck trousers, and an officer's cap at a natty angle. Belaye jauntily inspects his crew, who automatically line up before him. He straightens one of the sailor's neckerchiefs and tries to act as if he were oblivious to the admiring glances of the girls. Casually he touches Poll's cheek, and she steps back in a romantic daze.

The orchestra sounds a drum roll, and Belaye begins to dance. His merry, rapid dance depicts the routine of life at sea: he peers through an imaginary long glass, climbs imaginary ropes, and orders his crew about. The crew, who stand in back of him during this solo, throw their hats in the air at a final dazzling display of virtuosity by their commander. The girls rush to surround him. The tars take their swooning partners out of the square, lest they begin to devote all of their time to the side-whiskered captain. Poll is the last reluctant girl to leave the scene and whirls out of sight, dizzy with love for the captain.

Belaye is alone for a moment, but soon he is joined by a pretty overdressed young lady and her chaperone. This is Blanche, the girl he wants to marry, accompanied by her aunt, Mrs. Dimple. Blanche is all decked out in red, white, and blue and clearly is in love with her fiancé's navy. Mrs. Dimple, in black, wears a high feathered hat and brandishes an umbrella, which gets in the way every time the captain tries to speak to her or to Blanche. He and Blanche snatch a few moments together; he embraces her, and the music is romantic. But Mrs. Dimple is on the job again; the music mimics her busybody authority as she scolds the two lovers. They begin to dance together, but Mrs. Dimple good-humoredly interferes again and in the process drops her umbrella and shawl over and over again. When she turns away to look about the square, Belaye kisses Blanche; upon the return of the crowd, he escorts her and Mrs. Dimple to another part of the town.

Poll observes his departure disconsolately, and all the girls follow her example in a slow ensemble dance that is listless and despondent. The sailors try to cheer the girls up, but the girls will have none of them. The tars are a little angry now and play tug of war with their sometime sweethearts. When they end up flat on their backs, they vow vengeance on their handsome captain.

Good Captain Belaye dances back in at this point, and again the girls are in a daze. The sailors rage as the girls reach out to touch him and blow him kisses frantically. Belaye reprimands them as if they, too, were members of his crew, but the sailors are still jealous and threaten him. He dances in their midst and is tossed about by the men, as the girls continue flirting. Belaye dances gaily down through a line of adoring girls, who kneel and try to touch him as he passes, and the curtain falls.

SCENE TWO: THE QUAYSIDE Night has fallen. A drop curtain places us on a dock that stretches out into Portsmouth Harbor. H.M.S. *Hot Cross Bun* is seen at the right. Above the ship's anchor chain a nude figurehead winks amusingly. Across the water a lighthouse stands at the end of a long seaside quay, where the Lord Nelson Tavern and the customhouse face us. Captain Belaye strides across the scene and mounts the gangway, shaking his head at the impertinent lasses of Portsmouth town.

Pineapple Poll follows him. She knows that the *Hot Cross Bun* has been ordered back to sea and is sad that she will not see Belaye for some time. Then, on the right, at the foot of the gangway, she discovers a discarded sailor's uniform. Suddenly her face brightens and she rushes off into the wings.

Liberty has expired for the crew of the *Hot Cross Bun,* and in slow single file the sailors make their way across the dock to their ship. When they have disappeared up the gangway, Poll returns. She now wears white sailor's pants and her mood has changed completely:

And I went to Lieutenant Belaye (and he never suspected me!)
And I entered myself as a chap as wanted to go to sea.

Poll is delighted at the ruse, whirls happily, puts on the blue jacket, takes the ribbons out of her hair, and adjusts the sailor hat at a jaunty angle. Now she is ready for sea. She steps up the gangway with salty determination.

The music now sounds a pathetic strain, and Jasper arrives on the scene. He is looking for Poll and has come to the dock as a last resort. He cannot find her and, as he looks down at the water, he fears the worst. Suppose she has thrown herself into the sea, all for the love of Captain Belaye! Jasper doesn't quite believe it, but soon he finds it impossible to believe anything else: there on the dock is Poll's hair ribbon and there are her discarded clothes. Jasper shakes his fist at the *Hot Cross Bun* and weeps for his lost love. He knows she is dead. He holds Poll's dress against his shoulder, as if she were still dancing with him, and caresses the dress. Slowly he walks away.

SCENE THREE: ON BOARD H.M.S. HOT CROSS BUN  The curtain rises, the music brightens, and we find ourselves on the afterdeck of Captain Belaye's ship. In the back, under the poop deck, is the captain's cabin. The white ensign of the Royal Navy flies free in the wind. Belaye is at the helm. The crew lines up at quarters on deck, and Captain Belaye leaves the helm to put them through their paces. He dances before them, long glass in hand. The crew watch respectfully, all that is except the sailor Pineapple Poll, who adores her captain so much that she can barely keep in line. At Belaye's command, Poll spreads her arms wide and the rest of the crew, in a close line, turn around her, like an anchor chain winding around a capstan.

Although the crew seem to be exhausted and Poll is plainly seasick, Belaye has other tasks for them to do and orders them to aim one of the ship's guns at a target he spies in the distance. The crew haul out a cannon, set it in place, load it, and stand ready. Belaye walks over to fire the gun and is astonished to see his crew hold their hands to their ears and run to the starboard side. The cannon is delayed in firing, and when it finally explodes, Pineapple Poll falls back in a dead faint. The other sailors don't know what to do, and Belaye tries to revive this supersensitive member of his crew. He is holding Poll in his arms when she recovers, and this is sufficient to send her into another swoon.

At this point Belaye sees that the *Hot Cross Bun* has reached its destination: Portsmouth again! He takes a ring out of his pocket and smiles. He all but drops Poll, runs across the deck, and leaps over the side to the dock. Poll is left alone for a moment and assumes that all the crew will go ashore. But then she observes that the men are behaving in a curious fashion, very unlike the seafaring type, and a number of curious incidents come back to her:

We sailed that afternoon at the mystic hour of one,—
Remarkably nice young men were the crew of the *Hot Cross Bun*.
I'm sorry to say that I've heard that sailors sometimes swear,
But I never yet heard a Bun say anything wrong, I declare.

When Jack Tars meet, they meet with a "Messmate, ho! What Cheer?"
But here, on the *Hot Cross Bun*, it was "How do you do, my dear?"
When Jack Tars growl, I believe they growl with a big big D—
But the strongest oath on the *Hot Cross Bun* was a mild "Dear me!"

One sailor, striding across the deck with affected saltiness, stops to primp girlishly at the porthole of the captain's cabin. No wonder, Poll says to herself, that:

Belaye would admit that his men were no great use to him,
"But then," we would say, "there is little to do on a gunboat trim.
I can hand, and reef, and steer, and fire my big gun too—
And it is such a treat to sail with a gentle well-bred crew."

Poll begins to wonder where Captain Belaye has gone and picks up his long glass to train it on the town. One of the crew points out that she's looking through the wrong end and grabs the instrument to have a look himself. Captain Belaye leaps back aboard, and they are delighted at his return until they see that he is not alone. He lifts over the side his new bride, Blanche, and Mrs. Dimple.

When the sailors see Blanche in her wedding dress, they fall over in a mass faint. All but Poll, that is, who is so angry that she goes to the captain and claims him for her own. Blanche will not believe her, and Poll takes off her hat and jacket to prove that she has been intimate with Belaye on the ship. Belaye cannot believe his eyes. No one can believe their eyes when all the sailors tear off their false beards and turn out to be girls too!

Blanche now hates her new husband and will not listen when he tries to explain that he is surprised by all this. She is threatening to leave him when the real "Jack Tars," the real crew of the *Hot Cross Bun*, climb over the bulwarks to berate their captain for sailing away with their girls. Attacked from all sides, Belaye can do nothing. Some of the girls swoon and fall over the helm. But the sailors will have no more nonsense. They grab the girls, throw them on the deck, and stand over them triumphantly. Belaye leaves with his Blanche and her aunt.

The girls seem delighted at this reconciliation and rock contentedly back and forth in their sailors' arms. Now Jasper enters with Poll and they dance together happily. Poll is joyful that at least one man can be constant in his affections! Captain Belaye and his new wife have now settled their argument and they enter with Mrs. Dimple. Belaye is in full-dress uniform—gold epaulets and cocked hat. Mrs. Dimple carries his regular jacket and cap; she goes and presents them to Jasper. The potboy puts both of them on. Poll kisses him, admires his appearance, and they leave the scene to the sailors.

The crew of the *Hot Cross Bun* dance a vigorous, rowdy number and then hail the return of Jasper. Poll joins Jasper; he lifts her high in his arms, then releases her, and Poll dazzles the assembled crowd with rapid, whipping turns on point. Belaye and Blanche return; Poll circles the stage swiftly and then rejoins Jasper. The crew and their girls stand aside as Jasper and Belaye, arm in arm, lead the procession of principals. When these two come to the front of the stage, they separate and stretch between them a large Union Jack, which they drape about Mrs. Dimple's shoulders. She kneels between the two happy couples, umbrella in one hand, trident in the other. Some of the sailors move forward and lift her high over the deck. They begin to turn her as the other sailors and their girls circle them, and the curtain falls as Mrs. Dimple, ruling Britannia with all her might, smiles down upon all the happy lovers.

# A POEM FORGOTTEN

*Music by Wallingford Riegger. Choreography by Eliot Feld. Scenery and costumes by José-Luis Cuevas. Lighting by Jules Fisher. First presented by the American Ballet Company at the Brooklyn Academy of Music, New York, October 22, 1970, with Daniel Levans, Edward Henkel, Christine*

*Kono, Cristina Stirling, Elizabeth Lee, Larry Grenier, James Lewis, and Richard Munro. Conductor: Isaiah Jackson.*

A recollection of childhood, boyhood, and youth, *A Poem Forgotten* is a narrative work to the *Concerto for Piano and Wind Quintet* of Wallingford Riegger. The curtain rises, and we see on stage, his back to us at first, a boy, naked to the waist, going through the ritual of being born. He falls back, sucking his thumb, his father helps him, and gradually he learns to crawl, jump, and walk. No sooner does he do so, however, than his mother emerges with a little sister for him. The two children play as the parents make love. Against a backdrop of boyhood images, the father carries the mother away and the children are alone.

A red beanie on the back of his head, the boy now jumps down from a bench and tests his adolescent strength. His sister, fascinated also by her growing attractions, sits on the bench while the boy enjoys seduction by a girl in purple. When she goes, however, the boy hides his face in shame and wants to cry out. He joins his sister on the bench and wiggles his thumb.

After an interval, he and the sister sit rocking as three rowdy boys play roughly. He joins them: there is some trouble, but the girl in purple breaks it up. This scene is caught in a frozen tableau, with the boy stretched out on the floor. The three hoodlums now attack the girl in purple as the sister, watching, lifts her dress above her waist, wishing it were her. The boy goes to lie at his sister's feet as his father re-enters, carrying the boy's mother.

NOTES   Anna Kisselgoff in the New York *Times* called *A Poem Forgotten* "a brilliant, personally phrased essay on a young man's memories of his adolescence. Its idiom . . . is really expressive, not expressionist, and this is not a minor ballet . . . Daniel Levans, so obviously slated to become an exceptional dancer, was outstanding."

## POÈME DE L'EXTASE (Poem of Ecstasy)

*Music by Alexander Scriabin. Choreography by John Cranko. Designed by Jürgen Rose. First presented by the Stuttgart Ballet at the Württemberg State Theatre, Stuttgart, March 24, 1970, with Margot Fonteyn, Jan Stripling, Bernd Berg, Heinz Clauss, Richard Cragun, and Egon Madsen in principal roles. First presented in the United States by the same ensemble at the Metropolitan Opera House, New York, July 21, 1971.*

The choreographer John Cranko expressed the essence of his ballet, derived from a story by Colette, in his own words: "At a party given by a great diva, there appears among the guests a young man who falls in love with her. At first she is flattered, then she remembers, more and more vividly, her former lovers, realizes that her life is already fulfilled and finally sends him away."

The ballet is set to the *Poème de l'Extase* of Scriabin and also to that composer's *Sonata No. 9*, orchestrated by Wolfgang Fortner.

The American critic Hubert Saal wrote in *Newsweek* (August 2, 1971): "Fonteyn is wonderful. In that frenetic atmosphere, she stands out as the one distinct figure, delicate but strong, nobly resigned to age. 'What I like about the ballet,' she says, 'is that it's all one piece—the decor, the music, the choreography. It all goes together in a special period style and requires its own posing and line and fresh possibilities for *arabesques*. It's remarkable the number of different things you can do with *arabesques*. I suppose it's really the most important movement in ballet . . . Few ballerinas are lucky enough to get a new ballet, much less a role tailor-made for my personality. I can act my age. It's about someone looking back on her memories rather than forward to them. It's something I can put myself into easily, like a nice coat.'"

The British critic John Percival wrote at great length about *Poème de l'Extase* in *Dance and Dancers* magazine:

"Cranko's intention was to get away from the little-girl image to which ballerinas are mostly confined. They spend most of their lives playing sixteen-year-old princesses, adolescent peasant girls, neglected younger daughters, and other similar characters, with a whole host of our feathered friends (swans, firebirds, bluebirds) for light relief. As Cranko remarked, an actress as she grows up graduates to new and often more interesting roles, a dancer is stuck with much the same kind of role all her life. His first idea was to make a ballet based on *Medea* but he decided the story could not be made clear enough in dancing. So after various possibilities had been discussed, he announced that he had settled on a plot based on Colette's novel *Break of Day*. At the premiere, one disgruntled colleague complained of having read the book in preparation and found it completely irrelevant. I could not agree: the novel to my mind provides both the situation and the motivation—but the story has undergone a complete change of setting and therefore of emphasis and development in Cranko's treatment.

"The idea is, briefly, that a mature woman (not old, but past her youth) has a young man fall in love with her. After some hesitation, she rejects him because she has built a contented life for herself and carries with her the memory of her former lovers; she prefers to keep all that as something already achieved, and concentrate on her life now rather than risk a new adventure that might be disappointing. Don't run off to read the novel for an idea of what the ballet looks like—Colette's heroine lives in a cottage near the sea and works in her garden; Cranko's heroine is a fine lady with a salon, clearly in a fashionable town where there is lots of society. In a brief program note he describes her as a great stage star, but I don't think there is any real indication of this in the ballet—only that she is clearly much admired and respected by the guests who throng the room where the first scene takes place.

"I don't know whether the ballet's chosen style dictated the choice of music or vice versa, but they go marvelously together. A program note acknowledges that choreography and production draw their inspiration from the work of the painter Gustav Klimt (1862–1918), who was one of the practitioners of the style known variously as *Jugendstil* (so called after the Munich magazine which served as a rallying point for the movement) or Art Nouveau. Richly ornamented, sensuous, full of natural-looking forms organized in a very artificial way, it is a style well suited both to ballet and to today's taste, besides providing an apt parallel to the swirling, swooning, orgiastic music of Scriabin's *Poem of Ecstasy.*

"Cranko's designer, as on several earlier occasions, is Jürgen Rose, who has made the ballet as stunning visually as in every other respect. The settings have a remarkable amount of detail in them and much rich coloring, so that you might expect the dancers to be lost in the confusion, but in practice it is all so meticulously worked out that every detail remains clear. And the work evokes its chosen model without in any way losing its own individuality.

"The first scene—perhaps prologue would be more accurate—is set in an elaborately furnished period drawing room. The walls are champagne colored, with decorations in red and blue. Above a large round seat rises an ornate wire structure supporting a huge pale orange bowl from which curls a faint whiff of smoke suggesting incense; above this is a multi-colored hanging bowl lamp that mirrors its shape. At the side and in a recess at the back are smart black and white upright chairs.

"The people who enter are dressed in smart frocks with big hats, or in formal jackets with ties; the atmosphere is one of studied ease, very formal informality. Their movements are very artificial too, with particularly elaborate ways of holding or moving their hands. They move about like people at a party waiting for the real point of the party to arrive. A young man enters at the back, at first unnoticed by the others: more eager, more earnest and less affected than the rest, he seems slightly out of place, and clearly he feels a certain coolness on their part towards him, for he goes to sit alone in an alcove.

"Suddenly a woman enters quietly from the opposite corner. She has her back to us but at once we know that she is the one who has been awaited. Graciously and with studied charm she acknowledges the greetings of the assembled company. But now the youngster, too, comes to her, a little too warmly for a stranger, and she turns away from him, but he persists in paying attention to her. For a moment she seems rather annoyed, but her carefully held poise continues, and when he returns after everyone else has gone, she dismisses him with a single gesture of one arm. Alone, she lies on her couch . . .

"The lights dim; when they come up once more the walls of the room and all furniture except the couch have disappeared (and the couch vanishes, too, once she has got up from it). At the back of the stage, a vast curtain tumbles billowing from above, followed by another: they are painted with multi-colored swirling patterns of great beauty. The boy has returned; like the woman he is now dressed in a simpler, more stylized version of the realistic clothes they wore before. We have left reality for the world of her imagination, and now the visions of her past lovers come to her, wrapped in great cloaks of red, blue, black and white or white and gold. First all of them together; then they go and return one by one, this time appearing in turn from behind those great curtains. Without their cloaks they look almost naked, but their flesh-colored tights are embroidered each with a different jewel-like pattern. Each dances with her in turn, and each time the boy tries to intervene and take the place of this rival from the past, so that this part of the ballet (the greater part, in fact) becomes a tumultuous series of solos, duets and trios.

"Jan Stripling is the first to appear: tall, slim but strong, mature and quietly forceful in appearance and manner. Next Bernd Berg: smaller, more impetuous, in some respects a little like Egon Madsen, who plays the youngster; and this similarity is emphasized by giving them a kind of danced duel in which they echo each other's leaps and turns. Now Heinz Clauss, a little older than the others in appearance, and very gentle but with the air of a hard core of strength in reserve. Finally Richard Cragun, almost Bacchic in appearance and overwhelming in the youthful virility with which he hurtles round the stage.

"Now the boy is again alone with the woman and for a moment his hopes rise as she caresses his head while he kneels before her. But even while she pulls his head against her body, she is gazing across to where the four lovers have again returned, this time all together. They seize her and run with her held between them in a great circle round the stage; they lift her high above them, wrapped in their cloaks like a statue of winged victory. Then, two by two, they take the corners of those great curtains at the back and, as the music reaches its last orgasmic climax, run with them diagonally right across the stage. The curtains fall from where they hung, billowing behind the running men, right across the stage and out of sight. The light begins to dim. Realizing his fate, the boy backs away out of sight and out of the woman's life. She stands alone, looking after her visions and again raising one arm, this time to reach after them. But it is not a sad longing she feels, rather a sense of fulfillment. She raises both arms and curls them round her head, smoothing her face with a caressing movement, then her hands drop, first to her breasts and then to hang by her side. And as she stands there, a smile, a look of ineffable joy comes over her face.

"It is a marvelous role for Fonteyn. She has caught exactly the visual style of the ballet—that first entrance, her hands held at a slight angle, her arms curving gently down, her hip thrust a little to one side so that her dress also flows curvingly, her head alertly poised: you know at once that she is going to be exactly right. The personality too: even though she comes on with her back to you, there is not for a moment any doubt (and would not be, even if you did not recognize her) that here is the star—both in real life and in the character she is playing. But more than this: there is depth and warmth too, there is a living person there, not just a dancer, but a woman, not a conventional ballerina but a great dance-actress. And the best thing about this performance is that the humanity of it is achieved through the deliberately artificial style. It is not a question of two different aspects, a mannered exterior and a natural interior, nor a question of achieving humanity in spite of the artificiality, but actually through the elaborate artifice. The poses and movements, any one of which could have come from a painting of this period, are necessarily contrived, stylized, yet at the same time they express the emotions in a natural way. See how she stands with the back of one hand against her lips, her body and arms a carefully contrived pattern of curves and angles—it could look simperingly shallow, but it does not, it conveys the feelings of a woman who has accepted a certain way of life but can look within herself with truth and understanding.

"Fonteyn's dancing in *Poème* (and I must stress that it is a real dancing role, not just an acting part) is mainly in duets, trios or larger ensembles with her five partners. And what partners they are. All four of the visions are so strong, they look so handsome and manly, they dance with such fire and strength, they support her with such tenderness and firmness too; and each emerges also as a real individual. Cragun has the role needing most virtuosity (some of the leaps in which he swirls in the air are fantastically unexpected and yet done with such apparent ease)—but all of them have to dance hard, and they all do it well. You would be hard put to it to find another company which could cast these four roles successfully—and that is without mentioning Madsen in the lead, who has to keep up with all four of them right through the ballet, dancing like a dream—yet what you notice more than his dancing is the way he brings the boy to life, the eagerness of his admiration for the woman at the beginning, contrasted with the artificiality of the rest of the assembled company; his engaging mixture of diffidence and assertiveness; the way he responds to the challenge of each remembered rival; and the look of absolute brokenheartedness on his face at the end when he realizes he is defeated."

# PRESENCE

*Music by Bernd Alois Zimmermann. Choreography by John Cranko. Scenery and costumes by Jürgen Schmidt-Oehm. First presented by the Stuttgart Ballet at the Württemberg State Theatre, Stuttgart, May 16, 1968. First presented in the United States by the same ensemble at the Metropolitan Opera House, New York, June 20, 1969, with Marcia Haydée, Richard Cragun, and Heinz Clauss in the principal roles.*

A ballet for the well-read, *Presence* has as its main characters Don Quixote, Ubu Roi, and Molly Bloom. The choreographer has said that the characters are in no way intended as literal copies after Cervantes, Jarry, and Joyce, but are rather the omnipresent reflections of certain of their aspects common to us all.

*Presence*, said Cranko, "is a series of portrait-dialogues revealing the protagonists: Don Quixote, the Dreamer, who hardly knows whether he is a part of a dream or reality, whether he himself is the dream or is conceived by the dream of another; Roi (King) Ubu, the Mighty, a remorseful and naïve Cain who seeks to destroy everything that stands in his way; and with them, Molly, the Woman—Goddess, Prostitute, Virgin in one—the Mother of us all, and the Creation of us all." The ballet is in five episodes, each in the form of a pantomime.

In an interview in *Opera News* (October 11, 1969), in which he discussed much of his work in detail, John Cranko recalled that originally *Presence* "was an idea that came from the composer . . . It has no rhythm at all, just structures and textures; this bit's spiky and that bit's oily, this bit's flat and that bit's high. Zimmermann chose the three characters—Ubu, Molly Bloom and Don Quixote—and I used them in alternating sequences of pantomime and dance."

## PRINCE IGOR

*Ballet in one act. Music by Alexander Borodin. Choreography by Michel Fokine. Scenery and costumes by Nicholas Roerich. First presented by Diaghilev's Ballets Russes at the Théâtre du Châtelet, Paris, May 18, 1909, with Adolph Bolm, Sophie Fedorova, and Helen Smirnova in the principal parts. First presented in the United States by Diaghilev at the Century Theatre, New York, January 18, 1916, with Bolm, Lubov Tchernicheva, and Sophie Pfanz.*

Set to the music of the "Polovtsian Dances" from the second act of Borodin's opera *Prince Igor,* this is purely a dance ballet, without any connection with the plot of the opera. When it was first performed with full chorus and orchestra, the ballet served to introduce to Western Europe the unimagined color of Russian music and dancing combined in a striking single work.

The scene, when the curtain rises, is suffused in the violet light of the approaching dawn. The light of two campfires is thrown against two great tents made of animal skins. Gathered about the fires, the men and women of the Polovtsy tribe sleep soundly. In the distance, around other campfires, other members of the tribe are curled in sleep. A lone warrior stands on watch.

One of the sleeping girls begins to stir. She raises her arm, rises, and stretches. As soon as she is fully awake, she goes from group to group, gradually waking the whole tribe. The somnolent music becomes expectant in its rhythm, as the drowsy villagers prepare for their daily tasks. The sun rises, and the people's dark garments take on their vivid natural colors.

The girl moves forward, turns rapidly, and begins to dance to the music. Other girls join her dance; in the back a group of youths accompany them. The young warlike villagers are unable to contain the vigor which sleep has stored up within them; they seek to release their energy. The girls sit on the ground as one of the boys comes forward and dances with keen strength, spinning swiftly to the pulsating rhythm of the music. The girls surround him, gyrating with brilliant turns. As the youth concludes his dance, the girls fall at his feet.

A great warrior, the leader of the tribe, moves forward, brandishing a brilliant sword. A dozen girls appear, as if at his silent command, and dance softly. Their primitive costumes are embellished with flowing gauze, which follows their movements in dancing waves. A girl in white, with long braided hair, is among them. The music mounts in intensity; the girls sit on the ground and a brave warrior leaps over their heads. He dances fiercely, called by some distant battle call. The girls dance in a group, as a formation of warriors circle their leader. The warrior slides forward, brandishing his weapon, and the entire ensemble forms a warlike tableau to the insistent demand of the music.

The men gather in the center of the stage and dance around and around to the demanding tempo. The girls enclose them in a wide circle of whirling movement. Suddenly the music hesitates. The two groups cross the scene quietly, then the men move up behind the girls and lift them high. The youths slap their thighs in their enthusiasm for battle and they race back and forth across the stage.

Six of the Polovtsy girls come to the front and dance with an energy that emulates the warriors' strength. They are joined by the girls dressed in gauze, who reassert the femininity of their sex. But the warlike dancers take over again, stomping the ground with their feet and clapping their hands to the beat of the music. The finest warrior of them all comes forward and, as the entire tribe beats out the rhythm of his dance, the brave Polovtsian dances a whirling climax to the ballet. He comes forward to the footlights and continues his dance, turning like a persistent top. The whole tribe gathers behind him and turns with him. The scene is alive with whirling movement as the curtain falls.

## PRINTEMPS

*Music by Claude Debussy. Choreography by Lorca Massine. Costumes designed by Irene Sharaff. First presented by the New York City Ballet at the New York State Theatre, January 13, 1972, with Violette Verdy in the principal role.*

Describing *Printemps* in her review of the premiere in the New York *Post*, Frances Herridge said the ballet "was a picture of Spring, come gently to life— all innocence and sweet frolic, full of freshness and grace, and utterly feminine in the romantic spirit of time past. It was as though Isadora Duncan, inspired by Botticelli's *Primavera*, had gamboled with her girls to the lyrical music of Claude Debussy."

The dance indicates the years' remaking and shows how a new spring spirit can take over from the old.

## THE PRIVATE LESSON

*Music by Georges Delerue. Choreography by Flemming Flindt. Decor and costumes by Bernard Daydé. First presented at the Opéra Comique, Paris, April 6, 1964. First presented in the United States by the Royal Danish Ballet at the New York State Theatre, New York, December 17, 1965, with Mette Hønningen, Henning Kronstam, and Mona Kiil.*

Based on a play by Eugène Ionesco, *The Private Lesson* tells of a lesson given by a psychopathic ballet master.

The scene is the ballet master's classroom. His pianist is preparing for the day's lesson when the bell rings and a young girl arrives. She is shown to the dressing room. When she returns ready for her practice the ballet master enters. The lesson at first goes well, but with complicated exercises on *pointe*, the pupil has difficulties and complains. The pianist is sent away. The ballet master insists that the girl continue, becoming more and more incensed. The dancer is almost hypnotized by him. In the end, the ballet master loses his temper and strangles her.

The pianist returns and the ballet master behaves like a little boy who is sorry and asks for help. She reproaches him indulgently and together they carry the girl's body away. Again the pianist prepares for a lesson. She picks up some overturned chairs when suddenly the bell rings . . .

## PRODIGAL SON

*Ballet in three scenes. Music by Sergi Prokofiev. Choreography by George Balanchine. Scenery and costumes by Georges Rouault. First presented by Diaghilev's Ballets Russes at the Théâtre Sarah Bernhardt, Paris, May 21, 1929, with Serge Lifar in the title role, Felia Dubrovska as the Siren, Michael Fedorov as the Father, and Leon Woizikowski and Anton Dolin as Servants to the Prodigal Son. Revived by the New York City Ballet at the City Center, New York, February 23, 1950, with Jerome Robbins as the Prodigal Son, Maria Tallchief as the Siren, Michael Arshansky as the Father, and Herbert Bliss and Frank Hobi as Servants to the Prodigal Son. Lighting by Jean Rosenthal.*

The story of the prodigal son is told first in the Bible: ". . . A certain man had two sons. And the younger of them said to his father, Father give me the portion of goods that falleth to me. And he divided unto them his living. And not many days after the younger son gathered all together, and took his journey into a far country, and there wasted his substance with riotous living. And when he had spent all, there arose a mighty famine in that land; and he began to be in want . . . And he would fain have filled his belly with the husks that the swine did eat: and no man gave unto him. And when he came to himself he said, How many hired servants of my father's have bread enough to spare, and I perish with hunger! I will arise and go to my father, and will say unto him, Father, I have sinned against heaven and before thee, and am no more worthy to be called thy son: make me as one of thy servants. And he arose and came unto his father. But when he was yet a great way off, his father saw him, and had compassion, and ran, and fell on his neck, and kissed him. And the son said unto him, Father I have sinned against heaven, and in thy sight, and am no more worthy to be called thy son. But the father said to his servants, Bring forth the best robe, and put it on him; and put a ring on his hand, and shoes on his feet: And bring hither the fatted calf, and kill it; and let us eat, and be merry: For this my son was dead, and is alive again; he was lost, and is found . . ." (St. Luke, 15:11–24)

This ballet tells the parable dramatically, with certain necessary omissions from and additions to the original story, but with the central theme preserved.

SCENE ONE: HOME  The curtain rises almost immediately after the orchestra
has played the first few bars of a strong, high-spirited theme. The scene is
opulently colored. A painted backdrop depicts the distant view and imaginative sky line of the ancient Near East. A bright yellow sun hangs in a rich blue
sky over a port with a lighthouse watching over the sea. At the right, in the
back, is the opening to a tent; on the left, toward the front, stands a low picket
fence with a small gate. Two boys, friends to the prodigal son, are busy about
the scene, hurriedly arranging a store of large wine jugs as if they are preparing for a long journey. The prodigal son emerges from the tent, followed by
two sisters. He is dressed in a short blue tunic and an open vest. His sisters,
dressed in long, flowing garments, try to engage his attention, but the carefree
youth ignores them to greet his friends. He picks up one of the wine jugs and
throws it to one of them playfully. The music becomes terse in tempo, and the
prodigal son dances vigorously in response to its pounding rhythm. With robust gaiety he seems to act out for his friends the adventures in store for them
away from home and to reveal, at the same time, an innocent, headstrong
spirit that urges him to seek those adventures. His sisters are frightened at his
strong determination to leave home so selfishly and watch apprehensively. The
prodigal son leaps about the stage with boundless energy, oblivious to their
care. His dance stops in an open gesture when he looks up, to find himself face
to face with his father, who has come out of the tent. He is embarrassed for an
instant and steps back.

As a new, poignant melody begins, the father beckons to his children. They
come and sit before him, the son unwillingly, but obediently. The son's attention wanders, and the father patiently turns his head back to the family circle.
He holds up his arms over his children and looks upward in humble prayer.
He touches their heads softly. The son turns away in protest at the ritual, but
his father persists gently. When the son twists his body away, the father takes
the boy's hand and places it on his sisters' hands.

The tension between the son and the father increases; the son turns away in
disgust, leaps up, and flaunts his indifference in his father's face. The father
rises and stands motionless and unprotesting in his grief, as his son dances in
defiance before him. The son's temper is so high and his eagerness to leave
home so intense that his sisters watch in terror and sadness. His dance is
closely similar to his first dance, but here he is emboldened by anger. He ignores his family, beckons to his two friends, and points toward the open high-
way. They gather together their gear and run off through the gate, closing it
hastily behind them. In a final gesture of rebellion, the son turns rapidly in the
air before his father, dashes across the stage, and jumps high over the fence
after his companions. The sisters stand close to their father in sympathy, but
the old man walks forward slowly, raises his hand in unacknowledged farewell,
and stands for a moment watching. Then he motions his daughters to the tent
and follows them into their home. The scene blacks out.

SCENE TWO: IN A FAR COUNTRY  The backdrop has been changed when the
lights come up again. Still heavily colored, it now depicts an open tent
furnished with a festive table. The small, symbolic fence that figured in the

first scene stands as it was, on the left. A loud, crashing march heralds the arrival of a group of revelers, who enter on the left in a close line. They wear short tunics and white tights. All of them are bald. The manner in which they cross the stage to the raucous music is grotesque. As they separate, the beautiful, jubilant melody that will dominate the scene receives its first statement from the orchestra. They go over to the fence, turn it upside down, and we see that the prop is also a long black table. The table is moved back. The revelers form in short lines before it and hop across invisible lines toward each other, playing some fantastic game. Four of them lie down on the stage and spread their legs to form a star. One of the revelers lies across the middle of the star as the others move forward and rotate the pattern their companions have made. Their frolic is renewed until the prodigal son enters on the right with his two friends.

The revelers cease their play and gather in a close group on the other side of the stage; they are just as frightened as the intruders. The prodigal son doesn't see them at first. Then he approaches carefully, urging his friends to follow. They refuse, and he abandons his fears, to greet the strangers with open cordiality. He tries to shake hands with one of them, then with another, but all the revelers pull their hands back. He doesn't understand. They touch his rich clothes covetously and come closer. He hesitates and moves away apprehensively, but his friends force him back and he remembers the wine they have brought with them. He tells his companions to give the revelers drink, and immediately the situation changes. The revelers form a parade behind him, and the prodigal son is carried on the shoulders of his two friends. Everyone is now his friend. He is lifted up and, from above, shakes hands with all of his new companions. They throw him side to side in jovial welcome. Then he dances between his two fellows as everyone watches admiringly. He grasps their hands elatedly, and all the revelers rush to shake his hand. The whole group dances boldly and vigorously with the prodigal son. He jumps over the table as the dance ends, and all gather about him.

The siren comes in, dancing on point slowly and seductively to a tune of Oriental character. She wears a tight red tunic about her slim body, a high headdress, and from her shoulders there trails a crimson cape of velvet. The men watch her intently; the prodigal son is dazzled by her strange beauty and the confidence with which she fascinates. She turns slowly, wrapping the cape around the upper part of her body, then unwinds the garment. She handles the cape as if it were a part of her own body—an animate object obedient to her will. When the cape is fully extended behind her, the siren steps back over it, pulls it up between her legs, and winds it around them. Holding the cape with one arm, she dances proudly. She seems oblivious to the fact that she is being watched; this dance seems to please her more than it could please anyone else. She drops the cape and falls to her knees in an attitude of conventional despair. Then she rises, proud and assertive, to turn intricately on point. She throws the cape behind her, falls back on her arms, and, moving slowly on her hands and points, drags it across the floor. Then she kneels low and pulls the cape up over her head, covering her body completely.

The prodigal son, now helplessly attracted, moves from behind the table and pulls the cape away. The siren rises on point, unsurprised. He tosses the garment aside as she turns to look at him. The prodigal son becomes now as obedient to her desire as the castoff raiment. He stands transfixed as the siren dances before him. She turns with strong, sinuous grace and holds out her arms in a gesture of approval and welcome. She approaches him closely; the prodigal son places his hands on her waist; they move backward in response to her lead. The siren pushes him back against the table. The revelers gather about them, and the siren is thrown back high above the table, into the waiting arms of her accomplices. She sits in triumph over the suppliant prodigal son, who lies on the table beneath her.

The siren is lifted down and sits facing the prodigal son. His eyes look down. His two friends begin a dance to amuse the group. Relieved by this distraction, the prodigal son watches with the others, but glances at the siren when her eyes leave his face. The siren touches his hand and moves her fingers up his arm to caress the golden medallion that hangs about his throat. He looks her full in the face.

His friends finish their dance, kneel before the table, and everyone applauds. The siren and the prodigal son come forward, watching each other intimately. They stand apart. It is as if he were imitating her movements. The siren falls back in his arms. She repulses his caress and entwines her arms back around her neck, and the two dance forward. They pause, and he puts his head between her legs, rises, and the siren sits proudly on his shoulders. Then she slides down his back. She stands on point before him and coils her leg about him, holding him fast, as he turns her. She releases him, and he pulls her over his back; the siren's hands reach out for her feet so that her body forms a hoop about him. Her body snakes about him completely, and slowly she slides to the floor. He steps out of the coil, rolls the siren upright, and holds her under her arms. Her knees rest on his feet as he moves across the stage. Now the prodigal son becomes bold and caresses the siren openly. He sits at her feet, his knees drawn up. She approaches him and sits on his head while resting her feet firmly on his knees. Now she rises straight up, arrogant in her voluptuousness and power. She steps away, and the prodigal son lies supine. She lies back across his body; their legs tangle. Now powerless, the prodigal son lies entwined in the siren's grasp. She gestures in insidious exultation.

The music pounds and shrieks fiercely. The prodigal's two friends pull the couple apart. Their companions are now reveling in drunkenness and force the prodigal son to join them. They drag his exhausted body about the stage while the siren watches from the table. He seeks her help, but the profligates carry her above the table and she pours wine down his throat as he slides down the table beneath her. They lift him high and carry the siren under him. Both are held by the waist as their bodies fall back hideously. They embrace frantically, are finally released, and two drunkards crawl under their legs. The prodigal staggers from group to group in his intoxication and falls against the table, where he cannot distinguish one of his companions from another. The siren watches him expectantly. He rushes up on the table, but the revelers tilt it up high under him and he slides down it, all his strength spent. The siren places her pointed toe on his chest in triumph.

Maria Tallchief in *Firebird*. Photo by George Platt Lynes.

Edward Villella in *Brahms-Schoenberg Quartet*. Photo by Martha Swope.

Violette Verdy in *Liebeslieder Walzer*. Photo by Martha Swope.

Suzanne Farrell and Jacques d'Amboise in *Apollo*. Photo by Martha Swope.

Suzanne Farrell and Arthur Mitchell in *Agon*. Photo by Martha Swope.

Suzanne Farrell and Peter Martins in *Jewels* ("Diamonds").
Photo by Costas.

Violette Verdy, Carla Fracci, Eleanor D'Antuono, and Patricia McBride in *Pas de Quatre* at the Gala to Save the Dance Collection of the New York Public Library, 1972. Photo by Martha Swope.

Karin von Aroldingen in *A Midsummer Night's Dream*. Photo by Costas.

Sara Leland and Bart Cook in *Tchaikovsky Suite No. 3*. Photo by Costas.

Suzanne Farrell and Peter Martins in *Concerto in G*. Photo by Martha Swope.

Suzanne Farrell and Peter Martins in *Concerto in G*. Photo by Beverley Gallegos.

The table now stands up on end. The revelers conceal themselves behind it. The prodigal is shoved back against the table, where he rests helpless. Hands reach out from either side and move down his body. The friends rush out from behind, turn him upside down, shake him, and collect his gold greedily. They stand aside as the siren is carried out. She stands upright on a man's shoulders, her arms akimbo. She gets down and gathers up all the remaining gold. Now the thieves rob the prodigal of all his outer garments, even his shoes. He is still unaware of what they have done to him, and the debauchers celebrate by crawling over and under each other, like eels. The siren yanks off the prodigal's gold medallion, kisses it, and exits. Her companions leave the scene, running across the stage, back to back, like many-legged insects.

The prodigal son wakens slowly from his stupor. He slides down the table to the ground and falls on his face. He pulls himself back up, gripping the table with agonized effort. He looks down at his hands, then at his body. He remembers and holds his head in disbelief. Stretching his hand up plaintively in despair, he acknowledges the betrayal of his friends and his own self-betrayal. He falls to the ground, sees water, crawls to it, drinks, and curls up like a child. He rises, looks behind him at the scene of his debauchery, and struggles off on his knees.

The profligates return, bringing their loot with them. The siren follows. The table is now turned upside down to form the gate and fence. The siren's companions run to the fence, arrange themselves within it, and the siren joins them. One of the men lifts high the end of her crimson cape, others begin a rowing motion, and the table becomes a ship, the siren's cape its sail, and her arched body its figurehead. Her companions blow their trumpets, and the scene blacks out.

SCENE THREE: HOME   The stage is set as it was for the first scene. The prodigal son, covered now with a thin and tattered black cloak, crawls across the stage, supporting his exhausted body with a staff. The music is dark, almost funeral-like in its persistent beat. The traveler's progress is slow and, to him, endless, for he has no idea where he is. He looks about hopelessly. Suddenly he sees the gate to his home. He staggers toward it, reaches out his hand, touches it, and collapses with the effort.

His sisters emerge from the tent. One of them sees him and calls to the other. Together they go to him and open the gate to lead him in lovingly. The piercing melody of the music reflects their great joy. They stand on either side of their kneeling brother as their father comes out. They are so happy that they do not move. The father remains near the door of his home. The son slowly and hesitatingly raises his head and looks up at his father. He beseeches him with outstretched arms. The father does not move. The son twists away toward the fence, but he has no sooner moved than his father raises his hand to keep him. He turns back toward his home, bows his head to the ground, and stretches his arms out behind in self-denial. With head still bowed, he crawls toward his father slowly, wretchedly. He falls full length just as he nears him, reaches out to drag himself forward by grasping his father's feet. He pulls himself up, clinging to his father's arms. The father reaches out to gather him close in forgiveness, love, and protection and, holding him like a child, he covers his son with his cloak.

## THE PROSPECT BEFORE US

*Dramatic ballet in seven scenes. Music by William Boyce. Choreography by Ninette de Valois. Scenery and costumes by Roger Furse. First presented by the Sadler's Wells Ballet at the Sadler's Wells Theatre, London, July 4, 1940, with Pamela May, Mary Honer, Margaret Dale, Frederick Ashton, Robert Helpmann, and John Hart among the principals. First presented in the United States by the Sadler's Wells Theatre Ballet at the Pabst Theatre, Milwaukee, Wisconsin, November 3, 1951, with Svetlana Beriosova, Pirmin Trecu, Stanley Holden, Pauline Harrop, and Michael Hogan among the principals.*

The Prospect Before Us, or *Pity the Poor Dancers,* is a comedy based on eighteenth-century English art, music, and theatrical history. The art is that of the colorful caricaturist Thomas Rowlandson (1756–1827), one of whose drawings, entitled *The Prospect Before Us,* gives the ballet its name; the music is an arrangement by Constant Lambert of selections from the works of the English composer William Boyce (1710–79); and the history is taken from an incident related in John Eber's *History of the King's Theatre.*

The King's Theatre and its rival, the Pantheon, were popular London theatres of the time. Rowlandson's engraving shows us the stage of the Pantheon, where the celebrated French dancers Mademoiselle Théodore and Monsieur Didelot are dancing a ballet before an enthusiastic audience. But there were also enthusiastic audiences at the King's Theatre. The ballet *The Prospect Before Us* tells us the story of these two theatres—the intense rivalry of their managers, the resorting to any means to achieve success, the fierce competition for guest artists, and the pitiable condition of dancers who did not know from one day to the next on which stage they would appear.

SCENE ONE: THE STAGE OF THE KING'S THEATRE, 1789   After the orchestra has played a brief, charming overture, the curtain rises on a ballet rehearsal backstage at the King's Theatre. Five ladies of the ballet await the direction of Monsieur Noverre, the great ballet master, who stands on the right studying a choreographic chart. Madame Noverre sits in the background, knitting. Monsieur Didelot, the *premier danseur,* paces up and down, wondering when the devil Noverre will get on with the show. Mademoiselle Théodore, the *première danseuse,* wanders in. She sits down on the stage and blithely tries on one pair of dancing slippers after another while her fellow performers fret. Finally she finds a pair that suits her, and the rehearsal resumes. Monsieur Noverre pulls Monsieur Didelot into the rehearsal, and this *premier danseur* automatically supports Mademoiselle Théodore in a series of poses. He is not the least bit interested in dancing with her, and when he lifts her indifferently, the girl begins to complain. Didelot rages back at her.

Mr. Taylor, the manager of the King's Theatre, enters with a party of guests. The manager of the Pantheon Theatre, Mr. O'Reilly, wanders in to see what his chief competitor is up to. He trips over some of the dancers and watches the rehearsal with broken, humble envy. When the great Vestris is given a chance to rehearse his variation, he is so disdainful of these spectators that he merely indicates with his fingers the difficult steps he will dazzle them with in actual performance.

The visitors parade off the stage, and the rehearsal ends. When Mr. Taylor returns, Monsieur Noverre and his wife attack him with a demand for more money. As the three squabble over a contract, Mr. O'Reilly tries vainly to find out how much money Taylor is giving them. Finally Taylor accedes to Noverre's demands and he and his rival are alone.

Mr. Taylor and Mr. O'Reilly sit down on chairs at the back of the stage. Poor O'Reilly sits wrapped in thought as Taylor regales him with stories of the dancers, the unprecedented success they will have, and the money he will rake in. He brings out a bottle and offers his friend a drink. O'Reilly hardly notices his glass and drinks almost automatically as he sits sulking, thinking that all this might be his. But suddenly O'Reilly leaps up from his chair, claps his friend on the back, and is all expansive good humor. Taylor is bewildered by this change of mood, but listens patiently as O'Reilly gabbles about the beauty of the dancers and congratulates him on his good fortune. Soon O'Reilly staggers off and Mr. Taylor sits alone, wondering what on earth could have happened to change his rival's mood so quickly.

SCENE TWO: THE BURNING OF THE KING'S THEATRE    Mr. Taylor finds out the answer to his rival's strange behavior soon enough. It is June 17, 1789. A drop curtain depicting the burning of his theatre falls on the previous scene. Mr. Taylor ambles by, not noticing that anything is wrong. O'Reilly enters and calls his attention to a blazing wreckage. Taylor despairs. The dancers come into the street to watch the fire, and O'Reilly instantly directs them toward his theatre, the Pantheon, where new, profitable jobs await them. Mr. Taylor tries to get between his rival and his dancers, but O'Reilly steps over his back to welcome Monsieur Noverre and his wife and take them on to his theatre.

SCENE THREE: A LONDON STREET    Four kids in ragged clothes run into a street in the poor section of the city. A half-dressed harridan looks down from the window of a nearby house as they play aimlessly, tumbling and dancing and clapping hands. They hear a parade approaching and sit down, their backs to the footlights, as a strange procession enters. A horn player and drummer announce the arrival of a party of poor, impoverished dancers, who enter carrying a model of the Pantheon Theatre. Mr. O'Reilly is evidently not paying them very well, for written across the model of his theatre is the legend "Pray Remember the Poor Dancers."

SCENE FOUR: THE STAGE OF THE PANTHEON THEATRE    Mr. O'Reilly's opening night has come, and he sits watching the first performance of the ballet in a stage box on the left. Mr. Taylor observes his rival's success from the opposite box on the right. Dancers enter and, before a conventional pastoral backdrop, enact a *divertissement* with some semblance of plot. Mr. Taylor is anxiously looking for empty seats in the house and does not give his full attention to the ballet. Mr. O'Reilly is delighted with the dancing and when Monsieur Didelot wanders about the stage, anxiously looking for his love, does not in the least hesitate to direct him toward the right girl.

A girl in the *corps de ballet* stands in front of poor Mr. Taylor, obstructing his view of the stage. When another girl prevents Mr. O'Reilly from watching the stage, he flirts with her openly and outrageously, and all but pulls her into the box with him. Soon Mr. O'Reilly gets so carried away by the wonder and beauty of this performance in his own theatre that he, too, must become a part of the *divertissement*. He steps out of his box onto the stage and stumbles about awkwardly among the dancers. He is gradually enveloped by the *corps de ballet* and becomes, at the end of the ballet, a grotesque and embarrassed figure of the final tableau. The curtain falls as O'Reilly poses thus in triumph and Taylor, in his box, despairs at his rival's success.

SCENE FIVE: THE STAGE OF THE NEW KING'S THEATRE    Some time has passed: it is now 1790. Mr. Taylor has secured funds and has rebuilt the King's Theatre. The curtain rises on the stage of the new theatre, its equipment refurbished to duplicate the first scene of the ballet. The stage is dark. Four men stand near the footlights, disputing. Their shadows are thrown up against the back wall of the stage, making a comic enlargement of their obviously petty argument. One of the men is Mr. Taylor; the others are his lawyers, who prance about daintily examining a contract as they pursue their legal dialectic. The problem is: can Mr. Taylor, with his New King's Theatre, oblige Monsieur Noverre and his dancers to return, or has Mr. O'Reilly of the Pantheon a legal right to their continued services? O'Reilly observes the dispute.

The lawyers decide in favor of O'Reilly, who oddly enough is impatient with his advantage. He has grown tired of the whims, tempers, and persistent demands of the great choreographer and wishes to be rid of dancers forever.

SCENE SIX: THE BURNING OF THE PANTHEON    Hardly has Mr. O'Reilly had a chance to return to his theatre with his problem than the Pantheon catches on fire, and, as in Scene Two, we are treated to the pyrotechnical drop curtain. Mr. O'Reilly dances a jig of delight before his flaming theatre and sees himself happily released from the uncertainties of the world of ballet. He is so delighted with the fire that he turns around and warms his pants near its flames.

His dancers, the girls first, flee the burning wreckage. They flee with obvious pleasure: perhaps they, abetted by the dauntless Mr. O'Reilly, have had a hand in the holocaust! Mr. Taylor welcomes them with open arms. Monsieur Noverre and his wife are the last to accept their former manager's greetings and to accompany him back to the New King's Theatre. Mr. O'Reilly, his troubles now but a heap of ashes, looks upon the smoking scene with the uncontrolled relish a stepfather might feel in seeing off to school a thankless child. He will pay for it, in the end, but now he is happy.

SCENE SEVEN: THE STAGE OF THE NEW KING'S THEATRE  Back at Mr. Taylor's new theatre, Monsieur Noverre is again rehearsing his dancers on their home stage. Monsieur Vestris uses the back of one of the chairs for a bar and warms up for his solo, while the ballet master and his wife hover busily over the *corps de ballet*.

Mr. Taylor enters, followed by the inevitable parade of lawyers. Now that the Pantheon has burned down, there is no problem: the French artistes can return to the King's Theatre without fear of suit from Mr. O'Reilly. Mr. Taylor shakes hands with the lawyers one by one, and they dance about him joyfully.

In the midst of this celebration, Mr. O'Reilly stumbles in. He has lost his wig and his coat, and his stockings flap about his ankles: he is very drunk. Whether he is drunk because he is happy or drunk because he is sad, we cannot at first determine, but it soon appears that he has had second thoughts: again he is jealous of Mr. Taylor, who always seems to have all the luck, what with his faithful dancers, his friends to lend him money, and his brand-new theatre.

As soon as he sees the dancers, he begins to imitate them, ruthlessly and absurdly, burlesquing both the ladies and the gentlemen in their artificial poses. When they reprimand him, he apes their movements even more outrageously. Finally O'Reilly collapses on the floor, where he sits with affected dignity. Monsieur Noverre cannot quite believe that he can be so intoxicated. The rank odor of spirits that the besotted manager breathes upon him causes the dancing master almost to swoon. The dancers are aghast at this scandalous interruption to their rehearsal and exit in a huff, followed by Monsieur Noverre and his wife. O'Reilly hoots at them, and as Madame Noverre passes, he grabs hold of her skirt and almost pulls her to the floor.

Mr. Taylor sees nothing for it but to give his unfortunate friend more to drink: it would be useless to *stop* him from drinking. The two sit side by side, as they did at the end of Scene One, Mr. Taylor happy and triumphant, bragging of his good fortune, whispering stories about the dancers, and clapping poor Mr. O'Reilly on the back again and again to display his bumptious good nature. After all, business is business, he seems to say, one must not cast out one's rivals. And business is business, also, to Mr. O'Reilly, who all of a sudden, drunk as he is, comes to. He slaps Taylor on the back and staggers about the stage, almost falling into the orchestra, wholly possessed with a new and brilliant idea. He clutches his rival's bottle of whisky in his arms and, zigzagging, nearly tripping, he stumbles off into the wings. Mr. Taylor, left alone, recalls that O'Reilly was similarly jubilant some while back, when, just as now, he had no right to be. Drunk as O'Reilly is, could he be plotting another ruse? Could he? After all, there is a limit to the number of new King's Theatres. The curtain falls.

# PULCINELLA

*Dramatic ballet in one act. Music by Igor Stravinsky, based on scores by Giambattista Pergolesi. Choreography by Leonide Massine. Scenery and*

*costumes by Pablo Picasso. First presented by Diaghilev's Ballets Russes
at the Théâtre National de l'Opéra, Paris, May 15, 1920, with Leonide Massine as* Pulcinella, *Tamara Karsavina as* Pimpinella, *Vera Nemtchinova as*
Rosetta, *Lubov Tchernicheva as* Prudenza, *Stanislas Idzikowski as* Caviello,
*Nicholas Zverev as* Florindo, *Enrico Cecchetti as* Il Dottore. *First presented
in the United States by the New York Music Guild in Chicago, 1933, with
choreography by Laurent Novikoff.*

Stravinsky's score for *Pulcinella* is based on music by the great Neapolitan,
Giambattista Pergolesi. The story of the ballet is based on an early eighteenth-
century Italian manuscript found in Naples, and its principal characters are
taken from the *commedia dell'arte,* the popular Italian masked comedy,
which, beginning in the sixteenth century, captured the imagination of all of
Europe with its universal types: the pathetic Pierrot, the heartless and flirtatious Columbine, the deathless Pulcinella (Punch, to the English-speaking
world), and others. The ballet tells a new variation of Pulcinella's immortality.

A narrow street in Naples is the scene. A volcano can be seen in the distance, over the bay at the end of the street. The end house to the left is that of
Tartaglia, whose daughter, Rosetta, is beloved by the youth Caviello. The end
house to the right is that of *Il Dottore* (the doctor), whose daughter, Prudenza, is beloved by Florindo.

At the beginning of the ballet Caviello and Florindo enter to watch the
houses of their sweethearts. Soon Prudenza and Rosetta look out of their windows. They smile at their suitors, seemingly encouraging them, then pour
water out over their heads. The doctor, meanwhile, has discovered the presence of the boys and drives them away.

Pulcinella enters—the familiar figure with a long, pendulous red nose. He
dances in the street to the tune of a small violin he plays. His dance and his
music attract the girls. Prudenza, who clearly adores him, tries to embrace
him. Pulcinella chases her back into her house. Rosetta appears, properly
chaperoned by her father, Tartaglia. She tells him that she is in love with Pulcinella and must marry him. Tartaglia upbraids her for loving the ugly little
man, but Rosetta ignores him. She tries to interest Pulcinella, who is as
indifferent to her as he was to Prudenza. She dances before him. Enchanted,
Pulcinella kisses her and takes her for a partner in a dance.

Pimpinella, Pulcinella's wife, discovers the two dancing together. The husband protests that he is innocent, that he still loves only her; Pimpinella is at
length convinced of it, and the couple dance.

Meanwhile the two suitors, Caviello and Florindo, have been watching the
street. They have seen that Pulcinella is the favorite of both Rosetta and
Prudenza, and they are furious with jealousy. Their rage is still more inflamed
when it becomes obvious that Pulcinella dares to reject the advances of the
girls.

They attack Pulcinella, both jumping on him at once. Pimpinella screams for
help, and both Rosetta and Prudenza rush out to help. The boys flee, and poor
Pulcinella, left in the hands of three women, all eager to assist him, is almost
torn in two by their fierce sympathy.

Summoned by their fathers, the two girls return to their homes. Pulcinella dances with his wife.

Florindo and Caviello have been waiting for this moment. They re-enter the street, disguised in black cloaks, carrying swords. Just as they run for him, Pulcinella sees them. He crosses himself hurriedly and pushes his wife into their house. Before he can enter too, he is caught by the two boys. Florindo strikes him dead with his sword. The murderers leave. Pulcinella gets up as if nothing had happened to him. He turns down the street and disappears.

The stage is empty for a moment. Then an astonishing thing happens. Four little Pulcinellas enter, carrying on their shoulders a fifth Pulcinella, apparently dead. They lay the corpse down in the street and dance.

Tartaglia and the doctor come out with their daughters, to see what has happened. The two girls, horrified to see their Pulcinella lying thus in the street, helplessly hover over his body. The doctor examines Pulcinella and declares him dead.

A magician joins them and assures the girls that he can bring Pulcinella back to life. The four little Pulcinellas and the two girls anxiously await the result of his mysterious incantations. The two fathers stand aside, disbelieving. After pommeling Pulcinella's body thoroughly, the magician commands him to live again. Pulcinella gets up, and the onlookers rejoice. The two girls swear to him that he is their only love.

Their fathers, however, remain unconvinced, even by appearances. To prove these skeptics wrong, the magician takes off his long cloak and wig: *he* is the real Pulcinella! His friend, Fourbo, has been the body.

Fourbo and Pulcinella trick the two fathers into retreating into their homes. Pimpinella comes into the street and, seeing two Pulcinellas, runs away in horror. Fourbo, still alias Pulcinella, brings her back.

Now everyone tries to get into the act. Caviello and Florindo enter, wearing Pulcinella disguises, to renew their romances with Rosetta and Prudenza. The girls accept them. Pimpinella, Rosetta, and Prudenza are dancing with three fake Pulcinellas. The real Pulcinella intervenes and kicks each of his imitators. While his friend Fourbo seeks safety in the magician's costume, Pulcinella unmasks the other two impostors before their girls.

The doctor and Tartaglia, still astonished by the goings on, are persuaded by Fourbo, the magician, to permit their daughters to marry Florindo and Caviello. The fathers agree. Pulcinella dances joyfully with Pimpinella, and the magician declares that they and the other two couples are man and wife.

NOTES Massine's *Pulcinella* was first presented in the United States by the City Center Joffrey Ballet, in 1974. The New York première was at the City Center, October 9, 1974.

*Music by Igor Stravinsky. Choreography by Jerome Robbins and George Balanchine. Scenery and costumes by Eugene Berman. Lighting by Ronald Bates. First presented by the New York City Ballet at the Stravinsky Festival, 1972, at the New York State Theatre, Lincoln Center, June 23, 1972, with a cast headed by Edward Villella and Violette Verdy. Conducted by Robert Irving.*

I am proud that the painter Eugene Berman, who died December 14, 1972, soon after *Pulcinella* was completed, designed this ballet for us. His help, friendship, and collaboration were essential. I had long felt that the original idea of the ballet from the Diaghilev days was just not interesting enough for the stage any more. But Jerome Robbins and I loved the music. So did Stravinsky's friend Berman, who was of course almost an Italian, so immersed was he in Italy, living there, painting there, knowing that beautiful country, its art and its traditions and theater, too, in all its variations. Berman was a kind of specialist in the *commedia dell'arte,* the improvisational theater identified with the great natural mimicry of the clowns of Naples, what Lincoln Kirstein has called the "underground manual idiom of scurrilous tricks and gesture." It was just those tricks that inspired us to do this new ballet with Berman to Stravinsky's music and I am glad that we did it. Robbins and I enjoyed putting the piece on; we even enjoyed dancing in the first performances, and if the ballet doesn't last as we made it, both of us know that Berman's part in it ought to. Good painters go on forever.

You just have to read the story of the first *Pulcinella,* described above in the first version, to see how complicated it all was for the audience to understand. Our idea was to simplify so that everything would be clear, and we hit on a variation of not only the Pulcinella myths, but the Faust myth, too. We decided that Pulcinella, a Neapolitan scamp, would make a pact with the devil to save his skin. He would then, as would be expected, renege on his promise, but his girl would rescue him, in spite of his having given her a hard time all along. Jerome Robbins and I had worked together before on a compressed story ballet, *Tyl Ulenspiegel,* where he, as the hero, made the whole of a personal as well as political and religious plot idea wonderfully clear in a matter of minutes. (One of the reasons Robbins is such a great choreographer is his great gift as a dancer; we can't remember that too often.)

To see the ballet and enjoy it, I hope words are not really necessary. It might be good to hear the recording that Stravinsky conducted of his lovely music (Col. ML-4830) and to read Robert Craft's notes on that album. As for the action:

Berman's superb drop curtain of Pulcinella and Stravinsky's signature rises on a graveyard scene. Eight Pulcinellas as pallbearers bring to his tomb a white skeleton recumbent on a catafalque. The Pulcinellas are beside themselves with grief. They put the skeleton in the tomb, nevertheless, weeping and wailing all the time.

The Devil arrives. At the tomb, he obliges the skeleton to look over the list of sins the deceased Pulcinella has committed, etc. He then tempts the deceased to sign a pact by which he will rise from the dead if he obeys the Devil in the future. The skeleton signs and then, miraculously, comes out of the grave a full-fledged Pulcinella. His girl, who had despaired at his death, rejoices. She cannot believe that her love has been restored to her. Pulcinella, however, intent on a reunion with his fellow comics, repulses her cruelly. The Devil drags him away to meet several fascinating ladies. In a brief scene in a brothel, the ladies, at the Devil's command, respond to his desires.

Pulcinella leads on a group of his fellow clowns as the baby Pulcinellas watch. He dresses then in a woman's dress and in this disguise, suddenly becoming a beggar, is seen asking for alms at a street fair of acrobats. This is simply a disguise for thievery, of course. The police spot him. He eludes them, then just as the police think they have cornered him, all his identical Pulcinella friends turn up and they don't know *whom* they are chasing. Victorious over the law, Pulcinella passes out the loot among his friends. He gives too fast, however, and there is nothing left for himself! Alone, he laments. A skeleton appears, brought onto the scene by the Devil; Pulcinella shivers in terror at this reminder of the pickle the Devil got him out of. Now when his girl comes onto the scene, he does not dismiss her rudely. The chorus sings as the Devil gives him a scroll; this is the pact he has signed.

A funeral procession of another Pulcinella passes. The Devil reminds Pulcinella of the flames of hell that await him. Then a young boy appears, blond and attractive, especially to the Devil, who can't keep his eyes off the boy. Suddenly blind to all else, the Devil follows the boy. Pulcinella has again escaped.

He and his girl are reunited. Pulcinella indicates that for some reason he is terribly, terribly hungry; ravenous, in fact. So a long table and a huge pot are brought in. Quickly, a potful of pasta is produced out of the pot. Pulcinella and his friends eat so much they collapse. The Devil arrives with his scroll again. Before he knows what has happened to him, Pulcinella's pals put him in the pot and give the scroll to their friend.

The scene shifts now to a solo by the girl, followed by one for Pulcinella, dressed now all in a white costume festooned with black balls. The brass in the orchestra begins a richly melodic section and the *pas de deux* for the two lovers begins. A dance of celebration for all the villagers follows, after which Pulcinella and his girl come forward to the front of the stage, with all their friends, to blow kisses to the audience.

## PULCINELLA VARIATIONS

*Music by Igor Stravinsky. Choreography by Michael Smuin. Scenery by Jack Brown. Costumes by Stanley Simmons. First presented by American Ballet Theatre at the Metropolitan Opera House, New York, July 11, 1968.*

The program note reads: "Stravinsky, feeling sympathetic affinities with the music of Pergolesi, produced in this composition what is, in effect, a portrait of Pergolesi and his time." Similarly, the ballet presents, without a plot or story, a dance impression of the world of *commedia dell'arte,* the world of Punch and Harlequin and Columbine.

NOTES Writing of this production, Walter Terry in the *Saturday Review* said that "*Pulcinella Variations* turned out to be a delight, the best work of

choreography yet by Michael Smuin, a highly virtuosic dancer in the company
. . . What he has done is to retain the antic nature of the *commedia dell'arte*,
for he has choreographically distilled its very essence from all its many
flavors."

## PUSH COMES TO SHOVE

*Music by Franz Joseph Haydn and Joseph Lamb, arranged by David E.*
*Bourne. Choreography by Twyla Tharp. Costumes by Santo Loquasto.*
*Lighting by Jennifer Tipton. First presented by American Ballet Theatre*
*at the Uris Theatre, New York, January 9, 1976, with Mikhail Baryshnikov,*
*Marianna Tcherkassky, Martine van Hamel, Clark Tippet, and Christopher*
*Aponte as principals. Conductor: Akira Endo.*

A mix of old and new music, time past and present, new and old dance, *Push
Comes to Shove* displays the genius of the contemporary dancer in rare and
droll combinations. Doris Hering wrote in *Dance Magazine:* "It's like a giant
Euclidean doodle with a firm undercurrent of pure ballet logic."

*Push Comes to Shove* introduces ballet's first modern folk hero, in a
modified Chaplin style. He appears, in practice clothes and derby hat, in front
of the curtain as the piece begins and starts to react to Joseph Lamb's *Bohemian Rag 1919.* Two girls join him and under the palsy-walsy horseplay there
is a wry suggestion of feeling. Which doesn't last long. For before we know
it the stage picture has changed to a formal area, the music is Haydn's
*Symphony No. 82 in C,* and the vaudeville hero is now *premier danseur* and
acting and dancing like one for real. Except maybe he is a pugilist, ready to
knock 'em all out. The fancy girl dancers who take over the stage scare him off
and then another group of girls seizes the stage, dancing to Joseph Lamb
again. The hero comes and goes, there are dance situations that make jokes.
Both sides, as epitomized in the hero, part hoofer/beatnik/street crazy, part
*danseur noble,* are played off against each other. The hero dances this schizo-
phrenia for all he is worth. His derby hat, which is like an ever present talisman throughout the ballet, being played with and tossed about, reminds us of
the dual nature of what is happening: a modern audience watching a new
ballet danced by remarkable classical performers trained in an old technique.
*Push Comes to Shove* holds the mirror up to the audience and to the dancers
and the company they keep.

*Time* said that *Push Comes to Shove* "just might be the most important
dance event of the year." Frances Herridge wrote soon after the premiere in
the New York *Post:* "Baryshnikov is so irresistible with his Peck's Bad Boy insouciance and his spoofing of bombast that you don't notice at first how amusing the rest of the group is . . . There are speeded-up sequences reminiscent
of Mack Sennett. There are manipulated duets that made puppets of the ladies. And there are loose nuts everywhere. In short, there's not a dull moment."

Writing about the ballet in the *Times* of London, the critic John Percival
said: "At the heart of *Push Comes to Shove* is a hilarious performance by

Mikhail Baryshnikov. In effect, he is playing the Twyla Tharp role: the little bundle of nerves and muscles, glaring out from a moplike fringe. Sheer energy is his *métier* here, manifested in sudden bursts of wild spinning or fantastic jumps. But it is put over with an absolutely cool manner and a vaudeville comic's timing.

"In fact, Baryshnikov by no means carries the work alone. Martine van Hamel, just coming into bloom as a ballerina (I saw her charming Sylphide, and heard everyone raving about her Swan Queen and her Raymonda), has an aloof allure that is irresistible. Making up a trio of contrasted personalities, appearances and manners is Marianna Tcherkassky, small and pertly pretty.

"Those three principals dance a wickedly funny *pas de quatre* with a black bowler hat in the prelude, which is set to Joseph Lamb's *Bohemian Rag*, and each of them leads one movement of the main ballet, which is danced to Haydn's 'Bear' Symphony. Yes, the two musical styles do go together, thanks to the unfailing ingenuity of Tharp's invention. The mixture of tradition and irreverence even passes into Santo Loquasto's costume designs, which make the men wear woollen leg-warmers beneath their calf-length velvet pants."

## THE RAKE'S PROGRESS

*Dramatic ballet in six scenes. Music by Gavin Gordon. Choreography by Ninette de Valois. Book by Gavin Gordon. Scenery and costumes by Rex Whistler. First presented by the Sadler's Wells Ballet at the Sadler's Wells Theatre, London, May 20, 1935, with Walter Gore as the Rake and Alicia Markova as the Betrayed Girl. First presented in the United States by the Sadler's Wells Ballet at the Metropolitan Opera House, New York, October 12, 1949, with Harold Turner as the Rake and Margot Fonteyn as the Betrayed Girl.*

This ballet is based on the series of paintings of the same name by the great English satirist William Hogarth. Hogarth showed in this famous work the gradual corruption of an adventurous youth who suddenly found himself endowed with unlimited money. The scenery and costumes, the characters—their situation and their dancing—are a vivid reproduction of eighteenth-century London, its people, and their habits as Hogarth saw them. The music is an appropriate eighteenth-century style.

SCENE ONE  The curtain rises on a drop curtain that depicts a street in eighteenth-century London. Georgian houses, public buildings, and a church line both sides of a cobblestone street that extends into the distance. When this curtain rises, we find ourselves in the elegant apartment of the rake. There are doors left and right, and across the back there is a large window. The rake is a youth who has recently come into a fortune, and this morning all the merchants, hangers-on, and toughs who hope to profit by his good luck are paying their daily call. He is still in his night clothes, but this doesn't prevent a tailor from measuring a new coat for him. The rake seems to enjoy this attention, however, and is hardly disturbed when his jockey informs him that his horse won an important race the day before. Now a fencing master takes over and beseeches the rake to practice at his art. The rake obliges him briefly, then practices the horn under the direction of a musician.

The rake begins to dress, and all come to his assistance when needed. When he is fully dressed, he turns to his dancing master. The dancing master takes out a violin and, as he plays on the instrument, shows the rake fancy steps. The rake is not very agile, despite his youth; the truth is that he is not accustomed yet to the gestures of the youthful rich.

The dancing lesson is interrupted by an altercation at the door. There a determined old woman is arguing familiarly with the maid. She forces the maid, her daughter, into the room and follows after. The old harridan upbraids the rake for seducing her daughter and threatens blackmail. The pretty girl obviously does not approve of this procedure and is embarrassed when the rake gives her mother money. They leave the scene, and the dancing lesson continues. The drop curtain falls as the rake succeeds in affecting the manner, if not the skill, of the dance his teacher has set him.

SCENE TWO    Three ladies of the town, apparently on their way to a party, parade the street in front of the drop curtain. The rake's maid and her mother pass them. When the curtain rises, we find ourselves in a bedchamber. The room is hardly private, however, for the two women sitting at a table on the right are clearly of loose character. They are drinking and gossiping together. Three other winsome bawds are exchanging jokes in the center of the room; they guffaw lustily at the slightest innuendo. In the back, on the left, in a curtained alcove, is an unmade bed. A lush painting of Venus and Mars in a gilt frame hangs on the back wall, giving the room an air of hopeful respectability.

Soon a friend of the rake's swaggers into the room, followed by the rake himself. Rake he is determined to be: he is drunk and delighted with himself. The girls take immediate advantage of him and his friend, treating them as if they were the only attractive men in the world.

The guests are treated to *divertissements* by a professional dancer, who does an eighteenth-century version of the striptease by removing her stockings, and a female ballad singer, who creaks out a song. This song delights the drunken rake, who throws his arm about the ballad singer and insists upon joining her. The music goes to his head, unfortunately, and he begins to pass out.

He is revived, however, as the girls begin to dance. Soon everyone in the room is dancing, whirling and whirling about in a manner that reflects the rake's intoxication. The rake expresses his admiration for this display by throwing coins about the room. One of the rowdy girls scurries about trying to pick up all the money, while the others devote themselves to affected gaiety to amuse the rake. The curtain falls, leaving the rest of the bawdy scene to our imagination.

SCENE THREE    Before the drop curtain, three creditors lie in wait to accost the rake. He strolls in haughtily. They present their bills, which are long overdue, and demand payment. Evidently the rake has run through his inheritance rather rapidly, for he is not in the least condescending: he is afraid. The pretty maid whom we met in the first scene comes into the street. As we might have expected, from her annoyance with her demanding mother, she does not despise her seducer. On the contrary, she observes him with some sympathy and intercedes in his quarrel with the creditors. The poor serving maid tells the men that she will pay the bills! The rake appears to be unimpressed by this expression of love, but the creditors are pleased with her promise; they exit. The rake goes on down the street, immediately forgetting the trouble he has had. The girl does a dance that expresses her love for the rake and the impossibility of its fulfillment.

SCENE FOUR  The rake has seriously come down in the world, for this time the curtain rises on a low gambling dive. The rake, no longer dressed in finery, enters and joins three burly-looking characters in a game of cards. Cleaned out in the higher-class gaming rooms and brothels, he imagines that he can easily regain his losses among such ignorant folk. His fellow players are cleverer than he thinks, however, and luck seems to be against him. He begins to lose steadily. He clings to his few coins as if they were the last moments of a happy life. It is not difficult for us to imagine that the betrayed girl, the lovely chambermaid he has spurned, would have a great deal of pity for him. The poor devil cannot bear to lose: he loses not only his money, but his connection with reality, as he hopes that this last bet will bring back all the opulence of his former life—the tailors and jewelers and race-track touts indebted to *him* again, much wine, many women, and endless song. Simultaneously he sees that if he loses, he will enjoy none of these things: that leaves, for him, poor fellow, nothing. The last wager is made, the last card is turned up, the tables are turned; he is wiped out! Less rake than pauper, the unfortunate fellow collapses.

SCENE FIVE  Before the curtain, the betrayed girl dances alone, hoping that the rake, who has now been put in the debtor's prison, will be released and come back to her.

SCENE SIX  When the curtain comes up again the scene, like the rake's progress, has gone from bad to worse: we are in a madhouse, a dark place and damp, where therapy consists of filthy isolation. The more dangerous lunatics can be seen behind iron grilles, posing as kings and cardinals. Creatures less preoccupied sit in an open area. One of these men entertains himself and his fellow madmen by a grotesque dance with a rope, which outlines in the air the images that haunt him.

The outside door clangs open, and the rake is thrown into the cell. The men watch the new inmate while he tries, as they did, to escape. When he falls to the floor exhausted, they display their individual manias for his benefit. While the rake looks at them, we think for a moment that he is not really mad, that there has been some mistake: an eighteenth-century solution to a down-and-outer's problem, some gross misjudgment. But we are wrong. The rake rises and dances like a demon.

The girl he has betrayed comes to visit him and tries pathetically to make him remember her, but now this man's only thought is to escape from her, to escape from everyone, to get out. He attacks the door again, and again he falls to the floor. The lovely girl attempts to mend his agony by sweet and loving gestures that might give him some hope. Her thoughtfulness and devotion are contrasted vividly with the fashionable world that her lover has left, when some well-dressed ladies enter the asylum and observe the inmates for entertainment and diversion.

The rake becomes hysterical, catatonic, and thrashes about the floor uncontrollably. He dies in the midst of his paroxysms. The betrayed girl holds him close in her arms, weeping that her love might have saved him, weeping that he did not understand the path of self-destruction.

## RAPSODIE ESPAGNOLE

*Music by Maurice Ravel. Choreography by George Balanchine. First presented at the New York City Ballet's Hommage à Ravel at the New York State Theatre, Lincoln Center, May 29, 1975, with Karin von Aroldingen and Peter Schaufuss in leading roles.*

Ravel knew Spain well. The Spanish composer Manuel de Falla has recalled that "Ravel's Spain was a Spain ideally presented by his mother, whose refined conversation, always in excellent Spanish, delighted me, particularly when she would recall her youthful years spent in Madrid."

I found the music exciting for its vigor, clarity, and wonderful flamenco from the first and tried to arrange some expressive yet simple dances for passionate young persons.

## RAYMONDA

*Ballet in three acts. Music by Alexander Glazunov. Choreography by Marius Petipa. First presented at the Maryinsky Theatre, St. Petersburg, January 19, 1898. First presented in the United States in abbreviated form by the Ballet Russe de Monte Carlo at the City Center, New York, March 12, 1946, with choreography by Alexandra Danilova and George Balanchine. First presented complete by the Kirov Ballet at the Metropolitan Opera House, New York, September 16, 1964, with Irina Kolpakova as Raymonda, Vladilen Semenov as Jean de Brienne, and Gennady Selutsky as Abderachman.*

Glazunov's music for *Raymonda* contains some of the finest ballet music we have. And Petipa's original choreography, which I remember from student appearances at the Maryinsky Theatre, was superb. But his story was nonsense, difficult to follow, and, in the words of an old Russian balletomane Prince Lieven, "it has everything but meaning," as you will see. It takes place in medieval Hungary.

ACT ONE, SCENE ONE  Raymonda, betrothed to Jean de Brienne, who is away at war, celebrates her birthday at the home of her aunt, a countess. Jean sends his fiancée gifts, among them a tapestry portrait of himself, and announces that he will arrive the next day. But Abderachman, a Saracen chief, pays an unexpected visit to the castle. He admires Raymonda, attempts to lure her with rich gifts.

ACT ONE, SCENE TWO  Raymonda dreams that her lover descends from his portrait and leads her into the garden to dance a *pas de deux*. But this vision is dispelled and in Jean's place Raymonda finds the sinister Saracen, who renews his advances. Raymonda swoons.

ACT TWO  At a reception the countess gives in honor of the Saracen, Raymonda anxiously awaits Jean's arrival. But Abderachman approaches her passionately and insists that she dance with him. She accepts and the Saracen then commands his retinue to entertain Raymonda with jugglers and dancing. Moors and Spaniards join in a dance that becomes fierce with intensity; at its height the Saracen attempts to abduct Raymonda. At that point, who should arrive but Jean de Brienne, accompanied by his old father, King Andrew II of Hungary. Raymonda rushes to Jean's arms. He and his followers threaten Abderachman and his retinue, but the king intervenes and proposes single combat for the rivals. The ensuing duel is furious and Abderachman falls.

ACT THREE  A festival is being held at Jean de Brienne's castle to celebrate his marriage to Raymonda. The festival begins with a *grand pas hongrois* in which Raymonda dances a variation and Jean a final solo before the lovers are united forever.

NOTES  Rudolf Nureyev staged his version of the complete *Raymonda* with the Royal Ballet's touring company at the Festival of Two Worlds in Spoleto in 1964. Doreen Wells and Nureyev appeared in the principal roles. Act III of this production, with scenery and costumes by Barry Kay, was presented by the Royal Ballet at the Royal Opera House, Covent Garden, July 16, 1966, with Doreen Wells and David Wall. Alexander Bland, reviewing this and other ballets on the same program in *The Observer,* wrote that David Wall "finally and triumphantly established himself as the most promising British dancer since the war, heading for the international class. In *Les Sylphides* he gave . . . an almost faultless performance, very much in the Nureyev style; his young boy in *The Invitation* . . . was rather more than adequate: and finally he came up at the end of the evening to give his *Raymonda* solo a mixture of dash, control, musicality, and style of which any Kirov dancer could have been proud."

Nureyev staged *Raymonda* for the Australian Ballet in 1965. In 1972 he mounted it for the Zurich Ballet in a production designed by Nicholas Georgiadis, in 1975 for American Ballet Theatre. In Zurich, Nureyev and Marcia Haydée danced the first performance. Reviewing it in *Dance and Dancers* magazine, the British critic John Percival wrote:

"The Zurich Ballet is more used to appearing alone in some quite ambitious productions, but I doubt whether its dancers have tackled anything as taxing as Nureyev's *Raymonda*. This has been completely rethought and drastically changed since the two previous productions Nureyev has mounted. The good features of those productions remain: the marvelous Glazunov score, full of dreamy waltzes and exciting rhythms; some brilliant solos preserving Petipa's choreography; and the biggest of all classical roles for a ballerina (now even augmented beyond what we saw before). These virtues have been increased, too; the score is now played complete, and almost in the composer's original order, except for one change in Act Three to give the hero an extra solo; and the new choreography which Nureyev has added is well devised to show off the dancers and to make the best of the preserved Petipa.

"The trouble with *Raymonda* has always been the story . . . Nureyev has found a surprisingly simple way to make sense of the whole. He takes his cue from the fact that there was always a dream sequence, designed to allow Raymonda a duet with her admirer Jean de Brienne in the early part of the ballet, although the plot did not actually introduce him until near the end. Nureyev considerably enlarged this dream to cover not just one scene but a substantial part of Act One and almost the whole of Act Two.

"What happens now is that Raymonda is first seen playing with her friends (two girls and two troubadours) while preparations are going on all around for her marriage as soon as Jean gets back from the wars. Pretty soon he arrives with the King of Hungary (in whose forces he has been serving) and offers her a present: a tapestry banner he has brought back from the Crusades. Left alone, Raymonda imagines the dark Saracen warrior from whom Jean won this. She falls asleep, and in her dream the banner grows until it becomes the Saracen's tent. The traditional love duet with Jean remains, but in addition there are scenes alone with the Saracen, Abderachman; others in which he and Jean phantasmagorically exchange places; and others again in which both appear dancing with her and her friends. For a while Abderachman persuades Raymonda (and her girl friends) to remain with him, enjoying the divertissement of Spanish and oriental dances he provides; but at last the nobly retiring Jean is provoked into challenging his rival. They compete at archery, fight with lances on horseback, and finally engage in a duel with swords, in which Jean, with one mighty blow, shatters his enemy's helmet and wounds him, presumably fatally. Now Raymonda can unreservedly give Jean her heart and her hand—and at this point she wakes up to find him and her friends come to look for her. Thus Act Two ends happily, and Act Three is, as usual, the wedding celebration.

"This makes a more interesting story, for its own sake and also as a portrait of Raymonda's inner struggle. The presence of the troubadours, poetic exponents of the artificial conventions of courtly love, among her friends is evidence that she is not really ready, when the ballet starts, for the wedding which is imminent. Together the friends play at being in love, but Raymonda's games are still childish. Jean's devotion is at first too reticent to awaken her; only when her dreams conjure up the dark figure of her animus, and Jean proves able to defeat this imagined rival, does she come to terms with her hidden longings.

"The role of Raymonda thus becomes dramatically interesting, and Marcia Haydée (who danced the first four performances of the production) makes the most of this. But it is still, above all, an immensely demanding virtuoso role, with so many solos that I lost count, each showing off a different aspect of technique—leaps, turns, balances and so on. There is a beautiful lyric solo with a scarf; a solo in which she jumps repeatedly to land with a stabbing thrust on full point; and of course that haunting last-act solo with its hints of melancholy beneath a surface of surpassing grandeur."

Nureyev staged his production of *Raymonda* for American Ballet Theatre in New York in 1975. Cynthia Gregory and Nureyev danced the first performance. John T. Elson wrote in *Time* magazine:

"*Raymonda* is a two-hour experience in pure dance. And what dancing there is! . . . The incandescent Miss Gregory danced the role as if it had been created for her alone, carrying out variation after variation—six in all—with radiant confidence. The breathtaking pauses at the peak of her balances last only a second or so; yet they seem to embody T. S. Eliot's haunting lines in *Burnt Norton:* 'At the still point of the turning world . . . There the dance is, but neither arrest or movement.'"

Marius Petipa's original scenario for *Raymonda,* including his instructions to the composer, Glazunov, has been translated by Debra Goldman for *Ballet Review* (Vol. 5, No. 2).


## RAYMONDA VARIATIONS

*Music by Alexander Glazunov. Choreography by George Balanchine. Scenery by Horace Armistead. Costumes by Karinska. First presented by the New York City Ballet at the City Center, New York, December 7, 1961, with Patricia Wilde and Jacques d'Amboise in the leading roles.*

I have already mentioned in speaking of *Pas de Dix* how I have always liked the music Glazunov wrote for the ballet *Raymonda.* This ballet also has music taken from Glazunov's score for *Raymonda,* but it is music of an entirely different character from *Pas de Dix.* Originally called *Valse and Variations,* the ballet consists of dances for two principals, soloists, and a *corps de ballet.* There is no story, only the music to dance to.

When the curtain goes up, twelve girls stand posing in an elegant garden. They dance for us and then the principals, another girl and then a boy, join them. Next, the girl and the boy are alone for an adagio. This is followed by a series of nine variations, or solos, by five of the girls and the two principals. The ballet concludes with a coda and a finale by all the dancers.

To try to talk about these dances in any useful way outside the music is not possible; they do not have any literary content at all and of course have nothing to do with the story of the original ballet *Raymonda.* The music itself, its grand and generous manner, its joy and playfulness, was for me more than enough to carry the plot of the dances.

## THE REAL McCOY

*Music by George Gershwin. Choreography by Eliot Feld. Setting and costumes by Rouben Ter-Arutunian. Lighting by Thomas Skelton. First presented by the Eliot Feld Ballet at the New York Shakespeare Festival Public Theatre, December 7, 1974, with Eliot Feld in the leading role. Pianist: Gladys Celeste Mercader.*

*The Real McCoy* recaptures the past and projects it into the present. With the authenticity of George Gershwin's music as a floor to walk on, the action has other points to make, too, about the American Dream. The hero of the piece, a bright, brash young man, a mix of James Cagney and Fred Astaire, indicates at the start that any kid can be a star, like Astaire maybe. Perhaps he is, in fact, George Gershwin? The painted backdrop of rainbows reminds us that much is being sought after, in the '30s fashion.

A guy in a top hat, with cane, and a blonde on a chaise longue turn the sofa into a canoe and go paddling. They meet curious adventures. At the end, the hero dances frantically. Seeking a cocktail feeling of joy or experiencing the Real McCoy?

## REFLECTIONS

*Music by Peter Ilyich Tchaikovsky. Choreography by Gerald Arpino. Lighting by Jennifer Tipton. First presented by the City Center Joffrey Ballet at the City Center, New York, February 24, 1971, with Erika Goodman, Dana Sapiro, Denise Jackson, Glenn White, and Henry Berg as the principals. Cellist: Warren Lash. Conducted by Walter Hagen.*

Arranged to Tchaikovsky's *Variations on a Rococo Theme for Violoncello and Orchestra, Reflections* is a dance ballet with no plot beyond the beauties of the score. This music, not often enough heard, is of interest to those who know only Tchaikovsky's familiar works. There is, first of all, the statement of the theme, danced by a group of seven girls. Seven variations then follow, the first two danced by girls, the third a *pas de deux*, the fourth a *pas de trois* for three girls, the fifth another *pas de deux*, the sixth yet another, and the seventh an ensemble for all the dancers. There is no setting, only the dancers providing absorbing displays of reflected virtuosity to the music.

# THE RELATIVITY OF ICARUS

*Music by Gerhard Samuel. Text by Jack Larson. Choreography by Gerald Arpino. Set and costumes by Rouben Ter-Arutunian. Lighting by Thomas Skelton. First presented in New York City by the City Center Joffrey Ballet at the City Center, October 17, 1974, with Ann Marie DeAngelo as the Sun, Russell Sultzbach as Icarus, and Ted Nelson as Daedalus. Soprano: Joan Bell. Conducted by Seymour Lipkin.*

The story of two men, father and son, who escaped from the labyrinth on self-made wings, has been told many times. This ballet is a variation on that story, based on the poem by Jack Larson and the music by Gerhard Samuel.

Daedalus was the builder of the Labyrinth on the island of Crete. He and his son Icarus were later imprisoned in the Labyrinth. To escape from it and the Minotaur, the monstrous man-bull who dwelt there, they fashioned wings of feathers and wax, which enabled them to fly. Icarus, however, flew too near the sun, the wax on his wings melted, and he fell into the sea, thenceforth called Icarian.

The text by Jack Larson for the music that accompanies the action follows:

As it was with Icarus,
Imprisoned in the labyrinth of his father's creation
Punished by the echoes of a monster's satisfaction
He wished to escape in wings from the confusion of earth.
As it was with Icarus,
Wanting to fly from memories of a Minotaur's birth
Away from mutilated bodies of handsome young men
From the echoes of rape and massacre of young women:
As it was with Icarus,
Out of the labyrinth in wings of things of feathers and wax
Straining free of gravity into air currents that relax
He took flight into the transforming softness of the clouds.
As it was with Icarus,
Even the clouds mushroom in echoes of thunderous shrouds
And though he flies straight as light, like light he'll curve near the moon
And return to the labyrinth a trillion light years too soon.
As it was with Icarus,
Soar to the sun, it's only a mass of multiplied light
Transmuting its brilliance into the curvature of night
Like his too warm wings, the escape expands as it contracts.
And disappears from space as impermanent as wax.
As it was with Icarus,
So it is with all of us.*

The action of the ballet takes place in a remarkable luminous and reflecting setting that catches light and movement, expanding and focusing, deflecting and returning, in much the same way as interpretations of myth invariably return to the primal story.

First the Sun, a lovely girl, dances around a raised area on which Daedalus lies. The Sun reveals him to us and from Daedalus springs full-armed his son Icarus. Bound to his father by cords about his wrists, Icarus is taught to fly. The cords, however, make it impossible for him to fly free of Daedalus.

Daedalus is enamored now of the Sun, and would follow her, sensing even the danger he sees in loosening the cords and abandoning his son. But the boy is more deeply tempted than the father. To free himself, he strangles Daedalus. The liberated Icarus then plunges into an endless fall. The Sun turns again about the earth.

In a long, discursive essay, "Arpino's *Icarus:* Confrontations with the Fall," in *Dance Magazine* (January 1975), Richard Philp writes: "Nobody was unmoved by *Icarus* . . . I believe that we all seem to have seen something in the ballet which is familiar; it holds a mirror up before us and reflects experience which is difficult to reject, or accept . . .

"For one of the simplest interpretations, with which the ballet's strongest supporters are content to settle, I borrow a quote from Nietzsche's *Zarathustra:* 'Many a one hath cast away final worth when he hath cast away his servitude.'

"Wherever *Icarus* is danced, the ballet will continue to evoke comment and interpretation which will have to deal to some extent with the meaning of myth and the nature of human freedom. Visually, I think of *Icarus* and remember the struggling movements outwards, away from, beyond; conversely, there is also a sense of restriction, withdrawal, retreat. To rephrase Nietzsche: When Icarus casts off his servitude [to Daedalus], he is in effect casting away himself; Icarus, like many of us, cannot function without the flexing pressures of obligation."


# REMEMBRANCES

*Music by Richard Wagner. Choreography by Robert Joffrey. Set by Rouben Ter-Arutunian. Costumes by Willa Kim. Lighting by Jennifer Tipton. First presented by the City Center Joffrey Ballet at the City Center, New York, October 12, 1973, with Francesca Corkle and Jonathan Watts as principals. Conducted by Seymour Lipkin. Pianist: Stanley Babin. She, Who Sings: Donna Roll. She, Who Remembers: Jan Hanniford.*

*Remembrances* is a ballet about looking back. As a woman sings her recollections of past love, a woman who remembers remains at her side to watch and reach out toward a danced re-enactment of the past.

The program recalls that Richard Wagner, in 1849, having taken an active role in the revolutionary movement in Germany, was forced to flee with his wife, Minna, and to settle in Switzerland. There, in Zurich, he met a wealthy silk merchant, Otto Wesendonck, who, at his wife Mathilde's urging, became Wagner's patron. It was not long before "something dangerously like a love affair" developed between Mathilde and Wagner.

Some of Wagner's work is inextricably linked with his relationship to Mathilde. In 1853 he wrote for her personal album a sonata that is described by one of his biographers, Paul Bekker, as "a summary of the past and a promise for the future, a delicate act of homage to the woman who had inspired the music which was now to flow from him in an almost unbroken stream." Written on the manuscript of the sonata, as a motto, is the inscription: "Do you know what will follow?"

Mathilde Wesendonck and Wagner became artistic collaborators a few years later, when in 1857–58 he set to music five of her poems. The poems are entitled *Der Engel* (*The Angel*), *Stehe Still* (*Stand Still*), *Im Treibhaus* (*In the Greenhouse*), *Schmerzen* (*Tears*), and *Träume* (*Dreams*). Wagner said that *Im Treibhaus* and *Träume* could be described as "studies" for *Tristan und Isolde*.

In 1935 Arturo Toscanini discovered a lost, unpublished piece of Wagner's known as the *Porazzi Theme*, which the composer had played on the afternoon of his death. Dating from 1859, this theme had been jotted down on the back of a sketch for *Tristan*, relating to the lovers' invocation to the night.

These musical works of Wagner's are the score for the ballet and set the scene for its backward look.

The ballet carries as its motto this quotation from Shelley:

> Music, when soft voices die
> Vibrates in the memory.

The pianist begins the music in the dimly lit auditorium. The house slowly darkens with the quiet music. Soon a girl in a long dress walks slowly across the stage. She reaches out in a gesture of longing and sits down. Following her now comes another girl, her double, who is to sing what the first girl feels and acts as she watches the scene that flows before her.

A girl dances with a boy, it is apparently long ago and almost lost to the memory but soon other images come back, the lovers are among friends, four other couples. The scene appears to be a clearing high above a cavernous bay, the sea shimmering in the distance; the setting resembles an oculus that is focused on a far-off place, the sea, mountains, enclosed in a curved landscape of the memory.

Two couples dance to the music of the first song. Then later, the lead girl, alone, dances and seems to suffer, but her lover rejoins her.

There is a recognition between the woman who watches her past and the girl who dances it. Others now dance to the low threnody of strings. Finally, the girl is left by herself, kneeling. She rises; her partner returns. Later among the happy couples, the lovers seem to expire. She, Who Remembers reaches out to them and gestures to She, Who Sings. But her young image only looks back at her.

NOTES  Writing in *Dance and Dancers* about *Remembrances*, Patricia

Barnes referred to the ballet as "perhaps the best thing Robert Joffrey has yet achieved. . . . It is a lushly romantic work, matching the music's soul and passion. . . . Corkle has always been a brilliant young technician. In *Remembrances* Joffrey has seen another side of her. One is tempted to say that this ballet has made her a great dancer. She performed it as if her heart was on fire, with a sincerity and depth that were remarkable. In her movement there was a dramatic tension and in her musicality a wealth of understanding of what can transform a simple movement into art.

"Jonathan Watts . . . was here making his first stage appearance in nine years. . . . He is now dancing better than ever, even after such a long lay-off period. Always an immaculate stylist, in *Remembrances* he was superb, partnering with tenderness, possessing elegant *ports de bras* and unforced dignity."

## LES RENDEZVOUS

*Ballet* divertissement *in one act. Music by François Auber, arranged by Constant Lambert. Choreography by Frederick Ashton. Scenery and costumes by William Chappell. First performed by the Sadler's Wells Ballet at the Sadler's Wells Theatre, London, December 5, 1933, with a cast headed by Alicia Markova, Stanislas Idzikowski, Pearl Argyle, Ninette de Valois, and Robert Helpmann. Revived with new decor by William Chappell, November 16, 1937. First presented in the United States by the Sadler's Wells Theatre Ballet at the Northrop Auditorium, Minneapolis, Minnesota, November 7, 1951, with Elaine Fifield and Pirmin Trecu in the principal roles. First performed by the Royal Ballet at Covent Garden, London, May 7, 1959.*

*Les Rendezvous* is a dance entertainment set to music from Auber's *L'Enfant Prodigue*. In a private park, young couples promenade and dance to give appropriate expression to youthful sentiments that take hold of their ebullient spirits. There is no plot.

The curtain rises on a bright, sunny scene. A high white fence of wrought iron stands out against a light-green back cloth. The gate to the park, in the center, is open. The orchestra plays music that is light and charming, music suggestive of the good nature we always feel when we watch boys and girls show their happiness by dancing together. Trumpets sound a fanfare and the ballet begins.

Young couples out for a stroll dance into the park one by one from the corners of the stage. They are all dressed in white; the girls wear pink ribbons in their hair and pink sashes, and the boys wear belts of light blue. The young people move back and forth across the park. Finally there are six couples. They stand on either side of the gate, and a seventh couple enters. They pass down the line formed by their friends, greet them effusively, and then, more formally, shake hands.

Now the couples divide into different groups and fill the stage with shifting, quick movement. The boys dance alone briefly, then leave the stage to a couple who dance a short *pas de deux*. The boy lifts the girl off into the wings; the music is rapid and joyful, the lift is long and slow, and there is an effect of joyfulness mixed with romance. Other boys enter and lift their partners more rapidly, more in direct imitation of the music. Six girls surround the romantic couple when they return, and the introduction to the ballet finishes as the boy again lifts the girl into the wings.

Four girls dance a bright *pas de quatre*. They are joined by their partners and leave the stage as the boy of the lead couple enters and dances a bold leaping-and-turning variation to brilliant, flourishing music. The boy gestures toward the gate, his girl rejoins him there, and they leave the stage together. The other couples have returned and form three tableaux about the stage. The boy, reaching out to his partner who kneels below, comes back, leading his girl forward, and the two of them dance a slow, romantic duet. Four of the boys lift the girl to their shoulders as the adagio ends. There she poses gracefully, as the girls gather about her raised figure, hold hands, and enclose her with a circle of arabesques.

The music becomes saucy and bouncing. A girl bounds on stage with two partners, turning from the arms of one boy into the arms of the other. The two boys lift her high into the air, release her, and their steps quicken to the hastening music. The *pas de trois* finishes as all three kneel.

Next the lead girl dances alone. She leaps onto the scene, turns dizzily, delighting us with her deft, swift movement. She is very pretty, apparently in love, and enjoys showing off a little. Boys emerge from the wings one by one and bow to the girl, in tribute to her beauty and her masterful dance. She bows gratefully in return and leaves the stage on the left.

Rhythmic handclaps are heard off-stage. Six boys run into the park to dance in unison a strong, buoyant ensemble, dazzling with its long, high leaps, multiple turns, and the quick, steady certainty with which they finish their brilliant sequence of movement. A trumpet fanfare announces the arrival of six girls, who join their partners for a brief dance before the reappearance of the ballerina, who whirls about the stage. The *corps de ballet* returns and forms a background for another virtuoso variation by the ballerina's partner, who places his hands on his shoulders and spins like a top.

Four girls approach the boy and blindfold him. He plays their game for a moment, then turns in their midst and rushes off as the ballerina enters on the right to hop backward on point in a long diagonal. All the couples are now on stage. They bow to each other and bid their partners a fond farewell. One by one, they leave the park through the gate. When the ballerina disappears into the wings, her partner leaps after her in a high trajectory. Four girls, who remain in the park, pose amusingly, as if the fun has just begun.

# REQUIEM CANTICLES

*Music by Igor Stravinsky. Choreography by Jerome Robbins. Lighting by Ronald Bates. First presented by the New York City Ballet at the Stravinsky Festival, June 25, 1972, at the New York State Theatre, Lincoln Center,*

*New York, with Merrill Ashley, Susan Hendl, Bruce Wells, and Robert Maiorano as principals. Soprano: Elaine Bonazzi. Bass: William Metcalf. Conducted by Robert Craft.*

Stravinsky's *Requiem Canticles,* for contralto, soloists, and orchestra, first performed in 1966 at Princeton, New Jersey, was selected by Jerome Robbins as one of his ballets for our Stravinsky Festival in 1972. That event, which marked the composer's ninetieth birthday, also mourned his death as we hope he would have wished us to do, with celebration. *Requiem Canticles* was the final ballet of the Festival.

Stravinsky had earlier informed the New York City Ballet that he planned the *Requiem Canticles* "as an instrumental work originally, and I composed the threnody for wind instruments and muffled drums, now at the center of the work, first. Later I decided to use sentences from six texts of the traditional Requiem service, and that time I conceived the triangulate instrumental frame of the string *Prelude,* wind-instrument *Interlude,* and percussion *Postlude.* The *Requiem Canticles* are concert music, but the celebration of death is to be played in memory of a man of God, a man of the poor, a man of peace."

Robbins's *Requiem Canticles* was an appropriate finale in dance to what was, for many of us on both sides of the footlights, a memorable week.

A *Village Voice* critic said of the ballet: "Mr. Robbins's piece, conducted by Robert Craft, accentuated the energy heard in the music. Here were granite blocks of black-clothed dancers staring out at the audience in the *Prelude* and shaking in tight spasms. The choral sections followed, with the *Exaudi* bringing in slow gestures and walkings, the *Dies irae* frenzied with lifts and aimless striding, the *Tuba mirum* showing Bruce Wells as a sort of Angel Gabriel ready to call everyone to judgment, the non-vocal *Interlude* leaving the stage to four dancers full of expectation, *Rex tremendae* bringing back the corps in their block phalanxes, Merrill Ashley bursting out of a semicircle of corps in *Lacrymosa,* the *Libera me* letting the corps members converge on one another on their knees and making room for short solos by Miss Ashley and Susan Hendl before the group goes into asymmetric attitudes; and finally the drums and bells of the *Postlude* setting off a mechanism of ticking bodies, limbs, and finally just heads in open-mouthed, silent cries of fear and marvel."

# REVENGE

*Dramatic ballet in four scenes with prologue. Music by Giuseppe Verdi. Choreography by Ruth Page. Book by Ruth Page with the collaboration of Nicolas Remisov. Scenery and costumes by Antoine Clavé. First presented by Les Ballets des Champs-Élysées at the Théâtre de l'Empire, Paris, October 17, 1951, with Sonia Arova as Azucena, Vladimir Skouratoff as Manrico, Jacqueline Moreau as Leonora, and Gérard Ohn as the Count di Luna. First presented in the United States by Ruth Page Ballets at the Civic Opera House, Chicago, November 26, 1955, with Sonia Arova, Oleg Briansky, Alicia Markova, and Bentley Stone in the principal roles.*

Like the ballet *Carmen, Revenge* is also based on a great popular opera—Verdi's *Il Trovatore*. The ballet is faithful to the opera's theme of passionate revenge and condenses into a comparatively short space of time the principal elements of the musical drama. The time is the sixteenth century. The place is Spain.

PROLOGUE: THE COURTYARD OF THE CASTLE OF THE COUNT DI LUNA    The elderly Count di Luna has two infant sons, of whom he is very proud. One day an old gypsy woman is discovered hovering over the cradle of one of these boys. The child's nurse, suspecting sorcery, sounds the alarm, and the old count's servants capture the gypsy. The hag pleads that she meant no harm, that she was only interested in reading the child's fortune. She is driven out of the castle, but when the child becomes ill, she is brought back. At the count's order, she is burned at the stake for sorcery. His child recovers.

The old gypsy's young daughter, Azucena, dances in despair as the flames of her mother's burning light the distant sky. Gentlemen of the count's household stand on the steps of the courtyard watching the fire with indifference. Azucena vows to avenge her mother's horrible death. She steals the count's other son and flees into the night.

SCENE ONE: THE CASTLE    Twenty years have passed. The old Count di Luna is dead. On his deathbed he urged his remaining son never to abandon search for his brother. Unknown to the new count, his brother still survives as Manrico, whom Azucena has brought up as her own son.

Both the Count di Luna and Manrico are in love with the beautiful Leonora, lady in waiting to the queen. Leonora favors Manrico, and the count, enraged that the girl should prefer a ragged gypsy to a nobleman, is determined to separate them. Leonora escapes with Manrico to a gypsy camp.

SCENE TWO: THE GYPSY MOVEMENT    The Count di Luna traces the two lovers and comes in person to the gypsy camp. There he challenges Manrico to a duel. The young gypsy, warned by a premonition, reluctantly consents to this contest, and the two brothers, completely ignorant of their relationship, begin to fight. Manrico gains the upper hand and might easily slay the count. The premonition returns, and he stays his hand. Azucena regrets that her ward has not killed the count; after twenty years, she can still think only of revenge.

The count, enraged by jealousy and Manrico's contempt, is determined to force his love on Leonora. He sends her to prison with Manrico.

SCENE THREE: IN FRONT OF THE PRISON    The two lovers endure torture in prison by the count's order. Leonora, in desperation, promises that she will marry the count if he will set Manrico free.

SCENE FOUR: THE BETROTHAL    The marriage ceremony has been arranged. Manrico, who does not know that she has arranged for his release, accuses Leonora of faithlessness. But Leonora, unwilling to marry the count, has taken poison and urges Manrico to seek his freedom. Manrico discovers what she has done and weeps as she dies in his arms.

The Count di Luna orders Manrico's execution. The youth bids farewell to his foster mother, who despairs that her revenge means such a sacrifice. But when Manrico is dead, she weeps no more. She turns to the Count di Luna in fierce triumph. Glorying in her revenge, she holds out to him the locket that hung about the neck of his brother twenty years before. To the count's horror at this secret, Azucena responds with demoniac exultation: she has had her revenge at last.

# REVERIES

*Music by Peter Ilyich Tchaikovsky. Choreography by John Clifford. Costumes by Joe Eula. Lighting by Ronald Bates. First presented by the New York City Ballet at the New York State Theatre, December 4, 1969, with Conrad Ludlow, Anthony Blum, Johnna Kirkland, Gelsey Kirkland, and ensemble.*

The fourth ballet by John Clifford, *Reveries* uses music from Tchaikovsky's *Suite No. 1* (the first, third, fourth, and sixth movements). The plot of the ballet is the plot of the music.

The curtain rises after a brief orchestral introduction. The first movement, marked *Introduction and Fugue,* is staged for a boy and twelve girls who, dressed in flowing pink, surround their romantic hero. He is seen in a spotlight, center. Detached at first, he kneels and watches the girls dance, then joins them under the dark, starry sky. His dance is like magic, and they all seem to respond like flowers in the wind. He leaves the girls then to commence to dance to the fugue. The boy returns to dance and fall at the feet of his Muses. They soon leave, the scene darkens and he, too, departs.

To the third movement of Tchaikovsky's Suite, *Intermezzo,* the dance begins in a diagonal of light on a dark stage. Four boys and four girls face each other. The stage brightens, a boy lifts on a girl in white, and the orchestra plays a romantic theme. The couple dances, he catching her under the arms as she leaps. As the music ends, he kneels before her, then holds her as she falls into his arms. A brilliant soloist in blue dances in dynamic contrast to the lyricism of the lovers.

The *Marche Militaire* is led by a girl who matches the brilliance of Tchaikovsky's melody with the help of a small group of four girls. The finale, *Gavotte,* brings the four principals together in a climactic ensemble of complication and exuberance.

NOTES   Clive Barnes wrote in the New York *Times:* "*Reveries* is John Clifford's best piece to date, and is a lovely piece of choreography. . . . He really illuminates the music. There is a sumptuous and love-rapt *pas de deux* for Johnna Kirkland and Conrad Ludlow, and beautiful solos for Anthony Blum and Johnna's brilliant kid sister, Gelsey Kirkland. . . . The entire piece is elegant yet fun."

Arlene Croce, editor of *Ballet Review*, wrote of John Clifford in *Playbill* in 1969: "The youngest of the New York City Ballet's dancer-choreographers is twenty-one-year-old John Clifford. Clifford came to New York from Los Angeles and was awarded a scholarship to the School of American Ballet, where he entered the choreography workshop in 1966. He made his choreographic debut with *Stravinsky Symphony* in the spring of 1968 and has revised it steadily ever since. His second ballet, to Vaughan Williams' *Fantasia on a Theme of Thomas Tallis,* is a lyrical work about two real people and a dream couple whom the real people prefer to one another. Premièred early this year, *Fantasies* was a hit with both critics and audiences, and Clifford has been invited to stage his next ballet for the company's Sixth Annual Spring Benefit on May 8, on the same program with new works by George Balanchine and Jerome Robbins. Robbins, who returns this spring to choreograph for the company after more than a decade's absence, provided Clifford with his earliest inspiration. Shortly before spring rehearsals began, Clifford was to be found at the State Theatre, where Robbins was taking class.

" 'I've been watching Jerry work on his new piece,' he told an interviewer. 'I'm rehearsing it but I don't know if I'm going to be in it yet. The way he squeezes everything he can get out of you! I can't do that yet. He's a rhythm choreographer of course—he uses every last bit of rhythm. And he's so thorough. I think he thought about *The Cage* for years before he did it, thought it all out and knew exactly what he wanted to do. When I first joined the company I would watch every performance of *The Cage* and people would say, "Well, John, what did you like this time?" The first large-scale choreography I ever saw was the film of *West Side Story.* I've seen it more than twenty times. When it came out again recently, I went back. I think it affected my spatial concepts when I began to choreograph. I used to try and set bits of movement in the background that only ended up confusing the stage picture. I was choreographing selectively as if for a camera. I didn't realize that in the theater the spectator has to have a central focus because he's stationary; he can't move around like a camera picking up this and that. You know those funny, insectlike things the girls do in *The Cage?* Well, they do a lot with their arms and hands you really can't see, but only because the stage is so dark. I wish it could be brighter. I'd like to do a horror ballet like that some day. Actually, whether you do story ballets or not depends on the music. I consciously try to do something different in each piece. The Stravinsky—a neo-classical abstract work. Mr. B. thought it would be good for me to work with that score. Next, a long romantic piece with a bit of a story. Now I'm using Bernstein's *Prelude, Fugue and Riffs.* It's a jazz score from the same period as Stravinsky's *Ebony Concerto,* but it's not going to be set as a "jazz ballet" in that sense because it would look dated. I don't read music or have a record-player. I go to the library and listen to records. When I hear something I like, I file it away in the back of my mind. I hadn't heard the *Tallis* until about a year ago, on the Coast, when somebody played it for me. I didn't care for it too much then. But it came back to me for *Fantasies.* When I'm making a piece, I don't try to get the dancers to consciously project a meaning. I don't tell them what they're supposed to do except over coffee. Ideally, you just want the dancer to be. You try and get the ones you know will look right for the part in the first place, then things happen. . . . I have projects going all the time. This company is so full of terrific dancers but we have such an enormous rep they don't often have the energy to show off. Right now, in addition to the Bernstein, I'm choreographing a Bartók ballet over at the school, and a rock ballet—rock music. It's only a 7½-minute piece but it's the hardest thing I've ever done. I tried doing classical *pas de deux* movements but it didn't work, it looked too contrasty. Then I did regulation discothèque and hated it. Now, last night, I had them all just walk. It was better. I want to do all kinds of things—multimedia . . . using singers and speech . . . opera. I have this terrific idea but I won't talk about it. I think Lincoln Kirstein thinks I'm mad.'"

## RITE OF SPRING (*see* LE SACRE DU PRINTEMPS)

## RITUALS

*Music by Béla Bartók. Choreography by Kenneth MacMillan. Designer: Yolanda Sonnasend. First presented by the Royal Ballet at the Royal Opera House, Covent Garden, London, December 11, 1975, and introduced to the United States by the same ensemble April 27, 1976, at the Metropolitan Opera House, New York.*

Set to the *Sonata for Two Pianos and Percussion* of Bartók, *Rituals* is a dance ballet about Japanese formalized sport and theatre. The first scene shows the preparation for combat and self-defense for which movements have been derived from Japanese boxing, sumo wrestling, and a Japanese form of Tai-Chi. The second scene is inspired by the Bunraku Puppet Theatre and the third shows a "very emotional situation"—the birth of a child—in the impressive style of some forms of Japanese theatre.

The Royal Ballet visited Japan in 1975, which gave the choreographer Kenneth MacMillan an opportunity to watch the Kabuki theatre and Nō plays. The studied lack of emotion in the Japanese theatre inspired him to make a work of that character in ballet.

## THE RIVER

*Original score by Duke Ellington. Choreography by Alvin Ailey. Costumes by Frank Thompson. Lighting by Gilbert V. Hemsley, Jr. Special lighting by Nicholas Cernovitch. First presented by American Ballet Theatre at the New York State Theatre, Lincoln Center, New York, June 25, 1970, with a cast headed by John Prinz, Alexandra Radius, Hans Ebbelaar, Marcos*

*Paredes, Eleanor D'Antuono, Cynthia Gregory, Ivan Nagy, Dennis Nahat,*
*Sallie Wilson, and Keith Lee. Conducted by Jaime Leon.*

A quotation from the musician Duke Ellington prefaces the ballet: ". . . of
birth . . . of the well-spring of life . . . of reaffirmation . . . of the heavenly
anticipation of rebirth. . . ." The work itself is the result of collaboration between Duke Ellington and Alvin Ailey. In its musical entirety, the work consists of a *Prologue*, an *Epilogue*, and eleven sections. These are entitled:
*Spring, Spring Run, Meander, Giggling Rapids, Falls, Vortex, Lake, Main-*
*stream (Riba), Two Cities, The Sea (Mother)*, and *Spring*.

First presented by American Ballet Theatre in an unfinished state that was
later completed, on June 29, 1971, *The River* was appraised by critic Jean Battey Lewis of the Washington *Post* as a work with "an alive and joyous quality,
a life force that carries along its series of solos, duets and group dances in a
headlong sweep. . . . *The River* is not only a well-spring of free, unforced,
imaginative movement. It is also a tribute to Ailey's gifts as a director and
developer of talent that he has created passages which capture so sensitively
the strengths of some of Ballet Theatre's finest dancers."

Writing of *The River* soon after its première, in *The Saturday Review*, the
critic Walter Terry said: "The Ailey ballet *The River*, with an original score
by Duke Ellington, was not completed by première time, so for the season it
was given in part as 'six dances from a work in progress.' A full appraisal, of
course, must wait, but the Ailey dance brilliance—wonderful freshets of movement designs to delight the eye—are already there. There are patterns of mass
motion that are utterly beautiful, but there are also such choreographic concentrates as Eleanor D'Antuono's incredibly fast solo *Vortex;* Cynthia Gregory
(with either Ivan Nagy or Gayle Young) in a cool and graceful *pas de deux*,
surrounded by ensemble movements, called *Lake;* Dennis Nahat's jaunty
*Mainstream;* and the curiously haunting *Two Cities*, danced by Sallie Wilson
and Keith Lee, each in separate pools of light, each lonely, each reaching out
across the unseen barrier of river, of distance, of divisiveness, of solitary spirit,
however you care to interpret it, and, finally, bridging the abyss."

A year later, Deborah Jowitt wrote in the *Village Voice:* "Alvin Ailey has
added three more sections to *The River*. One, called *Sea*, certainly rounds the
whole piece out, since the sea people, Erik Bruhn and Natalia Makarova, can
now open the ballet by pulling away from the 'spring' (Keith Lee) in a receding wave and return at the end in a slow, coiling floor duet that seems to
spawn that wellspring again. *Meander*, for Mimi Paul, Ted Kivitt, and Ian
Horvath, is a playful, jazzy, carelessly sensuous *divertissement*—very nicely
danced, but not terribly compelling in its movement concept. *Giggling Rapids*
features Bruhn and Makarova in a fast, almost kittenish exchange. She has a
beautifully innocent body to go with her strength, and both are exuberant performers. As for the whole idea, well, the crowd loved seeing these two jazz it
up (so good-sporty of them), but watching Bruhn reminded me of Cathy Ber-
berian singing Beatles songs. Technique and persona not completely compatible with the material.

"There were other good things in *The River*. Dennis Nahat did marvelous

things with the rhythmic shape and impetus of his little solo in *Falls,* and
Eleanor D'Antuono has mastered *Vortex* completely, so that now her turns and
swirls unleash little spurts of power without obvious effort or preparation."

## RODEO

*Ballet in two scenes. Music by Aaron Copland. Choreography and book by*
*Agnes de Mille. Scenery by Oliver Smith. Costumes by Kermit Love. First*
*presented by the Ballet Russe de Monte Carlo at the Metropolitan Opera*
*House, New York, October 16, 1942, with a cast headed by Agnes de Mille*
*as the* Cowgirl, *Frederic Franklin as the* Champion Roper, *and Casimir*
*Kokitch as the* Head Wrangler. *Revived by Ballet Theatre at Rhine-am-Main*
*Air Force, Frankfurt, Germany, August 14, 1950.*

*Rodeo,* subtitled "The Courting at Burnt Ranch," is a love story of the American Southwest. The problem it deals with is perennial: how an American girl,
with the odds seemingly all against her, sets out to get herself a man. The girl
in this case is a cowgirl, a tomboy whose desperate efforts to become one of
the ranch's cowhands create a problem for the cowboys and make her the
laughingstock of womankind.

SCENE ONE   The corral of Burnt Ranch. The ballet's brief overture begins
with a crash of cymbals and continues with a rowdy, rhythmic melody reminiscent of the wild west. The music becomes quiet, and the curtain rises on the
corral of Burnt Ranch. The time is Saturday afternoon, the time of the weekly
rodeo, about the turn of the century. Against an orange-red sky whose intense
heat seems to bear down on the scene, a high wooden fence encloses the
parched, dusty ground of the corral. Half a dozen lazy cowhands stand about,
idling away the time. Among them stands the cowgirl, self-assertive in a bright
red shirt, brown hat tilted back over her head, and brown pants and boots.
Long pigtails hang down her back. One of the cowhands holds his hand up to
shield his eyes from the glaring sun and looks out into the distance. Another
cowboy rides in, twirling his arm over his head in a lassoing motion. The cowgirl hitches up her pants, as if to prepare for the rodeo that is about to begin.
The cowboys tell her that she can't come along and ride off rapidly. Not to be
outdone so easily, the cowgirl decides to follow them and rushes off to the
right, roping the air with a fast-turning arm.

Three cowhands ride on vigorously. Six of their fellows join them, and all
dance wildly, imitating in their movements the jolts and tricks of the rodeo.
The music is fierce and a challenge to the dancers. The cowgirl re-enters and
tries to join one of the groups. The cowgirl secretly hankers after the head
wrangler, and watches him anxiously. He and the others motion to her to go
away—she isn't wanted. The girl is used to this kind of treatment, however,
and stays put, trying to compete in the rodeo. She disgraces herself, and the
head wrangler is about to lose all patience with her.

But suddenly the corral is transfigured by the arrival of girls in city clothes—

Eastern friends of the rancher's daughter, who have come out with her to get a taste of ranch life. The cowboys slap their thighs in enthusiastic welcome; the girls wave to them with their handkerchiefs and giggle among themselves in feigned bashfulness. The cowgirl is both contemptuous and envious of their finery; she is visibly disgusted by their silly flirting.

The champion roper steps out to show off his skill before the girls. When the head wrangler steps over to them politely and takes off his hat to the rancher's daughter, the cowgirl can bear it no longer and rides off in a jealous fit of petulance. Four women from the ranch come out to watch the rodeo. They are entertained until the cowgirl rides in on what appears to be a bucking bronco. All the women raise their hands in despair at this foolish show-off. The cowgirl falls. The Eastern girls rush over to her and can't control their laughter: never in *their* born days has a *girl* done anything like that. The cowgirl is furious. She gets up and thumbs her nose at the women. Soon, alone with the cowboys, the girl sees that she's made a fool of herself all around; the women may laugh at her, but the men are worse: their silence makes her despair. She tries to regain her old familiarity with them. They ignore her and stare into the distance. The head wrangler jerks his thumb toward the house, telling her to leave the corral. He is the one man in the world the girl respects: smothering her tears, she obeys him.

The rodeo is over. The girls wave at the champion roper as he leaps away. The scene darkens, the music softens, the womenfolk cross the stage, moving slowly, bravely, yet wistfully, and there is created an impression of what home is like after a tiring, busy day. The cowboys cross the stage behind the women, and when the girls step backward, hesitating in their homeward march, the men move forward to them, place their arms about their waists, and move forward again with them.

The couples disappear. The cowgirl re-enters and tries to attract the head wrangler's attention. But it's as if she weren't even there: he goes to the rancher's daughter, who stands demure in her long blue dress with ribbons in her hair, lifts her softly, and takes her off into the night.

The cowgirl dances for a moment alone, trying to shake off what she knows has happened to her. She isn't any good as a woman and she's a miserable failure as a cowhand. The head wrangler returns. He doesn't understand what's wrong with this strange girl. A cowboy calls to him, and he leaves before the girl can tell him. The womenfolk try to call the girl home; she ignores them. The champion roper crosses the back of the corral, snapping his fingers in private anticipation of the Saturday night dance at the ranch house. He disappears. The cowgirl falls to the ground, all alone now with her problem. The stage blacks out around her.

A bright blue drop curtain, decorated with galloping wild horses, falls in front of the scene. Four couples rush out and begin a square dance. A caller shouts out directions to the dancers, and the couples respond by moving quickly into more intricate patterns as he commands. Soon they are out of breath, but turning still more rapidly and now shouting as they run around and around in a circle, faster and faster. They run off into the wings.

SCENE TWO   The ranch house. The curtain rises on the ranch house. The cowgirl is sitting alone on a bench at the left, watching three cowboys dance a jig to a jazzy piano accompaniment. One of the cowboys is the champion roper, dressed now in his Saturday-night best—violet shirt, a loud vest of cowhide, and striped yellow pants. He jumps high into the air and clicks his heels together repeatedly. The cowgirl, still dressed in the dusty clothes of the corral, feels out of place, though she is making an obvious effort to enjoy herself. The boys finish their jig. Three couples come in and dance about the room, oblivious to whether anyone is watching them. Two of the couples waltz into the parlor as the remaining pair quarrel: the boy kisses the girl, and she rushes out.

The boy despairs of women and sits down beside the cowgirl. She tries to comfort him, man to man. But another girl has come in looking for a partner. She sees the boy alone, lifts her dress flirtatiously, and runs out. He chases after her. The cowgirl can see no hope for such an idiot. The champion roper strides back in and notices the lonely girl. He doesn't know what the matter is; but since this is Saturday night and dancing time, he can see only one cure. He tells her to get up and dance. The cowgirl says she doesn't know how to dance. Well, first, he tells her, you'd better look a little cleaner. He tries to fix her face up and smacks the dust off her bottom.

Just as the girl is beginning to forget about the head wrangler, he comes in and goes over to the rancher's daughter. The cowgirl forgets all about the champion roper. He loses patience with her; after all, he's just as interested in other girls as she is in the head wrangler: He was only trying to make her have a good time. When the champion roper walks out on her, the girl begins to cry. She looks at the romantic dancing couple and falls to the floor in tears.

Gradually the room fills with people. The bench is moved back, and everybody gets ready for a community dance. The girls line up on one side, the boys on the other. Bravely, the girl decides to try again and hopefully stands in line with the girls. The boys approach and take their partners; the cowgirl is left standing alone! The music becomes sweet and lyrical; the couples form a circle; the boys lift the girls tenderly high above them; the girl turns away.

The champion roper dances in, jumping high in the air, clicking his heels together, breaking the romantic spell. When he finishes this bit of exhibitionism, he comes over and leans on the girl's shoulder. She stifles a sob. The other couples leave the scene. The roper puts his hand under her chin and tells her to cheer up, to try to dance with him again. He opens his arms wide, the girl smiles, hitches up her belt, comes close to him, and everything is all right for a few seconds while they dance.

Everything is spoiled, however, by the head wrangler and the rancher's daughter, who come back and remind the cowgirl of her real love. The roper catches her watching them; before he can do anything about it, she has run away. The roper sees a girl walking alone and pursues her into the wings.

All the cowboys and their girls dance now, filling the scene with violent color and vigorous movement. The couples clap their hands joyously in rhythm to the music. They stop dancing all at once and stare, as the cowgirl comes in, dressed from head to foot in bright red. The girls are shocked by this lack of taste; the boys are eager to find out what it means.

The champion roper goes to her, hitches up his pants, and asks her to dance. Even in her new dress the girl hitches up her clothes, too. They dance. The violins saw away at a square-dance theme, and the moving couples form a circle around them.

The cowgirl finds herself standing between the head wrangler and the roper. Both want to dance with her. The wrangler has forgotten the rancher's daughter long enough to notice the cowgirl. The roper and the wrangler throw the girl back and forth between them. She tries to escape, but the wrangler grabs her and tries to kiss her. The roper steps in and says, "No! She's my girl!" He takes her face in his hands and kisses her hard. He kisses her again, harder. Both of them wake up: they've both been wrong all along and didn't know what was happening. The head wrangler rejoins the rancher's daughter, and the whole group dances happily. As the curtain falls, the girls step into stirrups formed by the boys' hands and stand poised high over their heads. The cowgirl and the roper look into each other's eyes.

NOTES    *Rodeo* has been a steady favorite in the United States and on American Ballet Theatre's many tours abroad. That was proved especially true when the company revived the ballet in 1972, in New York, at their engagement at the City Center. Writing of that performance in *Dance Magazine*, the critic Nancy Mason said: "America was ripe for *Rodeo* when performed by Ballet Russe in 1942. We were at war; national feeling was running high. Although Women's Lib may now quibble about the theme—'How to get a man'—*Rodeo* isn't dated because it deals with basic emotions.

"The action's set on a ranch in the Southwest and concerns a tomboy (Christine Sarry) who prefers riding a horse to wearing a dress. She's the tagalong of the cowboys, desperately and unreciprocally in love with the Head Wrangler (Marcos Paredes). Aaron Copland's music offers rowdy and rhythmic accompaniment.

"There couldn't be better casting for the tomboy. Christine Sarry even looks the part with her cropped brown hair and stubborn expression. What's more, she's a superb actress and comedienne; a powerpacked little dynamo who can stir laughter or tears. One really feels for her plight and wishes her well. Projecting incredible energy, she'd meet any challenge by pushing back her hat, hitching up her trousers, then diving right in. Shyness underlies this gumption. Here's a girl more at home on the back of a horse than in any social situation.

"The turning point arrives at the Saturday night dance, where Chris is finally persuaded by the Champion Roper (Terry Orr, alternating with William Carter) to put on a dress and join the party. A few minutes later she dashes in and everything halts abruptly. Gone are the baggy trousers; in their place, a sensible red jumper and ankle-length boots; on her face, a triumphant, excited grin. The Head Wrangler does a double-take. Then there's a competition between him and the Champion Roper for her heart.

"In *Rodeo* virtuoso tap dancing was used for the first time in a ballet. It also focused international attention on utilizing American folk themes in ballets. It changed the course for the musical theater; the next year Agnes de Mille choreographed *Oklahoma.*

"What a happy thought that *Rodeo* is back in the active repertoire. The company performs it with infectious zeal and good feelings. It's a perfect vehicle for Christine Sarry; Terry Orr delights with his easygoing and confident Roper interpretation. And it's good to see William Carter. . . . He created an honest and charming 'big brother' feeling."

In his book *Inside American Ballet Theatre,* Clive Barnes records a long interview with Agnes de Mille on the origins of *Rodeo.*

## RODIN, MIS EN VIE

*Music by Michael Kamen. Choreography by Margo Sappington. Costumes by Willa Kim. First presented by the Harkness Ballet at the Harkness Theatre, April 17, 1974, with Jeanette Vondersaar, Chris Jensen, and Zane Wilson in principal roles.*

Rodin's sculpture come to life is the interesting idea behind this unusual ballet, which uses a specially commissioned score by Michael Kamen. Many familiar works by the great French artist (who once sculpted Nijinsky) are seen here in varied characterizations. The ebb and flow of the movement of sculptural bodies is seen to have a different quality from usual dance action and gesture. We are reminded of what must have attracted Rodin to dance and what must have generated some of his idealized figures as well as the power of his memorable studies and groupings. The work concludes in a dramatic tableaux with all of the figures "draped like some Dantesque vision," in Patricia Barnes's phrase, "over a vast scaffolding . . . It was particularly impressive."

## ROMANCE

*Music by Johannes Brahms. Choreography by Eliot Feld. Costumes by Stanley Simmons. Lighting by Jennifer Tipton. First presented by the American Ballet Company at the Brooklyn Academy of Music, New York, April 20, 1971, with Anna Laerkesen, Christine Sarry, Elizabeth Lee, Cristina Stirling, John Sowinski, Richard Munro, Daniel Levans, and Kenneth Hughes. Pianist: Harry Fuchs.*

A dance ballet for four girls and four boys to some of Brahms's later piano music, *Romance* has no narrative action. The drama of the piece and the atmosphere of each of the dances derive from the choreographer's response to the music and the response of his dancers to that impulse. The dances are accompanied by a pianist who sits at his instrument on the left side of the stage. There are benches on stage and the costumes and deportment of the dancers suggest a formal occasion. The four couples appear in various combinations and ensembles; at one point two boys perform a display piece. The music is drawn from nine piano works, mostly intermezzos (Opus 116, Opus 118, Opus 119, and a final *Capriccio*, Op. 76). These pieces are in many ways ideal for dances; they are brief, about three or four minutes each, and can be easily heard, and seen, as continuous, though there is no thematic connection.

A thematic connection, of course, can be given in dance form, and while romance is indeed the theme of the ballet and several couples are wrapt in it to the exclusion of everything but speed in conquest and fulfillment, the ballet plays its variations on the main subject: frustration, wrong matches, ill-fated meetings. The evocation here of different situations in love—tenderness, regret, jealousy—is what *Romance* is all about. If you do not know these piano pieces by Brahms, I commend them to you.


## ROMEO AND JULIET

Shakespeare's tragedy of *Romeo and Juliet* has been turned into dance by many choreographers. The six ballets described below are the most familiar:

*Ballet in three acts, based on the play by Shakespeare. Music by Sergei Prokofiev. Libretto by Leonid Lavrovsky, Sergei Prokofiev, and Sergei Radlov. Choreography by Leonid Lavrovsky. Décor by Pyotr Williams. First presented at the Kirov State Theatre of Opera and Ballet, Leningrad, January 11, 1940, with Konstantin Sergeyev and Galina Ulanova in the title roles, A. V. Lopukhov as Mercutio, and S. G. Karen as Tybalt. Revised and presented at the Bolshoi Theatre, Moscow, December 28, 1946. First presented in the United States by the Bolshoi Ballet at the Metropolitan Opera House, New York, April 16, 1959, with Galina Ulanova and Yuri Zhdanov in the title roles.*

The Soviet production relates Shakespeare's story in thirteen scenes, with a prologue and epilogue.

PROLOGUE   Friar Laurence, sage and philosopher, blesses the marriage of Romeo and Juliet. The three figures stand motionless in tableau in front of three arches.

ACT ONE, SCENE ONE: THE MAIN SQUARE OF VERONA   As dawn breaks, Romeo, son of Montague, is seen wandering alone about the deserted streets of Verona. Three servants leave the house of Capulet and walk across the square to join some girls in the inn. They are soon embroiled in a quarrel with two servants of Montague, the sworn enemy of their house. Swords are drawn and a fight starts. More and more people, including Benvolio, nephew of Montague, and Tybalt, nephew of Lady Capulet, join in the fray. Paris, who has come to Verona to seek the hand of Capulet's daughter, Juliet, reaches the square when the fighting is at its fiercest. Montague and his hated rival,

Capulet, unsheathe their swords and attack each other. The tocsin rings; its sound, reverberating through the city, brings crowds to the square. The prince of Verona then appears. He stops the fighting and an edict, forbidding disturbances in the city streets, is proclaimed. Tybalt leaves, cursing the Montagues.

Before the curtain, in a transitional *Front Scene,* the Capulet household is preparing for a ball. Juliet's nurse, carrying a beautiful dress, stops to reprimand some servants who have stolen food from the kitchen.

ACT ONE, SCENE TWO: JULIET'S ROOM   In her room, the walls covered with tapestries, Juliet plays hide-and-seek with her nurse instead of dressing for the ball. Lady Capulet comes into the room and tells Juliet that Paris has asked for her hand in marriage. Juliet protests that she is too young, but leading her to the mirror, her mother shows her that this is not so.

*Front Scene:* The preparations for the ball are almost finished. The servants carry in food and wine.

ACT ONE, SCENE THREE   The guests, including Verona's most illustrious citizens, troubadours, and many friends of Juliet's, arrive for the ball; among the last to come are Paris and his page.

*Front Scene:* Hearing music, Romeo's friends Mercutio and Benvolio decide to disguise themselves and go to Capulet's ball. They persuade Romeo to join them. He puts on a domino mask.

ACT ONE, SCENE FOUR: THE BALLROOM OF THE CAPULETS' PALACE   Juliet with all their guests awaits the arrival of her parents, who now enter. Paris presents Juliet with a bouquet. The ball now begins with a formal dance during which the men lay cushions at the feet of the ladies, kneel and kiss the hems of their skirts. The ladies and gentlemen then dance separately, followed by a slow and stately ensemble. Now Juliet, who has been arranging flowers and watching, dances herself. The dance of the guests is resumed briefly and then Juliet dances again. Romeo and his friends enter. He is enchanted by Juliet and approaches her. Paris, however, intercedes. Mercutio dances to distract the guests. As they dance together, Romeo tells Juliet how beautiful she is. His mask falls from his face and Juliet sees him for the first time. Juliet is captivated. This man she could really love. But then Tybalt appears and thinks he recognizes Romeo, a sworn enemy of the family. He tells old Capulet. Romeo quickly puts his mask back on. Although Tybalt there and then wishes to attack Romeo, Mercutio comes between them.

*Front Scene:* After the guests have left, Juliet learns from her nurse that it is none other than Romeo, son of her father's enemy Montague, with whom she has fallen in love.

ACT ONE, SCENE FIVE: THE GARDEN   Juliet cannot sleep and comes out on her moonlit balcony. She can only think of Romeo, whom she suddenly sees in the garden. They confess their love for each other and dance.

ACT TWO, SCENE ONE: THE MAIN SQUARE OF VERONA   Revelers throng the square. There are dances for the crowd and waitresses at the inn. A procession enters carrying an image of the Madonna. Benvolio and Mercutio flirt with ladies at the cafe and dance with the waitresses and there is another ensemble for the revelers. The nurse pushes her way through the crowds, looking for Romeo to give him a message from Juliet. He enters the square and the nurse whispers to him.

*Front Scene:* Romeo reads that Juliet has consented to be his wife and rapturously presses the letter to his heart.

ACT TWO, SCENE TWO: FRIAR LAURENCE'S CELL   On a simple table stand some flowers and a skull, which the friar is contemplating when Romeo enters. Romeo kneels before the friar and asks him to marry them secretly. Nervously waiting for Juliet to come, his hands play with the skull and the flowers. Juliet, wearing a black cape, rushes in. Friar Laurence marries them and hopes that their union will end the strife between the Montagues and Capulets.

*Front Scene:* The Montagues and Capulets are in the main square as the procession of the Madonna moves across. Mercutio buys fruit and gives it to his friends. Tybalt bursts into rage when a peddler's tray accidentally knocks into one of his companions. Both families are cruelly sensitive now to any possible offense.

ACT TWO, SCENE THREE: THE MAIN SQUARE OF VERONA   Revels continue in the square with a tambourine dance. Mercutio dances with waitresses at the inn. Tybalt enters and challenges Mercutio to a duel. Romeo tries to call it off and make peace but Tybalt mocks him and goads Mercutio into fighting. Mercutio is hit, struggles bravely against death but dies. Tybalt leaves, laughing. Romeo tries to hear Mercutio's heart and mourns. The body is borne out. Just as Romeo follows after, Tybalt comes back, insolent, swaggering. Romeo draws his sword, dashes up the stairs, and kills him. Romeo flees. The Capulets rush from their palace with the nurse. Lady Capulet so laments her kinsman's death that she is carried out gesturing wildly on his bier. The prince of Verona declares Romeo an exile for life.

ACT THREE, SCENE ONE: JULIET'S ROOM   At dawn the next morning, Romeo opens the curtain onto the balcony and watches the sun. Juliet pulls the curtain back and the two lovers dance an impassioned *pas de deux.* But the household is stirring and Romeo must go. He embraces Juliet for the last time. As he leaves by the balcony, Juliet's parents and Paris enter with the nurse. Paris tries to woo Juliet but is scorned. Hurt by Juliet's rebuff, Paris leaves. Juliet tells her parents that she will not marry him. They are angry and threaten to disown her. The mother and the nurse leave and the father tries to force Juliet to submit to his will. She dances in despair when he has finally left her alone. Then quickly she finds her cape and runs out.

*Front Scene:* Juliet rushes to Friar Laurence.

ACT THREE, SCENE TWO: FRIAR LAURENCE'S CELL   Juliet prays and relates her plight. She sees a dagger on the table and seizes it. Gently taking the dagger from her, Friar Laurence gives her instead a phial of sleeping potion which she must drink. She will then fall asleep, he tells her, and her parents, thinking her dead, will bury her in the family tomb. Meanwhile, Romeo, warned by Friar Laurence, will return under cover of darkness and take her away from Verona.

ACT THREE, SCENE THREE: JULIET'S BEDCHAMBER    It is evening and Juliet is with her family and Paris. She consents to marry Paris, they dance together, and her parents are jubilant. The nurse brings the wedding gown. Juliet is alone. She knows she must drink the potion but delays in a dance of indecision. She then quickly swallows the potion and falls back on the bed. Soon it is morning. Her friends come with troubadours to celebrate her engagement. Paris enters, eager to see his bride. But the wedding dress lies on a chair and Juliet still sleeps. Her mother comes and orders the nurse to waken her. She goes to the bed but starts back with a cry of terror. Juliet lies lifeless on the bed. All weep.

ACT THREE, SCENE FOUR: A STREET IN MANTUA    Romeo, alone, expresses his sorrow at his separation from Juliet. Outpacing Friar Laurence's messenger, Romeo's servant Balthasar arrives from Verona with the news that Juliet is dead. Stunned by grief, Romeo does not know what to do, then decides that he must go to his beloved.

ACT THREE, SCENE FIVE: THE CAPULET TOMB    Many attend Juliet's funeral and her body is placed in the family vault at the top of a flight of steps. Paris prays there and leaves. It grows dark. Romeo comes in, mounts the steps, removes her shroud and holds Juliet in his arms. He kisses her, then picks her up to carry her briefly down the steps. He ascends again, holding her high over his head, and places her on her tomb. He then drinks a phial of poison and dies, falling back down the steps. Juliet now awakes from her sleeping potion. She sees Romeo and at first thinks him perhaps asleep, as she has been, but he is dead. She takes his dagger at once and stabs herself. She falls back over his body.

EPILOGUE    Over the bodies of their children, the Montagues and the Capulets, followed by the populace, take each other's hands and swear to end their feud. All kneel.

NOTES    Prokofiev's score to *Romeo and Juliet* was completed September 8, 1935, soon after his return to Russia from Paris. It was first performed at a concert in Moscow in October of that year. Prokofiev's plan at that time was that the ballet should end happily, with Juliet resurrected in her tomb and a final joyous *pas de deux* for the two lovers. This idea received some criticism and the composer abandoned it. He said at the time: "I have taken special pains to achieve a simplicity that will, I hope, reach the hearts of all listeners. If people find no melody and no emotion in this work of mine, I shall be very sorry; but I feel that they will, sooner or later."

Some time elapsed before the score was first used for ballet, and this was in Brno, Czechoslovakia in 1938. Meanwhile, two suites arranged by Prokofiev were played in the U.S.S.R. and the United States.

The Soviet choreographer Leonid Lavrovsky published notes about his conception of the ballet, which was first produced in 1940: "The depths of passion and ideas, the intensity of feeling conveyed by the protagonists of Shakespeare's tragedy, demand the fusion of dance with mime. In ballet, words are absent and the effect of every phrase of mime must correspond with the spoken language of the stage characters. Mime should never descend to trivial, commonplace, imitative gestures, but become a genuine theatrical performance, in which characters, emotion, and passion are expressed by the movements of the body, instead of by the varied intonations of the voice. Ballet is a choreographic play in which the dancing must arise naturally from the mimed action, or the mimed action be the logical sequence of the dancing."

A film of Lavrovsky's *Romeo and Juliet* was produced in the U.S.S.R. in 1954, with Galina Ulanova.

When the Bolshoi's *Romeo and Juliet* was first presented in New York, Edwin Denby, writing about it for *The Hudson Review* (now included in his book *Dancers, Buildings and People in the Streets*), spoke of Ulanova's vividness:

"Bending her neck toward her partner in a lift of the Bedroom Scene, the gesture had the tragic quiet Pasternak speaks of. Or take the opposite kind of moment. Faced with marriage to County Paris, Juliet, her mantle flung round her, desperately rushes along the apron to Friar Laurence; armed by him with the sleeping potion, she flings the mantle round her again, and rushes desperately along the apron back home. The fling, the rush, the exact repeat are pure 'Perils of Pauline.' But Ulanova's art at that moment is so brilliant the audience breaks into delighted applause.

"You can find out something about Bolshoi style by trying the gymnastics of Ulanova's fling and rush yourself. Standing in the middle of the room, fling an arm across your chest, and at the same time raise the breastbone as high as it will go, bending it over at the top so it pushes the neck back. Don't let go, keep forcing the breastbone further, but in addition push the neck forward as hard as you can, and lift your head until you feel 'desperately resolved.' (It may make you cough.) And now, keeping the stance you are in unchanged, rush about the room with an incredible lightness and rapidity. If your family is watching, they will pick you off the floor, and urge you to try harder.

"The special stance of fling and rush you just tried (it involves a backbend between the shoulder-blades) is not classical. It has been called the pouter-pigeon silhouette by Walter Terry, and that is just how it looks. But when Ulanova does it, you feel it means, 'Here is my heart.'

"But if you notice that, you also notice her feet. In light runs on toe (bourrée steps) they seem to touch the floor sensitively. You see how keen the pointed foot looks in the air, during attitudes, arabesques, and passés, how clearly the leg defines and differentiates the different classic shapes. Below the waist Ulanova is a strict classicist; above the waist she alters the shape of classic motions now slightly, now quite a lot, to specify a nuance of drama (for example, the pouter-pigeon silhouette). Neither element—the lightness below or the weight above—is weakened for the sake of the other; the combined motion keeps fluid. And often while one movement is ebbing to its end, another seems already welling up in the midriff."

*Narrative ballet in one act, based on the play by Shakespeare. Music by Frederick Delius. Choreography by Antony Tudor. Scenery and costumes by Eugene Berman. First presented by Ballet Theatre at the Metropolitan Opera House, New York, April 6, 1943, with Alicia Markova as Juliet, Hugh Laing as Romeo, Nicolas Orloff as Mercutio, Antony Tudor as Tybalt, and Jerome Robbins as Benvolio.*

This dramatic ballet compresses into one vivid act the tragic love story of Romeo and Juliet. Within a single-unit setting representing the ordered golden beauty of the Italy of the Renaissance, the narrative proceeds without scenic interruption; and what might be spoken of as "scenes," in an ordinary dramatic spectacle, move together and coalesce with a flow that suggests the inevitability of the tragedy itself.

The score for the ballet is an arrangement by Antal Dorati of selected works by Delius: *Over the Hills and Far Away, The Walk to the Paradise Garden, Eventyr,* and *Brigg Fair.*

PROLOGUE   The curtain rises immediately on a drop curtain depicting the entrance to a palace in Verona. There are two great arches to the left and right, and in the center, cut out of the curtain, is a draped entry. A spotlight centers on this doorway, and Romeo steps out cautiously. He looks behind him, and Rosaline, a beautiful girl, follows him. Romeo takes her hand and attempts to embrace her. Rosaline warns him that he is too hasty, and Romeo follows her impatiently within.

Now members of the opposing families of Montague and Capulet dance onto the scene and challenge each other. The two leaders of the factions, Mercutio and Tybalt, are eager for a contest, and the two groups commence dueling. But the heads of the two houses at variance with each other enter with their wives and order their kinsmen to desist. The men reluctantly abandon their fighting and bow to the peers. It is apparent that their battle will be renewed at the first opportunity. Romeo and his friend Mercutio remain behind when the others have left. Only the entrance of the fair Rosaline persuades them that they have better business elsewhere.

BALL AT THE HOUSE OF THE CAPULETS   The drop curtain rises on a wide, open area of red marble enclosed by a decorative colonnade. Couples in richly embroidered costumes are dancing in elegant, courtly fashion. The music softens, and Juliet enters on the right. She lingers slightly, hesitating to step into the ballroom, for she knows what awaits her. She greets her parents warmly, yet formally. Capulet turns to introduce her to a young nobleman, Paris, but Juliet seeks instead the company of her cousin Tybalt. The understanding

Tybalt consoles her, but also reminds her of her duty and leads her to Paris. The assembled company begin to dance again, and Juliet accepts Paris as her partner.

Romeo enters on the right. He looks directly at Juliet. Juliet, her back to Paris for a moment, glances back at him. As Paris bends down to kiss her hand, Juliet looks across the room toward Romeo. The dance continues, and Romeo chooses a partner to join the ball. The two couples dance on opposite sides of the room. The set pattern of the dance separates them, and Juliet and Romeo despair of meeting. Soon the entire company circles the hall and the dance ends. The guests proceed to move toward the rear for refreshment, and Romeo and Juliet are alone.

Romeo falls at her feet and declares the overpowering love he has felt since he saw her. He rises, their faces touch, and they kiss. Then, formal again, the two bow to each other and begin to dance together a delicate, flowing measure. When the dance is over, they realize that they must separate and both say their farewells. But as they turn to go, they move together again and kneel.

Mercutio and Tybalt emerge from the banquet hall. Juliet's nurse urges her away, lest there be trouble. Tybalt warns Romeo and turns to Juliet questioningly, and all depart.

ROMEO WOOS JULIET IN THE CAPULET ORCHARD The lights dim. White drapes are drawn across the back colonnade. Four torchbearers enter on the right, followed by Romeo and Mercutio. Romeo is preoccupied and will not listen to his friend's appreciation of the beauty of the evening. Mercutio grows impatient and tells his friend that the romance he contemplates is out of the question. The music builds in intensity, and Romeo refuses to heed Mercutio's advice. Mercutio leaps to the back of one of the torchbearers and urges Romeo to follow them to a tavern. Romeo pretends to go, then conceals himself. The others return to look for him, but soon follow after Mercutio.

Two couples enter. Romeo holds his arm across his face, lest he be recognized. The couples disappear, and Romeo dances alone. Above the colonnade at the rear, Juliet looks down into the orchard and sees her lover. She is enchanted and rests her head sweetly on the balcony railing, wondering when he will look up and see her. Romeo glances up and blows kisses to her. She returns the kisses, but warns him away. Just as he hides behind a pillar on the right, Juliet's nurse comes into the garden. No sooner has she departed than Tybalt and Paris stroll by. When they are alone again, Romeo holds out his hands to Juliet and from above she gestures to him yearningly. Romeo gestures defiance of their families and proposes marriage. Juliet consents.

BETROTHAL OF ROMEO AND JULIET BY THE FRIAR Drapes are drawn across the colonnade, and Friar Laurence stands in his cell. Romeo enters. He is impatient and afraid and paces the floor. There is a sound at the door, and Romeo rushes to see who it is. Friar Laurence pulls him back warningly. Romeo's back is turned as Juliet runs into the room. He turns to her, and the two kneel before the friar, who blesses them. Juliet rises, turns rapidly, and falls low in Romeo's arms. Then she rushes off into the night, promising him that her nurse will bring him a message.

STREET SCENE   The curtains are drawn back, the friar disappears, and the open area becomes the street. It is still night. A cripple and a blind man enter, followed by the gay Mercutio and a friend. Romeo enters, followed by Juliet and her nurse. The nurse beckons Juliet away. The concern of the lovers is contrasted with the friction between their families, for Tybalt has entered and threatened Mercutio in earnest. The two fight, their kinsmen join the battle, and the music is ominous, like the sound of an approaching storm. Mercutio is stabbed by Tybalt and dies in Romeo's arms.

Romeo recovers from his grief and attacks Tybalt. He leaps to his back, forces him down, and stabs him to death. Now there is no hope of reconciling the two families. Romeo does not know what to do. Friar Laurence enters and takes the dagger from him. Finally the youth is persuaded that he must flee for his life.

Juliet and her nurse enter the square and see what has happened. Juliet weeps for Tybalt, but then, suddenly desperate, instructs the nurse to run to Romeo and reassure him.

ROMEO'S FAREWELL TO JULIET   The scene is Juliet's bedroom. Day is breaking. Juliet rises first and dances joyfully, with a sweet, youthful happiness, as Romeo watches her from the bed. She returns to him, he lifts her, and they embrace. Romeo prepares to leave. He must escape from Verona. They will meet elsewhere. Juliet weeps because of her happiness and its quick ending. They kiss. Romeo departs, and Juliet falls back on the bed, still weeping.

PREPARATIONS FOR THE WEDDING OF JULIET TO PARIS   Some time passes, and handmaidens to Juliet enter with her nurse to prepare her for the marriage her parents have insisted upon. They waken Juliet. Instantly she sits up and looks off into the direction that Romeo took when he left her. She cannot believe that this day she must marry another man. The nurse holds her in her arms and tries to comfort her. Juliet rises and protests to her father that she cannot marry Paris. Capulet refuses to listen to her or to his wife, who tries to intercede for Juliet.

Then, to the accompaniment of a melody almost unbearable in its sweetness and pathos, Juliet's four handmaidens form a tableau beside her. They hold before her a wedding dress of gold, and Juliet slips her arms into it as if the cloth were on fire.

When she is dressed, she weeps softly in her father's arms. Her father blesses her and places on her head a shining crown. She is presented with a bouquet of white flowers. Friar Laurence enters, and Juliet falls into his arms. When they are unobserved, the friar gives her a vial containing a secret drug and instructs her to drink it without delay: all may yet be well.

Juliet walks away, drinks the contents of the vial, whirls frantically, and swoons. Her family gathers about her. Six women bear slowly across the stage a great cloth trimmed in somber black.

PROCESSION TO THE TOMB   Two of Juliet's attendants head her funeral procession. Juliet lies on a bier carried high by her black-cloaked kinsmen. Her father and mother follow behind. When the procession has passed, the women holding up the cloth of mourning disappear to reveal another scene.

SCENE IN THE VAULT OF THE CAPULETS   We are in Juliet's tomb. She lies immobile on her bier, her hands pressed together at her breast. Romeo enters. He imagines that his beloved is dead and drinks a vial of poison. He falls at the foot of the bier.

Juliet gradually revives from the drug she has taken. She rises. Romeo sees her, pulls himself up with difficulty, reaches out for her, and—when Juliet comes to him—lifts her with his remaining strength. He falls. Juliet understands what has happened. She spins around and around frantically. Romeo rises again and lifts her in his arms. He holds her for a moment, then collapses across her bier. He dies. Juliet looks down upon him. She takes out his dagger, waits for a moment, and—rising suddenly on point, as if to meet the happiness only death can bring her—stabs herself in the heart. She falls across her lover's body and, with her last gesture, touches his face.

NOTES   Tudor's *Romeo and Juliet* was revived by American Ballet Theatre, July 22, 1971, at the New York State Theatre, Lincoln Center. The critic Deborah Jowitt wrote in the *Village Voice:* "What Antony Tudor did in his 1943 *Romeo and Juliet,* now revived by Ballet Theatre, makes it one of the most brilliant and interesting of recent ballets. In particular, he has worked with the structure of the play so as to situate it in the kind of Renaissance time and space with which Shakespeare's work has so many affinities.

"As Wylie Sypher pointed out in his *Four Stages of Renaissance Style,* the plot of *Romeo and Juliet* is an essay in symmetry and proportion. Capulet is weighed against Montague, Romeo's passion against Paris's suitability, love against hate, night against day, rashness against prudence, etc. Time is compressed into forty-two hours; space is defined and confined by the walls of Verona's chambers, gardens, piazzas. There is none of the depth, irregularity, or ripeness of the later *Hamlet* or *Macbeth.*

"Tudor has set his version of this sad and lyrical equation in what might be compared to a continuous Botticelli frieze. There is an emphasis on elegant, agitated, fastidiously sensual flow rather than on volume. It is as if Tudor had speeded up the heartbeat of the play, so tremulous is one's reaction to it. His space, like Botticelli's, is almost more medieval than Renaissance: depth is created by temporary hierarchies, events separated in time can coexist in space. When Romeo and Juliet wind through the pillars of the piazza in an ecstatic return from their wedding, they are small upstage figures, seen through the minor bustle of the square. When Juliet, enveloped by the nurse, weeps over Tybalt down left, their figures are balanced by those of Romeo and Friar Laurence consulting hastily down right. And the two tableaux are separated by a temporary 'wall' formed by two watching women. Tudor's use of these women is another odd detail. They witness the action from different positions, like those little faces in the corners of certain medieval paintings.

"The effect of all this compression on the spectator is fascinating. There is no blood, thunder, bombast; the action is drawn lightly over you like a veil while you sit in a state of almost febrile tension. Events, briefly sketched, flow out of each other; even what Tudor has chosen to show or not show is revealing. Nothing seems to have any preliminaries. The Montague boys' decision to attend the Capulet ball is conveyed to Mercutio's brusquely beckoning finger, while the powerful effect of the lovers' first meeting on Romeo and his friends is shown more fully. Letters are not delivered, potions are drunk, marriages are arranged at high speed and with pictorial clarity.

"Eugene Berman's marvelous pillars, archways and porticos hold and shape the action, add to the morbid delicacy of atmosphere. When a curtain is drawn to reveal the ball in progress, the dancers first appear cramped, too large for the space they inhabit—another painterly touch. Tudor's choice of excerpts from Delius is extremely unusual. The music meanders along its own path—painting a lush, summer atmosphere that is neither dramatically nor rhythmically assertive, but full of feeling. Often it creates a curious tension between its dreamy flow and the action of the play. For instance, the insistent little tappings and steppings of the court dances begin to be almost ominous against the inconclusive music.

"Since nothing in this ballet ever really stops, pauses for large scale 'dance numbers' would have been unthinkable. Tudor has built the dancing out of gesture so subtly and naturally that you are not aware of anything but the continuous unfolding of this lyrical disquisition on action. There is a ball scene, of course, quietly and slowly built up. There is no *grand pas de deux* for the balcony scene: alone on the stage floor, Romeo bursts into an exulting stammer of leaps and postures and wide-flung gestures, while Juliet on the balcony above returns his passion with slow and happy stretchings and curvings of her body and arms. Even the morning-after-the-wedding scene turns into a dance imperceptibly through a series of muted rushings, claspings, near-swoons.

"Because nothing seems calculated, no particular moments of dance can be easily isolated. Pointe work has a special expressive function. Juliet steps up onto pointe as if some delicate emotional balance were at stake, or as if she were on unfamiliar ground. In some of her steps, she might be swooning upward."

The critic Marcia Siegel wrote in the Boston *Globe:* "Antony Tudor's *Romeo and Juliet* is a beautiful ballet. An extraordinary ballet. I think it's the best new ballet I've seen this year, even though it's really a revival, originally choreographed in 1943 for the infant Ballet Theatre. Restaged July 22 by that company, with Carla Fracci and Ivan Nagy in the opening-night title roles, it's a deeply moving and interesting work. I don't know when I've seen a ballet with such clarity and distinction of detail.

"Tudor saw the perennial story in quite intimate terms, encompassed in one act with several scenes. This makes for a tighter production—the story moves quickly, building to its powerful tragic end, without the long interpolations of sword-play and ceremony that pad out more grandiose Romeo and Juliet ballets. There's considerably less display dancing, smaller crowds, and less exposition, but I think this makes sense. Tudor's ballet is about the star-crossed lovers. The John Cranko and Kenneth MacMillan versions we've seen here in recent years are about the spectacular possibilities of a full-length ballet based on Shakespeare's play—quite a different thing.

"Fracci and Nagy are splendid as the doomed couple. Fracci is one of our best actress-dancers, and Nagy, released by Tudor's unstereotyped movement from the conventional suffering nobility of his other roles, was more convincing, more alive to the dramatic situation than I've ever seen him. All their scenes together breathed wonder and changeableness, joy touched with disbelief, a sort of shining despair.

"Tudor set the ballet in the Italian Renaissance, and much of the movement looks like the paintings and court dances of the period—the men with one leg turned out and pointing a fashionable toe, the women tilting back with their weight thrust mincingly forward. At times the company looked awkward with these stylizations, but Bruce Marks as Tybalt, Rosanna Seravalli as Lady Capulet, and Bonnie Mathis as Rosaline showed me immediately what the shape of the movement is, how it works. What intelligent character dancers these three are!

"There's more in this ballet, both in its dancing and production, than I can discuss in one day, but Tudor's choice of Delius' music is indicative of his unusual concept. The elegaic, rich-textured, but not especially dancy score seems at first too impressionistic to support the tragedy. But in fact it reinforces the ballet's delicate romanticism and isn't overpowering as the more familiar Prokofiev *Romeo and Juliet* usually is.

"Eugene Berman's multilevel set suggests both the scaffolded flexibility of a Shakespearean stage and the columns and perspective of an Italian painting. . . .

"I went back to see Antony Tudor's *Romeo and Juliet,* given by American Ballet Theatre, and found it as fascinating as I had the first time. It's a ballet of ideas—not philosophical or moral preachings, but ideas about how to present a classic story.

"Ballets are produced in such quantity here, and with so little attention to durability, that they often seem to be a matter of choosing new spices to liven up the same old hamburger. Tudor's *Romeo* constitutes a rethinking of every aspect of the narrative ballet. He uses all theatrical elements to suggest the depth and universality of the theme, instead of just letting us recognize what we already know about it.

"Eugene Berman's opening drop shows a small Romanesque building, possibly a tomb, suspended against a blue sea or sky, just hanging there, a door to something insubstantial and timeless. Classical allusions keep recurring quietly. You notice during the principals' first duet that the other guests at the Capulets' ball have seated themselves beyond some pillars, at a dinner table in another room. Their backs are to the audience; they are too close to the stage for realism. They look flat, like the background of a Renaissance painting. Juliet's friends, dressed like Botticelli nymphs, lift a shroud across the stage where Juliet's drugged body lies, and stand there throughout the funeral procession, echoing the statues perched atop the colonnaded set.

"The changes of scene—there are about ten of them—are accomplished in a variety of ingenious ways, many involving characters in the ballet. In fact, two 'attendants' watch the whole ballet from a bench downstage, moving around to draw curtains and even, at one point, simulating a wall. They are spectators of the tragedy who also help present it to us, and at the same time they belong to the House of Capulet as servants. This is an Elizabethan device as well as a classical reference. Realistic theater didn't come along till the late nineteenth century, and Tudor isn't offering us a modern romance. Other critics have objected to the extremely stylized quality of this *Romeo*, as if that were a drawback, and as if *all* ballet weren't a stylization to begin with. I suggest that Tudor's concept of production has the same elevating effect on the story that Shakespeare's poetry has."*

*Ballet in eleven scenes with prologue, based on Shakespeare's play. Music by Sergei Prokofiev. Choreography by Frederick Ashton. Scenery and costumes by Peter Rice. First presented by the Royal Danish Ballet at the Royal Theatre, Copenhagen, May 19, 1955, with Mona Vangsaae and Henning Kronstam in the title roles. First presented in the United States by the Royal Danish Ballet at the Metropolitan Opera House, New York, September 26, 1956.*

Frederick Ashton's ballet follows this scenario:

At Verona there is constant feuding between the families of Montague and Capulet. A party of young men from Montague's household are present at an entertainment at Capulet's house. Among them is Romeo, who falls in love at first sight with Juliet, Capulet's only child. Romeo and Juliet declare their love for each other. They are secretly married by Friar Laurence. The brawls are continued. Romeo's friend Mercutio is killed by Tybalt, of the House of Capulet. Romeo kills Tybalt and is forced to flee. He takes refuge with Friar Laurence.

Meanwhile, old Capulet decides that Juliet shall marry Count Paris. The friar, hoping to bring about a reconciliation, advises Romeo to say farewell to Juliet and to hide in Mantua. When he learns of old Capulet's decision, he gives Juliet a sleeping draught which will produce a deathlike sleep. Juliet is believed dead, and is buried in the vault of her ancestors. The friar's message to Romeo miscarries. Supposing that his wife is indeed dead, Romeo hurries to the tomb, and commits suicide over her body. Juliet wakes too late, finds Romeo dead, and kills herself with his dagger.

*Ballet in three acts after William Shakespeare. Music by Sergei Prokofiev. Choreography and staging by John Cranko. Décor and costumes by Jürgen Rose. In the repertory of the National Ballet of Canada. First staged by John Cranko for the ballet of La Scala, Milan, at the Teatro Verde, in Venice,*

* Reprinted from Marcia B. Siegel's book, *At the Vanishing Point*, 1972.

*July 26, 1958; this production was extensively revised and first presented by the Stuttgart Ballet at the Württemberg State Theatre, Stuttgart, December 2, 1962. The Stuttgart Ballet production was first presented in the United States at the Metropolitan Opera House, New York, June 18, 1969, with Marcia Haydée as Juliet, Richard Cragun as Romeo, Jan Stripling as Tybalt, and Egon Madsen as Mercutio.*

The scene is Verona.

ACT ONE, SCENE ONE: THE MARKET PLACE   As day breaks, Romeo, son of Montague, is found declaring his love to the fair Rosaline. With the sunrise, the market place fills with townspeople, among whom are members of the two rival families, the Capulets and the Montagues. Tempers flare and a quarrel develops. The Duke of Verona appears and warns the two factions that death will be the ultimate punishment if the feud does not stop. Romeo and his friends Benvolio and Mercutio make reluctant peace with Tybalt, a kinsman of the Capulets.

ACT ONE, SCENE TWO: JULIET'S GARDEN IN THE CAPULETS' HOUSE   Juliet receives her first ball dress from her mother, Lady Capulet, and learns that she is to meet the noble Paris to whom she will be betrothed on the following day. Now she must bid farewell to her childhood.

ACT ONE, SCENE THREE: OUTSIDE THE CAPULETS' HOUSE   Guests appear for the Capulets' ball, among them Rosaline. Romeo and his friends, masked, follow her to the ball.

ACT ONE, SCENE FOUR: THE BALLROOM   Juliet dances with Paris but suddenly she and Romeo behold each other, and it is love at first sight. Tybalt, suspecting Romeo's identity, tries to start an argument but is prevented by Juliet's father who abides by the laws of hospitality.

ACT ONE, SCENE FIVE: JULIET'S BEDROOM   On the balcony outside her bedroom Juliet dreams of Romeo. He appears below in the garden. They declare their eternal love.

ACT TWO, SCENE ONE: THE MARKET PLACE   A carnival is in progress in the main square. Romeo, indifferent to the gaiety around him, is discovered by Juliet's nurse, who brings him a letter from her. She asks Romeo to meet her at the chapel of Friar Laurence.

ACT TWO, SCENE TWO: FRIAR LAURENCE'S CELL IN THE FOREST   In his cell, Friar Laurence joins the young lovers in marriage.

ACT TWO, SCENE THREE: THE MARKET PLACE   At the height of the carnival, Romeo returns to the square. Tybalt accosts him but Romeo declines to fight.

Mercutio, angered, engages in a duel with Tybalt, and dies at his hands. Romeo, distraught, turns on Tybalt and kills him.

ACT THREE, SCENE ONE: THE BEDROOM   In Juliet's bedroom the lovers are awakened by the sunrise, and Romeo, under sentence of exile, must leave Juliet and Verona. Lord and Lady Capulet enter with Paris, but Juliet rejects him.

ACT THREE, SCENE TWO: FRIAR LAURENCE'S CELL IN THE FOREST   Juliet, appealing for help to Friar Laurence, receives a potion from him that will place her in a deathlike sleep. He explains that Romeo will find her in the family tomb and both can escape together.

ACT THREE, SCENE THREE: THE BEDROOM   Juliet agrees to her marriage with Paris. After he leaves with her parents, she takes the sleeping draught and is thought to be dead when her family and friends discover her.

ACT THREE, SCENE FOUR: THE CAPULET FAMILY CRYPT   Romeo, who has never received Friar Laurence's message revealing the plan, believes Juliet to be dead and rushes to her tomb. There he finds the mourning Paris and kills him. Embracing Juliet for the last time, he plunges his dagger into his heart. Juliet awakens to find Romeo dead. Grief-stricken, she kills herself.

Reviewing a performance of Cranko's ballet by the Stuttgart Ballet at the Metropolitan Opera House in the spring of 1973, the critic Andrew Porter wrote in *The New Yorker:* "There can be little dispute that Prokofiev's *Romeo and Juliet* is the most successful full-length ballet score written since Tchaikovsky's. I have seen it set to movement in six different versions, and only one of them—Serge Lifar's, for the Paris Opéra—was without marked merit. John Cranko's, created for the Stuttgart Ballet in 1962, and chosen for the opening night, last week, of the company's current Metropolitan season, is a very successful dance drama that has worn well. It continues to display the special virtues and strongly individual character of the troupe for whom it was made, and provides extended, uncommonly telling roles for the major stars—Marcia Haydée, Egon Madsen, and Richard Cragun—that shine in the splendid ensemble. The Royal Ballet, they say, dances best in New York; perhaps the Stuttgarters do so, too. I was bowled over on the first night by the power and eloquence of their presentation, and certainly Jürgen Rose's *Romeo* scenery and costumes never look as handsome and striking as they do on the Metropolitan stage. Dramatic force, potent projection, is a mark of German dancing; in Stuttgart, with his international team of dancers, Mr. Cranko has combined this force with Royal Ballet 'school,' developed his artists by composing new works for and 'on' them, and created one of the world's leading companies.

"Approaches to a Shakespeare ballet are almost as diverse as those to a Shakespeare opera. Prokofiev in his *Romeo* score devised appropriate melodies and motifs for the characters and their attributes (Juliet as a girl, Juliet as a woman, Romeo's ardor, Mercutio's wit, etc.), wrote movements that mount to passionate climaxes in the right places, supplied the necessary (and some unnecessary) ensemble dances, and achieved all this with his wonted flair for theatre music. Leonid Lavrovsky did the original choreography; his version was first performed, in Leningrad, in 1940. He worked on the piece with Prokofiev (and once told me how tiresome and silly the composer had been—wanting, for a while, a happy ending, not wanting to lose a Dance of Carpet Sellers that he had somehow managed to bring in). While Prokofiev's 'libretto' was, so to speak, the plot, the characters, and their emotions, the choreographer added a more detailed attention to Shakespeare; in his version specific lines from the play seem often to ring out from the motion of the dancers: Romeo's 'O! she doth teach the torches to burn bright' when first he sees Juliet, his 'I do protest I never injur'd thee' to Tybalt, and then, after Mercutio's death, 'Fire-ey'd fury be my conduct now,' Juliet's 'My only love sprung from my only hate,' her 'Is there no pity sitting in the clouds?,' and many others. By comparison, Ashton's version for the Royal Danish Ballet, in 1955, to the same score, was a Lamb's Tale that became lyric poetry in the duets for the lovers. Kenneth MacMillan's *Romeo* for Covent Garden, ten years later, borrowed Cranko's solutions to the structural problems set by Prokofiev's ensembles, and acquired its special character from the detailed concentration on Juliet's development. In the monologues and duologues of MacMillan's version there is the same sense found in Lavrovsky's of words just below the surface of the dance. The successive quatrains and couplets of the antiphonal sonnet spoken by Romeo and Juliet when first they meet ('If I profane with my unworthiest hand') are transmuted into plastic imagery. Cranko's *Romeo* is more generalized, less intense in its close-ups. We do not follow the balcony and bedroom scenes 'line by line'; his approach, like Prokofiev's, is less literary. But the dances do not lack emotion, and they flow effectively. Cranko's presentation of the world around the tragedy—the street scenes, the assembly of Capulet's guests, the ball—is the most successful of all; a theatre flair kin to Prokofiev's is apparent in his handling. I miss Juliet's pas de deux with Paris on the wedding morning, a poignant moment in both the Lavrovsky and the MacMillan versions; the Friar Laurence scenes are rather skimpy, and Act III passes too swiftly. (Lavrovsky did well to insert a solo for Romeo in Mantua, corresponding to 'Is it even so? then I defy you, stars!') Comparisons are helpful in description; in its own right, Cranko's *Romeo* is an excellently vigorous, youthful, unrhetorical yet affecting work, couched in a fluent, eclectic choreography that I suppose could be called free-Fokine with modern ingredients, and very skillful in its theatrical shaping.

"The first night presented the nonpareil cast of Miss Haydée and Mr. Cragun in the title roles and Mr. Madsen as Mercutio. The second brought a new Juliet, the young Joyce Cuoco, touching and vulnerable, a promising actress and fleet technician—prone, in fact, to phrase some of the lyrical choreography too crisply. The Romeo and Mercutio swapped roles: Mr. Madsen now made a courteous, romantic Romeo, rather less boldly ardent than Mr. Cragun had been, while as Mercutio Mr. Cragun lacked only the twinkling beats with which Mr. Madsen had tripped through the Queen Mab solo. Jan Stripling's cold, strong Tybalt, the contrasted interpretations of Paris from Reid Anderson (a formal wooer) and Vladimir Klos (more tender), and Andrew Oxenham's bright Benvolio deserve mention; so do the unforced buoyancy, verve, and warmth with which the whole company took the stage."*

> *Ballet in three acts. Music by Sergei Prokofiev. Choreography by Kenneth MacMillan. Scenery and costumes by Nicholas Georgiadis. Lighting by William Bundy. First presented by the Royal Ballet at the Royal Opera House, Covent Garden, February 9, 1965, with Rudolf Nureyev and Margot Fonteyn as Romeo and Juliet. First presented in the United States by the Royal Ballet at the Metropolitan Opera House, New York, April 21, 1965.*

The English critic and editor Peter Williams has said, "The game of love and death is the theater's trump card, and Shakespeare was no fool about what made good theater, the rules of which have varied little in any language from the threshing floors of Greece until the present day." Kenneth MacMillan's version of *Romeo and Juliet*, while based on the Prokofiev score used by a number of choreographers, varies substantially in treatment and detail.

ACT ONE, SCENE ONE: THE MARKET PLACE   The curtain rises on a dark stage. Then, to pizzicato strings, the stage is gradually lighted, revealing the market place. It is early morning, and the market is not yet busy. Romeo enters and tries to declare his love for the lovely Rosaline, who rejects him. Romeo joins his friends Mercutio and Benvolio, and, as day breaks and the market begins to fill up with butchers and farmers, Romeo takes off his cape and watches idly. A girl tries to entice him away. With two other harlots, she becomes involved with Romeo and his friends. A quarrel now develops between Tybalt, a nephew of Capulet, and Romeo. The Capulets and Montagues are of course sworn enemies and a fight begins. The heads of the two families join the dispute and do not assist a solution. The Prince of Verona appears and is obliged to order them to cease their feuding. All place their swords on the ground at his command, in front of the slain, but the two families stand opposite each other, obstinate in their rage.

ACT ONE, SCENE TWO: JULIET'S ANTEROOM IN THE CAPULETS' HOUSE   After a brief musical interlude, the curtain rises on a bright and cheerful room. There are large bird cages to the right and left, and Juliet's nurse sits waiting. Juliet runs in and we are reminded at once that this girl who will become a tragic figure is at heart a child of fourteen. She plays with a doll. She reacts like a spoiled child, too, when her mother and father come in with Paris, whom she does not like. But Juliet is nevertheless interested somewhat in anyone who would express interest in marrying her; she yields to her father's insistence and is nice to him. When the Capulets and Paris leave, Juliet wants to resume her play with the doll, but the nurse points out that her childhood is over, that she

---

* From *A Musical Season* by Andrew Porter (Viking Press); © 1973 Andrew Porter. Originally in *The New Yorker*.

is a young woman now, about to be beloved. Juliet clutches her heart. The
curtain falls.

ACT ONE, SCENE THREE: OUTSIDE THE CAPULETS' HOUSE   Two huge iron gates
guard the entrance to the Capulet palace, where guests are arriving for a
masked ball. Romeo, Mercutio, and Benvolio, disguised in masks, enter.
Romeo flirts with a lady who drops a rose for him to pick up—the fair Rosaline.
Then he and his friends dance a vigorous, high-spirited *pas de trois*. They decide then to follow the lady into the ball. They are aware that they do so in
some danger.

ACT ONE, SCENE FOUR: THE BALLROOM   Romeo and his friends arrive at the
height of the festivities. Still infatuated with Rosaline, Romeo follows her. He
comes face to face with Juliet for a moment. As Juliet dances with Paris,
Romeo watches, bewitched. As Paris kneels to kiss her hand, Juliet turns, sees
Romeo, and is visibly disturbed. She is given a mandolin and strums it as six of
her friends dance. But their dance is interrupted by one for Romeo, as if Juliet
could not get him out of her mind. He dances marvelously for her alone, and
kneels at her feet, taking her mandolin. But Paris quickly intercedes and Juliet
dances. Romeo, irresistibly drawn to her, comes to join Juliet, catching her
about the waist. Mercutio, seeing that Romeo is entranced with Juliet, dances
to distract attention from him. Later, Tybalt recognizes Romeo and orders him
to leave, but Capulet intervenes and welcomes him as a guest in his house.

ACT ONE, SCENE FIVE: OUTSIDE THE CAPULETS' HOUSE   As the ball breaks up
and the guests depart, Tybalt follows Romeo out. Lord Capulet intervenes and
Tybalt is restrained from pursuing Romeo.

ACT ONE, SCENE SIX: JULIET'S BALCONY   Unable to sleep, Juliet comes out
on her balcony, throws off her scarf and leans against a column. She thinks of
Romeo. Suddenly he is there, below in the garden. She runs swiftly down the
long flight of steps to him. He drops his cloak and goes to her. He puts his
hand to her heart and then dances for her. Now they dance together, confess
their love, and the die is cast.

ACT TWO, SCENE ONE: THE MARKET PLACE   The market bustles with activity; buyers and sellers jostle together, hooded monks mingle with the crowd.
Romeo, who can think only of Juliet, watches as a wedding procession passes
and dreams of the day he will marry her. Her nurse enters on the right, seeking Romeo. She gives him a letter in which he rejoices: Juliet has consented to
marry him, but with their families so opposed, they must do this secretly.
Thinking only of his bride, Romeo dances joyfully, then embraces the nurse
and rushes out.

ACT TWO, SCENE TWO: THE CHAPEL   The music is somber as the curtain rises
on Friar Laurence's cell. The monk enters and prays. First Romeo and then
Juliet and the nurse come. All kneel before the monk. Friar Laurence joins the

hands of the two lovers, hoping that their union will end the strife between the Montagues and the Capulets. The nurse weeps.

ACT TWO, SCENE THREE: THE MARKET PLACE   Meanwhile, the crowd in the market place is still celebrating. Interrupting the revelry, Tybalt tries to pick a fight with Romeo. At such a time, Romeo will not duel his wife's kinsman. But Tybalt will be fought with and before anyone can intercede, Mercutio has accepted the challenge and the two enemies fight with swords. Romeo begs Mercutio to stop. Tybalt stabs Mercutio in the back. Mercutio staggers. He still tries to fight, but dies with gaiety, his sword becoming for a moment his guitar as he plays his own lament. As Mercutio dies, Romeo in revenge attacks Tybalt and kills him. Romeo is exiled. Lady Capulet holds the body of her nephew, swaying back and forth in her grief as her husband watches helplessly.

ACT THREE, SCENE ONE: JULIET'S BEDROOM   Romeo and Juliet lie together on a canopied bed. He kisses her as the sun comes through the window. She sleeps on for a bit but soon they rise to dance ecstatically of their mutual joy. At the end they are sick with sadness that they must part. After a long kiss Romeo rushes to the balcony and away, while Juliet hurries back to bed just as the nurse enters. Her parents soon follow with Paris. Juliet, to her father's rage, repulses Paris. The nurse begs her to bahave, but she cannot. She prays to her father to forget this marriage. When he will not she throws herself on the bed and cries like a child. But the family closes in on her, bearing down and insisting. Juliet seems to reconsider but instead of going to Paris and being nice to him she circles him on point. Capulet will tolerate this no longer; he and his wife take Paris away. They leave Juliet lying in despair. She sits up then at the foot of the bed, vulnerable yet sure, tormented but determined to find a way out for herself and her lover. She takes up her cloak, gestures toward the balcony as if that would bring Romeo back, prays frantically, and then rushes off to see Friar Laurence.

ACT THREE, SCENE TWO: THE CHAPEL   Juliet falls at the friar's feet and begs for help. He gives her a phial of sleeping potion which will make her fall into a deathlike sleep. The monk further undertakes to warn Romeo that Juliet has taken the potion and is not really dead but that she must be rescued from the family tomb.

ACT THREE, SCENE THREE: JULIET'S BEDROOM   Juliet, back in her room, hides the phial under the pillow. When her parents come, she begs her mother's pardon. Her father is pleased that she seems to have come to her senses. Juliet dances for Paris but resists any real contact with him. He kisses the hem of her dress. Her parents decide not to force matters and then Juliet is alone. She goes to the bed for the phial, but is frightened at the possible consequences of taking it. Suppose she will really die? What if the potion does not work at all and she is compelled to marry Paris anyway? She sits at the foot of the bed and again she is a child, younger than we saw even at the beginning, caught up in a fate beyond her. But she takes the phial, drinks the sleeping potion, and expires on the bed.

The next morning Juliet seems to be asleep when six friends of the bride enter with flowers. They remark how quiet she is and try to waken her. The nurse comes in with Juliet's wedding dress and then her parents arrive. The nurse falls full length beside the bed when Capulet declares that his daughter is dead. All lament.

ACT THREE, SCENE FOUR: THE CAPULET FAMILY CRYPT  The curtain rises on the grim interior of an underground cavern. Juliet lies on a bier in the center. Her family mourns and monks with candles lament her passing. Paris remains behind to bid farewell to Juliet, but Romeo, disguised as a monk, throws off his cloak and attacks him. Paris is killed. Believing Juliet to be dead (the message from Friar Laurence has miscarried), but not believing it possible, Romeo lifts her from the bier and holds her. He dances with the dead body of his beloved, trying to revive her, but she falls back always in his arms. He places her on the tomb, then drinks a phial of poison that he has brought with him. Juliet wakes, but as she moves off the tomb she sees Romeo's body. She takes his dagger, which he has dropped near Paris's body, plunges it into her breast, and embraces Romeo.

*Ballet in three acts. Music by Sergei Prokofiev. Choreography by John Neumeier. Scenery and costumes by Jürgen Rose. Lighting by Jorgen Mydtskov. Produced by John Neumeier assisted by Ray Barra and Henning Kronstam for the Royal Danish Ballet at the Royal Theatre, Copenhagen, December 20, 1974. First presented in the United States by the Royal Danish Ballet at the Metropolitan Opera House, New York, May 20, 1976.*

A compression of four crucial days in April of a Verona long ago, this *Romeo and Juliet,* after defining the strife between the two enemy families, shows the rise and fall of the love of the daughter of one for the son of the other. The frame of the ballet, while showing the background of the city and the carnage engendered by hatred, focuses on intimacy. The *pas de deux* govern the action.

ACT ONE: THE FIRST DAY  Crowds throng the market place of Verona in front of the house of the Capulets on the day before the Feast of San Zeno, the city's patron saint. Infatuated with Rosaline, Juliet's cousin, Romeo pays court to her. Servants of the rival houses of Capulet and Montague clash until the Prince of Verona insists upon a cessation of hostilities.

The Capulets, entertaining at a huge ball, introduce their daughter Juliet to the Count Paris, whom they have selected as her husband. Crashing the party, Romeo finds himself face to face with a creature unimaginable to him. Juliet responds in similar fashion and, after the ball, under her balcony, the two meet to declare their love under the moon.

ACT TWO: THE SECOND DAY   In the midst of celebrations in the city, Romeo proposes marriage to Juliet and they are wed in secret by Friar Laurence. Back in the center of the town, unaware of what has taken place elsewhere, cousins of the newly wed pair, Mercutio and Tybalt, fight a duel, in which Mercutio, of Romeo's family, is killed. Coming upon the action, Romeo, in horror, and unable to prevent this outcome, challenges Juliet's cousin Tybalt and kills him.

ACT THREE: THE THIRD DAY   Tybalt's funeral calls out all the Capulets. Romeo, after his wedding night with Juliet, is obliged to flee because of his part in the duel. Endeavoring to escape her marriage to Count Paris, Juliet consults Friar Laurence, who arms her with a potion that will cause her to appear dead for a day. Pretending to assent to her parents' will, Juliet takes the potion.

ACT FOUR: THE FOURTH DAY   Believing her dead, Juliet's parents mourn deeply. Her funeral is prepared. Romeo, on his way to Mantua, learns of her death and races back to Verona, seeking Friar Laurence, who might have explained the liberation he and Juliet had arranged. He fails to find him and goes to Juliet, who is laid out in her tomb. Believing her dead, he stabs himself. Awakening from her day's sleep, Juliet finds her beloved at her side. Finding him dead, she kills herself with his dagger.

The critic George Dorris has written an important essay, "Prokofiev and the Ballet," which examines in detail the scores of *Romeo and Juliet* and other ballets by that composer (*Ballet Review*, Vol. 4, No. 6).

# ROOMS

*Music by Kenneth Hopkins. Choreography by Anna Sokolow. First presented at the YM-YWHA, New York, February 24, 1955, with Beatrice Seckler, Eve Beck, Donald McKayle, Jeff Duncan, Jack Moore, Sandra Pine, Judith Coy, and Paul Sanasardo.*

Anna Sokolow has written of this work: "I wanted to do something about people in a big city. The theme of loneliness and non-communication evolved as I worked. I like to look into windows, to catch glimpses of unfinished lives. Then I ask: 'What is there, and why?' Then I thought of using chairs as if they were rooms, each dancer on his own chair, isolated from all the others though physically so close to them."*

*Rooms* has been danced by the Alvin Ailey Company, by the Netherlands Dance Theatre, and by the City Center Joffrey Ballet (September 7, 1967). Reviewing the latter production, Clive Barnes wrote in the New York *Times*:

* From *The Modern Dance, Seven Statements of Belief*, edited by Selma Jeanne Cohen, Wesleyan University Press, 1966.

"The pattern of *Rooms* is the pattern of a run-down rooming house. Eight straight-backed people are found sitting on eight straight-backed kitchen chairs. The chairs are their rooms, their patch of frightening privacy in an alien world. The people in the rooms, remote, removed, separate in the way of separateness of cities, are trying vainly to connect with life. They fail.

"Miss Sokolow shows us, with a series of dance images accurate enough to be painful, the shabbiness of their aspirations. A man dreams of escape, a girl dreams of love, a boy sees a false world as a flurry of jazz. Miss Sokolow forces us to peek into the windows of an apartment house we have all, however fleetingly, visited, but would prefer to forget."

## THE ROPES OF TIME

*Music by Jan Boerman. Choreography by Rudi van Dantzig. Scenery and costumes by Toer van Schayk. First presented by the Royal Ballet at the Royal Opera House, Covent Garden, London, March 2, 1970, with Rudolf Nureyev, Diana Vere, and Monica Mason in the principal roles. First presented in the United States by the same ensemble at the Metropolitan Opera House, New York, May 13, 1970, with the same principals.*

The ballet is prefixed by a quotation from the British writer and critic Richard Buckle: "Every journey we make is an adventure into the unknown; each arrival a birth and each departure a death." The characters in the ballet are a Traveller, Life, and Death.

The curtain rises on a dark stage. A man stands to the left, on top of a hemisphere, or egg, where he balances for a moment, then falls, to the sound of crashing glass. The pinnacle rises and out from under the Traveller is born. Dancing amidst ten boys young like himself, the Traveller becomes an individual and begins his life journey. Death enters and watches. So, too, does Life. The Traveller dances with her but Death cuts in and the Traveller is caught between. So begins the journey in which the two dominant figures accompany the venturing Traveller to the end. No sooner does he succeed in showing self-mastery than he is brought back, as it were, to earth. He returns at last to his birthplace to die.

In an interview about his ballet, Rudi van Dantzig said that the inspiration for it was a performing artist he much admires who has sustained a career well beyond the usual span, triumphing over age and adversity. The Traveller as performing artist, on trial before the public, is thus an important aspect of the ballet.

## A ROSE FOR MISS EMILY

*Music by Alan Hovhaness. Choreography by Agnes de Mille. Costumes and scenery by A. Christinia Giannini. Lighting by Gene Lowery. First presented at the North Carolina School of the Arts, Winston-Salem, October*

*24, 1970, with Gemze de Lappe and David Evans in leading roles. First presented by American Ballet Theatre at the City Center, New York, December 30, 1970, with Sallie Wilson and Bruce Marks in leading roles. Lighting by Tom Skelton.*

The choreographer Agnes de Mille has said of her ballet: "It is a story of narcissism . . . self-love, possessiveness and destruction. It is a story about a woman who eats up all the things she loves and then destroys herself."

Miss de Mille's program note reads: "Preoccupation with the morbid is a marked characteristic of the American psyche. It has passed into great literature with Edgar Allen Poe, William Faulkner, Ambrose Bierce and Shirley Jackson.

"This little melodrama, suggested by the masterpiece 'A Rose for Emily' by William Faulkner, seems, because of its stark terror, to lie outside normal experience; it is, however, universal.

"In every life there is an aspect of the personality sealed off and entombed, protected from the abrasive and healing effects of reality, cherished because it is safe, and because it is comforting. This buried person, this self-haunted mourner dotes on experiences and events that are ended, living on a febrile and false world of reflections. We call this sealing off memory; it can be and often is, a form of death."

The curtain rises to the ominous sound of low drum rolls and piano chords. A group of children stand in front of a house in the Old South. There is a jalousied porch, overgrown with creeping vines. The young persons act as if something mysterious has happened within; they seem to giggle in their dread of the unknown. A girl does an imitation of the la-de-da lady of the house, who can be seen dimly behind a scrim. The scrim rises and Miss Emily is seen, in a long gray dress. She dances but hobbles in her attempt to be glamorous. She suffers as a girl comes to give her a rose. The girl drops the flower before Miss Emily can take it and, giggling, leaves. Miss Emily places the rose on a couch, where a cover seems to hide a laid-out figure.

Now, looking in a mirror, the distraught woman recalls her past. A back curtain rises and we are in a scene recollecting her youth. Five girls in red are seen dancing. As Miss Emily looks back, the girls enclose her in a semi-circle, she embraces them and becomes, too, a girl in red—one of them. She is suddenly alone. A man comes to her. They dance together passionately, suppressed feeling rising to the surface. She crawls to his feet, asking for something he seems unable to give. She is embarrassed then and gets up. The man gives her a rose, which she secures at her shoulder, and the dance is resumed. It finishes as she claims the man, holding him fiercely in her arms.

There is silence as four masked couples enter. They appear to be a bit scandalized by what they see, but the man joins them. Miss Emily watches in horror as a young girl in pink blows him a kiss. Two other girls are attracted to him, too. Miss Emily tries to take him away, clinging to his back. She begs him; he rejects her; in suppressed fury she wraps her scarf around his neck and strangles him. He falls back on the couch, and dies. Her body trembles at his death, but she covers him and poses there, fascinated by a vision of her own glamour.

In a dance of triumph and self-justification, she relives the earlier scene, seeing herself and her lover as one of six happy couples. Putting back on now her old lady's dress of gray, she writhes on the floor in despair, reaching out for her lover.

The young people of the first scene return. They observe that Miss Emily has died. Placid at that discovery, they take up the body of Miss Emily and place it on the couch, on the blanket of rotten flowers that has covered the body of her lover all these years. One of them then lifts up a corner of the cover to look underneath.


## LA ROSE MALADE

*Music by Gustav Mahler. Choreography by Roland Petit. First presented by Les Ballets de Marseille at Le Palais des Sports, Paris, January 10, 1973, with Maya Plisetskaya. First presented in the United States by the Bolshoi Ballet at the Metropolitan Opera House, New York, September 18, 1974.*

Set to music from Mahler's *Symphonies No. 2* and *5*, this ballet is based on the poem by William Blake:

> O Rose, thou art sick!
>   The Invisible worm,
> That flies in the night,
>   In the howling storm,
>   Has found out thy bed
>     Of crimson joy;
>   And his dark secret love
>   Does thy life destroy.

The complete ballet, in three long parts, expands these eight lines into a dance work that has no plot but attempts to capture certain moods, feelings, and passions reflective of the poem. Only one of these parts was danced at the American premiere, by Plisetskaya and Alexander Godunov.

Choreographed especially for the Soviet ballerina by Roland Petit, *La Rose Malade* was created during Plisetskaya's residency in Paris with Petit's company in 1972.


## LE SACRE DU PRINTEMPS (The Rite of Spring)

*Ballet in two parts. Music by Igor Stravinsky. Choreography by Vaslav Nijinsky. Book by Igor Stravinsky and Nicholas Roerich. Scenery and costumes by Nicholas Roerich. First presented by Diaghilev's Ballets Russes at the Théâtre des Champs-Élysées, Paris, May 29, 1913, with Marie Piltz as the Chosen One. Rechoreographed by Leonide Massine and presented*

*by Diaghilev's Ballets Russes at the Théâtre des Champs-Élysées, 1920,*
*with Lydia Sokolova as the* Chosen One. *First presented in the United*
*States, with new choreography by Massine, at the Academy of Music, Phila-*
*delphia, April 11, 1930, under the auspices of the League of Composers.*
*Martha Graham danced the leading role in the first American presentation.*

Stravinsky has said that the "violent Russian spring" that seemed to begin in
an hour was like the whole earth cracking. . . . It was "the most wonderful
event of every year of my childhood." In 1910, when he was finishing *Fire-*
*bird,* the composer had an unexpected vision: "I saw in imagination a solemn
pagan rite: wise elders, seated in a circle, watching a young girl dance herself
to death. They were sacrificing her to propitiate the god of spring." The ballet
that resulted from this vision made musical and theatrical history. The score,
long a masterpiece of the modern repertoire, has become more popular in the
concert hall than in the theater, although there continue to be a number of
ballet versions (one by Kenneth MacMillan for the Royal Ballet, with scenery
and costumes by Sydney Noland, May 3, 1962, was introduced in North
America the following year, May 8, 1963).

Subtitled "Scenes of Pagan Russia in Two Parts," the ballet returns us to a
time when primitive rites dominated the lives of the Russian tribes. Every year
spring was consecrated by a human sacrifice.

FIRST TABLEAU: ADORATION OF THE EARTH   A musical prelude recalls man's
first relations with the world about him. The curtain rises. In a wasteland
scene dominated by great masses of stone, young girls and boys sit in separate
groups. They do not move, they wait and watch, as if expecting some sign
from the stone shafts they revere. The girls rise, as if drawn by the abundance
of Nature to which the music calls their attention. A wise man stands among
the dancers; the girls rush around and around him. Now he moves toward the
sacred mound of the enclosure. The girls follow and bow before him. The
opening phrase of the ballet—the quiet, plaintive cry of man against all-powerful Nature—is repeated.

The strings sound strong, persistent chords that rouse the young men. To
the virile beat of the music, they begin to dance, their movements accelerating
at its demand, their feet stamping, stamping the earth. The girls join in the
dance, the music becomes joyous, and the adolescents abandon themselves to
the swift, exuberant rhythms of the orchestra.

This music changes sharply. A new, penetrating melody shrieks warningly
and disturbs the young people. The happiness of the boys and girls shifts
abruptly to fierce savagery. They split into different groups; the boys face the
girls and move toward them. The boys seem bent on attack, but at the last
minute they hesitate; they move back and forth in an almost helpless effort,
ignorant of their own true intent. The rhythmic crescendos give place to the
soft trilling of flutes. Now the boys break their formation, and each carries a
girl away.

Four boys remain on the scene. They choose four girls, lift them up on their
backs, and dance slowly, bending low under the weight of their burdens in im-

itation of the plodding chords of the music. This "Round Dance of Spring" gradually increases in volume, and all the adolescents participate. All the dancers step back as the trilling flutes repeat their love call.

Drums herald the beginning of a contest between two rival tribes. Groups of men from each tribe engage in vigorous games. In the midst of their activity, the wise man, represented in the orchestra by a portentous melody on the tuba, tries to interrupt the games. The stronger theme of the games at first drowns out the wise man's theme, then recedes. The men turn to the wise man. There is a brief, taut silence, then all the men fall to the ground and worship the earth.

The drum rolls loudly, and all rise to dance, as if they had felt the pulse of the earth and been renewed by its power. The dance grows frenzied in its intensity. The curtain falls.

SECOND TABLEAU: THE SACRIFICE   Night is about to fall as this second scene begins; the setting sun has turned the sky scarlet. The girls sit near the wise man at a fire. One of these girls must be chosen by the others to make the sacrifice to the earth: this girl must dance herself to death. The music is calm; the figures on stage are quiet and they are unafraid. The girls regret what they have to do, but they are resigned to it with a kind of physical tiredness that the music reflects. They do not feel that they are victimized by Nature, but rather that they must obey what they believe to be its rules.

Soon the girls rise and move in the patterns of the "Dance of the Mysterious Circles." Their movements are trancelike, as if they themselves were not to make their dreadful decision. Their inspiration arrives, and they rush to the periphery of the scene; the chosen one stands alone in the center of the stage.

Now begins the dance that glorifies the victim. The chosen one remains motionless as the girls and men of the tribe whirl around her. All are transfixed at her power. They invoke the spirit of their ancestors, terrified anew by the force of Nature. Marking the relentless, sharp rhythms of the music with their feet, their dance reaches an ultimate expression of uncontrolled glory in sacrifice.

All the tribe members retire to watch the chosen one. The orchestra sounds strong, militant chords, trumpets blare harshly, cutting the air. The dance of the chosen one begins. The brutal savagery of the demanding music compels her to imitate it. Brief moments of comparative quiet, which seem at first to be periods of rest and release, are in reality more deadly because of the thrashing force that follows them. The girl is now wholly a part of the music, part of the earth. Hypnotized by her movements, the tribe joins in the violent dance. The chosen one begins to lose her strength, but—forced on by the convulsive violence of the music—is endowed with a new, superhuman compulsion. When it seems that Nature can demand no more, the girl is pushed into a fresh frenzy. Then she falls. She is dead.

The men of the tribe catch her up in their arms and hold her high over their heads before the sacred mound. The people of the tribe rush around her, holding up their arms. At the last slapping crescendo of the music, they fall to the earth.

NOTES  The first assistant to Nijinsky in the creation of the first version of *Le Sacre du Printemps,* Dame Marie Rambert, who later founded ballet in Britain and developed the gifts of Tudor, Ashton, de Mille and many others, has written in a way no one else can match of the background of this ballet in her autobiography, *Quicksilver* (1972):

"It was the painter Roerich who first suggested the subject of *Sacre du Printemps.* He then worked on the theme with Diaghilev, Stravinsky and Nijinsky. It was to be prehistoric Russia and represent the rites of spring. Stravinsky had finished his magnificent score by 1912, and we started the rehearsals with the company that same year.

"Nijinsky again first of all established the basic position: feet very turned in, knees slightly bent, arms held in reverse of the classical position, a primitive, prehistoric posture. The steps were very simple: walking smoothly or stamping, jumps mostly off both feet, landing heavily. There was only one a little more complicated, the dance for the maidens in the first scene. It was mostly done in groups, and each group has its own precise rhythm to follow. In the dance (if one can call it that) of the Wisest Elder, he walked two steps against every three steps of the ensemble. In the second scene the dance of the sacrifice of the Chosen Virgin was powerful and deeply moving. I watched Nijinsky again and again teaching it to Maria Piltz. Her reproduction was very pale by comparison with his ecstatic performance, which was the greatest tragic dance I have ever seen.

"The first night of that ballet was the most astonishing event . . . at the first sounds of the music, shouts and hissing started in the audience, and it was very difficult for us on the stage to hear the music, the more so as part of the audience began to applaud in an attempt to drown the hissing. We all desperately tried to keep time without being able to hear the rhythm clearly. In the wings Nijinsky counted the bars to guide us. Pierre Monteux conducted undeterred, Diaghilev having told him to continue to play at all costs.

"But after the interlude things became even worse, and during the sacrificial dance real pandemonium broke out. That scene began with Maria Piltz, the Chosen Virgin, standing on the spot trembling for many bars, her folded hands under her right cheek, her feet turned in, a truly prehistoric and beautiful pose. But to the audience of the time it appeared ugly and comical.

"A shout went up in the gallery:

" '*Un docteur!*'

"Somebody else shouted louder:

" '*Un dentiste!*'

"Then someone else screamed:

" '*Deux dentistes!*'

"And so it went on. One elegant lady leaned out of her box and slapped a man who was clapping. But the performance went on to the end.

"And yet now there is no doubt that, musically and choreographically, a masterpiece had been created that night. The only ballet that could compare with it in power was Bronislava Nijinska's *Los Noces,* created in 1923. She, like her brother, produced a truly epic ballet—so far unexcelled anywhere."

*Music by Igor Stravinsky. Choreography by Maurice Béjart. First presented
by the Ballet of the Twentieth Century at the Théâtre Royale de La Monnaie, in December 1959. First presented in the United States by the same
ensemble at the Brooklyn Academy of Music, New York, January 26, 1971,
with Tania Bari and Jorge Donn in principal roles.*

The choreographer of this version of *Le Sacre*, Maurice Béjart, has written:
"What is Spring but an immense primordial force, which after long sleeping
under the mantle of winter, suddenly bursts forth, kindling new life in all
things. . . . Human love, in its physical aspects, symbolizes the act by which
the divinity creates the Cosmos and the joy the divinity thereby derives. At a
time when the borders that divide the human spirit are gradually crumbling,
we must begin to speak in terms of the culture of all mankind. Let us avoid
folklore that is not universal and only retain the essential forces of mankind
which are the same the world over and throughout all periods of history.

"Let this ballet then be stripped of all the artifices of the picturesque in a
Hymn to this union of Man and Woman in the innermost depths of the flesh, a
union of heaven and earth, a dance of life and death, as eternal as Spring."

Rejecting, therefore, the original scenario of Stravinsky and Roerich, this
*Sacre* celebrates instead the mating of a young man and woman. Writing in
the New York *Times*, Anna Kisselgoff has said that Béjart's "use of group patterns and rhythmic pulse gives this *Sacre* an underivative look. . . . The chosen maiden is not sacrificed literally but thrown into a physical union with an
equally virginal male. . . . The Puritans did not ban Maypole-dancing in England for nothing and Béjart has given his strikingly designed fertility ritual the
primitive physical force it needs. It works."

The English critic Peter Williams has written in *Dance and Dancers* magazine: "The mass ritualistic movements leading up to the final orgasmic moment make pretty powerful theatre, in which the music plays a vital part."

Rudolf Nureyev danced Béjart's ballet on March 12, 1971, at the Palais des
Sports, Brussels.

John Taras choreographed a new version of *Le Sacre* for La Scala, Milan,
December 9, 1972. Natalia Makarova danced the principal role. Scenery and
costumes were designed by Marino Marini.

June 21, 1976, Glen Tetley's version of *Le Sacre*, created in 1975 for the
Munich Opera Ballet, was first presented in the United States by American
Ballet Theatre at the Metropolitan Opera House, New York. Scenery and cos-
tumes were by Nadine Baylis, lighting by John B. Read. The cast was led by
Mikhail Baryshnikov, Martine van Hamel, and Clark Tippet.

The action depicts a vernal sacrifice and renewal of the human spirit.

Bill Zakariasen wrote in the *Daily News* after the first performance in New
York: "Those expecting pagan rites of ancient Russia were no doubt disappointed, yet for the first time in my experience, the choreography matched the
elemental power of Stravinsky's music."

## SACRED GROVE ON MOUNT TAMALPAIS

*Music and lyrics by Alan Raph. Choreography by Gerald Arpino. Set designed by Robert Yodice from a concept by Ming Cho Lee. Costumes by David James. First presented by the City Center Joffrey Ballet at the City Center, New York, November 2, 1972, with Starr Danias, Russell Chambers, and Russell Sultzbach in leading roles. Conducted by Sung Kwak.*

From antique times, men and women have gone to sacred groves to celebrate the earth's renewal every spring. Mount Tamalpais, in Marin County, California, overlooking San Francisco Bay and the Pacific beyond, is the scene of this extensive dance ballet that explores the drive, innocence, and sophistication of contemporary youth. There is a pastoral marriage and evidence of other commitments ". . . to build from a moment onward/to build a beginning./ Come to the wall around you/Come through the wall around you./ Come and see/look and see/follow me." The score, with lyrics, which includes the *Canon in D* by Johann Pachelbel, was commissioned by the Foundation for American Dance, Inc.

The action depicts a wedding ceremony and the attendant celebration, followed by the birth of a son who represents a kind of prophet to the young persons on Mount Tamalpais.

NOTES   Writing about the ballet in the New York *Times,* Clive Barnes said that "Mr. Arpino has conceived his ballet as an exaltation of the human spirit. Californians (perhaps) in a Greek mood are dancing out fancies of renewal. Two lovers—Starr Danias and Russell Chambers—produce, quite suddenly, a full-grown son, Russell Sultzbach. . . . Miss Danias dances like a still thought in a quick world—there is a special quietness to her lyricism, a youthful melancholy, that Mr. Arpino so instinctively picks up. He creates beautifully for her, and Mr. Chambers, ardent and provocative, makes her a nicely matched partner. The assertive radiance of Mr. Sultzbach was also used to strong effect."

In a special portfolio by Olga Maynard on Gerald Arpino's "Berkeley ballets" for *Dance Magazine* (September 1973), the choreographer is quoted as saying that *Sacred Grove on Mount Tamalpais* polarizes its audiences: " 'For some (for whom the distance is too far from the real Mount Tamalpais, and the Berkeley life-style), the ballet is incomprehensible. It is not a work that should be approached intellectually, but as an experience. But people come to me, in every city that The Joffrey dances *Sacred Grove on Mount Tamalpais,* to say that it has made them feel beautiful again. I am very grateful for that. . . .

" 'The choreographer cannot deliberately make a ballet to appeal to an audience; he has to start from personal inspirations. He has to trust the ballet, to let it stand on its own strengths—or fall on its weaknesses. If it reaches the audience, then he is lucky that round!

" 'In *Trinity* and *Sacred Grove on Mount Tamalpais* I have been able to look at the world through the eyes of the young—to touch the heart of the matter of what it is to be young in this place and time. I could not have done this unless I had gone to Berkeley.

"'The choreographer (especially in the United States) needs Berkeley. Materialistic things, from which art cannot be separated, force us into certain perspectives, they sometimes narrow those perspectives, as tall buildings confine the sight of the sky. At Berkeley, The Joffrey had a true freedom, and our company was able to refresh and to replenish its spirit. Joffrey and I are very conscious of the free spirit that identifies this company; the dancers are very important to the company. They *are* The Joffrey.

"'As artists, they are very sensitive to an atmosphere and at Berkeley we all felt, very intensely, the free, open spirit that is the stamp of The Joffrey.'"

## SALTARELLI

*Music by Antonio Vivaldi. Choreography by Jacques d'Amboise. Scenery and costumes by John Braden. Lighting by Ronald Bates. Dedicated to the Drs. B. and L. Krynski. First presented by the New York City Ballet at the New York State Theatre, Lincoln Center, May 30, 1974, with Christine Redpath, Merrill Ashley, and Francis Sackett as principal dancers.*

The *saltarello*, an old Italian court dance, derived from the word for "jump," also had its popular manifestation among the people. Clive Barnes has said that it might be regarded as the Roman counterpart of the southern *tarantella*. This ballet by Jacques d'Amboise, a dance occasion without narrative, is performed on a *saltarello* base to music by Vivaldi (the *Concerto in D Minor* F.XI No. 19 and the *Concerto Grosso in D Minor*, Op. 3, No. 11). *Saltarelli* is a reworking of an earlier work mounted in 1973 for the Ballet de San Juan in Puerto Rico.

Writing in *The Record*, Barbara Archer said that the ballet "reflects the ease and breeziness Jacques d'Amboise usually brings to his own dancing. As its name suggests, the ballet transmits a constant energy."

Using seven dancers, the ballet varies lively presentation with quiet *pas de deux*. "There is a certain poetic touch," wrote Clive Barnes in the New York *Times*, "that through a chain of associations, can recall the tenderness and melancholy of Picasso's blue and rose periods."

## SARABANDE AND DANSE

*Music by Maurice Ravel. Choreography by Jacques d'Amboise. Costumes by John Braden. Lighting by Ronald Bates. First presented at the New York City Ballet's Hommage à Ravel at the New York State Theatre, Lincoln Center, May 29, 1975, with Colleen Neary in the principal role. Conductor: Robert Irving.*

Ravel wrote orchestrations of Debussy's *Sarabande* and *Danse* as a tribute to the great French composer who had died in 1918. Since the compositions are in effect dance works it was only natural that Jacques d'Amboise should have used them for our Ravel Festival in 1975. He did so for dance works expressive of the music without any specific narrative idea.

## SCÈNES DE BALLET

*Classic ballet in one act. Music by Igor Stravinsky. Choreography by Anton Dolin. First presented by Billy Rose at the Ziegfeld Theatre, New York, December 7, 1944, as part of the revue The Seven Lively Arts. Alicia Markova and Anton Dolin danced the leading roles. Presented by the Sadler's Wells Ballet at the Royal Opera House, Covent Garden, London, February 11, 1948, in a new version with choreography by Frederick Ashton and scenery and costumes by André Beaurepaire. Margot Fonteyn and Michael Somes were the principal dancers.*

Stravinsky wrote the music to this ballet after the forms of the classical dance, and the work consequently has no literary meaning or plot. In the composer's words, "The parts follow each other as in a sonata or in a symphony in contrasts or similarities."

The pattern of the ballet follows the divisions of the score. *Scènes de Ballet* is danced by two soloists and a *corps de ballet* of four boys and twelve girls. Stravinsky specified different dances for the eleven parts of his score.

The brief opening fanfare heralds an introduction by the *corps de ballet*, "Moderato." Now the ballerina dances a variation to bright, quick rhythms. After a brief pantomime section, "Lento," the *pas de deux* begins. In the Sadler's Wells production, the ballerina in the adagio is supported by five men. As they support her in pirouettes at one point, she keeps turning and another partner steps in to support her. A variation for the *danseur* "Risoluto," is followed by a variation for the ballerina. During her dance, her partner kneels before her and holds his hand to his heart; the four boys recline about him. There is another brief pantomime "Andantino," a final dance by the *corps de ballet*, "Con moto," and an apotheosis. Here the music gradually mounts in grandeur; the ballerina and her partner stand together in the center of the stage, and about them the *corps de ballet* are arranged in their original tableau.

*Music by Igor Stravinsky. Choreography by John Taras. First presented at the New York City Ballet's Stravinsky Festival, June 22, 1972, at the New York State Theatre, Lincoln Center, with Patricia McBride and Jean-Pierre Bonnefous in the leading roles.*

Well-known in Britain in Frederick Ashton's version, *Scènes de Ballet* is not familiar enough in America and my colleague John Taras at the New York City

Ballet made a new ballet to this music for our Stravinsky Festival. The dancing celebrates the beauty of the score, which was arranged originally as a
showpiece for an eminent dancer and her partner.

Writing in the *Daily News* after the premiere, the critic Sam Norkin said:
"Taras has devised sweeping, lyrical movement for his two soloists, Patricia
McBride and Jean-Pierre Bonnefous, who danced in the lavender mood of the
decor. The trumpet solo for their pas de deux was sensitively played by
Theodore Weis."

## SCHEHERAZADE

*Dramatic ballet in one act. Music by Nikolai Rimsky-Korsakov. Choreogra-
phy by Michel Fokine. Book by Alexandre Benois. Scenery and costumes
by Léon Bakst. First presented by Diaghilev's Ballets Russes at the Théâtre
National de l'Opéra, Paris, June 4, 1910, with Ida Rubinstein as Zobeide,
Vaslav Nijinsky as the Favorite Slave, and Enrico Cecchetti as the Chief
Eunuch. First presented in the United States by Gertrude Hoffman's Saison
Russe at the Winter Garden, New York, June 14, 1911.*

Color is the dominant element in this lavish ballet, color as brilliant and
resplendent as the Eastern sun—color in music and dancing, in lush decor, and
in the burning passions that consume the principal characters in the story.
Those who are familiar with Rimsky-Korsakov's music, which the ballet uses,
know that it is an orchestral suite—program music appropriate to a series of
stories told by the beautiful Scheherazade to fascinate her husband. The
makers of the ballet chose to abandon the composer's musical scheme and to
fashion a dance drama out of the first story in the *Arabian Nights,* a drama
that would embody all the mystery, passion, and violence that all these tales
contained.

The first movement of the suite, the section known as "The Sea and Sin-
bad's Ship," is played by the orchestra before the curtain rises. Its music insin-
uates an Oriental atmosphere, prognosticating the voluptuous adventure the
ballet relates and intimating the excitement and deadly risks attendant upon it.
The second movement begins; the curtain rises.

The scene is the great hall of an Oriental palace. Rich hangings of purple
and green and orange are looped from the ceiling, creating an impression of
abundant wealth that spends itself on every conceivable extravagance. On the
left a purple stairway carpeted with golden cloth leads to the upper reaches of
the palace. In the back there are three small blue doors decorated with silver
stars. The king, Shahriar, sits upon his royal cushion. He ignores the members
of his court as he turns constantly to caress Zobeide, his favorite concubine
and leader of his harem.

The scene is relaxed and luxurious, the music languid. Eight girls of the
harem recline lazily on multicolored cushions. Shahriar evidently wishes not to
be distracted from his dalliance as he rests in the cool, open room. But his
brother, Shah Zeman, who sits beside him, endeavors to engage his attention.

Shahriar's chief eunuch, an obese, conniving caricature of a man, waddles before him, unctuously suggesting entertainment. Shahriar grants him permission by his silence, and the chief eunuch claps his hands. Three girls dressed in gold run out, bow to their master, and sit down together to perform a preface to their specialty. Shahriar holds Zobeide in his arms and does not notice them. The girls rise and dance sinuously. No one is amused.

The chief eunuch and several attendants assist Shahriar to rise. He is a tall man, whose costume is covered with jewels; a high gold collar surrounds his proud bearded face. His brother looks with hatred upon Zobeide, who stands beside her lord and master, her supple, yielding body scarcely disguised in transparent gauze and myriad ropes of pearls. She pleads with Shahriar for a favor. He refuses and points off into the distance. He commands a hunt in the forest. Zobeide is enraged: she has been embarrassed before the entire harem. She stalks away and flops down on a cushion, to look on with sulking defiance.

Shah Zeman, suspicious of Zobeide's fidelity to his brother, seizes upon the sudden tension between the two lovers and whispers his fears to the king. Shahriar listens. Although he is annoyed by her behavior, he disbelieves the gossip about his favorite. Shah Zeman persists, and briefly the king is a willing listener. Zobeide turns away contemptuously. The king calls over several of his attendants and gives them secret instructions. They bow and retreat.

All the girls save Zobeide rise from their cushions to bid their lord farewell and to wish him luck on the hunt. Four of the girls circle him. He protests lightly, but when four others surround him, he bends down to kiss two of the concubines. The girls dress him for the hunt. Shahriar looks over at Zobeide, enraged by her rage and by her power over him.

The chief eunuch brings in silver halberds. The trumpeting music heralds the start of the expedition. Shahriar attempts to persuade Zobeide that she has no cause for her anger. The sullen concubine resists his explanation at first, then fondly bids him farewell. All the girls kneel and hold up their hands beseechingly as Shahriar walks past them with his entourage toward the waiting expedition. Several girls wave to him. The chief eunuch exits with his master.

Now free from care and eager to enjoy their own pleasure, the harem women gather together and whisper excitedly, like schoolgirls. The light dims. They run to the back of the room and peer through the keyholes of the locked doors. They consult again and exit, bringing with them chests of jewels. One of the girls pulls in the chief eunuch, who protests helplessly. The girls surround him and, by the movement of their bodies, try to secure a favor. The eunuch refuses. All the girls circle about him, but the adamant eunuch shoos them off. One of the girls steals the big ring of keys he carries at his waist. He chases her and takes them back. The girls kneel about him, and the eunuch's resistance begins to disappear. Shall he, or shall he not? The girls see that he requires a bribe and dangle dazzling necklaces before him. The eunuch consents.

He walks to the doors at the back and unlocks one of them. Three Negro slaves dash out, like quick stallions, to their waiting lovers and throw them down upon the cushions. The second door is unlocked; three other couples are reunited in heated, reclining embraces. It is as if the girls, each momentarily out of favor with the king, are rejoicing openly in their contempt for his fickle affection as they welcome the eager advances of their secret lovers. The slaves, who so seldom gain admittance to the harem, cover their bodies with frantic kisses.

Zobeide pleads with the chief eunuch to open the third door. He turns away. Zobeide stamps and insists. The eunuch demands payment. She takes up a necklace, throws it at his feet, and now, consumed by her desire, drags him impatiently toward the door. She stands beside it in a voluptuous pose, slithering like a cat. The door opens. The favorite slave sneaks out with wary delight. He sees Zobeide; she stands breathless, her head thrown back, as he touches her body intimately. The chief eunuch exits.

The girls of the harem and their lovers abandon themselves to riotous dancing. Servant boys enter. Zobeide and the favorite writhe together on the cushions. The favorite slave springs up, and everyone watches as he throws himself into a vigorous dance. Now the entire group moves about the stage in whirling circles. The music whips their natural excitement into a frenzy of pleasure. The favorite slave holds the group fascinated with his bold leaps and assertive passion. The room becomes a whirling mass of climactic, flashing color. Zobeide and her lover are lost to each other on the king's divan. At its height, Shahriar rushes in, his scimitar raised threateningly. The hunt was but a ruse designed by his brother to expose the unfaithfulness of Zobeide.

The group rushes away from him like a receding wave. The king's men stand poised, with their swords ready to strike them down. Zobeide and the slave are so involved in their ecstasy that at first they do not notice. The slave springs up as he sees the king; Zobeide gropes back toward the corner of the stairs and tries to press her body into the wall. The slave dashes across the stage. Shah Zeman cuts him down in mid-flight, and the slave falls. His legs rear up into the air, his body refusing to die. The shah strikes again, and the slave expires. The king's soldiers chase the slaves and the concubines, killing them mercilessly at his command. The eunuch is stabbed to death.

Zobeide pleads with the king for her life as his men close in on her with their scimitars. He orders them aside and the repentant woman kisses his hand. The king pulls his hand away. Zobeide reminds him of his devotion to her and her faithfulness to him. For a moment Shahriar believes her and is fascinated again by her loveliness. He embraces her and kisses her. As he raises his eyes, his brother kicks viciously at the body of Zobeide's secret lover and reminds him of her betrayal. He pushes her away. He hesitates. He does not wish to kill the woman he loves, despite her infidelity, for her repentance appears so genuine, but his kingly honor demands that a price be paid for his abused pride. He stands irresolute. His cohorts move toward Zobeide. Before they reach her, she pulls out a dagger and stabs herself in the belly. Her body doubles up over her arm. She is dead. The men drop their swords. Shahriar raises his arms in despair and weeps over her. His pride seems as nothing compared to his lost love.

NOTES   *Scheherazade,* the work that popularly identified the "new Russian Ballet" in the early days of Diaghilev's Ballets Russes, has managed to be in the active repertory of one company or another ever since. Its initial fame is understandable when we recall that its subject matter was new to its first audiences and when we remember its principal dancers. Tamara Karsavina soon took over the role of Zobeide, while Nijinsky continued in the part of the favorite slave. Carl Van Vechten wrote that "Karsavina's *Zobeide* is a suggestive picture of languorous lust, and Nijinsky, as the principal slave, alternates between surprising leaps into the air and the most lascivious gestures; like some animal, he paws the reclining Sultana." The librettist of the ballet, Alexandre Benois, wrote that Ida Rubinstein was "absolutely inimitable . . . in her proud, cunning and unrestrained passion" and that Nijinsky as the favorite slave was "half-cat, half-snake, fiendishly agile, feminine and yet wholly terrifying."

What has happened to *Scheherazade* since, is best reflected in a review by Edwin Denby in the New York *Herald Tribune:* "Seen on a ballet program today, *Scheherazade* . . . is an illustrious warhorse foundering in dishonor. Not that there isn't some kind of life left in the old girl. The bundling and the clinches are still fine for laughs and whistles and cries of 'Take it off' . . . A great many people register sex all over the stage with an earnestness that is disarming rather than embarrassing. But one wonders what *Scheherazade* looked like when it scandalized our parents or when Parisians swooned at the lushness of it in 1910. In the 1910 photographs the slave girls look soft and abandoned. Nijinsky bounded about them like a panther in thrilling spasms that grew to a paroxysm of death at the climax. Bakst the great decorator—the Berman of his day—dazzled the public by the sensual shock of the brilliant decor. And the 'slavic harmonies' of Rimsky's score dunked the orgy on the stage in a bath of gold.

"Nowadays the small orchestra, the clumsily executed decor, the earnest but overworked dancers can't create any sense of abandon. The trouble is that there is no dance form, nothing for them to do as dancers. There is only miming and hubbub, and that doesn't keep for thirty years. A dance ballet can keep fresh because of its form, because arms and legs stay arms and legs; but when the dancers have to pretend to be something they aren't, a ballet disintegrates into a charade."

The first production of *Scheherazade* in the United States was not rehearsed by Fokine and not authorized by him. It remained for Diaghilev's Ballets Russes to present the first authentic version in this country, January 17, 1916, at the Century Theatre, New York. Nijinsky danced *Scheherazade* with Diaghilev's company for the first time in the United States on April 15, 1916, at the Metropolitan Opera House.

## SCHERZO À LA RUSSE

*Music by Igor Stravinsky. Choreography by George Balanchine. Costumes by Karinska. First presented by the New York City Ballet at the Stravinsky Festival, June 21, 1972, at the New York State Theatre, Lincoln Center, New York, with Karin von Aroldingen and Kay Mazzo in leading roles.*

This is a lovely piece of music by Stravinsky that he originally composed for a movie in Hollywood but was never used. It lasts about five minutes but it is a charming, accurate evocation of an old Russian dance, and I liked very much arranging it for two girls and their girl friends in our Stravinsky Festival. It is certainly a Russian dance, as I recall such things from my childhood and my training in ballet there, but I do not mean the piece as any kind of sentimental gesture to the past. All of my dances to Stravinsky music are reflections of what he and I, together, might have done. My luck was that our working together lasted so long.

## SCHERZO FANTASTIQUE

*Music by Igor Stravinsky. Choreography by Jerome Robbins. First presented at the New York City Ballet's Stravinsky Festival, at the New York State Theatre, Lincoln Center, June 18, 1972, with Gelsey Kirkland, Bart Cook, Victor Castelli, Bryan Pitts, and Stephen Caras. Conducted by Robert Irving.*

At the beginning of our Stravinsky Festival at the New York State Theatre— the festival that celebrated the ninetieth birthday of the composer, who had died the previous year—I said that without music there can be no dance and that Stravinsky, more than any other composer, created music for dancers. The *Scherzo Fantastique*, an early work, first performed in 1909, gives us an idea not only of what the young composer most admired in those days but an idea of what he was to become. It is a piece for large orchestra lasting about sixteen minutes. The impresario Diaghilev heard the first performance, and it was this piece, and *Fireworks*, that interested him in the possibility of Stravinsky's composing music for ballet.

Jerome Robbins arranged to *Scherzo Fantastique* a dance for a girl and four boys, an exuberant work with no narrative that reflected the youth and brio of the score.

Writing about it in the *Daily News*, Sam Norkin said that "the ballet is appropriately swift and buoyant. The dancers spend most of their time spinning aloft, conceding to gravity only grudgingly. Gelsey Kirkland in filmy yellow was a delightful sprite in counterpoint to the men in the cast."

## SCHERZO FOR MASSAH JACK

*Music by Charles Ives. Choreography by Lar Lubovitch. Costume consultant, John Dayger. Lighting consultant, Beverly Emmons. First presented by American Ballet Theatre at the City Center, New York, January 17, 1973, with Daniel Levans, Ruth Mayer, Keith Lee, Bonnie Mathis, William Carter, Christine Sarry, and Ian Horvath in the leading roles. Assistant to Mr. Lubovitch: Ernest Pagano. Violin: Alexander Horvath. Piano: Howard Baer.*

An impressionistic dramatic dance about the Old South, *Scherzo for Massah Jack* presents and comments on aspects of antebellum plantation mythology and reality. The choreographer, Lar Lubovitch, describes his ballet as "a pure dance piece to illuminate the music of Charles Ives." The ballet develops its themes much as Ives developed the music for his *Trio*—by exploiting the variations possible on old American tunes and hymns. What Ives does with the song "My Old Kentucky Home" is similar to the choreographer's idea to probe and reveal new aspects of the familiar—here the pathos, absurdity, and tragedy of a familiar racist drama.

## SCHUBERTIADE

> *Music by Franz Schubert. Choreography by Michael Smuin. First presented by American Ballet Theatre at the City Center, New York, January 1, 1971, with Paula Tracy and Vane Vest, Cynthia Gregory and Gayle Young, Sallie Wilson and Marcos Paredes, Diana Weber and John Prinz, and Eleanor D'Antuono as principal dancers.*

A pianist plays Schubert waltzes and *Ländler* on stage for this dance ballet, named for what the Viennese call a Schubertiade—a civilized time at home for friends and family with fine music to play and dance to. And there is an intimate family atmosphere to the ballet, where children are present, too. Relationships between persons at the party become apparent as we go along; there is a sense of competitiveness among the boys, the girls are eager to outdress their peers, and it is clear how a number of the young couples feel about each other.

Writing in *Dance and Dancers* magazine, Patricia Barnes said that in *Schubertiade* "a mood is created and there is enough variety in the dancing to keep one's attention happily engaged. Diana Weber and John Prinz, in particular, have been given some of the most attractive choreography in the ballet. The brief, playful *pas de deux* was a delight and Prinz's virtuoso solo later on demonstrated his buoyance and excellent beats to fine effect. Weber, a meticulously precise young dancer, improves all the time . . . and it was nice to see Terry Orr, dashing and elegant, in another well-constructed male solo. Smuin, himself a brilliant dancer, really knows how to choreograph for men. Among the rest, Cynthia Gregory, Eleanor D'Antuono, Paula Tracy, Sallie Wilson and Gayle Young stood out, and at a later performance I was also impressed with the charm and delicacy of Karena Brock replacing D'Antuono."

## SCHUMANN CONCERTO

> *Ballet in three movements. Choreographic concerto by Bronislava Nijinska. Music by Robert Schumann (Piano Concerto in A minor). Scenery and costumes by Stewart Chaney. First presented by Ballet Theatre at the Metro-*

*politan Opera House, New York, September 27, 1951, with a cast headed by Alicia Alonso and Igor Youskevitch.*

The romantic mood of Schumann's music is the inspiration for this abstract ballet. Two central figures represent the romantic center of the ballet, and above this couple a *corps de ballet* of boys and girls dance as a background. The setting is romantic, too. Three gray stone arches draped with red cloth frame a backdrop that depicts a high, desolate cliff.

FIRST MOVEMENT: ALLEGRO AFFETTUOSO   When the curtain rises, after a long musical introduction, we see on stage the ballerina, who stands in an attitude of wistfulness. She is dressed all in white, in full romantic costume. To the right is her lover, who holds out his arms to her longingly. The couple and the small group of girls who stand to either side of them begin to dance. What they dance has no plot in any usual sense; they exit and re-enter, not continuing a pattern they have started, but simply dancing along with the dynamics of the music. The piano in the concerto represents no one in particular. When the music becomes vigorous, groups of boys cross the stage in high leaps. The *premier danseur* dances with one of these groups and exits. The ballerina now performs a variation. Her partner returns to watch as she circles the stage with rapid turns. They leave the stage to the *corps de ballet* briefly. The music becomes quiet; six of the girls form a tableau. The ballerina rejoins them, still turning, to the accompaniment of soft trills of the piano. Three of the boys lift her high, carry her around the stage and off into the wings. She and her partner return, as the last chords of the first movement begin, and join the *corps de ballet* to dance its final measures.

SECOND MOVEMENT: INTERMEZZO   The light dims. Eight girls in rust-color skirts covered with black net join other girls dressed in softly tinted dresses to form a backdrop for a *pas de deux* between the ballerina and her partner. Alternately, with the rhythm of the music, the *premier danseur* supports the ballerina in swift pirouettes that stop sharply with the music's hesitation and high lifts that end, again, with pirouettes. As the dance progresses, the ballerina turns more and more rapidly; her white dress seems to be in a perpetual whirl about her moving figure.

THIRD MOVEMENT: ALLEGRO VIVACE   The scene brightens, and a new backdrop reveals in the distance ancient ruins, overrun with moss and weeds and grass. A luminous yellow sun in a cloudless sky shines down on the nostalgic vista. The ballerina and her partner return. Three boys go to the front of the stage and recline to watch the ballerina dance. Soon they rise and, with a second group of men, stand at either side of the stage as the ballerina moves across it. She leaves the scene now to her partner, who dances brilliantly down a diagonal formed by the male *corps de ballet*. All the girls come back and reform a tableau, as the two principals dominate the scene. The ballerina encircles her lover with accelerated terms; he spins in the air, as the music reaches a crescendo of joyousness, and carries her off into the wings. The different units of the *corps de ballet* fill the stage with movement until the principals join in for the finale. The curtain falls as the ballerina is lifted high above the group. Her lover stands facing us with outstretched arms.


## SCOTCH SYMPHONY

*Classic ballet in three parts. Music by Felix Mendelssohn. Choreography by George Balanchine. Scenery by Horace Armistead. Costumes by Karinska and David Ffolkes. Lighting by Jean Rosenthal. First presented by the New York City Ballet at the City Center, New York, November 11, 1952, with Maria Tallchief, André Eglevsky, Patricia Wilde, Frank Hobi, and Michael Maule in the principal roles.*

When the New York City Ballet appeared at the Edinburgh Festival in August 1952, I had my first opportunity to see the great massed demonstration of parade units from the Scottish regiments in the famous nocturnal Military Tattoo. I greatly enjoyed this spectacle, as I also enjoyed seeing Scotland as a whole. It occurred to me that when my company returned to New York, we might do a Scottish ballet. Scotland, after all, was the scene of the first great romantic ballet, *La Sylphide,* and a new ballet might well recollect this fact as it also remounted dances in the Scottish manner. Mendelssohn, too, had written his *Scotch Symphony,* and this music seemed to me appropriate for the idea I had in mind.

Back in New York, we decided to do the ballet *Scotch Symphony* almost immediately, omitting the first movement of Mendelssohn's score, which is not appropriate for dance.

In the first movement of the ballet there are general dances by the ensemble, all in appropriate Scottish costume: there is a *pas de trois* by a girl and two boys, and there are solo passages for the girl.

The second movement is an adagio for a ballerina and her partner that represents, without a story, the general mood and atmosphere of the romantic ballet as epitomized in such ballets as *La Sylphide.*

The third movement is again an ensemble, in which the ballerina and her partner participate with *pas de deux* and variation, joining the soloists and *corps de ballet* in a finale.


## SEA CHANGE

*Music by Benjamin Britten. Choreography by Alvin Ailey. First presented by American Ballet Theatre at the Opera House, Kennedy Center for the Performing Arts, Washington, D.C., October 26, 1972, with Sallie Wilson and Royes Fernandez as principals.*

A dramatic dance for a girl and her drowned lover, *Sea Change* is introduced with two notes in the program: "Love transcends all bounds—including death," and a lyric from *The Tempest:*

> Full fathom five thy father lies;
> Of his bones are coral made;
> Those are pearls that were his eyes;
> Nothing of him that doth fade,
> But doth suffer a sea-change
> Into something rich and strange . . .

The action is divided into four parts, corresponding to the music of Benjamin Britten's *Four Sea Interludes* from *Peter Grimes,* the ballet's score.

In the first part, *Dawn,* the death of a fisherman at sea is mourned by his friends. In *Sunday Morning,* a girl, the dead man's wife, remote and detached, dances midst a vigorous dance by the young men of the village. In *Moonlight,* her love for the lost mariner is recapitulated as we see them dance together. In the final *Storm,* love appears to transcend death and the lovers are reunited.

The late John Cranko also made a ballet called *Sea Change.* Set to music by Sibelius, with scenery and costumes by John Piper and presented first by the Sadler's Wells Theatre Ballet at the Gaiety Theatre, Dublin, Ireland, January 18, 1949, the ballet told the story of another village situation. A ship goes to sea, there is a storm and all but one of the men return. While the villagers rejoice in their deliverance, the wife of the lost seaman, a young bride, interrupts the scene in a wild outpouring of grief. At the end, she scans the horizon in quiet despair. The critic Clive Barnes has called *Sea Change* "John Cranko's first major ballet."

## SEA SHADOW

*Music by Michael Colgrass. Choreography by Gerald Arpino. Setting by Ming Cho Lee. First presented by the Robert Joffrey Ballet at the Delacorte Theatre, Central Park, New York, September 5, 1963, with Lisa Bradley and Paul Sutherland. Music for the first performance was a movement of Ravel's Concerto in G for Piano and Orchestra.*

Called "a poem-in-dance," *Sea Shadow* is a dramatic *pas de deux* in which a sprite from the sea visits a dreaming boy on a beach. The ballet might be called a modern treatment of the Ondine theme, for attracted as the boy is by the sea sprite, it becomes clear that she will lead him not only to happiness but also to his death. In a mesmeric, underwater rhythm, the dance is performed to a score by the contemporary composer Michael Colgrass. The critic Walter Terry has called *Sea Shadow* "one of the most beautiful duets in all ballet."

# THE SEASONS

*Music by Alexander Glazunov. Choreography by Marius Petipa. First presented at the Hermitage Theatre, St. Petersburg, February 7, 1900. First presented by the Stuttgart Ballet, in a production by John Cranko, at the Württemberg State Theatre, Stuttgart, June 15, 1962. Completely revised by Mr. Cranko in a new version which was first presented in the United States at the Metropolitan Opera House, New York, April 30, 1971.*

While the first ballet to Glazunov's great score (one that is more familiar, from excerpts we know, than we suspect) included four danced tableaux of the seasons and an apotheosis, John Cranko's production also makes of the work a major opportunity for a reigning ballerina. He provides her with no less than three of the seasons—Winter, Summer, and Autumn. (Spring is led by two girls.) Each of these parts of the ballet is supported by soloists and *corps de ballet,* but the emphasis is on personal virtuosity and dance display. Summer and Autumn are both *pas de deux,* the latter rivaling the former in exuberance.

When *The Seasons* was first presented in America, Clive Barnes wrote in the New York *Times* that "Cranko has never choreographed with more authority. . . . The dancing has a range, scope and sheer bigness that have to be associated with the Bolshoi Ballet and nothing else. . . . Cranko's pure dance choreography has more vigor than it ever had. . . . The dancing is the best the Stuttgart has ever given us."

# SEBASTIAN

*Ballet in one act and three scenes. Music and libretto by Gian-Carlo Menotti. Choreography by Edward Caton. Scenery by Oliver Smith. Costumes by Milena. First presented by Ballet International at the International Theatre, New York, October 31, 1944, with Francisco Moncion in the title role. Restaged with new choreography by Agnes de Mille for American Ballet Theatre, May 27, 1957, with Lupe Serrano and John Kriza in principal roles. Restaged with new choreography by John Butler for the Netherlands Dance Theatre, Amsterdam, Autumn 1963, and introduced to the United States in 1966 by the Harkness Ballet, with Brunilda Ruiz, Lawrence Rhodes, Roderick Drew, Hester Fitzgerald, and Sarah Thomas in principal roles. Scenery and costumes by Jacques Noel, lighting by Nicholas Cernovich.*

This dramatic ballet is set in Venice at the end of the seventeenth century. The prince, in love with a notorious courtesan, has two possessive sisters who wish to break up the affair. They steal her veil, knowing that its possession will enable them to exercise black magic over her. Constructing a wax image of the courtesan, they cover it with her veil and plan to kill her by piercing the image with arrows. But the Moorish slave Sebastian, who has loved the courtesan, substitutes himself for the wax figure and takes the deadly arrows. By his self-sacrifice, he breaks the evil power, reuniting the prince with his beloved.

## SECRET PLACES

*Music by Wolfgang Amadeus Mozart. Choreography by Gerald Arpino. Setting by Ming Cho Lee. Lighting by Thomas Skelton. Pianist: Stanley Babin. Dedicated in living memory of Lorraine Squadron. First presented by the City Center Joffrey Ballet at the City Center, New York, February 20, 1968, with Lisa Bradley and Dermot Burke.*

A dance for two young lovers, *Secret Places* is performed to the second movement of Mozart's *Piano Concerto No. 21 in C Major* (K. 467). The dance begins in silence. The curtain rises on a dark woodland scene where the rays of the sun barely penetrate. On the left stand three golden trees. A girl enters. She walks through the glade, touches gently one of the trees, then goes. A boy comes from the opposite direction, looks about, leaves. The girl returns but this time as she starts to go her walk speeds up and becomes almost a dance step. Similarly with the boy; and as the two go and return yet again, just missing an encounter, their steps accelerate in speed and intensity so that there is an urgency in the air. Finally, as she leaps backward into the air, the boy is there to catch her, she is safe, they are together and the dance, with the music, begins.

Thoughtful and introspective with the score, the dance mirrors quiet joy, cautious discovery, exultation, and celebration of first love. At the end, the boy holds the girl high, she descends in a graceful pose, and they walk off into the forest.

## SEPHARDIC SONG

*Traditional music arranged by Manuel Valls. Choreography by Eliot Feld. Setting and costumes by Santo Loquasto. Lighting by Jennifer Tipton. First presented by the Eliot Feld Ballet at the New York Shakespeare Public Theatre, May 30, 1974, with Naomi Sorkin, George Montalbana, Suzanne Erlon, Valerie Felt, and Elizabeth Lee. Flute, Paul Dunkel; guitar, Fred Hand; soprano, Meria Sargon.*

This is a dance ballet performed to Iberian Jewish songs that are sung at the side of the stage. There is an atmosphere and feeling of the nearby sea in ropes or nets that are set against a sunset in the background. The persons who inhabit the ballet seem to be fisherfolk. There are different combinations. Four girls begin the piece, weaving in and out in a kind of chain to the songs that are being sung. Wives of fishermen at sea, they await their return. Later, one comes—or is he a lover?—to dance with one of the girls. The idea appears to be that everyone here is beloved—a friend, perhaps a lover—at any event all united and unafraid.

Reviewing the ballet for *Dance News*, the critic Nancy Goldner wrote: "This is one of those deceptively simple ballets, in which dancers 'just dance' . . . Feld has really caught the essence of lament because he discovers its neutrality—neither sad nor happy, but a mixture; in short, lyrical. As such it is a profound embodiment of the music, traditional Spanish songs, with their tantalizing off-key Flamenco mode."

In 1975 a new setting by Ming Cho Lee and costumes by Stanley Simmons replaced the first designs.


# SERENADE

*Classic ballet in four parts. Music by Peter Ilyich Tchaikovsky. Choreography by George Balanchine. Costumes by Jean Lurçat. First presented by students of the School of American Ballet at the estate of Felix M. Warburg, White Plains, New York, June 9, 1934. Presented by the producing company of the School of American Ballet at the Avery Memorial Theatre, Hartford, Connecticut, December 6, 1934, with Kathryn Mullowney, Heidi Vossler, and Charles Laskey in the principal roles.*

Named after its music—Tchaikovsky's *Serenade in C major for String Orchestra*—*Serenade* tells its story musically and choreographically, without any extraneous narrative. Because Tchaikovsky's score, though it was not composed for the ballet, has in its danceable four movements different qualities suggestive of different emotions and human situations, parts of the ballet seem to have a story: the apparently "pure" dance takes on a kind of plot. But this plot, inherent in the score, contains many stories—it is many things to many listeners to the music, and many things to many people who see the ballet.

Most people would agree that a nonprogrammatic piece of music doesn't have to have a story to be a pleasure: we enjoy symphonies by Tchaikovsky and Mozart just as much as we enjoy a symphony with a story, such as Beethoven's *Pastorale*. *Serenade* is programmatic only insofar as its music is programmatic.

To tell a story about something is simply a very human way of saying that we understand it. Making a ballet is a choreographer's way of showing how he understands a piece of music, not in words, not in narrative form (unless he has in mind a particular story), but in dancing.

The four movements of Tchaikovsky's score are danced in the following order, without interruption: (1) Piece in the Form of a Sonatina: *Andante non troppo, Allegro;* (2) Waltz; (3) Tema Russo: *Andante, Allegro con spirito;* (4) Elegy. Twenty-eight dancers in blue costumes dance the ballet before a blue background.

FIRST MOVEMENT  The orchestra plays the strong and spacious opening chords of the brief Andante section and repeats them deeply before the curtain rises. When we see the stage, a group of girls stand in a tableau of crossing lines. It is night. The shadowed light that shines upon them is soft. They are motionless at first, then respond to the music as the light brightens and the new melodious Allegro is heard.

The girls dance in small groups, forming patterns on the stage. One girl dances alone, turning, posing, leaping among the others. Others seem to imitate her originality, but then all are whirling faster and faster in a wide circle together. Suddenly, quickly, each girl stands motionless in the same tableau that opened the ballet, and the familiar chords of the introductory Andante are repeated.

One girl comes in late. She finds her place in the group and stands with the other girls. A boy enters at the back of the stage. As he walks forward toward the girl, her friends leave the stage.

SECOND MOVEMENT   A waltz begins as the boy reaches the girl. They begin to dance together, the girl moving away from him, then rejoining him. When her friends re-enter, the girl dances joyously among them; then she and her partner lead them in a dance, the boy lifting the ballerina high in front of the group. The waltz slowly and softly ends, and the group walks off to the tempo of its concluding rhythms.

THIRD MOVEMENT (the fourth movement in the original suite)   Five girls remain on stage. They sit together on the stage as the music is quiet, turning toward each other in gentle movements. They rise and, at the first sound of the brilliant Russian melody, respond immediately and dance with open gaiety. A boy rushes on and meets a girl; they dance together; and when the ensemble runs off, as the music finishes, we see that the girl has fallen to the floor, her head buried in her arms. She is alone.

FOURTH MOVEMENT   Another girl brings a boy to her. This girl walks behind the boy, guiding him forward: it is as if she moved him, as if he saw only what she wished. When they reach the fallen girl, the boy helps her to rise and now dances with the two of them. He remains with them, dancing with one of them alone, then both together, until there comes a time when he must choose. The girl who possessed him first, the girl who brought him to the other, claims him irrevocably and he leaves with her. The forsaken heroine collapses, revives briefly, and then is lost. Three boys lift her straight up above their shoulders. Her body arches back slowly as they carry her forward in a quiet procession; her arms open wide.

NOTES   *Serenade* was my first ballet in the United States. Soon after my arrival in America, Lincoln Kirstein, Edward M. M. Warburg, and I opened the School of American Ballet in New York. As part of the school curriculum, I started an evening ballet class in stage technique, to give students some idea of how dancing on stage differs from classwork. *Serenade* evolved from the lessons I gave.

It seemed to me that the best way to make students aware of stage technique was to give them something new to dance, something they had never seen before. I chose Tchaikovsky's *Serenade* to work with. The class contained, the first night, seventeen girls and no boys. The problem was, how to arrange this odd number of girls so that they would look interesting. I placed them on diagonal lines and decided that the hands should move first to give the girls practice.

That was how *Serenade* began. The next class contained only nine girls; the third, six. I choreographed to the music with the pupils I happened to have at a particular time. Boys began to attend the class and they were worked into the pattern. One day, when all the girls rushed off the floor area we were using as a stage, one of the girls fell and began to cry. I told the pianist to keep on playing and kept this bit in the dance. Another day, one of the girls was late for class, so I left that in too.

Later, when we staged *Serenade*, everything was revised. The girls who couldn't dance well were left out of the more difficult parts; I elaborated on the small accidental bits I had included in class and made the whole more dramatic, more theatrical, synchronizing it to the music with additional movement, but always using the little things that ordinarily might be overlooked.

I've gone into a little detail here about *Serenade* because many people think there is a concealed story in the ballet. There is not. There are, simply, dancers in motion to a beautiful piece of music. The only story is the music's story, a serenade, a dance, if you like, in the light of the moon.

*Serenade* has seen a number of different productions. It was produced by the American Ballet, the company made up of our dancers at the School of American Ballet, in its first season, at the Adelphi Theatre, New York, March 1–15, 1935. It was staged for the Ballet Russe de Monte Carlo, October 17, 1940, at the Metropolitan Opera House, with costumes by Lurçat and a cast headed by Marie-Jeanne, Igor Youskevitch, and Frederic Franklin. In 1941 *Serenade* was mounted for the South American tour of the American Ballet Caravan in a new production with costumes by Alvin Colt. In 1947 it was staged for the ballet of the Paris Opéra. On October 18, 1948, *Serenade* became part of the permanent repertory of the New York City Ballet. This production has costumes by Karinska.

The leading role in *Serenade* was first danced by a group of soloists, rather than by one principal dancer. In a number of productions, however, I arranged it for one dancer. But when the New York City Ballet was to make its first appearance in London, at the Royal Opera House, Covent Garden, in the summer of 1950, it seemed appropriate to introduce the company by introducing its principal dancers and the leading role was again divided and danced by our leading soloists.

*Serenade* is now danced by many ballet companies in the United States and abroad. A few years ago I finally succeeded in expanding the ballet so that it now uses all of the score of the Tchaikovsky "Serenade for Strings," something I had wanted to do for a long time. The interesting thing is that while some knowing members of the audience noticed this change and spoke to me about it, the critics didn't seem to notice at all! Perhaps they had seen the ballet too often!

Serenade was danced by students of the School of American Ballet at their annual program in 1974, at the Juilliard Theater, Lincoln Center, New York.

Don Daniels has written a long essay, "Academy: the New World of Serenade," in Ballet Review (Vol. 5, No. 1, 1975–76).


## SERENADE IN A

*Music by Igor Stravinsky. Choreography by Todd Bolender. Costumes by Stanley Simmons. Pianist: Madeleine Malraux. First presented at the New York City Ballet's Stravinsky Festival, June 21, 1972, at the New York State Theatre, Lincoln Center, with Susan Hendl, Robert Maiorano, Robert Weiss, and ensemble.*

Stravinsky's *Sonata in A for Piano* is dated 1925 and lasts twelve minutes—just long enough for each of the four movements to fill one side of a ten-inch recording in those days. Stravinsky never resented specifics about time. When we were working on new ballets together he always wanted to know precisely how long a particular dance or *pas d'action* would last, so that his music would be a perfect fit.

Todd Bolender arranged a dance ballet to the *Sonata* for our Stravinsky Festival. There are four movements—*Hymne, Romanza, Rondoletto,* and *Cadenza Finale.*

Writing after the premiere in the New York *Post*, the critic Frances Herridge said that "the solos and duets are lovely. The movement is softly romantic and stunningly danced by the long-legged Susan Hendl in one of her most important roles to date."

The New York City Ballet was fortunate to have the French pianist Madeleine Malraux play the music on this occasion.


## THE SEVEN DEADLY SINS

*Music by Kurt Weill. Choreography by George Balanchine. Libretto by Bertolt Brecht. First presented by Les Ballets 1933 at the Théâtre de Champs-Élysées, Paris, June 7, 1933, with Lotte Lenya and Tilly Losch in the leading roles. First presented in the United States by the New York City Ballet at the City Center, New York, December 4, 1958, with Lotte Lenya and Allegra Kent in the leading roles. Translation by W. H. Auden and Chester Kallman. Scenery and costumes by Rouben Ter-Arutunian.*

This is a ballet in song and dance about the seven deadly sins—sloth, pride, anger, gluttony, lust, avarice, and envy. The words and music were commissioned by Les Ballets 1933, for which I did the choreography. Twenty-five years later, when the New York City Ballet was about to celebrate its tenth anniversary at the City Center, Lincoln Kirstein, who had seen the original production, suggested that it might be revived.

Kurt Weill's Three-Penny Opera had been playing to full houses in New York for some years and the time seemed to be ripe for presentation of another important Weill-Brecht collaboration. When Lotte Lenya consented to participate and to sing the leading role again, I knew we would indeed have to do it.

I did not remember many details of the original production, which had been performed for only a few weeks in 1933, but working with Weill's score and the libretto, a great deal came back to me. Rouben Ter-Arutunian's setting and costumes were immensely helpful in making the work unified.

The ballet is the story of two Annies, a singing Annie who narrates the progress of a silent dancing Annie in her search for enough money to build a home for her family back in Louisiana. Annie travels to seven American cities, in each of which she encounters a sin. Annie I is the experienced alter ego of the innocent Annie II. Sings Annie I

"She's the one with the looks, I'm realistic;
She's just a little mad, my head is on straight.
You may think you can see two people,
But in fact you see only one
And both of us are Annie."

At the beginning, we see Annie's family gathered under a fringed lampshade, lamenting Annie's indolence. They call her "Lazy Bones," ask her to "think of us" and to send money for the "little home down by the Mississippi." In Scene 1, "Sloth," Annie I photographs Annie II compromising innocent passers-by for blackmail.

In Scene 2, "Pride," Annie works as a cabaret dancer in Memphis and talks about art, which Annie I deprecates. Speaking for Annie's family, she explains that

"When a man has paid for his evening,
He expects a good show in return . . .
Leave your pride to those who can well afford it . . ."

In Scene 3, "Anger," Annie is in Los Angeles working as a movie extra. While she is sickened at the cruelty she sees there, Annie I sings that "open disapproval of injustice is widely disapproved," and that "Unforgiving anger is from the Devil."

Scene 4, "Gluttony," takes place in Philadelphia, where Annie II does well as an acrobatic dancer. Because of her career, however, she must diet heavily. "Gluttons," sing the family, "never go to heaven."

Scene 5 is in Boston, where Annie is loved by a wealthy man but loves another. The singing Annie persuades her that love for love's sake is nothing but "Lust."

In Scene 6, "Envy," in San Francisco, Annie II envies others while Annie I sings:

"Don't let the flesh and its longings get you,
Remember the price a lover must pay,
And say to yourself when temptation besets you—

What is the use?
What is the use?
Beauty will perish and youth pass away."

Scene 7, "Avarice," sung by the family, shows Annie set up in Baltimore:

"She must be doing all right
And raking it in
To get in the news like that . . ."

After the seven years and the seven cities and the seven sins, the two Annies return to the little house in Louisiana. The family sings:

"Who fights the Good Fight and all Self subdues
Wins the Palm, gains the Crown."

## SHADOW OF THE WIND

*Ballet in six parts. Music by Gustav Mahler. Choreography by Antony Tudor. Scenery and costumes by Jo Mielziner. First presented by Ballet Theatre at the Metropolitan Opera House, New York, April 14, 1948, with Igor Youskevitch, Hugh Laing, Dimitri Romanoff, Alicia Alonso, John Kriza, Mary Burr, Ruth Ann Koesun, Crandall Diehl, Diana Adams, Nana Gollner, Muriel Bentley, and Barbara Fallis in principal roles.*

*Shadow of the Wind* is based on Mahler's *Song of the Earth,* a symphony for alto and tenor with orchestra. The critic Alfred Meyer has observed of this song cycle which is based on ancient Chinese texts: "It is not the earth that sings, and the poems deal less with the aspects of nature than with the philosophy of human existence."[*] The choreographer has said that his ballet symbolizes the impermanence of existence, the Chinese philosophy of accepting the mutations of life and bowing before them. Like the seasons, human experience is cyclical and has no sudden beginning or end.

In keeping with his interpretation of the score, the setting for Tudor's ballet is also Chinese. To the first song for solo tenor, "The Drinking Song of Earthly Woe," five men, one an old poet, another an old warrior, dance to the words: "O man, what is the span of thy life?/Not a hundred years art thou permitted to enjoy/The vanities of this earth!" The second song, for alto, about loneliness in autumn and the passing of life, is transposed in dance terms to be a presentation of an abandoned wife: "Autumn in my heart too long is lasting. O sun of love, never again wilt thou shine to dry my bitter tears?" The tenor's song of youth describes a pretty Chinese landscape with a green and white porcelain pavilion in a little pool that is reached by a bridge of jade. "My Lord Summons Me" is the name of the dance for a girl, a boy, and the ensemble. "The Lotus Gatherers" is the title of the next section, which is performed by a girl and the ensemble to a contralto solo about beauty, where youthful maidens

[*] See THE SONG OF THE EARTH, page 560.

pluck lotus flowers at the shore, where lovers play at longing. The fifth part, "Conversation with Winepot and Bird," is accompanied by the tenor lament that all life is woeful and wine the only reality. The final dance, "Poem of the Guitar," is performed to Mahler's "Farewell" for contralto: the poet waits for his friend for a last farewell but looks to the coming spring to waken the world anew.

## SHADOWPLAY

*Music by Charles Koechlin. Choreography by Antony Tudor. Scenery and costumes by Michael Annals. First presented by the Royal Ballet at the Royal Opera House, Covent Garden, January 25, 1967, with Anthony Dowell, Merle Park, and Derek Rencher in the principal roles. First presented in the United States by the Royal Ballet at the new Metropolitan Opera House, May 2, 1967, with the same principals.*

*Shadowplay* is an allegory about growing up. The scene is the jungle, where a Boy with Matted Hair sits alone. Creatures from the jungle world surround him and although he would prefer to be alone, he sees that he cannot remain passive to relationships. "Arboreals and Aerials"—monkeys and bright birds—come and then a dominating male figure called "Terrestrial" confronts the boy. He will not, however, submit to his will. The boy is then drawn to a "Celestial" figure, a beautiful goddess whose remoteness enchants him, but again masters his feelings after two close encounters. He is now a different person and his air of authority as he sits alone in the jungle affects the animals, too, who ape his civilized gestures and would copy his example. Then instinctively he copies theirs and scratches himself; the end is something like the beginning.

*Shadowplay* is set to music by the French composer Charles Koechlin (1867–1950), who wrote seven orchestral works on themes drawn from *The Jungle Book* by Rudyard Kipling. The score of the ballet consists of the last of these, *Les Bandar-Log*, and selections from *La Course de Printemps*. The ballet uses *The Jungle Book* situation as a point of departure for larger allegory. The critic Clive Barnes wrote after its New York *première* that the ballet "has as many meanings as an onion has layers, but basically it seems to be about the realms of experience and the attainment of grace . . . Tudor has produced a strange and engrossing work, a ballet that even at first glance has the look and feel of a major work."

*Shadowplay* was presented by American Ballet Theatre in 1975 for Mikhail Baryshnikov.

## SHÉHÉRAZADE

*Music by Maurice Ravel. Choreography by George Balanchine. Lighting by Ronald Bates. First presented by the New York City Ballet at the Hommage à Ravel at the New York State Theatre, Lincoln Center, May 22,*

*1975, with Kay Mazzo and Edward Villella as principals. Conducted by Robert Irving.*

Our plans for the Ravel Festival at the New York City Ballet were well advanced when I decided that I wished to add yet another work. *Shéhérazade* was Ravel's first piece composed for orchestra and one of his first works to be performed in public. His friend Tristan Klingsor, the painter and poet, had told Ravel tales of his travels in the East and the composer, attracted since his childhood to the exotic, the mysterious and fantastic, began work on an elaborate conception of an opera based on Galland's *A Thousand and One Nights*. He actually only finished the *Overture,* which is used for this ballet. Later, Ravel set three of Klingsor's poems as a song cycle, for yet another version of *Shéhérazade.*

The ballet's action is simple to describe—it is a dance for a girl and boy accompanied by two couples and eight girls. If it all seems to take place in another world remote from the present time, well, that is a way of thinking of Shéhérazade and the tales she told.


## SINFONIETTA

*Music by Malcolm Williamson. Choreography by Frederick Ashton. Costumes by Peter Rice. First presented by the Royal Ballet at the Royal Shakespeare Theater, Stratford-on-Avon, February 10, 1967, with Doreen Wells and David Wall in principal roles.*

*Sinfonietta* is a modern ballet with new music by one of England's leading young composers and a new design idea conceived by one of Britain's art colleges. Against the backdrop on stage moving shapes and light patterns are projected to accompany the dances. There is no story.

The ballet, like the music, is in three parts: toccata, elegy, and tarantella. The first is arranged for two couples, the second for a girl and five boys. This part, the elegy, has been called by the English critic Andrew Porter a "new Rose Adagio in a marvelous modern idiom." Here the girl is held and carried so that she seems never to touch the ground. The final movement is a brisk and gay tarantella for the ensemble from which one of the boys darts in and out to perform brilliant and challenging variations.

*Music by Paul Hindemith. Choreography by Jacques d'Amboise. Lighting by Ronald Bates. Dedicated to Bunny and Arthur Horowitz. First presented by the New York City Ballet at the New York State Theatre, Lincoln Center, January 9, 1975.*

The late Paul Hindemith, one of the half-dozen leading composers of the present century, came from Germany to teach at Yale University in 1940; he remained there the rest of his life. Lincoln Kirstein has noted that Hindemith, an extremely prolific composer, "was particularly interested in dancing." Among his earliest compositions were the famous *Triadic Ballet; Nobilissima Visione* (St. Francis): Massine/Tchelitchew (1938); and *Herodiade* for Martha Graham (1944). I myself greatly enjoyed working with Hindemith's music on several occasions. So, too, did Jacques d'Amboise in this ballet, arranged to the *Sinfonietta in E.* The work is a dance occasion, based on the music itself, without story.

## SITUATION

*Choreography by Hans van Manen. Decor and costumes by Jean-Paul Vroom. Lighting by Oliver Wood. First presented by the Netherlands Dance Theatre at the Circustheater, Scheveningen, Holland, April 20, 1970. First presented in the United States by the same ensemble at the Brooklyn Academy of Music, New York, April 1, 1972.*

*Situation* is a series of dances to a series of sounds, all set in a specific place, a room lined with graph paper, measuring 27 × 20 × 14 feet and with a digital clock on the wall, telling the precise time. This room contains its own story as the dancers come and go through one door to varied sounds: hunting, shooting, machine gun fire, a water tap, a bath filling, a jet engine, walking in gravel, rain on the street, and mosquitoes. The dancers are anonymous, stretching like gymnasts, coupling, responding to the sounds in different ways, responding too to brief periods of silence. Certain sounds appear to turn certain dancers on, others turn them off. There is rejection, satisfaction, unfulfillment, amusement, as the dance reflects the sounds in ways that appear individual to the performers.

## SLAUGHTER ON TENTH AVENUE

*Dramatic ballet within a musical revue. Music by Richard Rodgers. Choreography by George Balanchine. Scenery by Jo Mielziner. Costumes by Irene Sharaff. First presented by Dwight Deere Wiman in the musical revue* On Your Toes *(Richard Rodgers-George Abbott-Lorenz Hart) at the Imperial Theatre, New York, April 11, 1936, with Ray Bolger, Tamara Geva, and George Church as the principal dancers.*

The ballet *Slaughter on Tenth Avenue* was not a separate dance number in the great musical comedy *On Your Toes*, but a ballet that was part of the story. This story, a take-off on Russian ballet, had for its central theme a question very appropriate for its time: how could an American upstart hope to make good in a famous Russian ballet company?

Junior (Ray Bolger) was the American. Almost overnight he found himself a member of this famous Russian company when he successfully substituted for a dancer who had fallen ill. But young Junior didn't like the ballets the company danced. Sergei Alexandrovitch (Monty Woolley), the company's impresario, preferred ballets in the lush, pseudo-Russian, romantic style.

Junior thought he knew how to remedy this situation. He himself came from a vaudeville family, he knew a lot about music, and he tried to induce the company to accept an idea for a new kind of ballet. The ballerina (Tamara Geva) was all in favor of the idea, but the pompous Russian *premier danseur* (Demetrios Vilan) was jealous of Junior's talent and immediately began to plot against him. Only the enthusiasm of the company's rich patroness permitted Junior to proceed with his plan.

Rehearsals for the new ballet began. It was called *Slaughter on Tenth Avenue* and told a modern story of love and death. Junior himself was to dance the hero, a hoofer who one night visits a low dive on New York's West Side. Here he meets the strip-teaser (Tamara Geva), dances with her, and the two fall in love. But the girl is married to the big boss (George Church), who has been watching his wife dance so warmly with one of the customers. He breaks up the dance, fights with the hoofer, and pulls a knife on him. Accidentally he stabs the girl. She dies. The hoofer attacks the big boss and kills him. He dances around the body.

We learn that the ballet will end with the hoofer's suicide. He has killed the murderer, but is himself a murderer. The girl is dead; he has nothing to live for.

The day of the *première* of the new ballet approaches. Already *Slaughter* is popular with the company. But the *premier danseur* is determined that it shall fail and that Junior shall leave the company. To ensure his ends, he hires a group of gangsters, men very similar to the tough guys standing around the bar in the Tenth Avenue joint depicted in the ballet. The *danseur* gives these men tickets for a box near the stage for the opening night of the ballet, instructs them to eliminate Junior, and tells them how they can do it without being caught. At the end of *Slaughter on Tenth Avenue*, Junior is supposed to shoot himself. If they shoot him from the box, the ballet will end as planned, the curtain will fall, and no one will have any idea who committed the crime.

The gangsters agree. On the night of the *première*, they sit in a box in the theatre overlooking the stage. *Slaughter on Tenth Avenue* begins. We watch the action, are moved by the lyrical *pas de deux* danced by the hoofer and the girl, then see her murdered. As she dies in her lover's arms, the ballerina who is playing the girl speaks to Junior. She warns him of the plot against his life, which she overheard just before the rise of the curtain. She tells him that the gangsters will not dare to kill him if at the end of the ballet he keeps on dancing: he must change the ending and not shoot himself! The ballerina has called the police; they are sure to arrive in a matter of minutes.

When the big boss has been dispatched, Junior begins his dance of despair around the dead man's body. Then he improvises, dancing so artfully a frantic dance of death that the audience is unaware of any change. He moves faster and faster, incredibly spinning with ever greater energy, when his last strength seems to be spent. As he almost collapses on the stage from exhaustion, the police arrive. They arrest the frightened gangsters and the *premier danseur* amid tremendous applause for the new ballet. *Slaughter on Tenth Avenue* is a hit. Junior is the dancer of the hour. His success assured, the upstart hoofer marries the American girl he has loved all along and lives happily ever after.

NOTES   *On Your Toes* was the first musical I choreographed in the United States. Working with Lorenz Hart, Richard Rodgers, and George Abbott on this show made my job a pleasure from the start. The team of Rodgers and Hart represented for me, as it did for so many Americans, superb entertainment in the musical theatre. These men devised over the years a seemingly endless series of revues that were melodically and lyrically filled with great wit, touching humor, and eminent theatricality. After *On Your Toes*, it was my privilege to work with them on three other revues. *On Your Toes* was also my first association with the fine artist and comedian Ray Bolger, whose dancing throughout the show, and in *Slaughter*, will scarcely be forgotten by those who saw it.

# THE SLEEPING BEAUTY

*Classic ballet in three acts, with prologue. Music by Peter Ilyich Tchaikovsky. Choreography by Marius Petipa. Book by Marius Petipa and Ivan Vsevolojsky, after tales by Charles Perrault. Scenery and costumes by Ivan Vsevolojsky. First presented at the Maryinsky Theatre, St. Petersburg, Russia, January 15, 1890, with Carlotta Brianza as the Princess Aurora, Paul Gerdt as the Prince, Marie Petipa as the Lilac Fairy, Enrico Cecchetti as Carabosse, Varvara Nikitina as the Enchanted Princess, and Enrico Cecchetti as the Bluebird. First presented in Western Europe by Diaghilev's Ballets Russes at the Alhambra Theatre, London, November 2, 1921. Staged by Nicholas Sergeyev after the choreography of Marius Petipa. Additional choreography by Bronislava Nijinska. Orchestration of Prelude to Act Three and the Princess Aurora's variation in Act Three by Igor Stravinsky. Scenery and costumes by Léon Bakst. The cast included Olga Spessivtzeva as the Princess Aurora, Pierre Vladimiroff as the Prince, Lydia Lopokova as the Lilac Fairy, Carlotta Brianza as Carabosse, Felia Dubrovska, Lydia Sokolova, Bronislava Nijinska, Lubov Egorova, and Vera Nemtchinova as the Fairies, Ludmilla Shollar as the White Cat, Lydia Lopokova as the Enchanted Princess, and Stanislas Idzikowski as the Bluebird. Revived by the Sadler's Wells Ballet at the Sadler's Wells Theatre, London, February 2, 1939, in a new production staged by Nicholas Sergeyev after choreography by Marius Petipa. Scenery and costumes by Nadia Benois. The cast included Margot Fonteyn as the Princess Aurora, Robert Helpmann as the Prince, June Brae as the Lilac Fairy, and Mary Honer and Harold Turner as the Bluebirds. Revived by the Sadler's Wells Ballet in a new production under the supervision of Nicholas Sergeyev at the Royal Opera House, Covent Garden, February 20, 1946. Additional choreography by Frederick Ashton and Ninette de Valois. Scenery and costumes by Oliver Messel. Margot Fonteyn as the Princess Aurora, Robert Helpmann as the Prince, Beryl Grey as the Lilac Fairy, and Pamela May and Alexis Rassine as the Blue-*

birds *headed the cast. First presented in the United States by the Sadler's Wells Ballet at the Metropolitan Opera House, New York, October 9, 1949, with Margot Fonteyn and Robert Helpmann, Beryl Grey, Moira Shearer, and Alexis Rassine. Catherine Littlefield, Director of the Philadelphia Ballet, produced a complete version of* The Sleeping Beauty *with her own choreography at the Academy of Music, Philadelphia, February 12, 1937. This version was later produced at the Lewisohn Stadium, New York, July 29 and 30, 1937.*

The crashing, commanding chords of the brief overture to *The Sleeping Beauty* herald the special magic of the fairy tale the ballet relates, a fairy tale that is rich and formal in presentation, but warm and intimate in effect. Tchaikovsky and Petipa have so fashioned Perrault's story of the sleeping princess (*"La Belle au Bois Dormant,"* from *Mother Goose*) for the theater that notions of reality are suspended in favor of belief in characters who can live forever, in a curse of black magic that can put a forest to sleep for a hundred years, and in a beneficent fairy whose magic can rescue all goodness from evil. The time is unimportant, as is the place. The nameless mythical kingdom of the mythical King Florestan XXIV becomes the scene of our imagination.

The intensity of the music demands the attention, focusing it, as it were, on the splendor of the opening scene. The overture to *The Sleeping Beauty* also contains in miniature the story it introduces. Concealed within the opening regal chords is a theme that represents the fairy Carabosse, the evil fairy who will cast a spell upon the ballet's heroine and her family. This music is quickly interrupted by the melodious harp, which introduces a soft, slow, magical, compassionate theme—the melody of the Lilac Fairy, whose beauty and goodness will triumph over the evil fairy's challenge.

Now the music changes to a march tempo, quietly at first, then more assertively. The melody swells. The curtain rises.

PROLOGUE: THE CHRISTENING  The hall of King Florestan's palace is high-ceilinged. Great arches of stone cross the back of the stage; through them can be discerned the foliage of the garden. Drapery of resplendent color and ornament warms the spaciousness of the scene. On the right, on a small platform, stands the canopied cradle of the Princess Aurora, guarded by two nurses on each side. Two heralds stand at the back. Almost immediately the king's master of ceremonies, Cattalabutte, enters in elaborate full dress. With great flourish, he busies himself seeing that all is ready for the ceremony. Satisfied, he comes forward, gives a page his stick of office, and scans the list of guests who have been invited to attend the christening of the princess.

Twelve ladies in waiting enter the chamber. They circle the stage and ceremoniously ask Cattalabutte if they may see the child. He consents and leads them over to the cradle, where they hover over the princess. Cattalabutte directs a page to notify the king that all the preparations have been made and nervously unrolls the guest list again to check his memory. The ladies retire from the cradle and stand to one side. A fanfare sounds in the distance; it grows louder; three pages enter. To the blaring of trumpets, the king and

queen approach. They pause for a moment under the silk canopy that is held
high above them by Negroes dressed in gold and survey the scene. Then their
attendants drop their trains. The queen goes to the cradle. She kisses the princess and greets the ladies in waiting, who bow to her. She joins the king, who
stands in conference with Cattalabutte. After a brief consultation with their
servant, the two monarchs mount the steps to their thrones.

An arpeggio on the harp announces the arrival of the fairy godmothers of
the princess. The royal fairies are preceded by their pages, who enter two by
two and bow to their sovereigns. Five of the fairies enter in a group: the Fairy
of the Crystal Fountain, the Fairy of the Enchanted Garden, the Fairy of the
Woodland Glades, the Fairy of the Songbirds, and the Fairy of the Golden
Vine. Eight maids of honor attend them. Last of all comes the Fairy of the
Lilac, accompanied by six cavaliers, one for each of the fairies. The cavaliers
carry, on plush cushions, the gifts the fairies have chosen for their godchild.
The Lilac Fairy leads the group forward. The fairies bow low to the king and
queen, who welcome them cordially, and arrange themselves about the royal
cradle to bless the princess. They bow again to the king and queen and leave
the scene.

The maids of honor come forward in two lines and, to the syncopated
rhythm of a new melody, they dance in linear patterns. They are joined by the
cavaliers, who leap boldly in the air. The fairies return, and all dance together
briefly. The queen thanks the Lilac Fairy for the dance and asks the group to
continue. The Lilac Fairy bows.

A new tender theme is heard, accompanied by runs on the harp. The fairies
and their partners arrange themselves in five moving circles, the Lilac Fairy in
the center. Two of the girls in the back are lifted to their partners' shoulders
and turned around and around so that they appear to be swimming high in the
air. The fairies come forward to the footlights. One by one, the fairies pirouette rapidly and pose in attitude supported by their cavaliers. The maids of
honor lie at their feet in respectful obeisance.

The tableau is broken; the music subsides, then regains in volume; in a
hushed pause, the royal nurses bring the small princess to the center of the
stage. There is a magical rushing run on the harp, and the Lilac Fairy is lifted
high above the princess. She blesses the babe with her wand. The *pas de six* is
over. The harp plays for a moment, the tempo changes, and the fairies leave
the stage while the maids of honor dance a new sprightly measure in unison.

Now each of the fairies returns to perform a variation before the assembled
court. These variations are very short; they have no literal significance, and the
attributes of the different fairies cannot be read into them; but the different
music and different dances that Tchaikovsky and Petipa devised for the six
fairies gives each of the variations an individual, distinctive character. First is
the Fairy of the Crystal Fountain. She enters and waits for her music to begin.
Its movement is slow and leisurely; its melody, calm. The fairy dances forward
and moves back and forth across the stage on her points, her body in graceful
repose. As her feet mark the retarded rhythm of her music, her head and arms
depict the quiet sweetness of the melody. She kneels to the king and queen as
her variation ends and leaves the stage.

The Fairy of the Enchanted Garden emerges to dance with quick steps to a brighter tempo—music which carries her into swift pirouettes that accelerate as she moves across the stage. For the Fairy of the Woodland Glades, the music is characterized by a soft, tempered pizzicato. This fairy's skill in quiet, slow movement is revealed in the daring figure that highlights her dance: she dances forward on one foot, her other foot extended before her. With subdued brilliance her extended foot moves back, and the girl stands poised for a breathless moment in arabesque. This figure is repeated as she continues to move forward. Then her dance becomes luminous and light, with rapid dancing on point. She ends her variation standing on point, with open arms, one leg raised pertly before her.

In a flashing yellow costume, the Fairy of the Songbirds dances now to a hurried, tinkling melody, her arms moving ecstatically in simulated flight, her bright head turning to the shimmering elevation of the rhythm. She is followed by the Fairy of the Golden Vine, whose dance is characterized by the curt, staccato movement of her head and the quick pointing of the index fingers of both her hands—the so-called "Finger Variation." The tempo of the music increases sharply, and the brilliant fairy whirls to a quick, sudden stop.

The Lilac Fairy comes forward. She stands toward the back of the stage. The orchestra begins a sumptuously melodic waltz, and the Lilac Fairy accompanies its flowing line with extended, open movements in which her raised point traces small circles in the air. Then she turns in arabesque; she pauses briefly each time her body is seen in profile. In the rapid complexity of its movement and in the fullness of the magnificent waltz, the variation of the Lilac Fairy sums up in splendid grandeur the dances of all the other fairies.

Now the cavaliers dance. The maids of honor join them with light, precise movements. The fairies reassemble at the front of the stage. Their cavaliers hold them in attitude. The fairies' gifts are presented to the king and queen. The queen leaves the throne and delightedly examines the presents. There is a deep, rumbling sound, like an earthquake, off stage. Some of the courtiers imagine it to be only thunder, but the king is apprehensive. The queen trembles for the safety of her child, and the master of ceremonies cowers. A page rushes in and gestures helplessly to the king, pointing off to the left. The king understands suddenly and rushes over to Cattalabutte and demands to see the invitation list. He scans it rapidly, then dashes the scroll to the floor in a gigantic rage. Cattalabutte's fate is averted momentarily by the frightening appearance of two great rats, who emerge from the left and dance a few insidious steps. They run back out. Before the court has recovered, they return with other rats, pulling along behind them an enormous black coach. Standing majestically in the coach is the fairy Carabosse, the hunchbacked godmother of the Princess Aurora, whom the forgetful Cattalabutte has neglected to invite to the christening. She grasps at the air in her fury; her black chariot circles the stage, sweeping all the courtiers aside.

Assisted by her four rodent attendants, Carabosse steps down. The music gives a low warning. Her face is a hideous blue-white mask covered with moles and magical, shining spangles. Her long black dress is tattered and dusty, yet she wears it as if it were ermine. Carabosse hobbles forward on her stick and inquires fiercely of the king, by gesture, "Why was I forgotten? Do you realize what this will mean to the fate of your child?" Already, the king is afraid. He points to Cattalabutte as the real culprit. Carabosse approaches the cowardly master of ceremonies, who kneels at her feet. He throws up his hands, begging for mercy and to protect himself, but Carabosse reaches out her talonlike fingers and tears off his wig, which she throws at the hungry rats. Now, deprived of all his dignity, the courtier attempts to escape.

Carabosse raises her stick and, with a quick thrust in the small of his back, sends him flying. She caresses the rats, who form a small square about her as she dances blithely. She gestures to the royal couple, pointing to the cradle: "Your daughter will grow up . . . She will grow up to be a beautiful princess . . . the most beautiful princess of them all; and then"—Carabosse brings down her stick loudly; the music thunders—"and then . . . she will die! . . . She will prick her finger, no one will prevent it, and she will be a beautiful dead princess." The wicked fairy cackles with glee as the king tries to comfort the distraught queen. He motions Carabosse imperiously away, but the evil fairy persists in laughing at his discomfort. She whips her great black cape through the air to the sound of the harp.

The Lilac Fairy steps out. Carabosse tries to approach the cradle to repeat her curse. The Lilac Fairy holds up her wand in quiet defiance; Carabosse stumbles back. All the other fairies gather around her to guard the cradle. She threatens them with her stick, but the good fairies stand placidly impervious. The hideous, servile rats surround the grotesque Carabosse, and she dances a final, frantic jig, at the end of which she holds up her hand in triumph. She climbs back into her carriage; as she stands under its high roof of black plumes, shaking her fists at the whole court, the obedient rats draw the black chariot off. The thunder subsides.

The queen weeps in the king's arms. He cannot comfort her. The Lilac Fairy comes to them. The lovely melody that identifies this good fairy fills the hall. She gestures toward the cradle and gives them this message in pantomime: "Your daughter, the princess, will grow up to be beautiful, and it is true that she will prick her finger and seem to die . . . but in reality she will only go to sleep . . . she will sleep for a hundred years, and all the court with her . . . but one day a prince, as handsome as she is beautiful, will come to the princess . . . she will wake at his kiss, and all will live happily ever after."

The king and queen bow to the Lilac Fairy and thank her. The release from the evil curse of Carabosse causes the court to be joyful. All the fairies bow to the king and queen, and then the entire assembly turns toward the cradle of the Princess Aurora. The queen stands over her daughter; the ladies in waiting and the maids of honor kneel in homage, and the fairies stand in attitudes of infinite protectiveness. The curtain falls.

ACT ONE: THE SPELL   The scene is the garden of the palace. A colonnade of huge columns, topped by ancient statues, sweeps in a curve about a high fountain toward the right to support a great arch of stone over the back of the garden. Thrones for the king and queen are arranged at the right. On the left, a flight of wide stone steps leads up toward the palace. Peasants idle in the distance. Ladies in waiting and their cavaliers walk about the garden, marveling at its beauty and anticipating the day's festival. For today is the Princess Aurora's sixteenth birthday, and the king has decreed a celebration in her honor. The king has also invited the court and kingdom to entertain four foreign visitors: princes from England, India, Italy, and Spain, who have come long distances to meet the young princess and pay court to her.

Three old hags in black, their dark hoods concealing their faces, stoop together over spindles. As they sew, they keep looking about cautiously. Cattalabutte enters. He has aged somewhat in the sixteen years that have passed, but still flourishes his cape and stick at every opportunity. The old women dance away from him. Cattalabutte regards them suspiciously. They try to escape, but the master of ceremonies catches them. He takes the spindles from them forcibly and stands over them threateningly. The women cower at his feet as Cattalabutte reminds them that for sixteen years, ever since the curse of the wicked fairy Carabosse, the king has ordered that no spindles be brought within a mile of the Princess Aurora. He is interrupted by the arrival of the king and queen, who are followed by the four princes. The old women scurry into a corner.

The king greets Cattalabutte and wonders what his courtier holds concealed in the hand behind his back. Reluctantly Cattalabutte holds out the dread spindles. The king is shocked and furious. Cattalabutte points to the weird women; the king commands them to come forward. He tells them that they must hang for this offense; how otherwise can he protect his daughter from the spell of Carabosse? The women kneel at his feet and plead for forgiveness. The king is adamant. To a sudden crescendo of surging, pulsating music, the queen steps forward and asks the king to relent. After all, this is Aurora's birthday and the women are truly sorry. The king smiles and consents.

The king and queen mount their thrones, carrying fresh garlands. A group of peasant girls enters. They bow deeply to their lord. The courtiers gather on the steps, and the four princes stand to one side as the girls commence to dance to a flowing waltz. The girls weave in and out under the garlands and arrange themselves in circles that travel around the stage in opposite directions. Cattalabutte thanks them when the waltz is over, and they bow to the monarchs.

Four musicians enter, carrying golden instruments, followed by eight girls—friends of the princess. The four foreign princes stand ready to greet the guest of honor. The music is expectant. The four princes look toward the back of the garden and peer down the colonnade, hoping for a glimpse of the princess. Softly the music hesitates. In the distance, under the arch, we see a beautiful girl in a pink dress embellished with silver. She poses for an instant and disappears like an apparition. Then, brilliantly, to a burst of music, she is on stage, dancing joyfully with the sweet, innocent exuberance of youth. The four princes approach her. The princess goes to her mother, who embraces her warmly, then to the king, who kisses her on the forehead. The king then introduces her to the foreign princes, who bow low to her. She responds gently. The harp plays a rushing cadenza; all the other instruments are silent, waiting; there is a brief hush, a momentary interval of preparation like the soprano's measured intake of breath before a great aria commences. The "Rose Adagio" begins.

The four princes move to the front of the stage in a line. One by one, the princes support the Princess Aurora as she dances softly and openly her preparatory steps. Then she steps back; standing on point in attitude, she greets the first prince. Holding her right hand, he turns her in attitude, as she maintains the graceful pose. When she has come full circle, the prince releases her hand; both hands are raised to form a crown above her head for a moment of balance; then the second cavalier steps forward to hold her right hand. This design is repeated. Finally, as the last prince releases her, the princess extends her body in arabesque and holds this position with breath-taking equilibrium.

One of her suitors now supports Aurora, who modestly displays her dancing skill without conveying the least impression that she is unlike any other young girl who is beautiful and happens to be dancing. Sweetly holding her hands to her cheek, the princess leans forward. She is lifted high in the air. When she is released, she dances alone in a small circle, her arms invoking the melody of the music, her strong points tracing its rhythms.

Each of the enamored princes now presents Aurora with a freshly picked rose. The theme is played softly by the oboe. One prince supports her as the others come forward, one by one, with their gifts. The princess pirouettes swiftly as she accepts each of the flowers. Then, charmingly, she leaves her suitors and presents their flowers to the queen. She moves to the back of the stage and dances forward. Armed with fresh roses, the princes kneel at her feet. As she pirouettes past them, the princes hold out their flowers; the princess pauses in her turning to receive each rose. She holds the flower to her breast for a moment, then tosses them in the air as her dance continues.

The music approaches its fullest, final expression. One of the princes holds her hand as the princess stands again on point in attitude. He releases her, and she sustains her pose as if it were effortless. Then, moving only her arm, she takes the hand of the second prince, to prepare briefly for a second, longer balance. Her modest confidence in balance increases as the adagio comes to a conclusion. When the fourth prince releases her, she stands in what seems perpetually perfect balance until the final chord breaks the enchantment. She runs off into the garden.

The eight friends of the Princess Aurora dance to a tinkling, blithe melody. Soon the princess returns. The four princes beseech her to dance again. She turns to her mother, who encourages her with a smile, and the princess begins a *pas seul*. After posing in attitude and arabesque, she goes to the corner of the garden. She dances forward on point in a diagonal line with slow precision. Step by step, she bends her right knee and brings her right leg up so that it touches gently the back of her supporting leg. The diagonal completed, she dances backward toward the corner in a series of pirouettes, each of which ends in secure, perfect position. The princess circles the garden, with brilliant, accelerating spins, and leaves the stage.

When friends commence to dance, the princess comes back. She dances toward the front with high, broad leaps in which she kicks her front foot forward—a movement that gives her dance a new urgency. She circles the stage again, this time with open, free turns rapidly executed. The tempo of the music builds with her speed, with her joy in dancing.

On the right, in the corner, half concealed by the crowd, an old woman in black emerges. She watches the happy princess, and when Aurora circles near her, holds out a present to the princess. Aurora, barely stopping, takes it and dances on, delighted with the strange, new object. The gift is a spindle! The king rises in terror and warns the court. Everyone attempts to stop Aurora's dance and take the spindle from her. But the innocent, impetuous girl is so charmed by the spindle that she cannot cease to play with it. Suddenly, she pricks her finger. Instantly, she falls to the ground.

The king and queen rush to her. The angry monarch orders the court to find the criminal who presented the princess with the fatal spindle. The princess herself has no idea of what has happened. She stirs, looks into her father's disturbed face, and shakes her head slowly, as if to say, "Don't worry, nothing is wrong." Similarly she comforts her distraught mother. To prove that everything is all right, the anxious girl rises and begins to dance again. She moves rapidly, the music accelerates ominously, and there is a clap of thunder. The princess falls into her father's arms. The cymbals clash in evil triumph, and the old woman in black steps out. She throws aside her cape: she is the fairy Carabosse, come back to court to fulfill her prophecy. She cackles with delight. The princess seems to die. Armed courtiers chase the evil fairy as she runs into the garden.

A trumpet sounds, then the harp, and the melody of the Lilac Fairy is heard. She enters with her wand and comforts the king and queen, telling them that the princess, as she foretold, is not really dead, she is merely asleep, and this is the beginning of the spell that will last a hundred years. The king and queen thank the Lilac Fairy and bow humbly. Courtiers take up the princess and carry her slowly up the steps to the palace. The Lilac Fairy ascends the stairs; the last members of the court disappear. She holds out her wand, casting a spell over the kingdom.

The stage grows dark; the garden fades in the distance. From the ground, enormous shrubs, great branches of foliage rise magically and seem to entwine the garden and the palace, smothering them in sleep. In a small point of light, the Lilac Fairy can be seen dancing softly, waving her magic wand, as the palace and its people, obedient to her command, go to sleep for a hundred years.

ACT TWO: THE VISION   A brief orchestral introduction features the sound of hunting horns, and when the curtain rises on a wooded glen, we are prepared for the entry of the royal hunting party. The scene is the forest of King Florestan XXIV, a part of the forest remote from the sleeping palace; the time, one hundred years later. The setting sun glows in the distance over rocky hills that enclose a still stream. As the hunting party comes upon the scene, it is apparent that the style of dress has changed considerably. Duchesses and dukes, marchionesses and marquesse stride about the wood in their colorful riding habits. Gallison, tutor to Prince Florimund, the leader of the hunt, totters onto the stage exhausted. Prince Florimund follows. Dressed in red riding habit, with high red boots and a feathered hat, the prince bows to his guests. A countess approaches him and makes a suggestion. The prince responds lazily and motions her away gently. The persistent countess does not acknowledge the rebuff, however. She has in mind a game of blindman's buff and persuades the tutor to bind his eyes. The old man obliges her and chases after the royal couples, who egg him on by whipping their riding crops at his feet. He stumbles around, becomes dizzy, and takes the hand of what he imagines to be a beautiful lady. He is somewhat staggered as he takes the handkerchief from his eyes and finds himself embracing a peer.

The game has not amused the guests sufficiently and they turn to other entertainment. Reluctantly the prince yields to the countess' persuasion and takes her as his partner in a stately mazurka. Peasants enter the wood at the conclusion of the dance and perform a farandole, a round dance in which the boys and girls join hands and curve about the stage in a continuous serpentine line. Every member of the hunting party is diverted by the farandole except the prince, who is moody and preoccupied. The hunting horns sound again. Attendants bring in spears for the hunt, and the lords and ladies prepare to leave. But the prince has suddenly changed his mind and urges his guests to leave without him. He will remain in the forest for a little while and rejoin them later. The countess is visibly upset at her inability to attract the prince away; she attempts to change his mind; the prince dismisses her.

Now alone in the glen, the prince walks about. Night falls; the setting sun becomes the new moon. He stares out over the lake, hoping that the beautiful scene will settle his gloom. He turns away dejectedly and walks forward. Just as he turns his back, the theme of the Lilac Fairy is heard and a magical boat floats onto the lake from the right. Its gossamer sail hangs from a silver mast; motioning the boat forward is the Lilac Fairy, who stands with upraised wand in the great sea shell that forms the boat's hull. The boat stops at her command, and the fairy steps down to earth. Still preoccupied with his own thoughts, the prince does not see her. As he moves back toward the lake, he is astonished by her presence. He bows deeply.

The Lilac Fairy then begins to instruct the prince in the cause of his woe. In a palace not far from this forest, she tells him, sleeps a beautiful princess, a princess so lovely that his mind must have envisaged her all his life. This princess has been asleep for a hundred years, yet she is only sixteen. She will sleep forever unless she is kissed by a prince who loves her.

The prince is enchanted, but somewhat skeptical, and impatiently asks the Lilac Fairy to let him see the princess. The fairy consents to show him a vision of the Princess Aurora. She points her wand to the left, and concealed within a dark tree trunk we see a misty vision of the princess. The specter disappears as quickly as it came. The prince demands to see more of her; already he is enamored of Aurora. The Lilac Fairy now allows the vision of the princess to enter in person.

The princess comes in on the right. Still the beautiful young girl of the first act, her movements are now soft and romantic. A haunting melody begins, dominated by the cellos, lending the scene a dark, mysterious atmosphere. The prince lifts Aurora high off the ground and, when he lets her down, attempts to embrace her. Fairies who have followed the princess pull him away from her, and he watches as she dances alone. The fairies form a circular tableau in the center of the scene. The princess moves about this circle, momentarily disappearing from the prince's sight. He pursues her softly, patiently, yet never catches up to her. Finally he holds her for a brief moment in his arms. The vision relaxes against him for an instant and then leaves him, like a phantom. He beseeches the Lilac Fairy to call her back again.

The sixteen nymphs dance for a short interval, and suddenly the princess returns to their midst. The flowing music becomes strongly rhythmical. Standing in the center of the stage, she dances quickly, with staccatolike urgency, a brilliant variation that excites the prince's love for her. He holds out his arms and she vanishes.

The nymphs fill the scene again with their dancing, and the princess makes a final, spinning, illusory appearance. The prince asks the Lilac Fairy, "Where has she gone? Where can I find her again?" The Lilac Fairy calms his curiosity and tells him that to find the princess, they must sail across the lake to her father's palace, where the princess lies asleep. She motions for him to follow, and the curtain falls as the Lilac Fairy's magical boat disappears in the midst of the lake.

ACT THREE, SCENE ONE: THE AWAKENING The orchestra plays a long overture, the composition that was designed originally to accompany the journey of the Lilac Fairy and the prince toward the palace, a slowly paced interlude during which the fairy's magic barge passed slowly across the lake, surrounded by a panorama of dense forest and splendid vistas of the enchanted palace.

When the curtain rises, the Lilac Fairy and the prince have already disembarked. The fairy leads the prince across the stage from the right. He follows several paces behind her, looking about him cautiously, both amazed and delighted at the sleeping forest. Only shadows can be distinguished in the background. The two walk off at the left and reappear almost immediately behind a gauze curtain. Light emerges from behind; the palace can be seen, rising high on the summit in the distance. On the ground, two guards, frozen in an attitude of perpetual slumber, sleep away their watch. The prince stares at them, unbelieving. The Lilac Fairy leads him off; the light is extinguished, only to come up again in a moment in a high-vaulted chamber—the boudoir of the Princess Aurora. The Lilac Fairy enters first, holding her wand before her. She enters through a maze of great columns entangled with cobwebs, beckoning to the prince to follow. In the half-darkness, on the left, a silken bed canopied with royal drapes dominates the apartment. Guards stand in a line, motionless, sleeping against their upright spears.

The prince enters, marveling at the oppression of the sleeping rooms and the splendor they still contain. He glances incredulously at the sleeping guards. The Lilac Fairy motions him forward to the bed. In the dim light, he sees the sleeping princess. He hesitates, not wishing to disturb her sleeping beauty. The Lilac Fairy waves her wand, and he steps forward toward the bed. Curled in an attitude of peaceful contentment, the princess lies in deep slumber, her head on an ancient, dusty pillow. The prince bends down toward her face; the Lilac Fairy gestures with her wand; he kisses her softly. The music mounts to a vivid crescendo. The princess stirs, wakens, and rises slowly as the prince gathers her in his arms.

The light flashes out, and miraculously the giant spiders who hover over the chamber rise and vanish; the cobwebs are disentangled from the great pillars and gradually fall away. The light comes up slowly, royal pages stand against the high columns, and we see before us the great hall of King Florestan's palace.

ACT THREE, SCENE TWO: THE WEDDING   The lofty columns of stone support high-vaulting arches. In the distance, great, sweeping staircases climb up to the farther reaches of the castle. The thrones of the king and queen stand at the right.

With pomp and ceremony, as if he had not been disturbed by more than a night's sleep, the courtier Cattalabutte enters with all his old-time flourish. He struts about the hall as if he himself were responsible for the festivities that are about to follow.

The king and his queen enter regally. Cattalabutte bows to them and escorts them to the dais. Courtiers and ladies in waiting with their escorts dance in and promenade about the hall to the virile rhythms of a polonaise. Six other ladies enter. As the dance theme is repeated quietly, the special guests who have been invited to attend the wedding of Princess Aurora and Prince Florimund dance in to pay their respects to the parents of the bride.

These royal guests are perennial fairy tale characters. First comes the White Cat, held high on a pillow which her escorts carry on their shoulders. She paws the air plaintively and washes her face. Behind her comes Puss in Boots, who watches her possessively while waving his hat in greeting. Bluebeard and his wife, Goldilocks and her prince, Beauty and the Beast, and Florestan, the crown prince of the kingdom, and his two sisters follow behind. Last of all come the enchanted princess and the bluebird. Now, led by the Lilac Fairy, all six of the Princess Aurora's fairy godmothers enter in all their glory.

All the courtiers and guests arrange themselves in a great circle about the hall. Prince Florestan, Aurora's brother, and their two sisters step out and stand at the back of the stage toward the right. A lovely, lilting waltz begins; to its enchanting melody, the three dance a *pas de trois*. When the waltz ends, each of the two girls dances a short variation to music that is light and sparkling in its tinkling sound. Prince Florestan rejoins them, and all three leap off into the wings.

The next *divertissement* features the White Cat and Puss in Boots. This oboe mimes their mewing as Puss in Boots tries to ensnare the winsome cat in a love trap. The White Cat pretends to resist Puss's caresses, but actually she is delighted. Finally Puss can contain himself no longer and puts an end to the flirtation by carrying his ladylove off.

The Enchanted Princess enters with the Bluebird. Both flutter their arms in light, airy motions of flight and commence a *pas de deux*, perhaps the most dazzling dance duet of the entire ballet. The Bluebird, in his variation, seems to be suspended in soaring flight.

Another *divertissement* enacts the tale of Little Red Ridinghood. Four pages

in *Union Jack*. Photo by Beverley Gallegos.

Gelsey Kirkland and Edward Villella in *Tarantella*. Photo by Martha Swope.

Patricia McBride and Jean-Pierre Bonnefous in *Who Cares?* Photo by Rosemary Winckley.

Merrill Ashley, Renee Estopinal, and Susan Pilarre in *Concerto Barocco*. Photo by Costas.

Violette Verdy and Jean-Pierre Bonnefous in *Sonatine*. Photo by Martha Swope.

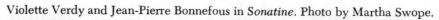

Patricia McBride and Edward Villella in *Dances at a Gathering*. Photo by Martha Swope.

Kay Mazzo and John Prinz in *Dances at a Gathering*. Photo by Martha Swope.

Peter Martins in *Tchaikovsky Pas de Deux*. Photo by Costas.

Peter Martins in *Coppélia*. Photo by Costas.

Kay Mazzo and Peter Martins in *Duo Concertante*. Photo by Martha Swope.

Suzanne Farrell and Peter Martins *Chaconne*. Photo by Martha Swope.

Helgi Tomasson in *A Midsummer Night's Dream*. Photo by Costas.

Allegra Kent and Jacques d'Amboise *Afternoon of a Faun*. Photo by Mar Swope.

bring small trees onto the stage. Red Ridinghood walks lightly through the wood, treading as softly as possible, glancing behind her at every turn. The wolf enters with a bold leap and conceals himself behind one of the trees. The girl passes; he steps out in front of her. Red Ridinghood tries to pretend that he is just another passer-by, like herself, and, holding her basket close, proceeds on her way. The wolf is fooled only for a moment: quickly he throws her over his shoulder and runs off.

Now the moment for which all the court has been waiting finally arrives. Princess Aurora and Prince Florimund enter. A spotlight brightens the brilliant white the bride wears for her wedding day, and all the lords and ladies bow. The royal couple come forward and begin to dance. Their *pas de deux* is gracious and formal. The Princess Aurora reveals, in her mastery of movement and balance, a maturity and perfection for which the "Rose Adagio" was but a youthful rehearsal. Still charming, the youthful princess is now about to be married, and her radiant poise reflects the lesson her love has taught. Prince Florimund supports his bride gallantly, lifting her effortlessly, holding her confidently—by each of his gestures and motions drawing the court's attention to her loveliness. As the *pas de deux* concludes, its tender music ascends to a pitch of everlasting joy. The princess turns with incredible speed on point and dives toward the floor. The prince catches her falling figure and holds her in the daring pose.

A final *divertissement* is offered by the Three Ivans, who perform a virile, stomping Russian dance for the bride and groom. The court is now at the height of good humor, and when the Princess Aurora returns to dance briefly alone, everyone is suddenly saddened by the fact that soon she will go away with her prince. But everyone watches closely this last dance of their princess; the entire assembly is infected by her happiness. Now the whole court—all the fairies, all the nobles, all the fairy tale figures—joins the bride and groom in a spirited mazurka, at the end of which the guests form a circle about the prince and princess who, standing in close embrace, become, in reality, a part of that fairy tale world that brought them together. Everyone kneels to them.

NOTES   The success of *The Sleeping Beauty* described here—as presented by the Royal Ballet (then the Sadler's Wells Ballet) in 1946, in London, and three years later in the United States—has led to many other productions. All of these, including new productions by the Royal Ballet itself, retain the main outlines of the story and the principal dances, while adding variations of character, new dances and ensembles to accompany changes in scenery and costume. Notable productions are those of the Leningrad Kirov Ballet (filmed in 1965, with Alla Sizova and Yuri Soloviev), the National Ballet of Washington (staged by Ben Stevenson), and the National Ballet of Canada (staged by Rudolf Nureyev). The latter, with Veronica Tennant as the Princess Aurora and, as guest artist, Rudolf Nureyev as Prince Florimund, was presented on film by Public Broadcasting Service television in the United States at Christmastime 1972 in color. Rudolf Nureyev first staged the ballet independently for La Scala, Milan, September 17, 1970, with scenery and costumes by Nicholas Georgiadis. Margot Fonteyn and Nureyev danced the première.

Nureyev has said of *The Sleeping Beauty* (in an interview in *Dance and Dancers*, January 1972): "It is really a kind of *Parsifal* of ballet and very important to the whole ballet world. It's very long and very lush, and there is nothing you can really cut. Since I had been brought up on the Kirov version, my production was naturally inspired by that."

In writing of Nureyev's *Sleeping Beauty* soon after its New York première in 1973, Andrew Porter in *The New Yorker* reviewed much of the ballet's history: "In ballet history, the usual order is reversed; the Romantic works come first, then the Classical. And the Petipa-Tchaikovsky *Sleeping Beauty*, first performed, in St. Petersburg, in 1890, is the grandest, fullest, and finest achievement of Classical ballet—its 'definitive statement' and an enduring inspiration to later choreographers. Balanchine, Ashton, and Kenneth MacMillan all proclaim their debt to the inventions of Petipa. Brought from Leningrad to London by Nicholas Sergeyev, *The Sleeping Beauty* became, in 1939, the foundation of the Royal Ballet's work, and the dancers, directors, ballet masters, and teachers who have gone out from Covent Garden to play leading roles in ballet across six continents have all been brought up on *Sleeping Beauty* as ballet's Bible. Meanwhile, in Leningrad itself, *The Sleeping Beauty* remains the work that shows Maryinsky-Kirov dancing at its purest and most poetic. The Kirov company brought its *Sleeping Beauty* to London twelve years ago, and left a new mark on all subsequent Western productions. The influence was continued, in a highly personalized variant, by the participation of the ex-Kirov dancer Rudolf Nureyev in the Royal Ballet performances and then by his own stagings of the work—at La Scala, in 1969, and now for the National Ballet of Canada. With a *Sleeping Beauty* 'produced, staged, and with additional choreography by Rudolf Nureyev after Marius Petipa,' the Canadian company made its Metropolitan début last week. It offered an exceedingly grand presentation of the piece—from a scenic point of view the grandest, in fact, that I have ever seen.

"When Auguste Bournonville, that great Romantic choreographer (whose *La Sylphide* is another work in the Canadian repertory), visited Petersburg in 1874, he was distressed by what he saw: 'Much as I wanted to, I could not discover action, dramatic interest, logical continuity, something that would even remotely remind one of common sense. And if, on occasion, I did succeed in finding a trace of something like it (as, for example, in Petipa's *Don Quixote*), the impression was immediately obscured by an endless number of monotonous bravura appearances.' Ivan Alexandrovich Vsevolozhsky, appointed Director of the Imperial Theatres in 1881, changed all that. He instituted production councils in which scenarist, choreographer, composer, and designer got together to plan a new work. Of *The Sleeping Beauty* he was both scenarist and costume designer; Tchaikovsky, 'in large letters,' dedicated the published score to him. Composer and choreographer worked closely together. Petipa told Tchaikovsky exactly how many measures he wanted for each episode, and specified the tempo, the style, even the scoring. Princess Aurora's first variation should be accompanied by violins and cellos pizzicato, and harps; at

Carabosse's unmasking, at the end of Act I, 'a chromatic scale must sound in the whole orchestra'; the Sapphire of Act III, being of pentahedral cut, required an accompaniment in 5/4 time. When, during rehearsals, the Panorama music of Act II came to an end before the great panorama of painted canvas had rolled its full course, Tchaikovsky composed extra music, whose length was determined, literally, by the yard. The three collaborators played each his different role in giving unity to the elaborate *féerie*. Vsevolozhsky had his conception of a glittering dance pageant mounting to its climax in an apotheosispaean to imperial splendor (a paean in the precise sense, since the ending would show Apollo costumed as Louis XIV). Petipa had his sharp-cut scheme for a balanced and well-varied sequence of dances. And Tchaikovsky? He always delighted in the evocation of past centuries. Petipa's blueprint checked his tendency to sprawly form. And he poured out his heart. It is Tchaikovsky's music that gives character to the heroine and expresses the 'inner theme' which raises *The Sleeping Beauty* above the level of a pretty divertissement.

"Most of the fairy tales that adults go to the theater to see again and again— *Swan Lake, Cinderella, Hansel and Gretel,* the *Ring*—symbolically enshrine truths about human experience and human behavior to make their pleasures more than incidental. *Swan Lake,* for example, is a drama involving conflict and character; it gives scope for dramatic expression, for acting, and for diverse striking interpretations. By comparison with Prince Siegfried in *Swan Lake,* Prince Florimund of *The Sleeping Beauty* is a cipher. What does he do to deserve his princess? The briar thicket surrounding his bride is no dangerous Magic Fire through which only the dauntless can pass. And similarly, by comparison with the brave, pathetic Odette and the formidable temptress Odile, Princess Aurora is a passive heroine played upon by circumstance. Can we find a moral in *The Sleeping Beauty* beyond that guest lists should be kept up-to-date lest awkwardness result? Perrault, who wrote the fairy tale on which the ballet is based, suggested, 'What girl would not forgo her marriage vows, at least for a while, to gain a husband who is handsome, rich, courteous, and kind?' Not enough! In a preface to the Penguin edition of Perrault, Geoffrey Brereton remarks that it is 'tempting to adopt the nature-myth interpretation and see the tale as an allegory of the long winter sleep of the earth'— but adds that 'the allegory, if it is one, is obscure.' Tchaikovsky's interpretation was simpler. His *Sleeping Beauty* is a struggle between good and evil, between forces of light and forces of darkness, represented by the benevolent Lilac Fairy and the wicked fairy Carabosse. The prelude, a straightforward exposition of the music associated with the two characters, suggests it; the consistent employment of melodies related to or derived from these themes—the Lilac Fairy's transformation of the Carabosse music at the close of Act I, the Carabosse figuration that propels Aurora's dance with the spindle, the opposition of the two themes in the symphonic entr'acte that precedes the Awakening—makes it clear. These two forces shape Aurora's destiny, and although she initiates nothing, with just a little stretching of the imagination we can accept the declaration of the Russian composer and critic Boris Asafiev that the heroine's three adagios (the Rose Adagio, in E flat; the Vision Scene appearance, in F; the Grand Pas de Deux, in C) tell 'the story of a whole life—the growth and development of a playful and carefree child into a young woman who learns, through tribulations, to know great love.' It is in this sense that Margot Fonteyn, since 1939 our leading Aurora, dances the role.

"That question 'Can we find a moral?' prompts others. Is it right to look for one? Does the 'meaning' of *The Sleeping Beauty* not lie simply in its patterns of movement, as does that of, say, *Ballet Imperial*, Balanchine's homage to Petipa and Tchaikovsky? While spectacle, pure dance, expressive dance, narrative, and symbolism must mix in any presentation of the work, what importance should be given to any single ingredient? Different productions have provided different answers. The Kirov's has modest décor; the dances shine as rich, perfectly cut jewels in a quiet, rather dowdy setting; this Leningrad *Beauty* is not a drama but a long, lyrical poem in varied metres, spun on a thread of radiant narrative. Kenneth MacMillan's presentation, at the German Opera, in Berlin, in 1967, was very grand indeed to look at (the epochs were moved forward, so that Aurora fell asleep in the reign of Catherine the Great and woke a century later, under Alexander II) and also rather dramatic—yet the main emphasis was again not on the story but on the dances, both Petipa's and those that MacMillan added, in brilliant emulation. The famous old Covent Garden version, which did more than twenty years' hard service (and in 1949 introduced the company to New York), balanced all the ingredients listed above, but toward the end it fell apart; though the central Petipa episodes were lovingly preserved, around them was a ragged patchwork. The 1968 replacement was softly romantic, lavishly sentimental in appearance, and did not last long; I have not seen its successor, which opened at Covent Garden in March.

"Nureyev's production for the National Ballet of Canada is different again. The décor, by Nicholas Georgiadis, is even more sumptuous than Barry Kay's in Berlin, though it does not sparkle so brightly. Mr. Kay produced a jewelled effect, of diamonds, rubies, sapphires, with the softer gleam of pearl and opal in the Vision Scene; Mr. Georgiadis prefers an impression of old gold, with touches of rich colors that are muted as if by a layer of fine dust; in the final scene the dominant tone becomes rust red. David Hersey's subtly elaborate lighting subdues the colors still further and blurs distinctions between them; a prevailing amber glow neutralizes all shades in the Vision Scene except when follow spots fall on the principals, or the attendant fairies enter pools of white light stage-front. Blackness at the back strikes an unsuitably sombre note at the christening party of the Prologue; Aurora's wedding, I think, also calls for a more splendid general blaze. All the same, the lighting is carefully and imaginatively wrought. There are some excellent stage effects: a streamer of red ribbon flies across the stage, to shape itself as Carabosse and her retinue; a boat for Florimund and the Lilac Fairy glides magically through the obstacles on the way to the palace. The tableau of sleeping courtiers through which the prince, marvelling, picks his way is a triumph for designer, producer, and lighter at once. Mr. Georgiadis's architecture, substantial and imposing, leaves plenty of space for the dance. His multitudinous costumes are beautiful both in detail and in massed effect. Only the cut of the tutus, which are large, floppy, and thus line-obscuring, is unhappy.

"Nureyev's handling of the piece is extremely elaborate, from the first moment of the fairies' entrée; they come on four at a time, *bourréeing* hand-in-hand, each group with an attendant cavalier, who then lifts the leader while she draws her companions through the mazes of a most un-Petipalike procession. The second fairy variation is danced in duplicate, which is unusual, but in the score the variation does bear the names of two characters (Coulante, Farine). Nureyev's main innovation in the Prologue is to divide the role of the Lilac Fairy into two: a 'Principal Fairy,' who does the dancing, and a Lilac Fairy 'proper,' who turns up at the party, last guest to arrive, only after Carabosse has spoken her curse. Crinolined and heavily draped, an ambulant tea cozy, this fairy can do little more than glide about and wave her wand. Carabosse is played by a woman, as she was by Natalia Dudinskaya in Leningrad a decade or so ago, and she is played by Celia Franca in terms of offended dignity rather than evil malice. Her retinue roughs up the good fairies in a rather infelicitous sequence. Amid all this complication, and with the roles of good and evil genies reduced, the point of the Prologue is not clearly made. The fact that the fairies are endowing young Aurora with the gifts characterized in their variations is unstated, and a newcomer might watch the scene without even becoming aware that a royal infant is the focus of the festivities. The knitting bee, at the start of Act I, becomes another production number, involving slatterns, cat's-paws, halberdiers, hangmen, and a good deal of fussy activity. At the close of the act, the four minor princes, lunging at Carabosse, run one another through. But Petipa's lovely inventions for Aurora are respected, even if eight minstrel girls figure too prominently in parts of the Rose Adagio. Veronica Tennant, Aurora at both performances I saw, places the choreography precisely, apart from a tendency to push forcefully into arabesque. She does not convey much sense of a developing character, and her dancing lacks, above all, legato—that feeling for a flowing line which links one image to the next. It is stop and start again—sequences chopped into short phrases. And this is a general company fault, observable in most of the solo dancing. The musical director, George Crum, has it, too; Tchaikovsky's long melodies do not flow smoothly enough. The anonymous orchestra is proficient but a bit short on strings. Some of Mr. Crum's rhythms are sludgy and undramatic.

"When, in Act II, Prince Florimund arrives, in the person of Rudolf Nureyev (who dances fourteen of the sixteen New York performances), he gives a splendid demonstration of that phrasing command which, so to speak, keeps the line going through the rests. In Petipa's original the Prince was not a large dancing role (the brilliant male technician of the Petersburg company, Enrico Cecchetti, created not the Prince but the Bluebird—and also Carabosse); Nureyev has enlarged it. He has given himself three variations in Act II, the second of them done to Panorama music shifted to an earlier point in the act. Aurora's second solo has been rewritten, without the alternating *relevés*, and not improved. The voyage to the palace and the Prince's entry are, as I said, strikingly achieved. After the Awakening, the climax of the story, there is a letdown. It is mainly Petipa's fault; here, surely, there should be a *pas de deux* for the Princess 'whose radiant beauty' (in Perrault's words) 'seemed to glow with a kind of heavenly light' and the Prince 'who hardly knew how to express his joy and gratitude'—but, instead, the curtain drops after a few bars. In the old Covent Garden version the difficulty was solved by moving straight into the wedding celebrations, and for the 1968 production Ashton composed a tender new *pas de deux* to the music of the entr'acte. In the Canadian version, on the opening night, Miss Tennant and Nureyev made things worse by expressing no great interest in one another. Reactions in this production were often inadequate. Earlier in Act II, the Prince showed little surprise when the Lilac Fairy joined him but behaved as if fairy apparitions were an everyday occurrence. Act III in the Canadian *Beauty* opens not brilliantly but quietly, with the Sarabande, originally the penultimate dance, brought forward. Then things follow much their usual course. The *pas de quatre* of Jewels becomes a *pas de cinq*, with the Diamonds a twin set. (The male Diamond is allotted Sapphire's 5/4 solo variation.) Bluebirds are placed before Cats; Red Ridinghood, Hop-o'-My-Thumb, and Cinderella are omitted; so, unfortunately, is the apotheosis. Again, the plot point—that all the characters of fairyland have assembled to pay homage to the royal couple—is not potently made, but again there is a display of dense dance patterns around the solos, with much rich 'doubling at the octave' in Nureyev's favored manner.

"The National Ballet of Canada was conceived when the Sadler's Wells/Royal Ballet, after its New York triumphs in 1949, went on to appear in Toronto. The official début was late in 1951; the company comes of age with a *Sleeping Beauty* that shows it need yield nothing in scale of presentation to the London company."*

March 15, 1973, the Royal Ballet produced a new version of *The Sleeping Beauty*. Designed by Peter Farmer, with lighting by William Bundy, the ballet used the choreography of Marius Petipa with new and additional dances by Kenneth MacMillan. Antoinette Sibley was the *Princess Aurora*, Anthony Dowell the *Prince*. The fairy variations were danced by Jennifer Penney, Laura Connor, Alfreda Thorogood, Anita Young, Lesley Collier, and Deanne Bergsma (the *Lilac Fairy*). Lesley Collier and Michael Coleman were the *Bluebirds*. Clement Crisp reviewed it in *The Financial Times*: "'A magical fantasy'—thus I. A. Vsevolozhsky, director of the Imperial Theatres and guiding spirit in the creation of *The Sleeping Beauty* as librettist and designer of the costumes, wrote to Tchaikovsky when he commissioned the score. *Beauty* is, of course, several things: the supreme achievement of Petipa's genius; the pinnacle of nineteenth-century ballet; a *ballet féerie* designed to delight a court audience and pay discreetly flattering homage to the Tsar, whose servants the artists of the Imperial Ballet were. For us it is the signature work of the Royal Ballet—symbol of the company's maturity in the 1946 staging, testimony to the international standing of the troupe at the triumphant New York opening in 1949.

* From *A Musical Season* (Viking Press); © 1973 Andrew Porter. Originally in *The New Yorker*.

"The 1946 staging was decorated by Oliver Messel, and after the austerities of the war it looked supremely opulent. Five years ago a new production, with designs by Henry Bardon and Lila de Nobili—*à la manière de Doré*—was a brave attempt at rethinking the piece; but it lacked airiness, space in which Petipa's inventions could breathe; and hence the new production by Kenneth MacMillan with designs by Peter Farmer, given at a gala in the presence of Her Majesty the Queen last night to pay tribute to the American Friends of Covent Garden whose generosity has paid for this much-needed revision.

"The result is entirely worthwhile. This new staging is Vsevolozhsky's 'magical fantasy,' with steps restored, some choreography renewed, other sections embellished. The *Beauty* has been reawakened, and the whole staging is a reassertion of MacMillan's love and understanding of the classic tradition of which he is a product. To detail the various innovations must wait until later viewings of the production; suffice it to say that the spirit of this great ballet is honored throughout. MacMillan has done his homework—*Beauty* is a well-documented ballet—and both the spirit of the piece and its choreographic structure have been honorably displayed.

"It is the special merit of Peter Farmer's settings that they give ample room for the dances. Each act of the ballet is conceived in one color: the Prologue is almost entirely blue—the most difficult shade to bring off on stage—and in amid the soaring arches of King Florestan's palace, which suggest a properly magical setting for a fairy tale, the arrival of the fairy godmothers had been staged with extraordinary skill as they enter down mysterious flights of stairs hidden from our eyes.

"For Act One we are in a garden setting which, at first viewing, seems too ingratiatingly pretty, but here—as throughout the evening—I was conscious of the care taken that nothing should obscure the impact of the dances. In the Prologue, the Fairy variations glittered diamond-sharp against the indigo darkness of the palace; with Aurora's appearance we could see the majesty of Petipa's inventions plain, and Antoinette Sibley was in superb form as the young princess, and later as the vision, and ultimately and most brilliantly as the bride.

"Carabosse—Alexander Grant, tremendous here as throughout the evening—is placed on stage under the guise of a courtier, and the spell is cast, and the Lilac Fairy intervenes, with a real feeling for the magical element that sustains the whole action of the piece. In this scene, as at every point during the action, there is a concern for dramatic credibility; MacMillan has reworked small incidents that have become dully traditional, and the action is carried forward with a nice appreciation for period style.

"The first two acts are set in a suitably fantastic and improbable realm of fairy enchantment; but with the hunting scene we enter a world which, as Vsevolozhsky intended, has some historical reality. The whole development of the staging moves from the imaginary, dream-like setting of Aurora's youth into the clarity and formal elegance of the age of Louis XIV in which she must awake from Carabosse's enchantment.

"The Prince Florimund is Anthony Dowell, princely in style and technique; his journey to Aurora's palace—with its use of panorama as demanded by

Tchaikovsky's music—is true theatrical magic and the celebrations of the final act are grand and beautiful. Further comment must wait until the *Beauty* enters the repertory next week: until then a welcome for the production, and for the excellence of the company's performance."

For a contemporary Soviet Russian appraisal of Marius Petipa's achievement in *The Sleeping Beauty*, an essay by Vera Krasovskaya in *Dance Perspectives*, No. 49, is of interest. Yuri Slonimsky's monograph, *Marius Petipa*, translated by Anatole Chujoy in *Dance Index* VI, Nos. 5 and 6 (1947), remains the classic account of that master's work, by the renowned Soviet critic and historian. Also of interest is *Russian Ballet Master: the Memoirs of Marius Petipa*, edited by Lillian Moore and translated by Helen Whittaker (New York, Macmillan, 1958).

Now the wheel has come full circle. The Sadler's Wells Ballet production of *The Sleeping Beauty*, designed by Oliver Messel, which introduced the ballet to the modern audience, has been mounted anew by American Ballet Theatre, which staged it at the Metropolitan Opera House, New York, June 15, 1976, with Natalia Makarova and Mikhail Baryshnikov. The production was staged by Mary Skeaping, after Petipa; the lighting was by Nananne Porcher.

Margot Fonteyn's performance in the original Messel production by the Sadler's Wells Ballet in New York in 1949 has been recalled by the critic Dale Harris in *Ballet Review* (Vol. 4, No. 6): "The ultimate proof of Fonteyn's skill was to make her last-act variation into the climax of the entire evening, to transform into the apex of Aurora's good fortune a simple dance designed to provide a lyrical contrast with the *grand adage* that precedes it and the strong male solo and boisterous coda that succeed it. In 1949 there was no male solo and the coda was used for the Three Ivans. Fonteyn's triumph was compounded of all her virtues: the slow opening section showed off her nobly proportioned body, its perfect placement, the pliancy of her back, the clarity and continuity of her line from fingertips to feet, the ballerina head and face which gave focus to the body's expressiveness by directing the audience's attention where she wanted it to be. In the sequence to the perky violin solo, as she flicked her wrists while raising her arms she would draw the rhythm taut by raising her eyes a fraction later than her arms. The same kind of rubato informed her phrasing of the *petits battements frappés* to the pizzicati, so that she seemed to be toying with the music, teasing it out, flirting with it. Yet in the final section her fast, sure *piqué* turns were thrilling precisely because they accorded so exactly with the music's strong, driving rhythm. Fonteyn's musicality was awesome."*

Clive Barnes in a long appraisal of American Ballet Theatre's revival of the ballet entitled "A Promise Fulfilled" (the New York *Times*, June 27, 1976) discussed the virtues of the Oliver Messel production and its meaning for the company's dancers and the contemporary audience.

The critic Tobi Tobias wrote an interesting historical overview of *The Sleep-*

* Reprinted by permission of *Ballet Review*, Marcel Dekker, publisher.

*ing Beauty* entitled "Inheritance" for the first issue of American Ballet Theatre's magazine *On Point,* Summer 1976.

## SMALL PARADES

*Music by Edgard Varèse. Choreography by Glen Tetley. Decor and costumes by Nadine Baylis. Lighting by John B. Read. First presented by the Netherlands Dance Theatre in March 1972. First presented in the United States by the same ensemble at the Brooklyn Academy of Music, New York, March 30, 1972.*

A dance ballet to contemporary music in a chaste, modern setting, *Small Parades* is performed to five famous pieces by Varèse: *Intégrales, Density 21.5, Octandre, Hyperprism,* and *Ionisation.* Arranged for ten dancers, the ballet is divided into five parts, like the music, and performed without interruption.

Writing after its U.S. premiere, Clive Barnes said in the New York *Times* that *Small Parades* "is a ballet of space and emotion. Its vocabulary is a perfect amalgam of classic ballet and modern dance, and its structure has a natural strength . . . Tetley uses classic dance here almost as a commentary on his modern-dance experience. These Dutch dancers are the perfect expression of this revealing choreographic ambiguity."

## SOLITAIRE

*Music by Malcolm Arnold. Choreography by Kenneth MacMillan. Scenery and costumes by Lawrence Shafer. First presented by the Sadler's Wells Theatre Ballet, June 7, 1956, with Margaret Hill, Sara Neil, and Donald Britton. First presented in the United States by the Royal Ballet at the Metropolitan Opera House, New York, September 17, 1957, with scenery and costumes by Desmond Healy.*

*Solitaire* is a playful *divertissement* arranged to the *English Dances* of Malcolm Arnold. Its choreographer calls the ballet "a kind of game for one" and the ballet follows the efforts of an attractive girl to be included in a group of other young people. Time and again she tries to join in their games but is always rebuffed. In the end, she is as alone as she was at the beginning. While this sounds somewhat sad, it is not, because both the music and the dances have a gaiety and warmth that suggest inner as well as conscious security. The girl is lovely, she dances superbly. It is perhaps the people she wants to be with who are missing something!

# SOME TIMES

*Music by Claus Ogerman. Choreography by Dennis Nahat. Scenery and costumes by Rouben Ter-Arutunian. Lighting by Nananne Porcher. First presented by American Ballet Theatre at the New York State Theatre, Lincoln Center, New York, July 14, 1972, with Mimi Paul, Martine van Hamel, Naomi Sorkin, Ian Horvath, and Dennis Nahat and ensemble.*

A ballet about young people in these times, this ballet, without a narrative, plots the interaction of the sexes in a series of dances. A lone girl moves through a social scene as if she were alone. Two boys and a girl fantasize together. The scene, an abstract one, might be any contemporary place in which young persons might be alone, and be themselves.

# SONATINE

*Music by Maurice Ravel. Choreography by George Balanchine. Lighting by Ronald Bates. First presented by the New York City Ballet at the Hommage à Ravel at the New York State Theatre, Lincoln Center, May 14, 1975, with Violette Verdy and Jean-Pierre Bonnefous. Pianist: Madeleine Malraux.*

This little dance ballet opened our Ravel Festival at the New York City Ballet in 1975. The year 1975 was the one hundredth anniversary of Ravel's birth. I have always loved his music, from the time I made a bit of a waltz from his *Valses Nobles et Sentimentales* in Russia, and so we thought it would be a good idea to celebrate this wonderful composer's life and work by arranging new dances to as many scores as we could. We did seventeen ballets, sixteen of them new. Some were very long, like *L'Enfant et les Sortilèges*, with lots of costumes and a big production. Others, like *Sonatine*, were only a few minutes long, simply using Ravel's music and making what we could of it.

The pianist and the dancers are on stage together when the curtain goes up on the ballet. The pianist begins to play; the girl and the boy stand and listen. They like what they hear, apparently, for they begin to move to it, following its line, and gradually becoming imbued with its spirit.

# THE SONG OF THE EARTH

*Music by Gustav Mahler. Choreography by Kenneth MacMillan. First presented by the Stuttgart Ballet Company, November 7, 1965. First presented in the United States by the Royal Ballet at the new Metropolitan Opera House, April 25, 1967, with Anthony Dowell, Donald MacLeary, Georgina Parkinson, Jennifer Penney, and Ann Jenner in leading roles.\**

\* See also SHADOW OF THE WIND.

Mahler regarded his *Das Lied von der Erde* as a "symphony in songs." The work is set for tenor, alto, and orchestra. Mahler found the text for his songs in a volume of translations of the Chinese poet Li-Tai-Po (702–763) and others. The poems speak of earthly woe, loneliness, youth, beauty, drunkenness and the spring, and farewell, not, in other words, celebrating nature so much as expressing a philosophy of a lifetime. To the last poem, the composer added these lines:

> The lovely earth, all, everywhere,
> Revives in spring and blooms anew,
> All, everywhere and ever, ever,
> Shines the blue horizon,
> Ever . . . ever . . .

The choreographer has said that his ballet is about Death. "This theme comes out very strongly. But I can't say that the man who moves among the dancers like Death actually is Death. That would be too specific. The Germans call him *der Ewige*, the one who is always there, and it is difficult to find an English equivalent. The direct translation would be The Eternal, but probably the best description is in the last line of the last poem, 'Forever . . . forever . . .'

"The Death figure is not at all evil. In fact, he is . . . just there, always hanging about. He wears a colorless mask without any marks on it, and it makes him look like the others, only just that much different. Basically the theme of the ballet is quite simple: a man and a woman; Death takes the man; they both return to her and at the end of the ballet—in the last poem—we find that in Death there is the promise of renewal."

While Kenneth MacMillan has said that people expecting a line by line translation in stage action of the text of the songs are bound to be disappointed, he has tried, as with *Images of Love*, to distill what is spoken, "and to find imagery for the ideas behind the words. My interest was to create movements to describe the essence of the poems."

Since the songs are sung in the theatre in German, a translation of them by Alfred H. Meyer is given here:

THE DRINKING SONG OF EARTHLY WOE

> Wine in the golden goblet is beckoning,
> But drink not yet, first I will sing you a song!
> The Song of Sorrow, let its mockery laugh itself into your soul.

> When sorrow approaches, the soul's gardens lie desolate,
> Joy and song wither and die.
> Dark is life, is death.

> Lord of this house!
> Thy cellar holds the fullness of golden wine!
> Here, this lute I call mine own!

To play upon the lute, to empty glasses,
These are things that fit each other.
At the proper time a goblet full of wine
Is worth more than all the kingdoms of this earth!
Dark is life, is death!

The firmament in its eternal blue, and the earth,
These will long endure, will blossom in springtime.
But thou, O man, what is the span of thy life?
Not a hundred years art thou permitted to enjoy
The idle vanities of this earth!

Look there below! In the moonlight upon the graves
There crouches a wild, ghostly figure—
An ape it is! Hark how his howling
Shrills out into the sweet airs of this our life!

Bring on the wine! The time has come, my comrades!
Drain your golden goblets to the dregs!
Dark is life, is death!

### THE LONELY ONE IN AUTUMN

The mists of autumn build their blue wall over the sea;
With hoarfrost covered, stands the grass;
It seems as if an artist had strewn the dust of jade over delicate blossoms.
The flowers' fragrance has spent itself;

A cold wind bows them to earth.
Soon the withered, golden leaves
Of lotus flowers will be scattered upon the waters.
My heart is weary. My little lamp
Has gone out, a-crackling, minding me of need for sleep,
I come to you, blest resting-place!
Yea, give me rest; for I need quickening!

I weep and weep in all my solitude.
Autumn in my heart too long is lasting.
O Sun of Love, never again wilt thou shine,
Gently to dry my bitter tears?

### OF YOUTH

Midway in the little pool
Stands a pavilion of green
And of white porcelain.

Like the back of a tiger
The bridge of jade arches
Across to the pavilion.

In the little house friends are seated,
Beautifully gowned, drinking, gossiping;
Some are writing verses.

Their silken sleeves glide
Backwards, their silken caps
Hang from the back of their necks.

On the smooth surface of the quiet pool
All is mirrored
Wondrously.

All stands upon its head
In the pavilion of green
And of white porcelain.

Like a half-moon stands the bridge,
Reversed in its bow. Friends,
Beautifully gowned, are drinking, gossiping.

OF BEAUTY

Youthful maidens are plucking flowers,
Plucking lotus flowers at the edge of the shore.
Between bushes and leaves are they sitting.
Gathering blossoms in their laps and calling
To each other in jest.
The golden sun plays about their forms,
Reflected in the quiet water.
The sun mirrors their slender limbs,
Their sweet eyes,
And a zephyr with gentlest caress raises the fabric
Of their sleeves, wafts the magic
Of their perfume through the air,
O see, beautiful youths at play
On fiery horses, over there at the edge of the shore,
Glistening from afar like rays of the sun;
Between the green branches of the willows
Fresh youth is making its way!
The steed of one whinnies for joy
And shies and rushes past.
Over flowers, grasses, gallop his hoofs,
Whose stormy stamping crushes the fallen blossoms.

Heigh! How his mane flies in the breeze,
How his nostrils dilate!

The golden sun plays about the forms,
Reflecting them in the quiet water.
And the loveliest of the maidens
Sends him long glances of yearning.
Her haughty bearing is no more than feigned.
In the sparkle of her wide eyes,
In the darkening of the eager glance,
Ascends the plaint of the passion of her heart.

## THE DRUNKEN ONE IN SPRINGTIME

If life is no more than a dream,
Why bother?
I'll drink, till drink no more I can,
The whole, live-long day!

And when no longer I can drink,
When throat and soul are full,
I'll stagger on till to my door,—
And sleep, and sleep, and sleep.

What hear I, awakening? List!
A bird sings in a tree.
I ask him whether Spring has come,
I feel as in a dream.

The birdling twitters, Yes! the Spring
Overnight has come!
In contemplation deep I brood,
While birdling sings and laughs!

Anew I fill my goblet
And drain it to the dregs
And sing until the moon shines bright
In the dark'ning firmament!

And when no longer I can sing
Again to sleep I'll go.
For what matters Spring to me?
Drunk only let me be!

### FAREWELL

The sun is sinking 'neath the hills.
Evening descends into the vales
With its cool, quiet shadows.
Behold! As a bark of silver
The moon rises into the blue heaven.
I feel the motion of a gentle wind
Behind the dark pines.

The brook sings its music through the dark.
The flowers grow pale in the twilight.
The earth breathes the quiet of rest and sleep.
All longing goes a-dreaming.
Weary humanity is homeward bound,
To seek anew in sleep
Forgotten fortune, youth.
Birds are perched upon their branches.
The world falls into sleep.
The cool wind is in the shadow of my pines.

I stand here and await my friend, for a last farewell.
I long, O friend, at thy side
To drink in the beauty of this evening.
Where are you? You leave me long in solitude!
I wander to and fro with my lute
On paths thick with soft grass.
O Beauty! O World, drunk with love eternal—life!

He climbed from his horse and gave his friend a farewell cup; asked him
Whither he was going, and why it needs must be.
He spoke, his voice choking: O, my friend, Fate in this world has not
    been kind to me!
Whither am I bound? I go, I wander into the mountains.
I seek rest for my lonely heart.
I am wand'ring toward my native place, my home.

I shall no longer seek the far horizon.
My heart is still and waits for its deliverance.
The lovely earth, all, everywhere,
Revives in spring and blooms anew,
All, everywhere and ever, ever,
Shines the blue horizon,
Ever . . . ever . . .

The English music and dance critic Andrew Porter has written:

"MacMillan has shaped his response to the score in pure movement. No decor. No costumes. No picturesque lighting. And no 'acting.'

"The music of *The Drinking Song of Earthly Woe* leaps up and the boys leap on in a bounding, unforced surge of invention, patterning the energy and the soaring, plunging emotional contours of the movement. The slow movement, *The Lonely One in Autumn,* is quietly and simply danced by four girls, sometimes partnered, sometimes not ('O Sun of Love, will you never shine again, gently to dry my bitter tears?'). There follow three scherzos. *Of Youth* tells verbally of a cultivated social scene, a pavilion of green and white porcelain where friends sit, chatter, write verses. MacMillan finds playful, exquisitely articulated invention—and when the tenor sings of the reflections in the little pool ('everything standing on its head') the soloist is momentarily inverted!

"In *Of Beauty* the choreographer keeps more specifically to the poet's narrative: the girls plucking flowers by the stream, the boys crashing in on their prancing horses; the love-glance that unites one couple. In *The Drunkard in Spring,* set for four boys, MacMillan has treated drunkenness with great delicacy. It could so easily be vulgar, but his handling is as poetic, as lyrical, as Li-Tai-Po's and Mahler's. There is a wonderful moment when a question is asked: no conventional mime-signal, but a new unforced image that seems to sing.

"Throughout, MacMillan works with extraordinary economy. Only twenty dancers are involved, and the second half of the finale, the *Farewell,* the longest movement, is set only for three: the ballerina, her human partner, and *der Ewige,* the eternal one. A half-mask sets him apart from the others, even while he joins in their dances.

> "Whither am I bound? I go, I wander into the mountains.
> I seek rest for my lonely heart.
> I am wandering toward my native place, my home.
>
> I shall never roam in foreign lands.
> My heart is at rest and waits its hour!

"And then Mahler adds the words already quoted. Solos, *pas de deux, pas de trois* succeed one another. Human parting, eternal beauty. It is all so simple, so clear, so poetic."

## SONG OF THE NIGHTINGALE

*Dramatic ballet in two scenes. Music by Igor Stravinsky. Choreography by Leonide Massine. Scenery and costumes by Henri Matisse. First presented by Diaghilev's Ballets Russes, February 2, 1920, Paris. Revived by Diaghilev's Ballets Russes, 1925, with choreography by George Balanchine and with Alicia Markova in the principal role.*

This work, based on the story of "The Nightingale" by Hans Christian Andersen, is both an opera and a ballet; it has also been arranged by the composer as a symphonic poem. First performed as an opera, the score was revised to exclude voices for ballet performance. The opera consisted of three acts. In the ballet the first act was omitted, but it is necessary to mention its contents here.

The scene of Act One is the home of the nightingale, a wood in China, near the palace of the emperor. A fisherman glides his boat across a lake. He sings to himself. As his boat goes into the distance, we hear the magical song of the nightingale. At the emperor's order, the imperial chamberlain and his followers come to the wood to hear the nightingale. As they seek its voice, they mistake other sounds for the song of the bird. They are led to the nightingale by a humble scullery maid. The courtiers are disappointed in the bird's ordinary appearance, but delighted at its song. The nightingale accepts their invitation to sing at court.

SCENE ONE: THE IMPERIAL PALACE    When preparations have been made for his arrival, the Emperor of China enters his court. The nightingale is brought before him. The bird waits until the emperor signals her to begin her song, then commences.

The emperor is so enchanted with the song that he tells the bird she may have anything she wants. The bird replies that she has moved the emperor to tears and that is all the favor she requires.

Now the noble ladies, noting the high favor in which the lowly nightingale is held by their emperor, try to imitate her song. They fail miserably.

A gift arrives from the Emperor of Japan: a mechanical nightingale, beautifully wrought in gold and set with gems. The song of the toy bird delights the emperor and his court, and they forget the presence of the real nightingale. When the emperor tires of the toy and turns to ask the bird to sing again, she has disappeared. The angry monarch thereupon banishes the bird from his kingdom and makes the toy bird principal songster at his court.

SCENE TWO: THE EMPEROR'S BEDCHAMBER    The mechanical nightingale stands by the emperor's bedside. The emperor is dying. Death stands ready to welcome the monarch, and courtiers prematurely prepare the way for his successor. Spirits taunt the emperor with a list of his good deeds and wrongdoings. He cannot bear their chatter and calls for music. He begins to expire.

The song of the nightingale is heard. The return of this beautiful music delights the emperor, and Death is so struck by the wonderful song of the nightingale that he asks the bird to continue to sing.

The bird consents if Death will permit the emperor to live. Death makes this bargain and vanishes as the nightingale again takes up her song.

The emperor recovers completely and again offers to do any favor the bird wishes. The nightingale replies that his tears are her best reward and that she will sing to him every night until the rise of the sun.

Officials of the court, come to continue the deathwatch, enter the bedchamber. They are astonished to find the emperor standing in all his majesty, ready to receive them.

NOTES  *Le Rossignol (The Nightingale)* was originally composed as an opera in three acts, which Serge Diaghilev presented for the first time at the Paris Opéra, May 26, 1914, under the direction of Pierre Monteux. Alexandre Benois designed the scenery and costumes. This work was first presented in the United States at the Metropolitan Opera House, New York, on March 6, 1926, with Marion Talley in the principal role.

Stravinsky revised his score for symphonic performances, eliminating the first act of the original. He was persuaded by Diaghilev that this new arrangement of his music might be suitable for ballet, and, now called *Le Chant du Rossignol*, the work was presented, with the choreography by Leonide Massine.

A new ballet to this music was my first assignment for Diaghilev's Ballets Russes, soon after I joined the company. I chose for the leading role in the ballet the young artist Alicia Markova, who had just joined Diaghilev's company, when she was only fourteen years old. We saw Markova dance in London, in 1924, at the studio of Serafima Asafieva, where she was a brilliant student. Diaghilev engaged her—the youngest dancer ever to belong to his company—immediately after seeing her dance.

*Music by Igor Stravinsky. Choreography by John Taras. Scenery and costumes by Rouben Ter-Arutunian. First presented at the New York City Ballet's Stravinsky Festival, June 22, 1972, at the New York State Theatre, Lincoln Center, with Gelsey Kirkland as the Nightingale, Elise Flagg as the Mechanical Nightingale, Francisco Moncion as the Emperor, Penny Dudleston as Death, and Peter Naumann as the Fisherman.*

When we were planning our celebration of Stravinsky's ninetieth birthday at the New York City Ballet, one of the composer's works that came immediately to mind was the *Song of the Nightingale*, which had been missing for too long a time from the ballet theatre. The ballet master John Taras undertook the choreography, which retells the lovely story in a most effective way. Writing after the premiere in the *Daily News*, the critic Sam Norkin said:

"John Taras' version of this fairy tale ballet with lavish, colorful decor by Rouben Ter-Arutunian was seen for the first time last night. This is the tale of the Chinese emperor who banishes his live nightingale in favor of a mechanical one, to his regret. Compassionately, the real bird returns in time to save the emperor from the throes of death. The intriguing character solos were beautifully designed and executed. The corps flourished long ribbons and there was a courtiers' pageant. This elegant new ballet belongs in the repertory."

## SONGS OF A WAYFARER

*Music by Gustav Mahler. Choreography by Maurice Béjart. First presented by the Ballet of the Twentieth Century at the Forest National Arena, Brussels, March 11, 1971, with Rudolf Nureyev and Paolo Bortoluzzi. First pre-*

*sented in the United States by Rudolf Nureyev and Friends at the Uris Theatre, New York, March 1, 1977, with Nureyev and Johnny Eliasen.*

It has been said that Mahler's songs are the way to his symphonic works. The *Lieder eines fahrenden Gesellen (Songs of a Wayfarer)* indeed leads thematically to sections of the First and Fourth Symphonies, but it is in the beautiful simplicity of the songs, the words here by Mahler himself, written after an unhappy love affair, that we begin to catch the complexities the composer was later to develop. The songs in this case, sung by a man accompanied by orchestra, tell the story of a young man who cannot forget the loss of a girl who marries another. This theme is another variation on Schubert's *Die Schöne Müllerin.* At first, the man is sick with grief and despair. Later, turning to nature, he is partially revived but in a wild impetuous third song the dagger that stabs his breast returns and he cannot escape the girl's dominion over him. The final song begins with the poet saying that eyes of blue are sweet but fill me with fear and I must say goodbye to all I hold dear. He continues to wander, lonely at night, finding rest under a linden tree, finally, where pain is forgotten.

It is important to know what the words are about, for although this ballet does not reproduce the suggested action of the poem, its subject is the hero's state of mind. The other dancer who moves with him is his alter ego, representing his states and shifts of mind. They are the only two performers, and the emotions the hero lives through in his loss constitute the choreographic fabric.

After the premiere of *Songs of a Wayfarer* in Brussels, the critic John Percival wrote to *Dance and Dancers* magazine that the character Nureyev portrays "exists pure and undiluted by any element of story telling, diversion or contrast—just fifteen minutes of sheer theatrical impact which holds the huge audience spellbound."

## LA SONNAMBULA (see NIGHT SHADOW)

## LA SOURCE

*Music by Leo Delibes. Choreography by George Balanchine. Costumes by Karinska. Lighting by Ronald Bates. First presented by the New York City Ballet at the New York State Theatre, Lincoln Center, November 23, 1968, with Violette Verdy and John Prinz in principal roles.*

My admiration for Delibes as a composer of music for ballet is no secret, I believe; with Tchaikovsky, who knew his music well, of course, and Stravinsky, he is for me one of the three great musicians of the dance. Some years ago, in 1950, to music from his superb ballet score *Sylvia,* I arranged a *pas de deux* that was danced by Maria Tallchief and André Eglevsky, and is still danced by others, with some success. This was later expanded into a *divertissement* for the New York City Ballet. That, however, was not enough and I kept wanting to use more of Delibes's music. The result is *La Source,* which uses music from that work and from *Naila,* too. *La Source* puts together an earlier *pas de deux* of that title with elements from the *Sylvia Pas de Deux and Divertissement.*

The ballet is in effect an extended *pas de deux,* with a soloist and a *corps de ballet* of eight girls. The curtain rises on an empty stage—only a blue background—soon after the music starts. A boy carries on a girl and their dance begins. After an adagio, each does a variation. The soloist and girls dance now to wonderfully familiar music by Delibes. In the midst of the ensemble, the couple return and the stage is left to them. The boy dances a second variation, as does the girl. The ensemble takes the stage again briefly, before the girl and boy return for a final flourish of dancing.

NOTES  Writing in *Dance and Dancers,* Patricia Barnes wrote of an early performance: "The two dancers, Violette Verdy and John Prinz, dance the work wonderfully well . . . The choreography and music for Prinz's second solo are strongly rhythmic, and the dancing given to him is pure virtuosity—as an example, a passage of whirling turns in *arabesque* which Prinz manages with admirable dexterity. This gives way to a precise pizzicato solo for Verdy ending in a *manège* of turns . . . Verdy gives the ballet just the right radiance, and Prinz in his first created leading role confirmed that he is one of the most interesting young dancers in America, or indeed, anywhere."

## SOUVENIRS

*Music by Samuel Barber. Choreography by Todd Bolender. Scenery and costumes by Rouben Ter-Arutunian. Lighting by Jean Rosenthal. First presented by the New York City Ballet at the City Center, New York, November 15, 1955, with Edith Brozak, Ann Crowell, Carolyn George* (Three Young Girls), *Arthur Mitchell* (Attendant), *Roberta Meier and Richard Thomas* (Husband and Wife), *Todd Bolender* (A Man About Town), *Roy Tobias* (Another Man About Town), *Jillana and Jonathan Watts* (A Lady and Her Escort), *Wilma Curley and Robert Barnett* (Bride and Groom), *Irene Larsson* (The Woman), *John Mandia* (The Man), *Jane Mason* (A Maid), *Herbert Bliss* (Man in Grey), *Patricia Savoia, Dido Sayers, Ronald Colton, Gene Gavin, Walter Georgov* (Hotel Guests), *and Eugene Tanner* (An Attendant).

The designer of *Souvenirs,* Rouben Ter-Arutunian, accurately sets the stage in a recollection published in *Dance Perspectives:* "The costumes were taken from the era of silent films and based on a set of fashion plates Todd Bolender had found . . . The ballet was a spoof of a certain aura of pre-World War I, and the set was more a series of prop pieces than a decor as such. There was the prop of the elevator; a few palms, suggesting the court of a European-type spa; a round banquette, found often in the vestibules of these hotels. Later there was a set of doors; a couch with a tiger, and a beaded curtain; then, at the end, a pole with banners and a virile lifeguard. There was a minimum of decor. The emphasis was on the costumes, which brought out the satire."

The time is 1914, the scene the Palm Springs Hotel. In six swift episodes the ballet shows us some of the guests and what they are up to: how they make their entrance to the hotel and try to get acquainted; how a bride and groom can get mixed up in a corridor with a Man About Town and his Lady; how girls at dances pine for partners and how one who is pretty can dance with four men at the same time; how a wife can make a new conquest over an argument with her husband; how a siren entices a Man About Town into her boudoir and feigns to protect herself with a gun; how, on the beach the next afternoon, a lifeguard is the center of attention.

The music for *Souvenirs*, originally composed as a suite for two pianos, uses old dance forms that were popular in the days before World War I. The work was orchestrated by the composer for the New York City Ballet.

# SPARTACUS

*Ballet in four acts. Music by Aram Khachaturian. Choreography by Yuri Grigorovich. Scenery and costumes by Simon Virsaladze. First presented in this version by the Bolshoi Ballet at the Bolshoi Theatre, Moscow, April 9, 1968, with Vladimir Vasiliev, Yekaterina Maximova, Maris Liepa, and Nina Timofeyeva in principal roles.*

Not the first Soviet ballet to this story, this one by Grigorovich appears to have attracted the most acclaim. A synopsis of the action, based on classical sources such as Plutarch, relating the fate of the Roman slave Spartacus, follows:

ACT ONE, SCENE ONE: SUBJUGATION   The Roman legions terrify their captive empire. The army leader is Crassus, cruel, ruthless, and coldly flamboyant. After campaigns in Thrace, where the land has been pillaged and burnt, he brings back Thracian captives to Rome to sell as slaves. Among them are Spartacus and his wife, Phrygia. Spartacus expresses his love of freedom and his refusal to be reconciled to his new state of slavery.

ACT ONE, SCENE TWO: THE SLAVE MARKET   The captives are left at the wall of the capital. Men and women are separated so that each will get a better price for the slave dealer from the Roman patricians. Phrygia is parted from Spartacus. Phrygia is desperate in her grief. Her beloved Spartacus has been reduced to slavery, and she herself is subject not only to Rome but the Roman master who has purchased her, and taken her from her husband forever.

ACT ONE, SCENE THREE: ORGY   Phrygia has been bought by Crassus, and taken to Crassus's villa in Rome. Aegina, Crassus's concubine, mocks Phrygia's unhappiness and fears. For her, wine, gold, lust, power, and murder are the only facts of pleasure. Crassus is holding an orgiastic party for his friends. As the climax to this, two masked gladiators are brought in. They are to fight blindfolded until one of them is killed. They fight with blind and deathly intensity until one is slain. The victor takes off his mask. It is Spartacus.

Spartacus looks down at his unwitting victim with a terrified compassion. He has been forced to murder a fellow man, a slave like himself. What has he done? What more will he be forced to do?

ACT ONE, SCENE FOUR: THE GLADIATORS' BARRACKS  Spartacus, returned to the Gladiators' Barracks, is full of remorse. He calls upon the gladiators to break their chains and escape from their shameful captivity. With superhuman efforts they do this, and overcoming their guards flee to freedom.

ACT TWO, SCENE ONE: THE APPIAN WAY  It is night. The gladiators, escaping in glory, meet shepherds resting by the wayside. Inflamed with the spirit of revolt they call the shepherds to join them, and Spartacus's band is joined by many brave men. It is now an army, dedicated to remove the yoke of Rome. Spartacus is proclaimed its leader.

Alone, Spartacus muses on his forced acceptance of power. He is determined to lead his slave army to victory and to free thousands of Rome's victims. But he realizes that he first must find Phrygia and release her from Crassus.

ACT TWO, SCENE TWO: CRASSUS'S VILLA  Spartacus discovers Phrygia in Crassus's villa to the south of Rome, and they are joyfully reunited. Meanwhile Crassus is giving a feast for the Roman patricians at which Aegina is also present.

Aegina contemplates Crassus and herself. She not only wants power over Crassus, but wishes to dominate the entire world. He tries to achieve it with power and cruelty, and she with cunning and duplicity. But they share the same ambitions—power, glory, and riches. Both need to acquire all and relinquish nothing.

ACT TWO, SCENE THREE: CRASSUS'S DEFEAT  The patricians pander to Crassus and praise his power and victories. But the praise is cut short by the terrifying news that the villa is all but encircled by the advancing army of Spartacus. Crassus, Aegina, and the patricians depart in defeat, leaving Spartacus in possession of the villa.

Spartacus ponders on his victory. The Roman legions' success rests solely on the weapons of the legionnaires and the submission of the conquered. The Roman leaders themselves are cowards.

ACT TWO, SCENE FOUR: THE CONTEMPTUOUS GENEROSITY OF SPARTACUS  Crassus has been captured and is brought before Spartacus, whom he recognizes as his former gladiator. The rebel soldiers want to execute the Roman general out of hand, but Spartacus asserts his authority and permits Crassus to save his life with the same kind of trial the tyrant imposed upon gladiators. But this time the singlehanded combat will not be blindfolded. The rebels are warriors, not murderers. Crassus fights Spartacus but is no match for him. At point of death Crassus pleads for mercy. With a gesture of contempt the rebel leader lets him go.

ACT THREE, SCENE ONE: CONSPIRACY  The dishonored Crassus swears revenge, and Aegina fans his hatred. He calls his soldiers once more into the field, and Aegina sees them off to battle. Left alone, Aegina is full of hatred for Spartacus, fearing she might lose Crassus. She vows vengeance.

ACT THREE, SCENE TWO: THE ENCAMPMENT OF SPARTACUS  Aegina steals into Spartacus's camp by night. Phrygia's fears are not helped by Spartacus's attempts to console her. Spartacus is told by a messenger that the Roman legions are advancing on him. He now puts forward his plan of battle, and the weaker among his captains are frightened by the daring of his tactics. Spartacus now calls upon all of them to take an oath of loyalty.

Spartacus, left to his thoughts, notes that the rebel forces will be defeated if there is dissension among their leaders. For all this death in battle is preferable.

ACT THREE, SCENE THREE: TREASON  The faithful captains of Spartacus await his signal to start the combat and follow him at once. Those of weaker mettle might have followed their example, but Aegina appears out of the darkness bringing wine and whores. They succumb to temptation and fall easily to the advancing vanguard of Crassus's army. Crassus himself rewards Aegina for her help.

Crassus now knows that his revenge will not be complete until Spartacus has been killed, for he cannot forgive the humiliating stain to his honor he suffered as the captive of a slave. He will overtake the remainder of Spartacus's army and annihilate it.

ACT THREE, SCENE FOUR: THE FINAL BATTLE  Spartacus's troops are encircled and his army is fast dwindling in the face of vastly superior forces. Spartacus is still fearless and begins to counterattack the legionnaires. Cunningly the Romans ambush him, triumphantly raising him on their spears as he dies a hero's death. Phrygia comes on to the battlefield to find his dead body. She is heartbroken.

NOTES  The first Soviet ballet *Spartacus* had choreography by Leonid Yacobson, music by Khachaturian, book by Nikolai Volkov, décor by Valentina Khodasevich, and was first presented at the Kirov State Theatre in Leningrad, December 27, 1956, with Makarov and Zubkovskaya in the principal roles of Spartacus and Phrygia. Another treatment of the same story was made by Igor Moiseyev, with designs by Alexander Konstinovsky, and given at the Bolshoi Theatre, Moscow, March 11, 1958. This version, presented in the United States at the Metropolitan Opera House, New York, September 12, 1962, by the Bolshoi Ballet, featured Dmitri Begak and Maya Plisetskaya in the main roles.

Writing in the British magazine *Dance and Dancers* about her impressions of the Grigorovich *Spartacus*, Patricia Barnes said: "Grigorovich's choreography and conception are brilliant. This is an immensely moving work, filled with imaginative theatrical strokes and performed with blazing intensity by Mikhail Lavrovsky, who at this performance dominated the ballet. The dances are fairly clearly divided between the coldly neo-classic steps given to Crassus and his armies and the more plastique work, expressive and eloquent, for Spartacus and his followers.

"Particularly successful has been the way Grigorovich has used his male dancers. Never have I seen an ensemble used with such sweep and grandeur, and rarely has a dance work on such an ambitious scale succeeded so well in putting across its ideas and dramatic theme with such a minimum of mimetic fuss.

"The opening is startlingly effective. Crassus is seen standing in the center of the stage, arm raised, the lower half of his body surrounded by a wall of shields. Seconds later it is seen as the soldiers of his army spill forward filling the vast stage in a profusion of silver uniforms, shields and swords.

"The tragic ending is in its way as admirable as the ballet's opening. The black-clad grieving figure of Phrygia is lifted high by the followers of Spartacus and the body of her husband is handed up to her, together with his battle shield. She lays the shield on his chest and, eyes cast down, sorrowfully contemplates the dead Spartacus. It is a beautifully conceived scene and brings the curtain down on a work of truly heroic dimensions.

"Mikhail Lavrovsky's Spartacus is a wonder to behold. It is a superbly thought-out role and Lavrovsky has explored every dramatic nuance of it. From our first view of him as a slave in bondage, through his moments of resolution as he vows to free the slaves in captivity, until his final battle, he never departs from a characterization that is deeply felt and powerfully projected.

"A particularly superb episode is a gladiator fight. Two men, blindfolded, are brought in for the entertainment of Crassus's court, and fight for their lives. One kills the other—he takes off his helmet, and it is Spartacus, grieving over the fellow slave he has been forced to kill. As he stands there his face reflects the bitter anguish of his heart and with it we see the beginnings of his revolt, the first stirrings of his determination to free himself and his fellow-slaves from his ruthless captors.

"Almost as impressive was the sweetly passionate portrayal of Phrygia by Natalia Bessmertnova. Her dancing, so extraordinarily individual, had the elegiac beauty of a poem and her dark eyes and pale face caught at the heart.

"In a role that was created by Maris Liepa (and one could see how brilliant he must have been), young Mikhail Gabovich was extraordinarily good. If he looked on the young side, he could hardly be blamed, being under twenty, and he nevertheless gave a portrayal of genuine power. He presented Crassus as a warrior both arrogant and heartless, and his dancing was lithely elegant.

"The last of the four principal roles, Aegina, is the least interesting, being rather more of a stereotype. It was performed on this occasion by Svetlana Adyrkhaeva, who danced with a sveltely voluptuous allure.

"Finally, the dancing of the company, for which no praise could be too high. The men in particular outdid themselves in convincing one that the stage was filled with hundreds. Their attack and technical mastery was constantly outstanding."

Clive Barnes in the magazine of the Friends of Covent Garden, *About the House,* said that the Grigorovich *Spartacus* was "undoubtedly the most successful Soviet ballet since *Romeo and Juliet.*" The Grigorovich *Spartacus* was performed by the Bolshoi Ballet in London for the first time July 17, 1969.

## LE SPECTRE DE LA ROSE

*Ballet in one act. Music by Carl Maria von Weber. Choreography by Michel Fokine. Book by J. L. Vaudoyer. Scenery and costumes by Léon Bakst. First presented by Diaghilev's Ballets Russes at the Théâtre de Monte Carlo, Monte Carlo, April 19, 1911, with Vaslav Nijinsky and Tamara Karsavina. First presented in the United States by Diaghilev's Ballets Russes at the Metropolitan Opera House, New York, April 3, 1916, with Alexander Gavrilov and Lydia Lopokova.*

This is a ballet danced by two people, a romantic *pas de deux.* The ballet has a simple story, but the story is so slight that we must refer to the actual dancing for an impression of the ballet. Its first performances convinced audiences that it was possible for two dancers, alone on a stage, to create a story and at the same time to create a mood in which that story could become real, like a lyric poem.

*Le Spectre de la Rose* is based on a poem, a poem by the nineteenth-century French poet and novelist and great critic of the ballet Théophile Gautier. Just as Gautier adapted the work of another poet, Heinrich Heine, to produce the romantic classic *Giselle,* so his own creative work gave to another age the inspiration for another romantic ballet. In Gautier's poem a rose addresses the girl who wore it to a ball. The rose is grateful for having danced with her all evening, grateful even for death on her breast, and tells the maiden that his ghost will continue to dance, at her bedside, all night long, to express his love.

The ballet *Le Spectre de la Rose* has a real setting but, as in *Giselle,* it is a dream that comes to life within this setting that creates its romanticism. The music is Carl Maria von Weber's *Invitation to the Dance,* as orchestrated by Hector Berlioz.

The curtain rises on a young girl's boudoir. The room is formal, high, and cool, with immense windows that look on to a garden. There is a bed on the right and on the left a small dressing table. The colors are blue and white, and as we look at the walls and the furniture and see the moon through the French windows, we imagine that the girl who lives here is demure and innocent. The room is uncluttered, plain in spite of its elegance; it makes you interested in the life it contains. The young girl enters. She is dressed formally, in a long white gown. She takes off the cape she wears about her shoulders, unties her bonnet, and we notice that she holds in her hand a red rose. She refuses to relinquish it as she moves about the room, turning slowly, dancing with an invisible partner, remembering the excitement of her first ball. She has come back from the dance to her familiar surroundings and finds the room a little old-fashioned; it has not changed as she imagines she has changed. She is in love. She presses her lover's rose against her cheek and sits down in a white chair near one of the windows. Half-asleep from fatigue, she still wishes to relive her first encounter with romance. But sleep soon overtakes her. Her hand falls from her face, and the red rose slips from her fingers to the floor.

There is almost no sound for a moment, and then suddenly, buoyantly, the orchestra plays at full volume a quick, intoxicating waltz. As this rush of sound fills the room, through the open window the spirit of the rose leaps in a high, smooth trajectory to stand poised behind the girl's chair. He dances alone as the girl sleeps, moving about the room effortlessly, seeming to touch the floor almost against his will, dancing with the lightness of the rose petals that adorn his body.

He touches the girl, and now—awake in her dream—she dances with him. When the two dance together to the soaring waltz, the young girl moves with the grace of the spirit she has invoked; as they glide and leap about the room, their dance is absolutely continuous, never-ending, unbroken in its flow of movement into movement; the only thing that can stop it is the music. The girl is inspired by her partner as naturally as she held the rose to her cheek and—with his strong, but tender, aid—she becomes not simply a beautiful young girl in love with love, but a part of the romantic night.

The dream cannot last. The waltz melody fades. The girl goes to her chair and sits as before, her arm limp at her side, pointing to the rose on the floor. The spirit of the rose hovers gently over her head in farewell and in a continuous movement rushes toward the window. He disappears into the oncoming dawn at the high point of a leap that seems never-ending.

The light of the sun disturbs the girl. She moves in her sleep, then wakens lazily, rubbing her eyes, not yet aware of where she is. She is still thinking of the spirit of the rose and looks for her mysterious partner. He is not there! She sees she is alone in her own room and that she must have been dreaming. Then she sees the rose on the floor at her feet. She picks it up gently and holds it against her breast, content that the dream is still with her.

Mikhail Baryshnikov first danced *Le Spectre de la Rose* at a performance during the first Hamburg Ballet Festival, dedicated to the memory of Nijinsky, June 22, 1975. Lynn Seymour was the girl. She had been advised on her role by Margot Fonteyn, who had known the recollections of Tamara Karsavina. Baryshnikov learned his role from André Eglevsky, the great *premier danseur* who had learned it from Fokine himself. John Percival reported to *Dance and Dancers* that he had never seen Baryshnikov "dance better in anything, and I have never seen this role so well done. It was a very demanding version of the choreography that he performed, but he danced at full strength throughout . . . His immensely powerful leaps were done with such soft strength, and he evoked perfectly the mixture of sensuousness and romance which is the ballet's essence." In 1976, Baryshnikov danced the role for the first time in the United States with American Ballet Theatre in a production with costumes by Stanley Simmons. Marianna Tcherkassky was the girl.

Nancy Goldner wrote in *Dance News* after the 1976 revival by American Ballet Theatre: "For once a legendary ballet made immediate sense. In a flash the story became important and full of implication. One could really see and feel the specter as an essence of nature and the sleeping beauty's shy, cautious, and finally rapturous acknowledgment of the rose as a story about maturation. As the dreamer, Tcherkassky was perfect . . . the perfect straight lady to Baryshnikov's more exotic role. He was a marvel of strength and clarity, but the fantastic aspect of his specter was that he reincarnates a historical style without looking mannered . . . The gentle but insistent way he insinuated himself into the girl's mind was a masterful fusion of contradictory impulses. Similarly, his approach to the steps was robust while his body was curling, introspective. Even in the big soaring jumps were his eyes and head lowered, somehow hidden. He was utterly manly, yet utterly a personification of spirit. One could recognize in this *Spectre* the Fokine who made the male solo in *Les Sylphides*."

On December 6, 1976, the American Ballet Theatre production was seen on WNET television in the program "In Performance at Wolf Trap."

In an account of his training for *Le Spectre de la Rose*, the dancer Mikhail Baryshnikov has recalled (in the book *Baryshnikov at Work*) that the ballet requires a very special style. He characterizes it as "a kind of broken, soft harmony. It calls for the dancer to dance in a less stretched-out way, almost a little 'off.'"

## SQUARE DANCE

*Music by Arcangelo Corelli and Antonio Vivaldi. Choreography by George Balanchine. Lighting by Nananne Porcher. Square Dance Caller: Elisha C. Keeler. First presented by the New York City Ballet at the City Center, New York, November 21, 1957, with Patricia Wilde and Nicholas Magallanes in the leading roles.*

Ballet and other forms of dance of course can be traced back to folk dance. I have always liked watching American folk dances, especially in my trips to the West, and it occurred to me that it would be possible to combine these two different types of dance, the folk and the classic, in one work. To show how close the two really are, we chose old music also based on ancient dances and a new setting, put the musicians on the stage on a platform like a bandstand, and invited the famous square dance caller Elisha C. Keeler to call out the dances. The dances he called out seem to be folk dances, but of course all the steps were purely classic. The spirit and nerve required for superb square dancing are close to what we always want in ballet performances, which is one way perhaps of explaining why so many American dancers are so gifted. The American style of classic dancing, its supple sharpness and richness of metrical invention, its superb preparation for risks, and its high spirits were some of the things I was trying to show in this ballet.

The music, all for strings, consists of Corelli's *Saraband*, *Gigg*, and *Badiniere*

from the *Suite for Strings,* and Vivaldi's *Concerti Grossi,* Op. 3 and Op. 10,
and the *Violin Concertos,* Op. 3 and Op. 12, *Concerto for Violin and Strings in
E major,* Op. 3, No. 12 (first movement), and *Concerto in B minor,* Op. 3, No.
10. Much of this eighteenth-century music was of course derived from old folk
dance forms and rhythms that were later refined for the courts of Europe.

In 1976 we decided to revive *Square Dance* at the New York City Ballet,
but with some changes, doing it without the caller and with the orchestra in
the pit. I also put in a new dance for the boy. Kay Mazzo and Bart Cook
danced the first performance of this revival, May 20, 1976, at the New York
State Theatre. The following day, Anna Kisselgoff in the New York *Times*
noted that while in the first version, you would have heard a call by Mr.
Keeler and the music would repeat with the dancers performing the step, now
the lead dancer calls the tune by dancing to it and the others follow him. "He
is the caller, but uses movement instead of words."

## SQUARES

*Music by Zoltan Szilassy. Choreography by Hans van Manen. Decor and
costumes by Bonies. First presented by the Netherlands Dance Theatre at
the Théâtre de la Ville, Paris, June 24, 1969. First presented in the United
States by the same ensemble at the Brooklyn Academy of Music, New York,
March 30, 1972.*

*Squares* is a way of looking at dance in a setting that frames the action. The
setting, on a raised platform, invariably a variation on the square, varies: it is
an enclosure, an upright outline, or a frame of light, fluorescent or ultraviolet.
It hems the ten dancers in, liberates them, or sets them off.

## STARS AND STRIPES

*Ballet in five campaigns. Music by John Philip Sousa, adapted and orches-
trated by Hershy Kay. Choreography by George Balanchine. Scenery and
lighting by David Hays. Costumes by Karinska. First presented by the New
York City Ballet at the City Center, New York, January 17, 1958, with Allegra Kent, Robert Barnett, Diana Adams, and Melissa Hayden and
Jacques d'Amboise in the leading roles.*

Ever since I came to the United States I have liked watching parades and listening to Sousa's marches. For many years in the back of my mind was the
hope that one day I might find an opportunity to do a ballet using his music.
The problem was always the arrangement of the music for dancing and it was
not until I had heard Hershy Kay's arrangement of Gottschalk's music for
*Cakewalk* that I thought I had found a solution. I talked about the possibility
with the composer, who was just as enthusiastic as I was about Sousa. We

went over all the pieces we might use and planned their arrangement together. Kay's score was just what I wanted.

We dedicated the ballet to the memory of Fiorello H. La Guardia, the late mayor of New York City who had epitomized America to so many of us for so many years.

The ballet is a kind of balletic parade, led by four "regiments." The five campaigns or movements feature each regiment in turn and at the end they all combine. In the first movement, to Sousa's *Corcoran Cadets* a majorette leads twelve girls. Another girl leads the second campaign in the *Rifle Regiment* march. *Thunder and Gladiator* march is danced by a regiment of boys, and the fourth, to the *Liberty Bell* and *El Capitan* marches, is a *pas de deux*. All regiments participate in the fifth campaign, the *Stars and Stripes* finale.

Karinska created brilliant costumes for this ballet and it seemed to me that David Hays's setting, and the final display of the American flag he arranged, were ideal.


## THE STEADFAST TIN SOLDIER

*Music by Georges Bizet. Choreography by George Balanchine. Setting and lighting by David Mitchell. Lighting by Ronald Bates. First presented by the New York City Ballet at the Saratoga Performing Arts Center, Saratoga, New York, in July 1975, with Patricia McBride and Peter Schaufuss. Conducted by Robert Irving.*

Hans Christian Andersen's stories are endlessly interesting. I am always coming back to them—sometimes for ballets. This particular story, which I first arranged in *Jeux d'Enfants* in 1955, tells of a toy soldier who goes through an endless series of trials and difficulties for the sake of a doll who does not pay any attention to him. At the end, both toys fall into a fire. What happens in the ballet is a little different, but I hope clear. The doll is an automaton ballerina, a bit like the toy made by Dr. Coppélius but with more soul. She is so enchanted with herself that she just keeps on rejoicing in her steps and gestures. She adores herself and ignores entirely the soldier, who presents her with his heart. Still, she ignores him. Her dancing so overheats her that she opens the window for relief. A draft rushes into the room and sends her up the chimney. The tin soldier mourns her and rejoins his platoon. All he has left is his paper heart.


## THE STILL POINT

*Music by Claude Debussy. Choreography by Todd Bolender. First presented by the Dance Drama Company, 1954, with Emily Frankel and Mark Ryder. First presented in New York, April 10, 1955, at the YMHA. Presented by the New York City Ballet, March 14, 1956, with Melissa Hayden and Jacques d'Amboise in leading roles. Presented by the City Center Joffrey*

*Ballet, September 24, 1970, with Pamela Johnson and Dennis Wayne. Lighting by Jennifer Tipton. Assistant to Mr. Bolender: John Mandia.*

*The Still Point,* which takes its title from T. S. Eliot's poem *Four Quartets,* is a dance drama arranged to music by Debussy—the first three movements of the *String Quartet,* Opus 10, transcribed for orchestra by Frank Black. The drama is about a young girl who, lonely at first and rejected, finds love. She endures jealousy, embarrassment, and torment as her girl friends rejoice in young love. Rejected by them, she rejects herself and suffers. She so wants a young man of her own that she dreams, too, and simply waits, fearing a little a real encounter. Finally, a boy comes, watches her as she dreams, then touches her shoulder. She reacts at first as if she had been stung and appears to resist him. Realizing that he has found an extraordinarily sensitive girl, the boy is gentle with her. She watches him dance, then they dance together, becoming closer, too, in thought, as they touch. They find in each other, at the end, the dreams they have had.

NOTES   Writing in *Dance Magazine* of *The Still Point,* the critic Doris Hering said that "Mr. Bolender has uncanny insight into the feelings of young women. His girl in *Mother Goose Suite,* his debutante in *Souvenirs,* and the tortured protagonist of *The Still Point* are all sisters under the skin—poignant sisters seeking fulfillment in romantic love. Of them all, the girl in *The Still Point* is the most touching because she is delineated with the most depth and at the same time with the most simplicity. In fact, simplicity is the prime virtue of this little ballet. Mr. Bolender has had the courage and the care to let the dancing speak out honestly without any mimetic overlay. And in Melissa Hayden and Jacques d'Amboise in the leading roles; and Irene Larsson, Roy Tobias, Jillana and John Mandia in secondary roles, he found responsive instruments. As the lonely girl, Melissa Hayden wove endless nuance and pathos into her portrayal, and yet the danced outlines were contained and beautifully clear. As her friend, Jacques d'Amboise communicated the steady masculinity that we have associated heretofore only with Igor Youskevitch."

# STIMMUNG

*Music by Karlheinz Stockhausen. Choreography by Maurice Béjart. First presented by the Ballet of the Twentieth Century at Brussels University, Brussels, Belgium, 1972. First presented in the United States at Carnegie Hall, New York, by the same ensemble, February 14, 1974.*

This ballet is a full-evening concert occasion based on the ambience of sound, a ballet that requires the attention of an evening's entertainment, without intermission. It was inspired by a piece of music, the title of which, *Stimmung,* carries a number of interesting meanings. Perhaps the best of these meanings, and the clearest for the dance involved here, is what might be called voiced atmosphere, or ambience. It is important to realize what the composer meant in thinking of the piece that accompanies the ballet and what the choreographer contemplated in the course of his composition to this music. Béjart describes his intention, plus the action:

"The ballet *Stimmung* is born from music and through music, and has no other purpose than to prolong in space, by tangible forms, the vibration which comes from the voice, the inner self, the absolute center of man—and which strives to touch this absolute vibration (which some call divinity).

"The ballet is ritual—'magic names'—and magic gestures. Doesn't every gesture which completely absorbs our being, and which is performed with complete concentration, have some impact on the total life of the cosmos? 'I raise my little finger,' said a Zen master, 'and the course of the stars is disturbed.'

"In *Stimmung* the gestures of life become gestures of dance as the dancers interpret and join daily life, inspired by the different intonations of the accompanying voices creating the diverse 'ambience' which succeed each other in the course of the day.

"As in life, from time to time man passes from sadness to joy; eroticism becomes prayer; joy transfigures the ritual; abstraction becomes lyricism; dance—mathematical equation; humor appears under each attitude and (visible or invisible) directs this ceremony which pretends to be serious without taking itself seriously.

"Ten dancers create the subject matter and its multiple combinations, such as the image of the 'Tekraktys' of Pythagoras, the triangle that contains the first ten numbers which are the basis of all mathematical combinations. The eleventh dancer in turn will incarnate himself in this interrogation until, when the cycle is completed, only the breath (which is the beginning and the end of everything) continues to exist.

"No improvisation is permitted, but each dancer finds himself or herself confronted by a series of possibilities which can be resolved differently each performance. The steps, which are 'regulated,' can be combined and repeated by each performer in a different way a number of times, which depends only on the imagination, the schemes, and the mutations which the act itself undergoes each performance according to the singers' inspiration."

The inspiration of the singers is, of course, largely dependent on what the composer has written. He has said that the work was built upon a series of "magic names" assembled for him by an American anthropologist, the names of some thirty deities from varied religions and cultures: Vishnu, Uranus, Uwoluwo, Rhea, Venus, et al. These names are invoked in the sung text. Stockhausen has recalled that the title of the piece, *Stimmung*, originally meant "harmony of pure intervals . . . In addition, and far from the least important, the German word 'Stimmung' corresponds to the notion of fluidity, of frame of mind (for example, one speaks of 'gute Stimmung'—good ambience— or of 'schlechte Stimmung'—bad ambience). It evokes the harmonious resonance of man and his environment. Finally the word 'Stimmung' includes 'Stimme,' meaning voice!"

The work is sung by six singers, who enter simultaneously with the dancers at the start of the piece. Seated about a lamp on a raised platform at the back of the stage, they sing meditatively, their voices amplified so that the softest nuances are heard. Each singer has a command of nine models and eleven magic names that he can, after a "scheme of form" and according to the context, introduce freely. "The others," writes the composer, "can react to these models and magic names with some 'transformations,' 'digressions variées,' 'oscillations,' 'unisson.' Nothing is directed.

"Surely *Stimmung* is meditative music. Time is abolished. One listens to the inside of the sound, to the inside of the harmonic spectrum, to the inside of a vocal INSIDE, with the most subtle undulations. It is scarcely explosive. All the senses are awakened and calm. In the sensuous beauty shines the beauty of the eternal."

## THE STONE FLOWER

*Ballet in three acts. Music by Sergei Prokofiev. Libretto by Mira Prokovieva, based on a story by Pavel Bashov. Choreography by Yuri Grigorovitch. Scenery and costumes by Simon Virsaladze. First presented by the Bolshoi Ballet at the Bolshoi Theatre, Moscow, February 12, 1954. Revised and presented by the Bolshoi Ballet at the Kirov State Theatre of Opera and Ballet, Leningrad, July 6, 1958. First presented in the United States by the Bolshoi Ballet at the Metropolitan Opera House, New York, May 4, 1959, with Vladimir Vasiliev, Marina Kondratieva, Maya Plisetskaya, and Vladimir Levashev in the principal roles.*

*The Stone Flower,* Prokofiev's last ballet, writes the choreographer Yuri Grigorovitch, "tells of the fate of the stone carver Danila who wishes to see the full power of stone and to show its beauty to the people. The creative urge which possesses Danila and the desire to create more perfect art is the leitmotif of the ballet."

ACT ONE   Danila, a young craftsman, desires to create a malachite vase that will be as simple and beautiful as a flower. He is not satisfied with one vase he has made; the secrets of the malachite seem to elude him. His mind is full of these problems as he meets his beloved Katerina and goes with her to their betrothal party. There Severyan, a bailiff, attempts to purchase the vase Danila has made, but the artist refuses to sell. In the course of the ensuing argument, Severyan becomes fascinated by Katerina and tries to embrace her. Danila and their friends defend the girl and force the bailiff to leave. There is a lyrical scene between the lovers and Katerina departs.

Danila smashes the vase and begins work on a new piece of malachite. The spirit of the malachite appears and with a touch of her hand shapes the stone, but as she disappears the stone resumes its original form. Danila pursues the spirit, who sometimes appears as a fairy, sometimes as a lizard, finally revealing herself to be the Mistress of the Copper Mountain. There she leads Danila to her underground realm where she is surrounded by maidens who are the spirits of the various precious stones. Danila is dazzled as he watches the blossoming of these fairy stone flowers.

ACT TWO   Katerina, missing Danila, dances pensively alone. Severyan attempts to seduce her, but she defends herself with a sickle and he is forced to leave. Danila, meanwhile, is learning the secret of the malachite as he works away in the palace of the Mistress of the Copper Mountain, who is enthralled by him. Katerina searches for Danila at the village fair. There again she is compelled to defend herself against Severyan, who tries to carry her off. The Mistress of the Copper Mountain now enters, transfixes Severyan, places him under a spell, and leads him to his death.

ACT THREE   Still searching for her beloved, Katerina comes into the forest. As she rests there beside a fire, a fair maiden emerges from the flames and leads her to the Copper Mountain. In the palace, Danila has realized his dream. He has created a stone flower. As the spirits of the stones dance in crystalline patterns, the mistress of the palace again tries to tempt him. But Danila's thoughts are only of Katerina. He realizes that he must leave the palace. Angered at his rebuff, the Mistress of the Copper Mountain decides that Danila will be turned into a statue and kept at the palace.

When the fire maiden brings Katerina, there is an emotional *pas de trois* between the boy and the two girls who love him. Danila in the end chooses Katerina and the fearlessness of their love obliges the Mistress of the Copper Mountain to release Danila from her spell. The young lovers return to their village, to share with them the joy of their love and the secret of creating beauty from stone. The Mistress of the Copper Mountain appears to bid them goodby, and vanishes.

NOTES   Describing the ballet, the choreographer has written:

"The foundation for the musical and choreographic structure of the ballet is the combination of the real-life scenes and fantastic dreams. The dance language is fundamentally based on folk choreography. The scene of the party, with the ceremonial features, is constructed in the form of a Ural dance rhapsody.

"Fantastic scenes utilize the classical dance. The movements of the classical dance characterizing the world of the Mistress of the Copper Mountain have a sharp, clean-cut style, emphasizing the nature of formation of stones and crystals. In the dances of the stones there should be reflected the sparkling, shining play of reflected beams. Dances of the main characters Katerina and Danila are also classic, the courage of the human heart showing broadly in the ballet. These dances are quite different from the dances of the stones, since we are dealing with a human quality. The dances of Katerina and Danila have elements of folk dancing and features of Russian painting technique.

"The classic dance also serves as a foundation for the character of the Mistress of the Copper Mountain. This fantastic creature personifies the splendor and beauty of nature. She has two faces; the face of powerful and strong secret force and the face of human justice, full of feminine charm. The author, Bazhov, makes her appear both as a lizard and as the spirit of malachite. This contradictive character determines the means for creating the character for the ballet. Her dances tend to be classic in style for the stone dances and must have very flexible elements for the sliding lizard so vividly created by Bazhov.

"A special role in the ballet is played by Severyan, the bailiff. He is a ruthless, soulless person—the only negative person in the story. Naturally the style varies from the style which outlines the other characters. Severyan, as with other characters of the ballet, must be expressed with full dance and plastic language which the choreographer must create."

## SUMMERSPACE

*Music by Morton Feldman. Choreography by Merce Cunningham. Scenery and costumes by Robert Rauschenberg. Lighting by Nicholas Cernovich. First presented by Merce Cunningham and his Dance Company at the American Dance Festival, Connecticut College, New London, Connecticut, August 17, 1958, with Merce Cunningham, Carolyn Brown, Viola Farber, Cynthia Stone, Marilyn Wood, and Remy Charlip. First presented by the New York City Ballet at the New York State Theatre, April 19, 1966, with Anthony Blum, Kay Mazzo, Patricia Neary, Sara Leland, Deni Lamont, and Carol Sumner. Lighting by Ronald Bates.*

*Summerspace*, which Merce Cunningham has subtitled "a lyric dance," is the second work by this distinguished modern dancer for the New York City Ballet (the first being *The Seasons*, created for Ballet Society in 1947). The music, a commissioned score, is composed in Morton Feldman's graph system. The background by Robert Rauschenberg is a pointillist skyscape and this idea is continued in the costumes. The choreographer revised his original work for the ballet idiom. There are six dancers—four girls and two boys.

Writing about his original production in *Dance Magazine*, Merce Cunningham recalled that the principal momentum behind the piece "was a concern for steps that carry one through space, and not only into it. Like the passage of birds, stopping for moments on the ground and then going on, or automobiles more relentlessly throbbing along turnpikes and under and over cloverleafs. This led to the idea of using kinds of movement that would be continuous, and could carry the dancer into the playing area, and out of it."

The resultant space-play is a continuum of movement that appears to swim in an intense haze of summer heat. The stage space here is a field, in fact, rather than the usual proscenium-enclosed space with a center of interest, and as the choreographer explains, since all points are of equal usage, "one does not lead to any particular other. The eye is not guided but allowed to jump throughout the space. The corners, in a conventional theatre stage, are nuggets that can sparkle. The momentum, too, is different. In a general way, the Balanchine dancers proceed in a vertical accent. 'He usually likes the accent down.' The force of *Summerspace* is horizontal. The stillnesses are dealt with as that, and not as positions in preparation." (From an interview with Merce Cunningham in *Ballet Review*, Vol. 1, No. 4.)

# SWAN LAKE

*Dramatic ballet in four acts. Music by Peter Ilyich Tchaikovsky. Book by
V. P. Begitchev and Vasily Geltzer. First presented, with choreography by
Julius Reisinger, at the Bolshoi Theatre, Moscow, March 4, 1877, with
Pauline Karpakova in the leading role. This incomplete and unsuccessful
production was superseded by a new choreographic version by Lev Ivanov
and Marius Petipa, which was presented for the first time in a complete,
four-act production at the Maryinsky Theatre, St. Petersburg, February 8,
1895, with Pierina Legnani in the double role of Odette-Odile. Act Two of
this version was presented for the first time at the Maryinsky Theatre, St.
Petersburg, February 29, 1894, with Legnani as Odette. Scenery by Botcharov and Levogt. First presented in western Europe in complete form in
Prague, Czechoslovakia, June 27, 1907, with choreography by Achille
Viscusi. First presented in the United States at the Metropolitan Opera
House, New York, December 20, 1911, with Catherine Geltzer as Odette-
Odile, Mikhail Mordkin as Prince Siegfried, and Alexandre Volinine as
Benno. This production was staged by Mordkin after the Petipa-Ivanov
choreography. Scenery by James Fox. First presented in England in complete form by the Sadler's Wells Ballet at the Sadler's Wells Theatre, London, November 29, 1934, with the Petipa-Ivanov choreography reproduced
by Nicholas Sergeyev; Alicia Markova as Odette-Odile, Robert Helpmann
as Prince Siegfried. Scenery and costumes by Hugh Stevenson. Presented
complete by the San Francisco Ballet, in a version staged by William Christensen, 1940. The revised Sadler's Wells production, with scenery and costumes by Leslie Hurry, was first presented in the United States October 20,
1949, with Margot Fonteyn and Robert Helpmann. Presented complete with
the original choreography of Lev Ivanov staged by David Blair, by the Atlanta Civic Ballet, August 24, 1965. Presented complete with Ivanov's choreography staged by David Blair by American Ballet Theatre at the Civic
Opera House, Chicago, February 16, 1967. Scenery by Oliver Smith. Costumes by Freddy Wittop. Lighting by Jean Rosenthal. Presented in varied
versions by many companies.*

Musically, and as a dance drama, Swan Lake is undoubtedly the most popular
of all classical ballets. It is possible to see at least a major portion of the complete Swan Lake—the famous second act—danced by almost every ballet company in the world. And the ballet is a favorite of ballerinas as well as audiences. All leading dancers want to dance Swan Lake at least once in their
careers, and all audiences want to see them dance it. To succeed in Swan Lake
is to become overnight a ballerina. Petipa and Ivanov are to the dancer what
Shakespeare is to the actor: if you can succeed in their choreography parts,
there is a suggestion that you can succeed at anything.

Why is it that Swan Lake has been so consistently popular with both audiences and dancers for so long a time? What about its chief rivals in the classi-

cal repertory—*Giselle, The Sleeping Beauty,* and *Coppélia*—why are they not as popular? If we set aside practical considerations (unlike *Swan Lake,* these other ballets cannot successfully be shortened into one-act versions; the part does not provide the spirit of the whole), we find the answer in *Swan Lake*'s romantic and tragic story and the music that accompanies its unfolding.

The heroines of these other classics all have some relation to the real world—they are peasant girls or princesses. Strange things may happen to them, but they live within determined conventions. The heroine of *Swan Lake* has another story. She is a princess of the night; she is all magic, a creature of the imagination.

On one level, her story is a girl-meets-boy story: girl meets boy, girl loses boy, girl gets boy, and then both are lost. What prevents this from being silly is the character of the girl. She is Queen of the Swans, a beautiful bird, except for the brief time—between midnight and dawn—when the mysterious sorcerer, Von Rotbart, allows her to become a beautiful woman. In the world of sky and water she is at home, but in the real world, where romance is possible, she seems to be irretrievably lost. The great love she comes to have for a worldly prince is doomed at its start; she has no control over her destiny.

The Swan Queen is the opposite of the Firebird, the bird triumphant; she is immediately pathetic, a creature whose initial fear and consuming love interest us immediately. The dignity and courage and authority she possesses as Queen of the Swans become, in the ballet, the dignity of the woman in love. Humanly speaking, even in this magical world she inhabits, she is never unreal or absurd to us, because we see that love does not shatter her dignity; rather, it ennobles her beauty and explains her universal appeal.

ACT ONE: THE GARDEN OF PRINCE SIEGFRIED'S CASTLE  Before the curtain rises, an overture warns us of the impending tragedy of the story. After the woodwinds have introduced the principal romantic theme, and the strings have taken it up, there is a faltering: a soft, gradually building questioning by the strings. And the answer comes in boldly asserted warnings by the crashing of cymbals and resounding trumpet calls. But soon, over these crescendos, the romantic theme returns at full, conquering volume. It quietens, and the curtain rises.

This is Prince Siegfried's twenty-first birthday, and the young prince is celebrating the occasion in the garden of his ancestral palace. Young people from the surrounding estates have come to pay tribute to him. Benno, friend to the prince, is talking to a group of twelve young men. Wolfgang, the prince's old tutor, comes in merrily and is almost immediately attracted to the bottles of wine that stand on a table at the right. The atmosphere is one of anticipation, and as the trumpets blare the climax of a spirited march, the host enters. The handsome prince is not haughty; neither is he familiar. He is delighted to see his friends, thanks them as they congratulate him, claps his old tutor on the back affectionately, and prepares to enjoy the festivities that have been arranged in his honor.

First there is a *pas de trois,* danced by two girls and a boy. (Since the Diaghilev company's second-act version of 1911, this *pas de trois* has often been performed as a *divertissement* in Act Two. Sometimes it is danced by Benno and two cygnets, sometimes by a first huntsman and two swan princesses, as in the production by the Sadler's Wells Theatre Ballet. Where the *pas de trois* is not interpolated in Act Two, the music for the variation of the *danseur* is almost invariably used for a variation by Benno.) For the dance of the two girls and a boy, the music is lightly melodic and flowing. Now each dances alone: the first girl performs to blithe, tripping music that increases in speed; the boy, to strongly accented rhythms that mark the precision of his *entrechats* and turns in the air; and the second girl, to a light, almost joking theme. Climactic music accompanies the final display of virtuosity that all three perform.

While most of the assembled guests have been watching the dance, the old tutor has been privately celebrating the prince's coming of age by drinking as much wine as possible. Just as everyone begins to enjoy the party, the conviviality is disturbed by the entrance of the princess mother and her four ladies in waiting. Siegfried goes to his mother and escorts her into the garden. She observes his friends with considerable disdain; there is an effort to hide the wine bottles, and poor old Wolfgang finds himself in obvious disfavor. The princess mother indicates to her son that his coming of age is hardly the occasion for levity. He responds to this opinion dutifully, but with apparent resistance. Siegfried is further disturbed when his mother points out to him that he must soon choose a wife. Her suggestion is in the nature of a command, and Siegfried turns stubbornly away. Tomorrow night, his mother reminds him, his birthday will be celebrated formally at a court ball, and there, from among the loveliest ladies of the land, he must select his future wife. Siegfried sees that argument is impossible; as he kisses his mother's hand and leads her out of the garden, he seems to bend to her will.

Wolfgang gestures his pleasure at the departure of the dominating princess mother. He attempts to restore the spirit of the happy occasion by claiming that, old as he is, he can dance better than any of the younger men. Everyone laughs at him, but Wolfgang is not to be outdone. He approaches one of the village maidens, who giggles as he takes her by the hand and begins to dance. The melody to which he partners her is subdued and charmingly sentimental, sweetly echoing the joys of youth. Soon Wolfgang is having such a good time that he tries to surpass himself by whirling his partner around and around. In the process he becomes dizzy and falls to the ground, taking his partner with him.

Now Prince Siegfried is convinced that the only thing to do is to enjoy himself to the utmost: tomorrow, after all, is another day. The prince signals that the celebration should continue. Wine is poured for all the guests, and village couples dance a vigorous polka that completely restores to the gathering its natural spirit of gaiety. Still Siegfried broods; the celebration has failed to dispel his apprehension in regard to the morrow.

Night begins to fall. Benno knows that Siegfried must be distracted for the remainder of the evening. He hears the sound of fluttering wings overhead, looks up, and sees in the sky beautiful wild swans in full flight. Against the sound of harp and strings, the oboe sounds softly the theme of these enchanted birds. Benno suggests that the prince form a hunting party and go in search of the swans. Siegfried consents; crossbows are brought, and flaming torches are provided to light the way through the woods. The village girls circle the stage and exit. Wolfgang alone is unwilling to accompany the hunting party. As the full orchestra takes up the mysterious and doomful theme that heralded the swans, Wolfgang tells Siegfried that he is too old, that he will remain in the garden. The young men bid him good-by and rush off into the night. The curtain falls as the old tutor stands alone in the center of the empty garden, his bottle his only friend.

ACT TWO: A LAKESIDE   While the curtain is lowered, the music continues to develop the theme of strange foreboding. Then all is quiet for a moment. As the music resumes, the curtain rises on a forest scene; a great lake, its shining surface undisturbed by the wind, shimmers in the moonlight. The music begins again. The hunting party enters, led by Benno. All carry crossbows. The men look above them through the trees, searching for the swans; they are astonished to see that the swans have settled on the lake and, within a few feet of them, are placidly gliding by. Leading the group of swans is a beautiful white bird, apparently their queen. The diamonds in her crown reflect spangles of light over the dark water.

A flourish from the orchestra heralds the arrival of the prince. The hunting party bows to him. Benno hastens to point out to Siegfried that the swans can be seen close by. The prince directs the men to hasten along the lakeside ahead of the swans; he is about to follow them off, when he sees something in the distance that gives him pause. He stops, close by the lakeside, then retreats hurriedly across the glade to conceal himself. He has seen something so strange and extraordinary that he must observe it closely in secret.

No sooner has Siegfried hidden himself than the most beautiful woman he has ever seen enters the quiet glade. He cannot believe his eyes, for the girl appears to be both swan and woman. Her lovely face is enclosed by swan feathers, which cling closely against her hair. Her pure white dress is embellished with soft, downy swan feathers, and on her head rests the crown of the Queen of the Swans. The young woman thinks she is alone. She poses in arabesque, then remains almost motionless, softly bending her cheek down against her shoulder in a gesture reminiscent of a swan smoothing its feathers. The music informs us of the pathos of this gesture, and Siegfried is so enchanted by the magical creature that he enters the glade. He moves quietly, lest he disturb her.

The girl is terrified, her whole body trembles, her arms press against her breast in an attitude of almost helpless self-protection; she backs away from the prince, moving frantically on points that drive desperately against the ground. Her arms seek the air for freedom, for escape. The prince, already in love, begs her not to fly away. The girl looks at him and gestures that she is afraid. Siegfried wonders why. She points to his crossbow and draws her arm back as if to let fly an arrow, then holds her arm over her face, cowering with fear. The prince indicates that he will never shoot her; he will protect her. The girl bows to him in gratitude.

The prince now asks her who she is, why she is here? The girl's hands enclose the crown on her head: she is Odette, Queen of the Swans. The prince salutes her and says that he will honor her, but how is it that she is the Swan Queen? The Swan Queen asks for his patience and points to the lake. The lake, she indicates, was made by her mother's tears. Her mother wept because an evil sorcerer, Von Rotbart, made her daughter into the Swan Queen. And swan she must always be, except between midnight and dawn, unless a man should love her, marry her, and never love another. Then she will be saved and be a swan no longer.

Siegfried holds his hands to his heart and says that he loves her, that he will marry her and never love another. He swears his faithfulness. Now angry at the fate of his love, he demands to know where this Von Rotbart hides himself. Just at this point, the magician appears at the lakeside. His owl-like face is a hideous mask; he reaches out his claws, beckoning Odette to return to him. [In one-act versions of *Swan Lake*, this lengthy mime passage is often shortened and the music is used to accompany a dance in which the prince, his bow set aside, follows the dancing Swan Queen, lifts her as they circle the stage, embraces her, and supports her gently in poses until she breaks away from him at the entrance of Von Rotbart.] Von Rotbart points menacingly at Siegfried. Odette moves between them, begging Von Rotbart for mercy. Trumpets sound in blaring, warning crescendo. The prince seizes his bow, kneels, and aims it at the magician. Odette beseeches him to stop and runs diagonally across the stage toward Siegfried. She touches his stretched bow and stands over it and her lover in extended arabesque. Von Rotbart disappears. Siegfried rises and embraces Odette. The music quietens. The prince puts his arm about the girl, and they go toward the forest.

The prince tells the girl that she must come the next evening to the court ball. He has just come of age and must marry and at the ball he will choose her as his bride. Odette replies that she cannot come to the ball until she is married—until Von Rotbart no longer has power over her—otherwise the magician will expose her and their romance will perish. She knows, she tells Siegfried, that Von Rotbart will stop at nothing to keep her in his power, that he will contrive artfully to make Siegfried break his promise to her, and that should he do so, should be be faithless, Von Rotbart will cause her own death. Siegfried again swears his faithfulness.

When the lovers have left the glade, Odette's charges, all the swans who, like herself, assume human form only between the hours of midnight and dawn, dance in from the lakeside. They form a single serpentine line that moves toward the front, then face the audience in a triangular grouping.

Soon Benno, the prince's friend, comes upon the dancing swans. They encircle him, rushing past him with their fluttering arms. Benno, unaware of the mystery of these creatures, thinks only of the hunt. The swans cower in fear and rush together in a close group by the lakeside. Benno hails the rest of the hunting party. The huntsmen marvel at his discovery and aim their crossbows at the swans. Suddenly the music crashes warningly; Siegfried runs in and behind him comes Odette. The Swan Queen stands before the group of trembling swans and stretches out her arms to protect them; the huntsmen must kill her first. As Odette begs the men for mercy, Siegfried orders them to lower their bows and to respect the magical birds. When the huntsmen have learned that, like Odette, the swans are really unfortunate girls in the hands of an evil magician, they remove their caps and bow in apology to the maidens.

Siegfried and Odette again vanish into the forest, the huntsmen leave the scene, and the swan maidens come forward in three columns to dance. They dance to a charming waltz; their ensemble is dominated by two swan maidens who emerge from the group to dance in unison between lines formed by their friends. When the dance is over, the swans gather together in picturesque groupings to form a final tableau.

Now the swan maidens gather at either side of the stage. Siegfried enters with Benno. The harp sounds a series of arpeggios. The prince searches for Odette among the swans. He does not find her. The huntsmen return and stand among the swan maidens. Siegfried stands with his friend in the center of the glade. At the back, behind them, Odette enters softly. She touches Benno's shoulder, poses for a brief second in arabesque, then comes forward. It is as if she had not seen the prince. The harp is plucked gently. Odette rises on point, then sinks slowly to the ground. She rests on her left knee, her right leg stretched before her. She bends down low, her arms reach forward like enclosing wings, and to the quiet rhythm of the music her body stirs expectantly. Siegfried comes forward, reaches down to her hands, and raises her. The solo violin begins quietly the wistfully romantic theme of the adagio. Odette pirouettes with slow, romantic adroitness in his arms. Now her love supports her as she bends low in a deep arabesque. Each of the huntsmen, observing the beauty of this love duet, now stands between two swan maidens, his arms about their waists.

Odette moves to Benno, and the prince admires her loveliness as his friend holds her in arabesque. The beautiful Swan Queen returns to her lover, moves in supported attitude, then rests for a moment against his breast. She moves now slightly away, rises on point, takes Siegfried's hand, and then—raising her right leg straight before her—removes her hand from his; for a fraction of a second, as she lifts both arms up, the idyllic nature of this dance is luminously clear: the relation of Odette and Siegfried is one of complete sweetness and absolute trust. Odette falls back, and Benno catches her gently in his arms as her right leg closes against her left. Benno lifts her up, she returns to the prince, nestles against his shoulder as he embraces her softly, and the movement is repeated a second time. Siegfried puts his arms about Odette at its conclusion and leads her toward the lakeside. The swan maidens turn in arabesque, to the gently hopping rhythm of the woodwinds, and cross the stage before the lovers. As the solo violin resumes, Odette and the prince run forward quietly between the swan maidens. Siegfried lifts Odette high in his arms to the violin's music; he lifts her again, and then she pirouettes in his arms. He continues to lift her effortlessly to the demand of the theme; she turns to his encircling arms, then moves away on point with a gesture of obeisance and love.

Now a number of the swan maidens are arranged in a diagonal line across the stage. The huntsmen, standing in back, lift some of the girls to their shoulders. The prince moves back. Odette goes to him, and Siegfried opens his arms to her. She turns away then and, hopping softly, moves in arabesque down the line formed by her charges. Siegfried follows her adoringly and, taking her about the waist, lifts her at arm's length high above his head. He lifts her again, releases her, and, as she reaches the end of the diagonal, lifts her to carry her to the right side of the stage. The violin repeats the theme of the first lifts of the adagio, and this time, to the melody, Odette executes supported arabesques followed swiftly by pirouettes that she terminates with an open pointing of her leg to the left. These movements are repeated with the music.

The swan maidens are now grouped on the left. After the final pirouette, Siegfried stands close behind Odette. She leans back softly against him and balances. The prince opens his arms as Odette opens hers and gently he moves her arms close to her body, as if he were quieting her frightened wings. Siegfried moves slightly from side to side, gently rocking his love. Odette rushes away, seemingly compelled to resist the embrace, and balances in arabesque, both arms encircling her head. From behind, the prince takes her arms, moves them back close to her body, and Odette leans back against him, now confessing the power of her love for him.

The adagio nears its end. Siegfried turns the Swan Queen slowly as she stands on point, her right foot trembling in *petits battements*. She turns a final series of slow pirouettes in his arms and then is held by the prince; both arms over her head, her left leg extended to the side. Siegfried holds her thus, then releases her; she balances for an instant and then, holding her pose, falls to the side; at the last breathless moment she is caught in the arms of her lover's friend. The adagio is over. The two lovers and Benno leave the stage.

Four cygnets appear and dance with bright, youthful precision a *pas de quatre* that is accompanied by lightly bouncing music of great charm. This is followed by a dance for two swan princesses. Here the music is openly joyous, uninhibited in its bounding, youthful expression of happiness in newfound love.

Just as this dance ends, we notice that dawn is approaching. Odette returns and dances a variation that is at first modestly lyrical; her arms stretch back and her neck arches backward as she balances in arabesques, and we feel that to this beautiful woman such a pose is the most beautiful and natural thing in the world. The music increases in momentum, and the variation finishes with a dazzling diagonal of rapid pirouettes across the stage.

The swan maidens are alerted by the coming light and prepare to return to the lake. Odette, in their midst, comes forward and—from the front of the stage toward the back—executes to the driving rhythm of the rapid music a series of quick, desperate movements that reflect her fear at her departure from her lover. Siegfried beseeches her to stay, but she cannot. Benno kneels before her. Now impelled to become again the Swan Queen, she rushes toward Benno and stands in full flight on his extended knee. Siegfried reaches out for her, lifts her down gently. The swan maidens have responded already to the return of the mysterious music that presaged the first appearance of the magical creatures: Odette and Siegfried are alone. Von Rotbart appears by the lakeside, beckoning Odette to come to him. She is helpless and must obey. She holds out her arms yearningly toward Siegfried, but her feet carry her back toward the lake. Her body trembles with helplessness, and she glides farther and farther away from him, to disappear in the new dawn. Siegfried reaches out toward her, unable to console himself by her promise to return.

The huntsmen enter the glade. Benno comforts the prince, and then, at the sound of wings overhead, all look up to see the swans in full flight, led by their queen. The curtain falls.

ACT THREE: THE GREAT HALL OF PRINCE SIEGFRIED'S CASTLE   The time is the following evening. The ball that the princess mother has arranged in honor of her son is about to take place. After a long and regal musical introduction, the curtain rises on the hall of the palace. There is a roll of drums, and a march begins. Here in the great hall, the royal thrones are placed on a dais to the right; on the left, with a short flight of steps leading down to the ballroom, is the formal entrance. Across the back, stretching into the distance, is a long, curved colonnade.

A flourish of music marks the entrance of two royal pages. The prince and his mother enter the room. The assembled guests bow to them as they proceed to the dais. The princess mother turns to speak to her son. Siegfried looks out over the ballroom with a blank stare; he is thinking of his meeting with Odette and his vow to be faithful to her. His mother, jealous of his preoccupation, addresses him somewhat in the manner of Gertrude upbraiding Hamlet: "Are you ill? You must pay attention to our guests; they are beginning to remark your strange behavior." The prince throws off his thoughts and assures his mother that he will not fail in his obligations.

Ambassadors from foreign lands, attired in colorful native costume, have come to pay tribute to the prince on his coming of age. A trumpet sounds a flourish, and a herald announces the arrival of six beautiful girls invited by the princess mother as prospective brides for her son. The girls are attired identically in stunning evening dresses and each carries a large feathered fan. The princess mother nods to them, and they begin to dance before the prince to the strains of a courtly waltz.

Siegfried pretends to watch them, but actually he thinks only of the lakeside glade and his meeting with Odette. His mother taps him on the arm and warns him that he must dance with his guests. The prince descends from the dais and dances briefly with each of the would-be brides. He dances automatically, with no interest, holding the girls casually about the waist and scarcely looking at his partners. The girls are dismayed at his indifference, but cannot display their displeasure too markedly lest their hostess be disappointed in them. Siegfried returns to the dais and again sinks into melancholy.

The princess mother rises and approaches the prospective brides. She thanks them for the lovely waltz and congratulates them on their beauty. Now she turns to the prince, asking him to confirm her opinion. Siegfried gestures that the girls are very pretty, indeed, but he does not wish to marry any of them. He loves another. He bows coldly to the girls. As his mother upbraids him, the music is interrupted suddenly.

Again the trumpet sounds a flourish. All the guests turn to watch the door. A herald hastens to inform the princess mother that a strange couple has arrived.

He does not know who they are, but avows that the woman is a creature of rare beauty. Siegfried looks expectantly toward the door. His mother orders that the guests be admitted. There is a crash of cymbals, the room darkens mysteriously, and the music hurries warningly into a repetition of the theme that marked the fate of the Swan Queen.

The light returns, and a tall bearded knight enters with his daughter. As the knight introduces himself and his daughter, Odile, to the princess mother, Siegfried—excited almost beyond control—stares at the beautiful girl. Although dressed in somber black, she is the image of his beloved Odette. [Although not originally designed for the same dancer, Odile for many years has been danced by the same ballerina who performs the role of Odette; Odette-Odile has become the most famous dual role in ballet.] Odile returns his stare with a steady glance of cold, but passionate, interest. In the distance, framed by an arch of the colonnade, Odette is seen holding out her hands to Siegfried. The prince is so enchanted by the girl he supposes to be the Swan Queen that he does not notice Odette's warning. The vision of the Swan Queen fades. Siegfried takes Odile by the hand. Now he foresees that the ball will be a happy occasion after all! He escorts Odile into the palace garden. Odile's father watches their departure with interest. Unknown to the prince, he is in reality not a knight at all, but Von Rotbart, the evil magician, who has transformed himself and his conniving daughter in order that Siegfried will be deceived and break his promise to Odette never to love another. Convinced that his trickery will doom Odette and Siegfried, Von Rotbart turns to the princess mother with a gracious smile. She is charmed by his flattery and—hopeful that her son will marry a lady of rank, as Odile appears to be—invites Von Rotbart to sit beside her on the dais.

Now the guests from foreign lands, who have come to honor the prince on his birthday, come forward to dance. First, two Spanish couples dance a quick and supple *divertissement* to the sound of music reminiscent of the melodies and rhythm of Spain. Next five Hungarian couples line up and, to the slow, anticipating measures of the music, commence a *czardas* that gathers in speed to end in a whirling finish. A vigorous Polish mazurka danced by eight couples concludes this series of *divertissements*. Von Rotbart indicates his appreciation of this entertainment to the princess mother and then suggests that his daughter, Odile, is the most beautiful dancer at the ball. Just as the princess mother is about to wonder where her son has taken Odile, Prince Siegfried appears with the stunning girl. Von Rotbart leaves the dais and tells Odile that the time has come for her to dance before the princess mother and Prince Siegfried. The orchestra sounds a rhythmic flourish, and the *pas de deux* between Odile and the prince begins. [When it is performed as a separate *divertissement*, this dance is known as the "Black Swan," or "Magic Swan," *pas de deux*. As a *divertissement*, the *pas de deux* necessarily lacks the dramatic impact it possesses as a part of the complete *Swan Lake*.]

This dance dramatically displays the cunning of Odile and the infatuation of the prince. In opposition to the adagio of Act Two, it has another kind of grace: it is full of pride and arrogance, rather than tenderness; it has the cold, dazzling light of a bright diamond. As Odile goes to Siegfried, Von Rotbart

stands on the right, watching with guile and satisfaction. The prince welcomes
his new love with joy: now his mother and the whole court will see how wonderful she is. Odile pirouettes across the ballroom floor, then turns rapidly in
Siegfried's arms. Von Rotbart calls to her, and she goes obediently to her father, standing in arabesque with her hand on his shoulder. Von Rotbart whispers in her ear. Odile looks back at the prince and nods. She has grown
confident with the success of her disguise and, when she returns to the prince,
is determined to display her power over him with even more breath-taking
skill. Siegfried supports her adoringly as she bends low in arabesque, but then
Odile lets go his hand to stand alone, poised, balanced, splendidly self-
sufficient. She goes back to Von Rotbart, and this time the impetuous prince
follows her. After receiving more instructions from her father, she rejoins her
lover, who supports her with glowing pride in bold and confident movements.
For a moment the two are separated. They promenade across the ballroom
floor, Odile walking with masterful authority and steely confidence, and meet
in the center of the stage to resume the dance. Suddenly Odette again appears
in the distant colonnade. Von Rotbart immediately notes her presence and signals to Odile, who steps between Siegfried and the vision. Odette extends her
clasped hands to Siegfried, despairing of her fate if he abandons her. The
enchanted Siegfried has no idea that she is there; the cunning Odile smiles at
him—a cold, even smile in which he can discern nothing but warmth for his
passion. The vision of Odette persists, and Odile becomes angry at this interference. She runs to Siegfried and places her hands over his eyes. Siegfried is
so infatuated that he regards this gesture as flirtatious and fails to see that
Odette, all hopes gone, has vanished, weeping, in the distance.

The *pas de deux* continues. Odile, now the winning seductress, carries her
conceit still farther, and the innocent prince is utterly in her hands. The dance
ends as the prince kneels before Odile and the proud, evil girl stands over him
in high, conquering arabesque. With the final note of the music, she gives a
curt, triumphant toss of her head.

The prince now dances a variation expressive of his great joy in rediscover-
ing the girl he supposes to be Odette. Odile follows with a quick final dance
designed to whip Siegfried's passion still further, and she succeeds in this
brilliantly. Her variation contains a dazzling circling of the stage with small,
swift turns, a series of quick, close movements performed in a straight line
from the front of the stage to the back, and finally a series of thirty-two
*fouettés*. These relentless, whipping turns sum up her power over the prince
and, with disdainful joy, seem to lash at his passion. Helplessly bewitched, he
rejoins his enchantress for a brief final dance.

Siegfried then approaches Von Rotbart and asks for Odile's hand in marriage. Von Rotbart immediately consents. Siegfried announces his decision to
his mother, and Odile bows before the princess mother. Von Rotbart, still un-
satisfied, addresses the prince further: he asks Siegfried to swear an oath of
fidelity of Odile, asks him to promise that he will never love another. Siegfried's love for Odile is so great that he is offended by this request, and then,
too, he knows that he has heard those words before. Why should they be
asked again, he wonders. He looks at Odile, and his fate hangs in the balance.

The music hesitates. He takes the oath. At that moment there is a crash of thunder. The ballroom darkens. The theme of the abandoned Odette screams above the orchestra. Quick flashes of light show the frightened courtiers fleeing the ballroom, the distraught princess mother, and Von Rotbart and Odile standing before the prince in a final triumph of self-revelation. Their hideous, cruel laughter Siegfried cannot bear, and he turns to see in the distance the pathetic figure of Odette, reaching out to him helplessly, her body racked with sobs. He falls to the floor in an agony of guilt.

ACT FOUR: THE LAKESIDE   The swan maidens have gathered by the side of the lake. They are sad and wistful at the fate of their queen. Their grief is reflected in the still tableaux they form with a group of small black swans who have joined them and in the dance the little swans do with their elders to soft, tender music. They yearn for the return of Odette. When she appears, weeping, they try to comfort her, but she tells them they do wrong to give her false hope. "I have been betrayed and I must die: the magician has won."

The music cries out with her grief, and she runs toward the lake. Two swan princesses intercept her and urge her to wait. They remind her that Siegfried is only human, that he could not have known the power of sorcery and thus could have had no suspicion of Von Rotbart's design. "You must wait," they advise her, "and hear the prince." "No," she gestures, "I have lost him and could not bear it."

Some of the swans hear Siegfried in the distance, calling for Odette, and tell her that he approaches. The Swan Queen orders a group of little swans to stand before her so that the prince will not discover her. Siegfried rushes into the clearing and frantically searches for Odette among the swans. Desperate, he asks the swans if they have seen her; he is about to abandon hope when the swans that surround Odette bend down and he sees her standing among them. He runs to her and takes her in his arms, asking for her forgiveness, swearing his infinite love. They go into the forest, and the swan maidens continue their dancing. When the lovers return, Odette has forgiven her lover, but she tells him—with tears streaming down her smiling face—it is no use, for what is her forgiveness alongside her death, which now must surely follow. "Von Rotbart is relentless. My life was forfeit if I should be betrayed. Only in death am I released from his power."

Now Odette dances to music that is tenderly beautiful. She moves softly in a long diagonal enclosed by the swans and, at the moment of her imminent death, expresses her undying love for the prince. Von Rotbart, enraged at Odette's delay, hovers over the scene disguised as a monstrous owl. He vows vengeance on her and all the swans. The swan maidens tremble as Siegfried defies Von Rotbart, who is momentarily overpowered by the strength of the prince's love for Odette.

The lovers embrace as Von Rotbart disappears. Odette then reminds the prince that only in death will she be released from Von Rotbart, only in death will she be free to love him forever. Her gestures are dramatic and sure as she tells him this, and suddenly she rushes across the stage in a swift diagonal to the shore's edge and throws herself into the lake as the music reaches a surging climax. Siegfried is motionless for a moment and stands helpless among the grieving swan maidens. Then, knowing that life without Odette will be nothing, he declares that he will follow her. He runs down the same diagonal that Odette took to the lakeside and drowns himself.

Siegfried's sacrifice of his love that Odette might not be destroyed by the evil magician has caused Von Rotbart's downfall. Again the malevolent owl-like creature appears, but only briefly. He lingers among the distraught swan maidens only long enough to see that love has triumphed in the end. He dies.

The stage darkens. The music softens. The swan maidens form two diagonal lines at the right, and as the light of day gradually rises in a soft glow, we see their figures bent low to the ground in grief at the loss of their queen and in gratitude for their own liberation from the evil sorcerer. Then, on the waters of the lake, a gleaming jeweled bark glides into view, its ornaments brilliant in the morning sun. Odette and Siegfried, clasped in each other's arms, move in the magical bark to a new and perpetually happy life. The swan maidens raise their heads, and their arms move softly, like ripples on the water, in quiet farewell to their queen.

NOTES   March 4, 1952, was the seventy-fifth anniversary of the first performance of *Swan Lake*. In observance of this occasion, Anatole Chujoy wrote the following authoritative article in the April 1952 issue of the informative and popular publication, *Dance News:* "Troubled less than it is in our days, a civilized world would have rested from its labors on March 4 to celebrate an important occasion in the history of ballet and music, the diamond jubilee of *Swan Lake*, the greatest romantic-classic ballet of all times.

"*Swan Lake*, as it were, stands at the highest point of the curve which represents the history of the source of all ballet as we know it today—the romantic-classic era which began with *Giselle* in 1841 and ended with *Les Sylphides* in 1909—the greatest period the classic dance has ever known. *Swan Lake* is often accepted as a strictly classic ballet; actually it is much more a romantic ballet. In conception, content, structure and emotion it is much closer to *Giselle*, for example, than to *The Sleeping Beauty*. In fact, it owes some of its choreographic invention to *Giselle*.

"*Swan Lake*, which has been variously called the greatest ballet of all times and an old war horse, was first presented on March 4, 1877, at the Moscow Imperial Bolshoi Theatre.

"Two years earlier, in the spring of 1875, the Director of the Bolshoi Theatre, V. P. Begitchev, commissioned Tchaikovsky to compose a score for a ballet then called *The Lake of the Swan*, based on a libretto written by the director himself, who was also a playwright of sorts, in collaboration with Vasily Geltzer (the future father of Catherine Geltzer, subsequently the famous prima ballerina of the Moscow Theatre [and the first to dance the complete *Swan Lake* in the United States]).

"Tchaikovsky hoped to create in *Swan Lake* a score that the Bolshoi Theatre would accept with the same regard as orchestras accepted his symphonic works. This hope was not realized. The choreographer assigned to the ballet was Julius Reisinger, a hack ballet master who possessed neither the talent nor the taste to choreograph a work to the music of a major composer.

"The ballerina, Pauline Karpakova, was a run-of-the-mill dancer past her bloom, who insisted upon interpolating sure-fire 'numbers' from other ballets in her repertoire to replace some of Tchaikovsky's music which she could not appreciate, understand or even count. The première of the ballet was to be a testimonial gala in her honor and she was not going to take any chances.

"When the première of *Swan Lake* took place it was a disappointment to everybody, especially to its composer. Herman Laroche, a well-known music critic, composer and friend of Tchaikovsky, wrote about the première as follows:

"'If during the creation of the ballet he [Tchaikovsky] had pictured fairy-tale splendor and brilliance he must have felt a bitter disappointment when he saw the work of the ballet master on the stage. I must say that I had never seen a poorer presentation on the stage of the Bolshoi Theatre.

"'The costumes, decor, and machines did not hide in the least the emptiness of the dances. Not a single balletomane got out of it even five minutes of pleasure. The greater, however, was the joy of the melomane. From the very first measures of the introduction one felt the hand of a true master; a few pages later we knew already that the master was in excellent humor, that he was fully at the height of his genius.'

"It cannot be said that *Swan Lake* was a total failure. It had a moderate success with the spectators and it remained on the stage until 1883 during which time it was given thirty-three performances.

"According to another contemporary of Tchaikovsky, N. Kashkin:

"'It [*Swan Lake*] was kept in the repertoire until the scenery was worn to shreds. The music also suffered a great deal. The substitution of the original numbers with others was practiced to an even greater extent, and toward the end almost a third of the music of *Swan Lake* had been substituted with that from other ballets, usually from the most mediocre ones.'

"When the scenery finally gave out the directorate of the Bolshoi Theatre took *Swan Lake* off the repertoire, and the ballet was not revived until January 1901, when Alexander Gorsky, a talented choreographer not sufficiently appreciated by his contemporaries and almost entirely neglected by historians, staged a new version of it.

"The version of *Swan Lake* which came down to our generation dates back to the St. Petersburg production choreographed by Lev Ivanov and Marius Petipa and first presented at the Maryinsky Theatre on January 17, 1895, more than a year after the death of Tchaikovsky.

"The production of *Swan Lake* at the Maryinsky came about in a rather unorthodox manner. The initiative for it stemmed from Ivanov, not from Petipa, as is generally supposed.

"After Tchaikovsky died of cholera on November 6, 1893, there was a general upsurge of interest in his work. His operas were being revived by Imperial and private opera houses, his orchestral compositions, even those which earlier had not been successful, were being played by symphonic organizations all over Russia.

"On March 1, 1894, an evening honoring the memory of Tchaikovsky was given at the Maryinsky Theatre. The program included several excerpts from the composer's operas and what is now called Act II of *Swan Lake,* independently staged for the occasion by Lev Ivanov, Marius Petipa's assistant who carried the unpretentious title of second ballet master and *regisseur,* the same Ivanov who had staged in 1892 Tchaikovsky's *The Nutcracker.*

"The role of Odette, the Swan Queen, was taken by Pierina Legnani, the great Italian ballerina, who had made her debut at the Maryinsky the year before in the ballet *Cinderella,* in which she introduced to St. Petersburg balletomanes her famous thirty-two *fouettés.* The short ballet caught the imagination of the audience.

"Petipa saw the performance and decided to profit by its success. He ordered a repetition of the performance at a gala evening and on that occasion placed his name alongside Ivanov's (and ahead of it) as choreographer. The second performance had an even greater success and Petipa decided to revive the whole ballet.

"Richard Drigo, the composer of the ballets *Talisman, The Magic Flute* and others, who was then conductor of the Maryinsky, was commissioned by Petipa to clean up the Moscow score. Drigo, on the whole, did a conscientious job, but found it necessary for some reason to eliminate several numbers from the ballet and substitute for them a few of Tchaikovsky's short 'salon pieces,' among them *Op. 72 Nos. 11, 12,* and *15,* as well as one number in Act III by an anonymous composer (Drigo himself, perhaps).

"Outside Russia there has often been speculation about what choreographer staged which part of the ballet. Indeed on several occasions the entire ballet, through sheer negligence, has been credited to Petipa, which is not only historically incorrect but also a great injustice to Ivanov. It has been established beyond any doubt that Petipa staged Act I (called Act I, Scene 1 in the original St. Petersburg version) and most of Act III (called Act II in the original version). Ivanov staged Act II, which constitutes the familiar one-act version (called Act I, Scene 2 in the original version), and Act IV (called Act III in the original version).

"Unlike the Moscow opening, eighteen years before, the St. Petersburg première on January 17, 1895, was a huge success. The occasion was also a testimonial gala for Pierina Legnani, who danced the double role of *Odette-Odile* and could not restrain herself from injecting her thirty-two *fouettés* from *Cinderella,* this time as the coda of her *pas de deux* in the ballroom scene (Act III).

"The two acts of *Swan Lake* which Lev Ivanov was permitted to stage were a great achievement for the choreographer and the culmination of his long but frustrated career at the Maryinsky, too little of which is known to the outside world.

"In staging the two acts Ivanov went contrary to the basic artistic direction in ballet during the second half of the nineteenth century, which aimed to demonstrate the technical proficiency of the dancer and the spectacular solution of complicated technological choreographic problems. Ivanov built Acts II and IV on musical principles, thus breaking a strong and generally accepted tradition. An excellent example of this is the adagio in Act II.

"In Petipa's ballets the adagio usually unfolds against the background of a picturesque backdrop or an immobile group of dancers who do not take part in the action. Ivanov's composition of the adagio in Act II is a duet with an active ensemble which accentuates and participates in the dance of the two principals. It is motivated entirely by the construction of the music, which was inspired, according to memoirs of Tchaikovsky's friends, by the vocal duet in his opera *Ondine*, the score for which he had destroyed before the opera was ever produced.

"This may sound less than revolutionary now, but in 1894 it was quite a step forward, so much so, in fact, that no choreographer dared to take a similar step until Michel Fokine, at the very height of his avant-garde Fronde'ism, utilized Ivanov's idea in *Les Sylphides* in 1909. Fokine also made use of some of Ivanov's choreography in *The Dying Swan* which he staged for Anna Pavlova in 1905.

"But Ivanov did more than just violate the canonical principles of the construction of the adagio by subordinating it to the problems of the musical themes. His two acts of *Swan Lake* very effectively dethroned the ballerina as the alpha and omega and, one might say, the *raison d'être* of the ballet. For some forty years Petipa constructed his ballets *ad majoram ballerinae gloriam*. The ballerina was all that mattered and everyone and everything else was on the third plane. Not so in *Swan Lake*. Here Ivanov treated the ballerina only as one of the protagonists. Here she either participates in the dances together with other dancers or alternates with them, or, if she performs a solo passage, the other dancers echo or accompany her. But no one leaves the stage for her variation, no one freezes into the painted backdrop.

"The adagio in Act II is a remarkable example of Ivanov's choreography, a testimonial to his choreographic and musical genius, but it is not the only example. One has but to think of the witty and compositionally perfect *pas de quatre* of the cygnets, the man's variation, and especially the entire last act to realize the great talent of Ivanov that was never allowed to achieve full bloom because of Petipa's dictatorial position in the Imperial Theatre.

"An appreciation of Lev Ivanov in English and an analysis of his work on *Swan Lake* and *The Nutcracker* is still to be done, and this writer hopes to do it before very long. It can be said here, however, that Ivanov's two acts of *Swan Lake* have been an inspiration to many contemporary choreographers whose origin was in prerevolutionary Russia. If one man can be considered the precursor of modern ballet, especially in the musical approach to choreography, that man was Lev Ivanov.

"Since its St. Petersburg première *Swan Lake* has never left the stage. The greatest ballerinas of prerevolutionary Russia, among them Mathilde Khessinska, Olga Preobrajenska, Anna Pavlova, Tamara Karsavina, and Olga Spessivtzeva, have vied for the privilege of dancing it.

"The current production of *Swan Lake* in Russia is based on the Ivanov-Petipa version, revived by Agrippina Vaganova in 1935. It is being given both in Moscow and Leningrad and is unquestionably the most popular ballet of the repertoire of both state theatres. It is also the ballet always presented on gala

occasions and it is safe to say that every American and Western European dip-
lomat and dignitary visiting Moscow has seen it.

"In Western Europe the full-length *Swan Lake* is only being given by the
two British companies, the Sadler's Wells Ballet and the International Ballet.
Both productions are based on the St. Petersburg version and both were staged
by Nicholas Sergeyev, a former *regisseur* of the Maryinsky Theatre.

"The familiar one-act version of *Swan Lake* dates back to the Diaghilev
Ballets Russes, which presented the ballet first in two acts [November 30,
1911, at the Royal Opera House, Covent Garden, London, with Mathilde
Kchessinska, *prima ballerina assoluta* of the Imperial Theatre and Vaslav
Nijinsky. Mischa Elman played the solo violin passages for these perform-
ances] and later in one act (ca. 1925). With the exception of the small French
groups, nearly all professional contemporary ballet companies in America
and Western Europe have a one-act version in their repertoire, based more or
less on the Ivanov choreography."

Swan Lake is always changing. That is as it should be. Tradition in performance is, unlike teaching, discontinuous, as my friend Lincoln Kirstein has said.
It is always interrupted, depends on shifts of directorships, changes of parts,
whims of choreographers, dancers, designers, musicians, and the public. Only
recently has a way been found to make permanent a record of a performance
and I imagine that in the future it will be possible to know about a number of
"definitive" *Swan Lakes*. But I also suspect that artists will want always to
change it, to remake it for themselves. That is what many of us have done, and
I hope will keep on doing.

My own version of Act Two, for example, first presented by the New York
City Ballet November 20, 1951, retained then only the central *adagio* and the
*pas de quatre*. But I have made many changes in the ballet since and we have
new scenery and costumes, too, by Rouben Ter-Arutunian.

In England, the Royal Ballet, which has revised its production a number of
times, has arrived at a useful compromise by retaining its older, Sergeyev version of the original in the repertory of its national touring company and
presenting newer versions at Covent Garden and on international tours. This
keeps the old well intact and at the same time makes possible innovation. One
of the major revisions in the Royal Ballet's production was December 12, 1963,
when Robert Helpmann staged a production with scenery and costumes by
Carl Toms that had new dances by Frederick Ashton and restagings of other
dances by Rudolf Nureyev and Maria Fay. Margot Fonteyn and David Blair
danced the principal roles.

The Bolshoi Ballet and the Kirov Ballet productions of the complete *Swan
Lake* have become familiar. Other productions of interest include a version by
Vladimir Bourmeister for the Moscow Stanislavsky Ballet (1953), Rudolf
Nureyev's staging for the Vienna State Opera (1964), with Margot Fonteyn
and himself, and Erik Bruhn's production for the National Ballet of Canada
(1967).

Bruhn's production was fortunately filmed for television in Canada. Produced and directed by Norman Campbell, with scenery and costumes by Desmond Healy, this National Ballet of Canada presentation featured Lois Smith, Erik Bruhn, and Celia Franca. In an hour and a quarter, Bruhn compressed for the television audience the entire ballet, employing new choreography and new arrangements, too, of the score. This version was presented in the United States by the Public Broadcasting Service, July 17, 1972, over Channel 13, New York.

On June 27, 1972, Natalia Makarova of American Ballet Theatre danced *Swan Lake* with the Royal Ballet in London. Clement Crisp wrote in London's *Financial Times:* "Odette and Odile are both magical beings, the one enchanted, the other an enchantress; the particular distinction of Natalia Makarova's interpretation was marvelously to convey this quality of magic.

"Her entrance as Odette is quite extraordinary; the Swan Queen is terrified, a fraught creature at Siegfried's appearance, trembling in his arms. Like Melisande when Golaud finds her, she is lost, a prey to unfathomable terrors, and throughout this first encounter we are made aware how heavily Von Rotbart's spell lies upon her. Infinitely pathetic, she seems not of this world and the menace of the enchanter's presence never seems to desert her during the whole of the act. The result is a profoundly moving characterization, expressed through dancing of exquisite perfection.

"With the Kirov, Makarova's Odette was a marvel; now it seems even more amazing. The great sound-act duet pours out in an unbroken cantilena, long-breathed, phrased with the inevitability of genius. The pure, classic schooling, the lightness that imbues her every movement, make the dancing float on the music—albeit Makarova demands slow tempi and is not, I would hazard, the most musical of dancers. But an *assoluta* is to be allowed her own way with the score, and the means amply justify the end when it results in an interpretation at once classically controlled, in the Kirov manner, and totally communicative of the Swan Queen's tragedy.

"In her Kirov performances, Makarova's Odile was something below the standard of her Odette; this is now no longer true. She plays the third act with prodigious brilliance; the choreographic variants she offers are acceptable since the enchantress in the ballroom shines with a hectic glitter that is totally compelling. No prince could resist this malign beauty, and Donald MacLeary's fine Siegfried is no exception. He is obsessed with her, and very properly so; Makarova's shining presence is hypnotically attractive—witness the fact that after prolonged stage calls following her variation, the truth of her impersonation seemed to carry right through them: we were not cheering a ballerina but Von Rotbart's creation.

"If the fourth act seemed slightly flat, I would blame the production rather than the interpreter; it is unfamiliar to Makarova, and not particularly effective anyway. What shone through the relative dullness of the staging here was the beauty of her style, with its delicacy and impeccable placing, the expressive force of her poses, and such small but thrilling things as a *pas de bourrée* which seems to meet the ground with a feathery lightness. I imagine that some viewers will consider Makarova 'cold' as Odette; her performance is still absolutely true to the canons of the Kirov style in which the very statement of the choreography must contain the essence of the role without any external 'acting' —and I find it entirely satisfying. My only hope is that her interpretation be preserved on film—it is essential for future generations to be able to study it, and to marvel at its magnificence."

There have been a number of films made of *Swan Lake*, or parts thereof (the Royal Ballet's Act Two, with Margot Fonteyn, for example). David Vaughan in *Ballet Review*, Vol. 4, No. 1, wrote at length of the Kirov Ballet's film.

When the first edition of this book of ballet stories first appeared, in 1954, there was only one complete four-act version of *Swan Lake* before the public in the West—the Royal Ballet's, described above. Since then, many other four-act productions have materialized, and in the United States it has been possible to see different versions by the National Ballet, American Ballet Theatre, in a notable staging by David Blair, the Bolshoi Ballet, the Kirov Ballet, the National Ballet of Canada, and the Stuttgart Ballet, among others. The one by John Cranko for the Stuttgart Ballet prompted these remarks by the choreographer: "I am always surprised by productions of *Swan Lake* that claim to have used all the music. Such a production would last about as long as *Die Meistersinger*. While opera lovers can take this length, balletomanes tend to enjoy shorter fare. Something must go and I have, therefore, cut the well-known waltzes and *pas de trois* from Act One and put in their place the equally beautiful but seldom performed *pas de six*. This gives Siegfried the opportunity to dance and also to develop the character. The Black Swan *Pas de Deux* remains in the place Tchaikovsky intended, and in the fourth act the Drigo *pas de deux*, which always seemed too slight for the situation, has been replaced by the beautiful *Elegy for Strings*. I have tried to base my own work on the classic/romantic style of Petipa, working freely and in my own manner, but not losing sight of the great man's direction. Consequently most of the second act has been retained in its usual form. For the opening of the fourth act and the famous elegiac entry of the swans I have 'borrowed' from various Soviet productions. However, all the musical repetitions have been cut and the drama has been strengthened accordingly so that the prince emerges as a living person who experiences a tragic ordeal, rather than being a human crane who simply lifts the ballerina. The national dances have been woven into an overall dramatic arrangement instead of being pointless *divertissements*. What of the ending? There have been many 'happy endings,' where the lovers are reunited after death in 'fairyland,' but I believe that Tchaikovsky intended to write a tragic ballet. Consider the situation: Siegfried proves unworthy, he breaks his vow and unconsciously confuses outward appearances with inner reality, . . . he is a tragic hero and must be vanquished. The tone of the music, especially in the fourth act, is tragic. In the imperial theatre the Tsar (surrounded by so many tragedies) made it an unwritten rule that everything must close happily. But Odette and Siegfried are not the sort of lovers who can 'live happily ever after.'"

Reviewing Margot Fonteyn's *Autobiography* in the New York *Times* (May 15, 1976), the critic Anna Kisselgoff recalled that the ballerina, on May 3, 1972, offered "at the age of 53 an unforgettable *Swan Lake* with Rudolf in

New York that surpassed the effort of any younger ballerina that season. The idea of a technique drenched in emotionalism (for this was the secret of that night's success) is not usually associated with the most regal of the Royal Ballet's ballerinas.

"Yet that is a notion about herself that she accepts fully. Writing of the early years of the Nureyev-Fonteyn partnership, she describes the contrast between the two dancers this way: 'It was paradoxical that the young boy everyone thought so wild and spontaneous in his dancing cared desperately about technique, whereas I, the cool English ballerina, was so much more interested in the emotional aspects of the performance.'"

## LA SYLPHIDE

*Ballet in two acts. Music by Jean Schneitzhoeffer. Choreography by Philippe Taglioni. Book by Adolphe Nourrit. Scenery by Pierre Ciceri. Costumes by Eugène Lami. First presented at the Théâtre de l'Académie Royale de Musique, Paris, March 12, 1832, with Marie Taglioni as La Sylphide and Mazilier as James. Marie Taglioni danced the title role when the ballet was introduced to London (1832), St. Petersburg (1837), and Milan (1841). A version of* La Sylphide *was presented in the United States for the first time on April 15, 1835, with Mademoiselle Céleste in the leading role. It was subsequently danced in the United States by the same ballerina; by Augusta Maywood (1838); Amélie Galster (1839), sister-in-law of Marie Taglioni; and by Fanny Elssler (1840). In 1836* Sylphiden *was presented by the Royal Danish Ballet in a version by Auguste Bournonville with music by Herman Løvenskjold. Lucile Grahn danced the Sylphide in the first performance of this version, which has been in the active repertory of the Royal Danish Ballet ever since. Taglioni's* La Sylphide *was revived in 1946 by the Ballets des Champs-Élysées, Paris, with choreography by Victor Gsovsky, scenery by Serebriakov, and costumes by Christian Bérard. Nina Vyroubova and Roland Petit danced the principal roles. The Royal Danish Ballet danced the ballet in the United States for the first time at the Metropolitan Opera House, New York, September 16, 1956. Harald Lander staged* La Sylphide *for American Ballet Theatre in San Antonio, Texas, November 11, 1964, with Toni Lander and Royes Fernandez. Music arranged and composed by Edgar Cosma after Løvenskjold. On May 20, 1967, Carla Fracci and Erik Bruhn danced in this production at the New York State Theatre. Erik Bruhn staged it for the National Ballet of Canada in Toronto, December 31, 1964, with Lois Smith and himself in the leading roles. These were later taken by Lynn Seymour and Rudolf Nureyev.*

Once a curiosity but now popular in repertories in the United States, Canada, England, and the continent, *La Sylphide* deserves continuing attention. Ballet history was changed completely by the work. Marie Taglioni who danced it and the men who created the role for her made a revolution in the art of dancing that we still witness whenever we go to the ballet and see a world of story

—of sylphs, ondine, swan queens, and firebirds—that is both real and fantasy, settings that are both ethereal and natural, costumes of flowing white, satin toe shoes, and dancers who rise on *pointe* and are lifted magically into the air by their partners. The era of the romantic ballet begun by this ballet is still much with us.

ACT ONE    The story of *La Sylphide* is a romance of old Scotland. The scene is the living room of a Scottish farmhouse. The time is 1830. The room is large and high. On the left a fire blazes in a great fireplace; a huge stone mantel rises from it to the rafters. The mantel is hung with trophies of the hunt—colorful stuffed birds, powder horns, and flintlocks. A staircase runs up the back of the room to the upper story, and a bright plaid decorates the banister. Near the first landing of the stairs is a high, peaked window through whose diamond-shaped translucent glass we can discern the break of day.

This is the wedding day of James Reuben, the young Scots peasant who lives in this house with his mother. The bridegroom sleeps restlessly in a high wing chair drawn close to the fire. He is dressed for his wedding: kilts, cap with high feather. His dark head stirs against the back of the chair; he is dreaming. His dream is with us in the room, and we understand his restlessness. For kneeling on the floor at his feet, her long white dress against the bridegroom's bright tartan, is the diaphanous, winged sylphide, who glances with quiet happiness about the room and seems with her penetrating gaze to look into the eyes of her dreaming lover.

Gurn, another young peasant, rests in a corner against the fireplace. In his deep sleep, Gurn is not disturbed by the realization of his friend's dream; he himself dreams of Effie, James's bride-to-be, and the love he will lose this day.

The sylphide rises effortlessly and circles about the chair. She looks down upon the sleeping James with wistful longing, moving around the room with a lightness and grace that make her wings more than a part of her costume. James turns his head as she dances about him; he is still asleep, but in his dream he watches every gesture she makes. Creature that she is from another world, the sylphide now seems a part of this room. Her smile is the considered smile of possession; she is both beautiful and serious, and her face tells us that her love is great enough to endure beyond James's dream. Should James respond to her love, we feel that this dream might become permanent.

James stirs in his sleep. He wakens suddenly and beholds the sylphide before him. He reaches out for her desperately. Frightened now by reality, the sylphide eludes his grasp. She rushes toward the fireplace. She disappears like the smoke from the dying embers. James moves his hand to his forehead in disbelief at the apparition: was she really there, after all? He becomes frantic and unable to understand the mystery and decides to question Gurn. He shakes his friend awake rudely. Did he see the beautiful vision? How long have we slept? Gurn is a little embarrassed at his own dream and is about to tell James yes, he saw the beautiful girl, but he sees that his friend is not talking about Effie, the bride, but about someone quite different. He wonders at his friend.

James is angry at Gurn for allowing himself to sleep so soundly. He is still trying to piece together the fragments of his dream when he hears his mother approach. She comes in from another room with Effie. Reminded by his bride's presence that he has scarcely thought of her, James is embarrassed. Gurn greets the bride first. The beautiful young lass smiles at him. Gurn can hardly control himself, he is so moved by her loveliness; meekly he presents her with a rare bird he killed yesterday while hunting. Effie accepts the gift, but turns to her fiancé. Why, she wonders, is he preoccupied? Has he no greeting for her? James shakes off his dream and kisses her fondly. They embrace. Effie cannot see James's face as he stares over her shoulder into the fireplace. His mother and Gurn watch him curiously.

Again James kisses his bride. Amused by his own formality, he kisses her hand and tells her that this is the day he has long awaited. Effie sees that he is sincere and his old self again. She is therefore a little annoyed when Gurn steps in, takes her hand and tries to kiss it too. She shakes her finger at him, and James, seeing that he has a rival in his friend, jokes with him about it. Gurn, however, is in no mood for jokes and walks away to nurture his private dream.

James's mother embraces her son and Effie. The lovers kneel before her; she blesses them and hopes for their eternal happiness. Effie and James look into each other's eyes; in her sight, he has forgotten his dream.

Now the music brightens and becomes festive with the arrival of Effie's bridesmaids. The young peasant girls, dressed in brilliant plaids, surround the lovers and wish them well. Gurn approaches. The girls giggle at his discomfiture: after all, he might choose one of them instead of Effie, who is already spoken for. The unhappy Gurn pleads with them to intercede for him; can't anything be done, he wonders, before it is too late? The girls put him off and bring out the wedding gifts they have for Effie: bunches of freshly picked flowers, decorative cloths, and simple jewelry. The bride is delighted with the presents, tries on the jewelry, and drapes the new material over her shoulder.

She and her friends do not notice James as he walks away from them and stares into the fire. Gurn watches him suspiciously. What can be wrong with his friend? James turns his head to look at the precise spot where he last saw the sylphide. He catches his breath and jumps back, startled. Someone is there! He reaches out his arms hopefully, and out of the dark corner steps not his sylphide, but a frightening figure: Old Madge, the village sorceress. The girls are pleased and run over to her. Old Madge stumbles forward, bent low over her crude walking stick. Her ragged clothes are filthy; her stringy gray hair hangs loose about her white, ghostly face. She cackles hideously and walks straight over to James and looks up into his face. His fear turns to anger. He orders her away. Madge cowers pathetically, and the girls are shocked at James's behavior.

The bridegroom stalks away. The girls persuade Madge to tell their fortunes. Effie is the first to hold out her hand. She asks the sorceress if her marriage will be a happy one? Effie does not really have any doubts; it is, after all, the conventional question. Old Madge nods her head and grins, "Yes, you will be happy in marriage." Emboldened by this answer, Effie asks another question: does James love her? James looks over at the group. The witch says,

"No," smiling the same toothless smile as she shakes her head. James will tolerate this no longer. Old Madge cackles ominously. He picks up a broom and drives the hag from the room.

Effie, reassured by James's indignation, tells him that she never doubted his love and that Old Madge is a proverbial liar. James believes her and is comforted. As long as Effie is with him and he can look into her eyes, he, too, has no doubt.

His mother comes to take Effie away. It is time for her to dress for the wedding. Mother Reuben laughs at her son when he doesn't want to let Effie go. She takes the girl by the hand and leads her and her bridesmaids up the stairs. Effie glances back at James, who smiles at her reassuringly.

But now, alone in the room, James has his doubts. He cannot get his dream out of his mind, though rationally he knows it is nonsense. Effie is his real love and so she will remain. But will the dream recur? What would he do if it did? Could such a vision really exist? As he asks himself these tormenting questions, he feels a draft. He turns around, and there—standing in the window—is the sylphide! She is leaning against the window frame; her hands are clasped before her; her expression is one of sweet sadness; and her eyes look down, refusing to meet James's glance. James goes to the window and asks her why she is so sad. Before she vanished so mysteriously, the sylphide was blithe and happy; what can be troubling so beautiful a girl? The sylphide replies that she loves someone who does not love her. James turns as if to move away, but the sylphide continues. He must know, she says, that she loves him. She is the one who brought him the beautiful dream; she is the one who will always watch over him and keep him from harm. Gurn, who has been sulking in a dark corner near the fireplace, emerges from the shadows to watch closely.

James reminds the sylphide that he is to be married this very day. The sylphide knows. Tears fall upon her cheeks. She murmurs that there can be no more beauty in her life: she must die. She starts to leave. James can suppress his secret no longer. He kneels before her and tells her that since she disappeared from his sight he has not been able to forget her for a single moment; he has tried, for he owed it to his love for his fiancée, but he could not: he has loved her as she loves him.

The sylphide dances about the room. James is enraptured to see his dream become real and to find the creature even more graceful in life. She moves toward the window, beckoning James to follow her. He does not move. She whispers softly into his ear. The unhappy bridegroom looks toward the stairs and hangs back. The sylphide watches him and sees the source of his anxiety. Lightly, without seeming to have the least idea of what it is, she takes up the plaid Effie has left behind on the chair, puts it around her shoulders, and poses demurely with downcast eyes as the bride. James can resist her no longer. When the sylphide kneels at his feet, he draws her to him and kisses her.

Gurn is now convinced of his friend's faithlessness and dashes up the stairs to Effie. James and the sylphide are frightened. Excited voices approach. Quickly the sylphide cuddles up in a corner of the huge chair. James throws the plaid over her just as Gurn and Effie, in her bridal gown, rush down the stairs. Her friends follow. Gurn accuses James of having kissed another woman in this room. But where is she? James asks him; he laughs and swears he has been quite alone. Effie and Gurn see no one, but Gurn notes the plaid that covers the chair. James trembles. Gurn pulls the plaid away, and underneath is . . . nothing! The sylphide was vanished! James is as surprised as his friend, but immediately reassures Effie, who now berates Gurn for allowing his jealousy to govern his sense of truth. The girls ridicule Gurn mercilessly, and he slinks out of the room.

James's mother enters with the wedding guests—her friends as well as the friends of the happy couple. Refreshments are served, toasts are made, the bagpipes tune up, and soon everyone is either dancing or talking volubly. Everyone, that is, except James. As all the other young men of the village surround the bride, James stands apart, reminded anew of the sylphide. Effie breaks away from her admirers and reminds the bridegroom that he has not asked her to dance. James is shocked at his forgetfulness, and the two begin to dance. The other guests stand back and watch them. The couple dance together happily until the formal pattern of the peasant dance forces them to separate for a moment. At this point the sylphide returns. She is seen only by James, and the other guests are astonished—when James rejoins Effie—to see him turn his head away from his bride. The *pas de deux* becomes a *pas de trois:* every movement of Effie's is imitated and elevated by the sprightly sylphide. The guests join Effie and James in a general dance, while the sylphide runs hither and yon, now visible, now concealed by the turning couples.

James tries not to lose sight of her and whirls Effie around and around as he frantically pursues the sylphide. Effie is so happy she doesn't notice his anxiety. The sylphide continually eludes him, and James can no longer see her. The dance stops, and some of the guests surround James and inquire about his strange behavior.

They are put off, however, by the beginning of the wedding ceremony. The guests stand in formal groups about the fireplace, where James and Effie stand with his mother. The ritual begins. The couple start to exchange wedding rings. James take off his own ring and holds it at Effie's finger tip. He moves to slip it on her finger, when the sylphide darts out from nowhere and takes the ring from his hand. The guests gasp at the sudden disappearance of the ring. James turns away from his bride. The sylphide whispers to him that she will die if he marries anyone else. James is so appalled at this possibility that he now sees his course: he must prevent such a tragedy. The sylphide beckons to him and stands there in the room by the window before his wedding guests; the bridegroom vanishes.

Effie dissolves in tears. No one can understand how or why James has abandoned her thus. Gurn rushes in and announces that he has just seen the bridegroom running across the moor with another woman. Effie will not believe it. Gurn tries to comfort her, assuring her that she can be certain of his love. Mother Reuben and all the guests gather about the troubled bride. Effie sits down in the chair by the fire. The plaid is placed around her shoulders, her wedding veil is removed. Gurn kneels beside her.

ACT TWO   Eerie music suggestive of an unnatural world marks the beginning of this second scene, which will unravel the mystery of the magical sylphide and confront the romantic James with his destiny. When the curtain rises, it is still night. On the left, a small fire throws grotesque shadows against the walls of a small, dark cave. The surrounding forest is impenetrably black. The witch, Old Madge, emerges from the cave and stands over the fire. Hovering over the flames, she invokes her demons, beseeching them to obey her commands. With her crooked walking stick, she draws a magic circle about the fire, then hurries into the shadows of the cavern. She returns with her sisters in witchcraft: hunchbacked, cackling hags who gather about the circle. The hideous women hang a huge black caldron over the fire and dance around and around it. Suddenly Old Madge orders silence and, walking up to stand over the caldron, she points her finger downward in unquestioning command. The other witches are silenced by this gesture and wait expectantly for some result. Old Madge orders them to dance again; as they circle the fire, smoke and steam and blue flame arise from the caldron, illuminating the forest for a few flashing moments. The conflagration in the caldron simmers down, and the old women crowd around to see what remains inside. With an imperious sweep of her arm, Old Madge tells them to stand back. The sun is about to rise, and they must hasten their work. Madge takes her stick and pokes it into the caldron; when she pulls it out, we see on the end of the stick, like a banner, a lovely shimmering scarf. The old women grab at it, but Madge holds it to her breast; only she is aware of the power of this beautiful scarf. She orders her sisters away, and all the witches disappear into the cave.

In the distance, the sun rises brightly over the fields of heather and we see a clearing in a thickly wooded glade. The green trees hang down over the scene, almost obscuring the witches' cave. Dew covers the ground as the morning mist settles on the earth.

On the right, James enters the forest. No longer dressed like a typical Scots peasant, James wears a costume befitting the bridegroom of his sylphide: white tights and a plaid vest. He carries a bird nest in his hand. Carefully he examines the colorful eggs and replaces them. He looks about the forest for his love, but she is not to be found. As he begins to approach the cave, he discovers the sylphide standing by his side. He is astonished at the suddenness of her appearance and asks her where she has been hiding. The lovely girl smiles back at him so beautifully that James leaves off his questioning. As if to show him how she appeared so swiftly and silently, she dances about the forest like a magical sprite; the tips of her toes seem to require only the air to support them in flight. James is bewitched anew by her charm and becomes apprehensive when the sylph darts in and out behind the trees. He holds out the bird's nest and tells her he has brought her a gift. The sylph shrinks back; and we see suddenly that she is not frightened because James has probably harmed the eggs in the nest, but because the living birds who fly about the forest are moved by a power quite different from the mysterious force that makes her a sylphide as well as a woman. The sylphide is afraid of the nest. Scrupulously she takes it between her hands and runs to place it high on an overhanging branch. James smiles warmly at what he believes to be her tenderness; lightly the sylphide moves her finger tips over her diaphanous white gown.

James draws her to his side. The sylphide places her head on his shoulder for a moment, and James moves to take her face in his hands. Before he can do so, the sylphide has danced away toward the back. James observes her as she calls forth a band of sylphs, who pay homage to her and to him. The sylphs surround the happy lovers, and James would dance with his bride; but every time he turns to take her in his arms, she is mysteriously gone and before him stands another sylphide. This happens repeatedly, and James becomes frantic in his search. Then, just as if nothing had happened, the sylphide is at his side again, looking up into his eyes. James is satisfied, but again the vision disappears: all the sylphs seem to fly away in the blazing light of the sun.

Alone, James considers that he has made a mistake. Yesterday, in his mother's house, the sylphide was always appearing and vanishing mysteriously, but that he could understand—for there he alone shared her secret; but here in the forest with her, with no one to see, why should she wish to escape *him?* She had sworn that she loved him and would love him eternally, and yet she would be loved only from afar. Was his love an illusion, he wondered?

On the left, close to where he last saw his beloved, the branches rustle. James is startled to see Old Madge come out of her cave. In his present state of mind, he greets her like an old friend. He remembers his rudeness of yesterday and hastens to apologize. Old Madge tells him not to mind, she understands the momentary follies of youth—but why is he here in the forest? What has happened?

James tells her briefly that he has run away with his true love, the most beautiful girl in the world. Why then does he look so dejected, Madge inquires? "Because," James tells her, "the sylphide is never with me: I search for her, and she is not to be found; I reach out to touch her beside me, and she eludes my embrace."

Madge offers to help him with her occult powers. James, willing to try any device to still the sylphide's flight, beseeches the witch to ease his state of mind and secure his permanent happiness. Old Madge holds out the bright magic scarf and offers it to James. She instructs him to place this scarf about the sylphide's shoulders, and then the sylphide will never fly again: her light, transparent wings will fall to the ground and flutter no more; she will be his, on earth.

James is delighted with this magic and kneels before the witch in gratitude. Old Madge's eyes gleam with triumph as she looks down upon him. Then she hurries away into the dark cavern as she sees the sylphide approaching. James runs to his bride and embraces her. She responds warmly to his affection and seems to be charmed by the gift he offers her. James places the scarf about her shoulders. As the cloth touches her flesh, the sylphide clutches at her heart in a spasm of agonizing pain. Her wings fall to the ground. She stumbles forward. James, struck dumb by this outcome, tries to hold her in his arms and comfort her. The dying sylphide looks at him in horror and pushes him away. Slowly her body relaxes, and she lies dead before him, like a leaf fallen from a tree.

As James kneels beside her, weeping, the mirthful cackle of Old Madge ricochets against the dark walls of her hidden cavern. The sylphide's winged sisters emerge from the trees above. They do not comfort the despairing hero, but take the sylphide tenderly in their arms. As they lift her from the ground, they themselves are lifted up; the branches of the trees overhead move back, and high into the clear sky the winged creatures carry their dead queen.

James is inconsolable in his grief. The softness of the music that has carried his ideal love away forever is interrupted by the shrill, open sound of joyous bagpipes, reminding him of his home and the happiness he might have found there. Across the forest, in the distance, we see a wedding procession moving over the moor. Gurn and Effie, arm in arm, lead the happy party, and the curtain falls as the faraway church bells sound their welcome.

NOTES   The National Ballet of Washington presented *La Sylphide* in the version by Elsa Marianne von Rosen in 1969. When Margot Fonteyn, dancing this ballet for the first time, appeared in this production October 3, 1969, the critic Clive Barnes wrote: "After seeing Dame Margot it seemed only remarkable that she had never danced the role before. It suited her perfectly, for she brings to these Romantic ballets a most exquisite sense of period style.

"The ballet is a kind of Victorian nosegay—sweet, sentimental and yet completely acceptable upon its own period terms. . . . Dame Margot fitted into its ardors with effortless grace. . . . she conveys the mystic character of the sylph with a seductive mixture of femininity and charm. It recalls her beguiling performance in Ashton's *Ondine*, all thoughtless wiles and innocent raptures."

When American Ballet Theatre staged a new production of *La Sylphide* in New York, July 8, 1971, the staging was by the Danish dancer, choreographer, and producer Erik Bruhn. Clive Barnes commented in the New York *Times* the next day: "By far the best aspect of the production is Mr. Bruhn's staging. This is far more authentic than the first production of *La Sylphide* he created for the National Ballet of Canada some years ago. Indeed, it follows the original fairly carefully and with considerable sensibility.

"The only major addition is a brief new solo for Effie, which is reasonable enough. As is common nowadays, the hero, James, dances the second male solo in this act, and his rival, Gurn, dances the first. Mr. Bruhn takes further than any other production the current trend to romanticize Gurn and to remove him from the original comic tradition, and I can see no harm in this, even though it eliminates some of the traditional pantomime.

"There were other details of the production I was less happy about. I would like to have seen more stage machinery used—this is part of that particular period. I regret the omission of some of the smaller touches that are usually introduced—such as the Sylphide, on persuading James to run away from home, bringing him his cap. There were even details of choreography missing—including James's quite celebrated turn-and-a-half, where he ends a sequence with his back to the audience facing his ballerina.

"These are quibbles, but perhaps the kind of details that give authenticity to the authentic. But at last Ballet Theatre has found a good and valid version of this very important classic, and it will fit well into the company's repertory.

"At this first performance, the Sylphide was danced by Carla Fracci, with Ted Kivitt as her swain, James. Miss Fracci, with her fugitive smile wreathing the corners of her mouth, her tarlatan skirt frothing, and her shy yet captivating manner, is the epitome of the Romantic ideal, when, poetically, women often meant to be more myth than reality. And her dancing had the right febrile grace.

"The Sylphide herself is all spirit—an image rather than a character, an unattainable sex symbol for an age that in polite literary terms had no explicit sex but merely its lost promise. James, the Highland lad, who, rather foolishly, throws away everything to follow her into the heather, has more of the dimensions of reality, and Mr. Kivitt acted with a simple forcefulness.

"Probably the most rewarding character in *La Sylphide* is that of Madge the Witch, who ruins James and insures all ends unhappily. This is now played by Dennis Nahat, who is wearing one of the two or three most interestingly twisted noses I have ever encountered, and glowers with genuine power. It is a good idea to have this role played by a man—it often is in Denmark—and Mr. Nahat, with his unfailing sense of style, is already good and will soon be even better."

Erik Bruhn performed the role of Madge in New York, in August 1974, in the production of *La Sylphide* he had staged for the National Ballet of Canada. Writing in *Dance Perspectives* about his famous roles in the essay "Beyond Technique," Erik Bruhn recalled the first time he appeared as James in *La Sylphide:* "It was a pretty difficult assignment—to do James at the age of 23. I would consider any age between 18 and 24 as the right age for James on the stage. Of course we are all that age at one time or another. But to play him that way is possible only if you can achieve and sustain an idea about how you see him. To play yourself or to play your own age is not enough; to play young when you are young is very hard. When you are mature you can look on youth from a certain distance and this makes you objective. But when you are terribly involved with what is happening to you at this age it is difficult to re-create this. Some people would say that when you look back it isn't the truth you are seeing anymore, it is what you think the truth is. Yes, the role is also what you think it is. It is what you bring to it—your thoughts, your mind. You give life to the role by bringing to it what is true for you at that moment.

"For me, James is the youngest in the gallery of Romantic ballet heroes. He is an idealist, a poet. In the end when he tries to grasp his ideal and tries to make her a real woman, he dies. Without this dream, this illusion, he can no longer exist. All he wants to catch is a dream which exists only in his head and which nobody else can see. He is a true escapist. Nobody can actually get hold of James. His mother, his fiancée—none of the real people understand him. But when he is alone with his dream he is quite himself; he is a total being. When the dream is gone, he must die with it. He believes only in this dream and it is sad that he could never grasp reality. James dies without knowing that he is licked, which becomes a very beautiful thing.

"Unlike James, Albrecht in *Giselle* is on the point of entering maturity. He realizes that he has done something terrible and that he must suffer. If he can survive his night of remorse he will come out the better for it. He pays the price as James never did. Therefore he can live."

For an interesting analysis of the difference between the Bournonville style and the classic style taught in Russia, as well as for a penetrating account of *La Sylphide*, readers are referred to the book *Baryshnikov at Work*, where the dancer describes with Charles Engell France characteristics of performances he has known.


## LES SYLPHIDES

*Classic ballet in one act. Music by Frédéric Chopin. Choreography by Michel Fokine. Scenery and costumes by Alexandre Benois. First presented by Diaghilev's Ballets Russes at the Théâtre de Châtelet, Paris, June 2, 1909, with Anna Pavlova, Tamara Karsavina, Maria Baldina, and Vaslav Nijinsky as the principal dancers. Fokine's first arrangement of this ballet was presented on March 21, 1908, in St. Petersburg, under the title* Chopiniana. *The dancers were members of the Imperial Ballet; Pavlova and Oboukoff danced a classical pas de deux to the "Waltz," which was the only part of the original production without a realistic setting or suggestion of plot. The second production, given by Fokine's students, April 6, 1908, was wholly classical; like the first "Waltz," it had no plot, and the musical structure was altered. Preobrajenska, Pavlova, Karsavina, Nijinsky, and Bekefify were the principal dancers. This second version was costumed in the long white ballet dress made popular by Marie Taglioni in* La Sylphide. *The title of this famous ballet of Taglioni's was Diaghilev's inspiration for the new name he applied to* Chopiniana *when it was first presented in Western Europe in substantially the same form as its second production. First presented in the United States in its authorized version by Diaghilev's Ballets Russes at the Century Theatre, New York, January 20, 1916, with a cast that included Lydia Lopokova, Lubov Tchernicheva, Xenia Maclezova, and Adolph Bolm. An unauthorized version, not credited to the choreographer and not supervised by him, was presented in the United States by Gertrude Hoffman's Saison des Ballets Russes on June 14, 1911, at the Winter Garden, New York, with Maria Baldina, Lydia Lopokova, and Alexandre Volinine as the principal dancers.*


No one knows exactly when the first *ballet blanc*, or white ballet, was first performed. It is probable that this kind of ballet, which involved a new conception of dance based on ethereal atmosphere, soft music, and diaphanous white costumes, was first performed before *La Sylphide;* but it was *La Sylphide,* and the dancing of its ballerina, Marie Taglioni, that made the *ballet blanc* famous. *Les Sylphides,* its twentieth-century namesake, has carried this fame into our time more than any other ballet.

For the *ballet blanc* did not remain popular. Théophile Gautier, who first used the phrase, was complaining in 1844 that since *La Sylphide* the Paris stage was so dominated by white gauze, by tulle and tarlatan, that the "shades became mists of snow in transparent skirts" and "white almost the only color in use."

And so the misty white ballets gradually passed out of fashion. The ballets that replaced them for half a century were more concerned with dancing than with mood—more devoted to elaborate, regal stage spectacle, and the development within this frame of the classic dance, than to simple stories of fantasy and ethereal romance.

*Les Sylphides* restored the *ballet blanc,* now embellished with the developed classic dance; but it did so without a story. Here, instead of characters with definite personalities and a narrative, we have simply dancers in long white dresses and a *danseur* in white-and-black velvet, whose movements to music invoke the romantic imagination to a story of its own. It is the music, and the care with which the classic dance embodies it, that tells us the story of these magical creatures who dance in the light of the moon.

The overture, *Prelude, Opus 28, No. 7,* to the ballet is quiet and contemplative. The curtain rises on a secluded wood near an ancient ruin, where lovely girls in white are grouped about the scene in a still, charming tableau. The light is bluish white, soft, and misty. As the *Nocturne, Opus 32, No. 2,* commences, some of the girls begin to dance to the light, airy melody. They are joined by the principal dancers, who stand in a cluster at the rear.

Now a girl dances a variation to a gentle but joyous waltz, music suggestive of beautiful and controlled happiness.

The next dance, like the *Mazurka, Opus 33, No. 3,* that accompanies it, is not as soft; it is bolder, more open and free, but still restrained in its exuberance as the ballerina bounds diagonally across the stage in *grand jetés,* over and over again.

A variation to another mazurka, *Opus 67, No. 3,* is danced by the *danseur* after the girls have formed a decorative tableau about the stage.

When the overture is repeated, the sylphs form picturesque groups, the girls kneeling about central figures. The *danseuse* who now enters comes softly, pauses, and seems to listen to a distant call. She moves among the groups adroitly and sweetly, but completely removed from them in her rapt attention to what she might hear.

The *Waltz, Opus 64, No. 2,* commences, and the *danseur* lifts the ballerina across the stage from the wings. She appears to be so light that it must require no effort to hold her. She is released, and the *pas de deux* begins. Throughout this dance, as the music increases in momentum, the girl responds with unhesitating swiftness and flight to the inspiration of the music and the night: she abandons herself to the air.

The stage is empty for a moment, there is no music; then, to the final buoyant *Waltz, Opus 18, No. 1,* the dancers return, move diagonally across the stage, mingle, brush past each other, and fill the stage with movement like the swift fluttering of butterfly wings. The principal dancers join them for short solos; and at the final chords, there is a swift, silent rush and all are standing still, in the same tableau in which we first saw them.

NOTES *Les Sylphides* is associated with many famous dancers. Fokine staged his work for the Royal Danish Ballet on October 21, 1925 (in a revised version), for René Blum's Ballet Russe de Monte Carlo in 1936, and for Ballet Theatre in 1940.

In the first Diaghilev production in Paris, the first solo, Waltz, was danced by Karsavina; the second, Mazurka, by Anna Pavlova; the third, Mazurka, by Nijinsky; the Prelude, by Maria Baldina; the *pas de deux*, Waltz, by Pavlova and Nijinsky; and the final Waltz, by all the soloists and the *corps de ballet*. Vaslav Nijinsky danced *Les Sylphides* in the United States on April 14, 1916, at the Metropolitan Opera House.

The music for Fokine's first arrangement of the ballet that was later to become *Les Sylphides* was orchestrated by Glazunov. Music for the second version was orchestrated by Keller and Glazunov. Music for the Diaghilev production was orchestrated by Stravinsky (his first Diaghilev commission), Tcherepnine, Glazunov, and Liadov. Later orchestrations include those of Vittorio Rieti and Lucien Caillet.

On January 13, 1972, *Chopiniana*, the work on which *Les Sylphides* was based, was presented for the first time outside Russia:

> *Music by Frédéric Chopin. Staged by Alexandra Danilova after Michel Fokine. Pianist: Gordon Boelzner. First presented by the New York City Ballet at the New York State Theatre, Lincoln Center, with Kay Mazzo, Peter Martins, Karin von Aroldingen, and Susan Hendl in the principal roles.*

The title *Chopiniana* derives from a suite of four piano pieces by Chopin, orchestrated by Alexander Glazunov (*Opus 46*, 1894). Fokine, planning these for a charity performance ballet, asked the composer to add the *C Sharp Minor Waltz* (for Anna Pavlova and Mikhail Oboukoff, Nijinsky's teacher). This first *Chopiniana* was danced March 21, 1908, comprising five scenes: a Polonaise in Polish court dress; an evocation of Chopin and his Muse who repels nightmares of dead monks in his Mayorquin monastery; a Mazurka for a peasant wedding; the Waltz; and, as finale, a Tarantella based on Fokine's memory of a Capri festival.

A second (this current) *Chopiniana* introduced April 16, 1908, used different piano pieces orchestrated by Maurice Keller, retaining Glazunov's Waltz but eliminating all character dancing and mime for a visualized abstraction. Set in three days, Fokine described: "Some of the *corps de ballet* groups accompanying the dancing of the soloists were staged by me, just before curtain time." Diaghilev produced it in his initial Paris ballet season, June 2, 1909, under his own title as *Les Sylphides*, with Pavlova, Karsavina, and Nijinsky, in a long blond wig which the designer Alexandre Benois said "seemed a trifle comic when I saw it on stage . . . his slightly caricatured appearance made the artist look like a figure from some old beaded reticule or painted lampshade." Some critics frowned on piano music in arrangements made then (and later) by Keller, Liadov, Rieti, Malcolm Sargent, Sokolov, Stravinsky, Taneef, Tcherepnine, etc. Scenery was by Benois; later by A. Socrate, Leon Zak, etc. In 1932, for René Blum's Ballets du Théâtre de Monte

Carlo under Balanchine's artistic direction, a Corot landscape was used. Fokine restaged his work for the Royal Danes in 1925 as *Chopiniana,* by which it was familiar in Russia before and since. In 1936, for Les Ballet Russes de Monte Carlo, he altered music and steps for the male solo. Other changes have crept in over sixty years, some due to individual dancers of which Fokine complained; others to the memories of rehearsalists after his death in 1942.

Costumes and scenery suggested the "romantic" (classic) lyricism of the 1830s. However much long skirts evoked Taglioni, Fokine's choreography surpassed any *tableaux vivants* inspired by static popular lithographs of the period. This was the first ballet as a whole (with precedents from Ivanov and Gorsky) in which movement itself projected from important music was a prime factor rather than a propulsive accompaniment. Fokine's fluent pattern held no pretext for virtuosity or pageantry. Layers of sentiment or sentimentality have tended to dull the force, logic, and ingenuity of this academic masterpiece. The original was planned for large opera house stages; later, scenic frames shrunk spatial possibilities due to the need for touring smaller theaters, while musical tempi increasingly decelerated. The present recension is not offered as a pious museum restoration but as a testimony of approximate efficiency in a context of its contemporary choreographic vitality.

Reviewing *Chopiniana* in *Dance News,* the critic Nancy Goldner wrote: "The decision to strip *Les Sylphides* of its scenery, costumes, orchestration, and by implication its sense of period, even genre—as the City Ballet has done with *Chopiniana*—will strike some as cantankerous and perverse; to others, like myself, a stroke of genius. While watching American Ballet Theatre's production during the last few seasons, I have been continually discovering that there is sturdy, tightly constructed, and subtle but unmistakable climax-building choreography underneath all the aspects that bring historicity to the ballet but have little to do with choreographic fact. One went to see *Les Sylphides* for great performances.

"Now we can more clearly see *Chopiniana* for great choreography as well. On the most obvious level, we can see what choreography is in the legs, since the girls wear short white tunics. It is easier to see that Fokine has been brilliantly economical. Alexandra Danilova's staging has also brought out the choreography's precision and deliberateness. The ensemble looks more vivid, more important. The placement of dancers now looks more linear, lending to the pretty formations a welcome touch of austerity. With this production, one also becomes more aware of lovely repetitions and the fact that *Chopiniana* is, in one aspect, a study on entrances and exits. The ballet is as beautiful as ever, but it is not of a genre. The City Ballet production, in other words, does not preclude style, just stylization. In its de-interpretation, it restores and preserves. This is useful."

NOTES    *Ballet Review* (Vol. 4, No. 5) published in 1973 an interview with the ballerina and teacher Alexandra Danilova that is of special interest in view of her part in the staging of the New York City Ballet revival of *Chopiniana:*

BALLET REVIEW    "How did you think the New York City Ballet's *Chopiniana* turned out?

ALEXANDRA DANILOVA   "Well, I think the first performance was beautiful, and I think the angle that we took is very interesting, and it was very clever of Mr. B. to suggest all these things, because *Chopiniana* is usually done with long skirts, blue flowers—

BR   "But this was really radical.

AD   "But it is not, if you think that from the beginning it was done with the piano. Chopin never orchestrated. And in Paris people said it was illogical to orchestrate Chopin when he wrote strictly for piano.

BR   "Was it the Glazunov orchestration?

AD   "Yes, it was Glazunov, then it was Stravinsky, then it was Dorati. So Mr. Balanchine wanted to go right back as like it was done, and now we have the ballet done with the piano, so this time they say why is it not with orchestra?

BR   "The principal criticism has been that the ballet was done for a particular reason with the costumes that it had, that when Fokine made the ballet the whole mood and the whole aura of the piece had a lot to do with the production and that these elements were very important to it.

AD   "I think a little bit different. I don't know what they wore originally because it was done for annual school performance, and they probably, like we have, just had that white wardrobe tutu past the knee. But then when Diaghilev bought *Sylphides* from Fokine he asked I think Benois to do the costumes, and Benois did the costumes which we wear for forty or fifty years, let's say. And then the time come when the costumes are not necessary, like the scenery is not necessary. So it is a good angle to put just in tunic to see all the beauty of the movement.

BR   "I, personally, thought it was very beautiful.

AD   "But it is always—you can't please everybody. Don't forget that all our geniuses go twenty-five years ahead of the audience. The beginning, people spit when Stravinsky *Petrouchka* and *Firebird* was played. And now it's the classic. It took twenty-five years for public to catch up, and they love *Petrouchka*. They have such a habit of having *Sylphides* done the way Diaghilev did, but why not to show another angle? I know some people wrote me a letter that they just can't go and see old *Sylphides;* they think it's too heavy.

BR   "I thought it was both interesting and beautiful, but many people thought a part of what the ballet meant to them was gone.

AD   "Well it's too bad if they take so personally, but a lot of times you come to the rehearsal and admire the ballet before it's done with the costumes, and sometimes costumes ruin the ballet. But this was absolutely pure like crystal. There was pure art of Chopin and pure choreography of Fokine."

# SYLVIA

*Ballet in three acts and four scenes. Music by Léo Delibes. Choreography by Louis Mérante. Book by Jules Barbier and the Baron de Reinach. Scenery by Chéret, Rubé, and Chaperon. Costumes by Lacoste. First presented at the Théâtre de l'Opéra, Paris, June 14, 1876, with Rita Sangalli as* Sylvia *and Louis Mérante as* Amyntas. *Revived at the Paris Opéra, by Léo Staats, December 19, 1919, with Carlotta Zambelli; by Serge Lifar, February 12, 1941, with Lycette Darsonval; by Albert Aveline, 1946. First presented in Russia at the Maryinsky Theatre, St. Petersburg, December 15, 1901, with Olga Preobrajenska in the title role. First presented in England in a one-act version, produced by C. Wilhelm, at the Empire Theatre, London, May 18, 1911, with Lydia Kyasht as* Sylvia.

Until recently, *Sylvia,* or *The Nymph of Diana,* was more familiar to the English-speaking world for its music than for its dancing. Its original choreography survives only at the Paris Opéra, where the production has long been one of the glories of France. To the rest of the world, selections from the ballet's score, selections such as the often-played *Valse Lente* and *Pizzicato Polka,* have been the principal reminders of the ballet's existence. These selections, as a matter of fact, are so familiar to us that we sometimes forget that they are part of a score for a three-act ballet and that this particular score was extraordinary for its time, as it remains for ours. The American critic Carl Van Vechten reminded us some years ago that before Delibes composed his ballets, "music for dancing, for the most part, consisted of tinkle-tinkle melodies with marked rhythm." Before *Sylvia* and *Coppélia,* Delibes' first great ballets, ballet music was universally subservient to the dancer: it had no drama to it and merely accompanied the steps of a dance with embellishing sound. Delibes changed all that, fusing drama with lyric melody, to become the father of modern ballet music, the inspiration of Tchaikovsky in his own ballet scores, and the precursor of Igor Stravinsky.

The story of Delibes' ballet *Sylvia* is a return to mythology. Sylvia, nymph of Diana, chaste goddess of the hunt, is loved by a mortal, Amyntas, the shepherd. The gods contrive against the romance until, with godlike privilege, they change their minds and the nymph and the mortal are united forever.

ACT ONE: A SACRED GROVE   The orchestra plays an Olympian prelude before the curtain rises. In this regal-sounding music—with its majestic trumpet calls suggestive of a royal hunt and its alternate light, open, joyous melody—we have a brief musical picture of the ballet's story.

The curtain rises on a grove sacred to the goddess Diana. Dominating the scene is a statue of Eros, the child god of love, armed with his bow and arrows. It is night. Magical creatures of the wood, fauns and dryads, cavort about by the light of the moon. The fauns flirt playfully with the dryads and finally succeed in ensnaring the creatures with garlands of flowers. But the sylvan lovers soon pause in their flirtations. A stranger is approaching! They conceal themselves to watch in secret.

Amyntas, the shepherd, enters the grove. He thought he had heard singing and dancing and looks about suspiciously. He sees nothing and cannot understand. Some nights ago he looked into this place and saw dancing a lovely nymph, the most beautiful girl he had ever beheld. Perhaps he was dreaming, but no—there is a soft horn call and soft, rustling, tripping music, as if a mysterious, unfelt wind had disturbed all the leaves of the forest.

Amyntas hides and observes the scene as his beautiful nymph, Sylvia, comes into the wood with her followers. They dance in honor of the chase, the pursuit of their patron goddess. Their innocent joy in the hunt seems to be curiously out of place as they dance before the statue of Eros, who would surely think them unnatural creatures to be so satisfied. Soon the girls tire and rest.

Now it happens they are observed by another. Orion, giant hunter of the forest, loves Sylvia in secret and wishes to abduct her. He is disturbed when some of the nymphs find the shepherd's crook and cloak lying on the ground and is immediately jealous. Sylvia orders her nymphs to seek out the intruder in the sacred grove, and Amyntas is brought before her. Enraged that a man has cast his eyes upon her and intent above all on preserving her purity, Sylvia determines that he must die. She draws her bow, though the young man is obviously in love with her. The love that he feels, Sylvia decides, he himself is not responsible for: it is some mischief of Eros. She therefore aims her bow at the statue.

Amyntas, shocked at this offense to the god who has inspired his love for her, runs across the wood and stands before the statue of Eros to protect it. But Sylvia has drawn her bow: her arrow sinks into the shepherd's breast, and he falls to the ground. Now the statue comes to life and Eros retaliates by aiming his arrow at Sylvia's heart. The girl collapses, clutching at her heart. Her nymphs gather about her, fearing that she is dead, but Sylvia holds out the arrow of Eros and says that she has not been hurt, it is nothing. She departs from the forest as day begins to dawn.

Villagers enter the forest and pay tribute to Eros. They do not notice the body of Amyntas. As soon as they depart, Orion enters in search of Sylvia. When he discovers the dead shepherd, he rejoices that he now has no rival and makes a new plan: he will capture Sylvia with a golden chain. Orion is observed by a straggling peasant, who remains on the scene in hiding to see what will happen.

Sylvia returns to the forest. Orion hides. The girl, remorseful at the death of the shepherd, hovers over his body. We wonder at her change of heart and then recall that she brushed off Eros' arrow too lightly. Orion takes advantage of her lack of vigilance, throws the chain of gold about her, lifts the struggling nymph into his arms, and runs toward the inner darkness of the forest.

A peasant who has seen all this is unable to help Sylvia. He runs to tell the other peasants that Amyntas is dead. His friends try to revive Amyntas, but the shepherd does not stir. An old magician comes forward and presses a rose to the shepherd's lips, and he returns to life. When he discovers, however, that Sylvia has disappeared, he wishes himself dead again. The sorcerer comforts him and tells him that perhaps Sylvia loves him; perhaps the arrow of Eros really touched her heart. Amyntas is then told of Sylvia's capture by the hunter Orion. He instantly prepares to save her; before departing, he bows to the statue of Eros. The statue again comes to life: Eros points the way to Orion's hiding place, and Amyntas sets out to rescue his beloved.

ACT TWO: THE CAVE OF ORION    Orion watches as his captive wakens. As soon as she opens her eyes and sees her abductor, Sylvia attempts to escape from him. But the weapons of the hunt have been taken from her, and she has no defense. She is impervious to his declarations of love, and the repulsed Orion grows angry. Sylvia placates him with wine, which the hunter has never tasted before. His servants willingly prepare it at their master's suggestion.

At first the wine merely increases Orion's passion, and the nymph dances before him to encourage him to drink more. He does so, but—tiring of the dance—seizes Sylvia in his arms. She easily eludes him, and the intoxicated giant falls to the ground.

Still she cannot escape. Orion has blocked the entrance to the cave with a huge boulder. The girl prays to Eros. The god appears to her, takes her by the hand, and leads her into the forest. There he turns around and, with an impatient godlike gesture, causes Orion, his grotto, and his servants to vanish into the earth.

The sound of a hunting horn causes her to rush to the nymphs she has abandoned, but Eros reminds her of Amyntas, who more than anyone grieves over her disappearance.

ACT THREE, SCENE ONE: A WOODED LANDSCAPE ON THE SEACOAST  Amyntas is still unaware of Sylvia's rescue; he enters lonely and dejected soon after the curtain rises on a celebration in honor of the god Bacchus. The sea stretches into the distance behind the trees; at the left is the sacred temple of Diana. Bacchantes dance and present grapes to the god of wine.

A ship is seen approaching the shore. A pirate captains this ship and as it reaches shore, he interrupts the festival and attempts to interest the natives in the purchase of slave girls. In reality, this pirate is Eros, who wishes to return Sylvia to Amyntas. Eros urges the veiled slave girls to surround the shepherd, but the moody Amyntas takes interest in only one of the girls, who seems to him strangely familiar. The girl dances before the youth to a pizzicato melody. He is completely delighted with her and when she removes her veil, he is overcome with happiness. He clasps Sylvia in his arms.

Orion bursts in on the scene. Eros has not been able to suppress the hunter, and Sylvia, knowing the giant's power, rushes into the temple of her patron goddess. Amyntas prepares to engage Orion in combat, but Orion runs past him to force the doors of the temple.

ACT THREE, SCENE TWO: THE TEMPLE OF DIANA  A distant roar that grows louder and louder reminds us of the anger of the gods. Lightning flashes. Within her temple, Diana, her bow drawn tight, stands over Sylvia, who kneels before her protectress. Orion dashes toward Sylvia. Diana releases her bow, and the evil hunter is pierced through the heart.

The angry goddess, who divines the real reason for Sylvia's fears, asks her how it has happened that she is in love. Sylvia confesses that Eros wounded her with one of his darts. Upon this declaration, Eros removes his disguise. Diana threatens him, but the god of love reminds her that once upon a time even she was grateful for his gift of love: the one time Diana was moved by his power and kissed the sleeping Endymion by the light of the moon.

The embarrassed goddess, confronted by her one fault, forgives Sylvia for breaking her vow never to love. She rises to her high seat in her temple with Eros. All her handmaidens bow low to the god and goddess, and the village peasants stand amazed as Amyntas and Sylvia—having received the blessing of Olympus—are transfigured by their love.

NOTES   Frederick Ashton revived *Sylvia* in London, September 3, 1952, with scenery and costumes by Robin and Christopher Ironside. Margot Fonteyn, Michael Somes, John Hart, and Alexander Grant danced the principal roles as they also did September 29, 1953, when the Sadler's Wells Ballet brought it to New York.

## SYMPHONIC VARIATIONS

*Classic ballet in one act. Music by César Franck. Choreography by Frederick Ashton. Scenery and costumes by Sophie Fedorovitch. First presented by the Sadler's Wells Ballet at the Royal Opera House, Covent Garden, London, April 24, 1946, with Margot Fenteyn and Michael Somes, Pamela May and Brian Shaw, and Moira Shearer and Henry Danton. First presented in the United States by the Sadler's Wells Ballet at the Metropolitan Opera House, New York, October 12, 1949, with the same cast but with John Hart replacing Henry Danton.*

This classic dance ballet is arranged to Franck's *Symphonic Variations* for piano and orchestra. There is no story, only a mood created by the setting and costumes, the music, and the dancers' response to it.

When the curtain rises, six dancers are on stage. Three girls stand forward in a line parallel to the front of the stage. In the back, turned away from us, are three boys. The backdrop is of abstract design: curved and slanting black lines on a light green cloth.

The orchestra begins. The dancers do not move: they stand quietly in youthful meditation on the music. Directly the piano begins, the girls commence to dance. As if activated only by the instrument, they pause as the orchestra takes up the theme. A variation on the theme is stated, and one of the boys comes forward. He takes turns dancing with the three girls, then remains still as they dance about him. Now he holds the girls, one by one, as they whirl in his arms.

The girls rest as the two other boys join the leading male soloist in a line similar to that which was formed at the beginning by the three girls. The three dance—the two boys on the outside miming in motion the part of the orchestra, while the soloist, in the center, takes the part of the piano. The boys dance now to the girls, who respond to their statement of a theme. Two of the girls dance alone, then with one of the boys. They retire; another boy takes the center of the stage and dances a variation.

The principal ballerina now comes forward and, while the boys in the background dance quietly, she moves with sweet splendor to the music of the piano. The male soloist joins her, and they dance a *pas de deux*.

After this romantic sequence, all six dancers move together. Now they are not so much separate individuals responding to the music, as one group animated by the same theme. The boys and girls divide, come together in couples, and make swift, open patterns about the stage while the music rushes toward its conclusion. Their swift ebullience is broken at the end, as the dancers resume the meditative poses with which the ballet began.

NOTES Ashton has said of his ballet and the time it was composed, just after World War II, in *Frederick Ashton and His Ballets*: "My mother died in 1939, just before the war. So I was independent at last, although it didn't do me any good. Almost as soon as the war started I had to go into the R.A.F. Everyone was being called up—all the dancers and everyone I knew in the theatre—and I wanted, I suppose, to share their agony. I must say, I thought it was the end of everything. It was a period of enormous frustration to me because I felt I hadn't said nearly enough to be ready to die on it.

"The importance of the war was that it gave me a period to think and read a good deal and also, because I was rather unhappy, I went in for mysticism. I read St. Theresa of Avila and St. John of the Cross and lots of books about mystics and mysticism. After all, one was told that it was the end of the world.

"During the war, the tendency in all the ballets seemed to become much too literary and dramatic. During the last part of the war, I was stationed at the Air Ministry as an Intelligence officer and I saw everything that was going on, although at this stage I couldn't do any work myself. It was very frustrating, and originally I think that *Symphonic Variations* was very much overchoreographed. I remember doing a tremendous amount of eliminating, especially in the finale; I pared and pared and pared until I got the kind of purity I wanted. You see, when I started I was going to do something very complicated, with lots of people and a sort of seasonal theme. But then I thought one day that six dancers would be enough. When one begins to do things one is apt to overcharge everything, and if things get too intense, one blurs the vision of the audience. By simplifying, you make it easier for an audience to take in your intentions.

"With *Symphonic Variations* I had to do a lot of experimenting to find the sort of movement that I wanted. That was what took the time, but once I had achieved it the rest went fairly well. I was able to ride on the music quite a bit because I knew it very well and I'd listened to it during the war. I'd always hoped I would get round to using it one day."

Margot Fonteyn has also written of the time of the creation of this ballet: "When *Symphonic Variations* was almost finished, Michael Somes had to have an operation on the cartilage in his knee. The first night of *Symphonic* was postponed for something like two months while Michael had his operation and got back into training.

"When we started to rehearse it all again Fred took out a lot of things and simplified and purified the choreography. Instead of having his usual deadline for the dress rehearsal and the first performance, he had time to reassess the choreography. I think that's one reason why it turned out to be one of his masterpieces. I remember a lot of discussion and all sorts of different ideas and versions and several different endings, and Sophie Fedorovitch at the rehearsals and coming in each day to say what she thought. A lot went into revising *Symphonic*. It's probably the only ballet he's ever had the opportunity to revise before the first night."

The critic and dancer David Vaughan, writing in *Ballet Review*, has said of this ballet: "The postponed première of Ashton's *Symphonic Variations* was for him a kind of manifesto similar to *Apollo*—a clearing away of literary and scenic paraphernalia, just six dancers on an open stage, given an illusion of even greater spaciousness by Fedorovitch's airy decor. If Ashton had shown at various times in his earlier career the influence of Nijinski and Massine, to say nothing of Pavlova and Duncan, there were moments in *Symphonic Variations* that inevitably, maybe coincidentally, suggested Balanchine's masterpiece, especially in the passages of supported adagio involving three women and one man. But more important was the final distillation of Ashton's own classicism: it marked the beginning of his exploration of various motifs that became trademarks of his *pas de deux* at that time—the skimming lifts with *batterie* or *pas de bourrée* just off the floor, the scissor-like movements, the *arabesques élançées*. Notable also was the courage to be simple, to leave out anything extraneous to the piece's lyric utterance: there is never any sense of strain after the ingeniously original lift or step, indeed, some of the most eloquent passages are the transitions when the dancers join hands in a simple run.

"*Symphonic Variations* was, then, a kind of summation, and a consummation, of Ashton's career up to that point, made possible, no doubt, by the kind of fallow period he had been obliged to go through during his war service, however frustrating that must have been at the time. From there he could move on to the inevitable next step in the development of British ballet—or at any rate of the Wells, as it acquired official recognition as the national ballet in the form of the royal charter—the creation of full-length ballets that could stand alongside the classics of the repertory, *Giselle, Swan Lake, Sleeping Beauty,* and the rest."

David Vaughan's biography *Frederick Ashton and His Ballets* examines in detail the making of this ballet and its subsequent history in performance.

The British writer James Monahan, whose admiration for this ballet is well known, has again described it in his book *The Nature of Ballet* (London, 1976).

## SYMPHONIE CONCERTANTE

*Classic ballet in three movements. Music by Wolfgang Amadeus Mozart. Choreography by George Balanchine. Scenery and costumes by James Stewart Morcom. Lighting by Jean Rosenthal. First presented by Ballet Society at the City Center, New York, November 12, 1947, with Maria Tallchief, Tanaquil LeClercq, and Todd Bolender in the principal roles.*

Set to Mozart's *Sinfonia Concertante in E flat major for Violin and Viola* (K. 364), this ballet follows closely the design of the music. It has no story. Its gold backdrop represents the formal classical frame into which both music and dancing fit. The three parts correspond to the three movements of the score. There are two ballerinas, corresponding to the solo instruments, a *danseur*, a group of six secondary soloists, and a *corps de ballet* of sixteen dancers.

FIRST MOVEMENT: ALLEGRO MAESTOSO   The curtain rises and the stage is empty. The music begins, allegro maestoso. After the opening chords, eight dancers emerge from either side of the stage, dancing to the light, quick rhythm of the music. They arrange themselves in a pattern that encloses the front part of the stage. The six soloists enter and dance in a close line. Now they move to the back and dance forward in rapid, crossing diagonals.

The introductory passage is over. Quietly the solo instruments are heard. All the dancers move to the sides of the stage, and slowly the ballerinas enter at the back. They meet in the center of the stage and dance together. Then, as the violin alone is heard against the orchestra, one of the ballerinas dances briefly alone. The other ballerina succeeds her as the viola returns with the same melody. The two dancers follow the turns of the solo instruments throughout the ballet, dancing together and alternately. They do not represent the instruments in any literal sense; their dances are simply accompanied by the instruments. The ballerinas leave the stage when the violin and viola are silent, returning when the instruments are heard again. Three girls enter with each of the ballerinas in turn and support them in brief, extended poses, after which the two dance together.

The opening section of the first movement is now repeated. The *corps de ballet* kneels, and the two ballerinas enter as they did at the beginning. The violin, which took priority over the viola, now takes a secondary position. The ballerinas dance closely together, almost touching, as the two instruments intertwine the melody. One of the ballerinas supports the other as the violin plays in the background against the dominant viola. Then both pirouette off while the *corps de ballet* accompanies the final orchestral bars. All kneel on the last chord.

SECOND MOVEMENT: ANDANTE   The six soloists remain on stage as the *corps* exits. The second movement begins, and the girls dance forward slowly. They separate and retire as the two ballerinas enter with the *danseur*, who supports each of the girls in turn to the music. When the principal theme of the movement is stated by the orchestra, the six soloists cross the stage with measured pace. The *danseur* leads the ballerinas to the back, the soloists dance, then the ballerinas move forward again to dance to the intricate alternation of violin and viola. The movement ends as softly as it began. As the three principals exit, the six soloists enclose them in a moving semicircle.

THIRD MOVEMENT: PRESTO   To the high-spirited, joyous finale, the two ballerinas and their partner take turns in dancing alone and in the brief duets and trios. The *corps de ballet* forms a moving background to their movements.

Each of the principals circles the stage brilliantly. The dancing becomes brisk with the clipped, delightful cheerfulness of the music. The girls flick their wrists elegantly as the movement draws to its conclusion, then dance together with the principals, who kneel before the group as the ballet ends.

NOTES   This ballet is a good example of how dancing might aid appreciation of the music. Mozart's *Sinfonia Concertante* is long and difficult; to the inexperienced listener it might be boring; perhaps only the musician likes it immediately. The ballet, on the other hand, fills the time measured by the music with movement and seems to shorten the length of the music. What seemed dull at a first *hearing*, is not so dull when the ballet is first *seen*.

It is interesting that although Mozart wrote no music for ballet, of all composers his music is most adaptable for ballet, of all composers his music is the most danceable. Children who hear Mozart's music without knowing what it is, instinctively wish to dance to it. They appreciate its true quality better than their elders, who are often too impressed by Mozart's greatness to listen to his work with unaffected ears.

## SYMPHONIE POUR UN HOMME SEUL (Symphony for a Man Alone)

*Score by Pierre Schaeffer and Pierre Henry. Choreography by Maurice Béjart. First presented by the Ballets de l'Étoile in 1955 with Michèle Seigneuret and Maurice Béjart in the principal roles. First presented in the United States by the Ballet of the Twentieth Century at the City Center, New York, November 30, 1971, with Suzanne Farrell and Jorge Donn in principal roles.*

One of the ballets that established the international fame of European choreographer Maurice Béjart and his subsequent ballet company, the Ballet of the Twentieth Century, *Symphony for a Man Alone* was the first dance work to use an electronic score, a popular complement to dance from that time forward. The signature of the ballet has been given by the choreographer himself. Béjart writes:

"How reply to the clamor of the crowd? . . . with violins? With oboes? And what orchestra can boast of rendering that other cry which man in his solitude is powerless to utter? Let us leave the sound of the violoncello, too easy for present-day man, his daily epic and collective anguish. Footsteps, voices and familiar sounds will suffice. Footsteps press upon him, voices go through him, who make love and war, the whistle of bombs or the tune of song . . . May the modern dancer, without costume or decor, be without drum or trumpet. To the rhythm of his own heart, if he is sincere, dance will be the more true."

The choreographer's response to the demands of his audience produces in this case the situation of a man, alone, entrapped, as in a prison, among strands of rope hanging from above. The man is haunted throughout the ballet by a girl, an illusive figure with whom he cannot establish any kind of permanent relationship. He tries, but the girl always at the crucial moment vanishes or escapes his grasp. At the end, he seems to despair. Man, alone, no matter what the quality of the music to accompany his solitude, seeks another.


# SYMPHONY IN C

*Classic ballet in four movements. Music by Georges Bizet. Choreography by George Balanchine. First presented under the title* Le Palais de Cristal *by the Paris Opéra Ballet at the Opéra, July 28, 1947, with Lycette Darsonval, Tamara Toumanova, Micheline Bardin, Madeleine Lafon, Alexandre Kaliujny, Roger Ritz, Michel Renault, and Max Bozzoni as principals. Scenery and costumes by Léonor Fini. First presented in the United States by Ballet Society at the City Center, New York, March 22, 1948, with Maria Tallchief, Tanaquil LeClercq, Beatrice Tompkins, Elise Reiman, Nicholas Magallanes, Francisco Moncion, Herbert Bliss, and Lew Christensen in the principal roles.*

*Symphony in C* is not based on a story, but on the music to which it is danced. Bizet's symphony is in four movements; each of these movements develops different themes, different melodies. Correspondingly, in the ballet, there is a different dance scheme and development for each of these four movements. Each movement has its own characteristic ballerina, *premier danseur,* and *corps de ballet.* Toward the end of the ballet, when the different groups have danced their special parts of the symphony, all the groups combine with their ballerinas for a kind of dance summing up of all that has gone before. There is no scenery, only a blue background; the dancers are dressed in classical ballet costumes.

FIRST MOVEMENT: ALLEGRO VIVO   The curtain rises before the music begins. Two small groups of girls begin to dance with the opening chord. As the orchestra plays the first theme and repeats it, the two groups dance in opposition, first dancing all together, then alternately following the movements of two leaders.

The ballerina appears as the second theme is announced by the oboe and strings. She dances forward in crisp, open movements to the rhythm of the melody, turning gracefully as she poses and balancing for a moment as she waits for the theme to begin anew. Her dance now becomes brisk and flourishing. She pirouettes swiftly as the two soloists join her, balances again briefly, and leaves the stage.

After the orchestra has given an intimation of the first theme and horns have played a short transition, two boys enter to support the soloists. The ballerina returns with her partner. She dances around the stage, retires to the rear, and, as the first theme of the movement returns, leads the ensemble. On the last clipped chord she stands supported in a quick, graceful pose.

SECOND MOVEMENT: ADAGIO   The *corps de ballet* moves slowly to the introductory passage. A second ballerina enters with her partner as the soft central theme of the movement is sounded by the oboe. She is lifted low off the floor and moves as if in slow motion, then is lifted high, her legs describing sweeping arcs in the air. Her partner supports her in long, slow lifts and held poses while the *corps de ballet* gathers about her. As the movement ends, the ballerina falls back in her partner's arms.

THIRD MOVEMENT: ALLEGRO VIVACE   Here the music is spirited and lively. Six girls, in a third *corps de ballet,* dance forward; two couples join them to leap across the stage; and, finally, a third ballerina and her partner enter to circle the stage in broad leaps. They dance together briefly, turning rapidly in the air together, and rush off into the wings. Soon they return, repeat their dance, and lead the *corps de ballet* to the bright, ebullient music. At one point the boy lifts the ballerina off the floor and drops her, pushing her forward, so that she seems to bounce to the music. The entire group joins in the final measures, the *corps de ballet* kneeling as the ballerina is held in a graceful pose at the last chord.

FOURTH MOVEMENT: ALLEGRO VIVACE   In the final movement, the principals of the first three movements join with a fourth ballerina and her partner in an exhilarating display of virtuosity that becomes at times a contest. The fourth ballerina and her accompanying group dance first. They are followed by the ballerina of the first movement and her *corps de ballet.* The ballerina of the Adagio movement appears next, then the ballerina of the third movement.

The thirty-two girls who have made up the four *corps de ballet* now line the stage at the sides and across the back. All four ballerinas dance in their midst, each executing the same brilliant steps. Their partners enter for their turn, while secondary soloists dance behind them. At the close, all forty-eight dancers—soloists and *corps de ballet*—join the principals in a brilliant finale. As the last chord of the music sounds, the ballerinas turn quickly and fall back over their partners' arms as the secondary soloists are lifted high behind them in a climactic tableau.

NOTES   *Symphony in C* was originally mounted for the Paris Opéra during my visit there as guest choreographer in 1947. For the Opéra, I staged revivals of three ballets: *Apollo, Le Baiser de la Fée,* and *Serenade,* and although the two latter ballets had never been seen in Paris before, at the end of my engagement I wished to stage a new work especially for the principal dancers of the Opéra.

It seemed fitting to select for this new work music by a French composer. I accordingly chose the little-known *Symphony in C Major* written by the French master Bizet when he was only seventeen years old. Composition of the ballet was completed in about two weeks.

The ballet was staged for Ballet Society in New York the following spring. When this company became the New York City Ballet seven months later, *Symphony in C* was the concluding ballet on the first program. The ballet has been a part of the permanent repertory of the New York City Ballet ever since.

In 1973, the New York City Ballet made a series of films for television in Berlin. Writing about the film of *Symphony in C* the critic Robert Greskovic said in *The Soho Weekly News*: "Though this and the 15-or-so other films of Balanchine's ballets were made for TV, this projected print made a dazzling image. Unlike the Tharp tape, the filming here plays no camera tricks. With the exception of some close-ups for the *adagio pas de deux* of the second movement, the camera maintains its eye as a transfixed spectator from an imaginary vantage point about the twentieth row center of a visionary theater. The familiar white tutus of the female dancers and (alas, equally familiar) black sequined leotards, tights and white sweat socks of the male dancers are neutrally and delicately set off by a consistently cool, pale olive background. The cast is Karin von Aroldingen, Jean-Pierre Bonnefous—first movement; Allegra Kent, Conrad Ludlow—second movement; Sara Leland, John Clifford— third movement; and Marnee Morris, Victor Castelli—fourth movement. The full-stage picture is always clear and yields the full force of this work by the company at its very best. With the brisk flow that Robert Irving's magic-wand baton makes of this symphony, Bizet via Balanchine strikes a focus/blend of perfection throughout. The careful camera make-up gives everyone in the cast a theatrical patina that glows and radiates a screen persona to the performance. (Especially glamorous here is von Aroldingen . . .) The angle of vision hovers slightly above the floor space, defining a steady rake to the dancing plane that opens at you like the palm of a hand extended in formal presentation. The depth of field grows physical as the choreographic/symphonic lines occupy more and more space with diagonal and flanking formations. The paths that the solo dances describe become lines of force that draw their length in after-images of energy. As the fourth movement shifts into the repeats of the finale, the space further deepens as it fills with the *corps de ballet* and soloists from the preceding three movements. That horse-shoe formation of ballerinas has never looked so precise and pure as legs and arms rapidly angle and arc in unison and frame the principals' and soloists' coda sections like a rainbow of warm white light."

## SYMPHONY IN E FLAT

*Music by Igor Stravinsky. Choreography by John Clifford. First presented at the New York City Ballet's Stravinsky Festival, June 20, 1972, at the New York State Theatre, Lincoln Center, with Gelsey Kirkland, Peter Martins, and ensemble.*

Stravinsky's first symphony, dedicated to "my dear teacher N. A. Rimsky-Korsakov," was first performed in 1907. The young dancer and choreographer John Clifford, who had done his first ballet to Stravinsky's *Symphony in C* for us, and other fine ballets since, was a natural to undertake the choreography for this work's presentation at the New York City Ballet's Stravinsky Festival. There are four movements—*Allegro moderato, Scherzo allegretto, Largo,* and

*Finale, Allegro molto.* The dancing is the choreographer's story of the music; what he sees happening in it.

Reviewing the ballet the next day in the *Daily News*, Sam Norkin wrote of *Symphony in E Flat:* "Intricate maneuvers and groupings are complemented by the expert pas de deux and solo sections for Gelsey Kirkland and Peter Martins. Tiny Gelsey is a fine lyric dancer who can turn into a pocket dynamo or fly away without warning. She is an exciting thing to observe."

## SYMPHONY IN THREE MOVEMENTS

*Music by Igor Stravinsky. Choreography by George Balanchine. First presented by the New York City Ballet at the Stravinsky Festival, 1972, at the New York State Theatre, Lincoln Center, June 18, 1972, with Helgi Tomasson, Sara Leland, and Edward Villella in principal roles. Lighting by Ronald Bates. Conducted by Robert Craft.*

I remember Stravinsky's talking to me about this music during World War II, when I visited him in Hollywood. It is a magnificent, major work, and I had wanted for many years to make a ballet to the music. The appropriate opportunity came in 1972, when we were preparing the Stravinsky Festival at the New York City Ballet.

The score is a short one for a symphony—about twenty-one minutes—and is in three movements. Stravinsky has written that "the formal substance of the symphony exploits contrasts of several kinds, one of them being the contrast between the principal instrumental protagonists, harp and piano. Each instrument has a large obbligato role in a movement to itself, and only at the turning-point fugue . . . do the two play together and unaccompanied."

"Composers combine notes," Stravinsky said. Choreographers combine movements and the ones I arranged for this music follow no story line or narrative. They try to catch the music and do not, I hope, lean on it, using it instead for support and time frame. If I were to try to relate that a boy and sixteen girls begin the ballet, that would not be very interesting, or that a girl in purple dances with eight others to music for clarinet, piano, and strings soon follows. What is really interesting is the complexity and variety of the music, from the propulsive drive and thrust of the vigorous opening (which also closes the ballet) to the developed use, almost like a concerto, of the piano in the first movement, the harp in the second and the two together in the finale.

The central movement, Andante, is a *pas de deux.* One writer has called this a "strangely quiet, sensuous, meditative interlude with a pronounced Eastern tinge." I had not thought of that but paraphrasing Stravinsky, how and in what form the things of this world are impressed upon my dance is not for me to say.

After the ballet was in our repertory, I heard that the first movement of the symphony was actually composed as a possible accompaniment for a film about China and that the second movement was also composed (but not used) for a film project—the apparition-of-the-Virgin scene for the film of Werfel's *Song of Bernadette*.

## TALES OF HOFFMANN

*Ballet in prologue, three acts, and an epilogue. Music by Jacques Offenbach, arranged and orchestrated by John Lanchbery. Choreography by Peter Darrell. Design by Alistair Livingstone. Lighting by John B. Read. Scenario by Peter Darrell from stories by E. T. A. Hoffmann. First presented by Scottish Theatre Ballet at the Kings Theatre, Edinburgh, Scotland, April 6, 1972, with Peter Cazalet as Hoffmann. First presented in the United States by American Ballet Theatre at the New York State Theatre, Lincoln Center, New York, July 12, 1973, with sets and costumes by Peter Docherty and with Cynthia Gregory and Jonas Kage in the principal roles.*

Those who are familiar with Offenbach's opera of this title, or with the popular film, will know all about E. T. A. Hoffmann, the German teller of tales whose stories have already made ballet history in *Coppélia* and *The Nutcracker*.

PROLOGUE: A TAVERN OUTSIDE AN OPERA HOUSE  Hoffmann is drinking with friends while awaiting the arrival of La Stella, his latest love, who is appearing at the opera. He is asked to explain the meaning of three souvenirs on his table but at first refuses. La Stella arrives and gives her maid a note for Hoffmann which, unseen by him, is intercepted by Counsellor Lindorf. Hoffmann, now a little drunk, agrees to tell the stories behind the three souvenirs and the tales proper begin:

ACT ONE (THE FIRST TALE): THE CONSERVATORY IN SPALANZANI'S HOUSE  Spalanzani, an inventor, has invited some friends to see his latest invention, the lifelike mechanical doll, Olympia. Hoffmann as a very young man observes Olympia from afar and tries to meet her. Spalanzani announces that Olympia will dance for his guests, but first insists that Hoffmann put on a pair of magic spectacles. Hoffmann immediately falls in love with Olympia and asks her to marry him. Spalanzani, delighted with the success of his deception, agrees at once. Hoffmann, whirling Olympia about in a dance, loses the magic pair of glasses. The doll thereupon falls apart and poor Hoffmann realizes he has been tricked.

ACT TWO (THE SECOND TALE): THE MUSIC ROOM OF ANTONIA'S HOME  Ten years have passed. Hoffmann, in love with Antonia, is taking music lessons from her father. Behind her father's back, Antonia flirts with Hoffmann while dancing to his playing. When they are discovered, the father warns Antonia that too much exertion will be fatal to her. Doctor Miracle suddenly appears. He promises to cure Antonia and hypnotizes her into believing that she is a great ballerina. Hoffmann returns and Antonia, enthralled by her vision, implores him to play so that she may dance again. Urged on by Doctor Miracle, Hoffmann reluctantly does so until, overcome, Antonia dies in his arms.

ACT THREE (THE THIRD TALE): DAPERTUTTO'S SALON   Now an older and more serious man, Hoffmann has turned to religion for comfort from his earlier disappointments. He finds himself in the salon of Dapertutto, who tries to lure him again to the enjoyment of sensual pleasures but without success until the arrival of Giulietta, a lovely courtesan. Encouraged by Dapertutto, Giulietta so seduces Hoffmann that he even renounces his faith. Then he realizes, when his reflection disappears in a mirror, that he has lost his immortal soul. In his anguish he prays that he may be forgiven and, as his reflection reappears, Giulietta and Dapertutto are drawn into the mirror and vanish.

EPILOGUE: THE TAVERN   Hoffmann, his stories told, is offered more drink by the sinister Counsellor Lindorf. La Stella emerges from the opera house looking for Hoffmann and finds him in a drunken sleep, her note crushed on the ground. Sad and disappointed, she is led away by Lindorf. Hoffmann, roused from his stupor, realizes that yet again he has been duped by the evil presence that has pursued him throughout his life.

## THE TAMING OF THE SHREW

> *Ballet in two acts after Shakespeare. Music by Kurt-Heinz Stolze after Domenico Scarlatti. Choreography and production by John Cranko. Scenery and costumes by Elizabeth Dalton. Lighting by Gilbert V. Hemsley, Jr. First presented by the Stuttgart Ballet at the Wurttembergische Staatstheater, Stuttgart, Germany, March 16, 1969, with Marcia Haydée and Richard Cragun in the principal roles. First presented in the United States by the same ensemble at the Metropolitan Opera House, New York, June 12, 1969.*

*The Taming of the Shrew* turns out to be just as amusing to see in dance form as it is in the spoken theater. The action of the ballet follows closely that of the play:

ACT ONE, SCENE ONE: OUTSIDE THE HOUSE OF BAPTISTA, A WEALTHY NOBLEMAN   Hortensio, a fop, Lucentio, a student, and Gremio, an elderly roué, serenade the beautiful Bianca, one of the nobleman's daughters. Their love songs are rudely interrupted by her sister, Katherine, who thinks herself just as beautiful. In addition, Baptista explains to the suitors that Kate, as the elder of the two, must be married first. Neighbors, awakened by the serenade and the rumpus, chase the thwarted lovers away.

ACT ONE, SCENE TWO: A TAVERN   Here Petruchio, a gentleman of more generosity than means, is robbed of his last penny by two ladies of the streets. The suitors suggest that he, therefore, might be interested in the charms and fortune of Katherine. He readily agrees.

ACT ONE, SCENE THREE: INSIDE BAPTISTA'S HOUSE   Bianca muses over her preferences among her three suitors. She is interrupted by a jealous outburst from Kate, a rowdy tomboy of a girl, who calls her a scheming flirt. This dispute is further interrupted by the arrival of Petruchio, who is accompanied by Bianca's suitors in disguise. Petruchio is none too favorably received by Kate. Alone with Bianca, the suitors throw off their disguises and continue their wooing in the form of singing, dancing, and music lessons. Bianca soon recognizes Lucentio as the most desirable.

Kate reacts violently against Petruchio's protestations of passion, thinking that they are a false mockery, but something in his manner convinces her, nevertheless, to accept his offer and they agree to get married.

ACT ONE, SCENE FOUR: A STREET   Here neighbors on their way to Kate's wedding treat the whole matter as a huge joke. The three suitors, now in high hopes that Bianca will soon be released to marry one of them, join them.

ACT ONE, SCENE FIVE: INSIDE BAPTISTA'S HOUSE   The guests have arrived. Kate in her bridal array is all expectant and waiting, but the bridegroom appears to have forgotten the day. When he does appear, in fantastic garb, Petruchio behaves very badly, ill-treating the priest and carrying off Kate before the wedding festivities have started.

ACT TWO, SCENE ONE: PETRUCHIO'S HOUSE   Kate is a fiery-tempered girl and Act Two shows what Petruchio aims to do about it. In the first scene he finds fault with the food and the girl has to go without her supper.

ACT TWO, SCENE TWO: A CARNIVAL   Meanwhile, in a scene at the carnival, two of Bianca's suitors, Gremio and Hortensio, encounter a masked and cloaked stranger. Both of them believing her to be Bianca are only too eager to take their marriage vows. Too late they discover that they have been duped and married to ladies of the street, who have been suitably briefed, bribed, and disguised by Lucentio.

ACT TWO, SCENE THREE: PETRUCHIO'S HOUSE   When Petruchio finds fault with the new clothes that he has ordered for Kate, her weary resistance finally crumbles and she capitulates, only to find that her master is a kinder, wittier husband than she thought possible.

ACT TWO, SCENE FOUR: ENROUTE TO BIANCA'S WEDDING   Petruchio indulges in more whims, fancies, and tricks, but Kate has learned her lesson and joins in the fun.

ACT TWO, SCENE FIVE: BAPTISTA'S HOUSE   At Bianca's wedding the action is all tied up. Gremio and Hortensio have found out that the joys of marriage are a mixed blessing, and even Lucentio has reason to fear that Bianca is not the angel that she appeared to be. Kate, on the other hand, and to everyone's astonishment, turns out to be the truest, most obedient, most loving of wives.

Which goes to show that women are not always what they appear to be or, in other words, never judge a book by its cover.

## TARANTELLA

*Music by Louis Moreau Gottschalk, reconstructed and orchestrated by Hershy Kay. Choreography by George Balanchine. Costumes by Karinska. First presented by the New York City Ballet at the New York State Theatre, January 7, 1964, with Patricia McBride and Edward Villella.*

This *pas de deux* is one of a long series of short ballets I have made for the gifts of specific dancers. The music is for solo piano and orchestra, based on the *Grande Tarantelle* of the New Orleans pianist-composer Louis Gottschalk who dazzled Europe and the United States with his recitals a hundred years ago. This work, which I asked Hershy Kay to orchestrate for us, is thought to be the first work for piano and orchestra ever composed by an American. It is a dazzling display piece, full of speed and high spirits. So, I hope, is the dance, which is "Neopolitan" if you like and "*demi-caractère.*" The costumes are inspired by Italy, anyhow, and there are tambourines.

## TCHAIKOVSKY CONCERTO NO. 2 (*see* BALLET IMPERIAL)

## TCHAIKOVSKY PAS DE DEUX

*Music by Peter Ilyich Tchaikovsky. Choreography by George Balanchine. Costumes by Karinska. First presented by the New York City Ballet at the City Center, New York, March 29, 1960, with Violette Verdy and Conrad Ludlow.*

When Tchaikovsky composed his ballet *Swan Lake*, some of the music did not fit in with the plans of Petipa, his choreographer, and was discarded. When I learned that this music had recently been discovered in the Bolshoi Theatre archives, I was naturally interested to see what it was like. Upon receiving the score through the Tchaikovsky Foundation, I decided at once that the pieces would form an accompaniment to a *pas de deux* for two of our leading dancers. As such, it is of course a display piece, based on the music and the maximum gifts of virtuoso performers. Once, after a successful first performance of a similar display *pas de deux*, one of our dancers said that she did not know if she would be able to do the piece again. Of course she did it again, and again and again, and better! What had seemed at the beginning a stretching of her capacities became easy second nature and she went on to new achievements. Violette Verdy and Edward Villella have appeared frequently in this *pas de deux*, which is also in the repertory of the Royal Ballet and other companies.

# TCHAIKOVSKY SUITE NO. 2

*Music by Peter Ilyich Tchaikovsky. Choreography by Jacques d'Amboise. Production designed by John Braden. Lighting by Ronald Bates. First presented by the New York City Ballet at the New York State Theatre, Lincoln Center, January 9, 1969, with Marnee Morris, John Prinz, Allegra Kent, Francisco Moncion, Linda Merrill, and John Clifford as principals. Conducted by Robert Irving.*

The first of a series of Tchaikovsky suites in the New York City Ballet, this dance ballet is performed to music from the composer's *Suite No. 2* for orchestra. In keeping with Tchaikovsky's music, which is fascinating in its Russian references, the ballet makes gestures to Russian, Georgian, and Ukrainian folklore or costumes, but the dances may be said to take place in any time and place. If you do not know this music of Tchaikovsky's, and it is no doubt the least famous of the four suites for orchestra, I with pleasure recommend that you become acquainted with it.

Reviewing the ballet for the New York *Times,* the critic Clive Barnes wrote: "Mr. d'Amboise, a strong dancer himself, of course, creates gratefully for dancers. Here in the first movement he has precisely caught in the delightfully skittish quality of Marnee Morris, the special lilt of laughter in her dancing, and contrasted this with the pouncing, very virile quality of John Prinz. Both dancers responded happily.

"The deep-set mystery of Allegra Kent and the somber power of Francisco Moncion have inspired the softer-toned second movement. Miss Kent showed just the right misty poetry, while Mr. Moncion, filled with a kind of animal nobility, made her an ideal partner.

"For the third movement the ballet reverts to the lighter-hearted tone of the beginning, and here Linda Merrill (in her first major created assignment) and John Clifford fly around blithely and impressively."

# TCHAIKOVSKY SUITE NO. 3

*Music by Peter Ilyich Tchaikovsky. Choreography by George Balanchine. Scenery and costumes by Nicolas Benois. Lighting by Ronald Bates. First presented by the New York City Ballet at the Saratoga Performing Arts Center, Saratoga, New York, July 23, 1970, with Karin von Aroldingen and Anthony Blum, Kay Mazzo and Conrad Ludlow, Marnee Morris and John Clifford, Gelsey Kirkland and Edward Villella in the principal roles.*

In 1947, for American Ballet Theatre, I did a ballet called *Theme and Variations* that used the last two movements of Tchaikovsky's *Suite No. 3 in G*

*Minor.* The first three movements of this *Suite* I have always liked, too, and so I decided in 1970 to make dances for them. Putting all the dances together, plus *Theme and Variations,* we had a new work, *Tchaikovsky Suite No. 3.* It is interesting that when this *Suite,* not envisioned as a dance score, was first performed in St. Petersburg (1885), it was an enormous success, while his ballet score to *Swan Lake* (1877) was considered "too symphonic" and his music for *The Sleeping Beauty* (1890) was judged simply "very nice" by the Tsar.

1. The curtain rises on the *Élégie* after the orchestra has established a pensive, romantic mood. We are in an empty, dark space, behind a scrim, perhaps a ballroom. Ghosts are possible. A boy kneels left. Seven girls appear to him. He seems to seek another and then before we are aware of it he is dancing with one of the girls. She, like him, barefoot, dances with him in ecstatic abandonment. Both sense that this will not last long, that he is bound to lose her. She rests her head on his shoulder and acknowledges this. And soon she is one of seven girls again. She is the last to leave him as he kneels before her in the abandoned room.

2. *Valse Mélancolique:* A *pas de deux* for another couple, again with a mysterious atmosphere, behind the scrim. Nothing is permanent. She disappears, returns, goes again.

3. The *Scherzo* is danced by a girl and boy and eight supporting girls. Here the vitality of the score supports a flowing animation in the *pas de deux* and there is an impression of endless speed. Here in a brighter light, we make out chandeliers in the distance. As the music ends, the scrim rises and brilliant lighting illuminates a grand ballroom.

4. *Tema con Variazioni* begins in this space. See *Theme and Variations,* page 636.

## TEXAS FOURTH

*Music: traditional songs by Harvey Schmidt arranged by David Baker and orchestrated by Elizabeth Myers. Choreography by Agnes de Mille. Scenery by Oliver Smith. Costumes by A. Christina Gianini. Lighting by Nananne Porcher. First presented by the Agnes de Mille Heritage Dance Theatre at the North Carolina School of the Arts, 1973. First presented by American Ballet Theatre at the New York State Theatre, Lincoln Center, July 8, 1976, with Dennis Nahat, William Carter, Rebecca Wright, Eric Nesbitt, George de la Pena, Buddy Balough, and Ruth Mayer in principal roles.*

A bicentennial celebration of memory and recollection, *Texas Fourth* reminds us what the Fourth of July was like in Texas back in 1936. It begins with four couples square-dancing on the plains while a fiddler calls the tune. A boy does a buck and wing. Next, we are in the midst of a razzmatazz Fourth in a small town. A vigorous batonist leads a troupe of drum majorettes and there is a girl who likes a boy. Everyone seems to be having a rousing, noisy great time when there is a time-stop. The girl sees the ghost of her mother and has a vision, too, of the people of *her* time, dancing and behaving in a quite different, decorous, polite, and genteel way. Texas was different then. But so is the girl, now! We are our ancestors but ourselves, too. Blessed by her mother, she rejoins the boy and the future begins.

After the first performance of *Texas Fourth* by American Ballet Theatre, Agnes de Mille was given the Handel Medallion, New York City's highest award for artistic achievement. She remarked in her acceptance speech that *Texas Fourth* is about "all those lovely, old-fashioned virtues." The action of the ballet takes place in Baird, Texas, her husband's birthplace, and the piece is dedicated to the memory of his grandmother, Roma Foy.

## THEATRE

*Music by Richard Strauss. Choreography by Eliot Feld. Costumes by Frank Thompson. Lighting by Jennifer Tipton. First presented by the American Ballet Company at the Brooklyn Academy of Music, New York, January 6, 1971, with Eliot Feld, Elizabeth Lee, and Edward Verso in the principal roles.*

*Theatre* is a tragic *commedia dell'arte* ballet. Here we see the classical figures Pierrot, Columbine, and Harlequin in a new combination. The character of the ballet is prefigured by a note in the program quoting John Keats:

I asked to see what brings the hollow brain
Behind environed; what high tragedy
In the dark secret chambers of her skull
Was acting.

The score is the *Burlesque for Piano and Orchestra* of Richard Strauss.

The central figure in *Theatre* is Pierrot, whom we first see sitting making up backstage. Naked to the waist, he stares out at us, as if we were his mirror, examining his face. His countenance is a pasty mask and it is difficult to imagine its being amused at anything. A curtain comes down, lights come up, and suddenly we are on stage, with Columbine and Harlequin and other dancers. The two lovers dance together; alongside their convivial happiness Pierrot is rejected, tearful. Harlequin dances in a kind of triumph and Pierrot joins in to play ball with them. Here, too, he fails. Pulcinella doesn't help matters by introducing a bag of money into the situation. Nothing will cure Pierrot's misery. As he dances alone now his deep despair seems almost overwhelming. As if to crush and release him simultaneously a shower of colored balls falls on Pierrot from above. Now the dancers return and the sad figure of Pierrot leaves the scene.

Writing of *Theatre* in *Dance and Dancers* magazine, Patricia Barnes said that "Feld is quite exceptional in the role of Pierrot, deeply poignant yet never sentimental. It is a performance I shall treasure. As Harlequin, Edward Verso has just the right air of cool mischief. His dancing, quickly precise, helped to create a character, and Elizabeth Lee was equally successful with her sleekly feminine Columbine.

"Among the major assets of the ballet were the incredibly beautiful costumes by Frank Thompson, which must be among the most successful created for an American company in recent years. In their color, cut and conception they were ravishing. While placed within the world of *commedia dell'arte,* they were nevertheless freshly and brilliantly realized and once again Jennifer Tipton's lighting helped enormously. Throughout the season Christopher Keene produced playing from the orchestra of a consistent high standard. He is a young conductor of immense talent, and has been of enormous help to this company."

## THEME AND VARIATIONS

*Classic ballet. Music by Peter Ilyich Tchaikovsky. Choreography by George Balanchine. Scenery and costumes by Woodman Thompson. First presented by Ballet Theatre at the City Center, New York, November 26, 1947, with Alicia Alonso and Igor Youskevitch in the leading roles.*

In addition to his ballet scores, Tchaikovsky composed a great deal of music ideal for dancing. This was perhaps natural for a man who had discovered in ballet a genuine inspiration. Between the time of his first ballet, *Swan Lake* (1877), and his second, *The Sleeping Beauty* (1890), Tchaikovsky wrote four orchestral suites. They were not composed for dancing, yet to listen to them is to think immediately of dancing. They remind us that it is a pity that the composer was not, during this period, a favorite of his contemporary choreographers.

In 1933 I arranged the ballet *Mozartiana* to the fourth of these orchestral suites. *Theme and Variations* is arranged to the final movement of the *Suite No. 3, in G.* This is a dance ballet; like *Ballet Imperial,* it evokes that great period in classical dancing when Russian ballet flourished with the aid of Tchaikovsky's music.

When the curtain rises, we see that the setting is formal: the scene is a great ballroom with huge, towering pillars decorated with vines, luxurious red draperies, and crystal chandeliers containing thousands of candles. A formal garden can be seen in the background. There is a *corps de ballet* of twelve girls arranged in two groups about the ballerina and the *premier danseur.* The girls are dressed in muted colors; the ballerina is in white with a coronol of white flowers. The *premier danseur* wears a blue costume and a blue beret embellished with a white plume.

The music begins, and the ballerina points her toe, dancing softly as the violins play the principal theme. Her steps are simple and graceful, like the melody, and with her feet she seems to point to the quiet charm of the music. Her partner similarly introduces the music and leaves the stage with the ballerina. The twelve girls move forward lightly. They dance a brief ensemble as the theme is repeated on insistent plucked strings to the accompaniment of flutes and clarinets.

Now the tempo increases. The ballerina returns and, surrounded by the *corps de ballet,* begins to display her virtuosity, whirling quickly and brightly in *fouettés* to a restatement of the theme which the strings treat like a *perpetuum mobile.*

The woodwinds announce the theme in a slower tempo; the *corps de ballet* of twelve girls divides into three close groups and describe shifting, flowing lines on the stage. The music becomes assertive again in the fourth variation. The full orchestra plays the theme with a flourish, and the *premier danseur* performs a graceful, yet animated, dance.

When the soloist has left the stage, the orchestra snaps the *corps de ballet* into movement with a sudden chord and plays a fast fugue to which the girls dance their first brilliant ensemble. Just as suddenly, the variation ends. The *premier danseur* now dances alone, describing diagonals across the stage with long, bold leaps. The music is staccato, the strings whirring in tarantella fashion to strong, persistent chords.

The seventh variation is a subdued and noble treatment of the theme. Four girls gather softly, hold hands, and move slowly on point. The ballerina enters. The girls cluster about her in a close semicircle. The English horn varies the theme, and the girls support the ballerina as she executes beautiful adagio movements.

The music trippingly accelerates. The ballerina separates herself from the *corps* and dances vigorously and joyously to the demanding rhythm, her pose changing with quick elegance to the beat of the music, her *pointes* stabbing at the floor in response to the sharp attack of the orchestra. She turns rapidly across the stage and pauses.

The *premier danseur* joins her. A solo violin sounds the melody, and a *pas de deux* begins. Its beginning is softly playful; but as a new variation sweeps the orchestra into a piercing, flowing melody, the dancing is noble and tender. To this theme of open joy and romance the ballerina, supported by her partner, executes slowly and perfectly movements—simple, yet also difficult—that display her full beauty.

When the two principals leave the stage, a drum roll sounds, followed by a bright fanfare on the horns. Eight boys enter with a flourish. The *corps de ballet* joins them, with the two principal dancers, as the orchestra announces with blaring pomp a regal polonaise. There are swift variations by the two principals—the ballerina accompanied by the girls; the *premier danseur,* by the boys—and rapid regroupings and shiftings of partners in the ensemble as the final variation increases in liveliness. The two principals, hand in hand, lead the dancers about the ballroom in a sweeping circle. There is vigorous dancing to the final crashes of music, and then, at the last chord, a tableau in which the ballerina is lifted high to her partner's shoulder while all her court salutes her.

# THE THREE-CORNERED HAT

*Dramatic ballet in one act. Music by Manuel de Falla. Choreography by Leonide Massine. Book by Gregorio Martínez Sierra. Scenery and costumes by Pablo Picasso. First presented by Diaghilev's Ballets Russes at the Al-*

*hambra Theatre, London, July 22, 1919, with Leonide Massine as the Miller, Tamara Karsavina as the Miller's Wife, Leon Woizikowski as the Corregidor, and Stanislas Idzikowski as the Dandy. First presented in the United States by the Ballet Russe de Monte Carlo at the St. James Theatre, New York, March 9, 1934, with Leon Woizikowski as the Miller and Tamara Toumanova as the Miller's Wife.*

*The Three-Cornered Hat* tells a love story of Spain with humor and warmth. The scene is a small Spanish village. The Spanish tone of the ballet is established immediately by the music, by cries of *"Olé! Olé! Olé! Olé!"* from behind the curtain, and by the sound of rhythmic castanets, dancing feet, and hand clapping.

The curtain rises on the village scene. The village miller stands before his house, whistling to a black bird who sits in a cage. The bird will not sing as he wishes it to. The miller's wife comes out of the house and teases her husband. He chases her and they embrace.

The couple go to the well to draw water. While the miller is busy at the well, a dandy passes by and blows kisses to his wife, who responds flirtatiously. The miller looks up and sees this exchange and chases the dandy off. He is not angry with his wife. He is delighted that other men find her as beautiful as he does. They are very much in love.

Now the governor of the province, the corregidor, enters with an escort. A doddering old fool, he looks absurd in his finery among the simple folk of the village. He wears a three-cornered hat, symbol of his class and position.

Almost immediately the corregidor eyes the miller's wife and decides that she must be his. The miller's wife is polite to him, but no more. He passes on. Noting that his wife is getting all the attention, the miller decides he'd better give another girl some favor. He playfully flirts with one of the lovely girls of the village. Now that both husband and wife have cause to be jealous, they are amused at each other and embrace.

The miller goes into the house. His wife, remaining outside, dances a brilliant *fandango*. The corregidor has come back and secretly watches her. Soon he approaches her and tries to make advances. The woman eludes him cleverly and flees. The old man, however, pursues her.

The miller has watched this scene from inside the house and runs out to help his wife. The corregidor can run no more and falls to the ground, exhausted. The miller and his wife pick him up, dust him off, and try to act as if it were all an accident, but the corregidor, furious with them, suggests that this is only the beginning of what they may expect of him. The husband and wife dance together.

Evening falls. The village folk come to the miller's house to join in a festival with the happy couple. The miller gives them wine and then dances alone a *farruca*, which everyone applauds. The villagers hear the approach of marching soldiers. The escorts of the corregidor enter. The men arrest the miller and take him off. Abandoned by her friends, the miller's wife is alone.

But not for long. The corregidor is back again, seeking her favor now with real determination. The miller's wife throws him to the ground as he clumsily holds her. He rises with difficulty and pursues her to the village bridge, which crosses a running stream. On the bridge, the corregidor again attempts to embrace the girl. In the process of pushing him away, the miller's wife pushes him off the bridge into the stream. She laughs at him, but helps the corregidor out of the water. But the old fool takes up the chase again. The miller's wife takes a gun from the house and, threatening the corregidor with buckshot, flees over the bridge away from the village.

The corregidor stands in front of the miller's house, alone, his clothes still dripping from the dunking he got in the stream. He takes off his outer garments and his three-cornered hat, lays them out to dry, and goes into the house to sleep.

Dawn comes. The miller has escaped the corregidor's henchmen and returns home. In front of his house he sees the corregidor's clothes and the three-cornered hat! Then he observes the corregidor himself, walking around in one of his own nightshirts! The miller decides there's only one thing to do. He will pursue the corregidor's wife, who is also young and beautiful! On the walls of his house he draws a caricature of the corregidor and leaves.

Now the poor corregidor is attacked by his own soldiers, who don't recognize him in the miller's nightshirt. He curses them, and the village folk come to see what the trouble is. The miller and his wife, who have found each other outside the town, come in. Their friends are told what the corregidor has tried to do, and in anger all the people rise up against the governor and his cohorts. The intruders are routed, and all dance triumphantly, led by the miller and his wife. A dummy representing the defeated corregidor is thrown higher and higher into the air by the crowd.

NOTES   Although Leon Woizikowski first danced the miller at the American première of *The Three-Cornered Hat,* Leonide Massine later danced the role in the United States. The ballet was revived by Massine for Ballet Theatre in 1943 and for the Sadler's Wells Ballet in 1947.

Tania Massine, the choreographer's daughter, assisted by Yurek Lazowski, staged a revival of *The Three-Cornered Hat* for the City Center Joffrey Ballet in New York, September 25, 1969. Luis Fuente was the *Miller,* Barbara Remington the *Miller's wife,* Basil Thompson the *Corregidor,* Rebecca Wright the *Corregidor's wife,* and Frank Bays the *Dandy.* The original Picasso designs were reconstructed by William Pitkin.

## THREE ESSAYS

*Music by Charles Ives. Choreography by Lar Lubovitch. First presented by American Ballet Theatre at the City Center, New York, January 15, 1974, with Warren Conover, Christine Sarry, Clark Tippet, and Ian Horvath in leading roles.*

Like an earlier work by the dancer-choreographer Lar Lubovitch for the same ensemble (see *Scherzo for Massah Jack*), this ballet is a period piece based on its score. The American master Charles Ives was, of course, remarkable in his many gifts, among them a memorable capacity to recollect the past, which is what the ballet here also aims to do. The composer's notations for the three parts of the music are embodied by the choreographer: "Elegy to Our Forefathers"; "The Rockstrewn Hills Join in the People's Outdoor Meeting"; "From Hanover Square North at the End of a Tragic Day (1915)."

What we see portrayed in dance terms is a commentary on these themes of the composer, and an ironic one, relating to World War I, and all that conflict meant, or seemed to mean, to Americans, together with its consequences.

Commenting in *Cue* magazine, the critic Robert Jacobson wrote: "Lubovitch's piece is marked by turbulence . . . and commands respect . . . His images are often memorable and he leaves you thinking."

## THREE VIRGINS AND A DEVIL

*Music by Ottorino Respighi. Scenario by Ramon Reed. Choreography by Agnes de Mille. Scenery and costumes by Motley. Setting designed by Arne Lundborg. First presented by Ballet Theatre at the Majestic Theatre, New York, February 11, 1941, with Agnes de Mille as the* Priggish One, *Lucia Chase as the* Greedy One, *Annabelle Lyon as the* Lustful One, *Eugene Loring as a* Devil, *and Jerome Robbins as a* Youth.

The critic Robert J. Pierce has called this ballet a burlesque in the form of a medieval morality play. Arranged to Respighi's *Ancient Dances and Airs for the Lute,* this *danse caractère* personifies three typical but differing young women and shows what happens to them under devilish circumstances.

After a short overture the curtain rises on a medieval landscape, a monastery gate at the right, with door shut; a grotto at the left, leading to a cave. Three girls come in. Their leader, a priggish lass, is trying to drag her friends to church. She displays maximum piety in this undertaking, trying to persuade the Greedy One, who is decked out in finery, to put her belongings in the alms box. Not to be overlooked, the Lustful One, a child of nature with a garland of flowers, sees the directions things are taking and decides to renounce her wreath. When a prancing Youth enters to find all the virgins swaying in prayer, he is clearly astonished at such unanimous piety. He cannot persuade any of the girls to join him.

Now a hermit enters, asking the Greedy One for money. The beggar is a peculiar sort of fellow, almost spastic in his movements as he seems to try to hide one of his feet under his cloak. The foot keeps trembling and bothering him. When he can bear it no longer, he throws off the cloak and reveals himself as a Devil, tail, horns, cloven foot, and all.

The virgins, in their uniform piety, are appalled, but when he brings out a sort of cello and starts to play, they all dance lustily to his tune. They get so carried away by their revels that when the Youth returns, again beckoning to the Lustful One, she jumps obligingly onto his back, whereupon he carries her swiftly into the grotto—a gate, of course, to hell.

The Devil tempts next the Greedy One, who responds to his offer of a bright jewel and follows her sister to the other world. The Priggish One, of course, is harder to tempt and the Devil has his own time of it getting from her the proper response. She mothers him and strikes terror into him by trying to get him into the monastery. Unable to bear such tactics any longer, he begins to chase her like a man possessed. In terror she flees, running from him in a wider and wider circle, but pursuing him, too, determined to have yet another convert. The widening circle of the chase leads to the grotto entrance, where the Devil stands aside and permits the lady to dash down to hell with her own momentum.

NOTES   Agnes de Mille first produced a ballet to this theme in London, in 1934, at the Palace Theatre, in the musical comedy *Why Not Tonight?* Greta Nissen, Elizabeth Schooling, and M. Braithwaite were the Girls and Stanislas Idzikowski the Devil. The music was by Walford Hyden.

American Ballet Theatre revived *Three Virgins and a Devil* at the New York State Theatre, Lincoln Center, New York, July 25, 1973, with Sallie Wilson (now called the Fanatical One), Ruth Mayer, and Christine Sarry as the Virgins, Dennis Nahat as a Devil, and Daniel Levans as a Youth. The conductor was Akira Endo and the lighting was by Nananne Porcher.

## TIL EULENSPIEGEL

*Ballet by Jean Babilée. Music by Richard Strauss. Choreography by Jean Babilée. Scenery and costumes by Tom Keogh. First presented by Les Ballets des Champs-Élysées, November 9, 1949, at the Théâtre des Champs-Élysées, Paris, with Jean Babilée in the title role. First presented in the United States by Ballet Theatre at the Metropolitan Opera House, New York, September 25, 1951, with a cast headed by Jean Babilée and Ruth Ann Koesun. Costumes by Helene Pons.*

Richard Strauss's score *Til Eulenspiegel's Merry Pranks* was not composed to be danced, but the fact that the music has a plot and relates incidents in the life of one of the most popular figures in European folklore has made it naturally attractive to choreographers. Til Eulenspiegel is the perennial prankster who never seems to get his comeuppance. Although he may hurt people when he tricks them, he really has no harmful intentions; he is a maker of fun motivated by his own innocent pleasure and not by cunning. Such a man sooner or later runs into trouble with the law, for much as we may admire his artfulness and daring, the law will be more impressed with the number of his misdemeanors.

This ballet shows us the roguery of Til—his inability to conform to convention and his contempt for the law. Here his pranks are so good-humored that even the law is inclined to forgive him.

The curtain rises as the music begins. The scene is an improvised impression of an ancient market place. Against a mottled gray background, five colorful booths are arranged in a semicircle. The light is dim; spotlights shine down on the brightly colored awnings over the booths. A girl enters. She is small, has long blond hair, and wears a flowing dress. She dances across the market place to the soft opening bars of the music and disappears.

Two by two, a group of ragamuffin merchants march out to stand behind their booths and wait for customers. As soon as they are all stationed at their jobs, they look in unison from right to left. A quiet, impudent theme is heard in the orchestra, and the men sense that something is going on behind their backs. They are right. Til Eulenspiegel dances in. His face is chalk-white beneath his orange hair, but this does not disguise his expression of impudence. His dance is spontaneously graceful and grotesque at the same time; we imagine already that anything he does will be funny.

As he runs about the market place, Til almost collides with a young girl. Immediately he begins to make up to her. He kneels before her, begging for a mere glance. The girl, dressed in formal medieval costume, will have none of his impertinence and repulses him. This only encourages Til, who encircles her in a tumbling dance that infuriates the girl. When he sees that she does not like him, Til makes fun of her behind her back. The merchants are delighted. The girl orders him away. The exuberant Til complies and jumps up backward to sit on one of the booths. There he watches the girl with what seems to be an innocent eye. But the cymbals crash, the music bursts into a loud ruckus. At a sudden signal from Til, all the merchants jump out from behind their booths. They grab the girl and toss her in the air. She crawls off, disheveled, on all fours—no longer a charming young lady: Til's magic has turned her into a witch.

Til and the merchants go back to their booths. A courtly theme is heard, and a gentleman enters with his lady. Til is very amused at their formal ways and laughs at the flowing feather in the gentleman's cap. They try not to notice him, but Til forces himself between them and tries to engage the lady's attention. He jumps up and down in his excitement to please her. He pleads with her to notice him and to send her escort away so that they may dance together alone. The lady, however, is shocked by this behavior. Unfortunately her escort cannot assist her, for just as he flirts with the lady, Til is also trying to humiliate the gentleman. He runs out and returns quickly, dressed in a hat filled with variously colored long-flowing feathers. When he bows to the lady, these absurd feathers reach to the floor. She now thinks him ridiculous as well as rude and will never respond to his advances. Til must have his good-humored revenge. He throws down his hat with a flourish at the lady's feet and challenges her lover to a duel. The lady is aghast as the two men assume dueling stances before her. The merchants applaud the combat. The two duelists rush each other, turn each other upside down in a cartwheel of movement, and roll over and over together, their bodies joined in a tumbling hoop. The gentleman has clearly had enough by this time and, seizing his lady by the hand, dashes off.

No sooner have they departed than a group of ragged hunchbacks come into the market place, begging for alms. The lights dim, Til runs out, and the merchants hide behind their booths. Now Til is back again, but dressed in a long black cape and a high-peaked hat. He, too, is a hunchback all of a sudden; he joins the pilgrimage of the stricken men. The men accept him as their equal in misery and marvel when by a quick miracle he is cured: the hump on his back has vanished! They congratulate him on his cure and, to ensure a cure for themselves, do what Til anticipated: they give him all their money and walk out of the square, certain that this tribute to one of their former fellows will hasten their own recovery. The wealthy Til rids himself of cap and cloak and counts his fortune.

His girl, Nell, the blonde who appeared at the beginning of the ballet, comes into the square. In the soft light, she and Til dance together. Now completely happy, he swings her around and around in the air. A distant trumpet call is heard; Til cups his hand to his ear for a moment to listen, but then continues with the dance. He and Nell rush off into the night together.

The trumpet theme grows in the orchestra. Til runs back in and circles the stage in leaps timed to its open, joyous melody. The merchants jump out from behind their booths, tear down the awnings, and—using the awning poles for lances—surround him in a mock military drill. Til, in the center, jumps up and down in glee. The merchants form a parade and rush around the stage. At the theme's fullest crescendo, Til leaps onto their backs and rides high above them in triumph.

But the theme is cut short sharply. There is a menacing drum roll, the theme of the gallows, and ominous, plodding music changes Til's ebullience into fear. Six soldiers dash in and rush him. Til runs for one of the booths, but the soldiers jump up after him. Til escapes between their legs and hides underneath. Til's impudent theme, sounded by the clarinet, laughs at the loud, heavy theme of the law. The soldiers gang up on him again; again he escapes and the music ridicules them. Finally they grab him and hold him securely after a long tussle.

One of the soldiers runs off. He returns with a judge and a hangman. Til's legs run in the air as he is held motionless; he wraps his legs around one of the soldiers in his fright. The judge flourishes a scroll and begins to read the indictment against Til for all his crimes. The criminal is led forward, his head bowed. A soldier kneels down to form the chopping block, and Til is placed across it. The hangman aims the ax. The sonorous theme of authority is sounded firmly; Til's merry theme reaches a high shriek of terror and disintegrates as it descends the scale. There is a moment of silence. Still the ax is posed above Til, but the executioner does not move. Nell enters on the right. The judge, the executioner, the soldiers—all turn to look at her. They pardon Til because of the reality of his love for her and imagine that with Nell he will lead a less prankish life. His head still on the block, Til anxiously feels the back of his neck. He looks up carefully. When he sees that they don't intend to execute him, after all, he rushes over to Nell and kneels to her in gratitude. He touches her hands then, and they dance briefly.

Now that everything is back to normal, now that he still has his neck and his Nell, Til reverts instantly to his old ways: he runs over, assaults the judge, and berates him for treating him like a common criminal! Before the judge can retaliate, Til has run off after Nell.

Babilée's *Til Eulenspiegel* was the second ballet based on Richard Strauss's famous score. The first was by Vaslav Nijinsky, whose last ballet it was. Nijinsky's *Til* was presented for the first time by Diaghilev's Ballets Russes at the Manhattan Opera House, New York, October 23, 1916. The scenery and costumes were by Robert Edmond Jones. Carl Van Vechten wrote of this performance:

"*Til Eulenspiegel* is the only new ballet the Russians have produced in America. In selecting this work and in his arrangement of the action Nijinsky was moved, no doubt, by consideration for the limitations of the company as it existed. The scenery and costumes by Robert E. Jones, New York, were decidedly diverting—the best work this talented young man has done, I think. Over a deep, spreading background of ultramarine, the crazy turrets of medieval castles leaned dizzily to and fro. The costumes were exaggerations of the exaggerated fashions of the Middle Ages. Mr. Jones added feet of stature to the already elongated peaked headdresses of the period. The trains of the velvet robes, which might have extended three yards, were allowed to trail the full depth of the Manhattan Opera House stage. The colors were oranges, reds, greens, and blues, those indeed of Bakst's *Scheherazade*, but so differently disposed that they made an entirely dissimilar impression. The effect reminded one spectator of a Spanish omelet.

"In arranging the scenario, Nijinsky followed in almost every detail Wilhelm Klatte's description of the meaning of the music, which is printed in programme books whenever the tone-poem is performed, without Strauss' authority, but sometimes with his sanction. Nijinsky was quite justified in altering the end of the work, which hangs the rogue-hero, into another practical joke. His version of this episode fits the music and, in the original *Til Eulenspiegel*, Til is not hanged, but dies in bed. The keynote of Nijinsky's interpretation was gaiety. He is as utterly picaresque as the work itself; he reincarnated the spirit of Gil Blas; indeed, a new quality crept into stage expression through this characterization. Margaret Wycherly, one of the most active admirers of the dancer, told me after the first performance that she felt that he had for the first time leaped into the hearts of the great American public, whose appreciation of his subtler art as expressed in *Narcisse*, *Petrouchka*, and even *Scheherazade*, had been more moderate. There were those who protested that this was not the Til of the German legends, but any actor who attempts to give form to a folk or historical character, or even a character derived from fiction is forced to run counter to many an observer's preconceived ideas."

## TILT

*Music by Igor Stravinsky. Choreography by Hans van Manen. Decor and costumes by Jean-Paul Vroom. First presented by the Netherlands Dance Theatre, January 21, 1972, at the Circustheater, Scheveningen, Holland. First presented in the United States by the same ensemble at the Brooklyn Academy of Music, New York, April 7, 1972.*

The choreographer, Hans van Manen, has described his own ballet: "Stravinsky's *Concerto in D for String Orchestra* [the same score Jerome Robbins used in 1951 for his ballet *The Cage*] is played in its entirety twice—the choreography being almost exactly the same for both versions. However, with the repeat of the music, as opposed to the first time it is played, the choreography for the six dancers is redistributed as follows:

—the first variation for six dancers is divided into three *pas de deux*
—the *pas de deux* is danced simultaneously by three couples
—the male variation is performed by three girls.

In the section that follows the sexes are transposed—the girls dance the parts of the men and the men those of the girls.

"The next three *pas de deux* remain unchanged but are danced by different couples. The finale is repeated in mirror-image with a change in each of the two *pas de deux*. Movement alone has no meaning for me in itself; it takes its significance only from the context in which it is placed."

## TIME PAST SUMMER

*Music by Peter Ilyich Tchaikovsky. Choreography by Benjamin Harkarvy. First presented by the Pennsylvania Ballet at the Academy of Music, Philadelphia, February 14, 1974, with Alba Calzada, Joanne Danto, and Lawrence Rhodes in leading roles.*

Eleven Tchaikovsky songs accompany this ballet, which looks back to the Russia of Chekhov and some of the characters in his memorable plays and stories. Writing in the *Dancing Times* the critic George Dorris said: "People at a Chekhovian garden party listen to two singers and think over their lives . . . An effective, moving ballet."

## LE TOMBEAU DE COUPERIN

*Music by Maurice Ravel. Choreography by George Balanchine. Lighting by Ronald Bates. First presented by the New York City Ballet at the Hommage à Ravel at the New York State Theatre, Lincoln Center, May 29, 1975. Conducted by Robert Irving.*

Ravel said that, in style, *Le Tombeau* is not so much a homage to the great French composer François Couperin as a tribute to eighteenth-century French music in general. The music, orchestrated from an original piano suite dedicated to friends of Ravel who had died in World War I, is in six parts: *Prélude, Fugue, Forlane, Rigaudon, Menuet,* and *Toccata.* The ballet that I arranged to this music doesn't say anything beyond the combination of these particular dancers moving to Ravel's lovely score, his memorial to Couperin.

These particular dancers are sixteen in number, eight couples divided into two quadrilles. They are mid-twentieth-century dancers moving to the work of a man who, in 1919, wrote tributes to a composer who flourished at the court of Louis XIV.

The American composer Norman Lloyd has written in the Golden Encyclopedia of Music that Couperin "is one of the greatest composers of the Baroque period, and one of the subtlest and most musicianly minds France has produced." I wholeheartedly agree; one of the pleasures this particular piece gave me as we made so many ballets so swiftly for our homage to Ravel in 1975 was my recollection of this master's work.

## TRACES

*Music by Gustav Mahler. Choreography by John Cranko. Scenery and costumes by Jürgen Rose. First presented by the Stuttgart Ballet at the Württemberg State Theatre, Stuttgart, Germany, April 7, 1973. First presented in the United States by the Stuttgart Ballet at the Metropolitan Opera House, New York, May 30, 1973, with Marcia Haydée, Heinz Clauss, and Richard Cragun in the principal roles. Conducted by Stewart Kershaw.*

*Traces* is a dramatic ballet about the past, as recalled in the present. The score is the *Adagio* from Mahler's *Tenth Symphony*. To its music a woman, released from obviously terrible captivity (a concentration camp?), adjusts to her new freedom while the past pulls at her memory.

The scene is an empty ballroom, with a sofa and chair. The woman enters. Her lover greets her, patient, understanding, warm. As they look together toward the back of the room, a group of dancers emerges. In the midst of their dance the woman sees a vision of a man in her past. He, a victim of persecution, head shaven, thin, in ragged clothes, draws her sympathy. In his spell her world seems to change completely. In the darkness the dead appear to waken. They rise slowly and crawl toward us. The man in her past stands out among them, leaping and springing in a kind of frantic agony. The woman joins him and comforts him when he collapses. Alternately drawn toward him and away from him, dreading yet cherishing the memory, the woman flings herself against the man. Now he leaves. She goes mad with grief. In the mass of prisoners he falls. They step over him—another victim, as they themselves shall likely be. The woman seeks refuge in her new lover's arms. She looks back at the prisoners, who turn suddenly and drop the rags from their backs to reveal numbers. They crouch down again and the ballroom dancers move among them. The woman dances with her new lover but is not to be comforted by his gentleness. Moving rigidly as in a trance, she walks slowly with him toward the back, toward a glowing circle of fire that might be the sun.

## TRIAD

*Music by Serge Prokofiev. Choreography by Kenneth MacMillan. Setting and costumes by Peter Unsworth. First presented by the Royal Ballet at*

Lawrence Rhodes in *At Midnight*. Photo by Martha Swope.

Lydia Abarca and Derek Williams in *Agon*. Photo by Anthony Crickmay.

Paul Russell in *Le Corsaire*. Photo by Martha Swope.

Trinette Singleton and Dermot Burke in *Astarte*. Photo by Herbert Migdoll.

Starr Danias and Dennis Wayne in *Sacred Grove on Mount Tamalpais*. Photo by Herbert Migdoll.

Paolo Bortoluzzi and Jörg Lanner in *Nijinsky, Clown of God*. Photo by Rosemary Winckley.

Suzanne Farrell in *Nijinsky, Clown of God*. Photo by Rosemary Winckley.

Jorge Donn in *Nijinsky, Clown of God*. Photo by Rosemary Winckley.

Marcia Haydée and Richard Cragun in *Daphnis and Chloë*. Photo by Beverley Gallegos.

*the Royal Opera House, Covent Garden, London, January 19, 1972, with
Antoinette Sibley, Anthony Dowell, and Wayne Eagling. First presented
in the United States by the Royal Ballet at the Metropolitan Opera House,
New York, in 1972.*

The three principal dancers in *Triad* are a girl, a boy, and his brother. The two
boys are devoted but from the start there is a problem. One of them is upset
and cries. A girl comes to them and dances. One brother tries to shield the
other from the effects of this dance of the girl's but the girl will not permit it.
Now one of the boys dances for the girl, then she again for *him*. After a dance
for all three, the girl tries to persuade one to come away with her. She goes
but he stays. The two boys dance, one continuing to try to shield the other.
But not for long. When three male "companions" enter, the stronger brother
throws the weaker to them, only to rescue him at the last minute. After a passionate *pas de deux* between the stronger boy and the girl, the younger
brother despairs. He leaves but returns, tries to separate them, fails, again despairs.

NOTES Writing in *Saturday Review* about *Triad*, the critic Walter Terry
said that while the ballet "may seem to some to have homosexual overtones, I
felt it to be rooted in something like the deep mystique of twins who are both
dual and one. MacMillan captures this feeling tastefully but, what is more,
imaginatively. The contours of his movements are generally balletic, but the
dynamism is that of modern dance; that is, indeed, a striking integration of the
elegance and dignity of classicism with the passionate, almost visceral, expres-
sivity of free dance.

"In the cast I saw, Dowell and Wayne Eagling were most appealing as the
brothers whose bond goes deeper than physicality, and Miss Sibley, as the girl,
touched the heart with a portrayal involving need, desire, rejection. A most rewarding, adult ballet, rich in striking designs as well as in dramatic intensity."

## TRINITY

*Music by Alan Raph and Lee Holdridge. Choreography by Gerald Arpino.
Lighting by Jennifer Tipton. Conductor: Walter Hagen. Rock Group: Virgin Wool. Organ: Hub Miller. Boys Choir: St. Luke's Chapel. First presented
by the City Center Joffrey Ballet, October 9, 1969, with Christian Holder,
Gary Chryst, Rebecca Wright, Dermot Burke, Donna Cowen, Starr Danias,
and James Dunne in principal roles.*

Named for its three parts, *Sunday, Summerland,* and *Saturday, Trinity* is a
homage to youth, joyful and aspiring. It uses for music themes reminiscent of
Gregorian chant and Baroque styles translated into rock, employing sections of
the regular orchestra, a boy's choir, and a rock group, "Virgin Wool." There are
two conductors, one for the orchestra and chorus, one who leads the rock
group from the organ.

Thirteen dancers participate in *Sunday*, which is heralded by a brass chorale before the curtain rises. The dancers enter gradually until finally all are present to respond to the throb of the rock organ. This is a group dance, exuberant, demanding in its rhythm and pulse, persistent, rejoicing in companionship and celebratory of youth. There are a number of solos and small ensembles as the mixture of rock and Baroque mounts in intensity. At the end, all lie in a circle on the floor as lead boy leaves.

In the part called *Summerland*, the pulse of the score slows down. The dancers rise from the circle and in varied ensembles suggest the sweetness of young love. Couple after couple now take the stage, one of them dancing a protracted adagio of affection. The accent here is on high spirits, too, shown in the many remarkable lifts in which the boys reach the girls up to the skies. All six couples rejoin as chimes sound twice and the boys carry the girls off.

*Saturday*, standing for the ancient Sabbath, begins as two boys enter the darkened scene carrying candles. The entire group follows, each bearing a lighted candle. They leave then and a boy comes forward to perform a dance to the hymn/rock beat, a version of the *Ite, missa est* that concludes the Latin Mass. He is joined by other male soloists and we have an impression that there is nothing on earth like lifting your arms and responding to the swell of the mighty organ that dominates the music here. The score intensifies in cracking crescendos of sound. All of the dancers then re-enter, each putting a candle on stage. The music gradually diminishes and the lights diminish, too, so that all we see on stage is the presentation of the candles.

NOTES  Speaking of his ballet to Anna Kisselgoff of the New York *Times*, the choreographer of *Trinity*, Gerald Arpino, said, "I think I'm in tune with my time. . . . This is my Aquarius ballet. I wanted the classic idiom with its escape from gravity—for the highest reach man can assume. I don't want to sound corny, but this is a ballet about man seeking his inner self. When the kids leave the candles on the floor, it's not meant to suggest just the literal peace marches. In the end, each individual must express himself. All he can leave is the light of himself."

The critic Andrew Porter reviewed *Trinity* at the time of the City Center Joffrey Ballet's London debut in May, 1971: "Gerald Arpino's *Trinity* made a whizzing start. For here the company seemed to be the 20th century's answer to the Bolshoi Ballet: which is to say nothing prissy, and nothing pretentious, but tremendous vigour and soaring virtuosity; flashing, exhilarating achievement rather than refined niceties; punch rather than polish. But—unlike the Bolshoi—an imagery both on stage and from the players that belongs to the present day: thoroughly demotic images supercharged into a buoyant art.

"The score, for the company's own group The Virgin Wool, choirboys, electric organ and orchestra, strikes into plain chant and Palestrina, and turns them into rock—not self-consciously but exuberantly. The dancing strikes into classicism at times, and breaks it into modern movement. The whole is heady and joyful, a celebration of a youth that can effortlessly encompass and transform the past."

John T. Elson in *Time* magazine wrote that *Trinity* "represents a throbbing fusion of classic dance with the sound of now. It perfectly epitomizes the jaunty style and passionate, youthful temperament of the New York City Center's Joffrey Ballet."

Patricia Barnes, in *Dance and Dancers*, wrote: "*Trinity* is a hard ballet to describe for its vitality, sincerity and passion, its dynamic coloring, both choreographic and musical, must be seen. Nor can words alone convey the personality and power of dancers such as Gary Chryst, Christian Holder and Dermot Burke; these three did a great deal to make *Trinity* the success it was. However, the whole cast had a splendid exuberance that made the ballet a pleasure to watch."

In the *Village Voice*, writing of the work of choreographer Gerald Arpino, Deborah Jowitt said: "His new ballet, *Trinity*, never lets go of you, never stops pounding and hurling fast, smart-alecky movement at you. He ignores—or perhaps uses—several basic dichotomies with magnificent ease. The Joffrey dancers are young and phenomenal. The best of them may grow in artistry or sensitivity, but they will probably never be more indomitable. Although they are young, they already have a discipline that very few people their age possess. I think it is the combination of discipline and vigor that excites Arpino. The three-part *Trinity* is set to some very good rock music (written by Alan Raph and Lee Holdridge and played by Virgin Wool), and the whole dance seems a taut by-play between the freedom inherent in rock and the control necessary for ballet. The dancers progress from the flung *développés* of Broadway to perfectly centered pirouettes rendered dangerous and exciting by fast, off-balance head circles or contrary arm gestures. This gives the movement an odd duality; ballet with a loose, whizzing quality in one part of the body only.

"Rock is heavy, ballet light. In *Trinity*, the dancers skid and wiggle on top of the beat; they punch it, but rarely drop onto it. Another interesting paradox. The movement is, for the most part, fast and very intricate—except for a slow ritual with votive candles in the last section and a softer second movement that features those stunning one-arm lifts that drove the crowd wild."

## THE TRIUMPH OF DEATH

*Dance drama in ten scenes after Eugène Ionesco by Flemming Flindt. Music by Thomas Koppel. Scenery and costumes by Poul Arnt Thomsen. Lighting by Jorgen Mydtskov. Music recorded by The Savage Rose. First presented by the Royal Danish Ballet at the Royal Theatre, Copenhagen, Denmark, February 19, 1972. First presented by the same ensemble at the Metropolitan Opera House, New York, May 27, 1976.*

A harsh and direct statement of the ills of this and other times, set to a score by a Danish rock group, this ballet sets out to deliver a message against all the destructive forces in the modern world, from pollution to political tyranny and human corruption. In a universal protest designed to force audiences to open their eyes, Flindt shows a materialistic society destroyed by corruptive influences.

# TROIS VALSES ROMANTIQUES

*Music by Emmanuel Chabrier. Choreography by George Balanchine. Costumes by Karinska. First presented by the New York City Ballet at the New York State Theatre, April 6, 1967, with Melissa Hayden and Arthur Mitchell, Gloria Govrin and Frank Ohman, and Marnee Morris and Kent Stowell in the principal roles.*

This is the third ballet I have done to music of Chabrier, a favorite composer of mine. I first heard music by this marvelous Frenchman soon after I left Russia and joined Diaghilev's Ballets Russes. In Paris I heard a concert of his music and liked it right away. I thought then that doing a ballet to Chabrier's music would be a pleasure and when the first opportunity presented itself some years later, I arranged *Cotillon*. The third of the *Trois Valses Romantiques* was included in that score. Then there was *Bourrée Fantasque*.

The ballet has no subject beyond the music and what it stands for to me. The first waltz is marked *Très vite et impétueusement*, the second *Mouvement modéré de valse* and the third *Animé*. The dances I arranged to these lovely pieces are simply expressive of the music as I see it, dances for a boy and a girl with two supporting couples, and a *corps de ballet* of six couples. The dances are about love and romance and what might happen.

# TWICE

*Music by Herbie Mann, Steve Miller Band, James Brown, and Santana. Choreography by Hans van Manen. Film visualization by Jean-Paul Vroom. Assistant film direction by Richard Brink. Costumes by Joop Stovkis. First presented by the Netherlands Dance Theatre at the Sadler's Wells Theatre, London, November 2, 1970. First presented in the United States by the same ensemble, April 2, 1972, at the Brooklyn Academy of Music.*

Like *Mutations*, the signature work of the Netherlands Dance Theatre in the early 1970s, *Twice* relies on both live dances and dance on film. Hans van Manen was responsible for the cine-choreography of *Mutations*, a technique he elaborates here. The title, originally *Sock It to Me*, applies to repeats in movement and to the mirroring of live movement in film.

*Twice* consists of four parts. The first, *Double*, to Herbie Mann's "Memphis Underground," is performed by an ensemble on stage whose movements are seen, too, on a movie screen high above the scene. The camera closes in on certain individuals and focuses the general attention on particular gestures and movement. In the second part, *Superimpositions*, a masked couple dance to the Steve Miller Band playing "Song for Our Ancestors." A flowing dance, the *pas de deux* yields to an ensemble, where other masked dancers pick up choreographic themes we have just seen.

*Theme*, the third part, is a solo for a boy to James Brown singing "Sex Machine." The dance begins slowly, builds to a frantic finish, and the scene blacks out. The finale, *Twice*, to music by Santana ("Savor"), gives the stage again to all twelve dancers, whose movements assume a brilliant staccato to the rhythm of strobe light.


## THE TWO PIGEONS

*An Allegory in two acts, based on the Fable by La Fontaine by Henry Regnier and Louis Mérante. Music by André Messager. Choreography by Louis Mérante. First presented at the Opéra, Paris, October 18, 1886. Presented by the Royal Ballet in a new version with choreography by Frederick Ashton at the Royal Opera House, Covent Garden, London, February 14, 1961. Scenery and costumes by Jacques Dupont. The principal roles were danced by Lynn Seymour, Christopher Gable, Elizabeth Anderson, and Johaar Mosaval. First presented in the United States by the Royal Ballet at the Metropolitan Opera House, New York, April 24, 1963, with Lynn Seymour, Alexander Grant, Georgina Parkinson, and Johaar Mosaval in the principal roles.*

The historian and critic Ivor Guest has noted that the discovery at the Royal Opera House of the score used for a 1906 presentation in London of *The Two Pigeons* prompted Frederick Ashton to stage a new version of the ballet. For this he discarded the scenario of the old ballet in favor of an allegorical treatment of the fable of his own devising. The story the ballet depicts is based on the poem *Les Deux Pigeons* by La Fontaine. While the two birds love each other, one tires of home and longs to roam abroad. When his love protests the pigeon replies that she is not to worry; after all, he will be gone only three days and just think of the adventures he will be able to tell! After his trip is over, the pigeon gratefully returns to his true love and they live happily ever after.

The choreographer has situated the action in Paris, where a young painter and his love live in an attractive garret. The painter is restless, however, and when a band of gypsies happens by, he is so enchanted by their free spirit—and also so interested in one of the girls—that he goes off. As his girl looks sadly after him from the balcony of the garret, a pigeon flies across the stage.

In the gypsy encampment, the boy learns that the transient life is not all moonlight and roses. He also learns that his affection for the gypsy lady has aroused the jealousy of her lover. There is much fiery gypsy dancing and appropriate displays of passion. The boy sees the gypsies have been kind to him only as a trick, but before he can escape they have tied him up and given him a rough time.

Meanwhile, back at the studio, his faithful love still sits on the balcony, awaiting his return. When she sees him her arms touchingly imitate the happy flapping of pigeon wings. They are reunited, dance ecstatically, and then rest by a chair, where first one pigeon comes to rest, and then another.

## TZADDIK

*Music by Aaron Copland. Choreography by Eliot Feld. "For My Grand-mother Bessie." Setting and costumes by Boris Aronson. Lighting by Jennifer Tipton. First presented in 1974 by the Eliot Feld Ballet at the Newman Theater, New York, with Eliot Feld in the leading role.*

There is a saying, Eliot Feld, the dancer and choreographer, reminds us: "A Jew without learning is incomplete." His ballet is a dramatic dance about an old rabbi and two students. The music is a trio, too: Copland's *Vitebsk*.

The students are two young men. Devoted to the master and anxious to do what he wishes, what they do is never enough for him. They are younger, after all, and represent the possibly dangerous and innovatively new. Amid the displayed exhortation it is easy to imagine the learned man's acquiring such knowledge of the young men that they are forever in his power, for their own good and the love of God. In the end, at his command, the sacred scrolls are unraveled. The students and their master are wound up in them, wholly committed to the sacred text.

Writing about *Tzaddik* in *Dance and Dancers* magazine, the English critic John Percival said: "This is an unusual theme for dancing, but it works, thanks to the striking imagery Feld has discovered for its expression. The movement is often hectic, small in scale and agitated. The impression is not of calm academic learning but an intense desire to convey beliefs deeply held . . . The performance by Feld as the teacher is intense and impassioned."

## TZIGANE

*Music by Maurice Ravel. Choreography by George Balanchine. Costumes by Joe Eula. Lighting by Ronald Bates. Solo violin: Lamar Alsop. Conducted by Robert Irving. First presented by the New York City Ballet at the Hommage à Ravel at the New York State Theatre, Lincoln Center, May 29, 1975, with Suzanne Farrell and Peter Martins as principals.*

The tziganes were Hungarian Gypsies who lived near Vienna. Haydn and Schubert, who summered nearby, both used elements of their music. Liszt, who was born in their midst, wrote that the tziganes played "as if suddenly given the power to express their pleasure, they flew to their violins and cymbals and began playing in a fury of excitement."

Ravel's music, for violin and piano originally (1924), was composed for the Hungarian violin virtuoso Yelly d'Aranyi. It was later orchestrated.

The ballet we made for our Hommage à Ravel to this exciting music tried to catch its atmosphere and dynamism. The first part is a solo for the ballet's heroine to the accompaniment of a long, pleading solo by the violin. A boy joins her. He and a small *corps de ballet* of eight dancers then gather for a cumulative dance of joy and exultation to the driving force of the music.


# UNDERTOW

*Ballet in one act with prologue and epilogue. Choreography by Antony Tudor. Music by William Schuman. Libretto by Antony Tudor, after a suggestion by John van Druten. Scenery and costumes by Raymond Breinin. First presented by Ballet Theatre at the Metropolitan Opera House, New York, April 10, 1945, with a cast headed by Hugh Laing as the* Transgressor, *Alicia Alonso as* Ate, *Diana Adams as* Cybele, *Nana Gollner as* Medusa, *Shirley Eckl as* Volupia, *Patricia Barker as* Aganippe, *and Lucia Chase as* Polyhymnia.

Modern ballets are continually enlarging the subject matter of the dance. It might seem strange to us now, but not until 1936—when Antony Tudor produced *Lilac Garden*—did we ever see on the ballet stage people, who looked and acted somewhat like ourselves, in a dramatic ballet. The women in *Lilac Garden* wore long party dresses, not romantic *tutus;* the men were anxious lovers, not mechanical cavaliers. And the characters in the ballet were caught up in a dramatic situation that was dominated by their inner feelings.

*Undertow* represents another effort to extend the dramatic dance. It attempts to show us why a young man, called the transgressor, commits murder. It shows us where he was born, the people he grew up with, and the people who influenced his life. All the characters in the ballet, except the hero, have names derived from mythology. They are thus not particular personalities, but universal characters recognizable in the life of every man. The time is the present.

PROLOGUE: BIRTH AND INFANCY   The light is dim. We make out Cybele, great mother of gods, in labor. She gives birth to a son, who creeps out from between her limbs and cries. The mother is revolted by the sight of her son and the agony she has suffered. She abandons him and seeks a lover—Pollux, the immortal youth who is born anew each day. Her son instinctively despises his mother and nurtures his grief. Even as a child, the transgressor discovers in the world no love.

THE CITY: ADOLESCENCE AND MANHOOD   The scene is a street in the slums of a huge city. We sense immediately the irony of the splendid statues that dominate the nearby square: great winged horses fly away from a place the inhabitants can never leave. Their life is so miserable that they cannot entertain the notion of accustoming themselves to anything else. A woman, made up hideously, stands pouting, waiting for someone to notice her. She is Volupia, here a bedraggled personification of sensual pleasure.

The transgressor, now a youth, enters with a pretty young girl. Her name is Aganippe and she is innocent inspiration. They appear to be having a good

time together until the boy notices the streetwalker. He is fascinated by her
and observes her with open curiosity. His girl abandons him. Volupia looks at
the boy contemptuously and smartens up for a man who now struts onto the
scene. He goes directly to her and follows, as she knowingly leads the way.

A rowdy bunch of boys race into the street. What seems to be playfulness
on their part is genuinely mean and cruel. They are aware of nothing else in
the world but the nuisance they may cause. The hero observes them. On the
surface he has no reaction; underneath we suspect that he despises his life and
is compelled to watch these people only because he seeks an explanation of
their grossness.

Volupia, her first mission over, comes back looking for another man. An old
man makes furtive advances toward her. He is so timid that the woman turns
on him and ridicules him. He leaves the scene.

The youth's companion, Aganippe, comes back into the street. She is accompanied by another girl, Nemesis, with whom she is playing a private game.
The man who has just recently finished his rendezvous with Volupia is attracted by Aganippe's beauty and innocence. He tries to strike up a conversation with her. The transgressor turns on him in a rage, orders him to leave
the girl alone, and chases him off.

Polyhymnia, the muse of sacred music, enters as an overcheerful, pious
busybody who is deluded into thinking she can change the lives of the people
in this slum with the right word. She is recruiting an audience for a prayer
meeting and invites all the passers-by to come. Several people join her: among
them, Pollux, still the handsome youth, who is now courting the modest
Pudicitia, and Ate, the hideous creature who would lead all men into evil.
Ate's body is demure and innocent, her face and gestures grotesquely obscene.
She accompanies the religious woman only out of malice and soon leaves.

Ate approaches the transgressor, but he is immune to her invitations and she
seeks the company of Aganippe's discouraged admirer. In vivid contrast to this
sordid couple, a bride and groom, Hymen and Hera, enter and—in a gay and
tender dance—suggest to the young hero the true power of love. The transgressor watches them enviously, then disbelieves in their happiness to conceal
his own misery.

Three lewd drunken women cavort about the scene noisily, braying and
bawling Polyhymnia's call to prayer. Ate comes back to seek more mischief
with the gang of dead-end kids. The transgressor and Aganippe watch her.
She runs off with the gang, and the two innocents look at the ground in disgust. When Ate re-enters, this time alone, the youth goes directly to her and
accosts her. He puts his hands around her neck and threatens to choke her to
death. Aganippe flees. The transgressor proceeds to kill Ate, but stops, frightened, when the girl Nemesis comes in, guiding home one of the besotted
women. Ate takes advantage of the youth's hesitation to elude him.

Still another kind of woman comes on the scene to disturb the hero.
Medusa, true to her name, seems to be attractive, but her beauty is empowered to turn men to stone. She is so different, and yet so like the streetwalker
and Ate, that the transgressor watches her with interest. She tries to take up
with Pollux, but this youth has sense enough to repulse her. Medusa looks to-

ward the transgressor: she must have someone. He is about to join her, when Polyhymnia begins to lead a revival meeting in the middle of the street. The youth participates in the meeting, hoping to escape. Medusa perceives this ruse and sends Polyhymnia and her crowd packing.

Now the transgressor is alone with a woman for the first time in his life. He is tense, expectant. The woman appears to control the youth as he responds to her advances. But gradually his true feelings become plain and we see that in reality he has control of the woman. Finally he can no longer conceal the hatred he has felt for women all his life. He becomes violent, and Medusa is afraid. The transgressor laughs. It is too late. He throws her to the ground, embraces her as she at first desired, and in the act, seizes her throat and chokes her viciously to death. The full orchestra is unleashed in a thundering, violent crescendo. The scene blacks out.

EPILOGUE: GUILT   The hero is alone on the scene. In the back, the misty panorama of the city and the winged horses of the square gradually rise into the sky, as if the very scene of the crime would flee from the criminal. The transgressor moves as if recovering from a hideous nightmare, the dream that has been his life. Yet in remembering the end of the dream, he sees that he has destroyed his life. He wonders what else he could have done, what other ending such a dream could have had. He finds no answer. But perhaps no one knows what he has done! Perhaps he can escape!

Curious people come into the street to watch him. He ignores them. Surely, in every way, he is better than they. Then Aganippe comes in, playing with a balloon. She stops and stares at him. The transgressor recalls their early friendship, smiles at her, and walks toward her. But the girl knows. She points at him, and everyone watches as her forgotten balloon rises in the sky. His guilt reaffirmed by the one person in the world he respects, the hero walks away to meet his end.

# UNFINISHED SYMPHONY

*Music by Franz Schubert. Choreography by Peter Van Dyk. Costumes by Kalinowski. Lighting by Nananne Porcher. First presented in Paris, 1958. First presented in the United States by American Ballet Theatre at the New York State Theatre, July 1971, with Cynthia Gregory and Michael Denard.*

A dance ballet to Schubert's great *Unfinished Symphony*, the choreographer has created here a dance for two persons. They are lovers but there is a sense of experience and apparent detached civilization in their approach to each other. There is no radical discontent but there is a continuing sense of potential drama about their relationship.

Writing in *Cue* magazine, the critic Greer Johnson wrote of the ballet: ". . . This is a full-bodied if serenely understated hymn to two mature lovers so responsive to one another that touch and gesture are transformed into literally metaphysical poetry. The work is quiet; it enfolds you; it flows and caresses to make its unhurried, knowingly sensual point."

Deborah Jowitt, writing of *Unfinished Symphony* in the *Village Voice*, found the ballet "a curiously hypnotic duet performed by Cynthia Gregory and Michael Denard. They're both in blue-gray, and the lighting creates a blue ambience, and they move quite slowly with a smooth, barely inflected dynamic. Everything they do looks thoughtful and deliberate; even the more abandoned poses are carefully charted. They might even be sleepwalkers. Once they look sharply at each other and then at one corner of the stage, and the contrast is startling. . . . The calm heroism of some of the poses at times suggests a dream battle in which they are both engaged—sometimes as colleagues, sometimes as antagonists. Both Gregory and Denard sustain the gliding, weightless choreography beautifully, and the Schubert music provides the plangent tension that keeps the somnambulism from being soporific."

## UNION JACK

*Music by Hershy Kay, adapted from traditional British music. Choreography by George Balanchine. Scenery and costumes by Rouben Ter-Arutunian. Lighting by Ronald Bates. Conducted by Robert Irving. First presented by the New York City Ballet at the New York State Theatre, Lincoln Center, New York, May 12, 1976, with Jacques d'Amboise, Helgi Tomasson, Sara Leland, Peter Martins, Kay Mazzo, Karin von Aroldingen, Suzanne Farrell, Patricia McBride, and Jean-Pierre Bonnefous as principals.*

It is no secret that I love England. Ever since I first went there, in the 1920s, soon after I left Russia and joined Diaghilev's great Ballets Russes, I liked London best of all the cities we visited. After Diaghilev died and I wanted to find the best place to make ballets, England was where I should have liked to remain. The immigration laws did not then permit such a step and when later Lincoln Kirstein came to see me and made it possible for me to come to America, I seized the independent alternative. I was lucky. Ever since, however, I have gone back to Britain whenever I could, and recall with affection the New York City Ballet's visits to London and Edinburgh and other cities. *Scotch Symphony* grew out of one of these visits and I shall never forget the long engagement the New York City Ballet had at Covent Garden in 1950. It was the longest period up to that time that we had had to dance on any one stage, and when we came back to the City Center the autumn of that year, everyone knew, I believe, that there was no stopping the objectives Lincoln Kirstein and I had set out to accomplish. So it is not only that I love Britain; we owe it a lot. When it was a question of what we as a ballet company should do to celebrate the American bicentennial, for me as for Lincoln Kirstein it was no question: we should celebrate as we could the English and what they have given us. We were helped in this ambition by many friends, from the composer Hershy Kay, our magnificent dancers, and the designer Rouben Ter-Arutunian, to our supporters, like Jacques d'Amboise's wonderful friends, the Leslie R. Samuelses. Making the ballet, for this time and place, was a pleasure.

As Lincoln Kirstein recalls, Americans and others in London at 11 A.M. precisely every morning may observe at Buckingham Palace the changing of the guard, a ritual of care that has its equivalent in Scotland and throughout the United Kingdom. It is a question of order and protection, perhaps only a symbol in these days of potential higher threats no guards could control, but for many of us it is the ultimate civilized gesture, as it has always been. My ballet is meant as a tribute to all that represents.

Our ballet is a three-part salute that acknowledges those ritual aspects of Britain as alive today in military ceremony and theatrical vitality as they have been for the past two centuries. It utilizes folk, military, naval, and music-hall themes for action as well as music. The music is composed by Hershy Kay on themes and variations drawn from the following sources, which by name and association give the best idea of associated action:

Part I: *Scottish Guards*. A procession of dancers to the music of "Keel Row," "Ye Banks and Braes o'Doon," "Caledonian Hunt's Delight," "A Hundred Pipers," "Dance wi' My Daddy," Regimental Tattoos: "Amazing Grace."

Part II: *Costermonger pas de deux* (Pearly King and Queen), a dance for the hero and heroine of the annual Cockney celebration for those born within the sound of the bells of St. Mary le Bow in the City of London, accompanied by: music-hall songs of London, 1890–1914, and "The Sunshine of Your Smile," "The Night the Floor Fell In," "Our Lodger's Such a Nice Young Man," "Following in Father's Footsteps," and "A Tavern in the Town."

Part III: *Horn Pipe*, with music based on "Rule, Britannia."

# LES VAINQUEURS

*Ceremony in five tableaux based on an idea of Richard Wagner's. Choreography by Maurice Béjart. Decor and costumes by Yahnele Toumelin. Lighting by Serge Apruzzese. First presented by the Ballet of the Twentieth Century, December 10, 1969, at the Théâtre de la Monnaie, Brussels. First presented in the United States by the same ensemble at the Brooklyn Academy of Music, New York, January 30, 1971.*

Few persons are aware of the importance of Buddhism in the life and work of Richard Wagner. The choreographer of this ballet about love and renunciation, Maurice Béjart, has said: "It is curious to observe the little importance that biographers of Richard Wagner place both on his discovery of Buddhism and the influence that Buddhism had on his life and work beginning in 1855. Yet it is only in full awareness of this development that his two greatest works *Tristan* and *Parsifal* can be musically and intellectually understood. The theory of the leitmotif carried to its logical conclusion reflects the psychological concept of the states of consciousness of Buddhism and their constant mutations.

"It is interesting to note, too, that many scholars have found great similarities between the Celtic cosmogony and myths and the Indo-Tibetan Buddhist. And the two works of Richard Wagner, *Tristan* and *Parsifal*, in which Buddhist influence is strongly present, are in fact based on Celtic lore.

"'*Parsifal* is a Buddhist scion transplanted to a Christian soil and climate, or, even more exactly, an attempt to correlate and fuse Buddhism and Christianity, but then the word "attempt" does not sit well on Wagner, so let us say, rather, an aim fairly well accomplished, for the duality of the religious sources does not bother the spectator and has not much concerned the critics.' (G. Leprince: *The Presence of Wagner*)

"If *Les Vainqueurs* has not been published, the reason could very well be *Tristan*. It is hard to bring forth two great works at one time: one will always end up swallowing the other: the night of *Tristan* has darkened the light of *Les Vainqueurs*. And if no sketch has been found of a subject on which he worked for so long a time, it is simply that the passion of Isolde absorbed the musical material of the love of Ananda for the pure Savitri.

"What is the meaning of this 'ceremony'? The dance is a rite. A ballet which descends to the roots of its origins is always a ceremony. Every work of art has multiple meanings. This is more so the case in a dance work where the idea transcends the word and the limits of the word, for dance belongs wholly and integrally to the world of form. Consequently what the public discovers in it is a reflection of its own thought.

"If people see nothing but a magic universe of shapes and colors, they are pretty nearly right. Whether they read into it a wondrous fairy tale, a romantic and exotic love story, the psychoanalytic version of the Tristan myth, or the initiation voyage toward illumination, will depend upon their own bent of mind. Some, to be sure, will see the work as a sacrilege, others, I hope, as an act of love, a love which for Wagner transcends human love, as 'it is the road which leads to elimination of the individuality, abjuration of the urge to live, achievement of the peace of Nirvana.' It is this cosmic love that makes Isolde declare at the end of the work:

> In the mass of waves
> of this sea of delights
> in the thunder, the clamor and the din
> waves of perfume
> breathing into ALL
> by the breath of the world,
> to sink, to drown, to lose consciousness,
> joy supreme."

Béjart uses as a signature for the ballet verses from the Buddhist Mantra:

> "Thou, the Victor, the Delivered, Deliver!
> Arrived upon the other shore,
> Cause the other there also to arrive."

The music of the ballet, as so often in the work of this choreographer, alternates in contrast, the one here between Wagner's score from *Tristan und Isolde* and Indo-Tibetan ragas.

A dramatic Buddha figure at the beginning of the ballet turns into a Tristan figure. He finds his love, there is a voyage, reminiscent of the action of the opera. The action then shifts to the contemporary, and there is a dance celebration by performers in jeans. Everything appears to be timeless.

Maurice Béjart has spoken of the libretto inspired by the life of Buddha that Wagner was writing at the same time he was working on *Tristan*. To a reporter for *The New Yorker*, Béjart said: "The libretto—which is also called *Les Vainqueurs*—exists, but nobody has ever discovered a note of the music. So I made a theory from my own experience as a choreographer. If you work on two ideas simultaneously and produce just one of them, the dominant work absorbs the ideas you prepared for the other one. I think that some of the music Wagner wrote for *Les Vainqueurs* ended up in *Tristan*, so I combined the two works. The final words of Isolde, when she says, 'I sought to dissolve myself in the ocean of life,' are very like a well-known Buddhist prayer."

## VALENTINE

*Music by Jacob Druckman. Choreography by Gerald Arpino. Lighting by Jennifer Tipton. Contrabass: Alvin Brehm. First presented by the City Center Joffrey Ballet at the City Center, New York, March 10, 1971, with Rebecca Wright and Christian Holder.*

*Valentine* is a dance for a girl and a boy accompanied by a double bass. The composer Jacob Druckman has said of the music for *Valentine*: "The work is one of the most difficult ever written for the contrabass and demands that the player attack the instrument with bow, tympany stick, both hands alternating percussive tapping on the body of the instrument with pizzicato harmonics, while the voice sustains tones, sings counterpoints, and punctuates accents. All of this necessitates the player's assaulting the instrument with an almost de Sade-like concentration (hence the title)."

That is the way of the dance, too, for the dancers are dressed and behave like competing boxers in the ring. They shadowbox, spar, stand off, get together, and react to the ferocity of the score.

## LA VALSE

*Ballet in two parts. Music by Maurice Ravel. Choreography by George Balanchine. Costumes by Karinska. Lighting by Jean Rosenthal. First presented by the New York City Ballet at the City Center, New York, February 20, 1951, with Tanaquil LeClercq, Nicholas Magallanes, and Francisco Moncion in the principal roles.*

Ravel called his composition *La Valse* a "choreographic poem." It was composed to be danced, "a sort of apotheosis of the Viennese waltz . . . the mad whirl of some fantastic and fateful carrousel." The ballet follows in outline the theatrical scheme Ravel imagined for his music: "At first the scene is dimmed by a kind of swirling mist, through which one discerns, vaguely and inter-

mittently, the waltzing couples. Little by little the vapors disperse, the illumination grows brighter, revealing an immense ballroom filled with dancers . . ."
Prior to this scene, the ballet makes use of another composition of Ravel's, *Valses Nobles et Sentimentales,* a group of eight short waltzes that introduces the ballroom scene and its principal dancers.

PART ONE: VALSES NOBLES ET SENTIMENTALES    The first waltz serves as the overture. Percussion instruments underline the liveliness of the animated waltz rhythm. The curtain rises, and the second waltz begins.

Three girls stand before a blue net curtain in formal dress. They hold their white-gloved hands in a light, mannered pose. The music is soft and beguiling. The girls bow low and begin to dance, at first somewhat wistfully, then coyly, but always their movements are as formal as their long white gloves, which seem to accent every one of their gestures. Underneath their slate-colored costumes their full skirts are brilliant red, and as they separate and move more freely, the whirling dresses color their dance. Far behind the blue net curtain, in the obscure distance, hangs a cluster of dimly lighted chandeliers. The girls exit modestly, their white-gloved arms before their faces.

A handsome couple, holding hands, dance out gaily to the tinkling tune of the third waltz. Their lighthearted duet is marked by quick, sprightly steps. They dance together closely and separate only as they exit at opposite sides of the stage.

The next waltz is more open in its melody, and to its rapid rhythms another couple dance boldly and freely. They run past each other in high, joyful leaps. The fifth waltz begins with subdued, romantic contrast. The girl who dances it moves gracefully and deliberately. Her partner kisses her hand and kneels. The music becomes blithe, and the ballerina dances before the boy with close, lighthearted steps. The boy marvels at her beauty and reaches out to claim her. This girl dances alone to the sixth waltz, after which her partner rejoins her.

As this couple exit toward the right, they are met by two girls. The couple pause, then the ballerina leaves the stage and a third girl takes her place. These are the same three girls who danced the first waltz. The seventh waltz begins. They claim the boy, covering him with their arms. One girl breaks away to dance, then another. The boy joins them, lifts them high as the music races its tempestuous theme. The four stand together, and one of the girls falls back in the boy's arms. He kneels as the girls run off. The music hesitates in its momentum, and the girls and boys of the earlier waltzes rush in and out, over and about him. He rises, turns swiftly, and the three girls confront him. He dances with them again as the waltz theme returns, then leaps off into the wings.

The stage is empty as the sinuous, final waltz commences. A girl in white emerges. She steps forward, opening her arms slowly; her body recoils slightly as she moves forward. She walks over to the right; her arms mime the flow of the expectant music. A boy enters at the back. They do not see each other. They exchange positions, then each bends backward and recognizes the other. They approach, touch hands warily, and with formal, sophisticated movements of her arms, the ballerina gives her partner her hand. They separate, pass, and come together back-to-back in the center of the stage, where they turn together, their arms entwined. Now they separate again and repeat their introduction. The boy lifts the ballerina slowly; her white dress flows with the final measures of the waltz. He lifts her off into the wings.

PART TWO: LA VALSE   The lights dim, the blue net curtain is raised, the distant chandeliers brighten, the music to La Valse begins. The music throbs low and mysteriously; light catch-phrases from a waltz hover over a deep, foreboding background of sound. A spotlight picks up a boy, who runs onto the stage in search of a girl he cannot find. He looks for her helplessly in the dark ballroom. Another boy enters with his dancing partner. They appear to be lost. Suddenly, on the opposite side of the stage, the spotlight shines on three girls, whose white-gloved arms are held up before their faces like masks. The boy chooses one of the girls and starts to dance with her, but the girl falls back strangely in his arms as they move in a circle. They exit. Another couple moves across the scene hurriedly, and three girls and three boys run on and off seeking their partners. All the dancers seem to be waiting for the waltz to emerge through the weird music that holds it in abeyance. The waltz rhythm pulsates; a sparkling rush of sound from the harp heralds its full waltz melody. The ballroom brightens; eight couples fill the stage.

They dance joyously in a large circle; the color of the girls' skirts contrasts vividly with the black walls of the room. As the couples swirl past, we see that the chandeliers are hung with crepe. The black cloth hangs low into the room. The couples change partners in the center of the circle and continue their tempestuous dance. A loud fanfare in rapid waltz rhythm announces the arrival of two new groups of dancers, who cross the stage diagonally as the others stand back. Two couples dance before the group, then the boys gather in the center of the circle, where they choose partners. Now there are two girls for each boy.

The ballerina of the fifth waltz enters with her partner, and the fierce, pounding waltz abates to a soft, mellifluous volume and tempo as they dance softly. The boy exits; the ballerina dances with a group of girls as the couples stand and watch. The cymbals clash, the momentum increases, and the ballerina in white enters. She leaps toward the front, all the dancers gathering on each side of the stage to form wide, opening doors of movement to heighten the speed of her dazzling entry. The dancers move toward the center of the room, where one of the girls is lifted high above them all; the group circles about her. In back, the black crepe swirls as the dancers pass.

The ballerina in white dances happily with her partner; the waltz is quiet again. The couples stand aside and converse and do not notice them. Their dance is slow at first; the ballerina's movements are retarded and she seeks to move more freely as the waltz attempts to resume its previous intensity. But the music hesitates overlong; it unwinds with a snap of sound like a spring that has been wound up too tightly. Disintegrating patterns of waltz melody and tempo struggle helplessly against the orchestra. The once brilliant theme sounds with the pathetic intensity of a hurdy-gurdy. The girl turns with despairing speed to her partner's arms. A staccato trumpet heralds a pause; the weird, warning first bars of *La Valse* cause all to stand aside. They all look toward the back.

A figure in black emerges beneath the funereal chandeliers. His head is bowed as he walks forward slowly. About his neck hangs a heavy black medal on a black chain. The girls kneel before him; their partners turn their faces away. The ballerina in white turns away in terror. The black specter is followed by a page, who holds in his arms a mirror and a black gown. The music whirls frantically in anticipation.

The girl in white staggers toward the man unwillingly, as if hypnotized by his presence; she goes to him recognizing her own fears of his fatal attraction. He presents her with a splendid necklace and holds the mirror before her. He waits anxiously for her reaction. The girl turns away in horror: the mirror is cracked black glass. Her horror turns to fascination as the waltz attempts to penetrate the mystery of sound and sight. It races suddenly to a desperate loud statement, falters away again. The man offers the girl a pair of long black gloves. He holds them open, and she slides her arms into them as the music sounds a booming, relentless crescendo. Presented now with a black gown, the girl slips into it delightedly and covers her white costume. The stranger rewards her finally with a black bouquet. He kisses her hand, takes her about the waist, and begins to turn her about the room.

The crescendo has now receded, and the waltz attempts again to come to life. The girl is moved faster and faster by her partner as the waltz resumes its momentum. She throws down her bouquet and begins to fall limp in his arms. He turns her faster; she cannot break away. The waltz reaches the peak of driving, irrevocable rhythm; crashes of its beauty tear the air. The girl falls back, then rises to the close embrace of the grotesque black figure. She dies. The specter disappears. Her lover drags her off.

The couples return to their dancing, now rushing about the cold, dark ballroom in frantic pursuit of the pleasure the music will no longer allow them. The exhausted waltz is now heard only in a climactic struggle of instruments. The boy enters in the back, carrying the dead girl in his arms. The boys lift her away from him to their shoulders. Her head falls back, her arms hang loose. Her lover attempts to embrace her, but she is lifted high above him. All of the dancers close in. The girl's body is turned around and around. About the circling center, the group races in a fateful, fantastic carrousel.

Elena Bivona, in an essay on Patricia McBride in *Ballet Review* (Vol. 3, No. 3), wrote of a performance of *La Valse:* "From a ballet of delicate suggestion she has extracted religious horrors without leaving a smudge on the delicate framework. In one performance, her first waltz had marvelously slow-sharp inflections of arm and hand; the gestures clawed and sank at the same time, brittlely artificial and softly demanding. As Bruhn can in *Giselle*'s last act, she interfused tension with luxuriance to make a dream-ridden girl innocent of her own evil but evil nonetheless. And against the articulate arms she countered a tense neck, the tight muscles keeping her head alert, watching without object, waiting half-aware. Another performance made the same waltz the world of a woman a thousand years old in corruption, her movements still and stretching, her vitality at a controlled scream-pitch ready to devour new adventures, and there are obviously none left but the destruction she finally conjures up, to her astonishment, fear, and joy. On this night, the girl was no innocent; she was the hostess, her white dress an obscenity of wit, her physical youth a Dorian Gray monstrosity, her corruption radiating as if it were beauty, and she is so fascinating she must feed on the fascination she draws to herself. Vampira. A monster—or two monsters, three, a slightly different one each time to find out who this death-lover in her, in Balanchine, in us, is.

"She met Death once with a hypnotized, terrified blankness, tight neck muscles hardened to a vise for her staring face, and her body a Bunraku doll's manipulated by a puppet master: fluent in her upper body, simple and a little jerky from the waist down. She could abandon that possibility another night to make her softness an all-knowing perverted eroticism, her presence so strong Death himself makes no impact until the moment, when he seizes her for their first dance, that his strength overpowers hers; and that, perhaps only because she and Death are a single identity and the recognition itself is what claims her, is what lets loose the chaos of the ballet's finale. *La Valse* that night became a circle of evil seeking its own face for which Death holding his mirror was the perfect metaphor."*

# VARIATIONS

*Music by Igor Stravinsky. Choreography by George Balanchine. Lighting by Ronald Bates. First presented by the New York City Ballet at the New York State Theatre, March 31, 1966, with Karin von Aroldingen, Karen Batizi, Diane Bradshaw, Marjorie Breler, Elaine Comsudi, Rosemary Dunleavy, Susan Hendl, Ruth Ann King, Jennifer Nairn-Smith, Delia Peters, Donna Sackett, Lynne Stetson, Robert Maiorano, Paul Meija, Frank Ohman, John Prinz, David Richardson, Michael Steele, and Suzanne Farrell.*

Stravinsky composed his *Variations for Orchestra* dedicated to the memory of Aldous Huxley in 1963–64. Soon afterwards I was able to see the score. I decided that as soon as possible I would like to do a ballet to the music. What kind of ballet it was to be, however, was not then clear. Stravinsky's work is concise, lasting only four minutes, forty-five seconds, which is not in the theatre a sufficient time to develop and hold the attention, not to mention the ears, of the audience. Stravinsky's music also demands to be heard not just once, but many times. I accordingly decided to have the music played three times for a set of three dances.

The curtain rises and twelve girls are seen on the stage. There is no setting. Stravinsky's piece was composed, he tells us, on a pitch series, a succession of twelve notes that came to his mind as a melody and was then seen as material for variations. As the music begins, the girls face the audience in two groups of six. There is a variation for twelve violins in the orchestra which is taken up in a different way by mixed strings, and later by twelve woodwinds. The dancers

* Reprinted by permission of *Ballet Review*, Marcel Dekker, publisher.

reflect these changes in the orchestra in different groupings and separations, each of the twelve dancing a little differently from the others. As the first part ends, the original two groups of six have become three groups of four. Stravinsky has said in a program note: "The halves . . . are unities as well as fragments, and are therefore divisible in turn, and invertible, reversible, mirror-invertible, mirror reversible."

The second playing of the music is danced by six boys, who stand at the beginning in two rows of three. They dance in various combinations, one of them at a certain point being singled out by the other five.

For the third playing, a girl dances on stage quickly. In yet another version of the same subject, she reflects the conciseness of Stravinsky's score.


## VARIATIONS FOR FOUR

*Music by Marguerite Keogh. Idea and choreography by Anton Dolin. Costumes by Tom Lingwood. First presented by Festival Ballet at Royal Festival Hall, London, September 1957. First presented in the United States by American Ballet Theatre at the Metropolitan Opera House, New York, September 25, 1958.*

Many ballet-goers are familiar with Anton Dolin's re-creation of the great nineteenth-century ballet *Pas de Quatre*, in which the four leading ballerinas of the day appeared together for a single performance of display and polite competition. Dolin, renowned as a *danseur* since his debut with Diaghilev's Ballets Russes, conceived the idea of staging a similar showpiece for four outstanding male soloists. The result is a popular work both here and abroad, where it has been performed by gifted *premiers danseurs*.

The bright music that raises the curtain heralds a festive occasion. The four dancers enter to a stately theme, pose and dance together briefly, then separate to perform independently their special skills in a series of variations. These vary in tempo and energy, building to a brilliant display of speed and virtuosity for all four. There is also a sustained *adagio* for one of the soloists, to remind us of the *danseur's* romantic role. All four participate in a rapid, flourishing finale.

NOTES    After its revival by American Ballet Theatre at the New York State Theatre, July 12, 1972, Clive Barnes wrote in the New York *Times*:

"Let me confess to a prejudice. I love Anton Dolin's *Variations for Four*. In classic ballet women have so much of it their own way. For years the male dancer has stood politely, sometimes sufferingly, behind his ballerina, flexing his muscles and practicing his humility. Dolin was one of the first great male dancers of the century—with Serge Lifar he was one of Diaghilev's last two premier danseurs, and he played a principal role in the development of both British and American ballet—and this pas de quatre is almost a charter of Men's Liberation in ballet. There are just four men dancing; brilliantly, competitively and with no apologies.

"Since the work was first created for London's Festival Ballet, a company Dolin himself formed, it has been in the repertory of many leading companies, including American Ballet Theatre. But on Wednesday night at the New York State Theatre the ballet had its first revival with the company since its original American production in 1958. It was exultantly danced.

"In some ways, rather like the Royal Danish Ballet, the male dancers of Ballet Theatre are more interesting than the women. Undeniably Ballet Theatre has gathered together a most unusual collection of men, and this *Variations for Four* can show some of them off in style. At the first performance it was danced by an immaculate Ted Kivitt, a forceful John Prinz, a gutsy Alexander Filipov and, in the final solo, Ballet Theatre's newest star, the Italian Paolo Bortoluzzi. Mr. Bortoluzzi needs to be careful of his fine Italian hands— he is at times too flamboyant for New York taste—but he is a magnificent dancer with a special pulse and arrogance of his own. He is like an Italian racing car—extravagant, different but powerful."

# VARIATIONS POUR UNE PORTE ET UN SOUPIR

*Sonority by Pierre Henry. Choreography by George Balanchine. Scenery and costumes by Rouben Ter-Arutunian. Lighting by Ronald Bates. First presented by the New York City Ballet at the New York State Theatre, Lincoln Center, January 17, 1974, with Karin von Aroldingen and John Clifford.*

*Variations for a Door and a Sigh* has an interesting score, or sonority, as the French composer Pierre Henry calls it. I first heard work by the composer when I visited him some years ago in Paris, at the suggestion of Nicolas Nabokov, and decided then that I would like to do a ballet to this piece one day. Henry was the first "traditionally oriented" composer to interest himself in electro-acoustical techniques. This particular piece makes maximum use of the whole gamut of sounds that can be associated with sighs and the opening and closing of doors. I picked out fourteen of the twenty-five variations Henry wrote for the original concert version, and arranged to them a *pas de deux*, a duet for the female door and the male sigh. The ballet begins with a sigh.

It is dark and silent as the curtain rises. A spotlight reveals a male figure all in white responding to the sound of sighs. We hear then the sound of a creaking door and the woman is revealed, also in white, but with a black silken skirt attached to her waist that stretches like a wide train across the whole stage. In its center, like the central support for a tent that has yet to rise, she dances to the door sounds. Her limbs open and close, creaking and slamming, about an invisible hinge. She approaches the man and then he dances again. They continue to alternate dances as a relationship becomes more intense. Her enveloping skirt is agitated and rises and falls in waves of blackness that engulf the stage. She is all cool control, he white heat. He achieves an ultimate sigh as her inundating black skirt enfolds him. He disappears in its folds; she, too, bows beneath it.

A number of persons have called *Variations* "the male liberation ballet." I prefer to think of it as an every-man-for-himself ballet. Maybe it shows, in a way, man's weakness—how he strives to get involved but, once there, doesn't know how to get out.

In 1965, in Brussels, Maurice Béjart arranged his own cycle of Pierre Henry's variations for seven dancers in homage to the visual talent of the artist Arman: "Seven dancers enter the stage to create a ballet in which choreography has no place." The dancers improvised their movement according to suggestions from the sonorous structure; each time sequence was propelled by the dancers themselves.

In 1972, in Glasgow for the Scottish Theatre Ballet, Peter Darrell staged his ballet *Variations for a Door and a Sigh*. A program note stated that the work "explores the realms of sexual behavior and the conflicts of personal commitment." Peter Darrell also alluded to a quotation from Tolstoy as the starting point for his ballet: "Man survives earthquakes, epidemics, terrible illnesses and every kind of spiritual suffering, but always the most poignant tragedy was, is and ever will be the tragedy of the bedroom."


## VESTRIS

*Music by Genaidi Banschikov. Choreography by Leonid Jacobson. First presented at the International Ballet Competition, Moscow, June 1969, with Mikhail Baryshnikov. First presented in the United States by American Ballet Theatre at the Kennedy Center of the Performing Arts, Washington, May 20, 1975, with Baryshnikov. Costume by Marcos Paredes. Conductor: David Gilbert.*


One of the greatest dancers of all time, Auguste Vestris appeared to be the natural subject for a ballet in which a young dancer might show, in a very short time, the complete range and versatility of his gifts, in dance and mime. The Soviet choreographer Leonid Jacobson accordingly responded to the young dancer Mikhail Baryshnikov and made for him a seven-minute display piece that sums up a forgotten but illustrious dancer in a forgotten time.

Vestris was born in Paris in 1760 and died there eighty-two years later. Famed for his elevation, pirouettes, and *batterie*, Vestris's performances enthralled Europe for many years, from his debut at age twelve until his retirement at fifty-six. Parliament recessed to watch him and his father, another virtuoso, in 1781. Vestris danced the first performances of great ballets by Noverre and later taught pupils who were to govern ballet in Europe: Didelot, Perrot, Auguste Bournonville, and Marie Taglioni. There are many lithographs and prints of Vestris in performance of many roles, all of which were studied by Jacobson and Baryshnikov as the ballet was being made.

The action is divided into seven brief sections and the basic idea is not to re-create Vestris historically so much as to give a notion of his time as another dancer displays a similar range of versatility. The seven parts are: "An Old

Man Dancing a Minuet," "The Coquette Dance," "The Preacher-Prophet," "Classical Dance Variations," "Prayer," "Laughter," and "Dying Man."

In formal ballet dress fashioned after the eighteenth century, with white wig, white jacket and tights, the star dancer acts his age, relives youth and shows what he is made of.

*Vestris* was performed at Wolf Trap, near Washington, in 1976, filmed for television, and broadcast first by WNET, New York, on December 6, 1976.

Reviewing the ballet in the New York *Times*, the critic Clive Barnes said "the dance itself is a perfect joy—a cameo impression of a dancer, of a style, of a period and of a man. Within its brief compass it manages to convey a whole sheaf of dramatic and choreographic messages."

In the book *Baryshnikov at Work*, the dancer recalls the genesis of the ballet, which has been recorded there in marvelous pictures by Martha Swope.

## VIOLIN CONCERTO

*Music by Igor Stravinsky. Choreography by George Balanchine. First presented by the New York City Ballet at the Stravinsky Festival, at the New York State Theatre, Lincoln Center, June 18, 1972, with Karin von Aroldingen, Kay Mazzo, Peter Martins, and Jean-Pierre Bonnefous in the leading roles. Lighting by Ronald Bates. Conducted by Robert Irving. Violin soloist: Joseph Silverstein.*

Stravinsky has written (see NOTES below) that he did not like the standard violin concertos. I myself have always preferred Stravinsky's. Some years ago, when the Original Ballet Russe happily gave me the opportunity, I made a ballet to this violin concerto of his. It was called *Balustrade*, largely after splendid scenery by the great artist Pavel Tchelitchew, who painted a décor that was dominated by a white balustrade in perspective in the background. *Balustrade* was first danced at the Fifty-first Street Theatre, New York, January 22, 1941, with Tamara Toumanova, Roman Jasinski, and Paul Petroff in the leading roles. I do not remember this ballet; but not, alas! What I did then was for *then*, and what I wanted to do to this same music for our Stravinsky Festival at the New York City Ballet represented more than thirty years' difference. The dancers were different and I liked the music even more.

The score is in four movements, the middle part being a center or core of two "Arias" enclosed by introductory Toccata and a final Capriccio.

And so is the ballet in four movements, the center being arranged as two *pas de deux* for different couples to accompany the Arias. The introductory Toccata introduces the principal dancers with a small *corps de ballet*. All four of the soloists participate in the Capriccio finale. The best guide to the character of these dances is a number of hearings of the music.

NOTES In the book *Dialogues and a Diary*, Stravinsky recalled that "The *Violin Concerto* was not inspired by or modeled on any example. I do not like the standard violin concertos—not Mozart's, Beethoven's, Mendelssohn's or

Brahms's. To my mind, the only masterpiece in the field is Schoenberg's, and
that was written several years after mine. The titles of my movements, Toccata, Aria, Capriccio, suggest Bach, however, and so to some extent, does the
musical substance. My favorite Bach solo concerto is the one for two violins, as
the duet with a violin from the orchestra in the last movement of my concerto
must show. But the *Violin Concerto* contains other duet combinations, too, and
the texture of the music is more often chamber music in style than orchestral.
I did not write a cadenza for the reason that I was not interested in violin virtuosity. Virtuosity for its own sake plays little part in my concerto, and the
technical difficulties of the piece are, I think, relatively tame.

"The ballet *Balustrade* (1940) by George Balanchine and Pavel Tchelitchew, and with the music of my *Violin Concerto,* was one of the most satisfactory visualizations of any of my theatre works. Balanchine worked out the
choreography as we played my recording together and I could actually watch
him imagine gesture, movement, combination, composition. The result was a
dance dialogue in perfect co-ordination with the dialogues of the music. The
dancers were few in number, and the whole second Aria was performed—and
beautifully performed—as a solo piece, by Toumanova. *Balustrade* was produced by Sol Hurok, that master judge of the *vox populi* (I imagine *Balustrade* must have been one of his few misjudgments in that sense). The set was
a very simple white balustrade across the back of the dark stage."

Reviewing *Violin Concerto* in *The Nation,* Nancy Goldner wrote of the
dance to the second Aria: "The duet for Kay Mazzo and Peter Martins is
amazingly complex and dense, as is most of the ballet. It churns and seems to
be a continuous process of knotting and unknotting. In their first phase, she
faces him for a second, grabs his waist and slides to the floor, resting on her
front haunch while her back leg is tensely stretched. He looks to the right. She
looks to the left, her arm partly covering her face. There is discord here, which
builds and builds as their sculptured and quickly changing poses become more
multi-dimensional. Too, their relationship with the music becomes increasingly
independent, until they finally seem to be in total counterpoint, though never
in disharmony. Perhaps that is one reason why Mazzo's simple big movement
to the one resounding chord in the score is such a shock. Another reason is that
nothing is simple between this couple. But as soon as she has made that simple
declaration the duet turns convoluted again. She collapses her knees inward
and rotates away from Martins, who is grasping her ankles. The choreography
is so innovative, intense and rich that detailed analysis of it, and clues as to
why it seems to be a profound embodiment of inner turbulence, must await
further performances. But first let me describe one luscious detail in it. Martins
rolls Mazzo from one foot to another. In this little air voyage, she starts out
with one foot pointed and the other flexed. With great deliberation and yet
speed, she simultaneously points the flexed foot and flexes the pointed one. We
can almost see each dot along the arced paths her feet trace. As the trip ends,
she lands on one foot and whips her flexed foot along the floor into a point.
This is an exclamation point to a juicy five-second game. Many choreographers
have played with flexed feet in classical ballet, but Balanchine's version is now
the definitive one."

# VIVA VIVALDI!

*Music by Antonio Vivaldi. Choreography by Gerald Arpino. First presented by the Robert Joffrey Ballet at the Delacorte Theatre, Central Park, New York, September 10, 1965, with Robert Blankshine, Jon Cristofori, Edwina Dingman, Luis Fuente, Ian Horvath, Margo Sappington, and Trinette Singleton in leading roles.*

This lively dance ballet with a Spanish flavor is set to music by Vivaldi (*Violin Concerto in D major, P. 151,* arranged for guitar and orchestra). A display piece for fine dancers, who perform both allegro and adagio roles, there is no story, only the tempo and melody of the score and the expression of the dance accompaniment.

# VOLUNTARIES

*Music by Francis Poulenc. Choreography by Glen Tetley. Designed by Rouben Ter-Arutunian. Lighting by John B. Read, executed by Gilbert V. Hemsley, Jr. First presented by the Stuttgart Ballet at the Württemberg State Theatre, Stuttgart, December 22, 1973, with Marcia Haydée and Richard Cragun in the leading roles. First presented in the United States by the same ensemble at the Metropolitan Opera House, Lincoln Center, New York, June 4, 1975, with the same principals.*

Created in memory of John Cranko, the Stuttgart Ballet's founder, *Voluntaries* is a dance tribute and valedictory by Glen Tetley. It was Tetley's first work for the company, of which he was appointed director in the winter of 1974 after Cranko's sudden death in the summer of 1973.

The choreographer's program note for the ballet tells us that, by musical definition, voluntaries are free-ranging organ or trumpet improvisations that are often played before, during, or after religious services. The Latin root of the word also connotes desire or flight. The choreographer says that the ballet is conceived as "a linked series of voluntaries." The music is Poulenc's *Concerto for Organ, Strings, and Percussion;* the soloists in New York were Calvin Hampton, organist, and Howard Van Hyning, timpanist.

The stage action is both a tribute and a dance celebration, a ritual of remembrance and rededication that looks forward rather than back. A stranger to the occasion would know only of the dance event itself and not of its sentimental pretext.

*Voluntaries* is danced before a painted backdrop of concentrated color and design that suggests liveliness, a kind of microscopic slide depicting continuity and no interruption. The stage action shows Cranko's principal dancers in combinations and permutations of movement that remember. They also look forward to the future!

Writing of the New York premiere, the critic Clive Barnes said in the New York *Times* that *Voluntaries* "is an outstanding amalgam of classic ballet and modern dance and, probably, Mr. Tetley's more purely beautiful and sinuous work to date . . . At the end the cheers for the company and Mr. Tetley engulfed the opera house."

## WALK TO THE PARADISE GARDEN

*Music by Frederick Delius. Choreography by Frederick Ashton. Setting by William Chappell. First presented by the Royal Ballet at the Royal Opera House, Covent Garden, November 15, 1972, with Merle Park, David Wall, and Derek Rencher.*

Frederick Ashton has called this brief ballet a *Liebestod*—or love-death. The music is from Delius' great lyric opera, *A Village Romeo and Juliet,* and it serves as the prelude to the final scene of that work, where the two lovers kill themselves. Similarly, in the ballet, the lovers, after ultimate expressions of joy in each other, discover no other course but suicide to perpetuate the depth of their passion. They meet white-robed Death, submit, and rejoice again.

Writing in *The Times* of London after the premiere, the critic John Percival said that this was "the first big part Ashton has created for Merle Park, and he reveals in her a lyricism and natural warmth her usual bravura roles have hidden. She and David Wall play a pair of lovers, entirely absorbed in each other . . . What they have to do includes some fantastically difficult things. Not only the familiar Bolshoi . . . tricks, like spinning the girl horizontally through the air and catching her again, but even a moment when she is held upside down high above his head. Yet Ashton sets these virtuoso tricks so smoothly into the dance, and they are so effortlessly done by this couple, that you hardly notice the difficulty, rather the rapture they express. Yet there is about the dance a sense of stolen time, an undertone of feeling that the moment cannot last, and at the end this manifests itself chillingly in the form of a stern angel all in stark white (Derek Rencher), who draws the lovers to him, parts them and allows them to be joined again only in death. Ashton has caught the mood of the Delius music perfectly, although seeing deeper into it than his audience perhaps expected. A handsome setting by William Chappell completes a small but perfectly-formed work."

In his authoritative biography of Frederick Ashton, David Vaughan describes the process of the ballet's creation in detail. He also remarks: "This dance was the most important role that Ashton ever choreographed for Merle Park, and as with so many other dancers he brought out reserves of passion that had been hidden until then."

# WALPURGIS NIGHT

*Music by Charles Gounod. Choreography by Leonid Lavrovsky. First presented by the Bolshoi Ballet at the Filial Theatre, Moscow, 1941. First presented in the United States by the Bolshoi Ballet at the Metropolitan Opera House, New York, April 23, 1959.*

The Walpurgis Night scene in Gounod's opera *Faust* occurs at the beginning of the last act. Here Mephistopheles brings Faust to witness the revels that traditionally take place on the eve of May Day at Brocken, highest point of the Hartz Mountains. There Mephistopheles summons the shades of famous courtesans. The ballet freely depicts the height of the revels.

# WATERMILL

*Music by Teiji Ito. Choreography by Jerome Robbins. Costumes by Patricia Zipprodt. Lighting by Ronald Bates. Décor by Jerome Robbins in association with David Reppa. First presented by the New York City Ballet at the New York State Theatre, Lincoln Center, February 3, 1972, with Edward Villella, Penny Dudleston, Hermes Conde, Jean-Pierre Frohlich, Bart Cook, Tracy Bennett, Victor Castelli, Deni Lamont, Colleen Neary, and Robert Maiorano in the principal roles. Musicians: Dan Erkkila, Genji Ito, Teiji Ito, Kansuke Kawase, Mara Purl, and Terry White.*

The score of *Watermill*, by the contemporary composer Teiji Ito, is radically different from the music we customarily hear in the ballet theater: it is quiet, full of pauses (what the composer calls "silent sounds") and stems mainly from the religious ceremonial and theatrical music of the Orient. It employs numerous percussion and wind instruments, including the Shakuhachi, a bamboo flute used in Japan in the thirteenth century. This flute was played mainly by Zen Buddhist priests whose compositions for the instrument still survive. These musical-religious works are usually contemplative evocations of nature and the seasons. So also is this ballet—a contemplation on a man's life as seen through the passage of the four seasons. However influenced by the music and theater of the East, the ballet—its world, people and events—are not to be taken as Oriental.

Writing of *Watermill*, Jacqueline Maskey in *High Fidelity/Musical America* aptly described the theme: a ritual of remembering.

"The man recalls: himself as a youth, light and graceful, boneless as a leaping fish; the ritual games that test and harden him; the perfections of love in which his partner seems woman, earth, moon-goddess; then the devils, irrational phantoms that tear and torment. Peasant figures—sowing, reaping, winnowing, gleaning—thread through his recollections. He recognizes, in a ceremony with grain stalks, nature and his oneness with it and, in a bent figure, the inevitability of old age. As he gazes, boys release curious and buoyant paper shapes which rise into nothingness as must his own dust, and the curtain falls.

"*Watermill* is a particular view of human existence, expressed in terms of the inexorable cycle of the seasons. Man matures and declines; the moon waxes and wanes; the earth is fruitful, then fallow; snow follows sun."

The six musicians, all in Japanese costume, enter and sit on the right of the stage. A framed scrim faces us. As the music begins with a plaintive sound, we discern behind it gradually three high mysterious shapes that we can't quite make out—they are not trees, for wasp-waisted, they spread out at the base, too; they are not giants or windmills. They stand in a field filled with mist under a crescent moon. As the mist lifts a bit, we see that they are high sheaves of grain, the stalks gathered in tightly at the middle. There is a fence in the distance, and before we know it, we see there is a man there, too, standing in the field in a long black cloak, his face hidden, a part of the natural landscape, too. What we have gradually seen here and made out patiently in the mist is characteristic of the voyage of recollection and discovery that now begins for this man and for us.

Slowly, slowly, looking up for a moment at the sky, the man comes toward us. He kneels, rises, leaving his cloak on the ground. He takes off his shoes then, and his shirt and trousers. Standing now almost naked, he stretches out his arms as figures bearing multicolored lanterns approach him. They come up to him closely, their lanterns poised at the end of long wands, as if to illumine his body fully, then go away. To a chanted song that rises from the music, the man begins to dance. But not for long. He sits down and youths enter with kites, an umbrella, etc.

A boy runs as men in the background till the fields. The man notices the boy, reaches out his hand to him, but the boy sees another man in the distance and goes to him. Five boys trot across the field, five more, too, these carrying sticks. The man walks among them. They do warlike gymnastics, as if preparing for battle. But the man runs off. He returns as the youths stop and remain motionless.

A woman enters in a long green dress and turban. In the background, a group of young persons arrange a picnic on the grass behind one of the sheaves of grain. The woman puts down a rug on the grass. There is a longer period of waiting. She lets fall her outer garment and her long hair, which she combs slowly. The man watches her some distance away. We have the impression that he is both with her and is remembering her, their contact is so close. She lies down to sleep; so does he. Darkness falls. A boy—the man in his youth?—enters and goes to the woman. He pulls her body to his and she stretches around him; to the light of the moon they embrace closely. They roll and undulate together on the blanket and stop. The picnickers in the back rise and go; the moon keeps on descending.

The man awakens and lifts his arm. The boy on the blanket raises his arm simultaneously. The girl, too, hails the descending moon. The man and the boy rise together; the man goes to the girl as the boy backs out. The man takes the girl's hand, then lies with his head in her lap as, on the right, the boy of the first scene sleeps. The girl gets up, takes her rug, and leaves as the man and boy sleep.

There is a menacing atmosphere. A bearded creature enters; two black figures follow. The man wakes up the boy, and to howls it seems of dogs and the beat of percussion, there is an attack of some sort. The man watches; the boy runs off. The man stretches out now as if dead. Figures enter with baskets to gather pebbles. Leaves flutter down in the autumn air. The man glances up, then sits bowed over, head on knees. Rose petals fall. Peasants enter, take shafts of wheat and let them balance and fall within their fingers. The moon rises and is seen in eclipse. The man kneels and watches the peasants as ever so slowly they wave the stalks of wheat in the still air, then return them to the shaft. One girl remains and gives the man two wheat stalks. He holds them aloft, balancing them carefully; they seem to be balanced extensions of his arms. Snow falls gently. The man dances as it were with the stalks of wheat; they quiver in the evening air. The man kneels within a cross they have made of the stalks. A girl and boy come in with more wheat stalks as the snow thickens. The man moves, holding the stalks; they seem extensions of his arms and tremble at his every movement. Snow falls. He dances as it were with the stalks of quivering wheat, crossing them and kneeling as they cross. A girl and a boy enter with wheat tassles. They soon leave and the man rises as the boy returns; the girl does, too. The man lays down the cross of wheat and the boy who died. The snow has stopped. The man is alone. He takes up his cloak and leaves as an aged figure with a stick comes in. So, also, do men who carry on their shoulders heavy burdens. They cross the stage, slowly, at the back. Suddenly their burdens begin to lift off their shoulders and rise into the air. The curtain falls.

NOTES Nancy Goldner reviewed *Watermill* for *Dance News:* "Jerome Robbins's *Watermill* is one of the most perfect productions I have seen. It is beautiful, by all means—but it is more than that. It is exquisite. The details are the thing, although the work deals with large themes. The ballet is a meditation on nature. There is a meditator. His world is populated by seeders, tillers, harvesters, and phenomena of nature—the moon, wind, snow, stalks of wheat. Even the music, written by Teiji Ito and played by him and friends on the side of the stage, is as natural sounding as it is sounds of music. But it is always the details. Some boys wave small kites; each bobs at a different altitude. They also carry lanterns at different heights. This sensitivity to slight variation is exciting and moving. Four of the lanterns are large, in primary colors. Two of them are tiny and white. They look so fragile next to the larger ones. In addition to going through its phases, the moon ascends and descends. It seems to move when you're not looking. Its changing aspects are always something of a surprise. The wind which causes the wheat bundles to rustle is slight; it becomes a presence, like the moon. When fall comes, the leaves float onto the stage one by one. Even the snow seems to have been sprinkled over the land by a Haiku poet-god, so gentle is the fall and isolated the flakes. The list could go on. . . .

"The Orientalisms are not only in the music, props, and use of props. The entire spirit of *Watermill* is Orientally meditative. It unfolds slowly. With the exception of the dance of the spring/youth figure and the running sequence, which in itself is a rare-faction of the action—the boys and protagonist do a trot-like stylization of a run—the dancers move slowly, very slowly. Time becomes thick, sliceable. Edward Villella, the meditator-dreamer, has a quality here that suggests great power beneath the stillness. It is this suggestion of action that makes him so compelling, and maddening. Like the wind and moon, he becomes a presence. Unlike the moon, he does not mark the passing of time but seems to be a second of time stretched into forever. You either settle into his state of consciousness, or go insane. Maybe you can settle on a compromise by coughing and fidgeting. But you can't go to sleep. Robbins gets at some part of you.

"There are some obscure sections. Some actions are not definable by line and verse, but they do make emotional sense. Some things make such sense that they become permanent images in the mind. One such moment was the sound of wind before the nightmare. It struck to the core. It was one of the great moments in the theater. Oddly enough, though, the nightmare itself hit sideways. For me, the totality of the piece was not equal to some of the parts. Not because the parts were unconnected to each other and to the larger theme; on the contrary, never have I seen a dance so perfectly interrelated. But because the ballet is not so much about nature, time, life cycles, and whatnot as it is 'about' a particular state of consciousness. And now I must confess that I was one of those who were going insane. The moments when I was thoroughly engrossed were the moments when I was most detached from the proceedings, when my attention was drawn away from the slow-moving dancers and from time. Only my aesthetic sense was engaged and heightened. Robbins wanted the whole being to be there. Those who find dwelling on a stalk of wheat exhilarating will find *Watermill* a masterpiece to end all masterpieces. I can only admire Robbins' essay."

Writing in *Dance and Dancers* magazine, Patricia Barnes said: "Every so often—but not that often—a ballet turns up which instantly convinces one of its place in dance history. It becomes a landmark. Such a one is Jerome Robbins's *Watermill*, a creation of such imagination, depth and profundity that no one seeing it can remain untouched in some way by it. The first night audience greeted it with a mixture of cheers and boos; some were clearly baffled by its newness and just sat looking stunned and perplexed. But it is not just that it is new and different: innovation alone does not make great art. *Watermill* is, in addition, a work of extraordinary beauty: a poetic and deeply felt work that seems to have been torn from the very soul of its creator. It has even been suggested that the ballet is part autobiographical, and certainly the title is the same as the island where Robbins has his country home.

"In 1964 Robbins studied the Noh technique, and clearly what he learned has been stirring in his mind ever since. *Watermill* incorporates much that can be traced to Noh—the deliberation, refinement and simplicity of movement, the stripping away of excessive gesture—but despite the influence of the music and theater of the East, this ballet's world, people and events, according to a program note, are universal and not to be construed as Oriental.

"Another influence on this particular world appears to be Robert Wilson, the fascinating and provocative young director who has forged a whole new theater style, and who recently performed in Paris with enormous success. But the creative genius of *Watermill* is Robbins alone. How incredible this choreographer is, never sitting back on the laurels of past successes, never choosing the easy way, but constantly challenged by new vistas and new ideas, a choreographer who can equally touch the heart and stimulate the intellect."

# A WEDDING BOUQUET

*Comic ballet in one act. Music by Lord Berners. Choreography by Frederick Ashton. Words by Gertrude Stein. Scenery and costumes by Lord Berners. First presented by the Vic-Wells Ballet at the Sadler's Wells Theatre, London, April 27, 1937, with Mary Honer as the Bride, Robert Helpmann as the Bridegroom, Margot Fonteyn as Julia, June Brae as Josephine, Julia Farron as Pépé, and Ninette de Valois as Webster. First presented in the United States by the Sadler's Wells Ballet at the Metropolitan Opera House, New York, October 25, 1949, with Margaret Dale as the Bride, Robert Helpmann as the Bridegroom, Moira Shearer as Julia, June Brae as Josephine, Pauline Clayden as Pépé, and Palma Nye as Webster.*

When *A Wedding Bouquet* was first presented, one critic called it a *ballet bouffe*. That is exactly what it is: a comic work that achieves some of its funniest farce by exposing the absurdity of great dignity and seriousness. Its subject, a wedding in a provincial French town near the turn of the century, presents a set of conventions that must not be upset; and at the cost of many laughs, all the conventions are observed. They are observed in the determined, apparently senseless fashion with which people in René Clair movies observe their conventions: everything seems to combine against them, but in the end everything is all right. It is possible to watch *A Wedding Bouquet* and see it as a continental comic equivalent to the Edwardian pathos of such a ballet as *Lilac Garden*. Gertrude Stein's commentary on the action is spoken during the ballet by an observing orator.

The curtain rises on the garden of a farmhouse near Bellay. There is a long table set out for the wedding feast, and the ballet begins as people scurry about preparing the refreshments. Webster, the maid, is certain that things will not be ready by the time the bride and groom arrive. On the right, sitting apart from the scene, is the orator. He pours himself a glass of champagne.

As the guests begin to arrive, the orator speaks over the music to tell us about some of them. In addition to the peasant girls and boys and the usual gate crashers, there are Josephine ("She may be wearing a gown newly washed and pressed") and her two friends, Paul ("Pleasant, vivacious, and quarrelsome") and John ("An elder brother who regrets the illness of his father"). There is the aggressive young lady Violet ("Violet, oh will you ask him to marry you?"), who eagerly pursues a young man named Ernest ("May be the victim of himself"). Ernest eagerly repulses Violet's advances.

Now Julia enters. The orator tells us that she "Is known as forlorn," and forlorn she certainly is. She can hardly walk, she is so dejected. Apparently the trouble is that the fickle bridegroom of the day has abandoned her. Tagging along behind Julia is her dog, a Mexican terrier called Pépé ("Little dogs resemble little girls"). Julia directs all her affections to Pépé, and Pépé switches her tail like a little girl honored with a lollipop. One of the men tries to cheer Julia up, but Pépé protects her mistress. It appears that Josephine is terribly sorry for Julia. She tries to comfort her like a true friend, and Julia sulks with lunatic pleasure.

The bridal party approaches. First, the bride ("Charming! Charming! Charming!"). The bridesmaids dance together under her bridal veil. The bridegroom is clearly harassed. ("They all speak as if they expected him not to be charming.") As if the silly wedding weren't enough, he must now deal with the guests ("They incline to oblige only when they stare") and with Julia. The sight of this demented past indiscretion of his makes the bridegroom despair. Patiently he poses with the bridal party for a photograph of the wedding group. Then he tries to act as if nothing had happened.

Julia won't let him. She hangs on him like a cat. She won't give him up! The guests titter and chatter among themselves, guessing at the bridegroom's situation. Pépé tries to distract the bride, who begins to be suspicious. The bridegroom tries to push Julia off, and she throws herself at his feet. The bride despairs.

Now Josephine, too, is crying in her beer. She is so upset, because Julia is upset, that she drinks far too much. She starts to make the inevitable scene and is asked to leave. The groom, alone with Julia and all the other girls he's been intimate with, dances a bright tango. When he observes all these demanding women, he is lighthearted: marriage has set him free at last! Apparently his new bride sees how lucky she is.

Night begins to fall and the guests start to leave ("Thank you. Thank you."). The bridegroom goes to his bride, and the unhappy Julia is left alone. She still has Pépé, however. The dog tries to comfort her as Julia stupidly stares off into space.

## WEEWIS

*Original commissioned score by Stanley Walden. Rock group: Virgin Wool. Choreography by Margo Sappington. Lighting by Jennifer Tipton. First presented by the Joffrey City Center Ballet at the City Center, New York, October 28, 1971, with Gary Chryst, James Dunne, Rebecca Wright, Christian Holder, Susan Magno, and Tony Catanzaro.*

The name of this ballet is a small mystery: it is the name of the choreographer's cat. *Weewis* is a dance ballet, a series of duets, performed to the music of a rock group. Writing of the ballet in *Time*, the critic John T. Elson said that the three couples "appear to exemplify the varying moods of love (definitely profane)." The first dance is for two boys. The second is for a girl and boy and shows the sinuous variations possible in sophisticated lovemaking. The third dance is a fierce apache number for another girl and boy.

## WESTERN SYMPHONY

*Ballet in three movements. Music by Hershy Kay. Choreography by George Balanchine. Scenery by John Boyt. Costumes by Karinska. First presented by the New York City Ballet at the New York City Center, September 7, 1954, with Diana Adams, Herbert Bliss, Janet Reed, Nicholas Magallanes, Patricia Wilde, Tanaquil LeClercq, Jacques d'Amboise, and others.*

My idea in this ballet was to make a formal work that would derive its flavor from the informal American West, a ballet that would move within the framework of the classic school but in a new atmosphere. Earlier ballets on American folk themes (*Billy the Kid, Rodeo,* et al.) have been based on cowboy lore, but these have been story ballets. I wanted to do a ballet without a story in an unmistakably native American idiom. To accomplish that, I needed a new score and turned to the young composer Hershy Kay.

*Western Symphony* was a close collaboration between us. I was neither interested in local atmosphere nor narrative pantomime and told Kay that I wanted to try a symphonic American dance work which, by the impetus of indigenous melodies, would help me to use the universal language of the classic ballet in a fresh way. He liked the idea and wrote a symphony to order, a work in four movements, based on themes like "Red River Valley," "Old Taylor," "The Gal I Left Behind Me," "Rye Whiskey," "Golden Slippers," and others. To these movements I arranged a series of dance ensembles that I hope have some of the sentiment and candor of the time and places where those tunes were first sung.

I have crossed the United States by car some dozen times, have camped in the open air in New Mexico and Wyoming, in Montana and South Dakota. The vast sweep of the land, the impression of the Rockies and the plains, and the vision of the men who crossed the mountains and worked the plains, on foot and on horseback, cannot fail to move any newcomer, particularly one who has fresh memories of Europe, most of which is closely settled and where there have been few empty natural spaces for thousands of years.

*Western Symphony* was originally presented in practice clothes without a set. This was regrettable but we had no money at that time and had to wait for the following season for the designs of John Boyt and Karinska to materialize. The original four movements of the ballet have since been cut to three, omitting the third movement. In 1956, in Paris, during our third European tour, the United States Information Agency made a color film of the ballet with all its four movements.

# THE WHIMS OF CUPID AND THE BALLET MASTER

*Music by Jens Lolle. Choreography by Vincenzo Galeotti. First presented by the Royal Danish Ballet at the Royal Theatre, Copenhagen, October 31, 1786. First presented in the United States by the Royal Danish Ballet at the Metropolitan Opera House, New York, September 22, 1956. Scenery and costumes by Ove Christian Pedersen.*

This is said to be the oldest ballet in the repertory. It has survived for almost two centuries at the Royal Theatre in Copenhagen and has never been omitted for such a length of time as to prevent several of the previous cast from assisting the new production, thus carrying on the original choreography by Galeotti in the proper spirit. Galeotti, who came to Denmark from Italy as early as 1775, is the first choreographer of importance to the Danish ballet.

The story is a comedy about lovers from many countries who come to pay tribute to the god Cupid. They dance before him the characteristic styles of their lands and then he plays a trick, blindfolding the couples. The curious matchmaking that results leads to hilarity and what the original program called a finale of "great confusion."

# WHO CARES?

*Music by George Gershwin, orchestrated by Hershy Kay. Choreography by George Balanchine. Costumes by Karinska. Lighting by Ronald Bates. Pianist: Gordon Boelzner. First presented by the New York City Ballet at the New York State Theatre, Lincoln Center, February 5, 1970, with Karin von Aroldingen, Patricia McBride, Marnee Morris, and Jacques d'Amboise as the principal dancers.*

This ballet is a set of dances to some songs by George Gershwin that I have always liked very much. "Who Cares?" goes back to 1931 and *Of Thee I Sing.* In Europe in the late 1920s and 1930s, we all knew Gershwin's music and loved it; it is beautiful, very American, too. Before I came to America I saw the Gershwin musical *Funny Face* in London and admired it. I did some work in musical comedies in London after that and continued to make dances for them after I came to New York. I don't think I would have done that if it had not been for George Gershwin's music. There are popular songs and popular songs; Gershwin's are special.

I was lucky enough to know Gershwin, who asked me to Hollywood to do dances for the movie *Goldwyn Follies.* Gershwin gave me a book of his songs, arranged in the way he used to do them in concerts. One day at the piano I played one through and thought to myself, Beautiful, I'll make a *pas de deux.* Then I played another, it was just as beautiful and I thought, A variation! And then another and another and there was no end to how beautiful they were.

And so we had a new ballet. No story, just the songs. Here they are, with the dancers who first danced them: "Strike Up the Band" (1927), Ladies and Gentlemen; "Sweet and Low Down" (1925), Ensemble; "Somebody Loves Me" (1924), Deborah Flomine, Susan Hendl, Linda Merrill, Susan Pilarre, Bettijane Sills; "Bidin' My Time" (1930), Deni Lamont, Robert Maiorano, Frank Ohman, Richard Rapp, Earle Sieveling; "'S Wonderful" (1927), Susan Pilarre and Richard Rapp; "That Certain Feeling" (1925), Deborah Flomine and Deni Lamont, Bettijane Sills, and Earl Sieveling; "Do Do Do" (1926), Susan Hendl and Frank Ohman; "Lady Be Good" (1924), Linda Merrill and Robert Maiorano; "The Man I Love" (1924), Patricia McBride and Jacques d'Amboise; "I'll Build a Stairway to Paradise" (1922), Karin von Aroldingen; "Embraceable You" (1930), Marnee Morris and Jacques d'Amboise; "Fascinatin' Rhythm" (1924), Patricia McBride; "Who Cares?" (1931), Karin von Aroldingen and Jacques d'Amboise; "My One and Only" (1927), Marnee Morris; "Liza" (1929), Jacques d'Amboise; "Clap Yo' Hands" (1926), Karin von Aroldingen, Patricia McBride, Marnee Morris, Jacques d'Amboise; "I Got Rhythm" (1930), Entire Cast.

NOTES  The first performance of *Who Cares?* had only an orchestral beginning ("Strike Up the Band") because the composer Hershy Kay, who was arranging the songs for us, was busy with a musical. Gordon Boelzner, the pianist, played all the other songs except for "Clap Yo' Hands," where we played a recording of Gershwin doing the piece himself. We still do.

We did not have much scenery for the ballet at the beginning. This was provided later by Jo Mielziner, November 21, 1970, who gave us a scrim with two layers of silhouetted skylines of New York in a kind of fan shape for the backdrop and, for the sides of the stage, skyscraper cliffs.

When *Who Cares?* was first done, Lincoln Kirstein wrote an extensive note for our program: "*Who Cares?* is both the name of a new ballet in the classical idiom by George Balanchine and an old song George and Ira Gershwin wrote in 1931 for *Of Thee I Sing*. The dictionary says *classic* means standard, leading, belonging to the highest rank of authority. Once it applied mainly to masterpieces from Greco-Roman antiquity; now we have boxing and horse racing classics, classic cocktail dresses and classic cocktails. Among classic American composers we number Stephen Foster, John Philip Sousa and George Gershwin (1898–1937). First heard fifty years ago, the best of the Gershwin songs maintain their classic freshness, as of an eternal martini—dry, frank, refreshing, tailor-made with an invisible kick from its slightest hint of citron. Nostalgia has not syruped their sentiment nor robbed them of immediate piquancy. We associate them with time past, but when well sung or played, or preferably both at once, they not only revive but transcend their epoch. Lovely in themselves they are by way of becoming art songs, which that beautiful singer Eva Gauthier long ago realized when she first sang them in concert well after they had become familiar hits. The Gershwins wrote hit songs which were art songs. Most art songs pretend to be love songs; the Gershwin genre seem to be about playmates more than lovers. It was not by accident the best dance team of the time, Fred and Adele Astaire, were brother and sister.

"To the musician George Gershwin, perhaps their most important element was their potential as piano pieces. He played energetically, long and magically at private parties and in public. His semi-improvisational style was taken seriously even by 'serious' critics. Gilbert Seldes, our first popularizer of what we now call pop art (in painting as well as theater), indeed complained that *The Rhapsody in Blue* was a masterpiece marred by Liszt-like extended cadenzas; certainly Gershwin was a hypnotic virtuoso as well as a knowing and generous analyst of the jazz style of which he was a master. This he traced to the individual ragtimers at the turn of the century whose collective ingenuities in piano playing built up a tradition which he inherited, and which he used with a new articulate sophistication, flexibility and brilliance.

"But there is another serious aspect of the Gershwin songs which marks their sturdy structure—words supporting the tunes, mainly by his brother Ira. The wit, tact, invention, metaphor and metric of Ira's rhymes meant that you not only left the theater whistling melodies, but singing words. His phrasing was simple enough, his phrases sharp enough to impose themselves at one hearing; once heard, they were almost infectiously memorable. Love & dove, June & moon, true & you long comprised the pidgin English of Tin Pan Alley. Ira Gershwin not only transubstantiated such base metal; with condescension or parody he created a new prosody, a new means for lyric writing which incorporated the season's slang, references to local events, echoes of the vernacular rhythms of ordinary speech in a frame of casual thrown-away elegance which was never false, insistent or self-conscious. He seemed to have stumbled on what was right, fitting, appropriate, surprising and charming, as if such had been coins tossed in his path. But such coinage is art, not accident, and Ira incidentally was a poet and a master of mnemonics. He was also a satirist; there had always been comic ballads, but it is odd to find in 'Strike Up the Band' (1927), an ostensibly patriotic hit tune, its almost Brechtian tang. . . . Ira Gershwin's lyric style involved his skill in manipulating repetition, shift of breath, perfect punctuation, instinct for vulgarism in a mosaic of unusual context, plus a laconic polish. His vocabulary was small; both Noel Coward and Cole Porter were more literary; Lorenz Hart's smashing pastiches depended on a wide reading. These three derived from Gilbert and Sullivan, a more operatic or light-operatic tradition. Ira was in the line of minstrelsy—the minstrel show and the ancient descent from troubador soloists. All the songs sang 'I love you,' but Ira's hummed it with a unique American, or rather Manhattan (cocktail), simplicity and savor. Lyrics are to be sung, not enunciated like patter songs, or launched—like arias. In love songs, intense emotion is usually in inverse proportion to the heartbreak clarity of words. George Gershwin's tunes were not impassioned but playful. Their pretext was not profound feelings, but sportive sex, flirtatious games, gallantry in a tennis tournament: love, set, match. George Gershwin took forms and archetypes as he received them and composed something unheard before out of formulae. He did not so much write parodies of Negro spirituals, barroom ballads or cowboy songs; he appropriated familiar atmospheres and by his mastery whipped them into the strict form of the hit song, as someone might break a green colt into a pacer. He alternated tenderness with ironic narcissism, or contrasted a smashing climax with the most delicate expression of loss or confusion. And Ira's lyrics were indeed—lyric: personal, enthusiastic, eminently singable. The Gershwins were showmen; they gloried in hits, show stoppers, grand finales with everybody shouting in the aisles, but their brashest choirs never obscured the fragility of certain solos when George almost seemed to be singing to himself. Idiosyncratic serenades, at once self-deprecatory and wistful, they were as elegant, athletic and lonely as he was in life, which no one knew better than his brother.

"This faintly confessional residue of George Gershwin is a touching legacy. In 1930, for *Girl Crazy*, he and Ira wrote a deliberately paced number for a chorus of dubious cowboys, dude ranch gigolos leaning on the fence of a Reno divorce ranch. The wrangler of 1930 had already become a drugstore cowboy on his way to becoming a midnight cowboy; but forty years ago he was more the dandy than the hustler. And in Ira's deft quotation of the titles of four popular songs in his introduction, we have his compliments to colleagues in the song writing industry, a delicious in-joke of the era, as well as a not unjustified boast of the Gershwin superiority, as aristocrats of American lyricism, masters of music to the American electorate. The Gershwins' beautiful manners and high style, their instant melange of insouciance and shrewd innocence, their just estimation of the imaginative elasticity of an elite audience which they had developed, have left a body of words and music which lives, unblurred by vulgar rhetoric or machine-made sentiment. To combine an intensely personal attitude with a flagrantly popular language is a feat which few popular artists manage, and it is appropriate that Balanchine has used the songs not as facile recapitulation of a lost epoch, but simply as songs, or melodies for classic, un-deformed, traditional academic dances, which in their equivalence of phrasing, dynamics and emotion, find their brotherly parallel."

Soon after the first performances, Arlene Croce, editor of *Ballet Review*, wrote about the ballet in the *Dancing Times*: "The title of Balanchine's Gershwin ballet, *Who Cares?*, has a double significance. It means, Who Cares what we call it ('as long as I care for you and you care for me'), and it suggests that the piece is an elegant throwaway. That's how it looks, too—like nothing much. The curtain goes up while the orchestra is playing 'Strike Up the Band' and we see a double exposure of Manhattan skylines projected in a pinkish haze on the backcloth. An excellent idea, but it stops there. The rest of the stage looks bleak. The girls wear their very well-cut Karinska tutus, this time in turquoise and lemon-yellow. The skirts have pleats and look 1920s and mini-mod at the same time. So do the boys' black bellbottom slacks. Like the title and the sky-line, everything has a double impact, with one effect or style superimposed on another—Now on Then, ballet dancing on show tunes. The two planes of meaning are so shuffled that we're never completely in one world or the other, we're in both at once. Or rather, we're in four worlds since *Who Cares?* scram-bles two elements, classical dancing and show dancing, and two eras, the Twenties and the Seventies, with equal paronomasiac facility. And since the Twenties was itself a period of classical revival, the play of references can grow almost infinitely complex. When Balanchine has five boys do double air turns (one boy at a time) in 'Bidin' My Time,' we're pleased with ourselves for thinking of the boys' variation in *Raymonda*, Act Three (the metrical swing of the music is pretty much the same), and even more pleased when we remember the masculine ensemble that made the song famous in *Girl Crazy*. That's simple enough. But when toward the end of the ballet his four stars fly across the stage to 'Clap Yo' Hands' in what is unmistakably a series of quotations from *Apollo*, we catch an unframeable glimpse of the multiple precedents *Who Cares?* is made of. It's then that we see, for just the flash of the moment that he gives us to see it, how comradely the links are between the Gershwin of *Lady Be Good!*, *Tip Toes*, *Oh, Kay!* and *Funny Face*, and the syncopated Stravinsky of *Apollon Musagete*. We notice that the dancers in the ballet wear necktie-belts in homage not only to Astaire but to the Chanel who in 1928 knotted men's striped cravats around the waists of Apollo's muses. But the allusion to 1928 isn't endstopped; it reverberates with *Apollo*'s own recapitulations of the Nineties and Marius Petipa—high noon at the Maryinsky—and so we are borne back ceaselessly into the past. To the question 'What is classicism?' Balanchine responds with a blithe shrug and a popular song. Classicism is the Hall of Fame viewed as a hall of mirrors. The Fun House. . . .

"The ballet suddenly . . . finds its own life—when the boys and girls start dancing out in pairs to ''S Wonderful,' 'That Certain Feeling,' 'Do Do Do,' and 'Lady Be Good'; the dance invention tumbles forth, so does the applause, and we realize that what we're going to see is not a clever foreigner's half-infatuated, half-skeptical view of a popular American art form, we're going to see the art form itself, re-energized. But this spectacle we see isn't like a musical comedy, it's more like a lieder recital with a few social mannerisms mostly in the pleasant, sappy, ingenue style of Old Broadway. Just when you think that maybe the dancers do represent a musical comedy chorus full of stock types (with Linda Merrill as the company's inevitable redhead), they vanish and another ballet, or musical, or recital begins.

"The second half of *Who Cares?* has an *Apollo*-type cast—one boy (Jacques d'Amboise) and three girls (Patricia McBride, Marnee Morris, and Karin von Aroldingen). Each girl dances once with the boy and once by herself and then the boy dances alone. They are all four together in the Apollonian coda. The music is the same parade of Gershwin hits that has been going on since the beginning, only now, with the lights blue and the stars out, we listen more intently. If this is a musical comedy world, it's the most beautiful one ever imagined. In 'Fascinatin' Rhythm,' Patricia McBride holds a high extension in second and then in two or three lightning shifts of weight refocuses the whole silhouette while keeping on top of the original pose. It's so charming to see in relation to that unexpected stutter in the music which unexpectedly recurs, that it hits the audience like a joke, but that's fascinating rhythm, and that's *Who Cares?* Classical syntax, jazz punctuation. I couldn't begin to say what d'Amboise's solo to 'Liza' is composed of, though—it suggests soft-shoe virtuoso tap and classical lift and amplitude all at once, and d'Amboise, whose style in classical ballet has characteristically a casual, crooning softness played against sudden monkey-like accelerandos and sharp bursts of detail, dances it in total splendor. Everywhere the tight choreography sustains an almost unbelievable musical interest.

"As if it weren't enough for Balanchine to give us dances of extreme tension and wit and elegance, he also gives us back the songs unadorned by their usual stagey associations. 'Stairway to Paradise' isn't a big production number; it's one girl (von Aroldingen) covering ground in powerful colt-like jumps and turns. And in the duets, the emotion is more serious (the sense of receding hopes, for example, in 'The Man I Love') for not being acted out. It isn't emotion that dominates the stage so much as a musical faith that the choreography keeps, and that's what convinces us that the songs are good for more than getting drunk at the St. Regis by—that they have theatrical momentousness and contemporary savor. Gershwin in 1970, in the age of Burt Bacharach, has no trouble sounding classical, and that is how Balanchine hears him.

"I am also persuaded that Balanchine hears Gershwin the way Gershwin composed, i.e. pianistically, and this brings up the subject of orchestration and Hershy Kay. Kay had been set the task of orchestrating sixteen of the seventeen songs that Balanchine uses in *Who Cares?* (one number, 'Clap Yo' Hands,' is a recording made by Gershwin himself at the piano), but because of commitments to the Broadway show *Coco,* Kay has so far orchestrated only the opening ('Strike Up the Band') and closing ('I Got Rhythm') songs. The remaining fourteen songs were played for the three performances of *Who Cares?* that were given this season, with his customary sensitivity and attack, by Gordon Boelzner, from Gershwin's own concert arrangements. These piano arrangements were unvaryingly simple: verse followed by chorus followed (sometimes twice) by chorus repeat. But they are also beautiful examples of Gershwin's highly developed keyboard technique. Gershwin's pianism was comparable in its own time to Gottschalk's, and I hope Kay's further orchestrations of Gershwin are as good as the ones he did for the Gottschalk ballet *Cakewalk,* by far his best orchestration for the ballet theater. To my disappointed ear, his 'Strike Up the Band' and 'I Got Rhythm' were in the vulgarized idiom of his 'Stars and Stripes'-hotcha added to heat; and while the musical format of *Who Cares?* precludes his 'symphonizing' in the style of *Western Symphony,* orchestral thickening could destroy the bone-dry delicacy, the tonal transparency of this music and should be avoided like temptation. The more so as Balanchine has taken such evident delight in choreographing the countermelodies, cross-rhythms and abrupt syncopations out of which Gershwin built his compositions—it isn't all razz-ma-tazz—and not since the heyday of Fred Astaire have such felicities been observed.

"Fred and Ginger, Fred and Adele, George and Ira, George and Igor . . . it's easy to be seduced by the nostalgia of it all, but the remarkable thing about *Who Cares?* is how infrequently it appeals to that nostalgia. It certainly makes no appeal on the basis of period glamor or period Camp. The multiple images, the visual punning, the sense of a classical perspective—all of that sweeps by with a strength of evocation more powerful than any individual moment of recognition. It's mysterious, the mythological intensity built up by a ballet that doesn't seem to have a thought in its airy head. No single cultural myth seems to be at the core of it. Manhattan in the Golden Twenties, penthouse parties, where composers of brilliance entertained at the baby grand until dawn, are lovely to think about but aren't the subject of *Who Cares?* any more than a rainbow on a wet afternoon is. To put it as simply as I can, this wonderful ballet enriches our fantasy life immeasurably, as works of art are meant to do. It's tonic, medicinal, too. Its fresh unclouded feeling seems to strike with special directness at the city's depressed spirits. Just before the première (on February 5), Balanchine received New York City's biggest award for cultural achievement, the Handel medallion, on the stage of the State Theatre. He made a number of jokes in the disreputable manner of his hero on such occasions, Bob Hope, had what they call in show business a 'good roll,' and then rang up the curtain on a Gershwin march. The Higher Seriousness didn't have a chance, but who cares?—the ballet was a beaut."

The critic Robert Sealy has also written at length of his impressions of the first performances of *Who Cares?* (in *Ballet Review*, Vol. 3, No. 3).

"*Who Cares?* is a brilliant high wire act: a classical ballet to Gershwin show tunes. It must have been difficult to get it all set, balanced and in focus, to keep it from becoming what it most definitely is *not:* nostalgia, show biz, Broadway, dear old Busby or anything, for that matter, to do with the past. It is to be danced at the moment, in the now of things. What it's really about is the inherent joy of being a man or a woman with a healthy body and the ability to *dance, dance, dance.* As usual, Balanchine has walked the wire over the falls.

"Like all strong, self-assured artists, Balanchine makes his intention clear right at the beginning; he puts his hands on your head and *makes* you see it his way. The principals do not appear in the *Raymonda* part. To emphasize that *Who Cares?* is a classical ballet, eight songs ('Strike Up the Band,' 'Sweet and Low Down,' 'Somebody Loves Me,' 'Bidin' My Time,' ''S Wonderful,' 'That Certain Feeling,' 'Do Do Do,' 'Lady Be Good') have been made into a suite of classical dances, by turns dainty, humorous, robust and romantic, and given to the ensemble. Many people squirm in their seats (as they would through the prologue to *The Sleeping Beauty* or the first act of *Swan Lake*) waiting for the stars; they object to this 'Eat your greens before dessert' attitude—but I think the greens are delicious. 'Somebody Loves Me,' the second number after the 'icebreaker,' is rather daring in that it is a *very* long pas de cinq. Four little girls who might be on the field hockey scrub team, led by Captain Bettijane Sills, twirl and kick over and over, so sweetly, so demurely, the sort of thing the swan girls do while waiting for Odette. It is very appealing, but it makes the audience rather cross. This is exactly the sort of thing in NYCB repertory where proper setting and lighting would help (a hockey field in Riverside Park just before spring dusk, for example). As it is, it must flounder about by itself and get crushed by the big kids. In the first 'act,' 'Bidin' My Time' is the crucial support of the piece, the stem of the flower: heavily masculine quotes from *Raymonda* danced by five men. Unfortunately, the boys are too willowy and not up to it. What is wanted is the easy coordination of a basketball team warming up, easily, almost languidly, the tension is ahead. The last four songs are one long dance with a fresh use of strutaways and rapid turns, especially in the breathless pas de quatre, 'That Certain Feeling.'

"A Gershwin *Apollon Musagéte*—behind the Metropolitan Museum certainly. This memorable quartet dances to eight songs: 'The Man I Love' (Apollo, Terpsichore); 'I'll Build a Stairway to Paradise' (Calliope); 'Embraceable You' (Apollo, Polyhymnia); 'Fascinating Rhythm' (Terpsichore); 'Who Cares?' (Apollo, Calliope); 'My One and Only' (Polyhymnia); 'Liza' (Apollo) and 'Clap Yo' Hands' (the fingers-to-chin, muscled roundabout, Apollo-and-the-muses-at-play part, before the call to Mount Olympus). I am afraid I must call it an affair of sentiment, retire before it and pass out. Never in a theater have I wanted so much to jump the moat and join in. It is pure, unmitigated, uncut joy, an open, palpitating, vulnerable heart on the sleeve. Patricia McBride as Terpsichore clears the high Petipa hurdles of 'Fascinating Rhythm' with room to spare; Jacques d'Amboise (who else?) as Apollo does the big solo leaps in yellow shoes and has a finish of arms-raised ecstasy; and the two of them in 'The Man I Love,' angular, cat-wary, in and out of each other's arms, alternately aloof and impassioned, alert to the rising and falling sounds from the piano, have the memory-burning dance of a lifetime. It is finally Gershwin's music itself, with its slight pretentiousness, its striving after The Better Things (this uniquely New York thing that makes 'Rhapsody in Blue' and *Porgy and Bess* rise above derivation, surpass eclecticism and become great light music) that jells the ballet, preserves Balanchine's fast-stepping, high-breasted, cheeky, slightly put-on attitudes and keeps the whole thing from becoming a dance cavalcade of evergreens."[*]

## WILLIAM TELL VARIATIONS

*Music by Gioacchino Rossini. Choreography by Auguste Bournonville. Staged by Hans Brenaa. Lighting by Thomas Skelton. First presented in the United States by the City Center Joffrey Ballet at City Center, New York, March 23, 1969, with Charthel Arthur and Luis Fuente as principals.*

This dance ballet by the great Danish ballet master has an interesting history. There are several versions of it, one claiming that the ballet originated in another form as a *divertissement* in the first production of Rossini's *William Tell* at the Paris Opéra, August 3, 1829, another that it derives from Bournonville's *Tyrolerne,* an idyllic one-act ballet with music by J. F. Frohlich first performed March 3, 1835. *Tyrolerne,* according to Clive Barnes, who knows the Danish ballet and its history extremely well, also had music by Rossini; it is his theory that Bournonville later expanded the Rossini score with music from *William Tell.* The ballerina Marie Taglioni danced a famed *Tyrolienne* at the first performance of Rossini's opera but the choreography for her dance was by Aumer, not Bournonville.

In any case, Bournonville's ballet is a treasure of the Danish tradition and was taught to Hans Brenaa, who staged the work, when he was a young student at the Royal Danish Ballet School.

It is a dance ballet for a girl and a boy and two supporting couples, an entertainment for the eye and ear to glorious music by Rossini.

[*] Reprinted by permission of *Ballet Review,* Marcel Dekker, publisher.

## THE WIND IN THE MOUNTAINS

*A Country Calendar. Music by Laurence Rosenthal. Choreography by Agnes de Mille. Costumes by Stanley Simmons. Lighting by Jean Rosenthal. First presented by the American Ballet Theatre at the New York State Theatre, March 17, 1965, with Joseph Carow, Karen Krych, Gayle Young, Judith Lerner, and William Glassman in the principal roles.*

To a score based largely on early American songs and folk tunes, this dance narrative traces the progress of the seasons in the country—"Traveling Weather," "Wind," "Ice," "Rain," "Natural Catastrophe," "All Clear," "Apotheosis." It begins with a cowboy shouting out to the mountains and the world, "Hello, there," and his words echo back from the hills. A pathfinder enters, then a young couple in love dance with their friends. A lady in red tries to lure the boy away, he follows her and his girl laments. Another suitor tries to cheer her up but she falls on the ice and is undone. Then in the rain she is alone and sad when she sees her lover. A man prays and the rain stops. A train is heard in the distance and in comes a stranger, a Wild West traveling salesman who delights the whole town. The ladies fall at his feet, except the girl, who remains faithful to the memory of the boy. The boy comes back. A square dance is called and around and around in a big circle to a hymnal tune the friends and neighbors go.

## WITCH BOY

*Music by Leonard Salzedo. Libretto and choreography by Jack Carter. Scenery and costumes by Norman McDowell. First presented by the Ballet der Lage Landen, Amsterdam, May 24, 1956, with Norman McDowell in the title role. First presented in the United States by the National Ballet at the Lisner Auditorium, Washington, D.C., March 29, 1971, with Gerard Sibbritt in the title role.*

Based on the American folk ballad of Barbara Allan and set in the Smoky Mountains about the turn of the century, *Witch Boy* is the work of British choreographer and dancer Jack Carter. Carter has said that the theme of the ballet "is that very nice, ordinary people can, by force of circumstances, be turned into a mob." *Witch Boy*'s story, of frontier days, tells of the unwelcome advances a Preacher makes to Barbara Allan, who flees to the mountains to escape him. There on the mountainside, she meets the Witch Boy, a possessed, handsome youth, child of the Conjureman. They fall in love.

Bringing the Witch Boy back to her home town, Barbara Allan finds that things are not so simple. Though the two join in the dancing they find there, her friends and relatives clearly think the Witch Boy an odd choice for her to make, particularly when the Preacher loves her. In addition to his quaint mountain garb, the Witch Boy behaves in a manic way that visibly makes all the townsfolk nervous. The Preacher, seizing the chance to put down the competition, craftily suggests to his parishioners that the boy is guilty of witchcraft. Their response is instantaneous and violent: they beat the boy and lynch him. As he hangs from a tree, the Conjureman returns, mourns, and by the magic he possesses, a new Witch Boy appears, born afresh to haunt the community and future Barbara Allans.

NOTES *Witch Boy* was an important vehicle for the English *premier danseur* John Gilpin, whose dramatic interpretation was much applauded. He first danced the part in the London Festival Ballet's production of November 27, 1957, with Anita Landa as Barbara Allan.

Talking with critic Jean Battey Lewis of the Washington *Post* at the time of *Witch Boy*'s American premier, in 1971, Jack Carter spoke of the power of classical ballet: "Putting on a ballet in sneakers and jeans doesn't make it original. And I don't think you need bare feet and dirty soles to show emotion. I think classical ballet technique is so strong it can absorb new discoveries in movement. I'm interested in movement to say something. Antony Tudor started me off. In *Lilac Garden* you can see people think through movement. I'm interested in people and the human relationship."

Reviewing the National Ballet's production, Clive Barnes wrote in the New York *Times* that *Witch Boy* "is a sensationally theatrical ballet, with a couple of parthenogenetic births, a hell-fire preacher and a lynch party. It is a very strong dramatic work with a wonderful part for the Witch Boy. Gerard Sibbritt danced with great dramatic strength, providing the role with febrile agony, and that animalistically evil quality, ill-defined but menacing, that the Witch Boy must possess." The part of the Preacher has been notably danced in England by Anton Dolin and by Frederic Franklin in the United States. Lydia Diaz-Cruz danced Barbara Allan in the National Ballet's production.

# PART TWO

## *How to Enjoy Ballet*

It is strange that many people think ballet is a difficult thing to enjoy. Ballet isn't any harder to enjoy than a novel, a play, or a poem—it's as simple to like as a baseball game.

Yet imagine a person who goes to a baseball game for the first time. He hasn't played the game, he doesn't know the rules, and he gets confused trying to watch everything at once. He feels out of place and annoyed because he isn't sure why everyone else is so excited.

If he had played baseball himself, he wouldn't have this problem. But he doesn't have to play to enjoy. Once he knows what it's all about, once he understands why the players run and slide and leap and catch as they do, he begins to appreciate the game. He becomes familiar with its elements, he enjoys it. The same thing is true of ballet.

Dancing is very popular here in America. Most of us learn to dance when we are young. And I don't mean ballet dancing. We hear music just about everywhere we go; we have a response to its rhythm and melody and want to express this response in a natural way, so we begin to dance. Ballet dancing is an entirely different thing from ballroom dancing, the dancing most familiar to us, though that, too, requires skill. Ballet also began in the ballroom, in the courts of Italy and France, but over the years it has been elevated to the stage and has become an art. This art is based on something natural to us, response to music, but it expresses this response in a specific, formalized way. Over the past four hundred years, dancers and ballet masters have built up a grammar of movement, a synthesis of what is anatomically possible and pleasing. This is the basic vocabulary of the dancer and the people who make ballets. They have to learn it like a language, from the elementary forms and words. The choreographer chooses certain elements he wants from ballet's extensive vocabulary, makes some new ones, and arranges all these in a new pattern to a meter he derives from music. But we don't have to understand this language in detail to enjoy ballet, any more than we have to know about the pigments of the painter or the complex meters of the poet.

Ballet takes our natural impulse to move, to make signs, to make ourselves as attractive and graceful as possible, and turns it into something new, something entirely different. Perhaps what we see the first time we go to the ballet we don't like at all. Dancers in strange costumes do nothing but move to a piece of music we're unfamiliar with; people who represent characters in an ancient Greek myth, for example, dance a story we don't remember much about; or characters in a modern story-ballet behave quite differently from the people next door. We come away saying that ballet's unnatural.

This is exactly true: ballet is unnatural, it has nothing to do with our daily lives in an immediate sense. What ballet does is to take movements we're all familiar with—running and jumping, turning and balancing, lifting and holding

—and mold attitudes that underlie these actions into a spectacle that entertains. The melodies we hear in music are very different from the natural noises we hear in the everyday world: the slamming of doors, running brooks, the sound of wind in the trees. Melody is artificial, it is made by man. Ballet is artificial in this same sense: its roots are in everyday life, but it is created by artists. What ballet takes from life it transforms.

Broadway at Times Square, for example, is certainly a kind of spectacle, but it doesn't always entertain. It depends on how good we are at seeing. A talented choreographer can see superbly: he can watch this same scene and, by showing us special patterns of movement and behavior, entertain us with a character ballet, make us laugh or make us sad. He makes order out of what seems to us crowded and chaotic, makes what is fleeting and transitory permanently interesting.

The choreographer can do this in a number of ways: in ballets with stories, in ballets that aim to create a certain mood, or simply in dance ballets, where the music provides the plot the dancers move to. I think it's important to understand these distinctions.

Story ballets are entirely different from the stories we read in books: or they should be. In a story depicted on the ballet stage, we *see* what happens, it can't be explained. The plot is simple, the characters easily identifiable, and what happens to them is luminously clear.

What I've called "mood" ballets don't necessarily tell any kind of story; usually, as in *La Valse,* they are ballets in which an outside force, like destiny, seems to control the movement of the dancers.

In dance ballets there is no story, no outside force, only the music. The choreographer works with the music he has chosen much as the poet works with his meters. Most ballets, indeed, are like dramatic or lyric poems: they are created in relation to music and sometimes set within a fable or story. In ballet, the clumsy becomes graceful, the hesitant, inarticulate thought is expressed in direct, eloquent gesture, and nothing appears impossible; love can triumph over everything. In many great ballets, love does.

If you say that all this is fantasy, all imagination, you are right. Some people try to persuade us that poetry and painting and music and dancing are like what we see and do every day. In order to convince us that art is interesting, they tell us that the rumble of drums and the loud crash of cymbals in a piece of music represents Fate, for example, or that a certain portrait painter has depicted a girl's coloring just as it was in real life.

These people, well intentioned as they often are, actually put a stumbling block in our path. They make art easy in the wrong way. If we're told a great deal about a moment of history represented in a painting, for instance, and learn the background of the historical event, our appreciation is severely limited. Our appreciation is intellectual, based on something besides the picture. We could much more profitably spend our time just *looking* at the picture.

Some works of art can be appreciated intellectually, but not many good ones. To enjoy the good ones, we must have an openness of mind in addition to information or their beauty will forever escape us. First of all, we must suspend our prejudices.

As adults, we are well informed about certain things and we have definite ideas on many subjects. But in a sense we are all prejudiced. The older most of us get, the more we have to unlearn in order to learn something new. For instance, many of us were introduced in school to only certain types of music, only certain forms of poetry, and only particular schools of painting. As a result we have a tendency to resist anything new, as well as innovations in something we have become fond of. Children don't have this problem. You can play a Bach suite or a Mozart serenade to a child, and she may very well dance to it. It doesn't occur to her that these composers are old and "classical" or dull and cold or different from what she hears over the radio. She realizes instinctively that the exciting thing about all the arts is that they don't confirm what we already know, so much as they inform us of something new. They contain, in words, in music, in movement, new visions of the world.

Just as a child has her ears open, she keeps her eyes open if you take her to the ballet. Don't be afraid that she will be bored—with no trouble at all she'll become part of the magical world ballet is portraying and she'll not resist its impact. She is not afraid of being afraid (she even enjoys it a little when a wicked fairy appears), she is capable of being moved by love, by the attitudes people have toward one another on the stage. She will sense instantly that a boy partnering a girl well is gentle, respectful, eager for the girl to be as beautiful as possible and that a boy who is a bit of a show-off is not right in his part. She is apt to know, in short, much more than we do.

In order to place ourselves in her position and learn what she knows instinctively, we must go to the ballet with an open mind. If we go often, if we learn gradually that we can't see everything on the stage at once, if we learn to identify dancers and see different dancers in the same part, we'll establish a familiarity with the art and begin to enjoy it. There's no sense in being like the man who says he doesn't know anything about dancing, but he knows what he likes. By saying this, he cheats himself, protects his prejudices from exposure, nurses his own stubbornness. He's not only unwilling to learn anything, he would be embarrassed to learn anything.

Where ballet is concerned, learning by doing is impossible for most of us. We can learn, however, by seeing and by listening; we can learn nothing if we don't go see the ballet, and our appreciation of it will be severely limited if we do not have an awareness of the music that is played there. For ballet is not dancing alone: it is a composite of music and dancing. The relation of dancing to music is not a literal one. It is not a matter of plotless interpretation, a note-by-note, bar-by-bar rhythmic picture of music. On the contrary, it is a complement to the music, something added that is in the mood and spirit of the music as a choreographer sees it. We all have certain emotions when we hear a piece of music. So does a choreographer. He expresses and orders his emotions by placing people on the stage in a particular fashion and arranging their movements so that they have a certain quality: they may be sad, for example, though there isn't always a story to give them a reason for this. The music is sometimes the story. If the choreographer has chosen his music well, we will appreciate the complement the dance makes to its sound: the music will be, as it were, the floor on which the dancer moves. It will not be an excuse for the imposition of literary ideas foreign to music.

But frequently a too sensitive awareness of music can be a disadvantage to the inexperienced balletgoer. Some music lovers are very stubborn, they know what they like, they hold certain things sacred and won't even entertain the notion that they might enrich their musical experience. Their ears are open to only a few pieces, or they think dance "violates" the pieces they love. It may be difficult in such cases to expect a music lover to keep both ears *and* eyes open. I know an intelligent young lady, for example, who walked out on a performance of *The Sleeping Beauty* because she didn't like Tchaikovsky; and a young man who said he loved Bach so much that he could not watch *Concerto Barocco*. Both these people missed a chance, I think, to see in ballet things that might have changed their minds. Love of music can be so intense with some of us that it is acutely private and we resent any intrusion on that privacy.

Ballet in many cases can show us how to appreciate music. The structure of a symphony, how a piece of music is put together, may be something we have no interest in now, but continual attendance at the ballet will cause us to think differently. Dancing is always pointing to music, showing it, making it visually interesting. If our eyes are entertained, we begin to listen in a new way.

Reading about the ballet can be of help to the balletgoer. The numerous story-ballets with complicated plots are not always intelligible when we see them the first time, and it is advisable to know what happens. After our appreciation has matured somewhat, we will find other books—histories and criticism —interesting. Some two or three books of criticism on dancing, such as Noverre's *Letters* and Gautier's ballet reviews, are among the finest works of art appreciation.

But until we have *seen,* no amount of reading will help us. There is no short cut to seeing. *What* you see is not important. Good ballet can be seen frequently throughout the United States. Ballet companies may not visit your community with any regularity, but many of the large cities have their own permanent ballet organizations. Nor does it matter which you see. You cannot tell who is or who is not a good dancer if you don't know anything about the subject, and it is absurd to let anyone tell you. He may very well be wrong, and you'll miss a great deal, perhaps never go back to the ballet because you thought he was right. Much antagonism toward ballet is often created by someone who tells us that so-and-so is the world's greatest dancer in such-and-such a ballet. The inexperienced balletgoer sees the ballerina, doesn't like her, and never goes again.

Certain people don't like "cold" dancers. They use this word as if it meant something bad, something negative. The strange thing is that this quality of "coldness," which some regard negatively, often achieves positive results. I think you will find that people who say they prefer "hot," fiery dancers tend to create their own image of what they want to see, instead of watching the stage and seeing that the dance has its own quality—which might be cool and clear as crystal or, like a diamond seen in different lights, first cold, then hot.

What is it, then, that we should appreciate about a dancer? What things should we watch for the first time we go?

You will often hear people talk about the technical accuracies of dancers. They will say, "It's not important how many *fouettés* a girl can do, it's important that her supporting foot remain in place" and "Male dancers must always point their toes while doing *entrechats*." These things are quite true, there are many other such things, many finer points of technique, and we learn them as we watch, but all these criticisms are only part of a general appearance and manner that we must watch for first.

We should be ready, too, to enjoy the artist who perhaps has not yet achieved great success. We may discover later on that we saw the first of many dances that made her eventually a ballerina. That will be exciting. However, the good dancer will not in performance remind us of this kind of success. Watching her dancing over the years, we will see and appreciate the movement, the victory she appears to achieve in executing effortlessly a particular step or gesture at a specific time in a specific place. Her dancing will refract and amplify and make spacious, as music does, the emotion a particular dance intends. She is not someone we are in love with, or someone we should like to love, though some of her dancing reminds us of the happiness, the understanding, the playfulness and tenderness love has.

Only the professional dancer can analyze a performance and tell us that a certain dancer missed something. Dancers are not automatons. Every performance is different. Dancers must adjust themselves at almost every performance to a new pair of shoes, just as the tennis champion adjusts his hand to a new racket and the violinist adjusts to a new bow. Moreover, the condition of the stage floor is crucial to all dancers. No dancer dances well on a stage with a bad floor. If you have been to ballet performances where famous ballerinas seemed to be holding something back, where all the members of the *corps de ballet* danced hesitantly, refusing to commit themselves wholly to the dance, it was probably because they were risking their professional lives on the floor they were dancing on. The ideal stage for dancing is unfinished pine, smoothed over: it is not glossy linoleum or highly polished hardwood or the shiny plastic distances we see in the movies, or wood laid over cement or linoleum. When the nineteenth-century French critic Gautier remarked that an Italian dancer's feet were "like two steel arrows rebounding from a marble pavement," he was able to make the simile because she was dancing on a wooden stage. The dancer feels most secure when she knows that her ballet slippers are in real contact with the floor when she wants them to be; when she can feel the friction of the floor as she turns in pirouettes; when she can descend from a jump without fear of sliding.

Some stages, too, are precariously raked, or pitched: the back of the stage is higher than the front. The designers of such stages had more consideration for the audience's ability to see than for the perfection of the performance that entertains the audience. The degree of rake differs from stage to stage in old theatres, and it is naturally extremely hard for dancers to adjust their balance to them. These are not excuses; they are the conditions under which every dancer works, and no dancer should be punished for them. In one recital a pianist plays millions of notes; if you aren't a pianist yourself, you won't know the ones he missed. The great pianist Anton Rubinstein once said that if he'd been paid a penny for every note he missed, he'd be a very rich man.

Ballet is now so advanced in the United States that very seldom do we see incompetence on the stage. Bad dancers appear less and less. Our dancers are professionals. Like professional ball players, they must possess a technique. Usually their technique is so great that however tired they are (and tired they often are, with eight performances a week), their exhaustion is invisible to the audience. Only the professional can see it.

The audience must watch technique as part of a performance, not as a separate thing. The stage illusion and the atmosphere created by the dancing are destroyed if you sit in your seat and count turns or stop-watch changes of position. We take it for granted that flowers are beautiful; we don't have to take them apart to see this. We take them as they are. The taking apart is the job of the botanist, just as the technical analysis of a performance is the job of the professional dancer.

Great technical ability is only part of being a great dancer. At first we might find ourselves applauding a feat that seems astonishing, and six months later, when we've seen dozens of dancers do the same thing with an equal amount of facility, we might applaud less. We have to see to know better. We have to compare. But what we will all like at the beginning and what will make us want to go again soon is a dancer who interests us in an extremely simple way: we will remember afterward what her dance looked like. We will remember the girl, but only because of the dance she showed us. No doubt she was attractive, but she didn't play on that and make us think of it. No doubt she did some steps that seemed incredibly hard, but she didn't stress this, she didn't try to hit us between the eyes with her skill as if to say, "Look! *This* is good." Instead, the big moments of the dance came with the same lack of effort and stress as the small ones. She will quietly and effortlessly seem to conquer the stage space in which she moves to the time of the music.

Where the dancing of dramatic roles is concerned, we must beware of standard images. Some people think that the heroine in *Swan Lake* must always be very slender, short, have black hair parted in the middle, and dance like a bird, with lyrical feeling. Actually, what they mean by lyricism is often lethargy. I have seen dozens of Swan Queens. Some of them looked like birds, others did not, and all gave fine performances. Great ballets were not devised for one type of dancer. Sometimes I hear people say, "But so-and-so wasn't like Pavlova." They forget that if Pavlova and other great dancers of the more distant past were here today, they would not be so sentimental. They were professionals. They would appreciate the greater technical difficulties of modern classical choreography and admire our dancers with an affectionate, professional understanding. If they were dancing today, they know, they would be trying to do the same things our dancers do.

Seeing great classical ballets of the past is like seeing great plays: we are so familiar with *Hamlet* and *Romeo and Juliet*, know the lines so well that we think we can say them with more understanding than any actor. We may see these plays many times and come away disappointed, but one day we experience an extraordinary thing. We hear an actor say the words that are so familiar to us, and suddenly they are no longer private quotations to us. The play becomes new and moving. The same thing happens at the ballet.

Like all the arts, ballet is many things to many people. It is high-brow and something to make fun of to some people because they are afraid to understand it. Others have no wish to understand it and go to the ballet merely to show off their clothes, to see their friends or to make new ones. Still others seek the fashionable and go to the theatre because a particular dance or dancer has been praised extravagantly. Finally, there are those who enjoy the ballet with no pretension at all. They are able to do this because they understand what ballet is as a particular form of entertainment, because they are not frightened by other people telling them that ballet is "important" and "significant." Ballet is important and significant, but first of all it is a pleasure.

When we first start going to the ballet, it is no more significant or important than most of the other things we enjoy watching. It may become significant later, after we have enjoyed it and been entertained by it, after it has become important to us in a personal way. But at first we should simply watch it, as we watch our friends swimming or ice-skating, or playing baseball or tennis.

Music, we all know, is an aural perception: reading notes is not sufficient, we must hear them. Ballet is a visual art, like painting or architecture. But unlike painting or architecture, ballet is a visual spectacle that moves: it is not static. We can always see famous paintings by going to museums or famous buildings. Ballet, by comparison, is transitory. We no sooner take in a particular movement in a ballet than it has become another movement. The movements accumulate rapidly, and if we don't watch carefully, we are lost. We must train ourselves to see.

I think we must do this for the same reason and in the same way that we train ourselves to enjoy any of the other arts. To read a book—and we all have experience with this—is not necessarily to understand it. Similarly, to listen is not always to *hear*, and to look not always to *see*. Often, when we want to say that we understand something, we say that we "see" it. Ballet, with application and attention, can be seen and not merely watched.

We go to the theatre to see ballet and watch dancers—people like ourselves, with bodies and heads and arms and legs, running and jumping and lifting to a piece of music. We ask ourselves, why should they do this? The answer is that ballet displays the most beautiful movement of which the human body is capable. The human body, of course, has its limitations. We can bend it and stretch it and lift it, but only to a certain degree. We can, however, decrease the body's limitations with practice. After we have learned to walk, we can run; after we have lifted light objects, we are able to lift heavy ones. The dancer's concern is to fulfill the maximum of what the body can do in a beautiful way.

But the skill of dancers is useless unless it is displayed in a certain form. No one would enjoy watching a group of dancers jump about the stage aimlessly, no matter how well they jumped. Ballet asks the body to move in time. Ballet uses music to indicate time.

Not only in its movement and transitory nature, then, is ballet different from other visual arts. It is two things at once: a composition, a unification of music and dancing. We must hear and see at the same time. This process is something like reading a poem or watching a movie. A poem says something to us, but it speaks in a certain rhythm, a certain time scheme, a certain music. In a movie, the continuous pictures the camera shows us are controlled in sequence and length by what the script specifies. Music is ballet's timekeeper.

To show dancers moving with ideal strength and grace requires beautiful people. Few dancers are beautiful when they begin to study, but when they dance well, they become beautiful. Beautiful dancers are easily associated with ideal characters in stories, with kings and queens and princesses, with love, victory over evil, and death. Many ballets have stories with such heroes and heroines. But sometimes there is no literal story at all in ballet, no narrative. Just as people in real life make different gestures and stand in different positions when they are in different moods, so do dancers in a ballet. A *pas de deux*, for example, is simply a dance for two people, a man and a woman; and even when it is performed on a bare stage with no surrounding story, a *pas de deux* is always a kind of romance. The man is tender and admiring as he lifts the woman and supports her in order to display her beauty, while she, in her reliance on his strength and assurance, admires him in return. This quality in the *pas de deux* may not be apparent to the newcomer to ballet, but the more often this kind of dance is seen, the clearer become its romance and tenderness.

Program music is very easy for most of us to understand. When a composer tells us that his symphony is about a thunderstorm, we immediately have something to compare it with. Some ballets are like program music. These ballets require program notes to tell us what the ballet is really about. Some things, of course, are impossible to represent clearly on stage without the spoken word, but the central idea of every dramatic ballet is clear the first time we see it.

Many ballets are like symphonies that only have identifying numbers. A *pas de deux* or a dance ballet may have to be seen a number of times before we begin to enjoy it. Then passages we were able to like at the beginning become connected with other passages we appreciate later; we soon retain in our minds all the different passages and detect their connections.

Here are a few final suggestions which I hope will enhance your enjoyment of this great art. All ballets are accompanied by music, but because it is hard to listen to music and watch dancers at the same time, play the music over before you go to the ballet or listen to it on records. This is particularly important, naturally, in ballets that do not have conventional stories, where the ballet is based on the music.

Many ballets have plots. There are stories taken from fairy tales (*The Sleeping Beauty*), from ancient myths (*Orpheus*), from the Bible (*Prodigal Son*), from poems (*Illuminations*), and from stories devised especially for particular ballets. Not all of these stories are simple, and brief program notes are often insufficient. As I have said, ideally the best stories for ballets are those that can be *shown*, stories that require no elucidation at all in the written word. But stories inevitably have their complications. These complications were cleared up in the old ballets by pantomime. People could understand this when these ballets were created, for they were familiar with the mime vocabulary, but today, when that vocabulary has gone out of fashion, miming on the stage is often obscure to us and we aren't sure what is happening. Read the stories through, then, and in the theatre you will not be looking down constantly at an incomplete program note. You will be watching the stage.

Many people who go to the ballet, and not only newcomers, feel there is something suspect about ballets without stories—about dance ballets pure and simple. They think there is a hidden meaning they don't grasp. The real point is that they are trying to appreciate ballet intellectually. They expect ballet always to be like the theatre or literature or the movies, which, quite naturally, it is not. Ballet is like nothing so much as dancing. To appreciate it you have to watch it, not think about it. If you only think about it, you'll probably miss the next step and miss something you might have liked very much.

Don't hesitate to go to see ballet companies that you don't think are first-class. Only by seeing *all* the companies can you compare, analyze, and discover what you prefer.

Another thing I'd like to mention is this. Many of us are interested in reading ballet criticism in newspapers and magazines. This criticism can be informative and revealing but I think it is important for us, if we read critics, to read *all* of them, and then go to the ballet and see for ourselves. You will often find that critics radically disagree. How can you discover which one is right unless you see the ballet in question? It also happens very often that dance critics change their minds. Dance critics, like music critics, review the same pieces year after year; what they disliked one year they sometimes like another. If you have read a particular dance critic or music critic over the years, you will discover this to be true.

And, finally, no one can enjoy the ballet if he decides he will go only a certain number of times. If you go only occasionally, once or twice every few years, say, you will never be fully entertained. You must go as many times as possible, as often as you read a novel, as often as you go to the movies or the theatre, as often as you look at paintings or listen to a concert or an opera. We come to enjoy all of these arts through persistent exposure to what each has to teach us about the pleasures that life contains. If we neglect the ballet, we are depriving ourselves of one of the greatest of these pleasures. Naturally, we can live without art: we can eat and sleep and live by our senses alone. But throughout history man has never been satisfied with the necessities of life. He has sought entertainment and enlightenment through art and has become a happier being.

# PART THREE

## *A Brief History of the Ballet*

Our word *ballet* comes from the Italian *ballare,* to dance, and it is to the courts of Italy at the height of the Renaissance that we trace the beginning of ballet as we know it today. Dancing as primitive ritual—as a form of hero worship and worship of gods, as glorification of the dead, as a means of celebrating the seasons and the elements—is fundamental in history. Dancing as a popular skill embodied in folk dances is familiar in every country. Dancing as a skill, as a refined human discipline, was developed in religious rites of Mediterranean countries and in the ancient Orient, where chosen persons were taught godlike gestures and movement in order to emulate and celebrate for the populace the drama of their common deities. In the choral dance of Greece, dancing as an art designed for entertainment grew out of the native ritualistic dance. Now the trained performer of a common ritual became the dedicated dancer who aimed to give pleasure to a nondancing audience.

Greek drama began with group or choral dances interrupted and embellished with storytelling. As the chorus of dancers began to sing and to participate in the action of the stories devised by poets, pantomime and meaningful movement evolved. The masks worn by the Greek chorus were a feature of the theatrical dance till late in the eighteenth century. The poet Aeschylus, whose plays were performed by two principal actors and a chorus, rehearsed his choruses in the postures, movements, and gestures proper to the dramatic situation. With his successors, Sophocles and Euripides, the importance of the chorus was proportionately reduced with introduction of a larger cast of characters, but a basic vocabulary of theatrically effective mimicry, attitude, and movement had been established.

What the Greeks achieved was extended by the Romans, who exploited the comic possibilities of mime and dance. The Romans combined the two with acrobatics and circus routines and used them to illustrate popular fables. Tumblers, jesters, and buffoons so humanized dancing that the ritualistic base of Greek tragedy was wholly forgotten.

The comic art of the Romans was reborn in sixteenth-century Italy by traveling players who embodied the *commedia dell'arte:* skilled popular comedians who improvised variations on stock characters—Pulcinella, Punch, Columbine, Pierrot, Harlequin, and others—in stock plots. The gestures, costumes, and characterization of these actors became comic archetypes for all of Europe, influencing many others—the dancers of Paris, the plays of Molière, the carnival puppet shows (*Punch and Judy, Petrouchka*) of the Western world.

While these troupes entertained the provinces of Italy and southern France, the capitals of the Renaissance saw splendid revivals of Roman opulence in the form of pageants and staged celebrations. The rulers of these capitals used every happy event—engagements, marriages, visits of notable persons, military victories—as an excuse for spectacular entertainment in poetry, painting, dance, song, and theatrical mechanics. Appropriate myths inherited from Rome were adapted for the particular occasion, depicted by artists, and danced by the masked members of the court. Interludes of dancing were performed at pageants between recitations and songs, between courses at banquets, and to accompany with appropriate representation the serving of rare dishes at great feasts.

Like the popular art of the *commedia dell'arte,* court dances also had special forms. The folk dances that the courts had sophisticated were further refined into precise floor patterns, simple set steps that required set preparations, and endings performed with elegant bows and flourishes. Popular court dances of this time were called *balletti* (diminutive of *ballo;* hence *ballet*); they were similar to the English morris dance. Castiglione, master of Renaissance manners, wrote in *The Courtier:*

"There are certain other exercises that can be practiced in public and in private, like dancing; and in this I think the Courtier ought to have care, for when dancing in the presence of many and in a place full of people, it seems to me that he should preserve a certain dignity, albeit tempered with a lithe and airy grace of movement; and although he may feel himself to be very nimble and a master of time and measure, let him not attempt those agilities of foot and double steps which we find very becoming in our friend Barletti, but which perhaps would be little suited to a gentleman. Yet in a room privately, as we are now, I think he may try both, and may dance morris-dances and brawls; but not in public unless he be masked, when it is not displeasing even though he be recognized by all." Within the aristocracy of the court a new aristocracy developed—the aristocracy of the best dancer.

Catherine de Médicis introduced the new Italian pageantry to France. Under her influence, Italian musicians and dancing masters came to Paris and staged for the court spectacles consisting of vocal and instrumental music, spoken dialogue, pantomime, dancing, and mechanical effects. The combination of these elements produced the *ballet de cour,* or court ballet, the European model for costly entertainment. With the assistance of their ladies, gentlemen of the court performed *masques*—allegorical plays with poetry and dancing—and *mummings*—colorful dances performed by masked figures among dancers at court balls.

Toward the end of the sixteenth century, Catherine de Médicis, with the assistance of an Italian musician turned dancing master, produced at her court an entertainment that superseded in extravagance and purpose all those previously seen in Europe. This work was called the *Ballet Comique de la Reine.* It employed all the familiar elements of the *ballet de cour* and Italian opera— music, singing, dancing, royal processions, declamation of verse, elaborate scenery and mechanical effects—but for the first time these elements were fused in a dramatic whole that made sense to the spectators: the disparate parts were not mere diversions at a court function, they represented a conscious design to entertain an audience with a unity of comedy, dance, music, and spectacle. The performance cost 3,600,000 francs, lasted for five hours, and was witnessed by some ten thousand people. Its success assured the future of dancing as a necessary part of regal entertainment. It was, in effect, the first ballet as we recognize the term today—a combination of music, dancing, plot, and design.

Seven years later there appeared in France a book that provided the first foundation for the establishment of dancing as a profession. Arbeau's *Orchésographie* (*The Writing of Dancing*) illustrated and gave directions for executing the popular court dances of the time. Arbeau also indicated the principles for the five basic positions of the feet that were to become the foundation of the classic dance. In an effort to teach the dances that had become so popular, it was necessary to arrive at principles upon which all teaching could be based: the limitations of the human body, how and in what directions it could move, and the fundamental steps that best prepared it for movement.

The popular dances of the continent had meanwhile become the courtly habit in England, where Queen Elizabeth appointed a gentleman to the post of Lord Chancellor because "he wore green bows on his shoes and danced the *pavane* to perfection." The poets Ben Jonson, Milton, and Campion, and the great designer Inigo Jones developed masques in imitation of the *ballet de cour*. The masques featured dancing by members of the court, but the real contribution England made to the development of ballet was in the antimasque, a pure dance that preceded the performance of the masque proper, danced by professionals. Ben Jonson thus addressed Queen Elizabeth in 1609:

"And because Her Majesty (best knowing that a principal part of life in these spectacles lay in their variety) had commanded me to think on some dance, or show, that might precede hers, and have the place of a foil, or false masque: It was careful to decline, not only from others, but mine own steps in that kind, since the last year, I had an *antimasque* of boys; and therefore now devised that twelve women, in the habit of hags or witches, sustaining the persons of Ignorance, Suspicion, Credulity, etc., the opposites to good Fame, should fill that part, not as a masque, but a spectacle of strangeness, producing multiplicity of gesture."

In France, dancing flourished at the court of Louis XIV, himself an accomplished dancer. In 1661 Louis XIV founded the first dancing academy in the world, an institution for the instruction of dancing that has continued down to the present day at the Paris Opéra. Under the direction of Beauchamp, the king's dancing master, and the Italian musician and dancer Jean Baptiste Lully, students were taught professionally, to perform on a stage. The great dramatists Molière and Corneille collaborated with Lully in the production of comedy and tragedy ballets that secured the admiration of court and public. The excellence of stage performance gradually superseded the court dances; the larger, freer movements possible in the theatre replaced the confined gestures of the ballroom. Louis Pécourt became the first *premier danseur,* the first dancer to excel in performances in a theatre. Soon women appeared as professional dancers for the first time.

Beauchamp specified the Five Positions of the classic dance, positions of the feet that became the prerequisite for a dancer's training at the French Academy and the instinctive basis for all performance. The positions are still the basis of ballet today. These positions are absolute in their anatomical authority: the ease with which they are taught to young students, the ease and security they allow the dancer on stage, and, most important of all, the variety of movement made possible by their use. They are as essential to ballet as fundamental techniques of sound structure are to architecture. The Five Positions, with their embodiment of the turned-out leg, distinguished ballet from all other forms of theatrical dance. Ballet dancing had now become a profession, one that could be taught and learned and mastered.

Now that there was fundamental agreement on the basis of the classic dance, there were quarrels about innovations of technique. While Lully in his years at the French Academy had devised dances that were complex in pattern and floor design, he had not considered dancing off the floor, dancing that aimed at elevation, at flight. His successor, Rameau, thought differently and encouraged his dancers to turn in the air and perform steps high off the floor. In Lully's time, when dancing was moved from the ballroom to the stage, it was quite natural for ballet to imitate the technique of dancing in a ballroom— where performers and spectators stood on the same level—but Rameau realized that on a raised stage the dancers were seen from an entirely different perspective by the spectators, that the dancers' feet were clearly visible for the first time, and, accordingly, that the dance must make an adjustment of technique to hold its audience. The conservative adherents of Lully, those who advocated a "horizontal" dance, contested the theories of the new, rebel "verticalists" of Rameau.

This contest between the Lullists and the Rameauists contained the basic argument that runs throughout the history of ballet down to the present: the argument between "tradition" and innovation, between strict classicism and expressiveness, between pure dance and "literary" ballets, between ballet and modern dance. This argument was embodied in two popular dancers of the time: Marie Camargo and Marie Sallé. Camargo, champion of the new *danse verticale,* was a brilliant technician, praised for her airiness and strength. She was the first *danseuse* to perform the *entrechat-quatre,* to execute high *cabrioles* and jumps. To display her skill, Camargo shortened the conventional cumbersome ballet dress so that her agile steps might be seen. A great innovator, Camargo was also a traditionalist, interested in technique rather than the human and dramatic elements of the dance.

Camargo's rival, Marie Sallé, "muse of gracious, modest gesture," exemplified in her refined and gracious dancing a spiritual rather than technical elevation. Here the accent was on nobility of posture and deportment and on characterization of a particular part for dramatic effect. Sallé did not dance simply for the sake of dancing. Her most famous role, that of the statue beloved by Pygmalion, she devised for herself. Called a *ballet-pantomime* in opposition to the rigid and formal opera-ballets of the Paris Opéra, Sallé's dancing in this work was faithful to the Greek style of its story. Effecting another innovation in costume, Sallé let her hair down and over her corset and petticoat wore only a muslin dress "draped about her in the manner of a Greek statue."

Rameau's ballets at the Paris Opéra accommodated both the new technique and dramatic expression within the frame of the opera-ballet, a series of danced *entrées* connected by a threadlike plot. The *entrées* depicted dances in various countries—Turkey, Peru, Persia, America—which allowed for spectacle as well as for occasional dramatic interest in stories imposed upon the natives. With their great geographical variety and concern for imitation of native dances throughout the world, Rameau's ballets brought down to earth the mythological characters with which the dance had been preoccupied since the Renaissance.

Another dancer wanted ballet to go still further. After Rameau's death, ballet at the Paris Opéra degenerated to the point where each of its elements—dancing, music, story, and spectacle—seemed to exist for its own sake. The dancers' technical proficiency was displayed, with marked contempt for music, in ridiculous dramas. Jean Georges Noverre, a student of Louis Dupré, a great admirer of Marie Sallé and of the English actor David Garrick, wanted to unify the elements of ballet into a dramatic whole. He wrote, in ballet's first critical text, *Letters on the Dance and Ballets,* that poetry, painting, and dancing should be a "faithful likeness of beautiful nature," that dancing should be united with pantomime to ensure dramatic expression, and that such expression must be related directly to music. Working with such musicians as Christoph Willibald Gluck, whose reforms in opera were closely allied to Noverre's in ballet; with such dancers as Gaetan Vestris, first great classical dancer in Europe; with Marie Allard and Madeleine Guimard, superb mimes as well as dancers; and with the patronage of such notable persons as Marie Antoinette—Noverre successfully initiated reforms in ballets that were seen and applauded all over Europe. His ballets were danced in London, Vienna, Paris, Milan, and St. Petersburg. All of Europe delighted in the new *ballet d'action*—works in which dancers reflected in their movement and gesture the dramatic intention of plot and music. Among Noverre's students were Vincenzo Galeotti, who became ballet master at the Royal Theatre, Copenhagen; Charles Didelot, the Frenchman who became "the father of Russian ballet" at the Imperial Theatre in St. Petersburg; and Jean Dauberval, who, in *La Fille Mal Gardée,* created what was perhaps the first comic ballet.

One of Dauberval's pupils, Salvatore Vigano, extended Noverre's reforms in spectacular ballets produced in his native Italy. At La Scala, Milan, Vigano mounted works that unified music, dancing, and mime as Noverre had never been able to do. Mime, Vigano regarded as the expression of the "movement of the soul: it is the language of all peoples, of all ages and times. It depicts better than words extremes of joy and sorrow . . . It is not sufficient for me to please the eyes. I wish to involve the heart." Indeed, he regarded mime with such importance that the composer Rossini remarked to Stendhal, the choreographer's great admirer, that Vigano's ballets had too much pantomime and not enough dancing. Vigano's idea was the *choreodrame,* ballets in which Noverre's principle of dramatically expressive embodiment was seen in every dancer on stage, in the *corps de ballet* as well as in the performances of principal dancers. Within particular settings and plots, Vigano worked tirelessly to arrange dances appropriate to drama and score. Under his direction, La Scala became the greatest ballet theatre in all of Europe.

This pre-eminence of Italian ballet was sustained by the dancer, choreographer, and teacher Carlo Blasis, student of Dauberval, who wrote—in his *Elementary Treatise upon the Theory and Practice of the Art of Dancing* (1820) and in the *Code of Terpsichore* (1829)—the first lexicons of the classic dance. Here the basic theories of all the great dancers and choreographers who preceded Blasis were tacitly assumed in general instructions to pupils and ballet masters and were embodied in detailed, illustrated instruction on practice: the proper execution of positions, poses, movements, and steps of elevation—all the resources known to the classic dancer. Blasis' work has been the foundation of all instruction in the classic dance ever since. The classic disciplines he insisted upon in his teaching at La Scala were precursors of the instruction that later dominated the Russian Imperial School at St. Petersburg and ballet everywhere.

Vincenzo Galeotti produced in 1786 in Copenhagen a ballet still in the current repertory, *The Whims of Cupid and the Ballet Master*. His most distinguished student, August Bournonville, who studied also in Paris under Vestris, advanced Galeotti's commitment to dramatic expression in ballet. Audiences at performances of the Royal Danish Ballet today recognize the importance of pantomime and drama that Bournonville introduced in the more than fifty ballets he choreographed for that company. They recognize, too, a vigorous dance style that Bournonville established and taught to Christian Johansson, the Swedish dancer who became in St. Petersburg the most celebrated *premier danseur* of his time. From 1860 until his death in 1903, Johansson taught in St. Petersburg all of the great dancers of the Russian ballet.

Founded in 1735 to teach court cadets the fashionable dances of Europe, the Russian Imperial School, adjunct of the Imperial Theatre, was directed by a series of French and Italian ballet masters, who produced in St. Petersburg the work of European choreographers and invited to the Russian capital foreign dancers to star in these works. The Frenchman Charles Didelot was the first to establish the Russian school and theatre on a firm base. Didelot, student of Noverre, Dauberval, and the *premier danseur* Auguste Vestris, was appointed ballet master at St. Petersburg in 1816. He established at the Imperial School a consistent foundation of classical instruction and mounted such excellent ballets at the Imperial Theatre that the poet Pushkin was moved to say that in Didelot's ballets there was more poetry than in all the French literature of that time. After Didelot's death (1837) the Russian Theatre continued to flourish, but principally as an opulent setting not for Russian, but for the finest ballets and dancers of Western Europe.

In Western Europe of the 1830s, the supremacy of Italian dance technique combined with the Romanticism that dominated the other arts of the time to produce a new kind of ballet. Romanticism in ballet, as in the other arts, was a rebellion against classical subject matter, classical technique, and classical attitudes. The Romantic ballet extended the classical dance technique with daring innovations: girls danced on their toes for the first time, and new steps of elevation were devised to display voluptuous real-life heroines who by theatrical magic became idealized, unattainable creatures of wood and glade. Heroines of ballets were no longer characters from classical mythology: wronged peasant girls and sylphs displaced the Medeas, the Junos, the Aphrodites. Audiences rejoiced in the theatrical display of the beauty of the broken heart. Paris, again, and London were the ballet capitals of the world.

Marie Taglioni, creator of the wistful *La Sylphide*, became the first famous dancer Europe had ever known. The ballet *Giselle*, inspired by the Romantic poet Gautier, superseded Taglioni's vehicle in excellence of plot and dance, and enthralled audiences from St. Petersburg to Boston. Taglioni's contemporaries—Carlotta Grisi, the first dancer of *Giselle;* the Danish ballerina Lucile Grahn; the lively Fanny Cerrito—appeared in a score of ballets on romantic themes, while the great Fanny Elssler, Taglioni's archrival, was so secure in her reputation that she could abandon the opera houses of Europe for two years and dance on tour throughout the United States. Elssler's phenomenal success in America in 1840–42 was typified by the reception tendered her by President Van Buren and his Cabinet at Washington and by the banquet given by members of Congress in her honor at the Capitol. In 1845 Jules Perrot, the Romantic ballet's finest choreographer and the one male dancer who managed to hold his own in this age of romanticism, staged in London a special dance for Taglioni and three of her rivals—Grisi, Cerrito, and Grahn. The success of this *Pas de Quatre* obliged *The Times* to call the ballet "the greatest Terpsichorean exhibition that ever was known in Europe."

While the triumphs of these first great ballet stars increased the popularity of the art, the art itself began to suffer. Interest in all performances was centered on the stars and what they danced; people cared less and less about the music they danced to, the plots they acted, or the productions that displayed them. Taglioni or Elssler, alone, was enough. Prospective dancers and choreographers therefore saw little profit in remaining in Paris and London. In Russia, they knew, the Tsar's court required spectacular entertainment. And it could support it by the most bountiful treasury in Europe.

In the year Taglioni retired (1847), a young Frenchman, Marius Petipa, was engaged as a dancer at the Russian Imperial Theatre. Petipa was successful as a dancer in St. Petersburg; there he watched the work of the French ballet masters Jules Perrot and Arthur Saint-Léon as they entertained a new avid audience of aristocratic balletomanes. Then suddenly there was an opportunity to create a ballet of his own. In 1860 he had restaged the Perrot-Coralli *Giselle*, the romantic ballet that seemed certain to remain a permanent fixture in the Russian repertory. But ballet by this time required a new impetus, which Petipa discovered in a reawakened classicism. He devised for his ballet a mass dance on a tremendous scale, with spectacular stage effects. Beginning in 1862, with his first great success, a four-act dance extravaganza set in the desert, with pyramids and colossal palaces of ancient Egypt, Petipa succeeded Jules Perrot as ballet master to the Imperial Theatre. His influence was to dominate the Russian ballet almost up to the time of his death fifty years later. His supremacy survived the reigns of four Tsars, who delighted in the entertainment he provided their courts and in the universal model of excellence he caused the Russian ballet to become. Petipa created fifty-seven full-length, evening-long ballets, devised countless shorter *divertissements*, restaged seventeen ballets by other choreographers, and mounted ballets in thirty-four operas during his years at the Imperial Theatre.

St. Petersburg was now the ballet capital of the world. The French ballet master Petipa welcomed to Russia dancers and teachers from Italy, France, Germany, and Scandinavia; with their assistance he made the Imperial Ballet School the greatest in the world. Petipa's school provided the standard for the dancer's training, as his theatre was the exemplar for the dancer's performance. Foreign dancers who came to Russia for guest engagements introduced diverse technical elements from all of Europe: brilliant classicists, who had been trained in Italy under the disciplines founded by Blasis, contributed to the growth of a new style. This style was not so much Russian as polygenous. It was historic in its all-inclusiveness, in its gigantic assimilation of classic dance techniques as they were practiced in all of Europe. It produced, toward the end of the nineteenth century, great Russian dancers, who danced in such ballets as *Swan Lake* and *The Nutcracker,* works by the Russian choreographer Lev Ivanov, who produced them under Petipa's direction, and Peter Ilyich Tchaikovsky. Tchaikovsky was commissioned by Petipa to write the score for the ballet that turned out to be the masterpiece of both men. *The Sleeping Beauty,* Russian ballet music, as well as Russian ballet and Russian dancers, was the accepted standard throughout the Western World.

Petipa died in 1910. Some years before his death, the classical ballet he had perfected had passed its zenith; it began to disintegrate as its elements became disassociated. A young dancer and choreographer, Michel Fokine, who in 1905 created for the ballerina Anna Pavlova the short lyric dance *The Dying Swan,* rebelled against the omnipotence of "tradition." Like Sallé, Noverre, and Vigano before him, Fokine aimed at unification of dancing, music, and design. He asserted that dancing was interpretative, expressive. "The ballet must no longer be made up of *numbers, entries,* and so on. It must show artistic unity of conception . . . Ballet must have complete unity of expression, a unity which is made up of harmonious blending of the three elements—music, painting, and plastic art." Fokine's suggested reforms were rejected by his superiors at the Imperial Theatre. They were championed by a man who understood music, painting, and dancing: Serge Diaghilev.

Diaghilev wished to take the Russian ballet to Paris. In 1907 he had presented Russian music to Western Europe for the first time, and he now wished Europeans to admire what he knew to be the finest dancing in the world. He chose Fokine as choreographer to a company to be known as Diaghilev's Ballets Russes. Anna Pavlova, Tamara Karsavina, and Vaslav Nijinsky secured leave from the Imperial Theatre to be his principal dancers. His dancers, his designers, his musicians, were the finest in Russia.

On May 18, 1909, Diaghilev's Ballets Russes opened their first season in Paris. In the new ballets of Fokine, ballets like *Prince Igor* and *Les Sylphides,* and in the quality of the dancing, the music, and theatrical design, the season was an unprecedented success. This pattern of success continued the next year, with the Stravinsky-Fokine *Firebird,* and the next, with the Stravinsky-Fokine *Petrouchka,* and the next, with the Debussy-Nijinsky *The Afternoon of a Faun* and the Fokine-Weber *Le Spectre de la Rose,* and so on, season after season, year after year, for twenty years of dance entertainment based on an inviolable rule of uniform excellence in choreography, music, decor, and performance.

Paris was again the world capital of dance. Diaghilev's Ballets Russes provided a center of artistic endeavor such as Europe had not known since the Medici courts of the Renaissance. And Diaghilev, like the Renaissance princes, not only perpetuated established talent, he discovered, encouraged, and developed talent. He numbered among his principal female dancers Pavlova, Karsavina, Lopokova, Spessivtzeva, Dubrovska, Nemtchinova, Sokolova, Tchernicheva, Egorova, Nijinska, Danilova, and Markova; among the men, Nijinsky, Fokine, Vladimiroff, Bolm, Mordkin, Novikoff, Volinine, Cecchetti, Massine, Woicikowski, Idzikowski, Dolin, and Lifar. Among his composers were Stravinsky, Debussy, Ravel, Richard Strauss, Fauré, Satie, Respighi, De Falla, Prokofiev, Poulenc, Auric, Milhaud, Dukelsky, Rieti, Lambert, Berners, Sauguet, and Nabokov. His designers were such painters as Benois, Roerich, Bakst, Soudeikine, Doboujinsky, Larionov, Picasso, Derain, Matisse, Braque, Gris, Utrillo, Miró, Tchelitchew, Di Chirico and Rouault. His choreographers were Fokine, Nijinsky, Massine, Nijinska, and myself.

Since the disbandment of Diaghilev's company following his death in 1929, his dancers and choreographers have influenced ballet throughout the world. Serge Lifar has been for many years ballet master at the Paris Opéra, which, with the Royal Danish Ballet at Copenhagen, continues the oldest traditions of teaching and performance in the free world. Ninette de Valois, a soloist with the Diaghilev company, founded a ballet company and an associated school in London which became in time the Royal Ballet, the national company of Great Britain. Massine and I were the first choreographers of the Ballet Russe de Monte Carlo, founded in Europe in 1932. In America, I founded with Lincoln Kirstein the American Ballet, precursor of the present New York City Ballet. The American Ballet's complementary group, Kirstein's Ballet Caravan, produced, in addition to classical works, ballets based on native American material—Filling Station, Billy the Kid, Yankee Clipper, etc.—with choreography by such American dancers as Lew Christensen, Eugene Loring, and William Dollar and with music by American composers. The New York City Ballet, with its associated school, the School of American Ballet, represents the result of many years of work toward the achievement of excellence in classical performance.

The Ballet Theatre, now the American Ballet Theatre, founded by Lucia Chase and Richard Pleasant, grew out of the New York ballet school of Mikhail Mordkin. Fokine, who had staged many of his own works for many ballet companies, supervised productions of his ballets by the Ballet Theatre and created his last ballet for this company in 1941. The English choreographer Antony Tudor, who—like Frederick Ashton, principal choreographer to the Sadler's Wells Ballet—had been a student in London of Marie Rambert, joined the Ballet Theatre at its inception. This company has produced many works by native American choreographers.

Many other companies have appeared since. The City Center Joffrey Ballet in New York, the Pennsylvania Ballet in Philadelphia, the Boston Ballet, the Dance Theatre of Harlem, the Eliot Feld Ballet are representative of the tremendous growth in the number and talent of our dance ensembles. In Canada, the National Ballet of Canada and the Royal Winnipeg Ballet have concurrently set high standards for performance. Companies from England, Denmark, Germany, Russia, France, Holland, Belgium, Australia, and other countries that visit North America regularly bring us new repertories. It is possible to compare.

Our schools for the teaching of ballet have established new criteria for excellence. You cannot really have a ballet company without a school to train the talent you require. Dancers from all over the world come to work at our schools when they visit us, just as we go to theirs. Ballet is a truly international art; everyone understands.

Nancy Hanks, chairman of the National Endowment for the Arts, acknowledged in 1976 that dance is "the fastest growing art in the nation." In New York it used to be that the summer was the doldrums and no ballet companies would appear. Now, it is almost impossible to find enough theatres for the companies who wish to perform here in the summer. The dance season is now a year-round affair that never stops.

Writing in the New York *Times* about ballet's soaring popularity, the critic Anna Kisselgoff noted: "In 1965, the report of the Rockefeller Panel on the Arts placed dance attendance in the United States at one million. For 1975, it was fifteen million, according to the Association of American Dance Companies . . . These are not fanciful figures. One has only to compute the number of seats and performances among the array of dance companies scheduled in New York between April and September 1976 to realize that close to one and a half million people will attend dance performances in this city in just the next four months."

With more persons watching dance performances regularly, knowledge of and concern for ballet have grown, too. Many companies, like the New York City Ballet, have wonderful subscribers—interested persons who have come to know what we represent, wish to keep up with it and to see more, regularly. Their support, needless to say, is vital to us. And I do not mean in terms of financial support, valuable as that is; I mean in terms of interest and response. They simply *know* more than those who come only occasionally and they are a most rewarding and perceptive audience. The more companies fortunate enough to have that kind of support, the better for all of dance. Ballet has come a long way from its beginnings at the court of Catherine de Médicis in the sixteenth century.

# PART FOUR

*Chronology of Significant Events in the History of Ballet*

Ballet, we have seen, is an art without nationality; it has a family history. The new ballets we see on the stage today come at the end of a long line of descent from the past. Dance has a living past in the dancers of today; its traditional theory of basic steps and movements is the foundation of its current practice. No one can learn to dance without a teacher, and that teacher was the student of an earlier master. In the eighteenth century, the Frenchman Noverre and the Italian Galeotti taught the Dane Antoine Bournonville, whose son Auguste was the master of the Swede Johansson, teacher of the Russians Pavlova and Fokine.

The dancers, teachers, and choreographers we are familiar with today are thus offshoots of a great international family tree—living embodiments of a precise tradition. Ballet's history is a record of teachers and students: what the teacher handed down, what the student learned, what he carried forward and extended, what he rejected, what he changed. In the gradual unfolding of this story, we see how the contributions of different individuals in different countries move forward, seem to falter, then converge in the ballet we know today.

1469   Lorenzo de' Medici, great patron of the arts, succeeds to the rule of Florence. His marriage to Clarice Orsini: grand procession, tournament; allegorical masque, executed by the foremost painters, poets, and sculptors of the time, depicts in song and spectacle the glories of antiquity.

1475   Grand tournament of Giuliano de' Medici is held at Florence: scene, costumes, and dance figures commemorated in the *Birth of Venus, Mars and Venus,* and *Primavera* of Botticelli.

c.1500   Development in Italy and southern France of the popular court dance form the *ballo,* social dances performed in a ballroom or in the open air. The *ballo* is freer, more animated, than the other variety of dance popular at this time, the *basse danse* (low dance). Originally Italian, the *basse danse* was a carefully prescribed court dance, the ancestor of the minuet. *Balletti* is the diminutive of *ballo,* and it is from this word that we derive *ballet.*

1512   The *masque,* variation of princely Italian masquerades, is introduced in England, at the court of Henry VIII. Social, rather than theatrical or dramatic, at first, the *masque* later includes songs, speeches, introductory dance, general dance, and finale of speech and chorus.

1523   Robert Copland's *The Manner of Dancing Basse Dances After the Use of France* appears in England.

1533   Catherine de Médicis arrives in France. Her marriage to Henry of Orleans (later Henry II) takes place: introduction of Italian pageantry to France.

c.1555   Baldassarino de Belgiojoso (Balthazar de Beaujoyeulx), Italian violinist, immigrates to France and becomes a member of the French Court: later develops French and Italian elements into the first modern ballet.

1558   Royal fete and ball is held on April 24 for the marriage of Francis, eldest son of Catherine de Médicis, and Mary Queen of Scots: spectacle with "*masques* and *mummeries,*" beginning of the *ballet de cour,* costly court entertainments consisting of vocal and instrumental music, spoken dialogue, pantomime, dancing, and mechanical effects. All dancers in these ballets wear masks. Ladies of the court participate, but principal roles are taken by men.

1570   Jean Antoine de Baïf, French poet, and Joachim Thibault de Courville, French musician, found the Academy of St. Cecilia in Paris to encourage the fusion of poetry, music, and movement after the manner of the ancients. Dancing to be in accord with music and song.

1571   Troupe of Italian comedians popularize in Paris the *commedia dell'arte* (Columbine, Harlequin, et al.), traditional native farces of Italy.

c.1575   Giovanni da Bologna's *Mercury*—inspiration for the *attitude,* basic prose of classic ballet. "On one occasion, performing the part of Mercury, I took, as I turned in my pirouette, the attitude of the statue of Mercury by Bologna." —Carlo Blasis, 1830.

1580   The history of ballet as we know it today begins on October 15, when Beaujoyeulx presents *Ballet Comique de la Reine* at the court of Catherine de Médicis on the occasion of the marriage of Marguerite of Lorraine, the Queen's sister, to the Duc de Joyeuse: assimilation of French and Italian elements of dance, music, and spectacle into a coherent dramatic whole. To its creator, this work was called a *ballet* because it presents "a geometrical arrangement of numerous people dancing together under a diverse harmony of many instruments"; it is *comique* "for the lovely, tranquil, and happy conclusion by which it ends, by the quality of the personages involved, who are almost all gods and goddesses." Beaujoyeulx's musico-dramatic synthesis of Italian opera and French *ballet de cour* originates the school of French ballet and opera that is to serve as the model in Europe for two centuries.

1588   Jehan Tabourot, priest of Langre, publishes—under the pseudonym Thoinot Arbeau—*Orchésographie* (writing of dancing), *treatise in the form of a dialogue whereby all manner of persons may easily acquire and practice the honorable exercise of dancing:* illustrations and directions on the proper execution of dances of the time (pavane, galliard, gavotte, etc.), and establishment of principles for the five absolute positions of the classic dance (*see* Glossary). Arbeau's work provides the potential technical base for instruction in dancing and assures French supremacy in the initial development of ballet.

1597   Thomas Morley's *Plaine and Easie Introduction to Practical Musick* details the differences between types of music for dancing, calling the pavane "a kind of staid musick ordained for grave dancing" and the galliard "a lighter and more stirring kind of dance." The pavane, galliard, allemande, sarabande, polonaise, minuet, jig, gavotte, etc., were originally dance tunes that originated among the peoples of Italy, France, Germany, Spain, and Poland in the sixteenth century or before. These popular or courtly dances soon gave rise to a new form in music, as composers stylized the contrasting moods of the dances in the writing of *suites.*

1605   Ben Jonson, English poet and dramatist, and the architect Inigo Jones collaborate on the production of the *Twelfth Night Masque:* unrivaled scenic and dramatic effect.

1607   *Orfeo,* opera by Monteverdi, is performed on February 24 at the Academia degl'Invaghiti, Mantua: development of principles of *ballet comique* in musical work; first opera to use accompaniment of full orchestra.

1608   First antimasque, in *The Hue and Cry after Cupid,* Jonson-Jones, surrounds heroic figures with sportive dancers to amuse spectators with "antic faces" and "ridiculous gesture."

1625 Ballet in France regresses to nondramatic dances introduced by poems or songs.

1632 Jean Baptiste Lully (Giovanni Battista Lulli), musician and dancer, is born in Italy on November 29.

1634 First performance of *Comus*, masque by John Milton.

1641 *Prosperity of the Arms of France*, ballet by Cardinal Richelieu, performed.

1645 Cardinal Mazarin, successor to Richelieu as Prime Minister, introduces Italian grand opera to Paris: France absorbs Italian mechanical stage devices to increase the spectacle of ballet.

1645 Louis XIV, at age seven, first dances publicly.

1653 Louis XIV appears as *Le Roi Soleil* (the Sun King) in the *Ballet de la Nuit*, composed partly by Lully.

1658 "Tragedy and ballet are two species of painting in which what is most illustrious in the world is placed on view," writes Abbé Michel de Pure in *Idée des Spectacles*.

1661 Académie de Danse is founded by Louis XIV in a room in the Louvre, Paris: "Although the art of dancing has always been recognized as one of the most honorable, and the most necessary for the training of the body, to give it the first and most natural foundations for all kinds of exercises and amongst others for those of arms; and as it is . . . many ignorant people have tried to disfigure the dance and to spoil it . . . we deemed it opportune to establish in our good town of Paris a Royal Academy of Dancing." On June 28, 1669, Louis XIV of France grants royal letters patent for the establishment of a theatre in which to present opera and drama with music: L'Académie de Musique et de Danse, the institution we know today as the Paris Opéra. Although the name of this institution has changed with different French regimes and it has occupied numerous buildings, the name on the Théâtre de l'Opéra in Paris is L'Académie de Musique et de Danse, representing almost three hundred years of uninterrupted history in teaching and performance.

1664 On January 29, in *Le Mariage Forcé*, Italian composer and dancer Lully begins collaboration with the French poet-playwright Molière; *commedia dell'arte* combined with the tradition of French court dancing in the creation of comedy ballets to incidental music. Louis XIV, Lully, and Pierre Beauchamp, first great French dancer, participate in performance.

1670 *Les Amants Magnifiques* is presented: comedy ballet by Molière and Lully in which the performers "by their steps, gestures, and movements, visibly expressed all things." On October 23 there is presented *Le Bourgeois Gentilhomme*, last collaboration between Molière and Lully: play includes overture, ten musical numbers, dialogue for soprano and contralto, a ballet in Act One (*Ballet des Nations*), and finale for solo and chorus. Lully dances at the first performance. Excerpt from the play: "All the ills of mankind, all the tragic misfortunes that fill the history books, all political blunders, all the failures of great commanders, have arisen merely from lack of skill in dancing . . . When a man has been guilty of a mistake, either in ordering his own affairs, or in directing those of the State, or in commanding an army, do we not always say: so-and-so has made a false step . . . ?"

1671 *Psyche*, tragedy ballet by Molière, Corneille, Lully, and Quinault, presented on January 17.

1671 The Paris Académie opens on March 19 with *Pomone*, a *pastorale* with music by Cambert, dances by Beauchamp, and text by the Abbé Perrin, director of the Académie.

1671    Pierre Beauchamp, dancing master to the King, becomes first ballet master of the Académie. Dancing begins to be a profession, rather than a court pastime.

1672    Lully succeeds to the directorship of the Académie as composer, conductor, and manager; dancing school inaugurated under Beauchamp. Under Lully's direction, formal court dance is adjusted to the stage: larger, more open movements of the theatre replace small, confined gestures of the ballroom.

1672    Louis Pécourt, pupil of Beauchamp, makes his debut at the Académie, becomes *premier danseur*, dancing principal roles in ballets by Lully and Beauchamp. He was "handsome and well made," danced "with all possible noblesse," appeared always "with grace, justness, and activity," and was "so agreeable in conversation that the greatest lords took pleasure in his company."

1681    *The Triumph of Love* (Lully) presented on January 21 at St. Germaine en Laye, the first ballet in which women appeared as professional dancers. Ladies of the French court dance the first performance on this work (but it was later danced at L'Académie Royale, when Mademoiselle Lafontaine, first *première danseuse* in the history of ballet, made her debut).

1682    Père Claude François Menestrier's *Ballets Ancient and Modern* becomes the first published history of dancing.

1684    *An Arrow against Profane and Promiscuous Dancing Drawn Out of the Quiver of the Scriptures,* by Increase Mather, is published in Boston.

1687    Lully dies on March 22. In the fifteen years he superintended the Académie, Lully produced twenty grand operas in addition to other works and firmly established the new school of opera-ballet, in which music and dancing shared equally in the drama. Italian grand operas of this time give dancing a secondary place and include ballets only as *divertissements*. Lully, violinist and dancer, leaves French lyric drama so successfully formulated that Paris is the theatre capital of the world, a universally accepted model of teaching and execution.

1687    Beauchamp retires as ballet master; he is succeeded by Louis Pécourt.

1689    *Dido and Aeneas,* opera by Purcell, is performed by Josias Priest's Singing and Dancing Academy in London.

1697    Birth of Louis Dupré, *Le Grand Dupré,* great French dancer: a "rare harmony in movement earned for the celebrated Dupré the glorious title of *'Dieu de la Danse':* and in fact this excellent dancer seemed a divinity rather than a man: the calm and flowing continuity of his every movement and the perfect coordination and control of every muscle made for a perfect ensemble."—Noverre.

c.1700    Pierre Beauchamp names the five basic positions of the classic dance (*see* Glossary). As a dancer, Beauchamp had also been a model for future technique in dancing; he was a virtuoso executant of *pirouettes* and *tours en l'air.*

1701    *Choreography, or the Art of Writing Dancing* is published in Paris. This early work on dance notation was edited by Raoul Ager Feuillet; it has been attributed to Louis Pécourt.

1705    Françoise Prévost succeeds Mademoiselle Lafontaine as *première danseuse* at the Académie. Rameau wrote that Prévost "put into one single dance all the rules we are able to give in our art and she puts them into practice with such grace, justness, and activity that she may be looked upon as a prodigy of her kind."

1707 Birth of Marie Sallé. Niece of the famous harlequin Francisque Moylin, and daughter of a tumbler, she is to endow her dancing with dramatic gesture and mimed expression and become a great *danseuse* of the century.

1708 At the Château of the Duchesse du Maine, two celebrated dancers from the Opéra, Françoise Prévost and Jean Balon, perform the final scene of Act Four of Corneille's *Horace* as a pantomime. The scene is acted in silence, "through gestures and bodily movements, among which was not a single all-too-pronounced dance step": early introduction of dramatic mime into ballet.

1710 Marie-Anne Cupis de Camargo, celebrated French dancer of Spanish descent, is born on April 15; she becomes the principal rival of Sallé.

1712 *Manual,* by John Rich, provides a series of exercises for facility in dancing based on the five basic positions indicated by Arbeau (1588) and specified by Beauchamp (c. 1700): beginning of a systematic foundation for the ideal execution of the classic dance.

1714 Birth of Christoph Willibald Gluck, German composer, the founder of modern opera.

1717 On March 2, John Weaver, English dancer and ballet master at the Drury Lane Theatre, London, presents a "new dramatic pantomime, after the manner of the ancient pantomimes," *The Loves of Mars and Venus.* This pantomime ballet with a plot is the first *ballet d'action* on record. Wrote Colley Cibber: "The fable of Mars and Venus was formed into a connected presentation of dances in character, wherein the passions were so happily expressed, and the whole story was so intelligibly told, by a mute narration of gesture only, that even thinking spectators allowed it both a pleasing and rational entertainment."

1721 *Anatomical and Mechanical Lectures upon Dancing,* by John Weaver, is published: establishment of an anatomical base for proper dance instruction. "Dancing is an elegant and regular movement, harmoniously composed of beautiful *Attitudes,* and contrasted graceful postures of the Body, and parts thereof."

1725 *The Dancing Master,* by Pierre Rameau, is published: descriptions of dances of the time and detailed instructions on the five absolute positions. "Dancing adds graces to the gifts which nature has bestowed upon us, by regulating the movements of the body and setting it in its proper positions. And, if we do not completely eradicate the defects with which we are born, it mitigates or conceals them. This single instance will suffice to explain its utility and to excite a desire to be skilled in it."

1725 Marie Sallé appears at John Rich's Lincoln's Inn Fields Theatre, London, in ballet-pantomimes. It was in England, rather than in the set, conventional pattern of ballet at the Paris Opéra, that Sallé could use freely the gestural dance that interested her. She was so popular, however, that the Opéra continually asked her to return. When she did so, the Opéra was obliged to produce the *ballets d'action* that she acted and danced with such expression. Thus popularity and intelligence combined to introduce a new kind of ballet to Europe.

1726 Marie Camargo makes her debut at the Opéra on May 5.

1726 First French dancing master is appointed to the Court of Denmark.

1727 Jean Georges Noverre is born on April 29.

1729 Gaetan Vestris is born in April, in Florence. He becomes the first *danseur* of his time, the first great classical dancer in Europe, a choreographer, mime, and ballet master; he is student of Louis Dupré.

c.1730    The *danse haute* (high dance) begins to replace the *danse terre à terre* (dance close to earth). The old court spectacles had been performed in rooms, with the audiences grouped about the dance area on raised platforms. In the theatre, the stage itself was raised and the audience watched from below. Lully's ballets, though making certain concessions to the theatre, still remained horizontal, describing dances on the horizontal plane of the stage floor as if it were still the ballroom and audiences were looking down on it. Rameau aimed at a vertical dance, where a theatre audience could be entertained by dancers who jumped and leaped. In the fierce controversy that raged between the Lullists and Rameauists, the latter found great support in the popularity of the spectacular *danse haute* of Marie Camargo, who about this time shortened the traditional ballet dress in order that the audience might see the *entrechat* and other remarkable steps of elevation. Camargo is credited with introducing the ninety-degree turnout for dancers and the *entrechat-quatre* (see Glossary).

1734    Marie Sallé creates in London the ballet-pantomime *Pygmalion.* "She has dared to appear in this *entrée* without pannier, skirt, or bodice, and with her hair down; she did not wear a single ornament on her head. Apart from her corset and petticoat she wore only a simple dress of muslin draped about her in the manner of a Greek statue."

1735    Opening of the Imperial Dancing Academy in St. Petersburg, Russia, as the Empress Anna Ivanovna orders that all cadets be taught to dance in order to replace foreign artists at the Russian court. A Frenchman, Lande, is appointed director and an Italian, Francesco Araya, is engaged to teach the cadets Italian dances.

1735    *Les Indes Galantes,* opera-ballet by J. P. Rameau, is presented at the Opéra on August 23 with Dupré, Camargo, and Sallé.

c.1737    The works of Jean Philippe Rameau begin to replace those of Lully at the Académie. At this time, the original thirty-seven members of the company have increased to one hundred and forty-nine.

1738    Imperial St. Petersburg Theatrical Academy (now the Leningrad Choreographic Academy) is founded.

1743    Jean Georges Noverre, pupil of Dupré, makes his debut at the Opéra Comique, Paris.

1745    *The Princess of Navarre,* lyric comedy ballet by Rameau, libretto by Voltaire, is produced.

1745    On December 29, Jean Barthélemy produces in Berlin his recollection of Marie Sallé's *Pygmalion.* The statue is danced by La Barberina (Barberina Campanini), Italian *danseuse* who popularizes the Italian pantomime in European dance. She appeared at the Opéra, where Rameau arranged dances for her, and in London at John Rich's theatre, where she acquired knowledge of English pantomime. C. H. Graun composes for this production of *Pygmalion* music that substitutes for the conventional dance numbers a free score related directly to the action: the first score of this kind. Among the dancers in this production is Jean Georges Noverre.

1746    "It is up to poetry, music, and dance to present to us the image of human actions and passions," writes Charles Batteux, *Les Beaux Arts reduit à un même principe.*

1748    The Royal Theatre, home of the Royal Danish Ballet, opens in Copenhagen.

1750    Noverre partners Camargo at Lyon.

c.1751  Noverre stages his first ballet, *Les Fêtes Chinoises* (*The Chinese Festivals*).

1751    Gaetan Vestris succeeds Louis Dupré as *premier danseur* at the Opéra.

1755    On February 5, Noverre signs contract with David Garrick to arrange dances at the Drury Lane Theatre, London. To Garrick, Noverre is "the Shakespeare of the Dance." To Noverre, Garrick is "the most handsome, the most perfect, and the most worthy of admiration of all actors; he may be regarded as the Proteus of our time, because he understood all styles and presented them with a perfection and truth which aroused not only the applause and praise of his countrymen, but also excited the admiration and encomiums of all foreigners. He was so natural, his expression was so lifelike, his gestures, features, glances were so eloquent and convincing, that he made the action clear even to those who did not understand a word of English."

1756    Marie Sallé dies. Writes her friend Noverre: "Mademoiselle Sallé . . . replaced tinsel glitter by simple and touching graces. Her physiognomy was noble, sensitive, and expressive. Her voluptuous dancing was written with as much finesse as lightness; it was not by leaps and frolics that she went to your heart."

c.1757  Gallini sees "the celebrated Dupré, at near the age of sixty, dance at Paris with all the agility and sprightliness of youth, and with such power of pleasing as if the graces in him had braved superannuation."

1757    "The dance still awaits a man of genius. It is in a bad state everywhere, for hardly anyone suspects the essence of it to be a kind of imitation . . . A dance is a poem. This poem should have its independent representation. It is an 'imitation' by virtue of the movements, an imitation which presupposes the collaboration of poet, painter, musicians, and pantomime-dancer."—Denis Diderot.

1760    On March 1, Noverre at Stuttgart, ballet master to the court of the Duke of Württemberg, begins reforms in the direction of the *ballet d'action*, pantomime ballet with definite plot, where dance is integrated with the action of the story.

1760    Auguste Vestris, great French dancer, son of Gaetan Vestris and the *danseuse* Marie Allard is born on March 27. Said his father, Gaetan: "Auguste is more skillful than I and the explanation is simple: Gaetan is his father—an advantage nature denied me." Auguste Vestris is credited with introducing the *entrechat-huit* and multiple pirouettes. He was the teacher of Charles Didelot, Jules Perrot, Carlotta Grisi, and Fanny Elssler, among others.

1760    Marie Allard makes her debut in June at the Opéra, Paris. Allard soon becomes a ballerina. She is a student of Gaetan Vestris.

1760    Noverre's *Letters on the Dance and Ballets* published in December in Lyon and Stuttgart: "Children of Terpsichore, renounce *caprioles, entrechats,* and overcomplicated steps; abandon grimaces to study sentiments . . . study how to make your gestures noble, never forget that is the lifeblood of dancing; put judgment and sense into your *pas de deux* . . . away with those lifeless masks, but feeble copies of nature; they hide your features, they stifle, so to speak, your emotions and thus deprive you of your most important means of expression; take off those enormous wigs and those gigantic headdresses . . . discard the use of those stiff and cumbersome hoops, which disfigure the elegance of your attitudes . . . Lully's dance music is cold, tedious, and devoid of character . . . What was compatible then is no longer so . . . A well-composed ballet is a living picture of the passions, manners, habits, ceremonies, and customs of all nations of the globe, consequently it must be expressive in all its details and speak to the soul through the eyes; if it be devoid of expression, of striking pictures, of strong situations, it becomes a cold and dreary spectacle. This form of art will not admit of mediocrity."

1761　On June 12 there takes place at the Opéra the debut of Dauberval, afterward *premier danseur* and choreographer of the first comic ballet; he was a student of Noverre.

1761　*Don Juan*, "pantomime ballet in the manner of the ancients," with music by Gluck and choreography by Gasparo Angiolini (1723–96), is presented on October 17. This work, created independently of Noverre, claims to be the first of its kind. Its music and dancing are subordinate to a plot; Gluck's score is composed in terms of stage action.

1762　The *première* of Gluck's *Orpheus and Eurydice* takes place on October 5 at the Burg Theatre, Vienna. This opera epitomizes for music what the new *ballet d'action* of Noverre accomplished for dancing. Just as Noverre wished to replace the virtuoso dancer with action and meaningful gesture, Gluck in *Orpheus* broke the tyranny of the virtuoso singer and replaced casually connected solos with musical drama. The first production of *Orpheus* has ballets by Angiolini; a later production, ballets by Noverre.

1763　*Jason and Medea, ballet d'action* by Noverre, to music by Rodolphe, is produced on February 11 at Stuttgart with Gaetan Vestris as Jason.

1766　Double pirouettes are introduced in Paris by the German ballerina Anna Heinel.

1767　Noverre is appointed ballet master to the Imperial Theatres in Vienna, dancing master to Empress Maria Theresa and her family, and teacher of her daughter, Marie Antoinette; this is the beginning of his collaboration with Gluck.

1767　Birth of Charles Louis Didelot, French dancer, choreographer, ballet master, "father of the Russian ballet."

1767　The first performance of *Alcestis*, opera by Gluck with ballet by Noverre, takes place on December 26 at the Burg Theatre, Vienna. In his dedication of the opera, Gluck applies Noverre's doctrine to opera: "I shall try to reduce music to its real function, that of seconding poetry by intensifying the expression of sentiments and the interest of situations without interrupting the action by needless ornament. I have accordingly taken care not to interrupt the singer in the heat of dialogue to wait for a tedious *ritournel*, nor do I allow him to stop on a sonorous vowel, in the middle of a phrase, in order to show the nimbleness of a beautiful voice in a long cadenza."

1768　John Durang, first American to become famous as a dancer, is born on January 6.

1769　Salvatore Vigano, Italian dancer, choreographer, teacher, and ballet master—student of Dauberval—is born on March 25. "It is not enough for me to please the eye; I wish to interest the heart."

1770　Gaetan Vestris revives Noverre's *Jason and Medea* on December 11 at the Opéra, Paris, with Marie Allard. Vestris discards the mask customarily worn by dancers, freeing the features for expressive mime and the dramatic expression essential to Noverre's *ballet d'action*. A member of the audience later wrote of Vestris' performance: "The particular merit of Vestris was his grace, his elegance, his delicacy. All his *pas* had a purity, a finish of which one can have no idea today, and it was not without reason that they compare his talent to that of Racine."

1771    Noverre produces on October 17 a second version of his ballet *Les Jalousies ou Les Fêtes du Serail* at the Teatro Regio Ducal, Milan, to music by Mozart. The ballet performed between the two acts of Mozart's festival production is *Ascanio in Alba.*

c.1772    "Ballet is an action explained by a dance" appears in the *Encyclopedia* of Diderot and D'Alembert.

1773    Maximilien Gardel, *premier danseur,* discards his mask in performances at the Opéra.

1774    Noverre becomes ballet master at Milan.

1775    Royal Theatre, Copenhagen, engages Vincenzo Galeotti as ballet master, choreographer, and *premier danseur.* A student of Noverre, Galeotti remained active in Denmark until 1816. He built up a repertory of some fifty ballets which have been performed more than two thousand times.

1776    Gaetan Vestris becomes ballet master at the Paris Opéra.

1776    Revival of Noverre's *Les Caprices de Galathée* in November at the Opéra, Paris, with Madeleine Guimard, Marie Allard, and Le Picq.

1776    Ernest Theodor Amadeus Hoffmann, German writer, composer, lawyer, and masterful writer of romances, is born on January 24. Hoffmann wrote many imaginative and supernatural stories, of which only a few are contained in Offenbach's opera *Tales of Hoffmann.* The ballets *Coppélia* and *The Nutcracker* are based on two of Hoffmann's stories.

1776    Noverre succeeds Gaetan Vestris as ballet master at the Opéra in August; appointed by his former pupil, Marie Antoinette, now Queen of France.

1778    First performance of *Les Petits Riens* (Mozart-Noverre) at the Opéra, Paris, on June 11.

1778    August 3: Teatro alla Scala opens in Milan. Five ballets are produced the first year.

1779    *Mirza, ballet d'action* by Maximilien Gardel, with Gardel, Dauberval, A. Vestris, Guimard, and Allard, is presented in Paris. Act Three of this work takes place in America; it is the first ballet with an American scene.

1779    On May 18, Gluck and Noverre produce *Iphigenia in Tauris* in collaboration.

1780    Noverre becomes ballet master at the King's Theatre, London.

1781    On October 13, Mozart, writing on opera in a letter to his father, reaffirms Noverre's principles: "Why do Italian comic operas please everywhere—in spite of their miserable libretti? . . . Just because in them music reigns supreme, and when one listens to it all else is forgotten. Why, an opera is sure of success when the plot is well worked out, the words written solely for the music and not shoved in here and there to suit some miserable rhyme (which, God knows, never enhances the value of any theatrical performance, be it what it may, but rather detracts from it) . . ."

1783    First English translation of Noverre's *Letters* is published.

1783    The Bolshoi Theatre, until 1889 the center of Russian ballet, opens in St. Petersburg on October 5.*

1786    *La Fille Mal Gardée* (Dauberval-Hertel), probably the first comic ballet, is presented.

1786    *Les Caprices du Cupidon et le Maître du Ballet* (Galeotti) is produced on October 31 at the Royal Theatre, Copenhagen. This ballet has been in the

---

* New Russian calendar dates are used throughout this book. Exceptions are those few instances where tradition or the preference of living persons dictates the use of the Old Style. Both Old and New Style dates are used in these few cases.

repertory of the Royal Danish Ballet since its first performance; it is the oldest ballet in existence with its original choreography intact. Harald Lander revived the ballet for the Paris Opéra on February 27, 1952.

1792     Alexander Placide and his wife dance a ballet, *The Bird Catcher,* on January 25 in New York. John Durang, first professional American dancer, is in the cast.

1795     *Jason and Medea,* great *ballet d'action* by Noverre, is produced in St. Petersburg by his student Le Picq.

1796     *Flore and Zéphire,* ballet by Didelot, is produced on July 7 in London: the first ballet in which a dancer is suspended on wire to simulate flight.

1796     *Danse,* by M. L. E. Moreau de Saint-Méry, is published in Philadelphia. Probably the first book on dancing published in the United States, *Danse* was freely quoted by Blasis thirty-four years later. Saint-Méry expressed the opinion that the principal object of the dance is "the same as that of music, the expression of sentiment and passions. A gesture is beautiful only when it depicts sadness, tenderness, pride—in a word, the soul."

1801     Charles Didelot becomes choreographer at the Imperial Russian Theatre. Pushkin, the great Russian poet, expresses the opinion that in Didelot's ballets there is more poetry than in all the French literature of the period. Didelot believed that ballet must have a plot; that dancers, in accordance with the action, must be able to solve their own problems, reconstruct the characters themselves: "A true dancer must be also a good actor and a poet at heart." His teachers were Auguste Vestris, Noverre, and Dauberval. Didelot is known as the "father of the Russian ballet."

1801     *The Creatures of Prometheus* (Beethoven-Vigano) is produced on March 28 at the Court Theatre, Vienna.

1803     Noverre's *Letters* is translated into Russian and Danish.

1804     Marie Taglioni, great ballerina of the Romantic era, is born on April 23.

1805     Hans Christian Andersen, Danish poet and fabulist, balletomane, is born on April 2. Andersen's fairy stories provide plots for many ballets.

1808     Gaetan Vestris dies on September 23.

1810     Noverre dies on October 19.

1810     Fanny Elssler, Romantic ballerina, is born on June 23.

1810     Jules Perrot, great *danseur* of the Romantic ballet and its finest choreographer, is born on August 18; creator, with Jean Coralli, of *Giselle, Pas de Quatre,* etc. In Perrot's view, ballet must be filled with dramatic action and presented as a realistic reflection of life. He was responsible for the integration of dance and pantomime that made possible the dramatic ballet as we know it today. His teachers were Auguste Vestris and Salvatore Vigano.

1811     Théophile Gautier, poet, novelist, critic, guiding spirit of the Romantic ballet, is born on August 31.

1812     The celebrated dancer and student of Dauberval, Salvatore Vigano, becomes ballet master at La Scala, Milan, and progress in the development of ballet shifts from France to Italy. Vigano's contribution was the *choreodrame,* or dance drama, a more complete development of Noverre's *ballet d'action* than had been realized in France. This was a dramatic spectacle that integrated principals, moving masses of dancers, and authentic backgrounds with music. His work anticipated Fokine's reforms and the mass spectacles of D. W. Griffith by a hundred years.

1815     Birth of Arthur Michel Saint-Léon, French dancer, choreographer, musician, and ballet master.

1816     Charles Didelot becomes first ballet master at the Imperial Russian Theatre.

He remains in Russia until his death in 1837. In addition to the many excellent ballets Didelot produces in Russia, he establishes in the Imperial School the teaching methods and techniques that are afterward to make it famous.

1816    Antoine Bournonville, pupil of Noverre, succeeds Galeotti as ballet master and choreographer at the Royal Theatre, Copenhagen.

1819    Birth of Carlotta Grisi, ballerina of the Romantic era, creator of *Giselle*.

1820    Carlo Blasis' *Elementary Treatise on the Theory and Practice of the Art of Dancing* is published in Milan. The first complete work on dance technique, this book is still the primary text of classical dancing today.

1820    This is the approximate beginning of the Romantic ballet.

1821    Fanny Cerrito, Romantic ballerina, is born.

1821    Lucile Grahn, Danish ballerina of the Romantic era, is born on June 30.

1821    Salvatore Vigano dies on August 10.

1821    Date of the first known print depicting a dancer *sur les pointes* (on toe). Dancing on *pointes* is the outstanding innovation in technique of the Romantic ballet.

1822    On February 6, gas lighting is first used at the Paris Opéra. The soft, misty quality of this lighting did much to support the ethereal scenes of the Romantic ballet.

1822    Marius Petipa, great choreographer and ballet master, the founder of Russian classicism, is born on March 24.

1822    Marie Taglioni makes her debut on June 10 at the Hoftheatre, Vienna, in a ballet created especially for her by her father, Philippe Taglioni: *The Reception of a Young Nymph at the Court of Terpsichore*. Another young dancer in the ballet who was also making her debut: Fanny Elssler.

1825    Birth of Augusta Maywood, first American ballerina to become internationally famous.

1825    The Bolshoi Theatre, Moscow, opens on January 18. The Moscow Ballet alone danced in this theatre until 1939, when it became the principal Soviet ballet theatre.

1826    Auguste Vestris gives his farewell performance at the Opéra.

1829    Auguste Bournonville succeeds his father, Antoine, as ballet master, choreographer, and *premier danseur* at the Royal Theatre, Copenhagen. Until his death, in 1879, Bournonville worked almost uninterruptedly in Denmark. He was the Royal Danish Ballet's greatest choreographic genius and also its finest organizer. He made ballet equivalent to opera and drama in importance at the Royal Theatre, developed Danish dancers, and enriched the Danish repertory with more than fifty original ballets. These works were not only romantic, in conformance with their time, but bright, comic ballets that depicted the life of the people. *Napoli,* his presentation of Italian life, is perhaps the finest of the ten ballets by Bournonville still performed in Copenhagen. A great dancer himself, the pupil of his father's friend Auguste Vestris and of Galeotti, Bournonville choreographed—in opposition to the French *ballet blanc*—for men as much as for women. Wrote Hans Christian Andersen: "When the Italian Galeotti died in Denmark, Terpsichore wept. Who was there that could supply his place as ballet composer? No one took his place; but a new one was born, who, like every true genius, made his own way—and that is Bournonville."

1829    Carlo Blasis' *Code of Terpsichore,* primary text for dancers, establishes fundamentals of the modern classic dance.

1830    The sylphide costume first appears, in Paris. This long, diaphanous ballet dress that reaches well below the knee, almost to the ankle, was named *post facto* for *La Sylphide*, the famous ballet created by Marie Taglioni in 1832. In its guise appeared many heroines of the Romantic ballet; the costume is still familiar in the second act of *Giselle*, in *Swan Lake*, and in *Les Sylphides*.

1830    Jules Perrot makes his debut at the Opéra.

1830    *Le Dieu et la Bayadère* (P. Taglioni-Auber-Scribe) is presented at the Opéra on October 13 with Marie Taglioni.

1831    Jean Coralli becomes ballet master at the Opéra.

1831    This is the probable date of the first *ballet blanc*, or white ballet, familiar today in *Giselle* (Act Two), *Les Sylphides*, et al., at the Paris Opéra.

1832    Marie Taglioni dances the title role in *La Sylphide* on March 12.

1832    *La Sylphide* is presented in London on July 26 at the Theatre Royal, Covent Garden, with Marie and Paul Taglioni.

1834    Birth of Lev Ivanov, first great Russian choreographer (*Swan Lake*, etc.).

1834    Edgar Degas, French painter of the ballet, is born on July 19.

1834    Fanny Elssler makes her debut at the Paris Opéra in September, in *La Tempête* (Coralli). Elssler's immediate and brilliant success begins at this point to challenge the supremacy of Marie Taglioni, whose rival she never ceased to be.

1835    Auguste Vestris, age seventy-five, partners Marie Taglioni in a minuet at a special performance at the Opéra on April 8.

1835    The first American performance of *La Sylphide*, by Céleste, takes place on April 15.

1835    Fanny Cerrito makes her debut at the San Carlo Theatre, Naples. "There must be youth, and that I found in Cerrito! It was something incomparably beautiful, it was a swallow flight in the dance, a sport of Psyche," writes Hans Christian Andersen.

1835    The first book of Hans Christian Andersen's *Fairy Tales* (*Eventyr*) is published in Copenhagen.

1836    Clément Philibert Léo Delibes, French composer, is born on February 21.

1836    Carlotta Grisi makes her London debut on April 12 in a *pas de deux* with her husband, Jules Perrot.

1836    Fanny Elssler appears in *Le Diable Boiteux* (*The Devil on Two Sticks*), ballet by Jean Coralli, at the Paris Opéra, on June 1.

1836    Auguste Bournonville stages *La Sylphide* for Lucile Grahn at the Royal Theatre, Copenhagen. This version, which had new music by the Danish composer Herman Løvenskjold, has been in the repertory of the Royal Danish Ballet since it was first produced.

1836    Théophile Gautier begins to write art and theatre criticism for *La Presse* in Paris.

1837    Carlo Blasis is appointed director of the Imperial Academy of Dancing and Pantomime at La Scala, Milan.

1837    Marie Taglioni makes her St. Petersburg debut on September 30, in *La Sylphide*. Taglioni remains in Russia until 1841.

1837    Augusta Maywood and Mary Ann Lee make their debuts in *The Maid of Cashmere* (*Le Dieu et la Bayadère*) on December 30 at the Chestnut Street Theatre, Philadelphia.

1838    Lucile Grahn makes her Paris debut.

1838    *La Sylphide* with Augusta Maywood in the title role and Mary Ann Lee as Flora is presented on March 17, at the Chestnut Street Theatre, Philadelphia.

c.1838 George Washington Smith, first American *danseur noble,* makes his debut at the Chestnut Street Theatre. Smith partners the American ballerinas Lee and Maywood, and Fanny Elssler. His popularity is such that he receives equal billing with all of his famous partners.

1839 Marius Petipa visits the United States with his father, Jean Antoine Petipa, in the ballet company of Madame Lacomte.

1839 *La Sylphide,* with Paul Taglioni and his wife Marie is presented on May 21, at the Park Theatre, New York.

1839 The American ballerina Augusta Maywood makes her debut on November 11 at the Paris Opéra.

1840 Carlotta Grisi makes her debut in Paris on February 28.

1840 Peter Ilyich Tchaikovsky is born on May 7/19.

1840 Fanny Elssler makes her American debut on May 14 at the Park Theatre, New York, in *La Tarentule* (Coralli) and a solo, *La Cracovienne.* Elssler's success is greater than that accorded any other European artist up to this time; she is received by President Van Buren, feted by Congress, and becomes the adored idol of millions.

1840 Fanny Elssler dances *La Sylphide* in New York on June 1.

1840 Marius Petipa first dances in Paris, at the Comédie Française, with Carlotta Grisi.

1841 In June, Fanny Cerrito dances *La Sylphide* in London.

1841 Christian Johansson, brilliant pupil of Auguste Bournonville, makes his debut at the Imperial Russian Theatre, on June 24, in a *pas de deux* with the ballerina Andreyanova. Johansson later becomes *premier danseur.*

1841 First performance of *Giselle* (Adam-Perrot-Coralli), greatest of all the Romantic ballets, takes place on June 28, with Carlotta Grisi and Lucien Petipa, at the Paris Opéra. Writes Théophile Gautier: "Carlotta danced with a perfection, a lightness, boldness and chaste and delicate voluptuousness which place her in the first rank between Taglioni and Elssler; as for pantomime she exceeded all expectations; not a conventional gesture, not a false movement; she was nature and artlessness personified. True, she has Perrot the Aerial for husband and teacher."

1842 Perrot is in London as dancer, choreographer, and ballet master; active there until 1848.

1842 Fanny Elssler dances *La Fille Mal Gardée* on July 1, during her last performance in the United States. The visit that had been scheduled to last only for a few months has been extended to more than two years.

1842 Marie Taglioni's farewell performance in St. Petersburg takes place on March 30.

1842 *Napoli,* masterpiece by Auguste Bournonville, is presented on March 29 by the Royal Danish Ballet. This ballet has been in the active repertory of this company ever since it was first produced.

1842 Auguste Vestris dies on December 5.

1843 Lucile Grahn makes her St. Petersburg debut in January, in *Giselle.*

1844 *Les Trois Graces* (*The Three Graces*), famous Romantic ballet print by Eugene Lejeune, is published in London on June 1. This lithograph is unique in its portrayal of three great dancers of the Romantic period: Taglioni as *La Sylphide,* Fanny Elssler as Florinda in *Le Diable Boiteux,* and Carlotta Grisi as Beatrix-Diane in *La Jolie Fille de Gand.* Elssler is the center and pre-eminent figure in the print—an acknowledgment of her supremacy over the older Taglioni and the younger Grisi. The identity of the designer and the accurate identity of all three Graces—overlooked for a hundred years—was not established until 1944 by George Chaffée, who related his findings in *Dance Index* (Vol. 3, Nos. 9–11).

1844    The American dancer Mary Ann Lee studies with Jean Coralli at the Paris Opéra.

1845    Taglioni, Grisi, Cerrito, and Grahn dance Jules Perrot's *Pas de Quatre* at Her Majesty's Theatre, London, on July 12.

1845    The Russian ballerina Andreyanova appears in Paris. Andreyanova studied with Taglioni when the latter visited Russia and in 1842 danced a version of *Giselle* in St. Petersburg. She was probably the first Russian dancer to appear in Paris.

1846    Taglioni, Grahn, and Cerrito appear as the Goddesses, Perrot as Mercury and Saint-Léon as Paris, in *The Judgment of Paris* (Perrot-Pugni) at Her Majesty's Theatre, London, on July 23.

1846    *Giselle* is presented for the first time in America on January 1, with Mary Ann Lee and George Washington Smith, at the Howard Atheneum, Boston.

1847    Marie Taglioni retires.

1847    Mazilier succeeds Coralli as ballet master at the Opéra.

1847    Marius Petipa arrives in St. Petersburg as *premier danseur* at the Imperial Theatre.

1848    *Première* of *Faust,* fantastic ballet in seven scenes, ballet by Jules Perrot, is held on February 12 at La Scala, Milan. Fanny Elssler dances the first performance of this ballet; the American ballerina Augusta Maywood, the second. Maywood, who is to remain in Europe and found her ballet company, shares with Elssler the highest title a dancer can have in Italy: *prima ballerina e prima mima assoluta.*

1848    Fanny Elssler makes her Russian debut on October 22, in *Giselle.*

1848    Jules Perrot dances for the first time at the Imperial Russian Theatre on October 31. Perrot was ballet master at the Imperial Theatre from 1851–59.

1850    Enrico Cecchetti, dancer and teacher, is born on June 21.

1850    Lev Ivanov becomes a dancer at the Imperial Russian Theatre on March 2. Dancer, musician, and choreographer, Ivanov becomes second ballet master at the Imperial Theatre in 1855; as such he is chief assistant to Marius Petipa, who entrusts to him the choreography of *The Nutcracker* and almost the whole of *Swan Lake.*

1851    Carlotta Grisi makes her Russian debut on October 20, in *Giselle;* she remains in Russia until 1853.

1851    Last appearance of Fanny Elssler, in Jules Perrot's ballet *Faust,* on June 21, in Vienna.

1851    Cesare Pugni, Italian composer, is appointed official ballet composer at the Imperial Russian Theatre. In his many years in St. Petersburg, Pugni turns out music for more than three hundred ballets. This music is completely subservient to dance and possesses little dramatic interest. Only with the ballet scores of Delibes and Tchaikovsky does ballet become a coherent musical and choreographic whole.

c.1854  Carlotta Grisi retires.

1855    Fanny Cerrito makes her St. Petersburg debut.

1857    Enrico Cecchetti, age seven, appears with his family in the Ronzani Ballet at the opening of the Academy of Music in Philadelphia.

1858    The Royal Opera House, Covent Garden, London, first opens in its present form. Since its reopening after World War II, Covent Garden has maintained two state-supported institutions: the Covent Garden Opera and the

Royal Ballet. Ballet was not regularly performed at Covent Garden until 1946.

1859   Arthur Michel Saint-Léon makes his debut at the Imperial Theatre, St. Petersburg, on October 19. Saint-Léon becomes ballet master and remains in Russia until 1867, when he is appointed ballet master at the Paris Opéra.

1860   The Maryinsky Theatre in St. Petersburg opens on October 14. This famous Russian theatre, today the Kirov State Academic Theatre of Opera and Ballet in Leningrad, was the home of the Imperial Russian Ballet from 1889 to 1939. Since the Bolshevik Revolution, the center of Soviet ballet has gradually shifted to Moscow and the Bolshoi Theatre, Moscow.

1860   Marius Petipa restages *Giselle* at the Imperial Russian Theatre, St. Petersburg, on October 20.

1860   Christian Johansson begins to teach at the Russian Imperial School. Johansson's fame as a teacher exceeds his fame as a dancer; what Petipa is to the theatre, Johansson is to the classroom. From 1860 until his retirement, soon after the turn of the century, Johansson is the master of all the great Russian dancers of this period. Pavlova and Fokine were but a few of his pupils.

1862   *The Daughter of Pharaoh* (Petipa-Pugni), first great success in Russia of Marius Petipa, is presented on January 30. This monumental spectacle, with scenes set in the desert, in pyramids, and in colossal palaces, introduces the mass dance on a large scale. Petipa stages the work in six weeks. With its success he becomes ballet master to the Imperial Theatre and begins that reign over Russian ballet that was to last almost until his death, nearly fifty years later.

1864   *The Humpbacked Horse* (Pugni/Saint-Léon), first ballet with a Russian theme, is produced by the Frenchman Saint-Léon in St. Petersburg on December 27.

1865   Lucien Petipa becomes ballet master at the Paris Opéra.

1866   Paul Gerdt becomes *premier danseur* at the Imperial Russian Theatre. He is twenty-two years old. Gerdt remains a first dancer in St. Petersburg for fifty years, until his retirement in 1916. He is Franz in Petipa's revival of *Coppélia* (1884) and the prince in the first productions of *The Sleeping Beauty* (1890) and *The Nutcracker* (1892). In 1907 he appears as a young man in *Le Pavillon d'Armide* (Fokine-Tcherepnine-Benois) with two of his famous pupils, Anna Pavlova and Vaslav Nijinsky. As classical dancer, partner, and mime, he is regarded by many as the finest *danseur noble* ever to appear on the Russian stage. As a teacher, he is in large part responsible for the excellence of the Imperial School in classes for mime and supported adagio. Among his pupils: Pavlova, Fokine, and Balanchine.

1866   *The Black Crook* is presented on September 12 at Niblo's Garden, New York City. Marie Bonfanti and Rita Sangalli, both students of Carlo Blasis, are among the dancers who appear in this popular musical extravaganza, which runs for 475 nights.

1867   Saint-Léon becomes ballet master at the Paris Opéra.

1869   Nicholas Legat, dancer, teacher, and choreographer, is born on December 27 in Moscow. Although he is a fine dancer, Legat becomes important principally as an excellent teacher. At the Imperial Ballet School and, later, in Europe, he trains many dancers who afterward become famous. Legat teaches in London after leaving Russia in 1914; the school he starts there is continued by his wife.

1870   The *première* of *Coppélia* (Saint-Léon/Delibes) takes place on May 25 at the Paris Opéra.

1870    Enrico Cecchetti makes his debut at La Scala, Milan.

1871    Birth of Carlotta Zambelli, ballerina, great teacher at the Paris Opéra.

1872    Serge Diaghilev is born on March 31.

1872    Théophile Gautier dies on October 23.

1875    The opening of the present Paris Opéra takes place on January 5. From the time of its founding in 1669, the Académie de Musique et de Danse has produced opera and ballet in twelve different buildings; this is its permanent home.

1876    *Sylvia, or The Nymph of Diana* (Mérante-Delibes) is first presented on June 14 at the Paris Opéra, with Rita Sangalli and Mérante.

1877    The first production of *Swan Lake* (Reisinger-Tchaikovsky) is presented on March 4 at the Bolshoi Theatre, Moscow.

1878    Isadora Duncan, American dancer, is born on May 27. "Man must speak, then sing, then dance. But the speaking is the brain, the thinking man. The singing is the emotion. The dancing is the Dionysian ecstasy which carries all away. It is impossible to mix in any way, one with the other."

1880    Michel Fokine, Russian dancer, choreographer and ballet master is born on May 8. "As a reformer, he is to the twentieth century what Noverre was to the eighteenth, for he has exerted a profound and beneficial influence in every branch of the art of ballet."—C. W. Beaumont.

1881    Anna Pavlova is born on January 15.

1882    Igor Stravinsky is born on June 17/29.

1882    Lev Ivanov is appointed *régisseur* of the Imperial Russian Ballet.

1883    The Metropolitan Opera House, New York, opens on October 22.

1884    Marie Taglioni dies in Marseille on April 23.

1884    Fanny Elssler dies on November 27.

1885    The Italian ballerina Virginia Zucchi, pupil of Carlo Blasis, first appears in Russia. Zucchi's dazzling technique compels the Imperial Ballet School to balance the softer French style of dancing with the brilliant grace of the more vigorous Italian style in its instruction.

1885    Paul Gerdt celebrates his twenty-fifth anniversary on the Russian Imperial stage, in *La Fille Mal Gardée*.

1885    Lev Ivanov is appointed second ballet master of the Imperial Russian Ballet.

1885    Birth of Tamara Karsavina.

1887    Enrico Cecchetti, Italian dancer, is engaged by the Imperial Theatre in St. Petersburg on November 23. As a dancer, as one of the second ballet masters (1890), and, most importantly, as a teacher at the Imperial School (1892–1902), in Diaghilev's Ballets Russes (1909), and at his own school in London (1918), Cecchetti instructs and influences many great dancers: Pavlova, Karsavina, Nijinsky, et al.

1889    On April 25, the Maryinsky Theatre, St. Petersburg, becomes the center of the Imperial Russian Ballet. This famous theatre (now the Kirov State Academic Theatre of Opera and Ballet) remains the official home of Russian ballet until 1939.

1889    Olga Preobrajenska is graduated from the Russian Imperial Academy. She is ballerina at the Maryinsky Theatre for many years, until 1917, and teacher, in Paris, of Irina Baronova, Tamara Toumanova, Tatiana Riabouchinska, and many others.

1890    The first performance of *The Sleeping Beauty* (Petipa-Tchaikovsky) takes place on January 27 at the Maryinsky Theatre, St. Petersburg.

1891    Léo Delibes dies on January 16.

1892    Jules Perrot dies on August 29.

1893    Peter Ilyich Tchaikovsky dies on November 6/17.

1894    Hans Beck becomes ballet master at the Royal Theatre, Copenhagen.

1895    The first presentation of the complete *Swan Lake,* with choreography by
        Lev Ivanov and Marius Petipa, is given on February 8 at the Maryinsky
        Theatre, St. Petersburg, for the benefit of the Italian ballerina Pïerina Leg-
        nani.

1895    A "class in perfection" is introduced at the Russian Imperial School for
        dancers who have been graduated and are dancing regularly at the
        Maryinsky Theatre. Christian Johansson is the first teacher of this class,
        which is taken later by Nicholas Legat.

1898    Michel Fokine makes his debut on May 8 at the Imperial Theatre.

1899    Carlotta Grisi dies on May 22.

1899    Anna Pavlova makes her debut on June 25 at the Maryinsky Theatre.

1899    Isadora Duncan makes her debut in Chicago. This recital is not a success,
        and it is not until the following year, when she first dances in Paris, that
        Duncan's innovations are appreciated.

1899    The magazine *World of Art* first appears in St. Petersburg. Founded by
        Serge Diaghilev, Léon Bakst, and Alexandre Benois, this magazine gives first
        expression to those ideas of modern art that are to dominate Diaghilev's
        Ballets Russes.

1900    Vaslav Nijinsky enters the Imperial Dancing Academy in St. Petersburg on
        September 1.

1901    Lev Ivanov dies; he was a Russian ballet master, dancer, and choreographer,
        the choreographer of *The Nutcracker* and *Swan Lake* (except for Act One
        and Act Three, which are the work of Petipa). Associated with the Imperial
        Russian Theatre from the time of his graduation from the Imperial School in
        1852 for almost fifty years, Ivanov remained inconspicuous because of
        jealousies and theatre intrigue.

1902    Tamara Karsavina makes her debut on May 13 at the Imperial Theatre.

1903    Anna Pavlova dances *Giselle* in St. Petersburg.

1904    Michel Fokine submits suggestions for reforms to the director of the Impe-
        rial Theatre: "Dancing should be interpretative. It should not degenerate
        into mere gymnastics. The dance should explain the spirit of the actors in
        the spectacle . . . it should express the whole epoch to which the subject of
        the ballet belongs. For such interpretative dancing, the music must be
        equally inspired. In place of the old-time waltzes, polkas, pizzicati and
        galops, it is necessary to create a form of music which expresses the same
        emotion as that which inspires the movements of the dancer. The ballet
        must no longer be made up of 'numbers,' 'entries,' and so on. It must show
        artistic unity of conception. The action of the ballet must never be inter-
        rupted to allow the *danseuse* to respond to the applause of the public . . .
        Ballet must have complete unity of expression, a unity which is made up of
        a harmonious blending of the three elements—music, painting, and plastic
        art." These suggestions are rejected.

1905    Michel Fokine creates the *pas seul Le Cygne* (*The Dying Swan*) for Anna
        Pavlova in St. Petersburg; this becomes the best known of all Pavlova's
        dances.

1905    Isadora Duncan makes her first appearance in Russia; her reforms in the
        dance, her dedication to music, and her contempt for the close-fitting cos-
        tume and the ballet slipper in her improvised dances, are approved by those
        who seek reform at the Imperial Theatre—among them, Michel Fokine.

1906 Anna Pavlova becomes *prima ballerina* after a performance of *Swan Lake* at the Maryinsky Theatre.

1907 Death of Lucile Grahn.

1907 Serge Diaghilev organizes a series of Russian concerts in Paris with the assistance of Rimsky-Korsakov, Scriabin, Rachmaninoff, and Chaliapin.

1907 Fokine produces, for a charity performance on March 8 at the Maryinsky Theatre, the ballet *Eunice,* dances in the manner of stylized movement depicted on ancient Greek vases; the dancers appear in flowing tunics, barefoot.

1907 *Le Pavillon d'Armide* (Fokine-Tcherepnine-Benois), is presented on December 8 at the Maryinsky Theatre, with Pavlova, Nijinsky, and Paul Gerdt.

1908 *Chopiniana,* Fokine's first version of *Les Sylphides,* is presented on March 21, with Pavlova and Oboukoff.

1908 Vaslav Nijinsky is graduated from the Imperial Ballet School in May; he appears with Ludmilla Shollar in Fokine's dances in *Don Giovanni.*

1909 Diaghilev's Ballets Russes makes its first appearance, at the Théâtre du Châtelet, Paris, on May 18: *Le Pavillon d'Armide* and *Prince Igor* (Fokine-Borodin-Roerich) create one of the most successful *premières* in history. This is the beginning of a new era in ballet, as Diaghilev makes possible the complete realization of Fokine's reforms and founds a ballet company dedicated to Fokine's ideal: unification of the three elements—music, painting, and dancing. Fokine is choreographer to Diaghilev.

1909 Diaghilev's Ballets Russes presents *Les Sylphides* on June 2, with Pavlova, Karsavina, and Nijinsky, at the Théâtre du Châtelet.

1909 Diaghilev appoints Enrico Cecchetti instructor to his Ballets Russes.

1910 Anna Pavlova and Mikhail Mordkin make their United States debut on February 28 in *Coppélia,* at the Metropolitan Opera House. "Her technique is of a sort to dazzle the eye. The most difficult tricks of the art of the dancer she executed with supreme ease . . . Grace, a certain sensuous charm, and a decided sense of humor are other qualities that she possesses. In fact, it would be difficult to conceive a dancer who so nearly realizes the ideal of this sort of dancing."—Carl Van Vechten in the New York *Times.*

1910 *Swan Lake* is performed in England for the first time, in May, at the London Hippodrome, with Olga Preobrajenska as Odette and George Kyaksht as Prince Siegfried.

1910 *Firebird* (Fokine-Stravinsky) is presented by Diaghilev's Ballets Russes on June 25.

1910 Pavlova and Mordkin dance *Giselle* on October 15 at the Metropolitan Opera House. "Grisi is said to have been gently melancholy in it, but Pavlova was probably more than that. Her poetic conception of the betrothed girl's madness when she finds that her lover has deceived her, and her death, come very close to being tragic. It is almost impossible to describe the poetry of her dancing in the second act, where as one of the *Wilis* she engages in the wildest sort of measures under the forest trees."—Carl Van Vechten in the New York *Times.*

1910 Tamara Karsavina succeeds Anna Pavlova as ballerina at the Imperial Theatre, St. Petersburg.

1910 Marius Petipa dies on July 14.

1911 Saison Russe is presented by Gertrude Hoffman in New York. Repertory includes first United States productions of *Les Sylphides* and *Scheherazade.* Gertrude Hoffman and Lydia Lopokova are the principal dancers. These versions of Fokine's ballets were not authorized by him.

1911    *Petrouchka* (Fokine-Stravinsky-Benois) is presented on June 13 in Paris by Diaghilev, with Karsavina, Nijinsky, Orlov, and Cecchetti.

1911    Diaghilev's Ballets Russes first appear in London on June 21.

1911    *Swan Lake* is presented in four acts on December 20 at the Metropolitan Opera House, with Catherine Geltzer, first dancer of the Moscow Imperial Opera, and Mikhail Mordkin.

1912    Nijinsky's *The Afternoon of a Faun* (Debussy) is presented by Diaghilev, Paris, on May 29.

1913    Anna Pavlova resigns from the Maryinsky Theatre; she never returns to Russia.

1914    In a letter to *The Times,* London, July 6, Fokine states the five principles of the New Ballet: (1) "Not to form combinations of ready-made and established dance steps, but to create in each case a new form corresponding to the subject, the most expressive form possible for the representation of the period and the character of the nation represented." (2) ". . . Dancing and mimetic gesture have no meaning in a ballet unless they serve as an expression of its dramatic action, and they must not be used as a mere *divertissement* or entertainment . . ." (3) "The new ballet admits the use of conventional gesture only when it is required by the style of the ballet, and in all other cases endeavors to replace gestures of the hands by mimetic of the whole body. Man can be and should be expressed from head to foot." (4) ". . . Expressiveness of groups and of ensemble dancing. In the older ballets the dancers were ranged in groups only for the purpose of ornament, and the ballet master was not concerned with the expression of any sentiment in groups of characters or in ensemble dances. The new ballet, on the other hand . . . advances from the expressiveness of the face to the expressiveness of the whole body, and from the expressiveness of the individual body to the expressiveness of a group of bodies and the expressiveness of the combined dancing of a crowd." (5) "Alliance of dancing with the other arts. The new ballet . . . does not demand 'ballet music' of the composer as an accompaniment to dancing; it accepts music of every kind, provided it is good and expressive. It does not demand of the scenic artist that he should array the ballerinas in short skirts and pink slippers. It does not impose any specific 'ballet' conditions . . . but gives complete liberty to their creative powers."

1915    Massine becomes choreographer to Diaghilev.

1916    The first American appearance of Diaghilev's Ballets Russes takes place at the Century Theatre, New York. The principal dancers are Pflanz, Bolm, Massine, Sokolova, Tchernicheva, Fedorova, and Cecchetti.

1916    Vaslav Nijinsky dances for the first time in the United States, in *Le Spectre de la Rose* and *Petrouchka,* with Diaghilev's Ballets Russes, on April 12 at the Metropolitan Opera House.

1916    The second New York season of Diaghilev's Ballets Russes opens on October 16 at the Manhattan Opera House with Nijinsky's *Til Eulenspiegel.* An American tour follows.

1917    *Parade* (Massine-Satie-Cocteau-Picasso) is presented by Diaghilev's Ballets Russes on May 18 at the Théâtre du Châtelet, Paris.

1917    *The Good-Humored Ladies* (Massine-Scarlatti-Bakst) is presented on April 12 by Diaghilev's Ballets Russes: the first major ballet by Massine.

1918    Enrico Cecchetti opens the Academy of Dancing in London.

1919    Nijinsky retires.

1920    The Royal Academy of Dancing is founded in London.

1921　The Fokine School opens in New York on January 1.

1921　Isadora Duncan is invited by the Soviet Government to open a school in Moscow.

1921　Diaghilev revives *The Sleeping Beauty* at the Alhambra Theatre, London, on November 2. Spessivtzeva, Lopokova, Egorova, and Trefilova alternate in the part of Princess Aurora. Pierre Vladimiroff is the Prince. Lopokova and Nijinska alternate as the Lilac Fairy. Parts of the fairies are taken by Dubrovska, Sokolova, Nemtchinova, Tchernicheva, Egorova, and Nijinska. Carlotta Brianza, the Princess Aurora of the original production of this ballet, is Carabosse. Stanislas Idzikowski and Lopokova dance the Bluebird *pas de deux* at the first performance. Ludmilla Shollar, Leon Woicikowski, and Anatole Vilzak are in the cast. This reaffirmation of the permanence of the classic dance fails with the ballet audience, which is accustomed to two or three ballets an evening, in the fashion made popular by Diaghilev himself.

1921　Bronislava Nijinska becomes choreographer to Diaghilev.

1922　On January 5, Enrico Cecchetti celebrates his fiftieth anniversary on the ballet stage by taking the part of Carabosse in Diaghilev's revival of *The Sleeping Beauty*.

1922　A *Manual of Classical Theatrical Dancing* (*Cecchetti Method*), by C. W. Beaumont and Stanislas Idzikowski, is published in London.

1923　"Dancing has forever been in existence as a spontaneous custom, a social discipline. Thus it is finally that dancing meets us not only as love, as religion, as art, but also as morals."—Havelock Ellis, *The Dance of Life*.

1923　*L'Âme et la Danse* (*Dance and the Soul*), dialogue by Paul Valéry, is published in Paris.

1924　Balanchine becomes choreographer to Diaghilev.

1924–25　Anna Pavlova and her company make their last American tour.

1925　*Petrouchka* is staged by Fokine for the Royal Danish Ballet on October 21 at the Royal Theatre, Copenhagen. With their careful attention to detail, respect for a choreographer's direction, and their scrupulous maintenance of tradition, the Royal Danish Ballet's production of this famous ballet is generally acknowledged to be the best in existence.

1925–26　Mikhail Mordkin and his Russian Ballet Company tour America.

1926　Martha Graham, dancer and choreographer, gives her first independent dance recital at the Forty-eighth Street Theatre, New York, on April 18. Like Isadora Duncan before her, Martha Graham has greatly influenced the theatrical dancing of her time, but more than Duncan—whose art was personal and inimitable—Martha Graham has developed in addition to a stage personality a new, nonballetic dance vocabulary expressive of inner tensions. This new system of dance can be imparted to others, can be taught with the same rigor as the classic ballet, and has become, under Martha Graham's tutelage, not only a contemporary contribution, but a lasting discipline.

1926　Ninette de Valois, former member of Diaghilev's Ballets Russes, establishes ballet school in London in May.

1926　Ballet Club (now Ballet Rambert), first permanent English company, presents at its first performance, on June 15, *A Tragedy of Fashion*, ballet by Frederick Ashton. Marie Rambert, the director of this company and its accompanying ballet school, was a student of Émile Jaques-Dalcroze and Cecchetti. Ashton, Tudor, De Mille, and Andrée Howard are a few of the celebrated choreographers who have studied under her direction.

1927 Isadora Duncan gives her last concert at the Théâtre Mogadon, Paris, on July 8.

1927 Isadora Duncan dies on September 14.

1928 *Apollo, Leader of the Muses* (Balanchine-Stravinsky-Bauchant) is presented by Diaghilev on June 12.

1928 Enrico Cecchetti dies on November 13.

1928 Ninette de Valois' Academy of Choreographic Art presents *Les Petits Riens* (De Valois-Mozart), on December 13, at the Old Vic Theatre, London.

1929 Atlanta Civic Ballet, oldest organization of its kind in the United States, founded as the Dorothy Alexander Concert Group.

1929 Serge Diaghilev in a letter to *The Times*, London, July 13, defends his Ballets Russes from charges that their dances are "extravagant, repellent, athletic, acrobatic": "The classical dance has never been and is not today the Russian Ballet. Its birthplace was France; it grew up in Italy, and has only been conserved in Russia. Side by side with the classical dance there has always existed the national or character dance, which has given the evolution of the Russian Ballet. I do not know of a single classical movement that was born of the Russian folk dance. Why have we got to take our inspiration from the minuet of the French Court and not from the Russian village festival? That which appears to you acrobatic is dilettante terminology for our national dance step. The mistake really, in fact, goes much deeper, because it is undoubtedly the Italian classical school which has introduced into ballet the acrobatic elements . . ."

1929 The last performance of Diaghilev's Ballets Russes takes place at Covent Garden, London, on July 26. The program includes: *Le Bal* (Balanchine-Rieti-Chirico), with Danilova and Dolin; *Prodigal Son* (Balanchine-Prokofiev-Rouault), with Lifar and Dubrovska; *Aurora's Wedding* (Petipa-Tchaikovsky-Bakst), with Danilova as Aurora, Lifar as the prince, and Markova and Dolin as the bluebirds.

1929 Serge Diaghilev dies in Venice on August 19.

1930 *Capriol Suite* (Ashton-Warlock-Chappell), ballet based on dances described in Arbeau's *Orchésographie* (1588), is presented by Marie Rambert Dancers in London.

1930 The American *première* of Massine's ballet to Stravinsky's *The Rite of Spring* is presented on April 11 at the Academy of Music, Philadelphia. Martha Graham dances the leading role. The music is performed by the Philadelphia Orchestra under Leopold Stokowski.

1930 Anna Pavlova makes her last public appearance on December 13 in *Giselle*, with Pierre Vladimiroff, London.

1931 Anna Pavlova dies at The Hague on January 23.

1931 Ninette de Valois opens a ballet school at the Sadler's Wells Theatre, London, on January 31. The Sadler's Wells Theatre at the time is under the direction of Lilian Baylis, director of the Old Vic Theatre.

1931 The Vic-Wells Ballet gives its first performance on May 5 at the Old Vic Theatre, London, under the direction of Ninette de Valois. Other performances are given at the Sadler's Wells Theatre, and the history of the Sadler's Wells Ballet begins.

1932 René Blum and Colonel W. de Basil found the Ballet Russe de Monte Carlo; its choreographers are Balanchine and Massine.

1932 Harald Lander becomes ballet master to the Royal Danish Ballet.

1932 Constant Lambert, English composer and conductor, becomes musical director of the Vic-Wells Ballet and begins to conduct ballet performances at the Sadler's Wells Theatre.

1933  The first performance of *Les Présages* (Massine-Tchaikovsky-Masson), at Monte Carlo on April 13. This "choreographic symphony" to Tchaikovsky's Fifth Symphony portrays man's battle with fate; it is the first ballet to a full symphony.

1933  The Jooss Ballet makes its first United States appearance.

1933  The first performance of Les Ballets 1933 (under the direction of George Balanchine) takes place in June at the Théâtre des Champs-Élysées, Paris.

1933  The Ballet Russe de Monte Carlo gives its first Paris performance in June at the Théâtre du Châtelet.

1933  Serge Lifar and his Russian Ballets appear in the United States.

1933  The School of American Ballet is founded in October by Lincoln Kirstein, George Balanchine, Edward M. M. Warburg, and Vladimir Dimitriev.

1933  First performance in the United States of the Ballet Russe de Monte Carlo on December 22 at the St. James Theatre, New York. The program: *La Concurrence* (Balanchine-Auric-Derain), *Les Présages* (Massine-Tchaikovsky-Masson), and *Le Beau Danube* (Massine-Strauss-Polunin). Among the dancers are Alexandra Danilova, Leonide Massine, Tamara Toumanova, Tatiana Riabouchinska, Irina Baronova, Leon Woicikowski, David Lichine, Yurek Shabelevsky, and André Eglevsky.

1934  The first all-English production of *Giselle* is presented on January 1 at the Old Vic Theatre, London, by the Vic-Wells Ballet, with Alicia Markova.

1934  The School of American Ballet opens on January 2 in New York.

1934  *Fundamentals of the Classic Dance*, by Agrippina Vaganova (1879–1951), is published in Russia. This is the crucial text of present-day Russian ballet technique (translated into English by Anatole Chujoy, 1946).

1934  Ruth Page is appointed ballet director and *première danseuse* of the Chicago Grand Opera Company.

1934  Vic-Wells Ballet produces the first complete *Swan Lake* staged in England, with Alicia Markova, on November 20.

1934  The School of American Ballet presents Balanchine's *Mozartiana, Serenade, Alma Mater,* and *Transcendence* on December 6 at the Avery Memorial Theatre, Hartford, Connecticut.

1935  In March, the American Ballet, founded by Lincoln Kirstein and Edward M. M. Warburg, opens a two-week season at the Adelphi Theatre, New York, with a repertory of ballets by George Balanchine. Tamara Geva and Paul Haakon are guest artists in a company that includes Ruthanna Boris, Gisella Caccialanza, William Dollar, Charles Laskey, Eugene Loring, Annabelle Lyon, and Elise Reiman, among others.

1935  The Littlefield Ballet is organized in Philadelphia by Catherine Littlefield (1904–1951): the first ballet company with an American director and American dancers. The following year this company becomes the Philadelphia Ballet. For this company, Catherine Littlefield choreographs a complete version of Tchaikovsky's *The Sleeping Beauty*.

1935  The American Ballet, under the direction of George Balanchine, becomes the resident ballet company at the Metropolitan Opera. Anatole Vilzak, Ruby Asquith, Harold and Lew Christensen, Erick Hawkins, Lillian Moore, and others join the company.

1935  *Dance: a Short History of Classic Theatrical Dancing*, by Lincoln Kirstein, is published in New York.

1936    *Lilac Garden* (Tudor-Chausson) is presented by the Ballet Club on January 26 at the Mercury Theatre, London.

1936    Ruth Page Ballets make their first appearance in New York on March 1.

1936    *Orpheus* (Balanchine-Gluck) is performed by the American Ballet on May 22 at the Metropolitan Opera House, with scenery and costumes by Pavel Tchelitchew.

1936    Ballet Caravan is organized in May by Lincoln Kirstein to provide opportunity for American dancers, choreographers, composers, and designers. Ballet Caravan tours the United States during three years, mounting new works by Lew Christensen, William Dollar, Erick Hawkins, and Eugene Loring to new music by Elliott Carter, Jr., Aaron Copland, Paul Bowles, etc. All the dancers, like those in the American Ballet, are students or graduates of the School of American Ballet; among them are Christensen, Marie-Jeanne, Caccialanza, Loring, and Danieli.

1936    A *Bibliography of Dancing* (Paul Magriel) is published in New York on August 2.

1937    The American Ballet stages a Stravinsky Festival on April 27 at the Metropolitan Opera House: *Apollo, Leader of the Muses; Card Game;* and *The Fairy's Kiss*—all with music by Stravinsky and choreography by Balanchine.

1937    The Philadelphia Ballet has a season at the Théâtre des Champs-Élysées, Paris, during the International Exposition: it is the first American ballet company to visit Europe.

1937    The San Francisco Ballet, with associated ballet school, is organized by William Christensen.

1938    *Billy the Kid* (Loring-Copland-Kirstein-French) is presented on October 16 by Ballet Caravan at the Chicago Opera House: the first successful ballet with an American subject portrayed in an American dance idiom.

1938    *Ballerina* (original title *La Mort du Cygne*), the first movie to deal in detail with ballet, is filmed in France, with Mia Slavenska and Yvette Chauviré. Many of the young students who appear in this film later become noted dancers.

1939    Nicholas Sergeyev's production of *The Sleeping Beauty* is presented by the Sadler's Wells Ballet on February 2 at the Sadler's Wells Theatre, London, with Margot Fonteyn, June Brae, and Robert Helpmann.

1939    Royal Winnipeg Ballet of Canada founded.

1940    Ballet Theatre's first performance takes place on January 11, at the Center Theatre, New York: *Les Sylphides, The Great American Goof* (Loring-Brant-Saroyan-Aronson), *Voices of Spring* (Mordkin-Strauss-Simonson). Among the dancers are Adolph Bolm, Patricia Bowman, Edward Caton, Lucia Chase, Karen Conrad, Leon Danielian, Agnes de Mille, Anton Dolin, William Dollar, Viola Essen, Nora Kaye, Andrée Howard, Hugh Laing, Eugene Loring, Annabelle Lyon, Dimitri Romanov, Nina Stroganova, Yurek Shabelevsky, and Antony Tudor. During its first season, Ballet Theatre presents eighteen ballets. Fokine stages his own ballets for the company.

1940    The Dance Notation Bureau is founded in New York for the purpose of recording ballets and dances in an intelligible dance notation.

1941    The American Ballet makes a South American tour. In its repertory are *Ballet Imperial, Concerto Barocco, The Bat, Billy the Kid, Time Table, Filling Station, Errante, Serenade, Apollo, Charade,* and *Pastorela.* Among the dancers are Marie-Jeanne, Lew Christensen, William Dollar, Nicholas Magallanes, Beatrice Tompkins, and Mary Jane Shea.

1941    Ballet Theatre makes its first transcontinental tour; Alonso, Baronova, Hightower, Markova, Osato, Robbins, and Skibine join the company.

1941    International Ballet is founded in England by Mona Inglesby. The repertory of this company includes the reproductions by Sergeyev of *Giselle, Coppélia, Swan Lake,* and *The Sleeping Beauty.*

1942    *Pillar of Fire* (Tudor-Schoenberg-Mielziner) is presented by Ballet Theatre on April 8 at the Metropolitan Opera House, with Nora Kaye, Hugh Laing, and Antony Tudor.

1942    Fokine dies on August 22.

1942    The first performance of *Rodeo* (De Mille-Copland-Smith) is presented by the Ballet Russe de Monte Carlo on October 16 at the Metropolitan Opera House, New York.

1944    The first American tour of the Mia Slavenska Company begins on January 3.

1944    *Fancy Free* (Robbins-Bernstein-Smith) is presented by Ballet Theatre on April 18 at the Metropolitan Opera House, New York.

1944    The first performance of Ballet International takes place on October 30 at the International Theatre, New York. The principal dancers are Viola Essen, Marie-Jeanne, André Eglevsky, and William Dollar. This company gives its last performance on December 23, 1944. Its founder, the Marquis George de Cuevas, established the Grand Ballet de Monte Carlo in Europe in 1947. This new company, which features many American dancers, returned to the United States for a four-week engagement at the Century Theatre, New York, November 1949, as the Marquis de Cuevas' Grand Ballet. The principal dancers are Rosella Hightower, André Eglevsky, Marjorie Tallchief, and George Skibine. This company returned to Europe in 1950.

1945    The first season of Les Ballets des Champs-Élysées, in Paris. Its managing director is Roger Eudes; artistic director, Boris Kochno; ballet master and choreographer, Roland Petit.

1946    In London, the Sadler's Wells Ballet reopens the Royal Opera House, Covent Garden (closed as a theatre during the war), on February 20, with a performance of *The Sleeping Beauty:* Sadler's Wells Ballet, as the first permanent resident company at Covent Garden, becomes the national ballet of Britain.

1946    The first full evening of ballet by the Sadler's Wells Theatre Ballet is given on April 8 at the Sadler's Wells Theatre, London. It consists of *Promenade* (De Valois-Haydn), *Assembly Ball* (Howard-Bizet), and *The Nutcracker.*

1946    Ballet Society, a "non-profit organization for the advancement of the lyric theatre by production of new works," is founded in New York in July for private, subscription audience. Musical Director, Leon Barzin; Secretary, Lincoln Kirstein; Executive Manager, Frances Hawkins; Technical Director, Jean Rosenthal; Artistic Director, George Balanchine.

1946    Ballet Theatre opens its first overseas engagement on July 4 at the Royal Opera House, Covent Garden, London, with *Les Sylphides, Fancy Free, Black Swan pas de deux,* and *Bluebeard.*

1946    Ballet Society gives its first performance in New York on November 20. The program: *The Four Temperaments* and *The Spellbound Child.* Among the dancers are Mary Ellen Moylan, Tanaquil LeClercq, Beatrice Tompkins, Elise Reiman, Fred Danieli, Nicholas Magallanes, Todd Bolender, Francisco Moncion, and Herbert Bliss.

1948    Alicia Markova, Anton Dolin, and Mia Slavenska join the Ballet Russe de Monte Carlo on September 16 as guest artists for a season at the Metropolitan Opera House.

1948    The first performance of *Orpheus* (Balanchine-Stravinsky-Noguchi) is given on April 28, with Nicholas Magallanes, Maria Tallchief, and Francisco Moncion, by Ballet Society, at the New York City Center.

1948    The first public performance of Ballet Society takes place on April 29 at the New York City Center: *Renard, Élégie, Orpheus, Symphonie Concertante.*

1948    The first performance of Les Ballets de Paris de Roland Petit, at the Théâtre Marigny, Paris, on May 22.

1948    The Paris Opéra Ballet opens its season at the New York City Center on September 21.

1948    The first performance of the New York City Ballet, on October 11, as Ballet Society becomes the resident company at the New York City Center of Music and Drama. The program consists of *Concerto Barocco, Orpheus,* and *Symphony in C.* The Musical Director is Leon Barzin; General Director, Lincoln Kirstein; Lighting by Jean Rosenthal; principal dancers, Maria Tallchief, Marie-Jeanne, Tanaquil LeClercq, Beatrice Tompkins, Nicholas Magallanes, Francisco Moncion, and Herbert Bliss; Artistic Director, George Balanchine.

1948    *Cinderella* (Ashton-Prokofiev-Malclès), first full-scale, three-act English ballet, is presented by the Sadler's Wells Ballet in London on December 23.

1949    *The Dance Encyclopedia,* compiled and edited by Anatole Chujoy, is published in New York on March 21.

1949    The Sadler's Wells Ballet makes its first appearance in the United States on October 11 at the Metropolitan Opera House, New York.

1949    Jerome Robbins becomes associate artistic director of the New York City Ballet in November.

1949    *Firebird* (Balanchine-Stravinsky-Chagall) is given its first performance, with Maria Tallchief and Francisco Moncion, by the New York City Ballet at the City Center, New York, on November 27.

1950    Vaslav Nijinsky dies in London on April 8.

1950    The Sadler's Wells Ballet observes its twenty-first birthday in a gala performance at the Sadler's Wells Theatre, London, on May 15. At this performance, Ninette de Valois, director, dances the part of Webster, the maid, in *A Wedding Bouquet* (Ashton-Berners-Stein) and Margot Fonteyn takes the part in which she first appeared as a soloist, on December 4, 1934: Young Treginnis, in *The Haunted Ballroom.*

1950    The New York City Ballet opens its first overseas engagement at the Royal Opera House, Covent Garden, London, on July 10 with *Serenade, The Age of Anxiety,* and *Symphony in C.*

1950    Ballet Theatre begins its first European tour, in August, at Frankfurt, Germany.

1950    The first season of Festival Ballet opens in London on October 24, with Alicia Markova and Anton Dolin.

1951    Nora Kaye and André Eglevsky join the New York City Ballet in January.

1951    Jean Babilée and Nathalie Philippart are guest artists with Ballet Theatre at the Metropolitan Opera House, New York.

1951    Ballet Theatre opens its first South American tour on May 21, in Rio de Janeiro.

1951    Ballet Rambert celebrates its twenty-fifth anniversary in London on July 29. This company, under the direction of Madame Marie Rambert, has been in continuous existence longer than any other English company.

1951    American Ballet Theatre School opens in New York on September 17.

1951    Sadler's Wells Theatre Ballet begins its first tour of Canada and the United States on October 5 at Quebec City, Canada.

1952    *The Classic Ballet* (Stuart-Dyer-Kirstein) is published in New York.

1952    The National Ballet of Canada is founded in Toronto.

1952    First European tour of the New York City Ballet opens in Barcelona, Spain, on April 15.

1953    The New York City Ballet ends a three-month engagement at the City Center, New York, on January 25: the longest run of any ballet company in the United States.

1953    First appearance outside Denmark of the Royal Danish Ballet—at the Royal Opera House, Covent Garden, London.

1953    Agnes de Mille Dance Theatre begins first tour of the United States.

1956    First tour of the United States by the Robert Joffrey Ballet.

1956    Royal Danish Ballet begins first United States tour at the Metropolitan Opera House, New York, September 16.

1956    First American Regional Ballet Festival takes place in Atlanta, Georgia.

1957    First overseas tour of the San Francisco Ballet.

1957    The Bolshoi Ballet begins first United States and Canadian tour.

1958    Les Grands Ballets Canadien founded in Montreal.

1960    American Ballet Theatre tours the U.S.S.R. for the first time.

1961    First United States and Canadian tour of the Leningrad Kirov Ballet.

1962    The New York City Ballet tours the U.S.S.R.

1963    First performances in Washington, D.C., of the National Ballet.

1963    The Robert Joffrey Ballet tours the U.S.S.R.

1963    Ford Foundation announces ten-year program for the long-range professional development of ballet in the United States.

1964    Opening of the New York State Theatre, designed by Philip Johnson for dance.

1965    Debut of the Harkness Ballet at Cannes, France.

1965    First United States government grants to dance.

1965    *Ballet Review* founded in New York by Arlene Croce.

1966    Robert Joffrey Ballet becomes City Center Joffrey Ballet.

1967    Association of American Dance Companies founded.

1969    First U.S. appearances of the Stuttgart Ballet.

1970    Eliot Feld forms a ballet company.

1971    First U.S. appearances of the Australian Ballet.

1972    Second Soviet tour of the New York City Ballet.

1973    First U.S. appearances of the National Ballet of Canada.

1976    American Ballet Theatre, City Center Joffrey Ballet, Alvin Ailey Dance Theatre, and the Eliot Feld Ballet assume control of the City Center Theatre, New York.

1976    Fiftieth anniversary of Martha Graham's first independent dance recital in New York, April 18.

1976    New York City Ballet, the Royal Ballet, the Royal Danish Ballet, American Ballet Theatre, and the Soviet folk-dance company appear at Lincoln Center, New York, in the spring and summer months.

The chronology of important events in the history of theatrical dance to be found in *Dance*, by Lincoln Kirstein (1935), is the master list upon which any chronology of the history of ballet must naturally be based, and I acknowledge my great indebtedness to it, as well as to the text of that monumental work. I am also indebted to numerous other sources, principal among which are: *The Dance Encyclopedia,* compiled and edited by Anatole Chujoy, the largest single collection of data on ballet in English; various contributors of articles to *Dance Index,* especially Lillian Moore, George Chaffée, Anatole Chujoy, and the late Dr. Artur Michel; numerous historical articles published in the indispensable magazine *Ballet,* which has unfortunately ceased publication; and the pioneer researches of C. W. Beaumont.

The scrupulous historical essays that appeared in *Dance Index* during that magazine's brief existence eloquently demonstrated that many writers on ballet have a cavalier tradition of carelessness and indifference to the accuracy of dates, names, places, and events. Insofar as possible, I have tried not to parrot previous errors and earnestly hope that, in the interest of accuracy, any readers who discern mistakes will be good enough to inform me of them in care of the publishers.

Marianna Tcherkassky and Ivan Nagy in *Giselle*. Photo by Martha Swope.

Mikhail Baryshnikov and Marianna Tcherkassky in *Le Spectre de la Rose*. Photo by Martha Swope.

Gelsey Kirkland in *La Sylphide*. Photo by Louis Péres.

Mikhail Baryshnikov and Natalia Makarova in *Don Quixote*. Photo by Rosemary Winckley.

Gelsey Kirkland and Jonas Kåge in *The Leaves Are Fading*. Photo by Martha Swope.

Rudolf Nureyev in *Le Corsaire*. Photo by Louis Péres.

Mikhail Baryshnikov in *Le Sacre du Printemps*. Photo by Beverley Gallegos.

Gelsey Kirkland and Mikhail Baryshnikov in *La Sylphide*. Photo by Beverley Gallegos.

## PART FIVE

# *How I Became a Dancer and Choreographer*

A dancer's history usually begins at the age of eight or nine. I myself began to study dancing, in Russia, when I was nine. In my case, this was almost accidental. My father was a musician, a composer, and we were naturally a musical family. My brother played the piano, my sister played the violin, and from the time I was five years old, I, too, studied the piano. There was no idea that I should be a musician; I only studied music because my parents felt I should be missing something important in life if I knew nothing about it.

Many men in my mother's family had been in the army, and for a while it was thought that I would become one of the Tsar's cadets. But one day my mother happened to be visiting the Imperial Ballet School in St. Petersburg. She had always loved dancing, and when one of the governors of the school suggested that she try to enter me, she agreed. After all, I could always go into the army if I didn't turn out to be good.

That was in 1914. In August of that year the Imperial School held its regular auditions for new pupils in St. Petersburg. These were auditions for the eight-year course in ballet, drama, and music. The final choice of which art the student would permanently pursue was made after he had learned something about each one. But these were not auditions in any real sense; we had never danced before, and there was very little they could tell. First, a doctor examined us briefly. He felt our muscles, listened to our hearts and our breathing, and sent us to the large auditioning room of the school. There were about a hundred and fifty boys seeking admittance and more than two hundred girls. In small groups, the boys and girls separately, we went in before the judges, who were seated at a table down at the end of the auditioning room. Karsavina was there, I remember. Even then I knew what a great ballerina Karsavina was and I was a little afraid. I thought I looked awkward.

The judges asked us to walk and observed our posture, our carriage. We knew absolutely no dancing and could not have executed a step if we'd been asked. The judges picked a few boys out of each group that came before them. I was picked out, but from the judges' manner I couldn't tell if this was because I was good or bad. We were told to go to another room, and after a long wait we were asked to come back. The judges watched us again, then divided the group, sending some of us to one side of the room. Again we waited. We had no idea who had been chosen or who had been eliminated. At the end of the day, they announced the names of those who had been selected as new students. I was one of seven or eight boys.

Until I actually entered the school, I didn't know whether to be pleased or not. Once in the Imperial School itself, I was decidedly displeased. I didn't like it. I was homesick, and the army seemed to me a much better idea than ballet.

The first year, we were all on trial at the school. Only if we passed that first year successfully would we be admitted as permanent students. I didn't care. All of us lived at the school, in Theatre Street, in St. Petersburg. We could go home only at Easter, Christmas, and during the summer; our parents could not visit us. The discipline was very strict: we all got up at the same time, washed at the same time (always in cold water, except on Friday before dinner), ate on a strict schedule, went to the same classes, and were sent to bed promptly at nine o'clock. We wore blue uniforms, with silver lyres on the stiff collar and on the cap.

And I did not like it. My fellow students knew this because I sulked so much. They didn't help matters by calling me "Rat" all the time. When I thought I couldn't stand it any more, I ran away. I knew my parents would be very angry, so I went to the home of an aunt who lived in St. Petersburg. She was understanding, but also she was firm with me. She took me back.

Still I hated the school. I was certain I had no aptitude for dancing and was wasting my time and the Tsar's money. The only people who thought differently then were Olga Preobrajenska, the great *prima ballerina* at the Maryinsky Theatre, who was very kind to me, and my favorite teacher, S. M. Andreanov, who instructed me in classic technique.

Every day at the Imperial School we had the same schedule: ballet class, lessons in character dancing, classes in Russian literature, French, arithmetic, music (we all had to play some instrument), and religion. We also took fencing lessons. This was a curriculum similar to that of any fine European school, except for the ballet classes. I liked the classes in religion and music best, but still, even though I was admitted as a permanent student after the first year, I thought I was in the wrong place. I remembered that there were other departments at the Imperial School—drama and music—and thought that I might be better off there.

Then everything changed. What happened was very simple. In the first year at the school, we went only to classes; we were not associated with the Imperial Theatre, the Maryinsky, in any way. The second year, as was customary, we became a part of the theatre, dancing in large groups with the *corps de ballet*. I first danced on the stage of the Maryinsky in the garland dance in *The Sleeping Beauty:* the waltz in the first act. I also appeared as a cupid on one of the carriages in the final act. The Maryinsky was a beautiful theatre, all blue and gold, and as children we were very excited about dancing on its stage, where almost any magical effect could be made: real waves, scores of swimming swans, fire, and great cascading fountains banked in tiers. We learned very early what it was to be a part of a theatre; the theatre became a home to us, a natural place to be.

The garland dance in *The Sleeping Beauty* was performed by scores of people in the regular *corps de ballet* of the Maryinsky, and we children were naturally unimportant, but that evening nevertheless changed my whole life. At that moment I saw that others had been right about what was good for me. I saw then what ballet was in terms of a theatre.

The Maryinsky production of *The Sleeping Beauty* was wonderfully elaborate, a real spectacle, the kind of thing Hollywood tries to achieve in its huge productions. Only here there was more magic. The Tsar's treasury could afford it! There were about two hundred and fifty dancers in the company; all were professionals. The first act of *The Sleeping Beauty* was marvelous in scenic effect: a huge garden with cascading fountains. When the wicked fairy Carabosse appeared in the prologue, her great coach was drawn by a dozen mice. Later, when she appeared in disguise and tricked the princess into pricking her finger, her appearance changed completely. She turned to the king and queen and said that the princess would die, and then, miraculously, her disguise disappeared into the floor and they saw before them the wicked fairy they had forgotten to invite to their daughter's christening. It was fantastic— there she was, a bent old lady, harmless, and the next moment her disguise had fallen through the floor and she was black and shiny, the wicked fairy. Fire came up all over the stage and everyone despaired. Of course, the Lilac Fairy then intervened and predicted that the princess would wake up in a hundred years. Then the whole palace went to sleep. From the stage floor, great trees and shrubbery arose and climbed higher and higher, vines entwined about the colonnades of the garden, so that the whole palace was overgrown and it was quiet, asleep.

Later, when the Lilac Fairy took the prince to the palace, there was a wonderful panorama scene, not an interval with music, as this part of the ballet is performed nowadays. The music was played slowly, as it should be, and the Lilac Fairy guided her boat across the stage. The scenery moved from left to right so that the boat really seemed to be moving over a lake in an enchanted forest. Then, in the finale, where the Princess Aurora is married, there was a spectacular apotheosis: the stage was deep and high, and from high up in the back down to the center of the stage there was a great flight of steps. On either side of the steps there was a flight of fountains, which spilled over, one into the other, so that there was a continuous waterfall. All the fairies were grouped on the stairs with their cavaliers, and they and all the court bowed in tribute to the princess. It was beautiful.

And so I began to like dancing very much. I started to work very hard. I wanted to dance more on the stage, and to do that I knew I had to be good, very good. I was only ten, but I was experiencing with ballet the same kind of lesson I had learned with music.

When I first took piano lessons, I hated them, too. For two years the only thing that would make me practice was the thought of being sent to bed without my supper. Then, when I was seven, I learned a part of a Beethoven sonata. I didn't play it well at first, but well enough to hear how lovely it sounded. I loved it and wanted to play it well, so then it would sound even more beautiful. And now I was learning the same thing about dancing: it took work, but when you saw what the work could produce, you wanted to work very badly.

Ballet performances at the Maryinsky in St. Petersburg were given only twice a week, on Wednesdays and Saturdays. The rest of the week, the theatre was devoted to opera. All of us looked forward to the ballet evenings, when the official court carriages would come to the school and take us to the theatre for our appearances. Only when we were brought back to the school, at midnight, did we have our supper. We were so excited about going on stage at the theatre that, young as we were, we were not hungry until it was all over.

As a child, I danced in all the ballets in the Maryinsky repertory that required a large male *corps de ballet:* in the first real Russian ballet, *The Humpbacked Horse;* in the Petipa classics *Paquita* and *Don Quixote;* in *The Nutcracker,* where I began as one of the toy soldiers and gradually danced bigger parts—the king of mice, the nutcracker prince, and dance parts in the *grand divertissement.*

In 1954 I finally arranged our own production of *The Nutcracker.* At the Maryinsky, the first act of this ballet was not merely a small family party with a miniature Christmas tree. There was an enormous Christmas tree with hundreds of presents under it. When the children had been sent to bed and little Clara tiptoed downstairs to rescue the nutcracker, her favorite gift, the stage picture changed completely. At the stroke of midnight, the toys under the tree came to life. The chief toy soldier became a general, challenging intruders. Mice invaded the room, and there on stage a great pitched battle between the soldiers and the rats took place. They fired muskets and shot off cannon balls of candy. Clara tried to help the soldiers, but only when her beloved nutcracker was transformed into a brave, handsome prince was the battle won. This kind of thing we do not see nowadays in revivals of *The Nutcracker.* People think of *The Nutcracker* as a "suite" rather than a ballet. First it was a ballet.

In the Maryinsky *Swan Lake,* too, there were marvelous stage effects. At the beginning of Act Two there was not just one swan swimming across the lake, as we see so often today: there were two dozen swans, gliding across what appeared to be real, rippling waves. Actually, each swan was secured to a long stick, which members of the Tsar's Finnish regiment maneuvered underneath the stage between the rippling canvas waves. Later, when the twenty-four swan maidens appeared on stage, the audience didn't have to guess who they were: they had already seen them.

In another Maryinsky production, Mazilier's famous ballet *Le Corsaire,* there was a real shipwreck. A gigantic ship was tossed high on the waves and completely demolished. The Tsar's Finnish regiment worked again here, moving large sheets of canvas so that they undulated like storm waves. After the ballet was over, the soldiers formed ranks and drilled out of the theatre with impeccable military style, as if their regiment had just won honors at a parade.

I've gone into some detail here about the Maryinsky production for two reasons: first, to give some idea of the natural excitement these ballets had for all of us at the Imperial Ballet School; and second, because I find that people in general are very curious about what they call "Russian ballet." There used to be a time, until very recently, in fact, when people thought that *Russian* ballet was all there was. That was wrong, of course. Only because the Tsar's treasury could afford it, only because the courts of the Tsar in the nineteenth century required opulent entertainment, and because schools had been provided to train people to provide it, did it happen that in Russia there was a great period in ballet. The Tsar's wealth created great theatres, schools were started to supply these theatres with dancers, and from all over Europe—the

Frenchmen Didelot, Perrot, and Petipa; the Italian Cecchetti; the Swede Johansson—ballet masters and teachers, dancers and musicians all came to embellish the Imperial courtly entertainment.

Contrary to the general belief, ballet was not taken very seriously by the Russian public. It was an entertainment almost exclusively for the aristocracy, among whom there were perhaps only a few gentlemen who were not primarily interested in what the ballerinas were doing after the performance. After the first performance of *The Sleeping Beauty*, Tsar Nicholas I said condescendingly to Tchaikovsky, "Very nice." The Tsar was familiar with every ballet in the repertory of his theatre and yet he had no idea that he had just heard the greatest ballet score the Russian theatre has ever produced. Like the rest of the Russian audience, he had a dilettante attitude toward ballet.

The Russians, as I have said, established ballet schools, and in these institutions the best teachers in Europe made great Russian dancers. All the influences—the French, the Italian, the Scandinavian—all the talent commingled to form in the nineteenth century in Russia the finest dancing academy in all the world.

By the time I first saw ballet at the Maryinsky Theatre, both Pavlova and Nijinsky had left Russia, never to return. But there were still in St. Petersburg many great dancers. Principal among these were Tamara Karsavina, our ballerina, and Pierre Vladimiroff, who had succeeded Nijinsky as *premier danseur*. We idolized these dancers and strove to perfect ourselves.

I worked very hard at the school, appeared in my first character role, a Spanish dance in Fokine's *Jota Aragonese*, in January 1916, and acted also on the stage of the Alexandrinsky, the Tsar's dramatic theatre. At the ballet school we were trained in acting, too, and mime, where we learned the importance of stage gesture. We learned how different stage appearance was from ordinary life, how to work within theatrical disciplines to create illusion. One of my teachers, Paul Gerdt, appeared as a young man in Fokine's *Pavillon d'Armide* with two of his students, Pavlova and Nijinsky. Gerdt was then sixty-three years old, but from his stage presence he appeared as young as his students.

At the Alexandrinsky Theatre, I acted the part of the young student in Andreyev's *Professor Storitsyn*, among other roles, and at the Mikhailovsky, the Imperial Theatre for opéra-comique, I danced and acted in *A Midsummer Night's Dream* to Mendelssohn's music and danced one of the Furies in the Meyerhold-Fokine *Orpheus*. Like all other students at the school, I was almost oblivious to what was going on in the world outside. Few of us knew there was a war.

When Tsar Nicholas II abdicated in March 1917, the Imperial Ballet School was closed down. I lived at my aunt's in St. Petersburg, waiting for the school to open again. I worked as a bank messenger, as a saddler's apprentice, and at nights played the piano for silent movies in neighborhood theatres. During the October Bolshevik Revolution later that same year, Lenin selected the balcony of the *prima ballerina assoluta* of the Imperial Theatre, Mathilda Kschessinska, from which to address the people. I remember hearing him that night. I had gone, with a group of my fellow students from the school, to see what was attracting the huge crowd. All of us thought the man on the balcony must be a lunatic. Then we were young; we did not understand the Revolution.

The Bolsheviks did not wish to reopen the Imperial Theatres: the theatres were, after all, aristocratic and "bourgeois" institutions. But Lunacharsky, the new Bolshevik Minister of Education, was a balletomane. He persuaded the Bolsheviks to use the Tsar's old theatres for party meetings and for speeches to the public. Party members and the public were compelled to attend. In 1918 Lunacharsky further persuaded the Bolsheviks to allow the old Imperial Ballet Company and students of the school to perform *divertissements* in the old Maryinsky after these official functions were over. And so we danced again, this time in a "state" theatre, though it was the same Maryinsky, and the school was reopened. There was no heat, either in the theatre or at the school, and food and clothing were very scarce. On stage, in flimsy costumes, we could see our breath almost freeze; in the audience, people wore fur coats. At the school, we burned the polished parquet floors to keep warm and made trousers out of the draperies. The Tsar's carriages, which had previously driven us to the theatre, were not available, and we had to walk to and from our performances.

We worked hard at taking up our studies again. A new course in Marxian history at the school seemed a small sacrifice for the resumption of training for our chosen profession. We were not paid, we were undernourished and ill-clothed, but still we studied and danced. When Lunacharsky came to take us to see Griffith's movie *Intolerance* in 1920, we still wore the remnants of our Imperial uniforms.

In 1921 I was graduated from what had become the Academy of Opera and Ballet (now the Kirov Academy of Opera and Ballet). I had been a government charge since I was ten years old, and the Bolsheviks, like the Tsar before them, expected all graduates of state schools to remain in state theatres until they were pensioned. As an honor graduate, I secured good roles in the theatre's repertory.

This same year, 1921, I entered the Conservatory of Music in St. Petersburg. The famous composer Glazunov was then director of the conservatory. My interest in music had not diminished during the years I had spent learning the theatrical arts; rather, it had greatly increased. I had played the piano regularly at the school and on vacations, and it now seemed to me time to learn even more about music. For three years at the Conservatory of Music I studied theory, composition, and piano while I continued to dance in the state ballet company at the old Maryinsky. I wanted to be a fine pianist as well as a good dancer.

Meanwhile I had become interested in choreography. I do not know how to explain this interest. I had learned to dance, to move, I loved music, and suddenly I wanted to move people to music, to arrange dances. In 1920 I had arranged my first ballet, a short ballet in the Fokine style, to the music from Rubinstein's *La Nuit*, which was danced by my fellow students at the school. The boys and girls who were in my ballet liked it very much, though its quality of movement was new to them. Our teachers did not like it at all. I saw immediately that I should never be able to convince the management of the state theatre to become interested in my work. I would have to present it myself.

This I did, in St. Petersburg, in 1923, in a program called "Evenings of the Young Ballet," which I organized with Vladimir Dimitriev, who has remained in Russia as a designer. In this program I was responsible for all the choreography. I tried to show the evolution of ballet in Russia from Petipa's classicism through Fokine's reforms to my own ideas of movement. The dancers were members of the state company who had been graduated with me. We had a hard time finding a place to put on this program, which was finally presented in the amphitheatre formerly occupied by the Tsar's State Duma (Parliament).

The "Evenings of the Young Ballet" were popular with the dancers who performed them and with the young people in the audience, but they were not liked by the directorate of the state theatre. The director informed my dancers that they could not appear in my ballets and continue as members of the state company. We were therefore compelled to stop our performances, and I was obliged to arrange dances elsewhere.

At the Mikhailovsky Theatre I arranged the dances for Ernst Toller's *Broken-Brow*, devised pantomime ballets to the Milhaud-Cocteau *Le Boeuf sur le toit* and to Alexander Blok's poem *The Twelve*, and began work on a ballet set to Stravinsky's *Pulcinella*, which had already been staged in Western Europe by Diaghilev's Ballets Russes. I also arranged a dance scene for a production of Bernard Shaw's *Caesar and Cleopatra* at the Mikhailovsky. (This was the opening scene, which I depicted as a cabaret. Later, when I knew English and could read Shaw in his own language, I saw what nonsense this was!)

All this time, I was still dancing at the old Maryinsky as a member of the state company. The modern ballets of the Diaghilev repertory were becoming a part of the traditional Russian repertory. These ballets excited me enormously: I loved their music and choreography and marveled at the imagination of a man like Serge Diaghilev, whose Russian company in France could produce so many masterpieces so consistently. Needless to say, no equivalent creativeness existed in the theatre at St. Petersburg.

In 1924 I thought it would be a good idea to take a small group of Russian dancers to Western Europe. We had some difficulty with the Soviet authorities, but in those days it was actually possible to leave Russia and the authorities thought the tour might well have propagandistic value. They consented, provided that we went to Europe on our summer vacation from the state theatre. We were called the "Soviet State Dancers." There were actually very few dancers—Alexandra Danilova, Tamara Geva, Nicholas Efimov, and myself. I was then twenty, the oldest of all. I arranged a number of ballets, among them pieces to the "Oriental Dance" from Mussorgsky's *Khovantchina* and a waltz of Kreisler's. We learned these dances perfectly and in June 1924 sailed from St. Petersburg (it had become Leningrad) on a German boat. We were bound for Berlin, where we had secured our first engagement.

In Berlin we danced with some success, then went on to perform in German watering places and at Mannheim. Then we accepted an invitation to dance at the Empire Theatre in London. From London we went to Paris. There we were fortunate enough to secure an audition with Serge Diaghilev, the genius impresario who had brought the Russian ballet to Europe fifteen years before and had caused the ballet capital of the world to shift from St.

Petersburg back to Paris. Diaghilev had seen one of our performances; he liked our dancing and our dances. He invited us to join his Ballets Russes.

When I became ballet master to Diaghilev's Ballets Russes, I was twenty-one years old. I was humble in this position in the most famous ballet company in the world and sought to learn everything possible from Diaghilev, the man who had fostered Fokine and Nijinsky and commissioned from Igor Stravinsky that great composer's first ballet scores, *Firebird* and *Petrouchka*. I had just arrived in Europe and, though I had learned European languages at the ballet school in St. Petersburg and knew the culture of Europe in general, I had much to learn.

Several years ago Anatole Chujoy's *Dance News* published an article of mine on Diaghilev to commemorate the twentieth anniversary of his death. What I said then seems just as true to me now:

"Perhaps it is only today, almost twenty-five years after his death, that all contemporary choreographers begin to realize the true proportions of the enormous artistic debt we all owe to Serge Diaghilev. If we analyze the work we have done since his death in 1929, we see that we are still following in his footsteps, still adhering to the principles laid down by him during the twenty years he guided the fortunes of his unique Ballets Russes. Were he alive today, Diaghilev would probably find a new direction in his beloved art form, a new approach to the creation and presentation of ballet. He was always twenty-five years ahead of his time.

"Diaghilev had the capacity to see not only the potentialities inherent in an artist, be he choreographer, composer, designer or dancer, he also knew what work, what style, what period, suited that artist best. Great though it was, his genius for discovery would not have been so overwhelming had he not had that innate and cultivated taste which alone distinguishes true artistic quality from a sense for novelty and craftsmanship.

"If I were to describe Diaghilev simply, I should say that he was a man of high culture. It so happened that he was a great ballet impresario, a patron of the arts, but he could just as easily have been a statesman, an ambassador: he could have held any post that required knowledge, intelligence, culture, taste. He was at home in world literature, music, painting and sculpture. He spoke three languages with the fluency and in the idiom of the native. Never a professional musician, he could read a musical score as one reads a book.

"Stravinsky has described Diaghilev's intimate musical knowledge in his *Autobiography* and Nicolas Nabokov, who also composed his first ballet for the Ballets Russes, has written of Diaghilev's great understanding of music in his book *Old Friends and New Music*. Never a choreographer or a dancer, Diaghilev knew what was exactly right and what was wrong about a particular ballet or in any portion of it. Never a painter, he possessed an unerring and intimate knowledge of art.

"These qualities made Diaghilev a creator, a real producer. He was not just the director or manager of a ballet company who guessed what the public would accept and what it would reject. He did not follow the public; the public followed him. He did not really care very much whether people agreed with him or not. What mattered to him was the work done by the best and most suitable choreographer, musician, designer and dancers. If they succeeded, their work was a success. Diaghilev so inspired the artists who worked under his direction that it is not too much to say that any ballet created for his company bore his personal stamp as well as that of the composer, painter and choreographer.

"Strangely enough, he did not interfere with work in progress. Before work began, he discussed projected ballets with their creators in great detail. We argued and recognized each other's points. Diaghilev had great respect for artistic integrity. By the time actual work began on ballets, every phase of their production represented a collaboration between artists and their producer.

"Even if we discount for the moment the fact that companies the world over are still using ballets created for the Diaghilev company (*Petrouchka, Les Sylphides,* etc.) and that much of what else there is in ballet today stems from the Diaghilev roots, we cannot escape the fact that it was Diaghilev who invented the formula of presenting three short ballets in one evening and thus made possible the presentation of ballet not only by big resident companies in the few opera houses of European capitals, but also by touring companies in big and small cities and towns in America and Europe.

"If it can be said at all that one man took ballet from the thin aristocratic stratum of society and gave it to the people at large, Diaghilev was the man who did it. To Diaghilev's additional credit, one is reminded that he never attempted to lower the artistic standard of ballet to the level of those who had no prior knowledge, taste or appreciation of the art form. On the contrary, by constant and painstaking work to present ballet of the highest calibre to the people to whom ballet was new, he succeeded in elevating the people to the appreciation of ballet, in developing their taste and increasing their enjoyment.

"Personally, I owe to Diaghilev my growth and development during the second period of my artistic life. The first part of it I owe to the Russian Imperial Theatre where I was brought up, to its strict discipline, to its classicism, the basis of all ballet, to its two-hundred-year-old tradition which instilled in me a love for ballet and a respect for its history and artistic principles.

"The second period of my artistic life began in the Diaghilev company, where I learned to recognize what was great and valid in art, where I acquired the ability and strength to analyze a work of art on its true merits and where, finally, I learned to be on my own, to do what my artistic sense prompted me to do—in short, to be an artist. All this I owe to Diaghilev without any reservation."

For Diaghilev's company, beginning in 1925, I rehearsed the repertory and danced with the company in addition to creating ten new ballets. I don't think there's any question that *Apollo* (1928) was the most important of these, certainly the most important for me personally, for I regard this ballet as the crucial turning point in my artistic life. In the first ballets I choreographed for Diaghilev I had been successful, I think, but for the wrong reasons. *Pastorale,* for instance, which I arranged to music by Georges Auric in 1925, contained diverse types of movement—at least ten different types—whereas only one type was sufficient for the piece: the others should have been set aside and the one proper type developed. Stravinsky's score for *Apollo* taught me that a ballet, like his music, must have a restraint and discipline. Stravinsky's music had a wonderful clarity and unity of tone, and I saw that gestures, the basic material of the choreographer, have family relations, like different shades in painting and different tones in music. Some are incompatible with others: one must work within a given frame, consciously, and not dissipate the effect of a ballet with inspirations foreign to the tone or mood one understands it must possess. *Apollo* depicted Stravinsky's music visibly.

*Prodigal Son* and *Le Bal* (with Danilova, Nikitina, Dolin, and Lifar) were my last ballets for Diaghilev. A few months after the first performance of *Le Bal*, Diaghilev died in Venice. His company disbanded: there then came to an end the most important and entertaining twenty years of creativity in music and painting and dancing that Europe had seen since the Renaissance.

After some months had passed, I accepted an engagement as ballet master at the Royal Theatre, Copenhagen, with the Royal Danish Ballet, which, with the Paris Opéra, has the oldest continuous tradition of instruction and performance in the world. After this, I worked in London on my first musical comedy and in France helped to organize the Ballet Russe de Monte Carlo and staged for them their first new ballets: *La Concurrence, Cotillon,* and *Le Bourgeois Gentilhomme.*

My own company, Les Ballets 1933, was formed soon after this. This company performed in Paris and in London. It was during performances of Les Ballets 1933 that the painter Pavel Tchelitchew introduced me to the young American Lincoln Kirstein, who with Edward M. M. Warburg invited me to come to the United States to found the ballet school he knew was necessary if the classic dance was ever to flourish in America. We opened the School of American Ballet in New York on January 2, 1934, in studios that had been used in years past by Isadora Duncan. The school has become, over the years, the largest institution for the training of professional dancers outside the European state schools. Students from this school have danced in every American ballet company and in many companies in Europe. More specifically, they have been the basis for the founding of ballet companies that Lincoln Kirstein and I have directed. These companies have evolved and matured in the New York City Ballet. Morton Baum, Chairman of the Executive Committee of the New York City Center of Music and Drama, and the directors of that corporation invited Kirstein and me to found in 1948 this permanent, resident ballet company at the New York City Center. It is not for me to comment on the New York City Ballet: this would be like a father telling you about his own children. I can only invite you to come and see it, as I urge you again to see all ballet companies in New York and on tour throughout America.

Writing about ballet is difficult for me, even talking about ballet is difficult for me; if I were naturally a writer or a lecturer, and expressed myself well in writing and speaking, I should not be a choreographer. But I have tried to make clear a number of things in this book that will be of help to the audience and to the potential dancer. This book, however, as I have said elsewhere, is no substitute for the ballet you can see on the stage. Only by seeing ballet repeatedly in the theatre can you understand why it has entertained audiences for three hundred years and how it has given some of us happiness because we have been able to provide some of that pleasure.

# PART SIX

*Ballet for Your Children*

People often come to me and ask questions about dancing. They want to know if they should send their sons and daughters to ballet school, when to send them, how long it will take them to become dancers, and what chances they have for a career in ballet. Others ask about choreography: how I work, what I think of first when I am about to produce a ballet, whether choreography can be taught. In this and the following two sections I have answered these questions and many others that seemed to me important for students, dancers, parents of dance students, and—last but not least—the ballet audience.

Ballet must be seen to be enjoyed, but many of us are more easily entertained if we have in advance some information about an art that happens to be strange to us. Most people may want to relax and make no effort when they go to the theatre, but I think the answers to questions about a dancer's training, for instance, might help convince them that all art requires a certain amount of effort and ability on the part of the audience, too.

To ensure maximum clarity, I have arranged my views on ballet for your children, on dancers and choreography, in the form of particular questions and answers.

QUESTION    What ballets should children be taken to see?

ANSWER    Some people think that only ballets about puppets, such as *Petrouchka* and *Coppélia,* are good for children. They are, of course, but I think you will find that children enjoy almost all good ballet. A friend of mine, I remember, thought that a full program of four ballets would be too much for her five-year-old nephew to sit through; she thought the child would get bored and squirm. She decided that they would see only the first two ballets and then leave. But the child didn't want to go. He saw that all the other people weren't leaving and that there was obviously going to be more. He stayed for all the ballets and loved every minute of it.

Children enjoy ballets without stories as much as narrative ballets. If the ballet company is a good one and the orchestra good, they will love these musical ballets. We must understand that children are flexible; they have more imagination, more feeling for fantasy, than grownups. Grownups analyze. They come into the theatre and say sometimes, "This bores me, it's taking up my time"; or they compare, "My wife is better-looking than that girl"; or they complain that they see nothing on stage similar to everyday life. Children are open, freer, not so prejudiced. They have a natural ability to imagine things that ballet sometimes releases. The fascination life has for them is based on enjoying movement and change; ballet, in its idealization of movement, fascinates them. A storyless ballet, simply movement to music, they like almost instinctively. They will certainly like anything that is good, if we only give them the chance.

QUESTION   When should a child begin ballet training?

ANSWER   Children should begin to study when they are eight, nine, or ten
years old—certainly not before they are eight. All you can really do with
children before the age of eight is permit them to run around, dance a little, and sing songs. This, of course, is recreation and produces no real result. Before the age of eight, ballet training can actually be harmful. It is
serious training and it is hard work physically. In ballet class the first
thing we teach the children are the basic ballet positions, positions that
are unnatural to them. Their hips, knees, and feet have to be turned out
in certain directions. Because the bones and joints are still soft at this early
age, we never force children into the basic ballet positions. If they can't
do them perfectly, we wait. If you overtrain the small, undeveloped muscles of children, the muscles become hard and don't develop properly
with the body and the child is apt to become deformed. So even when a
child begins at eight, we are very careful. Very often a mother will come
to me and say, "My child dances very well and she is musical too. I think
she is another Pavlova." The child is perhaps four years old! In all probability someone has advised the mother that the child should study ballet,
someone who wants to make money and naturally doesn't care what happens to the child afterward. If you take a child of four in a ballet class
and train her seriously, you may please her parents but you will seriously
harm the child. However, when a child is eight or nine years old, she can
take a certain amount of direction and you can really begin to teach her.

QUESTION   What is the age limit for starting ballet training?

ANSWER   This really depends on the individual case—on the person's build
and on the softness of his joints. Generally speaking, beginning students
with professional theatre careers in mind should certainly start before
they are fifteen years old—preferably earlier. If they start to study at
fifteen, they will probably not be ready for the stage until they are over
twenty, by which time most dancers have been professionals for some
years. But I repeat, it depends on the individual case. Usually, after the
age of twenty-two no satisfactory results can be obtained.

QUESTION   If you want your child to be a dancer, what is the best preparation
before the child begins to attend ballet class?

ANSWER   I would suggest reading the child fairy stories—Grimm, La Fontaine,
Gozzi, and many others—read them stories from Greek mythology and
the stories of E. T. A. Hoffmann. Most people know Hoffmann's stories
from the operetta by Offenbach, *Tales of Hoffmann*, but he wrote
a great many other wonderful stories. The story of the ballet *The
Nutcracker* is just one of them. And by all means read the stories of
the great Hans Christian Andersen. And I don't mean Andersen's stories,
or any others, as they are watered down, especially translated and con-
densed for children. Good fairy stories were always written for intelligent
people. Children are more intelligent than many of us think. Mickey
Mouse will interest a child for only a short time; you should move on to
fairy tales. It is well to remember that if a child continues to be interested
only in Mickey Mouse, it is probably because you have not introduced

him to something new. Children like to move on to new, more complicated things. They don't like to be talked down to; they like it very much if you respect their capacity for new experience.

You should also play music for your child. If you don't play an instrument yourself, play records at home. Play them all the time; make music a regular thing around the house, like bathing and brushing teeth. Don't bother with jazz or swing or popular records; the air is filled with it from morning to night, and children will hear enough of it. Play anything good. Don't bother to tell the children what you are playing; soon they will remember, hum the music, and whistle it. They won't care what it is especially, but they will surprise you when they recognize it. Then go on to play other things.

Don't expect children to like the music you play at once, don't coax them, don't even ask their opinion, just play it. If you think Mozart bores children, you may find out that Mozart is just boring you. Children are not so prejudiced: they don't have the barriers to enjoyment that so many of us grownups have. Children are more aware, more teachable, more vulnerable to entertainment. They have their ears open.

QUESTION   Where are the best ballet schools in the United States?

ANSWER   Excellent schools with fine teachers are to be found all over America —in New York, California, Chicago, everywhere—not only in the big cities, but in smaller communities. New York is the center of dance activity in the United States—in spite of the impressive growth of dance in cities throughout the country—and sooner or later, almost all dancers find themselves studying or working in New York, as all actors do. It often happens that dancers do not begin to study in New York until they have established some sort of reputation for themselves elsewhere and only continue their study in New York because it is convenient for their work.

QUESTION   If you had a son, would you send him to ballet school?

ANSWER   Yes. The people who ask me this question say they hesitate to send their boys to ballet school because they are afraid the boys will become "sissified" or perhaps will not develop strong, muscular bodies as they might in another activity. That isn't true. Male dancers must be very strong, not only for their own work but for partnering; their bodies must be flexible and they must have a great deal of endurance. This is the reason why many of our best dancers were good soldiers during the war. Of course, you can be strong and a "sissy" at the same time, but this has nothing to do with ballet: it is the person himself. We do not give ballet classes for boys and girls separately. They are together in class from the beginning. Perhaps if boys started to take dancing lessons early, they would appreciate the companionship and charm of girls even sooner than they ordinarily do!

QUESTION   How is a child selected for admittance to a ballet school?

ANSWER   About the only things you can judge a child on when she is eight or nine years old are her general appearance and her health. We can only tell whether a child's insteps are good, whether her limbs are in the right proportion, and whether they are flexible. We must be able to watch her in class, two lessons a week, for perhaps six months to come to a real decision. Also, at the beginning, talent is not always the first thing that a child shows. That might come much later, when she has learned to dance well enough to demonstrate talent. Some girls and boys at the beginning seem to be very good, but as time goes on it often happens that they just do not show progress or development. If they are satisfactory at the beginning and develop badly, we advise them not to continue.

It is good if a child is musical, if she knows how to keep time to music and reacts to it. But it often happens that it is impossible to make any judgment about this, too, until after some time has elapsed in training.

QUESTION   What is a child taught first at a ballet school?

ANSWER   At the beginning, each of the five ballet positions (*see* Glossary) is shown to the children and explained very simply and plainly. Then the children are placed facing the wall with both hands on the bar, so that their weight is evenly supported by both hands. Standing this way, they must first learn to stand in each of the Five Positions until they become completely familiar with them and can adopt one or another at will, but as yet without any connecting exercises. These first classes are taken slowly; children do these same exercises for a month or so and then they get used to it. Actually, an exercise is a memory of something, a spontaneous memory. Soon it becomes a part of your existence, of your body, and if you are trained well at the beginning, after a while you can move from one place to another in the right way without even thinking about it. The unnatural position, in other words, becomes natural. It's like reciting something. If you want to recite Shakespeare, you have to memorize. You repeat it for a hundred times perhaps, and then something happens in your brain. You can recite spontaneously.

The children's attention is drawn to correct posture at the beginning; they are taught to keep their backs straight, their shoulders down. Next they are taught to do *demi-pliés* (*see* Glossary, *Plié*) very slowly in each of the five positions, always paying strict attention to posture.

The training of children requires a long time, and trying to shorten it by hurrying the child does no good whatever. Children must be watched to see when they have had enough of each exercise. It is important never to strain them in order to speed their progress.

When the children are familiar with the Five Positions, they must learn how to change from one position to another by means of connecting movements. Next they learn *battements tendus* (*see* Glossary), beginning with the simplest: from first position to second position and back. They should be taught *battements* only in front, then only sideways, then in back, separately. All these exercises should be taught first with both hands on the bar, then with only one hand on the bar. At this point the children learn how the hand and fingers should be held. Then, away from the bar, in the center of the room, they are taught the arm positions.

QUESTION   Should parents watch their children in class?

ANSWER   No, or if they must, only very seldom, for it confuses things. The child's respect for his parent and his respect for his teacher are entirely different things, and until the child learns to dance well, I think it's a mistake to confuse the child with two kinds of authority. He will learn to respect his teacher and learn to dance much faster if parental concern is suspended during ballet class. At the School of American Ballet during a child's first two years, parents visit classes only once a month. We can all understand that parents are vitally interested in their children's progress, but when they have chosen a school and a teacher, they should trust their own judgment and have faith in the teacher.

QUESTION   How soon should girls studying ballet begin to dance on toe?

ANSWER   Children should not be allowed to dance on point until their fourth year of study—after they have completed three years of training. That is, if a child enters a school and begins regular training when she is eight years old, she is eleven before taking toe exercises. This period of preparation is vitally necessary because many foot and leg muscles must be developed properly before a child can dance on toe without injuring herself seriously. The child's soft bone structure may be irreparably harmed if she begins dancing on toe before she is ten or eleven. If a child of eight enters a school and takes daily lessons, two years of training will give her the proper preparation. No profit can come from permitting a child to dance on point before she is prepared. Her dancing future will be short and she will be harmed physically. Only competent teachers are in a position to judge exceptions to these rules.

QUESTION   Is toe dancing painful?

ANSWER   No, not if the proper muscles are trained well first. In good ballet schools we are always careful to do this. Naturally, at first the muscles ache from the unfamiliar movement, but to a dancer an aching muscle is a discovery: she knows that she is conquering something new.

If you have been to the ballet and seen dancers remain on stage for long periods of time in a difficult ballet, you have probably wondered at their physical endurance. Dancing, however, trains their muscles so that they are controlled or relaxed almost unconsciously. In a dancer's body there is no constant tension. Muscles must be relaxed until they are used. In modern choreography there are steps so fast that some muscles have to be relaxed instantly or the dancer will tire in a few minutes.

QUESTION   Can knock-knees and other defects be corrected at ballet school?

ANSWER   Some children are knock-kneed when they're very young, but by the time they are ten, their structure changes completely and they aren't as knock-kneed as you thought they would be. Then they can go on with their lessons, for we can control the appearance of the knees slightly. If the child continues to be very knock-kneed, it is best to give up the lessons. The parents of one little girl we had at our school were different sizes: the father was very, very tall and the mother very, very short. I guessed correctly that when the girl grew up, she would have very short legs and a very long torso. But she wanted to continue studying and did so until it was apparent that she had grown the wrong way. You can't do anything about a structural defect like this. You just have to wait, to hope, that the young children who start lessons when they are eight or nine will still be well proportioned when they grow up. I'm sure some parents think this is too big a chance to take, spending all that money when they can't be sure their children will develop correctly for a professional career. But this chance must be taken, for if the child does not start lessons soon enough, it will be difficult—if not impossible—for her to become a fine professional dancer.

QUESTION   How is discipline maintained in a ballet class?

ANSWER   This is a question parents often ask, and they are quite right to be interested in it. When children go to a strange ballet class with a new teacher, they are a little in awe of the instructor, quite naturally. But actually this makes them more anxious to follow directions, to repeat the positions and steps that the teacher shows them. If their parents directed them at home in this way, they would probably say, "No, I won't, I don't want to." Parents naturally don't want to force things; they think their children really don't want to and that they might cry. But the teacher doesn't care, even if the children do cry. He simply directs them, politely and firmly.

The teacher must direct his young pupils quietly: you can't scream and correct children all the time. You can scream once, twice, maybe three times, and the children will be scared and obey you; but if you yell at them any more, they won't be frightened. They'll get used to your yelling, and you'll find that you have to pretend not to see them misbehaving—so that you won't scream any more and embarrass your authority.

Children see everything. They certainly see how you react when you turn around suddenly and catch them misbehaving. They know you will think ill of them. But if you don't notice, they'll say to themselves, "He doesn't care, he looks straight at us when we're horsing around, we can do anything we want to!"

But to a certain extent with children in ballet class you can't notice everything. You have to pretend not to see some of their little tricks, because for a whole hour it's very hard to hold their attention. You can hold their attention by noticing their tricks only once in a while. Then be firm with them, and they will behave for a little while. The next week they are quieter and behave for longer periods of time. By the end of the first year they respect you. They behave like soldiers: they come on time, they know when to start, wait obediently for your directions, and, finally, when you tell them that the lesson is over and say, "Thank you," they acknowledge this with a bow which will be so important to them later when they bow gracefully on the stage. They become such good soldiers that they don't leave the class unless you do say, "Thank you."

You can't expect all children to like ballet classes. I certainly did not like them at first, and I think this is more or less true of most young pupils. Only gradually do they learn to like it. After some time has elapsed, they enjoy bring able to do what they are told in class. They like the music the pianist plays for them to move to. First he plays music just for the sound, for rhythm and keeping time, but after a while he plays them little pieces. To look at the children, you'd think that they didn't know the difference, but they remember, they notice everything, they memorize music. Slowly they become trained to move well and to listen, and from a few steps and exercises they are able to do simple dance sequences. They watch grown-up dancers in other classes, admire them, and want to move beautifully too, by imitating with the little technique they have.

I think all children like the idea of dancing. If you tell them they're taking lessons to become something they don't know about, they don't listen to you. But dancing is different: they like it and somehow suffer through the lessons at first. It's like holding up a candy bar and saying to a child, "No, not yet, you must wait." They will wait, they will endure the lessons so that they can move brilliantly and beautifully. It is a natural thing for children to want to move well, to move well in time, to catch a baseball at the right moment, to hate to drop things. Dancing is a discipline that perfects this natural inclination: it gives us control over our bodies so that we are in a position to conquer space, so to speak, in given periods of time. Some music is very rapid, very complicated, and to move to it well is difficult, but the dancer is able to conquer the complicated time element of the music, she is able to move freely within the discipline of time.

Once we had at our school a child whose mother was a psychiatrist. The mother came to the school and wanted to know how the classes were run, how the children were made to behave, because at home she could do nothing with her own child. The mother watched her child in class, and this little girl—the little brat who at home was always doing the wrong thing—she was perfect! Like all the other pupils, she did exactly what the teacher said and enjoyed it. Afterward the mother wanted to know how this could happen. She said, "In my job I advise parents about their children. I'm supposed to know all about child psychology." She was told that it is a matter of knowing how to teach, when to notice things and when not to notice, and that children have a certain respect for what the teacher represents. For the child, the teacher is connected with a strange thing called the art of dancing, and the child knows that what she can learn from him is wonderful.

The respect that a child has for his teacher and the good manners she learns in ballet class are a very important part of the tradition of ballet, which is an aristocratic tradition. I use the word aristocratic here seriously, not because ballet is open only to an exclusive class of people, but because it is an exclusive art, practiced and completely understood only by those who are willing to spend a great deal of time and effort on it. The Greek word for aristocracy means the rule of the best, not the rule of an exclusive class. Ballet in this sense is a democratic art, open to all who are willing to work and to learn.

QUESTION  How many different classes are there in ballet schools?

ANSWER  Most schools are divided into different sections for beginners, intermediate, advanced, and professional classes, or classes equivalent to these distinctions. Classes for children are given separately. When a student has finished all the children's classes, she moves on to the regular classes. Students who have had previous study or experience are placed in the proper class after auditions.

QUESTION   Do students receive grades at ballet school?

ANSWER   Some schools give their children grades, but many promote students simply on the basis of their progress and ability in acquiring technique. Age has nothing to do with promotion, nor has the length of time spent in previous study. Promotion, in other words, is not automatic. It depends on the student's development. If a child has studied for some time and shows no aptitude for dancing, her parents should be so advised.

QUESTION   Should children practice ballet at home?

ANSWER   While practicing at home is not generally harmful, it actually does very little good; children should certainly not be made to do it. At home there is no teacher to watch and correct them; only in a class can they practice with real profit. It seems to me better if at home they think occasionally about their lessons and practice only the fine points they want to improve—hand movements and mime, for example.

QUESTION   Is it necessary for a student to continue her practice during long vacations?

ANSWER   It is not only unnecessary, it is inadvisable. If a serious student has been scrupulous about attending classes daily for nine or ten months of the year, rest and relaxation are recommended.

QUESTION   How many years of training are necessary before a beginner is graduated from a ballet school?

ANSWER   Usually, five or six years. The period is longer if the student has not attended class daily (Monday through Saturday for a minimum of nine months each year), shorter if his ability is exceptional. Because few students are likely to make their professional debuts when they are fourteen years old, this is an additional reason for not beginning to study until after the age of eight. It must be stressed, however, that few schools have any graduating system. No dancer really finishes going to school. Even if she is a ballerina in a ballet company, she still takes classes.

QUESTION   Is the public admitted to ballet classes?

ANSWER   No. Many schools allow visitors in class, and there is nothing wrong with this, particularly when the dancers have reached the professional point and are appearing frequently on the stage. But when the dancers are younger, it isn't such a good idea. Visitors distract the teacher and, most important, distract the students, who will naturally play to such an audience and are tempted to show off. Actually, visitors should be respectful and considerate and just ask politely if they may come, just as they would if they wanted to visit a class in a public high school.

QUESTION   Can students at a ballet school watch classes other than their own?

ANSWER   Yes, certainly. In fact they should be encouraged to do so. Most children who come to ballet class like to spend time afterward looking in on other classes. A young student who watches a professional class sees there the technique she is aiming for. This reinforces her ambition and makes her more eager to learn.

QUESTION   How do you tell whether or not a teacher is good?

ANSWER   This is certainly a problem that confronts parents as well as prospective students. It sometimes seems to me that there are more bad teachers of dancing than of any other art. There is a great tendency to take advantage of people's ignorance, for it is impossible to make a judgment about a teacher unless you know something about dancing. You can visit a ballet class, perhaps, and like what you see, but you can hardly tell if the teacher is training the children properly. Over the years bad teachers have devised many so-called methods, short cuts to fame; they invent nonsense about muscular knowledge to confuse and exploit those interested in ballet training. In engineering and medicine it's hard to fool people in this way, and there are laws to protect the public from collapsing bridges and quack doctors. In ballet training, however, where there is no great physical danger, there are no laws to protect you from fake teachers.

There are no short cuts, no new "methods" to become a good ballet dancer. There is only one way, instruction in the classic dance as it has been codified over a period of three hundred years. All able instructors teach ballet in terms of this universal tradition.

I think the best thing to do in seeking a good teacher is to ask the advice of a well-known professional, an experienced dancer. If you admire a dancer, find out where she studied from *The Dance Encyclopedia* or write to her. There are many fine schools, many wonderful teachers.

QUESTION   Are all ballet classes taught by the same instructor in a ballet school?

ANSWER   In smaller schools, yes, because it is necessary, but in the larger schools this is never the case. Teachers' schedules change throughout the year, and most students have a chance to benefit from the special knowledge and experience that each teacher naturally possesses. Such a system exposes the young student to varied direction and tends to prevent him from unconsciously imitating one teacher.

QUESTION   Should dancers have stage experience while they are still studying?

ANSWER   Not until they have reached a stage of professional competence. Children who appear on the stages of state theatres in Europe are called upon to do only very minor roles: they are not allowed to take roles for which their learning and talent have not qualified them.

QUESTION   Do ballet schools provide room and board for students?

ANSWER   No, not unless these schools are attached to higher educational institutions such as colleges and universities.

QUESTION   Do some schools accept only professional dancers?

ANSWER   Most are open to all. Some schools, like the School of American Ballet in New York, are interested primarily in students who wish to become professionals; but this school also accepts serious students who do not have professional careers in mind. The state schools in Europe, of course, accept only those students who may graduate onto the stages of state theatres.

QUESTION  How do ballet schools in the United States differ from those in Europe?

ANSWER  There are private schools in Europe, but most of the famous schools are state-supported institutions associated with a state theatre. This is true in France, which has the oldest dancing academy in the world, in Denmark, and in Milan at La Scala; recently it has become the case in England. In Russia, the schools formerly supported by the Tsars are supported by the Soviet regime. Each of these schools is attached to a ballet company financed by the state—the ballet of the Paris Opéra, the Royal Danish Ballet; and England's Royal Ballet, the ballet of the Bolshoi and Kirov state theatres, etc. Students are selected on a competitive basis, the government pays their way, and, after graduation, the student is obliged to spend a certain period dancing only with the state ballet company. It is axiomatic that if a student successfully completes the course, she will graduate onto the stage of the state theatre and become a permanent member of the state ballet company. Because these schools are state-supported, no foreign students are admitted except under extraordinary circumstances.

Since students in the state-supported European schools are chosen at a very early age, the curriculum consists not only of dancing in many cases, but includes also courses that students would be expected to take in ordinary schools—languages, literature, history, science, geography, and courses related to the other arts.

Students begin in these schools when they are about nine years old. In France, at the Opéra, the oldest ballet school in the world, the young students remain in the *classes supplémentaires,* first and second, for five years, then move on to the *classes des quadrilles.* The *corps de ballet* of the ballet company at the Opéra is selected from these groups.

The Paris Opéra ballet itself is divided rigidly into classes: *élèves* (apprentices), the first *quadrilles* (equivalent to *corps de ballet*), *quadrilles secondes coryphées* (dancers who perform in smaller groups than the *corps de ballet,* but who are not yet soloists), *petits sujets* (minor soloists), *grand sujets, premières danseuses* and *premiers danseurs* and, finally, *étoiles* (prima ballerinas and leading male dancers). Dancers remain in these divisions until they are promoted by the examinations that are given every member of the company every year. It is the usual practice for all dancers to perform two variations specified in advance by the directorate. The *étoiles* and *premières danseuses* and *danseurs* do not take part in the examinations. The examinations are judged by a jury of administrators, dancers, and teachers, which changes from year to year.

All the ballet schools in the United States are private. This is, of course, also true of our ballet companies. A number of our ballet companies, however, have their own ballet schools, where the members of the companies take class scholarships alongside regular students. Here, of course, it is not axiomatic that successful completion of a course gives the dancer a job with the company associated with the school.

# PART SEVEN

*Careers in Ballet*

QUESTION  How are dancers selected for ballet companies?

ANSWER  By audition. The ballet master and other interested people in our ballet companies usually have these auditions when they need to replace some of their dancers or want additions to their companies. These auditions are held in New York and all over the country; the latter is particularly true of those ballet companies that travel.

Often, at an audition, the ballet master will ask the dancer to perform a variation that is familiar to her; then he may show her a dance she doesn't know and see how she performs it, because the one thing that the dancer may know very well is not the best clue to her real talent. Previous experience is good to have, but every year all our ballet companies take in new girls and boys whose familiarity with the stage is meager indeed.

Many of our American companies, in New York and throughout the country, today have their own schools, and it is mostly from these schools that new members of the companies are selected. This would be the ideal situation for every ballet company, for in this way—with a definite idea of what kind of dancer they desire—companies can train students within their own requirements. The advantage of this is obvious, of course—even before a student dances on the stage, she will have had, in class, a real idea of the company's style and artistic demands.

QUESTION  How tall should a dancer be?

ANSWER  Between five feet and five-feet-six inches for a grown-up girl. Grown-up boys can be taller, of course, between five-feet-six and six feet, but not over six feet. There are exceptions, but not many. If a girl is five-feet-eight, on toe she will be way over six feet tall and will look silly with any partner she dances with. Dancers who intend to be only soloists can naturally afford to be taller, because their greater height will not be distracting or ludicrous as they will not be with girls or boys of average height in the *corps de ballet*. I must point out, however, that tall or short dancers with distinctive personalities and abilities can certainly achieve success.

QUESTION  Should all dancers be musical?

ANSWER  It would be wonderful if they were. At some time in her life a dancer should play a musical instrument—the piano, violin, flute, any musical instrument. She may not have talent and may play badly, but this experience will make her participate in music: she will not always be passive in relation to it. She will understand something about what music is. That, like dancing, music is hard to perform well. If it isn't possible for her to play an instrument, she should at least know solfeggio: how to sing scales (*do, re, mi, fa* . . . etc.), how to read a little music and be able to sing from the notes.

But being musical, of course, is not just being able to play an instrument, even if you play it well. There are, for instance, many unmusical singers who can sing the proper notes, but who haven't the least idea what the song is all about. The dancer's relation to music is very similar to the singer's: an orchestra is accompanying what she does; she is always moving with the music. She can move to the music automatically, count to herself all the time, and never really listen. Afterward she won't remember the music, only the sequence of steps. Counting is necessary, particularly in learning a new ballet, where you are anxious to remember the precise moment for entrances, exits, and particular steps; but after these simple things are grasped, the dancer should not only count but should also listen very carefully. After all, there's no reason why the public should be obliged to sit and watch a dancer move to music that she thinks is dull. They will think it is dull, too. Perhaps being musical is something a dancer is born with—either she reacts to it or she doesn't—but I think that, with intelligent application, any student can develop certain sensitivities to music that will improve the quality of her dancing immeasurably. No advice will help her as much as going to concerts and recitals frequently and listening to as much music as possible.

If your children take piano lessons or learn to play some other musical instrument, it is proper to enforce a certain discipline about it for some time; but if after a few years a child shows no aptitude for the instrument, it is foolish to compel her to continue. She will begin to hate music and undo all your work. If she has studied for some time, acquired a certain skill and been exposed to what music is, and doesn't wish to go on with her studies, allow her to stop. If she really loves music, she will go back to it; if she doesn't like it, you will have done her no harm.

QUESTION   Should dancers go to college?

ANSWER   It would be nice if they could, but since students who wish to become *professionals* should be studying dancing every day, it becomes difficult. Serious dance students have—in addition to their regular ballet classes—classes in character dancing, modern dance, supported adagio, and so forth. This means that unless dance students go to college at night, or between their classes at ballet school, when they are no doubt tired from their work at dancing, they can't go at all.

There are many people who say that all dancers are stupid, and some give as a reason for this the fact that dancers are not properly educated. It would be nice if we could have complete dancing academies in America, where students could be taught an academic curriculum, music, and the other arts to complement their study of dancing; but we have no such institutions, and besides, I don't think it is true at all that dancers are stupid. My experience has been that they are, on the contrary, apt to be very intelligent. It is also my experience that there are many stupid college graduates. Intelligence is not entirely a matter of education.

QUESTION   Must all dancers first be members of the *corps de ballet?*

ANSWER   Usually this is the case. Directors of a ballet company who have not seen a young professional in school do not know how talented she may be until she has had a chance to display her gifts, and most young dancers are therefore engaged first for the *corps de ballet*. Many of them, also, are too young to be placed in anything else. If they evidence talent in the *corps*, they will soon be given larger roles. But it is only seldom that a member of the *corps de ballet* becomes a ranking soloist overnight. Ballet companies that are directly associated with their own ballet schools can watch students from day to day and discover soloists among them; these students need not be tried out in the *corps de ballet*. Most of the great Russian dancers became important soloists as soon as they were graduated, some before they were graduated. Tanaquil LeClercq, a ballerina of the New York City Ballet, began as a soloist and leading performer. But it is by no means "once in the *corps de ballet*, always in the *corps de ballet*." We must remember that André Eglevsky, *premier danseur*, joined the Ballet Russe de Monte Carlo when he was fourteen and was dancing leading roles six months later; that Alexandra Danilova began in the *corps de ballet* of the Maryinsky Theatre, advanced to soloist, and became a ballerina in Diaghilev's great Ballets Russes; that Alicia Markova took soloist roles in Diaghilev's company soon after she joined it at the age of fourteen; that Maria Tallchief joined the Ballet Russe de Monte Carlo as a member of the *corps* to become a soloist and a ballerina.

QUESTION   Is a dancing career incompatible with marriage?

ANSWER   By no means. Very often dancers retire when they marry, perhaps because they go to live with their husbands in places where there is little dancing or because they want to have large families, but many successful dancers continue their careers after marriage and their careers continue to be successful.

QUESTION   Must ballet dancers belong to a union?

ANSWER   There are several unions which a ballet dancer might conceivably join, depending on where the ballet company is performing. If the ballet company performs in a legitimate theatre or opera house, in all probability the dancer would join the American Guild of Musical Artists, because AGMA has agreements with virtually all companies who perform in these theatres.

QUESTION   How much are ballet dancers paid?

ANSWER   The minimum in 1977 was $200 a week for dancers in our *corps de ballet* at the New York City Ballet. In 1942 the minimum was $41.50, and it can be seen that the dancer's pay has risen with the times; it will certainly continue to do so. Soloists and leading dancers are naturally paid much more than the minimum, but there is no established rule for their wages; it is a matter decided by the individual companies and the individual dancers. Still, it is obvious that no one ever pursued a dancing career to make a great deal of money. Leading singers and actors receive a great deal more money for their services than leading dancers. It's strange that this should be the case, for when actors and singers aren't regularly employed they can work at outside jobs and keep in practice by private study at night. The unemployed dancer, however, must attend ballet class during the day and work at her art constantly to keep in perfect condition. She seldom has either time or energy left for an outside job. The dancer between engagements is thus apt to be very poor. Even when they are working, I think it is safe to say that all dancers are underpaid or overworked, or both.

QUESTION   How long does a dancer's career last?

ANSWER   This is not an easy question to answer. Usually, nowadays, dancers appear on the stage by their late teens, often when they are sixteen or seventeen. It is even possible for dancers to become very famous before they are twenty. Some years ago, when I brought Irina Baronova, Tatiana Riabouchinska, and Tamara Toumanova to the Ballet Russe de Monte Carlo, they were all under sixteen. They were the "baby ballerinas" and became famous overnight.

By the time they are thirty, dancers have more or less reached their peak: they have acquired just about all the technique that is possible for them. But after they are thirty they can, of course, develop what they have learned and become greater artists still. The great dancers of the past—Pavlova, Karsavina, Spessivtzeva—we remember not as young girls, but as mature women, beautiful and gracious. Pavlova never retired; she was fifty when she died. Karsavina danced in public for the last time when she was forty-seven. It's up to the individual dancer. They can dance only occasionally when they grow older, and only gradually will audiences detect a change in them. Naturally, it is a happier thing if dancers retire before their audiences compel them to.

QUESTION   Should dancers have children?

ANSWER   Certainly. It does no harm whatever. Many dancers have children. Many dancers are also naturally unwilling to sacrifice a year out of their careers in order to have them. It depends on the individual.

QUESTION   Are sports good for dancers?

ANSWER   Only as an occasional pleasure. Dancers must take good care of their bodies. I would say that it is dangerous to skate, for instance. In skating, the knees bend a different way and the ankles are used differently. Playing football would be particularly hazardous. In fact, any game in which you would have to kick a ball would not be good. If a toe is injured, a dancer may have to give up dancing and all those years of study will be wasted. Tennis is all right, I suppose, for a little pleasure and if not pursued too strenuously. Actually, too much athletic activity destroys the finesse of a dancer's gesture. The truth is, of course, that dancers are so busy working at their art and are usually so tired from their studies that they seldom have the time or energy for sports.

Nathan Milstein, the great violinist, doesn't like to carry his violin because of the weight of the case. He must curve his fingers around the handle, and he feels that this strains them. It doesn't, of course, strain them seriously, and he would naturally be able to play well in any case; but he has some fine reaction in his hand that makes him think he won't be able to play with complete refinement. Horowitz, too, cares for his hands, as do all great instrumentalists. The principal instruments of a dancer are, of course, her legs, and she must respect them.

QUESTION   How is ballet training beneficial to those who do not intend to pursue professional careers?

ANSWER   Training in ballet strengthens the general physical condition of the body and develops the muscular system. It also gives complete control—poise, grace, and balance—to the body. Many people do not know how to enter a room gracefully; dancers do. Notice sometime that most people, when they are in a room with other people, often unconsciously turn around to look over their shoulders. Actually, they are self-conscious, ill at ease with their own bodies. They hesitate to turn their backs. These people control their faces well enough and imagine that grace consists largely of facial beauty. Dancers don't worry about people watching them from behind. They move unself-consciously; their grace is confident, an attribute of the whole body. For this reason, ballet training is beneficial not only to those who intend to pursue professional careers, but to all people.

QUESTION   What careers are open to dancers after they retire?

ANSWER   Many of them become teachers. Certainly, experienced dancers who have appeared for many years on the stage are the best-equipped teachers. Many former dancers become ballet masters in our ballet companies. There they rehearse ballets, give classes, and preserve the artistic disciplines. Such a person must not only be an exceptional teacher, he must also have a good visual memory and be very musical. Others with talent become choreographers; perhaps they began to create ballets while they were still dancing. Still others continue to work in the theatre as character dancers and mimes. In this country we regard this as something of a comedown, but we really shouldn't. In the Royal Danish Ballet, for example, the dancers stay on in the company and are much respected. It is a wonderful thing to see a dancer who was once a ballerina doing a part such as the mother in *Giselle*. This sort of dancer is very familiar with the ballet and knows that the part is important. It is she and other dancers like her who hand down to younger people the old traditions, and not just in a gossipy way: they watch them rehearse, correct them tirelessly, make sure of every detail. In this way the original choreographer's intention is preserved, along with the steps he planned, and very old ballets survive intact. That is an exciting way for a dancer to pay her debt to her profession.

# PART EIGHT

*Notes and Comments on Dancers,
Dancing and Choreography*

QUESTION  What country produces the finest classical dancers?

ANSWER  Classical dancing isn't a nationalistic question, and for a very simple reason: it isn't nationalistic dancing. Native character or folklore has nothing to do with it. The ability to "turn out" properly, for example, has nothing to do with the country from which a dancer comes. Americans have a great deal of ability because their bodies are strong and also because they are a very musical people. Maybe it's because we hear music, all kinds of it, everywhere here. Children respond to this rhythmical music. They clap, dance, and develop rhythmical sense almost by nature. This sense of rhythm needs schooling, very good schooling; but with such a background in your students, you can develop very great dancers. In France there are also lots of strong, well-built dancers who are musical, and certainly the same is true of England, Italy, and other countries. In other words, people of all nationalities make wonderful classical dancers. The problem really narrows down to where the best schools are. Where you have the best teachers, you have the best dancers, no matter what their nationality.

QUESTION  Is there such a thing as purely American ballet?

ANSWER  In answer to this question and the two that follow, I'd like to paraphrase the comment that I made on these subjects in Serge Lido's *Ballet 2*, some years ago.

From the time ballet began, it has been influenced by *all* the countries where it developed, from Italy, to France, to Scandinavia, and it has adapted itself to the physical abilities of the different countries. The historical development of the art has been traced in another part of this book. I hope I have successfully shown that the classic dance is a fully developed art form, which has now become universal. It has a body of classified and organized techniques which will remain as the basis of the vocabulary of classical dance until such time as ballet is replaced by some other form of theatrical entertainment.

I think that if there is such a thing as purely American ballet, it is reflected not in style but in subject matter. For example, a ballet about cowboys might be called American, as a ballet about Sherlock Holmes might be called English, or the cancan might be called French. The latter case, however, is a question of national rather than classical dance.

QUESTION  Are there different styles of classical dancing for each country?

ANSWER  As for style of dancing for different countries, there are naturally some small differences in execution, but they are mainly differences of personality. For example, there may be ten different interpretations of *Swan Lake* or *Giselle* in England, France, Denmark, Italy, and the United States—all equally valid. Some people, whose taste is inclined toward the obvious, have come to expect certain stylistic clichés from dancers—as, for example, that the dancer should be warm and passionate—but a dancer does not necessarily have to be warm or passionate. Some people are readily inclined to look for the obvious on stage. There are two types of personalities, for example, which seem to be universally pleasing to audiences: one is the vampire, almost like a female Mephistopheles; the other personality is like the lyrical or the poetic one, often almost lethargic. Yet some very good dancers that I have seen in my life were beautifully cold, like birds with no warmth at all. Others were like Oriental queens; others, again, were like pure crystal. The technique of classical dance necessarily creates a certain uniformity in dancers, which has little or nothing to do with nationality, but which is certainly modified by the personality of the dancer. I am, of course, talking about dancers with talent. Talent is God-given: it is not given by a nation or a passport. A dancer must certainly have this gift, but the gift can manifest itself in forms as various as the universe. One cannot say that sunshine is better than shade, or that a glass of cold water is worse than a flaming chimney.

There are many so-called connoisseurs who try to dictate a certain style of ballet dancing, and they talk about a tradition that they never knew. Fortunately, this does not endanger the progress or development of ballet, because the real public—the people who sit in galleries, at a small admission price which most of them can ill afford—can distinguish good dancing from an inferior imitation of a style which was interesting a hundred years ago. Every performance demonstrates that this is the true ballet public, without prejudice or fake balletomanism.

I was brought up in St. Petersburg. The style of dancing there was very strict and precise. At the same time, in Moscow, six hundred kilometers away, the style of dancing was close to that of a circus performance. The Muscovites accused us in St. Petersburg of being cold, and we accused them of bad taste. History shows that the dancers and choreographers who later influenced ballet as a whole came mainly from St. Petersburg.

QUESTION   What is the future of ballet in America?

ANSWER   The future of ballet in America, as well as in the other countries, depends on the rise of new choreographers capable of furthering its development. A school of dancing is not enough. A school naturally perpetuates the technique, but it cannot lead to a new style in the ballet; nor can a new style of ballet be invented. Progress in any art is a slow and complex process, and therefore it cannot be generated by one person only. Many people are necessarily involved. In the field of ballet, it is not only the personality of the dancer and the art of the choreographer which achieve or create a style—one should not forget the composers. Delibes and Tchaikovsky are, I believe, as responsible for what is now traditionally known as classic ballet as its choreographers and dancers.

Any good company needs a professional choreographer, just as any good restaurant needs a good chef. If a ballet company does not develop successfully, the blame must be laid at the feet of its choreographer. If he was given all possibilities of choosing the best dancers, and if he was given the liberty to do what he wanted, he should not have failed in his task of achieving adequate results.

QUESTION How does a choreographer originate his ballets?

ANSWER This is a question I can only answer by telling you how I go about creating a new ballet, because, of course, different choreographers have different ways of proceeding with their work. When I am about to produce a ballet, I begin in one of two ways: either I begin with the idea and then look for suitable music, or I hear a certain piece of music which inspires me with an idea.

This idea need not be explicitly dramatic, as in a narrative ballet such as *Prodigal Son* or *Orpheus;* it need not have a written libretto. On the contrary, the idea might consist only in a *location,* a place, where I might wish dancing to take place, the particular people I want to dance there, and a special mood. *La Valse,* for instance, doesn't have a plot, but it is dramatic in its casting, its dancing, and the mood which action and music evoke.

If I begin with an idea, I much prefer to have the music specially written for me and to be in constant touch with the composer while he is writing it. I try to tell him exactly what I want, and together we conceive the general mood and we time some of the dance sequences. I have found that most ballet composers like to have a definite timing for a ballet: they like to know when such-and-such occurs and how long it will last, whether a sequence is a dance sequence or a *pas d'action,* and so forth. Like novelists, they are interested in structure first. In this way, they can start to compose at any point in the ballet and not begin at the beginning. Working on the story ballets *Prodigal Son* and *Orpheus* was a collaboration between the composers, Prokofiev and Stravinsky, and myself.

If I begin with the music, I familiarize myself with the score thoroughly and try to understand what the composer had in mind musically when writing it. When he wrote his *Concerto in D minor for Two Violins,* Bach had no idea of composing music for a ballet; but in listening to this music, it is possible to conceive of movement that harmonizes with the score. Actually, it seems to me that the music of Bach and Mozart is always very close to dancing. It would be wrong to say that all music should be danced, but I think the greatest music is never far from dancing. I agree with the poet who said that music rots when it is too far removed from the dance, just as poetry rots when it departs too far from music.

To familiarize myself thoroughly with a piece of music, I study the score and listen to it. If a piano transcription of the score exists, I play the piece over and over on the piano; if it does not exist, I make a transcription myself. Often I spend much more time learning a score than I do working out a ballet. The Mozart score for *Caracole,* for instance, I had in mind for three years, whereas setting the steps took only seven days.

There is always music that I wish to arrange dances to. Sometimes I make the ballets right away, if this is possible. One night, some years ago, the composer Alexei Haieff played me some pieces of his on the piano. I liked the music, but I didn't think of producing a ballet. Several days later, when this music kept running through my head, I wanted very badly to make dances to it. The result was *Divertimento*. If I were a poet, I'd probably have written a poem about what this music sounded like and looked like; but I am a choreographer, a dancer, and only in dancing do I express myself naturally. In other cases, I have known the music for many years and have kept it for the right moment. This was the case with *Symphonie Concertante*, music which has always seemed to me Mozart at his most beautiful; it was also true of *Symphony in C, Bourrée Fantasque*, and many other ballets.

Before beginning rehearsals, then, I have an idea of what the general scheme of a ballet will be. I never arrange any of the dances or movements until I actually rehearse the dancers. I discuss scenery and costumes with the designer, so that they will be in accord with the idea. I discuss the lighting, and I discuss the music with the composer and the conductor, but I don't discuss the ballet with my dancers unless we are doing a story ballet.

If the ballet has no story, there is no need to discuss their parts with the dancers in any detail; these parts the dancers work out by themselves, in individual practice. But in the case of a story ballet, I tell them what characters they are playing and what their relation is to the other characters.

Other choreographers, naturally, work differently. In working on story ballets, some choreographers spend lots of time talking to the dancers, explaining the story to them: the time the story took place, the history of that era, and so forth.

I have no fixed procedure. I don't come to rehearsals with any idea so definite and fixed that it can't be changed on the spot. I never write anything down. Often I try a step, or a series of movements, on a particular dancer and then I change it to something else. I indicate the steps first, and then the dancers repeat after me. It is very simple to mount a ballet using dancers you have worked with: they understand your smallest gesture and know what you want almost instinctively.

Sometimes I arrange the end of a ballet first; sometimes I commence in the middle. Rehearsal time is limited, and I can't always indulge in the extravagance of following the order of the music. If I have plenty of time, I work with each dancer until he or she is absolutely perfect; but the natural thing is for the dancers to want to practice the steps alone and perfect themselves. This they automatically do when there is little time, as in the case of *Prodigal Son*, which was produced in ten days in 1929, and with *Firebird*, which was produced in a week in 1949.

It has been my experience that dancers drop naturally into their parts; they gradually come to live them. Every detail is given: I show them every precise movement and the smallest mimed gesture and action.

QUESTION  Is it proper for the old classical ballets to be revived and revised by present-day choreographers?

ANSWER  Yes, I don't see why not, if the choreographers have respect for the original music and for the intention of the work as it has come down to us. This is a question that many people ask very seriously, as if it meant the life or death of ballet. They talk about tradition as a matter of remembering old steps accurately and reproducing them on the modern stage. The trouble is that no one can possibly remember all the steps of the ballets he saw years ago. A consistent form of accurate, intelligible dance notation has only recently been perfected—in 1940.

What, then, do these people mean when they talk of preserving the classics in their original state? They mean, very simply, nothing at all. They don't know, nor does anyone else, exactly what those ballets were like. They just take the word of so-and-so that the old ballets, in fact, looked like such-and-such. But this is just one man's impression, and surely a faulty one: our memories are not as accurate as the movie camera.

We can naturally accept this man's word in part if the revivals he produces entertain us, but there is no use in deceiving ourselves into thinking that now, in the middle of the twentieth century, we are watching dancing and acting precisely as they were done in the nineteenth century. Those ballets—and their music—were changed radically and materially by dancers, conductors, ballet masters, and choreographers within the lifetime of their original creators.

It doesn't make sense to ask for the original, in short, if you have no idea of what the original was. People who always talk about tradition in a narrow, limited sense remind me of the story of the young Russian tenor who was to sing a leading part in a revival of an opera. During rehearsals, he was instructed to interrupt the dramatic action of one of his scenes and almost conceal himself at the back of the stage before he began to sing a difficult aria. The young tenor thought this was senseless and complained about it. But he was told that Mr. X, who had been very famous in this role, used always to interrupt the action in this manner and that he, too, must do so. The singer did as he was told, though he thought it was very foolish indeed. Some time later he asked the famous old tenor why he had changed the action of the opera. The old tenor was surprised and amused; he said, "Well, confidentially, I found that aria very difficult and I always needed to spit before I started to sing it, so I walked upstage a little and no one saw me."

QUESTION  Can anyone be taught to be a choreographer?

ANSWER  No. To be a choreographer, it is first of all necessary to be a dancer, a good one. This was true of choreographers in the past, as it is today; all our distinguished choreographers have been dancers of real quality. To become a good dancer, you must study at a ballet school for some years. Then you join a ballet company. This ballet company will dance good and important things, old ones and new ones, and there you will associate with conductors, musicians, and designers—as well as dancers. They advise you and you begin to learn. It's not, in other words, a matter of just learning how to dance and then starting to choreograph. You have to go through a period of preparation. If I told fifty well-trained dancers to move, to dance, to entertain me, they would not know what to do.

You must go through tradition, absorb it, and become in a way a reincarnation of all the artistic periods that have come before you. For instance, you must be able to know and feel how people acted and moved in Molière's plays, what sense of humor those people had, what their stage looked like. If you are going to do an Italian ballet set in a certain period, you try to go to Italy and become a part of that world. Then you put everything together—your dancing technique, your preparation in tradition, your knowledge of music, your ability—and something happens. A ballet is born.

Sometimes nothing happens. Then, I'm afraid, nothing can be done. There is no school where you can learn to be a choreographer. People can be advised about technique, they can be told to do this or that differently, but you cannot advise a person to be talented. He is born talented. It is a strange thing: your life is made somewhere, you are pushed in a certain direction, and you move that way.

There's no school that can teach choreography, just as there is no school where you can learn to be a novelist or a poet. Schools can give you technique, but from that point on you are on your own. At ballet school you can learn to dance, just as you can learn to write correct English and poetic meters in other schools, but that is only the beginning. Nothing really helps but the person himself, what inclination he has, what talent. We ought to remember the story of the famous English novelist who wanted to bring his son up to be a novelist, too. He worked with the boy, made him notice details in the way people acted, tried to teach him all the things he had learned with so much difficulty. He was deadly earnest about all this. His son turned out to be not a novelist, but a sheep farmer in Australia.

A choreographer must also be a teacher. I learned this myself when I did my first ballet, a composition in the Fokine style. I was fifteen years old and I taught this little ballet to eight boys in my class at the Imperial Ballet School in St. Petersburg. They were very good dancers. To make them stretch and extend themselves the way I wanted, I had to show them how to execute movements altogether new to them.

Choreographic movement is used to produce visual sensations. It is quite different from the practical movement of everyday life, when we walk, lift things, stand up, and sit down. Movement in choreography is an end in itself: its only purpose is to create the impression of intensity and beauty. No one intends to produce beautiful movements when rolling barrels or handling trains or elevators. But in all these everyday movements there are important visual dynamics if you look for them. Choreographic movements are the basic movements that underlie all gesture and action, and the choreographer must train himself to discover them. It's only natural that these basic movements will seem at first affected and artificial to the body that is accustomed only to the practical movements of everyday life. The object of the dancer's technical training is to enable him to perform—with perfect ease—choreographic movements, movements not limited by considerations of practical, daily life.

People in love all over the world have a certain attitude of sweetness and tenderness in the way they look and talk and touch. A choreographer notices this and finds movements to portray not the romance of A and B, but romance in general. A choreographer must see things that other people don't notice, to cultivate his visual sense. He must understand the stage space in a particular setting and how to fill that space with interesting movement; and to do this well, he must know music—know how to play it, preferably, and how to read it. For ballet is all a matter of space and time—the space on the stage, the time of the music to which the dancer moves.

The structure of a ballet must be tight, compact, like the structure of a building; good ballets move in measured space and time, like the planets.

The choreographer frees his mind from the limitations of practical time in much the same way that the dancer has freed his body. He turns not away from life, but to its source. He uses his technical proficiency to express in movement his essential knowledge. Talent, inspiration, and personality are not sources which come to an artist in a flash and go away; they are the accumulated results of all he has felt, thought, seen, and done—the stories he heard as a child, the art he has enjoyed, his education, and his everyday life—and are always with him, capable of being reached by his technical ability and transformed into dynamic designs of the utmost intensity.

If movement is the main means, possibly the only way, of presenting the art of dancing in its fullest significance, it is easy to understand the importance of connecting movements to each other with subtle care, yet at the same time emphasizing, by contrast, their continuity. For example, very brief and small movements to a fast or slow tempo—in every angle or degree of angle—are developed in relation to subsequent broad, large movements in the identical tempo, and increased from their use by one dancer to their use by many dancers. A kaleidoscope of such movements lives within the choreographer's brain, not yet, of course, set to any tempo. They are as yet only abstract memories of form. Of these, silence, placidity, and immobility are perhaps the most powerful forces. They are as impressive, even more so, as rage, delirium or ecstasy. When the body remains transfixed and immobile, every part of it should be invisibly tense, and even in relaxation there should be an inner muscular control.

The steps which a dancer has learned (and after he has studied about ten years with good teachers, he should have an impressive vocabulary of movements) are, when separate, devoid of meaning; but they acquire value when they are co-ordinated in time and space, as parts of the continual, rhythmic flow of the whole.

The student choreographer should at first work out simple technical exercises: for example, fitting eight bars of movement to eight bars of music. Many different interpretations may be given to music; there is no single meaning behind it which the listener must discover, and the chore-ographic student can fit any number of combinations of movements to the same eight bars of music. On the other hand, he can fit the same combination of movements to several different pieces of music. Or he can fit bars of movement to silence, which has a tempo of its own. But if he uses music, he must be sure to fit the movements to it completely.

There is a lot of talk about counterpoint in dancing. It is generally believed that counterpoint is based on contrasts. Actually, counterpoint is an accompaniment to a main theme which it serves to enhance, but from whose unity it must not detract. The only kind of counterpoint that I can see in dancing is the movements of arms, head, and feet which are contrapuntal to the static—or vertical—position of the body. For instance, in the *croisé* position the body is vertical—but one arm is raised, the other horizontal; one foot points forward, while the other supports the body; and the head is inclined toward one of the shoulders. All this is an accompaniment to the main theme, which is the vertical position of the body. In dancing one should not strive to achieve counterpoint by contrasting the movements of two dancers or two groups of dancers on the stage. This results not in counterpoint, but in disunity. (There is no need to apply musical terms to the dance; but if it is done, their meaning must be clearly understood.)

The eye can focus perfectly only on objects which are in the center of its field of vision. Those objects which are not head-on are seen clearly only because the observer knows and imagines what they are, while he focuses on the center object. If some new or different form is placed in the secondary part of a composition, the eye instinctively changes its focus and convinces itself of the identity of each individual form. And as vision is the channel through which the art of choreography reaches its audience, this inevitably results in confusion and a loss of attention to the main theme. But the eye can follow the movements of a large group of dancers if these form a harmonious pattern within its central field of vision.

It is impossible for choreographers to work very satisfactorily unless they are associated with a ballet company. You can compose music without an orchestra, but you cannot create a ballet without working directly with dancers.

In ballet companies, too, you learn many other things. When I was new in the Diaghilev company, I didn't know anything about Italian painting. I had just left Russia. Diaghilev took me to see pictures all over Italy. At first I was bored, but soon I became very interested: I saw that these pictures had a relation to other traditions I had absorbed, and I began to love them.

Choreography, finally, becomes a profession. In making ballets, you cannot sit and wait for the Muse. Union time hardly allows it, anyhow. You must be able to be inventive at any time. You can't be like the cook who can cook only two dishes: you must be able to cook them all.

# PART NINE

*Glossary*

Familiarity with ballet terms is not really necessary when we first start going to the ballet. In fact, if we know too much about the terms, we'll be watching to see what they mean in action and we'll miss most of the performance—it would be like knowing the meters of poetry before enjoying a poem. But while familiarity with ballet phrases is not important at the outset, it becomes important later on, after we have seen something of dancing. When we go to the ballet often, we begin to remember different steps and poses and want to know their names. That is only natural.

The most fundamental steps and positions—from the point of view of the spectator—are described below; a number of additional terms, an understanding of which will increase the knowledge of inexperienced members of the audience, are also discussed briefly. Because ballet as we know it was born in France, French is the language of the vocabulary of the classic dance. As such, it is ballet's international language, just as English is the universal language of sport and Latin the universal language of medicine.

## BASIC POSITIONS

The five fundamental positions of the feet are learned by the ballet student just as we all learn the alphabet. These positions constitute the basis for all steps in the vocabulary of the classic dance and are learned by the student at the very beginning, so that they become instinctive. These basic positions were indicated by Thoinot Arbeau (1588), formally established by Pierre Beauchamp, first ballet master at the Paris Opéra (c.1700), and set down in writing by Pierre Rameau in *The Dancing Master* (1725). They have been in constant use ever since, as the ideal foundation for exercises and performance. Each of the positions features the characteristic that distinguishes the classic dance from all other forms of theatrical dance—the turned-out leg. In ballet, each leg is turned out from the hip at an angle of ninety degrees, so that the feet form a single straight line on the floor. The five absolute positions are performed with the feet flat on the floor, high on the ball of the foot (*sur les demi-pointes*) or on the toes (*sur les pointes*).

FIRST POSITION: Heels are together;
feet are turned out to make a single
straight line.

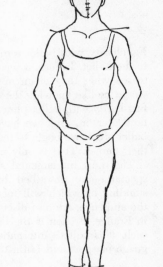

SECOND POSITION

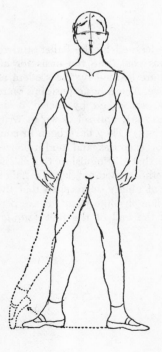

FIRST POSITION

SECOND POSITION: Feet are turned out to
form a straight line; heels are separated by
a distance equivalent to one of the feet.

THIRD POSITION: Both feet are turned
outward as in First Position; one foot
is placed in front of the other, each
heel touching the middle of the
opposite foot.

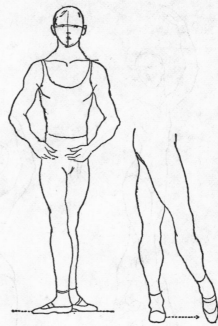

THIRD POSITION (LEFT)
AND TRANSITION INTO
FOURTH POSITION (RIGHT)

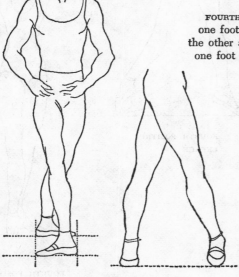

FOURTH POSITION: Feet are turned outward;
one foot is placed in front of and parallel to
the other at a distance of one foot. The toe of
one foot is in line with the heel of the other.

FOURTH POSITION
FRONT VIEW (LEFT) AND
SIDE VIEW (RIGHT)

FOURTH POSITION
CROISÉ

FOURTH POSITION
EFFACÉ

FOURTH POSITION
LEFT FOOT SUR LE POINTE

FIFTH POSITION: Feet are turned outward; one foot is placed in front of the other, the heels and toes touching so that the big toe of neither foot projects: the feet are boxed in.

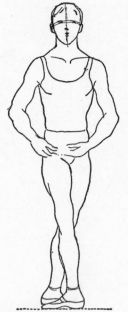

FIFTH POSITION

ADAGIO   As in music, a slow tempo: a dance in a slow tempo. The word is derived from the Italian *ad agio,* meaning at ease or in a leisurely manner. Adagios are danced by ballerinas and their partners. Adagios may occur in a ballet when the drama of the piece so dictates (*Swan Lake,* Act Two), as the central portion of a *grand pas de deux* (*Swan Lake,* Act Three), or simply as the music demands (*Symphony in C,* second movement). In adagio, the ballerina displays her beauty in slow, unfolding movements and sustained graceful poses. The principal quality of adagio is control.

Adagio is also the name for a section of any ballet class. Here the dancers practice—in the center of the room—slow, sustained exercises designed to give ease in the performance of dances that require balance, perfect line, and unquestionable authority in those who execute them.

The great Italian ballet master Carlo Blasis regarded the correct execution of adagio as the "touchstone of the dancer."

ALLEGRO   Dancing that is lively and fast, in comparison to adagio. All steps of elevation—jumps, *entrechats,* turns in the air, etc., are forms of allegro. An important quality of allegro is *ballon,* the ease with which a dancer remains in the air during a step in elevation and the ease with which he takes off and lands from a jump.

ARABESQUE   Set pose. In the most common form of arabesque, the dancer stands on one leg, with the other leg raised behind her and extended fully. The height of the raised leg is variable, as is the position of the arms.

BASIC ARABESQUE AND ARABESQUE PENCHÉ

ASSEMBLÉ   Literally, together. A step in which the dancer rises low off the floor, straightens both legs in the air, and returns to Fifth Position.

À TERRE   On the ground. *Par terre* is synonymous. Some dancers are called *terre à terre* dancers because they succeed best in steps that require no elevation, steps performed on the stage.

ATTITUDE   Basic pose of the classic dance, first described by Carlo Blasis (1829), who modeled it after the famous statue of Mercury by Bologna. In the basic attitude, the dancer stands on one leg and brings the other leg up behind at an angle of ninety degrees, with the knee bent.

BALLERINA   A leading female dancer of a ballet company. If the company is a large one, one or more principal ballerinas (*prima ballerinas*) stand at the top of the company's list of soloists. A dancer earns the title ballerina through years of hard work and by great dancing over the years in great roles. No matter what the standards of particular ballet companies, the dancer's lasting right to the title depends on continuous excellence in performance over a period of many years: we think of the great ballerinas of the past—Taglioni, Pavlova, Karsavina, Spessivtzeva—not as young girls, but as mature women. Few dancers possess the title ballerina with any secure permanence until they are thirty years old, at which time their native talent and artistry have usually been developed to the maximum. A ballerina is almost always associated with a particular role in a ballet—a role that has been created especially for her or a role in an accepted classic.

In the famous European ballet companies, which are state-supported and have their own ballet schools, the title ballerina (in France, *première danseuse*) stands

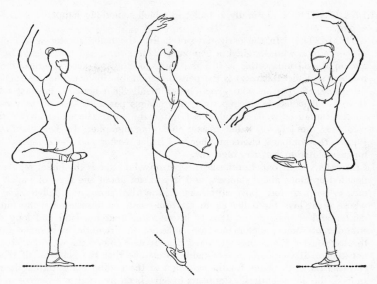

THREE VIEWS OF AN ATTITUDE

at the top of a rigorous hierarchy. Beneath this pinnacle are arranged major and minor soloists, *coryphées* (dancers who perform in small groups), and the numerous members of the *corps de ballet*. Above the rank of *prima ballerina* there sometimes reigns the *prima ballerina assoluta*. It is interesting that in the history of the Russian Imperial Theatre this title was used only twice: by Pierina Legnani, the Italian ballerina who created the leading role in the Petipa-Ivanov *Swan Lake* (1895), and by Mathilda Kschessinska, who succeeded to the title after Legnani left Russia in 1901. In the early years of this century, Olga Preobrajenska, Anna Pavlova, Vera Trefilova, Lubov Egorova, and Tamara Karsavina were all ballerinas at the Maryinsky Theatre in St. Petersburg; Kschessinska was the only *prima ballerina assoluta*. This did not mean that Kschessinska was a better dancer than all the others; it meant simply that she was a maturer artist, with years of experience and excellent performance. The hierarchies in the European state theatres were developed as a means of periodic appraisal of personnel, as a way of adjusting salaries. Dancing in these theatres is like the civil service: you are promoted according to your ability and your experience, and seniority is naturally important.

In America, where we have no such system, there really seems little need to use the Italian words *ballerina, prima ballerina,* etc., to indicate ranks we don't have. Moreover, so many inexperienced and unimportant dancers call themselves ballerinas in America that the term has little meaning. All our fine dancers are stars of our ballet companies; when the word *star* is used, we have a better idea of something special. The male equivalent of the rank of ballerina is *premier danseur.*

BALLET  From the Italian *ballare*, to dance, via *balleti*, the diminutive form of *balle,* a dance-song.

BALLET BLANC (white ballet)  Ballet in which girls wear long white gossamer costumes: *Les Sylphides, Giselle* (Act Two), etc.

**BALLET D'ACTION**    Literally, a ballet in which something happens: a ballet with a plot.

**BALLET MASTER**    In the early days of ballet, the ballet master was a choreographer, a man who designed or composed dances for a ballet company. In France and in Russia today, this is still the case. In England and America, the ballet master (or ballet mistress) is the person responsible for company instruction and discipline, the person who gives classes to all the company dancers, rehearses them in all ballets in the repertory, and assigns parts. He may or may not be a choreographer as well, though this is often the case. The name artistic director combines the jobs of ballet master and choreographer. In Diaghilev's Ballets Russes, the company choreographer was ballet master and the company instructor-disciplinarian was the *régisseur*.

**BALLETOMANE**    A ballet enthusiast: a person who attends the ballet regularly, has decided opinions about dancers, and is partisan about the type of ballet, music, etc., to be preferred above all others. In the ideal sense, the balletomane is one whose great love for ballet as an art transcends partisanship for the individual dancer and choreographer. It is to be regretted that the loud and long demonstrations of some balletomanes are sufficient to drive the newcomer from the theatre. Marian Eames has written: "Exactly who coined the word *balletomane* is not known. It would seem reasonable to assume that the behavior of the dance enthusiast was to blame for the selection of the ending *mane* rather than *phile*. Indeed, the dance enthusiast appears to have been frenzied to a degree in his devotion and often absurd. Yet his frenetic outbursts lacked the embarrassing hollowness of contemporary movie madness, for the idolatry lavished upon individual dancers was not born of a mere susceptibility to physical 'allure.' The adorer was moved by qualities and style which he could analyze and discuss; furthermore, his obsession with the art itself should not be confused with the easily bought allegiance of zealots who are beguiled less by the avowed object of their enthusiasm than by the glorious trappings which surround it."*

**BALLON**    A characteristic of *elevation* (dance in the air). The ease with which a dancer maintains in the air a position he normally holds on the ground; the ability to ascend lightly into the air and to land softly and smoothly. *Ballon* is the French word for *hand ball* and *balloon;* literally, it means *bouncing.* It is said that the term ballon was named after the French *danseur* Balon (active 1695), who possessed its qualities to a remarkable degree.

**BARRE (or bar)**    The round horizontal bar secured around the walls of a ballet classroom or rehearsal hall at a height of about three-and-a-half feet. The bar is usually placed opposite the long mirrors in which the dancer can watch what he is doing. Every ballet class begins with exercises at the bar, the dancer holding the bar for support as the daily elementary and constantly repeated exercises are performed; the lesson continues with exercises in the center of the room.

**BATTEMENT**    A nickname for an action of the leg. For example, the *battement tendu* (stretched beating), where the dancer—in the simplest form of this exercise —stands at the bar and extends her foot in front of her on the floor, or sideways, or back.

**BATTERIE**    The master term that applies to all movements in ballet in which one foot beats against the other, or in which the two feet beat together. Two types of this movement are distinguished: *grande batterie* (large, high beating steps) and *petite batterie* (small beating steps executed at a lower elevation).

---

* Foreword to "Russian Balletomania" by Anatole Chujoy, *Dance Index*, Vol. VII, No. 3.

BRISÉ Literally, a broken movement. A beating step of elevation in which the dancer rises from the floor, beats one leg against the other, and returns to the same Fifth Position—distinguishable from the *entrechat* in that only one leg beats.

CABRIOLE A movement of *grande batterie*. The cabriole develops the *battement*—in which one leg moves away from the supporting leg and returns—into a brilliant step of elevation: here both legs beat together in the air. One leg swings up to an angle of ninety degrees, the other leg rises, meets it, and both calves are beaten together (the feet do not cross); the legs are fully extended, knees straight, toes pointed. Cabrioles are also executed at an angle of forty-five degrees from the floor; they can be performed in any direction—front, back, and to the side.

CARACTÈRE The character dancer, or the dancer *en caractère*, performs national or folk dances—mazurkas, polkas, etc.—dances that are not performed on point. The dancer *en demi-caractère* performs popular dances such as the cancan, but may dance these on point; these are comic or semiserious dances, in other words, performed with some classical technique.

CHANGEMENT DE PIEDS (changing of the feet) Small jump from Fifth Position in which the dancer changes the position of both feet in the air.

CHASSÉ Literally, chased. A sliding step: the dancer jumps low off the floor, lands, and the working foot chases the landing foot out of position. A *chassé* embodies the same mechanical principle we see when we watch a horse canter. There the hind legs, moving together, displace the front legs.

CHOREOGRAPHER Someone who makes dances. The word means, etymologically, someone who records dances. It has come to mean simply the person responsible for the design of movement in a ballet. It is inaccurate to say that a choreographer "writes" a new ballet—for no choreographer sets down on paper what he wishes dancers to do from one moment to the next—but this is sometimes said.

All good choreographers have been good dancers. But to be a good dancer, of course, is not necessarily to be a choreographer. The dancer wishes *to be moved*, the choreographer wishes *to move*. To combine the two inclinations successfully is rare, but rare indeed are great choreographers. The choreographer is best compared to the poet: he is a man who uses the material of the classic dance that has been developed over hundreds of years, just as the poet uses the language he writes in. Like the poet, the choreographer finds new ways of saying things.

CLASSIC The word classic when applied to ballet is not the contrary of romantic. It applies to a rigorous basic vocabulary of steps and movements capable of infinite variation and a system of instruction that makes such variation possible for individual dancers. Classic ballets can be romantic, realistic, or mythological in subject matter. The classic dance is the dictionary of ballet and, as a method of instruction, it is also its grammar: basic steps and movements that must be learned and mastered if the student is to become an instrument of its possibilities. The classic dance is the fundamental material out of which new ballets are made; it constitutes the basic, instinctive knowledge that permits the dancer to perform them. As a system of instruction, the classic dance has been perfected through centuries of innovation and experiment. We know what is anatomically sound and physically possible. We know what must be taught first, how that must be learned so well that it becomes instinctive, what to teach next. We learn all this in schools, as dancers and teachers before us have learned it. Properly speaking, what we call the classic dance might be more easily understood if it were called the academic dance, after the academies in which it was evolved; but the word *classic* has come down to us, along with the tradition of the developed academic dance, and is now universally accepted. When we go to the ballet and see a ballet described as *classic* in the program, we know that the word doesn't imply something that is serious and perhaps not entertaining: classicism in dance is the basis for the finest entertainment.

CORPS DE BALLET   Dancers who appear only in large groups: the chorus, the backbone of every ballet company. Jean Georges Noverre (1759) advised the ballet master to "make your *corps de ballet* dance, but when it does so, let each member of it express an emotion or contribute to form a picture; let them mime while dancing so that the sentiments with which they are imbued might cause their sentiment to be changed at every moment." Until the present century, the function of the *corps de ballet* was merely decorative: as a group they embellished with their poses and did not distract from the performances of principal dancers. In dramatic ballets, they reacted with appropriate emotion to the dramatic situation (the death of Giselle, the huntsmen in *Swan Lake*).

The New Ballet of Michel Fokine, as he himself expressed it in 1914, "in developing the principle of expressiveness, advances from the expressiveness of face to the expressiveness of the whole body, and from the expressiveness of the individual body to the expressiveness of a group of bodies and the expressiveness of the combined dancing of a crowd." Every dancer in the crowd scene in the original production of *Petrouchka* (1911) had something to do at every moment, and each dancer was related in both action and reaction to the principals on stage. Ballet prior to Fokine was essentially linear: the stage was divided into

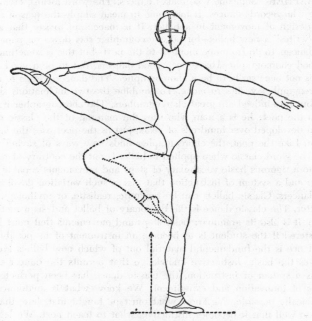

DÉVELOPPÉ À LA SECONDE

parts where the *corps de ballet* danced, where the soloists danced, where the ballerinas danced, and these established patterns were seldom violated. With

Fokine, movement on stage became orchestrated: each dancer on stage was an instrument contributing vitally to the general impression. Formerly it was only possible for a soloist to dance diagonally across the stage; now this is done by large groups of dancers: every dancer in such a group must be a soloist. Although every *corps de ballet* contains dancers of great talent who may eventually become principal dancers, and although it is wise for every soloist to have had experience in a *corps de ballet*, it is always possible in large state schools to discover talent early and not to permit it to idle long in the *corps*. This is the practice today with our ballet companies that are attached to schools. Talent is discovered early and used as soon as possible in appropriate roles. In ballet companies where the directors must first observe their new dancers in the *corps de ballet*, the *corps* itself becomes a kind of school, a testing ground, where talent is discovered. Experience in a *corps de ballet* gives a dancer invaluable lessons which are difficult to learn in any other way. Here she learns timing and precision; she learns also her relation to other dancers and other groupings of dancers on the stage. She learns, in fact, all the things that she must know to become a star.

DANCE (and danse) From the old high-German *danson*, meaning to drag or stretch.

DANSE D'ÉCOLE Literally, dance of the school. The classic dance, the academic dance based on the Five Positions and turnout (*see* Classic).

DANSEUR NOBLE A classical male dancer; partner of the ballerina in classical roles (Albrecht in *Giselle*, Siegfried in *Swan Lake*, etc.).

DÉVELOPPÉ From the French word that means, literally, to develop or to unfold. A gradual unfolding of the leg as it rises from the floor and is extended fully in the air. As it is raised toward complete extension, the foot of the working leg passes (*passé*) the knee of the supporting leg.

ENTRECHAT a, b

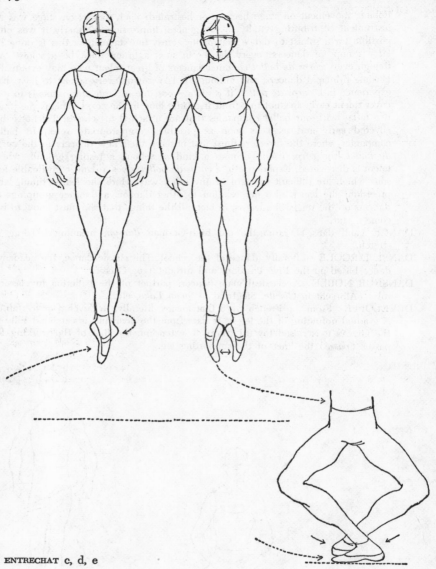

ENTRECHAT c, d, e

DIVERTISSEMENT  A dance or a series of dances for simple diversion and pleasure. A *divertissement* may be a whole number, like *Aurora's Wedding*, which contains plotless dance excerpts from *The Sleeping Beauty*, or it may be part of a whole ballet, like the folk dances that celebrate Prince Siegfried's birthday in the third act of *Swan Lake* or the series of character dances that come in the last act of *Coppélia*. A *grand pas de deux* taken out of a ballet and performed alone without its surrounding plot is a *divertissement*.

ÉCHAPPÉ  (from échapper, to escape or slip)  Step in which the dancer's feet escape from a closed position to an open position as she jumps upward. The movement is brisk and vigorous.

ELEVATION  The ability with which a dancer rises from the floor to perform jumps, and the capacity to remain in the air in the midst of these movements. The *danse d'élévation* was first popularized by Marie Taglioni (active 1822–48); within living memory, Vaslav Nijinsky (active 1908–19) still serves as a model conqueror of the air.

EN ARRIÈRE  Backward.

EN AVANT  Forward.

EN DEDANS  Inward.

EN DEHORS  Outward.

ENTRECHAT  Probably derived from the Italian *intrecciare*, to weave or braid. A beating step of elevation in which the dancer jumps straight into the air from *plié* and crosses his feet a number of times, making a weaving motion in the air. The term *entrechat* is compounded with numerals to indicate the number of movements of the legs: *entrechat-trois, entrechat-quatre, entrechat-cinq, entrechat-six, entrechat-sept, entrechat-huit*. Each leg moves once in a crossing: hence the term *entrechat-six* means six movements—counting both legs—or three crossings. *Entrechats* up to *entrechat-six* are movements of *petite batterie*, small beatings; *entrechat-six* and above are movements of *grande batterie*, large beatings.

FOUETTÉ  (from fouetter, to whip)  In *fouetté en tournant* (see illustration), a whipping motion of the free leg which propels the dancer around the supporting leg.

FOUETTÉ EN TOURNANT I, II (FROM RIGHT TO LEFT)

GLISSADE (glide)  A gliding movement from Fifth Position to an open position
and back to fifth position—usually seen as a preparatory step for jumps.

JETÉ (from jeter, to throw)  The word is derived from *jeter* rather than *sauter* (the
French word for jump) because in this movement, the dancer *throws* one leg
away and up in the air. This is a jump in which the weight of the body is thrown
from one foot to the other. There are small jumps in ballet (*assemblés, change-
ments, échappés*, etc.), but these are all preparations for the large aerial jumps
in which the dancer's body describes a swift, high trajectory in the air. In *grand
jeté* the dancer pushes off from the floor with one foot in a variety of preparatory
positions, holds a fleeting pose in flight, and lands softly on the other foot. It is
sometimes supposed by people who do not know French that the word *j'ter*

GRAND JETÉ

(which in English sounds like *shtay*) applies to a movement different from *jeter*. This is not the case. *J'ter*, of course, is simply a contraction which French-speaking people make of *jeter*—a contraction they make quite naturally.

LIBRETTO   The story line of a ballet; in a ballet without a plot, the idea on which the ballet is based. The ideal ballet story can be seen plainly and requires no extraneous explanation. The story of the *Prodigal Son* is a good example: once there was a boy who had everything, then he had nothing, then again he had everything.

NOTATION   The writing down of dances in a form sufficiently intelligible for their accurate reproduction. Dances were written down as early as the fifteenth century, but it is only recently—by the system devised by Rudolf von Laban—that the recording of dances and ballets has become universal (rather than arbitrary), accurate, and capable of the precision that permits them to be reproduced without the presence of the choreographer. The Dance Notation Bureau (founded in New York, 1940) has recorded many dances and ballets that have been faithfully reproduced on the basis of notation, and for the first time in dance history the copyrighting of choreography seems imminently possible.

PANTOMIME (from the Greek)   Literally, all-imitating *pantomimos*. A dumb show of significant gesture, ballet's way of indicating intricacies of plot. The players in the original Roman pantomimes wore masks and could express themselves only with their bodies. These pantomimes portrayed mythic characters, gods and goddesses. The *commedia dell'arte* of Italy reduced these formal theatrical pantomimes into a popular burlesque with a permanent set of characters—Harlequin, Columbine, Pierrot, etc.—what has come down to us as the Punch and Judy show. The vocabulary of mime was gradually absorbed into ballet, as traveling Italian comedians visited France and as dancers and ballet masters required the dance to express human emotions and situations. While it was said of Camargo (active 1726–35) that "she danced to dance, not to stir emotion," it was said of her rival, Marie Sallé (active 1718–40), that she "replaced tinsel glitter by simple and touching graces. Her physiognomy was noble, sensitive and expressive." The acting and miming of David Garrick was an inspiration to the French ballet master Noverre, the "Shakespeare of the dance." The mime vocabulary is now unknown to most of us because it is no longer taught as it used to be. It is rarely used in modern ballets, but in the older ballets (*Giselle, Coppélia, Swan Lake, Sleeping Beauty*) mime was essential; as we watch the older ballets, a knowledge of some of its elements is essential for us.

Mime is limited. There are some things it is foolish to try to indicate in a ballet: you cannot indicate your mother-in-law and be readily understood. But within the limits of pantomime, much can be expressed. Noverre wrote: "Gesture is the countenance of the soul, its effect must be immediate and it cannot fail to achieve its effect if it is true. . . . Dancers, like actors, should devote themselves to depict and feel: they have the same object to attain." Here are a few important mime expressions seen in ballet:

YOU: Point to person with open hand (with pointed finger when angry).

BEAUTIFUL (or GIRL): Circle the face gently with the back of the hand, letting the back of the middle finger outline the face.

PRINCESS: Lift arms and hold hands just over top of head, as if enclosing a crown.

DANCE: Circle the hands around each other above the head.

KISS: Touch lips with finger.

LOVE: Hold both hands over the heart.

MARRY: Point to wedding-ring finger with index finger of right hand.

ME: Point toward self with middle fingers of both hands simultaneously.

KING: With a flourishing gesture raise the right hand above the head, indicating the feather commonly worn in the hats of the nobility.

QUEEN: Let index finger of right hand touch top of forehead at points where crown touches.

STOP: Hold up hand, palm out.

ANGRY: Raise arms above the head, elbows front, and shake fists.

SAD: Let fingers trace tears as they fall down the face.

WEEP: Hide face in both hands, or rub eyes with clenched fists.

BEG MERCY: Hold arms out, palms together, as if praying.

NO: Hold arms at the side, then cross them before the body in a definite gesture as the head shakes.

OBEY: Point to floor with decided gesture.

FORGET: Hold out hands loosely, palms up, and shake the head slightly.

REMEMBER: Touch the temple with the index finger.

FRIENDS: Clasp hands together on a level with the waist.

BLESS: With the hand, touch the head of the person blessed.

DIE: Bring arms up to the side of the head, then bring them down quickly so that the hands, fists clenched, are crossed in front of the body.

SLEEP: Incline the head against the back of the hands.

CHILD: With both palms down, raise the hands in three steps, as if measuring the height of a growing child.

THANK YOU: Inclining the head simply, bring one hand down from the chest, extending it toward the person thanked.

PAS A pace, a formalized or measured step. The dancer's step, or *pas*, is very different from the ordinary step we take when walking: it is closer to the pace, which we take when we measure or consider something. A *pas* is a gesture of the whole body.

PAS D'ACTION Action in dancing—that part of a dramatic ballet, for example, where the relation of the characters is clarified. A *pas d'action* is not pure dancing and not pure mime, but a combination of the two, an integral part of the ballet spectacle. It's similar to many moments in opera where characters—after suspending the action for a while and singing a quintet—turn again to each other and resume their dramatic relation.

PAS DE DEUX A dance for two people. Although a *pas de deux* is any dance for two people, the usual, standard *pas de deux* consists of five parts: the *entrée*, in which the ballerina and the *premier danseur* make their appearance; the adagio, in which the *danseur* supports the ballerina in a slow, graceful dance; a variation of the ballerina; a variation of the *danseur;* and the coda, a concluding passage for both ballerina and *danseur* in which the dance is brought to a felicitous conclusion.

PAS DE TROIS A dance for three people. *Pas de quatre* is a dance for four people; *pas de cinq*, a dance for five; *pas de six*, for six; and so forth.

PIROUETTE A complete turn of the body on one foot. *Pirouette* used to be applied only to turns by men, while the term *tour* was reserved for turns by women. The terms are synonymous. Girls turn in pirouettes on *pointe*, boys on *demi-pointe*. Ideally, the body is vertical in pirouettes; the foot of the supporting leg remains in one place. The free leg can be lifted slightly off the floor, the knee bent, as in the most common form of pirouette; it can be raised in back, the knee straight, as in *pirouettes en arabesque;* or it can be raised in back, the knee bent, as in *pirou-*

PIROUETTE I, II (FROM RIGHT TO LEFT)

*ettes en attitude;* and so forth. Pirouettes have dazzled audiences since the history of ballet began, but multiple pirouettes were not introduced until 1766. At that time, three turns by a boy and two by a girl were considered spectacular. Turns performed off the floor are called *tours en l'air.*

PLIÉ (from plier, to bend)   In the classic dance, this is a bending of the knees, the knees wide open, the feet turned outward. The function of the *plié* in the dancer's body is like the function of springs in an automobile: it is necessary for the development of elasticity. *Demi-plié* is a half, or small, bending; *grand plié* is a deep bending of the knees.

POINTE   The dancer *sur les pointes* dances on her toes. This innovation of the Romantic ballet (c.1820) is now universally used by female dancers in ballet: men stand on their toes only in certain Russian folk dances. If the dancer has been properly trained, dancing on point is neither painful nor uncomfortable nor damaging. Although the classic ballet is the only form of dance that uses toe dancing consistently, ballet existed long before toe steps were introduced; dancing on *pointes* cannot be called the single hallmark of ballet. Dancing on *pointes* is actually an extension of a basic feature of the classic dance: the straight line formed by the stretched leg and the pointing foot when the free leg moves from the floor. The ballet slippers of Marie Taglioni, who popularized toe dancing, were unblocked. The toes of ballet slippers were later blocked with glue, as they are today, to give the dancer additional support. Every dancer darns the exterior of the toe of her ballet slipper—not for support, but to provide security of position while she dances and to prevent slipping. Dancing *sur la demi-pointe* is on the half-toe, where the dancer is supported high on the ball of the foot and under the toes.

PORT DE BRAS   Movement or carriage of the arms.

RELEVÉ (from relever, to lift again)   In ballet, the raising of the body onto *pointe* or *demi-pointe*.

RÉVÉRENCE   A deep bow.

ROMANTIC   Ballets that we call Romantic are a *kind* of classical ballet. *La Sylphide* (1832), which epitomized—until the masterpiece *Giselle* (1841)—what we recognize as Romanticism in ballet, was romantic in subject, temper, and mood; but both ballets expressed this, with innovations, in the vocabulary of the *classic* dance. Similarly, *Les Sylphides* (1909)—which embodies Romanticism in name, substance, and music—consists of classical steps and movements. What is classic in ballet is what has been developed over the years; what is romantic is a period through which that development passed. Romanticism in ballet, in other words, is not the opposite of classicism.

Romanticism was responsible for revolutionary innovations in classic technique and in the subject matter of ballets. Its desire for ethereal creatures caused dancers for the first time to rise on their toes, introduced the white ballet costume so familiar to us in *Giselle, Swan Lake,* and *Les Sylphides,* and caused the expansion of the dance vocabulary to meet the expressive requirements of elfin, unattainable heroines and heroes who aimed at—and so seldom secured—permanent happiness. As it contrasted real life with fantasy, the Romantic Ballet naturalized the pastoral theme that dominated earlier ballet. Where previously nymphs and shepherds were potential gods and goddesses, these pastoral characters now became realistic, only to escape later from realism's cruelty to supernatural kingdoms (Act Two of *La Sylphide* and *Giselle*).

The heroes of the Romantic movement in ballet are: Théophile Gautier (1811–1872), French poet, critic, and novelist, the librettist of *Giselle;* Jules Perrot (1810–1892), dancer and choreographer, collaborator on *Giselle* and creator of the *Pas de Quatre.* Its heroine is its great ballerina Marie Taglioni (1804–1884), creator of *La Sylphide.* The Romantic Ballet dominated the classic dance from about 1820 to 1870.

After this time, what we recognize as the great classical ballets—*Swan Lake, The Sleeping Beauty,* etc.—were created on the basis of a new uncovered, unconcealed technique and a more exacting dance discipline. Thus, unlike literature, music, and the other arts, ballet's great period of classicism came *after* the development of Romanticism.

ROND DE JAMBE   A rotary movement of the leg; the dancer describes circles in the air, or on the floor, with the pointed toe of the working foot. The *rond de jambe* is a basic exercise in the ballet class and a ballet step seen frequently on stage. The *rond de jambe en l'air* is executed away from the floor.

SAUTÉ (from sauter, to jump)   The word is used as a modifier to explain that a jump is involved in a step or pose: *sauté en arabesque, échappé sauté,* and so forth.

TOUR   *See* Pirouette.

TOUR EN L'AIR   A turn in the air. The dancer, standing in Fifth Position, rises from the floor from a *demi-plié,* executes a complete turn, and returns to original position. *Tours* may be doubled or tripled for spectacular effect, but three complete turns in the air is the maximum.

TURNOUT   The distinguishing characteristic of the classic dance: knees that face frontward in a normal standing position are turned out from the hip at an angle of ninety degrees (*see* Basic Positions). Because dancers wore heels on their shoes at the time the five absolute positions were established, the complete

TOUR EN L'AIR I, II (FROM RIGHT TO LEFT)

ninety-degree turnout was not perfected until some time later. Complete turnout is not forced in beginning students.

TUTU   Ballet skirt; a nickname for *tunique*, tunic. The so-called Romantic tutu, which reaches to about twelve inches above the floor, was made famous by Marie Taglioni in the first famous Romantic ballet, *La Sylphide;* it is still familiar to us in *Giselle* (Act Two) and *Les Sylphides.* Gradually, however, with the perfection of dance technique, the tutu has been shortened to make the whole leg visible.

VARIATION   A solo, a dance for one person. Synonym: *pas seul.*

# INDEX